Journalizing and Posting

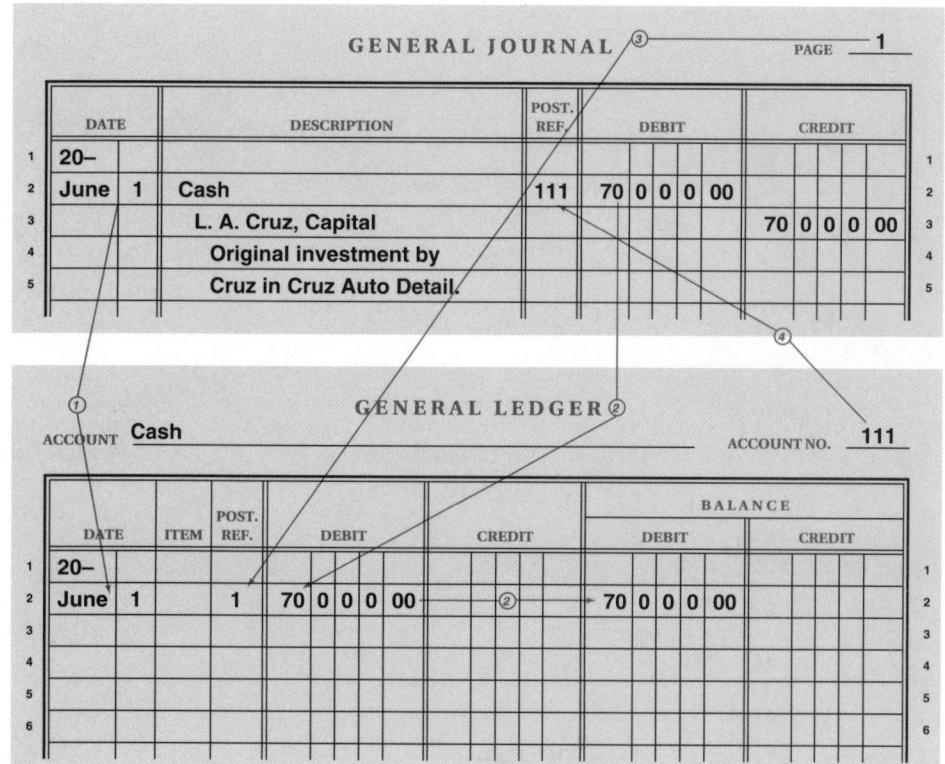

GENERAL JOURNAL ③   PAGE __1__

	DATE		DESCRIPTION	POST. REF.	DEBIT	CREDIT	
1	20–						1
2	June	1	Cash	111	70 0 0 0 00		2
3			L. A. Cruz, Capital			70 0 0 0 00	3
4			Original investment by				4
5			Cruz in Cruz Auto Detail.				5

① Date of transaction
② Amount of transaction
③ Page number of the journal
④ Ledger account number

GENERAL LEDGER ②

ACCOUNT **Cash**   ACCOUNT NO. **111**

	DATE	ITEM	POST. REF.	DEBIT	CREDIT	BALANCE DEBIT	BALANCE CREDIT	
1	20–							1
2	June 1		1	70 0 0 0 00		70 0 0 0 00		2
3								3
4								4
5								5
6								6

The Work Sheet

Account Name	Trial Balance Debit	Trial Balance Credit	Adjustments Debit	Adjustments Credit	Adjusted Trial Balance Debit	Adjusted Trial Balance Credit	Income Statement Debit	Income Statement Credit	Balance Sheet Debit	Balance Sheet Credit
	Assets				Assets				Assets	
		Liabilities				Liabilities				Liabilities
		Capital				Capital				Capital
	Drawing				Drawing				Drawing	
		Revenue				Revenue		Revenue		
	Expenses				Expenses		Expenses			

Steps in the Closing Process

R Close the Revenue accounts into Income Summary.
E Close the Expenses accounts into Income Summary.
I Close the Income Summary Account into the Capital Account, transferring the net income or net loss to the Capital Account.
D Close the Drawing account into the Capital Account.

College Accounting

Julie Boucher

Julie Boucher

College Accounting

SEVENTH EDITION 1–27

Douglas J. McQuaig

WENATCHEE VALLEY COLLEGE

Patricia A. Bille

HIGHLINE COMMUNITY COLLEGE

HOUGHTON MIFFLIN COMPANY   BOSTON   NEW YORK

Senior Accounting Editor: Bonnie Binkert
Associate Sponsoring Editor: Margaret E. Monahan
Editorial Associate: Damaris R. Curran
Senior Project Editor: Chere C. Bemelmans
Editorial Assistant: Elisabeth Kehrer
Senior Production/Design Coordinator: Carol Merrigan
Manufacturing Manager: Florence Cadran
Marketing Manager: Melissa Russell

This book is written to provide accurate and authoritative information concerning the covered topics. It is not meant to take the place of professional advice. The companies and financial information in this book have been created for instructional purposes. No reference to any specific company or person is intended or should be inferred. Any similarity with an existing company is purely coincidental.

Cover design: Rebecca Fagan
Cover image: John Sill

Comments about *College Accounting,* Seventh Edition, can be sent to the authors at the following e-mail address: pbille@uswest.net.

Credits

Introduction
p. 2, Tony Freeman/Photo Edit; p. 4, Michael Newman/Photo Edit; p. 5, Robert Brenner/Photo Edit.

Chapter 1
p. 8, Yvonne Hemser/Gamma Liaison; p. 10, Tony Freeman/Photo Edit; p. 15, Bob Daemmrich/Stock Boston.

Chapter 2
p. 37, S. Dooley/Gamma Liaison; p. 46, Charles Gupton/Stock Boston; p. 51, R. Rathe/Stock Boston.

(Credits continued on page C-1.)

Printed in the U.S.A.

Library of Congress Catalog Card No.: 96-76929

ISBN: 0-618-022791

3456789-VH-04 03 02 01

This text is sincerely dedicated to the students who will use it.

Every possible effort has been made to produce an understandable, up-to-date, and accurate presentation of the fundamentals of accounting.

This text is intended to be an important element in your course, as well as an invaluable future reference for you in the preparation of your career in business.

Best wishes for your success.

Douglas J. McQuaig

Patricia A. Bille

Contents

PART ONE

THE ACCOUNTING CYCLE FOR A SERVICE BUSINESS:
ANALYZING BUSINESS TRANSACTIONS

PART TWO

ACCOUNTING FOR CASH AND PAYROLL

PART THREE

THE ACCOUNTING CYCLE FOR A MERCHANDISING BUSINESS: USING SPECIAL JOURNALS

Chapter 18   **Ending Merchandise Inventory**   620

Appendix F
Estimating the Value of Inventories   647

Chapter 19   **Plant and Equipment**   658

Appendix G
The Voucher System of Accounting   695

PART SIX

ACCOUNTING FOR PARTNERSHIPS AND CORPORATIONS

PART SEVEN

ACCOUNTING FOR DECISION MAKING AND MANUFACTURING

Preface

The goals for the Seventh Edition of *College Accounting* are the same as they have been for the previous editions: to provide students with a strong basic knowledge of accounting terms, concepts, and procedures, always taking into consideration students' widely varying objectives, which include:

- preparation for entering the job market in accounting.
- a practical background in accounting for beginning other careers, such as clerical, secretarial, technical, sales, and management positions.
- retraining for career changes.
- preparation and background for more advanced studies in accounting.

Drawing from more than 60 years of combined teaching experience, we have developed an up-to-date, understandable, and teachable basic accounting text. The text is logically organized, liberally illustrated, and paced in a manner that is easy for students to read and understand. Based on extensive reviews, campus visits, and conversations with many accounting instructors and students, we have updated, revised, and improved both the text and the ancillary materials.

The accounting principles described are those endorsed by the Financial Accounting Standards Board.

CHARACTERISTICS OF COLLEGE ACCOUNTING

Focus on the Fundamentals

College Accounting, Seventh Edition presents the fundamentals of accounting in a practical, easy-to-comprehend manner. Great emphasis is placed on developing a firm foundation of fundamental procedures. Appropriate repetition enables students to develop confidence in themselves and to make progress in gradual stages. This repetition is accomplished through extensive use of examples and color-coded illustrations. Color photographs round out the text, which is designed to serve the wide range of student experiences.

Recording business transactions is directly related to the fundamental accounting equation. Each newly introduced transaction is fully illustrated and is supported with T account examples. Comprehensive reviews of T accounts, organized in relation to the fundamental accounting equation, appear in the Student Working Papers with Study Guide to assist as students review material and complete assignments.

Reading Comprehension

College Accounting, Seventh Edition is a very readable text. We write in short sentences and use many illustrations to help students relate the words to the procedures. Each chapter of *College Accounting* has been reviewed by business instructors who teach English as a Second Language courses and English for Special Purposes courses, as well as by students enrolled in these classes. With their assistance and advice, we have taken steps to ensure that the text is accessible to all readers.

Each chapter is limited to the presentation of one major concept, which is amply illustrated with business documents and report forms. As terms are introduced, they are defined thoroughly and are used in subsequent examples. Comprehension is also enhanced through the use of "Remember" and "FYI" statements. These short, marginal notes present a learning hint or a capsule summary of a major point made in preceding paragraphs as well as practical tips or information about the topic. End-of-chapter summaries review each performance objective presented in the chapter using text and illustrations.

Emphasis on Accounting Terminology

We firmly believe that accounting is the language of business and that learning new terminology is an essential part of a first course. Each key term is printed in green and is explained when it is first introduced. The end-of-chapter glossary repeats the definitions of the terms presented in the chapter. In addition, page numbers are included for each glossary term, making it easy for students to refer to a term in the chapter.

Questions, Exercises, and Problems   *College Accounting*, Seventh Edition provides a wealth of exercise and problem material that is supported by the Working Papers with Study Guide, offering instructors a wide choice for classroom illustrations and assignments. Each chapter ends with comprehensive review and study material consisting of a review of performance objectives; a glossary; discussion questions; exercises; several components—called Consider and Communicate, What If . . ., Critical Thinking, A Matter of Ethics, and Web Work—that foster problem solving and communication skills; and two sets of comparable A and B problems, progressing from simple to complex in difficulty.

- *Discussion Questions* Questions, based on the main points in the text and appropriate for either class discussion or for homework, are included at the end of each chapter.
- *Exercises* For practice in applying concepts, exercises are provided with each chapter. Each exercise is described briefly in the margin with a reference to the appropriate performance objective.
- *Consider and Communicate* Each Consider and Communicate question requires that students first think about the concepts presented in the chapter. Then they are asked to explain the concepts by applying what they have learned.
- *What If . . .* Each What If . . . assignment describes a set of accounting circumstances and asks students to use their knowledge of accounting, life experiences, and common sense to form a verbal or written response. These responses require a slightly higher level of thinking than the more basic Consider and Communicate feature.
- *Critical Thinking* Critical Thinking exercises provide an opportunity for students to develop their problem-solving skills and employ their knowledge of accounting to complete a task. The Critical Thinking feature is appropriate for individual or team responses and requires yet a higher level of thinking than the What If . . . feature.
- *A Matter of Ethics* In this exercise, a situation is described and students are asked to decide whether the action is ethical. Students are also asked to suggest what implications the described behavior might have. These

exercises are particularly valuable in fostering discussion by the class or in small groups.

- *Web Work* New to this edition, these assignments challenge students to browse the Web by suggesting topic-related descriptors in the URL or web address window. Students are further directed to look for certain details and then discuss or write about their discoveries.
- *Problems* Each chapter contains four A problems and four B problems. The A and B problems are parallel in content and level of difficulty. They are arranged in order of difficulty, with Problems 1A and 1B in each chapter being the simplest and the last problem in each series being the most comprehensive. Each problem is accompanied by a Check Figure so students can compare their total and correct errors in computation.

PROVEN COLOR-CODED PEDAGOGY

The Seventh Edition of *College Accounting* continues to implement a color-coded pedagogy that helps students recognize and remember key points. The pedagogical use of color also helps students understand the flow of accounting data and identify different types of documents and reports used in accounting. Finally, the use of color in this text helps students identify the performance objectives for each chapter, recognize the performance objectives called for in each exercise and problem, and review material efficiently and effectively.

- **Performance objectives** are highlighted in orange throughout the text. They are listed at the beginning of each chapter and restated alongside the related text discussion. They are referenced by a performance objective number in the chapter summary and in the exercises and problems.
- **Key terms** are printed in green. They are defined in the text and repeated in a glossary at the end of the chapter.
- **Remembers,** highlighted in blue, are learning hints or summaries placed in the margin of the text. These marginal notes often alert students to common procedural pitfalls and help them complete their work successfully.
- **FYIs,** highlighted in purple, are practical tips or information about accounting and business.
- **Tables,** outlined in purple, help students quickly identify material that must be examined as a unit and is not part of running text.

The Seventh Edition's consistent use of color extends to the treatment of accounting forms, financial statements, and documents in the text and end-of-chapter assignments.

- **Source documents,** such as invoices, bank statements, facsimiles, and other material that originates with outside sources, are shown in yellow.
- **Working papers, journals, ledgers, trial balances, and other forms and schedules** used as part of the internal accounting process are shown in green.
- **Financial statements,** including balance sheets, income statements, statements of owner's equity, and statements of cash flows, are shown in blue.

This distinctive treatment differentiates these elements and helps students see where each element belongs in the accounting cycle. Seeing these relationships helps students understand how accountants transform data into useful information.

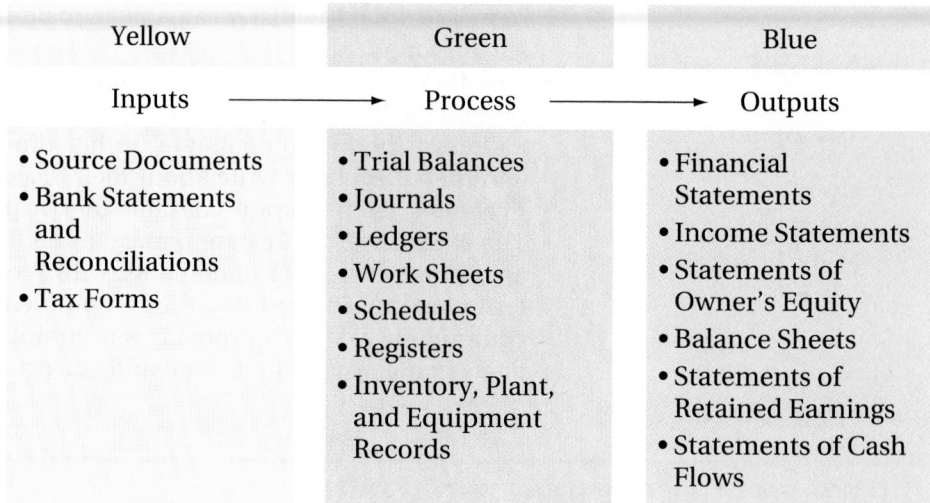

Yellow	Green	Blue
Inputs →	Process →	Outputs
• Source Documents • Bank Statements and Reconciliations • Tax Forms	• Trial Balances • Journals • Ledgers • Work Sheets • Schedules • Registers • Inventory, Plant, and Equipment Records	• Financial Statements • Income Statements • Statements of Owner's Equity • Balance Sheets • Statements of Retained Earnings • Statements of Cash Flows

GUARANTEE OF QUALITY MATERIAL

Successful use of an accounting text depends on more than the interesting and memorable presentation of material by the instructor and the text. The overall quality of the opening windows, examples, illustrations, color photographs, end-of-chapter questions, exercises, and problems, as well as ancillary materials, are critical to learning and retaining the facts and concepts covered in the course. Instructors and students must be assured that these materials are complete, consistent, and accurate.

Together with our publisher, we have taken a multistep approach to ensure quality materials for classroom use. The quality control system begins with in-depth reviews of the original manuscript and concludes with accuracy reviews of page proof by instructors who are actively teaching the course.

CHAPTER COVERAGE

College Accounting, Seventh Edition is designed primarily for use in a course extending two or three quarters or two semesters. The text is divided into parts: Chapters 1–5 cover the full accounting cycle for a sole proprietorship service business. Chapters 6–9 cover the combined journal, bank accounts, and payroll accounting. Chapters 10–14 cover special journals and the full accounting cycle for a merchandising firm. Chapters 15–19 cover notes payable and receivable as well as the valuation of receivables, inventories, and plant assets. Chapters 20–23 cover partnerships and corporations. Chapters 24–27 cover the statement of cash flows and financial statement analysis, as well as departmental and manufacturing accounting.

The following appendices expand content coverage and increase the instructor's options for structuring the course:

- *Appendix A: Methods of Depreciation (after Chapter 4)* This appendix describes methods of depreciation, including the Modified Accelerated Cost Recovery System.

- *Appendix B: Bad Debts (after Chapter 7)* This appendix covers the allowance and specific charge-off methods.
- *Appendix C: Inventory Methods (after Chapter 14)* This appendix describes methods of valuing inventories using weighted-average cost, FIFO, and LIFO.
- *Appendix D: The Statement of Cash Flows (after Chapter 14)* This appendix discusses the indirect method of determining cash flows.
- *Appendix E: Financial Statement Analysis (after Chapter 14)* This appendix describes percentages and ratios used to interpret information in financial statements.
- *Appendix F: Estimating the Value of Inventories (after Chapter 18)* Appendix F examines the retail and gross profit methods.
- *Appendix G: The Voucher System of Accounting (after Chapter 19)* This appendix illustrates the use of the voucher system as a means of internal control, particularly of cash.

Because many students take only one quarter or one semester of accounting, Appendices A through E offer a brief exposure to the basics of depreciation, the valuation of receivables and inventory, the statement of cash flows, and financial statement analysis.

Five of these appendices are developed more fully and presented as chapters in the second half of the text, as follows:

- Appendix A, Methods of Depreciation, is expanded into Chapter 19, Plant and Equipment.
- Appendix B, Bad Debts, is expanded into Chapter 17, Uncollectible Accounts.
- Appendix C, Inventory Methods, is expanded into Chapter 18, Ending Merchandise Inventory.
- Appendix D, The Statement of Cash Flows, is expanded into Chapter 24, The Statement of Cash Flows.
- Appendix E, Financial Statement Analysis, is expanded into Chapter 25, Comparative Financial Statements.

Appendices F and G, presented in the second half of the book, offer a brief exposure to the basics of estimating the value of inventories and the voucher system.

SPECIAL FEATURES AND ENHANCEMENTS FOR THE SEVENTH EDITION TEXT

- ***Complete Revision and Review*** The text and the end-of-chapter assignment materials have been thoroughly revised, updated, and reviewed.
- ***Full-Color Design with Photographs*** The Seventh Edition maintains its exciting full-color design, complete with two or three color photographs and accompanying captions in each chapter. These photographs help students visualize the concepts discussed in the chapter and glimpse them in practice.
- ***Drawings of Concepts*** Many chapters contain pictorial images to appeal to students' varied learning styles and enhance the text, color-coded forms, and rich illustrations.
- ***Transparent Acetate Pages*** New to Chapter 4, Adjusting Entries and the Work Sheet, we have created transparency overlays that allow students to

build a work sheet in stages, better visualizing the steps involved in the process.

- **Windows on the World Wide Web** New to this edition, these chapter openings provide a hands-on look at many of today's most well known businesses that are active on the Web. Each window first introduces students to the company and then asks a series of questions about the company that relate directly to the chapter topics. We provide web addresses for further investigation of the company. These questions and addresses are designed to prompt discussion, written responses, or additional questions surrounding the chapter.

- **Extended Examples** Cruz Auto Detail is integrated throughout Chapters 1–5 to illustrate the completion of the accounting cycle for a sole-proprietorship service business.

  Jackson Electric Supply is featured throughout Chapters 10–14 to illustrate the completion of the accounting cycle for a sole-proprietorship merchandising business using special journals.

  Jackson Electric Supply is reintroduced at appropriate points in Chapters 15–19.

- **Student Annotations** Additional Remembers and FYIs have been added to this edition. Remembers summarize key concepts for students, and FYIs are brief, interesting pieces of information about current business practice.

- **Continuous General Ledger Problem** A continuous general ledger problem featuring Like New, a sole proprietorship that renews furniture, begins in Chapter 3 by opening the accounting books for Like New. Students are required to enter into the software (for example, Peachtree, QuickBooks, or Houghton Mifflin's Windows General Ledger) the company name, company type, as well as the chart of accounts before journalizing and posting the first month's transactions and printing a trial balance. After Chapter 4 (Adjusting Entries and the Work Sheet), students continue with Like New by completing the end-of-the-month adjustments and printing the financial statements. After Chapter 5 (Closing Entries and the Post-Closing Trial Balance), students again work with Like New to close the books for the month and print a post-closing trial balance.

  Like New returns after Chapters 10–12 when the owner decides to add a line of merchandise and to introduce special journals for sales, purchases, cash receipts, and cash payments.

- **Icons** The following four icons accompany end-of-chapter assignments:

  The first icon on the left indicates exercises designed to enhance students' verbal and written communication skills as well as their group skills.

  The second icon on the left indicates assignments that involve critical thinking, to emphasize the importance of understanding how specific accounting procedures relate to accounting as a whole.

  Problems that can be solved using the Houghton Mifflin Windows General Ledger program are designated by the third icon on the left.

  Problems that can be worked using Spreadsheet Applications for *College Accounting* are identified by the fourth icon on the left.

- **New Web Assignments** Web Work exercises provide opportunities for students to do hands-on web browsing and sharpen their oral and written communication skills as well as their critical thinking skills.

- **Check Figures** Check Figures appear alongside every A and B problem in the text.

- **Cumulative Self-Checks** Questions (true/false, multiple choice, matching, and completion) and brief application problems follow every two to four chapters. These self-checks let students check their understanding of what they have read in the preceding chapters.

- *Accounting Cycle Review and Comprehensive Review Problem* These features give students the opportunity to apply accounting procedures to help them understand the process they have just studied in a series of chapters (1–5) and (7–14).

    In this edition, we have added a second Accounting Cycle Review Problem. Both Problems A and B involve the full accounting cycle, one for Fun World Waterslides and the other for Lakeland Indoor Sailboats, both sole-proprietorship service businesses.

    The Comprehensive Review Problem following Chapter 14 involves the full accounting cycle for Fine Fabrics, a sole-proprietorship merchandising business.

OTHER SPECIAL FEATURES AND ENHANCEMENTS FOR THE SEVENTH EDITION

Supplemental Learning Aids and Instructor's Support Package

Complete descriptions of all of the supplemental learning aids and support materials and of the following new items for students and instructors are included in the Instructor's Resource Manual with Solutions.

For Students

- *McQuaig/Bille Interactive Learning Center* The student web site, new to the Seventh Edition, expands the concepts and ideas presented in the text. The site offers interactive chapter quizzes that consist of 10 multiple choice and 10 true/false questions for each chapter, enabling students to test what they've learned and to find out why their answer is right or wrong. Suggested research activities, performance objectives, key terms, and company links are also offered on this site.
- *Study Materials in the Working Papers with Study Guide* The Working Papers with Study Guide contains rich discussions of the following topics to assist students in their study of accounting:

    Review of T Account Placement and Representative Transactions
    How to Study Accounting
    How to Solve Accounting Problems
    Ten-Key Skills Review
    Introduction to Spreadsheets
    Review of Business Mathematics
    How to Work a Practice Set
    Suggested Abbreviations for Account Titles

- *Suggested Homework Check Questions* Appearing in the Instructor's Resource Manual with Solutions, these questions, keyed to end-of-chapter assignments, provide students with the opportunity to practice the interpretive portion of the accounting process.
- *Houghton Mifflin Windows General Ledger Software* To accompany the Seventh Edition, Houghton Mifflin's new generic Windows general ledger program is available for student use. This package offers complete coverage of accounting concepts and procedures in an extremely simple and user-friendly computerized environment. Selected problems from *College Accounting*, Seventh Edition can be solved using this program.

- *Spreadsheet Applications for College Accounting* This innovative accounting software lets students solve end-of-chapter problems using Lotus 1-2-3 or Excel spreadsheet software. Students can select from prepared templates and use them to solve end-of-chapter problems accompanied by the spreadsheet icon. Instructions explaining how to convert Lotus templates to Excel and solve the problems are a feature of this program.
- *Practice Sets* A complete selection of manual and computerized practice sets is available for use with *College Accounting,* Seventh Edition. A complete listing and description of each practice set and its support package can be found in the Instructor's Resource Manual with Solutions.

  New to the Seventh Edition is the **Whitewater Kayaks Practice Set.** The practice set is based on a sole proprietorship and covers a one-month accounting period, enabling the student to acquire experience in dealing with the entire accounting cycle. In addition to a student text to complete the practice set manually, a CD-ROM gives the student the option of completing the practice set electronically using Peachtree 7.0, QuickBooks 2000, or Houghton Mifflin Windows General Ledger Software.

For Instructors

- *McQuaig/Bille Interactive Learning Center* The instructor web site, new to the Seventh Edition, offers additional instructor resource material. The site offers an enrichment manual designed to increase instructor options and to expand the flexibility of *College Accounting,* Seventh Edition. Teaching ideas and techniques, solutions to end-of-chapter problems, instructor outlines, performance objectives, and key terms are also offered on this site.
- *Instructor's Solutions Manual* to accompany **Whitewater Kayaks Practice Set** New to the Seventh Edition, the practice set is based on a sole proprietorship, covering a one-month accounting period, enabling the student to acquire experience in dealing with the entire accounting cycle. In addition to a student text to complete the practice set manually, a CD-ROM gives the student the option of completing the practice set electronically using Peachtree 7.0, QuickBooks 2000, or Houghton Mifflin Windows General Ledger Software.

Content Changes in the Seventh Edition

A complete list of content changes from the Sixth Edition to the Seventh Edition of *College Accounting* can be found in the Transition Guide, located in the Instructor's Resource Manual with Solutions. The following is a brief listing of the most important revisions and changes:

- *Introduction to Accounting* We have added the paraprofessional accountant as a section and a key term, and we now discuss the CMA certificate.
- *Chapter 1 Asset, Liability, Owner's Equity, Revenue, and Expense Accounts* We rewrote sample transactions to parallel the end-of-chapter problems. We added a section on numbering the chart of accounts when using a computer.
- *Chapter 2 T Accounts, Debits and Credits, Trial Balance, and Financial Statements* In Performance Objective 7, we eliminated (c) prepare a balance sheet containing the statement of owner's equity information. We edited the section entitled The T Account Form with Debits and Credits for

clarity (in the previous edition, this was called Recording Transactions in T Account Form). This section provides the procedures to follow in the earlier analysis for reference when working with each transaction.

- ***Chapter 4 Adjusting Entries and the Work Sheet*** We included a new section on journalizing adjusting entries.
- ***Chapter 6 Accounting for Professional Enterprises: The Combined Journal (Optional)*** This was Appendix B in the previous edition. We have added three Performance Objectives: Performance Objective 4—Prepare a work sheet for a professional enterprise; Performance Objective 5—Prepare financial statements for a professional enterprise; and Performance Objective 6—Record adjusting and closing entries in a combined journal.
- ***Chapter 8 Employee Earnings and Deductions*** This was Chapter 7 in the previous edition. We have updated the tax rules while adding a new key term: *withholding allowance*. A more precise distinction is now made between allowance and exemptions.
- ***Chapter 9 Employer Taxes, Payments, and Reports*** This was Chapter 8 in the previous edition. We have expanded Objective 8 to include end-of-year adjustments for accrued salaries and wages. Based on advice from our customers and reviewers, we deleted coverage of special deposit schedule rules (including four key terms: *monthly deposit schedule rule, semi-weekly deposit schedule rule, $100,000 one-day rule,* and *$500 rule*). We replaced the example Form 940 with Form 940EZ.
- ***Chapter 12 The Cash Receipts Journal and the Cash Payments Journal*** This was Chapter 11 in the previous edition. We inserted a section on Sales Returns and Allowances and Sales Discounts on an Income Statement.
- ***Chapter 13 Work Sheet and Adjusting Entries*** This was Chapter 12 in the previous edition. We changed the chapter title from Adjusting Entries to Work Sheet and Adjusting Entries and we relocated the expanded chart of accounts to Chapter 14.
- ***Chapter 14 Financial Statements, Closing Entries, and Reversing Entries*** This was Chapter 13 in the previous edition. This chapter now includes the expanded chart of accounts and an explanation on the arrangement of the accounts. We combined the discussion of Other Income with that of Other Expenses.
- ***Chapter 15 Notes Payable*** This was Chapter 14 in the previous edition. It now features an expanded section on Entry When Note Discounted at Bank Matures After End of Fiscal Period.
- ***Chapter 16 Notes Receivable*** This was Chapter 15 in the previous edition. We have expanded Performance Objective 1 to include: Write journal entries to record (e) renewal of a note at maturity and payment of interest; (f) renewal of a note with payment of interest and partial payment of principal; (g) a dishonored notes receivable; (h) collection of a note receivable formerly dishonored.
- ***Chapter 19 Plant and Equipment*** This was Chapter 18 in the previous edition. We have added new Performance Objective 6: Calculate the allowable depreciation for federal income tax returns using the Modified Accelerated Cost Recovery System. We revised our presentation of the double-declining balance method, and we expanded the section on Depreciation for Federal Income Tax, including Accelerated Cost Recovery System, and Modified Accelerated Cost Recovery System.
- ***Chapter 23 Corporate Bonds*** This was Chapter 22 in the previous edition. We have revised the section on coupon bonds.

• ***Chapter 26 Departmental Accounting*** This was Chapter 25 in the previous edition. We have deleted the discussion of Branch Accounting.

New

We introduce the following chapter in the Seventh Edition: Chapter 6 Accounting for Professional Enterprises: The Combined Journal (Optional).

SUPPLEMENTARY LEARNING AIDS FOR STUDENTS AND SUPPORT MATERIALS FOR INSTRUCTORS

For the Seventh Edition, we have assembled the most comprehensive package of student and instructor aids to complement a wide variety of teaching styles and course emphases. Detailed descriptions of each element of the support package are available in the Instructor's Resource Manual with Solutions.

For Students

• Working Papers with Study Guide 1–9
• Working Papers with Study Guide 1–14
• Working Papers with Study Guide 15–27
• McQuaig/Bille Interactive Learning Center
• Houghton Mifflin Windows General Ledger Software for Selected Problems
• Spreadsheet Applications for College Accounting
• Accounting Video Workshop
• Small Business Video
• Practice Sets:
> *Divesports* (after Chapter 3)
> *Sounds Abound,* Second Edition (after Chapter 5; can be used with Houghton Mifflin's General Ledger Software Program)
> *Let's Party* (after Chapter 5; can be used with Peachtree 3.5 or 5.0)
> *Lawson's Supply Center, Inc.* (after Chapters 8 and 9; can be used with Houghton Mifflin's General Ledger Software program)
> *Crystal Clean Maintenance* (after Chapter 9)
> *Oak Creek Canyon Jewelers* (after Chapter 9; can be used with Peachtree 3.5 or 5.0)
> *Rug Bug* (after Chapter 14; can be used with Peachtree 3.5 or 5.0)
> *Whitewater Kayaks* (after Chapter 14; can be used with Peachtree 7.0, QuickBooks 2000, or Houghton Mifflin's General Ledger Software program)
> *The Wax Works: A Cumulative Shoebox Practice Set with Business Papers* (after Chapter 14)
> *Verde Audio and Video* (after Chapter 16; can be used with Peachtree 3.5 or 5.0)
> *Camp Kits* (after Chapter 20)
> *Eagle Tea, Inc.* (after Chapter 23)
> *Carts Plus: A Three-in-One Practice Set* (after Chapter 25)

For Instructors

• Instructor's Resource Manual with Solutions
• Test Bank

- McQuaig/Bille Interactive Learning Center
- Computerized Test Bank
- Achievement Tests (A and B)
- Teaching and Solutions Transparencies
- Instructor's Guide to Accounting Video Workshop
- Instructor's Solutions Manuals for all practice sets

ACKNOWLEDGMENTS

We sincerely thank the editorial staff of Houghton Mifflin for their continuous support. Also, we thank our many students at Highline Community College for their observations and evaluations.

During the writing of the Seventh Edition, we consulted many users of the text throughout the country. Their constructive suggestions are reflected in the changes that have been made. Unfortunately, space does not permit mention of all those who have contributed to this volume. Some of those, however, who have been supportive and have influenced our efforts, are:

Joseph F. Adamo, CAZENOVIA COLLEGE
Clifford Bellers, WASHTENAW COMMUNITY COLLEGE
Catherine F. Berg, NASSAU COMMUNITY COLLEGE
Kenneth W. Brown, UNIVERSITY OF HOUSTON
Howard Bryan, SANTA ROSA JUNIOR COLLEGE
Theresa Capretta, TOMBALL COLLEGE
Carmela C. Caputo, EMPIRE STATE COLLEGE
Anthony R. Carbone, MASSACHUSETTS BAY COMMUNITY COLLEGE
C. P. Carter, UNIVERSITY OF MASSACHUSETTS–LOWELL
Janet Cassagio, NASSAU COMMUNITY COLLEGE
Michael S. Chaks, RIVERSIDE COMMUNITY COLLEGE
Frank Cress, BUTTE COLLEGE
Dana A. Crismond, MOUNTAIN EMPIRE COMMUNITY COLLEGE
Martha J. Curry, HUSTON-TILLOTSON COLLEGE
Carl Dauber, SOUTHERN OHIO COLLEGE–NORTH EAST
Allan Doyle, PIMA COLLEGE
Carl D. Erickson, INTERNATIONAL BUSINESS COLLEGE
William M. Evans, CERRITOS COLLEGE
Donald E. Foster, TACOMA COMMUNITY COLLEGE
Mary D. Foster, ILLINOIS CENTRAL COLLEGE
Lynne Fowler, HEALD BUSINESS COLLEGE
Walter A. Franklin, PALM BEACH COMMUNITY COLLEGE
Alan P. Fraser, RIO HONDO COLLEGE
William French, ALBUQUERQUE TECHNICAL-VOCATIONAL INSTITUTE
Theresa V. Gann, SAN JACINTO COLLEGE
Marlin Gerber, KALAMAZOO VALLEY COMMUNITY COLLEGE
Helen Gerrard, MIAMI UNIVERSITY–HAMILTON & MIDDLETOWN CAMPUSES
Charles F. Grant, SKYLINE COLLEGE
Harry Gray, INDIANA VOCATIONAL TECHNICAL COLLEGE
Gary Guinn, SKAGIT VALLEY COLLEGE
Julia F. Harrison, COLUMBUS STATE COMMUNITY COLLEGE
Robert Hartzell, COLORADO MOUNTAIN COLLEGE
C. Robert Hellmer, MILWAUKEE AREA TECHNICAL COLLEGE
Donald L. Holloway, LONG BEACH COMMUNITY COLLEGE

Jay S. Hollowell, COMMONWEALTH COLLEGE–VIRGINIA BEACH CAMPUS
Janis Hutchins, LAMAR UNIVERSITY–PORT ARTHUR
Thomas Jackson, CERRITOS COMMUNITY COLLEGE
Eugene Janner, BLINN COLLEGE
Edward H. Julius, CALIFORNIA LUTHERAN UNIVERSITY
James Kahl, LOWER COLUMBIA COLLEGE
Ann P. King, BRANELL INSTITUTE
Bobbie Krapels, MEMPHIS STATE UNIVERSITY
Ronald K. Kulhanek, GREAT LAKES JUNIOR COLLEGE
Joanne M. Landry, MASSASOIT COMMUNITY COLLEGE
Shirley Hsiang-ju Wen Leung, LOS MEDANOS COLLEGE
Kenneth Leibham, COLUMBIA GORGE COMMUNITY COLLEGE
Loren Long, ELGIN COMMUNITY COLLEGE
Gloria J. Lynch, MT. ALOYSIUS JUNIOR COLLEGE
Ted Lynch, HOCKING COLLEGE
Patricia McDaniel, CENTRAL PIEDMONT COMMUNITY COLLEGE
Shirl Mallory, COOSA VALLEY TECHNICAL INSTITUTE
Elizabeth Barnard Miller, COLUMBUS STATE COMMUNITY COLLEGE
Donald E. Morehead, HENRY FORD COMMUNITY COLLEGE
Robert S. Nash, HENRY FORD COMMUNITY COLLEGE
Jerome P. Neadly, MORTON COLLEGE
Dolores J. Osborn, CENTRAL WASHINGTON UNIVERSITY
Vincent Pelletier, COLLEGE OF DUPAGE
Joel C. Peralto, HAWAII COMMUNITY COLLEGE
Daniel J. Pike, ROCHESTER INSTITUTE OF TECHNOLOGY
Bernard Piwkiewicz, LANEY COLLEGE
Gray R. Ragsdale, CENTRAL TEXAS COLLEGE
Karen D. Richardson, TARRANT COUNTY JUNIOR COLLEGE–NORTHEAST CAMPUS
Fabiola Rubio, EL PASO COMMUNITY COLLEGE
Paul T. Ryan, JACKSON STATE COMMUNITY COLLEGE
Nelda Shelton, TARRANT COUNTY JUNIOR COLLEGE–SOUTH CAMPUS
Nancy Sheridan, BUCKS COUNTY COMMUNITY COLLEGE
Bill Smith, PORTLAND COMMUNITY COLLEGE
Harold R. Steinhauser, ROCK VALLEY COLLEGE
Nancy Stewart, ODESSA COLLEGE
Joseph Stoffel, WAUBONSEE COMMUNITY COLLEGE
Ron Summers, OKLAHOMA CITY COMMUNITY COLLEGE
Rahmat Ola Tavallali, WALSH COLLEGE
William G. Vendemia, YOUNGSTOWN STATE UNIVERSITY
Russell Vermillion, PRINCE GEORGE'S COMMUNITY COLLEGE
Florence G. Waldman, KILGORE COLLEGE
Martha Walty, SAN JOSE CITY COLLEGE
Dick D. Wasson, SOUTHWESTERN COLLEGE
Jim M. Weglin, NORTH SEATTLE COMMUNITY COLLEGE
Sharon Welch, PIMA COMMUNITY COLLEGE–WEST CAMPUS
Nancy T. Weller, GRAND RAPIDS JUNIOR COLLEGE
Bobby R. Williams, MCLENNAN COMMUNITY COLLEGE

A special note of thanks to the individuals who contributed greatly by reviewing page proofs and checking the end-of-chapter questions, exercises, and problems:

Gregory D. Barnes, CLARION UNIVERSITY
William A Barzen, ST. PETERSBURG JUNIOR COLLEGE–ST. PETERSBURG CAMPUS
Jennifer L. Berry, PARKS JUNIOR COLLEGE–SOUTH

Charles M. Betts, DELAWARE TECHNICAL AND COMMUNITY COLLEGE
Gary R. Bower, COMMUNITY COLLEGE OF RHODE ISLAND
Jay M. Bruns, TAMPA COLLEGE–PINELLAS
Ron Burnette, MACOMB COMMUNITY COLLEGE
Carolyn A. Byrd, ST. PETERSBURG JUNIOR COLLEGE–CLEARWATER CAMPUS
Lee Cannell, EL PASO COMMUNITY COLLEGE
Tim Carse, BARNES BUSINESS COLLEGE, DENVER
Henry Dalehite, HEALD COLLEGE
Mark Dawson, DUQUESNE UNIVERSITY
Steven M. Day, DIXIE COLLEGE
Diana Dewald, MANATEE COMMUNITY COLLEGE
Patricia A. Doherty, BOSTON UNIVERSITY SCHOOL OF MANAGEMENT
Richard Dugger, KILGORE COLLEGE
Nina Edgmand, SALT LAKE COMMUNITY COLLEGE
Hussein Emin, NASSAU COMMUNITY COLLEGE
Harry Gary, INDIANA VOCATIONAL TECHNICAL COLLEGE
Roxanne Gooch, CAMERON UNIVERSITY
Christine Uber Grosse, THUNDERBIRD, THE AMERICAN GRADUATE SCHOOL OF
    INTERNATIONAL MANAGEMENT
Dennis A. Gutting, ORANGE COUNTY COMMUNITY COLLEGE
Gloria M. Halpern, MONTGOMERY COLLEGE
Joyce Henzel, ROGERS STATE COLLEGE
Carla Hogan, SHORELINE COMMUNITY COLLEGE
Sally E. Huttemann, NATIONAL TECHNICAL INSTITUTE FOR THE DEAF AT ROCHESTER
    INSTITUTE OF TECHNOLOGY
Thomas L. Jackson, CERRITOS COLLEGE
David G. Jordan, BRYANT & STRATTON BUSINESS INSTITUTE
Jimmy King, MCLENNON COMMUNITY COLLEGE
Jacob V. Lamar, MONROE COLLEGE
Cathy Xanthaky Larson, MIDDLESEX COMMUNITY COLLEGE
Donald MacGilvra, SHORELINE COMMUNITY COLLEGE
George J. McGowan
Gail A. Mestas
Michael F. Monahan
Jenine Moscove, BRANFORD HALL CAREER INSTITUTE
Salah Negm, PRINCE GEORGE'S COMMUNITY COLLEGE
Daniel J. Pike, ROCHESTER INSTITUTE OF TECHNOLOGY
Linda L. Scott, INDIANA VOCATIONAL TECHNICAL COLLEGE
S. Murray Simons, MOUNT IDA COLLEGE
Elaine Simpson, ST. LOUIS COMMUNITY COLLEGE AT FLORISSANT VALLEY
Calvin L. Snyder, POLK COMMUNITY COLLEGE
Marion Taube, UNIVERSITY OF PITTSBURGH
Steven C. Teeter, UTAH VALLEY COMMUNITY COLLEGE
Josephine Vondras, ORANGE COUNTY COMMUNITY COLLEGE
Nicholas Walker, SAN JOAQUIN DELTA COLLEGE
Stan Weikert, COLLEGE OF THE CANYONS
Kay Westerfield, UNIVERSITY OF OREGON
Avalon White, BARTON COUNTY COMMUNITY COLLEGE

As always, we would like to thank our families for their understanding and cooperation. Without their support, this text would never have been written. Heartfelt appreciation is extended to Beverlie McQuaig for her detailed proofreading and good humor. Pertinent suggestions for updating the material were given by Judith McQuaig Britton, C.P.A., of Smith, Bunday, Berman,

Britton; John McQuaig, C.P.A., of McQuaig and Welk; and Laurie McQuaig Ramaley, D.C. We also express continued gratitude to Bruce Bille, Tracy Bille-Newkirk, James Newkirk, C.P.A., and Adeline Harris for their encouragement and assistance, and to the memory of Ryan Bille and Wesley Harris for their courage and inspiration.

Douglas J. McQuaig

Patricia A. Bille

College Accounting

Introduction to Accounting

Performance Objectives

After you have completed this introduction to accounting, you will be able to do the following:

1. Define *accounting*.

2. Explain the importance of accounting information.

3. Describe the various career opportunities in accounting.

Accounting is often called the language of business because, when confronted with events of a business nature, all people in society—owners, managers, creditors, employees, attorneys, engineers, and so forth—must use accounting terms and concepts to describe these events. Examples of accounting terms are *net, gross, yield, valuation, accrued, deferred*—the list could go on and on. So it is logical that anyone entering the business world should know enough of its "language" to communicate with others and to understand their communications.

As you acquire a knowledge of accounting, you will gain an understanding of the way businesses operate and the reasoning involved in making business decisions. Even if you are not involved directly in accounting activities, you will certainly need to be sufficiently acquainted with the "language" to be able to understand the meaning of accounting information, how it is compiled, how it can be used, and its limitations.

You may be surprised to find that you are already familiar with many accounting terms. Recalling your personal business activities and relating them to your study of accounting will be very helpful to you. For example, when you purchased this textbook, you exchanged cash or a promise to pay cash for the book. As you will see, this exchange is an accounting event. You are going to recognize many activities and terms as you begin your study of accounting.

DEFINITION OF ACCOUNTING

Objective 1

Define *accounting*.

Accounting is the process of analyzing, classifying, recording, summarizing, and interpreting business transactions in financial or monetary terms. A business transaction is an event that has a direct effect on the operation of an economic unit, is expressed in terms of money, and is recorded. Examples of business transactions are buying or selling goods, renting a building, paying employees, and buying insurance.

The primary purpose of accounting is to provide the financial information needed for the efficient operation of an economic unit. The term **economic unit** includes not only business enterprises but also not-for-profit entities, such as government bodies, churches and synagogues, clubs, and fraternal

Accounting is an important part of all types of businesses. These cruise ships require the same extensive recordkeeping as any large destination resort. The ship is a large floating hotel with guests, employees, management, recreational activities, restaurants, and shops.

organizations. Business enterprises or organizations may be called firms or companies. All of these entities require some type of accounting records. An **accountant** is a person who keeps the financial history of the transactions of an economic unit in written form.

Because it is important that all those who receive accounting reports be able to interpret them, a set of rules or guidelines for the accounting process has been developed. These guidelines or rules are known as **generally accepted accounting principles (GAAP)**.

Bookkeeping and Accounting

There are distinctions between bookkeeping and accounting. The two processes are closely related, but there is no universally accepted line of separation. Generally, bookkeeping involves the systematic recording of business transactions in financial terms. Accounting functions at a higher level. An accountant sets up the system that a bookkeeper uses to record business transactions. An accountant may supervise the work of the bookkeeper and prepare financial statements and tax reports. Although the bookkeeper's work is more routine, it is hard to draw a line where the bookkeeper's work ends and the accountant's begins.

IMPORTANCE OF ACCOUNTING INFORMATION

Objective 2

Explain the importance of accounting information.

Anyone who aspires to a position of leadership in business or government needs a knowledge of accounting. A study of accounting gives a person the necessary background and also gives him or her an understanding of the scope, functions, and policies of an organization. A person may not be doing the accounting work, but he or she will be continually dealing with accounting forms, language, and reports.

Users of Accounting Information

Owners Owners have invested their money or goods in a business organization. They desire information regarding the company's earnings, its prospects for future earnings, and its ability to pay its debts.

Managers Managers and supervisors have to prepare financial reports, understand accounting data contained in reports and budgets, and express future plans in financial terms. People who have management jobs must know how accounting information can be developed in order to evaluate performance in meeting goals.

Creditors Creditors lend money or extend credit to the company for the purchase of goods and services. The company's creditors include suppliers, banks, and other lending institutions, such as loan companies. Creditors are interested in the firm's ability to pay its debts.

Government agencies Taxing authorities verify information submitted by companies concerning a variety of taxes, such as income taxes, sales taxes, and employment taxes. Public utilities, such as electric and gas companies, must provide financial information to regulatory agencies.

Accounting and Technology

Before the invention of calculators and computers, all business transactions were recorded by hand. Now computers perform routine recordkeeping operations and prepare financial reports. Computers are used today in all types of businesses, both large and small. One question often arises: "Is the computer taking over accountants' jobs?" Actually, with the introduction of computers, more jobs have been created to fulfill management's need for more information.

Regardless of whether a business uses a computer, the nature of accounting is the same. The computer is a powerful tool of the accountant. However, as a tool, the computer is only as useful as the ability of the operator. The operator must be skilled to key the correct information into the computer program. Otherwise, as the saying goes, "garbage in, garbage out."

CAREER OPPORTUNITIES IN ACCOUNTING

Objective 3

Describe the various career opportunities in accounting.

To find job opportunities in accounting, all you need to do is read the newspapers' classified advertisements or browse the Internet. Although the jobs listed in these ads require varying amounts of education and experience, most of them are for positions as accounting clerks, general bookkeepers, or accountants. Let's take a look at the requirements and duties of these positions.

Accounting Clerk/Technician

An accounting clerk/technician does routine recording of financial information. The duties of accounting clerks vary with the size of the company. In small businesses, accounting clerks handle most of the recordkeeping functions. In large companies, clerks specialize in one part of the accounting system, such as payroll, accounts receivable, accounts payable, cash, inventory, or purchases. The minimum requirement for most accounting clerk positions is one term or semester of an accounting course.

General Bookkeeper

Many small- and medium-sized companies employ one person to oversee their bookkeeping operations. This person is called a general or full-charge bookkeeper. The general bookkeeper supervises the work of accounting clerks. Requirements for this job vary with the size of the company and the complexity of the accounting system. The minimum requirement for most general bookkeeper jobs is one or two years of accounting as well as experience as an accounting clerk.

Paraprofessional Accountant

To bridge a gap between the general bookkeeper and the professional accountant many firms are hiring **paraprofessional accountants**. They are able to manage the duties of the general bookkeeper as well as many of the duties of a professional accountant under that accountant's supervision. Qualifications generally include a two-year degree or certificate in accounting as well as appropriate prior experience.

Accountant

The term *accountant* describes a fairly broad range of jobs. The accountant may design and manage the entire accounting system for a business. The accountant may also prepare the financial statements and tax returns and perform audits. Many accountants enter the field with a four-year college degree in accounting; however, it is not unusual for accountants to start at entry-level positions and work their way up to management positions. Although accountants are employed in every kind of economic unit, they are classified into one of three categories: public accounting, managerial or private accounting, and not-for-profit accounting. We'll briefly look at these categories.

Accountants are employed in every kind of economic unit. Many start in entry level positions and work their way up to management.

Public Accounting Certified public accountants (CPAs) are independent professionals who provide services to clients for a fee. To become a CPA, a person must have a college degree, pass a rigorous examination, and generally complete a work-experience requirement. Public accountants design accounting systems, prepare tax returns, provide financial advice about business operations, and audit financial statements.

Managerial or Private Accounting Most people who are accountants are employed by private business organizations. These accountants (not necessarily CPAs) manage the accounting system, prepare budgets, determine costs of products, and provide financial information for managers and owners. Accountants have many opportunities to advance into top management positions. The Certified Management Accountant (CMA) exam has become an important partner to the CPA credentials.

Not-for-Profit Accounting Not-for-profit accounting is used for government agencies, hospitals, churches and synagogues, and schools. Accountants for these organizations prepare budgets and maintain records

Organizations that are in business to serve rather than make a profit require accounting procedures, just as do profit-making organizations. The difference is in the mission of the organization—profit or not-for-profit.

of revenues and expenses. It should be noted that some not-for-profit organizations do in fact make a profit; however, the profit is kept in the organization and not distributed. For example, a hospital makes a profit and then reinvests the profit in modern equipment. Local, state, and federal government bodies employ vast numbers of people in accounting positions.

CHAPTER REVIEW

Review of Performance Objectives

1. Define *accounting.*

   Accounting is the process of analyzing, classifying, recording, summarizing, and interpreting business transactions in financial or monetary terms. It is also an information system and the language of business.

2. Explain the importance of accounting information.

   A study of accounting gives a person the necessary background to understand the scope, functions, and policies of an organization.

3. Describe the various career opportunities in accounting.

   Accountants, paraprofessional accountants, bookkeepers, and accounting clerks will find employment opportunities in several areas—in the public sector, the private sector, or not-for-profit organizations.

GLOSSARY

Accountant A person who keeps the financial history of the transactions of an economic unit in written form; sometimes mistakenly called a bookkeeper. (2)

Accounting The process of analyzing, classifying, recording, summarizing, and interpreting business transactions in financial or monetary terms; sometimes mistakenly called bookkeeping. (1)

Economic unit Includes both business enterprises and not-for-profit entities, such as government bodies, churches and synagogues, clubs, and fraternal organizations. (1)

Generally accepted accounting principles (GAAP) The rules or guidelines used for carrying out the accounting process. (2)

Paraprofessional accountant A person who is qualified in accounting to assume the duties of a general bookkeeper as well as some of those of a professional accountant under that accountant's supervision. (4)

Transaction An event directly affecting an economic entity that can be expressed in terms of money and that must be recorded in the accounting records. (1)

1 Asset, Liability, Owner's Equity, Revenue, and Expense Accounts

WINDOWS ON | *THE WORLD WIDE WEB*

Just can't get enough Gap jeans or leather? Then you've already had experience with accounting. When you plunk down $48 for a pair of Gap jeans, to you it's an expense. To the store it's revenue. When you decide to use your MasterCard to buy the matching leather jacket for $198, you've incurred a liability—a promise to pay the credit card company for your purchases at a later date. All those pants and jackets sold at thousands of stores add up. How much revenue do you think Gap earned last year? Was it in millions or billions? What was Gap's equity, which is the difference between assets and liabilities? What are some of Gap's assets, the stores and businesses Gap owns? To find out check **www.gapinc.com/performance/annual_reports/pdf/fin_annual_98.pdf**.

Performance Objectives

After you have completed this chapter, you will be able to do the following:

1. Define and identify *asset, liability,* and *owner's equity* accounts.

2. Record a group of business transactions, in column form, involving changes in assets, liabilities, and owner's equity.

3. Define and identify *revenue* and *expense* accounts.

4. Record a group of business transactions, in column form, involving all five elements of the fundamental accounting equation.

As we stated in the Introduction, accounting is the process of analyzing, classifying, recording, and summarizing business transactions. We now introduce the analyzing, classifying, and recording steps in the accounting process.

ASSETS, LIABILITIES, AND OWNER'S EQUITY

The Fundamental Accounting Equation

Objective 1

Define and identify *asset, liability,* and *owner's equity* accounts.

Assets are properties or things of value, such as cash, equipment, copyrights, buildings, and land, owned and controlled by an economic unit or business entity. By the term business entity, we mean that the business is an economic unit in itself, and the assets or properties of the business are

When a company's liabilities are greater than its assets, it may be forced into bankruptcy. The money earned from a going-out-of-business sale is used to pay creditors.

completely separate from the owner's personal assets. However, the owner has a claim on the assets of the business and a responsibility for its debts. **The owner's right, claim, or financial interest is expressed by the word** equity **in the business.** Another term that could be used is **capital**. Whenever you see the term **owner's equity**, it means the owner's right to or investment in the business.

FYI

Other terms for equity are *investment, net worth,* or *proprietorship.*

Assets	=	**Owner's Equity**
Properties or things of value owned by the business		Owner's *right* to or investment in the business

Suppose the total value of the assets is $40,000 and the business entity does not owe any amount against the assets. Then,

Assets	=	**Owner's Equity**
$40,000	=	$40,000

Or suppose the assets consist of a truck that costs $28,000. The owner has invested $10,000 for the truck, and the business entity has borrowed the remainder from the bank, which is a **creditor** (one to whom money is owed). This business transaction or event can be shown as follows:

Assets	=	**Liabilities**	+	**Owner's Equity**
Items owned		Amounts owed to creditors		Owner's investment
$28,000	=	$18,000	+	$10,000

We have now introduced a new classification, **liabilities**, which represent debts. They are the amounts that the business entity owes its creditors. The debts may originate because the business bought goods or services on credit, borrowed money, or otherwise created an obligation to pay. The creditors' claims to the assets have priority over the claims of the owner.

An equation expressing the relationship of assets, liabilities, and owner's equity is called the **fundamental accounting equation (Assets = Liabilities + Owner's Equity)**. We'll deal with this equation constantly from now on. If we know two parts of this equation, we can determine the third. Let's look at some examples.

Determine Assets Ms. Jones has $9,000 invested in her travel agency, and the agency owes creditors $2,000; that is, the agency has liabilities of $2,000. Then,

Assets = Liabilities + Owner's Equity

   ?   = $2,000   + $9,000

We can find the amount of the business's assets by adding the liabilities and the owner's equity:

```
  $ 2,000  Liabilities
+   9,000  Owner's Equity

  $11,000  Assets
```

The completed equation now reads

Assets = Liabilities + Owner's Equity

$11,000 = $2,000   + $9,000

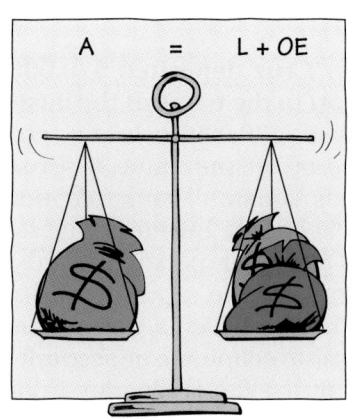

Like a teeter totter, the equation stays in balance by making equal or offsetting increases and decreases to one side or both sides.

Determine Owner's Equity Mr. Owen owns an auto lube shop. His business has assets of $36,000, and it owes creditors $5,000; that is, it has liabilities of $5,000. Then,

Assets = Liabilities + Owner's Equity

$36,000 = $5,000   +   ?

We find the owner's equity by subtracting the liabilities from the assets:

```
  $36,000  Assets
-   5,000  Liabilities

  $31,000  Owner's Equity
```

The completed equation now reads

Assets = Liabilities + Owner's Equity

$36,000 = $5,000   + $31,000

Determine Liabilities Mr. Cannon's insurance agency has assets of $42,000; his investment (his equity) amounts to $20,000. Then,

Assets = Liabilities + Owner's Equity

$42,000 =   ?   + $20,000

To find the firm's total liabilities, we subtract the equity from the assets:

```
  $42,000  Assets
-  20,000  Owner's Equity

  $22,000  Liabilities
```

The completed equation reads

Assets	=	Liabilities	+	Owner's Equity
$42,000	=	$22,000	+	$20,000

Recording Business Transactions

Objective 2

Record a group of business transactions, in column form, involving changes in assets, liabilities, and owner's equity.

As you know, business transactions are events that have a direct effect on the operations of an economic unit or enterprise and are expressed in terms of money. Each business transaction must be recorded in the accounting records. As business transactions are recorded, the amounts listed under the headings Assets, Liabilities, and Owner's Equity change. However, **the total of one side of the fundamental accounting equation must always equal the total of the other side.** The categories under these three main headings are called **accounts**.

Let's look at a group of business transactions. These transactions are typical of those seen in a service or professional type of business. In these transactions, let's assume that L. A. Cruz establishes her own business and calls it Cruz Auto Detail. Cruz Auto Detail is a **sole proprietorship**, or a one-owner business.

Assets owned by a business may be as small as its office supplies or as large as its delivery van or building.

Transaction (a) Cruz deposited $70,000 in a bank account in the name of the business. Cruz deposits $70,000 cash in a separate bank account in the name of Cruz Auto Detail. This separate bank account will help Cruz keep her business investment separate from her personal funds. This is an example of the **separate entity concept**, according to which a business is treated as a separate economic or accounting entity. The business is independent or stands by itself; it is separate from its owners, creditors, and customers.

The Cash account consists of bank deposits and money on hand. The business now has $70,000 more in cash than before, and Cruz's investment has also increased by $70,000. The account denoted by the owner's name followed by the word *Capital* records the amount of the owner's investment, or equity, in the business. The effect of this transaction on the fundamental accounting equation is as follows:

	Assets	=	Liabilities	+	Owner's Equity
	Items owned		Amounts owed to creditors		Owner's investment
	Cash	=			L. A. Cruz, Capital
(a)	+70,000	=			+70,000

Besides cash, an investment may be in the form of goods, such as equipment. The word *Capital* used under Owner's Equity therefore does not always mean that cash was invested.

Transaction (b) Bought equipment, paying cash, $43,000. Cruz's first task is to get her company ready for business; to do that, she needs the proper equipment. Accordingly, Cruz Auto Detail buys equipment whose cost is $43,000 and pays cash. **It is important to note at this point that Cruz does not invest any new money. She simply exchanges part of the business's cash for equipment.** Because equipment is a new type of property for the firm, a new account, Equipment, is created. Equipment is included under Assets. As a result of this transaction, the accounting equation changes:

	Assets	=	Liabilities	+	Owner's Equity	— *Elements*
	Items owned		Amounts owed to creditors		Owner's investment	
	Cash + Equipment =				L. A. Cruz, Capital	— *Accounts*
Initial Investment	70,000	=			70,000	
(b)	−43,000 +43,000					
New balances	27,000 + 43,000	=			70,000	
	70,000				70,000	

Transaction (c) Bought equipment on account from Williams Auto Supply, $7,000. Cruz Auto Detail buys equipment costing $7,000 on credit from Williams Auto Supply.

The Equipment account shows an increase because the business owns $7,000 more in equipment. There is also an increase in liabilities because the business now owes $7,000. The liability account **Accounts Payable** is used for short-term liabilities or charge accounts, usually due within thirty days. (The company to which we owe money is called a creditor.) There is now a total of $77,000 on each side of the equals sign. Because Cruz Auto Detail owes money to Williams Auto Supply, Williams Auto Supply is called a creditor of Cruz Auto Detail.

	Assets	=	Liabilities	+	Owner's Equity
	Items owned		Amounts owed to creditors		Owner's investment
	Cash + Equipment =		Accounts Payable +		L. A. Cruz, Capital
Previous balances	27,000 + 43,000	=			70,000
(c)	+ 7,000		+7,000		
New balances	27,000 + 50,000	=	7,000	+	70,000
	77,000			77,000	

Observe that the recording of each transaction must yield an equation that is in balance. For example, transaction (b) resulted in a minus $43,000 and a plus $43,000 *on the same side,* with nothing recorded on the other side, and transaction (c) resulted in a $7,000 increase to both sides of the equation. It does not matter whether you change one side or both sides. **The important point is that whenever a transaction is properly recorded, the accounting equation remains in balance.**

Transaction (d) **Paid Williams Auto Supply, a creditor, on account, $2,000.** Cruz Auto Detail pays $2,000 to Williams Auto Supply, to be applied against the firm's liability of $7,000.

With this payment, cash is being reduced. At the same time, the firm *owes* less than before, so the transaction should be recorded as a reduction in liabilities.

	Assets	=	Liabilities	+	Owner's Equity
	Items owned		Amounts owed to creditors		Owner's investment
	Cash + Equipment	=	Accounts Payable	+	L. A. Cruz, Capital
Previous balances	27,000 + 50,000	=	7,000	+	70,000
(d)	−2,000		−2,000		
New balances	25,000 + 50,000	=	5,000	+	70,000
	75,000			75,000	

Transaction (e) **Bought supplies on account from Rossi and Company, $800.** Cruz Auto Detail buys buffer pads, cleaners, and waxes from Rossi and Company for $800. Pads, cleaners, and waxes are listed under Supplies instead of under Equipment because a detailing company will use these items in a relatively short period of time. Equipment, on the other hand, normally lasts a number of years.

	Assets	=	Liabilities	+	Owner's Equity
	Items owned		Amounts owed to creditors		Owner's investment
	Cash + Equip. + Supp.	=	Accounts Payable	+	L. A. Cruz, Capital
Previous balances	25,000 + 50,000	=	5,000	+	70,000
(e)	+800		+800		
New balances	25,000 + 50,000 + 800	=	5,800	+	70,000
	75,800			75,800	

Accounting, as we said before, is the process of analyzing, classifying, recording, summarizing, and interpreting business transactions in terms of money. Look at the transactions thus far for Cruz Auto Detail and see if you recognize that we have gone through certain steps (in the form of questions). Let's illustrate these steps using transaction **(e),** bought supplies on account from Rossi and Company.

1. **What accounts are involved?** Supplies and Accounts Payable are involved.
2. **What are the classifications of the accounts involved?** Supplies is an asset and Accounts Payable is a liability.
3. **Are the accounts increased or decreased?** Supplies is increased because Cruz Auto Detail has more supplies than before. Accounts Payable is also increased because Cruz Auto Detail owes more than before.
4. **Is the equation in balance after the transaction has been recorded?** Yes.

Next, we record the transaction. We will stress this step-by-step process throughout the text. This example serves as an introduction to **double-entry accounting**. The "double" element is demonstrated by the fact that each transaction must be recorded in at least two accounts, keeping the accounting equation in balance.

Summary of Transactions

Let's summarize the business transactions of Cruz Auto Detail in column form, identifying each transaction by a letter of the alphabet. To test your understanding of the recording procedure, describe the nature of the transactions that have taken place.

	Assets			= Liabilities + Owner's Equity	
	Cash +	Equip. +	Supp. =	Accounts + Payable	L. A. Cruz, Capital
Transaction (a)	+70,000				+70,000
Transaction (b)	−43,000	+43,000			
Balance	27,000 +	43,000		=	70,000
Transaction (c)		+ 7,000		+7,000	
Balance	27,000 +	50,000		= 7,000 +	70,000
Transaction (d)	− 2,000			−2,000	
Balance	25,000 +	50,000		= 5,000 +	70,000
Transaction (e)			+800	+ 800	
Balance	25,000 +	50,000 +	800 =	5,800 +	70,000

75,800   75,800

The following observations apply to all types of business transactions:

1. Every transaction is recorded as an increase and/or decrease in two or more accounts.
2. One side of the equation is always equal to the other side of the equation.

In this chapter we are using a column arrangement as a practical device to show how transactions are recorded. This arrangement is useful for showing increases and decreases in various accounts as a result of the transactions. We also showed new balances after recording each transaction.

REVENUE AND EXPENSE ACCOUNTS

Objective 3

Define and identify *revenue* and *expense* accounts.

Revenues are the amounts earned by a business. Examples of revenues are fees earned for performing services, income from selling merchandise, rent income for the use of property, and interest income for lending money. Revenues may be in the form of cash or credit card receipts. Revenues may also result from credit sales to charge customers, in which case cash will be received at a later time.

Expenses are the costs that relate to earning revenue (or the costs of doing business). Examples of expenses are wages expense for labor performed, rent expense for the use of property, interest expense for the use of money, and advertising expense for the use of various media (for example, newspapers, radio, and direct mail). Expenses may be paid in cash when incurred (that is, immediately) or at a later time. Expenses to be paid at a later time involve Accounts Payable.

Revenues and expenses directly affect owner's equity. **If a business earns revenue, an increase in owner's equity occurs. When a business incurs or pays expenses, owner's equity decreases.** For the present, think of it this way: If the company makes money, the owner's equity is increased. If the company has to pay out money for the costs of doing business, then the owner's equity is decreased. Revenues and expenses fall under the umbrella of owner's equity: Revenue increases owner's equity; expenses decrease owner's equity.

Chart of Accounts

The **chart of accounts** is the official list of accounts *tailor-made* for the business. All the company's transactions must be recorded using the official account titles.

We now present the chart of accounts for Cruz Auto Detail. Some of the accounts are new to you, but they will be explained as we move along. When numbering account titles, the 100s are used for assets, the 200s are used for liabilities, the 300s are used for owner's equity accounts, the 400s are used for revenue accounts, and the 500s are used for expense accounts. You will encounter longer account numbers, but the first digit will usually be the same for any service business. In any case, use the exact account titles listed in the company's chart of accounts. Any changes must be approved by management.

Chart of Accounts

Assets

111 Cash
113 Accounts Receivable
115 Supplies
117 Prepaid Insurance
124 Equipment

Liabilities

221 Accounts Payable

Owner's Equity

311 L. A. Cruz, Capital
312 L. A. Cruz, Drawing

Revenue (increase in Owner's Equity)

411 Income from Services

Expenses (decrease in Owner's Equity)

511 Wages Expense
512 Rent Expense
513 Advertising Expense
514 Utilities Expense

Recording Business Transactions

Soon after the opening of Cruz Auto Detail, the first customers arrive, beginning a flow of revenue for the business. Let's examine more transactions of Cruz Auto Detail for the first month of operations.

Transaction (f) Sold services for cash, $3,520. Cruz Auto Detail receives cash revenue of $3,520 in return for services performed for customers over two weeks. In other words, the company earns $3,520 for services performed for cash customers. Revenue has the effect of increasing owner's equity, but because the company wants to know how much revenue is earned, we set up a special column for revenue. The revenue account for Cruz Auto Detail is called Income from Services. The accounting equation is affected as follows (PB stands for previous balance, and NB stands for new balance).

FYI

When setting up and maintaining the chart of accounts on a computer, you may find that you must reserve the 500 accounts for cost accounts (used in a merchandising business). You may need to number expenses as 600s. Read the setup instructions in your software package.

Objective 4

Record a group of business transactions, in column form, involving all five elements of the fundamental accounting equation.

	Assets			= Liabilities +	Owner's Equity	
	Cash +	Equipment +	Supplies	Accounts Payable	L. A. Cruz, + Capital	Revenue
PB (f)	25,000 + +3,520	50,000	+ 800 =	5,800	+ 70,000	
						+3,520 (Income from Services)
NB	28,520 +	50,000	+ 800 =	5,800	+ 70,000 +	3,520

79,320   79,320

(handwritten margin notes)

1) cash
   Rent Expense

2) cash – Asset
   Rent Exp – EQ

3) cash ↓
   Rent Exp

Transaction (g) Paid rent for the month, $900. Shortly after opening the business, Cruz Auto Detail pays the month's rent of $900. Rent is payment for the privilege of occupying a building.

It seems logical that, if revenue is added to owner's equity, then expenses (the opposite of revenue) must be subtracted from owner's equity. To be consistent, a separate column is set up for expenses.

We want to have a running total of the amount of expenses to be subtracted from owner's equity. To keep up this running total, as each new expense is incurred (or comes into being), it must be added to the previous total.

	Assets			= Liabilities +	Owner's Equity		
	Cash +	Equip. +	Supplies	Accounts Payable	L. A. Cruz, + Capital	Revenue −	Expenses
PB (g)	28,520 + −900	50,000 +	800 =	5,800	+ 70,000 +	3,520	
							+900 (Rent Expense)
NB	27,620 +	50,000 +	800 =	5,800	+ 70,000 +	3,520 −	900

78,420   78,420

Banks and other financial institutions sell their services to other businesses as well as to individuals.

Because the time period represented by the rent payment is one month or less, we record the $900 as an expense. If the payment covered a period longer than one month, we would record the amount under an asset called Prepaid Rent.

Let's review the mental process for formulating the entry by asking:

1. **What are the accounts involved?** In this transaction, they are Cash and Rent Expense.

2. **What are the classifications of the accounts involved?** Cash is an asset, and Rent Expense is an expense.

3. **Are the accounts increased or decreased?** Cash is decreased because after the payment we have less cash than we had before. Rent Expense is increased. Thus there is a $900 reduction in total owner's equity as a result of the expense.

4. **Is the equation in balance after the transaction has been recorded?** Yes.

[handwritten: has a value asset]

[handwritten: 1) cash ↓ ↑ prepaid ins ↑   2) Both assets]

Transaction (h) Bought insurance for one year, $360. Cruz Auto Detail pays $360 for a one-year liability insurance policy. At the time of payment, the company has not used up the insurance, so it is not yet an expense. As the insurance expires (is used), it will become an expense. **However, because it is paid in advance for a period longer than one month, it has value and is recorded as an asset.**

	Assets				= Liabilities +		Owner's Equity		
	Cash	+ Equip.	+ Supp.	+ Ppd. Ins.	= Accounts Payable	+ L. A. Cruz, Capital	+ Revenue	− Expenses	
PB	27,620	+ 50,000	+ 800		= 5,800	+ 70,000	+ 3,520	− 900	
(h)	−360			+360					
NB	27,260	+ 50,000	+ 800	+ 360	= 5,800	+ 70,000	+ 3,520	− 900	
		78,420					78,420		

At the end of the year or accounting period, an adjustment will have to be made to take out the expired portion (that is, coverage for the months that have been used up) and record it as an expense. We discuss this adjustment in a later chapter.

Observe that each time a transaction is recorded, the total amount on one side of the equation **remains equal** to the total amount on the other side. As proof of this equality, look at the following computation:

[handwritten: small glance of a financial statement]

Cash	$27,260	Accounts Payable	$ 5,800
Equipment	50,000	L. A. Cruz, Capital	70,000
		Revenue	3,520
Supplies	800		$79,320
Prepaid Insurance	360	Expenses	− 900
	$78,420		$78,420

Steps in Analyzing Transactions

Now that we have recorded transactions in all five classifications of accounts, let's pause to go through the steps we have followed:

Step 1 Read the transaction to understand what is happening and how it affects the business. For example, the business has more revenue, or has more expenses, or has more cash, or owes less to creditors.

Step 2 Identify the accounts involved and decide whether the accounts are increased or decreased. Look for Cash first; you will quickly recognize if cash is coming in or going out.

Step 3 Decide on the classifications of the accounts involved. For example, Equipment is something the business owns, and it's an asset; Accounts Payable is an amount the business owes, and it's a liability; Rent is an expense.

Step 4 After recording the transaction, make sure the accounting equation is in balance.

Transaction (i) Received a bill from *Valley News* for newspaper advertising, $400. Cruz Auto Detail receives a bill from the *Valley News* for newspaper advertising, $400. Cruz Auto Detail has simply received the bill for advertising; it has not paid any cash. Previously, we described an expense as money to be paid for the cost of doing business. An expense of $400 has now been incurred (or has taken place), and it should be recorded as an increase in expenses (Advertising Expense). Also, since the company owes $400 more than it did before and intends to pay at a later time, this amount should be recorded as an increase in Accounts Payable.

	Assets				= Liabilities +		Owner's Equity		
	Cash	+ Equip.	+ Supp.	+ Ppd. Ins.	Accounts Payable	L. A. Cruz, Capital	+ Revenue	− Expenses	
PB (i)	27,260	+ 50,000	+ 800	+ 360 =	5,800 +400	+ 70,000	+ 3,520	− 900 +400 (Advertising Expense)	
NB	27,260	+ 50,000	+ 800	+ 360 =	6,200	+ 70,000	+ 3,520	− 1,300	
			78,420				78,420		

Transaction (j) Sold services on account to Costello Taxi, $1,050. Cruz Auto Detail signs a contract with Costello Taxi to do detailing on credit. Cruz Auto Detail completes a detailing job and bills Costello Taxi $1,050 for services performed.

A company uses the **Accounts Receivable** account to record the amounts due from charge customers (legal claims against charge customers). Since Cruz Auto Detail's claim against Costello Taxi is $1,050 more than before the transaction took place, it seems logical to add $1,050 to Accounts Receivable. Revenue is earned (recognized) when the service is performed, so there is an increase in revenue. Keep in mind that Accounts Receivable is an asset. An asset is something that is owned, and Cruz Auto Detail owns a claim of $1,050 against Costello Taxi.

	Assets					= Liabilities +		Owner's Equity	
	Cash	+ Equip.	+ Supp.	+ Ppd. Ins.	+ Accts. Rec.	Accounts Payable	L. A. Cruz, Capital	+ Revenue	− Expenses
PB (j)	27,260	+ 50,000	+ 800	+ 360	+1,050 =	6,200	+ 70,000	+ 3,520 +1,050 (Income from Services)	− 1,300
NB	27,260	+ 50,000	+ 800	+ 360 +	1,050 =	6,200	+ 70,000	+ 4,570	− 1,300
			79,470					79,470	

When Costello Taxi pays the $1,050 bill in cash, Cruz Auto Detail will record this transaction as an increase in Cash and a decrease in Accounts Receivable. At that time, Cruz Auto Detail will not make an entry in the revenue account, because the revenue was earned and recorded when the service was performed.

Transaction (k) Paid on account to Williams Auto Supply, a creditor, $2,000. Cruz Auto Detail pays $2,000 to Williams Auto Supply, its creditor (the party to whom it owes money), as part payment on account.

	Assets					=	Liabilities +		Owner's Equity		
	Cash	+ Equip.	+ Supp.	+ Ppd. Ins.	+ Accts. Rec.		Accounts Payable	+	L. A. Cruz, Capital	+ Revenue	− Expenses
PB	27,260	+ 50,000	+ 800	+ 360	+ 1,050	=	6,200	+	70,000	+ 4,570	− 1,300
(k)	−2,000						−2,000				
NB	25,260	+ 50,000	+ 800	+ 360	+ 1,050	=	4,200	+	70,000	+ 4,570	− 1,300

77,470 = 77,470

Transaction (l) Received and paid a bill from Midwest Power, Inc., $160. Cruz Auto Detail receives a bill from Midwest Power, Inc., for $160. The accounting equation is affected as follows:

	Assets					=	Liabilities +		Owner's Equity		
	Cash	+ Equip.	+ Supp.	+ Ppd. Ins.	+ Accts. Rec.		Accounts Payable	+	L. A. Cruz, Capital	+ Revenue	− Expenses
PB	25,260	+ 50,000	+ 800	+ 360	+ 1,050	=	4,200	+	70,000	+ 4,570	− 1,300
(l)	−160										+160 (Utilities Expense)
NB	25,100	+ 50,000	+ 800	+ 360	+ 1,050	=	4,200	+	70,000	+ 4,570	− 1,460

77,310 = 77,310

Transaction (m) Paid on account to *Valley News*, a creditor, $400. Cruz Auto Detail pays $400 to the *Valley News* for advertising. Recall that this bill was recorded as a liability in transaction (i). The equation is as follows:

	Assets					=	Liabilities +		Owner's Equity		
	Cash	+ Equip.	+ Supp.	+ Ppd. Ins.	+ Accts. Rec.		Accounts Payable	+	L. A. Cruz, Capital	+ Revenue	− Expenses
PB	25,100	+ 50,000	+ 800	+ 360	+ 1,050	=	4,200	+	70,000	+ 4,570	− 1,460
(m)	−400						−400				
NB	24,700	+ 50,000	+ 800	+ 360	+ 1,050	=	3,800	+	70,000	+ 4,570	− 1,460

76,910 = 76,910

Transaction (n) Paid wages of a part-time employee, $1,400. Cruz Auto Detail pays wages of a part-time employee, $1,400.

	Assets					=	Liabilities +		Owner's Equity		
	Cash	+ Equip.	+ Supp.	+ Ppd. Ins.	+ Accts. Rec.		Accounts Payable	+	L. A. Cruz, Capital	+ Revenue	− Expenses
PB	24,700	+ 50,000	+ 800	+ 360	+ 1,050	=	3,800	+	70,000	+ 4,570	− 1,460
(n)	−1,400										+1,400 (Wages Expense)
NB	23,300	+ 50,000	+ 800	+ 360	+ 1,050	=	3,800	+	70,000	+ 4,570	− 2,860

75,510 = 75,510

Transaction (o) Bought equipment from Williams Auto Supply, $1,500, paying $600 in cash and placing the balance on account. Cruz Auto Detail buys additional equipment from Williams Auto Supply for $1,500, paying $600 down, with the remaining $900 on account. Because buying an item on account is the same as buying it on credit, both *on account* and *on credit* are used to describe such transactions.

	Assets					=	Liabilities +		Owner's Equity		
	Cash	+ Equip.	+ Supp.	+ Ppd. Ins.	+ Accts. Rec.	=	Accounts Payable	+	L. A. Cruz, Capital	+ Revenue	− Expenses
PB	23,300	+ 50,000	+ 800	+ 360	+ 1,050	=	3,800	+	70,000	+ 4,570	− 2,860
(o)	−600	+1,500					+900				
NB	22,700	+ 51,500	+ 800	+ 360	+ 1,050	=	4,700	+	70,000	+ 4,570	− 2,860
	76,410								76,410		

Cruz Auto Detail lists this $1,500 as an increase in assets. Note that three accounts are involved in this transaction: Cash, because cash was paid out; Equipment, because the company has more equipment than before; and Accounts Payable, because the company owes more than before.

Transaction (p) Received cash on account from Costello Taxi, a customer, $850. Cruz Auto Detail receives $850 from Costello Taxi to apply against the amount billed in transaction (j). Costello Taxi now owes Cruz Auto Detail less than it did, and so Cruz Auto Detail deducts the $850 from Accounts Receivable. An exchange of assets has no effect on the total of the equation.

	Assets					=	Liabilities +		Owner's Equity		
	Cash	+ Equip.	+ Supp.	+ Ppd. Ins.	+ Accts. Rec.	=	Accounts Payable	+	L. A. Cruz, Capital	+ Revenue	− Expenses
PB	22,700	+ 51,500	+ 800	+ 360	+ 1,050	=	4,700	+	70,000	+ 4,570	− 2,860
(p)	+850				−850						
NB	23,550	+ 51,500	+ 800	+ 360	+ 200	=	4,700	+	70,000	+ 4,570	− 2,860
	76,410								76,410		

Since Cruz Auto Detail had listed the amount as revenue, it shouldn't be recorded as revenue again. Think of paying income tax on the $850—once is enough.

Transaction (q) Sold services for cash, $2,700. Cruz Auto Detail receives cash revenue of $2,700 in return for services performed for customers for the rest of the month.

	Assets					=	Liabilities +		Owner's Equity		
	Cash	+ Equip.	+ Supp.	+ Ppd. Ins.	+ Accts. Rec.	=	Accounts Payable	+	L. A. Cruz, Capital	+ Revenue	− Expenses
PB	23,550	+ 51,500	+ 800	+ 360	+ 200	=	4,700	+	70,000	+ 4,570	− 2,860
(q)	+2,700									+2,700 (Income from Services)	
NB	26,250	+ 51,500	+ 800	+ 360	+ 200	=	4,700	+	70,000	+ 7,270	− 2,860
	79,110								79,110		

Transaction (r) Cruz withdrew cash for personal use, $3,000. At the end of the month, Cruz withdraws $3,000 in cash from the business for her personal living costs. A **withdrawal** is the taking of cash or other assets out of a business by the owner and is treated as a temporary decrease in owner's equity. Withdrawals are different from expenses. Expenses are paid to someone else for the cost of goods or services used in the business. Withdrawals are paid directly to the owner. A withdrawal may consist of cash or other assets.

Because the owner takes cash out of the business, there is a decrease of $3,000 in Cash. This also decreases Capital, because Cruz has reduced her equity. We record $3,000 as a minus under Capital and label it as Drawing.

	Assets					= Liabilities +		Owner's Equity		
	Cash	+ Equip.	+ Supp.	+ Ppd. Ins.	+ Accts. Rec.	Accounts Payable	L. A. Cruz, Capital	+ Revenue	− Expenses
PB	26,250	+ 51,500	+ 800	+ 360	+ 200	= 4,700	+ 70,000	+ 7,270	− 2,860
(r)	−3,000						−3,000 (Drawing)		
NB	23,250	+ 51,500	+ 800	+ 360	+ 200	= 4,700	+ 67,000	+ 7,270	− 2,860

$$76,110 \qquad\qquad\qquad\qquad 76,110$$

Summary of Transactions f Through r

Figure 1 on the opposite page summarizes business transactions f through r of Cruz Auto Detail, with the transactions identified by letter. To test your understanding of the recording procedure, describe the nature of the transactions.

CHAPTER REVIEW

Review of Performance Objectives

1. Define and identify *asset, liability,* and *owner's equity* accounts.

   Assets are cash, properties, or things of value owned by the business. *Liabilities* are amounts the business owes to creditors. *Owner's equity* is the owner's investment or net worth.

2. Record a group of business transactions, in column form, involving changes in assets, liabilities, and owner's equity.

   The accounting equation is stated as assets equals liabilities plus owner's equity. Under the appropriate classification, a separate column is set up for each account. Transactions are recorded by listing amounts as either additions to or deductions from the various accounts. The equation must always remain in balance.

3. Define and identify *revenue* and *expense* accounts.

   Revenue consists of amounts earned by a business, such as fees earned for performing services, income from selling merchandise, rent income for the use of property, and interest earned for lending money. *Expenses* are the costs of earning revenue—that is, of doing business—such as wages expense, rent expense, interest expense, and advertising expense.

4. Record a group of business transactions, in column form, involving all five elements of the fundamental accounting equation.

FIGURE 1

	Cash	+ Equip.	+ Supp.	+ Ppd. Ins.	+ Accts. Rec.	= Accounts Payable	+ L. A. Cruz, Capital	+ Revenue	− Expenses
Bal.	25,000	+ 50,000	+ 800			= 5,800	+ 70,000		
(f)	+3,520							+3,520 (Income from Services)	
Bal.	28,520	+ 50,000	+ 800			= 5,800	+ 70,000	+ 3,520	
(g)	−900								+900 (Rent Expense)
Bal.	27,620	+ 50,000	+ 800			= 5,800	+ 70,000	+ 3,520	− 900
(h)	−360			+ 360					
Bal.	27,260	+ 50,000	+ 800	+ 360		= 5,800	+ 70,000	+ 3,520	− 900
(i)						+400			+400 (Advertising Expense)
Bal.	27,260	+ 50,000	+ 800	+ 360		= 6,200	+ 70,000	+ 3,520	− 1,300
(j)					+ 1,050			+1,050 (Income from Services)	
Bal.	27,260	+ 50,000	+ 800	+ 360	+ 1,050	= 6,200	+ 70,000	+ 4,570	− 1,300
(k)	−2,000					−2,000			
Bal.	25,260	+ 50,000	+ 800	+ 360	+ 1,050	= 4,200	+ 70,000	+ 4,570	− 1,300
(l)	−160								+160 (Utilities Expense)
Bal.	25,100	+ 50,000	+ 800	+ 360	+ 1,050	= 4,200	+ 70,000	+ 4,570	− 1,460
(m)	−400					−400			
Bal.	24,700	+ 50,000	+ 800	+ 360	+ 1,050	= 3,800	+ 70,000	+ 4,570	− 1,460
(n)	−1,400								+1,400 (Wages Expense)
Bal.	23,300	+ 50,000	+ 800	+ 360	+ 1,050	= 3,800	+ 70,000	+ 4,570	− 2,860
(o)	−600	+1,500				+900			
Bal.	22,700	+ 51,500	+ 800	+ 360	+ 1,050	= 4,700	+ 70,000	+ 4,570	− 2,860
(p)	+850				−850				
Bal.	23,550	+ 51,500	+ 800	+ 360	+ 200	= 4,700	+ 70,000	+ 4,570	− 2,860
(q)	+2,700							+ 2,700 (Income from Services)	
Bal.	26,250	+ 51,500	+ 800	+ 360	+ 200	= 4,700	+ 70,000	+ 7,270	− 2,860
(r)	−3,000						−3,000 (Drawing)		
Bal.	23,250	+ 51,500	+ 800	+ 360	+ 200	= 4,700	+ 67,000	+ 7,270	− 2,860

Life Side of Equals Sign

Cash	$23,250
Equipment	51,500
Supplies	800
Prepaid Insurance	360
Accounts Receivable	200
	$76,110

Right Side of Equals Sign

Accounts Payable	$ 4,700
L. A. Cruz, Capital	67,000
Revenue	7,270
	$78,970
Expenses	−2,860
	$76,110

The accounting equation has been expanded and appears as follows:

Assets = Liabilities + Owner's Equity (Capital) + Revenue − Expenses

Accounts are classified and listed under each heading. Transactions are recorded by listing amounts as either additions to or deductions from the various accounts. The equation must always remain in balance.

Glossary

Accounts The categories under the Assets, Liabilities, and Owner's Equity headings. (10)

Accounts Payable A liability account used for short-term liabilities or charge accounts, usually due within thirty days. (11)

Accounts Receivable An account used to record the amounts owed by charge customers (legal claims against charge customers). (17)

Assets Cash, properties, and other things of value owned by an economic unit or business entity. (7)

Business entity A business enterprise, separate and distinct from the persons who supply the assets it uses. Property acquired by a business is an asset of the business. The owner is separate from the business and in fact has claims on it and a responsibility for its debts. (7)

Capital The owner's investment, or equity, in an enterprise. (8)

Chart of accounts The official list of account titles to be used to record the transactions of a business. (14)

Creditor One to whom money is owed. (8)

Double-entry accounting The system by which each business transaction is recorded in at least two accounts and the accounting equation is kept in balance. (12)

Equity The value of a right or claim to or financial interest in an asset or group of assets. (8)

Expenses The costs that relate to earning revenue (the costs of doing business); examples are wages, rent, interest, and advertising. They may be paid in cash, immediately or at a future time (accounts payable). (13)

Fundamental accounting equation (Assets = Liabilities + Owner's Equity) An equation expressing the relationship of assets, liabilities, and owner's equity. (8)

Liabilities Debts, or amounts owed to creditors. (8)

Owner's equity The owner's right to or investment in the business. (8)

Revenues The amounts a business earns; examples are fees earned for performing services, sales of merchandise, rent income, and interest income. They may be in the form of cash, credit card receipts, or accounts receivable (charge accounts). (13)

Separate entity concept The concept according to which a business is treated as a separate economic or accounting entity. The business stands by itself, separate from its owners, creditors, and customers. (10)

Sole proprietorship A one-owner business. (10)

Withdrawal The taking of cash or other assets out of a business by the owner for his or her own use. (This is also referred to as *drawing*.) A withdrawal is treated as a temporary decrease in owner's equity. (20)

QUESTIONS, EXERCISES, AND PROBLEMS

Discussion Questions

1. Define assets, liabilities, owner's equity, revenues, and expenses.
2. Explain the separate entity concept.
3. How do Accounts Receivable and Accounts Payable differ?
4. Describe two ways to increase owner's equity and two ways to decrease owner's equity.
5. How will the fundamental accounting equation change if supplies are purchased on account? Explain how this purchase will or will not change the owner's equity.
6. When an owner withdraws cash or goods from the business, why is this considered an increase to the Drawing account and not a wages account?
7. Define *chart of accounts,* and identify the categories of accounts.
8. What account titles might you suggest for the chart of accounts for a pet grooming shop owned by C. D. Tran? List the accounts by account category and include an appropriate account number for each.

Exercises

P.O. 1

Calculate missing items in the accounting equation.

Exercise 1-1 Complete the following equations:

a. Assets of $21,000 = Liabilities of $7,200 + Owner's Equity of $_____
b. Assets of $_____ − Liabilities of $19,000 = Owner's Equity of $28,000
c. Assets of $26,000 − Owner's Equity of $14,200 = Liabilities of $_____

P.O. 1

Calculate missing items in the accounting equation.

Exercise 1-2 Determine the following amounts:

a. The amount of the liabilities of a business that has $58,580 in assets and in which the owner has $34,300 equity.
b. The equity of the owner of a van that cost $28,000 who owes $6,200 on an installment loan payable to the bank.
c. The amount of the assets of a business that has $8,730 in liabilities and in which the owner has $21,500 equity.

P.O. 1

Formulate the accounting equation.

Exercise 1-3 Dr. J. O. Strain is an optometrist. As of December 31, Dr. Strain owned the following property that related to his professional practice, Strain Optical Clinic:

Cash, $1,040
Supplies, $950
Professional Equipment, $30,000
Office Equipment, $6,230

On the same date, he owed the following business creditors:

Borian Supply Company, $2,956
Ramirez Equipment Sales, $3,200

Compute the following amounts in the accounting equation:

Assets $_____ = Liabilities $_____ + Owner's Equity $_____

P.O. 1,3

Describe transactions affecting
the accounting equation.

Exercise 1-4 Describe a business transaction that will do the following:

a. Increase an asset and increase a liability
b. Decrease an asset and decrease a liability
c. Decrease an asset and increase an expense
d. Increase an asset and increase owner's equity
e. Increase an asset and decrease an asset
f. Increase an asset and increase revenue

P.O. 2

Describe various transactions.

Exercise 1-5 Describe a transaction that resulted in the following entries:

	Assets			=	Liabilities	+	Owner's Equity
	Cash	+ Supplies +	Equipment		Accounts Payable		L. Junko, Capital
(a)	+12,500						+12,500
(b)	−1,800		+1,800				
Bal.	10,700 +	+	1,800	=		+	12,500
(c)		+350			+350		
Bal.	10,700 +	350 +	1,800	=	350	+	12,500
(d)	−1,000		+5,000		+4,000		
Bal.	9,700 +	350 +	6,800	=	4,350	+	12,500
(e)	−1,500				−1,500		
Bal.	8,200 +	350 +	6,800	=	2,850	+	12,500

P.O. 1,3

Classify accounts.

Exercise 1-6 Label the following accounts as asset (A), liability (L), owner's equity (OE), revenue (R), or expense (E):

a. Office Supplies
b. Professional Fees
c. Prepaid Insurance
d. R. L. Osborn, Drawing
e. Accounts Payable
f. Service Income
g. R. L. Osborn, Capital
h. Rent Expense
i. Accounts Receivable
j. Wages Expense

P.O. 4

Describe various transactions.

Exercise 1-7 Describe a transaction that resulted in the following changes in accounts:

a. Rent Expense is increased by $930, and Cash is decreased by $930.
b. Advertising Expense is increased by $237, and Accounts Payable is increased by $237.
c. Accounts Receivable is increased by $226, and Service Income is increased by $226.
d. Cash is decreased by $390, and L. J. Miller, Drawing, is increased by $390.
e. Equipment is increased by $644, Cash is decreased by $200, and Accounts Payable is increased by $444.
f. Cash is increased by $370, and Accounts Receivable is decreased by $370.

P.O. 4

Describe various transactions.

Exercise 1-8 Describe the transactions that are recorded in the following equation.

	Assets			= Liabilities +	Owner's Equity		
	Cash +	Accounts Receivable +	Equipment	Accounts Payable	S. Yamamoto, + Capital	Revenue −	Expenses
(a)	+18,000		+6,000		+24,000		
(b)	−920						+920 (Rent Expense)
Bal.	17,080 +		+ 6,000 =	+	24,000 +	−	920
(c)		+2,900				+2,900 (Service Income)	
Bal.	17,080 +	2,900 +	6,000 =	+	24,000 +	2,900 −	920
(d)	−3,000		+12,000	+9,000			
Bal.	14,080 +	2,900 +	18,000 =	9,000 +	24,000 +	2,900 −	920
(e)	−2,400				−2,400 (Drawing)		
Bal.	11,680 +	2,900 +	18,000 =	9,000 +	21,600 +	2,900 −	920
	Total	32,580			Total	32,580	

CONSIDER AND COMMUNICATE

If a bookkeeper accidentally increased the Cash account by $450 when it should have been decreased after purchasing equipment for cash, what changes would take place in the equation? What other outcomes might there be in this situation?

WHAT IF . . .

The owner of a business needed cash for personal use, and there was enough cash in the account to cover the check. What if the owner then entered the transaction as a decrease to Cash and an increase to Wages Expense? Describe the effect on the fundamental accounting equation. Is it still in balance? Was this a correct recording of the transaction? If not, how should it have been recorded?

CRITICAL THINKING

Please read the following memorandum and follow the instructions set forth.

MEMORANDUM

TO:	Your Name	DATE:	July 31, 20—
FROM:	Kathy Dunn, Supervisor	SUBJECT:	Calculations for Lawrence Co.

Please provide the following ASAP (as soon as possible).

1. The balance of cash in Lawrence Company's checkbook shows $6,290. I need to know if this ties to or matches the Cash account

balance. I do know that total assets amount to $42,770, and Equipment amounts to $34,180. Other noncash assets are Supplies, $800, and Prepaid Insurance, $1,500.
2. C. Lawrence, the owner, wants to know the amount of her owner's equity. I pulled the outstanding bills, which amount to $6,174.
3. Please put the information in a memo addressed to me.
4. Thank you for your prompt response.

PROBLEM SET A

For additional help, see the demonstration problem at the beginning of each chapter in your Working Papers.

P.O. 1,2,3,4

Problem 1-1A In July of this year, B. R. Peters established a business called Sunshine Realty. The account headings are presented below. Transactions completed during the month follow.

Assets			= Liabilities +		Owner's Equity	
Cash +	Office Supplies +	Office Equipment	Accounts Payable	Capital	, + Revenue −	Expenses

a. Peters deposited $11,500 in a bank account in the name of the business.
b. Paid the office rent for the current month, $800, Ck. No. 1000 (Rent Expense).
c. Bought office supplies, paying cash, $253, Ck. No. 1001.
d. Bought office equipment on account from Brennan Computers, $3,485.
e. Received a bill from the *Weekly Journal* for advertising, $574 (Advertising Expense).
f. Paid on account to Brennan Computers, a creditor, $900, Ck. No. 1002.
g. Sold services for cash, $4,230 (Service Income).
h. Received and paid the bill for utilities, $296, Ck. No. 1003 (Utilities Expense).
i. Paid on account to the *Weekly Journal,* a creditor, $574, Ck. No. 1004.
j. Paid auto expenses, $341, Ck. No. 1005 (Auto Expense).
k. Peters withdrew cash for personal use, $1,150, Ck. No. 1006 (Drawing).

Check Figure

Left side of equals sign total, $15,154

Instructions

1. In the equation, write the owner's name above the term *Capital.*
2. Record the transactions and the balance after each transaction. Identify the account affected when the transaction involves revenue, expenses, or a withdrawal.
3. Write the account totals from the left side of the equals sign and add them. Write the account totals from the right side of the equals sign and add them. If the two totals are not equal, first check the addition and subtraction. If you still cannot find the error, reanalyze each transaction.

P.O. 1,2,3,4

Problem 1-2A In March, L. P. Sloan, M.D., established the Sloan Sports Medicine Clinic. The clinic's account headings are presented below. Transactions completed during the month of March follow.

Assets			=	Liabilities +		Owner's Equity	

Cash + Supplies + Professional +   Office   Accounts   , + Revenue − Expenses
                    Equipment   Equipment   Payable   Capital

a. Sloan deposited $25,000 in a bank account in the name of the business.
b. Paid the rent for the month, $1,100, Ck. No. 1000 (Rent Expense).
c. Bought supplies on account from Offices Inc., $850.
d. Bought professional equipment on account from Liu Company, $7,600.
e. Received a bill from the *Weekly Chronicle* for advertising, $585 (Advertising Expense).
f. Paid on account to Liu Company, a creditor, $2,860, Ck. No. 1001.
g. Sold professional services for cash, $5,455 (Professional Fees).
h. Received and paid the bill for utilities, $384, Ck. No. 1002 (Utilities Expense).
i. Paid the salary of the assistant, $1,800, Ck. No. 1003 (Salary Expense).
j. Bought a copy machine on account from Velos Office Equipment, $4,400.
k. Sloan withdrew cash for personal use, $2,500, Ck. No. 1004 (Drawing).

Check Figure

Cash, $21,811

Instructions

1. In the equation, write the owner's name above the term *Capital.*
2. Record the transactions and the balance after each transaction. Identify the account affected when the transaction involves revenue, expenses, or a withdrawal.
3. Write the account totals from the left side of the equals sign and add them. Write the account totals from the right side of the equals sign and add them. If the two totals are not equal, first check the addition and subtraction. If you still cannot find the error, reanalyze each transaction.

P.O. 1,2,3,4

Problem 1-3A P. K. Asher, Attorney at Law, opened her office on October 1. The account headings are presented below. Transactions completed during the month follow.

Assets				=	Liabilities +		Owner's Equity	

Cash + Office + Prepaid +   Office   + Library   Accounts   , + Revenue − Expenses
         Supplies   Insurance   Equipment   Payable   Capital

a. Asher deposited $20,000 in a bank account in the name of the business.
b. Bought office equipment on account from Norbert Equipment Company, $12,600.
c. Asher invested her personal law library, which cost $5,800. (Increase the account Library and increase the account P. K. Asher, Capital.)
d. Paid the office rent for the month, $850, Ck. No. 2000 (Rent Expense).
e. Bought office supplies for cash, $773, Ck. No. 2001.
f. Bought insurance for two years, $495, Ck. No. 2002.
g. Sold legal services for cash, $3,248 (Professional Fees).
h. Received and paid the telephone bill, $216, Ck. No. 2003 (Telephone Expense).
i. Paid the salary of the part-time receptionist, $890, Ck. No. 2004 (Salary Expense).
j. Bought gas and oil for the van, paying cash, $105, Ck. No. 2005 (Van Expense).

k. Sold legal services for cash, $2,240 (Professional Fees).
l. Paid on account to Norbert Equipment Company, a creditor, $1,800, Ck. No. 2006.
m. Asher withdrew cash for personal use, $2,150, Ck. No. 2007 (Drawing).

Check Figure

Right side of equals sign total, $37,877

Instructions

1. In the equation, write the owner's name above the term *Capital.*
2. Record the transactions and the balance after each transaction. Identify the account affected when the transaction involves revenue, expenses, or a withdrawal.
3. Write the account totals from the left side of the equals sign and add them. Write the account totals from the right side of the equals sign and add them. If the two totals are not equal, first check the addition and subtraction. If you still cannot find the error, reanalyze each transaction.

P.O. 1,2,3,4

Problem 1-4A R. C. Nye started Nye's Pest Service on May 1 of this year. The account headings are presented below. During May, Nye completed the transactions that follow.

Assets						= Liabilities +		Owner's Equity	
Cash +	Accounts Receivable	+ Supplies +	Prepaid Insurance	+ Truck +	Equipment	Accounts Payable	Capital	, + Revenue	− Expenses

a. Nye deposited $8,000 in a bank account in the name of the business.
b. Bought a used truck from Essen Motors for $15,650, paying $2,100 in cash, and placing the remainder on account.
c. Bought equipment on account from Granger Company, $2,800.
d. Paid the rent for the month, $850, Ck. No. 3001 (Rent Expense).
e. Bought insurance for the truck for the year, $825, Ck. No. 3002, Policy No. 311D.
f. Sold services for cash for the first half of the month, $3,264 (Service Income).
g. Bought supplies for cash, $462, Ck. No. 3003.
h. Sold services on account, $822 (Service Income).
i. Received and paid the bill for utilities, $188, Ck. No. 3004 (Utilities Expense).
j. Received a bill for gas and oil for the truck, $238 (Truck Expense).
k. Sold services for cash for the remainder of the month, $2,784 (Service Income).
l. Nye withdrew cash for personal use, $1,350, Ck. No. 3005.
m. Paid wages to the employees, $2,420, Ck. Nos. 3006–3008 (Wages Expense).

Check Figure

Cash, $5,853

Instructions

1. In the equation, write the owner's name above the term *Capital.*
2. Record the transactions and the balance after each transaction. Identify the account affected when the transaction involves revenue, expenses, or a withdrawal.
3. Write the account totals from the left side of the equals sign and add them. Write the account totals from the right side of the equals sign and add them. If the two totals are not equal, first check the addition and subtraction. If you still cannot find the error, reanalyze each transaction.

PROBLEM SET B

For additional help, see the demonstration problem at the beginning of each chapter in your Working Papers.

P.O. 1,2,3,4

Problem 1-1B On June 1 of this year, R. B. Ayala, Optometrist, established the Ayala Eye Clinic. The clinic's account names are presented below. Transactions completed during the month follow.

Assets			= Liabilities +		Owner's Equity		
Cash +	Office Supplies	+ Office Equipment	Accounts Payable	Capital	, + Revenue	− Expenses

a. Ayala deposited $12,000 in a bank account in the name of the business.
b. Paid the office rent for the month, $730, Ck. No. 1001 (Rent Expense).
c. Bought supplies for cash, $652, Ck. No. 1002.
d. Bought office equipment on account from Foster Company, $4,568.
e. Bought office equipment from Wesley Office Supply, $2,950, paying $500 in cash and placing the balance on account, Ck. No. 1003.
f. Sold professional services for cash, $1,540 (Professional Fees).
g. Paid on account to Wesley Office Supply, a creditor, $1,200, Ck. No. 1004.
h. Received and paid the bill for utilities, $242, Ck. No. 1005 (Utilities Expense).
i. Paid the salary of the assistant, $1,230, Ck. No. 1006 (Salary Expense).
j. Sold professional services for cash, $2,528 (Professional Fees).
k. Ayala withdrew cash for personal use, $1,530, Ck. No. 1007 (Drawing).

Check Figure

Left side of equals sign total, $18,154

Instructions

1. In the equation, write the owner's name above the term *Capital.*
2. Record the transactions and the balance after each transaction. Identify the account affected when the transaction involves revenue, expenses, or a withdrawal.
3. Write the account totals from the left side of the equals sign and add them. Write the account totals from the right side of the equals sign and add them. If the two totals are not equal, first check the addition and subtraction. If you still cannot find the error, reanalyze each transaction.

P.O. 1,2,3,4

Problem 1-2B On July 1 of this year, S. E. Taylor, D.C., established the Taylor Chiropractic Clinic. The organization's account headings are presented below. Transactions completed during the month of July follow.

Assets			= Liabilities +		Owner's Equity		
Cash +	Supplies +	Professional Equipment +	Office Equipment	Accounts Payable	Capital	, + Revenue	− Expenses

a. Taylor deposited $16,000 in a bank account in the name of the business.
b. Paid the office rent for the month, $1,000, Ck. No. 2001 (Rent Expense).
c. Bought supplies for cash, $685, Ck. No. 2002.
d. Bought professional equipment on account from Chiropractic Equipment Company, $18,435 (Professional Equipment).

e. Bought office equipment from Dotcom Computers, $3,295, paying $990 in cash and placing the balance on account, Ck. No. 2003.
f. Sold professional services for cash, $1,160 (Professional Fees).
g. Paid on account to Dotcom Computers, a creditor, $900, Ck. No. 2004.
h. Received and paid the bill for utilities, $227, Ck. No. 2005 (Utilities Expense).
i. Paid the salary of the assistant, $1,326, Ck. No. 2006 (Salary Expense).
j. Sold professional services for cash, $1,285 (Professional Fees).
k. Taylor withdrew cash for personal use, $1,600, Ck. No. 2007 (Drawing).

Check Figure

Cash, $11,717

Instructions

1. In the equation, write the owner's name above the term *Capital*.
2. Record the transactions and the balance after each transaction. Identify the account affected when the transaction involves revenue, expenses, or a withdrawal.
3. Write the account totals from the left side of the equals sign and add them. Write the account totals from the right side of the equals sign and add them. If the two totals are not equal, first check the addition and subtraction. If you still cannot find the error, reanalyze each transaction.

P.O. 1,2,3,4

Problem 1-3B A. P. Manley, a graphic artist, opened a studio for her professional practice on August 1. The account headings are presented below. Transactions completed during the month follow.

Assets					= Liabilities +		Owner's Equity		
Cash +	Office Supplies	+ Prepaid Insurance	+ Office Equipment	+ Library	Accounts Payable	Capital	, + Revenue	− Expenses

a. Manley deposited $15,500 in a bank account in the name of the business.
b. Bought office equipment on account from Specialized Equipment Company, $8,430.
c. Manley invested her personal library, $6,500. (Increase the account Library and increase the account A. P. Manley, Capital.)
d. Paid the rent for the month, $960, Ck. No. 1000 (Rent Expense).
e. Bought office supplies for cash, $836, Ck. No. 1001.
f. Bought insurance for two years, $890, Ck. No. 1002.
g. Sold graphic services for cash, $1,460 (Professional Fees).
h. Paid the salary of the part-time assistant, $800, Ck. No. 1003 (Salary Expense).
i. Received and paid the bill for telephone service, $182, Ck. No. 1004 (Telephone Expense).
j. Paid on account to Specialized Equipment Company, a creditor, $550, Ck. No. 1005.
k. Sold graphic services for cash, $1,548 (Professional Fees).
l. Paid cash for minor repairs to graphics equipment, $68, Ck. No. 1006 (Repair Expense).
m. Manley withdrew cash for personal use, $1,050, Ck. No. 1007 (Drawing).

Check Figure

Right side of equals sign total, $29,828

Instructions

1. In the equation, write the owner's name above the term *Capital*.
2. Record the transactions and the balance after each transaction. Identify the account affected when the transaction involves revenue, expenses, or a withdrawal.

3. Write the account totals from the left side of the equals sign and add them. Write the account totals from the right side of the equals sign and add them. If the two totals are not equal, first check the addition and subtraction. If you still cannot find the error, reanalyze each transaction.

P.O. 1,2,3,4

Problem 1-4B On March 1 of this year, L. P. Duong established Duong's Catering Service. The account headings are presented below. Transactions completed during the month follow.

			Assets			= Liabilities +		Owner's Equity	
Cash +	Accounts Receivable	+ Supplies +	Prepaid Insurance	+ Truck +	Equipment	Accounts Payable	Capital	, + Revenue −	Expenses

a. Duong deposited $15,000 in a bank account in the name of the business.
b. Bought a truck from Crandal Motors for $12,580, paying $2,500 in cash and placing the balance on account, Ck. No. 500.
c. Bought catering equipment on account from Castor Company, $2,520.
d. Paid the rent for the month, $695, Ck. No. 501 (Rent Expense).
e. Sold catering services for cash for the first half of the month, $1,810 (Catering Income).
f. Bought insurance for the truck for one year, $686, Ck. No. 502.
g. Bought catering supplies for cash, $285, Ck. No. 503.
h. Received and paid the heating bill, $140, Ck. No. 504 (Utilities Expense).
i. Received a bill from Quick Gas and Lube for gas and oil for the truck, $93 (Truck Expense).
j. Sold catering services on account, $927 (Catering Income).
k. Sold catering services for cash for the remainder of the month, $2,521 (Catering Income).
l. Paid the salary of the assistant, $1,342, Ck. No. 505 (Salary Expense).
m. Duong withdrew cash for personal use, $1,350, Ck. No. 506 (Drawing).

Check Figure

Cash, $12,333

Instructions

1. In the equation, write the owner's name above the term *Capital.*
2. Record the transactions and the balance after each transaction. Identify the account affected when the transaction involves revenue, expenses, or a withdrawal.
3. Write the account totals from the left side of the equals sign and add them. Write the account totals from the right side of the equals sign and add them. If the two totals are not equal, first check the addition and subtraction. If you still cannot find the error, reanalyze each transaction.

2

T Accounts, Debits and Credits, Trial Balance, and Financial Statements

Performance Objectives

After you have completed this chapter, you will be able to do the following:

1. Determine balances of T accounts having entries recorded on both sides of the accounts.

2. Present the fundamental accounting equation with the T account form, and label the plus and minus sides.

3. Present the fundamental accounting equation with the T account form, and label the debit and credit sides.

4. Record directly in T accounts a group of business transactions involving changes in asset, liability, owner's equity, revenue, and expense accounts for a service business.

5. Prepare a trial balance.

6. Prepare (a) an income statement, (b) a statement of owner's equity, and (c) a balance sheet.

7. Prepare (a) an income statement involving more than one revenue account and a net loss, and (b) a statement of owner's equity with an additional investment and either a net income or a net loss.

8. Recognize the effect of transpositions and slides on account balances.

We introduced the fundamental accounting equation as *Assets = Liabilities + Owner's Equity*. We also discussed the recording of transactions involving two new classifications of accounts: *Revenue* and *Expenses*. With the addition of Revenue and Expenses, the fundamental accounting equation was brought up to its full size of five account classifications. There are only five classifications; so, as far as you go in accounting—whether you are dealing with a small, one-owner business or a large corporation—there will be these five major classifications of accounts.

In this chapter, we will record the same transactions in T account form, and we will prove the equality of both sides of the fundamental accounting equation. We will do this by means of a trial balance, which we will discuss later in this chapter.

THE T ACCOUNT FORM

So far, we have recorded business transactions in a column arrangement. For example, the Cash account column in the books of Cruz Auto Detail is shown below.

Cash Account Column

Transaction	**(a)**	70,000
Transaction	**(b)**	−43,000
Balance		27,000
Transaction	**(d)**	−2,000
Balance		25,000
Transaction	**(f)**	+3,520
Balance		28,520
Transaction	**(g)**	−900
Balance		27,620
Transaction	**(h)**	−360
Balance		27,260
Transaction	**(k)**	−2,000
Balance		25,260
Transaction	**(l)**	−160
Balance		25,100
Transaction	**(m)**	−400
Balance		24,700
Transaction	**(n)**	−1,400
Balance		23,300
Transaction	**(o)**	−600
Balance		22,700
Transaction	**(p)**	+850
Balance		23,550
Transaction	**(q)**	+2,700
Balance		26,250
Transaction	**(r)**	−3,000
		23,250

Cash

	+		−
(a)	70,000	**(b)**	43,000
(f)	3,520	**(d)**	2,000
(p)	850	**(g)**	900
(q)	2,700	**(h)**	360
	77,070	**(k)**	2,000
		(l)	160
		(m)	400
		(n)	1,400
		(o)	600
Balance →	23,250	**(r)**	3,000
			53,820

Footings

As an introduction to the recording of transactions, the column arrangement had the following advantages:

1. In the process of analyzing the transaction, you
   a. Recognized the need to determine which accounts are involved.
   b. Determined the classification of the accounts involved.
   c. Decided whether the transaction resulted in an increase or a decrease in each of these accounts.

2. You further realized that, after each transaction had been recorded, the two sides of the fundamental accounting equation were in balance. In other words, the total of one side of the accounting equation equaled the total of the other side.

Now, instead of recording transactions in a column for each account, we will use a **T account form** for each account. *The T account form has the advantage of providing two sides for each account; one side is used to record increases in the account, and the other side is used to record decreases.*

After we record a group of transactions in a T account, we add both sides and record the totals in small, pencil-written figures called **footings**. Next, we subtract one footing from the other to determine the balance of the account. For the Cash account, shown previously, the balance is $23,250 ($77,070 − $53,820).

We now record the balance on the side of the account having the larger footing, which, with a few minor exceptions, is the plus (+) side. The plus side of a T account is the side that represents the **normal balance** of that account. The normal balance may, however, fall on either the left or the right side of an account, depending on what type of account it is. To review, we presented the T account for Cash; Cash is classified as an asset, and all assets look like the following T account:

Objective 1

Determine balances of T accounts having entries recorded on both sides of the accounts.

Assets

+	−
Left	Right

However, **not all classifications of accounts have the increase side on the left.**

Recall that we placed revenue and expenses under the "umbrella" of owner's equity. Revenue increases owner's equity, and expenses decrease owner's equity. The T accounts for this situation are as follows:

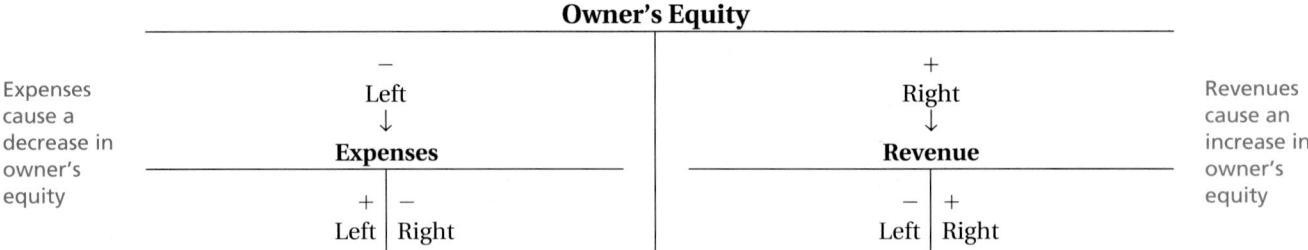

Increases in owner's equity are recorded on the right side of the account. Because revenue increases owner's equity, additions to revenue are also recorded on the right side.

Decreases in owner's equity are recorded on the left side of the account. Because expenses decrease owner's equity, additions to expenses are also recorded on the left side.

Using the five classifications of accounts, the fundamental accounting equation looks like this:

Assets = Liabilities +   Owner's Equity

Capital + Revenue − Expenses

■ ■ ■

Remember!

The entry for a business transaction may include any combination of pluses and minuses: pluses and pluses, pluses and minuses, or minuses and minuses.

Because revenue and expenses appear separately in the income statement, we will stretch out the equation to include them as separate headings, like this:

Assets = Liabilities + Capital + Revenue − Expenses

We can now restate the equation with the T forms and plus and minus signs for each account classification:

Assets	=	Liabilities	+	Owner's Equity	+	Revenue	−	Expenses
+ | −		− | +		− | +		− | +		+ | −
Left | Right		Left | Right		Left | Right		Left | Right		Left | Right

■ ■ ■

Objective 2

Present the fundamental accounting equation with the T account form, and label the plus and minus sides.

Before we go on, let us point out the increase, or plus, side of each account classification. You can recognize these in the accounting equation using T accounts.

Assets	The *left* side is the *increase* side.
Liabilities	The *right* side is the *increase* side.
Owner's Equity	The *right* side is the *increase* side
Revenue	The *right* side is the *increase* side.
Expenses	The *left* side is the *increase* side.

Because revenue is an addition to owner's equity, the placement of the plus and minus signs is the same as for owner's equity. On the other hand, because expenses are treated as deductions from owner's equity, the placement of the plus and minus signs is reversed. We will use this form of the fundamental accounting equation throughout the remainder of the text.

Your accounting background up to this point has taught you to analyze business transactions to determine which accounts are involved and to recognize that each amount should be recorded as either an increase or a decrease in these accounts. Now the recording process becomes a simple matter of knowing which side of the T accounts should be used to record increases and which should be used to record decreases. **Generally, you will not be using the minus side of the revenue and expense accounts, since transactions involving revenue and expense accounts usually result in increases in these accounts.** An exception to this statement is where errors have been made and require correction. Let's now add the last element to the T account before we record the familiar Cruz Auto Detail transactions.

THE T ACCOUNT FORM WITH DEBITS AND CREDITS

Objective 3

Present the fundamental accounting equation with the T account form, and label the debit and credit sides.

The left side of a T account is called the **debit** side; the right side is called the **credit** side. The T accounts representing the accounting equation now contain both the signs and the words *Debit* and *Credit*. There are only five classifications of accounts. These classifications are contained in the fundamental accounting equation:

Assets	=	**Liabilities**	+	**Owner's Equity**	+	**Revenue**	−	**Expenses**
+ −		− +		− +		− +		+ −
Debit Credit		Debit Credit		Debit Credit		Debit Credit		Debit Credit

The following table summarizes debits and credits and how they are affected by increases and decreases. **The critical rule to remember is that the amount placed on the debit side of one or more accounts MUST equal the amount placed on the credit side of another account or accounts.**

Debits Signify		**Credits Signify**	
Increases in	Assets Drawing Expenses	Decreases in	Assets Drawing Expenses
Decreases in	Liabilities Capital Revenue	Increases in	Liabilities Capital Revenue

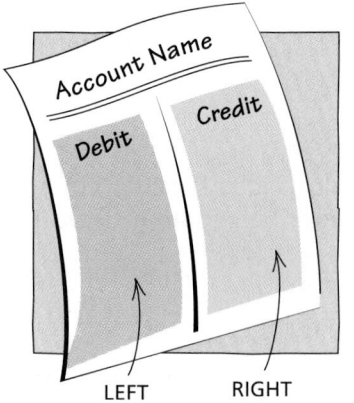

Debit is always the left side of the account, and credit is always the right side of an account. The + or −, however, changes with the type of account.

Before we begin recording, notice the new T account below the Capital account, L. A. Cruz, Drawing. Recall that the Capital account is increased when amounts are invested and decreased when amounts are taken out.

Capital

−	+
Debit	Credit
	Amounts in

Drawing

+	−
Debit	Credit
Amounts withdrawn	

We reserve the minus or debit side of the Capital account for permanent withdrawals, those made when the owner decides to reduce the size of the business permanently or when a net loss forces such a reduction. This concept is best illustrated by showing the Drawing T account under the umbrella of the Capital account.

Capital

−	+
Debit	Credit

Drawing

+	−
Debit	Credit

RECORDING BUSINESS TRANSACTIONS IN T ACCOUNTS

Objective 4

Record directly in T accounts a group of business transactions involving changes in asset, liability, capital, revenue, and expense accounts for a service business.

Our task now is to learn how to record business transactions in the T account form. First, let's review the steps in analyzing a business transaction.

1. **Decide which accounts are involved.**
2. **Classify the accounts involved** (asset, liability, capital, revenue, expense).
3. **Decide if the accounts involved are increased or decreased.**
4. **Decide which accounts are debited and which accounts are credited.**
5. **Check to see if the equation is in balance after the transaction has been recorded.**

For example, let's analyze the first transaction of the Cruz Auto Detail transactions using this five-step process. To formulate the entry, you must be able to visualize the fundamental accounting equation in the form of T accounts. With that in mind, the first transaction is as follows:

In transaction (a), Cruz deposited $70,000 cash in a bank account in the name of the business. This transaction results in an increase to Cash with a debit and an increase in the Capital account with a credit.

1. **Decide which accounts are involved.** The two accounts involved are Cash and L. A. Cruz, Capital.
2. **Classify the accounts involved (asset, liability, capital, revenue, expense).** Cash is an asset and L. A. Cruz, Capital, is an owner's equity account.
3. **Decide if the accounts involved are increased or decreased.** Cash is being deposited in the bank account, an increase to Cash. The owner has invested that cash in the business and has increased L. A. Cruz, Capital.
4. **Write the transaction as a debit to one account (or accounts) and a credit to another account (or accounts).** Since Cash is an asset and Cash is increased, Cash is debited. We now need an offsetting credit. L. A. Cruz, Capital, is an owner's equity account and is increased. L. A. Cruz, Capital, is credited. You now have a debit equal to a credit.
5. **Check:** There is at least one account debited and at least one account credited, *and* the total amount(s) debited equal the total amount(s) credited. **You now have a debit equal to a credit, a $70,000 debit to Cash and a $70,000 credit to L. A. Cruz, Capital.**

Stores such as this bike shop classify revenue accounts for each service activity—sales, repairs, and rentals. They may also classify expense accounts separately.

The resulting transaction in T account form follows:

Cash			L. A. Cruz, Capital	
+	−		−	+
Debit	Credit		Debit	Credit
(a) 70,000				(a) 70,000

In transaction (b), Cruz Auto Detail bought equipment, paying cash, $43,000. This transaction results in an increase to Equipment with a debit and a decrease to Cash with a credit.

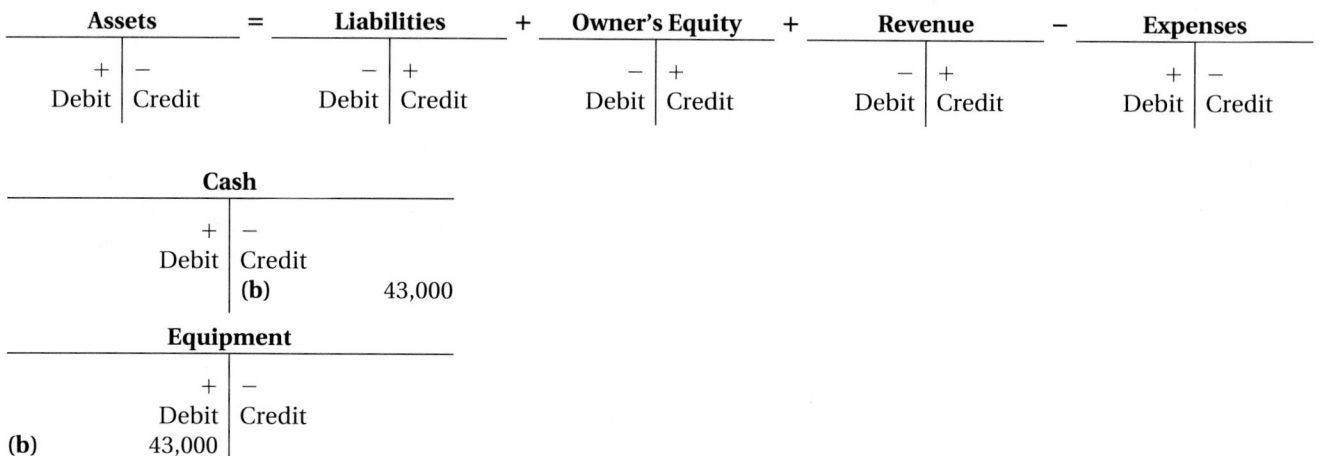

Assets		=	Liabilities		+	Owner's Equity		+	Revenue		−	Expenses	
+	−		−	+		−	+		−	+		+	−
Debit	Credit		Debit	Credit		Debit	Credit		Debit	Credit		Debit	Credit

Cash

+	−
Debit	Credit
	(b) 43,000

Equipment

+	−
Debit	Credit
(b) 43,000	

In transaction (c), Cruz Auto Detail bought equipment on account from Williams Auto Supply, $7,000. This transaction results in an increase to Equipment with a debit and an increase to Accounts Payable with a credit and is shown in T accounts as follows:

Assets		=	Liabilities		+	Owner's Equity		+	Revenue		−	Expenses	
+	−		−	+		−	+		−	+		+	−
Debit	Credit		Debit	Credit		Debit	Credit		Debit	Credit		Debit	Credit

Equipment		Accounts Payable	
+	−	−	+
Debit	Credit	Debit	Credit
(c) 7,000			(c) 7,000

In transaction (d), Cruz Auto Detail paid Williams Auto Supply, a creditor, $2,000. This transaction results in a decrease to Cash with a credit and a decrease to Accounts Payable with a debit.

Assets		=	Liabilities		+	Owner's Equity		+	Revenue		−	Expenses	
+	−		−	+		−	+		−	+		+	−
Debit	Credit		Debit	Credit		Debit	Credit		Debit	Credit		Debit	Credit

Cash		Accounts Payable	
+	−	−	+
Debit	Credit	Debit	Credit
	(d) 2,000	(d) 2,000	

In transaction (e), Cruz Auto Detail bought supplies on account from Rossi and Company, $800. This transaction results in an increase to Supplies with a debit and an increase to Accounts Payable with a credit.

Assets	=	Liabilities	+	Owner's Equity	+	Revenue	−	Expenses
+ | −		− | +		− | +		− | +		+ | −
Debit | Credit		Debit | Credit		Debit | Credit		Debit | Credit		Debit | Credit

Supplies	Accounts Payable
+ | −	− | +
Debit | Credit	Debit | Credit
(e) 800	**(e)** 800

Here is a restatement of the accounts after recording transactions (a) through (e). To test your understanding of the process, trace through the recording of each transaction and describe what happened in the transaction. Footings or subtotals (remember, always write the footings smaller than the entries and in pencil) are required to compute the balances of the accounts. The balances are written in the accounts on the side with the larger total.

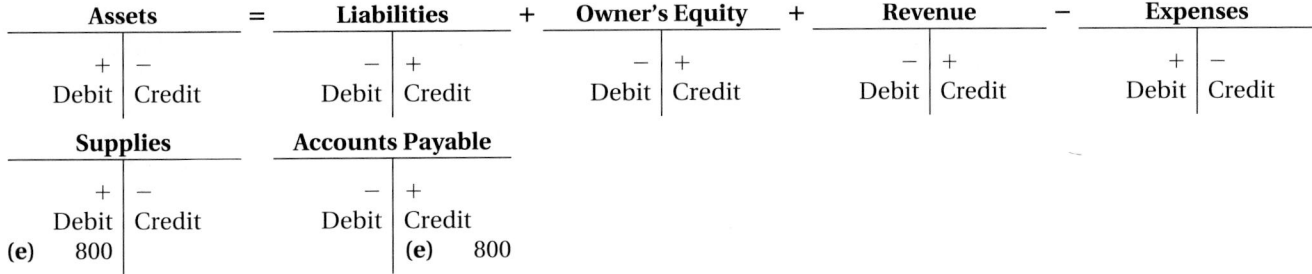

Assets	=	Liabilities	+	Owner's Equity	+	Revenue	−	Expenses
+ | −		− | +		− | +		− | +		+ | −
Debit | Credit		Debit | Credit		Debit | Credit		Debit | Credit		Debit | Credit

Cash

+	−
Debit	Credit
(a) 70,000	**(b)** 43,000
	(d) 2,000
	45,000
Bal. 25,000	

Accounts Receivable

+	−
Debit	Credit

Supplies

+	−
Debit	Credit
(e) 800	

Equipment

+	−
Debit	Credit
(b) 43,000	
(c) 7,000	
50,000	

Accounts Payable

−	+
Debit	Credit
(d) 2,000	**(c)** 7,000
	(e) 800
	7,800
	5,800

L. A. Cruz, Capital

−	+
Debit	Credit
	(a) 70,000

L. A. Cruz, Drawing

+	−
Debit	Credit

Income from Services

−	+
Debit	Credit

Wages Expense

+	−
Debit	Credit

Rent Expense

+	−
Debit	Credit

Advertising Expense

+	−
Debit	Credit

Utilities Expense

+	−
Debit	Credit

■ ■ ■

Remember!
The normal balance of an account classification is on the plus side.

■ ■ ■

FYI
The T account is not only a learning tool, but will serve you well as a problem-solving device when you need to analyze a transaction prior to recording it—manually or on a computer.

Let's pause to see if the two sides of the equation are equal by listing the balances of the accounts:

Account Name	Accounts with Normal Balances on the Left or Debit Side	Accounts with Normal Balances on the Right or Credit Side
	Assets Drawing Expenses	Liabilities Capital Revenue
Cash	$25,000	
Supplies	800	
Equipment	50,000	
Accounts Payable		5,800
L. A. Cruz, Capital		70,000
	$75,800	$75,800

In transaction (f), Cruz Auto Detail sold services for cash, $3,520. This transaction results in an increase to Cash with a debit and an increase to Income from Services with a credit.

Assets	=	Liabilities	+	Owner's Equity	+	Revenue	−	Expenses
+ | −		− | +		− | +		− | +		+ | −
Debit | Credit		Debit | Credit		Debit | Credit		Debit | Credit		Debit | Credit

Cash						Income from Services
+ | −						− | +
Debit | Credit						Debit | Credit
(f) 3,520						**(f)** 3,520

In transaction (g), Cruz Auto Detail paid rent for the month, $900. This transaction results in an increase to Rent Expense with a debit and a decrease to Cash with a credit.

Assets	=	Liabilities	+	Owner's Equity	+	Revenue	−	Expenses
+ | −		− | +		− | +		− | +		+ | −
Debit | Credit		Debit | Credit		Debit | Credit		Debit | Credit		Debit | Credit

Cash						Rent Expense
+ | −						+ | −
Debit | Credit						Debit | Credit
| **(g)** 900						**(g)** 900 |

In transaction (h), Cruz Auto Detail bought insurance for one year, $360. This transaction results in an increase to Prepaid Insurance with a debit and a decrease to Cash with a credit.

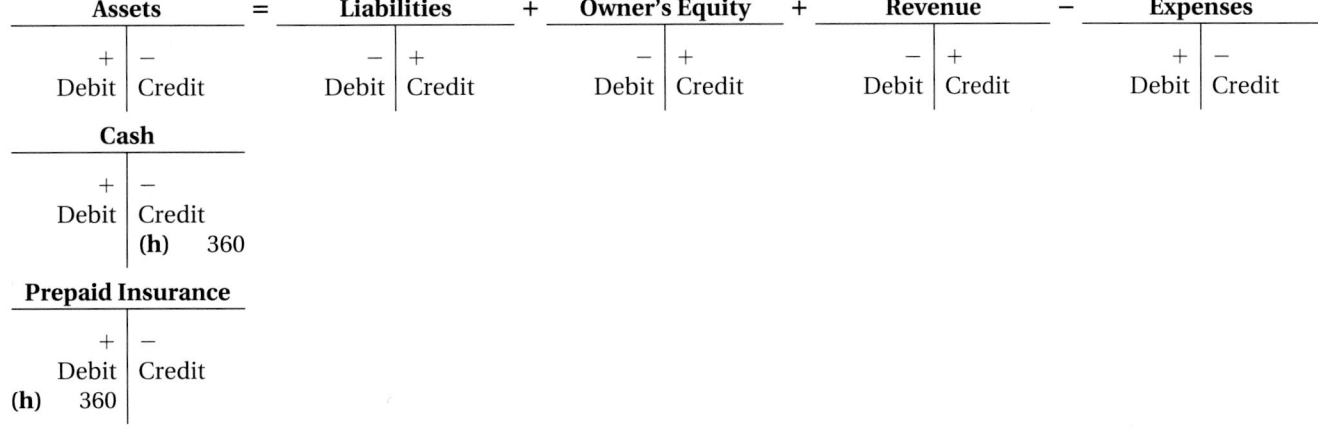

In transaction (i), Cruz Auto Detail received a bill from the *Valley News* for a newspaper advertisement, $400. This transaction results in an increase to Advertising Expense with a debit and an increase to Accounts Payable with a credit.

Assets	=	Liabilities	+	Owner's Equity	+	Revenue	−	Expenses
+ | −		− | +		− | +		− | +		+ | −
Debit | Credit		Debit | Credit		Debit | Credit		Debit | Credit		Debit | Credit

Accounts Payable

−	+
Debit	Credit
	(i) 400

Advertising Expense

+	−
Debit	Credit
(i) 400	

In transaction (j), Cruz Auto Detail sold services on account to Costello Taxi, $1,050. This transaction results in an increase to Accounts Receivable with a debit and an increase to Income from Services with a credit.

Assets	=	Liabilities	+	Owner's Equity	+	Revenue	−	Expenses
+ | −		− | +		− | +		− | +		+ | −
Debit | Credit		Debit | Credit		Debit | Credit		Debit | Credit		Debit | Credit

Accounts Receivable

+	−
Debit	Credit
(j) 1,050	

Income from Services

−	+
Debit	Credit
	(j) 1,050

In transaction (k), Cruz Auto Detail made a payment to Williams Auto Supply, a creditor, $2,000. This transaction results in a decrease to Cash with a credit and a decrease to Accounts Payable with a debit.

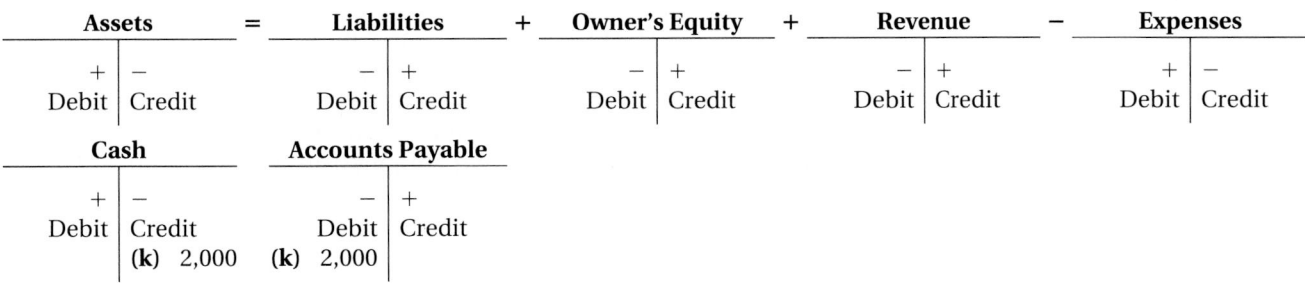

In transaction (l), Cruz Auto Detail received and paid a bill from Midwest Power, Inc., $160. This transaction results in an increase to Utilities Expense with a debit and a decrease to Cash with a credit.

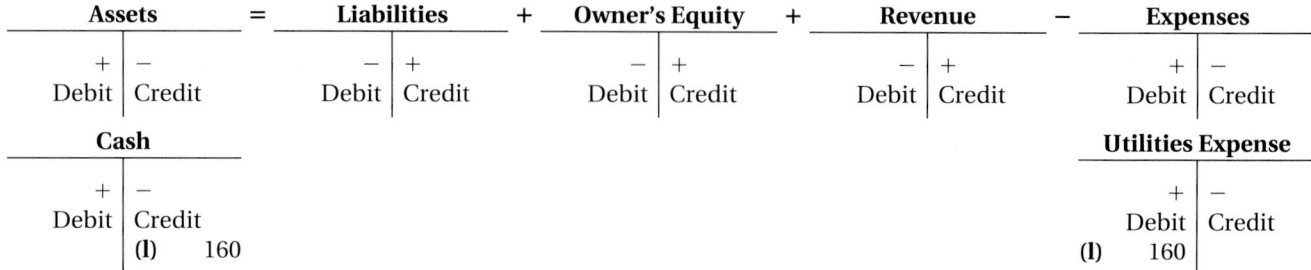

Assets	=	Liabilities	+	Owner's Equity	+	Revenue	−	Expenses
+ | −		− | +		− | +		− | +		+ | −
Debit | Credit		Debit | Credit		Debit | Credit		Debit | Credit		Debit | Credit

Cash

+	−
Debit	Credit
	(l) 160

Utilities Expense

+	−
Debit	Credit
(l) 160	

In transaction (m), Cruz Auto Detail made a payment on account to *Valley News,* a creditor, $400. This transaction results in a decrease to Accounts Payable with a debit and a decrease to Cash with a credit.

Assets	=	Liabilities	+	Owner's Equity	+	Revenue	−	Expenses
+ | −		− | +		− | +		− | +		+ | −
Debit | Credit		Debit | Credit		Debit | Credit		Debit | Credit		Debit | Credit

Cash

+	−
Debit	Credit
	(m) 400

Accounts Payable

−	+
Debit	Credit
(m) 400	

In transaction (n), Cruz Auto Detail paid wages of a part-time employee, $1,400. This transaction results in an increase to Wages Expense with a debit and a decrease to Cash with a credit.

Assets	=	Liabilities	+	Owner's Equity	+	Revenue	−	Expenses
+ | −		− | +		− | +		− | +		+ | −
Debit | Credit		Debit | Credit		Debit | Credit		Debit | Credit		Debit | Credit

Cash

+	−
Debit	Credit
	(n) 1,400

Wages Expense

+	−
Debit	Credit
(n) 1,400	

In transaction (o), Cruz Auto Detail bought equipment from Williams Auto Supply, $1,500, paying $600 in cash and placing the balance on account. This is called a **compound entry**; that is, more than one debit or more than one credit is recorded. The transaction results in an increase to Equipment with a debit, a decrease to Cash with a credit, and an increase to Accounts Payable with a credit.

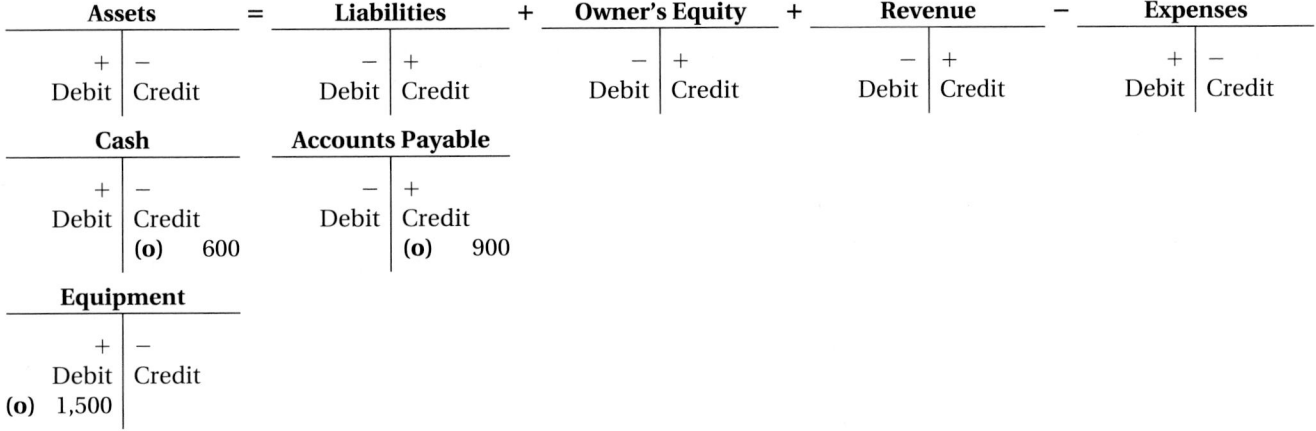

In transaction (p), Cruz Auto Detail received cash on account from Costello Taxi, a customer, $850. This transaction results in an increase to Cash with a debit and a decrease to Accounts Receivable with a credit.

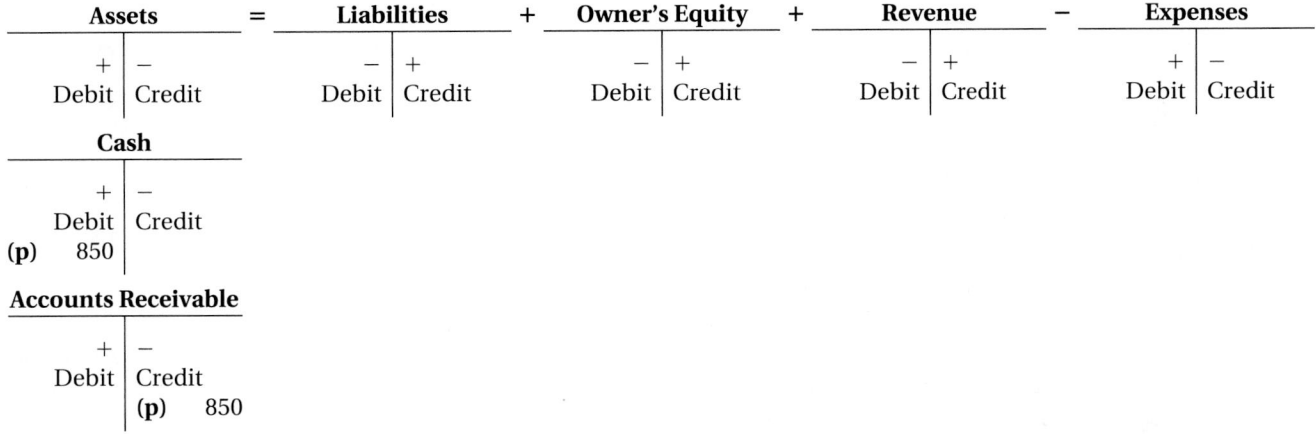

In transaction (q), Cruz sold services for cash to customers for the rest of the month, $2,700. This transaction results in an increase to Cash with a debit and an increase to Income from Services with a credit.

Assets	=	Liabilities	+	Owner's Equity	+	Revenue	−	Expenses
+ / −		− / +		− / +		− / +		+ / −
Debit / Credit		Debit / Credit		Debit / Credit		Debit / Credit		Debit / Credit

Cash

+	−
Debit	Credit
(q) 2,700	

Income from Services

−	+
Debit	Credit
	(q) 2,700

In transaction (r), Cruz withdrew cash for personal use, $3,000. This transaction resulted in an increase to Drawing with a debit and a decrease to Cash with a credit.

Assets	=	Liabilities	+	Owner's Equity	+	Revenue	−	Expenses
+ | −		− | +		− | +		− | +		+ | −
Debit | Credit		Debit | Credit		Debit | Credit		Debit | Credit		Debit | Credit

Cash

+	−
Debit	Credit
	(r) 3,000

L. A. Cruz, Drawing

+	−
Debit	Credit
(r) 3,000	

Summary of Transactions

The following T accounts show the transactions as they are ordinarily recorded. Footings are shown in color. You will notice that the balance of each account is normally on the plus side. Note that, in recording expenses, you place the entries only on the plus, or debit, side. Also, in recording revenue, you place the entries only on the plus, or credit, side.

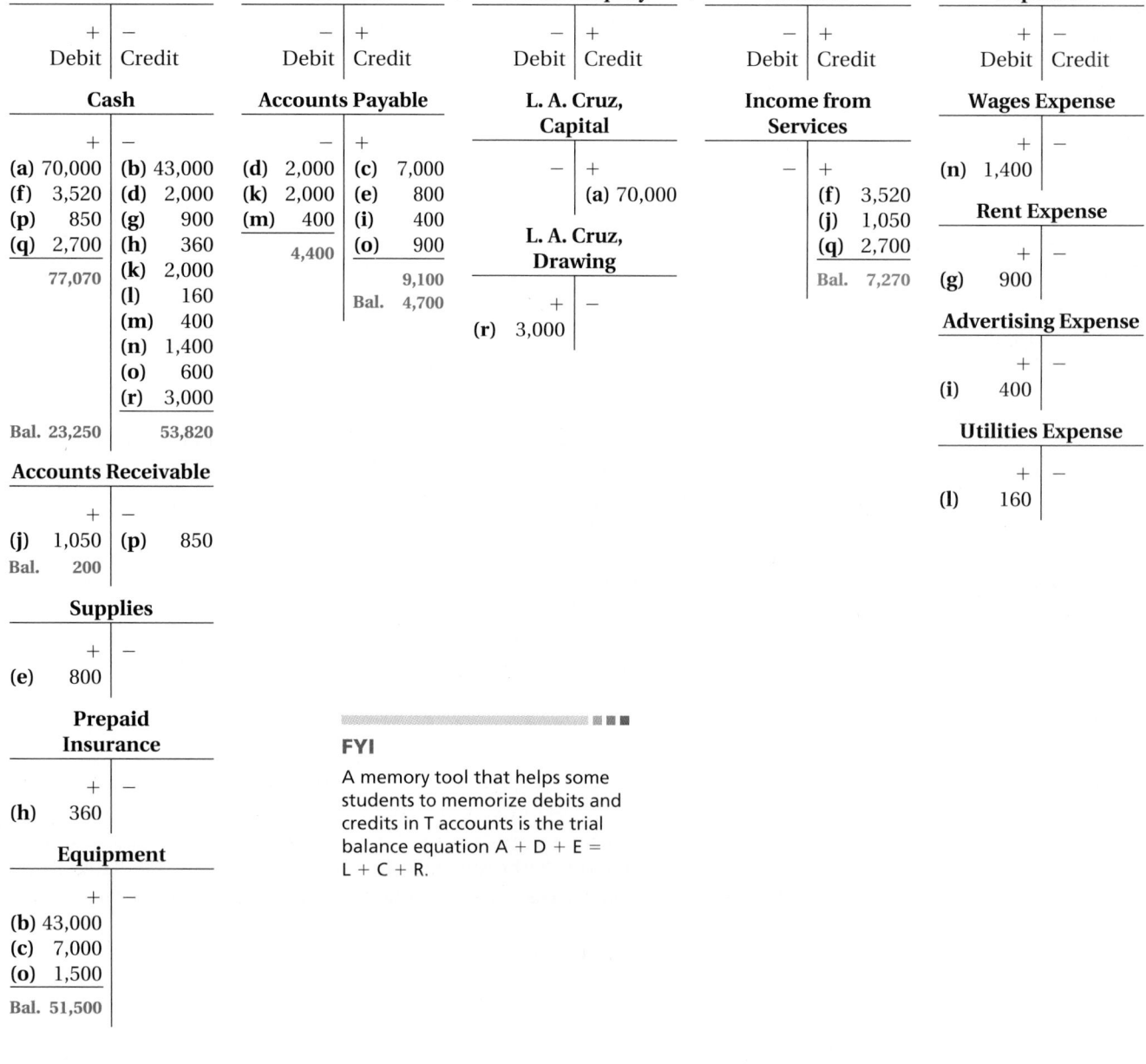

Assets	=	Liabilities	+	Owner's Equity	+	Revenue	−	Expenses
+ | −		− | +		− | +		− | +		+ | −
Debit | Credit		Debit | Credit		Debit | Credit		Debit | Credit		Debit | Credit

Cash

+	−
(a) 70,000	(b) 43,000
(f) 3,520	(d) 2,000
(p) 850	(g) 900
(q) 2,700	(h) 360
77,070	(k) 2,000
	(l) 160
	(m) 400
	(n) 1,400
	(o) 600
	(r) 3,000
Bal. 23,250	**53,820**

Accounts Receivable

+	−
(j) 1,050	(p) 850
Bal. 200	

Supplies

+	−
(e) 800	

Prepaid Insurance

+	−
(h) 360	

Equipment

+	−
(b) 43,000	
(c) 7,000	
(o) 1,500	
Bal. 51,500	

Accounts Payable

−	+
(d) 2,000	(c) 7,000
(k) 2,000	(e) 800
(m) 400	(i) 400
4,400	(o) 900
	9,100
Bal.	4,700

L. A. Cruz, Capital

−	+
	(a) 70,000

L. A. Cruz, Drawing

+	−
(r) 3,000	

Income from Services

−	+
	(f) 3,520
	(j) 1,050
	(q) 2,700
	Bal. 7,270

Wages Expense

+	−
(n) 1,400	

Rent Expense

+	−
(g) 900	

Advertising Expense

+	−
(i) 400	

Utilities Expense

+	−
(l) 160	

THE TRIAL BALANCE

Objective 5

Prepare a trial balance.

You can now prepare a trial balance by simply recording the balances of the T accounts in two columns. The **trial balance** is a listing of account balances in two columns—one labeled Debit and one labeled Credit—to prove that the total of all the debt balances equals the total of all the credit balances. A trial balance is not considered a financial statement; it is, as the name implies, a trial run by the accountant to prove that the debit balances equal the credit balances. This is evidence of the equality of the two sides of the fundamental accounting equation. The accountant must prove that the accounts are in balance before preparing the company's financial statements.

In preparing a trial balance, shown in Figure 1, record the accounts with balances in the same order as they are listed in the chart of accounts. The balance sheet accounts are listed first, followed by the income statement accounts.

- Assets
- Liabilities
- Owner's Equity
- Revenue
- Expenses

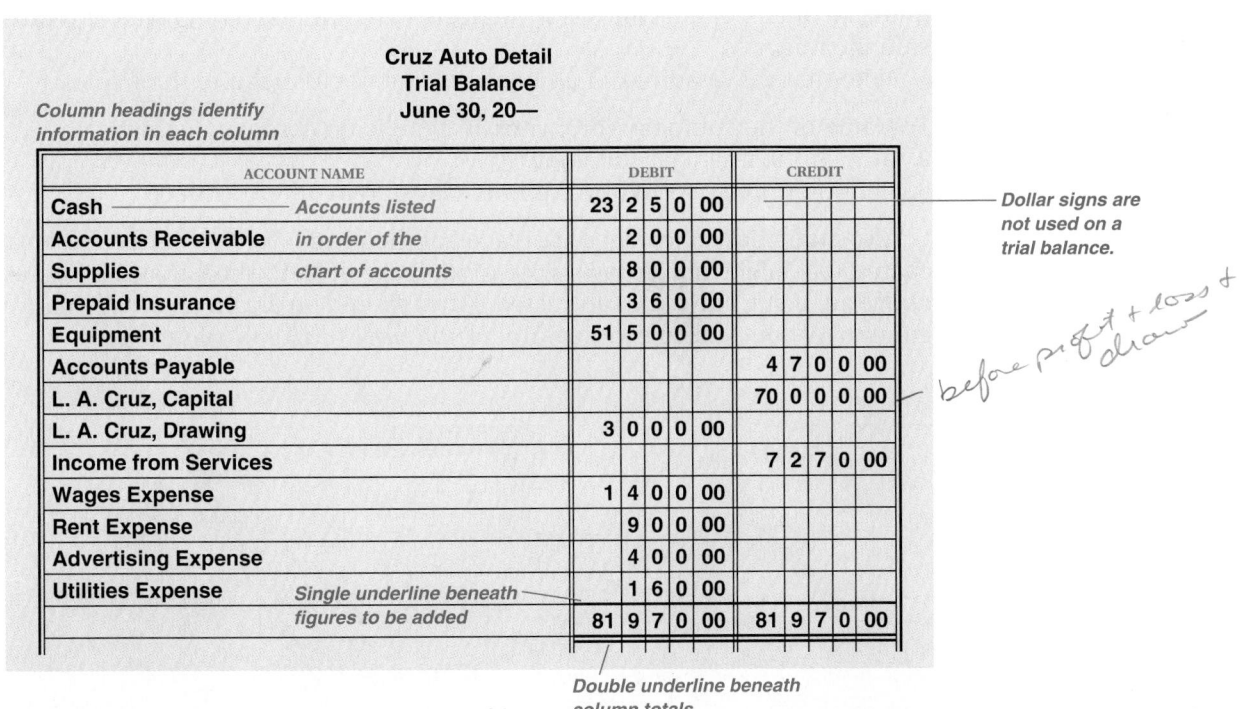

Cruz Auto Detail
Trial Balance
June 30, 20—

Column headings identify information in each column

ACCOUNT NAME		DEBIT		CREDIT	
Cash ——————— *Accounts listed*		23 2 5 0 00			
Accounts Receivable *in order of the*		2 0 0 00			
Supplies *chart of accounts*		8 0 0 00			
Prepaid Insurance		3 6 0 00			
Equipment		51 5 0 0 00			
Accounts Payable				4 7 0 0 00	
L. A. Cruz, Capital				70 0 0 0 00	
L. A. Cruz, Drawing		3 0 0 0 00			
Income from Services				7 2 7 0 00	
Wages Expense		1 4 0 0 00			
Rent Expense		9 0 0 00			
Advertising Expense		4 0 0 00			
Utilities Expense *Single underline beneath*		1 6 0 00			
figures to be added		81 9 7 0 00		81 9 7 0 00	

Dollar signs are not used on a trial balance.

before profit + loss + draw

Double underline beneath column totals

FIGURE 1

The normal balance of each account is on its plus side. Remember that when there is more than one entry in an account, we record the totals in footings and subtract one footing from the other to determine the balance. Record this balance on the side of the account with the larger footing. (Here we record the Drawing account balance in the debit column because it has a debit balance. We do not deduct Drawing from the Capital account when we prepare the trial balance.) The following table indicates where each of the account balances would normally be shown in a trial balance.

Account Titles	Trial Balance	
	Left or Debit Balances	**Right or Credit Balances**
	Assets	
		Liabilities
		Capital
	Drawing	
		Revenue
	Expenses	
Totals	<u>XXXX XX</u>	<u>XXXX XX</u>

■ MAJOR FINANCIAL STATEMENTS

Remember!

Accounting is defined as the process of analyzing, classifying, recording, and summarizing business transactions.

Remember!

The three-line heading of a financial statement answers the questions Who? What? and When?

A business's operating decisions are made from financial statements such as income statements.

Earlier we listed *summarizing* as one of the five basic tasks of the accounting process. To accomplish this task, accountants use financial statements. A **financial statement** is a report prepared by accountants to summarize the financial affairs of a business for managers and others, both inside and outside the business.

Note that the headings of all financial statements require three lines:

1. Name of the company (or owner, if there is no company name)
2. Title of the financial statement
3. Period of time covered by the financial statement, or its date

Also, note that dollar signs are placed at the head of each column and with each total. Single lines (drawn with a ruler) are used to show that the figures above are being added or subtracted. Lines should be drawn across the entire column. A double line is drawn under the final total in a column.

The financial statements are all interconnected. The income statement must be prepared first, followed by the statement of owner's equity, and then the balance sheet.

The Income Statement

The **income statement** shows total revenue minus total expenses, which yields the net income or net loss. The income statement shows the results of business transactions involving revenue and expense accounts—in other words, how the business has performed—over a period of time, usually a month or a year. When total revenue exceeds total expenses over the period, the result is **net income**, or profit. If the total revenue is less than the total expenses, the result is a **net loss**.

The income statement in Figure 2 shows the results of the first month of operations for Cruz Auto Detail.

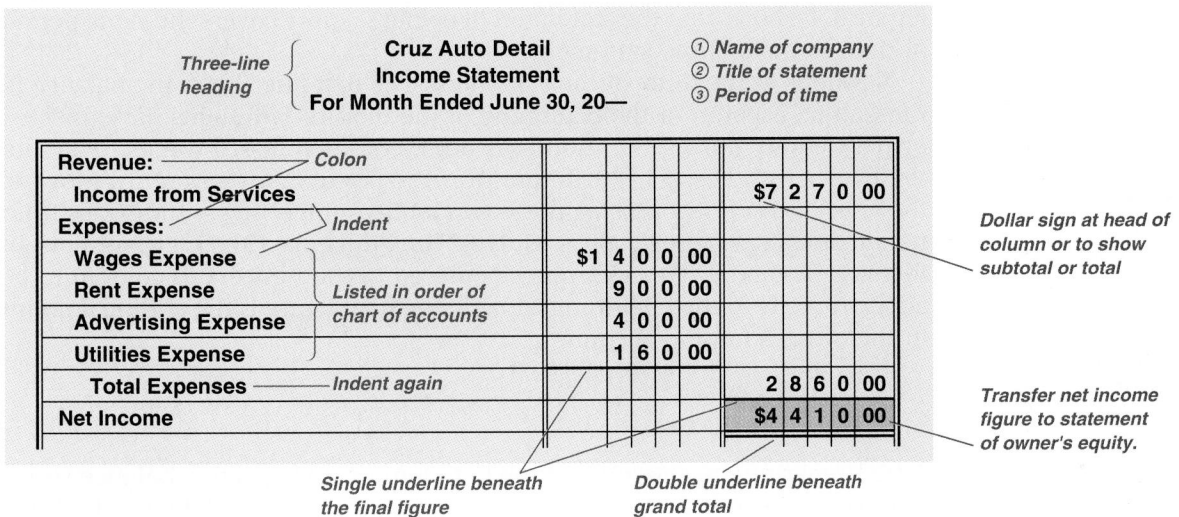

FIGURE 2

For convenience, the individual expense amounts are recorded in the first amount column. Thus, the total expenses ($2,860) may be subtracted directly from the total revenue ($7,270).

The income statement covers a period of time, whereas the balance sheet has only one date: the end of the financial period. On the income statement, the revenue for June, less the expenses for June, shows the results of operations—a net income of $4,410. To the accountant, the term *net income* means "clear" income, or profit after all expenses have been deducted. Expenses are usually listed in the same order as in the chart of accounts. Revenue and expense amounts are taken directly from the trial balance.

The Statement of Owner's Equity

We said that revenue and expenses are connected with owner's equity through the financial statements. Now let's demonstrate this by a statement of owner's equity, shown in Figure 3 (page 48), which the accountant prepares after he or she has determined the net income or net loss on the

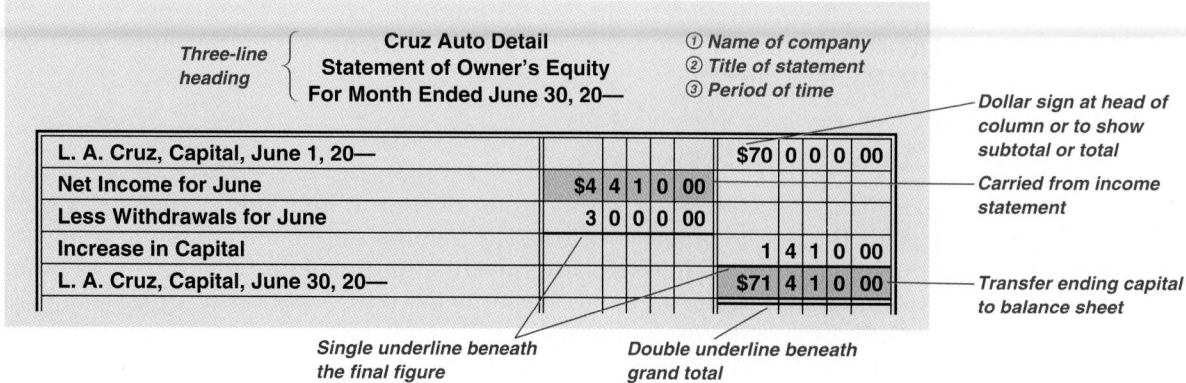

	Three-line heading	Cruz Auto Detail Statement of Owner's Equity For Month Ended June 30, 20—	① Name of company ② Title of statement ③ Period of time			
						Dollar sign at head of column or to show subtotal or total
L. A. Cruz, Capital, June 1, 20—					$70 0 0 0 00	
Net Income for June		$4 4 1 0 00				Carried from income statement
Less Withdrawals for June		3 0 0 0 00				
Increase in Capital					1 4 1 0 00	
L. A. Cruz, Capital, June 30, 20—					$71 4 1 0 00	Transfer ending capital to balance sheet

Single underline beneath the final figure

Double underline beneath grand total

FIGURE 3

income statement. The **statement of owner's equity** shows how—and why—the owner's equity, or Capital account, has changed over a stated period of time (in this case, the month of June). Notice the third line in the heading of Figure 3. It shows that the statement of owner's equity covers the same period of time as the income statement.

Now look at the body of the statement. The first line shows the balance in the Capital account at the beginning of the month. Two items have affected owner's equity during the month: A net income of $4,410 was earned, and the owner withdrew $3,000. To perform the calculations smoothly, move to the left-hand column and list these two items, subtracting withdrawals from net income ($4,410 − $3,000 = $1,410). The difference ($1,410) represents an increase in capital. This difference is placed in the right-hand column to be added directly to the beginning capital. The final figure is the ending amount in the owner's Capital account.

Remember!

The income statement is prepared first, so that net income can be recorded in the statement of owner's equity. The statement of owner's equity is prepared second, so that the ending amount of capital can be recorded in the balance sheet, which is prepared last.

The Balance Sheet

Objective 6c

Prepare a balance sheet.

After preparing the statement of owner's equity, we prepare a balance sheet. The **balance sheet** shows the **financial position**, or the condition of a business's assets offset by claims against them at a point in time. It summarizes the balances of the asset, liability, and owner's equity accounts on a given date (usually the end of a month or year). The balance sheet is, thus, like a snapshot—a picture of the financial condition of the business at that point in time.

The ending capital balance in the balance sheet is taken from the statement of owner's equity. Note that the accounts appear in the same order as in the chart of accounts.

In the **report form** of the balance sheet, the elements in the accounting equation are presented one on top of the other. A balance sheet prepared on June 30 for Cruz Auto Detail in report form would look like Figure 4.

Income Statement Involving More than One Revenue Account and a Net Loss

Objective 7a

Prepare an income statement involving more than one revenue account and a net loss.

When an organization has more than one distinct source of revenue, a separate revenue account is set up for each source. See, for example, the income statement of Rule Miniature Golf presented in Figure 5. Also note that expenses are greater than revenues, resulting in a net loss.

Cruz Auto Detail
Balance Sheet
June 30, 20—

Assets												
Cash	$23	2	5	0	00						
Accounts Receivable		2	0	0	00						
Supplies		8	0	0	00						
Prepaid Insurance		3	6	0	00						
Equipment	51	5	0	0	00						
Total Assets						$76	1	1	0	00	
Liabilities											
Accounts Payable						$4	7	0	0	00	
Owner's Equity											
L. A. Cruz, Capital						71	4	1	0	00	← Carried from statement of owner's equity
Total Liabilities and Owner's Equity						$76	1	1	0	00	

FIGURE 4

FIGURE 5

Rule Miniature Golf
Income Statement
For Month Ended September 30, 20—

Revenue:											
Admissions Income	$9	6	2	4	00						
Concessions Income	2	7	1	2	00						
Total Revenue						$12	3	3	6	00	
Expenses:											
Wages Expense	4	1	2	3	00						
Advertising Expense	3	1	7	00							
Total Expenses						13	4	7	5	00	
Net Loss						1	1	3	9	00	

Remember!

The amounts in the left column are used to calculate totals. Amounts in the right column are totals or grand totals.

Objective 7b

Prepare a statement of owner's equity with an additional investment and either a net income or a net loss.

Statement of Owner's Equity with an Additional Investment and a Net Income

Any additional investment by the owner during the period covered by the financial statements should be shown in the statement of owner's equity, since such a statement should show everything that has affected the Capital account from the *beginning* until the *end* of the period covered by the financial statements. For example, assume that the following information is true for the C. P. Walsh Company, which has a net income:

Balance of C. P. Walsh, Capital, on April 1	$87,000
Additional investment by C. P. Walsh on April 12	10,000
Net income for the month (from income statement)	2,600
Total withdrawals for the month	2,100

FIGURE 6

C. P. Walsh Company
Statement of Owner's Equity
For Month Ended April 30, 20—

C. P. Walsh, Capital, April 1, 20—		$87 0 0 0 00
Additional Investment, April 12, 20—		10 0 0 0 00
Total Investment		97 0 0 0 00
Net Income for April	$2 6 0 0 00	
Less Withdrawals for April	2 1 0 0 00	
Increase in Capital		5 0 0 00
C. P. Walsh, Capital, April 30, 20—		$97 5 0 0 00

The statement of owner's equity in Figure 6 shows this information.

The additional investment may be in the form of cash. Or the investment may be in the form of other assets, such as tools, equipment, and similar items. In the case of investments of assets other than cash, the assets should be recorded at their fair market value. **Fair market value** is the present worth of an asset, or the amount that would be received if the asset were sold to an outsider on the open market. Fair market value may differ greatly from the amount the owner originally paid for the asset.

Statement of Owner's Equity with an Additional Investment and a Net Loss

Assume the following for the L. N. Reems Company, which has a net loss:

L. N. Reems, Capital, on Oct. 1	$70,000
Additional investment by L. N. Reems on Oct. 25	6,000
Net loss for the month (from income statement)	250
Total withdrawals for the month	420

The statement of owner's equity in Figure 7 shows this information.

FIGURE 7

L. N. Reems Company
Statement of Owner's Equity
For Month Ended October 31, 20—

L. N. Reems, Capital, October 1, 20—		$70 0 0 0 00
Additional Investment, October 25, 20—		6 0 0 0 00
Total Investment		$76 0 0 0 00
Less: Net Loss for October	$ 2 5 0 00	
Withdrawals for October	4 2 0 00	
Decrease in Capital		6 7 0 00
L. N. Reems, Capital, October 31, 20—		$75 3 3 0 00

FYI

The information normally shown in the statement of owner's equity is sometimes included as part of the owner's equity section of the balance sheet in computerized general ledger systems.

ERRORS EXPOSED BY THE TRIAL BALANCE

Although using a computer greatly reduces the occurrence of addition and subtraction errors, it does not prevent the occurrence of other kinds of errors, such as recording transactions incorrectly.

If the debit and credit columns in a trial balance are not equal, then it is evident that we have made an error. Possible mistakes include the following:

- Making errors in arithmetic, such as errors in adding the trial balance columns or in finding the balances of the accounts.
- Recording only half an entry, such as a debit without a corresponding credit, or vice versa.
- Recording both halves of the entry on the same side, such as two debits rather than a debit and a credit.
- Recording one or more amounts incorrectly.

Procedure for Locating Errors

Suppose that you are in a business situation where you have recorded transactions for a month in the account books, and the accounts do not balance. To save yourself time, you need to have a definite procedure for tracking down the errors. The best method is to do everything in reverse, as follows:

- Look at the pattern of balances to see if a normal balance was placed in the wrong column on the trial balance.
- Re-add the trial balance columns.
- Check the transferring of the figures from the accounts to the trial balance.
- Verify the footings and balances of the accounts.

As an added precaution, form the habit of verifying all addition and subtraction as you go along. You can thus correct many mistakes *before* the time comes to prepare a trial balance.

When the trial balance totals do not balance, the difference might indicate that you forgot to record half of an entry in the accounts. For example, if the difference in the trial balance totals is $20, you may have recorded $20 on the debit side of one account without recording $20 on the credit side of another account.

Another possibility is to divide the difference by 2; this may provide a clue that you accidentally recorded half an entry twice. For example, if the difference in the trial balance is $600, you may have recorded $300 on the debit side of one account and an additional $300 on the debit side of another account. Look for a transaction that involved $300 and then see if you have recorded both a debit and a credit. By knowing which transactions to check, you can save a lot of time.

FYI

Even if debits equal credits, this does not necessarily mean that there were no errors in the recording of the transactions. For example, a transaction may have been forgotten, it may have been included twice, or it may have been written for an incorrect amount.

Transpositions and Slides

Objective 8

Recognize the effect of transpositions and slides on account balances.

If the difference is evenly divisible by 9, the discrepancy may be either a transposition or a slide. A **transposition** means that the digits have been transposed, or switched around, when the numbers were copied from one place to another. For example, one transposition of digits in 916 can be written as 619.

Correct Number	Number Copied	Difference	Difference Divided by 9
916	619	297	$297 \div 9 = 33$

A **slide** is an error in placing the decimal point; in other words, a slide in the decimal point. For example, $27,000 could be inadvertently written as $2,700:

Correct Number	Number Copied	Difference	Difference Divided by 9
27,000	2,700	24,300	$24,300 \div 9 = 2,700$

Or the error may be a combination of a transposition and a slide, as when $450 is written as $54:

Correct Number	Number Copied	Difference	Difference Divided by 9
450	54	396	$396 \div 9 = 44$

Again, the difference is evenly divisible by 9 (with no remainder).

CHAPTER REVIEW

Review of Performance Objectives

1. Determine balances of T accounts having entries recorded on both sides of the accounts.

   Add the amounts listed on each side of the T account. The totals are called footings. To get the account balance, subtract the total of the smaller side from the total of the larger side. Record the account balance on the larger side.

2. Present the fundamental accounting equation with the T account form, and label the plus and minus sides.

Assets	=	Liabilities	+	Owner's Equity	+	Revenue	−	Expenses
+ | −		− | +		− | +		− | +		+ | −
Left | Right		Left | Right		Left | Right		Left | Right		Left | Right

3. Present the fundamental accounting equation with the T account form, and label the debit and credit sides.

Assets	=	Liabilities	+	Owner's Equity	+	Revenue	−	Expenses
+ | −		− | +		− | +		− | +		+ | −
Left | Right		Left | Right		Left | Right		Left | Right		Left | Right
Debit | Credit		Debit | Credit		Debit | Credit		Debit | Credit		Debit | Credit

4. Record directly in T accounts a group of business transactions involving changes in asset, liability, capital, revenue, and expense accounts for a service business.

   The transactions are recorded by first recognizing and classifying the accounts involved. Next, decide whether the accounts involved are increased or decreased, and record the amounts as additions or subtractions in the accounts. The equation must always remain in balance.

5. **Prepare a trial balance.**

    A trial balance is a list of all account balances in two columns—one labeled Debit and one labeled Credit. The trial balance shows that both sides of the accounting equation are equal. The heading consists of the company name, Trial Balance, and the date.

6. **Prepare (a) an income statement, (b) a statement of owner's equity, and (c) a balance sheet.**

    (a) An income statement shows the results of operations of a business for a period of time. It includes revenue and expense accounts and reports either a net income or a net loss. (b) A statement of owner's equity shows the activity in the owner's equity, or Capital account, for a period of time. It includes the balance in the Capital account at the beginning of the period plus any additional investments and any increase or decrease in capital as the result of a net income (or a net loss) minus (or plus) any withdrawals. (c) A balance sheet shows the financial condition of a business at a point in time. It summarizes the balances of the asset, liability, and owner's equity accounts on a given date.

7. **Prepare (a) an income statement involving more than one revenue account and a net loss, and (b) a statement of owner's equity with an additional investment and either a net income or a net loss.**

    (a) An income statement containing more than one revenue account requires an additional line for each type of revenue, followed by a total amount of revenue. (b) A statement of owner's equity involving an additional investment requires a line for each additional investment beneath the beginning capital amount, followed by a total amount of investment.

8. **Recognize the effect of transpositions and slides on account balances.**

    An error in a trial balance may be a transposition or a slide. The clue is whether the difference in account balances or trial balance totals is evenly divisible by 9. With a transposition, some digits have been switched around. With a slide, the decimal point has been recorded in the wrong place.

Glossary

Balance sheet A financial statement showing the financial position of an organization on a given date, such as June 30 or December 31. The balance sheet lists the balances in the asset, liability, and owner's equity capital accounts. (48)

Compound entry A transaction that requires more than one debit or more than one credit to be recorded. (42)

Credit The right side of a T account; to credit is to record an amount on the right side of a T account. Credits represent increases in liability, capital, or revenue accounts and decreases in asset, drawing, or expense accounts. (36)

Debit The left side of a T account; to debit is to record an amount on the left side of a T account. Debits represent increases in asset, drawing, or expense accounts and decreases in liability, capital, or revenue accounts. (36)

Fair market value The present worth of an asset, or the amount that would be received if the asset were sold to an outsider on the open market. (50)

Financial position The resources or assets owned by an organization at a point in time, offset by the claims against those resources and owner's equity; shown on a balance sheet. (48)

Financial statement A report prepared by accountants that summarizes the financial affairs of a business. (46)

Footings The totals of each side of a T account, recorded in small, pencil-written figures. (34)

Income statement A financial statement showing the results of business transactions involving revenue and expense accounts over a period of time. (47)

Net income The result when total revenue exceeds total expenses over a period of time. (47)

Net loss The result when total expenses exceed total revenue over a period of time. (47)

Normal balance The plus side of a T account. (34)

Report form The form of the balance sheet in which assets are placed at the top and liabilities and owner's equity are placed below. (48)

Slide An error in placing the decimal point in a number. (52)

Statement of owner's equity A financial statement showing the activity in the owner's equity Capital account, over the financial period. (48)

T account form A form of account shaped like the letter T in which increases and decreases in the account may be recorded. One side of the T is for entries on the debit or left side. The other side of the T is for entries on the credit or right side. (34)

Transposition An error that involves interchanging, or switching around, digits during the recording of a number. (51)

Trial balance A list of all account balances to prove that the total of all the debit balances equals the total of all the credit balances. (45)

QUESTIONS, EXERCISES, AND PROBLEMS

Discussion Questions

1. Explain the difference between a balance sheet and a trial balance.
2. Does the term *debit* always mean "increase"? Does the term *credit* always mean "decrease"? Explain why.
3. What are footings?
4. Are the three financial statements presented in this chapter connected to each other? If so, how are they connected?
5. Describe a compound entry.
6. In a trial balance, if total debits equal total credits, what does this mean?
7. Give an example of a slide and a transposition. How can you determine whether an error involves a slide or a transposition?
8. What do we mean when we say that revenues and expenses are under the umbrella of owner's equity?

Exercises

P.O. 4

Describe transactions.

Exercise 2-1 During the first month of operation, Sherrard's Auto Supply recorded the following transactions. Describe what has happened in each of the transactions (a) through (k).

Cash			
(a)	3,300	(b)	435
(k)	1,125	(c)	98
		(e)	75
		(g)	900
		(i)	92
		(j)	325

Accounts Receivable	
(h)	915

Supplies	
(d)	280

Equipment	
(f)	3,850
(g)	1,835

Accounts Payable			
		(d)	280
		(g)	935

C. S. Sherrard, Capital			
		(a)	3,300
		(f)	3,850

C. S. Sherrard, Drawing	
(j)	325

Income from Services			
		(h)	915
		(k)	1,125

Rent Expense	
(b)	435

Utilities Expense	
(i)	92

Advertising Expense	
(c)	98

Miscellaneous Expense	
(e)	75

P.O. 1,2,3

Draw T accounts and record the plus and minus signs.

Exercise 2-2 On a sheet of paper, set up the fundamental accounting equation with T accounts under each of the five account classifications, noting plus and minus signs on the appropriate sides of each account. Under each of the five classifications, set up T accounts, again with the correct plus and minus signs and debit and credit, for each of the following accounts of Crystal Shoe Repair.

Cash
Accounts Receivable
Supplies
Equipment
Accounts Payable
K. Chan, Capital

K. Chan, Drawing
Income from Services
Rent Expense
Wages Expense
Utilities Expense
Miscellaneous Expense

P.O. 2,3,4

Record transactions in T accounts.

Exercise 2-3 T. M. Nestler operates Nestler Carpet Cleaners. The company has the following chart of accounts:

Assets

Cash
Accounts Receivable
Supplies
Prepaid Insurance
Cleaning Equipment
Truck
Office Equipment

Liabilities

Accounts Payable

Owner's Equity

T. M. Nestler, Capital
T. M. Nestler, Drawing

Revenue

Income from Services

Expenses

Wages Expense
Truck Expense
Utilities Expense
Advertising Expense

Using the chart of accounts above, record the following transactions in pairs of T accounts. Give the T account to be debited first and the account to be credited to the right. Show debit and credit and plus and minus signs. (Example: Received and paid the bill for the month's rent, $592.)

Rent Expense			Cash	
Dr.	Cr.		Dr.	Cr.
+	−		+	−
592				592

a. Received and paid the electric bill, $87.
b. Bought supplies on account, $238.
c. Paid for insurance for one year, $409.
d. Made a payment on account to a creditor, $605.
e. Received and paid the telephone bill, $47.
f. Sold services on account, $465.
g. Received and paid the gasoline bill for the truck, $109.
h. Received cash on account from customers, $787.
i. Nestler withdrew cash for personal use, $300.

P.O. 4

Classify accounts.

Exercise 2-4 List the classification of each of the following accounts as A (asset), L (liability), OE (owner's equity), R (revenue), or E (expense). Write Debit or Credit to indicate the increase side, the decrease side, and the normal balance side.

Account	Classification	Increase Side	Decrease Side	Normal Balance Side
0. Cash	A	Debit	Credit	Debit
1. Wages Expense				
2. Equipment				
3. K. Coe, Capital				
4. Service Revenue				
5. K. Coe, Drawing				
6. Accounts Receivable				
7. Rent Expense				
8. Fees Earned				
9. Accounts Payable				

P.O. 5

Prepare a corrected trial balance.

Exercise 2-5 Little Ones Day Care, owned by J. L. Little, hired a new book-keeper who is not entirely familiar with the process of preparing a trial balance. All the accounts have normal balances. Find the errors, and prepare a corrected trial balance for December 31 of this year.

Little Ones Day Care
Trial Balance
December 31, 20—

ACCOUNT NAME	DEBIT	CREDIT
Accounts Receivable		15 5 0 0 00
Cash	3 9 0 0 00	
Accounts Payable		9 7 0 0 00
Equipment	27 0 0 0 00	
J. L. Little, Capital		29 2 0 0 00
J. L. Little, Drawing		1 7 0 0 00
Prepaid Insurance		5 0 0 00
Income from Services		34 0 0 0 00
Rent Expense		3 5 0 0 00
Supplies	1 8 0 0 00	
Utilities Expense	3 6 0 0 00	
Wages Expense	15 4 0 0 00	
	72 9 0 0 00	75 2 0 0 00

P.O. 5,6,7a

Prepare trial balance and financial statements.

Exercise 2-6 During the first month of operations, Laslo Advertising Agency recorded transactions in T account form. Prepare a trial balance dated March 31 of this year. Prepare an income statement, statement of owner's equity, and balance sheet. *Note:* transaction (a) is original investment; (d) is additional investment.

	Cash		
(a)	5,100	(c)	350
(e)	3,500	(f)	600
(k)	7,580	(h)	175
		(i)	2,400
		(j)	2,200

Accounts Receivable

(g)	2,600	

Office Supplies

(c)	350	

Equipment

(b)	1,600	
(d)	3,200	

Accounts Payable

		(b)	1,600

O. D. Laslo, Capital

		(a)	5,100
		(d)	3,200

O. D. Laslo, Drawing

(j)	2,200	

Consulting Fees

		(e)	3,500
		(k)	7,580

Advertising Fees

		(g)	2,600

Salary Expense

(i)	2,400	

Rent Expense

(f)	600	

Utilities Expense

(h)	175	

P.O. 8

Exercise 2-7

Determine the effects of errors.

	Amount of Difference	Debit or Credit Column of Trial Balance Understated or Overstated
0. Example: A $282 debit to Accounts Receivable was not recorded.	$282	Debit column understated
a. A $32 debit to Supplies was recorded as $320.		
b. A $255 debit to Accounts Payable was recorded twice.		
c. A $79 debit to Prepaid Insurance was not recorded.		
d. A $63 credit to Cash was not recorded.		
e. A $180 debit to Equipment was recorded twice.		
f. A $54 debit to Supplies was recorded as $45.		

P.O. 8

Determine the effects of errors.

Exercise 2-8 Which of the following errors would cause a trial balance to have unequal totals? As a result of the errors, which accounts are overstated (by how much) or understated (by how much)?

a. A purchase of office equipment for $380 was recorded as a debit to Office Equipment for $38 and a credit to Cash for $38.
b. A payment of $140 to a creditor was debited to Accounts Receivable and credited to Cash for $140 each.
c. A purchase of supplies for $115 was recorded as a debit to Equipment for $115 and a credit to Cash for $115.
d. A payment of $86 to a creditor was recorded as a debit to Accounts Payable for $86 and a credit to Cash for $68.

CONSIDER AND COMMUNICATE

You are studying with a study buddy. Your study buddy can't accept that the left side of a T account is a debit and the right side is a credit in every part of the fundamental accounting equation. He just can't let go of his other definitions—he says, "But a credit memo is good, so I should always credit an account when increasing it." How would you respond to this confusion?

CRITICAL THINKING

The bookkeeper has made the following errors in recording transactions:

1. Recorded the entry to buy supplies for cash twice.
2. Did not enter the transaction to record the payment of the rent.
3. Recorded the amount paid for utilities as a debit to Salaries Expense instead of a debit to Utilities Expense.

Instructions

Explain the following things about *each* of these errors:

a. Will the error cause the trial balance to be out of balance?
b. How will this error change the financial statements; for example, will net income be overstated or understated or will assets be understated or overstated?
c. Explain how you would correct each error.

A MATTER OF ETHICS ▪▪▪

You had lunch with a friend who is an accounting clerk at a business near your office. During your conversation, your friend discusses the amount of cash the business has in the bank, how sales are not going very well, and the salaries of various employees. Is her revealing these details ethical or unethical?

WEB WORK ▪▪▪

Using an Internet web browser, type in the search box the phrase *accounting practices*. Search for an article or find a home page that will provide you with information about accounting practices or rules. Narrow your search by adding accounting terms to the search box—for example, accounting practices fair market value or accounting practices balance sheet. Discuss or prepare a written response of your findings.

PROBLEM SET A

For additional help, see the demonstration problems at the beginning of each chapter in your Working Papers.

P.O. 2,3,4

✶ **Problem 2-1A** During February of this year, D. O. Kent established Malcolm Leather Repair. The following asset, liability, and owner's equity accounts are included in the chart of accounts:

Cash	Office Equipment
Supplies	Accounts Payable
Shop Equipment	D. O. Kent, Capital
Store Equipment	

The following transactions occurred during the month of February:

a. Kent deposited $20,000 cash in a bank account in the name of the business.
b. Bought shop equipment for cash, $1,732, Ck. No. 1000.
c. Bought supplies on account from Melor Company, $413.
d. Bought store shelving for $808 from Kohler Hardware; payment is due in thirty days.
e. Bought office equipment from Stegal Office Supply, $399, paying $200 in cash and placing the balance on account, Ck. No. 1001.

f. Paid on account to Kohler Hardware, a creditor, $208, Ck. No. 1002.
g. Kent invested his personal leather working tools in the business with a fair market value of $300.

Check Figure

Cash balance, $17,860

Instructions

1. Write the account classifications (Assets, Liabilities, Owner's Equity, Revenue, Expense) in the fundamental accounting equation, as well as the plus and minus signs and Debit and Credit.
2. Write the account names on the T accounts under the classifications, place the plus and minus signs for each T account, and label the debit and credit sides of the T accounts.
3. Record the amounts in the proper positions in the T accounts. Write the letter next to each entry to identify the transaction.
4. Foot and balance accounts.

P.O. 1,2,3,4,5,7a

Problem 2-2A L. S. Quillan established the Quillan Copy Service during June of this year. The accountant prepared the following chart of accounts:

Assets

Cash
Supplies
Computer Software
Office Equipment
Electric Sign

Liabilities

Accounts Payable

Owner's Equity

L. S. Quillan, Capital
L. S. Quillan, Drawing

Revenue

Income from Services

Expenses

Advertising Expense
Rent Expense
Utilities Expense
Wages Expense
Miscellaneous Expense

The following transactions occurred during the month of June:

a. Quillan deposited $15,000 cash in a bank account in the name of the business.
b. Bought office equipment for cash, $685, Ck. No. 1001.
c. Bought computer software from Sysco Computer Center, $890, paying $200 in cash and placing the balance on account, Ck. No. 1002.
d. Paid current month's rent, $725, Ck. No. 1003 (Rent Expense).
e. Sold services for cash, $1,048 (Income from Services).
f. Bought an electric sign from Mory Sign Company, $1,325, paying $325 in cash and placing the balance on account, Ck. No. 1004.
g. Received bill from *The Times* for advertising, $434 (Advertising Expense).
h. Bought supplies on account from Jenkins Supply, $1,185.
i. Received and paid the electric bill, $188, Ck. No. 1005.
j. Paid on account to *The Times*, a creditor, $434, Ck. No. 1006.
k. Sold services for cash, $1,272.
l. Paid wages to an employee, $655, Ck. No. 1007.
m. Quillan invested his personal computer (Office Equipment) in the business with a fair market value of $1,200.
n. Quillan withdrew cash for personal use, $750, Ck. No. 1008.
o. Received and paid the bill for city business license, $35, Ck. No. 1009 (Miscellaneous Expense).

Check Figure

Trial balance total, $21,395

Instructions

1. Record the owner's name in the Capital and Drawing T accounts.
2. Correctly place the plus and minus signs for each T account, and label the debit and credit sides of the accounts.
3. Record the transactions in the T accounts. Write the letter of each entry to identify the transaction.
4. Foot the T accounts and show the balances.
5. Prepare a trial balance, with a three-line heading, dated June 30, 20—.

P.O. 1,2,3,4,5,6

Problem 2-3A T. D. Ming, a physical therapist, opened Ming Physical Therapy Clinic. Her accountant provided the following chart of accounts:

Assets

Cash
Accounts Receivable
Office Equipment
Office Furniture

Liabilities

Accounts Payable

Owner's Equity

T. D. Ming, Capital
T. D. Ming, Drawing

Revenue

Professional Fees
Consulting Fees

Expenses

Salary Expense
Rent Expense
Utilities Expense
Miscellaneous Expense

The following transactions occurred during July of this year:

a. Ming deposited $25,000 in a bank account in the name of the business.
b. Bought filing cabinets on account from Mead Office Supply (Office Equipment), $225.
c. Paid cash for chairs and carpets (Office Furniture) for the waiting room, $938, Ck. No. 1000.
d. Bought a photocopier from MJ's Office Equipment, $635, paying $135 in cash, placing the balance on account, Ck. No. 1001.
e. Received and paid the telephone bill, which included installation charges, $127, Ck. No. 1002.
f. Sold professional services on account, $1,723.
g. Ming invested her personal computer, printer, and scanner (Office Equipment) in the business with a fair market value of $2,300 (additional investment).
h. Received and paid the bill for the state physical therapy convention, $365, Ck. No. 1003 (Miscellaneous Expense).
i. Received and paid the electric bill, $84, Ck. No. 1004.
j. Received cash on account from credit customers, $789.
k. Paid on account to Mead Office Supply, a creditor, $155, Ck. No. 1005.
l. Paid the office rent for the current month, $680, Ck. No. 1006.
m. Sold consulting services for cash, $565.
n. Paid the salary of the receptionist, $715, Ck. No. 1007.
o. Ming withdrew cash for personal use, $1,075, Ck. No. 1008.

Check Figure

Net Income, $317

Instructions

1. Record the owner's name in the Capital and Drawing T accounts.
2. Correctly place the plus and minus signs for each T account, and label the debit and credit sides of the accounts.

3. Record the transactions in the T accounts. Write the letter of each entry to identify the transaction.
4. Foot the T accounts and show the balances.
5. Prepare a trial balance as of July 31, 20—.
6. Prepare an income statement for July 31, 20—.
7. Prepare a statement of owner's equity for July 31, 20— (Reminder: Additional investment).
8. Prepare a balance sheet as of July 31, 20—

P.O. 1,2,3,4,5,6,7b

✳ **Problem 2-4A** On July 1, N. B. Edgar opened Coin-Op Laundry. Edgar's accountant listed the following chart of accounts:

Cash
Supplies
Prepaid Insurance
Equipment
Furniture and Fixtures
Accounts Payable
N. B. Edgar, Capital
N. B. Edgar, Drawing
Laundry Revenue
Wages Expense
Rent Expense
Utilities Expense
Miscellaneous Expense

During July, the following transactions were completed:

a. Edgar deposited $20,000 in a bank account in the name of the business.
b. Bought tables and chairs for cash, $450, Ck. No. 1200.
c. Paid the rent for the current month, $705, Ck. No. 1201.
d. Bought washers and dryers from Eldon Equipment, $17,400, paying $4,000 in cash and placing the balance on account, Ck. No. 1202.
e. Bought laundry supplies on account from Borkal Distributors, $410.
f. Sold services for cash, $862.
g. Bought insurance for one year, $468, Ck. No. 1203.
h. Paid on account to Eldon Equipment, a creditor, $550, Ck. No. 1204.
i. Received and paid the electric bill, $118, Ck. No. 1205.
j. Paid on account to Borkal Distributors, a creditor, $145, Ck. No. 1206.
k. Sold services to customers for cash for the second half of the month, $881.
l. Received and paid the bill for the business license, $45, Ck. No. 1207.
m. Paid wages to an employee, $1,146, Ck. No. 1208.
n. Edgar withdrew cash for personal use, $875, Ck. No. 1209.

Check Figure

Net Loss, $271

Instructions

1. Record the owner's name in the Capital and Drawing T accounts.
2. Correctly place the plus and minus signs for each T account, and label the debit and credit sides of the accounts.
3. Record the transactions in the T accounts. Write the letter of each entry to identify the transaction.
4. Foot the T accounts and show the balances in each account.
5. Prepare a trial balance as of July 31, 20—.
6. Prepare an income statement for July 31, 20—.
7. Prepare a statement of owner's equity for July 31, 20—.
8. Prepare a balance sheet as of July 31, 20—.

PROBLEM SET B

For additional help, see the demonstration problem at the beginning of each chapter in your Working Papers.

P.O. 2,3,4

Problem 2-1B During December of this year, E. B. Romburg established Romburg's Aerobics. The following asset, liability, and owner's equity accounts are included in the chart of accounts:

Cash

Supplies

Exercise Equipment

Office Equipment

Video Equipment

Accounts Payable

E. B. Romburg, Capital

During December, the following transactions occurred:

a. Romburg deposited $28,000 in a bank account in the name of the business.
b. Bought exercise equipment for cash, $6,375, Ck. No. 1001.
c. Bought supplies on account from Hernandez and Company, $632.
d. Bought a printer (Office Equipment) on account from Office Warehouse, $824.
e. Bought exercise equipment on account from Donovan Company, $336.
f. Romburg invested his video equipment with a fair market value of $8,300 in the business.
g. Made a payment to Hernandez and Company, a creditor, $330, Ck. No. 1002.

Check Figure

Balance of Cash, ~~$20,959~~

21,295

Instructions

1. Write the account classifications (Assets, Liabilities, Owner's Equity, Revenue, Expense) in the fundamental accounting equation, as well as the plus and minus signs and Debit and Credit.
2. Write the account names on the T accounts under the classifications, place the plus and minus signs for each T account, and label the debit and credit sides of the T accounts.
3. Record the amounts in the proper positions in the T accounts. Write the letter of each entry to identify the transaction.
4. Foot and balance accounts.

P.O. 1,2,3,4,5

Problem 2-2B S. D. Orren established Orren's Cyber Service during November of this year. The accountant prepared the following chart of accounts:

Assets

Cash

Supplies

Computer Software

Office Equipment

Electric Sign

Liabilities

Accounts Payable

Owner's Equity

S. D. Orren, Capital

S. D. Orren, Drawing

Revenue

Income from Services

Expenses

Advertising Expense

Rent Expense

Utilities Expense

Wages Expense

Miscellaneous Expense

The following transactions occurred during the month:

a. Orren deposited $15,000 in a bank account in the name of the business.
b. Paid the rent for the current month, $630, Ck. No. 2001.
c. Bought office desks and filing cabinets for cash, $930, Ck. No. 2002.
d. Bought a computer and printer (Office Equipment) from Mega Computer Center for use in the business, $4,300, paying $2,500 in cash and placing the balance on account, Ck. No. 2003.
e. Bought an electric sign on account from Sign Works, $1,200.
f. Orren invested her personal computer software with a fair market value of $900 in the business.
g. Received a bill from *Business News* for newspaper advertising, $126.
h. Sold services for cash, $755.
i. Received and paid the electric bill, $158, Ck. No. 2004.
j. Paid on account to *Business News,* a creditor, $126, Ck. No. 2005.
k. Sold services for cash, $1,035.
l. Paid the wages to the employee, $742, Ck. No. 2006.
m. Received and paid the bill for the city business license, $35, Ck. No. 2007.
n. Orren withdrew cash for personal use, $550, Ck. No. 2008.
o. Bought printer paper and letterhead stationery on account from Office Suppliers, $86.

Check Figure

Trial balance total, $20,776

Instructions

1. Record the owner's name in the Capital and Drawing T accounts.
2. Correctly place the plus and minus signs for each T account, and label the debit and credit sides of the accounts.
3. Foot the T accounts and show the balances.
4. Prepare a trial balance with a three-line heading, dated November 30.

P.O. 1,2,3,4,5,6

Problem 2-3B B. D. Lander, an optometrist, opened a clinic in the name of B. D. Lander, O.D. Her accountant prepared the following chart of accounts:

Assets

Cash
Accounts Receivable
Office Equipment
Office Furniture

Liabilities

Accounts Payable

Owner's Equity

B. D. Lander, Capital
B. D. Lander, Drawing

Revenue

Professional Fees
Consulting Fees

Expenses

Salary Expense
Rent Expense
Utilities Expense
Miscellaneous Expense

The following transactions occurred during June of this year:

a. Lander deposited $18,000 in a bank account in the name of the business.
b. Bought a facsimile machine from Marshall's Equipment for $395, paying $100 in cash, and placing the balance on account, Ck. No. 1001.
c. Lander invested her personal office equipment in the business with a fair market value of $8,600 (additional investment).
d. Bought waiting room chairs and tables (Office Furniture), paying cash, $1,132, Ck. No. 1002

e. Bought an intercom system on account from Regal Office Supply (Office Equipment), $356.
f. Received and paid the telephone bill, $84, Ck. No. 1003.
g. Sold consulting fees on account, $1,287.
h. Received and paid the electric bill, $95, Ck. No. 1004.
i. Received and paid the bill for the State Optometric Convention, $250, Ck. No. 1005
j. Sold consulting fees on account, $1,836.
k. Paid on account to Mead Office Supply, a creditor, $165, Ck. No. 1006.
l. Paid the rent for the current month, $640, Ck. No. 1007.
m. Paid salary of the receptionist, $785, Ck. No. 1008.
n. B. D. Lander withdrew cash for personal use, $1,000, Ck. No. 1009.
o. Received $350 on account from patients who were previously billed.

Check Figure

Net Income, $1,269

Instructions

1   Record the owner's name in the Capital and Drawing T accounts.
2. Correctly place the plus and minus signs for each T account, and label the debit and credit sides of the accounts.
3. Record the transactions in the T accounts. Write the letter of each entry to identify the transaction.
4. Foot the T accounts and show the balances.
5. Prepare a trial balance as of June 30, 20—.
6. Prepare an income statement for June 30, 20—.
7. Prepare a statement of owner's equity for June 30, 20— (Reminder: additional investment).
8. Prepare a balance sheet as of June 30, 20—.

P.O. 1,2,3,4,5,6,7b

Problem 2-4B On May 1, C. O. Hobart opened Self-Service Laundry. Hobart's accountant listed the following chart of accounts:

Cash
Supplies
Prepaid Insurance
Equipment
Furniture and Fixtures
Accounts Payable
C. O. Hobart, Capital
C. O. Hobart, Drawing
Laundry Revenue
Wages Expense
Rent Expense
Utilities Expense
Miscellaneous Expense

During May the following transactions were completed:

a. Hobart deposited $20,000 in a bank account in the name of the business.
b. Bought chairs and tables (Furniture and Fixtures) paying cash, $354, Ck. No. 1000.
c. Bought laundry supplies on account from Fenton Supply Company, $248.
d. Paid the rent for the current month, $695, Ck No. 1001.
e. Bought washing machines and dryers from Walder Equipment Company, $11,500; paying $3,500 in cash, and placing the balance on account, Ck. No. 1002.
f. Sold services for cash for the first half of the month, $1,236.

g. Bought insurance for one year, $360, Ck. No. 1003.
h. Paid on account to Walder Equipment Company, a creditor, $500, Ck. No. 1004.
i. Received and paid electric bill, $88, Ck. No. 1005.
j. Sold services for cash for the second half of the month, $727.
k. Paid the wages to the employee, $1,221, Ck. No. 1006.
l. Hobart withdrew cash for his personal use, $940, Ck. No. 1007.
m. Paid on account to Fenton Supply Company, a creditor, $100, Ck. No. 1008.
n. Received bill from the county for sidewalk repair assessment, $120 (Miscellaneous Expense).

Check Figure

Net Loss, $161

Instructions

1. Record the owner's name in the Capital and Drawing T accounts.
2. Correctly place the plus and minus signs for each T account, and label the debit and credit sides of the accounts.
3. Record the transactions in the T accounts. Write the letter of each entry to identify the transaction.
4. Foot the T accounts and show the balances.
5. Prepare a trial balance as of May 31, 20—.
6. Prepare an income statement for May 31, 20—.
7. Prepare a statement of owner's equity for May 31, 20—.
8. Prepare a balance sheet as of May 31, 20—.

3 The General Journal and the General Ledger

WINDOWS ON | **THE WORLD WIDE WEB**

How do you keep track of the money you earn and spend? If you were keeping books for Sean "Puffy" Combs, the rapper, that would be quite a job! How much did Puff Daddy make in 1998? Check out this URL to find out: **http://asylum.aol.com/cgi-bin/news?&loadstory=938811701**.

Pretend you were to record his concert and record sales earnings, as well as his designer clothing purchases, in a general journal and general ledger. Compare his salary with the average salary of an accountant or auditor, which was $40,500 in 1999. When you finish school you may not be earning as much as a popular musician, but wouldn't it be helpful to know what the job you want might pay? Check out the following web site to find out about average salaries of the most popular careers: **http://www.aol.com/webcenters/workplace/career.adp**.

Performance Objectives

After you have completed this chapter, you will be able to do the following:

1. Record a group of transactions pertaining to a service enterprise in a two-column general journal.

2. Post entries from a two-column general journal to general ledger accounts.

3. Prepare a trial balance from the ledger accounts.

4. Correct entries using the ruling method.

5. Correct entries using the correcting entry method.

Recall that *recording* is a step in the definition of accounting. Here we introduce the *journal* as the official record of business transactions. We have recorded business transactions as debits and credits to T accounts. We introduced T accounts because, in the process of formulating debits and credits for business transactions, it's easier to visualize these debits and credits as the plus and minus sides of the T accounts involved. **Formulating the appropriate transaction debits and credits is the most important element in the accounting process.** It represents the very basic foundation of accounting, and all the structure represented by financial statements and other reports is entirely dependent upon it. After determining the debits and credits, the accountant records the transaction in a journal and a ledger.

The initial steps in the accounting process are

1. Record business transactions in a journal.
2. Post entries to accounts in the ledger.
3. Prepare a trial balance.

In this chapter, we present the general journal and the posting procedure.

THE GENERAL JOURNAL

We have seen that an accountant must keep a written record of each transaction. You could record the transactions directly in T accounts; however, only part of the transaction would be listed in each T account. A **journal** is a book in which business transactions are recorded as they happen. In the journal, both the debits and the credits of the entire transaction are recorded in one place. Actually, the journal is a diary for the business, in which you record in day-by-day order all the events involving financial affairs. A journal is called a *book of original entry.* In other words, a transaction is always recorded first in the journal. The process of recording a business transaction in the journal is called **journalizing**. The information about transactions comes from business papers, such as checks, invoices, receipts, letters, and memos. These **source documents** furnish proof (objective evidence) that a transaction has taken place, and they should be identified in the journal entry whenever possible. The basic form of journal is the **two-column general journal**. The term *two-column* refers to the two columns used for debit and credit amounts.

As an example of journalizing business transactions, let's use the transactions for Cruz Auto Detail. The pages of the journal are numbered in consecutive order. This is the first page, and so we write a 1 in the space for the page number. Also, we must write the date of each transaction. Let's begin with the first entry.

Objective 1

Record a group of transactions pertaining to a service enterprise in a two-column general journal.

Transaction (a) June 1: L. A. Cruz deposited $70,000 in a bank account in the name of Cruz Auto Detail.

First, we will show the complete journal entry.

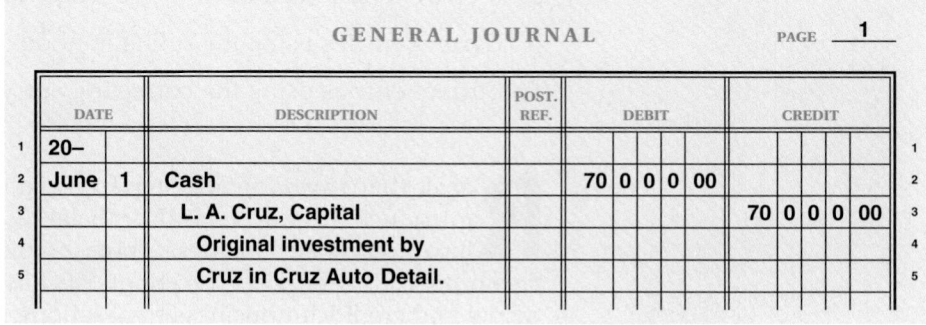

	DATE		DESCRIPTION	POST. REF.	DEBIT	CREDIT	
1	20–						1
2	June	1	Cash		70 0 0 0 00		2
3			L. A. Cruz, Capital			70 0 0 0 00	3
4			Original investment by				4
5			Cruz in Cruz Auto Detail.				5

To explain the entry, we break it down line by line. On the first line at the top of the page, we record the page number where indicated. On line one, we record the year in the left part of the Date column. On the second line, we record the month in the left part of the Date column and the day of the month in the right part of the Date column. We don't have to repeat the year and month until we start a new page, or until the year or month changes.

(Because our illustrations are separated, however, the month may be repeated to eliminate confusion.)

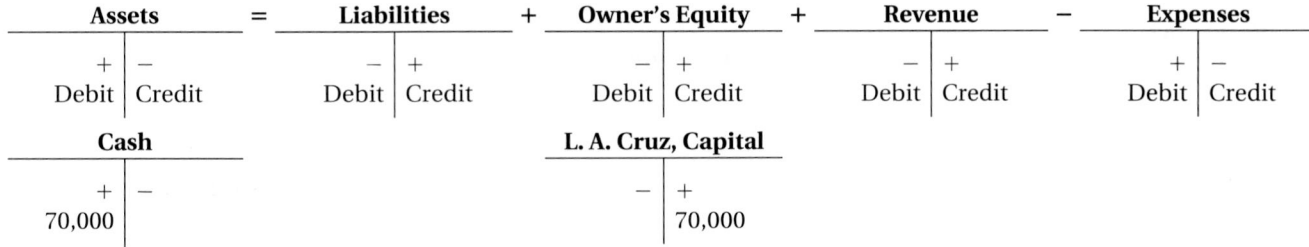

Decide which accounts should be debited and credited. We do this by first deciding which accounts are involved and whether they are increased or decreased. We then visualize the accounts and their plus and minus sides.

Cash is involved in our example. Cash is an asset because it falls within the definition of "things owned." Cash is increased, so we debit Cash.

L. A. Cruz, Capital, is involved. L. A. Cruz, Capital, is an owner's equity account because it represents the owner's investment. L. A. Cruz, Capital, is increased, so we credit L. A. Cruz, Capital. Let's show these entries by referring to our reliable fundamental accounting equation with the accompanying T accounts:

Assets	=	**Liabilities**	+	**Owner's Equity**	+	**Revenue**	−	**Expenses**
+ | −		− | +		− | +		− | +		+ | −
Debit | Credit		Debit | Credit		Debit | Credit		Debit | Credit		Debit | Credit

Cash		**L. A. Cruz, Capital**
+ | −		− | +
70,000 |		| 70,000

You perform this process mentally. If the transaction is more complicated, draw the T accounts on scratch paper. Using T accounts is the accountant's way of drawing a picture of the transaction. You must get into the T account habit; it will be a great help to you in the future.

Always record the debit part of the entry first. Enter the account title—in this case, Cash—in the Description column. Record the amount—$70,000—in the Debit amount column.

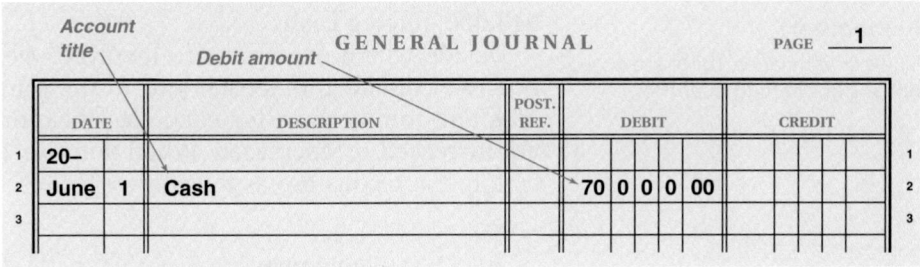

Next, record the credit part of the entry. Enter the account title—in this case, L. A. Cruz, Capital—on the line below the debit in the Description column, indented about one-half inch. On the same line, write the amount in the Credit column.

GENERAL JOURNAL   PAGE ___1___

	DATE		DESCRIPTION	POST. REF.	DEBIT	CREDIT	
1	20–						1
2	June	1	Cash		70 0 0 0 00		2
3			L. A. Cruz, Capital			70 0 0 0 00	3
4							4
5							5
6							6

Indent the account title that is credited

FYI

The explanation refers to the source document.

You should now write a brief explanation, in which you should refer to business papers, giving such information as check numbers, receipt numbers, or invoice numbers. You may also list names of charge customers or creditors, or terms of payment. Enter the explanation below the credit entry, indented an additional one-half inch.

GENERAL JOURNAL   PAGE ___1___

	DATE		DESCRIPTION	POST. REF.	DEBIT	CREDIT	
1	20–						1
2	June	1	Cash		70 0 0 0 00		2
3			L. A. Cruz, Capital			70 0 0 0 00	3
4			Original investment by				4
5			Cruz in Cruz Auto Detail.				5
6							6

Indent again for the explanation

Remember!

In the transaction, L. A. Cruz deposited $70,000 in a bank account in the name of Cruz Auto Detail.

Remember!

Like a trial balance, there are no dollar signs in journal entries.

For an entry in the general journal to be complete, it must contain (1) the date, (2) a debit entry, (3) a credit entry, and (4) an explanation. To anyone thoroughly familiar with the accounts, the explanation may seem quite obvious. Nevertheless, record the explanation as a required, integral part of the entry. To make the journal entries easier to read, leave one blank line between each transaction in your homework.

Transaction (b) June 2: Cruz Auto Detail bought equipment costing $43,000, paying cash.

Decide which accounts are involved. Next, determine which of the five possible classifications each part of the transaction applies to. Visualize the plus and minus signs for each classification. Decide whether the accounts are increased or decreased. When you use T accounts to analyze the transaction, the results are as follows:

Equipment		Cash	
+	–	+	–
Debit	Credit	Debit	Credit
43,000			43,000

Now journalize this analysis below the first transaction. Record the day of the month in the Date column. Remember, you do not have to record the month and year again until the month or year changes or you use a new journal page.

GENERAL JOURNAL

PAGE __1__

	DATE		DESCRIPTION	POST. REF.	DEBIT	CREDIT	
1	20–						1
2	June	1	Cash		70 0 0 0 00		2
3			L. A. Cruz, Capital			70 0 0 0 00	3
4			Original investment by				4
5			Cruz in Cruz Auto Detail.				5
6							6
7		2	Equipment		43 0 0 0 00		7
8			Cash			43 0 0 0 00	8
9			Bought equipment for cash.				9

Skip a line between entries in homework

Transaction (c) On June 3, Cruz Auto Detail bought equipment costing $7,000 on credit (on account) from Williams Auto Supply. Again start with the T accounts.

Equipment		Accounts Payable	
+	–	–	+
Debit	Credit	Debit	Credit
7,000			7,000

Remember!

In trying to figure out how a transaction should be recorded, first decide on the accounts involved. Then classify the accounts as A, L, OE, R, or E. Next, ask yourself whether the accounts are increased or decreased, and think of the related accounts with their plus and minus sides. Now the debits and credits of the transaction will fall into place.

After skipping a line in the journal, record the day of the month and then the entry. In journalizing a transaction involving Accounts Payable, always state the name of the creditor in the explanation. Similarly, in journalizing a transaction involving Accounts Receivable, always state the name of the customer who charged the amount in the explanation.

GENERAL JOURNAL

PAGE __1__

	DATE		DESCRIPTION	POST. REF.	DEBIT	CREDIT	
10							10
11		3	Equipment		7 0 0 0 00		11
12			Accounts Payable			7 0 0 0 00	12
13			Bought equipment on				13
14			account from Williams Auto				14
15			Supply.				15

When a business buys an asset, the asset should be recorded at the actual cost (the agreed amount of a transaction). This is called the **cost principle**. For example, suppose that the $7,000 that Cruz Auto Detail paid for the equipment from Williams Auto Supply was a bargain price, as Williams Auto Supply had been asking $8,500 for the equipment. The day after Cruz Auto Detail took possession of the equipment, it received an offer of $8,100 from another party, but the offer was declined. Cruz Auto Detail *should record the cost of the equipment as the actual amount paid in the transaction that occurred,* which is $7,000. This is true even though the fair market value may indeed be $8,100.

Transaction (d) On June 4, Cruz Auto Detail pays $2,000 to be applied against the firm's liability of $7,000. Picture the T accounts like this:

	Cash			Accounts Payable	
+	−		−	+	
Debit	Credit		Debit	Credit	
	2,000		2,000		

In this case, we see that cash is going out, so we record it on the minus side. We now have a credit to Cash and have completed half of the entry. Next, we recognize that Accounts Payable is involved. We ask ourselves, "Do we owe more or less as a result of this transaction?" The answer is "less," so we record it on the minus, or debit, side of the account.

Remember!

Get in the T account habit. Picture the T accounts in your mind, or draw T accounts on paper with their plus and minus signs. The T account habit is a must.

GENERAL JOURNAL   PAGE 1

	DATE	DESCRIPTION	POST. REF.	DEBIT	CREDIT	
16						16
17	4	Accounts Payable		2 0 0 0 00		17
18		Cash			2 0 0 0 00	18
19		Paid Williams Auto Supply				19
20		on account.				20
21						21
22						22
23						23
24						24
25						25
26						26

Now let's list the transactions for June for Cruz Auto Detail with the date of each transaction. The journal entries are illustrated in Figures 1, 2, and 3.

Heavy-duty ladders, spray painting machines, and a truck to carry it all in are part of the equipment used by these house painters.

FIGURE 1

GENERAL JOURNAL   PAGE ___1___

	DATE		DESCRIPTION	POST. REF.	DEBIT	CREDIT	
1	20–						1
2	June	1	Cash	111	70 0 0 0 00		2
3			L. A. Cruz, Capital	311		70 0 0 0 00	3
4			Original investment by				4
5			Cruz in Cruz Auto Detail.				5
6							6
7		2	Equipment		43 0 0 0 00		7
8			Cash			43 0 0 0 00	8
9			Bought equipment for cash.				9
10							10
11		3	Equipment		7 0 0 0 00		11
12			Accounts Payable			7 0 0 0 00	12
13			Bought equipment on				13
14			account from Williams Auto				14
15			Supply.				15
16							16
17		4	Accounts Payable		2 0 0 0 00		17
18			Cash			2 0 0 0 00	18
19			Paid Williams Auto Supply				19
20			on account.				20
21							21
22		4	Supplies		8 0 0 00		22
23			Accounts Payable			8 0 0 00	23
24			Bought buffer pads,				24
25			cleaners, and waxes on				25
26			account from Rossi and				26
27			Company.				27
28							28
29		7	Cash		3 5 2 0 00		29
30			Income from Services			3 5 2 0 00	30
31			Cash revenue.				31
32							32
33		8	Rent Expense		9 0 0 00		33
34			Cash			9 0 0 00	34
35			For month ended June 30.				35
36							36

June 1 Cruz invests $70,000 cash in her new business.

2 Buys equipment costing $43,000, paying cash.

3 Buys equipment costing $7,000 on credit from Williams Auto Supply.

4 Pays $2,000 to Williams Auto Supply, to be applied against the firm's liability of $7,000.

4 Buys buffer pads, cleaners, and waxes on account from Rossi and Company, $800.

7 Cash revenue received, $3,520.

8 Pays rent for the month, $900.

FIGURE 2

Remember!

You must enter the year and the month at the top of every page in the journal.

GENERAL JOURNAL PAGE ___2___

DATE		DESCRIPTION	POST. REF.	DEBIT	CREDIT	
20–						1
June	10	Prepaid Insurance		3 6 0 00		2
		Cash			3 6 0 00	3
		Premium for one-year vehicle				4
		insurance policy.				5
						6
	14	Advertising Expense		4 0 0 00		7
		Accounts Payable			4 0 0 00	8
		Received bill for advertising				9
		from Valley News.				10
						11
	15	Accounts Receivable		1 0 5 0 00		12
		Income from Services			1 0 5 0 00	13
		Billed Costello Taxi for				14
		services performed.				15
						16
	15	Accounts Payable		2 0 0 0 00		17
		Cash			2 0 0 0 00	18
		Paid Williams Auto Supply				19
		on account.				20
						21
	18	Utilities Expense		1 6 0 00		22
		Cash			1 6 0 00	23
		Paid bill for utilities, Midwest				24
		Power, Inc.				25
						26
	20	Accounts Payable		4 0 0 00		27
		Cash			4 0 0 00	28
		Paid Valley News in full.				29
						30
	24	Wages Expense		1 4 0 0 00		31
		Cash			1 4 0 0 00	32
		Paid wages of part-time				33
		employee.				34
						35

Remember!

Six types of information must be entered in the general journal for each transaction: the date, the title of the account to be debited, the amount of the debit, the title of the account to be credited, the amount of the credit, and the explanation.

June 10 Pays for a one-year vehicle insurance policy, $360.

14 Receives bill for newspaper advertising from *Valley News*, $400.

15 Cruz Auto Detail signed a contract with Costello Taxi to perform detailing work and then bills Costello Taxi $1,050 for services performed.

15 Pays $2,000 to Williams Auto Supply as part payment on account.

18 Receives and pays bill for utilities from Midwest Power, Inc., $160.

20 Pays *Valley News* for advertising, $400 in full. (This bill has been previously recorded.)

24 Pays wages of part-time employee, $1,400.

FIGURE 3

	DATE		DESCRIPTION	POST. REF.	DEBIT		CREDIT	
1	20–							1
2	June	26	Equipment		1 5 0 0 00			2
3			Cash			6 0 0 00		3
4			Accounts Payable			9 0 0 00		4
5			Bought equipment on					5
6			account from Williams Auto					6
7			Supply.					7
8								8
9		30	Cash		8 5 0 00			9
10			Accounts Receivable			8 5 0 00		10
11			Received from Costello Taxi					11
12			to apply on account.					12
13								13
14		30	Cash		2 7 0 0 00			14
15			Income from Services			2 7 0 0 00		15
16			Cash revenue.					16
17								17
18		30	L. A. Cruz, Drawing		3 0 0 0 00			18
19			Cash			3 0 0 0 00		19
20			Withdrawal for personal use.					20

GENERAL JOURNAL   PAGE __3__

Remember!

Every business transaction requires at least one debit and at least one credit. In a general journal, the debit part of the entry is recorded first. The credit part of the entry is recorded next, followed by a brief explanation of the transaction.

June 26 Buys additional equipment costing $1,500 from Williams Auto Supply, paying $600 down with the remaining $900 on account.

30 Receives $850 from Costello Taxi to apply on amount previously billed.

30 Cash revenue received, $2,700.

30 Cruz withdraws cash for personal use, $3,000.

POSTING TO THE GENERAL LEDGER

You can see that the journal is the *book of original entry.* Each transaction must first be recorded in the journal in full. However, it is difficult to determine the balance of any one account, such as Cash, from the general journal entries. So the ledger account has been devised to give us a complete record of the transactions recorded in each individual account. **The general ledger contains all the accounts.** It may be a loose-leaf binder so that you can add or remove pages. The process of transferring information from the journal to the ledger accounts is called posting.

The Chart of Accounts

The accounts in the ledger are arranged according to the chart of accounts, which is the official list of the ledger accounts in which transactions of a business are recorded. Assets are listed first, liabilities second, owner's equity

FYI

While charts of accounts vary from business to business, the beginning numbers for assets, liabilities, owner's equity, revenues, and expenses are standard for a service business. Some account numbers are much longer than three digits.

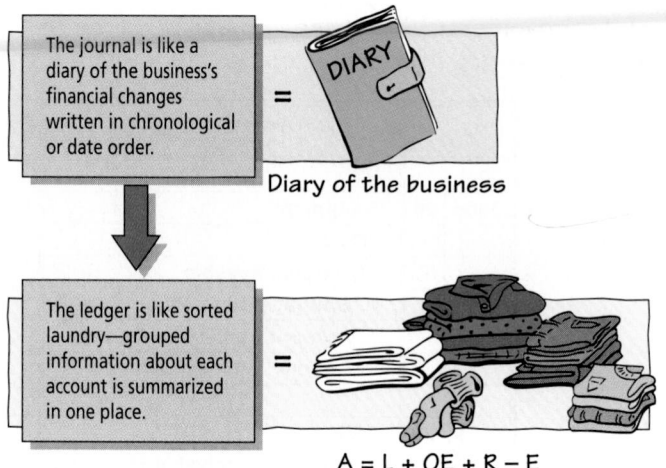

The journal is like a diary of the business's financial changes written in chronological or date order. =

Diary of the business

The ledger is like sorted laundry—grouped information about each account is summarized in one place. =

A = L + OE + R − E

third, revenue fourth, and expenses fifth. The chart of accounts for Cruz Auto Detail is as follows:

Chart of Accounts

Assets (100–199)

111 Cash
113 Accounts Receivable
115 Supplies
117 Prepaid Insurance
124 Equipment

Liabilities (200–299)

221 Accounts Payable

Owner's Equity (300–399)

311 L. A. Cruz, Capital
312 L. A. Cruz, Drawing

Revenue (400–499)

411 Income from Services

Expenses (500–599)

511 Wages Expense
512 Rent Expense
513 Advertising Expense
514 Utilities Expense

Notice that the arrangement of the chart of accounts consists of the balance sheet accounts followed by the income statement accounts. The numbers preceding the account titles are the **account numbers**. Accounts in the ledger are kept by numbers rather than by pages because it is hard to tell in advance how many pages to reserve for a particular account. When you use the number system, you can add sheets easily. The digits in the account numbers also indicate account *classifications*. For most companies, assets start with 1, liabilities with 2, owner's equity with 3, revenue with 4, and expenses with 5. The second and third digits indicate the positions of the individual accounts within their respective classifications.

The Ledger Account Form (Running Balance Format)

We have been looking at accounts in the simple T account form primarily because T accounts illustrate situations so well. The debit and credit sides are specifically labeled. The T account form is used to solve problems because it is such a good way to picture account activity. However, determining the balance of an account using the T account form is difficult. You must add both columns and subtract the smaller total from the larger. To overcome this disadvantage, accountants generally use the four-column account form with Balance columns in the general ledger. Let's look at the Cash account of Cruz Auto Detail in four-column form (Figure 4) compared with the T account form. *Leave the Post. Ref. column blank for now.*

FIGURE 4

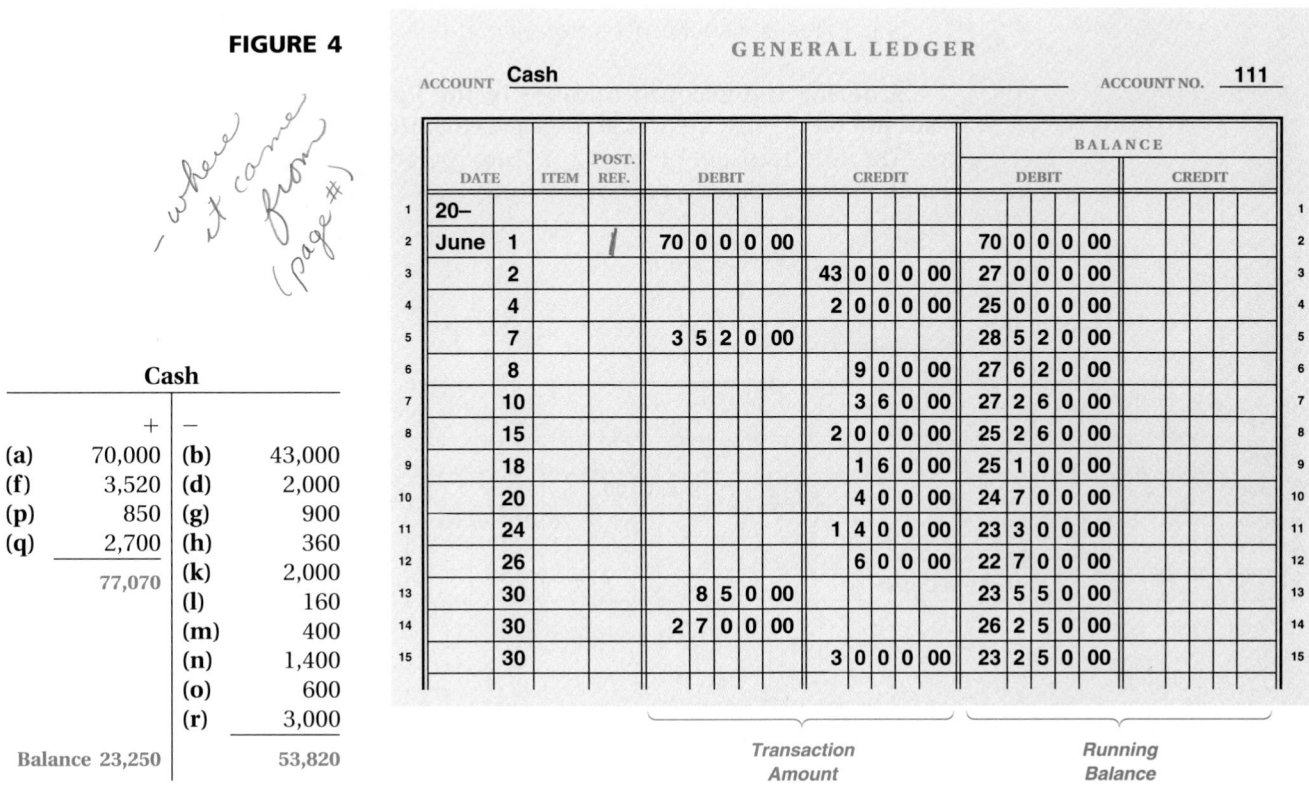

GENERAL LEDGER

ACCOUNT Cash   ACCOUNT NO. 111

	DATE	ITEM	POST. REF.	DEBIT	CREDIT	BALANCE DEBIT	BALANCE CREDIT	
1	20–							1
2	June 1		/	70 0 0 0 00		70 0 0 0 00		2
3	2				43 0 0 0 00	27 0 0 0 00		3
4	4				2 0 0 0 00	25 0 0 0 00		4
5	7			3 5 2 0 00		28 5 2 0 00		5
6	8				9 0 0 00	27 6 2 0 00		6
7	10				3 6 0 00	27 2 6 0 00		7
8	15				2 0 0 0 00	25 2 6 0 00		8
9	18				1 6 0 00	25 1 0 0 00		9
10	20				4 0 0 00	24 7 0 0 00		10
11	24				1 4 0 0 00	23 3 0 0 00		11
12	26				6 0 0 00	22 7 0 0 00		12
13	30			8 5 0 00		23 5 5 0 00		13
14	30			2 7 0 0 00		26 2 5 0 00		14
15	30				3 0 0 0 00	23 2 5 0 00		15

Transaction Amount   Running Balance

Cash

	+		–
(a)	70,000	(b)	43,000
(f)	3,520	(d)	2,000
(p)	850	(g)	900
(q)	2,700	(h)	360
	77,070	(k)	2,000
		(l)	160
		(m)	400
		(n)	1,400
		(o)	600
		(r)	3,000
Balance 23,250			53,820

Note the calculation of the running balance. In the abbreviated form, it looks like this:

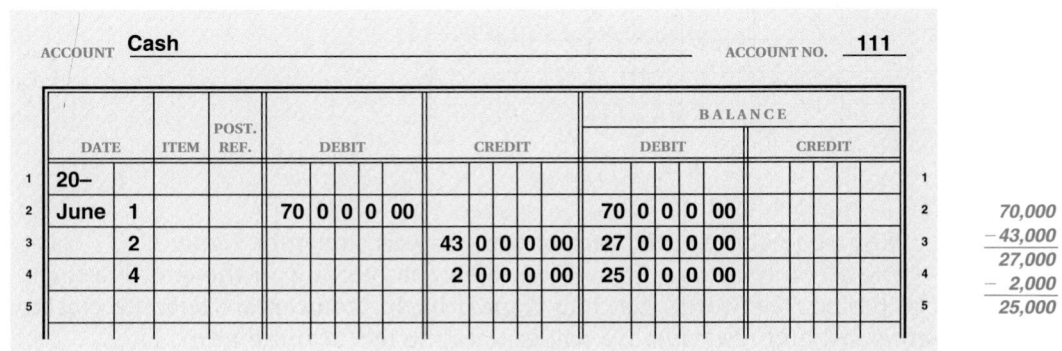

ACCOUNT Cash   ACCOUNT NO. 111

	DATE	ITEM	POST. REF.	DEBIT	CREDIT	BALANCE DEBIT	BALANCE CREDIT	
1	20–							1
2	June 1			70 0 0 0 00		70 0 0 0 00		2
3	2				43 0 0 0 00	27 0 0 0 00		3
4	4				2 0 0 0 00	25 0 0 0 00		4
5								5

70,000
– 43,000
27,000
– 2,000
25,000

The Posting Process

■■■

Objective 2

Post entries from a two-column general journal to general ledger accounts.

In the posting process, you must transfer the following information from the journal to the ledger accounts: the *date of the transaction,* the *debit and credit amounts,* and the *page number* of the journal. Post each account separately, using the following steps. Post the debit part of the entry first. After locating the account in the ledger, you need to do the following steps.

1. Write the date of the transaction in the account's Date column.
2. Write the amount of the transaction in the Debit or Credit column and enter the new balance in the Balance columns under Debit or Credit.
3. Write the page number of the journal in the Post. Ref. column of the ledger account. (This is a **cross-reference**; it tells where the amount came from.)
4. Record the ledger account number in the Post. Ref. column of the journal. (This is also a cross-reference; it tells where the amount was posted.)

Entering the account number in the Post. Ref. column of the journal should be the last step. It acts as a verification of the three preceding steps.

The first transaction for Cruz Auto Detail is illustrated in Figure 5. Let's look first at the debit part of the entry.

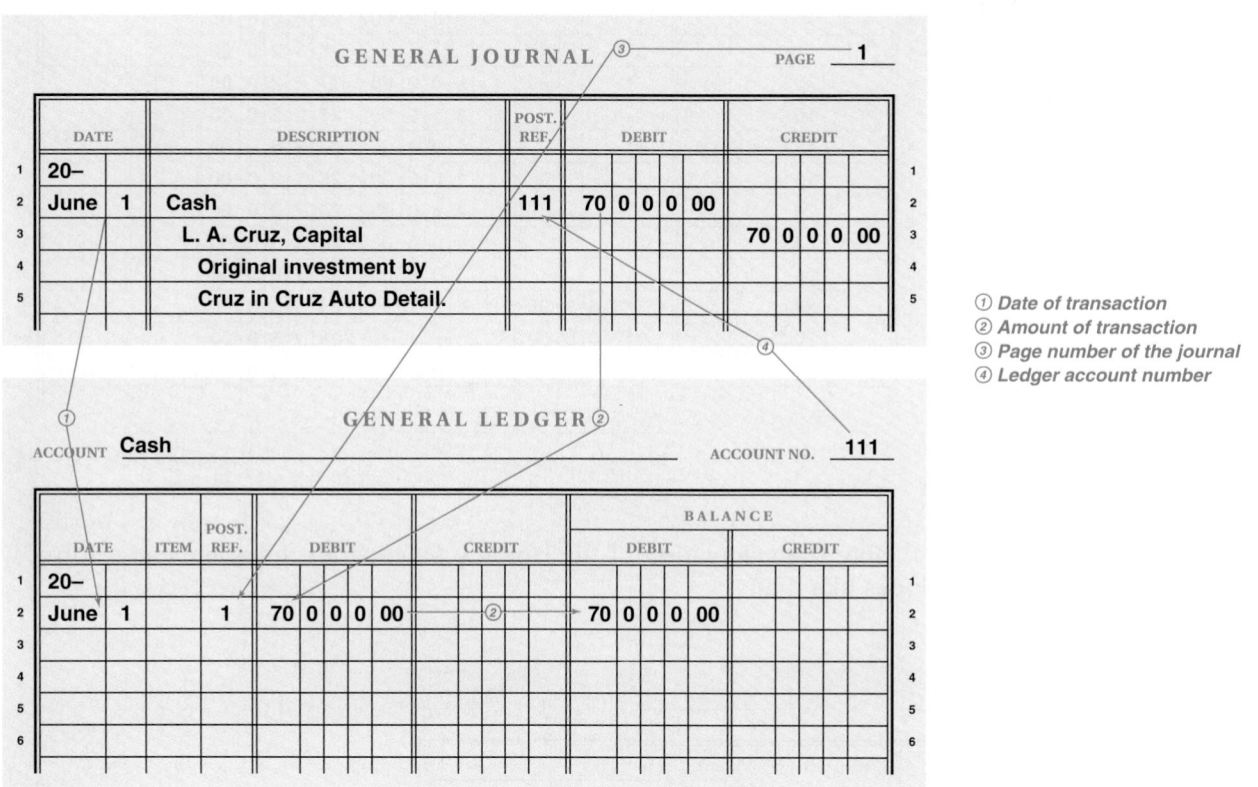

① Date of transaction
② Amount of transaction
③ Page number of the journal
④ Ledger account number

FIGURE 5

Next we post the credit part of the entry, as shown in Figure 6.

The accountant usually uses the Item column only at the end of a financial period. The words that may appear in this column are *balance, closing, adjusting,* and *reversing.* We will explain the use of these terms later.

Incidentally, some accountants use running balance–type ledger account forms that have only one balance column. However, we have used the two-balance-column arrangement to show clearly the appropriate balance of an account. For example, in Figure 5, Cash has a $70,000 balance recorded in the Debit column (normal balance). In Figure 6, L. A. Cruz, Capital, has a $70,000 balance recorded in the Credit column (normal balance).

In the recording of the second transaction, shown in Figure 7, see if you can identify in order the four steps in the posting process.

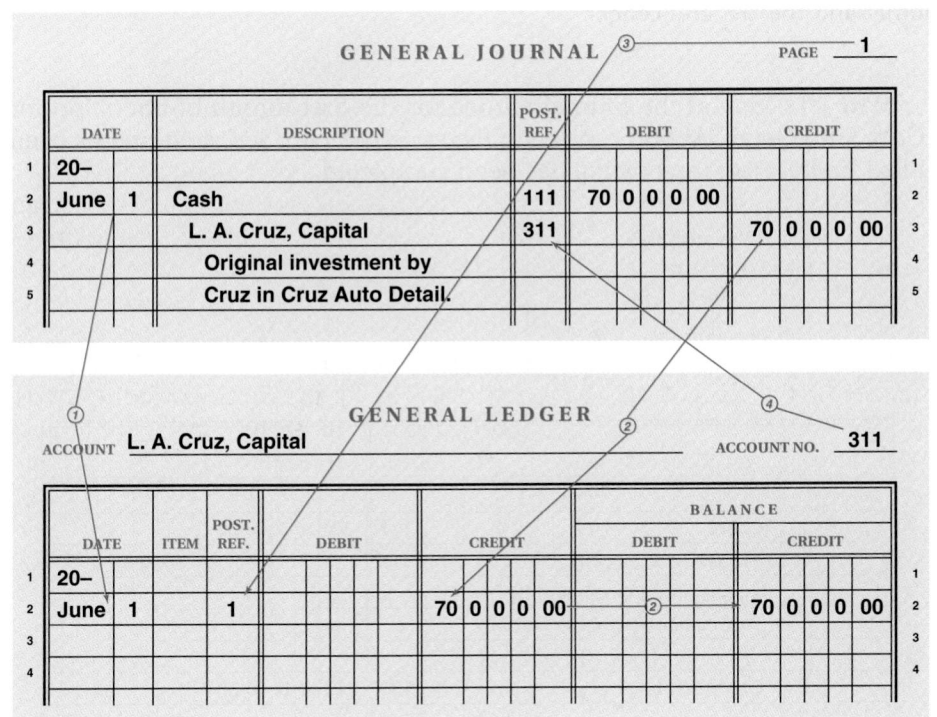

GENERAL JOURNAL PAGE 1

	DATE	DESCRIPTION	POST. REF.	DEBIT	CREDIT	
1	20–					1
2	June 1	Cash	111	70 0 0 0 00		2
3		L. A. Cruz, Capital	311		70 0 0 0 00	3
4		Original investment by				4
5		Cruz in Cruz Auto Detail.				5

① Date of transaction
② Amount of transaction
③ Page number of the journal
④ Ledger account number

GENERAL LEDGER

ACCOUNT L. A. Cruz, Capital ACCOUNT NO. 311

	DATE	ITEM	POST. REF.	DEBIT	CREDIT	BALANCE DEBIT	BALANCE CREDIT	
1	20–							1
2	June 1		1		70 0 0 0 00		70 0 0 0 00	2
3								3
4								4

FIGURE 6

FIGURE 7

GENERAL JOURNAL PAGE 1

	DATE	DESCRIPTION	POST. REF.	DEBIT	CREDIT	
7	2	Equipment	124	43 0 0 0 00		7
8		Cash	111		43 0 0 0 00	8
9		Bought equipment for cash.				9
10						10

Remember!

Do not record account numbers in the Post. Ref. column of the journal until the amounts have been posted to the ledger accounts as either debits or credits.

Remember!

Posting is simply transferring or copying exactly the same date and the debits and credits listed in the journal entry from the journal to the ledger.

GENERAL LEDGER

ACCOUNT Cash ACCOUNT NO. 111

	DATE	ITEM	POST. REF.	DEBIT	CREDIT	BALANCE DEBIT	BALANCE CREDIT	
1	20–							1
2	June 1		1	70 0 0 0 00		70 0 0 0 00		2
3	2		1		43 0 0 0 00	27 0 0 0 00		3

ACCOUNT Equipment ACCOUNT NO. 124

	DATE	ITEM	POST. REF.	DEBIT	CREDIT	BALANCE DEBIT	BALANCE CREDIT	
1	20–							1
2	June 2		1	43 0 0 0 00		43 0 0 0 00		2

Now let's look at the journal entries for the first month of operation for Cruz Auto Detail. As you can see in Figure 8, the Post. Ref. column has been filled in, because the posting has been completed.

FIGURE 8

GENERAL JOURNAL   PAGE ___1___

	DATE		DESCRIPTION	POST. REF.	DEBIT	CREDIT	
1	20–						1
2	June	1	Cash	111	70 0 0 0 00		2
3			L. A. Cruz, Capital	311		70 0 0 0 00	3
4			Original investment by				4
5			Cruz in Cruz Auto Detail.				5
6							6
7		2	Equipment	124	43 0 0 0 00		7
8			Cash	111		43 0 0 0 00	8
9			Bought equipment for cash.				9
10							10
11		3	Equipment	124	7 0 0 0 00		11
12			Accounts Payable	221		7 0 0 0 00	12
13			Bought equipment on				13
14			account from Williams Auto				14
15			Supply.				15
16							16
17		4	Accounts Payable	221	2 0 0 0 00		17
18			Cash	111		2 0 0 0 00	18
19			Paid Williams Auto Supply				19
20			on account.				20
21							21
22		4	Supplies	115	8 0 0 00		22
23			Accounts Payable	221		8 0 0 00	23
24			Bought buffer pads,				24
25			cleaners, and waxes on				25
26			account from Rossi and				26
27			Company.				27
28							28
29		7	Cash	111	3 5 2 0 00		29
30			Income from Services	411		3 5 2 0 00	30
31			Cash revenue.				31
32							32
33		8	Rent Expense	512	9 0 0 00		33
34			Cash	111		9 0 0 00	34
35			For month ended June 30.				35
36							36

**FIGURE 8
(continued)**

GENERAL JOURNAL   PAGE ___2___

	DATE		DESCRIPTION	POST. REF.	DEBIT	CREDIT	
1	20–						1
2	June	10	Prepaid Insurance	117	3 6 0 00		2
3			Cash	111		3 6 0 00	3
4			Premium for one-year vehicle				4
5			insurance policy.				5
6							6
7		14	Advertising Expense	513	4 0 0 00		7
8			Accounts Payable	221		4 0 0 00	8
9			Received bill for advertising				9
10			from Valley News.				10
11							11
12		15	Accounts Receivable	113	1 0 5 0 00		12
13			Income from Services	411		1 0 5 0 00	13
14			Billed Costello Taxi for				14
15			services performed.				15
16							16
17		15	Accounts Payable	221	2 0 0 0 00		17
18			Cash	111		2 0 0 0 00	18
19			Paid Williams Auto Supply				19
20			on account.				20
21							21
22		18	Utilities Expense	514	1 6 0 00		22
23			Cash	111		1 6 0 00	23
24			Paid bill for utilities, Midwest				24
25			Power, Inc.				25
26							26
27		20	Accounts Payable	221	4 0 0 00		27
28			Cash	111		4 0 0 00	28
29			Paid Valley News in full.				29
30							30
31		24	Wages Expense	511	1 4 0 0 00		31
32			Cash	111		1 4 0 0 00	32
33			Paid wages of part-time				33
34			employee.				34
35							35

GENERAL JOURNAL   PAGE ___3___

	DATE		DESCRIPTION	POST. REF.	DEBIT	CREDIT	
1	20–						1
2	June	26	Equipment	124	1 5 0 0 00		2
3			Cash	111		6 0 0 00	3
4			Accounts Payable	221		9 0 0 00	4
5			Bought equipment on				5
6			account from Williams Auto				6
7			Supply.				7

FIGURE 8 (continued)

	Date	Description	Post. Ref.	Debit	Credit
9	30	Cash	111	8 5 0 00	
10		Accounts Receivable	113		8 5 0 00
11		Received from Costello Taxi			
12		to apply on account.			
13					
14	30	Cash	111	2 7 0 0 00	
15		Income from Services	411		2 7 0 0 00
16		Cash revenue.			
17					
18	30	L. A. Cruz, Drawing	312	3 0 0 0 00	
19		Cash	111		3 0 0 0 00
20		For personal use.			

FYI

Computerized accounting programs also require journal explanations and will generate posting references.

In making journal entries, you will sometimes find that there are not enough lines at the bottom of a page to record the entire entry. In this case, do not split up the entry; instead, record the entire entry on the next journal page. The ledger entries for Cruz Auto Detail are shown in Figure 9.

FIGURE 9

GENERAL LEDGER

ACCOUNT **Cash** ACCOUNT NO. **111**

	DATE	ITEM	POST. REF.	DEBIT	CREDIT	BALANCE DEBIT	BALANCE CREDIT
1	20–						
2	June 1		1	70 0 0 0 00		70 0 0 0 00	
3	2		1		43 0 0 0 00	27 0 0 0 00	
4	4		1		2 0 0 0 00	25 0 0 0 00	
5	7		1	3 5 2 0 00		28 5 2 0 00	
6	8		1		9 0 0 00	27 6 2 0 00	
7	10		2		3 6 0 00	27 2 6 0 00	
8	15		2		2 0 0 0 00	25 2 6 0 00	
9	18		2		1 6 0 00	25 1 0 0 00	
10	20		2		4 0 0 00	24 7 0 0 00	
11	24		2		1 4 0 0 00	23 3 0 0 00	
12	26		3		6 0 0 00	22 7 0 0 00	
13	30		3	8 5 0 00		23 5 5 0 00	
14	30		3	2 7 0 0 00		26 2 5 0 00	
15	30		3		3 0 0 0 00	23 2 5 0 00	

ACCOUNT **Accounts Receivable** ACCOUNT NO. **113**

	DATE	ITEM	POST. REF.	DEBIT	CREDIT	BALANCE DEBIT	BALANCE CREDIT
1	20–						
2	June 15		2	1 0 5 0 00		1 0 5 0 00	
3	30		3		8 5 0 00	2 0 0 00	

**FIGURE 9
(continued)**

ACCOUNT **Supplies**   ACCOUNT NO. **115**

	DATE	ITEM	POST. REF.	DEBIT	CREDIT	BALANCE DEBIT	BALANCE CREDIT	
1	20–							1
2	June 4		1	8 0 0 00		8 0 0 00		2
3								3

ACCOUNT **Prepaid Insurance**   ACCOUNT NO. **117**

	DATE	ITEM	POST. REF.	DEBIT	CREDIT	BALANCE DEBIT	BALANCE CREDIT	
1	20–							1
2	June 10		2	3 6 0 00		3 6 0 00		2

ACCOUNT **Equipment**   ACCOUNT NO. **124**

	DATE	ITEM	POST. REF.	DEBIT	CREDIT	BALANCE DEBIT	BALANCE CREDIT	
1	20–							1
2	June 2		1	43 0 0 0 00		43 0 0 0 00		2
3	3		1	7 0 0 0 00		50 0 0 0 00		3
4	26		3	1 5 0 0 00		51 5 0 0 00		4

ACCOUNT **Accounts Payable**   ACCOUNT NO. **221**

	DATE	ITEM	POST. REF.	DEBIT	CREDIT	BALANCE DEBIT	BALANCE CREDIT	
1	20–							1
2	June 3		1		7 0 0 0 00		7 0 0 0 00	2
3	4		1	2 0 0 0 00			5 0 0 0 00	3
4	4		1		8 0 0 00		5 8 0 0 00	4
5	14		2		4 0 0 00		6 2 0 0 00	5
6	15		2	2 0 0 0 00			4 2 0 0 00	6
7	20		2	4 0 0 00			3 8 0 0 00	7
8	26		3		9 0 0 00		4 7 0 0 00	8
9								9
10								10
11								11

ACCOUNT **L.A. Cruz, Capital**   ACCOUNT NO. **311**

	DATE	ITEM	POST. REF.	DEBIT	CREDIT	BALANCE DEBIT	BALANCE CREDIT	
1	20–							1
2	June 1		1		70 0 0 0 00		70 0 0 0 00	2

**FIGURE 9
(continued)**

ACCOUNT L.A. Cruz, Drawing   ACCOUNT NO. 312

	DATE	ITEM	POST. REF.	DEBIT	CREDIT	BALANCE DEBIT	BALANCE CREDIT	
1	20–							1
2	June 30		3	3 0 0 0 00		3 0 0 0 00		2

ACCOUNT Income from Services   ACCOUNT NO. 411

	DATE	ITEM	POST. REF.	DEBIT	CREDIT	BALANCE DEBIT	BALANCE CREDIT	
1	20–							1
2	June 7		1		3 5 2 0 00		3 5 2 0 00	2
3	15		2		1 0 5 0 00		4 5 7 0 00	3
4	30		3		2 7 0 0 00		7 2 7 0 00	4
5								5
6								6

ACCOUNT Wages Expense   ACCOUNT NO. 511

	DATE	ITEM	POST. REF.	DEBIT	CREDIT	BALANCE DEBIT	BALANCE CREDIT	
1	20–							1
2	June 24		2	1 4 0 0 00		1 4 0 0 00		2
3								3

ACCOUNT Rent Expense   ACCOUNT NO. 512

	DATE	ITEM	POST. REF.	DEBIT	CREDIT	BALANCE DEBIT	BALANCE CREDIT	
1	20–							1
2	June 8		1	9 0 0 00		9 0 0 00		2

ACCOUNT Advertising Expense   ACCOUNT NO. 513

	DATE	ITEM	POST. REF.	DEBIT	CREDIT	BALANCE DEBIT	BALANCE CREDIT	
1	20–							1
2	June 14		2	4 0 0 00		4 0 0 00		2

ACCOUNT Utilities Expense   ACCOUNT NO. 514

	DATE	ITEM	POST. REF.	DEBIT	CREDIT	BALANCE DEBIT	BALANCE CREDIT	
1	20–							1
2	June 18		2	1 6 0 00		1 6 0 00		2

Preparation of the Trial Balance

Objective 3

Prepare a trial balance from the ledger accounts.

The trial balance is simply a list of the ledger accounts that have balances. A trial balance is presented in Figure 10.

Remember that the trial balance proves only that the total ledger debit balances equal the total ledger credit balances. Even when the debit and credit balances are equal, other types of errors may slip through—for example,

1. Posting the correct debit or credit amounts to the incorrect account.
2. Neglecting to journalize or post an entire transaction.

FIGURE 10

Cruz Auto Detail
Trial Balance
June 30, 20—

ACCOUNT NAME	DEBIT	CREDIT
Cash	23 2 5 0 00	
Accounts Receivable	2 0 0 00	
Supplies	8 0 0 00	
Prepaid Insurance	3 6 0 00	
Equipment	51 5 0 0 00	
Accounts Payable		4 7 0 0 00
L. A. Cruz, Capital		70 0 0 0 00
L. A. Cruz, Drawing	3 0 0 0 00	
Income from Services		7 2 7 0 00
Wages Expense	1 4 0 0 00	
Rent Expense	9 0 0 00	
Advertising Expense	4 0 0 00	
Utilities Expense	1 6 0 00	
	81 9 7 0 00	81 9 7 0 00

If the temporary balance of an account happens to be zero, insert long dashes through both the Debit Balance and the Credit Balance columns. We'll use another business, the Bessett Company, in this example. Its Accounts Receivable ledger account appears below.

ACCOUNT **Accounts Receivable**   ACCOUNT NO. **113**

	DATE		ITEM	POST. REF.	DEBIT	CREDIT	BALANCE DEBIT	BALANCE CREDIT	
1	20–								1
2	Oct.	7		96	1 4 0 00		1 4 0 00		2
3		19		97	2 3 8 00		3 7 8 00		3
4		21		97		1 4 0 00	2 3 8 00		4
5		29		98		2 3 8 00	—		5
6		31		98	1 6 2 00		1 6 2 00		6
7									7
8									8
9									9
10									10

Steps in the Accounting Process

1. **Record the transactions of a business in a journal (book of original entry or the day-by-day record of the transactions of a firm).** An entry should be based on some source document or evidence that a transaction has occurred, such as an invoice, a receipt, or a check.
2. **Post entries to the accounts in the ledger.** Transfer the amounts from the journal to the Debit or Credit columns of the specified accounts in the ledger. Use a cross-reference system. Accounts are organized in the ledger according to the account numbers assigned to them in the chart of accounts.
3. **Prepare a trial balance.** Record the balances of the ledger accounts in the appropriate column, Debit or Credit, of the trial balance form. Prove that the total of the debit balances equals the total of the credit balances.

Source Document

A source document can be an invoice, a receipt, a check, etc. We now add an important detail in the recording of a journal entry. This detail consists of listing the related source document number, which is used as a reference for the proof of a transaction. Figure 11 is an example of a source document followed by the journal entry (Figure 12) and ledger accounts (Figure 13). Note how the explanation differs from the one we showed earlier.

FIGURE 11

Williams Auto Supply   No. 4-962
220 East Ames Street
Detroit, Michigan 48222

Sold By: ___203___   Date: ___6/4/20—___
Name: Cruz Auto Detail
Address: 1701 East Delaware Street
               Detroit, Michigan 48228
Terms: Net 30 days

QUANTITY	DESCRIPTION	UNIT PRICE		AMOUNT	
36	Benton Car Wash, 64 oz	3	72	133	92
12	Benton Car Wax, 64 oz	12	21	146	52
12	Beetle Tire Dressing, 40 oz	5	16	61	92
12	Starr Leather Dressing, 8 oz	9	46	113	52
36	Buffer Pads, 9″	4	59	165	24
24	Beetle Upholstery Cleaner, 20 oz	3	76	90	24
24	Sponges	1	12	26	88
1	Bag Cloths	2	50	2	50
1	Buffer	59	26	59	26
	TOTAL			800	00

Record in the journal (Figure 12). Note how the explanation includes important information from the source document presented earlier.

	DATE	DESCRIPTION	POST. REF.	DEBIT	CREDIT	
		GENERAL JOURNAL			PAGE 1	
22	4	Supplies	115	8 0 0 00		22
23		Accounts Payable	221		8 0 0 00	23
24		Bought buffer pads,				24
25		cleaners, and waxes				25
26		from Williams Auto Supply,				26
27		Inv. No. 4-962.				27
28						28
29						29
30						30

FIGURE 12

Post to the ledger (Figure 13).

ACCOUNT **Supplies**   ACCOUNT NO. **115**

	DATE	ITEM	POST. REF.	DEBIT	CREDIT	BALANCE DEBIT	BALANCE CREDIT	
1	20–							1
2	June 4		1	8 0 0 00		8 0 0 00		2
3								3
4								4
5								5

ACCOUNT **Accounts Payable**   ACCOUNT NO. **221**

	DATE	ITEM	POST. REF.	DEBIT	CREDIT	BALANCE DEBIT	BALANCE CREDIT	
1	20–							1
2	June 3		1		7 0 0 0 00		7 0 0 0 00	2
3	4		1	2 0 0 0 00			5 0 0 0 00	3
4	4		1		8 0 0 00		5 8 0 0 00	4

Previous postings

FIGURE 13

CORRECTION OF ERRORS

Errors are occasionally made in recording journal entries and posting to the ledger accounts. Never erase them, because it might look as if you were trying to hide something. The method for correcting errors depends on how and when the errors were made. There are two manual methods for correcting errors; they are

1. The ruling method.
2. The correcting entry method.

Ruling Method

Objective 4

Correct entries using the ruling method.

You can use the ruling method to correct an error in the journal before posting or to correct an error in the ledger after an entry has been posted.

Correcting Errors Before Posting Has Taken Place When an error has been made in recording an account title in a journal entry, draw a line through the incorrect account title in the journal entry, and write the correct account title immediately above. Include your initials with the correction. For example, an entry to record payment of $700 rent was incorrectly debited to Salary Expense.

	DATE		DESCRIPTION	POST. REF.	DEBIT	CREDIT	
1	20–		~~Rent Expense~~				1
2	Mar.	1	~~Salary Expense~~ *DJM*		7 0 0 00		2
3			Cash			7 0 0 00	3
4			Paid rent for the month.				4

When an error has been made in recording an amount, draw a line through the incorrect amount in the journal entry, and write the correct amount immediately above. For example, an entry for a $230 payment for office supplies was recorded as $320. Include your initials with the correction.

	DATE		DESCRIPTION	POST. REF.	DEBIT	CREDIT	
1	20–				*pb* 2 3 0 00		1
2	Apr.	6	Office Supplies		~~3 2 0 00~~	*pb* 2 3 0 00	2
3			Cash			~~3 2 0 00~~	3
4			Bought office stationery.				4
5							5

Correcting Errors After Posting Has Taken Place When an entry was journalized correctly but one of the amounts was posted incorrectly, correct the error by drawing a single line through the amount and recording the correct

Whether you are preparing accounting records manually or on computer, accuracy is of primary importance. Rapid and accurate ten-key skills are a must for the accountant or bookkeeper.

amount above. For example, an entry to record cash received for professional fees was correctly journalized as $400. However, it was posted as a debit to Cash for $400 and a credit to Professional Fees for $4,000. In the Professional Fees account, draw a line through $4,000 and insert $400 above. Change the running balance of the account and initial the corrections.

FYI

Use a ruler to draw a line through an error.

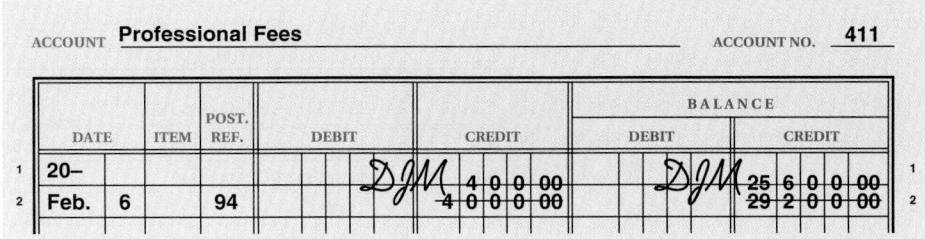

| ACCOUNT | Professional Fees | | | | | | ACCOUNT NO. | 411 |

	DATE	ITEM	POST. REF.	DEBIT	CREDIT	BALANCE DEBIT	BALANCE CREDIT	
1	20–				*DJM* 4 0 0 00	*DJM*	25 6 0 0 00	1
2	Feb. 6		94		~~4 0 0 0 00~~		29 2 0 0 00	2

Correcting Entry Method

Objective 5

Correct entries using the correcting entry method.

You should use the correcting entry method when incorrectly journalized amounts have been posted. There are two correcting entry methods; they are

1. One-step method. Simply make one entry that undoes the error and provides the correct account.
2. Two-step method. The first step reverses the error made by the original entry. The second step includes the correct entry.

The correcting entry should *always* include an explanation. For example, on January 9, a $620 payment for advertising was incorrectly journalized and posted as a debit to Miscellaneous Expense for $620 and a credit to Cash for $620.

FYI

How you correct an error on a computer depends on whether the entry has been posted or not. Before posting, most software programs allow you to replace the incorrect account number or amount. If the entry has been posted, you may have to make a correcting entry to reverse the error, and then record the correct entry.

	DATE		DESCRIPTION	POST. REF.	DEBIT	CREDIT	
1	20–						1
2	Jan.	27	Advertising Expense		6 2 0 00		2
3			Miscellaneous Expense			6 2 0 00	3
4			To correct error of January 9				4
5			in which a payment for				5
6			Advertising Expense was				6
7			debited to Miscellaneous				7
8			Expense.				8

For example, if the original entry was recorded as a debit to Miscellaneous Expense and a credit to Cash, then reverse this entry by debiting Cash and crediting Miscellaneous Expense.

	DATE		DESCRIPTION	POST. REF.	DEBIT	CREDIT	
1	20–						1
2	Jan.	27	Cash		6 2 0 00		2
3			Miscellaneous Expense			6 2 0 00	3
4			To reverse out an incorrect				4
5			entry recorded January 9.				5
6							6
7							7
8							8

	DATE		DESCRIPTION	POST. REF.	DEBIT	CREDIT	
1	20–						1
2	Jan.	27	Advertising Expense		6 2 0 00		2
3			Cash			6 2 0 00	3
4			To correct error of January 9				4
5			in which a payment for				5
6			Advertising Expense was				6
7			debited to Miscellaneous				7
8			Expense.				8

After the correcting entry has been journalized, the accounts are posted as for any other entry. After posting, the account balances should be correct.

CHAPTER REVIEW

Review of Performance Objectives

1. Record a group of transactions pertaining to a service enterprise in a two-column general journal.

   Based on source documents, the transactions are analyzed to determine the accounts involved and whether the accounts are debited or credited. For each transaction, total debits must equal total credits. The journal is a book of original entry in which a day-by-day record of business transactions is maintained. The parts of a journal entry consist of the transaction date, the title of the account(s) debited, the title of the account(s) credited, the amounts recorded in the Debit and Credit columns, and an explanation.

2. Post entries from a two-column general journal to general ledger accounts.

The ledger is a book that contains all the accounts, arranged according to the chart of accounts. Posting is the process of transferring information from the journal to the ledger accounts. The posting process consists of four steps:

1. Write the date of the transaction in the account's Date column.
2. Write the amount of the transaction in the Debit or Credit column, and enter the new balance in the Balance columns under Debit or Credit.
3. Write the page number of the journal in the Post. Ref. column of the ledger account.
4. Record the ledger account number in the Post. Ref. column of the journal.

3. Prepare a trial balance from the ledger accounts.

The trial balance consists of a listing of account balances in two columns, one labeled Debit and one labeled Credit. The balances come from the ledger accounts.

4. Correct entries using the ruling method.

The ruling method can be used if an error is discovered before or after an entry has been posted. Draw a line through the incorrect account title or amount, and write the correct account title or amount immediately above. Include your initials with the correction.

5. Correct entries using the correcting entry method.

This method is used if an error is discovered after an incorrectly journalized entry has been posted. If the error consists of the wrong account(s), an entry is made to cancel out or reverse the incorrect account(s) and insert the correct account(s). Initial the correction.

Glossary

Account numbers The numbers assigned to accounts according to the chart of accounts. (76)

Cost principle The principle that a purchased asset should be recorded at its actual cost. (72)

Cross-reference The ledger account number in the Post. Ref. column of the journal and the journal page number in the Post. Ref. column of the ledger account. (78)

General ledger A loose-leaf book containing the activity (by accounts) of a business. (75)

Journal The book in which a person makes the original record of a business transaction; commonly referred to as a *book of original entry*. (68)

Journalizing The process of recording a business transaction in a journal. (68)

Ledger account A complete record of the transactions recorded in an individual account. (75)

Posting The process of transferring figures from the journal to the ledger accounts. (75)

Source documents Business papers, such as checks, invoices, receipts, letters, and memos, that furnish proof that a transaction has taken place. (68)

Two-column general journal A general journal in which there are two amount columns, one used for debit amounts and one used for credit amounts. (68)

QUESTIONS, EXERCISES, AND PROBLEMS

Discussion Questions

1. Why is the journal called a book of original entry?
2. How does the ledger differ from the journal?
3. What is the purpose of having a ledger account for each account?
4. List by account classification the sequence of the accounts in the general ledger.
5. Arrange the following steps in the posting process in proper order:
   a. Write the ledger account number in the Post. Ref. column of the journal.
   b. Write the amount of the transaction.
   c. Write the date of the transaction.
   d. Write the page number of the journal in the Post. Ref. column of the ledger account.
6. What does cross-referencing in the posting process mean?
7. Why is a source document important to the journalizing process?
8. In a chart of accounts listed by account number, what is the first number for each of the following accounts:
   a. Professional Fees
   b. Utilities Expense
   c. J. R. Watson, Capital
   d. Accounts Receivable
   e. Accounts Payable

Exercises

P.O. 1
Label parts of a journal entry.

Exercise 3-1 In the two-column journal below, the capital letters represent where parts of a journal entry appear. Write the numbers 1 through 8 on a piece of paper. After each number, associate or match the capital letter where these items should appear with the number of the item.

GENERAL JOURNAL PAGE __1__

	DATE		DESCRIPTION	POST. REF.	DEBIT	CREDIT	
1	G						1
2	H	I	J	O	M		2
3			K	P		N	3
4			L				4
5							5

1. Year
2. Month
3. Explanation

4. Title of account debited
5. Ledger account number of account credited
6. Amount of debit
7. Day of the month
8. Title of account credited

Exercise 3-2 Architectural Consulting Service completed the following transactions. Journalize the transactions in general journal form, including brief explanations.

Oct.   7   Received cash on account from Walter Tauscher, a customer, Inv. No. 312, $890.
  15   Paid on account to Mason Brothers, a creditor, $265, Ck. No. 2242.
  20   M. L. Nguyen, the owner, withdrew cash for personal use, $1,230, Ck. No. 2243.
  23   Bought store supplies for $87 and office supplies for $36 on account from Wilber Office Supply, Inv. No. 1040.
  29   M. L. Nguyen, the owner, invested $4,500 cash and $5,500 of his personal equipment.

Exercise 3-3 Dupree Tutoring Service completed the following transactions. Journalize the transactions in general journal form, including brief explanations.

Mar.   1   Bought equipment for $9,000 from Educational Systems, paying $3,000 in cash and placing the balance on account, Ck. No. 3230.
  10   Paid the wages for the first week of March, $1,836, Ck. No. 3231.
  15   Sold services for cash to Central School District, $1,100, Sales Inv. 121.
  26   Sold services on account to Mason School, $1,240, Sales Inv. 122.
  31   Paid on account to Educational Systems, $500, Ck. No. 3232.

Exercise 3-4 The following May journal entries all involved cash.

Increases to Cash—Debits		Decreases to Cash—Credits	
5/1	10,000	5/3	900
5/9	1,700	5/8	700
5/16	5,400	5/12	3,200
5/23	700	5/25	4,600
5/30	4,300		

Post the amounts to the ledger account for Cash, Account No. 111. Assume that all transactions appeared on page 6 of the general journal.

Exercise 3-5 Arrange the following steps in the posting process in proper order:

a. The amount of the balance of the ledger account is recorded in the Debit Balance or Credit Balance column.
b. The amount of the transaction is recorded in the Debit or Credit column of the ledger account.

c. The ledger account number is recorded in the Post. Ref. column of the journal.
d. The date of the transaction is recorded in the Date column of the ledger account.
e. The page number of the journal is recorded in the Post. Ref. column of the ledger account.

P.O. 3

Prepare a corrected trial balance.

Exercise 3-6 The bookkeeper for Rains Company has prepared the following trial balance.

Rains Company
Trial Balance
June 30, 20—

ACCOUNT NAME	DEBIT	CREDIT
Cash		2 5 0 0 00
Accounts Receivable	8 3 0 0 00	
Supplies	6 0 0 00	
Prepaid Insurance	6 5 0 00	
Equipment	15 3 0 0 00	
Accounts Payable		2 7 0 0 00
D. Rains, Capital		12 5 0 0 00
D. Rains, Drawing	4 8 9 0 00	
Professional Fees		17 5 4 0 00
Rent Expense	5 0 0 00	
Miscellaneous Expense	1 8 0 0 00	
	32 0 4 0 00	35 2 4 0 00

The bookkeeper has asked for your help. In examining the company's journal and ledger, you discover the following errors. Use this information to construct a corrected trial balance.

a. The debits to the Cash account total $8,000, and the credits total $3,300.
b. A $500 payment to a creditor was entered in the journal correctly but was not posted to the Accounts Payable account.
c. The first two numbers in the balance of the Accounts Receivable account were transposed in copying the balance from the ledger to the trial balance.
d. The $1,500 amount withdrawn by the owner for personal use was debited to Miscellaneous Expense by mistake—it was correctly credited to Cash.

P.O. 4,5

Determine the effect of errors.

Exercise 3-7 Determine the effect of the following errors on a company's total revenue, total expenses, and net income. Indicate the effect by writing O for "Overstated (too much)"; U for "Understated (too little)"; or NA for "Not Affected."

Transactions	Total Revenue	Total Expenses	Net Income
Example: A check for $425 was written to pay on account. The accountant debited Rent Expense for $425 and credited Cash for $425.	NA	O	U
a. $320 was received on account from customers. The accountant debited Cash for $320 and credited Professional Fees for $320.			
b. The owner withdrew $1,000 for personal use. The accountant debited Wages Expense for $1,000 and credited Cash for $1,000.			
c. A check was written for $1,250 to pay the rent. The accountant debited Rent Expense for $1,520 and credited Cash for $1,520.			
d. $1,500 was received on account from customers. The accountant debited Cash for $1,500 and credited the Capital account for $1,500.			
e. A check was written for $125 to pay the phone bill received and recorded earlier in the month. The accountant debited Phone Expense for $125 and credited Cash for $125.			

P.O. 4,5

Journalize correcting entries.

Exercise 3-8 Journalize correcting entries for each of the following errors and include a brief explanation.

a. A cash purchase of office equipment for $510 was journalized as a cash purchase of store equipment for $510. (Use the ruling method; assume the entry has not been posted.)

b. An entry for a $250 payment for office supplies was journalized as $520. (Use the ruling method; assume the entry has not been posted.)

c. A $620 payment for repairs was journalized and posted as a debit to Equipment instead of a debit to Repair Expense. (Use the correcting entry method to journalize the correction.)

d. A $750 bill for vehicle insurance was received and immediately paid. It was journalized and posted as $570. (Use the correcting entry method to journalize the correction.)

CONSIDER AND COMMUNICATE

Your bookkeeper friend is telling you how sometimes she accidentally debits an incorrect expense account. Your friend says she doesn't have time to make the corrections; besides, the boss will never know the difference. How would you explain to her the impact of these errors?

WHAT IF . . .

Your employee hands you a balanced trial balance. What if you then find out that one transaction was left out completely, another was recorded twice, and a third entry was journalized as $25 instead of $250? Your employee argues that the trial balance is in balance, so it must be correct. How would you explain this situation to your employee?

CRITICAL THINKING

You work as an accounting clerk. You have received the following information supplied by a client from the client's bank, the client's tax returns, and a variety of other July documents. The client wants you to prepare an income statement, a statement of owner's equity, and a balance sheet for the month of July for Kristina L. Bialuski, Bialuski Company.

Income from Services	3,697	Rent Expense	1,500
Professional Fees	?	Wages Expense	2,850
Total Revenue	8,464	Utilities Expense	475
Beginning Capital	50,000	Drawing	1,100
Cash	20,350	Supplies	800
Truck	?	Equipment	18,630
Accounts Payable	?	Total Liabilities and Owner's Equity	55,530

WEB WORK

Using an Internet web browser, type in the search box the phrase *computerized accounting software* or *accounting software Peachtree*. Search for an article or find a home page that will provide you with information about computerized accounting. Narrow your search by adding accounting terms to the search box, for example, computerized accounting disadvantages or accounting practices manual. Discuss or write about your findings.

PROBLEM SET A

For additional help, see the demonstration problems at the beginning of each chapter in your Working Papers.

P.O. 1

Problem 3-1A The chart of accounts of the Brakke School is shown here, followed by the transactions that took place during October of this year:

Assets

111 Cash
113 Accounts Receivable
115 Prepaid Insurance
124 Equipment
127 Furniture

Liabilities

221 Accounts Payable

Owner's Equity

311 T. R. Brakke, Capital
312 T. R. Brakke, Drawing

Revenue

411 Tuition Income

Expenses

511 Salary Expense
512 Rent Expense
513 Gas and Oil Expense
514 Advertising Expense
515 Repair Expense
516 Telephone Expense
517 Utilities Expense
529 Miscellaneous Expense

Oct. 1   Bought liability insurance for one year, $1,540, Ck. No. 1527.
      3   Received a bill for advertising from the *Town Cryer*, $480.
      4   Paid the rent for the current month, $1,350, Ck. No. 1528.
      7   Received a bill for equipment repair from Fix-It Services, $186, Inv. No. 436.
      10 Received and deposited tuition from students, $4,603.
      11 Received and paid the telephone bill, $127, Ck. No. 1529.
      15 Bought desks and chairs from Bukola Furniture Company, $1,475, paying $775 in cash and placing the balance on account, Ck. No. 1530.
      18 Paid on account to the *Town Cryer,* a creditor, $480, Ck. No. 1531.
      21 T. R. Brakke withdrew $650 for personal use, Ck. No. 1532.
      24 Received a bill for gas and oil from Ott Oil Company, $358, Inv. 682.
      25 Received and deposited tuition from students $5,260.
      27 Paid the salary of the office assistant, $975, Ck. No. 1533.
      28 Bought a photocopier on account from Evergreen Office Machines, $1,300, Inv. No. 417.
      29 Received $600 tuition from a student who had charged the tuition on account last month.
      30 Received and paid the bill for utilities, $459, Ck. No. 1534.
      31 Paid for flower arrangements for front office, $48, Ck. No. 1535.
      31 T. R. Brakke invested his personal computer and printer, with a fair market value of $1,550, in the business.

Instructions

Record these transactions in the general journal, including a brief explanation for each entry. Number the journal pages 31, 32, and 33.

P.O. 2,3

Problem 3-2A The journal entries for August, Howell Car Care's second month of business, have been journalized in the general journal in your Working Papers. The balances of the accounts as of July 31 have been recorded in the general ledger in your working papers. Notice the word *Balance* in the Item column, the check mark in the Post. Ref. column, and that the amount is in the Balance column only.

Check Figure

Net Income, $10,503

Instructions

1. Write the owner's name, W. Howell, in the Capital and Drawing accounts.
2. Post the general journal entries to the general ledger accounts.
3. Prepare a trial balance as of August 31, 20—.
4. Prepare an income statement for the two months ended August 31, 20—.
5. Prepare a statement of owner's equity for the two months ended August 31, 20—.
6. Prepare a balance sheet as of August 31, 20—.

P.O. 1,2,3

Problem 3-3A Following is the chart of accounts of M. L. Haas, M.D.

Assets

111 Cash
113 Accounts Receivable
115 Supplies
117 Prepaid Insurance
124 Equipment

Liabilities

221 Accounts Payable

Owner's Equity

311 M. L. Haas, Capital
312 M. L. Haas, Drawing

Revenue

411 Professional Fees

Expenses

511 Salary Expense
512 Rent Expense
513 Laboratory Expense
514 Utilities Expense

Dr. Haas completed the following transactions during July:

July

1 Bought laboratory equipment on account from Stordeur Surgical Supply Company, $2,346, paying $1,500 in cash and placing the remainder on account, Ck. No. 1730.
3 Paid the office rent for the current month, $900, Ck. No. 1731.
5 Received cash on account from patients, $345.
6 Bought supplies on account from Turnbull Supply Company, $327, Inv. 3455.
7 Received and paid the bill for laboratory services, $874, Ck. No. 1732.
8 Bought insurance for one year, $1,135, Ck. No. 1733.
12 Performed medical services for patients on account, $2,368.
15 Performed medical services for patients for cash, $1,846.
16 Part of the equipment purchased on July 1 was found to be broken. Haas returned the damaged part and received a reduction in his bill, $168, Inv. 3162, Credit Memo No. 141.
18 Paid the salary of the part-time nurse, $985, Ck. No. 1734.
24 Received and paid the telephone bill for the month, $145, Ck. No. 1735.
28 Performed medical services for patients on account, $3,640.
29 Dr. Haas withdrew cash for his personal use, $1,800, Ck. No. 1736.

Check Figure

Trial balance total, $51,961

Instructions

1. Journalize the transactions for July in the general journal, beginning on page 21.
2. Write the name of the owner next to the Capital and Drawing accounts in the general ledger. The balances of the accounts as of June 30 have been recorded in the general ledger in your working papers. Notice the word *Balance* in the Item column, the check mark in the Post. Ref. column, and that the amount is in the Balance column only. This indicates a balance brought forward from a prior page or month.
3. Post the entries to the general ledger accounts.
4. Prepare a trial balance.

Instructions for General Ledger Software

1. Journalize the transactions in the general journal.
2. Post the entries to the general ledger.
3. Print a trial balance as of July 31.

P.O. 1,2,3

Problem 3-4A Vera's Landscaping Service has the following chart of accounts:

Assets

111 Cash
113 Accounts Receivable
115 Supplies
117 Prepaid Insurance
124 Equipment

Liabilities

221 Accounts Payable

Owner's Equity

311 V. Daily, Capital
312 V. Daily, Drawing

Revenue

411 Landscaping Income

Expenses

511 Salary Expense
512 Rent Expense
513 Gas and Oil Expense
514 Utilities Expense

The following transactions were completed by Vera's Landscaping Service:

Mar. 1 Daily deposited $20,000 in a bank account in the name of the business.
       4 Daily invested her personal gardening equipment, with a fair market value of $1,400, in the business.
       6 Bought a used trailer on account from Trailer Sales, $800, Inv. No. 314.
       7 Paid the rent for the current month, $485, Ck. No. 1000.
       9 Bought a used backhoe from Earth Equipment, $8,500, paying $4,000 in cash and placing the balance on account, Inv. No. 4166, Ck. No. 1001.
      10 Bought liability insurance for one year, $1,100, Ck. No. 1002.
      13 Sold landscaping services on account to Local Grocers, $1,225, Inv. 100.
      14 Bought supplies on account from Office Masters, $185, Inv. 5172.
      15 Sold landscaping services on account to C. Abrudan, $1,845, Inv. 101.
      17 Received and paid the bill from Grover Services for gas and oil for the equipment, $84, Ck. No. 1003.
      19 Sold landscaping services for cash to Chicz Company, $987, Inv. 102.
      22 Paid on account to Trailer Sales, a creditor, $600, Inv. 314, Ck. No. 1004.
      24 Received on account from Local Grocers, a customer, $500, Inv. 100.
      28 Sold landscaping services on account to Tsakuda Inc., $1,626, Inv. 103.
      29 Received and paid the telephone bill, $184, Ck. No. 1005.
      30 Paid the salary of the employee, $3,268, Ck. No. 1006.
      31 Daily withdrew cash for her personal use, $1,500, Ck. No. 1007.

Check Figure

Trial balance total, $31,968

Instructions

1. Journalize the transactions in the general journal, beginning on page 1. Write a brief explanation for each entry.
2. Write the name of the owner on the Capital and Drawing accounts.
3. Post the journal entries to the ledger accounts.
4. Prepare a trial balance dated March 31, 20—.

PROBLEM SET B

For additional help, see the demonstration problem at the beginning of each chapter in your Working Papers.

P.O. 1

Problem 3-1B The chart of accounts of the Bilson Language School is shown here, followed by the transactions that took place during December of this year:

Assets

111 Cash
113 Accounts Receivable
115 Prepaid Insurance
117 Supplies
124 Equipment
127 Furniture

Liabilities

221 Accounts Payable

Owner's Equity

311 T. L. Bilson, Capital
312 T. L. Bilson, Drawing

Revenue

411 Tuition Income

Expenses

511 Salary Expense
512 Rent Expense
513 Gas and Oil Expense
514 Advertising Expense
515 Repair Expense
516 Telephone Expense
517 Utilities Expense
529 Miscellaneous Expense

Dec. 1 Bought liability insurance for one year, $1,278, Ck. No. 1627.
      11 Received a bill for advertising from the *City News*, $590, Statement No. 4267.
      12 Paid the rent for the current month, $1,150, Ck. No. 1628.
      13 Received a bill for equipment repair from Repair Services, $286, Inv. No. 547.
      16 Received and deposited tuition from students, $3,970.
      17 Received and paid the telephone bill, $216, Ck. No. 1629.
      18 Bought desks and chairs from Siladke Furniture Company, $1,265, paying $600 in cash and placing the balance on account, Ck. No. 1630.
      20 Paid on account to the *City News*, a creditor, $590, Statement No. 4233, Ck. No. 1631.
      21 T. L. Bilson withdrew $750 for personal use, Ck. No. 1632.
      26 Received a bill for gas and oil from DeMers Oil Company, $247, Inv. 591.
      27 Received and deposited tuition from students, $4,370.
      31 Paid the salary of the office assistant, $955, Ck. No. 1633.
      31 Bought a fax machine on account from Central Office Machines, $899, Inv. 529.
      31 Received $700 tuition from a student who had put the tuition on account last month.
      31 Received and paid the bill for utilities, $348, Ck. No. 1634.
      31 T. L. Bilson invested her personal computer and printer, with a fair market value of $1,425, in the business.
      31 Bought supplies, $182, Ck. No. 1635.

Instructions

Record these transactions in the general journal, including a brief explanation for each entry. Number the journal pages 31, 32, and 33.

P.O. 2,3

Problem 3-2B The journal entries for May, Singh's Day Care's second month of business, have been journalized in the general journal in your working papers. The balances of the accounts as of April 30 have been recorded in the general ledger in your working papers. Notice the word *Balance* in the Item column, the check mark in the Post. Ref. column, and that the amount is in the Balance column only. This indicates a balance brought forward from a prior page or month.

Check Figure

Net Income, $5,538

Instructions

1. Write the owner's name, T. Singh, in the Capital and Drawing accounts.
2. Post the general journal entries to the general ledger accounts.
3. Prepare a trial balance as of May 31, 20—.
4. Prepare an income statement for the two months ended May 31, 20—.
5. Prepare a statement of owner's equity for the two months ended May 31, 20—.
6. Prepare a balance sheet as of May 31, 20—.

P.O. 1,2,3

Problem 3-3B Following is the chart of accounts of D. L. Sargeant, M.D.

Assets

111 Cash
113 Accounts Receivable
115 Supplies
117 Prepaid Insurance
124 Equipment

Liabilities

221 Accounts Payable

Owner's Equity

311 D. L. Sargeant, Capital
312 D. L. Sargeant, Drawing

Revenue

411 Professional Fees

Expenses

511 Salary Expense
512 Rent Expense
513 Laboratory Expense
514 Utilities Expense

Dr. Sargeant completed the following transactions during July:

July 1 Bought laboratory equipment on account from Brady Surgical Supply Company, $3,235, paying $1,235 in cash and placing the remainder on account, Inv. No. 2071, Ck. No. 1930.
3 Paid the office rent for the current month, $950, Ck. No. 1931.
5 Received cash on account from patients, $2,456.
6 Bought supplies on account from Kuschak Supply Company, $304, Inv. 3455.
9 Received and paid the bill for laboratory services, $945, Ck. No. 1932.
10 Bought insurance for one year, $1,045, Ck. No. 1933.
12 Performed medical services for patients on account, $2,470.
14 Performed medical services for patients for cash, $2,738.
18 Part of the equipment purchased on July 1 was found to be broken. Sargeant returned the damaged part and received a reduction in her bill, $243, Inv. 2071, Credit Memo No. 218.
20 Paid the salary of the part-time nurse, $990, Ck. No. 1934.
22 Received and paid the telephone bill for the month, $185, Ck. No. 1935.
24 Performed medical services for patients on account, $3,820.
30 Dr. Sargeant withdrew cash for her personal use, $1,500, Ck. No. 1936.

Check Figure

Trial balance total, $37,893

Instructions

1. Journalize the transactions for July in the general journal, beginning on page 21.
2. Write the name of the owner next to the Capital and Drawing accounts in the general ledger. The balances of the accounts as of June 30 have been recorded in the general ledger in your working papers. Notice the word *Balance* in the Item column, the check mark in the Post. Ref. column, and that the amount is in the Balance column only. This indicates a balance brought forward from a prior page or month.
3. Post the entries to the general ledger accounts.
4. Prepare a trial balance.

Instructions for General Ledger Software

1. Journalize the transactions in the general journal.
2. Post the entries to the general ledger.
3. Print a trial balance as of July 31.

P.O. 1,2,3

Problem 3-4B Bill's Landscaping Service maintains the following chart of accounts.

Assets

111 Cash
113 Accounts Receivable
115 Supplies
117 Prepaid Insurance
124 Equipment

Liabilities

221 Accounts Payable

Owner's Equity

311 W. Drake, Capital
312 W. Drake, Drawing

Revenue

411 Landscaping Income

Expenses

511 Salary Expense
512 Rent Expense
513 Gas and Oil Expense
514 Utilities Expense

The following transactions were completed by Drake:

Apr. 1 Drake deposited $18,000 in a bank account in the name of the business.

4 Drake invested his personal gardening equipment, with a fair market value of $1,500, in the business.

6 Bought a used trailer on account from Roadside Sales, $900, Inv. No. 415.

7 Paid the rent for the current month, $574, Ck. No. 100.

9 Bought a used bulldozer from Trekoe Equipment, $9,500, paying $4,000 in cash and placing the balance on account, Inv. No. 3255, Ck. No. 101.

10 Bought liability insurance for one year, $1,200, Ck. No. 102.

13 Sold landscaping services on account to Morgan Homes, $2,116, Inv. 100.

14 Bought supplies on account from Sanders Supply, $162, Inv. 4281.

15 Sold landscaping services on account to Baskett Inc., $2,736, Inv. 101.

17 Received and paid the bill from Le Services for gas and oil for the equipment, $84, Ck. No. 103.

Apr. 19 Sold landscaping services for cash to Marshall Company, $987, Inv. 102.

22 Paid on account to Roadside Sales, a creditor, $400, Inv. 415, Ck. No. 104.

24 Received on account from Morgan Homes, a customer, $500, Inv. 100.

28 Sold landscaping services on account to Hisayo Inc., $1,626, Inv. 103.

29 Received and paid the telephone bill, $145, Ck. No. 105.

30 Paid the salary of the employee, $2,268, Ck. No. 106.

30 Drake withdrew cash for his personal use, $1,400, Ck. No. 107.

Check Figure

Trial balance total, $33,127

Instructions

1. Journalize the transactions in the general journal that begins on page 1. Write a brief explanation for each entry.
2. Write the name of the owner on the Capital and Drawing accounts.
3. Post the journal entries to the general ledger accounts.
4. Prepare a trial balance dated April 30, 20—.

Continuous General Ledger Problem: Journalizing, Posting, and Trial Balance

J. Miracle, an expert art and furniture restorer, buys a studio where he has opened Like New, a sole proprietorship. His accountant has prepared the following chart of accounts. Some accounts may be unfamiliar to you at this time, but as you progress in your accounting education, these accounts will become necessary.

Chart of Accounts

Assets

111 Cash
113 Accounts Receivable
115 Supplies
117 Prepaid Insurance
142 Building
143 Accum. Dep., Building
144 Van
145 Accum. Dep., Van
146 Office Equipment
147 Accum. Dep., Office Equipment
148 Office Furniture
149 Accum. Dep., Office Furniture

Liabilities

211 Accounts Payable
212 Wages Payable
251 Mortgage Payable

Owner's Equity

312 J. Miracle, Capital
313 J. Miracle, Drawing
399 Income Summary

Revenue

411 Service Income

Expenses

511 Wages Expense
512 Utilities Expense
513 Advertising Expense
514 Repair Expense
519 Supplies Expense
520 Insurance Expense
521 Depr. Expense, Building
522 Depr. Expense, Van
523 Depr. Expense, Office Equip.
524 Depr. Expense, Office Furn.

Following are the transactions for May:

May
1   Miracle deposited $100,000 in a bank account in the name of the business, Dep. Slip No. 16262.
2   Miracle bought Like New for $125,400. The assets include a building, $90,000; van, $18,500; office equipment, $12,600; office furniture, $4,300. Paid $36,000 in cash (Ck. No. 1000) and placed the balance on a mortgage note. (Debit each asset separately and credit Cash and Mortgage Payable.)
4   Bought supplies on account from The Paint Pot, $2,290, Inv. 961.
5   Bought advertising on account from Adams Advertising, $841, Inv. 3162.

Note: The Continuous General Ledger Problem can be worked with Houghton Mifflin Windows General Ledger Package, Peachtree Release 5.01, QuickBooks 6.0, or other general ledger software packages.

May   7   Sold services on account to Adeline Harris, $1,256, Sales Inv. 2001.

          9   Sold services for cash to customers, $4,167, Cash Receipt Nos. 1100–1106.

      11   Bought insurance for the business from Drake Agency for one year, $1,153, Ck. No. 1001.

      12   Bought office equipment on account from Office Ready, $698, Inv. 6136.

      15   Paid wages of part-time assistant for the first half of the month, $850, Ck. No. 1002.

      16   Received on account from J. Wilson, a customer, $540, Cash Receipt No. 1107.

      17   Sold services for cash to customers, $5,173, Cash Receipt Nos. 1108–1116.

      18   The owner withdrew cash for personal use, $1,100, Ck. No. 1003.

      19   Received and paid the bill for repairs, $459, Ck. No. 1004.

      21   Bought additional office furniture on account from Au Furniture, $723, Inv. 475.

      22   Sold services on account to Jeff Isely, $1,536, Sales Inv. 2002.

      23   Sold services on account to Mike Willen, $2,314, Sales Inv. 2003.

      25   Received and paid for utility bill, $345, Ck. No. 1005.

      27   Paid $300 on account to Office Ready, a creditor, $300, Ck. No. 1006, Inv. 6136.

      31   Paid wages of part-time assistant for the second half of the month, $850, Ck. No. 1007.

Instructions

1. Open the general ledger software.
2. Create and save a new file as Likenew.
3. Print a copy of the chart of accounts for your convenience in planning journal entries.
4. Journalize the transactions in the general journal and post them to the general ledger.
5. Print the general journal.
6. Print the general ledger.
7. Print a trial balance.

Cumulative Self-Check: Chapters 1–3

PART I: MULTIPLE-CHOICE QUESTIONS

___ 1. Which of the following is not considered an account?

a. Cash
b. Prepaid Insurance
c. Equipment
d. Assets
e. Accounts Receivable

___ 2. In which of the following transactions would an expense be recorded?

a. Received a bill for utilities.
b. Paid on an account payable for the electric bill.
c. Received and paid a bill for repairs.
d. All of these should be recorded as an expense.
e. Only a and c should be recorded as an expense.

___ 3. The ending capital balance appears on which of the following statements?

a. Statement of owner's equity
b. Balance sheet
c. Income statement
d. Statement of owner's equity and balance sheet
e. Statement of owner's equity and income statement

___ 4. On a statement of owner's equity, if beginning capital is $41,000 and there are an additional investment of $6,000, a net loss of $8,000, and owner withdrawals of $15,000, the ending capital amount would be

a. $70,000.
b. $24,000.
c. $40,000.
d. $54,000.
e. none of these.

___ 5. If a $36 cash purchase of supplies is recorded as a $63 debit to Supplies and a $63 credit to Cash, the result will be that

a. the trial balance will be in balance.
b. the Supplies account will be overstated.
c. the Cash account will be understated.
d. Supplies will be overstated and Cash will be understated.
e. all of these will be true.

Note: Answers to the Cumulative Self-Check begin on page A-1.

____ 6. A person who wanted to know the balance of an account would look in

    a. the ledger.
    b. the chart of accounts.
    c. the journal.
    d. the source documents.
    e. none of these.

PART II: PRACTICAL APPLICATION

Journalizing, Posting, Trial Balance, and Financial Statements

The accounts and their balances, as of December 1 of this year, for Stanfill Services are listed below:

111 Cash	$18,900	311 D. Stanfill, Capital	$49,590
112 Accounts Receivable	6,300	312 D. Stanfill, Drawing	11,200
113 Supplies	870	411 Service Income	39,600
114 Prepaid Insurance	1,230	511 Wages Expense	10,450
124 Equipment	31,200	512 Utilities Expense	2,760
221 Accounts Payable	6,340	513 Rent Expense	12,620

Check Figure

Net income, $13,158

Instructions

1. Journalize the following December transactions in general journal form on journal page 31.

    Dec. 1 Stanfill deposited $10,000 in an account in the name of the business.
            4 Received and paid the bill for the rent for December, $900, Ck. No. 2331.
         11 Received $1,860 on account from customers, Cash Receipt Nos. 1430–1438.
         19 Sold services on account to M. Linares, $2,150, Sales Inv. No. 2591.
         22 Received and paid the bill for utilities, $197, Ck. No. 2332.
         23 Bought supplies on account from Staple Works, $248, Inv. No. 2606.
         31 Paid the wages for the month, $1,665, Ck. No. 2333.
         31 Stanfill withdrew $1,800 for personal use, Ck. No. 2334.

2. Label T accounts with the above account names.
3. Correctly place the plus and minus signs under all T accounts, and label the debit and credit sides of each T account.
4. Post the entries to the T accounts by date, and foot and balance the accounts.
5. Prepare a trial balance as of December 31.
6. Prepare an income statement for the year ended December 31.
7. Prepare a statement of owner's equity for the year ended December 31.
8. Prepare a balance sheet as of December 31.

4 Adjusting Entries and the Work Sheet

Performance Objectives

After you have completed this chapter, you will be able to do the following:

1. Define a *fiscal period*.

2. List the classifications of the accounts that occupy each column of a ten-column work sheet.

3. Complete a work sheet for a service enterprise, involving adjustments for supplies used, expired insurance, depreciation, and accrued wages.

4. Prepare an income statement, a statement of owner's equity, and a balance sheet for a service business directly from the work sheet.

5. Journalize and post the adjusting entries.

6. Prepare an income statement and a balance sheet for a business with more than one revenue account and more than one accumulated depreciation account.

Remember!

Accounting steps:

Analyzing: Which accounts are involved?

Classifying: assets, liabilities, capital, revenue, and expenses

Recording: journalizing

Summarizing: financial statements

Interpreting: drawing conclusions

R elating to the *summarizing* step in the definition of accounting, here we introduce the work sheet and the financial statements. Now that you are familiar with the classifying and recording phases of accounting for a service business, let's look at the remaining steps in the accounting process.

FISCAL PERIOD

A **fiscal period** is any period of time covering a complete accounting cycle. A **fiscal year** is a fiscal period consisting of twelve consecutive months. It does not have to coincide with the calendar year. If a business has seasonal peaks, it is a good idea to complete the accounting operations at the end of the most active season. At that time, management wants to know the results of the year and where the business stands financially. The fiscal year of a resort that operates during the summer may be from October 1 of one year to September 30 of the next. The government at some levels has a fiscal year from July 1 of one year to June 30 of the following year. Department stores often use a fiscal period from February 1 of one year to January 31 of the next. For income tax purposes, any period of twelve consecutive months may be selected. However, you have to be consistent and use the same fiscal period each year.

THE ACCOUNTING CYCLE

The **accounting cycle** represents the sequence of steps in the accounting process completed during the fiscal period. Figure 1 shows how we introduce these steps on a chapter-by-chapter basis. This outline brings you up to date on what we have accomplished so far and how each chapter fits into the steps in the accounting cycle.

FIGURE 1

Chapter 1
> Analysis of Business Transactions
> Assets = Liabilities + Owner's Equity
> Analysis of Business Transactions
> Assets = Liabilities + Capital + Revenue − Expenses

Chapter 2
> Analysis of Business Transactions
> Assets = Liabilities + Capital + Revenue − Expenses
> $+|-$ $-|+$ $-|+$ $-|+$ $+|-$

Chapter 3
> Journalize and Post Business Transactions.
> Prepare a Trial Balance.

Chapter 4
> Gather the Adjustment Data.
> Complete a Work Sheet.
> Prepare Financial Statements.
> Journalize and Post Adjusting Entries.

Chapter 5
> Journalize and Post Closing Entries.
> Prepare a Post-Closing Trial Balance.

THE WORK SHEET

The **work sheet** is a working paper used by accountants to record necessary adjustments and provide up-to-date account balances needed to prepare the financial statements. The work sheet is a tool that accountants use to help in preparing the financial statements. As a tool, the work sheet serves as a central place for bringing together the information needed to record the adjustments. With up-to-date account balances, the accountant can prepare the financial statements.

First, we present the work sheet form so that you can see the big picture. Next, we describe and show examples of adjustments. Finally, we show how the adjustments are entered on the work sheet and how the work sheet is completed.

For our purposes, we use a ten-column work sheet—so called because two amount columns are provided for each of the work sheet's five major sections. We will explain the function of each of these sections, again basing our discussion on the accounting activities of Cruz Auto Detail. But first we need to fill in the heading, which consists of three lines: (1) the name of the company, (2) the title of the working paper, and (3) the period of time covered.

Cruz Auto Detail
Work Sheet
For Month Ended June 30, 20—

ACCOUNT NAME	TRIAL BALANCE		ADJUSTMENTS		ADJUSTED TRIAL BALANCE		INCOME STATEMENT		BALANCE SHEET	
	DEBIT	CREDIT	DEBIT	CREDIT	DEBIT	CREDIT	DEBIT	CREDIT	DEBIT	CREDIT

Next, we want to point out the account classifications that are placed in each column. We start with the Trial Balance columns and then move across the work sheet, discussing each pair of columns separately.

The Columns of the Work Sheet

Trial Balance Columns When you use a work sheet, you do not have to prepare a trial balance on a separate sheet of paper. Instead, you enter the account balances from the general ledger in the first two amount columns of the work sheet. List the accounts that have balances in the Account Name column in the same order in which they appear in the chart of accounts. Assuming normal balances, the account classifications are listed in the Trial Balance Debit and Credit columns of the work sheet as shown at the top of the next page.

As we move along in this chapter, we will discuss the adjustments. The Adjusted Trial Balance columns contain the same account classifications as the Trial Balance columns. **The Adjusted Trial Balance columns are merely extensions of the Trial Balance columns, plus or minus any adjustment amounts.** If an adjustment is required, the amounts are carried from the Trial Balance columns through the Adjustments columns and into the Adjusted Trial Balance columns.

Account Name	Trial Balance		Adjustments		Adjusted Trial Balance		Income Statement		Balance Sheet	
	Debit	Credit	Debit	Credit	Debit	Credit	Debit	Credit	Debit	Credit
	Assets ——————→				Assets					
		Liabilities ——————→				Liabilities				
		Capital ——————→				Capital				
	Drawing ——————→				Drawing					
		Revenue ——————→				Revenue				
	Expenses ——————→				Expenses					

Income Statement Columns An income statement contains the revenues minus the expenses. Revenue accounts have credit balances, so they are recorded in the Income Statement Credit column. Expense accounts have debit balances, so they are recorded in the Income Statement Debit column.

Account Name	Trial Balance		Adjustments		Adjusted Trial Balance		Income Statement		Balance Sheet	
	Debit	Credit	Debit	Credit	Debit	Credit	Debit	Credit	Debit	Credit
	Assets ——————→				Assets					
		Liabilities ——————→				Liabilities				
		Capital ——————→				Capital				
	Drawing ——————→				Drawing					
		Revenue ——————→				Revenue ——————→		Revenue		
	Expenses ——————→				Expenses ——————→		Expenses			

Balance Sheet Columns As you recall, the balance sheet is a statement showing assets, liabilities, and owner's equity. Asset accounts have debit balances, so they are recorded in the Balance Sheet Debit column. Liability accounts have credit balances, so they are recorded in the Balance Sheet Credit column. The Capital account has a credit balance, so it is recorded in the Balance Sheet Credit column. Because the Drawing account is a deduction from Capital, it has a debit balance and is recorded in the Balance Sheet Debit column (the opposite column from that in which Capital is recorded).

Account Name	Trial Balance		Adjustments		Adjusted Trial Balance		Income Statement		Balance Sheet	
	Debit	Credit	Debit	Credit	Debit	Credit	Debit	Credit	Debit	Credit
	Assets ——————→				Assets ——————→				Assets	
		Liabilities ——————→				Liabilities ——————→				Liabilities
		Capital ——————→				Capital ——————→				Capital
	Drawing ——————→				Drawing ——————→				Drawing	
		Revenue ——————→				Revenue ——————→		Revenue		
	Expenses ——————→				Expenses ——————→		Expenses			

ADJUSTMENTS

Objective 3

Complete a work sheet for a service enterprise, involving adjustments for supplies used, expired insurance, depreciation, and accrued wages.

Adjustments are a way of updating the ledger accounts. They may be considered *internal transactions*. They have not been recorded in the accounts up to this time because no outside party has been involved. Adjustments are determined after the trial balance has been prepared.

Only a few accounts are adjusted. After you have acquired experience in accounting, these accounts will be easy to recognize. To describe the reasons for making adjustments, let's return to Cruz Auto Detail. First, we select the accounts that require adjustments. Next, we show the adjustments recorded in T accounts so you can see the effect on the accounts. **However, bear in mind that the adjustments are first recorded on the work sheet.**

Supplies

In the trial balance, the Supplies account has a balance of $800. When Cruz Auto Detail bought supplies, Cruz wrote the entry as a debit to Supplies and a credit to Accounts Payable. Thus she recorded the purchase of supplies as an increase in the Supplies account.

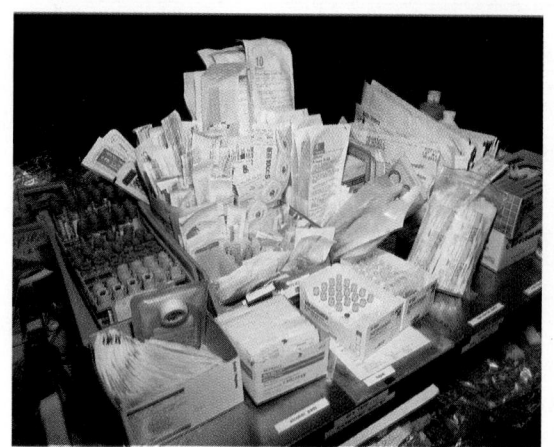

As long as supplies are unused, they are considered an asset. But we have not taken into consideration the fact that any business continually uses up supplies in the process of carrying on its activities. For Cruz Auto Detail, the items recorded under Supplies consist of buffer pads, cleaners, waxes, etc. Rather than going to the trouble of journalizing the supplies used each day, Cruz Auto Detail waits until the end of the month and then takes a physical count of the supplies left. **To find the amount of supplies used, subtract the amount left from the total supplies that were available.**

When Cruz counts the supplies on June 30, she finds that there is $260 worth of supplies left. The situation looks like this:

All businesses continually use up supplies in the process of doing business. Supplies that are unused, though, are considered an asset.

Balance of Supplies account $800	−	Amount of supplies left $260	=	Amount of supplies used and the adjusting entry amount $540

To record the amount of the supplies used, Cruz has to make an adjusting entry. The purpose of an **adjusting entry** is to bring the books up to date at the end of the accounting period. The journalizing of these adjustments is shown on page 125. Let's look at this in T account form. We need to take the amount of supplies used ($540) out of the Supplies account (credit Supplies) because we no longer have that much of the asset. Also, we need to put the amount of supplies used ($540) in the Supplies Expense account (debit Supplies Expense) because we have incurred this expense.

Remember!

For the adjustment of supplies, first find the amount used by subtracting the amount left from the balance of the Supplies account. In the adjusting entry, take the amount used out of Supplies and put it into Supplies Expense.

(a)

		Supplies						Supplies Expense		
			+	−					+	−
(Old)	Balance	800		Adjusting	540		Adjusting	540		
(New)	Balance	260								

Drawing T accounts on scratch paper is an excellent way of organizing the adjusting entry. By making this entry, Cruz Auto Detail has taken the amount used out of Supplies and put it into Supplies Expense. The new balance of Supplies, $260, represents the cost of supplies that are on hand and should therefore appear in the balance sheet. The $540 in Supplies Expense represents the cost of supplies that have been used and should therefore appear in the income statement.

Prepaid Insurance

The $360 balance in Prepaid Insurance represents the premium paid in advance for a one-year liability insurance policy. One month of the twelve months of premium has now expired, which amounts to $30.

$$12 \text{ months } \overline{)\$360} \quad \$\,30 \text{ per month}$$

In the adjustment, Cruz Auto Detail deducts the expired or used portion from Prepaid Insurance and adds it to Insurance Expense.

(b)	Prepaid Insurance			Insurance Expense		
		+	−		+	−
(Old)	Balance	360	Adjusting 30	Adjusting	30	
(New)	Balance	330				

The new balance of Prepaid Insurance, $330 ($360 − $30), represents the cost of insurance that remains paid in advance and should therefore appear in the balance sheet. The $30 figure in Insurance Expense represents the cost of insurance that has expired and should therefore appear in the income statement.

Depreciation of Equipment

We have followed the policy of recording durable items, such as appliances and fixtures, under Equipment because they will last longer than one year. The benefits of these assets will eventually be used up (the assets will either wear out or become obsolete). Therefore, we should systematically spread out the cost of these assets over their useful lives. That is, we allocate the cost of the equipment as an expense *over its estimated useful life* and call this **depreciation** because such equipment loses its usefulness. A part of this depreciation expense is allotted to each fiscal period. In the case of Cruz Auto Detail, the Equipment account has a balance of $51,500. Suppose we estimate that the equipment will have a useful life of seven years, with a trade-salvage value of $7,820 at the end of that time. Using **straight-line depreciation**, we can allocate the cost of an asset, less any trade-in value, evenly over the useful life of the asset. Depreciation for one month is figured like this:

1. Subtract the trade-in (salvage) value from the cost to get the full depreciation.

$$\$51,500 - \$7,820 = \$43,680$$

2. Divide the full depreciation by the number of years in the asset's useful life to get the depreciation for one year.

$$\frac{\$\ 6{,}240 \text{ per year}}{7 \text{ years }\ )\$43{,}680 \text{ full depreciation}}$$

3. Divide the depreciation for one year by 12 to get the depreciation for one month.

$$\frac{\$\ 520 \text{ per month}}{12 \text{ months }\ )\$6{,}240}$$

When depreciation is recorded, we do not subtract it directly from the asset account. In asset accounts, such as Equipment or Building, we must keep the original cost recorded in the account. Consequently, the amount of depreciation has to be recorded in another account; that account is Accumulated Depreciation.

Always record the adjusting entry for depreciation as a debit to Depreciation Expense (an income statement item) and a credit to Accumulated Depreciation (a balance sheet item), which increases both accounts required. The adjustment in T account form would appear as follows:

(c) Depreciation Expense, Equipment	Accumulated Depreciation, Equipment
+ | −	− | +
Adjusting 520 |	| Adjusting 520

On the balance sheet, the balance of Accumulated Depreciation is deducted from the balance of the related asset account as illustrated on the following partial balance sheet for Cruz Auto Detail. The net figure shown, $50,980, is referred to as the book value of the asset. Thus, **book value** (or **carrying value**) is the cost of an asset minus accumulated depreciation.

FYI

If we had a Building account, the adjusting entry would be a debit to Depreciation Expense, Building, and a credit to Accumulated Depreciation, Building. Building and Accumulated Depreciation, Building, would be listed separately on the balance sheet.

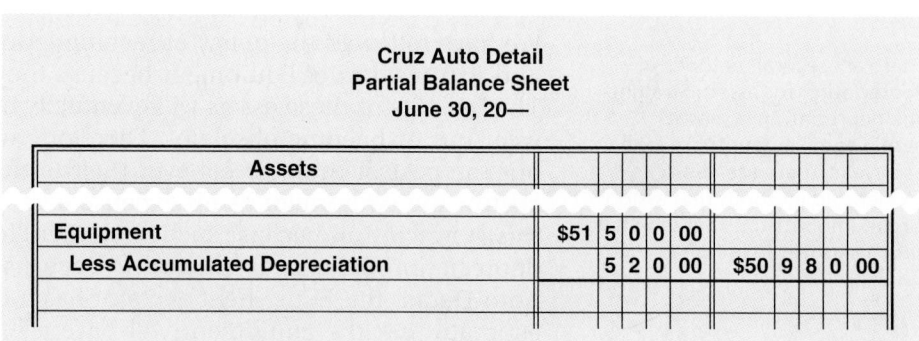

Cruz Auto Detail Partial Balance Sheet June 30, 20—			
Assets			
Equipment	$51 5 0 0 00		
Less Accumulated Depreciation	5 2 0 00	$50 9 8 0 00	

Accumulated Depreciation, Equipment, is contrary to, or a deduction from, Equipment, so we call it a **contra account.** To show the accounts under their proper headings, let's look at the fundamental accounting equation. Brackets indicate that Accumulated Depreciation, Equipment, is a deduction from the Equipment account. Note that the plus and minus signs are opposite.

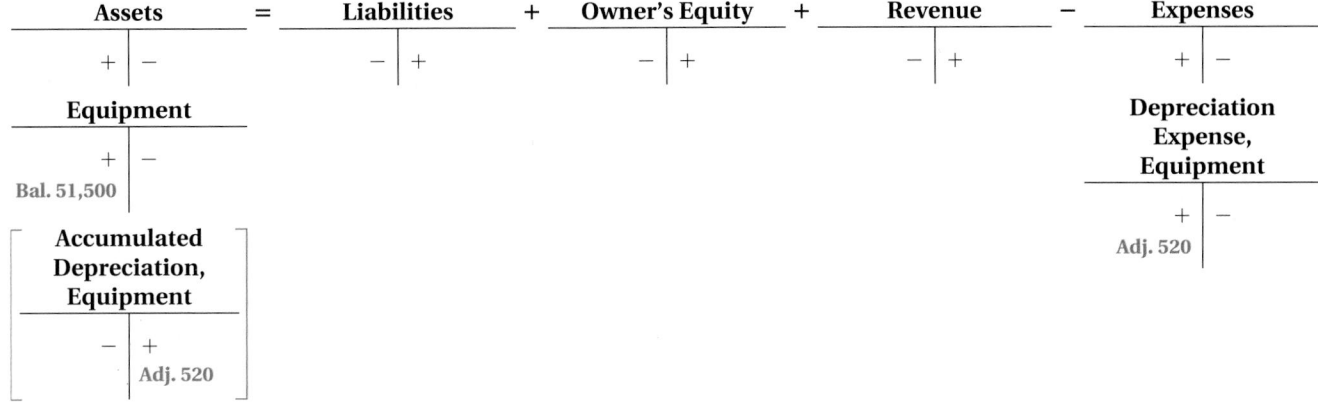

Accumulated Depreciation, Equipment, as the title implies, is the total depreciation that the company has taken since the original purchase of the asset. Rather than crediting the Equipment account, Cruz Auto Detail keeps track of the total depreciation taken since it first acquired the asset in a separate account. The maximum depreciation it could take would be the cost of the equipment, $51,500, less trade-in value of $7,820. So, Accumulated Depreciation, Equipment, will increase at the rate of $520 per month, assuming that no additional equipment has been purchased. For example, at the end of the second month, Accumulated Depreciation, Equipment, will amount to $1,040 ($520 + $520), and the book value will be $50,460 ($51,500 − $1,040).

Wages Expense

The end of the fiscal period and the end of the employees' payroll period rarely fall on the same day. A diagram of the situation looks like this:

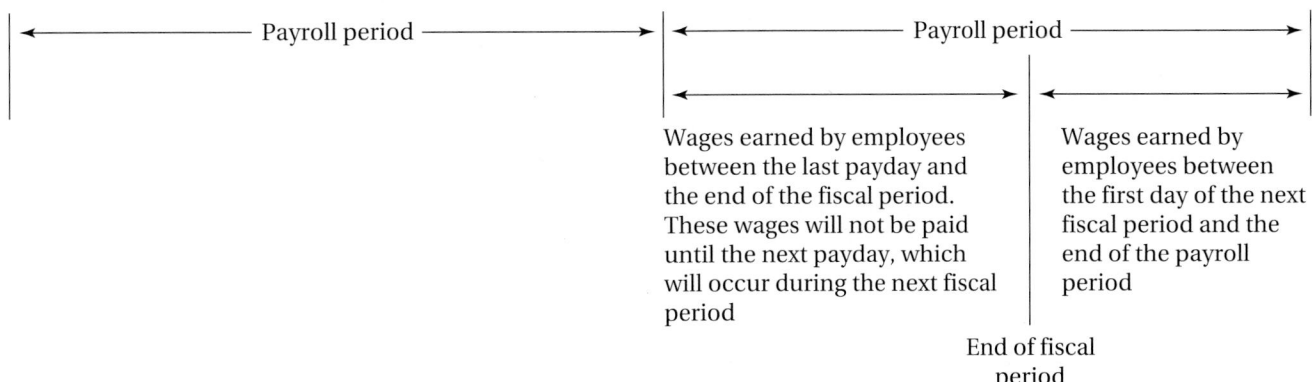

Since the last day of the fiscal period falls in the middle of the payroll period, we have to split up the wages earned in that payroll period between the fiscal period just ending and the next fiscal period. We will use another company for this example.

Assume that this firm pays its employees a total of $400 per day and that payday falls on Friday throughout the year. The employees work a five-day week. When the employees pick up their paychecks on Friday, the amount of the checks includes their wages for that day and for the preceding four days. Suppose that the last day of the fiscal period falls on Wednesday, December 31. The diagram on the following page illustrates this situation.

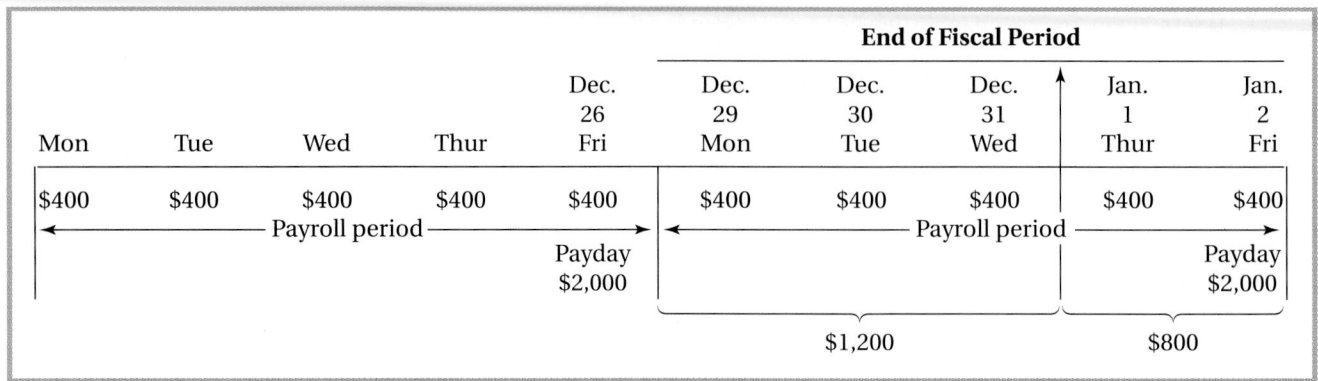

					End of Fiscal Period				
				Dec. 26	Dec. 29	Dec. 30	Dec. 31	Jan. 1	Jan. 2
Mon	Tue	Wed	Thur	Fri	Mon	Tue	Wed	Thur	Fri
$400	$400	$400	$400	$400	$400	$400	$400	$400	$400

← Payroll period →   Payday $2,000   ← Payroll period →   Payday $2,000

$1,200 $800

Remember!

If the end of the fiscal period (or end of the fiscal year) occurs during the middle of a payroll period, Wages Expense must be adjusted to bring it up to date. In the adjusting entry, add the amount employees have earned between the end of the last payroll period and the end of the fiscal period.

December						
S	M	T	W	T	F	S
	1	2	3	4	⑤	6
7	8	9	10	11	⑫	13
14	15	16	17	18	⑲	20
21	22	23	24	25	㉖	27
28	29	30	31			

— Paydays

To have the Wages Expense account show an accurate balance for the fiscal period, you need to add $1,200 for the cost of labor between the last payday, December 26, and the end of the year, December 31 ($400 for December 29; $400 for December 30; $400 for December 31). Because the $1,200 will not be paid at this time but is owed to the employees as of December 31, you also need to add $1,200 to Wages Payable, a liability account, because the company owes this amount to employees.

Wages Expense

	+	–
(Old) Balance 104,000		
Adjusting 1,200		
(New) Balance 105,200		

Wages Payable

–	+
	Adjusting 1,200

Returning to our illustration of Cruz Auto Detail, the last payday was June 24. Between June 24 and the end of the month, Cruz Auto Detail owes an additional $290 in wages to its employee. Accountants refer to this extra amount that has not been recorded at the end of the month as **accrued wages**. In accounting terms, **accrual** means recognition of an expense or a revenue that has been incurred (expense) or earned (revenue) but has not yet been recorded.

Remember!

In the adjusting entry for accrued wages, increase both the Wages Expense and the Wages Payable accounts.

(d)   Wages Expense

	+	–
(Old) Balance 1,400		
Adjusting 290		
(New) Balance 1,690		

Wages Payable

–	+
	Adjusting 290

The Financial Picture Before Adjustments

The Financial Picture After Adjustments

Without adjustments, the financial statements would be out of focus. Adjustments fine tune the financial picture of the business.

You record the adjusting entry for accrued wages as a debit to Wages Expense and a credit to Wages Payable because both accounts need to be increased.

Placement of Accounts in the Work Sheet

We have to enter the adjustments on the work sheet, but before doing so, let's briefly discuss the Drawing and Accumulated Depreciation accounts, as well as net income, and their effect on the work sheet.

Capital and Drawing Account Balances The Drawing account is a contra account (contrary to Capital). In the statement of owner's equity, Drawing is deducted from Capital. To show one account as a deduction from another, the plus and minus signs are switched around. The T accounts look like this:

L.A. Cruz, Capital		L.A. Cruz, Drawing	
−	+	+	−
Debit	Credit	Debit	Credit
	Balance	Balance	

The normal balance for the Capital account is recorded in the Credit columns of the Trial Balance, the Adjusted Trial Balance, and the Balance Sheet sections. The normal balance for the Drawing account is recorded in the Debit columns of the Trial Balance, the Adjusted Trial Balance, and the Balance Sheet sections.

Equipment and Accumulated Depreciation, Equipment, Account Balances The Accumulated Depreciation, Equipment, account is a contra account (contrary to Equipment). In the balance sheet, Accumulated Depreciation, Equipment, is deducted from Equipment. The T accounts look like this:

Equipment		Accumulated Depreciation, Equipment	
+	−	−	+
Debit	Credit	Debit	Credit
Balance			Balance

The normal balance for the Equipment account is recorded in the Debit columns of the Trial Balance, the Adjusted Trial Balance, and the Balance Sheet sections. The normal balance for the Accumulated Depreciation, Equipment, account is recorded in the Credit columns of the Trial Balance, the Adjusted Trial Balance, and the Balance Sheet sections.

Net Income

Net income (or net loss) is the difference between revenue and expenses. It is used to balance the Income Statement columns; since revenue is normally larger than expenses, the balancing amount must be added to the expense side. Net income (or net loss) is also used to balance the Balance Sheet columns. As on the statement of owner's equity, you add net income to the owner's beginning Capital balance. Since the Capital balance is located in the Balance Sheet Credit column, net income must also be added to that side. The following diagram shows these relationships:

Account Name	Trial Balance		Adjustments		Adjusted Trial Balance		Income Statement		Balance Sheet	
	Debit	Credit	Debit	Credit	Debit	Credit	Debit	Credit	Debit	Credit
	A + Draw. + E	Accum. Depr. + L + Cap. + R			A + Draw. + E	Accum. Depr. + L + Cap. + R	E	R	A + Draw.	Accum. Depr. + L + Cap.
Net Income							NI			NI

Remember!

A net income amount is entered in the Income Statement Debit column and the Balance Sheet Credit column (same side as the increase side of Capital). A net loss is entered in the Income Statement Credit column and the Balance Sheet Debit column (same side as the decrease side of Capital).

On the other hand, if expenses are larger than revenue, the result is a net loss. You must add net loss to the revenue side to balance the Income Statement columns. Also, because a net loss is deducted from the owner's beginning Capital balance, you must include net loss in the debit side of the Balance Sheet columns, thereby balancing these columns. To show this, let's look at the Income Statement and Balance Sheet columns diagrammed here.

	Income Statement		Balance Sheet	
	Debit	Credit	Debit	Credit
			A + Draw.	Accum. Depr. + L + Cap.
	E	R		
Net Loss		NL	NL	

Summary of Adjustments by T Accounts

To test your understanding, describe why the following adjustments are necessary. The answers are shown below the accounts.

(a)	Supplies					Supplies Expense	
	+	−				+	−
Balance	800	Adjusting	540	Adjusting		540	

(b)	Prepaid Insurance					Insurance Expense	
	+	−				+	−
Balance	360	Adjusting	30	Adjusting		30	

(c)	Depreciation Expense, Equipment			Accumulated Depreciation, Equipment		
	+	−		−	+	
Adjusting	520				Adjusting	520

(d)	Wages Expense			Wages Payable		
	+	−		−	+	
Balance	1,400					
Adjusting	290				Adjusting	290

a. To record the cost of supplies used during June, $540.
b. To record the insurance expired during June, $30.
c. To record the depreciation for the month of June, $520.
d. To record accrued wages owed at the end of June, $290.

Remember!

The amount of the adjusting entry for supplies used equals the balance of the Supplies account minus the amount of the supplies inventory (left over).

Remember!

Each of the accounts that is adjusted has a companion account. Supplies—companion account is Supplies Expense. Prepaid Insurance—companion account is Insurance Expense. Depreciation Expense—companion account is Accumulated Depreciation. Wages Expense—companion account is Wages Payable.

Mixed Accounts At this point, take special notice of the fact that **each adjusting entry contains an income statement account (revenue or expense) and a balance sheet account (asset, contra asset, or liability).** Accountants refer to these accounts as mixed accounts—accounts with balances that are partly income statement amounts and partly balance sheet amounts. The income statement and balance sheet accounts involved are separate accounts that have a part of their name in common, like Supplies Expense (an expense account) and Supplies (an asset account). For example, Supplies is recorded as $800 in the Trial Balance, but after adjustment, this amount is split up or apportioned as $540 in Supplies Expense in the Income Statement columns and $260 in Supplies in the Balance Sheet columns. Similarly, Prepaid Insurance is recorded as $360 in the Trial Balance columns but is apportioned as $30 in Insurance Expense in the Income Statement columns and $330 in Prepaid Insurance in the Balance Sheet columns. In other words, portions of these trial balance amounts are recorded in each section.

In the previous examples, we used T accounts to explain how to handle adjustments. T accounts help organize any type of accounting entry into debits and credits. But now it is time to record the adjustments on the work sheet. To help you remember which classifications of accounts appear in each column of the work sheet, we will label the columns with letters specifying each classification of accounts; for example, A for assets and L for liabilities as shown in Figure 2 on the following page.

Cruz Auto Detail
Work Sheet
For Month Ended June 30, 20—

	ACCOUNT NAME	TRIAL BALANCE			ADJUSTMENTS	
		DEBIT	CREDIT Accum. Deprec.		DEBIT	CREDIT
		A + Draw. + E	+ L + C + R			
1	Cash	23 2 5 0 00				
2	Accounts Receivable	2 0 0 00				
3	Supplies	8 0 0 00				(a) 5 4 0 00
4	Prepaid Insurance	3 6 0 00				(b) 3 0 00
5	Equipment	51 5 0 0 00				
6	Accounts Payable		4 7 0 0 00			
7	L. A. Cruz, Capital		70 0 0 0 00			
8	L. A. Cruz, Drawing	3 0 0 0 00				
9	Income from Services		7 2 7 0 00			
10	Wages Expense	1 4 0 0 00			(d) 2 9 0 00	
11	Rent Expense	9 0 0 00				
12	Advertising Expense	4 0 0 00				
13	Utilities Expense	1 6 0 00				
14		81 9 7 0 00	81 9 7 0 00			
15	Supplies Expense				(a) 5 4 0 00	
16	Insurance Expense				(b) 3 0 00	
17	Depreciation Expense, Equipment				(c) 5 2 0 00	
18	Accumulated Depreciation, Equipment					(c) 5 2 0 00
19	Wages Payable					(d) 2 9 0 00
20					1 3 8 0 00	1 3 8 0 00

FIGURE 2

Steps in the Completion of the Work Sheet

Before we complete the work sheet, let's list the recommended steps to follow.

1. Complete the Trial Balance columns, total, and rule.
2. Complete the Adjustments columns, total, and rule.
3. Complete the Adjusted Trial Balance columns, total, and rule.
4. Record balances in the Income Statement and Balance Sheet columns and total each column.
5. Record net income or net loss in the Income Statement columns by subtracting the smaller side from the larger side and adding the difference to the smaller side, total, and rule.
6. Record net income or net loss in the Balance Sheet columns by subtracting the smaller side from the larger side and adding the difference to the smaller side (the amount should be the same as the difference between the Income Statement column totals—if not, there is an error), total, and rule.

Step 1: Trial Balance Columns Note that the trial balance in Figure 2 is the same trial balance for Cruz Auto Detail presented earlier. You will be able to follow the completion of the entire work sheet for Cruz Auto Detail in Figures 3 through 6 by turning the transparent pages, thus adding the next stage of its completion, and in Figure 7 on pages 122–123.

Remember!

After the first fiscal period, Accumulated Depreciation will have a balance, so it will be listed immediately below the asset being depreciated (which in this example is Equipment). Consequently, Accumulated Depreciation will not appear at the bottom of next month's work sheet.

Remember!

Supplies is adjusted for the amount used.

Insurance is adjusted by adding the amount expired to Insurance Expense while deducting the same amount from Prepaid Insurance.

Depreciation is added to both Depreciation Expense and Accumulated Depreciation.

Accrued wages are added to both Wages Expense and Wages Payable.

Depreciation can occur from wear and tear of everyday use or assets can simply become obsolete.

Step 2: Adjustments Columns When we enter the adjustments, we identify them as **(a), (b), (c),** and **(d)** to indicate the relationships between the debit and credit sides and the sequence of the individual adjusting entries (see Figure 4).

Note that Supplies Expense; Insurance Expense; Depreciation Expense, Equipment; Accumulated Depreciation, Equipment; and Wages Payable did not appear in the trial balance because there were no balances in the accounts at that time. We wrote them below the Trial Balance totals to complete the work sheet.

Here is a brief review of the adjustments:

a. To record the $540 cost of supplies used during June.
b. To record the $30 cost of insurance expired during June.
c. To record $520 depreciation for the month of June.
d. To record $290 of accrued wages owed at the end of June.

Now let's look at the work sheet shown in Figure 7 (pp. 122–123). To reinforce the idea of adjusting entries, see the brief explanation of each adjustment at the right of the work sheet. Again, the completed work sheet is shown on the transparent pages (Figures 3–6) between pages 120–121.

After the first fiscal period, Accumulated Depreciation will always have a balance until the related asset is sold or disposed of. Consequently, it will be listed in the Trial Balance columns immediately below the appropriate asset (Equipment, in this case).

Regarding the work sheet, again, we emphasize that it is strictly a working paper or tool used to gather together all the up-to-date information needed to prepare the financial statements. **The adjustments are always recorded in the work sheet first.**

Step 3: Adjusted Trial Balance Columns Once the Adjustments columns are totaled and ruled, extend each Trial Balance amount, plus or minus any adjustment from the Adjustments columns, to the Adjusted Trial Balance columns as shown in Figure 5 or Figure 7.

Step 4: Income Statement and Balance Sheet Columns Extend the balances in the Adjusted Trial Balance columns to either the Income Statement or the Balance Sheet columns (see Figure 6).

Step 5: Net Income or Net Loss—Income Statement Columns Total each of the two Income Statement columns. Subtract the smaller side from the larger side, and write the difference under the smaller Income Statement column total, total and rule as shown in Figure 6.

Step 6: Net Income or Net Loss—Balance Sheet Columns Total each of the two Balance Sheet columns. Subtract the smaller side from the larger side, and write the difference under the smaller Balance Sheet column total (the amount should be the same as the difference between the Income Statement column totals—if not, there is an error), total and rule as shown in Figure 6.

If there is a net income, the credit side of the Income Statement columns will be larger than the debit side—more revenue than expenses. In this case, write Net Income in the Account Name column on the same line as the difference you calculated.

If there is a net loss, the debit side of the Income Statement columns will be larger than the credit side—more expenses than revenue. In this case,

FIGURE 7

	ACCOUNT NAME	TRIAL BALANCE			
		DEBIT		CREDIT	
				Accum. Deprec.	
		A + Draw. + E		+ L + C + R	
1	Cash	23 2 5 0 00			
2	Accounts Receivable	2 0 0 00			
3	Supplies	8 0 0 00			
4	Prepaid Insurance	3 6 0 00			
5	Equipment	51 5 0 0 00			
6	Accounts Payable			4 7 0 0 00	
7	L. A. Cruz, Capital			70 0 0 0 00	
8	L. A. Cruz, Drawing	3 0 0 0 00			
9	Income from Services			7 2 7 0 00	
10	Wages Expense	1 4 0 0 00			
11	Rent Expense	9 0 0 00			
12	Advertising Expense	4 0 0 00			
13	Utilities Expense	1 6 0 00			
14		81 9 7 0 00		81 9 7 0 00	
15	Supplies Expense				
16	Insurance Expense		Step 1		
17	Depreciation Expense, Equipment				
18	Accumulated Depreciation, Equipment				
19	Wages Payable				
20					
21	(a) Supplies used, $540				
22	(b) Insurance expired, $30				
23	(c) Depreciation of equipment, $520				
24	(d) Accrued wages, $290				

write Net Loss in the Account Name column on the same line as the difference you calculated.

Work Sheet Requiring Two Pages

If a large number of accounts is involved, it may be necessary to continue the work sheet to a second page.

■ ■ ■

Remember!

When a work sheet requires two pages, the totals at the bottom of the first sheet do not have to be equal. Debits must equal credits by the end of the second page.

(First Page)

Account Name	Trial Balance		Adjustments	
Wages Expense	3,240 00		(c) 220 50	
Totals carried forward	98,312 00	91,146 10	962 50	126 50

Cruz Auto Detail
Work Sheet
For Month Ended June 30, 20—

	ADJUSTMENTS		ADJUSTED TRIAL BALANCE		INCOME STATEMENT		BALANCE SHEET		
	DEBIT	CREDIT	DEBIT A + Draw. + E	CREDIT Accum. Deprec. + L + C + R	DEBIT E	CREDIT R	DEBIT A + Draw.	CREDIT Accum. Deprec. + L + C	
1			23 250 00		*No adjustment, so carry over amount directly*				
2			200 00				↓		
3	(a) 540 00		260 00		*Adjustment involved, subtract $540 (used) from $800*				
4		(b) 30 00	330 00		*Adjustment involved, subtract $30 (expired) from $360*				
5			51 500 00		*No adjustment, so carry over amount directly*				
6				4 700 00					
7				70 000 00					
8			3 000 00						
9				7 270 00			↓		
10	(d) 290 00		1 690 00		*Adjustment involved, add $290 (accrued) to $1,400*				
11			900 00		*No adjustment, so carry over amount directly*				
12			400 00						
13			160 00				↓		
14					*This line is blank because of the trial balance total*				
15	(a) 540 00		540 00		*Adjustment involved, carry $540 over to the same column*				
16	(b) 30 00			30 00	*Adjustment involved, carry $30 over to the same column*				
17	(c) 520 00		520 00		*Adjustment involved, carry $520 over to the same column*				
18		(c) 520 00		520 00	*Adjustment involved, carry $520 over to the same column*				
19		(d) 290 00		290 00	*Adjustment involved, carry $290 over to the same column*				
20	1 380 00	1 380 00	82 780 00	82 780 00					
21									
22	*Step 2*		*Step 3*						
23									
24									

Note that the totals at the bottom of the first page are labeled "Totals carried forward" in the Account Name column. At the top of the second page, the totals are repeated and labeled "Totals brought forward" in the Account Name column. Continue listing account names and balances below the totals brought forward.

(Second Page)

Account Name	Trial Balance		Adjustments	
	Debit	Credit	Debit	Credit
Totals brought forward	98,312 00	91,146 10	962 50	126 50
Wages Payable				(c) 220 50

Finding Errors in the Income Statement and Balance Sheet Columns

As you have seen, the amount of the net income or net loss must be recorded in both an Income Statement column and a Balance Sheet column. Suppose that, after the net income is added to the Balance Sheet Credit column, the Balance Sheet columns are not equal. To find the error, follow this procedure:

1. Check to see that the amount of the net income or loss is recorded in the correct columns. For example, net income is placed in the Income Statement Debit column and the Balance Sheet Credit column.
2. Verify the addition of all the columns.
3. Look to see if the appropriate amounts have been recorded in the Income Statement and Balance Sheet columns. For example, asset amounts should be listed in the Balance Sheet Debit column, expense amounts should be listed in the Income Statement Debit column, and so forth.
4. Verify, by adding or subtracting across each line, that the amounts carried over from the Trial Balance columns through the Adjustments columns into the Adjusted Trial Balance columns are correct.
5. The correct amounts of the revenue and expense accounts are transferred to the income statement columns.
6. The correct amounts of assets, liabilities, and owner's equity accounts are transferred to the balance sheet columns.

Generally, one of these steps will expose the error.

Completion of the Financial Statements

Objective 4

Prepare an income statement, a statement of owner's equity, and a balance sheet for a service business directly from the work sheet.

As we stated, the purpose of the work sheet is to help the accountant prepare the financial statements. Since we have completed the work sheet for Cruz Auto Detail, we can now prepare the income statement, the statement of owner's equity, and the balance sheet by taking the figures directly from the work sheet. These statements are shown in Figure 8 on the facing page.

Note that you record Accumulated Depreciation, Equipment, in the asset section of the balance sheet as a direct deduction from Equipment. As we have said, accountants refer to this as a *contra asset account* because it is contrary to its companion account. The difference, $50,980, is called the book value or carrying value because it represents the cost of the asset after Accumulated Depreciation has been deducted.

When preparing the statement of owner's equity, always remember to check the beginning balance of Capital against the balance shown in the Capital account in the general ledger. An additional investment may have been made during the fiscal period, and you need to record any such additional investment in the statement of owner's equity.

JOURNALIZING ADJUSTING ENTRIES

Objective 5

Journalize and post the adjusting entries.

To change the balance of a ledger account, you need a journal entry as evidence of the change. So far, we have been listing adjustments only in the Adjustments columns of the work sheet. The work sheet is not a journal, so we must journalize the adjustments to update the ledger accounts. **Take the information for these entries directly from the Adjustments columns of the work sheet, debiting and crediting exactly the same accounts and amounts in the journal entries.**

FIGURE 8

Cruz Auto Detail
Income Statement
For Month Ended June 30, 20—

Revenue:											
Income from Services							$7	2	7	0	00
Expenses:											
Wages Expense	$1	6	9	0	00						
Rent Expense		9	0	0	00						
Advertising Expense		4	0	0	00						
Utilities Expense		1	6	0	00						
Supplies Expense		5	4	0	00						
Insurance Expense			3	0	00						
Depreciation Expense, Equipment		5	2	0	00						
Total Expenses							4	2	4	0	00
Net Income							$3	0	3	0	00

Cruz Auto Detail
Statement of Owner's Equity
For Month Ended June 30, 20—

L. A. Cruz, Capital, June 1, 20—							$70	0	0	0	00
Net Income for June	$3	0	3	0	00						
Less Withdrawals for June		3	0	0	0	00					
Increase in Capital									3	0	00
L. A. Cruz, Capital, June 30, 20—							$70	0	3	0	00

Cruz Auto Detail
Balance Sheet
June 30, 20—

Assets											
Cash							$23	2	5	0	00
Accounts Receivable								2	0	0	00
Supplies								2	6	0	00
Prepaid Insurance								3	3	0	00
Equipment	$51	5	0	0	00						
Less Accumulated Depreciation		5	2	0	00		50	9	8	0	00
Total Assets							$75	0	2	0	00
Liabilities											
Accounts Payable	$4	7	0	0	00						
Wages Payable		2	9	0	00						
Total Liabilities							$4	9	9	0	00
Owner's Equity											
L. A. Cruz, Capital							70	0	3	0	00
Total Liabilities and Owner's Equity							$75	0	2	0	00

In the Description column of the general journal, write "Adjusting Entries" before you begin making these entries. This can eliminate the need to write an explanation for each entry. The adjusting entries for Cruz Auto Detail are shown in Figure 9.

FIGURE 9

GENERAL JOURNAL PAGE ___4___

	DATE		DESCRIPTION	POST. REF.	DEBIT	CREDIT	
1	20–		**Adjusting Entries**				1
2	June	30	**Supplies Expense**	515	5 4 0 00		2
3			**Supplies**	115		5 4 0 00	3
4							4
5		30	**Insurance Expense**	516	3 0 00		5
6			**Prepaid Insurance**	117		3 0 00	6
7							7
8		30	**Dep. Expense, Equipment**	517	5 2 0 00		8
9			**Accum. Dep., Equipment**	125		5 2 0 00	9
10							10
11		30	**Wages Expense**	511	2 9 0 00		11
12			**Wages Payable**	212		2 9 0 00	12

Remember!

Each adjusting entry consists of an income statement account and a balance sheet account.

When you post the adjusting entries to the ledger accounts, write the word "Adjusting" in the Item column of the ledger account. The adjusting entry for Supplies is posted as follows:

GENERAL LEDGER

ACCOUNT **Supplies** ACCOUNT NO. **115**

	DATE		ITEM	POST. REF.	DEBIT	CREDIT	BALANCE DEBIT	BALANCE CREDIT	
1	20–								1
2	June	4		1	8 0 0 00		8 0 0 00		2
3		30	Adj.	4		5 4 0 00	2 6 0 00		3
4									4

ACCOUNT **Supplies Expense** ACCOUNT NO. **515**

	DATE		ITEM	POST. REF.	DEBIT	CREDIT	BALANCE DEBIT	BALANCE CREDIT	
1	20–								1
2	June	30	Adj.	4	5 4 0 00		5 4 0 00		2
3									3
4									4

FYI

Many businesses produce monthly financial statements. Adjustments must be made every time a financial statement is done.

FIGURE 10

Karl Veterinary Clinic
Income Statement
For Year Ended December 31, 20—

Revenues:												
Professional Fees	$	111	7	2	0	00						
Boarding Fees		22	0	8	0	00						
Total Revenues							$	133	8	0	0	00
Expenses:												
Salaries Expense	$	84	0	0	0	00						
Depreciation Expense, Building		6	4	8	0	00						
Depreciation Expense, Equipment		3	8	4	0	00						
Supplies Expense		3	7	2	0	00						
Insurance Expense			7	2	0	00						
Miscellaneous Expense		2	1	6	0	00						
Total Expenses								100	9	2	0	00
Net Income							$	32	8	8	0	00

In the adjusted accounts, notice that the intent is to make sure that the expenses recorded match up or compare with the revenues for the same period of time. In other words, for the month of June, we record all the revenues for June and all the expenses for June. Thus the revenues and expenses for the same time period are matched. This is called the **matching principle**.

Objective 6

Prepare an income statement and a balance sheet for a business with more than one revenue account and more than one accumulated depreciation account.

Businesses with More than One Revenue Account and More than One Accumulated Depreciation Account

The only revenue account for Cruz Auto Detail is Income from Services. However, a business may have several distinct sources of revenue. For example, Karl Veterinary Clinic has two revenue accounts: Professional Fees and Boarding Fees. Figure 10 illustrates the placement of these accounts in the income statement.

In Figure 10, also note that the company has two assets subject to depreciation: Building and Equipment. In the financial statements, Depreciation Expense and Accumulated Depreciation must be listed for each asset.

Prepaid insurance is an asset that expires as time goes on. You make adjustments using the Prepaid Insurance and Insurance Expense accounts. For the insurance company, however, prepaid insurance is a liability.

Land supposedly lasts forever, so land is not depreciated. Adjustments would have been made in the work sheet for depreciation of the equipment and the building. The balance sheet for Karl Veterinary Clinic is shown in Figure 11.

FIGURE 11

Karl Veterinary Clinic
Balance Sheet
December 31, 20—

Assets										
Cash						$	6	2	4	0	00
Supplies							2	0	0	00
Land							4	4	0	0	00
Building	$117	7	0	0	00					
Less Accumulated Depreciation	36	4	0	0	00	81	3	0	0	00
Equipment	$ 42	6	0	0	00					
Less Accumulated Depreciation	29	2	0	0	00	13	4	0	0	00
Total Assets						$105	5	4	0	00
Liabilities										
Accounts Payable						$	2	8	0	0	00
Owner's Equity										
Doris P. Karl, Capital						102	7	4	0	00
Total Liabilities and Owner's Equity						$105	5	4	0	00

CHAPTER REVIEW

Review of Performance Objectives

1. Define *fiscal period* and *fiscal year.*

   A fiscal period is any period of time covering a complete accounting cycle. A fiscal year consists of twelve consecutive months.

2. List the classifications of the accounts that occupy each column of a ten-column work sheet.

Trial Balance Debit	Assets + Drawing + Expenses
Trial Balance Credit	Accum. Deprec. + Liabilities + Capital + Revenue
Adjustments Debit	Expenses
Adjustments Credit	Assets + Liabilities
Adjusted Trial Balance Debit	Assets + Drawing + Expenses
Adjusted Trial Balance Credit	Accum. Deprec. + Liabilities + Capital + Revenue
Income Statement Debit	Expenses
Income Statement Credit	Revenue
Balance Sheet Debit	Assets + Drawing
Balance Sheet Credit	Accumulated Depreciation + Liabilities + Capital

3. Complete a work sheet for a service enterprise, involving adjustments for supplies used, expired insurance, depreciation, and accrued wages.

    Adjustment for supplies used: debit Supplies Expense and credit Supplies.
    Adjustment for expired insurance: debit Insurance Expense and credit Prepaid Insurance.
    Adjustment for depreciation: debit Depreciation Expense and credit Accumulated Depreciation.
    Adjustment for accrued wages: debit Wages Expense and credit Wages Payable.

4. Prepare an income statement, a statement of owner's equity, and a balance sheet for a service business directly from the work sheet.

    Prepare the income statement directly from the amounts listed in the Income Statement Debit and Credit columns. The net income should equal the net income previously determined on the work sheet. For the statement of owner's equity, use the amount of the beginning capital listed in the Balance Sheet Credit column after checking the general ledger for any additional investment(s), the amount of the net income from the Balance Sheet Credit column, and the amount of Drawing from the Balance Sheet Debit column. Prepare the balance sheet directly from the amounts listed in the Balance Sheet Debit and Credit columns (except Drawing and Capital).

5. Journalize and post the adjusting entries.

    Adjusting entries are taken directly from the Adjustments columns of the work sheet.

6. Prepare an income statement and a balance sheet for a business with more than one revenue account and more than one accumulated depreciation account.

    Businesses that have more than one source of revenue or more than one type of asset that is subject to depreciation must show a separate account for each on the income statement and the balance sheet.

Glossary

Accounting cycle The sequence of steps in the accounting process completed during the fiscal period. (109)

Accrual Recognition of an expense or a revenue that has been incurred or earned but has not yet been recorded. (116)

Accrued wages The amount of unpaid wages owed to employees for the time between the end of the last pay period and the end of the fiscal period. (116)

Adjusting entry An entry to help bring the books up to date at the end of the fiscal period. (112)

Adjustments Internal transactions that bring ledger accounts up to date, as a planned part of the accounting procedure. They are first recorded in the Adjustments columns of the work sheet. (112)

Book value or **carrying value** The cost of an asset minus the accumulated depreciation. (114)

Contra account An account that is contrary to, or a deduction from, another account; for example, Accumulated Depreciation is listed as a deduction from Equipment. (114)

Depreciation An expense based on the expectation that an asset will gradually decline in usefulness due to time, wear and tear, or obsolescence; the cost of the asset is therefore spread out over its estimated useful life. A part of depreciation expense is apportioned to each fiscal period. (113)

Fiscal period Any period of time covering a complete accounting cycle, generally consisting of twelve consecutive months. (109)

Fiscal year A fiscal period consisting of twelve consecutive months. (109)

Matching principle The principle that the revenue for one time period is matched up or compared with the related expenses for the same time period. (127)

Mixed accounts Certain accounts that appear in the trial balance with balances that are partly income statement amounts and partly balance sheet amounts—for example, Prepaid Insurance and Supplies. (119)

Straight-line depreciation A means of calculating depreciation in which the cost of an asset, less any trade-in value, is allocated evenly over the useful life of the asset. (113)

Work sheet A working paper used by accountants to record necessary adjustments and provide up-to-date account balances needed to prepare the financial statements. (110)

QUESTIONS, EXERCISES, AND PROBLEMS

Discussion Questions

1. What is the purpose of a work sheet?
2. What is the purpose of adjusting entries?
3. What is a mixed account? Give an example. What is a contra account? Give an example.
4. In which column of the work sheet—Income Statement (IS), Balance Sheet (BS)—would the adjusted balances of the following accounts appear?

Account	IS or BS?	Account	IS or BS?
a. Prepaid Insurance		e. Accumulated Depreciation, Equipment	
b. Supplies		f. T. Oglevan, Drawing	
c. Wages Payable		g. Insurance Expense	
d. Income from Services		h. Depreciation Expense, Equipment	

5. Why is it necessary to make an adjustment if wages for work performed for the pay period Monday through Friday are paid on Friday and the accounting period ends on a Wednesday?
6. Define depreciation as it relates to a truck you bought for your business.
7. What is the amount of the adjustment for supplies if the balance of supplies bought is $1,450 but the amount left when counted is $860?
8. Why is it necessary to journalize adjusting entries that you have prepared on the work sheet?

Exercises

P.O. 2

List account classifications in work sheet columns.

Exercise 4-1 List the following classifications of accounts in all the columns in which they appear in the work sheet, with the exception of the Adjustments columns. (Example: Assets.)

Assets

Accumulated Depreciation (with previous balance)

Liabilities

Capital

Drawing

Revenue

Expenses

Write Net Income in the appropriate columns.

Account Name	Trial Balance		Adjustments		Adjusted Trial Balance		Income Statement		Balance Sheet	
	Debit	Credit	Debit	Credit	Debit	Credit	Debit	Credit	Debit	Credit
Assets					Assets				Assets	
Net Income										

P.O. 2

Classify accounts and indicate normal balances and statement columns.

Exercise 4-2 Classify each of the accounts listed below as assets (A), liabilities (L), owner's equity (OE), revenue (R), or expenses (E). Indicate the normal debit or credit balance of each account. Indicate whether each account will appear in the Income Statement columns (IS) or the Balance Sheet columns (BS) of the work sheet. Item 0 is given as an example.

Account	Classification	Normal Balance	IS or BS Columns
0. Example: Wages Expense	E	Debit	IS
a. Prepaid Insurance			
b. Accounts Payable			
c. C. Kronenberg, Capital			
d. Accounts Receivable			
e. Accumulated Depreciation, Building			
f. C. Kronenberg, Drawing			
g. Rental Income			
h. Equipment			
i. Depreciation Expense, Equipment			
j. Supplies			

that your type of to be adjusted

P.O. 3

Choose accounts that require adjustment.

Exercise 4-3 Place a check mark next to any account(s) requiring adjustment. Explain why those accounts must be adjusted.

✓	Account Name (in trial balance order)	Reason for Adjusting This Account
	a. Cash	
	b. Accounts Receivable	
	c. Supplies	
	d. Prepaid Insurance	
	e. Equipment	
	f. Accumulated Depreciation, Equipment	
	g. Accounts Payable	
	h. G. L. Johnson, Capital	
	i. G. L. Johnson, Drawing	
	j. Wages Expense	

P.O. 3

Prepare adjustments in the work sheet.

only Plot adjustments

Exercise 4-4 Below is a partial work sheet for Megan's Place. Prepare the following adjustments in this work sheet:

a. Supplies inventory (left or unused), $135—calculate the expired or used-up supplies.

b. Expired or used-up insurance, $300.

c. Depreciation expense on equipment, $850—remember to credit the accumulated depreciation account for equipment, not Equipment.

d. Wages accrued or earned since the last payday, $124 (owed and to be paid on the next payday).

	ACCOUNT NAME	TRIAL BALANCE DEBIT	TRIAL BALANCE CREDIT	ADJUSTMENTS DEBIT	ADJUSTMENTS CREDIT
1	Cash	5 6 2 1 00			
2	Supplies	3 8 5 00			
3	Prepaid Insurance	9 0 0 00			
4	Equipment	4 6 8 0 00			
5	Accumulated Depreciation, Equipment		1 2 5 0 00		
6	Accounts Payable		2 6 4 9 00		
7	M. Megan, Capital		4 6 2 4 00		
8	M. Megan, Drawing	2 2 0 0 00			
9	Service Income		6 8 4 7 00		
10	Rent Expense	9 5 6 00			
11	Wages Expense	5 6 0 00			
12	Miscellaneous Expense	6 8 00			
13		15 3 7 0 00	15 3 7 0 00		
14					

P.O. 3

Prepare adjustments and adjusted trial balance.

Exercise 4-5 Complete the work sheet through the adjusted trial balance using the following adjustment information:

a. Supplies inventory (left or unused), $148—calculate the expired or used-up supplies.
b. Expired or used-up insurance, $450.
c. Depreciation expense on equipment, $970—remember to credit the accumulated depreciation account for equipment, not Equipment.
d. Wages accrued or earned since the last payday, $221 (owed and to be paid on the next payday).

	ACCOUNT NAME	TRIAL BALANCE DEBIT	TRIAL BALANCE CREDIT	ADJUSTMENTS DEBIT	ADJUSTMENTS CREDIT	ADJUSTED TRIAL BALANCE DEBIT	ADJUSTED TRIAL BALANCE CREDIT
1	Cash	4 6 2 0 00					
2	Supplies	3 6 7 00					
3	Prepaid Insurance	1 1 0 0 00					
4	Equipment	5 6 7 8 00					
5	Accumulated Depreciation,						
6	Equipment		1 4 5 6 00				
7	Accounts Payable		1 9 7 5 00				
8	D. Lyon, Capital		6 1 2 6 00				
9	D. Lyon, Drawing	1 8 0 0 00					
10	Service Fees		5 7 3 6 00				
11	Rent Expense	8 6 5 00					
12	Wages Expense	7 8 5 00					
13	Miscellaneous Expense	7 8 00					
14		15 2 9 3 00	15 2 9 3 00				
15							
16							
17							
18							
19							
20							
21							
22							
23							
24							
25							
26							
27							
28							

P.O. 3

Calculate the missing adjustments.

Exercise 4-6 Journalize the four adjusting entries from the partial work sheet on the following page for the month ended May 31. (*Hint:* Use what you know about extending numbers to the four statement columns.)

ACCOUNT NAME	INCOME STATEMENT		BALANCE SHEET		
	DEBIT	CREDIT	DEBIT	CREDIT	
1 Cash			4 7 3 1 00		1
2 Supplies			2 6 6 00		2
3 Prepaid Insurance			8 4 1 00		3
4 Equipment			5 8 3 2 00		4
5 Accumulated Depreciation, Equipment				1 8 2 0 00	5
6 Accounts Payable				9 8 5 00	6
7 C. Peak, Capital				6 8 1 0 00	7
8 C. Peak, Drawing			2 1 5 0 00		8
9 Professional Fees		8 6 7 3 00			9
10 Salary Expense	2 7 8 7 00				10
11 Rent Expense	1 2 0 0 00				11
12 Miscellaneous Expense	1 3 4 00				12
13					13
14 Supplies Expense	1 1 8 00				14
15 Insurance Expense	1 8 5 00				15
16 Depreciation Expense, Equipment	3 6 4 00				16
17 Salaries Payable				3 2 0 00	17
18	4 7 8 8 00	8 6 7 3 00	13 8 2 0 00	9 9 3 5 00	18
19 Net Income	3 8 8 5 00			3 8 8 5 00	19
20	8 6 7 3 00	8 6 7 3 00	13 8 2 0 00	13 8 2 0 00	20
21					21

P.O. 5

Journalize adjusting entries from the work sheet.

Exercise 4-7 Journalize the adjustments for the Jama Company as of August 31.

ACCOUNT NAME	TRIAL BALANCE		ADJUSTMENTS	
	DEBIT	CREDIT	DEBIT	CREDIT
1 Cash	3 9 7 1 00			
2 Supplies	4 6 2 00			(a) 2 0 1 00
3 Prepaid Insurance	4 8 7 3 00			(b) 2 6 5 00
4 Equipment	5 6 7 8 00			
5 Accumulated Depreciation, Equipment		6 4 5 00		(c) 2 0 6 00
6 Accounts Payable		8 4 3 00		
7 A. Jama, Capital		12 5 5 1 00		
8 A. Jama, Drawing	2 0 0 0 00			
9 Service Fees		4 6 8 3 00		
10 Rent Expense	7 9 5 00			
11 Wages Expense	8 6 5 00		(d) 1 6 8 00	
12 Miscellaneous Expense	7 8 00			
13	18 7 2 2 00	18 7 2 2 00		
14 Supplies Expense			(a) 2 0 1 00	
15 Insurance Expense			(b) 2 6 5 00	
16 Depreciation Expense, Equipment			(c) 2 0 6 00	
17 Wages Payable				(d) 1 6 8 00
18			8 4 0 00	8 4 0 00
19				

P.O. 5
Journalize adjusting entries.

Exercise 4-8 Journalize the following adjusting entries that were included in the work sheet for the month ended December 31. Assume the financial statements have been prepared.

Dec. 31 Supplies inventory (left or unused), $196. The cost of supplies in the unadjusted trial balance was $534. The amount in the Adjustments column of the work sheet is $338 (verify).

31 Salaries for two days are unpaid at December 31, $1,600 (verify). Salaries are $4,000 for a five-day week.

31 Insurance was bought on September 1 for $1,800 for 12 months' coverage. Four months' coverage has expired, $600 (verify).

31 Depreciation for the month on equipment, $50, based on an asset costing $4,500 with a trade-in value of $1,500 and an estimated life of 5 years (verify).

CONSIDER AND COMMUNICATE

Assume that you have completed the income statement, but the net income is not the same as you calculated on your work sheet. What should you check?

WHAT IF . . .

You find that your accounting clerk forgot to adjust for $300 in wages earned since the last payday. The next payday is in the next accounting period. Will this omission affect the ledger accounts, income statement, statement of owner's equity, and balance sheet? If so, how?

CRITICAL THINKING

Your supervisor has just handed you the partial work sheet (on the following page) for the month ended July 31 and asked you to journalize the adjusting entries. He apologizes for having spilled liquid on the first six columns of the work sheet.

WEB WORK

Select a major company in which you are interested. Using your web browser, key in the name of the company; for example jcpenney. Or, if you know the web address of the company, key it into the Location box; for example, gapinc.com. Once you are on the home page, search for phrases like *company information* or *about us*. Write a summary of the information you find about the company including the company's product, its mission or goals, sales information, and any other financial information you discover, including the web address where you found the information.

	ACCOUNT NAME	INCOME STATEMENT DEBIT E						INCOME STATEMENT CREDIT R						BALANCE SHEET DEBIT A + Draw.						BALANCE SHEET CREDIT Accum. Depr. + L + C						
1	Cash													3	2	5	4	00								1
2	Supplies														2	0	2	00								2
3	Prepaid Insurance														5	5	0	00								3
4	Equipment													4	6	9	7	00								4
5	Accumulated Depreciation, Equipment																			1	8	3	8	00		5
6	Accounts Payable																				9	6	1	00		6
7	E. Walia, Capital																			5	1	1	5	00		7
8	E. Walia, Drawing													1	2	0	0	00								8
9	Service Income							4	5	8	7	00														9
10	Rent Expense	8	9	7	00																					10
11	Wages Expense	7	2	6	00																					11
12	Miscellaneous Expense		3	7	00																					12
13																										13
14	Supplies Expense	2	5	6	00																					14
15	Insurance Expense	3	4	0	00																					15
16	Depreciation Expense, Equipment	6	0	0	00																					16
17	Wages Payable																				2	5	8	00		17
18		2	8	5	6	00		4	5	8	7	00		9	9	0	3	00		8	1	7	2	00		18
19	Net Income	1	7	3	1	00														1	7	3	1	00		19
20		4	5	8	7	00		4	5	8	7	00		9	9	0	3	00		9	9	0	3	00		20

For additional help, see the demonstration problem at the beginning of each chapter in your Working Papers.

P.O. 3

Problem 4-1A The trial balance for the Reckis Insurance Agency as of August 31, after the firm has completed its first month of operations, follows:

Reckis Insurance Agency
Trial Balance
August 31, 20—

ACCOUNT NAME	DEBIT A + Draw. + E					CREDIT Accum. Depr. + L + C + R				
Cash	3	4	2	7	00					
Accounts Receivable	1	3	1	9	00					
Prepaid Insurance		3	6	2	00					
Supplies		4	9	2	00					
Office Equipment	4	9	3	9	00					
Accounts Payable						1	0	7	1	00
M. Reckis, Capital						9	0	2	0	00
M. Reckis, Drawing		9	0	0	00					
Commissions Earned						2	5	2	0	00
Rent Expense		6	9	5	00					
Travel Expense		2	2	5	00					
Utilities Expense		1	9	8	00					
Miscellaneous Expense			5	4	00					
	12	6	1	1	00	12	6	1	1	00

Check Figure

Net Income, $161

Instructions

1. Record the amounts in the Trial Balance columns of the work sheet and record the owner's name in the Capital and Drawing accounts.
2. Complete the work sheet by making the following adjustments and lettering each adjustment:
   a. Expired or used-up insurance, $86.
   b. Supplies inventory (left or unused), $91—calculate the amount of supplies used up.
   c. Depreciation expense on office equipment, $700—remember to credit the accumulated depreciation account for office equipment, not Office Equipment.

P.O. 4,5

Problem 4-2A The completed work sheet for Wong Design for the month of March is in your Working Papers.

Check Figure

Total Assets, $15,480

Instructions

1. Prepare an income statement.
2. Prepare a statement of owner's equity. Assume that no additional investments were made in March.
3. Prepare a balance sheet.
4. Journalize the adjusting entries.

P.O. 3,5

Problem 4-3A The trial balance of The Fashion Center for the month ended September 30 is presented below.

The Fashion Center
Trial Balance
September 30, 20—

ACCOUNT NAME	DEBIT	CREDIT
Cash	2 3 7 8 00	
Supplies	8 6 4 00	
Prepaid Insurance	1 3 4 5 00	
Equipment	32 9 7 8 00	
Accumulated Depreciation, Equipment		16 2 3 5 00
Accounts Payable		2 7 5 1 00
C. Barkley, Capital		45 2 0 8 00
C. Barkley, Drawing	22 4 4 5 00	
Income from Services		43 7 9 1 00
Wages Expense	29 7 6 1 00	
Rent Expense	14 9 3 2 00	
Utilities Expense	1 5 7 3 00	
Telephone Expense	1 2 7 1 00	
Miscellaneous Expense	4 3 8 00	
	107 9 8 5 00	107 9 8 5 00

Data for the adjustments are as follows:

a. Supplies inventory (left or unused), $227—calculate the expired or used-up supplies.
b. Expired or used-up insurance, $320.

c. Depreciation expense on equipment, $2,800—remember to credit the accumulated depreciation account for equipment, not Equipment.
d. Wages accrued or earned since the last payday, $468 (owed and to be paid on the next payday).

Check Figure

Net Loss, $8,409

Instructions

1. Complete the work sheet.
2. Journalize the adjusting entries.

P.O. 3,4,5,6

Problem 4-4A The trial balance for Wrye's Putt Putt Golf on June 30 is shown below.

Wrye's Putt Putt Golf
Trial Balance
June 30, 20—

ACCOUNT NAME	DEBIT	CREDIT
Cash	4 5 3 2 00	
Supplies	3 4 6 00	
Prepaid Insurance	1 2 8 4 00	
Equipment	23 6 8 7 00	
Accumulated Depreciation, Equipment		1 2 7 8 00
Repair Equipment	6 2 8 9 00	
Accumulated Depreciation, Repair Equipment		1 4 8 5 00
Accounts Payable		9 6 0 00
T. Wrye, Capital		23 0 1 0 00
T. Wrye, Drawing	1 5 6 5 00	
Golf Fees Income		12 3 8 7 00
Concessions Income		2 8 6 3 00
Wages Expense	2 1 6 3 00	
Rent Expense	1 3 5 0 00	
Utilities Expense	3 5 7 00	
Repair Expense	2 7 1 00	
Miscellaneous Expense	1 3 9 00	
	41 9 8 3 00	41 9 8 3 00

Data for month-end adjustments are as follows:

a. Supplies inventory (left or unused), $208 (calculate the expired or used-up supplies).
b. Expired or used-up insurance, $350.
c. Depreciation expense on Equipment, $800 (remember to credit the accumulated depreciation account for equipment, not Equipment).
d. Depreciation expense on Repair Equipment, $1,240 (remember to credit the accumulated depreciation account for repair equipment, not Repair Equipment).
e. Wages accrued or earned since the last payday, $385 (owed and to be paid on the next payday).

Check Figure

Net Income, $8,057

Instructions

1. Complete the work sheet for the month.

2. Prepare an income statement, a statement of owner's equity, and a balance sheet. Assume that no additional investments were made during June.
3. Journalize the adjusting entries.

Instructions for General Ledger Software

1. Journalize the adjusting entries in the general journal. (No work sheet is required.)
2. Post the adjusting entries.
3. Print an income statement, a statement of owner's equity, and a balance sheet. Assume that no additional investments were made during the month.

PROBLEM SET B

For additional help, see the demonstration problem at the beginning of each chapter in your Working Papers.

P.O. 3

Problem 4-1B The trial balance of the Marshall Insurance Agency as of September 30, after the firm has completed its first month of operations, follows:

Marshall Insurance Agency
Trial Balance
September 30, 20—

ACCOUNT NAME	DEBIT A + Draw. + E					CREDIT Accum. Depr. + L + C + R				
Cash	3	5	3	7	00					
Accounts Receivable	1	2	2	8	00					
Prepaid Insurance		6	7	5	00					
Supplies		3	8	7	00					
Office Equipment	5	2	4	6	00					
Accounts Payable						1	2	6	7	00
N. Marshall, Capital						9	6	2	8	00
N. Marshall, Drawing	1	1	0	0	00					
Commissions Earned						2	8	4	3	00
Rent Expense		7	8	5	00					
Travel Expense		4	8	8	00					
Utilities Expense		2	2	7	00					
Miscellaneous Expense			6	5	00					
	13	7	3	8	00	13	7	3	8	00

Check Figure

Net Income, $298

Instructions

1. Record the amounts in the Trial Balance columns of the work sheet and record the owner's name in the Capital and Drawing accounts.
2. Complete the work sheet by making the following adjustments and lettering each adjustment:
   a. Expired or used-up insurance, $100.
   b. Supplies inventory (left or unused), $107—calculate the amount of supplies used up.

c. Depreciation expense on office equipment, $600—remember to credit the accumulated depreciation account for office equipment, not Office Equipment.

P.O. 4,5

Problem 4-2B The completed work sheet for Clark Design for the month of March is in your Working Papers.

Check Figure

Total Assets, $20,458

Instructions

1. Prepare an income statement.
2. Prepare a statement of owner's equity. Assume no additional investments were made in March.
3. Prepare a balance sheet.
4. Journalize the adjusting entries.

P.O. 3,5

Problem 4-3B The trial balance of Quick Cleaners for the month ended September 30 is presented below.

Quick Cleaners
Trial Balance
September 30, 20—

ACCOUNT NAME	DEBIT	CREDIT
Cash	2 4 8 9 00	
Supplies	7 5 2 00	
Prepaid Insurance	1 2 3 6 00	
Equipment	22 7 5 2 00	
Accumulated Depreciation, Equipment		14 3 5 7 00
Accounts Payable		2 6 4 7 00
D. Stevenson, Capital		28 1 6 9 00
D. Stevenson, Drawing	20 3 5 9 00	
Income from Services		40 8 5 0 00
Wages Expense	24 9 8 3 00	
Rent Expense	10 6 7 3 00	
Utilities Expense	1 1 5 4 00	
Telephone Expense	1 2 4 4 00	
Miscellaneous Expense	3 8 1 00	
	86 0 2 3 00	86 0 2 3 00

Data for the adjustments are as follows:

a. Supplies inventory (left or unused), $345 (calculate the expired or used-up supplies).
b. Expired or used-up insurance, $895.
c. Depreciation expense on equipment, $3,200 (remember to credit the accumulated depreciation account for equipment, not Equipment).
d. Wages accrued or earned since the last payday, $595 (owed and to be paid on the next payday).

Check Figure

Net Loss, $2,682

Instructions

1. Complete the work sheet.
2. Journalize the adjusting entries.

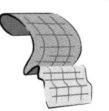

P.O. 3,4,5,6

Problem 4-4B The trial balance for Scott's Game Town on July 31 is shown below.

Scott's Game Town
Trial Balance
July 31, 20—

ACCOUNT NAME	DEBIT	CREDIT
Cash	3 6 2 1 00	
Supplies	2 5 7 00	
Prepaid Insurance	1 2 9 5 00	
Equipment	28 6 4 2 00	
Accumulated Depreciation, Equipment		2 3 8 7 00
Repair Equipment	1 8 6 5 00	
Accumulated Depreciation, Repair Equipment		7 8 0 00
Accounts Payable		8 4 2 00
T. Scott, Capital		23 9 7 1 00
T. Scott, Drawing	1 0 0 0 00	
Golf Fees Income		8 9 5 4 00
Concessions Income		2 7 5 2 00
Wages Expense	1 2 6 8 00	
Rent Expense	9 8 0 00	
Utilities Expense	2 4 6 00	
Repair Expense	3 8 0 00	
Miscellaneous Expense	1 3 2 00	
	39 6 8 6 00	39 6 8 6 00

Data for month-end adjustments are as follows:

a. Supplies inventory (left or unused), $136 (calculate the expired or used-up supplies).
b. Expired or used-up insurance, $245.
c. Depreciation expense on equipment, $650 (remember to credit the accumulated depreciation account for equipment, not Equipment).
d. Depreciation expense on repair equipment, $450 (remember to credit the accumulated depreciation account for repair equipment, not Repair Equipment).
e. Wages accrued or earned since the last payday, $315 (owed and to be paid on the next payday).

Check Figure

Net Income, $6,919

Instructions

1. Complete the work sheet for the month.
2. Prepare an income statement, a statement of owner's equity, and a balance sheet. Assume that no additional investments were made during July.
3. Journalize the adjusting entries.

Instructions for General Ledger Software

1. Journalize the adjusting entries in the general journal. (No work sheet is required.)
2. Post the adjusting entries.
3. Print an income statement, a statement of owner's equity, and a balance sheet. Assume no additional investments were made during the month.

Continuous General Ledger Problem: Adjustments

Adjustment information for Like New is listed below.

Adjustment information:

a. Wages accrued or earned since the last payday, $42.50 (owed and to be paid on the next payday).

b. Depreciation expense on office furniture, $1,100—remember to credit the accumulated depreciation account for office furniture, not Office Furniture.

c. Depreciation expense on office equipment, $890—remember to credit the accumulated depreciation account for office equipment, not Office Equipment.

d. Depreciation expense on van, $1,100—remember to credit the accumulated depreciation account for van, not Van.

e. Depreciation expense on building, $3,500—remember to credit the accumulated depreciation account for building, not Building.

f. Expired or used-up insurance, $96.08.

g. Supplies inventory (left or unused), $1,336—calculate the amount of the expired or used-up supplies.

Instructions

1. Launch the accounting software and open the file you saved as Likenew.
2. Journalize and post the adjusting entries.
3. Print an income statement, statement of owner's equity, and balance sheet.
4. Print the general journal (if you can filter the entries, print only the adjusting entries).
5. Print the general ledger (if you can filter the entries, print only the accounts affected by the adjusting entries).
6. Save the file as Likenew2.

Note: The Continuous General Ledger Problem can be worked with Houghton Mifflin Windows General Ledger Package, Peachtree Release 5.01, QuickBooks 6.0, or other general ledger software packages.

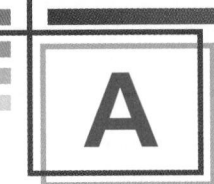

A Methods of Depreciation

Performance Objectives

After you have completed this appendix, you will be able to do the following:

1. Prepare a schedule of depreciation using the straight-line method.

2. Prepare a schedule of depreciation using the sum-of-the-years'-digits method.

3. Prepare a schedule of depreciation using the double-declining-balance method.

4. Prepare a schedule of depreciation for five-year property under the Modified Accelerated Cost Recovery System.

Three methods of depreciation will be illustrated using the example of a delivery truck. Assume that the truck was bought at the beginning of Year 1 and at a cost of $12,000. The truck is estimated to have a useful life of five years and a trade-in value of $3,000 at the end of the five-year period. The three methods to be described are straight-line, sum-of-the-years'-digits, and double-declining-balance.

STRAIGHT-LINE METHOD

Objective 1

Prepare a schedule of depreciation using the straight-line method.

We showed this method in Chapter 4, providing for an equal amount of depreciation each year.

$$\text{Yearly depreciation} = \frac{\text{Cost of asset} - \text{Trade-in value}}{\text{Years of life}} = \frac{\$12,000 - \$3,000}{5 \text{ years}}$$

$$= \frac{\$9,000}{5 \text{ years}} = \$1,800 \text{ per year}$$

Year	Depreciation for the Year	Accumulated Depreciation	Book Value (Cost Less Accumulated Depreciation)
1	$9,000 ÷ 5 years = $1,800	$1,800	$12,000 − $1,800 = $10,200
2	9,000 ÷ 5 years = 1,800	$1,800 + $1,800 = 3,600	12,000 − 3,600 = 8,400
3	9,000 ÷ 5 years = 1,800	3,600 + 1,800 = 5,400	12,000 − 5,400 = 6,600
4	9,000 ÷ 5 years = 1,800	5,400 + 1,800 = 7,200	12,000 − 7,200 = 4,800
5	9,000 ÷ 5 years = 1,800	7,200 + 1,800 = 9,000	12,000 − 9,000 = 3,000
	$9,000		

SUM-OF-THE-YEARS'-DIGITS METHOD

Objective 2

Prepare a schedule of depreciation using the sum-of-the-years'-digits method.

Add the number of years and use the sum as the denominator of the fractions. As numerators in the fractions, use the years in reverse order.

$$1 + 2 + 3 + 4 + 5 = 15$$

$$\frac{5}{15} + \frac{4}{15} + \frac{3}{15} + \frac{2}{15} + \frac{1}{15} = \frac{15}{15}$$

Year	Depreciation for the Year	Accumulated Depreciation	Book Value (Cost Less Accumulated Depreciation)
1	$9,000 × ⁵⁄₁₅ = $3,000	$3,000	$12,000 − $3,000 = $9,000
2	9,000 × ⁴⁄₁₅ = 2,400	$3,000 + $2,400 = 5,400	12,000 − 5,400 = 6,600
3	9,000 × ³⁄₁₅ = 1,800	5,400 + 1,800 = 7,200	12,000 − 7,200 = 4,800
4	9,000 × ²⁄₁₅ = 1,200	7,200 + 1,200 = 8,400	12,000 − 8,400 = 3,600
5	9,000 × ¹⁄₁₅ = 600	8,400 + 600 = 9,000	12,000 − 9,000 = 3,000
15	¹⁵⁄₁₅ $9,000		

DOUBLE-DECLINING-BALANCE METHOD

Objective 3

Prepare a schedule of depreciation using the double-declining-balance method.

The term *double* refers to double the straight-line rate. With an estimated useful life of five years, the straight-line rate is ⅕, or .2. Twice, or double, the straight-line rate is ⅖ (⅕ × 2) or .4. **The trade-in value is not taken into account until the end of the schedule.** In calculating declining balance method depreciation, double the straight-line rate is multiplied by the book value without subtracting trade-in value. This differs from the straight-line and sum-of-the-years'-digits methods where the trade-in value is subtracted from the original cost to calculate periodic depreciation expense. Multiply *book value* at beginning of year by twice the straight-line rate. Notice that an asset cannot be depreciated below its trade-in value. In year 3, only the amount of depreciation expense—$1,320 or $4,320–3,000—necessary to reduce the asset to its trade-in value is allowed. No further depreciation expense is permitted in years 4 and 5.

Year	Depreciation for the Year	Accumulated Depreciation	Book Value (Cost Less Accumulated Depreciation)
1	$12,000 × .4 = $4,800	$4,800	$12,000 − $4,800 = $7,200
2	$7,200 × .4 = 2,880	$4,800 + $2,880 = 7,680	12,000 − 7,680 = 4,320
3	$4,320 − $3,000 = 1,320	7,680 + 1,320 = 9,000	12,000 − 9,000 = 3,000
4	0	9,000	12,000 − 9,000 = 3,000
5	0	9,000	12,000 − 9,000 = 3,000
	$9,000		

ASSETS PLACED IN SERVICE AFTER DECEMBER 31, 1986

Objective 4

Prepare a schedule of depreciation for five-year property under the Modified Accelerated Cost Recovery System.

As long as the method is used consistently, companies may choose any of the three methods for their own financial statements. However, for tax purposes, the Internal Revenue Service stipulates certain rates for specific classes of assets. The rates also vary depending on the time the assets were placed in service. We will show the most recent rates.

Most businesses use the Modified Accelerated Cost Recovery System (MACRS) as defined by the Internal Revenue Service for federal income tax purposes. The Accelerated Cost Recovery System (ACRS) first took effect in 1981 and was later modified for assets placed in service after December 31, 1986, by the Tax Reform Act of 1986. The term *recovery* is used because MACRS is a means of recovering or deducting the cost of an asset. According to MACRS, property is divided into nine classes, as follows:

3-year property—certain horses and tractor units for use over the road

5-year property—autos, trucks, computers, typewriters, and copiers

7-year property—office furniture and fixtures and any property that does not have a class life and that is not, by law, in any other class

10-year property—vessels, barges, tugs, and similar water transportation equipment

15-year property—wharves, roads, fences, and any municipal wastewater treatment plants

20-year property—certain farm buildings and municipal sewers

27.5-year residential rental property—rental houses and apartments

31.5-year real property—office buildings and warehouses

39-year property—nonresidential real property placed in service after May 13, 1993

Under MACRS, trade-in value is ignored.

Our light truck qualifies as five-year property. The approximate rates (rounded for the sake of this illustration) are: first year, 20 percent; second year, 32 percent; third year, 19 percent; fourth year, 15 percent; fifth year, 14 percent. Congress may change the lives of property and/or the rates at which property is taxed.

Year	Depreciation for the Year	Accumulated Depreciation	Book Value (Cost Less Accumulated Depreciation)
1	$12,000 × .20 = $2,400	$ 2,400	$12,000 − $ 2,400 = $9,600
2	12,000 × .32 = 3,840	$ 2,400 + $3,840 = 6,240	12,000 − 6,240 = 5,760
3	12,000 × .19 = 2,280	6,240 + 2,280 = 8,520	12,000 − 8,520 = 3,480
4	12,000 × .15 = 1,800	8,520 + 1,800 = 10,320	12,000 − 10,320 = 1,680
5	12,000 × .14 = 1,680	10,320 + 1,680 = 12,000	12,000 − 12,000 = 0

For federal income tax purposes, a company must use either the current MACRS for assets placed in service after December 31, 1986, or an alternative straight-line depreciation method, which differs slightly from the method presented in the text.

PROBLEMS

P.O. 1

Check Figure

Year 1 depreciation, $3,000

Problem A-1 A delivery van was bought for $15,000. The estimated life of the van is four years. The trade-in value at the end of four years is estimated to be $3,000. Prepare a depreciation schedule for the four-year period using the straight-line method.

P.O. 2

Check Figure

Year 2 depreciation, $3,600

Problem A-2 Using the information in Problem A-1, prepare a depreciation schedule using the sum-of-the-years'-digits method.

P.O. 4

Check Figure

Year 3 depreciation, $2,850

Problem A-3 Assume the van was purchased after January 1, 1991. Using the information in Problem A-1, prepare a schedule of depreciation under MACRS.

5 Closing Entries and the Post-Closing Trial Balance

WINDOWS ON | *THE WORLD WIDE WEB*

Why would a company's accounting staff need to close or zero out the balance of revenues and expenses at the end of each year? Why not just keep a running total the entire time the firm is in business? How does this help the company prepare for a new accounting period? What advantage does annual reporting give investors? By the end of the 1990s, the clothing manufacturer, Tommy Hilfiger Corporation, reported net revenues of more than $800 million. What figure represents the year-end revenues for the present year? How would you record the financial data for this company if you were in charge of accounting for Tommy Hilfiger Corporation? What would be the difference between Tommy Hilfiger Corporation's trial balance and post-closing trial balance? Look up the financial highlights of Tommy Hilfiger Corporation at **http://www.tommypr.com/corporate/index5.htm**.

Performance Objectives

After you have completed this chapter, you will be able to do the following:

1. List the steps in the accounting cycle.

2. Journalize and post closing entries for a service enterprise.

3. Prepare a post-closing trial balance.

4. Define the following methods of accounting: accrual basis, cash-receipts-and-disbursements basis, modified cash basis.

5. Prepare interim statements.

Objective 1

List the steps in the accounting cycle.

Let's review the steps in the accounting cycle for an entire fiscal period. Remember that a fiscal period is generally twelve consecutive months, but can also consist of other time frames like three months or six months.

1. **Analyze source documents and record business transactions in a journal.**

2. **Post journal entries to the accounts in the ledger.**

3. **Prepare a trial balance.**

4. **Gather adjustment data and record the adjusting entries on a work sheet.**

5. **Complete the work sheet.**

6. **Prepare financial statements from the data on the work sheet.**

7. **Journalize and post the adjusting entries from the data on the work sheet.**

8. **Journalize and post the closing entries.**

9. **Prepare a post-closing trial balance.**

This chapter explains the procedure for completing the final steps: closing entries and the post-closing trial balance.

Adjusting entries, closing entries, and a post-closing trial balance are prepared at the end of a fiscal period. The number of months in a fiscal period varies. To introduce you to these final steps in the accounting cycle, we assume here that the fiscal period for Cruz Auto Detail is one month. We make this assumption so that we can thoroughly cover the material and give you a chance to practice its application. The entire accounting cycle is outlined in Figure 1.

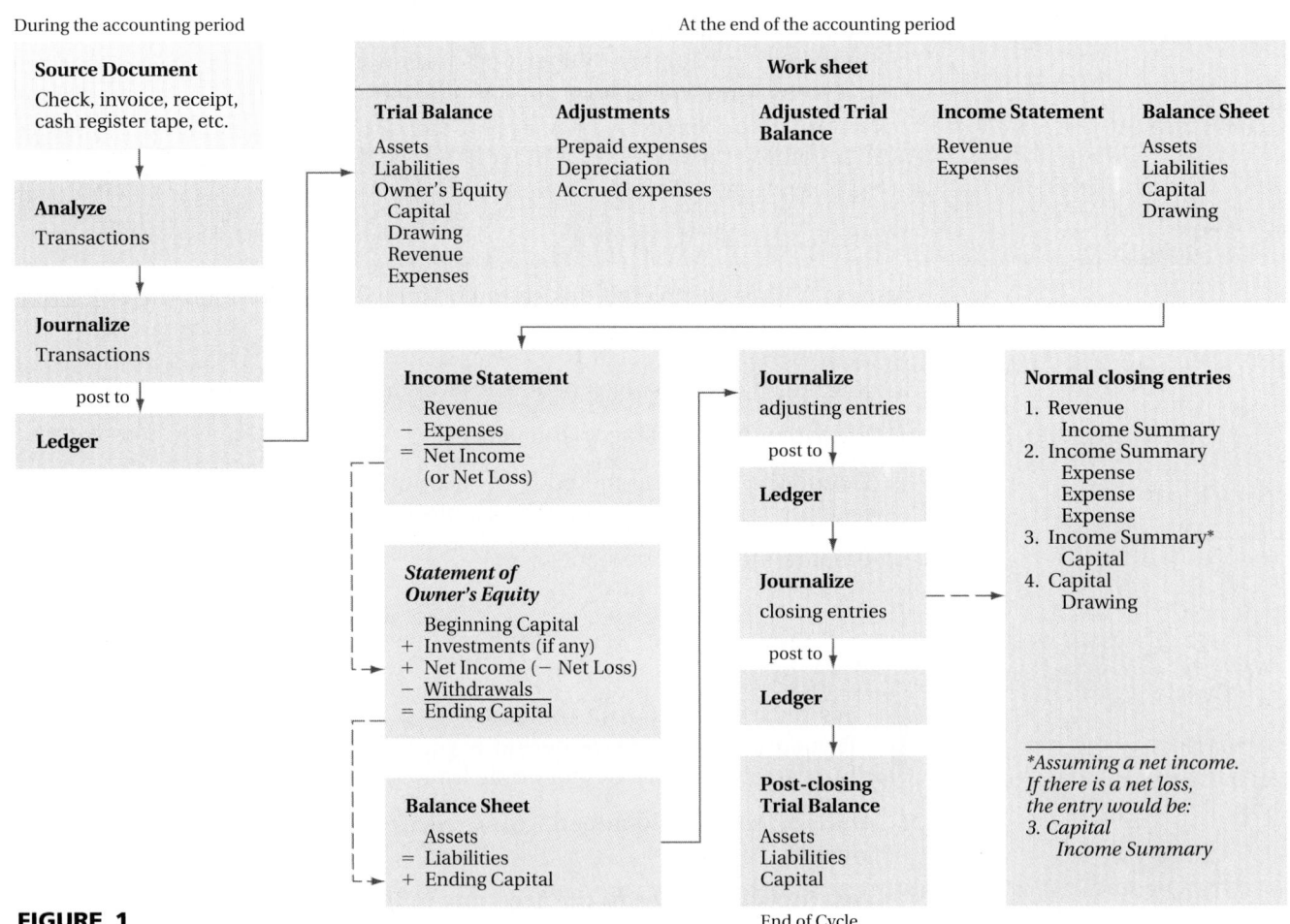

FIGURE 1

CLOSING ENTRIES

To help you understand the reason for the closing entries, let's repeat the fundamental accounting equation:

$$\text{Assets} = \text{Liabilities} + \text{Owner's Equity} + \text{Revenue} - \text{Expenses}$$

We know that the income statement, as stated in the third line of its heading, covers a period of time. The income statement consists of revenue minus expenses for this period of time only. So, when the next fiscal period begins, we should start with zero balances. We start all over again each period.

Closing entries empty or zero out temporary owner's equity accounts and prepare the accounts for the new accounting period—emptying out folders for one year so they can be filled with the new year's revenue and expenses.

Purpose of Closing Entries

This brings us to the *purpose* of the **closing entries**, which is to close (or clear) the temporary-equity or nominal accounts (revenue, expense, and drawing accounts). We do this because their balances apply to only one fiscal period. Closing entries are made after the last adjusting entry. With the coming of the next fiscal period, we want to start from zero, recording revenue and expenses for the new fiscal period. The closing entries also update the owner's Capital account.

Accountants also refer to closing the accounts as clearing the accounts. For income tax purposes, this is certainly understandable. No one wants to pay income tax more than once on the same income, and the Internal Revenue Service doesn't allow you to count an expense more than once. So now we have this:

$$\text{Assets} = \text{Liabilities} + \underset{\text{(Capital)}}{\text{Owner's Equity}} + \overset{\text{(closed)}}{\cancel{\text{Revenue}}} - \overset{\text{(closed)}}{\cancel{\text{Expenses}}}$$

The assets, the liabilities, and the owner's Capital account remain open. The balance sheet gives the present balances of these accounts. The accountant carries the asset, liability, and Capital account balances over to the next fiscal period.

Remember!

The matching principle is why we close revenue, expense, and drawing accounts.

Objective 2

Journalize and post closing entries for a service enterprise.

Procedure for Closing

The procedure for closing is simply to balance off the account; in other words, to make the balance *equal to zero*. This meets our objective, which is to start from zero in the next fiscal period. Let's illustrate this first with T accounts. Suppose an account to be closed has a debit balance of $960; then, to make the balance equal to zero, we *credit* the account for $960.

Debit		Credit	
Balance	960	Closing	960

At the end of a fiscal period, closing entries allow a business to start a new income statement period with a clean slate. Revenue and expense accounts are closed.

Now suppose an account to be closed has a credit balance of $1,200; then, to make the balance equal to zero, we *debit* the account for $1,200.

Debit		Credit	
Closing	1,200	Balance	1,200

Remember, every entry must have both a debit and a credit. So, to record the other half of the closing entry, we bring into existence the **Income Summary**. The Income Summary account does not have plus and minus signs, just debit and credit.

There are four steps in the closing procedure:

1. **Close the revenue accounts into Income Summary.**
2. **Close the expense accounts into Income Summary.**
3. **Close the Income Summary account into the Capital account, transferring the net income or loss to the Capital account.**
4. **Close the Drawing account into the Capital account.**

To illustrate, we return to Cruz Auto Detail. For the purpose of the illustration, assume that Cruz Auto Detail's fiscal period consists of one month. We have the following T account balances in the revenue and expense accounts after the adjustments have been posted.

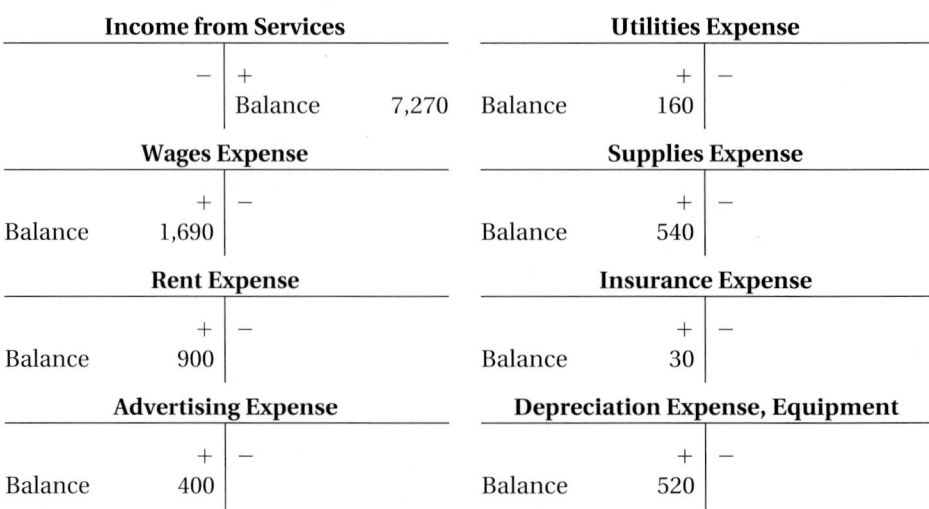

Step 1 Close the revenue account or accounts into Income Summary. In order to make the balance of Income from Services equal to zero, we *balance it off,* or debit it, in the amount of $7,270. Because we need an offsetting credit, we credit Income Summary for the same amount. Notice that there are no signs in Income Summary, only Debit and Credit like the other accounts.

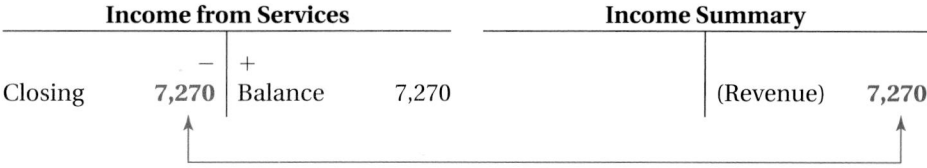

The balance of Income from Services is transferred to Income Summary.

Step 2 Close the expense accounts into Income Summary. To make the balances of the expense accounts equal to zero, we need to balance them off, or credit them. Again the T accounts are useful for formulating this journal entry.

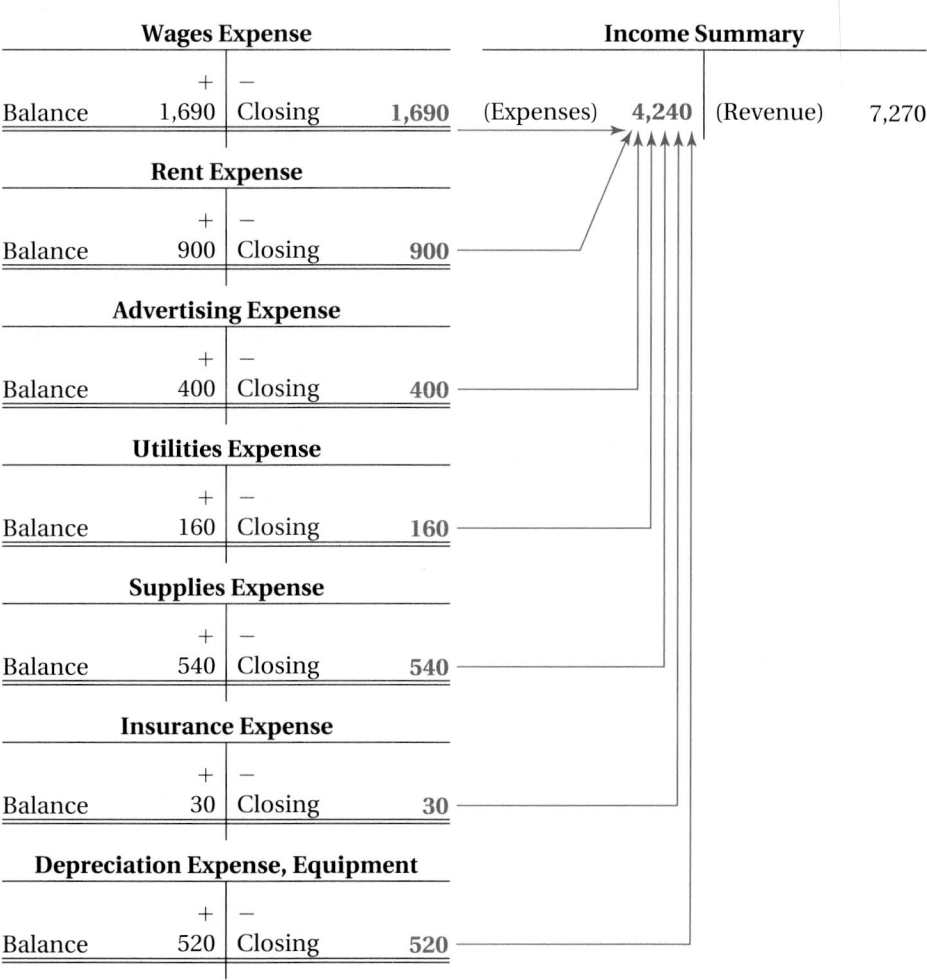

Step 3 Recall that we created Income Summary so that we could have a debit and a credit in each closing entry. Now that it has done its job, we close it out. We use the same procedure as before, in that we make the balance equal to zero, or balance off the account. We transfer, or close, the balance

of the Income Summary account into the Capital account, as shown in the T accounts and in Figure 2.

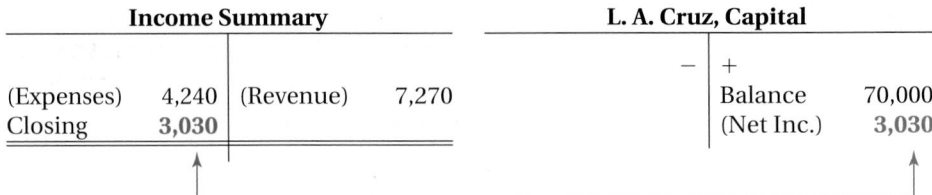

Income Summary		L. A. Cruz, Capital

Income Summary:
(Expenses)	4,240	(Revenue)	7,270
Closing	**3,030**		

L. A. Cruz, Capital:
−	+	
	Balance	70,000
	(Net Inc.)	**3,030**

Income Summary is always closed into the Capital account by the amount of the net income (Revenue minus Expenses) or the net loss. Comparing net income or net loss on the work sheet with the closing entry for Income Summary can serve as a check point or verification for you.

FIGURE 2

GENERAL JOURNAL   PAGE __4__

	DATE	DESCRIPTION	POST. REF.	DEBIT	CREDIT	
14	Step	Closing Entries				14
15	1 30	Income from Services		7 2 7 0 00		15
16		Income Summary			7 2 7 0 00	16
17						17
18	30	Income Summary		4 2 4 0 00		18
19		Wages Expense			1 6 9 0 00	19
20		Rent Expense			9 0 0 00	20
21	Step	Advertising Expense			4 0 0 00	21
22	2	Utilities Expense			1 6 0 00	22
23		Supplies Expense			5 4 0 00	23
24		Insurance Expense			3 0 00	24
25		Depreciation Expense,				25
26		Equipment			5 2 0 00	26
27						27
28	30	Income Summary		3 0 3 0 00		28
29		L. A. Cruz, Capital			3 0 3 0 00	29

Net income is added (credited) to the Capital account because, as shown in the statement of owner's equity, net income is treated as an addition. Net loss, on the other hand, is subtracted from (debited) to the Capital account, because net loss is treated as a deduction in the statement of owner's equity. Here's how to close Income Summary for J. Doe Company (net loss of $200):

Income Summary		J. Doe, Capital

Income Summary:
(Expenses)	900	(Revenue)	700
		Closing	**200**

J. Doe, Capital:
	−	+	
(Net Loss)	**200**	Balance	30,000

The entry to close Income Summary into Doe's Capital account would look like the following.

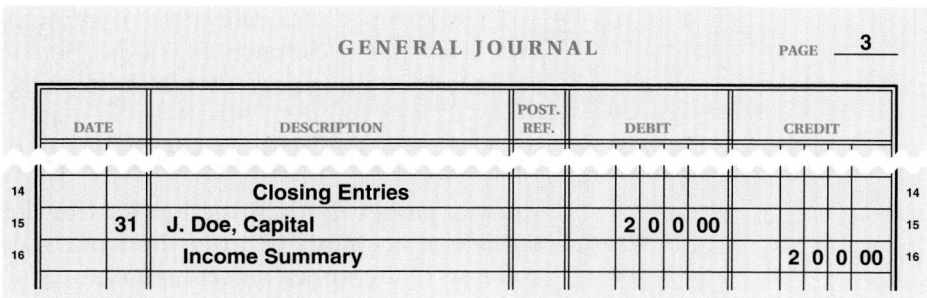

Step 4 Let's return to the example of Cruz Auto Detail. The Drawing account applies to only one fiscal period, and so it too must be closed. Drawing is not an expense because it did not help the business generate revenue. And because Drawing is not an expense, it cannot affect net income or net loss. It appears in the statement of owner's equity as a deduction from the Capital account, so it is closed directly into the Capital account. We balance off the Drawing account, or make the balance of it equal to zero. The balance of Drawing is transferred to the Capital account.

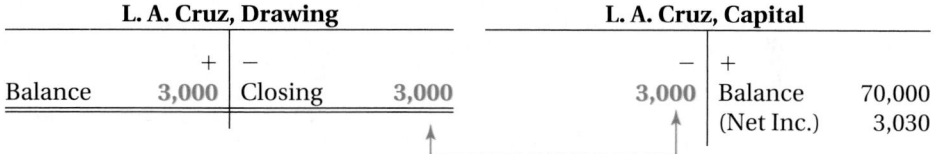

	L. A. Cruz, Drawing					L. A. Cruz, Capital	
	+	–			–	+	
Balance	3,000	Closing	3,000	3,000	Balance	70,000	
					(Net Inc.)	3,030	

The journal entries in the closing procedure are shown in Figure 3.

FIGURE 3

GENERAL JOURNAL PAGE 4

	DATE	DESCRIPTION	POST. REF.	DEBIT	CREDIT	
14	Step	**Closing Entries**				14
15	1 { 30	Income from Services		7 2 7 0 00		15
16	{	Income Summary			7 2 7 0 00	16
17						17
18	{ 30	Income Summary		4 2 4 0 00		18
19		Wages Expense			1 6 9 0 00	19
20		Rent Expense			9 0 0 00	20
21	Step	Advertising Expense			4 0 0 00	21
22	2 {	Utilities Expense			1 6 0 00	22
23		Supplies Expense			5 4 0 00	23
24		Insurance Expense			3 0 00	24
25		Depreciation Expense,				25
26	{	Equipment			5 2 0 00	26
27						27
28	Step { 30	Income Summary		3 0 3 0 00		28
29	3 {	L. A. Cruz, Capital			3 0 3 0 00	29
30						30
31	Step { 30	L. A. Cruz, Capital		3 0 0 0 00		31
32	4 {	L. A. Cruz, Drawing			3 0 0 0 00	32

FYI

As a memory tool for the sequence of steps in the closing procedure, use the letters of the closing elements, **REID**: **R**evenue, **E**xpenses, **I**ncome Summary, **D**rawing.

These closing entries show that Cruz Auto Detail has net income of $3,030, the owner has withdrawn $3,000 for personal expenses, and $30 has been retained in the business, thereby increasing capital.

Closing Entries Taken Directly from the Work Sheet

You can gather the information for the closing entries either directly from the ledger accounts or from the work sheet. Since the Income Statement columns of the work sheet consist entirely of revenues and expenses, you can pick up the figures for three of the four closing entries from these columns. Figure 4 shows a partial work sheet for Cruz Auto Detail.

	ACCOUNT NAME	TRIAL BALANCE DEBIT	TRIAL BALANCE CREDIT	ADJUSTMENTS DEBIT	ADJUSTMENTS CREDIT	INCOME STATEMENT DEBIT	INCOME STATEMENT CREDIT
1	Cash	23 2 5 0 00					
2	Accounts Receivable	2 0 0 00					
3	Supplies	8 0 0 00			(a) 5 4 0 00		
4	Prepaid Insurance	3 6 0 00			(b) 3 0 00		
5	Equipment	51 5 0 0 00					
6	Accounts Payable		4 7 0 0 00				
7	L. A. Cruz, Capital		70 0 0 0 00				
8	L. A. Cruz, Drawing	3 0 0 0 00					
9	Income from Services		7 2 7 0 00				7 2 7 0 00
10	Wages Expense	1 4 0 0 00		(d) 2 9 0 00		1 6 9 0 00	
11	Rent Expense	9 0 0 00				9 0 0 00	
12	Advertising Expense	4 0 0 00				4 0 0 00	
13	Utilities Expense	1 6 0 00				1 6 0 00	
14		81 9 7 0 00	81 9 7 0 00				
15	Supplies Expense			(a) 5 4 0 00		5 4 0 00	
16	Insurance Expense			(b) 3 0 00		3 0 00	
17	Depreciation Expense,						
18	Equipment			(c) 5 2 0 00		5 2 0 00	
19	Accumulated Dep.,						
20	Equipment				(c) 5 2 0 00		
21	Wages Payable				(d) 2 9 0 00		
22				1 3 8 0 00	1 3 8 0 00	4 2 4 0 00	7 2 7 0 00
23	Net Income					3 0 3 0 00	
24						7 2 7 0 00	7 2 7 0 00
25							
26							

FIGURE 4

You may plan the closing entries by balancing off all the figures that appear in the Income Statement columns. For example, in the Income Statement Credit column, there is a credit for $7,270 (Income from Services), so we debit that account for $7,270 and credit Income Summary for $7,270.

There are debits for $1,690, $900, $400, $160, $540, $30, and $520 (expense accounts). So now we *credit* these accounts for the same amounts, and we debit Income Summary for their total ($4,240).

Next, we close Income Summary into Capital, using the net income figure already shown on the work sheet in Figure 4.

We do, of course, have to get the last closing entry from the Balance Sheet columns to close Drawing.

Incidentally, accountants call the accounts that are to be closed (such as revenue, expenses, Income Summary, and Drawing) **nominal** or **temporary-equity accounts**. These accounts are *temporary* in that their balances apply to only one fiscal period. The *equity* aspect pertains because these accounts all come under the umbrella of owner's equity.

On the other hand, accountants call the accounts that remain open (such as assets, liabilities, and Capital) **real** or **permanent accounts**. These accounts have balances that will be carried over to the next fiscal period. They are *permanent* because as long as the company exists, there will be balances in these accounts.

■ ■ ■

Remember!

The temporary-equity accounts (revenue, expenses, Drawing, and Income Summary) are closed out because they apply to only one fiscal period.

Posting the Closing Entries

In the Item column of the ledger account, we write the word *Closing*. To show that the balance of an account is zero, we draw a line through both the Debit Balance and the Credit Balance columns.

After we have posted the closing entries, the Capital, Drawing, Income Summary, revenue, and expense accounts of Cruz Auto Detail appear as follows:

GENERAL LEDGER

ACCOUNT **L. A. Cruz, Capital**   ACCOUNT NO. **311**

	DATE		ITEM	POST. REF.	DEBIT	CREDIT	BALANCE DEBIT	BALANCE CREDIT	
1	20–								1
2	June	1		1		70 0 0 0 00		70 0 0 0 00	2
3		30		4		3 0 3 0 00		73 0 3 0 00	3
4		30		4	3 0 0 0 00			70 0 3 0 00	4

ACCOUNT **L. A. Cruz, Drawing**   ACCOUNT NO. **312**

	DATE		ITEM	POST. REF.	DEBIT	CREDIT	BALANCE DEBIT	BALANCE CREDIT	
1	20–								1
2	June	30		3	3 0 0 0 00		3 0 0 0 00		2
3		30	Closing	4		3 0 0 0 00	———	———	3

ACCOUNT **Income Summary**   ACCOUNT NO. **313**

	DATE		ITEM	POST. REF.	DEBIT	CREDIT	BALANCE DEBIT	BALANCE CREDIT	
1	20–								1
2	June	30		4		7 2 7 0 00		7 2 7 0 00	2
3		30		4	4 2 4 0 00			3 0 3 0 00	3
4		30	Closing	4	3 0 3 0 00		———	———	4

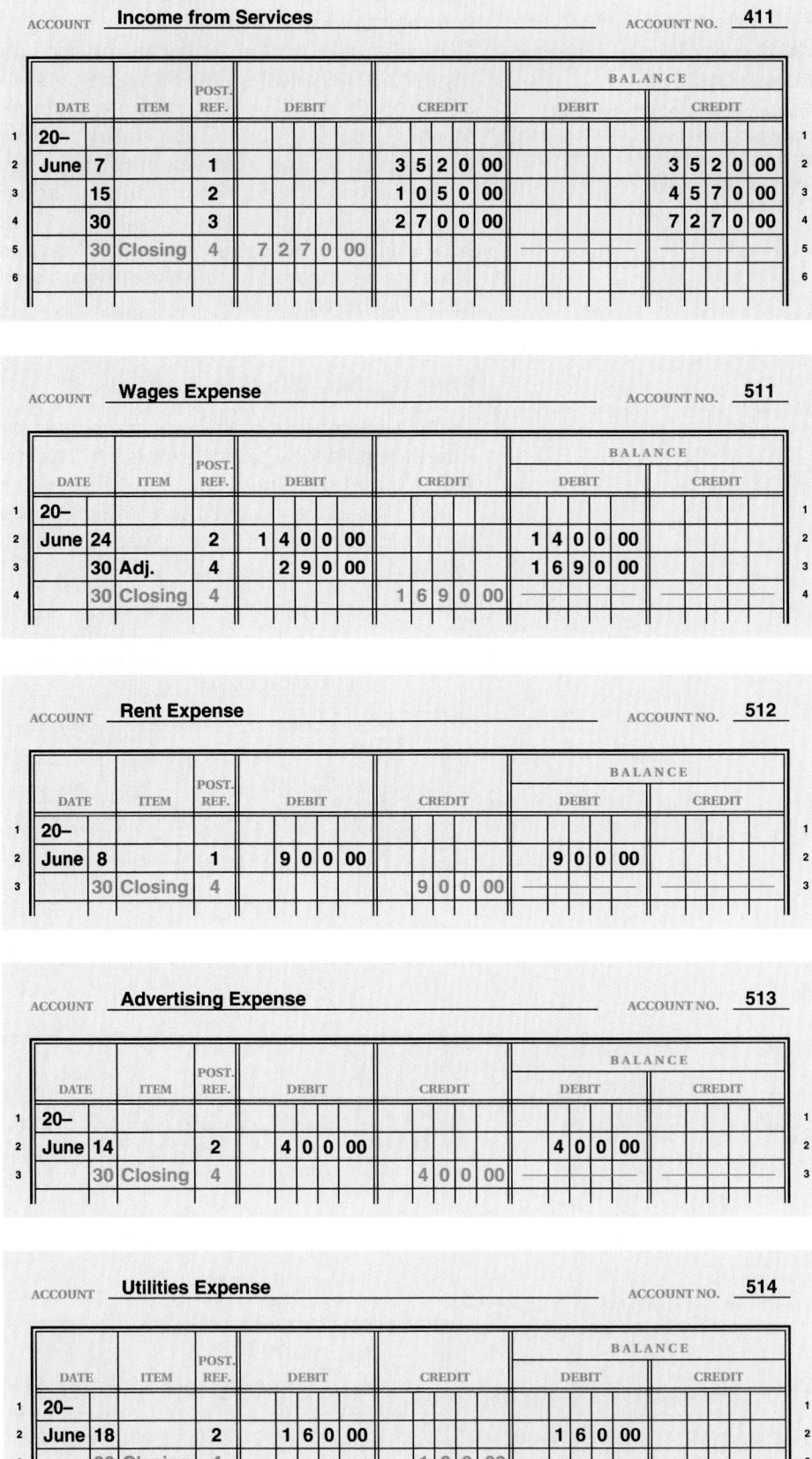

ACCOUNT   **Income from Services**   ACCOUNT NO. 411

	DATE	ITEM	POST. REF.	DEBIT	CREDIT	BALANCE DEBIT	BALANCE CREDIT	
1	20–							1
2	June 7		1		3 5 2 0 00		3 5 2 0 00	2
3	15		2		1 0 5 0 00		4 5 7 0 00	3
4	30		3		2 7 0 0 00		7 2 7 0 00	4
5	30	Closing	4	7 2 7 0 00		—	—	5
6								6

ACCOUNT   **Wages Expense**   ACCOUNT NO. 511

	DATE	ITEM	POST. REF.	DEBIT	CREDIT	BALANCE DEBIT	BALANCE CREDIT	
1	20–							1
2	June 24		2	1 4 0 0 00		1 4 0 0 00		2
3	30	Adj.	4	2 9 0 00		1 6 9 0 00		3
4	30	Closing	4		1 6 9 0 00	—	—	4

ACCOUNT   **Rent Expense**   ACCOUNT NO. 512

	DATE	ITEM	POST. REF.	DEBIT	CREDIT	BALANCE DEBIT	BALANCE CREDIT	
1	20–							1
2	June 8		1	9 0 0 00		9 0 0 00		2
3	30	Closing	4		9 0 0 00	—	—	3

ACCOUNT   **Advertising Expense**   ACCOUNT NO. 513

	DATE	ITEM	POST. REF.	DEBIT	CREDIT	BALANCE DEBIT	BALANCE CREDIT	
1	20–							1
2	June 14		2	4 0 0 00		4 0 0 00		2
3	30	Closing	4		4 0 0 00	—	—	3

ACCOUNT   **Utilities Expense**   ACCOUNT NO. 514

	DATE	ITEM	POST. REF.	DEBIT	CREDIT	BALANCE DEBIT	BALANCE CREDIT	
1	20–							1
2	June 18		2	1 6 0 00		1 6 0 00		2
3	30	Closing	4		1 6 0 00	—	—	3

Office supplies consist of a wide variety of items that are used up and reordered frequently in the course of doing business. W. B. Mason delivers all kinds of office supplies to keep businesses productive.

ACCOUNT **Supplies Expense**   ACCOUNT NO. **515**

	DATE	ITEM	POST. REF.	DEBIT	CREDIT	BALANCE DEBIT	BALANCE CREDIT	
1	20–							1
2	June 30	Adj.	4	5 4 0 00		5 4 0 00		2
3	30	Closing	4		5 4 0 00			3

ACCOUNT **Insurance Expense**   ACCOUNT NO. **516**

	DATE	ITEM	POST. REF.	DEBIT	CREDIT	BALANCE DEBIT	BALANCE CREDIT	
1	20–							1
2	June 30	Adj.	4	3 0 00		3 0 00		2
3	30	Closing	4		3 0 00			3

ACCOUNT **Depreciation Expense, Equipment**   ACCOUNT NO. **517**

	DATE	ITEM	POST. REF.	DEBIT	CREDIT	BALANCE DEBIT	BALANCE CREDIT	
1	20–							1
2	June 30	Adj.	4	5 2 0 00		5 2 0 00		2
3	30	Closing	4		5 2 0 00			3

THE POST-CLOSING TRIAL BALANCE

Objective 3

Prepare a post-closing trial balance.

After posting the closing entries and before going on to the next fiscal period, verify the balances of the accounts that remain open. To do so, prepare a **post-closing trial balance**, using the final balance figures from the ledger accounts. The purpose of the post-closing trial balance is to make sure that the debit balances equal the credit balances.

Note that the accounts listed in the post-closing trial balance (assets, liabilities, and Capital) are the *real* or *permanent accounts* (see Figure 5). The accountant carries forward the balances of the permanent accounts from one fiscal period to another.

FIGURE 5

Cruz Auto Detail
Post-Closing Trial Balance
June 30, 20—

ACCOUNT NAME	DEBIT	CREDIT
Cash	23 2 5 0 00	
Accounts Receivable	2 0 0 00	
Supplies	2 6 0 00	
Prepaid Insurance	3 3 0 00	
Equipment	51 5 0 0 00	
Accumulated Depreciation, Equipment		5 2 0 00
Accounts Payable		4 7 0 0 00
Wages Payable		2 9 0 00
L. A. Cruz, Capital		70 0 3 0 00
	75 5 4 0 00	75 5 4 0 00

Contrast this to the handling of *nominal* or *temporary-equity accounts* (revenue, expenses, Income Summary, and Drawing), which are closed at the end of each fiscal period.

If the total debits and total credits of the post-closing trial balance are not equal, here's a recommended procedure for tracking down the error.

1. Re-add the trial balance columns.
2. Check to see that the figures were correctly transferred from the ledger accounts to the post-closing trial balance.
3. Verify the posting of the adjusting entries and the recording of the new balances.
4. Make sure that the closing entries have been posted and that all revenue, expense, Income Summary, and Drawing accounts have zero balances.

THE ACCRUAL BASIS

Objective 4

Define the following methods of accounting: accrual basis, cash-receipts-and-disbursements basis, modified cash basis.

Up to this time, we have been using the accrual basis of accounting. **When we use the accrual basis, we record revenue when it is earned and expenses when they are incurred.** Revenues are inflows of assets, cash, or accounts receivable that result from selling goods or services. Expenses are outflows of used assets that result from selling goods or services. Revenues are recorded by the seller in the period that the buyer accepts delivery of the goods or services from the seller. Expenses are recorded by the seller in the same period in which the related revenue was recognized by the seller. This concept is called the *matching principle*. Cruz Auto Detail's transactions were recorded on the accrual basis. Let's recall two transactions.

Companies using accrual basis accounting, like Apple Computer, Inc. would debit Accounts Payable and credit Cash for this advertising expense. Smaller or professional firms that use a modified cash basis would debit Advertising Expense and credit Cash.

Transaction (i) Received the bill for newspaper advertising, $400. The expense was recorded before it was paid in cash. The expense was matched up with the fiscal period in which it was incurred.

Advertising Expense		Accounts Payable	
(i) 400		**(i)** 400	

Transaction (j) Entered into a contract with Costello Taxi to perform detailing services on a credit basis. Billed Costello Taxi for services performed, $1,050.

Accounts Receivable		Income from Services	
(j) 1,050		**(j)** 1,050	

The revenue was recorded before it was received in cash. It was matched up with the fiscal period in which it was earned. Accountants feel strongly that the accrual basis gives the most realistic picture of the revenue and expense accounts and, hence, the net income. (Net income equals total revenue minus total expenses.)

CASH-RECEIPTS-AND-DISBURSEMENTS BASIS

When the **cash-receipts-and-disbursements basis** is used, all revenue is recorded only when it is received in cash, and all expenses are recorded only when they are paid in cash. *The cash-receipts-and-disbursements basis is not appropriate for most business firms.* This is true because most companies do have some equipment, and the Internal Revenue Service requires that equipment be depreciated over a period of years, resulting in an expense that does not involve cash.

The cash-receipts-and-disbursements basis is used mainly by individuals for their personal tax returns. Here, revenue in the form of salaries or wages, interest, and similar items is reported only when received in cash, and expenses to be included as personal deductions are reported only when paid in cash.

MODIFIED CASH BASIS

Professional enterprises and many small businesses, particularly service firms, use a **modified cash basis**. **Revenue is not recorded by the firm until it receives cash** from the customer. Here we are concerned with situations in which services are performed in one fiscal period, but the cash for these same services is not received until a later fiscal period. Under the modified cash basis, the revenue is recorded in the later period, when the cash is actually received.

Most expenses also are recorded only when they are paid in cash. An expense may be incurred in one fiscal period and paid in a later period.

Under the modified cash basis, the expense is recorded in the later period, when it is actually paid. For example, an employee's earnings for the month of December are paid on January 5. Under this basis, no entry is made for accrued salaries, but on January 5, an entry is made debiting Salary Expense and crediting Cash.

However, **under the modified cash basis, exceptions are made for expenditures on items having an economic life of more than one year and on some prepaid items.** Examples of such expenditures and prepaid items are equipment, supplies, and insurance. Costs of these items must be prorated or spread out over their useful lives, and so adjusting entries are made for depreciation of equipment, supplies used up, and expiration of insurance. As we stated, there is no need to make additional adjusting entries, such as an adjustment for accrued salaries or other accrued adjustments that we will introduce later. The Internal Revenue Service publications refer to the modified cash basis as a hybrid method because it combines some of the characteristics of both the accrual basis and the cash-receipts-and-disbursements basis of accounting.

Remember!

Under the modified cash system, exceptions are made for recording supplies expense, insurance expense, and depreciation expense.

Accrual Basis vs. Modified Cash Basis

As an illustration, we will show selected transactions of another business, so that you can see how these transactions are recorded using both the accrual basis and the modified cash basis. (Assume that the transactions recorded in T accounts on page 161 have first been journalized.) Abbreviated income statements are shown at the top of page 162.

	Accounting Basis	
Transaction	**Accrual**	**Modified Cash**
a. Billed customers for services rendered, $2,600.	Journalized (Revenue is recorded at this point.) Dr. Accounts Receivable Cr. Income from Services	Not journalized (Cash has not been received.)
b. Received bill for advertising from *Milton Daily World*, $220.	Journalized (Expense is recorded at this point.) Dr. Advertising Expense Cr. Accounts Payable	Not journalized (Cash has not been paid.)

c. Bought equipment on account from Stanton Company, $1,940.	Journalized
	
	Dr. Equipment
	    Cr. Accounts Payable
		Journalized (Cash will be paid later.)
		
		Dr. Equipment
		    Cr. Accounts Payable

d. Received $2,000 from charge customers previously billed.	Journalized (Revenue was recorded previously.)
	
	Dr. Cash
	    Cr. Accounts Receivable
		Journalized (Cash has been received.) (Revenue is recorded at this point.)
		
		Dr. Cash
		    Cr. Income from Services

	Transaction	Accounting Basis	
		Accrual	**Modified Cash**
e.	Paid $100 to *Milton Daily World* for advertising previously billed.	Journalized (Expense was recorded previously.)	Journalized (Cash has been paid.) (Expense is recorded at this point.)

		Dr. Accounts Payable
		    Cr. Cash
			Dr. Advertising Expense
			    Cr. Cash

f.	Paid wages for the period, $1,400.	Journalized (Expense is recorded at this point.)	Journalized (Cash has been paid.) (Expense is recorded at this point.)

		Dr. Wages Expense
		    Cr. Cash
			Dr. Wages Expense
			    Cr. Cash

g.	Recorded depreciation of equipment for the period, $380.	Journalized (Expense is recorded at this point.)	Journalized (Depreciation is an exception.) (Expense is recorded at this point.)

		Dr. Depreciation Expense
		    Cr. Accumulated Depreciation
			Dr. Depreciation Expense
			    Cr. Accumulated Depreciation

These journal entries are posted in the following T accounts.

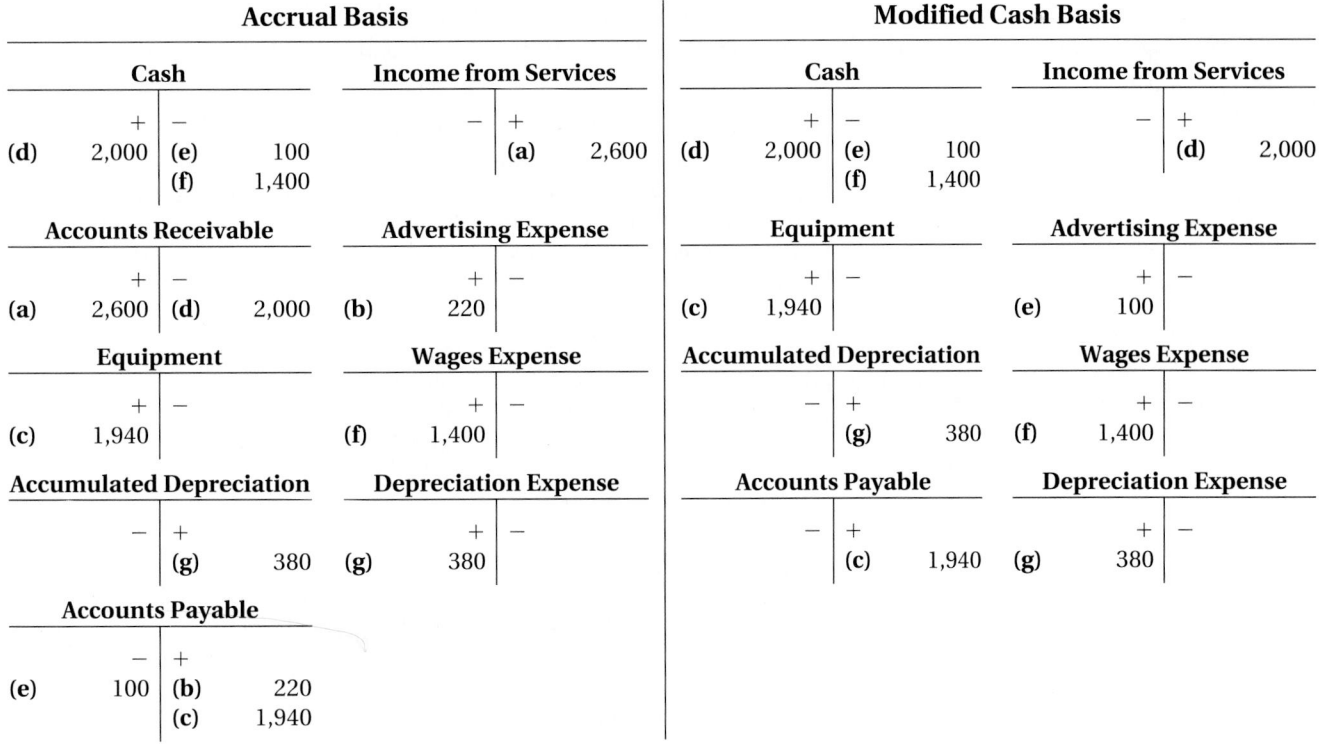

Here's a comparison of the income statements under the accrual basis and the modified cash basis.

Accrual Basis		
Income Statement		
Revenue:		
Income from Services		$2,600
Expenses:		
Advertising Expense	$ 220	
Wages Expense	1,400	
Depreciation Expense	380	
Total Expenses		2,000
Net Income		$ 600

Modified Cash Basis		
Income Statement		
Revenue:		
Income from Services		$2,000
Expenses:		
Advertising Expense	$ 100	
Wages Expense	1,400	
Depreciation Expense	380	
Total Expenses		1,880
Net Income		$ 120

INTERIM STATEMENTS

Objective 5

Prepare interim statements.

As we said previously, a firm's fiscal year generally consists of twelve consecutive months. However, it is understandable that the owner of the business does not want to wait until the end of the twelve-month period to determine whether the company made a profit or a loss. Instead, most owners want financial statements at the end of each month. Financial statements prepared during the fiscal year, for periods of less than twelve months, are called **interim statements**. (They are given this name because they are prepared within the fiscal period.) For example, a business may prepare the income statement, the statement of owner's equity, and the balance sheet *monthly.* These statements provide up-to-date information about the results and status of operations. For example, a company might have the following interim statements:

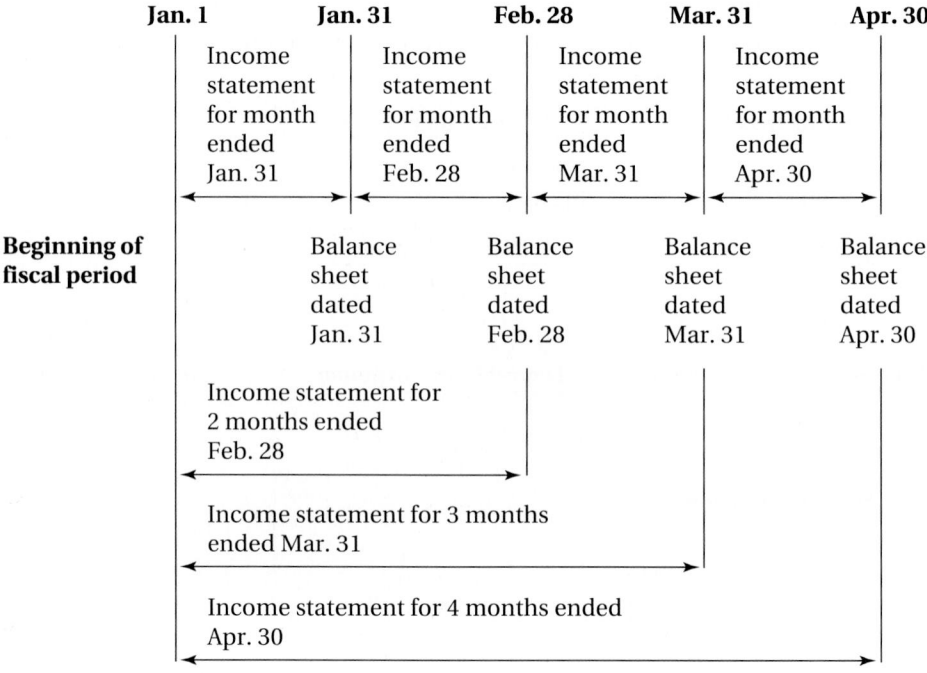

In this case, the accountant would prepare a work sheet at the end of each month. Next, based on these work sheets, he or she would prepare the financial statements. *However, the remaining steps—journalizing the adjusting and closing entries and preparing the post-closing trial balance—would be performed only at the end of the year.*

CHAPTER REVIEW

Review of Performance Objectives

1. List the steps in the accounting cycle.

   1. Analyze source documents and record business transactions in a journal.
   2. Post journal entries to the accounts in the ledger.
   3. Prepare a trial balance.
   4. Gather adjustment data and record the adjusting entries on a work sheet.
   5. Complete the work sheet.
   6. Prepare financial statements from the data on the work sheet.
   7. Journalize and post the adjusting entries from the data on the work sheet.
   8. Journalize and post the closing entries.
   9. Prepare a post-closing trial balance.

2. Journalize and post closing entries for a service enterprise.

   The four steps in the closing procedure are as follows:

   1. Close the revenue accounts into Income Summary.
   2. Close the expense accounts into Income Summary.
   3. Close the Income Summary account into the Capital account, transferring the net income or loss to the Capital account.
   4. Close the Drawing account into the Capital account.

3. Prepare a post-closing trial balance.

   A post-closing trial balance consists of the final balances of the accounts remaining open. It is the final proof that the debit balances equal the credit balances before the posting for the new fiscal period commences.

4. Define the following methods of accounting: accrual basis, cash-receipts-and-disbursements basis, modified cash basis.

   Under the *accrual basis* of accounting, revenue is recorded when earned, even if cash is received at a later date, and expenses are recorded when incurred, even if cash is to be paid at a later date. Under the *cash-receipts-and-disbursements basis*, revenue is recorded only when cash is received, and expenses are recorded only when paid in cash. This basis is used mainly by individuals for their income taxes.

   Under the *modified cash basis*, revenue is recorded only when cash is received, and most expenses are recorded only when paid in cash. However, exceptions are made for certain expenses, such as depreciation, supplies used, and insurance expired, allowing adjusting entries.

5. Prepare interim statements.

   Interim statements consist of year-to-date income statements, statements of owner's equity, and balance sheets as of various dates during the fiscal period.

Glossary

Accrual basis An accounting method under which revenue is recorded when it is earned, regardless of when it is received, and expenses are recorded when they are incurred, regardless of when they are paid. (158)

Cash-receipts-and-disbursements basis An accounting method under which all revenue is recorded only when it is received in cash, and all expenses are recorded only when they are paid in cash. (159)

Closing entries Entries made at the end of a fiscal period to close off the revenue, expense, and drawing accounts—that is, to make the balances of the temporary-equity accounts equal to zero. Closing is also called *clearing the accounts.* (149)

Income Summary An account brought into existence in order to have a debit and credit in each closing entry. The revenue and expense account balances are transferred to this account to allow calculations of net income or net loss. (150)

Interim statements Financial statements prepared during the fiscal year, covering a period of time less than twelve months. (162)

Modified cash basis An accounting method under which revenue is recorded only when it is received in cash. Most expenses are recorded only when they are paid in cash. However, exceptions are made for expenditures on items having a useful life of more than one year and for certain prepaid items. Expenditures for supplies and insurance premiums can be *prorated,* or spread out over the fiscal periods covered. Expenditures for long-lived items are recorded as assets and later depreciated as an expense over their useful lives. (159)

Nominal or **temporary-equity accounts** Accounts that apply to only one fiscal period and that are to be closed at the end of that fiscal period, such as revenue, expense, Income Summary, and Drawing accounts. This category may also be described as all accounts except assets, liabilities, and the Capital account. (155)

Post-closing trial balance The listing of the final balances of the real accounts at the end of the fiscal period. (157)

Real or **permanent accounts** The accounts that remain open (assets, liabilities, and the Capital account in owner's equity) and that have balances that will be carried over to the next fiscal period. (155)

QUESTIONS, EXERCISES, AND PROBLEMS

Discussion Questions

1. Number in order the following steps in the accounting cycle.
   - *3* a. Prepare a trial balance on the first two columns of the work sheet.
   - *2* b. Post journal entries to accounts in the ledger.
   - *7* c. Journalize and post adjusting entries.
   - *1* d. Analyze source documents and record transactions in the journal.
   - *6* e. Prepare financial statements.

4   f. Gather adjusting data and write adjusting entries on the work sheet.

8   g. Journalize and post closing entries.

9   h. Prepare a post-closing trial balance.

5   i. Complete the work sheet.

2. List the steps in the closing procedure.

3. What is the purpose of closing entries?

4. What are the two sources from which you can make closing entries?

5. What are real accounts? What are nominal accounts? Explain how they differ.

6. What is the purpose of the Income Summary, and how does it relate to the revenue and expense accounts?

7. What is the purpose of the post-closing trial balance? What is the difference between a trial balance and a post-closing trial balance?

8. Write the third closing entry to transfer the profit or loss to the P. Thompson, Capital, account for July 31, assuming the following:

   a. A profit of $3,847
   b. A loss of $1,278

Exercises

P.O. 2

Classify accounts and show where they are listed on the work sheet.

Exercise 5-1 Classify the accounts listed below as real (permanent) or nominal (temporary), and indicate with an x whether the account is closed. Also, indicate the financial statement in which each account will appear. The Building account is given as an example.

Account Title	Real	Nominal	Closed Yes	Closed No	Income Statement	Balance Sheet
0. Example: Building	X			X		X
a. Prepaid Insurance	X			X		X
b. Accounts Payable	X			X		X
c. Wages Payable	X			X		X
d. Services Income		X	X		X	
e. Rent Expense		X	X		X	
f. Supplies Expense		X	X		X	
g. Accum. Depr., Equip. *accl*	X			X		X

P.O. 2

Journalize closing entries from T account balances.

Exercise 5-2 Number the closing entries as steps 1 through 4. Journalize the closing entries on the following page.

Assets	=	Liabilities	+	Owner's Equity	+	Revenue	−	Expenses
Dr. | Cr.		Dr. | Cr.		Dr. | Cr.		Dr. | Cr.		Dr. | Cr.
+ | −		− | +		− | +		− | +		+ | −

Prepaid Insurance

Bal. 990 | (c) 360
Bal. 630 |

Accum. Depr., Equipment

| Bal. 3,200
| (b) 700
| 3,900 Bal.

Wages Payable

| (a) 210

L. Dempsy, Capital

560 | Bal.
500 | 24,000
1,060 | Bal. 2,560

L. Dempsy, Drawing

Bal. 500 | 500

Income Summary

4,210 | 3,650
560 | 560

Professional Fees

3,650 | Bal. 3,650

Wages Expense

Bal. 2,800 | 3,010
(a) 210 |
3,010 |

Insurance Expense

(c) 360 | 360

Depr. Expense, Equipment

(b) 700 | 700

Misc. Expense

Bal. 140 | 140

Exercise 5-3 As of December 31, the end of the current year, the ledger of Diggs Company contained the following account balances after adjustment. All accounts have normal balances. Journalize the closing entries.

Cash	$ 8,540	W. O. Ryan, Drawing	$1,698
Equipment	11,486	Professional Fees	6,875
Accumulated Depreciation,		Wages Expense	1,468
Equipment	2,687	Rent Expense	990
Accounts Payable	1,574	Depreciation Expense,	
Wages Payable	658	Equipment	1,243
W. O. Ryan, Capital	13,876	Miscellaneous Expense	245

Exercise 5-4 The Income Statement columns of the work sheet of R. Douglas Company for the fiscal year ended June 30 appear below. During the year, R. Douglas withdrew $4,100. Journalize the closing entries.

	ACCOUNT NAME	INCOME STATEMENT	
		DEBIT	CREDIT
1	Service Income		6 8 9 7 00
2	Rental Income		2 6 7 6 00
3	Rent Expense	2 7 0 0 00	
4	Wages Expense	1 9 5 4 00	
5	Utilities Expense	3 6 5 00	
6	Miscellaneous Expense	1 5 9 00	
7		5 1 7 8 00	9 5 7 3 00
8	Net Income	4 3 9 5 00	
9		9 5 7 3 00	9 5 7 3 00

Exercise 5-5 The Income Statement columns of the work sheet of R. Mandel Company for the fiscal year ended December 31 appear below. During the year, R. Mandel withdrew $28,000. Journalize the closing entries.

ACCOUNT NAME	INCOME STATEMENT			
	DEBIT		CREDIT	
1 Service Income			32 7 4 0 00	
2 Rental Income			12 0 0 0 00	
3 Wages Expense	43 5 2 0 00			
4 Utilities Expense	4 6 3 0 00			
5 Miscellaneous Expense	15 2 0 0 00			
6	63 3 5 0 00		44 7 4 0 00	
7 Net Loss			18 6 1 0 00	
8	63 3 5 0 00		63 3 5 0 00	

P.O. 2

Journalize closing entries three and four from account balances.

Exercise 5-6 After all revenue and expenses have been closed at the end of the fiscal period ended December 31, Income Summary has a debit of $35,450 and a credit of $31,430. On the same date, A. Morrison, Drawing, has a debit balance of $11,300, and A. Morrison, Capital, has a credit balance of $68,320.

a. Journalize the entries necessary to close the remaining temporary accounts.
b. What is the new balance of A. Morrison, Capital, after closing the remaining temporary accounts?

P.O. 5

Place accounts on financial statements.

Exercise 5-7 Indicate with an X whether each of the following would appear on the income statement, statement of owner's equity, or balance sheet. The first item is provided as an example.

Item	Income Statement	Statement of OE	Balance Sheet
0. Example: The total liabilities of the business at the end of the year.			X
a. The amount of the owner's Capital balance at the end of the year.		X	X
b. The amount of depreciation expense on equipment during the year.	X		
c. The amount of the company's net income for the year.	X	X	
d. Supplies on hand at the end of the year.			X
e. The book value of the equipment.			X
f. Total insurance expired during the year.	X		
g. Total accounts receivable at the end of the year.			X
h. Total withdrawals by the owner.		X	
i. The cost of supplies used during the year.	X		
j. The amount of the owner's Capital balance at the beginning of the year.		X	

P.O. 5

Prepare a statement of owner's equity from T accounts.

Exercise 5-8 Prepare a statement of owner's equity for VonBehren Veterinary Clinic for the year ended December 31. P. VonBehren's capital amount on January 1 was $140,000, and there was an additional investment of $8,000 on May 12 and withdrawals of $21,500 for the year. Net income for the year was $4,198.

CONSIDER AND COMMUNICATE

A friend of yours owns a small business and has completed part of an accounting class—through the chapter on adjustments. He is about to start a new fiscal period, and he sees no need for closing. Explain why the closing entries are so important to the accounting cycle and to his records.

CRITICAL THINKING

Your bookkeeper has submitted the following trial balance, marked "Post-Closing." Assume that the totals are correct.

a. Study the trial balance and prepare a response to what you have reviewed.
b. Journalize the closing entries. Prepare additional entries, if needed.
c. What is the net income or net loss for the period?
d. Was there an increase or a decrease in Capital?
e. What would be the ending amount of Capital?
f. What is the balance of the post-closing trial balance after posting the closing entries?

Post-Closing Trial Balance

ACCOUNT NAME	DEBIT A + Draw. + E	CREDIT Accum. Deprec. + L + C + R
Cash	2 3 2 7 00	
Accounts Receivable	9 1 9 00	
Prepaid Insurance	1 4 6 2 00	
Supplies	3 9 2 00	
Office Equipment	5 3 3 9 00	
Accounts Payable		
C. Horn, Capital		9 0 2 0 00
C. Horn, Drawing	1 0 0 0 0 00	
Commissions Earned		3 1 2 0 00
Rent Expense	7 9 5 00	
Advertising Expense	5 2 5 00	
Utilities Expense	2 9 8 00	
Miscellaneous Expense	1 5 4 00	
	13 2 1 1 00	13 2 1 1 00

A MATTER OF ETHICS

You are completing the accounting cycle for the company for which you work. You have made a post-closing trial balance, but it doesn't balance. You are tired, and besides, you don't think they pay you for this kind of headache.

You decide to increase the balance of an asset account to make the totals balance. Discuss this behavior and whether it is ethical or illegal.

WEB WORK

Using an Internet web browser, type the word *spreadsheets* in the search box. Search for an article or find a home page that provides information about computerized spreadsheets. Narrow your search by adding accounting terms to the search box, for example, *computerized* spreadsheet or *accounting tools*. Discuss or write about your findings.

PROBLEM SET A

For additional help, see the demonstration problem at the beginning of each chapter in your Working Papers.

P.O. 2

Problem 5-1A After the accountant posted the adjusting entries for M. Tigard, Designer, the general ledger contained the following account balances on May 31:

	ACCOUNT NAME	ADJUSTED TRIAL BALANCE	
		DEBIT A + Draw. + E	CREDIT Accum. Deprec. + L + C + R
1	Cash	2 3 1 8 00	
2	Accounts Receivable	1 2 0 8 00	
3	Prepaid Insurance	9 8 7 00	
4	Supplies	3 8 1 00	
5	Office Equipment	5 7 9 0 00	
6	Accumulated Depreciation, Equipment		1 3 6 4 00
7	Accounts Payable		8 8 0 00
8	M. Tigard, Capital		8 2 4 7 00
9	M. Tigard, Drawing	1 8 0 0 00	
10	Commissions Earned		3 6 9 7 00
11	Rent Expense	7 9 0 00	
12	Depreciation Expense, Equipment	5 2 0 00	
13	Utilities Expense	2 7 6 00	
14	Miscellaneous Expense	1 1 8 00	
15		14 1 8 8 00	14 1 8 8 00

Check Figure

Net Income, $1,993

Instructions

a. Write the owner's name on the Capital and Drawing T accounts.
b. Record the account balances in the T accounts for owner's equity, revenue, and expenses.
c. Journalize the closing entries with the four steps in correct order. Number the closing entries 1–4.
d. Post the closing entries to the T accounts right after you journalize each one to see the effect of the closing entries. Number the closing entries 1–4.

P.O. 2

Problem 5-2A The partial work sheet for Kingman Consulting for the month of May is as follows:

ACCOUNT NAME	INCOME STATEMENT DEBIT E	INCOME STATEMENT CREDIT R	BALANCE SHEET DEBIT A + Draw.	BALANCE SHEET CREDIT Accum. Depr. + L + C	
1 Cash			2 2 4 8 00		1
2 Supplies			2 2 0 00		2
3 Prepaid Insurance			8 5 9 00		3
4 Equipment			5 7 3 1 00		4
5 Accumulated Depreciation, Equipment				2 3 7 9 00	5
6 Accounts Payable				8 4 1 00	6
7 K. Kingman, Capital				2 4 1 5 00	7
8 K. Kingman, Drawing			1 8 0 0 00		8
9 Consulting Income		8 5 4 6 00			9
10 Rent Expense	8 0 0 00				10
11 Wages Expense	1 6 3 3 00				11
12 Miscellaneous Expense	1 6 8 00				12
13					13
14 Supplies Expense	1 4 5 00				14
15 Insurance Expense	2 6 4 00				15
16 Depreciation Expense, Equipment	7 0 0 00				16
17 Wages Payable				3 8 7 00	17
18	3 7 1 0 00	8 5 4 6 00	10 8 5 8 00	6 0 2 2 00	18
19 Net Income	4 8 3 6 00			4 8 3 6 00	19
20	8 5 4 6 00	8 5 4 6 00	10 8 5 8 00	10 8 5 8 00	20
21					21

Check Figure

Debit to Income Summary, second entry, $3,710

Instructions

a. Write the owner's name on the Capital and Drawing T accounts.
b. Record the account balances in the T accounts for owner's equity, revenue, and expenses.
c. Journalize the closing entries with the four steps in correct order. Number the closing entries 1 through 4.
d. Post the closing entries to the T accounts right after you journalize each one to see the effect of the closing entries. Number the closing entries 1 through 4.

P.O. 1,2,3

Problem 5-3A The completed work sheet for Kathy's Tour Company as of December 31 is presented in your Working Papers, along with the general ledger as of December 31 before adjustments.

Check Figure

Post-closing trial balance total, $7,520

Instructions

1. Write the name of the owner in the Capital and Drawing accounts.
2. Write the balances from the unadjusted trial balance in the general ledger.
3. Journalize and post the adjusting entries.
4. Journalize and post the closing entries with the four steps in the correct order.
5. Prepare a post-closing trial balance.

Problem 5-4A The account balances of Morrow Tutoring Service as of June 30, 20—, the end of the current fiscal year, are as follows:

	ACCOUNT NAME	TRIAL BALANCE	
		DEBIT	CREDIT
1	Cash	5 4 9 1 00	
2	Accounts Receivable	6 2 4 00	
3	Supplies	3 2 7 00	
4	Prepaid Insurance	1 2 8 0 00	
5	Equipment	6 4 9 7 00	
6	Accumulated Depreciation, Equipment		2 6 7 2 00
7	Van	18 6 7 4 00	
8	Accumulated Depreciation, Van		4 3 6 8 00
9	Accounts Payable		1 0 3 6 00
10	B. Morrow, Capital		4 8 4 8 00
11	B. Morrow, Drawing	12 0 0 0 00	
12	Fees Earned		53 2 8 0 00
13	Salary Expense	18 0 0 0 00	
14	Advertising Expense	1 2 0 0 00	
15	Van Operating Expense	6 0 5 00	
16	Utilities Expense	1 2 4 8 00	
17	Miscellaneous Expense	2 5 8 00	
18		66 2 0 4 00	66 2 0 4 00

Check Figure

Net income, $28,468

Instructions

1. Complete the work sheet:

   Data for the adjustments:
   a. Supplies inventory (left or unused), $180 (calculate the expired or used up supplies).
   b. Expired or used up insurance, $320.
   c. Depreciation expense on equipment, $890 (remember to credit the accumulated depreciation account for equipment, not Equipment).
   d. Depreciation expense on the van, $1,860 (remember to credit the accumulated depreciation account for the van, not Van).
   e. Salary accrued (earned) since the last payday, $284 (owed and to be paid on the next payday).

2. Prepare an income statement.
3. Prepare a statement of owner's equity; assume there was an additional investment of $2,000.
4. Prepare a balance sheet.
5. Journalize the adjusting entries.
6. Journalize the closing entries with the four steps in the proper sequence.

Instructions for General Ledger software

1. Print a trial balance.
2. Journalize the adjusting entries in the general journal and post to the general ledger. (No work sheet is required on the computer.)

3. Print an income statement, a statement of owner's equity, and a balance sheet.
4. Journalize the closing entries in the general journal.
5. Post the closing entries.
6. Print a post-closing trial balance.

PROBLEM SET B

For additional help, see the demonstration problem at the beginning of each chapter in your Working Papers.

P.O. 2

Problem 5-1B After the accountant posted the adjusting entries for K. Lu, Designer, the general ledger contained the following account balances on May 31:

	ACCOUNT NAME	ADJUSTED TRIAL BALANCE	
		DEBIT	CREDIT Accum. Deprec.
		A + Draw. + E	+ L + C + R
1	Cash	2 4 2 9 00	
2	Accounts Receivable	8 8 6 00	
3	Prepaid Insurance	1 4 6 0 00	
4	Supplies	5 7 0 00	
5	Office Equipment	4 6 7 2 00	
6	Accumulated Depreciation, Equipment		1 2 5 3 00
7	Accounts Payable		9 4 3 00
8	K. Lu, Capital		6 5 2 0 00
9	K. Lu, Drawing	1 6 5 0 00	
10	Commissions Earned		4 6 7 9 00
11	Rent Expense	8 9 5 00	
12	Depreciation Expense, Equipment	4 6 7 00	
13	Utilities Expense	2 6 4 00	
14	Miscellaneous Expense	1 0 2 00	
15		13 3 9 5 00	13 3 9 5 00

Check Figure

Net Income, $2,951

Instructions

a. Write the owner's name on the Capital and Drawing T accounts.
b. Record the account balances in the T accounts for owner's equity, revenue, and expenses.
c. Journalize the closing entries with the four steps in correct order. Number the closing entries 1 through 4.
d. Post the closing entries to the T accounts right after you journalize each one to see the effect of the closing entries. Number the closing entries 1 through 4.

P.O. 2

Problem 5-2B The partial work sheet for Colfeld Consulting for the month of June is as follows.

	ACCOUNT NAME	INCOME STATEMENT DEBIT E	INCOME STATEMENT CREDIT R	BALANCE SHEET DEBIT A + Draw.	BALANCE SHEET CREDIT Accum. Depr. + L + C	
1	Cash			6 1 0 4 00		1
2	Supplies			2 9 6 00		2
3	Prepaid Insurance			1 3 4 4 00		3
4	Equipment			6 7 5 1 00		4
5	Accumulated Depreciation, Equipment				3 3 9 3 00	5
6	Accounts Payable				1 3 5 6 00	6
7	D. Colfeld, Capital				1 3 6 7 00	7
8	D. Colfeld, Drawing			2 4 0 0 00		8
9	Consulting Income		15 0 6 0 00			9
10	Rent Expense	1 1 0 0 00				10
11	Wages Expense	1 9 0 8 00				11
12	Miscellaneous Expense	2 4 0 00				12
13						13
14	Supplies Expense	1 3 6 00				14
15	Insurance Expense	3 4 5 00				15
16	Depreciation Expense, Equipment	9 0 0 00				16
17	Wages Payable				3 4 8 00	17
18		4 6 2 9 00	15 0 6 0 00	16 8 9 5 00	6 4 6 4 00	18
19	Net Income	10 4 3 1 00			10 4 3 1 00	19
20		15 0 6 0 00	15 0 6 0 00	16 8 9 5 00	16 8 9 5 00	20
21						21

Check Figure

Debit to Income Summary, second entry, $4,629

Instructions

a. Write the owner's name on the Capital and Drawing T accounts.
b. Record the account balances in the T accounts for owner's equity, revenue, and expenses.
c. Journalize the closing entries with the four steps in correct order. Number the closing entries 1 through 4.
d. Post the closing entries to the T accounts right after you journalize each one to see the effect of the closing entries. Number closing entries 1–4.

P.O. 1,2,3

Problem 5-3B The completed work sheet for Dunn Insurance Agency as of December 31 is presented in your Working Papers, along with the general ledger as of December 31 before adjustments.

Check Figure

Post-closing trial balance total, $9,024

Instructions

1. Write the name of the owner in the Capital and Drawing accounts.
2. Write the balances from the unadjusted trial balance in the general ledger.
3. Journalize and post the adjusting entries.
4. Journalize and post the closing entries with the four steps in the correct order.
5. Prepare a post-closing trial balance.

P.O. 1,2,3

Problem 5-4B The account balances of Morton Company as of June 30, the end of the current fiscal year, are as follows.

ACCOUNT NAME	TRIAL BALANCE DEBIT	TRIAL BALANCE CREDIT
1 Cash	4 3 8 1 00	
2 Accounts Receivable	5 7 8 00	
3 Supplies	3 9 7 00	
4 Prepaid Insurance	1 1 3 8 00	
5 Equipment	5 7 1 3 00	
6 Accumulated Depreciation, Equipment		2 4 8 7 00
7 Van	12 6 7 8 00	
8 Accumulated Depreciation, Van		3 3 1 8 00
9 Accounts Payable		9 9 7 00
10 S. Morton, Capital		5 9 6 4 00
11 S. Morton, Drawing	18 0 0 0 00	
12 Professional Fees		48 3 1 7 00
13 Salary Expense	16 0 0 0 00	
14 Advertising Expense	8 8 7 00	
15 Van Operating Expense	4 6 2 00	
16 Utilities Expense	6 8 5 00	
17 Miscellaneous Expense	1 6 4 00	
18	61 0 8 3 00	61 0 8 3 00

Check Figure

Net income, $27,127

Instructions

1. Complete the work sheet.

   Data for the adjustments:
   a. Supplies inventory (left or unused), $160 (calculate the expired or used up supplies).
   b. Expired or used up insurance, $482.
   c. Depreciation expense on equipment, $590 (remember to credit the accumulated depreciation account for equipment, not Equipment).
   d. Depreciation expense on the van, $1,032 (remember to credit the accumulated depreciation account for the van, not Van).
   e. Salary accrued (earned) since the last payday, $651 (owed and to be paid on the next payday).
2. Prepare an income statement.
3. Prepare a statement of owner's equity; assume there was an additional investment of $2,000.
4. Prepare a balance sheet.
5. Journalize the adjusting entries.
6. Journalize the closing entries with the four steps in the proper sequence.

Instructions for General Ledger software

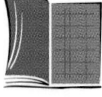

1. Print a trial balance.
2. Journalize the adjusting entries in the general journal and post to the general ledger. (No work sheet is required on the computer.)
3. Print an income statement, a statement of owner's equity, and a balance sheet.
4. Journalize the closing entries in the general journal.
5. Post the closing entries.
6. Print a post-closing trial balance.

Continuous General Ledger Problem:
Closing Entries

Check Figure

Post-Closing Trial Balance total
$202,602.92

Instructions

1. Open the accounting software and open the file you saved as Likenew2.
2. Journalize and post the closing entries. Some software packages do not require that you journalize closing entries; you need only select a menu item to cause closing entries to happen. Check your software's menus and/or documentation.
3. Print the general journal (if you can filter the entries, print only the closing entries).
4. Print the general ledger (if you can filter the entries, print only the accounts affected by the closing entries).
5. Print a trial balance (a post-closing trial balance).
6. Save the file as Likenew3.

Note: The Continuous General Ledger Problem can be worked with Houghton Mifflin Windows General Ledger Package, Peachtree Release 5.01, QuickBooks 6.0, or other general ledger software packages.

Cumulative Self-Check: Chapters 4–5

PART I: MULTIPLE-CHOICE QUESTIONS

_b._ 1. The net income appears on all of the following statements except

    a. the statement of owner's equity.
    b. the balance sheet.
    c. the income statement.
    d. all of these.
    e. none of these.

_d._ 2. Which of the following entries records the withdrawal of cash for personal use by Dolan, the owner of a business firm?

    a. Debit Cash and credit Drawing.
    b. Credit Cash and debit Salary Expense.
    c. Debit Cash and credit Salary Expense.
    d. Credit Cash and debit Drawing.
    e. None of these.

_d._ 3. Which of the following errors, considered individually, would cause the trial balance totals to be unequal?

    a. A payment of $62 for supplies was posted as a debit of $62 to Supplies and a credit of $26 to Cash.
    b. A payment of $763 to a creditor was posted as a debit of $763 to Accounts Payable and a debit of $763 to Cash.
    c. Cash received from customers on account was posted as a debit of $480 to Cash and a credit of $48 to Accounts Receivable.
    d. All of these.
    e. None of these.

_a._ 4. The balance in the Prepaid Insurance account before adjustment at the end of the year is $480. This represents six months' insurance paid on November 1. The adjusting entry required on December 31 is

    a. debit Insurance Expense, $160; credit Prepaid Insurance, $160.
    b. debit Prepaid Insurance, $80; credit Insurance Expense, $80.
    c. debit Prepaid Insurance, $420; credit Insurance Expense, $420.
    d. debit Insurance Expense, $420; credit Prepaid Insurance, $420.
    e. none of these.

_a._ 5. If an accountant fails to make an adjusting entry to record expired insurance at the end of a fiscal period, the omission will cause

    a. total expenses to be understated.
    b. total revenue to be understated.
    c. total assets to be understated.
    d. all of these.
    e. none of these.

Note: Answers to Cumulative Self-Check begin on page A-1.

b. 6. Faulkner Company bought equipment on January 2 of this year for $7,600. At the time of purchase, the equipment was estimated to have a useful life of eight years and a trade-in value of $400 at the end of eight years. Using the straight-line method, the amount of depreciation for the first year is

    a. $1,000.
    b. $900.
    c. $800.
    d. $950.
    e. none of these.

c. 7. If expenses are greater than revenue, the Income Summary account will be closed by a debit to

    a. Cash and a credit to Income Summary.
    b. Income Summary and a credit to Cash.
    c. Capital and a credit to Income Summary.
    d. Income Summary and a credit to Capital.
    e. none of these.

c. 8. In preparing closing entries, it is helpful to refer to which of the following columns of the work sheet first?

    a. The Balance Sheet columns
    b. The Adjusted Trial Balance columns
    c. The Income Statement columns
    d. Both the Adjusted Trial Balance and the Income Statement columns
    e. None of these

PART II: PRACTICAL APPLICATION

On December 31, the ledger accounts of Hanley's Upholstery Shop have the following balances after all adjusting entries have been posted.

Cash	$1,200
Supplies	1,900
Equipment	5,400
Accumulated Depreciation, Equipment	1,100
Accounts Payable	300
T. L. Hanley, Capital	6,500
T. L. Hanley, Drawing	16,400
Income Summary	
Income from Services	$25,900
Wages Expense	1,500
Rent Expense	2,400
Utilities Expense	1,000
Depreciation Expense, Equipment	500
Supplies Expense	2,200
Miscellaneous Expense	900

Instructions

Journalize the four closing entries in the proper order.

PART III: MATCHING QUESTIONS

_b._ 1. Creditor

_h._ 2. Business entity

_m._ 3. Fundamental accounting equation

_q._ 4. Income statement

_D._ 5. Owner's equity

_k._ 6. Accounts Receivable

_u._ 7. Net loss

_w._ 8. Ledger

_o._ 9. Credit

_s._ 10. Compound entry

_e._ 11. Trial balance

_f._ 12. Journalizing

_i._ 13. Posting

_n._ 14. Cross-reference

_a._ 15. Journal

_t._ 16. Work sheet

_X._ 17. Book value

_p._ 18. Depreciation

_y._ 19. Accounting cycle

_v._ 20. Fiscal year

_j._ 21. Contra account

_c._ 22. Mixed accounts

_r._ 23. Temporary-equity accounts

_L._ 24. Real accounts

_g._ 25. Debit

a. The book of original entry

b. One to whom money is owed

c. Accounts that are partly income statement and partly balance sheet accounts

d. Assets − Liabilities

e. A listing of the ending balances of all ledger accounts that proves the equality of total debits and total credits

f. The process of recording transactions in a journal

g. The left side of a T account

h. A business enterprise, separate and distinct from the person who owns its assets

i. The process of transferring accounts and amounts from the journal to the ledger

j. An account that is deducted from another account

k. Amounts owed by charge customers

l. Balance sheet accounts

m. Assets = Liabilities + Owner's Equity

n. A bookkeeping device for referring from journal to ledger or ledger to journal

o. The right side of a T account

p. Allocation of the cost of a plant asset over its estimated life

q. Financial statement that shows the net results of operations

r. Accounts that belong to only one fiscal period and are closed out at the end of each fiscal period

s. A transaction that has two or more debits and/or credits

t. Paper used to record adjustments and provide balances to prepare financial statements

u. Excess of total expenses over total revenues

v. A period of 12 consecutive months

w. A book containing all the accounts of a business

x. The cost of an asset minus its accumulated depreciation

y. Steps in the accounting process, completed during the fiscal period

Accounting Cycle Review Problem A

This problem is designed to enable you to apply the knowledge you have acquired in the preceding chapters. In accounting, the ultimate test is being able to handle data in real-life situations. This problem will give you valuable experience.

Chart of Accounts

Assets

111 Cash
112 Accounts Receivable
113 Supplies
114 Prepaid Insurance
121 Land
122 Building
123 Accumulated Depreciation, Building
124 Pool/Slide Facility
125 Accumulated Depreciation, Pool/Slide Facility
126 Pool Furniture
127 Accumulated Depreciation, Pool Furniture

Liabilities

221 Accounts Payable
222 Wages Payable
223 Mortgage Payable

Owner's Equity

311 K. Taylor, Capital
312 K. Taylor, Drawing
313 Income Summary

Revenue

411 Income from Services
412 Concessions Income

Expenses

511 Pool Maintenance Expense
512 Wages Expense
513 Advertising Expense
514 Utilities Expense
515 Interest Expense
516 Supplies Expense
517 Insurance Expense
518 Depreciation Expense, Building
519 Depreciation Expense, Pool/Slide Facility
520 Depreciation Expense, Pool Furniture
522 Miscellaneous Expense

You are to record transactions in a two-column general journal. Assume that the fiscal period is one month. You will then be able to complete all the steps in the accounting cycle.

When you are analyzing the transactions, think them through by visualizing the T accounts or by writing them down on scratch paper. For unfamiliar types of transactions, specific instructions for recording them are included. However, reason them out for yourself as well. Check off each transaction as it is recorded.

July 1 Taylor deposited $156,000 in a bank account for the purpose of buying Fun World Waterslides. The business is a public recreation area offering three large waterslides (called "tubes"), one children's slide, an inner tube run, and a hot tub area.

2 Bought Fun World Waterslides in its entirety for a total price of $540,800. The assets include pool furniture, $2,500; the pool/slide facility (includes filter system, pools, pump, and slides), $147,800; building, $95,500; and land, $295,000. Paid $133,000 down and signed a mortgage note for the remainder. (Debit the assets, and credit Cash and Mortgage Payable.)

July 2 Received and paid the bill for a one-year premium for insurance, $10,036.

2 Bought 125 inner tubes from Wright's Tires for $3,125, paying $1,500 down, with the remainder due in twenty days. (Debit Supplies instead of an Equipment account because inner tubes generally last only a month or so.)

3 Signed a contract with a video game company to lease space for video games and to provide a food concession. The rental income agreed upon is 10 percent of the revenues generated from the machines and food, with the estimated monthly rental income paid in advance. Received cash payment for July, $380. (Debit Cash and credit Concessions Income.)

5 Received bills totaling $1,190 for the grand opening/Fourth of July party. The bill from Party Promotions for the promotional handouts, balloons, decorations, and prizes was $620, and the newspaper advertising bills from the *City Star* were $570. (These expenses should all be considered advertising expense.)

6 Signed a year contract for the pool maintenance with Crystal Clean Maintenance and paid the maintenance fee for July of $506.

6 Paid cash for employee picnic food and beverages, $103.24. (Debit Miscellaneous Expense.)

7 Received $14,056 in cash as income for the use of the facilities.

9 Bought parts for the filter system on account from Applewood Pool Supply, $956. (Debit Pool Maintenance Expense.)

14 Received $9,182 in cash as income for the use of the facilities.

15 Paid wages to employees for the period ending July 14, $10,080.

16 Paid $1,190 on account for promotional expenses recorded on July 5.

16 Taylor withdrew cash for personal use, $2,000.

17 Bought additional pool furniture from Leisure Products for $2,126; payment due in thirty days.

18 Paid cash to seamstress for alterations and repairs to the character costumes, $49.60. (Debit Miscellaneous Expense.)

21 Received $12,150 in cash as income for the use of the facilities.

21 Paid cash to Wright's Tires as partial payment on account, $812.50.

23 Received a $225 reduction of our account from Leisure Products for lawn chairs received in damaged condition.

25 Received and paid telephone bill, $176.

30 Paid wages for the period July 15 through 29 of $11,560.

31 Received $13,970 in cash as income for the use of the facilities.

31 Paid cash to Applewood Pool Supply to apply on account, $478.

31 Received and paid water bill, $2,029.

July 31 Paid cash as an installment payment on the mortgage, $4,788. Of this amount, $1,710 represents a reduction in the principal, and the remainder is interest. (Debit Mortgage Payable, debit Interest Expense, and credit Cash.)

31 Received and paid electric bill, $979.

31 Bought additional inner tubes from Wright's Tires for $536, paying $100 down, with the remainder due in thirty days.

31 Taylor withdrew cash for personal use, $2,500.

31 Sales for the video and food concessions amounted to $5,670, and 10 percent of $5,670 equals $567. Since you have already recorded $380 as concessions income, record the additional $187 revenue due from the concessionaire (cash was not received).

Check Figures

Trial balance total, $615,642.50
Net income, $15,122.16

Instructions

1. Journalize the transactions, starting on page 1 of the general journal.
2. Post the transactions to the ledger accounts.
3. Prepare a trial balance in the first two columns of the work sheet.
4. Complete the work sheet. Data for the adjustments are as follows:
   a. Insurance expired during the month, $836 (rounded off).
   b. Depreciation of building for the month, $350.
   c. Depreciation of pool/slide facility for the month, $570.
   d. Depreciation of pool furniture for the month, $50.
   e. Wages accrued at July 31, $589.
   f. Inner tubes on hand (supplies) at July 31, $1,960.
5. Prepare the income statement.
6. Prepare the statement of owner's equity.
7. Prepare the balance sheet.
8. Journalize adjusting entries.
9. Post adjusting entries to the ledger accounts.
10. Journalize closing entries.
11. Post closing entries to the ledger accounts.
12. Prepare a post-closing trial balance.

assets
576928.66

Post closing
577898.66

Accounting Cycle Review Problem B

This problem is designed to enable you to apply the knowledge you have acquired in the preceding chapters. In accounting, the ultimate test is being able to handle data in real-life situations. This problem will give you valuable experience.

Chart of Accounts

Assets

111 Cash
112 Accounts Receivable
114 Prepaid Insurance
121 Land
125 Pool Structure
126 Accumulated Depreciation, Pool Structure
127 Fan System
128 Accumulated Depreciation, Fan System
129 Sailboats
130 Accumulated Depreciation, Sailboats

Liabilities

221 Accounts Payable
222 Wages Payable
223 Mortgage Payable

Owner's Equity

311 J. Moore, Capital
312 J. Moore, Drawing
313 Income Summary

Revenue

411 Income from Services
412 Concessions Income

Expenses

511 Sailboat Rental Expense
512 Wages Expense
513 Advertising Expense
514 Utilities Expense
515 Interest Expense
516 Insurance Expense
517 Depreciation Expense, Pool Structure
518 Depreciation Expense, Fan System
519 Depreciation Expense, Sailboats
522 Miscellaneous Expense

You are to record transactions in a two-column general journal. Assume that the fiscal period is one month. You will then be able to complete all the steps in the accounting cycle.

When you are analyzing the transactions, think them through by visualizing the T accounts or by writing them down on scratch paper. For unfamiliar types of transactions, specific instructions for recording them are included. However, reason them out for yourself as well. Check off each transaction as it is recorded.

June 1 Moore deposited $83,200 in a bank account for the purpose of buying Lakeland Indoor Sailboats, a business offering the use of small sailboats to the public at a large indoor pool with a fan system that provides wind.

2 Bought Lakeland Indoor Sailboats in its entirety for a total price of $213,300. The assets include sailboats, $20,800; fan system, $8,500; pool structure, $144,000; land, $40,000. Paid $64,400 down, and signed a mortgage note for the remainder. (Debit each asset and credit Cash and the mortgage payable.)

3 Received and paid bill for newspaper advertising, $148.

June 3 Received and paid bill for a one-year premium for insurance, $1,036.

  3 Bought additional boats from A and M Manufacturing Co. for $6,520, paying $3,200 down, with the remainder due in thirty days.

  3 Signed a contract with a vending machine service to lease space for vending machines. The rental income agreed upon is 10 percent of the sales generated from the machines, with the estimated total rental income payable in advance. Received estimated cash payment for June, $180. (Debit Cash and credit Concessions Income.)

  3 Received bill from Quick Printing for promotional handouts, $368 (Advertising Expense).

  3 Signed a contract for leasing sailboats from Kelsey Boat Co. and paid rental fee for June, $632.

  5 Paid cash for miscellaneous expenses, $92.44.

  8 Received $2,632.50 in cash as income for the use of the boats.

  9 Bought an addition for the fan system on account from Stanwood Pool Supply, $836.

  15 Paid wages to employees for the period ending June 14, $4,200.

  16 Paid on account for promotional handouts already recorded on June 3.

  16 Moore withdrew cash for personal use, $1,052.

  16 Bought additional sails from Bergen Products, Inc., $854; payment due in thirty days. (Debit Sailboats.)

  16 Received $3,043 in cash as income for the use of the boats.

  19 Paid cash for miscellaneous expenses, $42.64.

  20 Paid cash to A and M Manufacturing Co. as part payment on account, $480.

  22 Received $5,082 in cash for the use of the boats (Income from Services).

  23 Received a reduction in the outstanding bill from A and M Manufacturing Co. for a boat received in a damaged condition, $452. (Debit Accounts Payable, credit Sailboats.)

  24 Received and paid telephone bill, $84.

  29 Paid wages for period June 15 through 28, $4,652.

  30 Paid cash to Stanwood Pool Supply to apply on account, $418.

  30 Received and paid electric bill, $42.

  30 Paid cash as an installment payment on the mortgage, $1,880. Of this amount, $680 represents a reduction in the principal, and the remainder is interest. (Debit Mortgage Payable, debit Interest Expense, and credit Cash.)

  30 Received and paid water bill, $432.

  30 Bought additional boats from Stanski and Son for $4,852, paying $452 down, with the remainder due in thirty days.

June   30   Moore withdrew cash for personal use, $1,156.

  30   Received $4,632 in cash as income for the use of the boats.

  30   Sales from vending machines for the month amounted to $2,320. Ten percent of $2,320 equals $232. Since you have already recorded $180 as concessions income, list the additional $52 revenue earned from the vending machine operator. (Cash was not received.)

Check Figures

Net income, $1,379.42; total of post-closing trial balance, $240,914.42

Instructions

1. Journalize the transactions, starting on page 1 of the general journal.
2. Post the transactions to the ledger accounts.
3. Prepare a trial balance in the first two columns of the work sheet.
4. Complete the work sheet. Data for the adjustments are as follows:
   a. Insurance expired during the month, $86 (rounded off).
   b. Depreciation of pool structure for the month, $600.
   c. Depreciation of fan system for the month, $163.
   d. Depreciation of sailboats for the month, $804.
   e. Wages accrued at June 30, $696.
5. Prepare the income statement.
6. Prepare the statement of owner's equity.
7. Prepare the balance sheet.
8. Journalize adjusting entries.
9. Post adjusting entries to the ledger accounts.
10. Journalize closing entries.
11. Post closing entries to the ledger accounts.
12. Prepare a post-closing trial balance.

6 Accounting for Professional Enterprises: The Combined Journal (Optional)

Performance Objectives

After you have completed this chapter, you will be able to do the following:

1. Describe the accounting records for a professional enterprise.

2. Record transactions for both a professional and a service enterprise in a combined journal.

3. Post from the combined journal and determine the cash balance.

4. Prepare a work sheet for a professional enterprise.

5. Prepare financial statements for a professional enterprise.

6. Record adjusting and closing entries in a combined journal.

A professional enterprise offers a specialized service for a fee. The fee may be charged on a per hour basis, a per visit basis, or a per job or task basis. **Professional enterprises** include practices of medicine, dentistry, law, architecture, engineering, optometry, and so forth. Your knowledge of accounting procedures can be readily applied to professional enterprises. Professional enterprises generally use a modified cash basis.

EXAMPLE: RECORDS OF A DENTIST

To understand the modified cash system used by a professional enterprise, let's look at the records of Dr. S. A. Ogden, a dentist. The basic records used in his office are the appointment record and the patient's ledger record. Following is the chart of accounts for the office:

Chart of Accounts

Assets

111 Cash
112 X-ray Supplies
113 Dental Supplies
114 Office Supplies
115 Prepaid Insurance
121 Dental Equipment
122 Accumulated Depreciation, Dental Equipment
123 Office Furniture and Equipment
124 Accumulated Depreciation, Office Furniture and Equipment

Liabilities

211 Notes Payable

Owner's Equity

311 S. A. Ogden, Capital
312 S. A. Ogden, Drawing
313 Income Summary

Revenue

411 Professional Fees

Expenses

511 Dental Instruments Expense
512 Laundry and Cleaning Expense
513 Salary Expense
514 Laboratory Expense
515 Dental Supplies Expense
516 Rent Expense
517 Depreciation Expense, Dental Equipment
518 Depreciation Expense, Office Furniture and Equipment
519 X-ray Supplies Expense
521 Office Supplies Expense
522 Insurance Expense
523 Telephone Expense
524 Utilities Expense
525 Repairs and Maintenance Expense
526 Miscellaneous Expense

Appointment Record

The dentist's receptionist keeps a daily appointment record, showing the time of each appointment and the name of the patient, and gives a copy of the appointment record to the dentist the day before the scheduled appointments. Dr. Ogden's appointment record is shown in Figure 1.

Patient's Ledger Record

The receptionist also maintains a **patient's ledger record** card for each patient. One side of this card shows a daily record of the services performed, amount of any cost estimate given, plan of payment, and information regarding collections. This side of the card is shown in Figure 2 on page 188.

The other side of the card contains a diagram of the patient's teeth and a space for personal information about the patient.

FIGURE 1

APPOINTMENT RECORD

DATE 12/1/20—

HOUR	PATIENT	SERVICE RENDERED	FEES		RECEIPTS	
8:00	Ella Berger					
15	John Lyons					
30						
45	Carlos Reyes					
9:00						
15						
30						
45	Donna Heller					
10:00	L. A. Corrick					
15						
30						
45	Ralph Warfield					
11:00	Peter Smithson					
15						
30						
45						
1:00	Donald C. Kraft					
15						
30	N. C. Byers					
45						
2:00	Mrs. N. D. West					
15						
30	John F. Piper					
45	Nolan F. Sanderson					
3:00						
15	Nancy Stacy					
30						
45	C. D. Harper					
4:00						
15	Ardis Holcomb					

After Dr. Ogden completes the work, he (or an assistant) describes the services performed and writes the amount of the fees in the debit column. The card is returned to the receptionist, who records the services rendered and the fees charged on the appointment record.

The patient's ledger record for L. A. Corrick is shown in Figure 2, on the next page. **As with Accounts Receivable, debits mean increases in the amounts owed by patients, and credits mean decreases in the amounts owed by patients.** The Balance column shows the amount owed by the patient at the time of the latest entry.

The services to be performed may require a number of appointments. Some patients may make partial payments each time they have an appointment. Others may pay the entire amount at—or after—the last appointment. Patients' bills are compiled directly from the patient's ledger record.

FIGURE 2

L. A. Corrick
2416 Bryan Ave., E
Chicago, IL 60644

360-365-2619
Account No. 46-4128

DATE		SERVICE RENDERED	TIME	DEBIT	CREDIT	BALANCE
June	15	#31—M.O.D. (4)	10:00	1 0 5 00		1 0 5 00
July	4	Ck.			1 0 5 00	
	16	#27—D.O. (Amal.)	9:15	9 4 00		9 4 00
Aug.	5	Ck.			9 4 00	
Sept.	24	#25—P.J.C.	10:00	7 4 0 00		7 4 0 00
Oct.	6	Ck.			1 2 0 00	6 2 0 00
	18	#24—D. (Porc.)	9:00	8 0 00		7 0 0 00
Nov.	3	Ck.			1 2 0 00	5 8 0 00
	9	#18—full gold crown	10:00	5 5 0 00		1 1 3 0 00
Dec.	1	B. W. X-rays (6)	10:00	9 6 00		1 2 2 6 00
		Full upper denture		9 0 0 00		2 1 2 6 00
	1	Ck.			2 0 0 00	1 9 2 6 00

PLAN OF SERVICE	PLAN OF PAYMENT	COLLECTION EFFORTS
1–2 surf. ⎫ amalgam	30-day basis	
2–3 surf. ⎬ 1 full gold crown	or $100 per month	
1–1 surf. ⎭ 1 ceramic crown		
2 anterior porcelain		

ESTIMATE IF ANY		
$900 upper denture (6 appt.)	$150 per month	

The dentist or receptionist regularly reviews the patients' ledger records to determine which accounts are past due. Figure 3 shows the statement that was mailed to L. A. Corrick at the end of December.

Receipt of Payments from Patients

Depending on the size of the office, the person who receives payments may be the receptionist or the cashier in the accounting office. Whoever receives the payments issues a written receipt for all incoming cash, filled out in duplicate, sending the first copy to the patient and filing the second copy as evidence of the transaction. Receipts should be prenumbered so that they can be accounted for. The payment is recorded in the Receipts column of the appointment record.

When a patient sends in a payment, the receptionist records the amount on the appointment record and on the patient's ledger record in the credit column on the day the payment was received.

The form in Figure 4 on page 190 is a typical appointment record for a day, showing services rendered, fees (recorded by the dentist on the patients' ledger records), and payments received (recorded by the receptionist). The receptionist deposits $1,349 in the bank. A journal entry would now be made debiting Cash and crediting Professional Fees for $1,349.

■ ■ ■
Remember!

The fees charged are not recorded in the Professional Fees account until they are received in cash.

FIGURE 3

S. A. OGDEN, D.D.S.
1710 CARTER AVE., E
CHICAGO, IL 60642

STATEMENT

L. A. Corrick
2416 Bryan Ave., E
Chicago, IL 60644

December 31, 20—
Account No. 46-4128

DATE	PROFESSIONAL SERVICE	CHARGES		PAYMENTS		BALANCE	
6/15	#31—MOD (4)	105	00			105	00
7/4	Ck.			105	00	—	
7/16	#27—DO (Amal.)	94	00			94	00
8/5	Ck.			94	00	—	
9/24	#25—PJC	740	00			740	00
10/6	Ck.			120	00	620	00
10/18	#24—D (Porc.)	80	00			700	00
11/3	Ck.			120	00	580	00
11/9	#18—full gold crown	550	00			1,130	00
12/1	B.W. X-rays (6)	96	00			1,226	00
	Full upper denture	900	00			2,126	00
12/1	Ck.			200	00	1,926	00

PAY LAST AMOUNT IN BALANCE COLUMN. ◄

Summary of Procedures

1. Patients request appointments.
2. Receptionist records appointments on appointment record: date, time, and name of patient.
3. Receptionist furnishes dentist with appointment record for the day, plus the patients' ledger records.
4. Dentist performs services and records descriptions of the services performed on each patient's ledger card, listing the fees to be charged in the Debit column.
5. Receptionist accepts payments from patients both in the office and through the mail and records receipt of payments in the Receipts column of the appointment record. Any difference between the fee charged amount and the insurance company approved amount for the services rendered can be shown in the Debit column and a note made in the Service Rendered column. (For purposes of this text, cash receipts are recorded weekly.)
6. At the end of the day, receptionist deposits cash received in the bank.
7. Receptionist lists the description of services and the amount charged on the appointment record.
8. Receptionist records payments received on the patients' ledger cards in the Credit column. The source is the appointment record.
9. Receptionist compiles monthly statements directly from patient's ledger records.

FIGURE 4

APPOINTMENT RECORD

DATE 12/1/20—

HOUR	PATIENT	SERVICE RENDERED	FEES		RECEIPTS	
8:00	Ella Berger	Extraction	50	00		
15	John Lyons	Three amalgam fillings				
30		D.O. (3)	306	00	70	00
45	Carlos Reyes	Gold inlay filling	425	00		
9:00						
15						
30						
45	Donna Heller	Amalgam filling D.O.	92	00		
10:00	L. A. Corrick	B.W. X-rays (6)	96	00	200	00
15		Denture—full upper				
30		(6 appointments)	900	00		
45	Ralph Warfield	Prophylaxis	72	00	72	00
11:00	Peter Smithson	Endodontia treatment	220	00	50	00
15						
30						
45						
1:00	Donald C. Kraft	Amalgam filling M.O.D.	104	00	52	00
15						
30	N. C. Byers	Ceramco crown	585	00		
45						
2:00	Mrs. N. D. West	Extraction	50	00		
15						
30	John F. Piper	Amalgam filling 1 surf.	75	00		
45	Nolan F. Sanderson	Prophylaxis and full-				
3:00		mouth X-ray (14)	134	00		
15	Nancy Stacy	Fixed bridge 3 units				
30		(Gold) (5 appointments)	1,640	00	125	00
45	C. D. Harper	Prophylaxis & bitewing				
4:00		X-rays	92	00		
15	Ardis Holcomb	Periodontal treatment	284	00		
30						
45						
5:00						
15						
	Ronald T. McCaw				120	00
	Helen Bower				110	00
	Eugene Sampson				136	00
	Sidney Weeks				54	00
	C. D. Sanderson				186	00
	Roger Lindsay				74	00
	Gilbert Rae				100	00
			5,125	00	1,349	00

This procedure may vary, depending on the size of the office staff. Also, the monthly statement may consist of a duplicate copy of the patient's ledger card. If the size of the office staff is sufficiently large, the function of accepting and depositing money should be separated from the function of recording payments.

Here is a list of Dr. Ogden's transactions for December, the last month of the fiscal period. **To save time and space, cash receipts are recorded on a weekly basis.**

Dec. 1 Issued Ck. No. 416 for rent for December, $2,000.

1 Issued Ck. No. 417 for telephone bill for November, $71.

1 Issued Ck. No. 418 for electric bill for November, $112.

3 Issued Ck. No. 419 to First-Rate Printing for patient statement forms, $132.

5 Issued Ck. No. 420 to Milner Dental Supply for drills, $254.

5 Total cash received from patients during the week, $7,144.

8 Issued Ck. No. 421 to Garcia Office Supply for repair of copier, $92.

9 Issued Ck. No. 422 to S. A. Ogden for personal use, $750.

11 Issued Ck. No. 423 to Reliable Cleaning Service for janitorial service, $140.

We will first record these transactions in general journal form (Figure 5). However, since our objective is to introduce the combined journal, we will also record the same transactions in a combined journal.

FIGURE 5

GENERAL JOURNAL

DATE		DESCRIPTION	POST. REF.	DEBIT	CREDIT
20—					
Dec.	1	Rent Expense		2 0 0 0 00	
		Cash			2 0 0 0 00
		Rent for December,			
		Ck. No. 416.			
	1	Telephone Expense		7 1 00	
		Cash			7 1 00
		Telephone bill for November,			
		Ck. No. 417.			
	1	Utilities Expense		1 1 2 00	
		Cash			1 1 2 00
		Electric bill for November,			
		Ck. No. 418.			
	3	Office Supplies		1 3 2 00	
		Cash			1 3 2 00
		First-Rate Printing for			
		statement forms, Ck. No. 419.			

**FIGURE 5
(continued)**

5	Dental Instruments Expense		2 5 4 00			
	Cash				2 5 4 00	
	Milner Dental Supply for					
	drills, Ck. No. 420.					
5	Cash	7 1 4 4 00				
	Professional Fees				7 1 4 4 00	
	For period Dec. 1 through 5.					
8	Repairs and Maint. Expense		9 2 00			
	Cash				9 2 00	
	Garcia Office Supply, for					
	repair of copier, Ck. No. 421.					
9	S. A. Ogden, Drawing		7 5 0 00			
	Cash				7 5 0 00	
	For personal use, Ck. No. 422.					
11	Laundry and Cleaning Expense		1 4 0 00			
	Cash				1 4 0 00	
	Reliable Cleaning Service,					
	Ck. No. 423.					

THE COMBINED JOURNAL

Objective 2

Record transactions for both a professional and a service enterprise in a combined journal.

The **combined journal** is designed to make the recording and posting of transactions more efficient. It is used widely by professional and service enterprises, where **it replaces the general journal.** No explanations are given in the combined journal. **Special columns** are set up to record accounts that are used frequently by a particular business. Most transactions can be recorded on one line.

Compare the first nine transactions in the combined journal in Figure 6 (pages 194 and 195) with the same transactions recorded in the general journal in Figure 5. In the first transaction (paid rent for the month, $2,000), the entry is a debit to Rent Expense and a credit to Cash. There is a Cash Credit column in the combined journal, so you list $2,000 in this column; that $2,000 will be posted as part of the column total. The Other Accounts columns are used to record any accounts for which there are no special columns. Since there is no Rent Expense Debit column, the $2,000 debit to Rent Expense must be recorded in the Other Accounts Debit column. Notice that the Other Accounts column does not tell you where to post the $2,000. Therefore, you need to write the title of the account to be posted in the Account Name column. This amount is posted separately.

In the December 5 entry to record professional fees received in cash, special columns are available to handle both the debit to Cash and the credit to Professional Fees. In cases where the special columns can handle both the entire debit and credit amounts, it is not necessary to use the Account Name

Owners of dry cleaners and service stations as well as doctors and lawyers can buy premade combined journals targeted directly for their own professions. These combined journals are set up to help channel routine transactions into the journal.

column. To show that the Account Name column has not been overlooked, we draw a long line through it and put a dash in the Post. Ref. column. The individual amounts are posted as parts of the totals of the special columns. The rest of the month's transactions follow:

Dec. 12 Total cash received from patients during the week, $2,411.

16 Issued Ck. No. 424 to Davies Dental Supply for miscellaneous dental supplies, $432.

16 In payment of salaries, issued Ck. No. 425 to C. R. Jarvis, $970 and Ck. No. 426 to D. C. Smith, $970. (Use two lines.)

19 Bought new dental chair from Milner Dental Supply, $5,779. Issued Ck. No. 427 as a downpayment, $1,779. The balance is to be paid in ten monthly payments of $400 each (Notes Payable). (Use two lines.)

19 Total cash received from patients during the week, $1,120.

22 Issued Ck. No. 428 to S. A. Ogden for personal use, $810.

23 Issued Ck. No. 429 to Nollen Dental Laboratory for laboratory expense, $296.

23 Issued Ck. No. 430 to Milner Dental Supply as a contract payment (Notes Payable) on dental equipment purchased in October, $400.

27 Total cash received from patients during the week, $1,396.

29 Ogden wrote Ck. No. 431 payable to Briggs Automotive for repairing his car, $226 (to be recorded as Drawing).

31 Issued Ck. No. 432 to Milner Dental Supply for miscellaneous dental supplies, $219.

31 In payment of salaries, issued Ck. No. 433 to C. R. Jarvis, $970 and Ck. No. 434 to D. C. Smith, $970. (Use two lines.)

31 Issued Ck. No. 435 to S. A. Ogden for personal use, $1,190.

31 Issued Ck. No. 436 to Jersey Publishers Service for magazines for the office, $54.

31 Issued Ck. No. 437 to Clement Linen Supply for laundry services, $84.

31 Total cash received from patients this week up until last day of year, $1,976.

After you have added all columns at the end of the month, prove on scratch paper that the sum of the debit totals equals the sum of the credit totals.

Column	Debit totals	Credit totals
Cash	$14,047.00	$12,921.00
Other Accounts	8,840.00	4,000.00
Dental Supplies	651.00	
S. A. Ogden, Drawing	2,976.00	
Professional Fees		14,047.00
Laundry and Cleaning Expense	224.00	
Salary Expense	3,880.00	
Laboratory Expense	296.00	
Miscellaneous Expense	54.00	
	$30,968.00	$30,968.00

COMBINED JOURNAL

	CASH DEBIT	CASH CREDIT	CK. NO.	DATE	ACCOUNT NAME	POST. REF.	OTHER ACCOUNTS DEBIT	OTHER ACCOUNTS CREDIT
1				20—				
2		2 0 0 0 00	416	Dec. 1	Rent Expense	516	2 0 0 0 00	
3		7 1 00	417	1	Telephone Expense	523	7 1 00	
4		1 1 2 00	418	1	Utilities Expense	524	1 1 2 00	
5		1 3 2 00	419	3	Office Supplies	114	1 3 2 00	
6		2 5 4 00	420	5	Dental Instruments Expense	511	2 5 4 00	
7	7 1 4 4 00			5	————————	—		
8		9 2 00	421	8	Repairs and Maintenance Expense	525	9 2 00	
9		7 5 0 00	422	9	S. A. Ogden	—		
10		1 4 0 00	423	11	Reliable Cleaning Service	—		
11	2 4 1 1 00			12	————————	—		
12		4 3 2 00	424	16	Davies Dental Supply	—		
13		9 7 0 00	425	16	C. R. Jarvis	—		
14		9 7 0 00	426	16	D. C. Smith	—		
15				19	Dental Equipment	121	5 7 7 9 00	
16		1 7 7 9 00	427	19	Notes Payable	211		4 0 0 0 00
17	1 1 2 0 00			19	————————	—		
18		8 1 0 00	428	22	S. A. Ogden	—		
19		2 9 6 00	429	23	Nollen Dental Laboratory	—		
20		4 0 0 00	430	23	Notes Payable	211	4 0 0 00	
21	1 3 9 6 00			27	————————	—		
22		2 2 6 00	431	29	Briggs Automotive	—		
23		2 1 9 00	432	31	Milner Dental Supply	—		
24		9 7 0 00	433	31	C. R. Jarvis	—		
25		9 7 0 00	434	31	D. C. Smith	—		
26		1 1 9 0 00	435	31	S. A. Ogden	—		
27		5 4 00	436	31	Jersey Publishers Service	—		
28		8 4 00	437	31	Clement Linen Supply	—		
29	1 9 7 6 00			31	————————	—		
30	14 0 4 7 00	12 9 2 1 00		31			8 8 4 0 00	4 0 0 0 00
31	(1 1 1)	(1 1 1)					(X)	(X)

END OF MONTH
Post the column totals to the Cash account in the general ledger at the end of the month. The account number in parentheses at the foot of each column indicates that posting has been completed.

DAILY
Post each amount in the Other Accounts columns to an account in the general ledger. The account number recorded in the Post. Ref. column indicates that posting has been completed. The (X) indicates that the column total is not to be posted.

FIGURE 6

PAGE __12__

	DENTAL SUPPLIES	S. A. OGDEN, DRAWING	PROFESSIONAL FEES	LAUNDRY AND CLEANING EXPENSE	SALARY EXPENSE	LABORATORY EXPENSE	MISC. EXPENSE	
	DEBIT	DEBIT	CREDIT	DEBIT	DEBIT	DEBIT	DEBIT	
								1
								2
								3
								4
								5
								6
			7 1 4 4 00					7
								8
		7 5 0 00						9
				1 4 0 00				10
			2 4 1 1 00					11
	4 3 2 00							12
					9 7 0 00			13
					9 7 0 00			14
								15
								16
			1 1 2 0 00					17
		8 1 0 00						18
						2 9 6 00		19
								20
			1 3 9 6 00					21
		2 2 6 00						22
	2 1 9 00							23
					9 7 0 00			24
					9 7 0 00			25
		1 1 9 0 00						26
							5 4 00	27
				8 4 00				28
			1 9 7 6 00					29
	6 5 1 00	2 9 7 6 00	14 0 4 7 00	2 2 4 00	3 8 8 0 00	2 9 6 00	5 4 00	30
	(1 1 3)	(3 1 2)	(4 1 1)	(5 1 2)	(5 1 3)	(5 1 4)	(5 2 6)	31
								32
								33
								34

END OF MONTH
Post the column totals to
their general ledger accounts.
Account numbers in
parentheses indicate that
posting has been completed.

Objective 3

Post from the combined journal and determine the cash balance.

Remember!

Special columns are posted as one total. Amounts in Other Accounts columns are posted individually.

Posting from the Combined Journal

The person who keeps records posts items in the Other Accounts columns individually, usually daily, using the specific transaction date. **After posting the ledger account, the person records the ledger account number in the Post. Ref. column of the combined journal.** This procedure is similar to posting from a general journal.

Special columns, used only for debits or credits to specific accounts, are posted as totals at the end of the month. **After posting the ledger account, you record the ledger account number in the special column immediately below the total.** The account number is placed in parentheses. The total of the Cash Debit column in Figure 6 on pages 194–195 is an example. After the Cash account in the general ledger has been debited for $14,047.00, the account number of Cash (111) is placed in parentheses below the total of the Cash Debit column in the combined journal. Notice the X's in parentheses below the totals of the Other Accounts columns. These totals were not posted because the individual amounts recorded in the columns were posted separately to the accounts listed in the Account Name column. The separate amounts listed in the Other Accounts columns should not be posted twice.

The Cash, Dental Supplies, and Rent Expense accounts from Dr. Ogden's completed general ledger are shown in Figure 7 to illustrate the posting process.

FIGURE 7

A combined journal allows businesses to set up special columns for frequently used accounts, such as Dental Supplies for this professional firm.

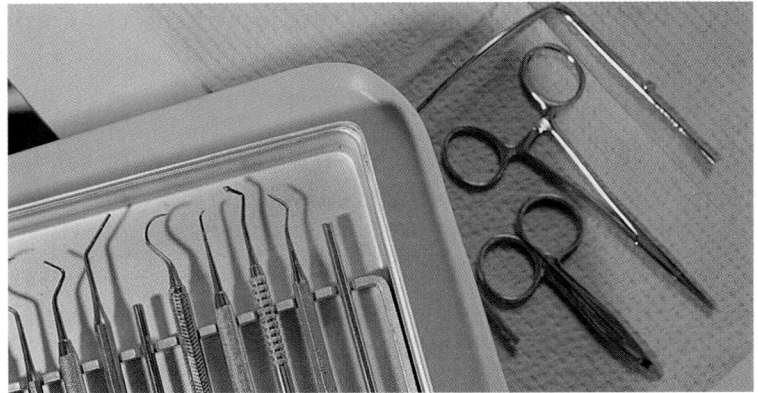

Determining Cash Balance

The cash balance may be determined at any time during the month by taking the beginning balance of cash, adding the total cash debits so far during the month, and subtracting the total cash credits so far during the month. For example, to determine the balance of cash on December 5:

COMBINED JOURNAL   PAGE **12**

	CASH DEBIT	CASH CREDIT	CK. NO.	DATE		ACCOUNT NAME
1				20—		
2		2 0 0 0 00	416	Dec.	1	Rent Expense
3		7 1 00	417		1	Telephone Expense
4		1 1 2 00	418		1	Utilities Expense
5		1 3 2 00	419		3	Office Supplies
6		2 5 4 00	420		5	Dental Instruments Expense
7	7 1 4 4 00				5	————————
8	7 1 4 4 00	2 5 6 9 00				

Beginning balance (Dec. 1)	$ 6,693
Add cash debits	7,144
Total	$13,837
Less cash credits	2,569
Ending balance (Dec. 5)	$11,268

Work Sheet for a Professional Enterprise

Objective 4

Prepare a work sheet for a professional enterprise.

Assume that Dr. Ogden's receptionist posted the journal entries to the ledger accounts and recorded the trial balance in the first two columns of the work sheet. Dr. Ogden uses the modified cash basis of accounting, recording revenue only when he has received it in cash and recording expenses only when he has paid for them in cash. However, when Dr. Ogden buys an item that is going to last a number of years, he records this item as an asset and writes it off or depreciates it by making an adjusting entry each year of its useful life. He also makes adjusting entries for expired insurance and for supplies used. Data for the adjustments are given below.

a. Additional depreciation on dental equipment, $8,400.
b. Additional depreciation on office furniture and equipment, $1,520.
c. Inventory of x-ray supplies, $618 (ending balance).
d. Inventory of dental supplies, $1,616 (ending balance).
e. Inventory of office supplies, $196 (ending balance).
f. Insurance expired, $1,836.

With these adjusting entries, the rest of the work sheet can be completed as shown in Figure 8. First the balances of the accounts that were adjusted are brought up to date in the Adjusted Trial Balance columns. Then these amounts are carried forward to the remaining columns.

FIGURE 8

	ACCOUNT NAME	TRIAL BALANCE DEBIT	TRIAL BALANCE CREDIT
1	Cash	7 8 4 6 00	
2	X-ray Supplies	2 7 6 2 00	
3	Dental Supplies	5 4 8 0 00	
4	Office Supplies	1 3 0 8 00	
5	Prepaid Insurance	2 4 4 8 00	
6	Dental Equipment	115 2 3 4 00	
7	Accumulated Depreciation, Dental Equipment		17 2 0 0 00
8	Office Furniture and Equipment	7 8 0 0 00	
9	Accum. Depr., Office Furniture and Equipment		4 2 0 0 00
10	Notes Payable		7 6 0 0 00
11	S. A. Ogden, Capital		71 4 9 8 00
12	S. A. Ogden, Drawing	46 2 8 0 00	
13	Professional Fees		161 0 2 4 00
14	Dental Instruments Expense	1 9 8 2 00	
15	Laundry and Cleaning Expense	3 0 2 4 00	
16	Salary Expense	40 8 0 0 00	
17	Laboratory Expense	5 8 5 6 00	
18	Rent Expense	18 0 0 0 00	
19	Telephone Expense	4 1 2 00	
20	Utilities Expense	7 7 8 00	
21	Repairs and Maintenance Expense	8 8 8 00	
22	Miscellaneous Expense	6 2 4 00	
23		261 5 2 2 00	261 5 2 2 00
24	Depreciation Expense, Dental Equipment		
25	Depreciation Expense, Office Furn. and Equipment		
26	X-ray Supplies Expense		
27	Dental Supplies Expense		
28	Office Supplies Expense		
29	Insurance Expense		
30			
31	Net Income		
32			
33			

Remember!

In adjusting for supplies, deduct the amount of the ending inventory from the amount recorded as Supplies.

Medical professionals have their uniforms or lab coats cleaned by outside services. Their work sheets are likely to include an account for Laundry and Cleaning Expense.

S. A. Ogden, D.D.S.
Work Sheet
For Year Ended December 31, 20—

	ADJUSTMENTS		ADJUSTED TRIAL BALANCE		INCOME STATEMENT		BALANCE SHEET		
	DEBIT	CREDIT	DEBIT	CREDIT	DEBIT	CREDIT	DEBIT	CREDIT	
			7 8 4 6 00				7 8 4 6 00		1
		(c) 2 1 4 4 00	6 1 8 00				6 1 8 00		2
		(d) 3 8 6 4 00	1 6 1 6 00				1 6 1 6 00		3
		(e) 1 1 1 2 00	1 9 6 00				1 9 6 00		4
		(f) 1 8 3 6 00	6 1 2 00				6 1 2 00		5
			115 2 3 4 00				115 2 3 4 00		6
	(a) 8 4 0 0 00			25 6 0 0 00				25 6 0 0 00	7
			7 8 0 0 00				7 8 0 0 00		8
		(b) 1 5 2 0 00		5 7 2 0 00				5 7 2 0 00	9
				7 6 0 0 00				7 6 0 0 00	10
				71 4 9 8 00				71 4 9 8 00	11
			46 2 8 0 00				46 2 8 0 00		12
				161 0 2 4 00		161 0 2 4 00			13
			1 9 8 2 00		1 9 8 2 00				14
			3 0 2 4 00		3 0 2 4 00				15
			40 8 0 0 00		40 8 0 0 00				16
			5 8 5 6 00		5 8 5 6 00				17
			18 0 0 0 00		18 0 0 0 00				18
			4 1 2 00		4 1 2 00				19
			7 7 8 00		7 7 8 00				20
			8 8 8 00		8 8 8 00				21
			6 2 4 00		6 2 4 00				22
									23
	(a) 8 4 0 0 00		8 4 0 0 00		8 4 0 0 00				24
	(b) 1 5 2 0 00		1 5 2 0 00		1 5 2 0 00				25
	(c) 2 1 4 4 00		2 1 4 4 00		2 1 4 4 00				26
	(d) 3 8 6 4 00		3 8 6 4 00		3 8 6 4 00				27
	(e) 1 1 1 2 00		1 1 1 2 00		1 1 1 2 00				28
	(f) 1 8 3 6 00		1 8 3 6 00		1 8 3 6 00				29
	18 8 7 6 00	18 8 7 6 00	271 4 4 2 00	271 4 4 2 00	91 2 4 0 00	161 0 2 4 00	180 2 0 2 00	110 4 1 8 00	30
					69 7 8 4 00			69 7 8 4 00	31
					161 0 2 4 00	161 0 2 4 00	180 2 0 2 00	180 2 0 2 00	32

Objective 5

Prepare financial statements for a professional enterprise.

Financial Statements

From the work sheet, Dr. Ogden's accountant prepares the financial statements shown in Figure 9. In this case, there was no additional investment made by S. A. Ogden during the year.

Adjusting and Closing Entries

Objective 6

Record adjusting and closing entries in a combined journal.

Dr. Ogden (or his receptionist) records the adjusting and closing entries entirely in the Other Accounts columns of the combined journal. These entries must be posted individually, so the special columns are never used for them.

FIGURE 9

S. A. Ogden, D.D.S.
Income Statement
For Year Ended December 31, 20—

Revenue:			
Professional Fees			$161 0 2 4 00
Expenses:			
Dental Instruments Expense	$ 1 9 8 2 00		
Laundry and Cleaning Expense	3 0 2 4 00		
Salary Expense	40 8 0 0 00		
Laboratory Expense	5 8 5 6 00		
Dental Supplies Expense	3 8 6 4 00		
Rent Expense	18 0 0 0 00		
Depreciation Expense, Dental			
Equipment	8 4 0 0 00		
Depreciation Expense, Office			
Furniture and Equipment	1 5 2 0 00		
X-ray Supplies Expense	2 1 4 4 00		
Office Supplies Expense	1 1 1 2 00		
Insurance Expense	1 8 3 6 00		
Telephone Expense	4 1 2 00		
Utilities Expense	7 7 8 00		
Repairs and Maintenance Expense	8 8 8 00		
Miscellaneous Expense	6 2 4 00		
Total Expenses			91 2 4 0 00
Net Income			$ 69 7 8 4 00

S. A. Ogden, D.D.S.
Statement of Owner's Equity
For Year Ended December 31, 20—

S. A. Ogden, Capital, January 1, 20—		$71 4 9 8 00
Net Income for Year	$69 7 8 4 00	
Less Withdrawals for Year	46 2 8 0 00	
Increase in Capital		23 5 0 4 00
S. A. Ogden, Capital, December 31, 20—		$95 0 0 2 00

Remember!

Whenever you are preparing a statement of owner's equity, always check the Capital account in the general ledger to see if any additional investment was recorded.

FIGURE 9
(continued)

S. A. Ogden, D.D.S.
Balance Sheet
December 31, 20—

Assets													
Cash									$	7	8	4	6	00
X-ray Supplies											6	1	8	00
Dental Supplies										1	6	1	6	00
Office Supplies											1	9	6	00
Prepaid Insurance											6	1	2	00
Dental Equipment	$115	2	3	4	00									
Less Accumulated Depreciation	25	6	0	0	00				89	6	3	4	00	
Office Furniture and Equipment	$	7	8	0	0	00								
Less Accumulated Depreciation		5	7	2	0	00			2	0	8	0	00	
Total Assets									$102	6	0	2	00	
Liabilities														
Notes Payable									$	7	6	0	0	00
Owner's Equity														
S. A. Ogden, Capital									95	0	0	2	00	
Total Liabilities and Owner's Equity									$102	6	0	2	00	

The adjusting and closing entries are shown in Figure 10 on pages 202–203, two pages of a shortened combined journal. These adjusting and closing entries are shown here on two pages to make the concept clear. In practice, the closing entries would be written right below the adjusting entries. Be careful not to split up any individual entry between two pages. The totals are included because it is customary to show totals of all columns of a combined journal. In the Account Name column, accounts to be credited do not have to be indented.

DESIGNING A COMBINED JOURNAL

Remember!

A combined journal can be used for either the accrual or the modified cash basis of accounting.

Since the combined journal is widely used in professional offices and service business firms, it is interesting to look over the varieties of combined journals available at stores selling office supplies. Some are bound journals; others are loose-leaf books. The number of columns varies from six to twenty, and they are available with or without column headings. Those that have printed column headings represent a "canned" type of combined journal. These journals are available for service stations, dry cleaners, doctors' offices, and many other types of businesses.

Combined journals with blank columns can be customized to meet the specific requirements of a given business. Prior to labeling the columns, first study the operations of the business and make up a chart of accounts. Next, identify those accounts that are likely to be used frequently to record typical transactions of the business. Naturally, if these accounts are used over and over, you need to set up special columns for them.

COMBINED JOURNAL

CASH		CK. NO.	DATE	ACCOUNT NAME	POST. REF.	OTHER ACCOUNTS	
DEBIT	CREDIT					DEBIT	CREDIT
			20—	**Adjusting Entries**			
			Dec. 31	Depr. Expense, Dental Equipment	517	8 4 0 0 00	
				Accum. Depr., Dental Equipment	122		8 4 0 0 00
			31	Depreciation Expense, Office			
				Furniture and Equipment	518	1 5 2 0 00	
				Accumulated Depreciation, Office			
				Furniture and Equipment	124		1 5 2 0 00
			31	X-ray Supplies Expense	519	2 1 4 4 00	
				X-ray Supplies	112		2 1 4 4 00
			31	Dental Supplies Expense	515	3 8 6 4 00	
				Dental Supplies	113		3 8 6 4 00
			31	Office Supplies Expense	521	1 1 1 2 00	
				Office Supplies	114		1 1 1 2 00
			31	Insurance Expense	522	1 8 3 6 00	
				Prepaid Insurance	115		1 8 3 6 00
			31			18 8 7 6 00	18 8 7 6 00
						(X)	(X)

FIGURE 10

CHAPTER REVIEW

Review of Learning Objectives

1. Describe the accounting records for a professional enterprise.

   The records for a professional enterprise generally consist of an appointment record, a recording of charges levied for services rendered, and patients' or clients' (customers') ledger cards. A combined journal is generally used to record transactions that are posted to a general ledger.

2. Record transactions for both a professional and a service enterprise in a combined journal.

   Special columns are set up to record transactions involving frequently used accounts. Transactions involving other accounts are recorded in the Other Accounts columns. A long line in the Account Name column and a dash in the Post. Ref. column indicate that all debits and credits for a transaction have been entered in special columns.

3. Post from the combined journal and determine the cash balance.

COMBINED JOURNAL

	CASH		CK. NO.	DATE		ACCOUNT NAME	POST. REF.	OTHER ACCOUNTS	
	DEBIT	CREDIT						DEBIT	CREDIT
1				20—		Closing Entries			
2				Dec.	31	Professional Fees	411	161 0 2 4 00	
3						Income Summary	313		161 0 2 4 00
4					31	Income Summary	313	91 2 4 0 00	
5						Dental Instruments Expense	511		1 9 8 2 00
6						Laundry and Cleaning Expense	512		3 0 2 4 00
7						Salary Expense	513		40 8 0 0 00
8						Laboratory Expense	514		5 8 5 6 00
9						Dental Supplies Expense	515		3 8 6 4 00
10						Rent Expense	516		18 0 0 0 00
11						Depr. Expense, Dental Equipment	517		8 4 0 0 00
12						Depr. Expense, Office Furniture			
13						and Equipment	518		1 5 2 0 00
14						X-ray Supplies Expense	519		2 1 4 4 00
15						Office Supplies Expense	521		1 1 1 2 00
16						Insurance Expense	522		1 8 3 6 00
17						Telephone Expense	523		4 1 2 00
18						Utilities Expense	524		7 7 8 00
19						Repairs and Maintenance Expense	525		8 8 8 00
20						Miscellaneous Expense	526		6 2 4 00
21					31	Income Summary	313	69 7 8 4 00	
22						S. A. Ogden, Capital	311		69 7 8 4 00
23					31	S. A. Ogden, Capital	311	46 2 8 0 00	
24						S. A. Ogden, Drawing	312		46 2 8 0 00
25					31			368 3 2 8 00	368 3 2 8 00
26								(X)	(X)

FIGURE 10 (continued)

Combined Journal
Posting Procedure

Amounts in the Other Accounts columns are posted separately, usually on a daily basis.

Amounts in the special columns are posted as column totals at the end of the month.

An account number in the Post. Ref. column indicates that the amount in the Other Accounts column has been posted; a dash in that column indicates that the amount is being posted as part of a column total. Below the totals of the Other Accounts columns, an X in parentheses indicates that the column total was not posted; accounts were posted individually. Below the totals of the special columns, the account numbers in parentheses indicate that each column has been posted.

4. Prepare a work sheet for a professional enterprise.

The work sheet for a professional enterprise is the same as the work sheet presented in Chapter 4 for a service enterprise.

5. Prepare financial statements for a professional enterprise.

The financial statements for professional enterprises are the same as the financial statements presented previously for service enterprises, except for some new account titles.

6. Record adjusting and closing entries in a combined journal.

Adjusting and closing entries are recorded in the Account Name column and the Other Accounts Debit and Credit columns. The closing entries may be recorded immediately below the adjusting entries. However, if it is necessary to carry over any one entry to a second page, you should not split up the entry.

Glossary

Combined journal A journal format widely used by professional and service enterprises in place of a general journal; designed to make the recording and posting of transactions more efficient. (192)

Patient's ledger record A record of amounts charged to patients, amounts received from patients, estimates given, and the remaining amounts owed by patients, which are called debit balances. In the event that a patient overpaid, the remainder is called a credit balance, which indicates a liability exists to the patient. (186)

Professional enterprise A business that provides a highly specialized service for a fee. (185)

Special columns Columns in a journal that are used to record amounts that occur frequently. (192)

QUESTIONS, EXERCISES, AND PROBLEMS

Discussion Questions

1. Why do small businesses find the combined journal convenient to use?
2. Name four columns that should always appear in a combined journal.
3. What types of transactions are recorded in the Other Accounts Debit and Other Accounts Credit columns?
4. In the Post. Ref. column of a combined journal, what does a dash signify and what does a number indicate?
5. What is the meaning of X's and numbers in parentheses under the column totals of a combined journal?
6. When an amount is placed in the Other Accounts Debit or Other Accounts Credit column, why is it necessary to complete the Account Name column?
7. You have been asked to design a combined journal for Andrea's Hair Salon. Customers pay in cash only. The business buys supplies on account from creditors. Rent and utilities are paid monthly. Employees are paid wages weekly. The owner, Andrea Wilke, makes withdrawals weekly. The firm advertises frequently. List the special columns needed plus the four columns that always appear in a combined journal.
8. Describe the process of proving the combined journal at the end of the month.

Exercises

P.O. 1

Record receipt of cash under modified cash basis.

Exercise 6-1 On June 4, the appointment record for a chiropractor shows that the total of the fees column is $326 and the total of the receipts column is $197. At the end of the day, $197 is deposited in the bank. Record the journal entry for the deposit in the general journal. Assume that the modified cash basis is used.

P.O. 2

List the columns to record transactions.

Exercise 6-2 The Brandon Advertising Agency uses a combined journal with the following columns. Assume that the accrual basis of accounting is used.

Cash Debit	Accounts Receivable Debit
Cash Credit	Accounts Receivable Credit
Ck. No.	Accounts Payable Debit
Date	Accounts Payable Credit
Account Name	Commissions Income Credit
Post. Ref.	Salary Expense Debit
Other Accounts Debit	Utilities Expense Debit
Other Accounts Credit	

List the columns in which each of the following would be recorded.

a. Payment of rent for the month.
b. Charging a client a commission.
c. Payment of an electric bill.
d. Investment of equipment by the owner.

P.O. 2

Designate columns to record transactions.

Exercise 6-3 T. L. Lee, an attorney, uses a combined journal with the columns listed below. Indicate which columns would be used to enter the following transactions.

a. Cash Debit
b. Cash Credit
c. Other Accounts Debit
d. Other Accounts Credit
e. Accounts Receivable Debit
f. Accounts Receivable Credit
g. Fees Earned Credit
h. Office Supplies Debit
i. Salary Expense Debit
j. Travel Expense Debit

1. Issued a check for $249 for the purchase of a filing cabinet.
2. Sold services on account, $5,440.
3. Received and paid the electric bill, $98.
4. Received and paid the bill for airline ticket, $356.
5. Sold services for cash, $100.
6. Received and paid the bill for rent for the month, $1,000.
7. Received $4,200 on account from customers.
8. T. L. Lee withdrew $1,500 for personal use.
9. Issued a check for $50 payment of court fees on behalf of the client (client owes us).

P.O. 2

Designate columns to record transactions.

Exercise 6-4 The books of Binyon and Associates, Certified Public Accountants, are kept on a modified cash basis. The client record of Alice Benson is presented on the following page.

BINYON AND ASSOCIATES
CERTIFIED PUBLIC ACCOUNTANTS
242 SELVA AVENUE
MIAMI, FLORIDA 32906

CLIENT RECORD

Alice Benson
1429 Garfield Avenue
Miami, Florida 32909

DATE		SERVICE	CHG		REC		BAL	
20—								
May	6	Tax prep.	164	00			164	00
June	2				90	00	74	00

Record the June 2 transaction in a combined journal.

P.O. 2
Journalize a withdrawal.

Exercise 6-5 Assume that on June 14, Binyon and Associates issues business check number 311 for $950 to Miami National Bank for payment on N. Binyon's home mortgage. Explain how the transaction would be recorded in a combined journal.

P.O. 2
List the special columns to accommodate a situation.

Exercise 6-6 Baxter Dental Laboratory maintains charge accounts for nine dentists. The owner is R. A. Baxter. Frequent payments include supplies, salaries, delivery, and owner's withdrawals. List the special columns you would suggest for a combined journal.

P.O. 2
Describe the posting procedure.

Exercise 6-7 Kroyer Landscaping Services uses a combined journal that includes the following columns:

Cash Debit
Cash Credit
Other Accounts Debit
Other Accounts Credit
Fees Income
Truck Expense Debit
Supplies Expense Debit
Wages Expense Debit
Miscellaneous Expense Debit

Indicate the columns that are posted individually and those that are posted as a column total. Indicate the columns that are posted daily and those that are posted at the end of the month.

P.O. 3
Determine up-to-date cash balance.

Exercise 6-8 Determine the cash balance after November 8.

Cash	
Beginning Nov. 1 Bal. 642.50	

	CASH		CK.	DATE	
	DEBIT	CREDIT	NO.		
1				20—	
2	9 2 1 64			Nov.	1
3		7 5 42	121		3
4	3 8 9 00				5
5		4 1 6 20	122		8
6	8 4 0 00	2 1 9 00	123		9
7		8 4 59	124		11

CONSIDER AND COMMUNICATE

You do the bookkeeping for a veterinarian. She has no formal accounting system yet, but she does save all source documents.

1. Convince her of the benefits of a combined journal.
2. Design the format for a combined journal with debit or credit columns and headings to accommodate the entries for a veterinarian using the modified cash basis.

WHAT IF . . .

Your friend has been using a general journal for his sole proprietorship business. He needs a better journal solution because he does the accounting himself. Discuss how you think a combined journal could be the answer he is looking for.

A MATTER OF ETHICS

It is Friday at 5 P.M. It is your responsibility to count the money in the cash register, prepare the deposit slip for the bank, and lock up. You have counted the money, prepared the bank deposit, and cleared the cash register, when a customer comes in to buy something. You finish the sale for $9.50. The customer had the exact change. You are in a hurry and do not want to redo the deposit, so you put the $9.50 in your bag (the safe is locked and you don't have the combination). You intend to add it to Monday's deposit. Over the weekend you run out of gas and need the $9.50 for gas. Discuss the situation.

WEB WORK

Using an Internet web browser, type in the search box the phrase *professional business* or *service business accounting*. Search for an article or find a home page that provides information about accounting for small businesses. Summarize your findings in a 1–2 paragraph memorandum to the owner of a small business. Plan a short oral presentation for your class.

PROBLEM SET A

For additional help, see the demonstration problem at the beginning of each chapter in your Working Papers.

P.O. 2

Problem 6-1A M. L. Janes, M.D., uses the following chart of accounts:

Assets

111 Cash
112 Medical Supplies
113 X-ray Supplies
114 Office Supplies
121 Medical Equipment
122 Accumulated Depreciation, Medical Equipment
123 Office Furniture and Equipment
124 Accumulated Depreciation, Office Furniture and Equipment
125 Vehicle
126 Accumulated Depreciation, Vehicle

Liabilities

211 Notes Payable

Owner's Equity

311 M. L. Janes, Capital
312 M. L. Janes, Drawing
313 Income Summary

Revenue

411 Professional Fees

Expenses

511 Nurse Salary Expense
512 Office Salary Expense
513 Equipment Rental Expense
514 Rent Expense
515 Medical Supplies Expense
516 X-ray Supplies Expense
517 Laboratory Expense
518 Cleaning Expense
519 Office Supplies Expense
521 Depreciation Expense, Medical Equipment
522 Depreciation Expense, Office Furniture and Equipment
523 Depreciation Expense, Vehicle
524 Vehicle Expense
525 Insurance Expense
526 Telephone Expense
527 Utilities Expense
528 Miscellaneous Expense

Dr. Janes's records consist of an appointment record book, examination and charge reports, patients' ledger records, a combined journal, and a general ledger. The doctor fills out an examination and charge report each time a patient visits. The report contains a description or listing of the treatments and tests administered, and also the amounts of the charges. The charges are then recorded in the patient's ledger record. Monthly statements based on the patient's ledger record are mailed to the patient. Dr. Janes's books are kept on the modified cash basis. These transactions took place during April:

Apr. 1 Paid Krebs Realty for rent for the month, $1,680 (Ck. No. 636).

2 Paid salary to M. Lewis (part-time office person), $875 (Ck. No. 637).

4 Bought medical supplies for cash from Pike Medical Supply Co., $460 (Ck. No. 638).

6 Received cash from patients during week, $7,920.

9 Paid telephone bill to Acme Telephone Company, $97 (Ck. No. 639).

12 Paid Techno-Labs for laboratory expense, $465 (Ck. No. 640).

13 Total cash received from patients during week, $5,470.

15 Dr. M. L. Janes withdrew $850 for personal use (Ck. No. 641).

17 Bought x-ray supplies for cash from Tilly Supply Company, $214 (Ck. No. 642).

18 Paid Terry's Service Station for gas and oil for vehicle used in business, $87 (vehicle expense) (Ck. No. 643).

Apr. 20 Received cash from patients during week, $2,986.

23 Bought postage stamps for cash at post office, $10 (Miscellaneous Expense) (Ck. No. 644).

24 Paid $104 for laundry service to Crystal Laundry (Cleaning Expense) (Ck. No. 645).

27 Paid King News Service for magazines, $76.75 (Miscellaneous Expense) (Ck. No. 646).

30 Paid salary for the month to C. Doane (nurse), $2,010 (Ck. No. 647).

30 Paid Best Janitorial, $132 (Cleaning Expense) (Ck. No. 648).

30 Received cash from patients (April 21 through 30), $2,158.

30 Dr. M. L. Janes withdrew $1,820 for personal use (Ck. No. 649).

Check Figure

Total debits, $27,414.75

Instructions

1. Record these transactions on page 9 of the combined journal. Insert the name of the Drawing account.
2. Prove the equality of the debit and credit totals in the Account Name column below the totals.

P.O. 6

Problem 6-2A The completed work sheet for S. R. Lindell, Psychologist, is shown in Figure 11 on pages 210 and 211.

Check Figure

Total Other Accounts Debit column, $173,211.40

Instructions

Record the adjusting and closing entries in the combined journal. Remember to total the columns and insert an X in parentheses below each total.

P.O. 2,3

Problem 6-3A Dr. Terrence T. Cascone operates the Cascone Allergy Clinic. The transactions described below were completed during September of this year. His chart of accounts is as follows:

Assets

111 Cash
112 Accounts Receivable
113 Supplies
114 Prepaid Insurance
121 Equipment
122 Accumulated Depreciation, Equipment

Liabilities

221 Accounts Payable

Owner's Equity

311 T. T. Cascone, Capital
312 T. T. Cascone, Drawing
313 Income Summary

Revenue

411 Professional Fees

Expenses

511 Salary Expense
512 Rent Expense
513 Laboratory Expense
514 Utilities Expense
515 Depreciation Expense, Equipment
516 Miscellaneous Expense

Sept. 2 Bought medical equipment on account, $1,680, from Wing Medical Supplies. (Use two lines.)

2 Paid Jayco Realty for office rent for month, $1,050 (Ck. No. 516).

2 Received cash on account from patients, $829: D. R. Calvin, $152.50; Diane Stillman, $272; Jackson Niles, $317; Teresa Garrett, $87.50. (Dr. Cascone uses the accrual basis. Use four lines, recording individual amounts in both the Cash Debit column and the Accounts Receivable Credit column. List each patient's name in the Account Name column.)

FIGURE 11

	ACCOUNT NAME	TRIAL BALANCE DEBIT	TRIAL BALANCE CREDIT	
1	Cash	6 2 7 0 00		
2	Supplies	5 2 6 0 00		
3	Office Equipment	56 4 1 0 25		
4	Accumulated Depreciation, Office Equipment		16 9 8 4 16	
5	S. R. Lindell, Capital		38 8 7 2 94	
6	S. R. Lindell, Drawing	24 7 8 5 00		
7	Professional Fees		70 9 2 9 20	
8	Salary Expense	16 3 2 4 60		
9	Advertising Expense	4 5 7 5 10		
10	Rent Expense	7 6 7 0 00		
11	Vehicle Expense	2 0 6 2 75		
12	Travel Expense	2 2 4 1 32		
13	Entertainment Expense	7 9 6 12		
14	Miscellaneous Expense	3 9 1 16		
15		126 7 8 6 30	126 7 8 6 30	
16	Depreciation Expense, Office Equipment			
17	Supplies Expense			
18				
19	Net Income			
20				
21				

Sept. 3 Received cash for professional services rendered, $2,419.

5 Received and paid electric bill to Mid-State Power, $147.52 (Ck. No. 517).

8 Received and paid telephone bill to Western Telephone Company for month, $73 (Ck. No. 518).

9 Recorded fees charged to patients on account for professional services rendered $766.50: F. Radewan, $396.50; M. Parkhill, $370. (Use two lines.)

15 Paid salary of L. Macy (assistant), $757.50 (Ck. No. 519).

19 Received cash for professional services, $598.

23 Returned part of the equipment purchased on September 2 and received a reduction on the bill, $75.

28 Billed patients on account for professional services rendered, $1,133: C. C. Robbins, $575; Meredith Capwell, $316.50; Drew Hanson, $241.50.

30 Paid salary of C. Bates (part-time assistant), $820.75 (Ck. No. 520).

30 Paid salary of R. Cato (receptionist), $1,120 (Ck. No. 521).

30 Dr. Cascone withdrew $1,688.50 cash for personal use (Ck. No. 522).

Check Figure

Total debits, $13,157.77

Instructions

1. Record these transactions in the combined journal, page 37.
2. Prove the equality of the debit and credit totals in the Account Name column below the totals.

S. R. Lindell, Psychologist
Work Sheet
For Year Ended December 31, 20—

ADJUSTMENTS		ADJUSTED TRIAL BALANCE		INCOME STATEMENT		BALANCE SHEET		
DEBIT	CREDIT	DEBIT	CREDIT	DEBIT	CREDIT	DEBIT	CREDIT	
		6 2 7 0 00				6 2 7 0 00		1
	(b) 5 8 5 20	4 6 7 4 80				4 6 7 4 80		2
		56 4 1 0 25				56 4 1 0 25		3
	(a) 5 9 8 2 80		22 9 6 6 96				22 9 6 6 96	4
			38 8 7 2 94				38 8 7 2 94	5
		24 7 8 5 00				24 7 8 5 00		6
			70 9 2 9 20		70 9 2 9 20			7
		16 3 2 4 60		16 3 2 4 60				8
		4 5 7 5 10		4 5 7 5 10				9
		7 6 7 0 00		7 6 7 0 00				10
		2 0 6 2 75		2 0 6 2 75				11
		2 2 4 1 32		2 2 4 1 32				12
		7 9 6 12		7 9 6 12				13
		3 9 1 16		3 9 1 16				14
								15
(a) 5 9 8 2 80		5 9 8 2 80		5 9 8 2 80				16
(b) 5 8 5 20		5 8 5 20		5 8 5 20				17
6 5 6 8 00	6 5 6 8 00	132 7 6 9 10	132 7 6 9 10	40 6 2 9 05	70 9 2 9 20	92 1 4 0 05	61 8 3 9 90	18
				30 3 0 0 15			30 3 0 0 15	19
				70 9 2 9 20	70 9 2 9 20	92 1 4 0 05	92 1 4 0 05	20
								21

3. Fill in owner's equity accounts and post to the accounts in the general ledger.
4. Prepare a trial balance.

P.O. 2

Problem 6-4A On September 1 of this year, T. W. Binford started a limousine service serving the local area. The following transactions related to Luxury Limousine Service were completed during September.

Sept. 1 Binford opened an account in the Golden State Bank in the name of the business and deposited $34,000.
2 Bought two used limousines from Laughlin Motors for $80,900, paying $20,900 down, with the balance payable in 30 days (Ck. No. 1).
3 Bought heavy-duty vacuum and car-cleaning equipment for $359 from Gehrig E. Schaums, paying cash (Ck. No. 2).
4 Paid Valley Service for gas and oil for limousines, $172 (Ck. No. 3).
5 Paid rent for subletting office space, $235 (Ck. No. 4).
7 Paid wages to L. Bain, $454 (Ck. No. 5).
7 Received revenue for the week, $1,214.
9 Paid for city business license, $86 (Ck. No. 6).
11 Bought desk and filing cabinet on account from Murray Office Supply, $279.
14 Paid for telephone answering service for the month, $136 (Ck. No. 7).

Sept. 14 Paid wages to L. Bain, $469 (Ck. No. 8).
 14 Binford withdrew $750 for personal use (Ck. No. 9).
 14 Received revenue for the week, $1,340.
 17 Paid Laughlin Motors $3,000 as part payment on account (Ck. No. 10).
 18 Paid $142 for advertising in the telephone directory (Ck. No. 11).
 18 Paid Valley Service for gas and oil for limousines, $214 (Ck. No. 12).
 20 Paid utilities for the month, $106 (Ck. No. 13).
 21 Received revenue for the week $1,439.
 23 Paid wages to L. Bain, $471 (Ck. No. 14).
 30 Received revenue for the week, $1,010.
 30 Paid Security Insurance Agency for vehicle insurance for six months, $757.
 30 Paid wages to L. Bain, $444 (Ck. No. 15).
 30 Binford withdrew $1,000 for personal use (Ck. No. 16).

Check Figure

Total debits, $128,977

Instructions

1. By reviewing the transactions for Luxury Limousine Service, develop a chart of accounts. The company will use the modified cash basis. All revenue is in the form of cash.
2. Label the appropriate columns in the combined journal. Next to the Date column, list a Ck. No. column and record checks beginning with number 1.
3. Record the transactions in the combined journal beginning with page 1.
4. Show proof of the equality of debit and credit totals in the Account Name column below the totals.

Instructions for General Ledger Software

1. Prepare a bank reconciliation as of July 31. Errors made by the company or the bank, as well as service charges, must be entered as debit or credit memos.
2. Print the bank reconciliation.
3. Record the necessary journal entries.
4. Print the journal entries.

PROBLEM SET B

For additional help, see the demonstration problem at the beginning of each chapter in your Working Papers.

P.O. 2

Problem 6-1B The following chart of accounts is used by C. Stevenson, M.D.:

Assets

111 Cash
112 Medical Supplies
113 X-ray Supplies
114 Office Supplies
121 Medical Equipment
122 Accumulated Depreciation,
    Medical Equipment

123 Office Furniture and
    Equipment
124 Accumulated Depreciation,
    Office Furniture and
    Equipment
125 Vehicle
126 Accumulated Depreciation,
    Vehicle

Liabilities

211 Notes Payable

Owner's Equity

311 C. Stevenson, Capital
312 C. Stevenson, Drawing
313 Income Summary

Revenue

411 Professional Fees

Expenses

511 Salary Expense
512 Rent Expense
513 Equipment Rental Expense
514 Medical Supplies Expense
515 X-ray Supplies Expense
516 Laboratory Expense
517 Cleaning Expense
518 Office Supplies Expense
519 Depreciation Expense, Medical Equipment
521 Depreciation Expense, Office Furniture and Equipment
522 Depreciation Expense, Vehicle
523 Vehicle Expense
524 Insurance Expense
525 Telephone Expense
526 Utilities Expense
527 Miscellaneous Expense

Dr. Stevenson's records consist of an appointment record book, examination and charge reports, patients' ledger records, a combined journal, and a general ledger. The doctor fills out an examination and charge report each time a patient visits. The reports contain a description or listing of the treatments and tests administered, along with the amounts of the charges. The charges are then recorded in the patient's ledger record. Monthly statements based on the patients' ledger records are mailed to patients. Dr. Stevenson's books are kept on the modified cash basis.

The following transactions took place during November:

Nov.   1   Bought medical supplies for cash from Mason Surgical Supply, $521.50 (Ck. No. 214).

1   Paid Kelsey Realty for rent for the month, $1,350 (Ck. No. 215).

4   Paid salary to C. Ortiz (part-time office person), $935 (Ck. No. 216).

6   Received cash from patients during the week, $8,412.

7   Bought an examination table from Shelly Surgical Supply, costing $1,680, paying $480 in cash and agreeing by contract to pay the balance in three monthly installments of $400 each (credit Notes Payable). (Issued Ck. No. 217.)

8   Paid Ruiz Laboratories for laboratory expense, $354 (Ck. No. 218).

9   Paid telephone bill to Region Telephone Company, $96 (Ck. No. 219).

13   Total cash received from patients during the week, $6,111.

16   Dr. C. Stevenson withdrew $1,000 for personal use (Ck. No. 220).

16   Bought x-ray supplies for cash from Saling's Supply Company, $198.50 (Ck. No. 221).

20   Total cash received from patients during the week, $2,595.

23   Bought postage stamps for cash at post office, $15 (Miscellaneous Expense) (Ck. No. 222).

26   Paid Sharkie's Service Station for gas and oil, $100.25 (Vehicle Expense) (Ck. No. 223).

28   Paid Strong and Company for janitorial service, $85 (Cleaning Expense) (Ck. No. 224).

30   Paid salary to L. Mackey (nurse), $2,305 (Ck. No. 225).

30   Dr. C. Stevenson withdrew $1,620 for personal use (Ck. No. 226).

30   Paid $102.10 to Economy Laundry for laundry service through November 30 (Cleaning Expense) (Ck. No. 227).

FIGURE 12

	ACCOUNT NAME	TRIAL BALANCE										
		DEBIT					CREDIT					
1	Cash	8	1	0	5	00						
2	Supplies	2	2	4	2	40						
3	Equipment	35	2	1	9	00						
4	Accumulated Depreciation, Equipment							7	4	9	0	00
5	T. R. Berman, Capital						27	9	4	5	40	
6	T. R. Berman, Drawing	14	8	8	0	00						
7	Professional Fees						65	9	5	2	00	
8	Salary Expense	31	3	1	5	00						
9	Advertising Expense	1	0	6	0	80						
10	Rent Expense	1	8	3	0	00						
11	Vehicle Expense	1	9	7	5	00						
12	Travel Expense	3	1	2	4	60						
13	Entertainment Expense		9	3	5	00						
14	Miscellaneous Expense		7	0	0	60						
15		101	3	8	7	40	101	3	8	7	40	
16	Depreciation Expense, Equipment											
17	Supplies Expense											
18												
19	Net Income											
20												
21												

Check Figure

Total debits, $27,480.35

P.O. 6

Check Figure

Total Other Accounts Debit column, $150,045.40

P.O. 2,3

Instructions

1. Record these transactions in the combined journal, page 26. Insert the name in the Drawing account.
2. Prove the equality of the debits and credits in the Account Name column below the totals.

Problem 6-2B The completed work sheet for Berman Development Company is shown in Figure 12 above.

Instructions

Record the adjusting and closing entries in the combined journal. Remember to total the columns and insert an X in parentheses below each total.

Problem 6-3B Teresa K. Muller, D.C., operates the Muller Chiropractic Clinic. The transactions described on pages 215–216 were completed during September of this year. Her chart of accounts is as follows:

Assets

111 Cash
112 Accounts Receivable
113 Supplies
114 Prepaid Insurance
121 Equipment
122 Accumulated Depreciation, Equipment

Liabilities

221 Accounts Payable

Owner's Equity

311 T. K. Muller, Capital
312 T. K. Muller, Drawing
313 Income Summary

Berman Development Company
Work Sheet
For Month Ended December 31, 20—

	ADJUSTMENTS		ADJUSTED TRIAL BALANCE		INCOME STATEMENT		BALANCE SHEET		
	DEBIT	CREDIT	DEBIT	CREDIT	DEBIT	CREDIT	DEBIT	CREDIT	
1			8 1 0 5 00				8 1 0 5 00		1
2		(b) 2 0 4 0 40	2 0 2 00				2 0 2 00		2
3			35 2 1 9 00				35 2 1 9 00		3
4		(a) 1 2 2 1 00		8 7 1 1 00				8 7 1 1 00	4
5				27 9 4 5 40				27 9 4 5 40	5
6			14 8 8 0 00				14 8 8 0 00		6
7				65 9 5 2 00		65 9 5 2 00			7
8			31 3 1 5 00		31 3 1 5 00				8
9			1 0 6 0 80		1 0 6 0 80				9
10			1 8 3 0 00		1 8 3 0 00				10
11			1 9 7 5 00		1 9 7 5 00				11
12			3 1 2 4 60		3 1 2 4 60				12
13			9 3 5 00		9 3 5 00				13
14			7 0 0 60		7 0 0 60				14
15									15
16	(a) 1 2 2 1 00		1 2 2 1 00		1 2 2 1 00				16
17	(b) 2 0 4 0 40		2 0 4 0 40		2 0 4 0 40				17
18	3 2 6 1 40	3 2 6 1 40	102 6 0 8 40	102 6 0 8 40	44 2 0 2 40	65 9 5 2 00	58 4 0 6 00	36 6 5 6 40	18
19					21 7 4 9 60			21 7 4 9 60	19
20					65 9 5 2 00	65 9 5 2 00	58 4 0 6 00	58 4 0 6 00	20
21									21

Revenue

411 Professional Fees

Expenses

511 Salary Expense
512 Rent Expense
513 Laboratory Expense
514 Utilities Expense
515 Depreciation Expense,
    Equipment
516 Miscellaneous Expense

Sept. 1 Bought x-ray equipment on account from Radiological Associates, $1,680. (Use two lines.)
2 Paid N. Barnes for office rent for the month, $925 (Ck. No. 423).
2 Received cash on account from patients, $816: Ralph Whitehall, $285; Eileen Butterick, $321; Anthony Clark, $210. (Dr. Gilman uses the accrual basis. Use three lines, recording individual amounts in both the Cash Debit column and the Accounts Receivable Credit column. List each patient's name in the Account Name column.)
4 Received cash for professional services rendered, $1,890.50.
6 Received and paid electric bill to Universal Electric, $135.50 (Ck. No. 424).
7 Received and paid telephone bill for month to Southern Telephone Company, $42 (Ck. No. 425).

Sept. 9 Recorded fees charged to patients on account for professional services rendered, $891.50: T. R. Swenson, $420; Hubert Cooke, $471.50. (Use two lines.)

15 Paid salary of A. Olivera (assistant), $1,120 (Ck. No. 426).

19 Received cash for professional services, $585.

22 Returned part of equipment purchased on September 1 and received a reduction on the bill, $175.

27 Billed patients on account for professional services rendered, $690: N. R. Cranston, $160; J. R. Perez, $285; S. N. Appleton, $245.

30 Paid salary of D. Curry (part-time assistant), $522.50 (Ck. No. 427).

30 Paid salary of V. Green (receptionist), $1,040 for the month (Ck. No. 428).

30 Dr. Muller withdrew $1,520 cash for personal use (Ck. No. 429).

Check Figure

Total debits, $12,033

Instructions

1. Record these transactions in the combined journal, page 43.
2. Prove the equality of the debit and credit totals in the Account Name column below the money column totals.
3. Fill in owner's equity accounts and post to the accounts in the general ledger.
4. Prepare a trial balance.

P.O. 2

Problem 6-4B On July 1 of this year, K. A. Boehm started a landscaping business. The following transactions relating to Boehm's Landscaping were completed during July.

July 1 Boehm opened an account at the Carter National Bank in the name of the business and deposited $15,000.

1 Paid rent for office and warehouse space for the month, $525 (Ck. No. 1).

2 Bought a used truck from Nielsen Motors for $18,200, paying $4,000 as a downpayment, with the balance on account due in 30 days (Ck. No. 2).

3 Bought landscaping equipment from Greene Equipment for $3,500, paying $1,500 as a downpayment, with the balance due in 30 days (Ck. No. 3).

3 Paid Zippie's Fast Serve for gas and oil for the truck, $149 (Ck. No. 4).

4 Received and paid bill for advertising from the *City Lights Review*, $158 (Ck. No. 5).

4 Bought fertilizers on account from Date's Lawn and Garden Store, $1,060.

4 Bought beauty bark from O&P Distributing Company on account, $300.

6 Received revenue for the week, $1,492.

7 Paid wages to part-time employee, $292 (Ck. No. 6).

7 Paid for telephone answering service for the week, $144 (Ck. No. 7).

10 Paid Zippie's Fast Serve for gas and oil for the truck, $135 (Ck. No. 8).

13 Received revenue for the week, $1,601.

17 Boehm withdrew $1,020 for personal use (Ck. No. 9).

20 Received revenue for the week, $1,288.

July 21 Paid wages to part-time employee, $312 (Ck. No. 10).
27 Paid $67 for city business license (Ck. No. 11).
27 Paid utilities for the month, $126 (Ck. No. 12).
30 Paid Nielsen Motors $2,000 to apply on account (Ck. No. 13).
30 Paid Zippie's Fast Serve for gas and oil for the truck, $45, plus $95 for a tune-up (Ck. No. 14).
31 Received revenue for the week, $1,625.
31 Paid wages to part-time employee, $321 (Ck. No. 15).
31 Boehm withdrew $850 for personal use (Ck. No. 16).

Check Figure

Total debits, $50,305

Instructions

1. By reviewing the transactions for Boehm's Landscaping, formulate a chart of accounts. Boehm will use the modified cash basis of accounting.
2. Label the appropriate columns in the combined journal. Next to the Date column, list a Ck. No. column and record checks beginning with number 1.
3. Record the transactions in the combined journal beginning with page 1.
4. Show proof of the equality of debit and credit totals in the Account Name column below the totals.

Instructions for General Ledger Software

1. Prepare a bank reconciliation as of July 31. Errors made by the company or the bank, as well as service charges, must be entered as debit or credit memos.
2. Print the bank reconciliation.
3. Record the necessary journal entries.
4. Print the journal entries.

7 Bank Accounts and Cash Funds

Performance Objectives

After you have completed this chapter, you will be able to do the following:

1. Describe the procedure for depositing checks.

2. Reconcile a bank statement.

3. Record the required journal entries directly from the bank reconciliation.

4. Record journal entries to establish and reimburse a Petty Cash Fund.

5. Complete petty cash vouchers and petty cash payments records.

6. Record the journal entries to establish a Change Fund.

7. Record journal entries for transactions involving Cash Short and Over.

A very important aspect of any system of financial accounting, either for an individual or for a business enterprise, is the accurate and efficient management of cash. For a business of any size, all cash received during a work day should be deposited at the end of the day, and all disbursements—with the exception of payments from Petty Cash—should be made by check. When we talk about cash, we mean currency, coins, checks, money orders, traveler's checks, and bank drafts or bank cashier's checks. Personal checks are accepted conditionally—that is, based on the condition that they are valid. In other words, we consider checks to be good until they are otherwise proven not to be good.

In this chapter, besides discussing bank accounts, we are going to talk about **cash funds**—petty cash funds and change funds—which are separately held reserves of cash set aside for specific purposes.

Internal control of cash is a critical activity in a business. Divide the cash activities among several people to deter mishandling.

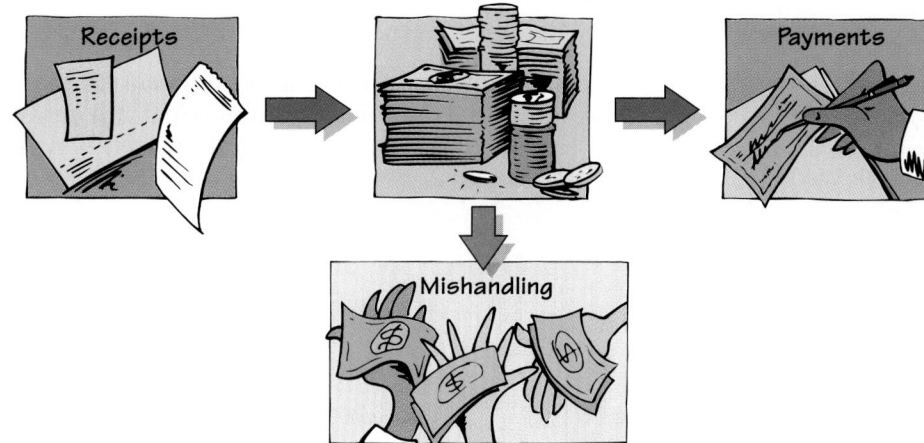

USING A CHECKING ACCOUNT

Although you may be familiar with the process of opening a checking account, making deposits, and writing checks, let's review these and other procedures associated with opening and maintaining a business checking account. We will discuss signature cards, deposit slips, automated teller machines, night deposits, and endorsements.

Signature Card

When Roberta C. Bryan founded Bryan Floral, a full-service florist, she opened a checking account in the name of the business. When she made her first deposit, she filled out a **signature card** for the bank's files. Bryan gave her assistant, Maria R. Figueroa, the right to sign checks too, so the assistant also signed the card. The signature card gives the bank a copy of the official signatures of any persons authorized to sign checks. The bank can use it to verify the signatures on any checks of Bryan Floral presented for payment. This card helps the bank detect forgeries. Figure 1 shows a typical signature card.

FIGURE 1

Title **Bryan Floral**		Account Number **5008-3007**

In consideration of the acceptance by BARNETT NATIONAL BANK of my/our account of the type indicated below, I/we agree to be bound by such rules and regulations and/or such schedules of interest, fees and charges applicable to such account as may now or hereafter be adopted and in effect at said Bank, and also by the provisions printed hereon. It is understood that the acceptance by said Bank of my/our account is subject to the receipt by said Bank of satisfactory credit information.

(1) Sign Here *Roberta C. Bryan*

(2) Sign Here *Maria R. Figueroa*

Address **1424 Garber Avenue**

City **San Diego**   State **California**   Zip **92109**

☑ CHECKING   ☐ MULTIPLE MATURITY   ☐ CASH MANAGER

☐ SAVINGS   ☐ GUARANTEED INTEREST (Multiple Maturity)   ☐ SAFE DEPOSIT   ☐ OTHER _____

IF THIS IS A JOINT ACCOUNT, BOTH OWNERS MUST SIGN ABOVE

Each of the signers guarantees the genuineness of the signature of the other. Each signer also agrees with the other and the Bank that deposits now or hereafter made to this account may be withdrawn in whole or part by either or survivor, and that each may endorse for deposit to this account any instrument payable to the order of either or both. Provisions respecting this agreement shall be modified only upon receipt by the Bank of written notice, signed by both.

Deposit Slips

Objective 1

Describe the procedure for depositing checks.

The bank provides printed **deposit slips** or deposit tickets on which customers record the amount of coins and currency they are depositing and list each individual check being deposited. A typical deposit slip is shown in Figure 2.

FIGURE 2

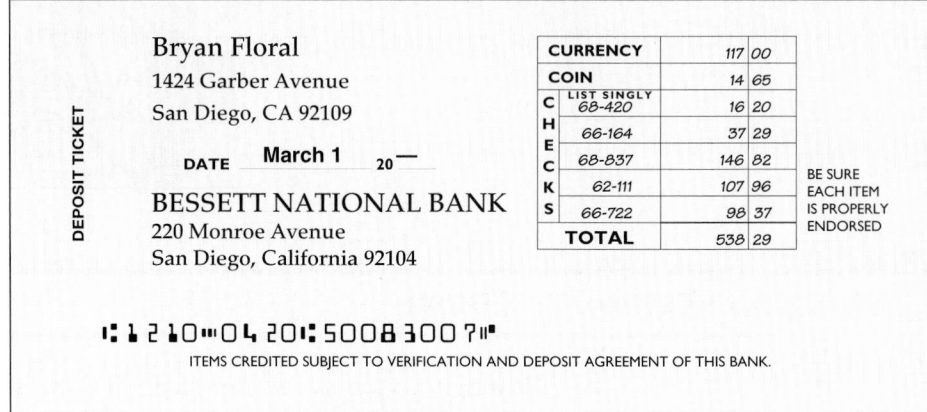

Each check should be listed according to its American Bankers Association (ABA) transit number. The **ABA number** is the small fraction located in the upper right corner of a check. The numerator (top of the fraction) indicates the city or state in which the bank is located and the specific bank on which the check is drawn. The denominator (bottom of the fraction) indicates the Federal Reserve District in which the check is cleared and the routing number used by the Federal Reserve Bank. For example,

$$\frac{68\text{-}420}{1210}$$

FYI

The 12 in the denominator represents the Twelfth Federal Reserve District, and the 10 represents the routing number used by the Federal Reserve Bank.

The 68 identifies the city or state, and the 420 indicates the specific bank within that area (see Figures 3 and 5).

For a business account, the depositor fills out the deposit slip in duplicate, giving the original to the bank teller and keeping the copy. (This procedure may vary from bank to bank.)

When the bank receives the deposited checks, it prints the amount of each check on the lower right side of the check in a very distinctive script called **MICR**, which stands for *magnetic ink character recognition*. The routing number (as well as the depositor's number) used by the Federal Reserve Bank was printed on the lower left side of the blank check before it was sent to the account holder. The reason banks use this MICR script is that the electronic equipment used to process the checks is able to rapidly read the script identifying the bank on which the check is drawn and the amount of the check.

Automated Teller Machines

Deposits, withdrawals, and transfers can be made at all hours at banks with **ATMs** (automated teller machines). Each depositor uses a plastic card that contains a code number. The amount to be deposited, withdrawn, or transferred is keyed in by the depositor. To make a deposit, the customer inserts an envelope containing cash and/or checks and a copy of the deposit slip into the ATM. To make a withdrawal, the customer requests an amount, the ATM dispenses it, and the customer removes the cash. In addition to deposits and withdrawals, a customer may transfer amounts from one account to another (for example, from savings to checking).

Night Deposits

Most banks also provide night depositories so that firms and individuals can make deposits after regular banking hours. Depositories are secured chutes into which a firm's representative can drop a bag of cash and checks, knowing that the day's receipts will be safe until the bank opens in the morning.

Endorsements

The bank may not accept for deposit a check made out to a firm until someone from the firm has endorsed the check. The endorsement may be made by signature or by stamp. The endorsement should appear on the back of the left end of a check, as it does in Figure 3. The **endorsement** (1) transfers title to the money and (2) authorizes the payment of the check. In other words, if the check is not good, NSF (not sufficient funds), then the bank, in order to protect itself, will deduct the amount of the check from the depositor's account.

FIGURE 3

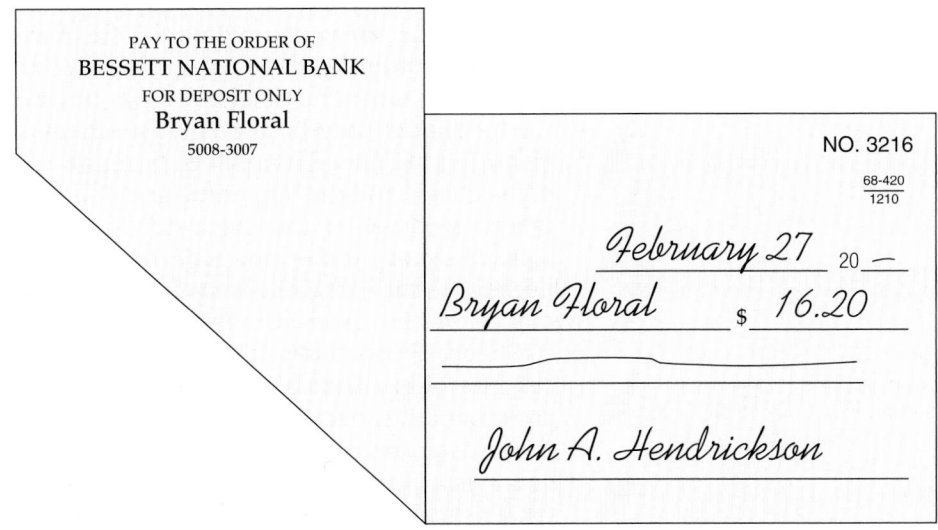

Restrictive Endorsement
```
PAY TO THE ORDER OF
BESSETT NATIONAL BANK
FOR DEPOSIT ONLY
Bryan Floral
5008-3007
```

```
NO. 3216
68-420
1210
February 27   20 —
Bryan Floral       $ 16.20

John A. Hendrickson
```

Restrictive Endorsement All checks made payable to Bryan Floral are endorsed by stamping on the back of the checks "Pay to the Order of Bessett National Bank, For Deposit Only, Bryan Floral." This is called a **restrictive endorsement** because it restricts or limits any further transfer of the check. This endorsement also forces the deposit of the check, because the endorsement is not valid for any other purpose.

Blank Endorsement When the party to whom a check is made payable (the payee) endorses the check by signing only her or his name on the back of the check, this is known as a **blank endorsement** (Figure 4). With a blank endorsement, there are no restrictions attached.

FIGURE 4

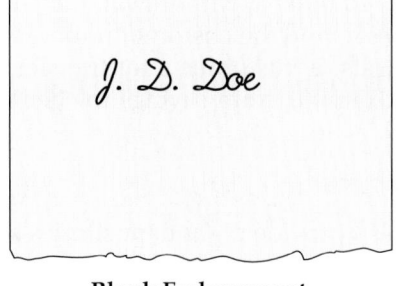

Blank Endorsement   Qualified Endorsement

Qualified Endorsement A third type of endorsement is a **qualified endorsement** (see Figure 4), which generally includes the phrase "Pay to the order of," followed by the name of the person to whom the check is being transferred, and then followed by the phrase "without recourse." Such an endorsement frees the endorser from future liability in case the drawer of the check does not have sufficient funds to cover the check.

WRITING CHECKS

People generally use a check to withdraw money from a bank checking account. The party who writes the check is called the **drawer**. A check represents an order by the drawer, directing the bank to pay a designated person or company. The party to whom payment is to be made is the **payee**.

The checks may be attached to check stubs. Each stub has spaces for recording the check number and amount, the date and payee, the purpose of the check, and the beginning and ending balances of cash. *Note:* The information recorded on the check stub is the basis for the journal entry, so check stubs are vitally important. A person in a hurry or under pressure sometimes neglects to fill in the check stubs. Therefore, it is best to record all the information on the check stub *before making out the check.*

Checks should be written carefully so that no dishonest person can successfully alter them. Write the payee's name on the first long line. Write the amount of the check in figures close to the dollar sign, then write the amount in words at the extreme left of the line provided for this information. Write cents as a fraction of 100. For example, write $727.50 as "seven hundred twenty-seven 50/100," or $89.00 as "eighty-nine and NO/100." From a legal standpoint, if there is a discrepancy between the amount in figures and the written amount, the written amount prevails. However, as a general practice, the bank gets in touch with the drawer and asks what the correct amount should be.

Computerized firms print their checks electronically. Some firms use a **check writer**, which is a machine that imprints the amount in figures and words on the check itself. Using this machine neatly prevents anyone from altering the amount of the check.

Finally, the drawer's signature on the face of the check should match that on the signature card on file at the drawer's bank.

Figure 5 is a check, with the accompanying stub, drawn on the account of Bryan Floral.

A description of the script appears in Figure 6.

FIGURE 5

FIGURE 6

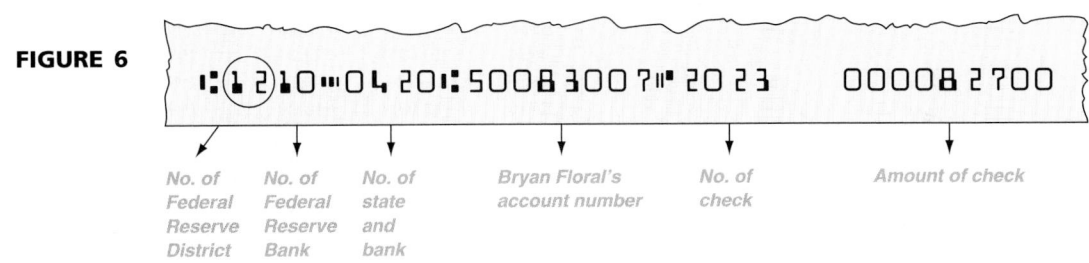

No. of Federal Reserve District	No. of Federal Reserve Bank	No. of state and bank	Bryan Floral's account number	No. of check	Amount of check

BANK STATEMENTS

Once a month the bank sends each of its customers a **bank statement**. This statement provides the following information about customers' cash accounts:

- The balance at the beginning of the month
- Additions in the form of deposits and credit memos
- Deductions in the form of checks and debit memos
- The final balance at the end of the month

A bank statement for Bryan Floral is shown in Figure 7 on page 224. The following legend of symbols is listed on the bottom of the statement:

- **CM (credit memo)** Increases in or credits to the account, such as notes or accounts left with the bank for collection.
- **DM (debit memo)** Decreases in or debits to the account, such as NSF checks, ATM withdrawals, and service charges. Service charges are based on the number of items processed and the average account balance. Special charges may also be levied against the account for collections and other services performed, including check printing.
- **PBP (pay by phone)** Transactions made by telephone using the number keypad instead of writing checks.

BESSETT NATIONAL BANK
220 Monroe Avenue
San Diego, California 92104

STATEMENT OF ACCOUNT	**Bryan Floral** **1424 Garber Avenue** **San Diego, CA 92109**	ACCOUNT NUMBER **5008-3007** STATEMENT DATE **September 30, 20 — – October 31, 20 —** TAX ID NUMBER **83-424 9732**

	SUMMARY	
	Balance Last Statement	$7,089.13
	Amount of Checks and Debits	$25,154.91
	Number of Checks	66
	Amount of Deposits and Credits	$27,031.78
	Number of Deposits	23
	Balance This Statement	$8,966.00

CHECKS/ OTHER DEBITS	CHECKS	CHECK NUMBER	DATE POSTED	AMOUNT	CHECK NUMBER	DATE POSTED	AMOUNT
		1952	10-01	50.00	1988	10-17	61.22
		1953	10-01	200.00	1989	10-17	463.29
		1954	10-01	400.00	1990	10-18	520.00
		1955	10-02	46.00	1991	10-19	14.57
		1956	10-02	174.23	1992	10-19	23.98
		1957	10-02	671.74	1993	10-19	115.16
		1958	10-03	846.20	1994	10-20	117.37
		1984	10-14	664.56	2018	10-30	126.70
		1985	10-15	719.00	2019	10-30	943.64
		1986	10-16	61.68	2020	10-31	843.17
		1987	10-16	591.84	2021	10-31	21.92

OTHER DEBITS	DESCRIPTION	DATE POSTED	AMOUNT
	DM NSF check from D. M. Scott	10-15	125.00
	DM Automated Teller Trans. 062142 customer N3162241 at terminal 30962—cash	10-16	20.00
	DM Service charge	10-31	5.50

DEPOSITS/ OTHER CREDITS	DEPOSITS	DATE POSTED	AMOUNT	DATE POSTED	AMOUNT
		10-01	921.00	10-17	873.19
		10-02	1,476.22	10-18	946.78
		10-03	463.62	10-21	329.49
		10-04	789.44	10-22	1,116.27
		10-07	1,063.14	10-23	734.13
		10-08	1,211.96	10-26	227.69
		10-14	992.27	10-28	439.45
		10-15	759.41	10-29	611.12
		10-16	641.33	10-30	764.35

OTHER CREDITS	DESCRIPTION	DATE POSTED	AMOUNT
	CM Note collected, principal $600, interest $6	10-29	606.00

PLEASE EXAMINE THIS STATEMENT CAREFULLY. REPORT ANY POSSIBLE ERRORS IN 10 DAYS.

CODE SYMBOLS

CM Credit Memo	OD Overdraft
DM Debit Memo	EC Error Correction
PBP Pay by Phone	

FIGURE 7

- **OD (overdraft)** The withdrawal of more than the cash balance in the account, resulting in a negative balance.
- **EC (error correction)** Corrections of errors made by the bank, such as mistakes in transferring figures.

The bank statement is a valuable aid to efficiency and accuracy because it provides a double record of the Cash account. If a business entity deposits all cash receipts in the bank and makes all payments by check, then the bank is keeping an independent record of the firm's cash. You might think that the two balances—the firm's and the bank's—should be equal, but this is unlikely. Some transactions may have been recorded in the firm's account before being entered in the bank's records. In addition, there are unavoidable delays (by either the firm or the bank) in recording transactions. Ordinarily, there is a delay of one or more days between the date on which a check is written and the date when it is presented to the bank for payment. Also, banks may not record deposits until the following business day. During this time lag, deposits made or checks written are recorded in the firm's checkbook, but they are not yet listed on the bank statement.

The bank mails statements to its depositors each month. The **canceled checks** (checks that have been paid or cleared by the bank) are listed on the bank statement. They are called *canceled checks* because they are canceled by a stamp or perforation, indicating that they have been paid. Debit or credit memos are generally mailed with the statement.

Remember!

Debit memos represent deductions from and credit memos represent additions to a bank account.

Recording Deposits or Withdrawals

Each business entity keeps its accounts from its *own* point of view. As far as the bank is concerned, each customer's deposits are liabilities, in that the bank owes the customer the amount of the deposits. Using T accounts, it looks like this:

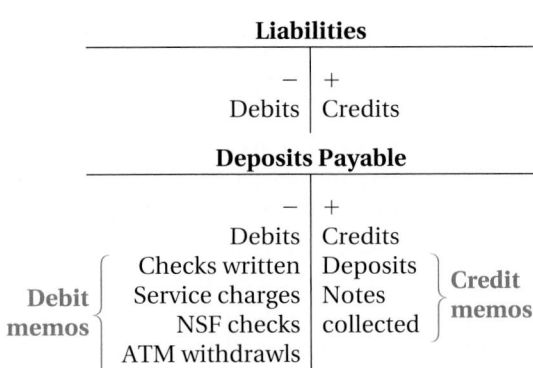

When the bank receives a cash deposit from a customer, the bank credits Deposits Payable, because it owes more to its customer. When the bank cashes a check (pays out) for a customer, the bank debits Deposits Payable, because it owes less to its customer.

The customer, on the other hand, uses the account titled Cash, or Cash in Bank, or simply the name of the bank. Deposits are recorded as debits, and withdrawals are recorded as credits in the account. On a bank reconciliation, the balance of the account is listed as the **ledger balance of cash** before reconciliation with the bank statement.

Need for Reconciling Bank Balance and Ledger Balance

Objective 2

Reconcile a bank statement.

Since the bank statement balance and the ledger balance of cash are not equal, a firm prepares a **bank reconciliation** to uncover the reasons for the difference between the two balances and to correct any errors that may have been made by either the bank or the firm. This makes it possible to arrive at the same balance in each account, which is called the *adjusted balance,* or *true balance,* of the Cash account.

There are a variety of reasons for differences between the bank statement balance and the customer's cash balance. Here are some of the more common ones:

FYI

When a bank agrees to accept payments on behalf of a customer, the fee the bank charges does not necessarily mean that the bank will follow up on collection of a payment or notify the customer that the payment is late.

- **Deposit in transit** A deposit made after the bank statement was issued. The depositor has naturally already added the amount to the Cash account in his or her books, but the deposit has not been recorded by the bank (this is also called a *late deposit*).

- **Outstanding checks** Checks that have been written by the company but not yet received for payment by the time the bank sends out its statement. The company employee, when writing checks, deducted the amounts from the Cash account in the company's books, which explains the difference.

- **Collections** When the bank acts as a collection point for its customers by accepting payments on their behalf, it adds the proceeds to the customer's bank account and sends a credit memorandum to notify the customer of the transaction or includes it on the next bank statement.

- **Interest income** Some checking accounts are interest bearing or earning. The depositor will not learn how much interest the bank has credited to the bank account until the bank statement is received.

- **NSF (not sufficient funds) check** When a bank customer deposits a check, it is recorded as cash on the customer's books. Occasionally, however, a check is not paid (bounces). When the bank notifies the customer of this, the customer must make a deduction from the Cash account. Simultaneously, the depositor records an increase in accounts receivable because the client's debt to the depositor remains unpaid. An NSF check may also be called a *dishonored check.*

- **Service charge** A bank charge for services rendered: for handling checks, for collecting money, for receiving payment of notes turned over to it by the customer for collection, for check printing, and for other such services. The bank immediately deducts the fee from the balance of the bank account and notifies the depositor with a debit memorandum.

- **Errors** In spite of internal controls and systems designed to double-check to prevent errors, sometimes either the customer or the bank makes a mistake. Often these errors do not become evident until the bank reconciliation is performed.

Steps in Reconciling the Bank Statement

Follow these steps to reconcile a bank statement:

1. **Canceled checks**
   a. Compare the amount of each canceled check with the bank statement and note any differences. The amount of the machine-readable characters should appear at the lower right-hand corner of the check, which should match the amount written on the check and the bank statements.

b. In the checkbook beside the check number, list the date of the bank statement. In some cases, a bank may not pay a check until one or two months after it was written. If a question arises as to whether or not you have paid a particular bill, you can look at the checkbook. Then you can refer directly to the bank statement to pick up the accompanying canceled check as proof of payment.

2. **Deposits**
   a. Compare the deposits in transit (not recorded by the bank at the time of the statement) listed on last month's bank reconciliation with the deposits shown on the bank statement. All of last month's deposits in transit should be listed on this month's bank statement. If they are not, notify the bank immediately.
   b. Compare the remaining deposits listed on this month's bank statement with deposits written in the company's accounting records. Consider any deposits not shown on the bank statement as deposits in transit.

3. **Outstanding checks**
   a. Arrange the canceled checks in order by check number.
   b. Look over the list of outstanding checks left over from last month's bank reconciliation, and note the checks that have now been returned or cleared.
   c. For each canceled check, compare the amount recorded in MICR numbers at the lower right-hand corner of the check with the amount recorded in the checkbook. Next, compare the canceled checks with the numerical listing in the statement. Use a check mark (✓) to indicate that the check has been paid and that the amount is correct. Any payments that have not been marked off, including the outstanding checks from last month's bank reconciliation, are the present outstanding checks.
   d. Review the endorsements on the backs of the checks to verify that money has been sent to the correct payee.

4. **Bank memoranda** Trace the credit memos and debit memos to the journal. If the memos have not been recorded, make separate entries for them.

A large firm should require that the reconciliation be prepared by an employee who is not involved in recording business transactions or in handling cash receipts and disbursements.

Besides their core activities of providing financial transactions, many banks are actively committed to community service by supporting various causes, such as Chase Manhattan Bank's sponsorship of the Chase Corporate Challenge.

Examples of Bank Reconciliations

Let's go through the reconciliation process for two firms, L. A. Chapton Company and Bryan Floral.

L. A. Chapton Company The bank statement of L. A. Chapton Company indicates a balance of $2,119 as of March 31. The balance of the Cash account in Chapton's ledger as of that date is $1,552. Chapton's accountant has taken the following steps:

1. Verified that canceled checks were recorded correctly on the bank statement.
2. Noted that the deposit made on March 31 was not recorded on the bank statement, $762.
3. Noted outstanding checks: no. 921, $626; no. 985, $69; no. 986, $438.
4. Noted credit memo: note collected by the bank from S. Ellers, $200, not recorded in the journal.
5. Noted debit memo: collection charge and service charge not recorded in the journal, $4.

The note received from S. Ellers is called a promissory note. A **promissory note** is a written promise to pay a definite amount at a definite future time. Let's assume that L. A. Chapton Company received the sixty-day non-interest-bearing note from S. Ellers for services performed. In recording the transaction, Chapton's accountant debited Notes Receivable and credited Income from Services. (The account Notes Receivable is similar to Accounts Receivable. However, Accounts Receivable is reserved for customer charge accounts, with payments usually due in thirty days.) Next, L. A. Chapton Company turned the note over to its bank for collection.

The bank will use a credit memo form to notify L. A. Chapton Company that the note has been collected and that the company's bank account has been increased by the amount of the note. Based on the credit memo, Chapton's accountant will make a journal entry debiting Cash and crediting Notes Receivable.

Think of the bank reconciliation in terms of the following:

1. Bring the bank statement balance up to date by recording the events that we knew about but the bank did not know about when it prepared the statement (deposits in transit and outstanding checks as shown in our checkbook, for example).
2. Bring the balance of the Cash account up to date by recording the events that the bank knew about but we did not know about until we received the statement (debit memos and credit memos as shown on the bank statement, for example).

The bank reconciliation may be prepared on a separate sheet of paper or on the back of the bank statement. Figure 8 shows L. A. Chapton's bank reconciliation. The items in the reconciliation that require journal entries are shown in color, and the entries are shown below.

Objective 3

Record the required journal entries directly from the bank reconciliation.

Note that the journal entries are based on the items used to adjust the ledger balance of Cash. These items represent the transactions that the bank has knowledge of but the firm does not. According to the bank reconciliation, the true balance of Cash is $1,748, which is the balance we wish to show on the firm's books. We can't change the balance of an account unless we first make a journal entry and then post the entry to the accounts involved. **Consequently, we have to make journal entries for items in the Ledger Balance**

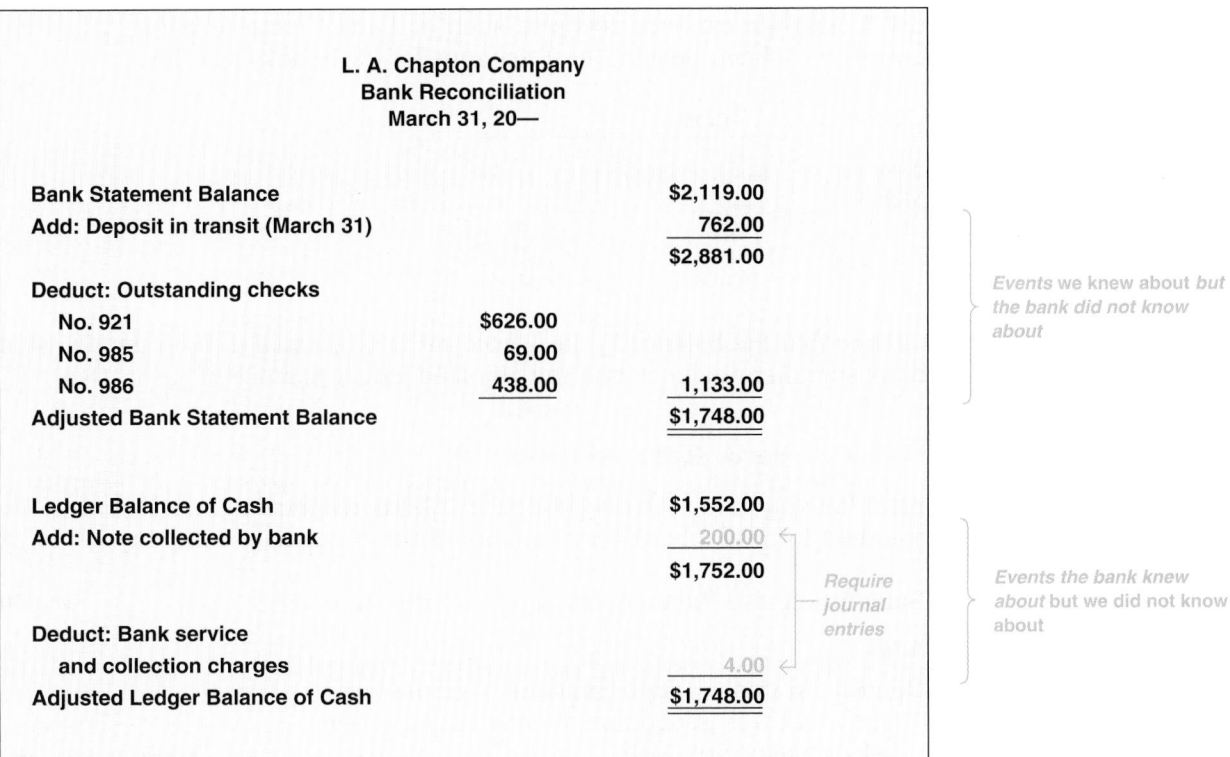

L. A. Chapton Company
Bank Reconciliation
March 31, 20—

Bank Statement Balance		$2,119.00
Add: Deposit in transit (March 31)		762.00
		$2,881.00
Deduct: Outstanding checks		
No. 921	$626.00	
No. 985	69.00	
No. 986	438.00	1,133.00
Adjusted Bank Statement Balance		$1,748.00
Ledger Balance of Cash		$1,552.00
Add: Note collected by bank		200.00
		$1,752.00
Deduct: Bank service		
and collection charges		4.00
Adjusted Ledger Balance of Cash		$1,748.00

Events we knew about but the bank did not know about

Require journal entries

Events the bank knew about but we did not know about

FIGURE 8

of Cash section of the bank reconciliation. In the Ledger Balance of Cash section, the additions are debited to the Cash account, and the deductions are credited to the Cash account. L. A. Chapton Company records the entries in its general journal:

GENERAL JOURNAL   PAGE _____

DATE		DESCRIPTION	POST. REF.	DEBIT	CREDIT
20—					
Mar.	31	Cash		2 0 0 00	
		Notes Receivable			2 0 0 00
		Non-interest-bearing note			
		signed by S. Ellers was			
		collected by the bank.			
	31	Miscellaneous Expense		4 00	
		Cash			4 00
		Service charge and collection			
		charge levied by bank.			

Here bank service and collection charges are recorded in Miscellaneous Expense because the amounts are relatively small. Some accountants may use a separate expense account, such as Bank Charge Expense. After the entries have been posted, the T account for Cash looks like this:

Cash			
Balance	1,552	Mar. 31	4
Mar. 31	200		
	1,752		
Bal. 1,748			

Note that the balance in the T account is now equal to both the adjusted bank statement balance and the adjusted ledger balance of cash.

Form of Bank Reconciliation

Now that you have seen an example of a bank reconciliation, let's look at the standard form of a bank reconciliation for an imaginary company.

Bank Statement Balance (last figure on the statement)		$4,000
Add		
Deposits in transit (deposits made after the bank statement was issued and already added to the ledger balance of Cash)	$300	
Bank errors (that understate balance)	20	320
		$4,320
Deduct		
Outstanding checks (they have already been deducted from the Cash account)	$960	
Bank errors (that overstate balance)	40	1,000
Adjusted Bank Statement Balance (the true balance of Cash)		$3,320
Ledger Balance of Cash (the latest balance of the Cash account if it has been posted up to date; otherwise take the beginning balance of Cash, plus cash receipts and minus cash payments)		$2,850
Add		
Credit memos (additions by the bank not recorded in the Cash account, such as collections of notes)	$500	
Book errors (that understate balance)	40	540
		$3,390
Deduct		
Debit memos (deductions by the bank not recorded in the Cash account, such as service charges or collection charges and NSF checks)	$ 20	
Book errors (that overstate balance)	50	70
Adjusted Ledger Balance of Cash (the true balance of Cash)		$3,320

Remember!

When placing each item on the bank reconciliation, ask yourself if it has been recorded only by the bank or only by the depositor. If an item has been recorded by both the bank and the depositor, there is nothing to do. If an item has been recorded only by the bank, then record it in a similar manner in the Ledger Balance of Cash section. If an item has been recorded only by the depositor, then record it in a similar manner in the Bank Statement Balance section.

Bryan Floral The bank statement of Bryan Floral shows a final balance of $8,966 as of October 31 (see Figure 9). The present balance of the Cash account in the ledger, after Bryan's accountant has posted from the journal, is $8,030.50. The accountant took the following steps:

1. Verified that canceled checks were recorded correctly on the bank statement.
2. Discovered that a deposit of $1,003 made on October 31 was not recorded on the bank statement.
3. Noted outstanding checks: no. 1916, $461; no. 2022, $119; no. 2023, $827; no. 2024, $67.
4. Noted that a credit memo for a note collected by the bank from Lee and Brock, $600 principal plus $6 interest, was not recorded in the journal.
5. Found that check no. 2001 for $523, payable to Davis, Inc., on account, was recorded in the journal as $532. (The correct amount is $523.)
6. Noted that a debit memo for a collection charge and service charge of $5.50 was not recorded in the journal.
7. Noted that a debit memo for an NSF check for $125 from D. M. Scott was not recorded.
8. Noted that a $20 personal withdrawal by Roberta C. Bryan, the owner, using an ATM, was not recorded.

Look at Figure 9 to see how each step relates to the bank reconciliation.

The accountant makes journal entries for the items indicated in Figure 9 to change the balance of the Cash account from its present balance of

FIGURE 9

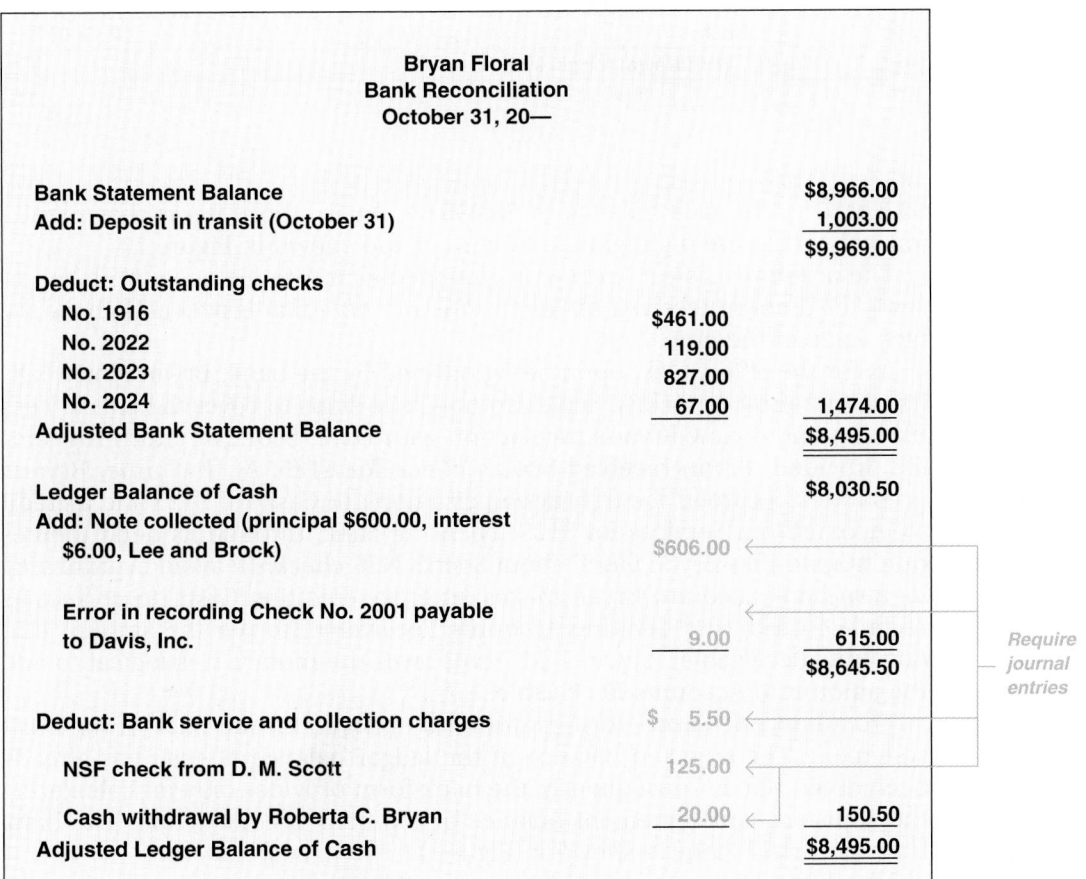

Bryan Floral
Bank Reconciliation
October 31, 20—

Bank Statement Balance		$8,966.00
Add: Deposit in transit (October 31)		1,003.00
		$9,969.00
Deduct: Outstanding checks		
No. 1916	$461.00	
No. 2022	119.00	
No. 2023	827.00	
No. 2024	67.00	1,474.00
Adjusted Bank Statement Balance		$8,495.00
Ledger Balance of Cash		$8,030.50
Add: Note collected (principal $600.00, interest $6.00, Lee and Brock)	$606.00	
Error in recording Check No. 2001 payable to Davis, Inc.	9.00	615.00
		$8,645.50
Deduct: Bank service and collection charges	$ 5.50	
NSF check from D. M. Scott	125.00	
Cash withdrawal by Roberta C. Bryan	20.00	150.50
Adjusted Ledger Balance of Cash		$8,495.00

Require journal entries

FIGURE 10

GENERAL JOURNAL   PAGE _____

DATE		DESCRIPTION	POST. REF.	DEBIT	CREDIT
20—					
Oct.	31	Cash		6 0 6 00	
		Notes Receivable			6 0 0 00
		Interest Income			6 00
		Bank collected note signed			
		by Lee and Brock.			
	31	Cash		9 00	
		Accounts Payable			9 00
		Error in recording check no.			
		2001 payable to Davis, Inc.			
	31	Miscellaneous Expense		5 50	
		Cash			5 50
		Bank service charge and			
		collection charge.			
	31	Accounts Receivable		1 2 5 00	
		Cash			1 2 5 00
		NSF check received from			
		D. M. Scott			
	31	R. C. Bryan, Drawing		2 0 00	
		Cash			2 0 00
		Withdrawal for personal use.			

$8,030.50 to the true balance of $8,495.00. Again, those items that require journal entries are highlighted in Figure 9 and shown in Figure 10.

The account Interest Income is classified as a revenue account. It represents the amount received on the promissory note that is over and above the face value of the note.

As for the NSF check, upon being notified by the bank, Bryan Floral calls its customer (D. M. Scott). Scott can now take steps to cover the check. Let's back up and review Bryan's transaction with D. M. Scott. In return for service provided, Bryan received Scott's check for $125. At that time, Bryan's accountant recorded the transaction as a debit to Cash for $125 and a credit to Income from Services for $125. Then the bank, through its debit memorandum, notifies Bryan Floral about Scott's NSF check. To avoid overdrawing its own bank account, Bryan makes an entry crediting Cash (to correct its record of Cash) and debiting Accounts Receivable (to put the amount into Accounts Receivable). Since D. M. Scott owes the money, it is logical to add the amount to Accounts Receivable.

A bank reconciliation form is ordinarily printed on the back of the bank statement. The adjusted balance of the ledger balance of cash has already been determined. Consequently, the bank form provides only for calculating the adjusted bank statement balance of the bank reconciliation. The bank form for Bryan Floral is shown in Figure 11.

Remember!

When you are reconciling a bank statement, always double-check for any outstanding checks or deposits from previous statements that have been carried forward. Also double-check for any bank service charges.

**THIS FORM IS PROVIDED TO HELP YOU BALANCE
YOUR BANK STATEMENT**

CHECKS OUTSTANDING—NOT
CHARGED TO ACCOUNT

NO.		$	
1916		$	461	00
2022			119	00
2023			827	00
2024			67	00
TOTAL		$	1,474	00

BEFORE YOU START—

PLEASE BE SURE YOU HAVE ENTERED IN YOUR CHECKBOOK ALL AUTOMATIC TRANSACTIONS SHOWN ON THE FRONT OF YOUR STATEMENT.

YOU SHOULD HAVE ADDED IF
ANY OCCURRED:

1. Loan advances.
2. Credit memos.
3. Other automatic deposits.

YOU SHOULD HAVE SUBTRACTED
IF ANY OCCURRED:

1. Automatic loan payments.
2. Automatic savings transfers.
3. Service charges.
4. Debit memos.
5. Other automatic deductions and payments.

BANK BALANCE SHOWN ON THIS STATEMENT	$ 8,966.00
ADD	
DEPOSITS NOT SHOWN ON THIS STATEMENT (IF ANY)	$ 1,003.00
TOTAL	$ 9,969.00
SUBTRACT—	
▶ CHECKS OUTSTANDING	$ 1,474.00
BALANCE	$ 8,495.00

SHOULD AGREE WITH YOUR CHECKBOOK
BALANCE AFTER DEDUCTING SERVICE CHARGE
(IF ANY) SHOWN ON THIS STATEMENT.

Please examine immediately and report if incorrect. If no reply
is received within 15 days the account will be considered correct.

FIGURE 11

THE PETTY CASH FUND

Day after day, business firms are confronted with transactions requiring small immediate payments, such as paying for delivery charges, a birthday card, or a new toner cartridge. If the firm had to go through the usual procedure of making all payments by check, the time consumed would be frustrating and the whole process would be unduly expensive. For many firms, the cost of writing each check is more than $10; this includes the cost of an employee's time for writing and reconciling the check. Suppose you buy 5 stamps from an employee for $1.65, and you want to reimburse her for that money. To write a check would not be practical. It only makes sense to pay in cash, using the **Petty Cash Fund**. *Petty* means "small," so the firm sets a maximum amount that can be paid immediately out of petty cash. Payments that exceed this maximum must be processed by regular check through the journal.

Establishing the Petty Cash Fund

Objective 4

Record journal entries to establish and reimburse Petty Cash Fund.

After the firm has set the maximum amount of a payment from petty cash, next step is to estimate how much cash will be needed during a given period of time, such as a month. It is also important to consider the element of security when keeping cash in the office. If the risk is great, the amount kept in the fund should be small. Bryan Floral decides to establish a Petty Cash Fund of $50 and put it under the control of the assistant. Accordingly, Bryan's accountant writes a check, cashes it at the bank, and records this transaction in the journal as follows:

	GENERAL JOURNAL			PAGE _____
DATE	DESCRIPTION	POST. REF.	DEBIT	CREDIT
20—				
Sept. 1	Petty Cash Fund		5 0 00	
	Cash			5 0 00
	Established a Petty Cash			
	Fund.			

T accounts for the entry look like this:

Petty Cash Fund			Cash	
+	−		+	−
50				50

Because the Petty Cash Fund is an asset account, it is listed on the balance sheet immediately below Cash.

Once the fund has been created, it is not debited again unless the original amount is not large enough to handle the necessary transactions. In that case, the accountant has to increase the Petty Cash Fund—perhaps from $50 to $75. **But, barring such a change in the size of the fund, Petty Cash Fund is debited only once.**

The check is written to the assistant, say, "John Doe, Petty Cash Fund." He or she converts it into convenient **denominations**, which are varieties of coins and currency, such as quarters and dimes and $1 and $5 bills. Then the assistant puts the money in a locked drawer and will not pay anything larger than $5 (or whatever is the agreed-upon amount) out of petty cash.

Remember!

The Petty Cash Fund account is debited only once, and this happens when the fund is first established.

Payments from the Petty Cash Fund

Objective 5

Complete petty cash vouchers and petty cash payments records.

The assistant now takes the responsibility for the Petty Cash Fund. He or she is designated as the only person who can make payments from it. In case of his or her illness, some other employee should be named as stand-in. A **petty cash voucher** must be used to account for every payment from the fund. The voucher constitutes a receipt signed by the person who authorized the payment and by the person who received payment as well as the purpose of the petty cash payment. Thus, even for small payments of $5 or less, there would have to be collusion between the payee and the assistant for any theft to occur. Figure 12 is a petty cash voucher.

FIGURE 12

PETTY CASH VOUCHER	
No. __1__	Date __September 2, 20—__
Paid to __Mark Delivery Service__	$ __2.00__
For __Delivery__	
Account __Delivery Expense__	
Approved by M. Figueroa	*Payment received by* D. Stanton

Petty Cash Payments Record

A petty cash fund is an effective and efficient way to deal with small cash payments that need to be made immediately. These caterers, delivering food for an office party, can be paid on the spot, saving their own company the expense of billing and the recipient the expense of writing a check.

Some firms prefer to have a written record on one sheet of paper, so they keep a **petty cash payments record**. In a petty cash payments record, petty cash vouchers and the accounts that are to be charged are listed as well as the purpose of the expenditure. Special columns for frequent types of expenditures are included in the Distribution of Payments section. The petty cash payments record is not a journal.

Bryan Floral made the following payments from its Petty Cash Fund during September:

Sept.
2   Paid $2 to Mark Delivery Service, voucher no. 1.
3   Bought pencils and pens, $3.09, voucher no. 2.
5   Paid local newspaper for advertising, $5, voucher no. 3.
7   Paid postage on incoming packages, $2.90, voucher no. 4.
10 Roberta C. Bryan, the owner, withdrew $5 for personal use, voucher no. 5.
14 Reimbursed employee for stamps, $1.65, voucher no. 6.
21 Bought stick-on tabs, $4.10, voucher no. 7.
22 Paid $3 to Mark Delivery Service, voucher no. 8.
26 Paid for mailing packages, $3.80, voucher no. 9.
27 Paid $3.50 to Fast Way Delivery, voucher no. 10.
29 Bought memo pads, $4.40, voucher no. 11.
29 Paid for making duplicate keys, $2.60, voucher no. 12.
30 Paid $3.20 to Mark Delivery Service, voucher no. 13.
30 Paid for trash removal, $5, voucher no. 14.

Figure 13 on pages 236–237 shows how these payments are recorded.

Petty Cash Payments Record
Month of September 20—

	DATE	VOU. NO.	EXPLANATION	PAYMENTS			OFFICE SUPPLIES		
1	Sept. 1		Established fund, check no. 90, $50						
2	2	1	Mark Delivery Service		2	00			
3	3	2	Pencils and pens		3	09		3	09
4	5	3	Local newspaper		5	00			
5	7	4	Postage on incoming mail		2	90			
6	10	5	Roberta C. Bryan		5	00			
7	14	6	Reimburse employee for stamps		1	65			
8	21	7	Stick-on tabs		4	10		4	10
9	22	8	Mark Delivery Service		3	00			
10	26	9	Postage for mailings		3	80			
11	27	10	Fast Way Delivery		3	50			
12	29	11	Memo pads		4	40		4	40
13	29	12	Making duplicate keys		2	60			
14	30	13	Mark Delivery Service		3	20			
15	30	14	Trash removal		5	00			
16	30		Totals	4	9	24	1	1	59
17			Balance in Fund $ .76						
18			Reimbursed check no. 136 49.24						
19			Total $50.00						
20									
21									

FIGURE 13

Reimbursement of the Petty Cash Fund

To bring the fund back up to the original amount when it is nearly exhausted (for instance, at the end of the month), the accountant reimburses the fund for expenditures made. Consequently, the Petty Cash Fund may be considered a revolving fund. If the amount initially put in the Petty Cash Fund is $50 and at the end of the month only $.76 is left, the accountant puts $49.24 in the fund as a reimbursement, thereby bringing the fund back up to $50 to start the new month.

Bear in mind that the petty cash payments record is only a supplementary record for gathering information. A less formal way of compiling the information concerning petty cash payments might consist of collecting one month's petty cash vouchers, then sorting them by accounts, such as Office Supplies, Delivery Expense, and the like. Then run a calculator tape for each account. At the end of the month, the accountant makes a summarizing entry to officially journalize the transactions that have taken place. The journal and T accounts of Bryan Floral are shown at the bottom of page 237.

Note that, in the summarizing entry, the accountant debits the accounts on whose behalf the payments were made and credits the Cash account. She or he leaves the Petty Cash Fund account alone. Then the assistant cashes a check for $49.24 and puts the cash in a locked place, thereby restoring the amount in the Petty Cash Fund to the original $50.

Remember!

The petty cash payments record or calculator tapes are not journals; they are simply used as a basis for compiling information for the journal entry. Remember, to change an account, we have to make a journal entry.

PAGE ___1___

DISTRIBUTION OF PAYMENTS

	DELIVERY EXPENSE	MISCELLANEOUS EXPENSE	OTHER ACCOUNTS — ACCOUNT	AMOUNT	
1					1
2	2 00				2
3					3
4			Advertising Expense	5 00	4
5	2 90				5
6			R. C. Bryan, Drawing	5 00	6
7		1 65			7
8					8
9	3 00				9
10	3 80				10
11	3 50				11
12					12
13		2 60			13
14	3 20				14
15		5 00			15
16	18 40	9 25		10 00	16
17					17
18					18
19					19
20					20
21					21

GENERAL JOURNAL   PAGE _____

	DATE		DESCRIPTION	POST. REF.	DEBIT	CREDIT	
1	20—						1
2	Sept.	30	Office Supplies		11 59		2
3			Delivery Expense		18 40		3
4			Miscellaneous Expense		9 25		4
5			Advertising Expense		5 00		5
6			R. C. Bryan, Drawing		5 00		6
7			Cash			49 24	7
8			Reimbursed the Petty Cash				8
9			Fund, Ck. No. 136.				9
10							10

Cash		R. C. Bryan, Drawing		Miscellaneous Expense	
+	−	+	−	+	−
	49.24	5.00		9.25	

Office Supplies		Delivery Expense		Advertising Expense	
+	−	+	−	+	−
11.59		18.40		5.00	

THE CHANGE FUND

Anyone who has ever tried to pay for a small item with a $20 bill knows that any firm that carries out numerous cash transactions needs a **Change Fund**.

Establishing the Change Fund

Objective 6

Record the journal entries to establish a Change Fund.

Before setting up a Change Fund, you have to decide two things: (1) how much money needs to be in the fund, and (2) what denominations of bills and coins are needed. Like the Petty Cash Fund, **the Change Fund is debited only once: when it is established.** It is left at the initial figure unless the person in charge decides to make it larger. The Change Fund account, like the Petty Cash Fund account, is an asset. It is recorded in the balance sheet immediately below Cash. If the Petty Cash Fund account is larger than the Change Fund account, it precedes the Change Fund.

The owner of Bryan Floral, Roberta C. Bryan, decides to establish a change fund; she decides this at the same time she sets up the company's petty cash fund. The entries for the two transactions look like this:

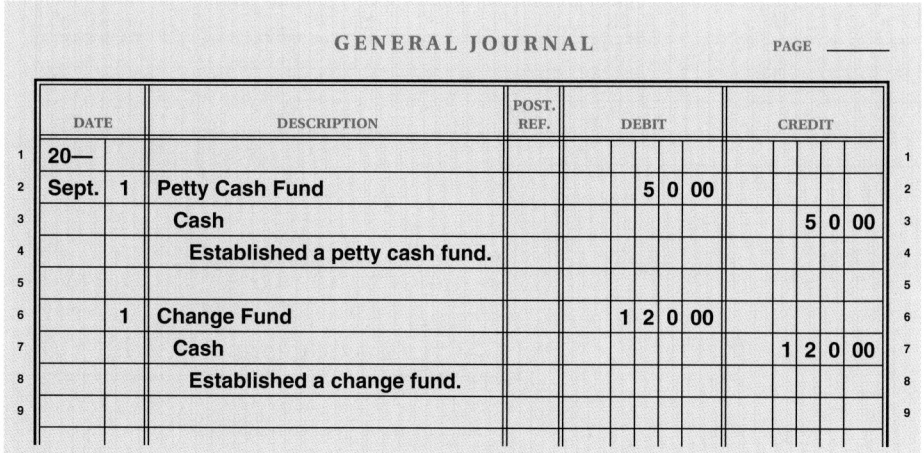

	DATE		DESCRIPTION	POST. REF.	DEBIT	CREDIT	
1	20—						1
2	Sept.	1	Petty Cash Fund		5 0 00		2
3			Cash			5 0 00	3
4			Established a petty cash fund.				4
5							5
6		1	Change Fund		1 2 0 00		6
7			Cash			1 2 0 00	7
8			Established a change fund.				8
9							9

(GENERAL JOURNAL   PAGE _____)

The T accounts for establishing the fund are as follows:

Change Fund			Cash	
+	−		+	−
120				120

Bryan cashes a check for $120 and gets the money in several denominations. She is now prepared to make change for any normal business transactions.

Depositing Cash

At the end of each business day, Bryan deposits the cash taken in during the day, but she holds back the amount of the Change Fund, being sure that it is in convenient denominations. Let's say that on September 1, Bryan Floral had $425 on hand at the end of the day.

$425 Total cash count
− 120 Change fund

$305 New cash deposit

The T accounts look like this:

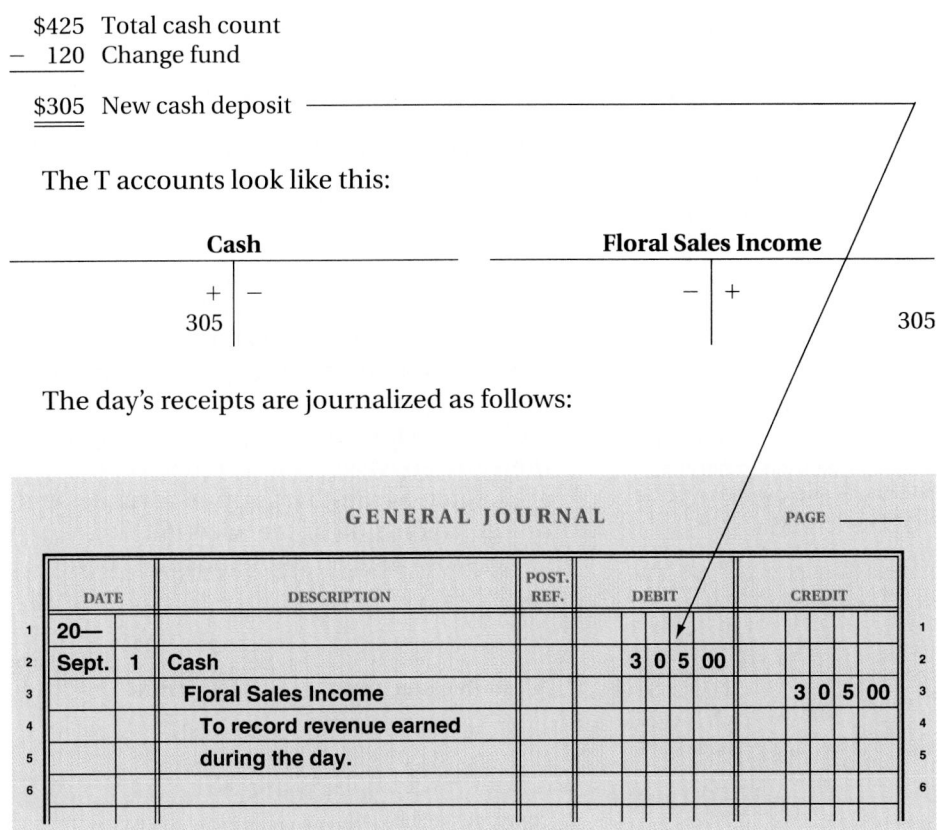

	Cash		Floral Sales Income	
+	−		−	+
305				305

The day's receipts are journalized as follows:

GENERAL JOURNAL   PAGE _____

	DATE		DESCRIPTION	POST. REF.	DEBIT	CREDIT	
1	20—						1
2	Sept.	1	Cash		3 0 5 00		2
3			Floral Sales Income			3 0 5 00	3
4			To record revenue earned				4
5			during the day.				5
6							6

The amount of the cash deposit is the total cash count less the amount of the Change Fund. This should be equal to the income earned.

On September 9, the cash count is $537. So Bryan deposits $417 ($537 − $120). Bryan's accountant makes the following entry to record the day's receipts:

GENERAL JOURNAL   PAGE _____

	DATE		DESCRIPTION	POST. REF.	DEBIT	CREDIT	
1	20—						1
2	Sept.	9	Cash		4 1 7 00		2
3			Floral Sales Income			4 1 7 00	3
4			To record revenue earned				4
5			during the day.				5
6							6

Some businesses label the Cash account *Cash in Bank* and label the Change Fund *Cash on Hand.*

CASH SHORT AND OVER

There is an inherent danger in making change: Human beings make mistakes, especially when there are many customers to be waited on or when the business is temporarily short-handed. Because mistakes do happen, accounting records must be set up to cope with the situation. One reason that a business uses a cash register is to detect mistakes in handling cash. **If, after removing the Change Fund, the day's receipts are less than the register reading, then a cash shortage exists. Conversely, when the day's receipts are greater than the register reading, a cash overage exists.** Both shortages and overages are recorded in the same account, which is called Cash Short and Over. Shortages are considered an expense of operating a business, and therefore shortages are recorded on the debit side of the account. Overages are treated as another form of revenue, and therefore overages are recorded on the credit side of the account.

Let's say that on September 14, Bryan Floral is faced with the following situation:

Cash Register Tape	Cash Count	Amount of the Change Fund
$490	$607	$120

After deducting the $120 in the Change Fund, Bryan will deposit $487 ($607 − $120). Note that this amount is $3 less than the amount indicated by the cash register ($490 − $487); therefore, a $3 cash shortage exists. The following T accounts show how Bryan entered this transaction into the books:

Cash	Floral Sales Income	Cash Short and Over
+ −	− +	
487	490	3

The next day, September 15, the pendulum happens to swing in the other direction:

Cash Register Tape	Cash Count	Amount of the Change Fund
$559	$680	$120

The amount to be deposited is $560 ($680 − $120). This figure is $1 greater than the $559 in floral sales income indicated by the cash register tape. Thus, there is a $1 cash overage ($560 − $559). The analysis of this transaction is shown in the following T accounts:

Cash	Floral Sales Income	Cash Short and Over
+ −	− +	
560	559	1

Bryan Floral's revenue for September 14 and 15 is recorded in the general journal as follows:

A scanner can speed counting and costing of goods, whether for the customer at the checkout counter or taking inventory of goods still on the shelves. The scanner, however, is only as accurate as the amount for each item entered in the computer.

GENERAL JOURNAL   PAGE _____

	DATE		DESCRIPTION	POST. REF.	DEBIT	CREDIT	
1	20—						1
2	Sept.	14	Cash		4 8 7 00		2
3			Cash Short and Over		3 00		3
4			Floral Sales Income			4 9 0 00	4
5			To record revenue earned				5
6			for the day involving a				6
7			cash shortage of $3.				7
8							8
9		15	Cash		5 6 0 00		9
10			Floral Sales Income			5 5 9 00	10
11			Cash Short and Over			1 00	11
12			To record revenue earned				12
13			during the day involving a				13
14			cash overage of $1.				14

As far as errors are concerned, one would think that shortages would be offset by overages. However, customers receiving change are more likely to report shortages than overages. **Consequently, the firm usually experiences a greater number of shortages.** A firm may set a tolerance level for the cashiers. If the shortages consistently exceed the level of tolerance, either fraud is being committed or somebody is making entirely too many careless mistakes.

Now let's summarize our discussion of the Cash Short and Over account by drawing the following conclusions from the illustration:

1. At the close of the business day, the firm deposits the difference between the amount in the cash drawer and the amount in the Change Fund.
2. The firm records the amount shown on the cash register tape as its floral sales income.
3. If the amount of the cash deposit disagrees with the record of receipts, Cash Short and Over makes up the difference. In the first situation just described, there was a shortage of $3, and so there was a debit to Cash Short and Over. In the second situation, there was an overage of $1, and so there was a credit to Cash Short and Over. It is apparent that, as a result of these transactions, the account looks like this:

Cash Short and Over		
Shortage	3	Overage	1

Throughout any fiscal period, the accountant must continually record shortages and overages in the Cash Short and Over account. Let's say that Bryan's final balance is $21 on the debit side. Bryan winds up with a net shortage of $21.

At the end of the fiscal period, **if the account has a debit balance or net shortage, the accountant classifies it as an expense and credits Cash Short and Over and debits Miscellaneous Expense, so that the amount is put in the income statement under Miscellaneous Expense.** The T account would look like this:

Cash Short and Over

Short		Over	
	3		1
	4		1
	3		2
	7		2
	5		1
	2		2
	3		1
	4		10
Bal. 21	31		

Conversely, **if the account has a credit balance or net overage, the accountant classifies it as a revenue account and debits Cash Short and Over and credits Miscellaneous Income, so that the amount is put in the income statement under Miscellaneous Income.** This is an exception to the policy of recording accounts under their exact account title in financial statements. Rather than attaching plus and minus signs to the Cash Short and Over account immediately, we wait until we find out its final balance, then make a journal entry to send the balance to the correct account classification.

CHAPTER REVIEW

Review of Performance Objectives

1. Describe the procedure for depositing checks.

   The procedure for depositing checks consists of first endorsing each check and then completing a deposit slip. On the deposit slip, record the date, the amount of currency to be deposited, the amount and ABA number of each check, and the total amount to be deposited. The checks to be deposited should accompany the deposit slip.

2. Reconcile a bank statement.

   The standard form for a bank reconciliation is as follows:

   Bank Statement Balance

   Add

   Deposits in transit
   Bank errors that understate bank statement balance

   Deduct

   Outstanding checks
   Bank errors that overstate bank statement balance

   Adjusted Bank Statement Balance

Ledger Balance of Cash

Add

Notes collected
Interest income earned
Checkbook errors that understate the ledger balance of cash
Bank credit memos

Deduct

Bank service charges
Checkbook errors that overstate the ledger balance of cash
NSF checks
Bank debit memos

Adjusted Ledger Balance of Cash

3. Record the required journal entries directly from the bank reconciliation.

   Journal entries for the Ledger Balance of Cash section are required. The entry for notes and interest collected is a debit to Cash and credits to Notes Receivable and Interest Income. The entry for a bank service charge is a debit to Miscellaneous Expense and a credit to Cash. The entry for an NSF check is a debit to Accounts Receivable and a credit to Cash.

4. Record journal entries to establish and reimburse Petty Cash Fund.

   The entry to establish a Petty Cash Fund is a debit to Petty Cash Fund and a credit to Cash. The entry to reimburse the Petty Cash Fund consists of debits to the items for which payments from the Petty Cash Fund were made and one credit to Cash for the total payments.

5. Complete petty cash vouchers and petty cash payments records.

   A petty cash voucher is made out for each payment from the Petty Cash Fund. In the petty cash payments record, each voucher is listed and a notation is made concerning the accounts involved; also, an explanation of why the money was paid out is recorded. The petty cash payments record is used as a source of information for making the journal entry to reimburse the Petty Cash Fund.

6. Record the journal entries to establish a Change Fund.

   The entry to establish the Change Fund is a debit to Change Fund and a credit to Cash.

7. Record journal entries for transactions involving Cash Short and Over.

   The Cash Short and Over account provides a way to keep a record of errors in making change. A debit balance in Cash Short and Over denotes a shortage, which is listed as Miscellaneous Expense; the entry is a debit to Miscellaneous Expense and a credit to Cash Short and Over. A credit balance in Cash Short and Over denotes an overage, which becomes Miscellaneous Income; the entry is a debit to Cash Short and Over and a credit to Miscellaneous Income.

Glossary

ABA number The number assigned by the American Bankers Association to a given bank. The first part of the numerator denotes the city or state in which the bank is located; the second part denotes the bank on which the check is drawn. The denominator indicates the Federal Reserve District in which the check is cleared and the routing number used by the Federal Reserve Bank. (220)

ATM (automated teller machine) A machine that enables depositors to make deposits, withdrawals, and transfers using a coded plastic card. (220)

Bank reconciliation A process by which an accountant determines whether and why there is a difference between the balance shown on the bank statement and the balance of the Cash account in the firm's general ledger. The object is to determine the adjusted (or true) balance of the Cash account. (226)

Bank statement A periodic statement that a bank sends to the drawer/depositor of a checking account listing deposits received and checks paid by the bank, debit and credit memos, and beginning and ending balances. (223)

Blank endorsement An endorsement in which the holder (payee) of a check simply signs her or his name on the back of the check. There are no restrictions attached. (221)

Canceled checks Checks issued by the depositor that have been paid (cleared) by the bank and listed on the bank statement. They are called canceled checks because they are canceled by a stamp or perforation, indicating that they have been paid. (225)

Cash funds Separately held reserves of cash set aside for specific purposes. (218)

Change Fund A cash fund used by a firm to make change for customers who pay cash for goods or services. (238)

Check writer A machine that imprints the amount of a check in figures and words on the check itself. (222)

Collections Payments collected by the bank and added to the customer's bank account in the form of a credit memorandum. (226)

Denominations Varieties of coins and currency, such as quarters, dimes, and nickels and $1 and $5 bills and so on. (234)

Deposit in transit A deposit not recorded on the bank statement because the deposit was made between the time of the bank's closing date for compiling items for its statement and the time the statement is received by the depositor; also known as a *late deposit*. (226)

Deposit slips Printed forms provided by a bank on which customers can list all items being deposited; also known as *deposit tickets*. (220)

Drawer The party who writes the check. (222)

Endorsement The process by which the payee transfers ownership of the check to a bank or another party. A check must be endorsed when deposited in a bank, because the bank must have legal title to it in order to collect payment from the drawer of the check (the person or firm who wrote the check). In case the check cannot be collected, the endorser guarantees all subsequent holders (*exception:* an endorsement "without recourse"). (221)

Ledger balance of cash The balance of the Cash account in the general ledger before it is reconciled with the bank statement. (225)

MICR Magnetic ink character recognition; the characters the bank uses to print the number of the depositor's account and the bank's number at the bottom of checks and deposit slips. The bank also prints the amount of the check in MICR when the check is deposited. A number written in these characters can be read by electronic equipment used by banks in clearing checks. (220)

NSF (not sufficient funds) checks Checks drawn against an account in which there are *not sufficient funds* and returned by the payee's bank to the drawer's bank because of nonpayment; also known as *dishonored checks*. (226)

Outstanding checks Checks that have been written by the drawer and deducted on his or her records but have not reached the bank for payment and are not deducted from the bank balance by the time the bank issues its statement. (226)

Payee The person to whom a check is payable. (222)

Petty Cash Fund A cash fund used to make small immediate cash payments. (234)

Petty cash payments record A record indicating the amount of each petty cash voucher, the accounts to which it should be charged, and the purpose of the expenditure. (235)

Petty cash voucher A form stating who requested cash from the Petty Cash Fund, signed by (1) the person in charge of the fund and (2) the person who received the cash, and indicating the purpose of the petty cash payment. (235)

Promissory note A written promise to pay a definite sum at a definite future time. (228)

Qualified endorsement An endorsement in which the holder (payee) of a check avoids future liability, in case the drawer of the check does not have sufficient funds to cover the check, by adding the words "Pay to the order of" and "without recourse" to the endorsement on the back of the check. (222)

Restrictive endorsement An endorsement, such as "Pay to the order of (name of bank), for deposit only," that restricts or limits any further negotiation of a check. It forces the check's deposit, because the endorsement is not valid for any other purpose. (221)

Service charge The fee the bank charges for handling checks, collections, and other items. It is in the form of a debit memorandum. (226)

Signature card The form a depositor signs to give the bank a copy of the official signatures of any persons authorized to sign checks. The bank can use it to verify the depositors' signatures on checks. (219)

QUESTIONS, EXERCISES, AND PROBLEMS

Discussion Questions

1. What is the purpose of a signature card?
2. What are the purposes served by endorsing checks?
3. Why is there generally a difference between the balance in the Cash account on the company's books and the balance on the bank statement?
4. On the bank statement reconciliation, what is the similarity between outstanding checks and NSF checks?
5. Indicate whether the following items in a bank reconciliation should be (1) added to the Cash account balance, (2) deducted from the Cash account balance, (3) added to the bank statement balance, or (4) deducted from the bank statement balance.
   a. NSF check
   b. Deposit in transit
   c. Outstanding check
   d. Bank error charging the firm's account with another company's check
   e. Bank service charge

6. Why is it unnecessary to make general journal entries for the bank statement side of the bank reconciliation?

7. a. Explain the purpose served by a Petty Cash Fund.

   b. Describe the entries to establish and reimburse the fund.

8. a. What does a debit balance in Cash Short and Over represent?

   b. Where does a debit balance in Cash Short and Over appear in the financial statements?

   c. What does a credit balance in Cash Short and Over represent?

   d. Where does a credit balance in Cash Short and Over appear in the financial statements?

Exercises

P.O. 2

Determine missing amounts on a bank reconciliation.

Exercise 7-1 Fill in the missing amounts for the following bank reconciliation:

Bank Reconciliation March 31, 20—		
Bank Statement Balance		$3,754.00
Add: Deposit in transit		267. (a)
		$4,021.00
Deduct: Outstanding checks		
No. 210	$210.00	
No. 224	321. (b)	
No. 227	320.00	851.00
Adjusted Bank Statement Balance		3170. (c)
Ledger Balance of Cash		$2,840.00
Add: Note collected by bank		427.00
		3267. (d)
Deduct: Bank service charge	12. (e)	
NSF check from customer	85.00	97.00
Adjusted Ledger Balance of Cash		3170. (f)

P.O. 3

Journalize entries from a bank reconciliation.

Exercise 7-2 The Ledger Balance of Cash section of the bank reconciliation for Jeon Company for July 31 is shown below.

Ledger Balance of Cash		$6,357.00
Add: Note collected (principal, $700.00, interest $41, signed by L. Hyde)	$741.00	
Error in recording Ck. No. 2225 payable to Fenton Company (recorded check for $18 too much)	18.00	759.00
		$7,116.00
Deduct: NSF check from J. Kelton	$ 85.00	
Bank service and collection charges	21.00	106.00
		$7,010.00

Journalize the entries required to bring the general ledger up to date as of July 31 of this year.

P.O. 2

Determine amount of outstanding checks.

Exercise 7-3 When the bank statement is received on December 3, it shows a balance of $3,000 as of November 30, before reconciliation. After reconciliation, the adjusted balance is $2,500. If there was one deposit in transit amounting to $500, what was the total of the outstanding checks, assuming that there were no other adjustments to be made to the bank statement?

P.O. 2

Place items on a bank reconciliation.

Exercise 7-4 Write a check mark in the column that indicates the location of each item that would be found on a bank reconciliation. The checks are written correctly.

Item	Add to Bank Statement Balance	Subtract from Bank Statement Balance	Add to Ledger Balance of Cash	Subtract from Ledger Balance of Cash
a. A check-printing charge				
b. An outstanding check				
c. A deposit for $187 listed incorrectly on the bank statement as $178				
d. A collection charge the bank made for a note it collected for its depositor				
e. A check written for $40.73 and recorded incorrectly in the checkbook as $40.37				
f. A deposit in transit				
g. An NSF check received from a customer				
h. A check written for $72.39 and recorded incorrectly in the checkbook as $720.39				

P.O. 2

Determine the adjusted ledger balance of cash.

Exercise 7-5 The Mysung Company's Cash account shows a balance of $752.00 as of August 31 of this year. The balance on the bank statement on that date is $1,250.50. Checks for $263.70, $437.05, and $327.00 are outstanding. The bank statement shows a check issued by another depositor for $237.25 (in other words, the bank made an error and charged Mysung Company for a check written by another company). The bank statement also shows an NSF check for $280.00 received from one of Mysung's customers. Service charges for the month were $12.00. What is the adjusted ledger balance of cash as of August 31?

P.O. 4

Journalize entries pertaining to a Petty Cash Fund.

Exercise 7-6 Make entries in general journal form to record the following:

a. Established a Petty Cash Fund, $150. Issued Ck. No. 857.
b. Reimbursed the Petty Cash Fund for expenditures of $102: Store Supplies, $28; Office Supplies, $36; Miscellaneous Expense, $38. Issued Ck. No. 889.
c. Increased the amount of the fund by an additional $25. Issued Ck. No. 891.

d. Reimbursed the Petty Cash Fund for expenditures of $91.84: Store Supplies, $45.92; Delivery Expense, $36.00; Miscellaneous Expense, $9.92. Issued Ck. No. 936.

P.O. 6,7

Journalize entry for the receipt of cash.

Exercise 7-7 At the end of the day, the cash register tape lists $827.27 as total income from services. Cash on hand consists of $15.27 in coins, $694.00 in currency, $80 in traveler's checks, and $236.00 in customers' checks. The amount of the Change Fund is $200. In general journal form, record the entry to record the day's cash revenue.

P.O. 6,7

Describe entries related to the Change Fund and Cash Short and Over.

Exercise 7-8

a. Describe the entries that have been posted to the following accounts after the Change Fund was established.

Change Fund		Sales		Cash	
200			Jan. 3 1,521	Jan. 3 1,523	
			Jan. 4 1,420	Jan. 4 1,419	
			Jan. 6 1,663	Jan. 6 1,660	

Cash Short and Over			
Jan. 4	1	Jan. 3	2
Jan. 6	3		

b. How will the balance of Cash Short and Over be reported on the income statement?

CONSIDER AND COMMUNICATE

Your friend owns a small clothing alterations business. To make change for a customer, your friend must take money out of her own wallet. How would you explain the separate entity concept, along with how a Change Fund account might help the situation?

CRITICAL THINKING

William Croxton, a college student, plans to provide résumé and thesis typing services to graduate students at the university near his home. He must determine how much money to deposit initially in his business account to pay for the start-up costs of the new business. After start-up costs, he must be left with a balance of $5,000 in his business account. He plans to buy a computer and printer and a copier for $3,500, and he will make a down payment of $1,500. The fax machine and telephone system he needs are available for $360 cash. He will buy paper for the copier, printer, and fax machine for $325 on account.

1. How much should William's investment be on May 1 if he plans to meet his goal of having $5,000 in his business account after the anticipated transactions?
2. Prepare a balance sheet for William's business as of May 15, 20—.

Transaction	Cash	Equipment	Supplies	Accounts Payable	W. Croxton, Capital
a. Make beginning investment (unknown at this time)					
Balance					
b. Buy computer/printer/copier for $3,500, paying $1,500 down, and placing the rest on account.					
Balance					
c. Bought fax/telephone for $360 cash.					
Balance					
d. Bought paper supplies for $325 on account.					
Balance					

A MATTER OF ETHICS

You work as a cashier in a service business. Some days you are short of cash at the end of the day, and some days you have more cash than the cash register tape says was earned. You are embarrassed when your cash is short and don't want the owner to know, so you take money from your wallet and make up the difference. On days when you are over, you keep the difference to help pay back what you paid to cover your shortages. Comment on this practice.

WEB WORK

Using an Internet web browser, type the phrase *small business accounting* or *sba.gov* for the home page of the Small Business Administration in the search box. Search for information about embezzlement or internal control systems. Discuss your findings in a five-minute presentation to your class, or summarize them in a one-page memorandum.

PROBLEM SET A

For additional help, see the demonstration problem at the beginning of each chapter in your Working Papers.

P.O. 2,3

Problem 7-1A Carver Men's Shop deposits all receipts in the bank each evening and makes all payments by check. On September 30 its Cash in Bank account has a balance of $2,041.60. The bank statement of September 30 shows a balance of $2,268.43. The following information pertains to reconciling the bank statement:

a. The reconciliation for August, the previous month, showed three checks outstanding on August 31: no. 1516 for $75; no. 1519 for $65.40, and no. 1520 for $120. Checks no. 1516 and 1520 were returned with the September bank statement; however, check no. 1519 was not returned.

b. Checks no. 1599 for $87.50, no. 1616 for $18.61, no. 1617 for $52.87, and no. 1618 for $40.79 were written during September and have not been returned by the bank.

c. A deposit of $442.34 was placed in the night depository on September 30 and did not appear on the bank statement.

d. The canceled checks were compared with the entries in the checkbook, and it was observed that check no. 1587, for $89, payable to C. T. Carver, the owner, for personal use, was written correctly but was recorded in the checkbook as $108.

e. There is a bank debit memo for service charges, $13.

f. There is a bank credit memo for collection of a note signed by J. L. Yung, $398, including $380 principal and $18 interest.

Check Figure

Adjusted ledger balance of cash, $2,445.60

Instructions

1. Prepare a bank reconciliation as of September 30, assuming that the debit and credit memos have not been recorded.
2. Record the necessary entries in general journal form, page 12.

P.O. 4,5

Problem 7-2A On July 1, Driskol and Company established a Petty Cash Fund. The following petty cash transactions took place during the month:

July	1	Cashed check no. 1956 for $125 to establish a Petty Cash Fund, and put the $125 in a locked drawer in the office.
	3	Bought postage stamps, $13.60, voucher no. 1 (Miscellaneous Expense).
	4	Issued voucher no. 2 for taxi fare, $18 (Miscellaneous Expense).
	6	Issued voucher no. 3 for delivery charges on outgoing parts, $3.80.
	9	N. Driskol withdrew $18 for personal use, voucher no. 4.
	13	Paid $6.80 for postage, voucher no. 5 (Miscellaneous Expense).
	19	Bought pens for office, $12.15, voucher no. 6.
	23	Paid $2.18 for a box of staples, voucher no. 7.
	28	Paid $22 for window cleaning service, voucher no. 8 (Miscellaneous Expense).
	29	Paid $12.18 for pencils for office, voucher no. 9.
	31	Issued for cash check no. 1974 for $108.71 to reimburse Petty Cash Fund.

Check Figure

Office Supplies, $26.51

Instructions

1. Journalize the entry establishing the Petty Cash Fund in the general journal, page 3.
2. Record the disbursements of petty cash in the petty cash payments record, page 1.
3. Journalize the summarizing entry to reimburse the Petty Cash Fund.

P.O. 6,7

Problem 7-3A M. Cho, owner of Cho's Crafts, makes bank deposits in the night depository at the close of each business day. The following information for the last three days of June is available.

	June		
	28	**29**	**30**
Cash register tape	$756.18	$835.60	$ 912.50
Cash count	854.97	934.40	1,014.70

Check Figure

Cash Short and Over, June 30, $2.20 over

P.O. 2,3

Instructions

In general journal form, record the cash deposit for each day, assuming that there is a $100 Change Fund.

Problem 7-4A On August 31, Kravsnik Company receives its bank statement. The company deposits its receipts in the bank and makes all payments by check. The debit memo for $149 is for an NSF check written by N. Carlton. Check no. 1924 for $336, payable to Garner Company (a creditor), was incorrectly recorded in the checkbook and journal as $200.

   The balance of the Cash account as of August 31 is $1,509. Outstanding checks as of August 31 are: no. 1928, $119; no. 1929, $243. The accountant notes that the deposit of August 31 for $261 did not appear on the bank statement.

Check Figure

Adjusted ledger balance of cash, $1,212

Instructions

1. Prepare a bank reconciliation as of August 31, assuming that the debit memos have not been recorded.
2. Record the necessary journal entries.
3. Complete the bank form to determine the adjusted balance of cash.

PEABODY NATIONAL BANK

Kravsnik Company
416 Seneca Avenue
Kansas City, Missouri 64102

ACCOUNT NO.
152-6 55-217

STATEMENT DATE
August 1–31, 20—

SUMMARY		
Balance Last Statement	$1,360.00	
Amount of Checks and Debits	$2,698.00	
Number of Checks	11	
Amount of Deposits and Credits	$2,651.00	
Number of Deposits	7	
Balance This Statement	$1,313.00	

CHECKS/OTHER DEBITS	CHECKS	CHECK NUMBER	DATE POSTED	AMOUNT	CHECK NUMBER	DATE POSTED	AMOUNT
		1917	8-04	172.00	1923	8-09	621.00
		1918	8-04	76.00	1924	8-17	336.00
		1919	8-05	146.00	1925	8-17	14.00
		1920	8-07	206.00	1926	8-23	533.00
		1921	8-07	139.00	1927	8-28	94.00
		1922	8-08	200.00			

OTHER DEBITS	DESCRIPTION		DATE POSTED	AMOUNT
	DM NSF check		8-31	149.00
	DM Service charge		8-31	12.00

DEPOSITS/OTHER CREDITS	DEPOSITS	DATE POSTED	AMOUNT	DATE POSTED	AMOUNT
		8-02	326.00	8-18	419.00
		8-05	412.00	8-24	398.00
		8-09	437.00	8-28	291.00
		8-14	368.00		

PLEASE EXAMINE THIS STATEMENT CAREFULLY. REPORT ANY POSSIBLE ERRORS IN 10 DAYS.

CODE SYMBOLS

CM Credit Memo   DM Debit Memo   OD Overdraft   EC Error Correction

Instructions for General Ledger Software

1. Prepare a bank reconciliation as of August 31. Errors made by the company or the bank, as well as service charges, must be entered as debit or credit memos.
2. Print the bank reconciliation.
3. Record the necessary journal entries.
4. Print the journal entries.

PROBLEM SET B

For additional help, see the demonstration problem at the beginning of each chapter in your Working Papers.

P.O. 2,3

Problem 7-1B The Malamura Company deposits all receipts in the bank and makes all payments by check. On November 30 its Cash account has a balance of $2,289.00. The bank statement on November 30 shows a balance of $2,894.00. You are given the following information with which to reconcile the bank statement:

a. A deposit of $320.00 was placed in the night depository on November 30 and did not appear on the bank statement.
b. The reconciliation for October, the previous month, showed three checks outstanding on October 31: no. 1727 for $81.30, no. 1730 for $127.40, and no. 1732 for $62.40. Checks no. 1727 and 1730 were returned with the November bank statement; however, check no. 1732 was not returned.
c. Check no. 1742 for $98.50, no. 1743 for $46.27, no. 1744 for $37.92, and no. 1745 for $200.91 were written during November but were not returned by the bank.
d. You compare the canceled checks with the entries in the checkbook and find that check no. 1737 for $58, payable to C. R. Malamura, the owner, for her personal use, was written correctly. However, the check was recorded in the checkbook as $85.
e. Included in the bank statement was a bank debit memo for service charges, $12.
f. A bank credit memo was also enclosed for the collection of a note signed by L. B. Norman, $464, including $436 principal and $28 interest.

Check Figure

Adjusted ledger balance of cash, $2,768.00

Instructions

1. Prepare a bank reconciliation as of November 30, assuming that the debit and credit memos have not been recorded.
2. Record the necessary entries in general journal form, page 4.

P.O. 4,5

Problem 7-2B On March 1 of this year, the Stenn Company established a Petty Cash Fund, and the following petty cash transactions took place during the month:

Mar. 1 Cashed check no. 1314 for $110 to establish a Petty Cash Fund, and put the $110 in a locked drawer in the office.
4 Issued voucher no. 1 for taxi fare, $14 (Miscellaneous Expense).
7 Issued voucher no. 2 for memo pads, $4.10.

Mar. 9 Paid $17.50 for an advertisement in a college basketball program, voucher no. 3.

16 Bought postage stamps, $16, voucher no. 4 (Miscellaneous Expense).

20 Paid $18.50 to have snow removed from office front sidewalk, voucher no. 5 (Miscellaneous Expense).

25 Issued voucher no. 6 for delivery charge, $3.45.

28 R. C. Do, the owner, withdrew $19 for personal use, voucher no. 7.

29 Paid $3.50 for postage, voucher no. 8 (Miscellaneous Expense).

30 Paid $8.40 for delivery charge, voucher no. 9.

31 Issued for cash check no. 1372 for $104.45 to reimburse Petty Cash Fund.

Check Figure

Office Supplies, $4.10

Instructions

1. Journalize the entry establishing the Petty Cash Fund in the general journal, page 3.
2. Record the disbursements of petty cash in the petty cash payments record.
3. Journalize the summarizing entry to reimburse the Petty Cash Fund.

P.O. 6

Problem 7-3B Melissa Smith, owner of Melissa's Beauty Salon, makes bank deposits in the night depository at the close of each business day. The following information for the first three days of April is available.

	April		
	1	**2**	**3**
Cash register tape	$358.20	$418.52	$424.79
Cash count	457.28	520.55	523.59

Check Figure

Cash Short and Over, April 3, $1.20 short

Instructions

In general journal form, record the cash deposit for each day, assuming that there is a $100 Change Fund.

P.O. 2,3

Problem 7-4B On August 2, Eastside Hotel receives its bank statement. The company deposits its receipts in the bank and makes all payments by check. The debit memo for $137 is for an NSF check written by T. N. Klein. Check no. 1617 for $63.80, payable to Wrye Company (a creditor), was incorrectly recorded in the checkbook and journal as $36.80.

The balance of the Cash account as of July 31 is $2,167.40. Outstanding checks as of July 31 are: no. 1631, $21.64; no. 1632, $91.23; no. 1633, $154.29. The accountant notes that the July 31 deposit of $268 did not appear on the bank statement.

Check Figure

Adjusted ledger balance of cash, $1,990.30

Instructions

1. Prepare a bank reconciliation as of July 31, assuming that the debit memos have not been recorded.
2. Record the necessary journal entries.

3. Complete the bank form to determine the adjusted balance of cash.

STANTON NATIONAL BANK

Eastside Hotel
410 W. Lang Street
Rockford, Illinois 61104

ACCOUNT NO.
761-145-792

STATEMENT DATE
July 1–31, 20—

SUMMARY		
Balance Last Statement	$2,168.50
Amount of Checks and Debits	$2,707.21
Number of Checks	14
Amount of Deposits and Credits	$2,528.17
Number of Deposits	7
Balance This Statement	$1,989.46

CHECKS/OTHER DEBITS

CHECKS	CHECK NUMBER	DATE POSTED	AMOUNT	CHECK NUMBER	DATE POSTED	AMOUNT
	1617	7-03	63.80	1624	7-08	120.00
	1618	7-03	167.00	1625	7-09	429.60
	1619	7-03	124.20	1626	7-12	37.40
	1620	7-05	137.20	1627	7-14	38.49
	1621	7-06	236.25	1628	7-22	182.71
	1622	7-06	159.89	1629	7-25	96.87
	1623	7-08	244.50	1630	7-26	19.20

OTHER DEBITS

	DESCRIPTION	DATE POSTED	AMOUNT
DM	NSF check	7-22	137.00
DM	Service charge	7-31	13.10

DEPOSITS/OTHER CREDITS

DEPOSITS	DATE POSTED	AMOUNT	DATE POSTED	AMOUNT
	7-03	491.50	7-15	291.76
	7-06	415.72	7-18	142.90
	7-09	439.16	7-28	368.93
	7-11	378.20		

PLEASE EXAMINE THIS STATEMENT CAREFULLY. REPORT ANY POSSIBLE ERRORS IN 10 DAYS.

CODE SYMBOLS

CM Credit Memo   DM Debit Memo   OD Overdraft   EC Error Correction

---

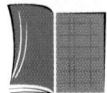

Instructions for General Ledger Software

1. Prepare a bank reconciliation as of July 31. Errors made by the company or the bank, as well as service charges, must be entered as debit or credit memos.
2. Print the bank reconciliation.
3. Record the necessary journal entries.
4. Print the journal entries.

B Bad Debts

Performance Objectives

After you have completed this appendix, you will be able to do the following:

1. Prepare the adjusting entry for bad debts using the allowance method, based on a percentage of credit sales.

2. Prepare the entry to write off an account as uncollectible when the allowance method is used.

3. Prepare the entry to write off an account as uncollectible when the specific charge-off method is used.

As you know, not all credit customers pay their bills. In this appendix, we turn our attention to the accounts receivable that will not be collected. There are two basic methods of providing for writing or charging off credit customers' accounts that are considered uncollectible. They are the allowance method and the specific charge-off method.

ALLOWANCE METHOD

The allowance method provides for bad debt losses in advance, by estimating them. Though there are a number of ways to estimate the amount of future losses from open accounts, we will base our estimate on a percentage of credit sales.

For example, based on its experience with bad debt losses, the Mosier Company estimates that 1 percent of its revenue from services on account for the year will be uncollectible. Obviously, Mosier does not know which credit customers will not pay their bills. If the company were certain that a particular customer would not pay his or her bill, then it wouldn't perform services without requiring cash in advance.

Adjusting Entry and Writing Off an Account

Objective 1

Prepare the adjusting entry for bad debts using the allowance method, based on a percentage of credit sales.

Mosier's total income from services on account for last year was $300,000. One percent of $300,000 is $3,000. On its work sheet, Mosier makes an adjusting entry. We show this in T account form.

Bad Debts Expense			Allowance for Doubtful Accounts		
	+	−		−	+
Dec. 31				Dec. 31	
Adjusting	3,000			Adjusting	3,000

Allowance for Doubtful Accounts is treated as a deduction from Accounts Receivable. Consequently, Allowance for Doubtful Accounts is a contra account. The adjusting entry is similar to the entry for depreciation in that there is a debit to an expense account and a credit to a contra account. In T account form, the adjustment for depreciation looks like this:

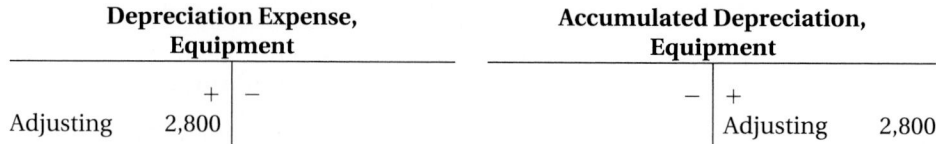

	Depreciation Expense, Equipment				Accumulated Depreciation, Equipment	
	+	−		−	+	
Adjusting	2,800				Adjusting	2,800

Assume that Mosier Company's balance of Accounts Receivable is $90,000 and its balance of Equipment is $75,000. Let's show the accounts and the adjusting entries in T account form.

Assets	=	Liabilities	+	Owner's Equity	+	Revenue	−	Expenses
+ −		− +		− +		− +		+ −

Accounts Receivable

+	−
Bal. 90,000	

Allowance for Doubtful Accounts

−	+
	Bal. 170
	Adj. 3,000
	Bal. 3,170

Equipment

+	−
Bal. 75,000	

Accumulated Depreciation, Equipment

−	+
	Bal. 7,000
	Adj. 2,800
	Bal. 9,800

Income from Services

−	+
	Bal. 300,000

Bad Debts Expense

+	−
Adj. 3,000	

Depreciation Expense, Equipment

+	−
Adj. 2,800	

The Depreciation Expense, Equipment, account comes into existence as an adjusting entry at the end of the year. It is closed immediately after being brought into existence. The same thing happens to Bad Debts Expense; it comes into existence as an adjusting entry, and then it is immediately closed during the closing process.

Objective 2

Prepare the entry to write off an account as uncollectible when the allowance method is used.

As certain charge customers' accounts are determined to be uncollectible and are written off, the losses are taken out of Allowance for Doubtful Accounts. Think of the Allowance for Doubtful Accounts as a reservoir. By means of the adjusting entry, the account is filled up at the end of the year and then is gradually drained off (reduced) during the next year by write-offs of charge customer accounts. The $170 balance in Allowance for Doubtful Accounts at the end of the year indicates that less accounts receivable were actually written off as uncollectible during the year than previously estimated. As a result, Bad Debts Expense in the period was overstated and therefore net income understated.

Let's go on to the next year. On January 2, the Mosier Company finally gives up on its attempts to collect $720 from its credit customer A. N. Brady, which is included in Accounts Receivable. The Mosier Company now writes off the account in the amount of $720, shown below in T account form.

Accounts Receivable		Allowance for Doubtful Accounts	
+ | −		− | +	
Bal. 90,000 | Jan. 2		Jan. 2 | Bal. 3,170	
(write-off) 720		(write-off) 720	
Bal. 89,280 |		| Bal. 2,450	

As you can see, the write-off has reduced both the balance of Accounts Receivable and the balance of Allowance for Doubtful Accounts but has not changed the net realizable value of accounts receivable. The general journal entry is shown below.

PAGE _____

	DATE		DESCRIPTION	POST. REF.	DEBIT	CREDIT	
1	20—						1
2	Jan.	2	Allowance for Doubtful Accounts		7 2 0 00		2
3			Accounts Receivable			7 2 0 00	3
4			Wrote off the account of				4
5			A. N. Brady as uncollectible.				5
6							6

An Advantage and a Disadvantage of the Allowance Method

The allowance method is consistent with the accrual basis of accounting in that it matches revenues of one year with expenses of the same year. The bad-debt loss potential is provided in the same year in which the revenue is earned. The conformity with the matching principle places the allowance method in compliance with generally accepted accounting principles as recognized by the FASB. However, the allowance method cannot be used for federal income tax purposes. This means that if a business uses the allowance method, the net income shown on the company's income statement will differ from the net income shown on its federal income tax return.

SPECIFIC CHARGE-OFF METHOD

Objective 3

Prepare the entry to write off an account as uncollectible when the specific charge-off method is used.

Under the specific charge-off method, when a credit customer's account is determined to be uncollectible, the account is simply written off. The terms *write-off* and *charge-off* mean the same thing. No allowance account is used with the specific charge-off method because no estimate of uncollectible accounts receivable is calculated. As an illustration, Walton Company uses the specific charge-off method. On May 5, Walton Company writes off the account of L. C. Garber, $220. For the purpose of this example, we will use a separate Accounts Receivable account for L. C. Garber. T accounts pertaining to Garber's account look like this:

Accounts Receivable				Bad Debts Expense		
	+	−			+	−
Balance	220	May 5 (write-off) 220		May 5 (write-off) 220		

The general journal entry is shown below.

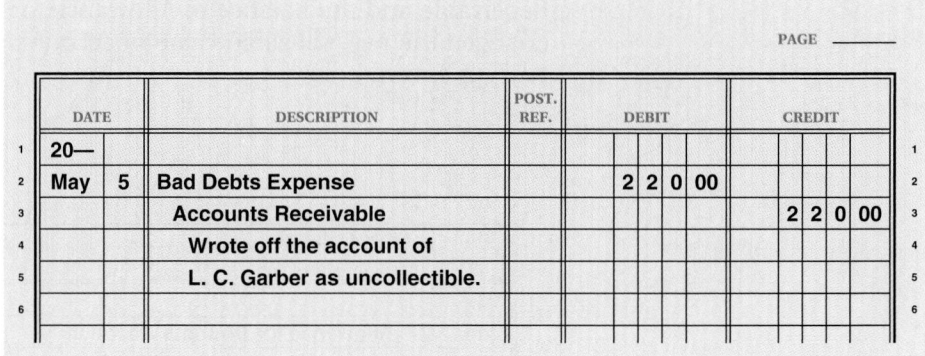

Under this method, entries will be made directly into the Bad Debts Expense account during the year. No adjusting entry is needed, and Allowance for Doubtful Accounts is not used.

Advantage of the Specific Charge-off Method

The main advantage is that the method may be used for federal income tax purposes. It is not necessary to make an adjusting entry. Also, one less account (Allowance for Doubtful Accounts) is required.

Disadvantage of the Specific Charge-off Method

This method is not consistent with the accrual basis of accounting (recognizing revenue when it is earned and expenses when they are incurred). The method does not match up the revenue of one year with the expense of the same year. This lack of conformity with the matching principle places the specific charge-off method in violation of generally accepted accounting principles. For example, the sale of services on account to L. C. Garber could have been made four years ago. Since the account receivable will never be collected, the revenue for that year was too high (overstated). Consequently, net income is also overstated during that year. Now, four years later, $220 is written off as an expense. So net income for this year is too low (understated) because of the added expense.

PROBLEMS

P.O. 1,2

Check Figure

Adjusting entry amount, $3,620

Problem B-1 Ramos Company's total sales on account for the year amounted to $362,000. The company, which uses the allowance method, estimated bad debts at 1 percent of its charge sales. Journalize the following selected entries:

2000
Dec.   31   The adjusting entry.

2001
Mar.   2   Write-off of the account of B. L. Hulse as uncollectible, $264.

June   6   Write-off of the account of A. P. Tolland as uncollectible, $341.

P.O. 1,2

Check Figure

Adjusting entry amount, $1,431.53

Problem B-2 Harron's Landscape Service's total revenue on account for 2000 amounted to $286,305. The company, which uses the allowance method, estimates bad debts at ½ percent of total revenue on account. Journalize the following selected entries:

2000
Dec.   12   Performed services on account for D. A. Wagner, $114.
        31   The adjusting entry for Bad Debts Expense.
        31   The closing entry for Bad Debts Expense.

2001
Feb.   18   Wrote off the account of D. A. Wagner as uncollectible, $114.

P.O. 3

Check Figure

Name of debit account, Bad Debts Expense

Problem B-3 Jump City uses the specific charge-off method for recording bad debts. Journalize the following selected entries:

2000
Apr.   10   Write-off of the account of J. C. Sonja as uncollectible, $195.

July   27   Write-off of the account of B. R. West as uncollectible, $142.

8 Employee Earnings and Deductions

WINDOWS ON | **THE WORLD WIDE WEB**

When you graduate from college, where will you work? What will you earn? Will you be paid by the hour, by commission, or with a salary? If you land a job at a large corporation like Microsoft, you can expect to receive benefits such as employer-paid coverage for medical, dental, and vision care for you and your family members. In addition, you will be entitled to life insurance, a 401K plan, and even free soft drinks, as well as discounts on Microsoft products at the company store.

If your job were in Microsoft's accounting department, you would need to keep records on payroll taxes paid and employee income tax withholding. You'd want to make sure paychecks were processed on time and were accurate. For more information on Microsoft benefits and job opportunities, go to **http://www.microsoft.com/jobs/**.

Performance Objectives

After you have completed this chapter, you will be able to do the following:

1. Calculate total earnings based on an hourly, piece-rate, or commission basis.

2. Determine deductions from tables of employees' income tax withholding.

3. Complete a payroll register.

4. Journalize the payroll entry from a payroll register.

5. Maintain employees' individual earnings records.

U p to now, we've been recording employees' earnings as a debit to Salaries or Wages Expense and a credit to Cash, but we've really been talking only about **gross pay**: the total amount of an employee's pay before deductions. We haven't mentioned the various deductions that we all know are taken out of our gross pay before we get to the **net pay**, or take-home pay. In this chapter, we talk about types of deductions and how to enter them in the payroll records, and about journal entries to record the payroll and pay the employees.

OBJECTIVES OF PAYROLL RECORDS AND ACCOUNTING

There are two primary reasons to maintain accurate payroll records. First, we must collect the data necessary to compute the compensation for each employee for each payroll period.

Second, we must provide the information needed to complete the various government reports—federal and state—required of all employers. All business enterprises, both large and small, are required by law to withhold certain amounts from employees' pay for taxes, to make payments to government agencies by specific deadlines, and to submit reports on official forms. Because governments impose penalties if the requirements are not met, employers are vitally concerned with payroll accounting. Anyone going into accounting or involved with the management of any business should be thoroughly acquainted with payroll accounting.

The employer is required to keep records of the following information:

1. **Personal data on employee** Name, address, Social Security number, date of birth

2. **Data on wage payments** Dates and amounts of payments, and payroll periods

3. **Amount of taxable wages paid** Dates and amount earned year to date for the calendar year involved

4. **Amount of tax withheld from each employee's earnings by pay period**

EMPLOYER/EMPLOYEE RELATIONSHIPS

FYI

Examples of independent contractors include a self-employed appliance repair person, plumber, or CPA.

Payroll accounting is concerned with employees and their compensation, withholdings, records, reports, and taxes. There is a distinction between an employee and an independent contractor. An **employee** is one who is under the direction and control of the employer, such as a secretary, bookkeeper, salesclerk, vice president, controller, and so on. An **independent contractor** is engaged for a definite job or service and may choose her or his own means of doing the work. Payments made to independent contractors are in the form of fees or charges. Independent contractors submit bills or invoices for the work they do. The payment is not subject to any withholding or payroll taxes by the person or firm paying that invoice.

HOW EMPLOYEES GET PAID

Employees may be paid a salary or wages, depending on the type of work and the period of time covered. Money paid to a person for managerial or administrative services is usually called a salary, and the time period covered is generally a month or a year. Money paid for either skilled or unskilled labor is usually called wages, and the time period covered is hours or weeks. Wages may also be paid on a piecework basis. A company may supplement an employee's salary or wage by commissions, bonuses, cost-of-living adjustments, and profit-sharing plans. As a rule, employees are paid by check, in cash, or by a direct deposit to their bank account. However, their compensation may take the form of merchandise, lodging, meals, or other property as well. When the compensation is in these forms, you have to determine the fair value of the property or service given in payment for an employee's labor.

Calculating Total Earnings

Objective 1

Calculate total earnings based on an hourly, piece-rate, or commission basis.

When compensation is based on the amount of time worked, the accountant has to have a record of the number of hours worked by each employee. When there are only a few employees, this can be accomplished by means of a time book. When there are many employees, time clocks or other electronic time-keeping systems are used.

FIGURE 1

TIME CARD

Name ___Asino, Matte E.___

Week ending ___Oct. 7, 20—___

Day	In	Out	In	Out	Hours Worked	
					Regular	Overtime
M	7:57	12:00	12:20	4:32	8	
T	7:56	12:06	12:36	4:37	8	
W	7:57	12:02	12:31	4:31	8	
T	8:00	12:11	12:40	6:32	8	2
F	8:00	12:03	12:33	5:33	8	1
S	7:59	11:02				3
S						

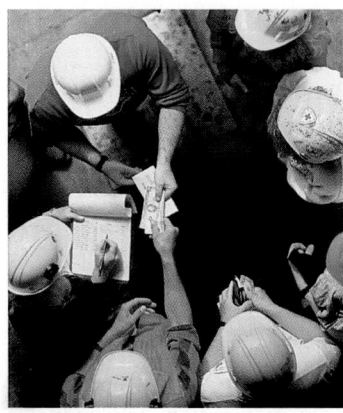

Although wages are more often paid by check or direct deposit, some industries or companies still pay employees in cash. From an internal control point of view, however, it is better to have a permanent record, which a check or direct deposit slip provides.

Employees may be paid weekly, biweekly, semimonthly, or monthly. Biweekly is every two weeks. Semimonthly is twice a month.

Wages

Consider Matte E. Asino, who works for Greg Company. His regular rate of pay is $22.84 per hour. The company pays time-and-a-half for hours worked in excess of 40 per week. In addition, it pays him double time for any work he does on Sundays and holidays. Asino has a ½-hour lunch break during an 8½-hour day. He is not paid for the lunch break nor is he paid for minutes before 8 AM or after 4:30 PM unless hours of overtime were authorized in advance. His time card for the week is shown in Figure 1.

Asino's gross wages can be computed by one of two methods. The first method works like this:

40 hours at straight time	40 × $22.84 per hour =	$ 913.60
2 hours overtime on Thursday	2 × $34.26 per hour =	$ 68.52
1 hour overtime on Friday	1 × $34.26 per hour =	$ 34.26
3 hours overtime on Saturday	3 × $34.26 per hour =	$ 102.78
Total gross wages	46	$1,119.16

FYI

Minimum wages are set by Congress or state legislature—whichever is higher. Originally, the minimum wage was $.25 per hour.

The second method of calculating gross wages is often used when it is necessary to identify or track overtime premium.

46 hours at straight time: 46 × $22.84 per hour = $1,050.64
Overtime premium:
6 hours × $11.42 per hour premium =   68.52

Total gross wages $1,119.16

How Employees Get Paid   **263**

Salaries

Employees who are paid a regular salary may also be entitled to extra pay for overtime. It is necessary to figure out their regular hourly rate of pay before you can determine their overtime rate. Consider R. Helvi, who gets a salary of $2,250 per month. She is entitled to overtime pay for all hours worked in excess of 40 during a week at the rate of 1½ times her regular hourly rate. This past week she worked 44 hours, so we calculate her overtime pay as follows:

$2,250 per month $\times$ 12 months = $27,000 per year
$27,000 per year $\div$ 52 weeks = $519.23 per week
$519.23 per week $\div$ 40 hours = $12.98 per regular hour

Earnings for 44 hours:
40 hours at straight time	40 $\times$ $12.98 =	$519.20
4 hours overtime	4 $\times$ $19.47 =	$ 77.88
Total gross earnings		$597.08

Piece Rate

Workers under the piece-rate system are paid at the rate of so much per unit of production. For example, Bob Faulk, a pear picker, gets paid $9 for picking a bin of pears. If he picks 6 bins during the day, his total earnings are 6 $\times$ $9 = $54.

Commissions

Some salespersons are paid on a purely commission basis. However, a more common arrangement is a salary plus a commission or bonus. Assume that Lena Breski receives an annual salary of $18,000. Her employer agrees to pay her a 5 percent commission on all sales during the year in excess of $100,000. Her sales for the year total $240,000. Her commission is $7,000 ($140,000 $\times$ .05). Therefore, her total earnings are $25,000 ($18,000 + $7,000).

Workers paid by the piece-rate system are paid according to how much they produce. The number of heads of lettuce picked or shirts sewn determines the worker's total compensation.

DEDUCTIONS FROM TOTAL EARNINGS

Anyone who has ever earned a paycheck has encountered some of the many types of deductions. Total earnings minus deductions equal net pay. The most usual deductions are for

1. Federal income tax withholding
2. State income tax withholding
3. FICA tax (Social Security and Medicare), employee's share
4. Purchase of U.S. savings bonds
5. Union dues
6. Medical and life insurance premiums
7. Contributions to a charitable organization
8. Repayment of personal loans from the company credit union
9. Savings through the company credit union

Employees' Federal Income Tax Withholding

FYI

Federal tax rates change frequently, but the procedure stays the same. We will use the tax table given in this chapter for all computations.

Employers are required not only to withhold employees' taxes and then pay them to the Internal Revenue Service, but also to keep records of the names and addresses of persons employed, their **taxable earnings** (the earnings subject to tax) and withholdings, and the amounts and dates of payment. The employer has to submit reports to the Internal Revenue Service quarterly (Form 941) and to the employee annually (W-2 form). With few exceptions, this requirement applies to employers of one or more persons.

The amount of federal income tax withheld from an employee's earnings depends on the amount of her or his total earnings, marital status, and the number of withholding allowances claimed. A **withholding allowance** is an amount of an individual's earnings that is exempt from income taxes (nontaxable). An employee is entitled to one personal allowance for the taxpayer, one for his or her spouse, and one for each dependent. An **exemption** is an amount of an employee's annual earnings not subject to income tax. Each employee has to fill out an **Employee's Withholding Allowance Certificate (Form W-4)**, shown in Figure 2.

The employer retains this form as authorization to withhold money for the employee's federal income tax.

Circular E, Employer's Tax Guide

Objective 2

Determine deductions using tables of employees' income tax withholding.

FYI

Circular E is sometimes referred to as the payroll bible.

Circular E contains withholding tables for federal income, Social Security, and Medicare taxes, along with the rules for depositing these taxes. It is regularly updated to reflect changes in tax laws and withholding rates. It also describes filing requirements for official employer reports. Circular E is provided free of charge by the Internal Revenue Service. Accountants responsible for preparation of payroll registers and forms should be familiar with the contents of Circular E.

The **wage-bracket tax tables** cover monthly, semimonthly, biweekly, weekly, and daily payroll periods. The tables are also subdivided on the basis of marital status. First locate the wage bracket in the first two columns of the table. Next, find the column for the number of allowances claimed and read down this column until you get to the appropriate wage-bracket line. A portion of the weekly federal income tax withholding table for married persons is reproduced in Figure 3 on page 266.

Form **W-4** Department of the Treasury Internal Revenue Service	**Employee's Withholding Allowance Certificate** ▶ For Privacy Act and Paperwork Reduction Act Notice, see page 2.	OMB No. 1545-0010 **20XX**

1 Type or print your first name and middle initial **Matte E.**	Last name **Asino**	2 Your social security number **5 4 3 2 4 1 6 8 0**
Home address (number and street or rural route) **6242 Baxter Drive**	3 ☐ Single ☒ Married ☐ Married, but withhold at higher Single rate. **Note:** *If married, but legally separated, or spouse is a nonresident alien, check the Single box.*	
City or town, state, and ZIP code **Bangor, Maine 04412**	4 If your last name differs from that on your social security card, check here. **You** must call 1-800-772-1213 for a new card . . . ▶ ☐	

5 Total number of allowances you are claiming (from line H above or from the worksheets on page 2 if they apply) . **5** 0

6 Additional amount, if any, you want withheld from each paycheck . . . . **6** $

7 I claim exemption from withholding for 1999, and I certify that I meet **BOTH** of the following conditions for exemption:
- Last year I had a right to a refund of **ALL** Federal income tax withheld because I had **NO** tax liability **AND**
- This year I expect a refund of **ALL** Federal income tax withheld because I expect to have **NO** tax liability.

If you meet both conditions, write "EXEMPT" here . . . . ▶ **7**

Under penalties of perjury, I certify that I am entitled to the number of withholding allowances claimed on this certificate, or I am entitled to claim exempt status.

Employee's signature (Form is not valid unless you sign it) ▶ *Matte E. Asino* **Date** ▶ *October 7, 20–*

8 Employer's name and address (Employer: Complete 8 and 10 only if sending to the IRS)	9 Office code (optional)	10 Employer identification number

FIGURE 2

Assume that Matte E. Asino, who claims zero allowances as of the October 7 payroll, has gross wages of $1,119.16 for the week. As $1,119.16 falls in the $1,110–$1,120 bracket, you can see from the table that $148 should be withheld.

Note the headings of the bracket columns: "At least" and "But less than." A strict interpretation of the $1,110–$1,120 bracket really means $1,110–$1,119.99. Therefore, if Asino's salary were $1,120, it would fall into the $1,120–$1,130 bracket.

Employees' State Income Tax Withholding

Many states that levy state income taxes also furnish employers with withholding tables. Other states use a fixed percentage of the federal income tax withholding as the amount to be withheld for state taxes. In our illustration, we assume that the amount of each employee's state income tax deduction is 20 percent of that employee's federal income tax deduction.

Employees' FICA Tax Withholding (Social Security and Medicare)

The Federal Insurance Contributions Act provides for retirement pensions after a worker reaches age 62, disability benefits for any worker who becomes disabled (and for her or his dependents), and a health insurance program after age 65 (Medicare). Both the employee and the employer have to pay **FICA taxes**, which are commonly referred to as **Social Security taxes** and **Medicare taxes**. The employer withholds FICA taxes from employees' wages and pays them to the U.S. Treasury Department.

FICA tax rates apply to the gross earnings of an employee during the **calendar year** (January 1 through December 31). After an employee has paid

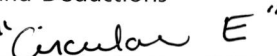 "Circular E"

MARRIED Persons—WEEKLY Payroll Period

If the wages are— At least	But less than	0	1	2	3	4	5	6	7	8	9	10
		The amount of income tax to be withheld is—										
$740	$750	93	85	78	70	62	54	46	39	31	23	15
750	760	95	87	79	71	63	56	48	40	32	25	17
760	770	96	88	81	73	65	57	49	42	34	26	18
770	780	98	90	82	74	66	59	51	43	35	28	20
780	790	99	91	84	76	68	60	52	45	37	29	21
790	800	101	93	85	77	69	62	54	46	38	31	23
800	810	102	94	87	79	71	63	55	48	40	32	24
810	820	104	96	88	80	72	65	57	49	41	34	26
820	830	105	97	90	82	74	66	58	51	43	35	27
830	840	107	99	91	83	75	68	60	52	44	37	29
840	850	108	100	93	85	77	69	61	54	46	38	30
850	860	110	102	94	86	78	71	63	55	47	40	32
860	870	111	103	96	88	80	72	64	57	49	41	33
870	880	113	105	97	89	81	74	66	58	50	43	35
880	890	114	106	99	91	83	75	67	60	52	44	36
890	900	116	108	100	92	84	77	69	61	53	46	38
900	910	118	109	102	94	86	78	70	63	55	47	39
910	920	121	111	103	95	87	80	72	64	56	49	41
920	930	124	112	105	97	89	81	73	66	58	50	42
930	940	126	114	106	98	90	83	75	67	59	52	44
940	950	129	115	108	100	92	84	76	69	61	53	45
950	960	132	117	109	101	93	86	78	70	62	55	47
960	970	135	120	111	103	95	87	79	72	64	56	48
970	980	138	123	112	104	96	89	81	73	65	58	50
980	990	140	126	114	106	98	90	82	75	67	59	51
990	1,000	143	129	115	107	99	92	84	76	68	61	53
1,000	1,010	146	131	117	109	101	93	85	78	70	62	54
1,010	1,020	149	134	120	110	102	95	87	79	71	64	56
1,020	1,030	152	137	122	112	104	96	88	81	73	65	57
1,030	1,040	154	140	125	113	105	98	90	82	74	67	59
1,040	1,050	157	143	128	115	107	99	91	84	76	68	60
1,050	1,060	160	145	131	116	108	101	93	85	77	70	62
1,060	1,070	163	148	134	119	110	102	94	87	79	71	63
1,070	1,080	166	151	136	122	111	104	96	88	80	73	65
1,080	1,090	168	154	139	125	113	105	97	90	82	74	66
1,090	1,100	171	157	142	128	114	107	99	91	83	76	68
1,100	1,110	174	159	145	130	116	108	100	93	85	77	69
1,110	1,120	177	162	148	133	119	110	102	94	86	79	71
1,120	1,130	180	165	150	136	121	111	103	96	88	80	72
1,130	1,140	182	168	153	139	124	113	105	97	89	82	74
1,140	1,150	185	171	156	142	127	114	106	99	91	83	75
1,150	1,160	188	173	159	144	130	116	108	100	92	85	77
1,160	1,170	191	176	162	147	133	118	109	102	94	86	78
1,170	1,180	194	179	164	150	135	121	111	103	95	88	80
1,180	1,190	196	182	167	153	138	124	112	105	97	89	81
1,190	1,200	199	185	170	156	141	126	114	106	98	91	83
1,200	1,210	202	187	173	158	144	129	115	108	100	92	84
1,210	1,220	205	190	176	161	147	132	117	109	101	94	86
1,220	1,230	208	193	178	164	149	135	120	111	103	95	87
1,230	1,240	210	196	181	167	152	138	123	112	104	97	89
1,240	1,250	213	199	184	170	155	140	126	114	106	98	90
1,250	1,260	216	201	187	172	158	143	129	115	107	100	92
1,260	1,270	219	204	190	175	161	146	131	117	109	101	93
1,270	1,280	222	207	192	178	163						
1,280	1,290	224	210	195	181	166						
1,290	1,300	227	213	198	184	169						
1,300	1,310	230	215	201	186	172						
1,310	1,320	233	218	204	189	175						
1,320	1,330	236	221	206	192	177						
1,330	1,340	238	224	209	195	180						
1,340	1,350	241	227	212	198	183						
1,350	1,360	244	229	215	200	186						
1,360	1,370	247	232	218	203	189						
1,370	1,380	250	235	220	206	191						
1,380	1,390	252	238	223	209	194						

$1,390 and over

1 (b) MARRIED person—

If the amount of wages (after subtracting withholding allowances) is: The amount of income tax to withhold is:

Not over $124 . . . . . $0

Over—	But not over—		of excess over—
$124	—$899 . .	15%	—$124
$899	—$1,855 . .	$116.25 plus 28%	—$899
$1,855	—$3,084 . .	$383.93 plus 31%	—$1,855
$3,084	—$5,439 . .	$764.92 plus 36%	—$3,084
$5,439	. . . . . .	$1,612.72 plus 39.6%	—$5,439

Use Table 1(b) for a **MARRIED person**

FIGURE 3

FYI

At one time, Social Security and Medicare were not separated for tax computation, and at a later date there was a $125,000 limit on Medicare taxable earnings. Now all earnings are taxable for Medicare.

Social Security tax on the maximum taxable earnings, the employer stops deducting Social Security tax until the next calendar year begins. Congress has frequently changed the schedule of rates and taxable incomes.

In this text, we assume a Social Security rate of 6.2 percent of the first $68,400 for each employee and a Medicare rate of 1.45 percent of all earnings for each employee. Both tax rates apply to earnings during the calendar year. (Tables for Social Security and Medicare tax withholdings are available in the Internal Revenue Service Circular E, Employer's Tax Guide, also called Publication 15.)

Let's return to Matte E. Asino, who had gross wages of $1,119.16 for the week ending October 7. Suppose that his total accumulated gross wages earned this year prior to this payroll period are $32,890. Asino's total gross wages including this payroll period were $34,009.16 ($32,890 + $1,119.16). Since the Social Security tax applies to the first $68,400 and the Medicare tax applies to all earnings, Asino's earnings are subject to both taxes. For Asino's Social Security tax, multiply $1,119.16 by 6.2 percent ($1,119.16 × .062 = $69.39). For Asino's Medicare tax, multiply $1,119.16 by .0145 = $16.23.

Here's another example. Assume that Sharlet Wilson had cumulative earnings of $70,400 at the beginning of the pay period. During this pay period, she earned $4,000. Since her cumulative earnings are greater than $68,400, she is exempt from the Social Security tax. However, because the Medicare tax applies to all earnings, she is not exempt from the Medicare tax. Her Medicare tax is $58 ($4,000 × .0145).

PAYROLL REGISTER

Objective 3

Complete a payroll register.

The **payroll register** is a multicolumn form prepared for each payroll period listing the earnings, deductions, and net pay for each employee. In Figure 4 (shown on the next page) we see a payroll register that shows the data for each employee on a separate line. This would be suitable for a firm, like Greg Company, that has a small number of employees.

First, we'll show the entire payroll register, then we'll break it down and explain it column by column. The number at the foot of each column refers to the related text description.

The payroll period shown in Figure 4 covers October 1 through October 7. The first part consists of employees' names, hours worked, beginning cumulative earnings, and taxable earnings.

(1) **Total Hours**—Taken from employees' time cards.
(2) **Beginning Cumulative Earnings**—The amount each employee has earned between January 1 and September 30 (the last day of the previous payroll period). It is taken from each employee's individual earnings record. (See Figure 7, pages 274–275.)
(3) **Regular Earnings**—Earnings for hours worked up to and including 40. In other words, the first 40 hours multiplied by each employee's regular hourly rate.
(4) **Overtime Earnings**—Hours in excess of 40 (relative to a 40-hour week) worked by each employee, multiplied by that employee's overtime rate.
(5) **Total Earnings**—Regular earnings plus overtime earnings.
(6) **Ending Cumulative Earnings**—Beginning Cumulative Earnings plus Total Earnings.

| | TOTAL HOURS | BEGINNING CUMULATIVE EARNINGS | EARNINGS | | | ENDING CUMULATIVE EARNINGS | "FUTA" |
NAME			REGULAR	OVERTIME	TOTAL		UNEMPLOYMENT
1 Asino, Matte E.	46	32,890 00	913 60	205 56	1,119 16	34,009 16	
2 Boritsky, Olga	45	6,192 00	619 20	116 10	735 30	6,927 30	735 30
3 Dray, Greg G.	49	6,846 00	684 60	231 05	915 65	7,761 65	154 00
4 Foulkes, Bob L.	40	38,637 00	1,073 25	0 00	1,073 25	39,710 25	
5 Groyer, Milli K.	40	68,000 00	1,888 89	0 00	1,888 89	69,888 89	
6 Kramer, Ada A.	40	68,100 00	1,891 67	0 00	1,891 67	69,991 67	
7 Minkowitz, John L.	55	36,840 00	1,023 33	575 63	1,598 96	38,438 96	
8 Orleons, Janet C.	40	45,783 00	1,271 75	0 00	1,271 75	47,054 75	
9 Pinkovich, Mark S.	44	46,970 00	1,304 72	195 71	1,500 43	48,470 43	
10 Romero, Sheila J.	45	54,978 00	1,527 17	286 34	1,813 51	56,791 51	
11 Tivoli, Jake T.	40	42,078 00	1,168 83	0 00	1,168 83	43,246 83	
12 Wilson, Sharlet D.	52	68,600 00	1,905 56	857 50	2,763 06	71,363 06	
13		515,914 00	15,272 57	2,467 89	17,740 46	533,654 46	889 30
14	(1)	(2)	(3)	(4)	(5)	(6)	(7A)
15							

15,272.57 + 2,467.89 = 17,740.46

515,914.00 + 17,740.46 = 533,654.46

FIGURE 4

(7) **Taxable Earnings**—The amount of earnings subject to taxation, **not the tax itself.** We'll use these columns later to figure the amount of each tax. In other words, **Taxable Earnings is the base on which to figure the tax. Taxable Earnings multiplied by the tax rate equals the amount of the tax.**

(7A) **Unemployment Taxable Earnings**—In our illustration, we are using a maximum of $7,000 for unemployment tax liability on the employer for each employee. This column represents the previously untaxed portion remaining of the $7,000 for the individual employees. **Unemployment tax is paid only by the employer in most states. An unemployment tax may be paid both to the state and to the federal government.** Actually, states may use different maximum earnings and different rates than does the federal government. However, many states use $7,000, which at the time of this writing is the amount used by the federal government. There are three possibilities for Unemployment Taxable Earnings, as follows:

a. **Employee's cumulative earnings including this pay period have not reached $7,000.** When an employee's cumulative earnings so far during the calendar year (since January 1) are less than $7,000, we record the total earnings for the payroll period in the Unemployment Taxable Earnings column. For example, Olga Boritsky's cumulative earnings before this week were $6,192. Olga's cumulative earnings after this week are $6,927.30 ($6,192 + $735.30). Because Olga's cumulative earnings are still less than $7,000, the entire $735.30 in wages earned during this pay period is listed in the Unemployment Taxable Earnings column.

PAYROLL REGISTER FOR WEEK ENDED   October 7, 20—

(7) TAXABLE EARNINGS		(8) DEDUCTIONS						
SOCIAL SECURITY	MEDICARE	FEDERAL INCOME TAX	STATE INCOME TAX	SOCIAL SECURITY TAX	MEDICARE TAX	MEDICAL INSURANCE	OTHER	
1 119 16	1 119 16	177 00	35 40	69 39	16 23	11 19		
735 30	735 30	90 00	18 00	45 59	10 66	11 03	UW	12 00
915 65	915 65	103 00	20 60	56 77	13 28	13 73	UW	15 00
1 073 25	1 073 25	122 00	24 40	66 54	15 56	16 10		
400 00	1 888 89	394 44	78 89	24 80	27 39	28 33		
300 00	1 891 67	395 30	79 06	18 60	27 43	28 38	UW	10 00
1 598 96	1 598 96	312 24	62 45	99 14	23 18	23 98	UW	12 00
1 271 75	1 271 75	222 00	44 40	78 85	18 44	19 08	UW	20 00
1 500 43	1 500 43	284 65	56 93	93 03	21 76	22 51		
1 813 51	1 813 51	372 31	74 46	112 44	26 30	27 20	AR	50 00
1 168 83	1 168 83	176 00	35 20	72 47	16 95	17 53	UW	25 00
	2 763 06	665 43	133 09		40 06	41 44	UW	30 00
11 896 84	17 740 46	3 314 37	662 88	737 62	257 24	260 50	174 00	
(7B)	(7C)	(8A)	(8B)	(8C)	(8D)	(8E)	(8F)	

3,314.37 + 662.88 + 737.62 + 257.24 + 260.50 + 174.00 = 5,406.61

PAGE   68

TOTAL	(9) PAYMENTS		(10) EXPENSE ACCOUNT DEBITED		
	NET AMOUNT	CK. NO.	SALES WAGES EXPENSE	OFFICE WAGES EXPENSE	
3 09 21	8 09 95	931	1 119 16		1
1 87 28	5 48 02	932	735 30		2
2 22 38	6 93 27	933	915 65		3
2 44 60	8 28 65	934		1 073 25	4
5 53 85	1 335 04	935	1 888 89		5
5 58 77	1 332 90	936		1 891 67	6
5 32 99	1 065 97	937	1 598 96		7
4 02 77	8 68 98	938		1 271 75	8
4 78 88	1 021 55	939	1 500 43		9
6 62 71	1 150 80	940	1 813 51		10
3 43 15	8 25 68	941	1 168 83		11
9 10 02	1 853 04	942	2 763 06		12
5 406 61	12 333 85		13 503 79	4 236 67	13
(8G)	(9A)	(9B)	(10A)	(10B)	14

5,406.61 + 12,333.85 = 17,740.46   13,503.79 + 4,236.67 = 17,740.46

FYI

Social Security and Medicare taxes are recorded separately in the payroll register because there is no limit on Medicare as there is on Social Security.

    b. **Employee's cumulative earnings were less than $7,000 before this week and are more than $7,000 after this week.** Look at the line for Greg Dray and notice that his cumulative earnings before this week were $6,846. Dray's new cumulative earnings (ending) are $7,761.65 ($6,846 + $915.65), putting him over the $7,000 maximum. Therefore, to bring Dray up to the $7,000 limit, $154 ($7,000 − $6,846) of his earnings for the week are taxable. After this week, none of Dray's earnings for the remainder of this calendar year will be taxable for unemployment.

    c. **Employee's cumulative earnings before this week were more than $7,000.** After an employee's earnings top $7,000 during the calendar year, record a dash in the Unemployment Taxable Earnings column to indicate that the column has not been forgotten or overlooked. For example, Matte Asino's total earnings before the payroll period ended October 7 (beginning) were $32,890 (as shown in his individual earnings record in Figure 7). Since he had previously earned more than $7,000 this year, we record a dash in the Unemployment Taxable Earnings column.

(7B) **Social Security Taxable Earnings**—The first $68,400 for each employee. We assume a Social Security tax rate of 6.2 percent of the first $68,400 paid to each employee during the calendar year.

    a. **Employee's cumulative earnings including this pay period have not reached $68,400.** When an employee's cumulative earnings so far during the year are less than $68,400, we record the total earnings for the payroll period in the Social Security Taxable Earnings column. For example, Olga Boritsky's cumulative earnings so far this year amount to $6,192. Because Olga's total earnings are less than $68,400, the entire $735.30 of wages earned during this pay period is listed in the Social Security Taxable Earnings column. Note that this is true of all the employees except Sharlet Wilson.

    b. **Employee's cumulative earnings before the week were more than $68,400.** After an employee's earnings top $68,400 during the calendar year, record a dash to indicate that the column has not been forgotten or overlooked. (Use the same procedure as for the Unemployment Taxable Earnings column.) For example, Sharlet Wilson's cumulative earnings before the payroll period ended October 7 were $68,600. Since she had previously earned more than $68,400, we record a dash in the Social Security Taxable Earnings column.

(7C) **Medicare Taxable Earnings**—All earnings for this period. We have assumed a Medicare tax rate of 1.45 percent on all earnings that are paid to each employee during the calendar year. Therefore, all earnings for this period are taxable and are recorded in the Medicare Taxable Earnings column.

(8) **Deductions**—Amounts taken away (withheld) from total earnings.

(8A) **Federal Income Tax Deductions**—The amount of the federal income tax deduction for each employee can be located directly on the wage bracket tables or calculated on a percentage basis as shown.

(8B) **State Income Tax Deductions**—States that impose income taxes also provide wage-bracket tables. The state tax deduction for each employee can be located directly in the appropriate table. As stated previously, we are assuming a rate of 20 percent of the federal income tax.

(8C) **Social Security Tax Deductions**—For each employee's Social Security tax deduction, we first go to the Social Security Taxable Earnings column and note the amount subject to tax. Next, we multiply the Social Security taxable earnings by 6.2 percent. For example, Boritsky's

The United Way is a huge charitable organization that collects and compiles contributions from companies and individuals and allocates funds to various agencies under its umbrella. United Way agencies reach out to all ages as well as providing funding for research on many health issues.

taxable earnings are $735.30, and her Social Security tax deduction is $45.59 ($735.30 × .062).

(8D) **Medicare Tax Deductions**—For each employee's Medicare tax deduction, we go to the Medicare Taxable Earnings column and note the amount subject to tax. Next, we multiply the Medicare taxable earnings by 1.45 percent. For example, Boritsky's taxable earnings are $735.30, and her Medicare tax deduction is $10.66 ($735.30 × .0145).

(8E) **Medical Insurance Deductions**—Premiums paid by the employee through payroll withholding. The amount of the premium for each employee depends on the number of dependents claimed. For example, Boritsky's premium is $11.03 per week.

(8F) **Other Deductions**—Employees' voluntary withholdings. In our illustration, UW represents the United Way, and AR stands for Accounts Receivable (employee pays charge account to the company). For example, Sheila Romero paid $50 on her charge account.

(8G) **Total Deductions**—The combined total of each employee's deductions for taxes, insurance, and other. For example, Boritsky's total deduction is $187.28 ($90.00 + $18.00 + $45.59 + $10.66 + $11.03 + $12.00).

(9) **Payments**—The amount of each employee's payroll check (take-home pay).

(9A) **Net Amount**—Each employee's Total Earnings minus Total Deductions. For example, Boritsky's net amount is $548.02 ($735.30 − $187.28).

(9B) **Ck. No.**—The number of each employee's payroll check.

(10) **Expense Account Debited**—Columns used for distributing each amount into the appropriate wages expense account. Greg Company uses Sales Wages Expense and Office Wages Expense. The sum of these two columns equals the total earnings.

(10A) **Sales Wages Expense**—Amounts earned by employees involved in sales activities.

(10B) **Office Wages Expense**—Amounts earned by employees involved in office activities.

THE PAYROLL ENTRY

Because the payroll register summarizes the payroll data for the period, it is used as the basis for recording the payroll in the ledger accounts. Since the payroll register does not have the status of a journal, a journal entry is necessary. Figure 5 shows the entry in general journal form.

FIGURE 5

			GENERAL JOURNAL												PAGE __31__	
	DATE		DESCRIPTION	POST. REF.	DEBIT					CREDIT							
1	20–																1
2	Oct.	7	Sales Wages Expense		13	5	0	3	79								2
3			Office Wages Expense			4	2	3	6	67							3
4			Employees' Federal Income														4
5			Tax Payable							3	3	1	4	37			5
6			FICA Tax Payable								9	9	4	86			6
7			Employees' State Income Tax														7
8			Payable								6	6	2	88			8
9			Employees' Medical Insurance														9
10			Payable								2	6	0	50			10
11			Employees' United Way														11
12			Payable								1	2	4	00			12
13			Accounts Receivable									5	0	00			13
14			Wages Payable							12	3	3	3	85			14
15			Payroll register, page 68,														15
16			for week ended October 7.														16

■ ■ ■

Remember!

The totals from the payroll register are the amounts used in the payroll entry.

Note that the accountant records the total cost to the company for services of employees as debits to the Wages Expense accounts.

Also note that the total Social Security tax deductions ($737.62) and the total Medicare tax deductions ($257.24) are combined to become FICA Tax Payable of $994.86 ($737.62 + $257.24). The two tax deductions are combined into the one liability account because they are paid together at the same time. Social Security and Medicare taxes are recorded separately in the payroll register because they must be listed separately on each employee's W-2 form (Wage and Tax Statement).

To pay the employees from the company's regular checking account, the accountant now makes the following journal entry:

■ ■ ■

Remember!

The amount shown as Wages Payable is the employees' take-home pay.

17		8	Wages Payable		12	3	3	3	85								17
18			Cash—M. Asino								8	0	9	95			18
19			Cash—O. Boritsky								5	4	8	02			19
20			Cash—G. Dray								6	9	3	27			20
21			Cash—B. Foulkes								8	2	8	65			21
22			Cash—M. Groyer							1	3	3	5	04			22
23			Cash—A. Kramer							1	3	3	2	90			23
24			Cash—J. Minkowitz							1	0	6	5	97			24
25			Cash—J. Orleons								8	6	8	98			25
26			Cash—M. Pinkovich							1	0	2	1	55			26
27			Cash—S. Romero							1	1	5	0	80			27
28			Cash—J. Tivoli								8	2	5	68			28
29			Cash—S. Wilson							1	8	5	3	04			29

Special Payroll Bank Account—An Alternative

FYI

A company with a small number of employees would probably use its regular bank account to issue a check to each employee.

A firm with a large number of employees would probably open a special **payroll bank account** with its bank. One check drawn on the regular bank account is made payable to the special payroll account for the amount of the total net pay for a payroll period. All payroll checks for the period are then written on the special payroll account. To record this, the accountant makes the following journal entry. In this book, assume the entry to debit Cash—Payroll Bank Account and to credit Cash has already been made.

FYI

With the use of the special payroll bank account, if employees delay cashing their paychecks, then the checks do not have to be listed on the bank reconciliation of the firm's regular bank account. Balances of Employees' Medical Insurance Payable, Employees' United Way Payable, and other employee deductions are paid out of the firm's regular bank account.

GENERAL JOURNAL   PAGE __1__

	DATE	DESCRIPTION	POST. REF.	DEBIT	CREDIT	
17	8	Wages Payable		12 3 3 3 85		17
18		Cash—Payroll Bank Account			12 3 3 3 85	18
19		Paid wages for week				19
20		ended October 7.				20
21						21
22						22
23						23
24						24
25						25
26						26

Paycheck

All the data needed to make out a payroll check are available in the payroll register. Matte E. Asino's paycheck is shown in Figure 6.

FIGURE 6

EMPLOYEE	TOTAL HOURS	O.T. HOURS	REG. PAY	O.T. PREM. PAY	GROSS PAY	FED INC. TAX	STATE INC. TAX	SOCIAL SECURITY TAX	MEDICARE TAX	MEDICAL INSURANCE	OTHER	TOTAL DED.	NET PAY
Matte E. Asino	46	6	913.60	205.56	1119.16	177.00	35.40	69.39	16.23	11.19	—	309.21	809.95

CENTRAL NATIONAL BANK   98-461 / 252

Payroll Account

Greg Company
610 First Avenue
Bangor, Maine 04412

October 8 20 __ No. 931

PAY TO THE ORDER OF   *Matte E. Asino* $ *809.95*

Eight hundred nine and 95/100 _____ DOLLARS

Ella D. Greg

⑆252⑈0461⑆

EMPLOYEE'S INDIVIDUAL EARNINGS RECORD

NAME **Matte E. Asino**
ADDRESS **6242 Baxter Drive**
Bangor, Maine 04412

EMPLOYEE NO. **5**
SOC. SEC. NO. **543-24-1680**
PAY RATE **$22.84**
EQUIVALENT HOURLY RATE **$22.84**

MALE **X** FEMALE _____
MARRIED **X** SINGLE _____
PHONE NO. **663-2556** DATE OF BIRTH **9/19/72**

DATE TERMINATED _____
CLASSIFICATION FOR WORKERS' COMPENSATION INSURANCE **Sales floor**

	PERIOD ENDED	DATE PAID	HOURS WORKED REG	HOURS WORKED O.T.	EARNINGS REGULAR	EARNINGS OVERTIME	EARNINGS TOTAL	ENDING CUMULATIVE EARNINGS	FEDERAL INCOME TAX	STATE INCOME TAX
40	9/3	9/4	40	8	913 60	274 08	1187 68	28721 70	167 00	33 40
41	9/10	9/11	40	2	913 60	68 52	982 12	29703 82	114 00	22 80
42	9/17	9/18	40	2	913 60	68 52	982 12	30685 94	114 00	22 80
43	9/24	9/25	40	5	913 60	171 30	1084 90	31770 84	139 00	27 80
44	9/30	10/1	40	6	913 60	205 56	1119 16	32890 00	148 00	29 60
45	10/7	10/8	40	6	913 60	205 56	1119 16	34009 16	177 00	35 40

FIGURE 7

Employees' Individual Earnings Records

Objective 5

Maintain employees' individual earnings records.

To comply with government regulations, a firm has to keep current data on each employee's accumulated earnings, deductions, and net pay. The information contained in the payroll register is recorded each payday in each **employee's individual earnings record**. Figure 7 shows a portion of the earnings record for Matte E. Asino.

CHAPTER REVIEW

Review of Performance Objectives

1. Calculate total earnings based on an hourly, piece-rate, or commission basis.

   Earnings calculated on an *hourly basis* equal the hourly rate multiplied by the number of hours worked. Earnings calculated on a *piece-rate basis* equal the total number of products produced multiplied by the rate per unit of product. Earnings calculated on a *commission basis* equal the total number of units sold or the price of units sold multiplied by the commission rate.

2. Determine deductions using tables of employees' income tax withholding.

   Using the appropriate income tax withholding table in IRS Circular E, first determine marital status and payroll period and then locate the wage bracket containing the amount of earnings. Next, on the same horizontal line, select the vertical column containing the number of allowances claimed.

3. Complete a payroll register.

   List the employees' names, hours worked, and beginning cumulative earnings. Add the total earnings to the beginning cumulative earnings to get ending cumulative earnings. The Unemployment Taxable Earnings column is used for the first $7,000 of each employee's earnings for FUTA and SUTA. The Social Security Taxable Earnings column is used for an assumed first $68,400. The Medicare Taxable Earnings column is used for all earnings. Under the Deductions columns, list the

DATE EMPLOYED __2/1/—__

NO. OF EXEMPTIONS __2__

PER HOUR ___X___   PER DAY _____

PER WEEK _____   PER MONTH _____

	DEDUCTIONS							PAID		
	SOCIAL SECURITY TAX	MEDICARE TAX	MEDICAL INSURANCE	CODE	OTHER AMOUNT		TOTAL	NET AMOUNT	CK. NO.	
	73 64	17 22	11 19	UW		5 00	307 45	880 23	877	
	60 89	14 24	11 19	UW			223 12	759 00	889	
	60 89	14 24	11 19	UW		5 00	228 12	754 00	901	
	67 26	15 73	11 19	UW			260 98	823 92	913	
	69 39	16 23	11 19	UW		5 00	279 41	839 75	925	
	69 39	16 23	11 19	UW			309 21	809 95	931	

income taxes withheld, the Social Security taxes withheld, the Medicare taxes withheld, and other deductions. The Social Security tax deduction equals the Social Security taxable earnings multiplied by an assumed rate of 6.2 percent. The Medicare tax deduction equals the Medicare taxable earnings multiplied by an assumed rate of 1.45 percent. Net amount equals total (gross) earnings minus total deductions. The Expense Account Debited columns are used to distribute salary and wages expense to the appropriate accounts.

4. Journalize the payroll entry from a payroll register.

Totals are taken directly from the payroll register. For the following entry, assume that one check is made payable to a special payroll bank account. The entry to transfer the cash to the payroll bank account is not shown here.

GENERAL JOURNAL   PAGE __31__

	DATE		DESCRIPTION	POST. REF.	DEBIT	CREDIT	
1	20–						1
2	Oct.	7	Sales Wages Expense		13 50 3 79		2
3			Office Wages Expense		4 23 6 67		3
4			Employees' Federal Income				4
5			Tax Payable			3 31 4 37	5
6			FICA Tax Payable			9 94 86	6
7			Employees' State Income Tax				7
8			Payable			6 62 88	8
9			Employees' Medical Insurance				9
10			Payable			2 60 50	10
11			Employees' United Way				11
12			Payable			1 24 00	12
13			Accounts Receivable			5 00	13
14			Wages Payable			12 33 3 85	14
15			Payroll register, page 68,				15
16			for week ended October 7.				16

The following entry is used to pay the employees:

18	8	Wages Payable	12 3 3 3 85		18
19		Cash		12 3 3 3 85	19
20		Paid wages for week			20
21		ended October 7.			21
22					22
23					23
24					24

5. Maintain employees' individual earnings records.

In the employees' individual earnings records, list the personal data for each employee. Based on the information contained in the payroll register, record the earnings and deductions for each payroll period.

Glossary

Calendar year A twelve-month period beginning on January 1 and ending on December 31 of the same year. (265)

Employee One who works for compensation under the direction and control of the employer. (261)

Employee's individual earnings record A supplementary record for each employee showing personal payroll data and yearly cumulative earnings, deductions, and net pay. (274)

Employee's Withholding Allowance Certificate (Form W-4) A form that specifies the number of allowances claimed by each employee and gives the employer the authority to withhold money for an employee's federal income taxes and FICA taxes. (264)

Exemption An amount of an employee's annual earnings not subject to income tax for the taxpayer, taxpayer's spouse, and dependents (usually children). (264)

FICA taxes Social Security taxes plus Medicare taxes, paid by both employee and employer under the provisions of the Federal Insurance Contributions Act. The proceeds are used to pay old-age and disability pensions and to fund the Medicare program. (265)

Gross pay The total amount of an employee's pay before any deductions. (260)

Independent contractor Someone who is engaged for a definite job or service, and who may choose her or his own means of doing the work. This person is not an employee of the firm for which the service is provided. (261)

Medicare taxes Federal government taxes levied on employees and employers; proceeds are used for medical insurance for eligible people age 65 or over. (265)

Net pay Gross pay minus deductions. Also called *take-home pay*. (260)

Payroll bank account A special checking account used to pay a company's employees. (273)

Payroll register A multicolumn form prepared for each payroll period listing the earnings, deductions, and net pay for each employee. (267)

Social Security taxes Federal government taxes levied on employees and employers; proceeds are used for old-age pensions and disability benefits. (265)

Taxable earnings The amount of an employee's earnings subject to a tax. (264)

Wage-bracket tax tables A chart providing the amounts to be deducted for income taxes based on amount of earnings, marital status, and number of allowances claimed. (264)

Withholding allowance An amount of an employee's annual earnings not subject to income tax. (264)

QUESTIONS, EXERCISES, AND PROBLEMS

Discussion Questions

1. What is the purpose of the employee's individual earnings record, and how is it related to the payroll register?
2. What is the purpose of the payroll register?
3. What information is included in an employee's individual earnings record?
4. Explain how gross earnings differ from net earnings for a payroll period.
5. Describe how a special payroll bank account is useful in paying the wages and salaries of employees.
6. List three required deductions and four voluntary deductions from an employee's total earnings.
7. What is the difference between an employee and an independent contractor? List three examples of an independent contractor.
8. What information is included in a wage-bracket withholding table? Are there overlapping amounts of gross earnings in the table?

Exercises

P.O. 1

Calculate gross pay.

Exercise 8-1 Determine the gross pay for each employee listed below.

a. Gary Dillon is paid time-and-a-half for all hours over forty. He worked forty-five hours during the week. His regular pay rate is $10.40 per hour.
b. Mai Do worked fifty-two hours during the week. She is entitled to time-and-a-half for all hours in excess of forty per week. Her regular pay rate is $12.30 per hour.
c. Latisha Morgan is paid a commission of 9 percent of her sales, which amounted to $10,474.
d. May Belski's yearly salary is $40,400. During the week, Belski worked forty-two hours, and she is entitled to time-and-a-half for all hours over forty.

P.O. 1,2

Determine gross pay and withholding.

Exercise 8-2 Lester Ramirez works for Pell Company, which pays its employees time-and-a-half for all hours worked in excess of forty per week. Ramirez's pay rate is $15.50 per hour. His wages are subject to federal income tax, a Social Security tax deduction at the rate of 6.2 percent, and a Medicare tax deduction at the rate of 1.45 percent. He is married and claims three allowances. Ramirez has a half-hour lunch break during an eight-and-one-half-hour day. He is paid for hours between 8 and 4:30 and overtime for increments greater that 30 minutes on a given day. Ramirez's beginning cumulative earnings are $36,722.

Complete the following using Ramirez's time card shown below:

a. ___40___ hours at straight time × $15.50 per hour — $ _620_

b. ___10___ hours overtime × $_23.25_ per hour — _232.50_

c. Total gross pay — $_852.50_

d. Federal income tax withholding (from tax tables in Figure 3, page 266) — $ _86_

e. Social Security tax withholding at 6.2 percent — _52.86_

f. Medicare tax withholding at 1.45 percent — _12.36_

g. Total withholding — _151.22_

h. Net pay — $_701.28_

TIME CARD

Name: Ramirez, Lester

Week ending: March 11, 20—

Day	In	Out	In	Out	Regular	Overtime
M	756	1209	1239	432	8	
T	752	1205	1235	504	8	½
W	759	1220	1240	503	8	½
T	800	1208	1238	434	8	
F	756	1209	1239	633	8	2
S	800	1201	1240	340		7
S						

Hours Worked

FIGURE 8

NAME	BEGINNING CUMULATIVE EARNINGS	EARNINGS			ENDING CUMULATIVE EARNINGS	TAXABLE EARNINGS		
		REGULAR	OVERTIME	TOTAL		UNEMPLOYMENT	SOCIAL SECURITY	MEDICARE
	245 7 5 4 00	6 7 2 4 00	1 2 2 0 00	7 4 9 4 00	253 2 4 8 00	2 4 5 6 00	7 9 4 4 00	7 9 4 4

P.O. 2,3

Determine net pay.

Exercise 8-3 Using the income tax withholding table in Figure 3, page 266, for each employee of Tri-State Company, determine the net pay for the week ended January 21. Assume a Social Security tax of 6.2 percent and a Medicare tax of 1.45 percent. All employees have cumulative earnings of less than $68,400. Assume all employees are married.

Employee	Allowances	Total Earnings	Social Security Tax Withheld	Medicare Tax Withheld	Federal Income Tax Withheld	Union Dues Withheld	Medical Insurance Withheld	Net Pay
a. Alster, C. A.	1	$ 880	$ 54.56	$ 12.76	$ 106.	$ 25	$ 30	$ 651.68
b. Drake, R. N.	2	820	50.84	11.89	90.	25	26	616.27
c. Finn, T. C.	3	1,010	62.62	14.65	110.	—	30	792.73
d. Handy, L. O.	0	1,075	66.65	15.59	166	25	30	771.76
e. Nguyen, M. E.	2	930	57.66	13.49	106	25	30	697.85
Totals		$4,715	$292.33	$ 68.38	$ 578.	$100	$146	$3530.29

P.O. 3

Locate errors in a payroll register.

Exercise 8-4 For the week ended September 7, the totals of the payroll register for Brennan, Inc., are presented in Figure 8. The regular and overtime earnings are correct. List six errors that exist. All earnings are subject to Social Security and Medicare taxes.

P.O. 3

Determine taxable earnings.

Exercise 8-5 For tax purposes, assume that the maximum taxable earnings are $68,400 for Social Security and $7,000 for the unemployment tax, and that all earnings are taxable for Medicare. For the payroll register for the month of November in Figure 9 (page 280), determine the taxable earnings for each employee.

	DEDUCTIONS					PAYMENTS		WAGES EXPENSE
FEDERAL INCOME TAX	SOCIAL SECURITY TAX	MEDICARE TAX	UNION DUES	MEDICAL INSURANCE	TOTAL	NET AMOUNT	CK. NO.	DEBIT
9 4 9 00	4 2 9 53	1 1 5 19	1 9 3 00	2 9 2 00	2 0 8 3 00	5 4 5 6 00		7 4 9 4 00

EMPLOYEE	BEGINNING CUMULATIVE EARNINGS	TOTAL EARNINGS	ENDING CUMULATIVE EARNINGS	TAXABLE EARNINGS UNEMPLOYMENT	SOCIAL SECURITY	MEDICARE
Alston, J.	63 1 7 3 00	4 7 6 7 00	67 9 4 0 00			
Ely, B.	33 2 1 9 00	3 8 3 0 00	37 0 4 9 00			
Glenn, C.	30 5 5 0 00	2 7 3 0 00	33 2 8 0 00			
Johns, A.	3 7 5 1 00	1 4 6 3 00	5 2 1 4 00			
Newkirk, J.	5 4 3 6 00	1 2 8 4 00	6 7 2 0 00			

FIGURE 9

P.O. 3,4

Determine FICA withholdings and journalize payroll entry.

Exercise 8-6 On January 21, the column totals of the payroll register for Kraal Company showed that its sales employees had earned $14,280, its driver employees had earned $9,340, and its office employees had earned $7,484. Social Security taxes were withheld at an assumed rate of 6.2 percent, and Medicare taxes were withheld at an assumed rate of 1.45 percent. Other deductions consisted of federal income tax, $3,732; medical insurance, $1,561; union dues, $486. Determine the amount of Social Security and Medicare taxes withheld, and record the general journal entry for the payroll, crediting Salaries Payable for the net pay. All earnings were taxable.

P.O. 1,2

Determine missing amounts.

Exercise 8-7 Lien Labs has two employees. The information shown below was taken from their individual earnings records for the month of September. Determine the missing amounts, assuming that the Social Security tax is 6.2 percent and the Medicare tax is 1.45 percent. All earnings are subject to Social Security and Medicare taxes. Round amounts to nearest dollar.

	Bandor	Ringness	Total
Regular earnings	$1,600	$?	$?
Overtime earnings	?	105	?
Total earnings	$1,740	$?	$?
Federal income tax withheld	$ 330	$?	$?
State income tax withheld	?	85	?
Social Security tax withheld	108	92	?
Medicare tax withheld	25	22	?
Medical insurance withheld	104	98	?
Total deductions	$ 679	$ 476	$?
Net pay	$?	$1,009	$?

P.O. 4

Journalize the payroll entry.

Exercise 8-8 Assume that the employees in Exercise 8-7 are paid from the company's regular bank account (check numbers 931 and 932). Record the payroll entry in general journal form, dated September 30.

CONSIDER AND COMMUNICATE

Nguyen Company pays its employees weekly by issuing checks on its regular bank account. The owner thinks it would be too much trouble to have a second checking account. Respond to the owner's concern.

WHAT IF . . .

You have just completed the payroll register for this week's payroll. You have crossfooted the register—that is, you have added the columns vertically and horizontally. There is just one problem: The total of the Net Amount column does not equal the total of the Gross Amount column minus the total of the Total Deductions column. How could this happen? What would you do to obtain correctly crossfooted totals?

A MATTER OF ETHICS

An employee who is married and has two children submits a W-4 form to his employer indicating that he is single and claims zero deductions. Is this action ethical, unethical, or illegal? Explain your reasoning.

WEB WORK

Using an Internet web browser, type in the search box the phrase *payroll accounting* for the home pages of firms that specialize in payroll services. Search for information about payroll services. Discuss your findings in a small group. Write a one-page recommendation to the owner of a business.

PROBLEM SET A

For additional help, see the demonstration problem at the beginning of each chapter in your Working Papers.

P.O. 1,2

Problem 8-1A Vadim Barsk, an employee of Myer Company, worked forty-six hours during the week of February 9 through 15. His rate of pay is $15.50 per hour, and he gets time-and-a-half for work in excess of forty hours per week. He is married and claims one allowance on his W-4 form. His wages are subject to the following deductions:

a. Federal income tax (use the table in Figure 3, page 266).
b. Social Security tax at 6.2 percent.
c. Medicare tax at 1.45 percent.
d. Union dues, $10.00.
e. Medical insurance, $12.00.

Check Figure

Net pay, $592.40

Instructions

Compute his regular pay, overtime pay, gross pay, and net pay.

P.O. 1,3,4

Problem 8-2A Rutger Homes has the following payroll information for the week ended February 21:

Name	Earnings at End of Previous Week	Daily Time							Pay Rate	Federal Income Tax
		S	M	T	W	T	F	S		
Ager, A. C.	1,920.00	8	8	8	8	8			10.65	30.00
Bell, D. R.	2,030.00			8	8	8	8	8	10.50	37.00
Cole, H. A.	2,064.00	8	8	8			8	8	10.95	39.00
Field, P. N.	628.00				8	8			20.00	15.00
Gray, L. B.	2,597.00	8	8	8			8	8	10.90	47.00
Harris, G. W.	2,075.00	8	8		8	8	8	8	10.00	27.00

Taxable earnings for Social Security are based on the first $68,400. Taxable earnings for Medicare are based on all earnings. Taxable earnings for federal and state unemployment are based on the first $7,000. Employees are paid time-and-a-half for work in excess of forty hours per week.

Check Figure

Net Amount, $2,169.16

Instructions

1. Complete the payroll register, page 37. The Social Security tax rate is 6.2 percent, and the Medicare tax rate is 1.45 percent.
2. Prepare a general journal entry to record the payroll. The firm's general ledger contains a Wages Expense account and a Wages Payable account.
3. Assuming that the firm transfers funds from its regular bank account to its special payroll bank account, and that that entry has been made, prepare a general journal entry to record the payment of wages. Begin payroll checks with no. 206.

P.O. 1,2,3,4

Problem 8-3A The Toler Company pays its employees time-and-a-half for hours worked in excess of forty per week. The information available from time cards and employees' individual earnings records for the pay period ended October 14 is shown in the chart at the top of page 283.

Taxable earnings for Social Security are based on the first $68,400. Taxable earnings for Medicare are based on all earnings. Taxable earnings for federal and state unemployment are based on the first $7,000.

Name	Earnings at End of Previous Week	Daily Time						Pay Rate	Income Tax Allowances
		M	T	W	T	F	S		
Baxter, J. C.	42,827.00	8	8	8	8	8	0	19.30	2
Choy, A. K.	43,539.00	8	8	8	8	10	8	19.60	1
Dray, W. L.	43,225.00	8	8	10	8	8	0	19.50	1
Gary, S. P.	49,831.00	8	8	8	8	8	0	20.00	3
Nye, M. B.	44,985.00	8	8	8	8	8	4	19.40	3
Otis, N. B.	41,131.00	8	8	8	8	8	0	19.00	1
Rega, J. B.	6,529.00	8	8	8	8	8	4	18.50	1
Sange, P. W.	43,013.00	8	8	8	8	8	4	19.25	2

Check Figure

Net Amount, $5,559.28

Instructions

1. Complete the payroll register, page 72, using the wage-bracket income tax withholding table in Figure 3 (page 266). The Social Security tax rate is 6.2 percent, and the Medicare tax rate is 1.45 percent. Assume that all employees are married.
2. Prepare a general journal entry to record the payroll. The firm's general ledger contains a Wages Expense account and a Wages Payable account.
3. Assuming that the firm has transferred funds from its regular bank account to its special payroll bank account, and that this entry has been made, prepare a general journal entry to record the payment of wages. In the payroll register, begin payroll checks with number 942.

P.O. 3,4

Problem 8-4A The information for the Saranga Company, shown in the chart at the top of page 284, is available from Saranga's time cards and the employees' individual earnings records for the pay period ended December 22.

Taxable earnings for Social Security are based on the first $68,400. Taxable earnings for Medicare are based on all earnings. Taxable earnings for federal and state unemployment are based on the first $7,000.

Check Figure

Net Amount, $6,953.41

Instructions

1. Complete the payroll register, page 56, using a Social Security tax rate of 6.2 percent and a Medicare tax rate of 1.45 percent. (The total of Social Security tax deduction and Medicare tax deduction for D. C. Lang is $62.63. Check this figure.) Concerning Other Deductions, AR refers to Accounts Receivable and UW refers to United Way. Begin payroll checks in the payroll register with number 971.
2. Prepare the general journal entry to record the payroll.

Name	Hours Worked	Earnings at End of Previous Week	Total Earnings	Class.	Federal Income Tax	Other Deduct.	
Coy, C. E.	44	32,950	750	Sales	79.00	UW	16.50
Dara, V. A.	40	37,410	850	Sales	102.00	AR	80.00
Farr, J. P.	40	36,860	838	Sales	99.00	UW	16.50
Gant, N. D.	44	32,490	735	Office	85.00	UW	15.00
Jong, J. W.	48	36,980	840	Office	108.00	UW	16.00
Lang, D. C.	40	67,750	1,540	Office	295.00	UW	12.00
Mory, R. G.	40	36,860	836	Sales	91.00	AR	54.00
Nge, P. M.	40	36,750	830	Sales	107.00	UW	16.00
Orr, T. B.	44	33,480	760	Sales	96.00	UW	16.50
Tye, K. C.	42	47,000	1,070	Sales	136.00	UW	18.00

3. Prepare the general journal entry to pay the payroll. Assume that funds for this payroll have been transferred to Cash—Payroll Bank Account and that this entry has been made.

PROBLEM SET B

For additional help, see the demonstration problem at the beginning of each chapter in your Working Papers.

P.O. 1,2

Problem 8-1B Inez Parr, an employee of Kellen Company, worked forty-four hours during the week of October 11 through 17. Her rate of pay is $17.50 per hour, and she receives time-and-a-half for all work in excess of forty hours per week. Parr is married and claims two allowances on her W-4 form. Her wages are subject to the following deductions:

a. Federal income tax (use the table in Figure 3, page 266).
b. Social Security tax at 6.2 percent.
c. Medicare tax at 1.45 percent.
d. Union dues, $15.25.
e. Medical insurance, $34.75.

Check Figure

Net pay, $606.42

Instructions

Compute her regular pay, overtime pay, gross pay, and net pay.

P.O. 1,3,4

Problem 8-2B Hagen Company has the following payroll information for the pay period ended May 14:

| Name | Earnings at End of Previous Week | Daily Time | | | | | | Pay Rate | Federal Income Tax |
		M	T	W	T	F	S		
Gilam, N. C.	7,455.00	8	8	8	8	8	0	8.80	27.00
Hardt, A. L.	6,513.00	8	8	8	8	8	0	8.50	33.00
Loren, D. R.	6,843.00	0	8	8	8	8	8	8.60	25.00
Ngo, N. A.	9,536.00	8	8	8	0	8	8	9.80	41.00
Sorley, B. M.	6,632.00	8	8	8	8	8	8	8.90	36.00
Unger, P. R.	7,467.00	0	8	8	8	8	8	9.20	21.00

Taxable earnings for Social Security are based on the first $68,400. Taxable earnings for Medicare are based on all earnings. Taxable earnings for federal and state unemployment are based on the first $7,000. Employees are paid time-and-a-half for work in excess of forty hours per week.

Check Figure

Net Amount, $1,903.01

Instructions

1. Complete the payroll register, page 34. The Social Security tax rate is 6.2 percent, and the Medicare tax rate is 1.45 percent.
2. Prepare a general journal entry to record the payroll.
3. Assuming that the firm has transferred funds from its regular bank account to its special payroll bank account, and that this entry has been made, prepare a journal entry to record the payment of wages. Begin payroll checks with No. 744.

P.O. 1,2,3,4

Problem 8-3B The Sorelle Company pays its employees time-and-a-half for hours worked in excess of forty per week. The information in the chart at the top of page 286 is available from time cards and employees' individual earnings records for the pay period ended September 21.

Taxable earnings for Social Security are based on the first $68,400. Taxable earnings for Medicare are based on all earnings. Taxable earnings for federal and state unemployment are based on the first $7,000.

Check Figure

Net Amount, $5,740.49

Instructions

1. Complete the payroll register, page 72, using the wage-bracket income tax withholding table in Figure 3 (page 266). The Social Security tax rate is 6.2 percent, and the Medicare tax rate is 1.45 percent. Assume that all employees are married.

Name	Earnings at End of Previous Week	Daily Time						Pay Rate	Income Tax Allowances
		M	**T**	**W**	**T**	**F**	**S**		
Brit, A. C.	6,565.00	8	8	8	10	8	0	17.50	1
Dorn, B. N.	35,338.00	8	8	8	8	8	0	23.25	2
Gorst, A. J.	33,250.00	8	10	8	8	8	0	22.00	2
Ingle, D. G.	36,224.00	8	8	8	8	8	4	24.00	3
Jeon, H. O.	34,655.00	8	8	8	8	8	0	23.00	0
Lemer, J. E.	28,827.00	8	8	9	8	8	0	18.50	2
Orse, D. W.	6,843.00	8	8	8	9	9	4	18.70	1
Worfe, W. L.	26,386.00	8	8	10	8	8	0	18.30	1

2. Prepare a general journal entry to record the payroll. The firm's general ledger contains a Wages Expense account and a Wages Payable account.
3. Assuming that the firm has transferred funds from its regular bank account to its special payroll bank account, and that this entry has been made, prepare a general journal entry to record the payment of wages. In the payroll register, begin payroll checks with Ck. No. 863.

PO 3,4

Problem 8-4B For the Saranga Company, the information in the chart on the following page is available from the time books and employees' individual earnings records for the pay period ended December 29.

Taxable earnings for Social Security are based on the first $68,400. Taxable earnings for Medicare are based on all earnings. Taxable earnings for federal and state unemployment are based on the first $7,000.

Check Figure

Net Amount, $7,183.23

Instructions

1. Complete the payroll register, page 56, using a Social Security tax rate of 6.2 percent and a Medicare tax rate of 1.45 percent. (The total of Social Security tax deduction and Medicare tax deduction for D. C. Lang is $22.33. Check this figure.) Concerning Other Deductions, AR refers to Accounts Receivable, and UW refers to United Way. Begin payroll checks in the payroll register with check no. 914.
2. Prepare the general journal entry to record the payroll.
3. Prepare the general journal entry to pay the payroll. Assume that funds for this payroll have been transferred to Cash—Payroll Bank Account and that this entry has been made.

Name	Hours Worked	Earnings at End of Previous Week	Total Earnings	Class.	Federal Income Tax	Other Deduct.	
Coy, C. E.	44	33,700	750.00	Sales	79.00	AR	75.00
Dara, V. A.	42	38,260	910.00	Sales	111.00	UW	16.50
Farr, J. P.	40	37,698	838.00	Sales	99.00	UW	16.50
Gant, N. D.	44	33,225	735.00	Office	85.00		
Jong, J. W.	48	37,820	840.00	Office	108.00	UW	16.00
Lang, D. C.	40	69,290	1,540.00	Office	295.00	UW	12.00
Mory, R. G.	43	37,696	926.00	Sales	105.00	UW	16.00
Nge, P. M.	40	37,580	830.00	Sales	107.00		
Orr, T. B.	44	34,240	760.00	Sales	96.00	AR	16.50
Tye, K. C.	42	48,070	1,070.00	Sales	136.00	UW	18.00

9 Employer Taxes, Payments, and Reports

Performance Objectives

After you have completed this chapter, you will be able to do the following:

1. Calculate the amount of payroll tax expense and journalize the related entry.

2. Journalize the entry for the deposit of employees' federal income taxes withheld and FICA taxes (both employees' withheld and employer's matching share) and prepare the deposit coupon.

3. Journalize the entries for the payment of employer's state and federal unemployment taxes.

4. Journalize the entry for the deposit of employees' state income taxes withheld.

5. Complete Employer's Quarterly Federal Tax Return, Form 941.

6. Prepare W-2 and W-3 forms and Form 940.

7. Calculate the premium for workers' compensation insurance, and prepare the entry for payment in advance.

8. Determine the amount of the end-of-the-year adjustments for (a) workers' compensation insurance and (b) accrued salaries and wages, and record the adjustments.

W e have talked about computing and recording such payroll data as gross pay, employees' income tax withheld, employees' FICA tax withheld, and various deductions requested by employees. Now we will pay these withholding liabilities and the taxes levied on the employer based on the total payroll.

EMPLOYER IDENTIFICATION NUMBER

Everyone who works must have a Social Security number, a vital part of federal income tax returns. An employer's counterpart to the Social Security number is the **employer identification number** assigned by the Internal Revenue Service. Employers of one or more persons are required to have such a number, and it must be listed on all reports and payments of employees' federal income tax withholding and FICA taxes.

EMPLOYER'S PAYROLL TAXES

An employer's payroll taxes are based on the gross wages paid to employees. Payroll taxes—like property taxes—are an expense of doing business. Greg Company records these taxes in the **Payroll Tax Expense** account and debits the account for the company's portion of FICA taxes and for state and federal unemployment taxes. In T account form, Payroll Tax Expense for Greg Company would look like the following example.

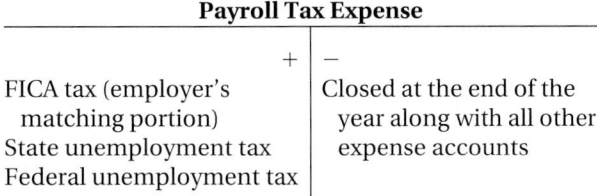

Payroll Tax Expense

+	−
FICA tax (employer's matching portion)	Closed at the end of the year along with all other expense accounts
State unemployment tax	
Federal unemployment tax	

As you can see, **FICA tax (employer's share), state unemployment tax, and federal unemployment tax are included under the umbrella of Payroll Tax Expense.** In most states, the unemployment taxes are levied on the employer only.

Employer's Matching Portion of FICA Tax (Social Security Plus Medicare)

FICA tax is imposed equally on both employer and employee. After the firm's accountant deducts the employee's share from gross wages and records it in the payroll entry under FICA Tax Payable, he or she then determines the

The skyrocketing costs of Medicare have caused Congress to try to make sweeping reforms. The issues are far-reaching, however, because Medicare affects such a large percentage of the population—who fear their benefits may be reduced.

employer's share by multiplying the employer's tax rates (assumed to be 6.2 percent for Social Security and 1.45 percent for Medicare) by the taxable earnings (assumed to be $68,400 for Social Security and all earnings for Medicare). The same tax rates apply to both the employer and the employees.

The accountant gets the Social Security and Medicare taxable earnings amounts from the payroll register. In Figure 1 we present the Taxable Earnings columns taken from the payroll register for the week ended October 7.

Before we look at the journal entry to record the employer's share of FICA tax, let's look at the entry in T account form.

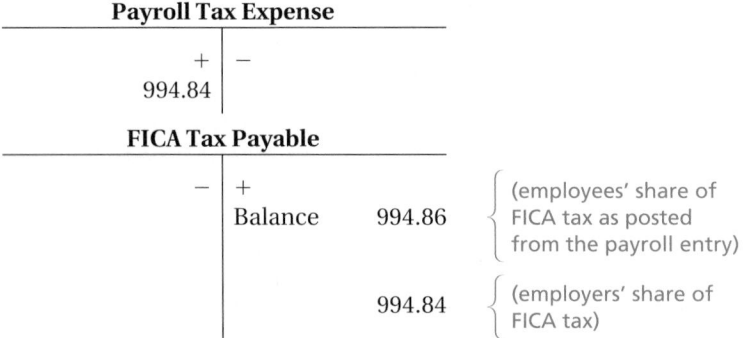

Note particularly that the FICA Tax Payable account is often used for both the tax liability of the employer and the amounts withheld from the employees. This is logical because both FICA taxes are paid at the same time

Amount of employees' earnings for the period that has not, as yet, been taxed as part of the $7,000 maximum liability

Amount of employees' earnings that are less than $68,400 per employee for the year

Amount of all employees' earnings

	NAME	TOTAL HOURS	TOTAL	ENDING CUMULATIVE EARNINGS	(7) TAXABLE EARNINGS		
					UNEMPLOYMENT	SOCIAL SECURITY	MEDICARE
1	Asino, Matte E.	46	1 1 1 9 16	34 0 0 9 16		1 1 1 9 16	1 1 1 9 16
2	Boritsky, Olga	45	7 3 5 30	6 9 2 7 30	7 3 5 30	7 3 5 30	7 3 5 30
3	Dray, Greg G.	49	9 1 5 65	7 7 6 1 65	1 5 4 00	9 1 5 65	9 1 5 65
4	Foulkes, Bob L.	40	1 0 7 3 25	39 7 1 0 25		1 0 7 3 25	1 0 7 3 25
5	Groyer, Milli K.	40	1 8 8 8 89	69 8 8 8 89		4 0 0 00	1 8 8 8 89
6	Kramer, Ada A.	40	1 8 9 1 67	69 9 9 1 67		3 0 0 00	1 8 9 1 67
7	Minkowitz, John L.	55	1 5 9 8 96	38 4 3 8 96		1 5 9 8 96	1 5 9 8 96
8	Orleons, Janet C.	40	1 2 7 1 75	47 0 5 4 75		1 2 7 1 75	1 2 7 1 75
9	Pinkovich, Mark S.	44	1 5 0 0 43	48 4 7 0 43		1 5 0 0 43	1 5 0 0 43
10	Romero, Sheila J.	45	1 8 1 3 51	56 7 9 1 51		1 8 1 3 51	1 8 1 3 51
11	Tivoli, Jake T.	40	1 1 6 8 83	43 2 4 6 83		1 1 6 8 83	1 1 6 8 83
12	Wilson, Charles D.	52	2 7 6 3 06	71 3 6 3 06			2 7 6 3 06
13			17 7 4 0 46	533 6 5 4 46	8 8 9 30	11 8 9 6 84	17 7 4 0 46

FIGURE 1

Employer's state unemployment tax
$889.30 × .054 = $48.02

Employer's Social Security tax
$11,896.84 × .062 = $737.60

Employer's Medicare tax
$17,740.46 × .0145 = $257.24

Employer's federal unemployment tax
$899.30 × .008 = $7.19

Combined Employer's FICA tax
($737.60 + $257.24) = $994.84

and to the same place. There may be a slight difference between the employer's and the employees' share of FICA taxes because of the rounding process. For the employees' share, the accountant uses the total of the employees' Social Security and Medicare tax deductions. For the employer's share, the accountant multiplies the total taxable earnings (Social Security and Medicare) by the tax rates.

Employer's State Unemployment Tax

The state unemployment tax (SUTA) is levied only on the employer in most states, the proceeds to be used to pay subsistence benefits to unemployed workers. The rate of the state unemployment tax varies considerably among the states. Assume that Greg Company is subject to a rate of 5.4 percent of the first $7,000 of each employee's earnings (the same base amount as for the federal unemployment tax). As shown in the portion of the payroll register illustrated in Figure 1, $889.30 of earnings are subject to the state unemployment tax. Accordingly, by T accounts, the state unemployment tax based on taxable earnings is as follows.

Payroll Tax Expense	State Unemployment Tax Payable
+ −	− +
(889.30 × .054)	(889.30 × .054)
48.02	48.02

Employer's Federal Unemployment Tax

The federal unemployment tax (FUTA) is paid only by the employer. Congress may from time to time change the rate. Let's assume a rate of .8 percent (.008) of the first $7,000 earned by each employee during the calendar year. For the weekly payroll period for Greg Company, the tax liability is $7.11 ($889.30 of unemployment taxable earnings, taken from the payroll register, multiplied by .008, the tax rate). The T account is as follows:

Payroll Tax Expense	Federal Unemployment Tax Payable
+ −	− +
(889.30 × .008)	(889.30 × .008)
7.11	7.11

━━━━━━━━━━━━━━━ ▬ ▬ ▬

Objective 1

Calculate the amount of payroll tax expense and journalize the related entry.

To make things clearer, figures for the three employer's payroll taxes have been presented separately. Now let's combine all of this information into one entry, which follows the regular payroll entry. Greg Company pays its employees weekly, so it also makes its Payroll Tax Expense entry weekly.

	DATE		DESCRIPTION	POST. REF.	DEBIT	CREDIT	
17	Oct.	7	Payroll Tax Expense		1 0 4 9 97		17
18			FICA Tax Payable			9 9 4 84	18
19			State Unemployment Tax				19
20			Payable			4 8 02	20
21			Federal Unemployment Tax				21
22			Payable			7 11	22
23			To record employer's share				23
24			of FICA tax and employer's				24
25			state and federal				25
26			unemployment taxes.				26
27							27
28							28
29							29
30							30
31							31

JOURNAL ENTRIES FOR RECORDING PAYROLL

At this point, let's restate in general journal form the entries that have already been recorded. We'll do this so that you can see the sequence of the payroll entries. First, the entry to record the payroll is journalized.

	DATE		DESCRIPTION	POST. REF.	DEBIT	CREDIT	
1	20–						1
2	Oct.	7	Sales Wages Expense		13 5 0 3 79		2
3			Office Wages Expense		4 2 3 6 67		3
4			Employees' Federal Income				4
5			Tax Payable			3 3 1 4 37	5
6			FICA Tax Payable			9 9 4 86	6
7			Employees' State Income Tax				7
8			Payable			6 6 2 88	8
9			Employees' Medical Insurance				9
10			Payable			2 6 0 50	10
11			Employees' United Way				11
12			Payable			1 2 4 00	12
13			Accounts Receivable			5 0 00	13
14			Wages Payable			12 3 3 3 85	14
15			Payroll register, page 68,				15
16			for week ended October 7.				16
17							17

Next, the entry to record the employer's payroll taxes is journalized.

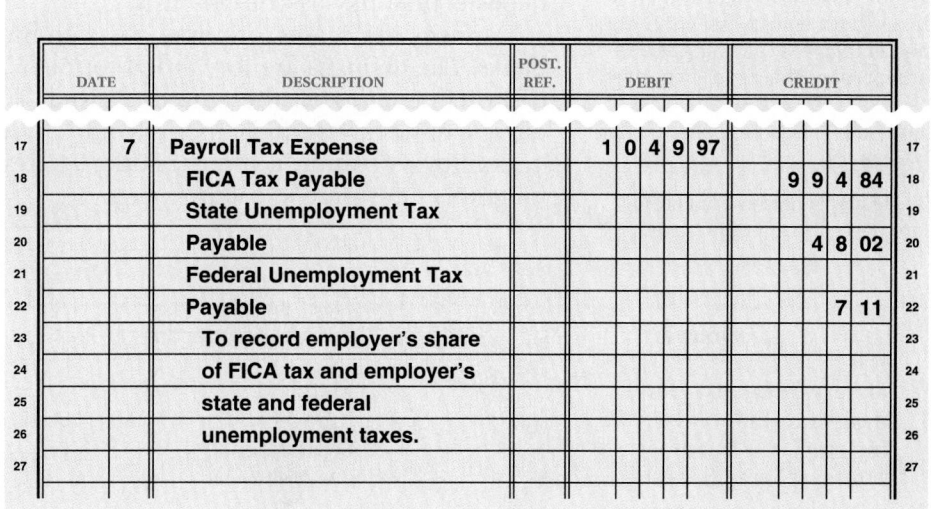

	DATE		DESCRIPTION	POST. REF.	DEBIT	CREDIT	
17		7	Payroll Tax Expense		1 0 4 9 97		17
18			FICA Tax Payable			9 9 4 84	18
19			State Unemployment Tax				19
20			Payable			4 8 02	20
21			Federal Unemployment Tax				21
22			Payable			7 11	22
23			To record employer's share				23
24			of FICA tax and employer's				24
25			state and federal				25
26			unemployment taxes.				26
27							27

Finally, the entry to pay the employees is journalized. Greg Company issues one check payable to a payroll bank account. To pay its employees, it will draw separate payroll checks on this payroll account. (The entry to transfer cash to the payroll bank account is not shown here.)

	DATE		DESCRIPTION	POST. REF.	DEBIT	CREDIT	
27		8	Wages Payable		12 3 3 3 85		27
28			Cash—Payroll Bank Account			12 3 3 3 85	28
29			Paid salaries for week				29
30			ended October 7.				30
31							31

As stated previously, in the first payroll entry, small employers will credit Cash directly instead of Wages Payable. These employers issue separate checks out of their regular bank accounts for each employee.

Next, we describe the entries for paying withholdings for employees' federal income tax and FICA tax and the employer's matching share of FICA tax. We also show the entries for paying the federal and state unemployment taxes and the withholdings for employees' state income tax.

PAYMENTS OF FICA TAX AND EMPLOYEES' FEDERAL INCOME TAX WITHHOLDING

Objective 2

Journalize the entry for the deposit of employees' federal income taxes withheld and FICA taxes (both employees' withheld and employer's matching share) and prepare the deposit coupon.

FYI

There are penalties applied for late deposits of federal taxes.

After paying employees, the employer must make payments in the form of federal tax deposits. A deposit includes the combined total of three items: (1) employees' federal income taxes withheld, (2) employees' FICA taxes withheld, and (3) employer's share of FICA taxes. Employers make these deposits on a pay-as-you-go basis.

Deposits are made to authorized commercial banks or Federal Reserve banks. The deposits are forwarded to the U.S. Treasury. The timing of these deposits depends on the amounts owed. The calendar year is broken into days, semiweekly periods, months, and **quarters** (3 consecutive months).

Employers submit a return, Form 941, every quarter. The due dates for filing this return are as follows:

Quarter	Ending Date of Quarter	Due Date for Form 941
January–February–March	March 31	April 30
April–May–June	June 30	July 31
July–August–September	September 30	October 31
October–November–December	December 31	January 31

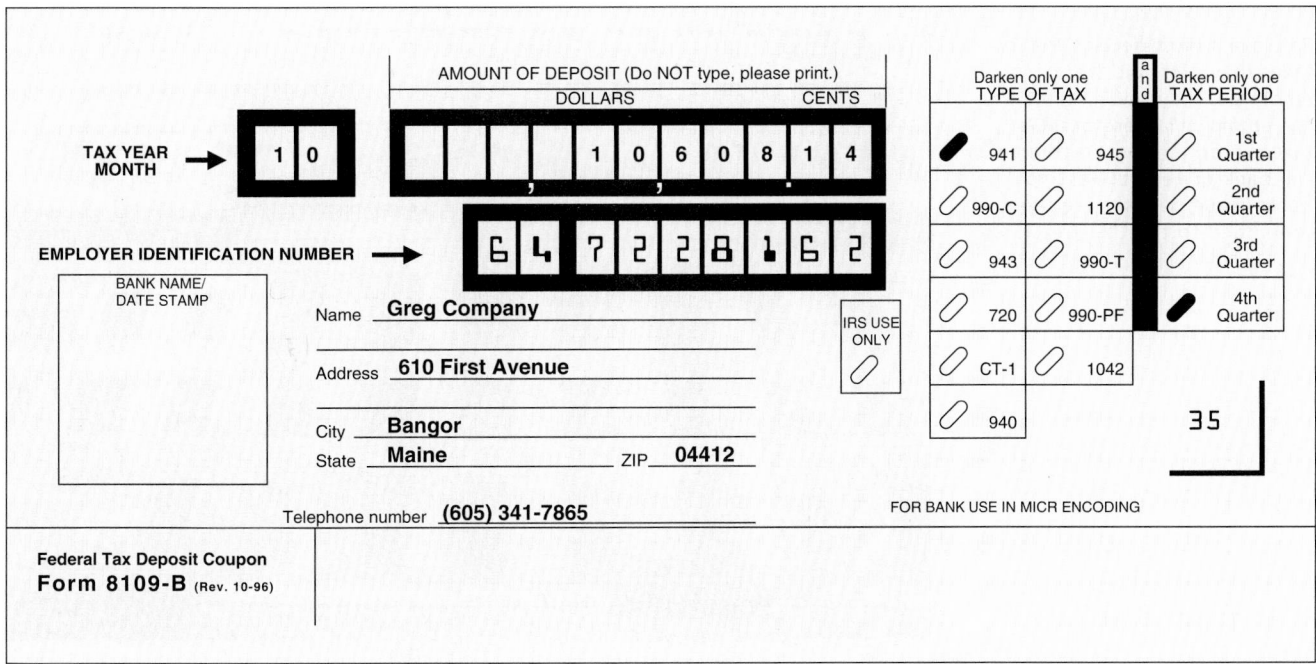

FIGURE 2

Federal Tax Deposit Coupon

Let's go back to Greg Company, where taxes were previously paid up to date. From the payroll of October 7, the following federal taxes are owed:

Employees' federal income taxes withheld	$3,314.37
Employees' FICA taxes withheld	994.86
Employer's share of FICA taxes	994.84
Total federal undeposited taxes	$5,304.07

We continue on for the next payroll period, ended October 14:

	Oct. 7	Oct. 14	Total
Employees' federal income taxes withheld	$3,314.37	$3,314.37	$ 6,628.74
Employees' FICA taxes withheld	994.86	994.86	1,989.72
Employer's share of FICA taxes	994.84	994.84	1,989.68
Total federal undeposited taxes	$5,304.07	$5,304.07	$10,608.14

Greg Company, which deposits monthly, receives a federal tax deposit card (printed with the company's name and tax number) from the Internal Revenue Service (Figure 2).

The accountant records the amount of the deposit, the employer identification number, the type of tax, the tax period, and the name and address of the company. The entry in general journal form to record the deposit of two weeks' taxes looks like the following.

Employers must deposit the taxes they withhold from employees' paychecks, as well as the employer's share of FICA taxes, in an authorized commercial bank or Federal Reserve bank. These deposits are then forwarded to the U.S. Treasury.

	DATE		DESCRIPTION	POST. REF.	DEBIT	CREDIT	
1	20–						1
2	Nov.	15	Employees' Federal Income Tax				2
3			Payable		6 6 2 8 74		3
4			FICA Tax Payable		3 9 7 9 40		4
5			Cash			10 6 0 8 14	5
6			Issued check for federal tax				6
7			deposit, Bangor Bank.				7
8							8

PAYMENTS OF STATE UNEMPLOYMENT INSURANCE

Objective 3

Journalize the entries for the payment of employer's state and federal unemployment taxes.

As we stated before, states differ with regard to both the rate and the taxable base for unemployment insurance. In our example, we assume that the state tax is 5.4 percent of the first $7,000 paid to each employee during the calendar year. **The state tax is usually paid quarterly and is due by the end of the month following the end of the quarter (the same as the due dates for Form 941).** Here's the entry in general journal form made by Greg Company for the first quarter (covering the months of January, February, and March). We assume that $60,436 was taxable for the quarter. The amount of the tax is $3,263.54 ($60,436 × .054).

	DATE		DESCRIPTION	POST. REF.	DEBIT					CREDIT					
1	20–														1
2	Apr.	30	State Unemployment Tax												2
3			Payable		3	2	6	3	54						3
4			Cash							3	2	6	3	54	4
5			Issued check for payment of												5
6			state unemployment tax.												6
7															7

The T accounts are as follows:

Cash		State Unemployment Tax Payable
+	–	–	+
	Apr. 30 3,263.54	Apr. 30 3,263.54	Mar. 31
			Balance 3,263.54

The balance in State Unemployment Tax Payable is the result of weekly entries recording the state unemployment portion of payroll tax expense.

PAYMENTS OF FEDERAL UNEMPLOYMENT TAX

The FUTA tax is calculated quarterly, during the month following the end of each calendar quarter and is used to administer the funds. **If the accumulated tax liability is greater than $100, the tax is deposited in a commercial bank or Federal Reserve bank, accompanied by a preprinted federal tax deposit card** like that used to deposit employees' federal income tax withholding and FICA taxes. The due date for this deposit is the last day of the month following the end of the quarter, the same as the due dates for the Employer's Quarterly Federal Tax Return and for state unemployment taxes.

Here is the entry in general journal form made by Greg Company for the first quarter. In our example, since the FUTA and state unemployment taxable earnings are the same (the first $7,000 for each employee), we assume that $60,436 was taxable for the quarter. The amount of the tax is $483.49 ($60,436 × .008).

	DATE		DESCRIPTION	POST. REF.	DEBIT				CREDIT				
1	20–												1
2	Apr.	30	Federal Unemployment Tax										2
3			Payable		4	8	3	49					3
4			Cash						4	8	3	49	4
5			Issued check for deposit of										5
6			federal unemployment tax.										6
7													7

The T accounts are as follows:

Cash			Federal Unemployment Tax Payable		
+	−		−	+	
	Apr. 30 483.49	Apr. 30	483.49	Mar. 31	
				Balance 483.49	

The balance in Federal Unemployment Tax Payable is the result of weekly entries recording the federal unemployment portion of payroll tax expense.

DEPOSITS OF EMPLOYEES' STATE INCOME TAX WITHHOLDING

Objective 4

Journalize the entry for the deposit of employees' state income taxes withheld.

Assume that the withholdings for employees' state income taxes are deposited on a quarterly basis, payable at the same time as state unemployment tax. Also, as of March 31, the credit balance of Employees' State Income Tax Payable is $1,526.08. The entry in general journal form to record the payment for the first quarter looks like this:

	DATE		DESCRIPTION	POST. REF.	DEBIT	CREDIT	
1	20–						1
2	Apr.	30	Employees' State Income Tax				2
3			Payable		1 5 2 6 08		3
4			Cash			1 5 2 6 08	4
5			Issued check for state				5
6			income tax deposit.				6
7							7

The T accounts are as follows:

Cash			Employees' State Income Tax Payable		
+	−		−	+	
	Apr. 30 1,526.08	Apr. 30	1,526.08	Mar. 31	
				Balance 1,526.08	

EMPLOYER'S QUARTERLY FEDERAL TAX RETURN (FORM 941)

Objective 5

Complete Employer's Quarterly Federal Tax Return, Form 941.

The purpose of Form 941 is to report the tax liability for withholdings of employees' federal income tax and FICA taxes, and also the employer's share of FICA taxes. Total tax deposits are also listed. As the title implies, the time period is three months. Remember that the due dates for the calendar year are: first quarter, April 30; second quarter, July 31; third quarter, October 31; fourth quarter, January 31.

A completed Form 941 for Greg Company is shown in Figure 3. Note that there are three main sections, which may be completed in the order

Form 941
(Rev. January 1999)
Department of the Treasury
Internal Revenue Service

Employer's Quarterly Federal Tax Return

► See separate instructions for information on completing this return.

Please type or print.

Enter state code for state in which deposits were made ONLY if different from state in address to the right ► (see page 2 of instructions).

Name (as distinguished from trade name)	Date quarter ended **December 31, 20—**
Trade name, if any **Greg Company**	Employer identification number **64-7228162**
Address (number and street) **610 First Avenue**	City, state, and ZIP code **Bangor, Maine 04412**

OMB No. 1545-0029

T	
FF	
FD	
FP	
I	
T	

If address is different from prior return, check here ►

IRS Use

1 1 1 1 1 1 1 1 1 1   2   3 3 3 3 3 3 3 3   4 4 4   5 5 5
6   7   8 8 8 8 8 8 8   9 9 9 9 9   10 10 10 10 10 10 10 10 10 10

If you do not have to file returns in the future, check here ► ☐ and enter date final wages paid ►
If you are a seasonal employer, see **Seasonal employers** on page 1 of the instructions and check here ► ☐

1	Number of employees in the pay period that includes March 12th . ►	**1**	12	
2	Total wages and tips, plus other compensation	**2**	216,252	00
3	Total income tax withheld from wages, tips, and sick pay	**3**	39,768	00
4	Adjustment of withheld income tax for preceding quarters of calendar year	**4**	—	
5	Adjusted total of income tax withheld (line 3 as adjusted by line 4—see instructions) . . .	**5**	39,768	00

FED (handwritten, right margin)

6	Taxable social security wages	**6a**	130,080 00	× 12.4% (.124) =	**6b**	16,129	92
	Taxable social security tips	**6c**		× 12.4% (.124) =	**6d**	—	
7	Taxable Medicare wages and tips . . .	**7a**	216,252 00	× 2.9% (.029) =	**7b**	6,271	31

8	Total social security and Medicare taxes (add lines 6b, 6d, and 7b). Check here if wages are not subject to social security and/or Medicare tax . . . . ► ☐	**8**	22,401	23
9	Adjustment of social security and Medicare taxes (see instructions for required explanation) Sick Pay $ _____ ± Fractions of Cents $ _____ ± Other $ _____ =	**9**	—	
10	Adjusted total of social security and Medicare taxes (line 8 as adjusted by line 9—see instructions)	**10**	22,401	23

FICA (handwritten, right margin)

11	**Total taxes** (add lines 5 and 10)	**11**	62,169	23
12	Advance earned income credit (EIC) payments made to employees	**12**	—	
13	Net taxes (subtract line 12 from line 11). If $1,000 or more, this must equal line 17, column (d) below (or line D of Schedule B (Form 941))	**13**	62,169	23
14	Total deposits for quarter, including overpayment applied from a prior quarter	**14**	62,169	23
15	**Balance due** (subtract line 14 from line 13). See instructions	**15**	—0—	
16	**Overpayment.** If line 14 is more than line 13, enter excess here ► $ _____ and check if to be: ☐ Applied to next return **OR** ☐ Refunded.			

- **All filers:** If line 13 is less than $1,000, you need not complete line 17 or Schedule B (Form 941).
- **Semiweekly schedule depositors:** Complete Schedule B (Form 941) and check here . . . . ► ☐
- **Monthly schedule depositors:** Complete line 17, columns (a) through (d), and check here . . . . ► ☑

17 Monthly Summary of Federal Tax Liability. Do not complete if you were a semiweekly schedule depositor.

(a) First month liability	(b) Second month liability	(c) Third month liability	(d) Total liability for quarter
18,236.45	20,956.56	22,976.22	62,169.23

Sign Here

Under penalties of perjury, I declare that I have examined this return, including accompanying schedules and statements, and to the best of my knowledge and belief, it is true, correct, and complete.

Signature ► *Ellen D. Greg*   Print Your Name and Title ► *Ellen D. Greg, Owner*   Date ► *Jan. 31, 20—*

For Privacy Act and Paperwork Reduction Act Notice, see back of form.   Cat. No. 17001Z   Form **941** (Rev. 1-99)

FIGURE 3

presented below. (The Internal Revenue Service has frequently changed the arrangement and questions on Form 941.)

Heading

Once an employer has secured an identification number and has filed her or his first return, the Internal Revenue Service sends forms directly to the employer. These forms have the employer's name, address, and identification number filled in.

Monthly Summary of Federal Tax Liability

For each month, list the combined total of employees' federal income and FICA taxes withheld and employer's share of FICA.

Questions Listed on Form 941 (Figure 3)

Read each question line by line.

1. Total number of employees.
2. Total wages and tips, plus other compensation, subject to federal tax withholding.
3. Total federal income tax withheld—shown as credits in the Employees' Federal Income Tax Payable account.
4. Adjustment of withheld income tax for preceding quarters of calendar year.
5. Adjusted total of income tax withheld—the total of income tax withheld after any adjustment for withheld income tax for preceding quarters.
6. Taxable Social Security wages paid—total of the Social Security Taxable Earnings listed in the payroll register for the three-month quarter; 12.4 percent equals the employees' 6.2 percent plus the employer's 6.2 percent.
   Taxable Social Security tips—refers to customer tips reported by employees; the employer withholds 6.2 percent.
7. Taxable Medicare wages and tips—total of the Medicare Taxable Earnings listed in the payroll register for the three-month quarter; 2.9 percent equals the employees' 1.45 percent plus the employer's 1.45 percent.
8. Total Social Security and Medicare taxes—shown as credits in the FICA Tax Payable account.
9. Adjustment of Social Security and Medicare taxes—used to record corrections in Social Security taxes reported on earlier returns and for rounding differences.
10. Adjusted total of Social Security and Medicare taxes.
11. Total taxes—the total of various taxes withheld from employees' pay and the taxes imposed on the employer.
12. Advance earned income credit (EIC) payments—payments made in advance to qualified employees for earned income credit. For qualifying low-income taxpayers, the earned income credit is a deduction from income tax owed.
13. Net taxes—the total federal tax liability for the quarter (this is the same amount as the total of the Monthly Summary of Federal Tax Liability section).
14. Total deposits for quarter—total of the debits to the Employees' Federal Income Tax Payable and the FICA Tax Payable accounts for the three-month quarter.

15. Balance due.
16. Overpayment.

The amount of wages subject to tax may differ in blocks 1, 3, 5, 17, and 20. Qualified employee contributions to retirement plans, such as 401k and 403b plans, reduce the amount of wages subject to federal income tax but not social security tax or Medicare tax. Whether employee retirement contributions reduce taxable state and local wages depends upon the appropriate state and local laws.

Wage Withholding Statements for Employees (Forms W-2)

Objective 6

Prepare W-2 and W-3 forms and Form 940.

After the end of a year (December 31) and by the following January 31, the employer must furnish for each employee a Wage and Tax Statement, known as **Form W-2**. This form contains information about the employee's earnings and tax deductions for the year. The source of the information used to complete Form W-2 is the employee's individual earnings record. The amounts used to complete Matte E. Asino's W-2 form (in Figure 4) represent the amounts taken from his earnings record at the end of the calendar year, December 31.

FIGURE 4

a Control number 22222 Void ☐	For Official Use Only ▶ OMB No. 1545-0008		
b Employer identification number 64–7228162	**1** Wages, tips, other compensation 46,330		**2** Federal income tax withheld 8,573
c Employer's name, address, and ZIP code	**3** Social security wages 46,330		**4** Social security tax withheld 2,872.46
Greg Company 610 First Avenue Bangor, Maine 04412	**5** Medicare wages and tips 46,330		**6** Medicare tax withheld 671.79
	7 Social security tips 0		**8** Allocated tips 0
d Employee's social security number 543–24–1680	**9** Advance EIC payment 0		**10** Dependent care benefits 0
e Employee's name (first, middle initial, last) Matte E. Asino	**11** Nonqualified plans 0		**12** Benefits included in box 1 0
6242 Baxter Drive Bangor, Maine 04412	**13** See instrs. for box 13		**14** Other
f Employee's address and ZIP code	**15** Statutory employee ☐ Deceased ☐ Pension plan ☐ Legal rep. ☐ Hshld. emp. ☐ Subtotal ☐ Deferred compensation ☐		
16 State Employer's state I.D. No. ME 464–729	**17** State wages, tips, etc. 46,330	**18** State income tax 1,735	**19** Locality name 0 **20** Local wages, tips, etc. 0 **21** Local income tax 0

Department of the Treasury—Internal Revenue Service

Form **W-2** **Wage and Tax Statement** **2000**

For Privacy Act and Paperwork Reduction Act Notice, see separate instructions.

Copy A For Social Security Administration–Send this entire page with Form W-3 to the Social Security Administration; photocopies are **Not** acceptable.

Cat. No. 10134D

Block 9 shows the total paid to the employee as advance earned income credit (EIC) payments. Block 13 is used for miscellaneous items, such as sick pay that is not included in income because the employee contributed to the sick pay plan. This box is also used for employer-provided group term life insurance in excess of $50,000. Box 14 may include the value of noncash fringe benefits, such as providing a vehicle for the employee. In box 15, statutory employees are life insurance and traveling salespersons, and legal representatives include attorneys and parents.

The accountant will prepare at least four copies of the W-2 form for each employee.

Copy A—Employer sends to the Social Security Administration.
Copy B—Employer gives to employee to be attached to the employee's individual federal income tax return.
Copy C—Employer gives to employee to be kept for his or her personal records.
Copy D—Employer keeps this copy as a record of payments made.

If state and local income taxes are withheld, the employer prepares additional copies to be sent to the appropriate tax agency.

Employer's Annual Federal Income Tax Reports (Form W-3)

Accompanying copy A of the employees' W-2 forms, Greg Company sends **Form W-3**, Transmittal of Wage and Tax Statements, to the Social Security Administration. This form is due on February 28, following the end of the calendar year.

For all employees, Form W-3 shows the total wages and tips, total federal income tax withheld, total Social Security and Medicare taxable wages, total Social Security and Medicare tax withheld, and other information. These amounts must be the same as the grand totals of the W-2 forms and the four quarterly 941 forms for the year. Greg Company's completed Form W-3 is presented in Figure 5.

Some boxes deserve an explanation. Box d, establishment number, may be used for a company that has separate establishments, with each establishment filing W-2 and W-3 forms separately. Box 9 is used for recording the amount of advance earned income credits shown on W-2 forms for qualified employees. Box h is used by a company that had more than one employer identification number (EIN) during the year.

To sum up thus far: The employer must submit the following at the end of the calendar year: Employer's Quarterly Federal Tax Return, Form 941, for the fourth quarter by January 31; Wage and Tax Statements, Form W-2, for all employees by January 31; Transmittal of Wage and Tax Statements, Form W-3, by February 28.

FYI

A copy is also sent (if applicable) to the state and/or local tax department, and a copy is given to the employee to attach to the state/local tax return.

REPORTS AND PAYMENTS OF FEDERAL UNEMPLOYMENT TAX

Remember!

If the accumulated FUTA tax liability at the end of a quarter is greater than $100, a deposit must be made.

As we stated previously, generally all employers are subject to the Federal Unemployment Tax Act. These employers must submit an Employer's Annual Federal Unemployment Tax Return, Form 940, not later than January 31 following the close of the calendar year. This deadline may be extended until February 10 if the employer has made deposits paying the FUTA tax liability

DO NOT STAPLE

a Control number		
	33333	For Official Use Only ▶ OMB No. 1545-0008

b	941	Military	943	1 Wages, tips, other compensation	2 Federal income tax withheld
Kind of Payer ▶	[X]	[ ]	[ ]	865,008	103,801
	CT-1 [ ]	Hshld. emp. [ ]	Medicare govt. emp. [ ]	3 Social security wages 778,836	4 Social security tax withheld 52,557.90

c Total number of Forms W-2 12	d Establishment number ———	5 Medicare wages and tips 865,008	6 Medicare tax withheld 12,542.62

e Employer identification number 64-7228162	7 Social security tips 0	8 Allocated tips 0

f Employer's name **Greg Company**	9 Advance EIC payments 0	10 Dependent care benefits 0

610 First Avenue

Bangor, Maine 04412

	11 Nonqualified plans 0	12 Deferred compensation 0

13

14

g Employer's address and ZIP code

h Other EIN used this year 0	15 Income tax withheld by third-party payer 0

i Employer's state I.D. no.
464-729

Contact person **Ellen D. Greg**	Telephone number (605) 341-7865	Fax number (605) 341-1463	E-mail address **GregCo@not.com**

Under penalties of perjury, I declare that I have examined this return and accompanying documents, and, to the best of my knowledge and belief, they are true, correct, and complete.

Signature ▶ *Ellen D. Greg*   Title ▶ *Owner*   Date ▶ *2/27/20–*

Form **W-3** Transmittal of Wage and Tax Statements 2000   Department of the Treasury
Internal Revenue Service

**Send this entire page with the entire Copy A page of Forms W-2 to the Social Security Administration. Photocopies are NOT acceptable.
Do not** send any remittance (cash, checks, money orders, etc.) with FORMS W-2 and W-3.

FIGURE 5

in full. **Form 940** shows total wages paid to employees, total wages subject to federal unemployment tax, and other information.

Using Greg Company as our example, federal unemployment taxable earnings by quarter are as follows:

Federal Unemployment Tax	1st Quarter	2nd Quarter	3rd Quarter	4th Quarter	Cumulative Total
Taxable earnings	$60,436	$9,536	$10,427	$3,601	$84,000
Tax rate	× .008	× .008	× .008	× .008	× .008
Tax liability	$483.49	$76.29	$ 83.42	$28.80*	$672.00

* Rounding

We now repeat the journal entry for the first quarter, in which $483.49 was deposited on April 30.

DATE		DESCRIPTION	POST. REF.	DEBIT	CREDIT	
20–						1
Apr.	30	Federal Unemployment Tax				2
		Payable		4 8 3 49		3
		Cash			4 8 3 49	4
		Issued check for deposit of				5
		federal unemployment tax.				6
						7

During the second quarter, many employees' total earnings passed the $7,000 limit of taxable earnings, and the firm's tax liability was reduced accordingly. Because Greg's total accumulated liability ($76.29) was less than $100, a deposit covering that quarter was not made. However, because of an expansion of the company, three new employees were hired during the middle of the quarter.

For the third quarter, the tax liability amounted to $83.42. The total cumulative tax liability was now $159.71 ($76.29 second quarter plus $83.42 third quarter). Consequently, $159.71 was deposited on October 31.

By the end of the fourth quarter, each of the twelve employees' earnings passed the $7,000 mark. The total liability for the quarter is $28.80. This amount will be paid by January 31, accompanied by the completed Employer's Annual Federal Unemployment Tax Return, Form 940.

The T account for Federal Unemployment Tax Payable follows. The credits to the account were part of the entries to record the federal unemployment tax portion of Payroll Tax Expense for each payroll period.

Federal Unemployment Tax Payable

	–	+	
Apr. 30 deposit	483.49	1st quarter (liability)	483.49
Oct. 31 deposit	159.71	2nd quarter (liability)	76.29
		3rd quarter (liability)	83.42
Jan. 31 deposit	28.80	4th quarter (liability)	28.80

Employer's Annual Federal Unemployment (FUTA) Tax Return (Form 940)

Figure 6 shows a completed Form 940-EZ for Greg Company. This form has three sections. (Bear in mind that this form changes from time to time.)

Part I Line 1 Record total wages paid.
Line 2 Record certain exempt wages—this includes such items as agricultural labor, family employment, and the value of meals and lodging.

Form **940-EZ**			**Employer's Annual Federal Unemployment (FUTA) Tax Return**		OMB No. 1545-1110
Department of the Treasury Internal Revenue Service (99)			▶ See separate **Instructions for Form 940-EZ** for information on completing this form.		**2000**

					T	
Name (as distinguished from trade name)		Calendar year 20—		FF	
				FD	
Trade name, if any **Greg Company**				FP	
				I	
Address and ZIP code **610 First Avenue Bangor, Maine 04412**	Employer identification number 64 ⁞7228162			T	

Answer the questions under **Who May Use Form 940-EZ** *on page 2. If you cannot use Form 940-EZ, you must use Form 940.*

A Enter the amount of contributions paid to your state unemployment fund. (See separate instructions.) . . . ▶ $ _____

B (1) Enter the name of the state where you have to pay contributions . . . . ▶ _____
      (2) Enter your state reporting number as shown on your state unemployment tax return▶

If you will not have to file returns in the future, check here (see **Who Must File** in separate instructions),**and complete and sign the return.** ▶ ☐

If this is an Amended Return, check here . . . . ▶ ☐

Part I   Taxable Wages and FUTA Tax

1	Total payments (including payments shown on lines 2 and 3) during the calendar year for services of employees	**1**	865,008	00
2	Exempt payments. (Explain all exempt payments, attaching additional sheets if necessary.) ▶ _____ **2** _____			
3	Payments of more than $7,000 for services. Enter only amounts over the first $7,000 paid to each employee. Do not include any exempt payments from line 2. The $7,000 amount is the Federal wage base. Your state wage base may be different. **Do not use your state wage limitation** **3**	781,008 00		
4	Total exempt payments (add lines 2 and 3)	**4**	781,008	00
5	**Total taxable wages** (subtract line 4 from line 1) . . . . ▶	**5**	84,000	00
6	**FUTA tax.** Multiply the wages on line 5 by .008 and enter here. **(If the result is over $100, also complete Part II.)**	**6**	672	00
7	Total FUTA tax deposited for the year, including any overpayment applied from a prior year	**7**	672	00
8	**Balance due** (subtract line 7 from line 6). Pay to the "United States Treasury" . . . . ▶	**8**	————	
	If you owe more than $100, see **Depositing FUTA tax** in separate instructions.			
9	**Overpayment** (subtract line 6 from line 7). Check if it is to be: ☐ **Applied to next return or** ☐ **Refunded** ▶	**9**	————	

Part II   Record of Quarterly Federal Unemployment Tax Liability (Do not include state liability.) Complete only if line 6 is over $100.

Quarter	First (Jan. 1 – Mar. 31)	Second (Apr. 1 – June 30)	Third (July 1 – Sept. 30)	Fourth (Oct. 1 – Dec. 31)	Total for year
Liability for quarter	483.49	76.29	83.42	28.80	672.00

Under penalties of perjury, I declare that I have examined this return, including accompanying schedules and statements, and, to the best of my knowledge and belief, it is true, correct, and complete, and that no part of any payment made to a state unemployment fund claimed as a credit was, or is to be, deducted from the payments to employees.

Signature ▶ *Ellen D. Greg*   Title (Owner, etc.) ▶ *Owner*   Date ▶ *1/31/20—*

For Privacy Act and Paperwork Reduction Act Notice, see separate instructions.   Cat. No. 10983G   Form **940-EZ** (2000)

DETACH HERE

FIGURE 6

Line 3   Record exempt wages paid—wages paid to each employee over and above $7,000 for the calendar year.

Line 4   Total exempt payments.

Line 5   Total taxable wages.

Line 6   Computation of tax due.

Line 7   Total FUTA tax deposited.

Line 8   Balance due.

Line 9   Overpayment.

Part II   Record of Quarterly Federal Unemployment Tax Liability.

WORKERS' COMPENSATION INSURANCE

Objective 7

Calculate the premium for workers' compensation insurance, and prepare the entry for payment in advance.

Most states require employers to provide **workers' compensation insurance** or industrial accident insurance for employees killed or injured on the job, either through plans administered by the state or through private insurance companies authorized by the state. The employer usually has to pay all the premiums. The premium rate varies with the amount of risk the job entails and the company's claims history. For example, handling molten steel ingots is much more dangerous than typing reports. Thus, it is very important that employees be identified properly in terms of the insurance premium classifications. The rates as percentages of the payroll may be .15 percent for office work, .5 percent for sales work, and 3.5 percent for industrial labor in heavy manufacturing. These same rates may be expressed as $.15 per $100 of the salaries or wages for office work, $.50 per $100 for sales work, and $3.50 per $100 for industrial labor.

Remember!

Workers' compensation for the year is first estimated based on the anticipated year's payroll; debit Prepaid Insurance, Workers' Compensation, and credit Cash. At the end of the year, when the actual payroll is known, the exact insurance premium is calculated; debit Workers' Compensation Insurance Expense and credit Prepaid Insurance, Workers' Compensation, for the amount paid at the beginning of the year.

If the amount of the estimated payroll is less than the actual payroll, debit Workers' Compensation Insurance Expense and credit Workers' Compensation Insurance Payable for the difference between the actual premium and the estimated premium.

Generally, the employer pays a premium in advance, based on the estimated payroll for the year. After the year ends, the employer knows the exact amount of the payroll and can calculate the exact premium. At that time, depending on the difference between the estimated and the exact premium, the employer either pays an additional premium or gets a credit for overpayment.

At Greg Company, there are two work classifications: office work and sales work. At the beginning of the year, the firm's accountant computed the estimated annual premium as follows:

Classification	Predicted Payroll	Rate (Percent)	Estimated Premium
Office work	$187,000	.15	$187,000 × .0015 = $ 280.50
Sales work	663,000	.50	663,000 × .0050 = 3,315.00
			Total estimated premium $3,595.50

As shown by T accounts, the accountant made the following entry.

Prepaid Insurance, Workers' Compensation		Cash	
+	−	+	−
Jan. 10 3,595.50			Jan. 10 3,595.50

Then, at the end of the calendar year, the accountant calculated the exact premium:

Classification	Exact Payroll	Rate (Percent)	Exact Premium
Office work	$192,000	.15	$192,000 × .0015 = $ 288.00
Sales work	673,000	.50	673,000 × .0050 = 3,365.00
			Total exact premium $3,653.00

Workers' compensation premiums are based upon the level of risk involved. A rating is given to the employer for each type of job.

Therefore, the amount of the unpaid premium is

$3,653.00	Total exact premium
$3,595.50	Less total estimated premium paid
$ 58.00	Additional premium owed

Objective 8a

Determine the amount of the end-of-the-year adjustment for workers' compensation insurance, and record the adjustment.

Now the accountant makes an adjusting entry, similar to the adjusting entry for expired insurance; this entry appears on the work sheet. The accountant then makes an additional adjusting entry for the extra premium owed. By T accounts, the entries are as follows:

Prepaid Insurance, Workers' Compensation			
	+	−	
Jan. 10 Bal.	3,595.00	Dec. 31 Adj.	3,595.00

Workers' Compensation Insurance Payable		
−	+	
	Dec. 31 Adj.	58.00

Workers' Compensation Insurance Expense		
	+	−
Dec. 31 Adj.	3,595.00	
Dec. 31 Adj.	58.00	

FYI

Workers' compensation premiums are based upon the level of risk involved. A rating is given to the employer for each type of job.

Greg Company will pay $58.00, the amount of unpaid premium, in January, together with the estimated premium for the next year.

ADJUSTING FOR ACCRUED SALARIES AND WAGES

Objective 8b

Determine the amount of the end-of-the-year adjustment for accrued salaries and wages, and record the adjustment.

Assume that $1,000 of salaries accrue for the time between the last payday and the end of the year. An adjusting entry is necessary.

	DATE		DESCRIPTION	POST. REF.	DEBIT	CREDIT	
1	20–		**Adjusting Entry**				1
2	Dec.	31	Salary Expense		1 0 0 0 00		2
3			Salaries Payable			1 0 0 0 00	3
4							4

Salaries Payable is considered a liability account, as are employees' withholding taxes and deductions payable. Federal income tax and FICA tax levied on employees do not become legal obligations until the employees are paid. Therefore, for the purpose of recording the adjusting entry, the entire liability of the gross salaries and wages is included under Salaries Payable or Wages Payable. In other words, in the adjusting entry, such accounts as Employees' Income Tax Payable, FICA Tax Payable (employees' share), and Employees' Union Dues Payable are not used.

Adjusting Entry for Accrual of Payroll Taxes

As you have seen, the following taxes come under the umbrella of the Payroll Tax Expense account: the employer's share of the FICA tax, the state unemployment tax, and the federal unemployment tax. The employer becomes liable for these taxes only when the employees are actually paid, rather than at the time the liability to the employees is incurred. From the standpoint of legal liability, there should be no adjusting entry for Payroll Tax Expense.

TAX CALENDAR

Now let's put it all together. To keep up with the task of paying and reporting the various taxes, the accountant compiles a chronological list of the due dates. We are including only the payroll taxes here, but sales taxes and property taxes should also be listed. When you think about the penalties for non-payment of taxes by the due dates, this chronological list seems to be well worth the effort.

Jan. 10 Pay estimated annual premium for workers' compensation insurance. (This is an approximate date, as it varies among the states.)

15 Make federal tax deposit for employees' income tax withholding, employees' FICA taxes withheld, and employer's FICA taxes for wages paid during the month of December.

31 Complete Employer's Quarterly Federal Tax Return, Form 941, for the fourth quarter.

31 Issue copies B and C of Wage and Tax Statement, Form W-2, to employees.

31 Pay state unemployment tax liability for the previous quarter, and submit state return, employer's tax report.

31 Pay any remaining federal unemployment tax liability for the previous year, and submit Form 940, Employer's Annual Federal Unemployment Tax Return.

31 Make state deposit for employees' state income tax withholding and submit any required state payroll reports. (Timing and required reports may differ from state to state.)

Feb. 15 Make federal tax deposit for employees' income tax withholding, employees' FICA tax withholding, and employer's FICA tax for wages paid during the month of January.

28 Complete Transmittal of Wage and Tax Statements, Form W-3, and attach copy A of W-2 forms for employees.

Mar. 15 Make federal tax deposit for employees' income tax withholding, employees' FICA tax withholding, and employer's FICA tax for wages paid during the month of February.

Compiling a chronological list of tax due dates helps accountants keep up with paying and reporting the various taxes.

Apr. 15   Make federal tax deposit for employees' income tax witholding, employees' FICA tax withholding, and employer's FICA tax for wages paid during the month of March.

30   Pay state unemployment tax liability for the previous quarter and submit state return, employer's tax report.

30   Complete Employer's Quarterly Federal Tax Return, Form 941, for the first quarter.

30   Make federal tax deposit for federal unemployment tax liability if it exceeds $100.

30   Make state deposit for employees' state income tax withholding.

CHAPTER REVIEW

Review of Performance Objectives

1. Calculate the amount of payroll tax expense and journalize the related entry.

   Payroll tax expense consists of the employer's matching portion of FICA taxes, plus the state unemployment tax, plus the federal unemployment tax. The *FICA tax* consists of Social Security and Medicare taxes. *Social Security tax* equals total Social Security taxable earnings multiplied by .062 (6.2 percent assumed rate) on the taxable earnings. For this text, the maximum taxable is $68,400. Total *Medicare tax* equals Medicare taxable earnings multiplied by .0145 (1.45 percent assumed rate). There is no maximum limit for Medicare—all earnings are taxable. *State unemployment tax* equals unemployment taxable earnings multiplied by .054 (5.4 percent assumed rate). *Federal unemployment tax* equals unemployment taxable earnings multiplied by .008 (.8 percent assumed rate). The related journal entry is as follows:

	DATE		DESCRIPTION	POST. REF.	DEBIT	CREDIT	
17	Oct.	7	Payroll Tax Expense		1 0 4 9 97		17
18			FICA Tax Payable			9 9 4 84	18
19			State Unemployment Tax				19
20			Payable			4 8 02	20
21			Federal Unemployment Tax				21
22			Payable			7 11	22
23			To record employer's share				23
24			of FICA tax and employer's				24
25			state and federal				25
26			unemployment taxes.				26
27							27

2. Journalize the entry for the deposit of employees' federal income taxes withheld and FICA taxes (both employees' withheld and employer's matching share) and prepare the deposit coupon.

	DATE		DESCRIPTION	POST. REF.	DEBIT	CREDIT	
1	20–						1
2	Nov.	15	Employees' Federal Income Tax				2
3			Payable		6 6 2 8 74		3
4			FICA Tax Payable		3 9 7 9 40		4
5			Cash			10 6 0 8 14	5
6			Issued check for federal tax				6
7			deposit, Bangor Bank.				7
8							8
9							9
10							10
11							11

3. Journalize the entries for the payment of employer's state and federal unemployment taxes.

State unemployment tax is paid on a quarterly basis. Payment is due by the end of the next month following the end of the calendar quarter.

	DATE		DESCRIPTION	POST. REF.	DEBIT	CREDIT	
1	20–						1
2	Apr.	30	State Unemployment Tax				2
3			Payable		3 2 6 3 54		3
4			Cash			3 2 6 3 54	4
5			Issued check for payment of				5
6			state unemployment tax.				6
7							7
8							8
9							9
10							10

If the amount of the accumulated federal unemployment tax liability exceeds $100 at the end of any quarter, the tax is due by the end of the next month following the end of the quarter. If the federal unemployment tax payable is less than $100 at the end of the year, it is due by January 31 of the next year.

	DATE		DESCRIPTION	POST. REF.	DEBIT	CREDIT	
1	20–						1
2	Apr.	30	Federal Unemployment Tax				2
3			Payable		4 8 3 49		3
4			Cash			4 8 3 49	4
5			Issued check for deposit of				5
6			federal unemployment tax.				6
7							7

4. Journalize the entry for the deposit of employees' state income taxes withheld.

   Employees' state income taxes withheld are paid on a quarterly basis or as required by your state. Payment may be due by the end of the next month following the end of the calendar quarter.

	DATE		DESCRIPTION	POST. REF.	DEBIT	CREDIT	
1	20–						1
2	Apr.	30	Employees' State Income Tax				2
3			Payable		1 5 2 6 08		3
4			Cash			1 5 2 6 08	4
5			Issued check for state				5
6			income tax deposit.				6
7							7

5. Complete Employer's Quarterly Federal Tax Return, Form 941.

   Form 941 is illustrated on page 299.

6. Prepare W-2 and W-3 forms and Form 940.

   W-2 form (Wage and Tax Statement) is illustrated on page 301. W-3 form (Transmittal of Wage and Tax Statements) is illustrated on page 303. Form 940 is illustrated on page 305.

7. Calculate the premium for workers' compensation insurance, and prepare the entry for payment in advance.

   Rates vary depending on the degree of physical risk involved in different occupations. The amount of the premium equals the predicted annual payroll multiplied by the premium rate. The entry is a debit to Prepaid Insurance, Workers' Compensation, and a credit to Cash.

8. Determine the amount of the end-of-the-year adjustments for (a) workers' compensation insurance and (b) accrued salaries and wages, and record the adjustments.

When the total annual payroll is known, the exact cost of workers' compensation insurance can be determined by multiplying the total payroll by the premium rate. Two adjusting entries are required. The first adjusting entry records the expired insurance as a debit to Workers' Compensation Insurance Expense and a credit to Prepaid Insurance, Workers' Compensation. The second adjusting entry records the difference between the estimated and the actual premiums. If the actual premium is greater than the premium that was paid in advance, the entry is a debit to Workers' Compensation Insurance Expense and a credit to Workers' Compensation Insurance Payable. The adjustment for accrued salaries and wages accounts for the additional amount of salaries or wages paid in the next payroll that are incurred in the current fiscal period—a debit to Wages (or Salaries) Expense. The credit to Salaries (or Wages) Payable accounts for the additional amount of liability incurred in the current period that will be paid with the next payroll that occurs in the following fiscal period.

Glossary

Employer identification number The number assigned each employer by the Internal Revenue Service for use in the submission of reports and payments for FICA taxes and federal income tax withheld. (289)

Federal unemployment tax (FUTA) A tax levied only on the employer, equal to .8 percent of the first $7,000 of total earnings paid to each employee during the calendar year. This tax is used to administer the funds. (292)

Form 940 An annual report filed by employers showing total wages paid to employees, total wages subject to federal unemployment tax, total federal unemployment tax, and other information. Also called the *Employer's Annual Federal Unemployment Tax Return.* (303)

Form 941 A quarterly report showing the tax liability for withholdings of employees' federal income tax and FICA tax and the employer's share of FICA tax. Total tax deposits made in the quarter are also listed on this Employer's Quarterly Federal Tax Return. (298)

Form W-2 A form containing information about employee earnings and tax deductions for the year. Also called *Wage and Tax Statement.* (301)

Form W-3 An annual report sent to the Social Security Administration listing the total wages and tips, total federal income tax withheld, total Social Security and Medicare taxable wages, total Social Security and Medicare tax withheld, and other information for all employees of a firm. Also called the *Transmittal of Wage and Tax Statements.* (302)

Payroll Tax Expense A general expense account used for recording the employer's matching portion of the FICA tax, the federal unemployment tax, and the state unemployment tax. (289)

Quarters Three consecutive months, also referred to as *calendar quarters.* (294)

State unemployment tax (SUTA) A tax levied only on the employer in most states. Rates differ among the various states; however, they are generally 5.4 percent or higher of the first $7,000 of total earnings paid to each employee during the calendar year. The proceeds are used to pay subsistence benefits to unemployed workers. (291)

Workers' compensation insurance This insurance, primarily paid for by the employer, provides benefits for employees injured or killed on the job. The rates vary according to the degree of risk inherent in the job. The plans may be sponsored by states or by private firms. The employer pays the premium in advance at the beginning of the year, based on the estimated payroll. The rates are adjusted after the exact payroll is known. (306)

QUESTIONS, EXERCISES, AND PROBLEMS

Discussion Questions

1. What payroll taxes are included under the Payroll Tax Expense account?
2. List the correct sequence of the steps for recording payroll entries, and identify the specific source of information for each entry.
3. Explain the deposit requirement for federal unemployment tax.
4. What is the purpose of Form 941? How often is it prepared, and what are the due dates?
5. How many copies are made of a Form W-2, and who uses the copies of the W-2 form?
6. What is the purpose of Form 940? How often is it prepared, and what is the due date?
7. Generally, what is the time schedule for payment of workers' compensation insurance premiums?
8. Explain the advantage of establishing a tax calendar.

Exercises

P.O. 1

Journalize the entry for payroll tax expense.

Exercise 9-1 West Company's partial payroll register for the week ended January 7 is shown below.

| | NAME | BEGINNING CUMULATIVE EARNINGS | TOTAL EARNINGS | ENDING CUMULATIVE EARNINGS | TAXABLE EARNINGS | | |
					UNEMPLOYMENT	SOCIAL SECURITY	MEDICARE
1	Bonner, R. S.		895 00	895 00	895 00	895 00	895 00
2	Falk, M. C.		567 00	567 00	567 00	567 00	567 00
3	Hagen, W. O.		483 00	483 00	483 00	483 00	483 00
4	Lien, Loan		679 00	679 00	679 00	679 00	679 00
5	Parker, S. J.		578 00	578 00	578 00	578 00	578 00
6	Tinker, E. B.		446 00	446 00	446 00	446 00	446 00
7			3648 00	3648 00	3648 00	3648 00	3648 00
8							
9							
10							
11							

Assume that the payroll is subject to a Social Security tax of 6.2 percent of the first $68,400 and a Medicare tax of 1.45 percent on all earnings. Also assume that the federal unemployment tax is .8 percent of the first $7,000, and the state unemployment tax is 5.4 percent of the first $7,000. Give the entry in general journal form to record the payroll tax expense.

P.O. 1

Journalize the entry for payroll tax expense.

Exercise 9-2 On January 14, at the end of the second week of the year, the totals of Kwan Company's payroll register showed that its store employees' wages amounted to $30,432 and its warehouse wages amounted to $12,360. Withholdings consisted of federal income taxes, $4,152; Social Security taxes at the rate of 6.2 percent of the first $68,400; Medicare taxes at the rate of 1.45 percent on all earnings; union dues, $811.

a. Calculate the amount of Social Security and Medicare taxes to be withheld, and write the general journal entry to record the payroll.
b. Write the general journal entry to record the employer's payroll taxes, assuming that the federal unemployment tax is .8 percent of the first $7,000 and the state unemployment tax is 5.4 percent of the same base, and that no employee has surpassed the $7,000 limit.

P.O. 1

Journalize the payroll entries.

Exercise 9-3 File Systems had the following payroll data for wages for the week ended February 5:

		TAXABLE EARNINGS			DEDUCTIONS			
TOTAL EARNINGS	ENDING CUMULATIVE EARNINGS	UNEMPLOYMENT	SOCIAL SECURITY	MEDICARE	FEDERAL INCOME TAX	STATE INCOME TAX	SOCIAL SECURITY TAX	MEDICARE TAX
6 7 5 0 00	72 8 3 0 00	6 7 5 0 00	6 7 5 0 00	6 7 5 0 00	8 2 2 00	1 5 5 00	4 1 8 50	9 7 88

a. Write the general journal entry to record the payroll.
b. Write the general journal entry to record the employer's payroll taxes. Assume rates of .8 percent for federal unemployment tax and 5.4 percent for state unemployment tax based on the first $7,000 for each employee and that no employee has earned more than $7,000.

P.O. 1

Journalize the entry for payroll tax expense.

Exercise 9-4 The following information on earnings and deductions for the pay period ended December 14 is from Lamba Company's payroll records:

Name	Gross Pay	Beginning Cumulative Earnings
Bremer, A. F.	$ 310	$ 6,620
Dugger, L. D.	760	38,100
Spulak, C. R.	1,080	62,800
Recknagle, L. W.	290	38,700
Carlisle, M. E.	590	62,400
Stevenson, D. H.	950	6,810

For each employee, the Social Security tax is 6.2 percent of the first $68,400, and the Medicare tax is 1.45 percent on all earnings. The federal unemployment tax is .8 percent of the first $7,000 of earnings of each employee. The state unemployment tax is 5.4 percent of the same base. Determine the total taxable earnings for unemployment, Social Security, and Medicare. Prepare a general journal entry to record the employer's payroll taxes.

P.O. 2

Journalize entries for payment of federal payroll taxes.

Exercise 9-5 Selected columns of Lau Company's payroll register for the month of January are as follows. The employees' FICA taxes are matched by the employer.

Payment Date	Employees' Federal Income Tax	Employees' Social Security Tax	Employees' Medicare Tax
Jan. 7	1,092.00	485.00	114.25
14	1,124.00	510.14	120.31
21	1,205.00	562.62	126.24
28	1,431.00	581.27	141.26

Lau Company deposits taxes monthly. Record the entry for payment of FICA and federal income taxes for employees and employer in general journal form.

P.O. 2,3

Journalize entries for payment of payroll taxes.

Exercise 9-6 On September 30, Krabb Company's selected account balances are as follows:

Employees' Federal Income Tax Payable	$ 2,169
FICA Tax Payable (employer and employee)	2,319
State Unemployment Tax Payable	1,308
Federal Unemployment Tax Payable	201
Salaries Payable	1,906
Salary Expense	32,738
Payroll Tax Expense	2,126

In general journal form, prepare the entries to record the following:

Oct. 15 Payment of liabilities for FICA and federal income tax.
31 Payment of liability for state unemployment tax.
31 Payment of liability for federal unemployment tax.

P.O. 2,3

Journalize entries for payment of payroll taxes.

Exercise 9-7 On September 30, Michilak Company's selected payroll accounts are as follows.

	FICA Tax Payable			State Unemployment Tax Payable	
−	+		−	+	
	Sept. 30	2,213.86		Sept. 30	1,217.83
	Sept. 30	2,213.86			

	Federal Unemployment Tax Payable			Employees' Federal Income Tax Payable	
−	+		−	+	
	Sept. 30	201.14		Sept. 30	3,312.74

Prepare general journal entries to record the following:

Oct. 15 Payment of federal tax deposit of FICA and federal income tax.
31 Payment of state unemployment tax.
31 Payment of federal unemployment tax.

P.O. 7,8

Journalize entries for workers' compensation insurance.

Exercise 9-8 Mayeno Company received a premium notice on January 2 for workers' compensation insurance stating the rates for the new year. Estimated employees' earnings for the year are as follows:

Classification	Estimated Wages and Salaries	Rate Per Hundred	Estimated Premium
Office clerical	$ 91,000	.11	$ 100.10
Warehouse work	28,000	.92	257.60
Manufacturing	$265,000	1.20	3,180.00
			$3,537.70

At the end of the year, the exact figures for the payroll are as follows:

Classification	Estimated Wages and Salaries	Rate Per Hundred	Exact Premium
Office clerical	$ 92,000	.11	$ 101.20
Warehouse work	27,000	.92	248.40
Manufacturing	$268,000	1.20	3,216.00
			$3,565.60

a. Record the entry in general journal form for payment of the estimated premium.
b. Record the adjusting entries on December 31 for the insurance expired and for the additional premium.

WHAT IF . . .

The payroll clerk is working on the payroll register, specifically the Taxable Earnings columns for federal and state unemployment taxes and FICA taxes. The problem is that several employees' gross earnings are about to exceed the limits for unemployment and FICA taxes. For each employee whose cumulative earnings were near the limit, the payroll clerk multiplied the tax rate by the amount by which the employee's earnings exceeded the tax ceiling (not the amount between the beginning cumulative earnings and the tax limit). Comment on this procedure.

CRITICAL THINKING

It is December 15, and you are the payroll clerk for Listel Company. The owner has come to you for help; two employees have asked for a 4 percent pay raise, and the owner wants to know how much more such a raise will cost her next year. Present gross salaries are as follows:

Employee A
$40,000/year   Married, with 2 allowances   Paid weekly

Employee B
$42,000/year   Married, with 1 allowance   Paid weekly

Assume the following tax rates and limits:

Social Security, 6.2 percent with a limit of $68,400
Medicare, 1.45 percent with no limit (all earnings taxable)
SUTA, 5.4 percent with a limit of $7,000
FUTA, .8 percent with a limit of $7,000

What will be the cost to the employer of giving Employee A and Employee B the pay raise?

A MATTER OF ETHICS

An employer prepares the payroll and correctly computes the necessary withholding taxes. The employer pays accumulated employment taxes on the fifteenth of the next month. Payday is the last day of the month. However, between the end of one month and the fifteenth day of the next month, the balance in the employer's business bank account has been getting smaller and smaller. The employer has used the funds withheld from employees to pay some of the business's bills. He anticipates that enough of the customers who owe him money will pay their outstanding debts. If this assumption is true, the checking account will have enough in it to pay the federal deposit on the fifteenth of the month. Is the employer acting ethically, because he intends to have enough money in the account for the deposit?

WEB WORK

Using an Internet web browser, type *employment laws* in the search box and search for information about laws of hiring and firing in your state. Discuss or write your findings.

PROBLEM SET A

For additional help, see the demonstration problem at the beginning of each chapter in your Working Papers.

P.O. 1

Problem 9-1A Mezistrano Labs had the following payroll for the week ended February 28:

Salaries		Deductions	
Technicians' salaries	$6,842.00	Federal income tax withheld	$ 684.00
Office salaries	2,064.00	Social Security tax withheld	552.17
		Medicare tax withheld	129.14
Total	$8,906.00	Union dues withheld	180.00
		Medical insurance	460.00
		Total	$2,005.31

Assumed tax rates are as follows:

a. FICA: Social Security, 6.2 percent (.062) on the first $68,400 for each employee, and Medicare, 1.45 percent (.0145) on all earnings for each employee.

b. State unemployment tax, 5.4 percent (.054) on the first $7,000 for each employee.

c. Federal unemployment tax, .8 percent (.008) on the first $7,000 for each employee.

Check Figure

Payroll Tax Expense, $1,067.20

Instructions

Record the following entries in general journal form:

1. The payroll entry as of February 28.
2. The entry to record the employer's payroll taxes as of February 28, assuming that the total payroll is subject to the FICA tax (combined Social Security and Medicare) and that $6,224.00 is subject to unemployment taxes.
3. The payment of the employees on March 2 (assume that the company has transferred cash to Cash—Payroll Bank Account for this payroll).

P.O. 1

Problem 9-2A Temp Services has the following payroll information for the week ended December 7.

	NAME	BEGINNING CUMULATIVE EARNINGS	TOTAL EARNINGS	DEDUCTIONS	
				FEDERAL INCOME TAX	STATE INCOME TAX
1	Barker, T. C.	6 8 2 0 00	4 8 0 00	4 6 00	5 52
2	Ellis, M. R.	6 8 4 0 00	4 7 0 00	4 5 00	5 40
3	Fisk, B. L.	36 3 2 0 00	7 4 0 00	8 5 00	1 0 20
4	Janus, V. O.	26 2 0 0 00	5 4 0 00	5 5 00	6 60
5	Lenski, A. D.	68 5 2 3 00	1 3 8 9 00	2 3 8 00	2 8 56
6	Mais, E. G.	28 4 2 6 00	6 0 5 00	6 4 00	7 68
7					
8					
9					
10					
11					
12					
13					
14					

Assumed tax rates are as follows:

a. FICA: Social Security, 6.2 percent (.062) on the first $68,400 for each employee, and Medicare, 1.45 percent (.0145) on all earnings for each employee.
b. State unemployment tax, 5.4 percent (.054) on the first $7,000 for each employee.
c. Federal unemployment tax, .8 percent (.008) on the first $7,000 for each employee.

Check Figure

Payroll Tax Expense, $258.10

Instructions

1. Complete the payroll register, page 72.
2. Prepare a general journal entry to record the payroll as of December 7.
3. Prepare a general journal entry to record the payroll taxes as of December 7.
4. Journalize the entry to pay the payroll on December 9. (Assume that the company has transferred cash to the Cash—Payroll Bank Account for this payroll.) Payroll checks begin with Ck. No. in the payroll register.

P.O. 5

Problem 9-3A For the third quarter of the year, Jiang Company, 6227 Circle Avenue, Chicago, Illinois 60652, received Form 941 from the Internal Revenue Service. The identification number of Jiang Company is 76-4213171. Its payroll for the quarter ended September 30 is as follows.

NAME	TOTAL EARNINGS	TAXABLE EARNINGS			DEDUCTIONS		
		UNEMPLOYMENT	SOCIAL SECURITY	MEDICARE	FEDERAL INCOME TAX	SOCIAL SECURITY TAX	MEDICARE TAX
1 Bailey, D. D.	6 5 7 9 00	4 2 1 00	6 5 7 9 00	6 5 7 9 00	6 4 6 00	4 0 7 90	9 5 40
2 Carter, L. E.	8 4 2 8 00		8 4 2 8 00	8 4 2 8 00	7 5 2 00	5 2 2 54	1 2 2 21
3 Dravski, P. A.	4 7 1 2 00	5 1 4 4 00	4 7 1 2 00	4 7 1 2 00	5 6 8 00	2 9 2 14	6 8 32
4 Gregor, V. O.	3 6 2 7 00	3 6 2 7 00	3 6 2 7 00	3 6 2 7 00	3 9 5 00	2 2 4 87	5 2 59
5 Temple, T. C.	7 8 3 0 00		7 8 3 0 00	7 8 3 0 00	7 0 2 00	4 8 5 46	1 1 3 54
6 Vorisky, O. T.	5 0 6 0 00		5 0 6 0 00	5 0 6 0 00	6 3 2 00	3 1 3 72	7 3 37
7	36 2 3 6 00	9 1 9 2 00	36 2 3 6 00	36 2 3 6 00	3 6 9 5 00	2 2 4 6 63	5 2 5 42

The company has had six employees throughout the year. Assume that the Social Security tax is 6.2 percent of the first $68,400, and that the Medicare tax is 1.45 percent of all earnings. The employer matches the employees' FICA (Social Security and Medicare) taxes. There are no taxable tips, adjustments, backup withholding, or earned income credits. Jiang Company has submitted the following federal tax deposits and written the accompanying checks:

On August 15 for the July Payroll

Employees' income tax withheld	$1,280.00
Employees' Social Security and Medicare tax withheld	851.10
Employer's Social Security and Medicare tax contributed	851.10
	$2,982.20

On September 15 for the August Payroll

Employees' income tax withheld	$1,392.00
Employees' Social Security and Medicare tax withheld	875.92
Employer's Social Security and Medicare tax contributed	875.92
	$3,143.84

On October 15 for the September Payroll

Employees' income tax withheld	$1,023.00
Employees' Social Security and Medicare tax withheld	1,045.03
Employer's Social Security and Medicare tax contributed	1,045.03
	$3,113.06

Check Figure

Total taxes, $9,239.10

P.O. 1,2,3

Instructions

Complete Form 941 dated October 31 for the owner, Byung Jiang.

Problem 9-4A The Lautman Company has the following balances in its general ledger as of June 1 of this year:

a. FICA Tax Payable (liability for May), $1,806.42.
b. Employees' Federal Income Tax Payable (liability for May), $998.00.
c. Federal Unemployment Tax Payable (liability for April and May), $180.36.
d. State Unemployment Tax Payable (liability for April and May), $1,306.84.
e. Employees' Medical Insurance Payable (liability for April and May), $1,282.00.

The company completed the following transactions involving the payroll during June and July:

June 13 Issued check for $2,804.42, payable to Security Bank, for the monthly deposit of May FICA taxes and employees' federal income tax withheld.

  30 Recorded the payroll entry in the general journal from the payroll register for June. The payroll register has the following column totals:

Sales salaries	$10,130.00	
Office salaries	4,068.00	
Total earnings		$14,198.00
Employees' federal income tax deductions	$ 1,422.00	
Employees' Social Security tax deductions	880.28	
Employees' Medicare tax deductions	205.87	
Employees' medical insurance deductions	710.00	
Total deductions		3,218.15
Net pay		$10,979.85

  30 Recorded payroll taxes. Employer matches the employees' FICA taxes. State unemployment tax is 5.4 percent, and federal unemployment tax is .8 percent. At this time, all employees' earnings are taxable for FICA and unemployment taxes.

  30 Issued check for $10,979.85 from Cash—Payroll Bank Account to pay salaries for the month.

July 14 Issued check for $1,992, payable to Careso Insurance Company, in payment of employees' medical insurance for April, May, and June.

  14 Issued check for $3,594.30, payable to Security Bank, for the monthly deposit of June FICA taxes and employees' federal income tax withheld.

  31 Issued check for $2,073.53, payable to the State Tax Commission, for state unemployment tax for April, May, and June. The check was accompanied by the quarterly tax return.

  31 Issued check for $293.94, payable to Security Bank, for the deposit of federal unemployment tax for the months of April, May, and June.

Check Figure

Payroll Tax Expense, $1,966.42

Instructions

Record the transactions in the general journal, page 77.

Instructions for General Ledger Software

1. Record the transactions in the general journal.
2. Print the journal entries.

PROBLEM SET B

For additional help, see the demonstration problem at the beginning of each chapter in your Working Papers.

P.O. 1

Problem 9-1B Kovach Company had the following payroll for the week ended March 21:

Salaries		**Deductions**	
Sales salaries	$7,420.00	Federal income tax withheld	$ 790.00
Office salaries	1,791.00	Social Security tax withheld	571.08
		Medicare tax withheld	133.56
Total	$9,211.00	State income tax withheld	186.00
		U.S. savings bonds	200.00
		Total	$1,880.64

Assumed tax rates are as follows:

a. FICA: Social Security, 6.2 percent (.062) on the first $68,400 for each employee, and Medicare, 1.45 percent (.0145) on all earnings for each employee.
b. State unemployment tax, 5.4 percent (.054) on the first $7,000 for each employee.
c. Federal unemployment tax, .8 percent (.008) on the first $7,000 for each employee.

Check Figure

Payroll Tax Expense, $999.76

Instructions

Record the following entries in general journal form:

1. The payroll entry as of March 21.
2. The entry to record the employer's payroll taxes as of March 21, assuming that the total payroll is subject to the FICA tax (combined Social Security and Medicare) and that $4,760 is subject to unemployment taxes.
3. The payment of the employees on March 23. (Assume that the company has transferred cash to Cash—Payroll Bank Account for this payroll.)

P.O. 1

Problem 9-2B Kuo Agency has the following information for the week ended December 14:

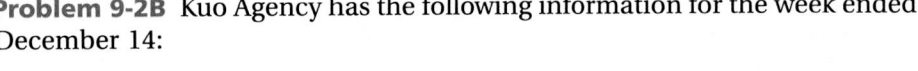

	NAME	BEGINNING CUMULATIVE EARNINGS	TOTAL EARNINGS	DEDUCTIONS	
				FEDERAL INCOME TAX	STATE INCOME TAX
1	Born, R. E.	10 6 5 0 00	4 6 0 00	4 3 00	5 00
2	Gorzel, T. S.	38 8 2 0 00	9 7 0 00	1 2 3 00	2 7 00
3	Junko, E. G.	67 8 0 4 00	1 0 9 5 00	1 5 7 00	4 2 00
4	Long, P. D.	6 7 5 0 00	3 8 5 00	3 1 00	1 5 00
5	Phillips, S. D.	31 6 7 0 00	6 9 4 00	7 8 00	1 8 00
6	Quinn, D. L.	48 9 6 1 00	1 0 4 0 00	1 4 3 00	3 5 00
7					

Assumed tax rates are as follows:

a. FICA: Social Security, 6.2 percent (.062) on the first $68,400 for each employee, and Medicare, 1.45 percent (.0145) on all earnings for each employee.

b. State unemployment tax, 5.4 percent (.054) on the first $7,000 for each employee.

c. Federal unemployment tax, .8 percent (.008) on the first $7,000 for each employee.

Check Figure

Payroll Tax Expense, $339.83

Instructions

1. Complete the payroll register, page 72.
2. Prepare a general journal entry to record the payroll as of December 14. The company's general ledger contains a Salary Expense account and a Salaries Payable account.
3. Prepare a general journal entry to record the payroll taxes as of December 14.
4. Journalize the entry to pay the payroll on December 16. (Assume that the company has transferred cash to the Cash—Payroll bank account for this payroll.) Payroll checks begin with Ck. No. 923 in the payroll register.

P.O. 5

Problem 9-3B For the third quarter of the year, Freeman Construction, of 7144 Stone Boulevard, San Francisco, California 94421, received Form 941 from the District Office of the Internal Revenue Service. The identification number for Freeman Construction is 77-6271161. Its payroll for the quarter ended September 30 is as follows:

	NAME	TOTAL EARNINGS	TAXABLE EARNINGS			DEDUCTIONS		
			UNEMPLOYMENT	SOCIAL SECURITY	MEDICARE	FEDERAL INCOME TAX	SOCIAL SECURITY TAX	MEDICARE TAX
1	Brinnon, D. L.	3 3 8 7 00	6 5 2 00	3 3 8 7 00	3 3 8 7 00	3 1 0 00	2 0 9 99	4 9 11
2	Finn, J. A.	6 7 5 3 00		6 7 5 3 00	6 7 5 3 00	7 0 4 00	4 1 8 69	9 7 92
3	Harrell, N. E.	7 7 8 0 00		7 7 8 0 00	7 7 8 0 00	8 2 0 00	4 8 2 36	1 1 2 81
4	Kelly, T. L.	6 2 4 3 00		6 2 4 3 00	6 2 4 3 00	6 6 0 00	3 8 7 07	9 0 52
5	Morton, S. M.	4 2 1 5 00	7 8 5 00	4 2 1 5 00	4 2 1 5 00	3 8 4 00	2 6 1 33	6 1 12
6	Rieck, A. J.	10 2 6 4 00		10 2 6 4 00	10 2 6 4 00	1 2 2 4 00	6 3 6 37	1 4 8 83
7		38 6 4 2 00	1 4 3 7 00	38 6 4 2 00	38 6 4 2 00	4 1 0 2 00	2 3 9 5 81	5 6 0 31

The company has had six employees throughout the year. Assume that the Social Security tax is 6.2 percent of the first $68,400 and that the Medicare tax is 1.45 percent of all earnings. The employer matches the employees' FICA (Social Security and Medicare) taxes. There are no taxable tips, adjustments, backup withholding, or earned income credits. Freeman Construction has submitted the following federal tax deposits and written the accompanying checks:

On August 15 for the July Payroll		On September 15 for the August Payroll		On October 15 for the September Payroll	
Employees' income tax withheld	$1,452.00	Employees' income tax withheld	$1,378.00	Employees' income tax withheld	$1,272.00
Employees' Social Security and Medicare tax withheld	984.80	Employees' Social Security and Medicare tax withheld	1,138.40	Employees' Social Security and Medicare tax withheld	832.92
Employer's Social Security and Medicare tax contributed	984.80	Employer's Social Security and Medicare tax contributed	1,138.40	Employer's Social Security and Medicare tax contributed	832.92
	$3,421.60		$3,654.80		$2,937.84

Check Figure

Total taxes, $10,014.24

P.O. 1,2,3

Instructions

Complete Form 941 dated October 29 for the owner, Tony Freeman. *Note:* The .01 difference is recorded on line 9, Fraction of Cents.

Problem 9-4B The Deupree Company has the following balances in its general ledger as of March 1 of this year:

a. FICA Tax Payable (liability for February), $1,405.20.
b. Employees' Federal Income Tax Payable (liability for February), $815.00.
c. State Unemployment Tax Payable (liability for January and February), $975.40.
d. Federal Unemployment Tax Payable (liability for January and February), $140.60.
e. Employees' Medical Insurance Payable (liability for January and February), $940.00.

The company completed the following transactions involving the payroll during March and April:

Mar. 12 Issued check for $2,220.20 payable to Coastal Bank, for monthly deposit of February FICA taxes and employees' federal income tax withheld.

31 Recorded the payroll entry in the general journal from the payroll register for March. The payroll register had the following column totals:

Sales salaries	$7,426.00	
Office salaries	1,837.00	
Total earnings		$9,263.00
Employees' federal income tax deductions	$ 752.00	
Employees' Social Security tax deductions	574.31	
Employees' Medicare tax deductions	134.31	
Employees' medical insurance deductions	490.00	
Total deductions		1,950.62
Net pay		$7,312.38

Mar. 31 Recorded payroll taxes. Employer matches the employees' FICA taxes. State unemployment tax is 5.4 percent. Federal unemployment tax is .8 percent. At this time, all employees' earnings are taxable for FICA and unemployment taxes.

31 Issued check for $7,312.38 from Cash—Payroll Bank Account to pay the salaries for the month.

Apr. 3 Issued check for $1,430, payable to Angel Insurance Company, for employees' medical insurance for January, February, and March.

14 Issued check for $2,169.24, payable to Coastal Bank, for monthly deposit of March FICA taxes and employees' federal income tax withheld.

30 Issued check for $1,475.60, payable to State Department of Revenue, for state unemployment tax for January, February, and March. The check was accompanied by the quarterly tax return.

30 Issued check, payable to Coastal Bank, for deposit of federal unemployment tax for January, February, and March, $214.70.

Check Figure

Payroll Tax Expense, $1,282.92

Instructions

Record the transactions in the general journal, page 77.

Instructions for General Ledger Software

1. Record the transactions in the general journal.
2. Print the journal entries.

Cumulative Self-Check: Chapters 7–9

PART I: COMPLETION

1. Checks issued by the depositor that have been paid or have cleared the bank are called _____ checks.

2. A deposit that is not recorded on the bank statement because it was made after the bank's closing date for preparation of bank statements is called a(n) _____.

3. The process by which the payee transfers ownership of the check to a bank or other party is called a(n) _____.

4. The person to whom a check is payable is called the _____.

5. A cash fund used to make small immediate cash payments is called a(n) _____.

PART II: APPLICATION

1. Cora Thomas's salary is $1,775 per month. If she works more than 40 hours in one week, she is entitled to overtime pay at the rate of 1½ times her regular hourly rate. During the current week, she worked 45 hours. Calculate her gross pay.

2. On June 30, the column totals of Midway Cleaning's payroll register showed that its cleaning employees had earned $9,000 and its office employees had earned $3,000. Social Security taxes were withheld at 6.2 percent, and Medicare taxes were withheld at 1.45 percent. All earnings are taxable. Other deductions consisted of federal income tax, $1,500; U.S. savings bonds, $500; and medical insurance, $962. Determine the amount of Social Security and Medicare taxes that should be withheld. Record the general journal entry to record the payroll, crediting Salaries Payable for the net pay.

3. Rensel Company's payroll for the week ended December 31 is as follows:

Gross earnings of employees	$155,000
Social Security taxable earnings	143,000
Medicare taxable earnings	155,000
Federal unemployment taxable earnings	22,000
State unemployment taxable earnings	22,000

Note: Answers to the Cumulative Self-Check begin on page A-1.

Assume that the payroll is subject to Social Security tax of 6.2 percent (.062), Medicare tax of 1.45 percent (.0145), federal unemployment tax of .8 percent (.008), and state unemployment tax of 5.4 percent (.054). Write the entry in general journal form to record the employer's payroll tax expense.

PART III: TRUE/FALSE

T   F   1. There is no limit on the amount of taxable earnings for Medicare.

T   F   2. When journalizing the entry to reimburse the Petty Cash Fund, include a credit to Petty Cash Fund.

T   F   3. When journalizing the entry to account for a customer's NSF check, debit Accounts Payable.

T   F   4. An employee's net pay is the result of subtracting his or her deductions from gross pay.

T   F   5. The gross pay for an employee who works 45 hours, earns $8.50 per hour, and receives time and a half for hours worked past 40 hours is $402.75.

10 | The Sales Journal

WINDOWS ON | **THE WORLD WIDE WEB**

If you bought a four-door Ford Explorer, Eddie Bauer edition, for around $35,000, Ford bookkeepers would record the transaction in a sales journal. If you changed your mind the next day and returned the Explorer to buy a Dodge Durango for $31,000 instead, Ford's records would need to show a sales return. Sales tax would have to be accounted for in the return as well. Your return of the Explorer affects numbers on Ford's income statement. And the dealership will have to make a journal entry to reduce sales totals for the month. Compare the price of new sport utility vehicles with financial statements for Ford Motor Company. For new car Blue Book values, visit Kelley Blue Book at **http://www.kbb.com/**. See Ford's annual reports at **http://www.ford.com/default.asp?pageid=37F**.

Performance Objectives

After you have completed this chapter, you will be able to do the following:

1. Describe the specific accounts used by a merchandising firm.

2. Record transactions in sales journals.

3. Post from sales journals to an accounts receivable ledger and a general ledger.

4. Prepare a schedule of accounts receivable.

5. Journalize sales returns and allowances, including credit memorandums and returns involving sales tax, and post to the ledger account.

6. Locate errors.

7. Post directly from sales invoices to an accounts receivable ledger and journalize and post a summarizing entry in the general journal.

By now you have had enough experience to complete the full accounting cycle for service and professional enterprises. To increase your accounting knowledge, let's introduce accounting systems for merchandising enterprises. This chapter describes specific accounts of merchandising firms; a merchandising firm can be anything from a dress shop to a supermarket. The sales journal and the accounts receivable ledger are also presented. We will use Jackson Electric Supply as a continuing example of a merchandising business.

SPECIAL JOURNALS

Any accounting system must be as efficient as possible. As a matter of fact, accounting is a means by which to measure efficiency in a business. Consequently, you should take shortcuts wherever possible without sacrificing internal control.

Special journals are books of original entry in which specialized types of repetitive transactions are recorded. Using a two-column general journal for recording transactions that take place over and over, day after day, is extremely time-consuming, because each individual debit and credit entry must be posted separately. Special journals save time by making it easier to handle specialized repetitive transactions and to divide up work.

The four most commonly used special journals are the sales journal (S) for sales of merchandise on account only, the purchases journal (P) for purchases of merchandise on account only (Ch. 11), the cash receipts journal (CR) for cash received (Ch. 12), and the cash payments journal (CP) for cash paid out (Ch. 12). If any or even all of these four journals are used, the general journal must still be used to record any *non*specialized transactions—in other words, any transactions that the special journals cannot handle. When a business uses more than one journal, it is necessary to use a letter in addition to the page number of the journal when posting to the ledger. **The letter designation for the general journal is J.**

SPECIFIC ACCOUNTS FOR MERCHANDISING FIRMS

Objective 1

Describe the specific accounts used by a merchandising firm.

A service or professional enterprise depends on the sale of its services for its revenue. Thus, a service or professional enterprise uses such accounts as Income from Services or Professional Fees. A merchandising business, on the other hand, depends on the sale of goods or merchandise for its revenue, recording the amount as credits to the Sales account.

Merchandise inventory consists of a stock of goods that a company buys and intends to resell, in the same physical condition, at a profit. Merchandise should be differentiated from other assets, such as equipment and supplies, that are acquired for use in the business and are not for resale.

Because the merchandising firm has to record transactions involving the purchase, handling, and sale of its merchandise, it uses accounts and procedures that we have not yet discussed. Let's look at the fundamental accounting equation with the new T accounts that are introduced in this and subsequent chapters.

The **Sales account** is a revenue account used for recording sales of merchandise.

The **Purchases account** is used strictly to record the cost of merchandise bought for resale. The plus and minus signs are the same as the signs for Merchandise Inventory. Purchases is placed under the heading of Expenses only because the accountant closes it along with the expense accounts at the end of the fiscal period.

The **Sales Returns and Allowances account** is used to record the physical return of merchandise by customers or a reduction in a bill because merchandise was damaged. It is treated as a deduction from Sales.

The **Purchases Returns and Allowances account** is used to record the company's returns of merchandise it has purchased from suppliers or reductions in bills because of damaged merchandise. It is treated as a deduction from Purchases.

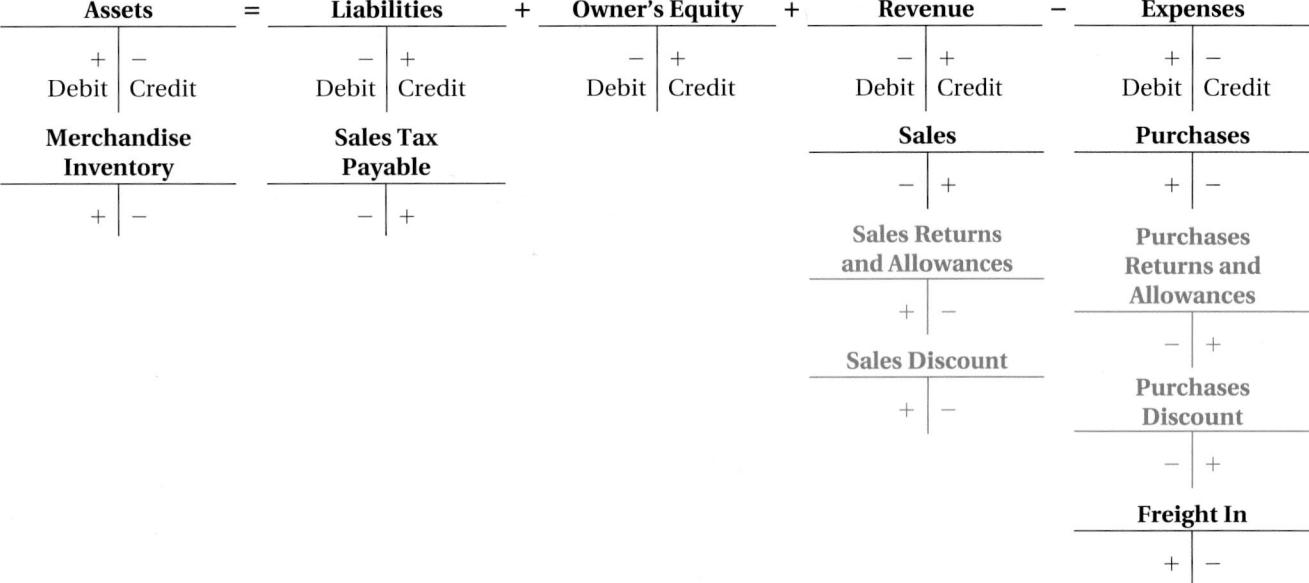

Assets	=	Liabilities	+	Owner's Equity	+	Revenue	−	Expenses
+ | −		− | +		− | +		− | +		+ | −
Debit | Credit		Debit | Credit		Debit | Credit		Debit | Credit		Debit | Credit
Merchandise Inventory		**Sales Tax Payable**				**Sales**		**Purchases**
+ | −		− | +				− | +		+ | −
						Sales Returns and Allowances		**Purchases Returns and Allowances**
						+ | −		− | +
						Sales Discount		**Purchases Discount**
						+ | −		− | +
								Freight In
								+ | −

The **Sales Discount account** and **Purchases Discount account** are used to record cash discounts granted for prompt payments, in accordance with the credit terms.

The **Freight In account** is used to record the transportation charges on incoming merchandise intended for resale. Debits to this account increase the cost of purchases.

The T accounts for returns and allowances and for discounts are shown in green to emphasize that we are treating them as deductions from the related accounts placed above them. We list these accounts as deductions because they appear as deductions in the financial statements. Their relationship is similar to that between the Drawing account and the Capital account; remember that we deduct Drawing from Capital in the statement of owner's equity.

The type of transaction most frequently encountered in a merchandising business is the sale of merchandise. Some businesses sell on a cash-and-carry basis only; others sell only on credit. Many firms offer both arrangements. The same general types of entries pertain to retail and wholesale enterprises.

Merchandising firms such as Sam Goody's must differentiate merchandise—or goods bought to be resold at a profit—from other assets like equipment and supplies (goods used in the business but not resold).

RECORDING SALES ON ACCOUNT

Sales are recorded only in response to a customer order. The routines for processing orders and recording sales vary with the type and size of the business. However, a sale of merchandise on credit, such as a sale for $200, would be entered in a sales journal. Here's what this sale would look like in T accounts as a debit to Accounts Receivable and a credit to Sales.

Accounts Receivable			Sales	
+	−		−	+
200				200

In a retail business, a salesperson usually prepares a sales ticket in either duplicate or triplicate for a sale on account. One copy goes to the customer and another to the accounting department, where it serves as the basis for an entry in the sales journal. A third copy may be used as a record of sales—to compute sales commissions or control inventory, for example.

In a wholesale business, the company usually receives a written order from a customer or from a salesperson who obtained the order from the customer. The credit department approves the order, then sends it to the billing department, where the sales invoice is prepared.

Invoices are prepared in multiple copies. Figure 1 shows one possible distribution of sales invoice copies to various parties.

Our model business, Jackson Electric Supply, is a wholesaler. One of its invoices is shown in Figure 2.

We introduce the sales journal by looking at three transactions on the books of Jackson Electric Supply:

Aug. 1 Sold merchandise on account to L. A. Long Company, invoice no. 320, $424.00.

FIGURE 1

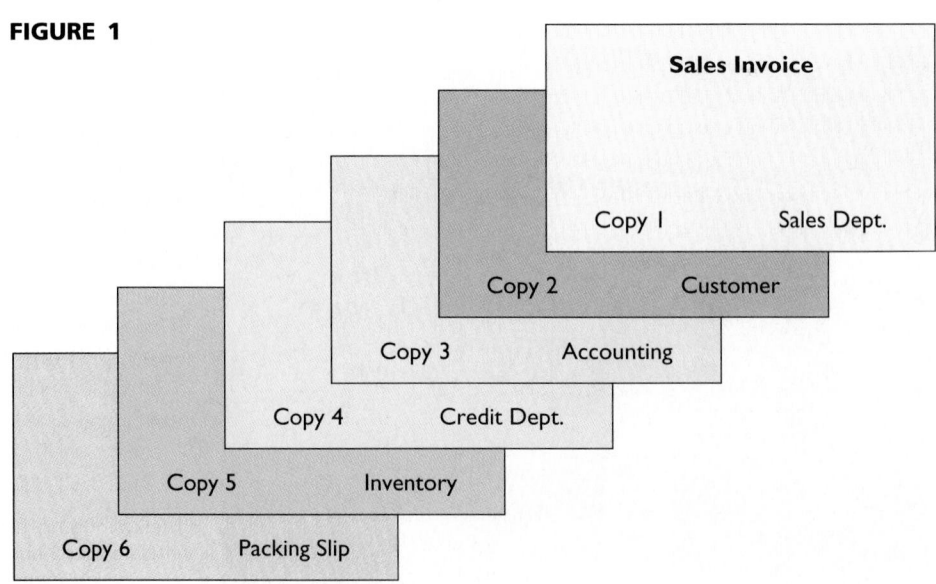

FIGURE 2

Jackson Electric Supply
625 N.E. Manor Avenue
Portland, Oregon 97201

INVOICE

SOLD TO	L. A. Long Company	DATE: **August 1, 20–**
	620 S.W. Kennedy Street	INVOICE NO.: **320**
	Portland, OR 97110	ORDER NO.: **5384**
		SHIPPED BY: **Their truck**
		TERMS: **2/10, n/30**

QUANTITY	DESCRIPTION	UNIT PRICE	TOTAL
1000	Ivory duplex outlet cover	32	320 00
50	Ceiling junction box	96	48 00
40	Junction box (stud mount)	1 40	56 00
		TOTAL	424 00

Aug. 3 Sold merchandise on account to Marin, Inc., invoice no. 321, $116.

6 Sold merchandise on account to Arreloa Construction, invoice no. 322, $394.

We can use T accounts to visualize these transactions:

Accounts Receivable			Sales	
+	−		−	+
424.00				424.00
116.00				116.00
394.00				394.00

If the transactions were recorded in a general journal, they would appear as they do in Figure 3 on the following page.

Next, the journal entries would be posted to the accounts in the general ledger (see Figure 3). As the last step in the posting process, the ledger account numbers would be recorded in the Post. Ref. column of the journal. (In each of the following ledger accounts, assume that there are no beginning balances.)

Obviously, there is a great deal of repetition in both journalizing and posting. The credit sales require three separate journal entries, three debit postings to Accounts Receivable, and three credit postings to Sales. We have presented all of this to show the advantages of the sales journal, which eliminates all this repetition.

FIGURE 3

GENERAL JOURNAL

PAGE ___23___

	DATE		DESCRIPTION	POST. REF.	DEBIT	CREDIT	
1	20–						1
2	Aug.	1	Accounts Receivable	113	4 2 4 00		2
3			Sales	411		4 2 4 00	3
4			Invoice no. 320, L. A. Long				4
5			Company.				5
6							6
7		3	Accounts Receivable	113	1 1 6 00		7
8			Sales	411		1 1 6 00	8
9			Invoice no. 321, Marin, Inc.				9
10							10
11		6	Accounts Receivable	113	3 9 4 00		11
12			Sales	411		3 9 4 00	12
13			Invoice no. 322, Arreloa				13
14			Construction.				14
15							15
16							16
17							17

GENERAL LEDGER

ACCOUNT **Accounts Receivable**

ACCOUNT NO. ___113___

	DATE		ITEM	POST. REF.	DEBIT	CREDIT	BALANCE DEBIT	BALANCE CREDIT	
1	20–								1
2	Aug.	1		23	4 2 4 00		4 2 4 00		2
3		3		23	1 1 6 00		5 4 0 00		3
4		6		23	3 9 4 00		9 3 4 00		4
5									5
6									6
7									7

ACCOUNT **Sales**

ACCOUNT NO. ___411___

	DATE		ITEM	POST. REF.	DEBIT	CREDIT	BALANCE DEBIT	BALANCE CREDIT	
1	20–								1
2	Aug.	1		23		4 2 4 00		4 2 4 00	2
3		3		23		1 1 6 00		5 4 0 00	3
4		6		23		3 9 4 00		9 3 4 00	4
5									5
6									6
7									7

THE SALES JOURNAL

Objective 2

Record transactions in sales journals.

The **sales journal** records sales of merchandise *on account only.* This specialized type of transaction calls for debits to Accounts Receivable and credits to Sales. Let's see how to record the three transactions for Jackson Electric Supply in the sales journal *instead of* in the general journal.

Remember!

The sales journal is a book of original entry. Do not duplicate the transaction in the general journal.

	SALES JOURNAL				PAGE __38__	
	DATE	INV. NO.	CUSTOMER'S NAME	POST. REF.	ACCOUNTS RECEIVABLE DR. SALES CR.	
1	20–					1
2	Aug. 1	320	L. A. Long Company		4 2 4 00	2
3	3	321	Marin, Inc.		1 1 6 00	3
4	6	322	Arreloa Construction		3 9 4 00	4
5						5

Because *one* money column is headed Accounts Receivable Dr./Sales Cr., each transaction requires only a single line. Repetition is avoided, and all entries for sales of merchandise on account are found in one place. Listing the invoice number makes it easier to check the details of a particular sale at a later date.

Posting from the Sales Journal

Objective 3

Post from sales journals to an accounts receivable ledger and a general ledger.

Using the sales journal also saves time and space in posting to the ledger accounts. The transactions involving the sales of merchandise on account for the entire month of August are shown in Figure 4 on page 336.

Because every entry is a debit to Accounts Receivable and a credit to Sales, you can make a single posting to these accounts for the amount of the total as of the last day of the month. This entry is called a **summarizing entry** because it summarizes one month's transactions. In the Post. Ref. columns of the ledger accounts, the letter S designates the sales journal.

A grocery store may have several sales accounts—one for groceries, one for produce, and one for meats, as well as one for sales tax.

FIGURE 4

	DATE	INV. NO.	CUSTOMER'S NAME	POST. REF.	ACCOUNTS RECEIVABLE DR. SALES CR.	
1	20–					1
2	Aug. 1	320	L. A. Long Company		4 2 4 00	2
3	3	321	Marin, Inc.		1 1 6 00	3
4	6	322	Arreloa Construction		3 9 4 00	4
5	9	323	Markam Service Company		9 6 1 00	5
6	11	324	Colmer Company		7 7 2 24	6
7	16	325	Howard and Sons, Inc.		4 4 1 00	7
8	20	326	Hazen Electric		7 1 0 00	8
9	23	327	Baker Company		3 8 4 00	9
10	24	328	Colmer Company		2 9 3 22	10
11	28	329	Howard and Sons, Inc.		4 8 7 00	11
12	30	330	Baker Company		6 1 4 00	12
13	31	331	L. A. Long Company		3 7 5 50	13
14	31	332	F. A. Barnes, Inc.		8 6 1 00	14
15	31				6 8 3 2 96	15
16					(113)(411)	16
17						17

SALES JOURNAL PAGE **38**

GENERAL LEDGER

ACCOUNT **Accounts Receivable** ACCOUNT NO. **113**

	DATE	ITEM	POST. REF.	DEBIT	CREDIT	BALANCE DEBIT	BALANCE CREDIT	
1	20–							1
2	Aug. 31		S38	6 8 3 2 96		6 8 3 2 96		2
3								3
4								4
5								5

ACCOUNT **Sales** ACCOUNT NO. **411**

	DATE	ITEM	POST. REF.	DEBIT	CREDIT	BALANCE DEBIT	BALANCE CREDIT	
1	20–							1
2	Aug. 31		S38		6 8 3 2 96		6 8 3 2 96	2
3								3
4								4
5								5

After posting the total of the Sales Journal to the Accounts Receivable account in the general ledger, write the account number of Accounts Receivable at the left below the total of the Sales Journal. Repeat the process of posting for the total of the Sales Journal to the general ledger, placing the account number of Sales at the right below the total of the sales journal. **Don't record these account numbers until you have completed the postings.**

If you should find an error, do not erase it. The same procedure for error correction that you learned earlier applies to special journals. If you catch the error in the journal entry before it is posted to the ledger, draw a single line through the error with a ruler, write in the correct information, and add your initials. If an amount is entered in the ledger incorrectly (although the journal entry is correct), follow the same procedure. However, if an entry included the wrong accounts, you must prepare a new journal entry to correct the first entry.

Sales Journal Provision for Sales Tax

Most states and some cities levy a **sales tax** on retail sales of goods and services. The retailer collects the sales tax from customers and later pays it to the tax authorities.

When goods or services are sold on credit, the sales tax is charged to the customer and recorded at the time of the sale. The sales journal must be designed to handle this type of transaction. For example, if a retail store sells an item for $100 and the sales tax is 4 percent, the transaction would be recorded in T accounts like this:

Accounts Receivable	Sales	Sales Tax Payable
+ −	− +	− +
104	100	4

Incidentally, when the sales tax is paid to the state, the accountant debits Sales Tax Payable and credits Cash.

Because we want to illustrate a sales journal for a retail merchandising firm operating in a state that has a sales tax, we will talk about the transactions of Freel Toy Center, another company. Its sales journal follows.

SALES JOURNAL   PAGE __96__

	DATE	INV. NO.	CUSTOMER'S NAME	POST. REF.	ACCOUNTS RECEIVABLE DEBIT	SALES TAX PAYABLE CREDIT	SALES CREDIT	
1	20–							1
2	Apr. 1	9382	D. E. Bates		1 6 64	64	1 6 00	2
3	1	9383	Center Child Care		2 2 88	88	2 2 00	3
4	1	9384	Randy Kelley		5 2 00	2 00	5 0 00	4
5	2	9385	R. M. Kale		1 2 48	48	1 2 00	5
18	30	10121	L. O. Link		1 2 4 80	4 80	1 2 0 00	18
19	30				2 5 1 8 80	9 6 80	2 4 2 2 00	19
20					(1 1 3)	(2 1 4)	(4 1 1)	20
21								21
22								22

A/R – daily   monthly   monthly
GL – monthly

The total of each column is posted to the ledger accounts at the end of the month. After posting the figures, the accountant records the account numbers in parentheses immediately below the totals. Note that Freel Toy Center's charge customers owe the total amount of the sales plus the sales tax, $2,518.80 ($2,422 + $96.80 = $2,518.80).

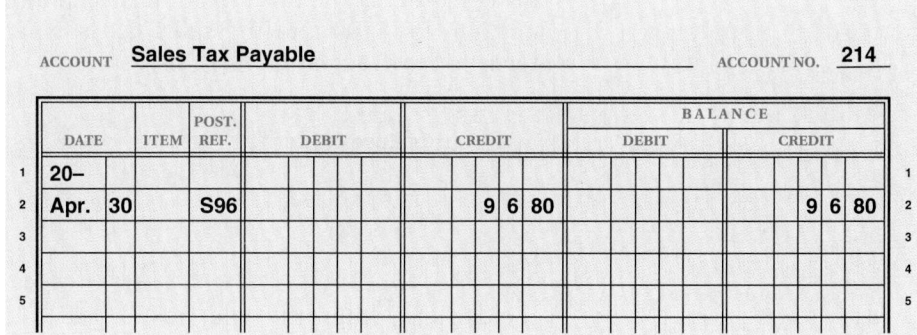

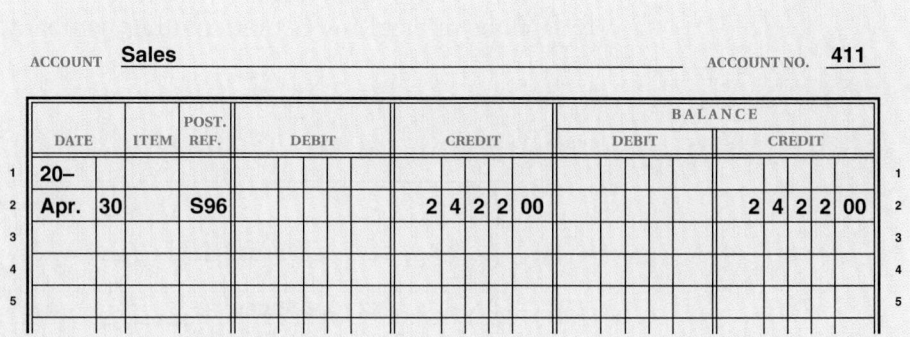

THE ACCOUNTS RECEIVABLE LEDGER

Accounts Receivable represents the total amount owed to a business by its charge customers. The information in this account is incomplete, however. The business can't tell at a glance *how much each* individual charge customer owes. To correct this shortcoming, businesses keep a separate account for each charge customer.

When a business has very few charge customers, it is possible to have a separate Accounts Receivable account in the general ledger for each charge customer. However, when there are many charge customers, which is usually the case, this arrangement is too cumbersome. Listing each charge customer's account makes the trial balance very long and there is a greater likelihood of errors.

It is more practical to have a separate book containing a list of all the charge customers with their respective balances. This is called the accounts receivable ledger. In the accounts receivable ledger, the individual charge customer accounts are listed in either alphabetical or numerical order. If the company's accounting system is not computerized, accountants prefer a loose-leaf binder, so that they can insert accounts for new customers and remove closed accounts.

The Accounts Receivable account in the general ledger should still be maintained. When all the postings are up to date, the balance of this account should equal the total of all the charge customers' individual balances. The Accounts Receivable account in the general ledger is called a controlling account. The accounts receivable *ledger,* containing the accounts of all the charge customers, is really a special ledger, called a subsidiary ledger. Figure 5 diagrams the interrelationship of these ledgers.

FIGURE 5

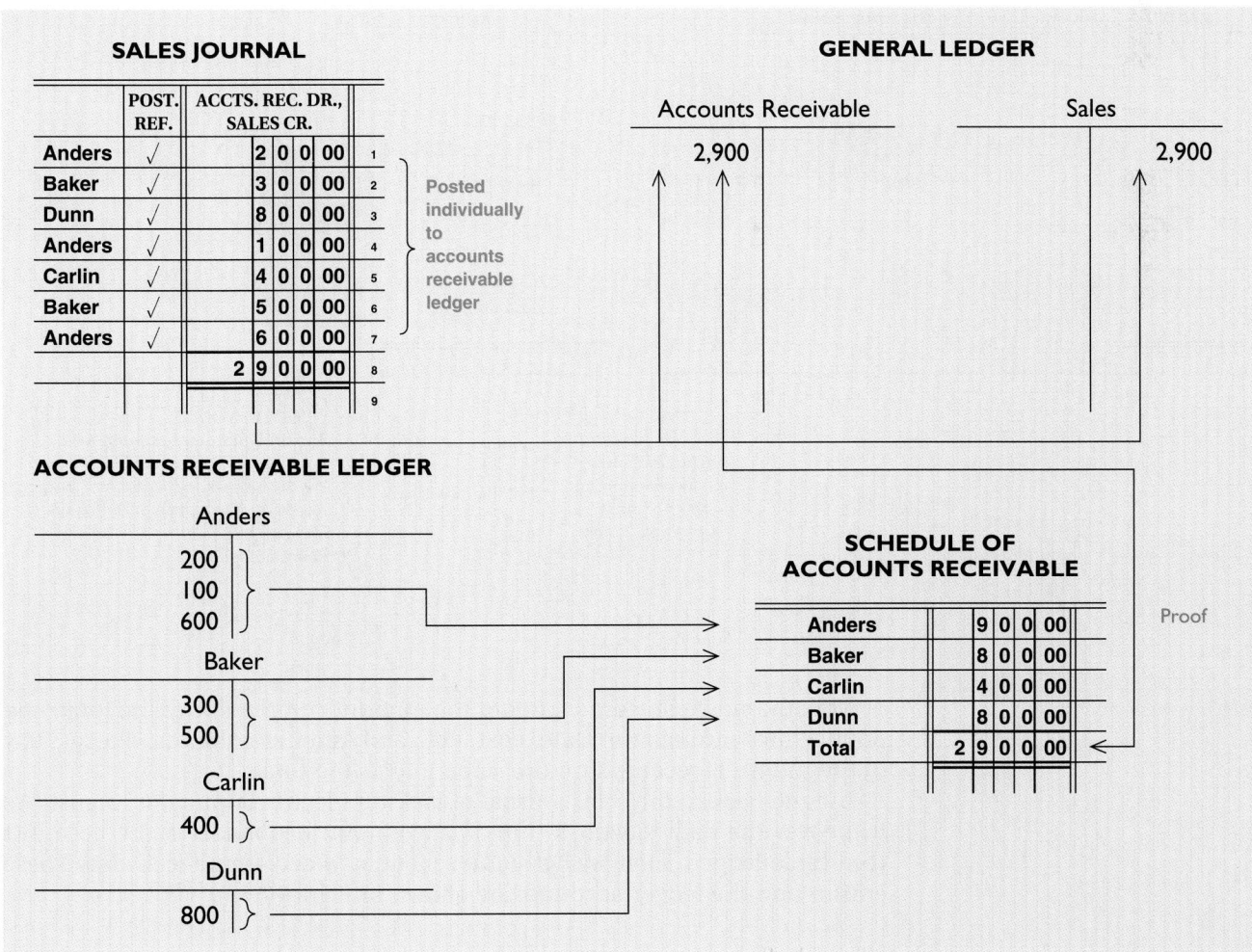

The accountant posts the individual amounts to the accounts receivable ledger every day, so that this ledger will have up-to-date information. At the end of the month, the accountant posts the total of the sales journal of $2,900 (in Figure 5) to the general ledger accounts as a debit to the Accounts Receivable controlling account and a credit to the Sales account. The schedule of accounts receivable is merely a listing of charge customers' individual balances.

In the simplified illustration in Figure 5, it just so happens that, since no payments were received from charge customers, the total of the sales journal equals the balance of Accounts Receivable. However, if $1,200 had been received from charge customers, both the balance of the Accounts Receivable controlling account and the total of the schedule of accounts receivable would be $1,700 ($2,900 − $1,200). The total of the sales journal would still be $2,900.

After you post an amount from the sales journal to a charge customer's account in the accounts receivable ledger, put a check mark (✓) in the Post. Ref. column of the sales journal. Figure 6 shows the posting procedure for a single-column sales journal.

FIGURE 6

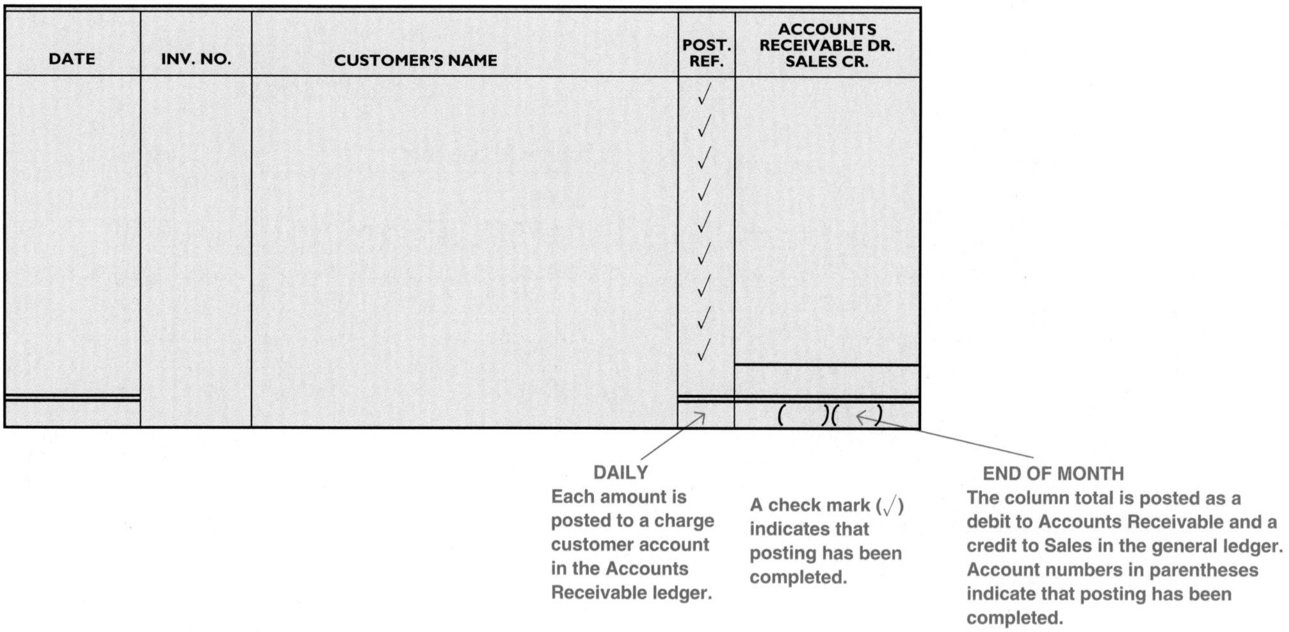

DAILY
Each amount is posted to a charge customer account in the Accounts Receivable ledger.

A check mark (√) indicates that posting has been completed.

END OF MONTH
The column total is posted as a debit to Accounts Receivable and a credit to Sales in the general ledger. Account numbers in parentheses indicate that posting has been completed.

Note the single line drawn under the Amount column above the total, and double lines through the Date, Post. Ref., and Amount columns. The last day of the month is recorded on the same line as the total.

Let's go back to the sales journal of Jackson Electric Supply for August. We will cover the daily postings that its accountant has made to the accounts receivable ledger. Then we'll see the schedule of accounts receivable. These entries and the ledger accounts are shown in Figure 7.

FIGURE 7

				SALES JOURNAL		PAGE __38__						
	DATE		INV. NO.	CUSTOMER'S NAME	POST. REF.	ACCOUNTS RECEIVABLE DR. SALES CR.						
1	20–											1
2	Aug.	1	320	L. A. Long Company	✓		4	2	4	00		2
3		3	321	Marin, Inc.	✓		1	1	6	00		3
4		6	322	Arreloa Construction	✓		3	9	4	00		4
5		9	323	Markam Service Company	✓		9	6	1	00		5
6		11	324	Colmer Company	✓		7	7	2	24		6
7		16	325	Howard and Sons, Inc.	✓		4	4	1	00		7
8		20	326	Hazen Electric	✓		7	1	0	00		8
9		23	327	Baker Company	✓		3	8	4	00		9
10		24	328	Colmer Company	✓		2	9	3	22		10
11		28	329	Howard and Sons, Inc.	✓		4	8	7	00		11
12		30	330	Baker Company	✓		6	1	4	00		12
13		31	331	L. A. Long Company	✓		3	7	5	50		13
14		31	332	F. A. Barnes, Inc.	✓		8	6	1	00		14
15		31				6	8	3	2	96		15
16							(113)(411)					16
17												17
18												18
19												19

ACCOUNTS RECEIVABLE LEDGER

NAME   **Arreloa Construction**
ADDRESS **1016 Broad Street, S.W.**
         Seattle, WA 98102

DATE		ITEM	POST. REF.	DEBIT				CREDIT				BALANCE			
20–															
Aug.	6		S38	3	9	4	00					3	9	4	00

NAME   **Baker Company**
ADDRESS **271 N. Kinman Street**
         Bishop, WA 98792

DATE		ITEM	POST. REF.	DEBIT				CREDIT				BALANCE			
20–															
Aug.	23		S38	3	8	4	00					3	8	4	00
	30		S38	6	1	4	00					9	9	8	00

FIGURE 7 (continued)

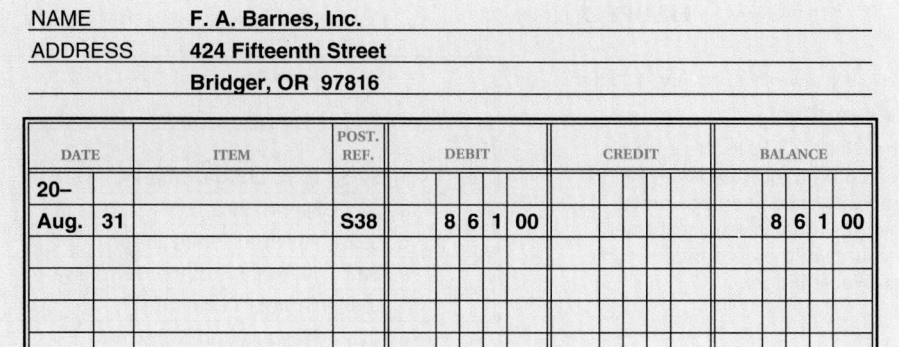

NAME   **F. A. Barnes, Inc.**

ADDRESS   **424 Fifteenth Street**

                   Bridger, OR 97816

DATE		ITEM	POST. REF.	DEBIT	CREDIT	BALANCE
20–						
Aug.	31		S38	8 6 1 00		8 6 1 00

NAME   **Colmer Company**

ADDRESS   **2168 Tenth Street**

                   Southridge, WA 98206

DATE		ITEM	POST. REF.	DEBIT	CREDIT	BALANCE
20–						
Aug.	11		S38	7 7 2 24		7 7 2 24
	24		S38	2 9 3 22		1 0 6 5 46

NAME   **Hazen Electric**

ADDRESS   **1620 Salazar Road**

                   Brighton, OR 97414

DATE		ITEM	POST. REF.	DEBIT	CREDIT	BALANCE
20–						
Aug.	20		S38	7 1 0 00		7 1 0 00

NAME   **Howard and Sons, Inc.**

ADDRESS   **4142 Lucientes Avenue**

                   Pender, OR 97512

DATE		ITEM	POST. REF.	DEBIT	CREDIT	BALANCE
20–						
Aug.	16		S38	4 4 1 00		4 4 1 00
	28		S38	4 8 7 00		9 2 8 00

FIGURE 7 (continued)

NAME   L. A. Long Company

ADDRESS   620 S.W. Kennedy Street

Portland, OR 97110

DATE		ITEM	POST. REF.	DEBIT	CREDIT	BALANCE
20–						
Aug.	1		S38	4 2 4 00		4 2 4 00
	31		S38	3 7 5 50		7 9 9 50

NAME   Marin, Inc.

ADDRESS   1457 Megler Avenue

Gabriola, OR 97316

DATE		ITEM	POST. REF.	DEBIT	CREDIT	BALANCE
20–						
Aug.	3		S38	1 1 6 00		1 1 6 00

NAME   Markam Service Company

ADDRESS   2720 N.W. 43rd Ave.

Portland, OR 97210

DATE		ITEM	POST. REF.	DEBIT	CREDIT	BALANCE
20–						
Aug.	9		S38	9 6 1 00		9 6 1 00

Objective 4

Prepare a schedule of accounts receivable.

Next, the accountant prepares a schedule of accounts receivable, listing each charge customer's balance. For this example, we assume that these were the only transactions involving charge customers.

Jackson Electric Supply
Schedule of Accounts Receivable
August 31, 20—

Arreloa Construction	3 9 4 00
Baker Company	9 9 8 00
F. A. Barnes, Inc.	8 6 1 00
Colmer Company	1 0 6 5 46
Hazen Electric	7 1 0 00
Howard and Sons, Inc.	9 2 8 00
L. A. Long Company	7 9 9 50
Marin, Inc.	1 1 6 00
Markam Service Company	9 6 1 00
Total Accounts Receivable	6 8 3 2 96

Again assume that there were no previous balances in the customers' accounts. The Accounts Receivable controlling account in the general ledger will have the same balance, $6,832.96, as the schedule of accounts receivable.

GENERAL LEDGER

ACCOUNT **Accounts Receivable** ACCOUNT NO. **113**

	DATE	ITEM	POST. REF.	DEBIT	CREDIT	BALANCE DEBIT	BALANCE CREDIT	
1	20–							1
2	Aug. 31		S38	6 8 3 2 96		6 8 3 2 96		2
3								3
4								4
5								5

SALES RETURNS AND ALLOWANCES

Objective 5

Journalize sales returns and allowances, including credit memorandums and returns involving sales tax, and post to the ledger accounts.

The Sales Returns and Allowances account handles two types of transactions having to do with merchandise that has previously been sold. A *return* is a physical return of the goods. An *allowance* is a reduction from the original price because the goods were defective or damaged. It may not be economically worthwhile to have customers return the goods; each situation is a special case. To avoid writing a separate letter each time to inform customers of their account adjustments, businesses use a special form called a **credit memorandum**. A credit memorandum (Figure 8) is a written statement indicating a seller's willingness to reduce the amount of a buyer's debt.

FIGURE 8

Jackson Electric Supply
625 N.E. Manor Avenue
Portland, Oregon 97201

CREDIT MEMORANDUM   No. 69

CREDIT TO: Baker Company
271 N. Kinman Street
Bishop, WA 98792

DATE: September 2, 20–

WE CREDIT YOUR ACCOUNT AS FOLLOWS:

QUANTITY	DESCRIPTION	TOTAL
1	Entrance panel circuit breaker, 100 amp 120v-12 circuits	54 00

The Sales Returns and Allowances account is a deduction from Sales. Using an account separate from Sales provides a better record of the total returns and allowances. Accountants deduct Sales Returns and Allowances from Sales on the income statement.

Using T accounts, here's an example of a return. The original sale is shown first, followed by the issuance of a credit memorandum.

Transaction (a) On August 30, Jackson Electric Supply sold merchandise on account to Baker Company, $614, and recorded the sale in the sales journal.

Transaction (b) On September 2, Baker Company returned $54 worth of the merchandise. Jackson Electric Supply issued credit memorandum no. 69 (see Figure 8).

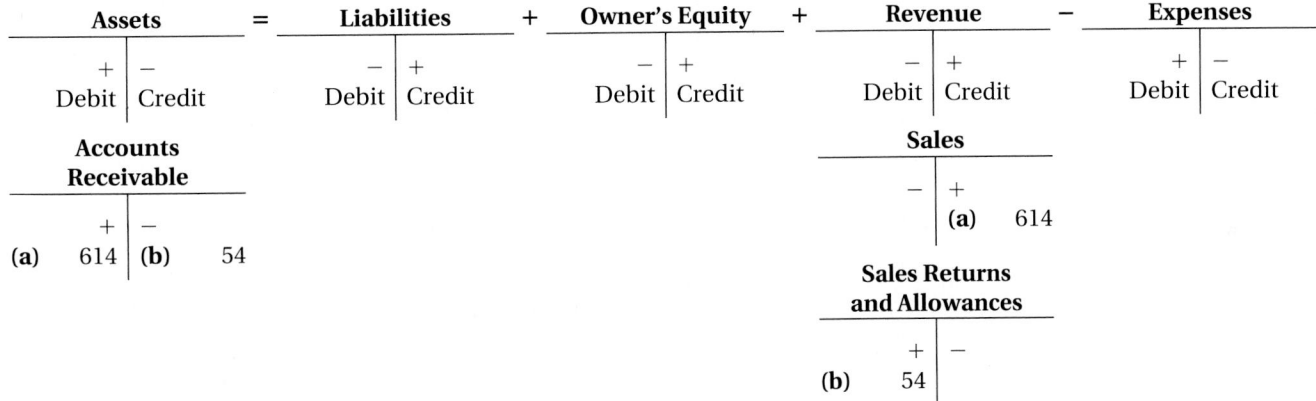

Jackson Electric Supply's accountant debits Sales Returns and Allowances because Jackson Electric Supply has more returns and allowances than it had before. The accountant credits Accounts Receivable because the charge customer, Baker Company, owes less than before.

You use the word *credit* in "credit memorandum" because the seller has to credit Accounts Receivable. Suppose that Jackson Electric Supply issues two credit memoranda during September and makes the following entries in the general journal:

	DATE		DESCRIPTION	POST. REF.	DEBIT	CREDIT	
1	20–						1
2	Sept.	2	Sales Returns and Allowances		5 4 00		2
3			Accounts Receivable,				3
4			Baker Company			5 4 00	4
5			Issued credit memo no. 69.				5
6							6
7		2	Sales Returns and Allowances		1 2 7 00		7
8			Accounts Receivable,				8
9			Markam Service Company			1 2 7 00	9
10			Issued credit memo no. 70.				10

GENERAL JOURNAL   PAGE 27

■ ■ ■

Remember!

When a credit memo is issued, it means we have given the customer permission to return the goods or to receive an allowance.

The general journal entry serves as the posting source for crediting the Accounts Receivable controlling account in the general ledger. It also serves as the posting source for updating the accounts receivable ledger and therefore includes the name of the charge customer. If the balance of the Accounts Receivable controlling account is to equal the total of the individual balances in the accounts receivable ledger, you must post the amount to *both* the Accounts Receivable account in the general ledger *and* the account of Baker Company in the accounts receivable ledger. To take care of this dual posting, draw a slanted line in the Post. Ref. column. When the amount has been posted as a credit to the general ledger account, write the account number of Accounts Receivable in the left part of the Post. Ref. column. After the amount has been posted as a credit to the account of Baker Company, draw a check mark in the right portion of the Post. Ref. column. Sales Returns and Allowances is posted in the usual manner. Here are the entries after posting is complete:

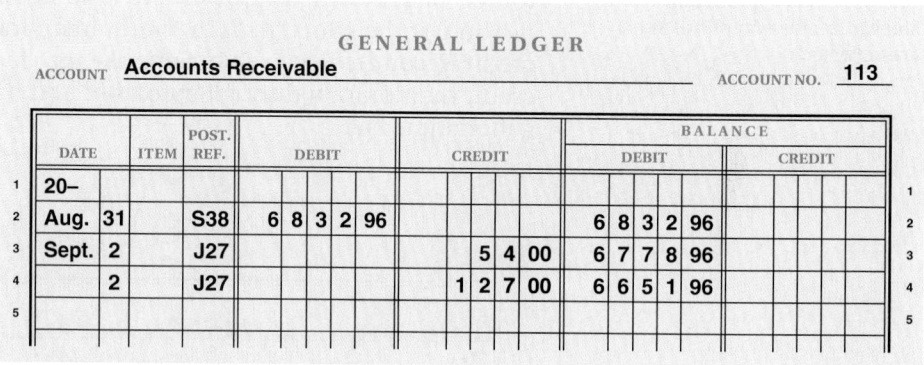

GENERAL JOURNAL   PAGE 27

	DATE		DESCRIPTION	POST. REF.	DEBIT	CREDIT	
1	20–						1
2	Sept.	2	Sales Returns and Allowances	412	5 4 00		2
3			Accounts Receivable,				3
4			Baker Company	113 ✓		5 4 00	4
5			Issued credit memo no. 69.				5
6							6
7		2	Sales Returns and Allowances	412	1 2 7 00		7
8			Accounts Receivable,				8
9			Markam Service Company	113 ✓		1 2 7 00	9
10			Issued credit memo no. 70.				10

GENERAL LEDGER

ACCOUNT **Accounts Receivable**   ACCOUNT NO. 113

	DATE	ITEM	POST. REF.	DEBIT	CREDIT	BALANCE DEBIT	BALANCE CREDIT	
1	20–							1
2	Aug. 31		S38	6 8 3 2 96		6 8 3 2 96		2
3	Sept. 2		J27		5 4 00	6 7 7 8 96		3
4	2		J27		1 2 7 00	6 6 5 1 96		4
5								5

ACCOUNT **Sales Returns and Allowances**   ACCOUNT NO. 412

	DATE	ITEM	POST. REF.	DEBIT	CREDIT	BALANCE DEBIT	BALANCE CREDIT	
1	20–							1
2	Sept. 2		J27	5 4 00		5 4 00		2
3	2		J27	1 2 7 00		1 8 1 00		3

ACCOUNTS RECEIVABLE LEDGER

NAME   **Baker Company**

ADDRESS   **271 N. Kinman Steet**

Bishop, WA 98792

DATE		ITEM	POST. REF.	DEBIT	CREDIT	BALANCE
20–						
Aug.	23		S38	3 8 4 00		3 8 4 00
	30		S38	6 1 4 00		9 9 8 00
Sept.	2		J27		5 4 00	9 4 4 00

NAME   **Markam Service Company**

ADDRESS   **2720 N.W. 43rd Ave.**

Portland, OR 97210

DATE		ITEM	POST. REF.	DEBIT	CREDIT	BALANCE
20–						
Aug.	9		S38	9 6 1 00		9 6 1 00
Sept.	2		J27		1 2 7 00	8 3 4 00

When a customer returns merchandise bought on account, the business issues a credit memorandum, which is a written statement that the seller is willing to reduce the buyer's debt. The entry is entered in the general journal if the sale was on account.

Sales Return Involving a Sales Tax

If a customer who returns merchandise to a retail store was originally charged a sales tax, the sales tax must be returned to the customer. Refer back to the sales journal of Freel Toy Center on page 337, which included sales taxes. On April 3, assume that D. E. Bates returns the merchandise bought on April 1 for $16 plus $.64 sales tax. Following is the general journal entry required for this type of return:

GENERAL JOURNAL   PAGE **12**

	DATE		DESCRIPTION	POST. REF.	DEBIT	CREDIT	
1	20–						1
2	Apr.	3	Sales Returns and Allowances		1 6 00		2
3			Sales Tax Payable		64		3
4			Accounts Receivable, D. E. Bates			1 6 64	4
5			Issued credit memo no. 371.				5
6							6
7							7

Procedure for Locating Errors

Suppose you are facing a situation where the total of the schedule of accounts receivable does not equal the balance of the Accounts Receivable controlling account. To locate possible errors, do everything in reverse. Here is a suggested order:

1. Re-add the schedule of accounts receivable.
2. Check the balances transferred from the customer accounts in the accounts receivable ledger to the schedule of accounts receivable.
3. Verify the balances of the customer accounts in the accounts receivable ledger.
4. Verify the postings from the sales and general journals to the Accounts Receivable controlling account.
5. Re-add the sales journal.
6. Check the postings from the sales and general journals to the customer accounts in the accounts receivable ledger.

POSTING DIRECTLY FROM SALES INVOICES (AN ALTERNATIVE TO USING A SALES JOURNAL)

Objective 7

Post directly from sales invoices to an accounts receivable ledger and journalize and post a summarizing entry in the general journal.

Companies that have a large volume of sales on account sometimes use duplicate copies of their sales invoices as a sales journal. The accountant posts daily to the charge customer accounts in the accounts receivable ledger, working directly from the copies of the sales invoices or sales slips. He or she writes the invoice number rather than the journal page in the Post. Ref. column of the customer's account. A file is maintained for the copies of the sales invoices. Then, at the end of the month, the accountant brings the Accounts Receivable controlling account up to date by totaling all the sales invoices for the month and then making a general journal entry debiting Accounts Receivable and crediting Sales.

Let's use a different firm to show how this procedure works. Gordon Sports Equipment Company posts directly from its sales invoices; the total of its sales invoices for December is $37,426. Its accountant journalizes and posts the entry as follows:

Remember!

Posting directly from sales invoices is an alternative to the special sales journal; don't do both.

GENERAL JOURNAL   PAGE __36__

	DATE		DESCRIPTION	POST. REF.	DEBIT	CREDIT	
1	20–						1
2	Dec.	31	Accounts Receivable	113	37 4 2 6 00		2
3			Sales	411		37 4 2 6 00	3
4			Summarizing entry for the total				4
5			of the sales invoices for the				5
6			month.				6
7							7

GENERAL LEDGER

ACCOUNT **Accounts Receivable**   ACCOUNT NO. __113__

	DATE	ITEM	POST. REF.	DEBIT	CREDIT	BALANCE DEBIT	BALANCE CREDIT	
1	20–							1
2	Dec. 31		J36	37 4 2 6 00		37 4 2 6 00		2
3								3
4								4
5								5

ACCOUNT **Sales**   ACCOUNT NO. __411__

	DATE	ITEM	POST. REF.	DEBIT	CREDIT	BALANCE DEBIT	BALANCE CREDIT	
1	20–							1
2	Dec. 31		J36		37 4 2 6 00		37 4 2 6 00	2
3								3
4								4
5								5

This journal entry is a *summarizing entry* because it summarizes the credit sales for one month. Because the accountant posts the entry to the accounts in the general ledger, there is no need for a sales journal; the one summarizing entry in the general journal records the total sales for the month.

One invoice and the corresponding entry in the accounts receivable ledger might look like Figure 9 and the accompanying ledger account on the following page. The $855 is posted to the general ledger as a part of the total in the monthly summarizing entry.

FIGURE 9

Gordon Sports Equipment Company
1620 Santa Rosa Avenue
San Francisco, California 94133

INVOICE

SOLD TO Norton Sporting Goods
225 N.W. Satsop Ave.
Portland, OR 97201

DATE: Dec. 4, 20–
INVOICE NO.: 6075
ORDER NO.: 359
SHIPPED BY: Express Collect
TERMS: 2/10, n/30

QUANTITY	DESCRIPTION	UNIT PRICE	TOTAL
10	Fentris cartop bicycle carrier No. 561N	85 50	855 00

ACCOUNTS RECEIVABLE LEDGER

NAME   Norton Sporting Goods
ADDRESS   225 N.W. Satsop Ave.
Portland, OR 97201

DATE		ITEM	POST. REF.	DEBIT	CREDIT	BALANCE
20–						
Dec.	4		6075	8 5 5 00		8 5 5 00

CHAPTER REVIEW

Review of Performance Objectives

1. Describe the specific accounts used by a merchandising firm.

   The Merchandise Inventory account is an asset account representing the cost of goods bought for resale. The Sales Tax Payable account is a liability account representing amounts owed to each appropriate entity. The Sales account is a revenue account representing the total sales of merchandise. The Sales Returns and Allowances account is a deduction from the Sales account, representing amounts allowed for returns of merchandise and damaged goods. The Sales Discount account is a deduction from the Sales account, representing amounts deducted for prompt payments. The Purchases account is a cost (expense) account representing the costs of goods bought for resale. The Purchases Returns and Allowances account is a deduction from the Purchases account, representing amounts granted by suppliers for the return of merchandise or damaged goods. The Purchases Discount account is a deduction from the Purchases account, representing amounts suppliers allow for prompt payments. The Freight In account is a cost representing the transportation charges on incoming merchandise.

2. Record transactions in sales journals.

   The sales journal is used to record sales of merchandise on account only. An entry can be recorded on one line. The date, invoice number, and customer's name are listed, along with the amount of the invoice in the Accounts Receivable Dr./Sales Cr. column. In states where there is a sales tax an additional column exists called Sales Tax Payable Cr. In this multicolumn sales journal the sales plus the sales tax represents the amount owed by the customer.

3. Post from sales journals to an accounts receivable ledger and a general ledger.

   The entries are posted daily to the accounts receivable ledger. At the end of the month, the total is posted to the general ledger as a debit to the Accounts Receivable controlling account and a credit to the Sales account.

4. Prepare a schedule of accounts receivable.

   The schedule of accounts receivable consists of a listing of the individual account balances of the charge customers taken from the accounts receivable ledger.

5. Journalize sales returns and allowances, including credit memorandums and returns involving sales tax, and post to the ledger accounts.

When a customer returns merchandise, or when his or her bill is reduced owing to an allowance for defective or damaged merchandise, the Sales Returns and Allowances account is debited and the Accounts Receivable account is credited. The entry is recorded in the general journal and posted to both the general ledger and the accounts receivable ledger.

6. Locate errors.

   If, at the end of the month, the balance of the Accounts Receivable controlling account does not equal the total of the schedule of accounts receivable, accountants must retrace their steps to locate the errors.

7. Post directly from sales invoices to an accounts receivable ledger and journalize and post a summarizing entry in the general journal.

   Another shortcut is using sales invoices or sales slips as a sales journal, thereby doing away with the sales journal. Post to the charge customer accounts in the accounts receivable ledger directly from the sales invoices. At the end of the month, add all the sales invoices and make a summarizing entry in the general journal for the amount of the total. This entry is a debit to Accounts Receivable and a credit to Sales.

Glossary

Accounts receivable ledger A subsidiary ledger that lists the individual accounts of charge customers in either alphabetical or numerical order, with their respective balances. (339)

Controlling account An account in the general ledger that summarizes the balances of a subsidiary ledger. (339)

Credit memorandum A written statement indicating a seller's willingness to reduce the amount of a buyer's debt. The seller records the amount of the credit memorandum in the Sales Returns and Allowances account. (344)

Freight In account The account used to record transportation charges on incoming merchandise intended for resale. (331)

Merchandise inventory A stock of goods (an asset account) that a company buys and intends to resell, in the same physical condition, at a profit. (330)

Purchases account An account for recording the cost of merchandise acquired for resale. (330)

Purchases Discount account An account that records cash discounts granted by suppliers in return for prompt payment; it is treated as a deduction from Purchases. (331)

Purchases Returns and Allowances account An account that records a company's return of merchandise it has purchased or a reduction in the bill because of damaged merchandise; it is treated as a deduction from Purchases. (331)

Sales account A revenue account for recording the sale of merchandise. (330)

Sales Discount account An account that records a deduction from the original price, granted by the seller to the buyer for the prompt payment of an invoice. (331)

Sales journal A special journal for recording the sale of merchandise on account only. (335)

Sales Returns and Allowances account The account a seller uses to record the physical return of merchandise by customers or a reduction in a bill because merchandise was damaged. Sales Returns and Allowances is treated as a deduction from Sales. This account is usually evidenced by a credit memorandum issued by the seller. (330)

Sales tax A tax levied by a state or city government on the retail sale of goods and services. The tax is paid by the consumer but collected by the retailer. (337)

Special journals Books of original entry in which specialized types of repetitive transactions are recorded. (330)

Subsidiary ledger A group of accounts representing individual subdivisions of a controlling account. (339)

Summarizing entry An entry made to post the column totals of a special journal to the appropriate accounts in the general ledger. It is also used when individual sales invoices are posted directly to the accounts receivable ledger. (335)

QUESTIONS, EXERCISES, AND PROBLEMS

Discussion Questions

1. What information typically appears on a sales invoice?
2. Describe the posting procedure for totaling and ruling the sales journal.
3. What is the purpose of a schedule of accounts receivable?
4. Describe the procedure for posting from the sales journal to the accounts receivable ledger.
5. What is the difference between a sales return and a sales allowance?
6. Why is it worthwhile to set up an account for sales returns and allowances, when one could just debit the Sales account for any transaction involving a return or an allowance?
7. Why is an accounts receivable ledger necessary for a business with a large number of charge customers?
8. Describe the method of posting directly from sales invoices.

Exercises

P.O. 3

Post to general and accounts receivable ledgers.

Exercise 10-1 Describe how this sales journal would be posted to the ledgers:

SALES JOURNAL   PAGE **94**

	DATE	INV. NO.	CUSTOMER'S NAME	POST. REF.	ACCOUNTS RECEIVABLE DR. SALES CR.	
1	20–					1
2	Oct. 3	414	Henderson Company		5 4 3 24	2
3	4	415	R. T. Holcomb		1 4 2 6 90	3
4	7	416	Gray Company		1 5 4 7 00	4
5	11	417	Mercer Mobil		3 2 1 2 16	5
6	16	418	J. L. Anthony		2 0 3 0 00	6
7	22	419	C. A. Goldman		1 8 4 4 05	7
8	31	420	F. A. Baumann		2 8 9 1 00	8
9	31				13 4 9 4 35	9
10						10

P.O. 5

Record sales return.

Exercise 10-2 Using the following source document (credit memo issued by Heald Electronics), record the transaction in general journal form on the books of Heald Electronics.

Heald Electronics
4160 Broad Street
Chicago, Illinois 60627

CREDIT MEMORANDUM   No.   **121**

DATE: **November 6, 20—**

CREDIT TO:

The Merchandise Mart

2241 Sullivan Street

Chicago, Illinois   60632

Your account has been credited for:

    1 Benton 27" color TV (1xf27)   **$623.00**

P.O. 5

Entries involving sales returns and allowances.

Exercise 10-3 Record the following transactions in a general journal for Denley Company:

Oct.   10   Mayer Company returned $520 of merchandise (wrong color) previously purchased on account. Issued credit memo no. 104. Mayer's original purchase was for $2,930.

17   Dolen Company returned $260 of defective merchandise previously purchased on account. Issued credit memo no. 105. Dolen's original purchase was for $720.

23   Denley Company issued credit memo no. 106 to Kily Company for $230 as an allowance for damaged merchandise. Kily's original purchase was for $3,530.

P.O. 5

Post to general and accounts receivable ledgers.

Exercise 10-4 Post the following entry to the general ledger and subsidiary ledger:

GENERAL JOURNAL   PAGE **52**

	DATE	DESCRIPTION	POST. REF.	DEBIT	CREDIT	
1	20—					1
2	June 16	Sales Returns and Allowances		2 4 1 27		2
3		Accounts Receivable, R. D. Moen			2 4 1 27	3
4		Issued credit memo no. 131.				4
5						5

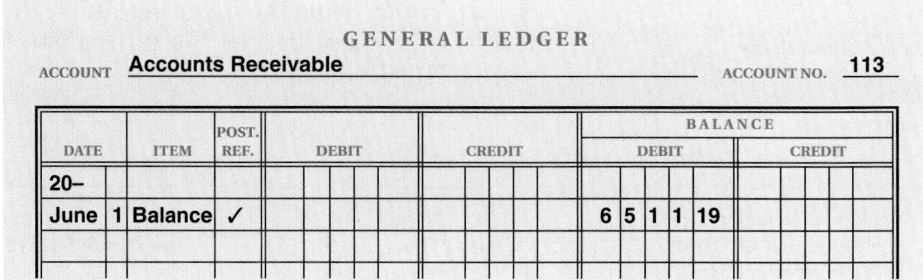

GENERAL LEDGER

ACCOUNT **Accounts Receivable**   ACCOUNT NO. **113**

DATE	ITEM	POST. REF.	DEBIT	CREDIT	BALANCE DEBIT	BALANCE CREDIT
20–						
June 1	Balance	✓			6 5 1 1 19	

ACCOUNT **Sales Returns and Allowances**   ACCOUNT NO. **412**

DATE	ITEM	POST. REF.	DEBIT	CREDIT	BALANCE DEBIT	BALANCE CREDIT
20–						
June 1	Balance	✓			3 1 4 60	

ACCOUNTS RECEIVABLE LEDGER

NAME   **R. D. Moen**

ADDRESS   **416 Fifth Avenue**

Dallas, Texas 75204

DATE	ITEM	POST. REF.	DEBIT	CREDIT	BALANCE
20–					
May 31		S26	3 1 2 60		3 1 2 60

P.O. 3,5

Describe transactions involving a sale, a return, and a payment.

Exercise 10-5 Describe the transactions recorded in the following T accounts:

Cash	
(c) 541	

Sales Tax Payable	
(b) 8.20	(a) 49.20

Sales Returns and Allowances	
(b) 100	

Accounts Receivable	
(a) 649.20	(b) 108.20
	(c) 541

Sales	
	(a) 600

P.O. 5

Entries involving a sale, a return, and a receipt of cash.

Exercise 10-6 Record the following transactions in general journal form:

a. Sold merchandise on account to C. C. Hall, $360 plus $18.00 sales tax (invoice no. D446).

b. Hall returned $90 of the merchandise. Issued credit memo no. 114 for $94.50 ($90 for the amount of the sale plus $4.50 for the amount of the sales tax).

c. Received $283.50 from C. C. Hall in full payment of account.

P.O. 6

Corrections involving a sales journal and an accounts receivable ledger.

Exercise 10-7 An accountant made the following errors in journalizing sales of merchandise on account in a single-column sales journal and in posting to the general ledger and the accounts receivable ledger. The errors were discovered at the end of the month before the closing entries were journalized and posted. Describe how to correct the errors.

a. The sales journal was footed correctly as $31,180, but it was posted as a debit and credit for $31,810.

b. A sale correctly recorded at $84 to N. P. Hale was posted to his account as $8.40.

c. A sale correctly recorded at $26 to N. A. Ales was posted to her account as $62.

P.O. 7

Summarizing entries for direct posting of sales and sales returns.

Exercise 10-8 A business uses copies of its sales invoices to record sales of merchandise on account and copies of its credit memorandums to record sales returns and allowances. During November the company issued 427 invoices for $148,941.20 and 16 credit memorandums for $9,427.18. Present the summarizing entries, dated November 30, in general journal form to record the sales and sales returns and allowances.

CONSIDER AND COMMUNICATE

After you finished the month's posting, the total of the schedule of accounts receivable matched the balance of the Accounts Receivable (controlling) account in the general ledger. You therefore mailed the statements to customers. You have received a phone call from Customer A, who is irritated and claims he was overcharged $43.97. Customer B calls to ask why her statement does not include her purchase of a blender for $43.97. She says she lost her original sales slip and needs a copy of the itemized bill so that she can return the item. Assume that the customers are correct. Explain how this could happen.

CRITICAL THINKING

TO: Accounting Clerk SUBJECT: Errors in trial balance
FROM: Senior Accountant DATE: April 1, 20—

Following is a trial balance prepared just before you were hired. There are two accounts missing, and the amount for Sales is off. Here are a few facts to consider. Our business is in a state that collects sales tax. I ran some totals, and we collected $1,400 in sales tax. Customers returned $800 in goods, which would reduce the above sales tax by $70. Our books need to reflect these events. The former accounting clerk said she did record everything— somewhere. Please determine the missing accounts and correct the accounts that are off.

Newkirk Retail Outlet
Trial Balance
March 31, 20—

ACCOUNT NAME	DEBIT	CREDIT
Cash	8 9 4 0 00	
Accounts Receivable	4 8 0 00	
Supplies	1 7 5 00	
Store Equipment	9 4 6 0 00	
Accounts Payable		9 5 8 00
D. Newkirk, Capital		11 9 5 9 00
D. Newkirk, Drawing	4 4 8 0 00	
Sales		18 0 0 0 00
Rent Expense	2 4 0 0 00	
Wages Expense	4 8 6 4 00	
Miscellaneous Expense	1 1 8 00	
	30 9 1 7 00	30 9 1 7 00

1. Think about where these amounts might have been put, think about what accounts are missing, and use T accounts to solve the problems.
2. Prepare a corrected trial balance.

A MATTER OF ETHICS

Ms. Hopper, an employee, accidentally dropped a pallet of boxes containing televisions off the forklift she was driving in the warehouse. No one saw what happened. She couldn't see (or hear) any damage to the televisions, so she reloaded the boxes and did not tell her supervisor. Is Ms. Hopper behaving in an ethical manner when she withholds this information? Assume that the sets were damaged and were delivered to customers. How would this damage affect the income statement?

WEB WORK

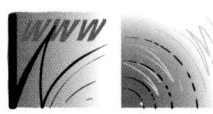

Using an Internet web browser, type *accounting* in the search box and search for information about a major company that interests you. Specifically look for sales information on the income statement. Discuss your findings in a small group. Write a one-page summary of your findings.

PROBLEM SET A

For additional help, see the demonstration problem at the beginning of each chapter in your Working Papers.

P.O. 2,3,4,5

Problem 10-1A Landon's Beauty Supplies had the following sales of merchandise on account and sales returns and allowances during November:

Nov. 5 Sold merchandise on account to The Hair Stop, invoice no. 71, $153.70.

9 Sold merchandise on account to Shear Touch, invoice no. 72, $218.87.

11 Sold merchandise on account to The Coiffure Center, invoice no. 73, $338.46.

15 Sold merchandise on account to Lia's Hair Design, invoice no. 74, $370.50.

16 Issued credit memo no. 14, $85.18, to Shear Touch for merchandise returned.

21 Sold merchandise on account to The Hair Stop, invoice no. 75, $495.72.

22 Issued credit memo no. 15, $37.15, to The Coiffure Center for merchandise returned.

26 Sold merchandise on account to Lia's Hair Design, invoice no. 76, $318.42.

28 Sold merchandise on account to Shear Touch, invoice no. 77, $296.38.

29 Sold merchandise on account to The Hair Stop, invoice no. 78, $107.64.

30 Issued credit memo no. 16 to Lia's Hair Design for damage done to merchandise during shipping, $18.92.

Check Figure

Sales account balance, $8,615.89 credit

Instructions

1. Record these sales of merchandise on account in the sales journal (page 34). Record the sales returns and allowances in the general journal (page 59).
2. Immediately after recording each transaction, post to the accounts receivable ledger.
3. Post the amounts from the general journal daily. Post the sales journal amounts as a total at the end of the month: 113, Accounts Receivable; 411, Sales; 412, Sales Returns and Allowances.
4. Prepare a schedule of accounts receivable. Compare the balance of the Accounts Receivable controlling account with the total of the schedule of accounts receivable.

P.O. 2,3,4,5

Problem 10-2A Bradey Company sells electrical supplies on a wholesale basis. The following transactions took place during April of this year:

Apr. 1 Sold merchandise on account to Mayhew Company, invoice no. 761, $573.21.

5 Sold merchandise on account to L. R. Friedel Company, invoice no. 762, $301.46.

6 Issued credit memo no. 50 to Mayhew Company for merchandise returned, $51.50.

10 Sold merchandise on account to Danson Hardware, invoice no. 763, $551.41.

14 Sold merchandise on account to Benson Company, invoice no. 764, $838.33.

17 Sold merchandise on account to Porter Company, invoice no. 765, $511.27.

21 Issued credit memo no. 51 to Benson Company for merchandise returned, $81.36.

Apr. 24 Sold merchandise on account to Overall Company, invoice no. 766, $627.89.

26 Sold merchandise on account to Danson Hardware, invoice no. 767, $736.32.

30 Issued credit memo no. 52 to Danson Hardware for damage to merchandise, $101.40.

Check Figure

Accounts Receivable account balance, $5,075.05 debit

Instructions

1. Record these sales of merchandise on account in the sales journal (page 39). Record the sales returns and allowances in the general journal (page 74).
2. Immediately after recording each transaction, post to the accounts receivable ledger.
3. Post the amounts from the general journal daily. Post the sales journal amounts as a total at the end of the month: 113, Accounts Receivable; 411, Sales; 412, Sales Returns and Allowances.
4. Prepare a schedule of accounts receivable. Compare the balance of the Accounts Receivable controlling account with the total of the schedule of accounts receivable.

Instructions for General Ledger Software

1. Record these transactions in either the sales journal or the general journal and post.
2. Print the entries from the general journal.
3. Print the entries from the sales journal.
4. Print a schedule of accounts receivable and compare its total with the Accounts Receivable account.

P.O. 2,3,4,5

✓**Problem 10-3A** Mandel Florists sells flowers on a retail basis. Most of the sales are for cash; however, a few steady customers have charge accounts. Mandel's sales staff fills out a sales slip for each sale. The state government levies a 5 percent retail sales tax, which is collected by the retailer. The following represent Mandel Florists' charge sales for March:

Mar. 4 Sold potted plant on account to C. Milo, sales slip no. 242, $48, plus sales tax of $2.40, total $50.40.

6 Sold floral arrangement on account to R. Droy, sales slip no. 243, $46, plus sales tax of $2.30, total $48.30.

12 Sold corsage on account to B. Carr, sales slip no. 244, $16, plus sales tax of $.80, total $16.80.

16 Sold wreath on account to American Club, sales slip no. 245, $65, plus sales tax of $3.25, total $68.25.

18 Sold floral arrangements on account to Troy Funeral Home, sales slip no. 246, $214, plus sales tax of $10.70, total $224.70.

21 Troy Funeral Home returned a flower spray. Delivery of the spray occurred after the funeral was over. Mandel allowed full credit on the sale of $98 and the sales tax of $4.90 Credit memo no. 27.

23 Sold flower arrangements on account to Piedmont Savings and Loan Association for its anniversary, sales slip no. 247, $120 plus sales tax of $6, total $126.

24 Allowed Piedmont Savings and Loan Association credit, $28, plus $1.40 tax, because of withered blossoms in floral arrangements, credit memo no. 28.

Check Figure

Schedule of Accounts Receivable total, $540.37

Instructions

1. Record these transactions in either the sales journal (page 23) or the general journal (page 57).
2. Immediately after recording each transaction, post to the accounts receivable ledger.
3. Post the amounts from the general journal daily. Post the sales journal amounts as a total at the end of the month: 113, Accounts Receivable; 411, Sales; 214, Sales Tax Payable; 412, Sales Returns and Allowances.
4. Prepare a schedule of accounts receivable and compare its total with the Accounts Receivable account.

P.O. 4,7

Problem 10-4A Rory Sporting Goods uses duplicate copies of its charge sales invoices as a sales journal and posts to the accounts receivable ledger directly from the sales invoices. At the end of the month, the accountant totals the invoices and makes an entry in the general journal summarizing the charge sales for the month. The charge sales invoices for December are as follows:

Dec. 3 R. A. Finch Company, invoice no. 5214, $580.
       9 C. T. Baker, invoice no. 5237, $792.
     11 Soro Athletic Supply, invoice no. 5245, $326.
     13 Jason Company, invoice no. 5261, $1,137.
     17 Matthews, Inc., invoice no. 5277, $732.
     19 Travalina Company, invoice no. 5291, $564.
     23 Richard and Company, invoice no. 5309, $1,015.
     30 Soro Athletic Supply, invoice no. 5322, $1,238.

Check Figure

Schedule of Accounts Receivable total, $7,163.00

Instructions

1. Post to the accounts receivable ledger directly from the sales invoices, listing the invoice number in the Post. Ref. column.
2. Record the summarizing entry in the general journal (page 33) for the total amount of the sales invoices.
3. Post the general journal entry to the appropriate accounts in the general ledger: 113, Accounts Receivable; 411, Sales.
4. Prepare a schedule of accounts receivable and compare its total with the Accounts Receivable account.

PROBLEM SET B

For additional help, see the demonstration problem at the beginning of each chapter in your Working Papers.

P.O. 2,3,4,5

Problem 10-1B Darnold Beauty Supplies had the following sales of merchandise on account and sales returns and allowances during November.

Nov. 2 Sold merchandise on account to The Hair Stop, invoice no. 91, $267.52.
      8 Sold merchandise on account to Shear Touch, invoice no. 92, $236.40.
     10 Sold merchandise on account to The Coiffure Center, invoice no. 93, $317.31.

Nov. 15 Sold merchandise on account to Lia's Hair Design, invoice no. 94, $215.80.

16 Issued credit memo no. 12, $65.70, to Shear Touch, for merchandise returned.

21 Sold merchandise on account to The Hair Stop, invoice no. 95, $235.64.

23 Issued credit memo no. 13, $120.40, to The Coiffure Center, for merchandise returned.

26 Sold merchandise on account to Lia's Hair Design, invoice no. 96, $135.36.

28 Sold merchandise on account to Shear Touch, invoice no. 97, $247.21.

29 Sold merchandise on account to The Hair Stop, invoice no. 98, $57.48.

30 Issued credit memo no. 14, $36.72, to Lia's Hair Design for merchandise damaged in transit.

Check Figure

Sales account balance, $8,028.92 credit

Instructions

1. Record these sales of merchandise on account in the sales journal (page 34). Record the sales returns and allowances in the general journal (page 59).
2. Immediately after recording each transaction, post to the accounts receivable ledger. Fill in the names of companies where necessary.
3. Post the amounts from the general journal daily. Post the sales journal amount as a total at the end of the month: 113, Accounts Receivable; 411, Sales; 412, Sales Returns and Allowances.
4. Prepare a schedule of accounts receivable. Compare the balance of the Accounts Receivable controlling account with the total of the schedule of accounts receivable.

P.O. 2,3,4,5

Problem 10-2B Mandelli Company sells food supplies on a wholesale basis. The following transactions took place during November of this year:

Apr. 3 Sold merchandise on account to Mayhew Company, invoice no. 822, $530.19.

7 Sold merchandise on account to L. R. Friedel Company, invoice no. 823, $418.40.

8 Sold merchandise on account to Danson Hardware, invoice no. 824, $281.16.

13 Issued credit memo no. 61 to L. R. Friedel Company for merchandise returned, $49.95.

15 Sold merchandise on account to Benson Company, invoice no. 825, $723.88.

21 Sold merchandise on account to Porter Company, invoice no. 826, $792.53.

24 Issued credit memo no. 62 to Benson Company for merchandise returned, $87.41.

26 Sold merchandise on account to Overall Company, invoice no. 827, $576.34.

28 Issued credit memo no. 63 to Danson Hardware for damage to merchandise, $44.84.

30 Sold merchandise on account to Danson Hardware, invoice no. 828, $831.92.

Check Figure

Accounts Receivable account balance, $5,141.64 debit

Instructions

1. Record these sales of merchandise on account in the sales journal (page 39). Record the sales returns and allowances in the general journal (page 74).
2. Immediately after recording each transaction, post to the accounts receivable ledger.
3. Post the amounts from the general journal daily. Post the sales journal amount as a total at the end of the month: 113, Accounts Receivable; 411, Sales; 412, Sales Returns and Allowances.
4. Prepare a schedule of accounts receivable. Compare the balance of the Accounts Receivable controlling account with the total of the schedule of accounts receivable.

Instructions for General Ledger Software

1. Record these transactions in either the sales journal or the general journal and post.
2. Print the entries from the general journal.
3. Print the entries from the sales journal.
4. Print a schedule of accounts receivable and compare its total with the balance of Accounts Receivable.

P.O. 2,3,4,5

Problem 10-3B Scarvaglierri Florists sells flowers on a retail basis. Most of the sales are for cash; however, a few steady customers have charge accounts. Scarvaglierri's sales staff fills out a sales slip for each sale. The state government levies a 5 percent retail sales tax, which is collected by the retailer. Scarvaglierri Florists' charge sales for January are as follows:

Mar. 4 Sold floral arrangement on account to C. Milo, sales slip no. 236, $44, plus sales tax of $2.20, total $46.20.

7 Sold potted plant on account to R. Droy, sales slip no. 237, $19, plus sales tax of $.95, total $19.95.

12 Sold wreath on account to American Club, sales slip no. 238, $72, plus sales tax of $3.60, total $75.60.

17 Sold flower spray on account to Troy Funeral Home, sales slip no. 239, $190, plus sales tax of $9.50, total $199.50.

20 Troy Funeral Home returned the flower spray. Delivery of the spray occurred after the funeral was over. Scarvaglierri allowed full credit on the sale of $190 and the sales tax of $9.50, credit memo no. 27.

21 Sold flower arrangements on account to Piedmont Savings and Loan Association for it's anniversary, sales slip no. 240, $180, plus sales tax of $9, total $189.

22 Allowed Piedmont Savings and Loan Association credit, $25 plus $1.25 tax, because of withered blossoms in floral arrangements, credit memo no. 28.

27 Sold corsage on account to B. Carr, sales slip no. 241, $12, plus sales tax of $.60, total $12.60.

Check Figure

Schedule of Accounts Receivable total, $455.32

Instructions

1. Record these transactions in either the sales journal (page 23) or the general journal (page 57).
2. Immediately after recording each transaction, post to the accounts receivable ledger.

3. Post the amounts from the general journal daily. Post the sales journal amount as a total at the end of the month: 113, Accounts Receivable; 411, Sales; 214, Sales Tax Payable; 412, Sales Returns and Allowances.

4. Prepare a schedule of accounts receivable and compare its total with the balance of Accounts Receivable.

P.O. 4,7

Problem 10-4B Cullen Sporting Goods uses duplicate copies of its charge sales invoices as a sales journal and posts to the accounts receivable ledger directly from the sales invoices. The invoices are totaled at the end of the month, and an entry is made in the general journal to summarize the charge sales for the month. The charge sales invoices for December are as follows:

Dec. 4 R. A. Finch Company, invoice no. 5216, $562.
      9 C. T. Baker, invoice no. 5240, $658.
    11 Soro Athletic Supply, invoice no. 5242, $452.
    18 Jason Company, invoice no. 5267, $370.
    24 Matthew's, Inc., invoice no. 5287, $502.
    27 Travalina Company, invoice no. 5294, $567.
    28 Richard and Company, invoice no. 5311, $345.
    31 Soro Athletic Supply, invoice no. 5317, $205.

Check Figure

Schedule of Accounts Receivable total, $4,440.00

Instructions

1. Post to the accounts receivable ledger directly from the sales invoices, listing the invoice number in the Post. Ref. column.

2. Record the summarizing entry in the general journal (page 33) for the total amount of the sales invoices.

3. Post the general journal entry to the appropriate accounts in the general ledger: 113, Accounts Receivable; 411, Sales.

4. Prepare a schedule of accounts receivable and compare its total with the balance of Accounts Receivable.

Continuous General Ledger Problem: Sales Journal

The Like New sole proprietorship began as a service business, selling its services as an art and furniture restorer. It is owned by J. Miracle. The books were adjusted and closed on May 31, 2000. Following is the trial balance for Like New on May 31, 2000, after closing.

	Like New General Ledger Trial Balance As of May 31, 2000		
Account	**Account Description**	**Debit Amt**	**Credit Amt**
111	Cash	68,823.00	
113	Accounts Receivable	4,566.00	
115	Supplies	1,336.00	
117	Prepaid Insurance	1,056.92	
142	Building	90,000.00	
143	Accum. Depreciation, Building		3,500.00
144	Van	18,500.00	
145	Accum. Depreciation, Van		1,100.00
146	Office Equipment	13,298.00	
147	Accum. Depr., Office Equipment		890.00
148	Office Furniture	5,023.00	
149	Accum. Depr., Office Furniture		1,100.00
211	Accounts Payable		4,252.00
212	Wages Payable		42.50
251	Mortgage Payable		89,400.00
312	J. Miracle, Capital		102,318.42
	Total:	**202,602.92**	**202,602.92**

Like New has decided to sell restored artwork and furniture in addition to its restoration services. Miracle has decided to add a sales journal to the records along with the general journal. The sales journal will receive entries for sales of merchandise on account only.

As the accountant for Like New, you will journalize and post the following June transactions. Journalize all sales of merchandise on account in the sales journal. The remainder of the journal entries will be journalized in the general journal.

If this is the first time you have worked for Like New, you will need to do a company setup on the general ledger accounting package you are using. This would include company information, customer names and balances, the chart of accounts, and beginning general ledger balances. Notice that the expense

Note: The Continuous General Ledger Problem can be worked with Houghton Mifflin Windows General Ledger Package, Peachtree Release 5.01, QuickBooks 6.0, or other general ledger software packages.

accounts are in the 600 category to leave 500-level accounts for the purchase of merchandise in the next chapter. Following are the transactions for June:

June
1   Miracle invested his personal facsimile machine, $269 (Office Equipment).

2   Bought supplies on account from the Paint Pot, $374, Inv. 980.

4   Sold two rocking chairs on account to Gail Murdock, $1,142, Sales Inv. 2004.

5   Sold four frames on account to Image Place, $392, Sales Inv. 2005.

6   Paid $500 on account to the Paint Pot, Ck. No. 1008.

7   Paid $300 on account to Au Furniture, Ck. No. 1009.

8   Paid the remaining $398 on account to Office Ready, Ck. No. 1010.

10   Sold one desk on account to Baker Inn, $897, Sales Inv. 2006.

11   Paid $1,140 interest (debit Interest Expense) and $261 on the principal of the mortgage (debit Mortgage Payable), $1,401, Ck. No. 1011.

12   Sold a clock on account to Adeline Harris, $947, Sales Inv. 2007.

13   Issued a credit memorandum to Image Place for one frame, $54, CM No. 1 (debit Sales Returns and Allowances and credit Accounts Receivable/Image Place).

14   Sold two tapestries on account to Baker Inn, $1,281, Sales Inv. 2008.

15   Paid wages of part-time assistant for the first half of the month, $850, Ck. No. 1012 (debit Wages Expense $807.50, debit Wages Payable $42.50).

16   Sold services for cash to customers, $6,476, Cash Receipt Nos. 1117–1124.

19   The owner withdrew cash for personal use, $1,644, Ck. No. 1013.

22   Received cash on account from Adeline Harris, $1,256, Cash Receipt No. 1125.

23   Received cash on account from Jeff Isely, $500, Cash Receipt No. 1126.

24   Sold a coat tree on account to Baker Inn, $128, Sales Inv. 2009.

25   Issued a credit memorandum to Baker Inn for one tapestry, $480, CM No. 2 (debit Sales Returns and Allowances and credit Accounts Receivable/Baker Inn).

26   Received cash on account from Mike Wallen, $1,000, Cash Receipt No. 1127.

28   Paid $841 on account to Adams Advertising, Ck. No. 1014.

30   Paid wages of part-time assistant for the second half of the month, $850, Ck. No. 1015.

Instructions

1. Launch the general ledger software.
2. Create a new file called likenews (*s* for sales journal). Enter the company name, chart of accounts (change the expenses to begin with a 6, e.g., 611 for Wages Expense), customer names and balances, vendor names and balances, and beginning general ledger balances.
3. Print a copy of the chart of accounts for your convenience in planning journal entries.
4. Journalize and post the transactions in either the general journal or the sales journal.
5. Print a trial balance ($212,166.42).
6. Print a schedule of accounts receivable ($6,063). Compare this number with the balance of Accounts Receivable in the trial balance in Direction 5. Are they the same? They should be.

11 The Purchases Journal

Performance Objectives

After you have completed this chapter, you will be able to do the following:

1. Journalize transactions in a three-column purchases journal.

2. Post from a three-column purchases journal to an accounts payable ledger and a general ledger.

3. Journalize transactions involving purchases returns and allowances in a general journal.

4. Prepare a schedule of accounts payable.

5. Journalize transactions in a multicolumn purchases journal.

6. Post from a multicolumn purchases journal to an accounts payable ledger and a general ledger.

7. Post directly from purchase invoices to an accounts payable ledger and journalize and post a summarizing entry in the general journal.

We have been talking about the procedures, accounts, and special journals used to record the *sale* of merchandise. Now let's talk about those same elements as they apply to *buying* merchandise. We will be dealing with the Purchases account and with Purchases Returns and Allowances. In this chapter, you'll see that Accounts Payable, like Accounts Receivable, is a controlling account.

PURCHASING PROCEDURES

When you think of the great variety of types and sizes of merchandising firms, it should come as no surprise to learn that there is also considerable variety in the procedures used to buy goods for resale. Some purchases may be for cash; however, in most cases, purchases are on a credit basis. In a small retail store, the owner may do the buying. In large retail and wholesale concerns, department heads or division managers do the buying, after which the Purchasing Department goes into action: It places purchase orders, follows up the orders, and sees that deliveries are made to the right departments. The Purchasing Department also acts as a source of information on current prices, price trends, quality of goods, prospective suppliers, and reliability of suppliers.

The Purchasing Department normally requires that any requests to buy merchandise be in writing, in the form of a **purchase requisition**. After the purchase requisition is approved, the Purchasing Department sends a purchase order to the supplier. A **purchase order** is the company's written offer to buy certain goods. The accountant does not make any entry at this point because the supplier has not yet indicated acceptance of the order. A purchase order has at least four copies. The original goes to the supplier; copies go to the Purchasing Department (as proof of what was ordered), the department that issued the requisition (telling it that the goods it wanted have been ordered), and the Accounting Department, and a blind copy (with quantities omitted) goes to Receiving.

To continue with the accounts of Jackson Electric Supply, the Cable Department submits a purchase requisition to the Purchasing Department, as shown in Figure 1.

FIGURE 1

Jackson Electric Supply	No. C-726
625 N. E. Manor Avenue	
Portland, Oregon 97201	

PURCHASE REQUISITION

DEPARTMENT Cable	DATE OF REQUEST July 2, 20—
ADVISE ON DELIVERY C. Carson	DATE REQUIRED Aug. 5, 20—

QUANTITY	DESCRIPTION
10	Jacketed copper cable, 6 ga., 65 amp. (100' roll)

APPROVED BY *R. L. Schmidt*   REQUESTED BY *J. C. Garcia*

FOR PURCHASING DEPT. USE ONLY

PURCHASE ORDER NO. __7918__   ISSUED TO: Draper, Inc.

DATE __July 5, 20—__   1614 Olivera St.

San Francisco, CA 94129

FIGURE 2

Jackson Electric Supply
625 N. E. Manor Avenue
Portland, Oregon 97201

PURCHASE ORDER

TO:	Draper, Inc.	DATE:	July 5, 20—
	1614 Olivera St.	ORDER NO.:	7918
	San Francisco, CA 94129	SHIPPED BY:	
		TERMS:	2/10, n/30

QUANTITY	DESCRIPTION	UNIT PRICE	TOTAL
10	Jacketed copper cable, 6 ga., 65 amp. (100' roll)	39	390 00
	Total		390 00

R. L. Schmidt

The Purchasing Department completes the rest of the purchase requisition and then sends out the purchase order shown in Figure 2.

The seller then sends an **invoice** to the buyer. The invoice is a business form prepared by the seller that lists the items shipped, their cost, the terms, and mode of shipping. This invoice should arrive before the goods (or at least *with* the goods). From the seller's point of view, this is a sales invoice. If the sale is on credit, the seller's accountant makes an entry debiting Accounts Receivable and crediting Sales. To the buyer, this is a purchase invoice. Customarily, when the merchandise is received, the buyer's accountant makes an entry debiting Purchases and crediting Accounts Payable. Jackson Electric Supply receives the invoice shown in Figure 3 on page 368 from Draper, Inc.

Below are T accounts used in buying and selling goods.

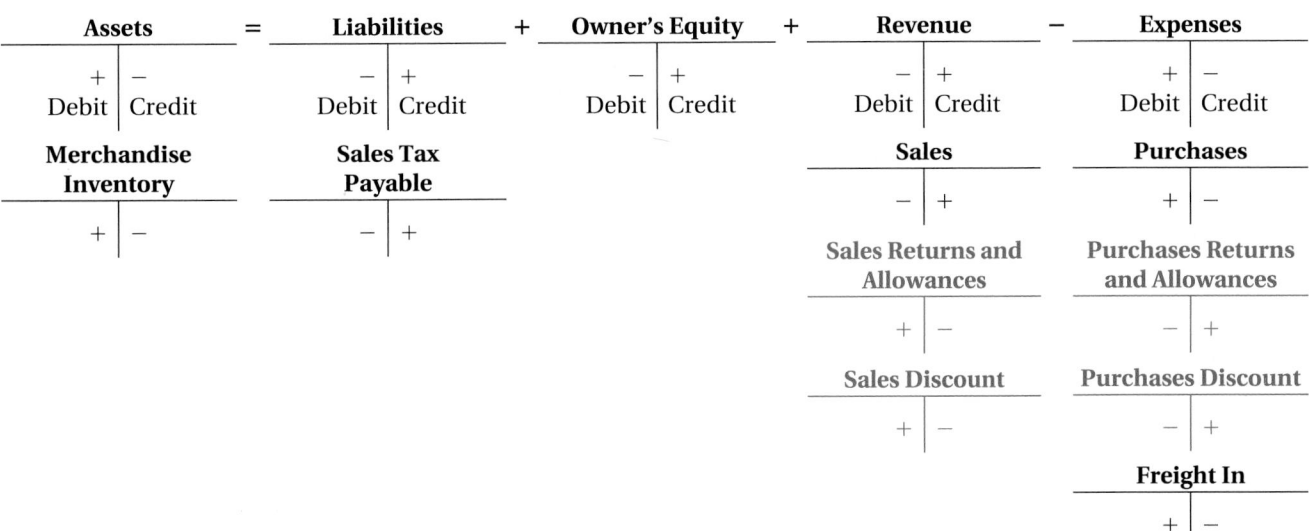

FIGURE 3

	Draper, Inc.	No. 2706
	1614 Olivera Street	
	San Francisco, CA 94129	

INVOICE

SOLD TO Jackson Electric Supply
625 N. E. Manor Avenue
Portland, Oregon 97201

DATE: July 31, 20—
ORDER NO.: 7918
SHIPPED BY: Pacific Freight Line
TERMS: 2/10, n/30

YOUR ORDER NO.	SALESPERSON	TERMS
7918	*C. L.*	2/10, n/30

DATE SHIPPED	SHIPPED BY	FOB
July 31, 20—	Pacific Freight Line	San Francisco

QUANTITY	DESCRIPTION	UNIT PRICE	TOTAL	
10	Jacketed copper cable, 6 ga., 65 amp. (100' roll)	39	390	00
	Freight		30	00
	Total		420	00

Bear in mind that the Purchases account is used exclusively for merchandise intended for resale. *If the firm buys anything else, the accountant records the amount under the appropriate asset or expense account.* At the end of the fiscal period, the balance in the Purchases account represents the total cost of merchandise bought during the period. Remember that Purchases is classified as an expense only for the sake of convenience. The classification is permissible because Purchases is closed along with the expense accounts at the end of the fiscal period.

Purchases Returns and Allowances is a deduction from Purchases. A separate account is set up to keep track of the amount of returns and reductions in bills because of damaged merchandise. On the income statement, we treat Purchases Returns and Allowances and Purchases Discount as deductions from Purchases; therefore, for consistency, they are presented below Purchases in the fundamental accounting equation just shown.

Freight Charges on Incoming Merchandise

Companies use the Freight In account to keep a record of all separately charged delivery costs on incoming merchandise.

Freight costs are expressed as FOB (free on board) destination or shipping point. **(Destination is the buyer's location; shipping point is the seller's location.)** In both cases, the supplier loads the goods free on board the carrier. Beyond that point, there must be an understanding as to who is responsible for paying the freight charges. **If the seller assumes the entire cost of transportation, without any reimbursement from the buyer, the terms are FOB destination.** In this case, title or ownership changes hands when the

To record the transportation costs of merchandise purchased for resale such as automobiles, accountants use an expense account called Freight In (also called Transportation In).

buyer receives the goods. **If the buyer is responsible for paying the freight cost, the shipping terms are called** FOB shipping point. In this case, title or ownership changes hands when goods are transferred to a common carrier (freight company).

Briefly, when goods are shipped FOB destination, the freight charges are not stated, and the seller simply pays the amount of the freight. Suppose Jackson Electric Supply (remember, it's in Portland) buys merchandise from a supplier in Chicago with shipping terms of FOB Portland listed on the invoice. The total of the invoice is $1,740, and there is no separate listing of freight charges. In other words, the seller has included the transportation costs in the price.

On the other hand, when goods are shipped FOB shipping point, with the buyer responsible for paying the freight charges, transportation costs may be handled in two ways:

1. The buyer may pay the freight charges directly to the transportation company. For example, an automobile dealer in Houston buys cars FOB Detroit. In this case, the automobile dealer makes one check payable to the manufacturer and another check payable to the carrier for the freight charges. (FOB Detroit is the same as FOB shipping point.)

2. The transportation costs may be listed separately on the invoice. For example, suppose a person orders a refrigerator from a mail order company. The mail order company has prepaid (paid in advance) the freight charges as a favor or convenience for the buyer. However, the freight charges are listed on the bill or invoice, and the buyer is responsible for reimbursing the mail order company for the freight charges. Similarly, when a business buys merchandise, the amount of the freight charges may be prepaid by the seller and listed separately on the invoice.

Look again at the invoice of Draper, Inc. Note that the freight cost is listed separately, and so the terms are FOB shipping point (San Francisco). Draper paid the transportation cost, but Jackson must reimburse Draper for this cost.

Let's proceed with three other transactions for Jackson Electric Supply. We first record the transactions in a general journal. Then, as a means of reemphasizing the advantages of special journals as opposed to a general journal, we record the same transactions in a special journal. In practice, the transactions would be recorded in only one journal, not both.

During the first week in August, the following transactions took place:

Aug. 2 Bought merchandise on account from Draper, Inc., $390, its invoice no. 2706, dated July 31; terms 2/10, n/30; FOB San Francisco; freight prepaid and added to the invoice, $30 (total $420).

3 Bought merchandise on account from Reilly and Peters, $708, its invoice no. 982, dated August 2; terms net 30 days; FOB Cleveland; freight prepaid and added to the invoice, $52 (total $760).

5 Bought merchandise on account from Adkins Manufacturing Company, $692, its invoice no. 10611, dated August 3; terms 2/10, n/30; FOB Los Angeles.

Notice that the transactions with Draper, Inc., and Reilly and Peters are both FOB shipping point with the freight charges listed separately. Consequently, the buyer (Jackson) must reimburse the sellers for the transportation costs by paying the total of the invoices. However, in the transaction with Adkins Manufacturing, which is FOB shipping point without freight charges listed, the buyer (Jackson) must pay the freight costs separately, perhaps when the goods are delivered.

For now, we are concerned with journalizing the three purchases. Let's visualize these transactions using T accounts.

Purchases			Freight In			Accounts Payable		
+	−		+	−		−	+	
Aug. 2 390		Aug. 2 30					Aug. 2 420	
3 708		3 52					3 760	
5 692							5 692	

If these transactions are journalized in a general journal, they look like Figure 4. The general journal entries are then posted to the general ledger.

FIGURE 4

GENERAL JOURNAL PAGE __22__

	DATE		DESCRIPTION	POST. REF.	DEBIT	CREDIT	
1	20–						1
2	Aug.	2	Purchases	511	3 9 0 00		2
3			Freight In	514	3 0 00		3
4			Accounts Payable	221		4 2 0 00	4
5			Draper, Inc., its invoice				5
6			no. 2706, dated July 31,				6
7			terms 2/10, n/30.				7
8							8
9		3	Purchases	511	7 0 8 00		9
10			Freight In	514	5 2 00		10
11			Accounts Payable	221		7 6 0 00	11
12			Reilly and Peters, its				12
13			invoice no. 982, dated				13
14			August 2, terms net 30 days.				14
15							15
16		5	Purchases	511	6 9 2 00		16
17			Accounts Payable	221		6 9 2 00	17
18			Adkins Manufacturing Co.,				18
19			its invoice no. 10611, dated				19
20			August 3, terms 2/10, n/30.				20
21							21

GENERAL LEDGER

ACCOUNT __Accounts Payable__ ACCOUNT NO. __221__

	DATE		ITEM	POST. REF.	DEBIT	CREDIT	BALANCE DEBIT	BALANCE CREDIT	
1	20–								1
2	Aug.	1	Balance	✓				3 5 6 00	2
3		2		J22		4 2 0 00		7 7 6 00	3
4		3		J22		7 6 0 00		1 5 3 6 00	4
5		5		J22		6 9 2 00		2 2 2 8 00	5

FIGURE 4 (continued)

ACCOUNT __Purchases__   ACCOUNT NO. __511__

	DATE		ITEM	POST. REF.	DEBIT	CREDIT	BALANCE DEBIT	BALANCE CREDIT	
1	20–								1
2	Aug.	1	Balance	✓			20 6 1 2 00		2
3		2		J22	3 9 0 00		21 0 0 2 00		3
4		3		J22	7 0 8 00		21 7 1 0 00		4
5		5		J22	6 9 2 00		22 4 0 2 00		5
6									6

ACCOUNT __Freight In__   ACCOUNT NO. __514__

	DATE		ITEM	POST. REF.	DEBIT	CREDIT	BALANCE DEBIT	BALANCE CREDIT	
1	20–								1
2	Aug.	1	Balance	✓			1 5 0 2 00		2
3		2		J22	3 0 00		1 5 3 2 00		3
4		3		J22	5 2 00		1 5 8 4 00		4
5									5

Let's take a minute to explain the terms in the transactions. The notation "net 30 days" or "n/30" means that the bill is due within 30 days after the date of the invoice. The notation "2/10, n/30" refers to the **purchases discount** or cash discount. It means that the seller offers a 2 percent discount if the bill is paid within 10 days after the date of the invoice. Otherwise, the gross amount must be paid within 30 days after the invoice date.

PURCHASES JOURNAL (THREE-COLUMN)

Objective 1

Journalize transactions in a three-column purchases journal.

The repetition illustrated in our example can be avoided if the accountant uses a **purchases journal** instead of the general journal. This purchases journal is used to record the purchase of merchandise *on account only*. Some businesses prefer multicolumn purchases journals, which include all purchases on accounts. We look at this journal later in the chapter.

PURCHASES JOURNAL   PAGE __29__

	DATE		SUPPLIER'S NAME	INVOICE NO.	INVOICE DATE	TERMS	POST. REF.	ACCOUNTS PAYABLE CREDIT	FREIGHT IN DEBIT	PURCHASES DEBIT	
1	20–										1
2	Aug.	2	Draper, Inc.	2706	7/31	2/10, n/30		4 2 0 00	3 0 00	3 9 0 00	2
3		3	Reilly and Peters	982	8/2	n/30		7 6 0 00	5 2 00	7 0 8 00	3
4		5	Adkins Manufacturing Co.	10611	8/3	2/10, n/30		6 9 2 00		6 9 2 00	4
5											5

Posting from the Purchases Journal to the General Ledger

Figure 5 shows the journal entries for all transactions involving the purchase of merchandise on account for August and the related ledger accounts for the same time period. In the Post. Ref. column of the ledger accounts, P designates the purchases journal. After posting the column totals for the month to the ledger accounts, the accountant goes back to the purchases journal and records the account numbers in parentheses directly below the total.

FIGURE 5

PURCHASES JOURNAL PAGE ___29___

	DATE		SUPPLIER'S NAME	INVOICE NO.	INVOICE DATE	TERMS	POST. REF.	ACCOUNTS PAYABLE CREDIT	FREIGHT IN DEBIT	PURCHASES DEBIT	
1	20–										1
2	Aug.	2	Draper, Inc.	2706	7/31	2/10, n/30		4 2 0 00	3 0 00	3 9 0 00	2
3		3	Reilly and Peters	982	8/2	n/30		7 6 0 00	5 2 00	7 0 8 00	3
4		5	Adkins Manufacturing Co.	10611	8/3	2/10, n/30		6 9 2 00		6 9 2 00	4
5		9	Sullivan Products Co.	B643	8/6	1/10, n/30		1 6 5 00	1 0 00	1 5 5 00	5
6		18	T. R. Wetzel	46812	8/17	n/60		2 2 8 00		2 2 8 00	6
7		25	Donaldson and Farr	1024	8/23	2/10, n/30		3 7 6 00	1 4 00	3 6 2 00	7
8		26	Draper, Inc.	2801	8/25	2/10, n/30		4 0 6 00	2 2 00	3 8 4 00	8
9		31						3 0 4 7 00	1 2 8 00	2 9 1 9 00	9
10								(2 2 1)	(5 1 4)	(5 1 1)	10
11											11
12											12

GENERAL LEDGER

ACCOUNT ___Accounts Payable___ ACCOUNT NO. ___221___

	DATE	ITEM	POST. REF.	DEBIT	CREDIT	BALANCE DEBIT	BALANCE CREDIT	
1	20–							1
2	Aug. 1	Balance	✓				3 5 6 00	2
3	31		P29		3 0 4 7 00		3 4 0 3 00	3
4								4

ACCOUNT ___Purchases___ ACCOUNT NO. ___511___

	DATE	ITEM	POST. REF.	DEBIT	CREDIT	BALANCE DEBIT	BALANCE CREDIT	
1	20–							1
2	Aug. 1	Balance	✓			20 6 1 2 00		2
3	31		P29	2 9 1 9 00		23 5 3 1 00		3
4								4

If a company were to purchase office supplies on account from a store like this, the company would not use a purchases journal unless it intended to then resell the supplies. Instead, the company would record the transaction in an accounts payable ledger.

FIGURE 5 (continued)

ACCOUNT **Freight In**   ACCOUNT NO. **514**

	DATE	ITEM	POST. REF.	DEBIT	CREDIT	BALANCE DEBIT	BALANCE CREDIT	
1	20–							1
2	Aug. 1	Balance	✓			1 5 0 2 00		2
3	31		P29	1 2 8 00		1 6 3 0 00		3
4								4

THE ACCOUNTS PAYABLE LEDGER

Remember!

Creditors are companies or individuals to whom we owe money.

Remember!

Increases in Accounts Payable are recorded in the Credit column. Decreases in Accounts Payable are recorded in the Debit column.

You know that the Accounts Receivable account in the general ledger is a controlling account, and that the accounts receivable ledger consists of an individual account for each charge customer. You also know that the accountant posts to the accounts receivable ledger every day.

Accounts Payable is a parallel case; it, too, is a controlling account in the general ledger. **The accounts payable ledger is a subsidiary ledger, and it consists of individual accounts for all the creditors.** Again, posting to the accounts payable ledger is usually done daily. After posting to the individual creditors' accounts, the accountant puts a check mark (✓) in the Post. Ref. column of the purchases journal. After the accountant has finished all the posting to the controlling account at the end of the period, the total of the schedule of accounts payable should equal the balance of the Accounts Payable (controlling) account. The three-column form is used for the accounts payable ledger.

Now let's look at the purchases journal (Figure 6) and the postings to the ledger (Figure 7) on page 374. Note that in the accounts payable ledger—as in the accounts receivable ledger—the accounts of the individual creditors are listed in either alphabetical or numerical order. Firms that handle all of their bookkeeping and accounting on computer may assign an account number to each individual account.

PURCHASES JOURNAL

PAGE **29**

	DATE		SUPPLIER'S NAME	INVOICE NO.	INVOICE DATE	TERMS	POST. REF.	ACCOUNTS PAYABLE CREDIT	FREIGHT IN DEBIT	PURCHASES DEBIT	
1	20–										1
2	Aug.	2	Draper, Inc.	2706	7/31	2/10, n/30	✓	4 2 0 00	3 0 00	3 9 0 00	2
3		3	Reilly and Peters	982	8/2	n/30	✓	7 6 0 00	5 2 00	7 0 8 00	3
4		5	Adkins Manufacturing Co.	10611	8/3	2/10, n/30	✓	6 9 2 00		6 9 2 00	4
5		9	Sullivan Products Co.	B643	8/6	1/10, n/30	✓	1 6 5 00	1 0 00	1 5 5 00	5
6		18	T. R. Wetzel	46812	8/17	n/60	✓	2 2 8 00		2 2 8 00	6
7		25	Donaldson and Farr	1024	8/23	2/10, n/30	✓	3 7 6 00	1 4 00	3 6 2 00	7
8		26	Draper, Inc.	2801	8/25	2/10, n/30	✓	4 0 6 00	2 2 00	3 8 4 00	8
9		31						3 0 4 7 00	1 2 8 00	2 9 1 9 00	9
10								(2 2 1)	(5 1 4)	(5 1 1)	10

FIGURE 6

A/P daily   monthly   monthly
GL - monthly

FIGURE 7

ACCOUNTS PAYABLE LEDGER

NAME **Adkins Manufacturing Company**
ADDRESS **254 Calle Mancha**
Los Angeles, CA 90025

DATE		ITEM	POST. REF.	DEBIT	CREDIT	BALANCE
20–						
Aug.	5		P29		6 9 2 00	6 9 2 00

NAME **Draper, Inc.**
ADDRESS **1614 Olivera Street**
San Francisco, CA 94129

DATE		ITEM	POST. REF.	DEBIT	CREDIT	BALANCE
20–						
Aug.	2		P29		4 2 0 00	4 2 0 00
	26		P29		4 0 6 00	8 2 6 00

NAME **Donaldson and Farr**
ADDRESS **2426 Reilly Way, N.E.**
Seattle, WA 98102

DATE		ITEM	POST. REF.	DEBIT	CREDIT	BALANCE
20–						
Aug.	25		P29		3 7 6 00	3 7 6 00

FIGURE 7 (continued)

NAME   Reilly and Peters

ADDRESS   2154 Springer St.

Boston, MA 02107

DATE		ITEM	POST. REF.	DEBIT	CREDIT	BALANCE
20–						
July	27		P28		1 8 0 00	1 8 0 00
Aug.	3		P29		7 6 0 00	9 4 0 00

NAME   Sullivan Products Company

ADDRESS   142 Grant Road

Cleveland, OH 44102

DATE		ITEM	POST. REF.	DEBIT	CREDIT	BALANCE
20–						
Aug.	9		P29		1 6 5 00	1 6 5 00

NAME   T. R. Wetzel

ADDRESS   1620 Minard St.

San Jose, CA 95101

DATE		ITEM	POST. REF.	DEBIT	CREDIT	BALANCE
20–						
July	29		P28		1 7 6 00	1 7 6 00
Aug.	18		P29		2 2 8 00	4 0 4 00

PURCHASES RETURNS AND ALLOWANCES

Objective 3

Journalize transactions involving purchases returns and allowances in a general journal.

As its title implies, the Purchases Returns and Allowances account handles either a return of merchandise previously purchased or an allowance made for merchandise that arrived in damaged condition. In both cases, there is a reduction in the amount owed to the supplier. The buyer sends a letter or printed form to the supplier, who acknowledges the reduction by sending a credit memorandum. The buyer should wait for notice that the deduction has been agreed to before making an entry.

The Purchases Returns and Allowances account is considered a deduction from Purchases. Using a separate account provides a better record for management of quality control of the total returns and allowances. Purchases Returns and Allowances is deducted from the Purchases account on the income statement. (We'll talk about this point later.) For now, let's look at an example consisting of two entries on the books of Jackson Electric Supply.

Transaction (a) On August 5, bought merchandise on account from Adkins Manufacturing Company, $692, its invoice no. 10611 of August 3; terms 2/10, n/30; FOB Los Angeles. Recorded this as a debit to Purchases and a credit to Accounts Payable. On August 6 returned merchandise costing $70. Made no entry.

Transaction (b) On August 8, received credit memorandum no. 629 from Adkins Manufacturing Company for $70. Recorded this as a debit to Accounts Payable and a credit to Purchases Returns and Allowances.

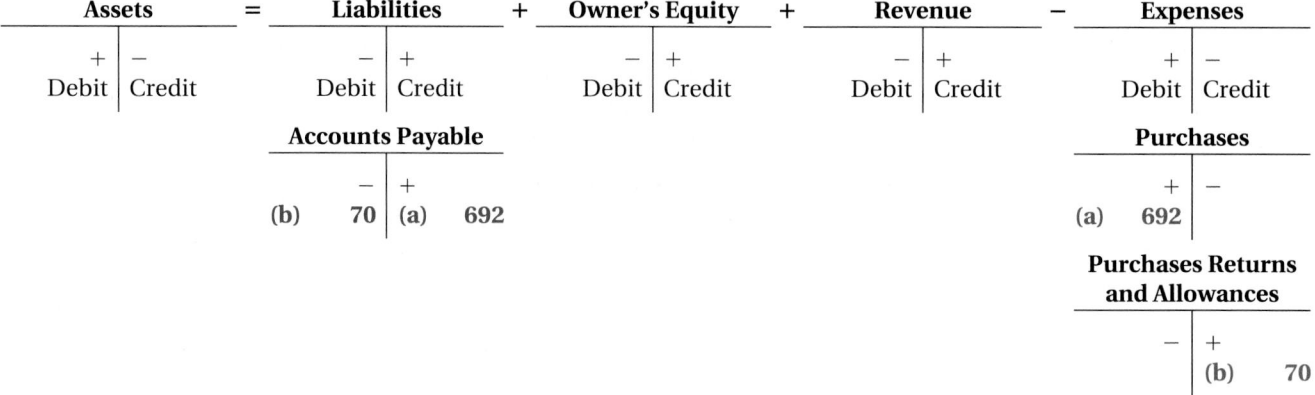

Purchases Returns and Allowances is credited because Jackson Electric Supply's returns and allowances have increased. Accounts Payable is debited because Jackson Electric Supply owes less than before.

On August 12, suppose that Jackson Electric Supply also received credit memo no. 482 from Sullivan Products Company for $36 as an allowance for damaged merchandise. The entries in the general journal for journalizing the two credit memos are as follows:

GENERAL JOURNAL   PAGE __27__

	DATE		DESCRIPTION	POST. REF.	DEBIT	CREDIT	
1	20–						1
2	Aug.	8	Accounts Payable, Adkins				2
3			Manufacturing Company		7 0 00		3
4			Purchases Returns and				4
5			Allowances			7 0 00	5
6			Credit memo no. 629 for				6
7			return of merchandise.				7
8							8
9		12	Accounts Payable, Sullivan				9
10			Products Company		3 6 00		10
11			Purchases Returns and				11
12			Allowances			3 6 00	12
13			Credit memo no. 482 as an				13
14			allowance for damaged				14
15			merchandise.				15

Remember!

A credit memo received by the buyer means a reduction in the amount the buyer owes.

In these entries, Accounts Payable is followed by the name of the individual creditor's account. **The accountant must post the amount to both the Accounts Payable control account and the individual creditor's account in the accounts payable ledger.** The journal entries are shown here as they appear when the posting is completed. The account numbers in the Post. Ref. column indicate postings to the accounts in the general ledger, and the check marks indicate postings to the accounts in the accounts payable ledger.

Remember!

From the viewpoint of the buyer, a credit memo is journalized as a debit to Accounts Payable and a credit to Purchases Returns and Allowances. From the viewpoint of the seller, a credit memo is journalized as a debit to Sales Returns and Allowances and a credit to Accounts Receivable.

GENERAL JOURNAL   PAGE __27__

	DATE		DESCRIPTION	POST. REF.	DEBIT	CREDIT	
1	20–						1
2	Aug.	8	Accounts Payable, Adkins				2
3			Manufacturing Company	221 ✓	7 0 00		3
4			Purchases Returns and				4
5			Allowances	512		7 0 00	5
6			Credit memo no. 629 for				6
7			return of merchandise.				7
8							8
9		12	Accounts Payable, Sullivan				9
10			Products Company	221 ✓	3 6 00		10
11			Purchases Returns and				11
12			Allowances	512		3 6 00	12
13			Credit memo no. 482 as an				13
14			allowance for damaged				14
15			merchandise.				15

GENERAL LEDGER

ACCOUNT **Accounts Payable**   ACCOUNT NO. __221__

	DATE	ITEM	POST. REF.	DEBIT	CREDIT	BALANCE DEBIT	BALANCE CREDIT	
1	20–							1
2	Aug. 1	Balance	✓				3 5 6 00	2
3	8		J27	7 0 00			2 8 6 00	3
4	12		J27	3 6 00			2 5 0 00	4
5								5

ACCOUNT **Purchases Returns and Allowances**   ACCOUNT NO. __512__

	DATE	ITEM	POST. REF.	DEBIT	CREDIT	BALANCE DEBIT	BALANCE CREDIT	
1	20–							1
2	Aug. 1	Balance	✓		7 0 00		6 4 0 00	2
3	8		J27		3 6 00		7 1 0 00	3
4	12		J27				7 4 6 00	4

Many computer stores charge a 15 percent restocking fee to anyone who returns a computer. This helps reduce handling costs. The Purchases Returns and Allowances account is used to record this fee.

ACCOUNTS PAYABLE LEDGER

NAME   Adkins Manufacturing Company

ADDRESS 254 Calle Mancha

            Los Angeles, CA 90025

DATE		ITEM	POST. REF.	DEBIT	CREDIT	BALANCE
20–						
Aug.	5		P29		6 9 2 00	6 9 2 00
	8		J27	7 0 00		6 2 2 00

NAME   Sullivan Products Company

ADDRESS 2154 Springer St.

            Boston, MA 02107

DATE		ITEM	POST. REF.	DEBIT	CREDIT	BALANCE
20–						
Aug.	9		P29		1 6 5 00	1 6 5 00
	12		J27	3 6 00		1 2 9 00

Schedule of Accounts Payable

Objective 4

Prepare a schedule of accounts payable.

Assuming that no other transactions involved Accounts Payable, the schedule of accounts payable would appear as follows. Note that the balances of the creditors' accounts, with the exception of the accounts for Adkins Manufacturing Company and Sullivan Products Company, are taken from the accounts payable ledger shown in Figure 7 on pages 374–375.

Jackson Electric Supply
Schedule of Accounts Payable
August 31, 20—

Adkins Manufacturing Company	$	6 2 2 00
Draper, Inc.		8 2 6 00
Donaldson and Farr		3 7 6 00
Reilly and Peters		9 4 0 00
Sullivan Products Company		1 2 9 00
T. R. Wetzel		4 0 4 00
Total Accounts Payable	$3	2 9 7 00

The Accounts Payable controlling account in the general ledger is now posted up to date.

GENERAL LEDGER

ACCOUNT **Accounts Payable**   ACCOUNT NO. **221**

	DATE	ITEM	POST. REF.	DEBIT	CREDIT	BALANCE DEBIT	BALANCE CREDIT	
1	20–							1
2	Aug. 1	Balance	✓				3 5 6 00	2
3	8		J27	7 0 00			2 8 6 00	3
4	12		J27	3 6 00			2 5 0 00	4
5	31		P29		3 0 4 7 00		3 2 9 7 00	5

SUBSIDIARY LEDGERS

The place of subsidiary ledgers in the accounting cycle is shown in Figure 8. The figure also shows how the schedules of accounts receivable and accounts payable fit into the accounting cycle.

FIGURE 8

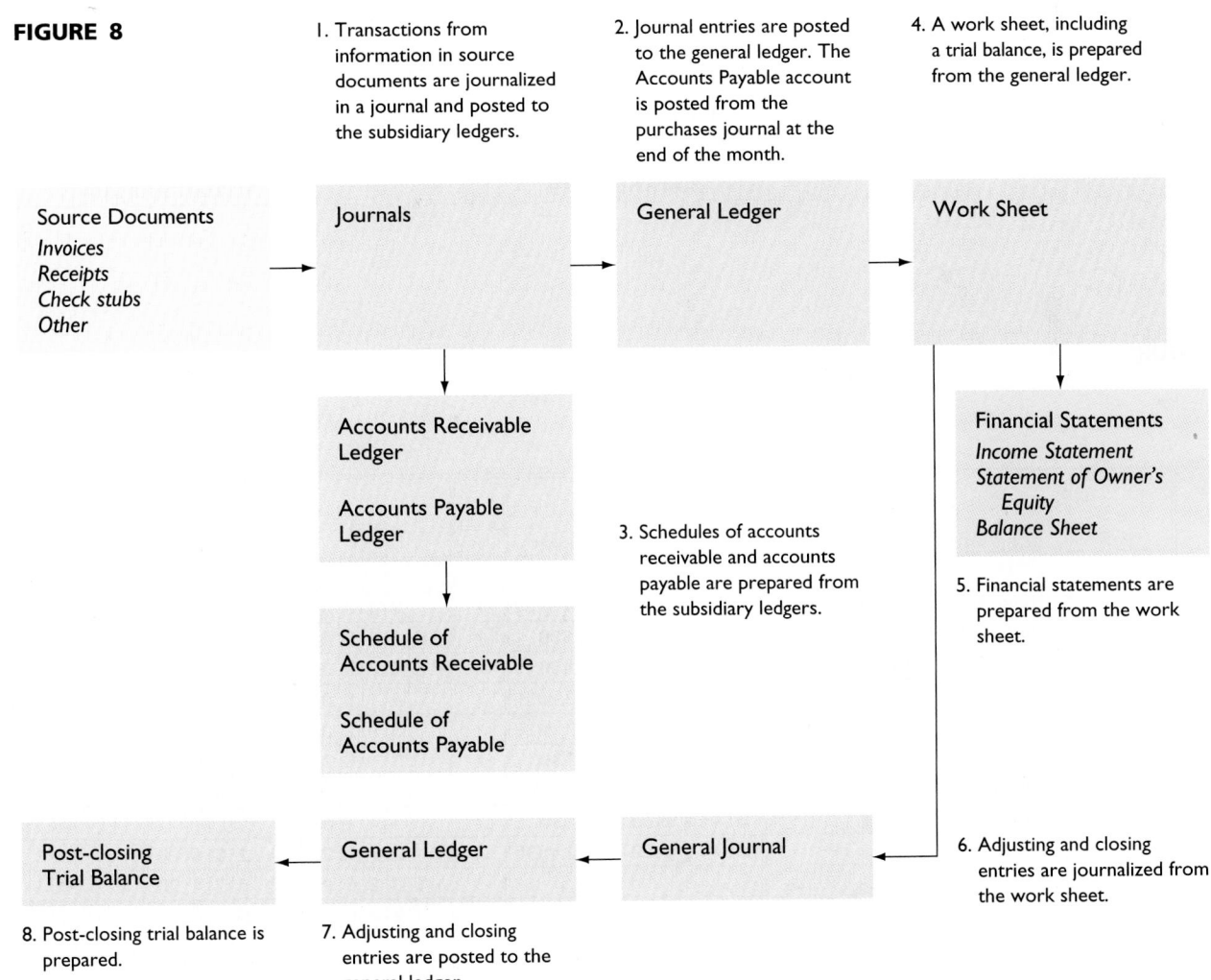

1. Transactions from information in source documents are journalized in a journal and posted to the subsidiary ledgers.

2. Journal entries are posted to the general ledger. The Accounts Payable account is posted from the purchases journal at the end of the month.

4. A work sheet, including a trial balance, is prepared from the general ledger.

Source Documents
Invoices
Receipts
Check stubs
Other

Journals

General Ledger

Work Sheet

Accounts Receivable Ledger

Accounts Payable Ledger

Schedule of Accounts Receivable

Schedule of Accounts Payable

3. Schedules of accounts receivable and accounts payable are prepared from the subsidiary ledgers.

Financial Statements
Income Statement
Statement of Owner's Equity
Balance Sheet

5. Financial statements are prepared from the work sheet.

Post-closing Trial Balance

General Ledger

General Journal

6. Adjusting and closing entries are journalized from the work sheet.

8. Post-closing trial balance is prepared.

7. Adjusting and closing entries are posted to the general ledger.

MULTICOLUMN PURCHASES JOURNAL (INVOICE REGISTER)

Objective 5

Journalize transactions in a multicolumn purchases journal.

Instead of the three-column purchases journal, some businesses prefer to use a multicolumn purchases journal or invoice register, which handles not only freight charges and purchases of merchandise but anything bought on account. Items other than merchandise usually consist of supplies and equipment acquired for use in the firm. The advantage of a multicolumn purchases journal is that all types of purchases on account are journalized in one journal.

As an illustration, let's use another company, Cortez's Gift Shop. Here are three transactions that occurred during the first week in May:

May 2 Bought merchandise on account from Chase Specialty Company, $610, its invoice no. L311, dated May 1; terms 2/10, n/30; FOB shipping point, freight prepaid and added to the invoice $36 (total $646).

Purchases		Freight In		Accounts Payable	
+	−	+	−	−	+
610		36			646

May 4 Bought packaging material on account from Benton Paper Products, its invoice no. 962D, dated May 4; terms n/30, $98.

Store Supplies		Accounts Payable	
+	−	−	+
98			98

FIGURE 9

PURCHASES JOURNAL

	DATE		SUPPLIER'S NAME	INVOICE NO.	INVOICE DATE	TERMS	POST. REF.	ACCOUNTS PAYABLE CREDIT	PURCHASES DEBIT	FREIGHT IN DEBIT	
1	20–										
2	May	2	Chase Specialty Company	L311	5/1	2/10, n/30	✓	6 4 6 00	6 1 0 00	3 6 00	
3		4	Benton Paper Products	962D	5/4	n/30	✓	9 8 00			
4		5	Lee Cabinet Shop	4273	5/5	n/30	✓	6 2 9 00			
5		9	C. B. Boles Company	C-349	5/7	1/10, n/30	✓	4 1 6 00	4 0 4 00	1 2 00	
6		16	Gable and Son	124-9	5/15	2/10, n/30	✓	3 9 2 00	3 9 2 00		
7		24	Moore Office Machines	N92	5/23	n/30	✓	5 1 5 71			
8		27	Curtis, Inc.	517R	5/26	1/15, n/60	✓	3 0 4 00	3 0 4 00		
9		30	Coe Office Supplies	5119	5/30	n/30	✓	4 2 36			
10		31	Brice Corporation	D274	5/29	2/10, n/30	✓	2 7 7 20	2 6 4 20	1 3 00	
11		31						3 3 2 0 27	1 9 7 4 20	6 1 00	
12								(2 2 1)	(5 1 1)	(5 1 4)	
13											

A/P-daily   monthly   monthly
GL-monthly

Remember!

To save time in posting, special columns are set up for frequently used accounts.

May 5 Bought a display case on account from Lee Cabinet Shop, its invoice no. 4273, dated May 5; terms n/30, $629.

Store Equipment			Accounts Payable	
+	−		−	+
629				629

These transactions, as well as others during the month, are now journalized in the multicolumn purchases journal shown in Figure 9.

For each transaction journalized in the multicolumn purchases journal, the amount to be credited is entered in the Accounts Payable Credit column. The next three columns are used to journalize the particular accounts most frequently affected. These are called special columns because each column has its own special account name. The final set of columns, under the heading Other Accounts Debit, is used to journalize the purchase of items that are not provided for in the special debit columns.

Posting from the Multicolumn Purchases Journal

Objective 6

Post from a multicolumn purchases journal to an accounts payable ledger and a general ledger.

Posting to the creditors' accounts in the accounts payable ledger from a multicolumn purchases journal is similar to posting from a three-column purchases journal. Posting is done daily, and the check marks (✓) in the Post. Ref. column indicate that the amounts have been posted separately.

The amounts listed in the Other Accounts Debit column are posted separately—usually on a daily basis. The posting process is the same as for posting from a general journal. The account numbers recorded in the Post. Ref. column indicate that the amounts have been posted.

At the end of the month, first prove that the sum of the debit totals equals the total of the Accounts Payable Credit column by making sure that debits equal credits horizontally for each entry and vertically as totals. This process is referred to as **crossfooting** the journal.

PAGE ____62____

STORE SUPPLIES DEBIT	OTHER ACCOUNTS DEBIT				
	ACCOUNT	POST. REF.	AMOUNT		
					1
					2
9 8 00					3
	Store Equipment	125	6 2 9 00		4
					5
					6
	Office Equipment	127	5 1 5 71		7
					8
4 2 36					9
					10
1 4 0 36			1 1 4 4 71		11
(1 1 4)			(X)		12
					13

monthly   *daily*

	Debit Totals		**Credit Total**
Purchases	$1,974.20	Accounts Payable	$3,320.27
Freight In	61.00		
Store Supplies	140.36		
Other Accounts	1,144.71		
	$3,320.27		

Next, the accountant posts the special columns as totals. After posting the total amount, he or she records the ledger account number in parentheses below the total in the appropriate column. The (X) placed below the total of the Other Accounts Debit column means "this amount was not posted"— because the figures have already been posted separately.

POSTING DIRECTLY FROM PURCHASE INVOICES (AN ALTERNATIVE TO USING A PURCHASES JOURNAL)

Objective 7

Post directly from purchase invoices to an accounts payable ledger and journalize and post a summarizing entry in the general journal.

Posting from purchase invoices is a shortcut, like posting from sales invoices. Daily, the accountant posts to the individual creditors' accounts, working directly from the purchase invoices. The suppliers' invoice numbers rather than journal page numbers are recorded in the Post. Ref. column. The Accounts Payable controlling account in the general ledger is brought up to date at the end of the month by making a summarizing entry in the general journal. The accountant debits Purchases and Freight In, and also the appropriate asset account for any goods and services the company bought on account, and credits Accounts Payable.

Since posting directly from purchase invoices is a variation of the accounting system, we will use a different example: Don's RV Service. This firm sorts its invoices for the month and finds that the totals are as follows: purchases of merchandise, $9,164; freight charges on merchandise, $291; store supplies, $168; office supplies, $126; and store equipment, $520. The accountant then makes a summarizing entry in the general journal as follows:

	GENERAL JOURNAL			PAGE 37

	DATE		DESCRIPTION	POST. REF.	DEBIT	CREDIT	
1	20–						1
2	Oct.	31	Purchases	511	9 1 6 4 00		2
3			Freight In	514	2 9 1 00		3
4			Store Supplies	114	1 6 8 00		4
5			Office Supplies	115	1 2 6 00		5
6			Store Equipment	125	5 2 0 00		6
7			Accounts Payable	221		10 2 6 9 00	7
8			Summarizing entry for total				8
9			purchase of goods on				9
10			account.				10

The accountant posts the above entry to the general ledger accounts.

GENERAL LEDGER

ACCOUNT **Store Supplies**   ACCOUNT NO. **114**

	DATE	ITEM	POST. REF.	DEBIT	CREDIT	BALANCE DEBIT	BALANCE CREDIT	
1	20–							1
2	Oct. 31		J37	1 6 8 00		1 6 8 00		2
3								3

ACCOUNT **Office Supplies**   ACCOUNT NO. **115**

	DATE	ITEM	POST. REF.	DEBIT	CREDIT	BALANCE DEBIT	BALANCE CREDIT	
1	20–							1
2	Oct. 31		J37	1 2 6 00		1 2 6 00		2
3								3

ACCOUNT **Store Equipment**   ACCOUNT NO. **125**

	DATE	ITEM	POST. REF.	DEBIT	CREDIT	BALANCE DEBIT	BALANCE CREDIT	
1	20–							1
2	Oct. 31		J37	5 2 0 00		5 2 0 00		2
3								3

ACCOUNT **Accounts Payable**   ACCOUNT NO. **221**

	DATE	ITEM	POST. REF.	DEBIT	CREDIT	BALANCE DEBIT	BALANCE CREDIT	
1	20–							1
2	Oct. 31		J37		10 2 6 9 00		10 2 6 9 00	2
3								3

ACCOUNT **Purchases**   ACCOUNT NO. **511**

	DATE	ITEM	POST. REF.	DEBIT	CREDIT	BALANCE DEBIT	BALANCE CREDIT	
1	20–							1
2	Oct. 31		J37	9 1 6 4 00		9 1 6 4 00		2
3								3

| | ACCOUNT | Freight In | | | | | | | ACCOUNT NO. | 514 | |

| | DATE | ITEM | POST. REF. | DEBIT | CREDIT | BALANCE | |
						DEBIT	CREDIT
1	20–						
2	Oct. 31		J37	2 9 1 00		2 9 1 00	
3							

This procedure does away with the need for a purchases journal, and it includes the buying of any goods or services on account in the same summarizing entry. An example of an invoice is shown in Figure 10.

Don's RV Service posts the amount of the invoice to the account of the supplier in the accounts payable ledger:

ACCOUNTS PAYABLE LEDGER

NAME Bingham Mobile Home Sales and Service

ADDRESS 9600 Madera St.

San Francisco, CA 94132

DATE	ITEM	POST. REF.	DEBIT	CREDIT	BALANCE
20–					
Oct. 7		13168		1 7 6 00	1 7 6 00

FIGURE 10

Bingham Mobile Home Sales and Service
9600 Madera St.
San Francisco, CA 94132

INVOICE

SOLD TO Don's RV Service
2716 Brighton Road
Burlingame, CA 94011

Rec'd October 7, 20–

DATE: Oct. 4, 20—
NO.: 13168
ORDER NO.: 1635
SHIPPED BY: Pacific Express Co.
TERMS: 1/10, n/30
FOB Burlingame

QUANTITY	DESCRIPTION	UNIT PRICE	TOTAL
20	TV antennas	8 80	176 00
	Total		176 00

Don's RV Service also includes the $176 figure in the summarizing entry recorded in the general journal, debiting Purchases and crediting Accounts Payable. Note that the supplier's invoice number is recorded in the Post. Ref. column in the Bingham Mobile Home Sales and Service account in the Accounts Payable ledger.

TRANSPORTATION CHARGES ON THE BUYING OF GOODS AND SERVICES OTHER THAN MERCHANDISE

Remember!

Freight In is used only to record the incoming transportation charges on merchandise intended for resale.

Any freight charges incurred when buying any other assets, such as supplies or equipment, should be debited to the respective asset accounts. Let's return to Jackson Electric Supply and assume that this company bought display cases on account from Coster Cabinet Shop, at a cost of $2,700 plus freight charges of $90. The seller of the display cases prepaid the transportation costs for Jackson Electric Supply and then added the $90 to the invoice price of the cases. Let's visualize this with T accounts.

Store Equipment	Accounts Payable
+ −	− +
2,790	2,790

If Jackson Electric Supply had paid the freight charges separately, the entry for the payment would be a debit to Store Equipment for $90 and a credit to Cash for $90.

INTERNAL CONTROL

You know that the efficient management of cash is critical to a firm. All payments should be made either by check or from the petty cash fund, and all cash received should be deposited in the bank at the end of the day. The handling of cash in this manner is an example of **internal control**. Internal control embraces plans and procedures for the control of operations as a part of the accounting system. This is necessary when the owner or management must delegate authority. The owner has to take measures to (1) protect assets against fraud and waste, (2) provide for accurate accounting data, (3) promote an efficient operation, and (4) encourage adherence to management policies.

Internal Control of Purchases

Purchases is one of the areas in which internal control is essential. Efficiency and security require most companies to work out careful procedures for buying and paying for goods. This is understandable, as large sums of money are usually involved. The control aspect generally involves the following measures:

1. Purchases are made only after proper authorization is given. Purchase requisitions and purchase orders are all prenumbered, so that each form can be accounted for.

2. The receiving department carefully checks all goods upon receipt for count, damages, and description. Later, the report of the receiving department is verified against the purchase order and the purchase invoice.

3. The person who authorizes the payment is neither the person doing the ordering nor the person actually writing the check. Payment is authorized only after verifying the purchase invoice data with the receiving report and purchase order.

4. The person who actually writes the check has not been involved in any of the foregoing purchasing procedures.

CHAPTER REVIEW

Review of Performance Objectives

1. Journalize transactions in a three-column purchases journal.

   The three-column purchases journal handles the purchase of merchandise on account and freight charges that are prepaid by the seller and included in the invoice total. A transaction is journalized on one line including the date, supplier's name, invoice number, invoice date, terms, Accounts Payable Credit, Freight In Debit, and Purchases Debit.

2. Post from a three-column purchases journal to an accounts payable ledger and a general ledger.

   Amounts in the Accounts Payable Credit column are posted daily to the accounts payable ledger. At the end of the month, the totals are posted to the general ledger as a debit to Purchases, a debit to Freight In, and a credit to Accounts Payable.

3. Journalize transactions involving purchases returns and allowances in a general journal.

   When a credit memo is received for the return of merchandise or as an allowance for damaged merchandise, the buyer credits Purchases Returns and Allowances. If the merchandise was bought on account, the buyer debits Accounts Payable. The transaction is journalized in the general journal.

4. Prepare a schedule of accounts payable.

   A schedule of accounts payable, listing the balance of each individual creditor's account, is prepared from the accounts payable ledger.

5. Journalize transactions in a multicolumn purchases journal.

   A multicolumn purchases journal handles transactions involving the buying of anything on account, as well as freight charges prepaid by suppliers on behalf of the buyer. Most transactions can be journalized on one line. There are special columns for the most frequently used accounts and an Other Accounts Debit column for all other purchases on account.

6. Post from a multicolumn purchases journal to an accounts payable ledger and a general ledger.

   Amounts in the Accounts Payable Credit column are posted daily to the accounts payable ledger. Amounts in the Other Accounts Debit column are posted daily to the general ledger. At the end of the month, the totals of the special columns are posted to the general ledger.

7. Post directly from purchase invoices to an accounts payable ledger and journalize and post a summarizing entry in the general journal.

As a further shortcut, the firm may post to the accounts of the individual creditors in the accounts payable ledger directly from invoices of purchases of merchandise bought on credit. At the end of the month, the accountant makes a summarizing entry in the general journal, debiting Purchases, Freight In, and assets that were acquired and crediting Accounts Payable for the total of the invoices.

Glossary

Accounts payable ledger A subsidiary ledger that lists the individual accounts of creditors in either alphabetical or numerical order. (373)

Crossfooting Horizontal and vertical addition of column totals to prove that the total debits equal the total credits vertically and horizontally. (381)

FOB destination Shipping terms under which the seller pays the freight charges and includes them in the selling price. Title or ownership changes hands when the buyer receives the goods. (368)

FOB shipping point Shipping terms under which the buyer pays the freight charges between the point of shipment and the destination. Payment may be made directly to the carrier upon receiving the goods or to the supplier, if the supplier prepaid the freight charges on behalf of the buyer. Title or ownership changes hands when goods are transferred to the freight company. (369)

Internal control Plans and procedures built into the accounting system with the following objectives: (1) to protect assets against fraud and waste; (2) to provide accurate accounting data; (3) to promote an efficient operation; and (4) to encourage adherence to management policies. (385)

Invoice A business form prepared by the seller that lists the items shipped, their cost, the terms of the sale, and the mode of shipment. It may also state the freight charges. The buyer considers it a purchase invoice; the seller considers it a sales invoice. (367)

Purchase order A written order from the buyer of goods to the supplier, listing the items wanted and the terms of the transaction. (366)

Purchase requisition A form used to request that the Purchasing Department buy something. This form is intended for internal use within a company. (366)

Purchases discount A cash discount allowed for prompt payment of an invoice; for example, 2 percent if the bill is paid within 10 days. (371)

Purchases journal A special journal used to record the buying of goods on account. It may be used to record the purchase of merchandise only. It may also be a multicolumn journal, or invoice register, used to record the buying of anything on account. (371)

QUESTIONS, EXERCISES, AND PROBLEMS

Discussion Questions

1. How can a computer be considered merchandise by one company and office equipment by another?

2. Explain the purpose of the purchase requisition, the purchase order, and the purchase invoice. Which form is used as the basis for a journal entry?

3. What special account columns in a purchases journal would you recommend in situations in which a company frequently buys merchandise and the seller pays the freight charges as a convenience to the buyer and lists the amounts in the purchase invoices?

4. Why is it good practice to post daily to the accounts payable ledger?

5. Explain the meaning and importance of the shipping terms *FOB destination* and *FOB shipping point*. Who has title to the goods once they have been shipped?

6. Describe the four procedures that most companies follow to maintain internal control of purchases.

7. Explain the procedure of posting directly from purchase invoices.

8. Explain the process of proving the totals of a multicolumn purchases journal. What is this process called?

Exercises

P.O. 1

Record journal entries relating to purchases FOB shipping point and FOB destination.

Exercise 11-1 Journalize the following transactions in general journal form:

a. Bought merchandise on account from Berg Company, invoice no. 711N, $941; net 30 days; FOB shipping point.

b. Paid West Express for shipping charges on Berg Company purchase, $64.

c. Bought merchandise on account from Anders, Inc., invoice no. D312, $1,342; net 30 days; freight prepaid and added to invoice, $112 (total $1,454).

d. Paid Berg Company account in full, invoice no. 711N.

e. Paid Anders, Inc., account in full, invoice no. D312.

P.O. 3

Describe entries involving a purchase and return.

Exercise 11-2 Describe the transactions in the T accounts.

Cash			Purchases		
	(c)	750	(a)	760	

Accounts Payable			Purchases Returns and Allowances		
(b)	50	(a) 800		(b)	50
(c)	750				

Freight In		
(a)	40	

P.O. 3

Record journal entries for a purchase and return.

Exercise 11-3 Journalize the following transactions in general journal form:

a. Bought merchandise on account from Westro, Inc., invoice no. C229; net 30 days; FOB destination, $1,010.

b. Received credit memo no. 117 from Westro, Inc., for merchandise returned, $102.

c. Issued a check to Westro, Inc., in full payment of account.

P.O. 3

Post to accounts payable ledger and general ledger.

Exercise 11-4 Post the following entry to the general ledger and the subsidiary ledger:

GENERAL JOURNAL   PAGE ___92___

	DATE		DESCRIPTION	POST. REF.	DEBIT	CREDIT	
1	20–						1
2	July	14	Accounts Payable, Bullock and				2
3			Hendricks		1 9 2 30		3
4			Purchases Returns and				4
5			Allowances			1 9 2 30	5
6			Credit memo no. 942 for				6
7			return of merchandise.				7
8							8

GENERAL LEDGER

ACCOUNT **Accounts Payable**   ACCOUNT NO. ___221___

			POST.			BALANCE	
	DATE	ITEM	REF.	DEBIT	CREDIT	DEBIT	CREDIT
1	20–							1
2	July 1	Balance	✓				2 7 6 1 24	2
3								3

ACCOUNT **Purchases Returns and Allowances**   ACCOUNT NO. ___512___

			POST.			BALANCE	
	DATE	ITEM	REF.	DEBIT	CREDIT	DEBIT	CREDIT
1	20–							1
2	July 1	Balance	✓				2 3 0 16	2
3								3

ACCOUNTS PAYABLE LEDGER

NAME **Bullock and Hendricks**
ADDRESS **542 Roselle Blvd.**
Richmond, CA 94879

	DATE		ITEM	POST. REF.	DEBIT	CREDIT	BALANCE	
	20–							
	June	13		P73		2 1 8 00	2 1 8 00	

P.O. 7

Record and post purchases directly from invoices.

Exercise 11-5 A business firm posts directly from its purchase invoices. After the invoices for the month have been sorted, the totals are as follows: purchases of merchandise, $9,583; freight charges on merchandise, $162; store supplies, $187; office supplies, $115; store equipment, $1,347. Journalize the summarizing entry in the general journal.

P.O. 3

Record journal entries for purchase and return of assets.

Exercise 11-6 Journalize the following transactions in general journal form:

a. Moi Company buys five different cash registers for use by cashiers on account from Reo Business Machines, invoice 142N, $10,416; net 30 days; FOB shipping point.
b. Paid Fastgo Freight Lines $204 for shipping charges on Reo Business Machines purchase.
c. One of the cash registers purchased for $2,010 is defective and is returned to the supplier. Reo Business Machines paid the freight charges. Moi Company received a credit memorandum from Reo Business Machines.
d. Paid Reo Business Machines in full, invoice no. 142N.

P.O. 2

Determine how errors will be exposed.

Exercise 11-7 The following errors were made in recording transactions in the purchases journal or in posting from it. How will each error come to the attention of the accountant?

a. An invoice of $470 for merchandise from Bellow Company was incorrectly recorded as having been received from Behlo Company.
b. A credit of $720 to the Holst Company account in the accounts payable ledger (controlling account) was posted as $270.
c. The Accounts Payable column of the purchases journal was overstated by $100.

P.O. 3

Correct journal entries.

Exercise 11-8 Journalize entries in general journal form to correct each error described below. Assume that the incorrect entries had been posted, and that the corrections are recorded in the same fiscal period in which the error occurred.

a. A $317 cash purchase of merchandise from L. B. Cho Company was journalized as a purchase on account.
b. The $1,810 cost of defective office equipment returned to the supplier was journalized as a credit to Purchases Returns and Allowances.
c. Transportation cost of $62 incurred on store equipment bought for use in the business was debited to Freight In.
d. Store supplies bought on account costing $91 were journalized as Purchases.

CONSIDER AND COMMUNICATE

You are the bookkeeper at a small merchandising firm. You are comparing the income statements from the last three years. You notice that the Purchases Returns and Allowances account (as a percentage of net sales) has been increasing at an alarming rate. If you were a manager, who would you speak to in the organization to help you understand why?

WHAT IF . . .

You have asked your client, a florist, to prepare a list of her accounts receivable by customer name, so that you may compare the balance with the balance of the control account in the general ledger.

She sent you the following list: Wholesome Florists, $750; Floral Supply, $505; Pretty Petals, $840.

You recognize the names as those of her suppliers, not her customers. You ask her again for the accounts receivable list, and she sends the same list, adding that those are the people who need to *receive* a payment from her. When you list a few of her customers' names, she tells you that these are the accounts payable because those are people who need to *pay* her.

Is she confused? If so, explain how she is confused about accounts receivable and accounts payable. Also suggest ways to avoid communication problems in the future.

A MATTER OF ETHICS

You work in a retail store selling computers. One of the employees asks you to write up the sales invoice for the sale of a computer to him at cost without the owner's approval. This employee knows that the owner sometimes sells computers to the employees at a discount and insists that it will not be any money out of the owner's pocket if you do this. Can you do this for the employee? If the owner would approve the sale only at a smaller discount, are you behaving ethically if you write up the sale at cost?

WEB WORK

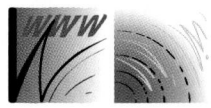

Using an Internet web browser, type *inventory* in the search box and search for information about a major company that interests you. Specifically look for the percentage of Cost of Goods Sold that Purchases and Merchandise Inventory represent. Discuss your findings or write about them in a memo to the CFO (chief financial officer).

PROBLEM SET A

For additional help, see the demonstration problem at the beginning of each chapter in your Working Papers.

P.O. 1,2,4

Problem 11-1A Melor Appliance uses a three-column purchases journal. The company is located in Oakland, California. On January 1 of this year, the balances of the ledger accounts are Accounts Payable, $756.87; Purchases, zero; Freight In, zero. In addition to a general ledger, Melor Appliance also uses an accounts payable ledger. Transactions for January related to the buying of merchandise are as follows:

Jan. 2 Bought eighty 12-inch, 3-speed Brisk Oscillating Fans from Sueto Company, $995.50, invoice no. 268J, dated January 2; terms net 60 days; FOB Oakland.

4 Bought ten Cool Humidifiers from Meeker Company, $1,840, invoice no. 39426, dated January 2; terms 2/10, n/30; FOB Denver, freight prepaid and added to the invoice, $70 (total $1,910).

7 Bought ten Airy Window Fans from Tolan Company, $310, invoice no. 452A, dated January 6; terms 1/10, n/30; FOB Oakland.

Jan. 10 Bought twenty-four 2-speed Ceiling Fans, Model 2760, from Akel Company, $3,527, invoice no. 7742, dated January 7; terms 2/10, n/30; FOB Napa, freight prepaid and added to the invoice, $102 (total $3,629).

14 Bought four Sharpie Electric Hedge Trimmers from Grass Products, $182, invoice no. 2542, dated January 13; terms net 30 days; FOB Oakland.

22 Bought forty Pesty Electric Bug Killers from Sueto Company, $2,570, invoice no. 392J, dated January 22; terms net 60 days; FOB Oakland.

28 Bought ten Breezy Electric Blowers from Grass Products, $736, invoice no. 2691, dated January 27; terms net 30 days; FOB Oakland.

30 Bought ten Apex Powered Attic Ventilators from Poe Manufacturing, $356, invoice no. 664C, dated January 27; terms 2/10, n/30; FOB Seattle, freight prepaid and added to the invoice, $51 (total $407).

Check Figure

Accounts Payable account balance, $11,496.37

Instructions

1. Open the following accounts in the accounts payable ledger and record the January 1 balances, if any, as given: Akel Company; Grass Products; Meeker Company, $185.20; Poe Manufacturing Company, $250.07; Sueto Company; Tolan Company, $321.60. For the accounts having balances, write "Balance" in the Item column and place a check mark in the Post. Ref. column.

2. Record the balance of $756.87 in the Accounts Payable controlling account as of January 1. Write "Balance" in the Item column and place a check mark in the Post. Ref. column.

3. Journalize the transactions in the three-column purchases journal beginning on page 81.

4. Post to the accounts payable ledger daily.

5. Post to the general ledger at the end of the month.

6. Prepare a schedule of accounts payable, and compare the balance of the Accounts Payable controlling account with the total of the schedule of accounts payable.

P.O. 3,4,5

Problem 11-2A Rascal Boutique is located in New York City. The company had the following purchases of merchandise and other assets and related returns and allowances during May of this year.

May 4 Bought merchandise on account from Velour, Inc., $818.41, invoice no. 24812, dated May 2; terms 2/10, n/30; FOB New York.

6 Bought merchandise on account from Festival, Inc., $557.27, invoice no. L123, dated May 4; terms net 30 days; FOB Fort Lee, freight prepaid and added to the invoice, $41 (total $598.27).

9 Bought store supplies on account from Roja Company, $214.86, invoice no. B1164, dated May 8; terms net 30 days; FOB New York.

11 Bought office supplies on account from Jet Office Supply, $196.41, invoice no. 2465, dated May 10; terms net 30 days; FOB New Rochelle, freight prepaid and added to the invoice, $11 (total $207.41). (Record Office Supplies for $207.41.)

14 Received credit memo from Pelon Company for merchandise returned, $45, credit memo no. 772.

May 16   Bought merchandise on account from Velour, Inc., $1,484.27, invoice no. 26453, dated May 16; terms 2/10, n/30; FOB New York.

21   Bought merchandise on account from Kim Company, $913.46, invoice no. H2695, dated May 19; terms net 30 days; FOB Newark, freight prepaid and added to the invoice, $51 (total $964.46).

26   Bought merchandise on account from Delo Company, $813.43, invoice no. 52478, dated May 24; terms 2/10, n/30; FOB New York.

29   Received a credit memo from Festival, Inc., for merchandise returned, $91, credit memo no. 344.

30   Bought merchandise on account from Pelon Company, $1,342.86, invoice no. B8042, dated May 28; terms 2/10, n/30; FOB Newark, freight prepaid and added to the invoice, $118 (total $1,460.86).

31   Bought merchandise on account from Delo Company, $274.27, invoice no. 61994, dated May 30; terms 2/10, n/30; FOB New York.

31   Bought merchandise on account from Festival, Inc., $505.36, invoice no. L285, dated May 29; terms net 30 days; FOB Fort Lee, freight prepaid and added to the invoice, $35 (total $540.36).

Check Figure

Accounts Payable account balance, $11,378.68

Instructions

1. Open the following accounts in the general ledger and enter the balances as of May 1.

114 Store Supplies	$ 396.41	511 Purchases	$7,683.19
115 Office Supplies	192.85	512 Purchases Returns	
221 Accounts Payable	4,138.08	and Allowances	296.41
		514 Freight In	591.52

For the accounts having balances, write "Balance" in the Item column and place a check mark in the Post. Ref. column.

2. Open the following accounts in the accounts payable ledger and record the May 1 balances, if any, as given: Delo Company, $1,246.87; Festival, Inc.; Jet Office Supply; Kim Company; Pelon Company, $1,432.92; Roja Company; Velour, Inc., $1,458.29. For the accounts having balances, write "Balance" in the Item column and place a check mark in the Post. Ref. column.

3. Journalize the transactions either in the general journal, starting on page 27, or on page 6 of the multicolumn purchases journal as appropriate.

4. Post the entries to the creditors' accounts in the accounts payable ledger immediately after you make each journal entry.

5. Post the entries in the general journal and the Other Accounts Debit column of the purchases journal immediately after you make each journal entry.

6. In the space below the purchases journal, show proof that the sum of the debit totals equals the total of the Accounts Payable Credit column.

7. Post the totals of the special columns of the purchases journal at the end of the month.

8. Prepare a schedule of accounts payable, and compare the balance of the Accounts Payable controlling account with the total of the schedule of accounts payable.

P.O. 7

Problem 11-3A The Dole Products Company of Dallas, Texas, records sales of merchandise daily by posting directly from its sales invoices to the accounts receivable ledger. At the end of the month, a summarizing entry is made in the general journal. The purchase of goods on account is recorded in a similar manner. Each day's posting is done directly from the invoices to the accounts payable ledger, and a summarizing entry is made in the general journal at the end of the month. Sales of merchandise and purchases of goods on account during May of this year were as follows.

Sales of Merchandise on Account

May	4	Lemon and Fay, no. 3522, $536.41.
	7	C. L. Favor, Inc., no. 3523, $1,232.30.
	11	P. R. Kevo and Company, no. 3524, $687.91.
	15	Mako Company, no. 3525, $392.74.
	22	C. D. Swick, no. 3526, $232.81.
	24	Lester Jaco, no. 3527, $494.88.
	25	Shelley Tai, no. 3528, $767.45.
	28	Milo Corporation, no. 3529, $844.97.
	30	Howard and Company, no. 3530, $936.54.
	31	C. L. Favor, Inc., no. 3531, $1,127.22.

Purchases of Merchandise, Supplies, and Equipment on Account

May	3	Russel Company, merchandise, $231.46; FOB Dallas.
	9	Galer Manufacturing Company, merchandise, $645.54; FOB Dallas.
	11	Quick Supply Company, office supplies, $118.49; FOB Dallas.
	19	Goodrow Company, merchandise, $3,427; FOB Houston, freight prepaid and added to the invoice, $86 (total $3,513).
	21	Turow Company, store supplies, $210.40; FOB Dallas.
	27	Wilson Specialty Products, merchandise, $2,467.10; FOB Dallas.
	31	Spring Distributing Company, store equipment, $1,010; FOB Dallas.

Check Figure

Total Sales, $7,253.23

Instructions

1. Journalize the summarizing entry for sales of merchandise on account in the general journal, page 27.
2. Journalize the summarizing entry for the purchase of goods on account in the general journal.

P.O. 1,2,3,4

Problem 11-4A The following transactions relate to the Stellar Company of Atlanta during April of this year. Terms of sale are 2/10, n/30.

Apr.	2	Sold merchandise on account to Stroud and Company, invoice no. 1126, $836.
	4	Bought merchandise on account from Plagge Manufacturing Company, invoice no. 16521, $657; terms 1/10, n/30; dated April 2; FOB Atlanta.
	9	Sold merchandise on account to Plover and Lee, invoice no. 1127, $1,265.
	12	Bought merchandise on account from Vick Company, invoice no. L8552, $2,143; terms 2/10, n/30; dated April 11; FOB Rome, freight prepaid and added to the invoice, $51 (total $2,194).
	15	Received credit memo no. 79 for merchandise returned to Keller Company, for $127.
	17	Sold merchandise on account to C. N. Horn, Inc., invoice no. 1128, $1,002.
	19	Issued credit memo no. 34 to Plover and Lee for merchandise returned, $89.

Apr. 26 Bought merchandise on account from M. R. Penn, Inc., invoice no. 7447, $1,686; terms 2/10, n/30; dated April 23; FOB Macon, freight prepaid and added to the invoice, $41 (total $1,727).

29 Bought office supplies on account from Taylor Stationery Company, invoice no. S336, dated April 29, $187; terms net 30 days.

29 Sold merchandise on account to Spencer Company, invoice no. 1129, $2,643.

30 Issued credit memo no. 35 to Spencer Company for merchandise returned, $171.

Check Figure

Accounts Payable account balance, $5,205.00

Instructions

1. Open the following accounts in the accounts receivable ledger and record the balances, if any, as of April 1: C. N. Horn, Inc.; Plover and Lee, $516; Spencer Company, $884; Stroud and Company. For the accounts having balances, write "Balance" in the Item column and place a check mark in the Post. Ref. column. Total the amounts and record the balance in the controlling account in the general ledger. (Verify: $1,400.)

2. Open the following accounts in the accounts payable ledger and record the balances, if any, as of April 1: Keller Company, $371; M. R. Penn, Inc., $196; Plagge Manufacturing Company; Taylor Stationery Company; Vick Company. For the accounts having balances, write "Balance" in the Item column and place a check mark in the Post. Ref. column. Total the amounts and record the balance in the controlling account in the general ledger. (Verify: $567.)

3. Journalize the transactions in the sales, purchases, or general journal, as appropriate (sales journal, page 24; purchases journal, page 18; general journal, page 68).

4. Post the entries to the accounts receivable ledger daily.

5. Post the entries to the accounts payable ledger daily.

6. Post the entries in the general journal immediately after you make each journal entry.

7. Post the totals from the special journals at the end of the month.

8. Prepare a schedule of accounts receivable.

9. Prepare a schedule of accounts payable.

10. Compare the totals of the schedules with the balances of the controlling accounts.

Instructions for General Ledger Software

1. Journalize the transactions in the sales, purchases, or general journal.

   a. For efficiency, analyze the transactions, indicate into which journal each transaction goes, and key the entries in three batches—the sales journal, the purchases journal, and the general journal.

   b. If the program uses a single-column purchases journal, add the amount of the freight to the amount of purchases.

2. Print the journals.

3. Post the amounts from the sales, purchases, and general journals to the subsidiary ledgers and to the general ledger.

4. Print the general ledger.

5. Print a schedule of accounts receivable and compare the total with the balance of the Accounts Receivable control account.

6. Print a schedule of accounts payable and compare the total with the balance of the Accounts Payable control account.

PROBLEM SET B

For additional help, see the demonstration problem at the beginning of each chapter in your Working Papers.

P.O. 1,2,4

Problem 11-1B The Urban Bicycle Shop uses a three-column purchases journal. The company is located in Oak Park, Illinois. On January 1 of this year, the balances of the ledger accounts are Accounts Payable, $542.14; Purchases, zero; Freight In, zero. In addition to a general ledger, the company also uses an accounts payable ledger. Transactions for January related to the purchase of merchandise are as follows:

Jan. 4 Bought sixty 10-speed bicycles from Nagara Company, $5,986, invoice no. 26145, dated January 3; terms net 60 days; FOB Oak Park.

7 Bought tires from Biggs' Tire Company, $931, invoice no. 9763, dated January 5; terms 2/10, n/30; FOB Oak Park.

8 Bought bicycle lights and reflectors from Gannon Products, $341, invoice no. 17317, dated January 6; terms net 30 days; FOB Oak Park.

11 Bought hand brakes from Best, Inc., $361, invoice no. 291GE, dated January 9; terms 1/10, n/30; FOB Chicago, freight prepaid and added to the invoice, $21 (total $382).

19 Bought handle grips from Gannon Products, $184.60, invoice no. 17520, dated January 17; terms net 30 days; FOB Oak Park.

24 Bought thirty 5-speed bicycles from Nagara Company, $1,518, invoice no. 26942, dated January 23; terms net 60 days; FOB Oak Park.

29 Bought knapsacks from Minsky Manufacturing Company, $315.10, invoice no. 762AC, dated January 26; terms 2/10, n/30; FOB Oak Park.

31 Bought locks from Laker Security, $310.41, invoice no. 27712, dated January 26; terms 2/10, n/30; FOB Chicago, freight prepaid and added to the invoice, $12 (total $322.41).

Check Figure

Accounts Payable account balance, $10,522.25

Instructions

1. Open the following creditor accounts in the accounts payable ledger and record the January 1 balances, if any, as given: Best, Inc.; Biggs' Tire Company, $211; Gannon Products; Laker Security, $181.04; Minsky Manufacturing Company, $150.10; Nagara Company. For the accounts having balances, write "Balance" in the Item column and place a check mark in the Post. Ref. column.
2. Record the balance of $542.14 in the Accounts Payable controlling account as of January 1. Write "Balance" in the Item column and place a check mark in the Post. Ref. column.
3. Journalize the transactions in the three-column purchases journal beginning with page 81.
4. Post to the accounts payable ledger daily.
5. Post to the general ledger at the end of the month.
6. Prepare a schedule of accounts payable, and compare the balance of the Accounts Payable controlling account with the total of the schedule of accounts payable.

P.O. 3,4,5

Problem 11-2B World Camera is located in Portland. The company bought the following merchandise and supplies and had the following returns and allowances during April of this year.

Apr. 3 Bought merchandise on account from Draeger Imports, $855, invoice no. C4581, dated April 1; terms 2/10, n/30; FOB Chicago, freight prepaid and added to the invoice, $30 (total $885).

4 Bought merchandise on account from Ness Company, $805, invoice no. 561AM, dated April 2; terms 1/10, n/30; FOB Portland.

7 Bought merchandise on account from Ross Photo Supply, $592, invoice no. 65872, dated April 5; terms net 30 days; FOB Portland.

11 Bought office supplies on account from Mackey, Inc., $290, invoice no. 5639, dated April 11; terms net 30 days; FOB Portland.

13 Received a credit memo from Ness Company for merchandise returned, $36, credit memo no. 617.

16 Bought merchandise on account from Askey Company, $805, invoice no. 41832, dated April 15; terms 1/10, n/30; FOB Phoenix, freight prepaid and added to the invoice, $38 (total $843).

22 Bought equipment on account from Robo Company, $992, invoice no. L21654, dated April 19; terms net 30 days; FOB Portland.

27 Bought merchandise on account from Ness Company, $765, invoice no. 598AM, dated April 25; terms 1/10, n/30; FOB Portland.

28 Received a credit memo from Ross Photo Supply for merchandise returned, $82, credit memo no. 922.

29 Bought merchandise on account from Draeger Imports, $1,428, invoice no. C4721, dated April 27; terms 2/10, n/30; FOB Chicago, freight prepaid and added to the invoice, $102 (total $1,530).

30 Bought store supplies on account from N. D. Rice, Inc., $86, invoice no. 61875, dated April 29; terms net 30 days; FOB Portland.

30 Bought merchandise on account from Askey Company, $570, invoice no. 42003, dated April 27; terms 1/10, n/30; FOB Phoenix, freight prepaid and added to the invoice, $41 (total $611).

Check Figure

Accounts Payable account balance, $9,866.00

Instructions

1. Open the following accounts in the general ledger and enter the balances as of April 1.

114 Store Supplies	$ 352.00	511 Purchases	$8,467.91
115 Office Supplies	180.00	512 Purchases Returns	
124 Equipment	10,420.00	and Allowances	310.05
221 Accounts Payable	2,585.00	514 Freight In	506.50

For the accounts having balances, write "Balance" in the Item column and place a check mark in the Post. Ref. column.

2. Open the following accounts in the accounts payable ledger and enter the April 1 balances, if any, as given: Askey Company, $1,220.10; Draeger Imports, $850.30; Mackey, Inc.; Ness Company; N. D. Rice, Inc.; Robo Company; Ross Photo Supply, $514.60. For the accounts having balances, write "Balance" in the Item column and place a check mark in the Post. Ref. column.

3. Journalize the transactions in either the general journal, starting on page 27, or the multicolumn purchases journal, on page 6, as appropriate.

4. Post the entries to the creditors' accounts in the accounts payable ledger immediately after you make each journal entry.

5. Post the entries in the Other Accounts Debit column of the purchases journal and in the general journal immediately after you make each of those journal entries.
6. In the space below the purchases journal, show proof that the sum of the debit totals equals the total of the Accounts Payable Credit column.
7. Post the totals of the special columns of the purchases journal at the end of the month.
8. Prepare a schedule of accounts payable, and compare the balance of the Accounts Payable controlling account with the total of the schedule of accounts payable.

P.O. 7

Problem 11-3B Hatch Products, Houston, records sales of merchandise daily by posting directly from its sales invoices to the accounts receivable ledger. At the end of the month, it makes a summarizing entry in the general journal. It records purchases of goods on account the same way, posting directly from the invoices to the accounts payable ledger daily and making a summarizing entry in the general journal at the end of the month. Sales of merchandise and purchases of goods on account during September of this year were as follows.

Sales of Merchandise on Account

Sept.	4	Stacy Corp., no. 2818, $1,348.41.
	7	I. D. Kent, no. 2819, $939.29.
	11	M. R. Braskey Company, no. 2820, $1,050.11.
	15	The Place, no. 2821, $686.57.
	21	Frank R. Baldwin, no. 2822, $899.51.
	23	C. R. Kelly, no. 2823, $527.32.
	25	Dave P. Hill, no. 2824, $716.82.
	26	Brisko C. Johns, no. 2825, $421.20.
	28	R. A. Casey, no. 2826, $227.94.
	29	Harry C. Wells, no. 2827, $332.92.
	30	C. P. Cole, no. 2828, $118.99.

Purchases of Merchandise, Supplies, and Equipment on Account

Sept.	3	Peel Corporation, merchandise, $3,740.50; FOB Houston.
	7	Landry Company, merchandise, $2,518.42; FOB San Francisco, freight prepaid and added to the invoice, $116 (total $2,634.42).
	9	Sutton Manufacturing Company, merchandise, $1,298.18; FOB Houston.
	17	Hess, Inc., store supplies, $427; FOB Houston.
	22	Peel Corporation, merchandise, $814.20; FOB Houston.
	26	Castor Specialty Products, merchandise, $3,471.14; FOB Boston, freight prepaid and added to the invoice, $152 (total $3,623.14).
	30	Jenson Office Furnishings, office equipment, $918.30; FOB Houston.
	30	D. C. Cane, Inc., merchandise, $1,210.50; FOB Houston.

Check Figure

Total Sales, $7,269.08

Instructions

1. Journalize the summarizing entry for the sales of merchandise on account in the general journal, page 27.
2. Journalize the summarizing entry for the purchase of goods on account in the general journal.

P.O. 1,2,3,4

Problem 11-4B The following transactions relate to Crest Products during April of this year. Terms of sale are 2/10, n/30. The company is located in Los Angeles.

Apr. 1 Sold merchandise on account to Hagen Hardware, invoice no. 5522, $672.00.

4 Bought merchandise on account from Sely Manufacturing Company, invoice no. C1142, $438; terms 1/10, n/30; dated April 2; FOB San Diego, freight prepaid and added to the invoice, $32 (total $470).

9 Sold merchandise on account to Becker Stores, invoice no. 5523, $1,118.

11 Bought merchandise on account from Barns Products, invoice no. 8990, $1,732.65; terms 2/10, n/30; dated April 11; FOB San Francisco, freight prepaid and added to the invoice, $72 (total $1,804.65).

16 Sold merchandise on account to B. R. Akers, invoice no. 5524, $845.32.

19 Issued credit memo no. 32 to Becker Stores for merchandise returned, $86.

24 Bought merchandise on account from Ashland Manufacturing Company, invoice no. P1981, $1,450.70; terms 2/10, n/30; dated April 22; FOB Santa Rosa, freight prepaid and added to the invoice, $87 (total $1,537.70).

27 Bought office supplies on account from Castle's, invoice no. E621A, dated April 25, $97.41; net 30 days.

28 Sold merchandise on account to Graham Specialty Company, invoice no. 5525, $3,960.00.

29 Issued credit memo no. 33 to B. R. Akers for allowance on damaged merchandise, $91.

30 Received credit memo no. 356 for merchandise returned to Boswell, Inc., for $155.86.

Check Figure

Accounts Payable account balance, $4,198.22

Instructions

1. Open the following accounts in the accounts receivable ledger and record the balances as of April 1: B. R. Akers; Becker Stores, $481.10; Graham Specialty Company, $327.50; Hagen Hardware, $836.00. For the accounts having balances, write "Balance" in the Item column and place a check mark in the Post. Ref. column. Total the amounts and record the balance in the controlling account in the general ledger. (Verify: $1,644.60.)

2. Open the following accounts in the accounts payable ledger and record the balances as of April 1: Ashland Manufacturing Company; Barns Products, $186.40; Boswell, Inc., $257.92; Castle's; Sely Manufacturing Company. For the accounts having balances, write "Balance" in the Item column and place a check mark in the Post Ref. column. Total the amounts and record the balance in the controlling account in the general ledger. (Verify: $444.32.)

3. Journalize the transactions in the sales, purchases, or general journal, as appropriate (sales journal, page 24; purchases journal, page 18; general journal, page 68).

4. Post the entries to the accounts receivable ledger daily.

5. Post the entries to the accounts payable ledger daily.

6. Post the entries in the general journal immediately after you make each journal entry.

7. Post the totals from the special journals at month end.
8. Prepare a schedule of accounts receivable.
9. Prepare a schedule of accounts payable.
10. Compare the totals of the schedules with the balances of the controlling accounts.

Instructions for General Ledger Software

1. Record the transactions in the sales, purchases, or general journal.
   a. For efficiency, analyze the transactions, indicate into which journal each transaction goes, and key the entries in three batches—the sales journal, the purchases journal, and the general journal.
   b. If the program uses a single-column purchases journal, add the amount of the freight to the amount of purchases.
2. Print the journals.
3. Post the amounts from the sales, purchases, and general journals.
4. Print the general ledger.
5. Print a schedule of accounts receivable and compare the total with the balance of the Accounts Receivable control account.
6. Print a schedule of accounts payable and compare the total with the balance of the Accounts Payable control account.

Continuous General Ledger Problem: Purchases Journal

Last month, Like New began to sell restored artwork and furniture in addition to selling its restoration services. Miracle also added a sales journal to the records last month to receive entries for sales of merchandise on account only. This month, Miracle has added a purchases journal to the records to receive entries for purchases of merchandise (for resale) on account only. As the accountant for Like New, you are to journalize and post the following July transactions. All sales on account are 2/10, n/30.

July 1 Sold merchandise on account to Baker Inn, Sales Inv. 2010, $688.

2 Paid $1,140 interest (debit Interest Expense) and $261 on the principal of the mortgage (debit Mortgage Payable), $1,401, Ck. No. 1016.

3 Bought merchandise on account from Frame Co., Inv. no. 1000, $436; terms 2/10, n/30; dated July 3; freight prepaid and added to the invoice, $24 (total $460).

8 Sold merchandise on account to Adeline Harris, Sales Inv. 2011, $327.

10 Bought merchandise on account from Unique Furniture, Inv. no. 3455, $1,261; terms 2/10, n/30; dated July 10; freight prepaid and added to the invoice, $64 (total $1,325).

15 Sold merchandise on account to Gail Murdock, Sales Inv. 2012, $844.60.

16 Paid wages of part-time assistant for the first half of the month, $850, Ck. No. 1017.

20 Issued credit memo no. 3 to Adeline Harris for merchandise returned, $86, Sales Inv. 2011.

23 Bought merchandise on account from Au Furniture, Inv. no. 494, $1,522.50; terms 2/10, n/30; dated July 23; freight prepaid and added to the invoice, $83 (total $1,605.50).

27 Bought supplies on account from The Paint Pot, Inv. no. 998, dated July 26, $46.36; net 30 days.

28 Paid the utility bill for two months, $247, Ck. No. 1018.

29 Sold merchandise on account to Mike Wallen, Sales Inv. 2013, $2,459.

30 Issued credit memo no. 4 to Gail Murdock as an allowance on damaged merchandise, $94, Sales Inv. 2012.

31 Received credit memo no. 17 for merchandise returned to Au Furniture, Inv. no. 494, $144.42.

31 Paid wages of part-time assistant for the second half of the month, $850, Ck. No. 1019.

Note: The Continuous General Ledger Problem can be worked with Houghton Mifflin Windows General Ledger Package, Peachtree Release 5.01, QuickBooks 6.0, or other general ledger software packages.

Instructions

1. Launch the general ledger software.
2. Open the likenew (June) file and rename it for July.
3. Add the following new accounts:

511 Purchases	512 Purchases Returns and Allowances
612 Utilities Expense	

4. Add the following vendor names and their current balances:

The Paint Pot	$2,164	Au Furniture	$423

5. Journalize and post the transactions in either the general journal or one of the two special journals—Sales Journal or Purchases Journal.
6. Print a trial balance ($219,660.88).
7. Print a schedule of accounts receivable ($10,201.60). Compare the total with the Accounts Receivable account in the trial balance. They should be the same. If not, there is an error; reverse the process until you find the error.
8. Print a schedule of accounts payable ($5,879.44). Compare the total with the Accounts Payable account in the trial balance. They should be the same. If not, there is an error; reverse the process until you find the error.

12 The Cash Receipts Journal and the Cash Payments Journal

WINDOWS ON | **THE WORLD WIDE WEB**

The next time you write out a check at your favorite hair salon or barbershop, think about the salon's cash receipts journal and how your sale might be recorded. If you pay by credit card, the salon must pay a bank credit-card expense to cover processing fees for your charge. The Redken highlighter or hair dye used on your hair may have been purchased by the salon at a discount. L'Oréal may give hair salons a trade discount on its Redken brand of hair-care products. Yet if you want to stock up on Redken styling products you will have to pay full price unless you take out a bank loan and open your own shop. So how well is L'Oréal doing financially, despite giving trade discounts? See L'Oréal's web site to find out at **http://www.loreal.com/us/group/index.asp**.

Performance Objectives

After you have completed this chapter, you will be able to do the following:

1. Journalize transactions for a retail merchandising business in a cash receipts journal.

2. Post from a cash receipts journal to a general ledger and an accounts receivable ledger.

3. Determine cash discounts according to credit terms, and record cash receipts from charge customers who are entitled to deduct the cash discount.

4. Journalize transactions in a cash payments journal for a service enterprise.

5. Post from a cash payments journal to a general ledger and an accounts payable ledger.

6. Journalize transactions involving cash discounts in a cash payments journal for a merchandising enterprise.

7. Journalize transactions in a check register.

8. Journalize transactions involving trade discounts.

We have seen that using a sales journal and a purchases journal enables an accountant to carry out the journalizing and posting processes much more efficiently. These special journals make it possible to post column totals rather than individual figures. They also make the division of labor more efficient because the journalizing functions can

403

be delegated to different persons. The *cash receipts journal* and the *cash payments journal* further extend these advantages.

THE CASH RECEIPTS JOURNAL

The **cash receipts journal** contains all transactions in which cash is received, or increases. When a cash receipts journal is used, all transactions in which cash is debited *must* be recorded in it. It may be used for a service as well as a merchandising business. Let's list some typical transactions of a retail merchandising business that result in an increase in cash. To get a better picture of the transactions, let's first record them in T accounts.

May 3 Sold merchandise for cash, $100, plus $8 sales tax.

Cash	Sales	Sales Tax Payable
+ –	– +	– +
108	100	8

May 4 Sold merchandise, $100, plus $8 sales tax, and the customer used a bank charge card. The bank issuing the card bills the customer directly each month. The business, on the other hand, deposits the bank credit card receipts every day. The bank *deducts a discount* and credits the firm's account with cash. We will assume that the discount is 4 percent. The firm therefore records the amount of the discount under Credit Card Expense: $108.00 × .04 = $4.32 credit card expense; $100.00 + $8.00 − $4.32 = $103.68.

Cash	Credit Card Expense	Sales Tax Payable	Sales
+ –	+ –	– +	– +
103.68	4.32	8.00	100.00

May 5 Collected cash on account from L. R. Reed, a charge customer, $216.

Cash	Accounts Receivable
+ –	+ –
216	216

May 7 The owner, G. H. Hall, invested cash in the business, $4,000.

Cash	G. H. Hall, Capital
+ –	– +
4,000	4,000

May 8 Sold equipment for cash at cost, $150.

Cash	Equipment
+ –	+ –
150	150

A customer using a bank charge card is actually borrowing the money (the total of the sale plus the sales tax) from the issuing bank. The merchandiser is still responsible for remitting the sales tax to the state revenue department.

The same transactions are shown in general journal form as follows:

					GENERAL JOURNAL				PAGE _____		
	DATE		DESCRIPTION	POST. REF.	DEBIT			CREDIT			
1	20–										1
2	May	3	Cash		1 0 8	00					2
3			Sales					1 0 0	00		3
4			Sales Tax Payable						8	00	4
5			Sold merchandise for cash.								5
6											6
7		4	Cash		1 0 3	68					7
8			Credit Card Expense			4 32					8
9			Sales					1 0 0	00		9
10			Sales Tax Payable						8	00	10
11			Sold merchandise involving								11
12			a bank charge card.								12
13											13
14		5	Cash		2 1 6	00					14
15			Accounts Receiv., L. R. Reed					2 1 6	00		15
16			Collected cash on account.								16
17											17
18		7	Cash		4 0 0 0	00					18
19			G. H. Hall, Capital					4 0 0 0	00		19
20			Owner invested cash.								20
21											21
22		8	Cash		1 5 0	00					22
23			Equipment					1 5 0	00		23
24			Sold equipment at cost.								24
25											25

UPS regularly uses an electronic tablet to record a customer's signature. This provides an instantaneous record to verify delivery. No paper is generated, and the signature can be read by customer service representatives who may have to respond to customer queries.

Now let's analyze these five transactions: The first three would occur frequently; the last two would occur less frequently. When designing a cash receipts journal, it is logical to include a Cash Debit column because all the transactions involve an increase in cash. If a business regularly collects cash from charge customers, there should be an Accounts Receivable Credit column. If a firm often sells merchandise for cash and collects a sales tax, there should be a Sales Credit column and a Sales Tax Payable Credit column. If the business honors bank charge cards and wants to record the amount of the discount at the time of each transaction, there should be a Credit Card Expense Debit column for the amount deducted by the bank.

However, the credit to G. H. Hall, Capital, and the credit to Equipment occur very seldom, so it would not be practical to set up special columns for these credits. They can be handled adequately by an Other Accounts Credit column, which can be used for credits to all accounts that have no special column.

CASH RECEIPTS JOURNAL   PAGE __41__

DATE		ACCOUNT CREDITED	POST. REF.	OTHER ACCOUNTS CREDIT	ACCOUNTS RECEIVABLE CREDIT	SALES CREDIT	SALES TAX PAYABLE CREDIT	CREDIT CARD EXPENSE DEBIT	CASH DEBIT	
1	20–									1
2	May 3	————				1 0 0 00	8 00		1 0 8 00	2
3	4	————				1 0 0 00	8 00	4 32	1 0 3 68	3
4	5	L. R. Reed			2 1 6 00				2 1 6 00	4
5	7	G. H. Hall,								5
6		Capital		4 0 0 0 00					4 0 0 0 00	6
7	8	Equipment		1 5 0 00					1 5 0 00	7
8										8

FIGURE 1

Now let's record these transactions in a cash receipts journal (see Figure 1). First, we repeat the transactions:

Remember!

The amount of credit card expense is based on the total of sales *plus* sales tax payable.

May 3 Sold merchandise for cash, $100, plus $8 sales tax.
  4 Sold merchandise, $100, plus $8 sales tax, and the customer used a bank charge card. Discount charged by the bank is 4 percent of the total of sales plus sales tax.
  5 Collected cash on account from L. R. Reed, a charge customer, $216.
  7 The owner, G. H. Hall, invested cash in the business, $4,000.
  8 Sold equipment for cash at cost, $150.

Remember!

Special journals include a sales journal, a purchases journal, a cash receipts journal, and a cash payments journal. They are used to save time by posting totals of the special columns rather than individual amounts to the general ledger.

As an alternative, many firms postpone recording the amount of bank credit card expense until they actually receive notification from their bank on their bank statement. For example, total credit card sales for a restaurant for a time period amount to $1,600 plus 6 percent sales tax. The entry is as follows:

Cash	Sales	Sales Tax Payable
+ | –	– | +	– | +
1,696	1,600	96

The restaurant's next bank statement includes a debit memorandum for credit card charges of $67.84, using an assumed 4 percent discount rate ($1,696.00 × .04). The firm handles this in a similar manner to a check service charge:

Credit Card Expense	Cash
+ | –	+ | –
67.84	67.84

Posting from the Cash Receipts Journal

Here are some other transactions made during the month that involve increases in cash. (Remember that these transactions are for a retail business.)

May 11 Borrowed $300 from the bank, receiving cash and giving the bank a promissory note.

16 Sold merchandise for cash, $200, plus $16 sales tax.

21 Sold merchandise, $50, plus $4 sales tax; customer used a bank charge card. Credit card expense charge is 4 percent of sales plus sales tax.

26 Collected cash from B. Sanchez, a charge customer, on account, $62.40.

28 Sold merchandise for cash, $40, plus $3.20 sales tax.

31 Sold merchandise, $150, plus $12 sales tax; customer used a bank charge card. Credit card expense charge is 4 percent of sales plus sales tax.

31 Collected cash from T. Nguyen, a charge customer, on account, $26.

In the transaction of May 11, in which $300 was borrowed from the bank, the bank was given a **promissory note** (a written promise to pay a specified amount at a specified time) as evidence of the debt. The account **Notes Payable**, instead of Accounts Payable, is used to represent the amount owed on the promissory note. The Accounts Payable account is reserved for charge accounts with creditors, which are normally paid on a thirty-day basis.

Let's assume that all the month's transactions involving debits to Cash have now been recorded in the cash receipts journal. The cash receipts journal (see Figure 2 on the following page) and the T accounts following it illustrate the postings to the general ledger and the accounts receivable ledger.

Individual amounts in the Accounts Receivable Credit column of the cash receipts journal are usually posted daily to the accounts receivable ledger. Individual amounts in the Other Accounts Credit column are usually posted daily.

At the end of the month, we can post the special column totals in the cash receipts journal to the general ledger accounts. These columns include Accounts Receivable Credit, Sales Credit, Sales Tax Payable Credit, Credit Card Expense Debit, and Cash Debit.

In the Post. Ref. column, the check marks (✓) indicate that the amounts in the Accounts Receivable Credit column have been posted to the individual charge customers' accounts as credits. The account numbers show that the amounts in the Other Accounts Credit column have been posted separately to the accounts described in the Account Credited column. An (X) goes under the total of the Other Accounts Credit column; it means "do not post— the figures have already been posted separately." This column is totaled to make it easier to prove that the debits equal the credits.

Note the ruling. A single rule is placed above the column totals, and double rules extend through all but the Account Credited column. Also, on the last line, the last day of the month is recorded in the Date column.

Let's say it's the end of the month. Total the columns first. Then begin **crossfooting** the journal by proving that the sum of the debit totals equals the sum of the credit totals. This process must be done before you post the totals to the general ledger accounts.

Objective 2

Post from a cash receipts journal to a general ledger and an accounts receivable ledger.

FYI

The dash is a placeholder indicating that nothing has been left out or forgotten.

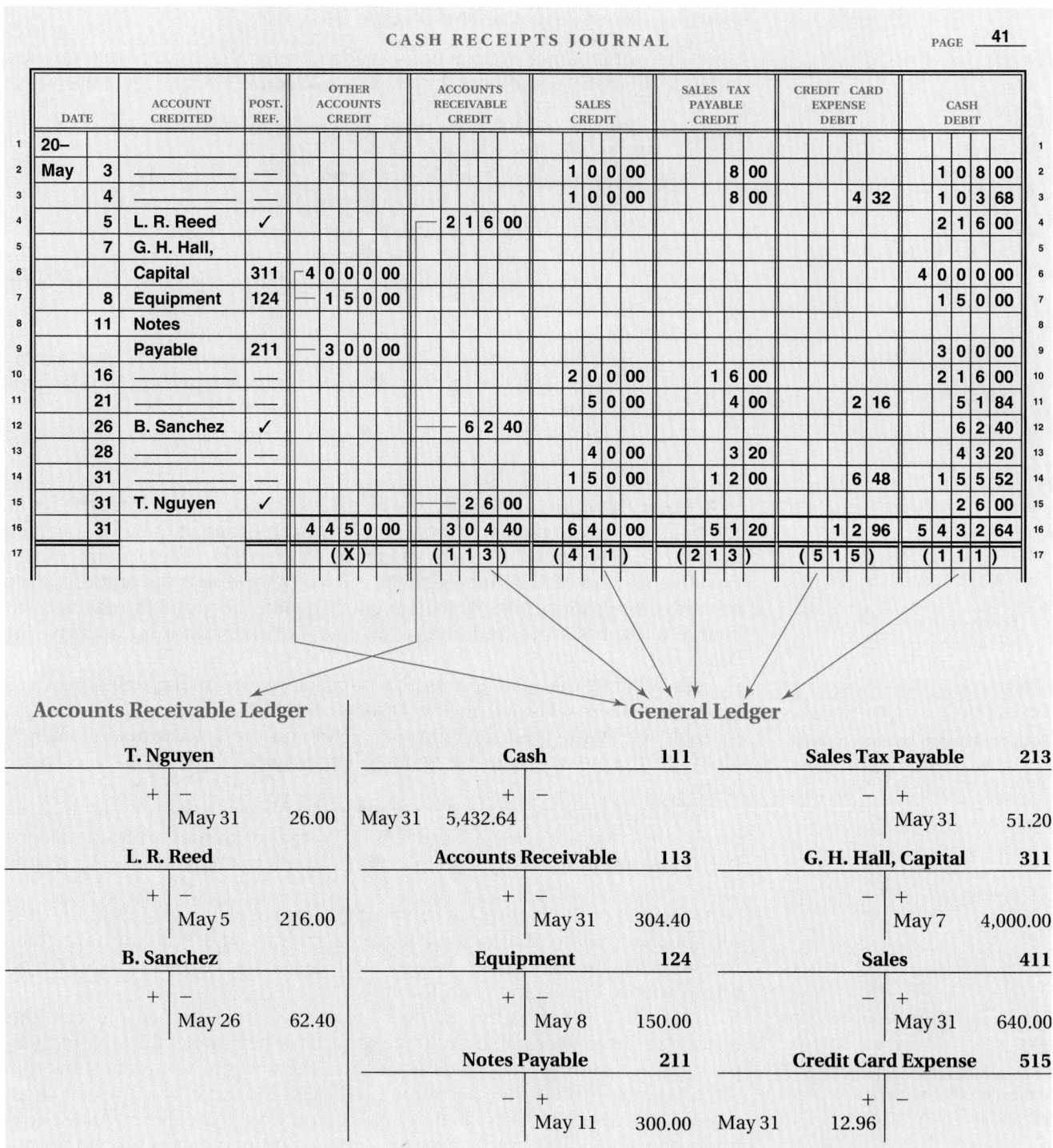

CASH RECEIPTS JOURNAL   PAGE **41**

	DATE	ACCOUNT CREDITED	POST. REF.	OTHER ACCOUNTS CREDIT	ACCOUNTS RECEIVABLE CREDIT	SALES CREDIT	SALES TAX PAYABLE CREDIT	CREDIT CARD EXPENSE DEBIT	CASH DEBIT	
1	20–									1
2	May 3	————	—			1 0 0 00	8 00		1 0 8 00	2
3	4	————	—			1 0 0 00	8 00	4 32	1 0 3 68	3
4	5	L. R. Reed	✓		2 1 6 00				2 1 6 00	4
5	7	G. H. Hall,								5
6		Capital	311	4 0 0 0 00					4 0 0 0 00	6
7	8	Equipment	124	1 5 0 00					1 5 0 00	7
8	11	Notes								8
9		Payable	211	3 0 0 00					3 0 0 00	9
10	16	————	—			2 0 0 00	1 6 00		2 1 6 00	10
11	21	————	—			5 0 00	4 00	2 16	5 1 84	11
12	26	B. Sanchez	✓		6 2 40				6 2 40	12
13	28	————	—			4 0 00	3 20		4 3 20	13
14	31	————	—			1 5 0 00	1 2 00	6 48	1 5 5 52	14
15	31	T. Nguyen	✓		2 6 00				2 6 00	15
16	31			4 4 5 0 00	3 0 4 40	6 4 0 00	5 1 20	1 2 96	5 4 3 2 64	16
17				(X)	(1 1 3)	(4 1 1)	(2 1 3)	(5 1 5)	(1 1 1)	17

Accounts Receivable Ledger

T. Nguyen

+	–
	May 31 26.00

L. R. Reed

+	–
	May 5 216.00

B. Sanchez

+	–
	May 26 62.40

General Ledger

Cash   111

+	–
May 31 5,432.64	

Accounts Receivable   113

+	–
	May 31 304.40

Equipment   124

+	–
	May 8 150.00

Notes Payable   211

–	+
	May 11 300.00

Sales Tax Payable   213

–	+
	May 31 51.20

G. H. Hall, Capital   311

–	+
	May 7 4,000.00

Sales   411

–	+
	May 31 640.00

Credit Card Expense   515

+	–
May 31 12.96	

FIGURE 2

Debit Totals		Credit Totals	
Cash	$5,432.64	Other Accounts	$4,450.00
Credit Card Expense	12.96	Accounts Receivable	304.40
		Sales	640.00
		Sales Tax Payable	51.20
	$5,445.60		$5,445.60

Post the special column totals to the general ledger, using the letters CR as the posting reference. Next, write the general ledger account number in parentheses below the total in the appropriate column.

Advantages of a Cash Receipts Journal

1. Transactions generally can be recorded on one line.
2. All transactions involving debits to Cash are recorded in one place.
3. It eliminates much repetition in posting when there are numerous transactions involving Cash debits. The Cash Debit side can be posted as one total.
4. Special columns can be used for specialized transactions and posted as one total.

CREDIT TERMS

Objective 3

Determine cash discounts according to credit terms, and record cash receipts from charge customers who are entitled to deduct the cash discount.

The cash receipts journal and the cash payments journal are used by both service and merchandising businesses to record all transactions in which cash comes into or goes out of the business.

The seller always stipulates credit terms: How much credit can a customer be allowed? And, how much time should the customer be given to pay the full amount? The **credit period** is the time the seller allows the buyer before full payment has to be made. Retailers generally allow twenty-five to thirty days.

Wholesalers and manufacturers often specify a **cash discount** in their credit terms. A cash discount is an amount that a customer can deduct if a bill is paid within a specified time. The discount is based on the *total amount of the invoice after any returns and allowances and freight charges billed on the invoice have been deducted.* Naturally, this discount acts as an incentive for charge customers to pay their bills promptly.

Let's say that a wholesaler offers customers credit terms of 2/10, n/30. These terms mean that the customer gets a 2 percent discount if the bill is paid within ten days after the invoice date. The discount period begins the day after the invoice date. If the bill is not paid within the ten days, the entire amount is due within thirty days after the invoice date. Other cash discounts that may be used are the following:

- **1/15, n/60** The seller offers a 1 percent discount if the bill is paid within fifteen days after the invoice date, and the whole bill must be paid within sixty days after the invoice date.
- **2/10, EOM, n/60** The seller offers a 2 percent discount if the bill is paid within ten days after the end of the month, and the whole bill must be paid within sixty days after the last day of the month.

A wholesaler or manufacturer that offers a cash discount adopts a single cash discount as a credit policy and makes this available to all its customers. The seller considers cash discounts as sales discounts; the buyer, on the other hand, considers cash discounts as purchases discounts. In this section we are concerned with the sales discount. *The Sales Discount account, like Sales Returns and Allowances, is a deduction from Sales.*

To illustrate, we return to Jackson Electric Supply. We record the following transactions in T accounts.

Transaction (a) August 1: Sold merchandise on account to L. A. Long Company, invoice no. 320; terms 2/10, n/30; $424.

Transaction (b) August 10: Received check from L. A. Long Company for $415.52 in payment of invoice no. 320, less cash discount ($424.00 × .02 = $8.48; $424.00 − $8.48 = $415.52).

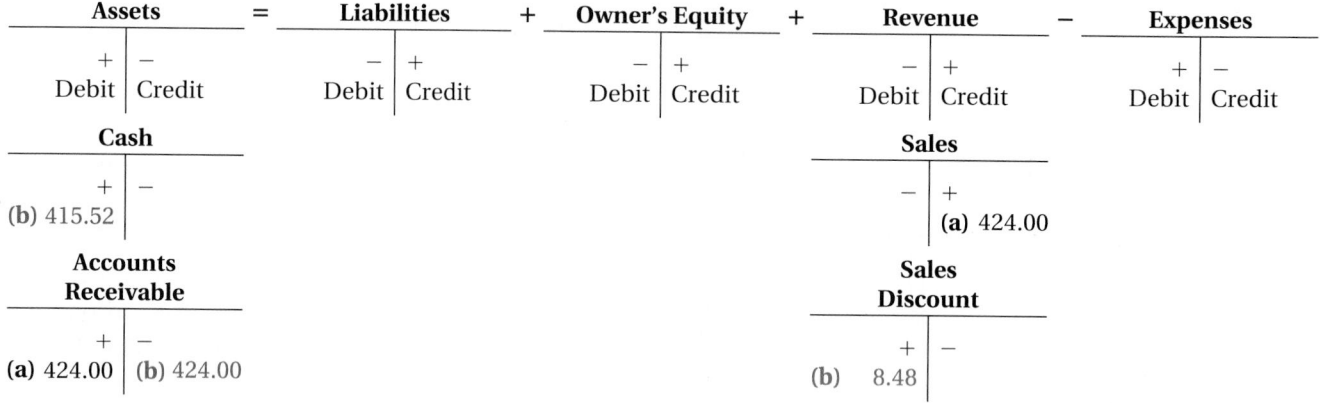

Since Jackson Electric Supply offers this cash discount to all its customers, and since charge customers often pay their bills within the discount period, Jackson Electric Supply sets up a Sales Discount Debit column in the cash receipts journal. Note that Jackson Electric Supply is a wholesaler. Therefore, a column for Sales Tax Payable is not used, since few states levy a tax on sales at the wholesale level.

CASH RECEIPTS JOURNAL   PAGE ___18___

	DATE		ACCOUNT CREDITED	POST. REF.	OTHER ACCOUNTS CREDIT	ACCOUNTS RECEIVABLE CREDIT	SALES CREDIT	SALES DISCOUNT DEBIT	CASH DEBIT	
1	20–									1
2	Aug.	10	L. A. Long Company			4 2 4 00		8 48	4 1 5 52	2
3										3

Several other transactions of Jackson Electric Supply during August involve increases in cash. Remember that the standard credit terms for all charge customers are 2/10, n/30.

Aug. 15 Cash sales for first half of the month, $1,460.
  16 Received check from Arreloa Construction for $386.12 in payment of invoice no. 322, less cash discount ($394.00 − $7.88 = $386.12).
  17 Received payment on a promissory note given by Nancy Turner, $300 principal, plus $3 interest. (The amount of the interest is recorded in Interest Income.)

Aug. 21 Received a check from Colmer Company for $756.80 in payment of invoice no. 324, less cash discount ($772.24 − $15.44 = $756.80).

23 Sold equipment for cash at cost, $126.

26 N. C. Jackson, the owner, invested an additional $4,000 cash in the business.

26 Received a check from Howard and Sons, Inc., for $432.18 in payment of invoice no. 325 less the cash discount ($441.00 − $8.82 = $432.18).

30 Received a check from Hazen Electric for $695.80 in payment of invoice no. 326, less cash discount ($710.00 − $14.20 = $695.80).

31 Cash sales for second half of the month, $1,620.

31 Received a check from Marin, Inc., in payment of invoice no. 321, for $116. (This is longer than the ten-day period, so Marin missed the cash discount.)

Jackson Electric Supply records these transactions in its cash receipts journal (Figure 3).

The company's accountant then proves the equality of debits and credits:

Remember!

When journalizing a cash receipt involving a sales discount, be sure to credit Accounts Receivable for the total amount of the sales transaction.

Debit Totals		Credit Totals	
Cash	$10,311.42	Other Accounts	$ 4,429.00
Sales Discount	54.82	Accounts Receivable	2,857.24
		Sales	3,080.00
	$10,366.24		$10,366.24

FIGURE 3

CASH RECEIPTS JOURNAL PAGE 18

	DATE	ACCOUNT CREDITED	POST. REF.	OTHER ACCOUNTS CREDIT	ACCOUNTS RECEIVABLE CREDIT	SALES CREDIT	SALES DISCOUNT DEBIT	CASH DEBIT	
1	20–								1
2	Aug. 10	L. A. Long Company	✓		4 2 4 00		8 48	4 1 5 52	2
3	15		—			1 4 6 0 00		1 4 6 0 00	3
4	16	Arreloa Construction	✓		3 9 4 00		7 88	3 8 6 12	4
5	17	Notes Receivable	112	3 0 0 00					5
6		Interest Income	422	3 00				3 0 3 00	6
7	21	Colmer Company	✓		7 7 2 24		1 5 44	7 5 6 80	7
8	23	Equipment	124	1 2 6 00				1 2 6 00	8
9	26	N. C. Jackson, Capital	311	4 0 0 0 00				4 0 0 0 00	9
10	26	Howard and Sons, Inc.	✓		4 4 1 00		8 82	4 3 2 18	10
11	30	Hazen Electric	✓		7 1 0 00		1 4 20	6 9 5 80	11
12	31		—			1 6 2 0 00		1 6 2 0 00	12
13	31	Marin, Inc.	✓		1 1 6 00			1 1 6 00	13
14	31			4 4 2 9 00	2 8 5 7 24	3 0 8 0 00	5 4 82	10 3 1 1 42	14
15				(X)	(1 1 3)	(4 1 1)	(4 1 3)	(1 1 1)	15
16									16
17									17

daily   A/R–Daily monthly daily   monthly
G.L.–monthly   GL monthly

SALES RETURNS AND ALLOWANCES AND SALES DISCOUNTS ON AN INCOME STATEMENT

In the fundamental accounting equation, to be consistent with the income statement, we placed Sales Returns and Allowances and Sales Discounts under Sales with the plus and minus signs reversed. Both accounts are contra revenue accounts, so we subtract their totals from Sales on the income statement. Here is the Revenue from Sales section of the annual income statement of Jackson Electric Supply.

Jackson Electric Supply
Income Statement
For Year Ended December 31, 20—

Revenue from Sales:					
Sales			$235 1 8 0 00		
Less: Sales Returns and Allowances	$ 8 4 0 00				
Sales Discounts	1 8 8 0 00		2 7 2 0 00		
Net Sales				$232 4 6 0 00	

THE CASH PAYMENTS JOURNAL: SERVICE ENTERPRISE

The **cash payments journal**, as the name implies, is a special journal used to record all transactions in which cash goes out, or decreases. When the cash payments journal is used, all transactions in which cash is credited *must* be recorded in it. This journal may be used for either a service or a merchandising business.

To get acquainted with the cash payments journal, let's list some typical transactions of a service firm (such as a dry cleaner or a bowling alley) or a professional enterprise (such as a lawyer's office) that result in a decrease in cash. To illustrate, we record the following transactions in T accounts:

May 2 Paid L. N. Brown Company, a creditor, on account, Ck. No. 63, $1,220.

Accounts Payable		Cash	
−	+	+	−
1,220			1,220

May 4 Paid cash for supplies, Ck. No. 64, $190.

Supplies		Cash	
+	−	+	−
190			190

May 5 Paid wages for two weeks, Ck. No. 65, $1,216 (previously recorded in the payroll entry).

Wages Payable		Cash	
−	+	+	−
1,216			1,216

May 6 Paid rent for the month, Ck. No. 66, $950.

Rent Expense		Cash	
+	−	+	−
950			950

The same transactions are now shown in general journal form.

GENERAL JOURNAL   PAGE _____

	DATE		DESCRIPTION	POST. REF.	DEBIT	CREDIT	
1	20−						1
2	May	2	Accounts Payable,				2
3			L. N. Brown Co.		1 2 2 0 00		3
4			Cash			1 2 2 0 00	4
5			Paid on account, Ck. No. 63.				5
6							6
7		4	Supplies		1 9 0 00		7
8			Cash			1 9 0 00	8
9			Paid cash for supplies,				9
10			Ck. No. 64.				10
11							11
12		5	Wages Payable		1 2 1 6 00		12
13			Cash			1 2 1 6 00	13
14			Paid wages for two weeks,				14
15			Ck. No. 65.				15
16							16
17		6	Rent Expense		9 5 0 00		17
18			Cash			9 5 0 00	18
19			Paid rent for month,				19
20			Ck. No. 66.				20

Let's analyze these four transactions. The first one would occur frequently, as payments to creditors are made several times a month. Of the last three transactions, the debit to Wages Payable might occur twice a month, the debit to Rent Expense once a month, and the debit to Supplies only occasionally.

It is logical to include a Cash Credit column in a cash payments journal because all transactions recorded in this journal involve a decrease in cash. Since payments to creditors are made often, there should also be an

Accounts Payable Debit column. You can set up any other column that is used often enough to warrant it. Otherwise, an Other Accounts Debit column takes care of all the other transactions.

Now let's record these same transactions in a cash payments journal and include a column titled Ck. No. If you think a moment, you will see that this is consistent with good management of cash. All expenditures except Petty Cash expenditures should be paid for by check. Let's repeat the transactions.

Objective 4

Journalize transactions in a cash payments journal for a service enterprise.

May 2 Paid L. N. Brown Company, a creditor, on account, Ck. No. 63, $1,220.
4 Paid cash for supplies, Ck. No. 64, $190.
5 Paid wages for two weeks, Ck. No. 65, $1,216 (previously recorded in the payroll entry).
6 Paid rent for the month, Ck. No. 66, $950.

CASH PAYMENTS JOURNAL PAGE **62**

	DATE	CK. NO.	ACCOUNT DEBITED	POST. REF.	OTHER ACCOUNTS DEBIT	ACCOUNTS PAYABLE DEBIT	CASH CREDIT	
1	20–							1
2	May 2	63	L. N. Brown Co.			1 2 2 0 00	1 2 2 0 00	2
3	4	64	Supplies		1 9 0 00		1 9 0 00	3
4	5	65	Wages Payable		1 2 1 6 00		1 2 1 6 00	4
5	6	66	Rent Expense		9 5 0 00		9 5 0 00	5
6								6

Other transactions involving decreases in cash during May are as follows:

May 7 Paid a one-year premium for fire insurance, Ck. No. 67, $360.
9 Paid Morris, Inc., a creditor, on account, Ck. No. 68, $418.
11 Issued Ck. No. 69 in payment of delivery expense, $62.
14 Paid Russet and Son, a creditor, on account, Ck. No. 70, $110.
16 Issued Ck. No. 71 to the Logan State Bank for a Note Payable, $660, $600 on the principal and $60 interest.
19 Voided Ck. No. 72.
19 Bought equipment from Snyder Company for $200. Issued Ck. No. 73.
20 Paid wages for two weeks, Ck. No. 74, $1,340 (previously recorded in the payroll entry).
22 Issued Ck. No. 75 to Scheel Advertising Agency for advertising, $94 (not previously recorded).
26 Paid telephone bill, Ck. No. 76, $26.
31 Issued check for freight bill on equipment purchased on May 19, Ck. No. 77, $28.
31 Paid Lynn and Trask, a creditor, on account, Ck. No. 78, $160.

You should list all checks in consecutive order, even those checks that must be voided. In this way, *every* check is accounted for, which is necessary for internal control.

These transactions are recorded in the cash payments journal illustrated in Figure 4. Notice that an (X) is placed under the Other Accounts column. That means "do not post—the individual figures have already been posted."

FIGURE 4

CASH PAYMENTS JOURNAL   PAGE ___62___

	DATE	CK. NO.	ACCOUNT DEBITED	POST. REF.	OTHER ACCOUNTS DEBIT	ACCOUNTS PAYABLE DEBIT	CASH CREDIT	
1	20–							1
2	May	2 63	L. N. Brown Co.	✓		1 2 2 0 00	1 2 2 0 00	2
3		4 64	Supplies	113	1 9 0 00		1 9 0 00	3
4		5 65	Wages Payable	214	1 2 1 6 00		1 2 1 6 00	4
5		6 66	Rent Expense	512	9 5 0 00		9 5 0 00	5
6		7 67	Prepaid Insurance	114	3 6 0 00		3 6 0 00	6
7		9 68	Morris, Inc.	✓		4 1 8 00	4 1 8 00	7
8		11 69	Delivery Expense	513	6 2 00		6 2 00	8
9		14 70	Russet and Son	✓		1 1 0 00	1 1 0 00	9
10		16 71	Notes Payable	211	6 0 0 00			10
11			Interest Expense	518	6 0 00		6 6 0 00	11
12		19 72	Void	—				12
13		19 73	Equipment	121	2 0 0 00		2 0 0 00	13
14		20 74	Wages Payable	214	1 3 4 0 00		1 3 4 0 00	14
15		22 75	Advertising					15
16			Expense	515	9 4 00		9 4 00	16
17		26 76	Telephone					17
18			Expense	516	2 6 00		2 6 00	18
19		31 77	Equipment	121	2 8 00		2 8 00	19
20		31 78	Lynn and Trask	✓		1 6 0 00	1 6 0 00	20
21		31			5 1 2 6 00	1 9 0 8 00	7 0 3 4 00	21
22					(X)	(2 2 1)	(1 1 1)	22

At the end of the month, after totaling the columns, check the accuracy of the footings by proving that the sum of the debit totals equals the sum of the credit totals. Since you have posted the individual amounts in the Other Accounts Debit column to the general ledger, the only posting that remains is the credit to the Cash account for $7,034 and the debit to the Accounts Payable (controlling) account for $1,908.

Debit Totals		**Credit Totals**	
Other Accounts	$5,126.00	Cash	$7,034.00
Accounts Payable	1,908.00		
	$7,034.00		$7,034.00

Objective 5

Post from a cash payments journal to a general ledger and an accounts payable ledger.

The posting process for the cash payments journal is similar to the posting process for the cash receipts journal. Individual amounts in the Accounts Payable Debit column are usually posted daily to the subsidiary ledger. After posting, put a check mark (✓) in the Post. Ref. column. Individual amounts in the Other Accounts Debit column are usually posted daily to the general ledger. Post these figures individually, then place the account number in the Post. Ref. column. Totals of the Cash Credit column and the Accounts Payable Debit column are posted to the general ledger accounts at the end of the month. Write the appropriate general ledger account number in parentheses below the column totals. Print an (X) below the total of the Other Accounts Debit column to indicate that the total amount is not posted. The posting letter designation for the cash payments journal is CP.

The advantages of the cash payments journal are similar to the advantages of the cash receipts journal:

1. Transactions generally can be recorded on one line.
2. All the transactions involving credits to Cash are recorded in one place.
3. For numerous transactions involving Cash credits, the Cash Credit side can be posted as one total.
4. Special columns can be used for specialized transactions and posted as one total.

THE CASH PAYMENTS JOURNAL: MERCHANDISING ENTERPRISE

Objective 6

Journalize transactions involving cash discounts in a cash payments journal for a merchandising enterprise.

There is one slight difference between the cash payments journal for a merchandising enterprise and that for a service enterprise. This difference has to do with the cash discounts available to a merchandising business. Recall that a cash discount is the amount that the buyer may deduct from the bill; this acts as an incentive to get the buyer to pay the bill promptly. The buyer considers the cash discount to be a purchases discount, because it relates to the buyer's purchase of merchandise. The Purchases Discount account, like Purchases Returns and Allowances, is treated as a deduction from Purchases on the buyer's income statement.

Let's return to Jackson Electric Supply and assume that the following transactions take place. To demonstrate the debits and credits, we show some typical transactions in the form of T accounts.

Transaction (a) August 2: Bought merchandise on account from Draper, Inc., $420, its invoice no. 2706, dated July 31; terms 2/10, n/30; FOB San Francisco, freight prepaid and added to the invoice, $30 (total invoice $450).

Transaction (b) August 8: Issued Ck. No. 76 to Draper, Inc., in payment of invoice no. 2706 less the cash discount of $8.40, $441.60 ($450.00 − $8.40), which is recorded in the cash payments journal. Notice that the discount applies only to the amount billed for the merchandise (2 percent of $420). Here are the transactions shown in T accounts:

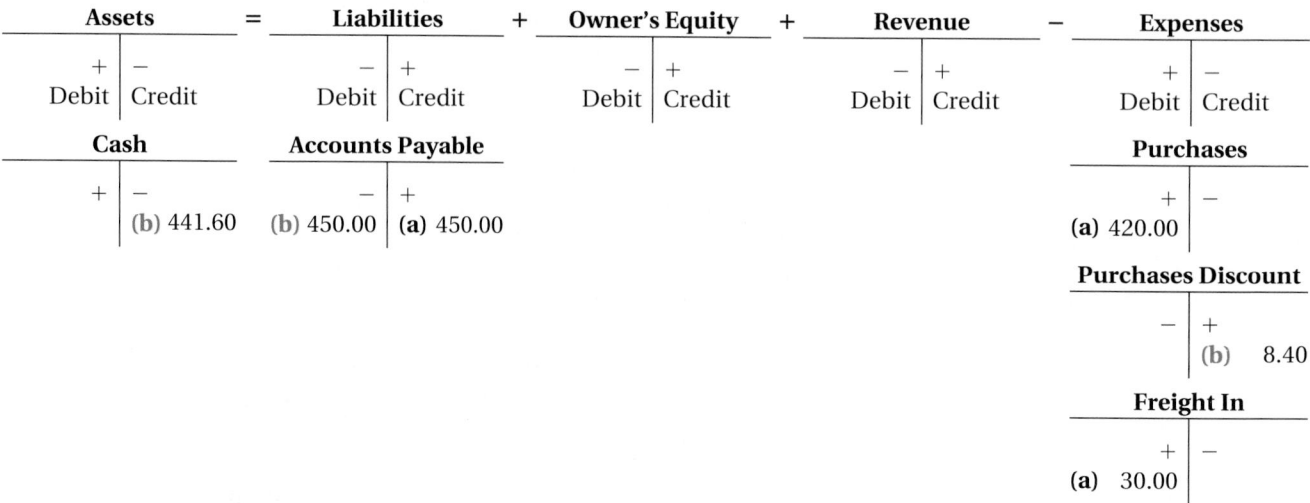

Any well-managed business takes advantage of a purchases discount whenever possible. So, if a discount is generally available to the business, it is worthwhile to set up a special Purchases Discount Credit column in the cash payments journal. Transaction **(b),** August 8, looks like this in the cash payments journal:

					OTHER ACCOUNTS DEBIT	ACCOUNTS PAYABLE DEBIT	PURCHASES DISCOUNT CREDIT	CASH CREDIT	
	DATE	CK. NO.	ACCOUNT DEBITED	POST. REF.					
1	20–								1
2	Aug. 8	76	Draper, Inc.			4 5 0 00	8 40	4 4 1 60	2
3									3

CASH PAYMENTS JOURNAL — PAGE 26

Here are some other transactions of Jackson Electric Supply involving decreases in cash during August. Note that credit terms vary among the different creditors. Detailed information on the purchase invoices paid below is available in the purchases journal on page 372.

Aug. 10 Paid wages for two-week period, Ck. No. 77, $1,680 (previously recorded in the payroll entry).

11 Issued Ck. No. 78 to Adkins Manufacturing Company, in payment of invoice no. 10611 ($692), less return ($70); less cash discount, 2/10, n/30; $609.56 ($692 − $70 = $622; $622.00 × .02 = $12.44; $622.00 − $12.44 = $609.56).

12 Bought supplies for cash; issued Ck. No. 79 payable to Dillon Office Supplies, $70.

15 Issued Ck. No. 80 to Sullivan Products Company in payment of its invoice no. B643 ($165) less return ($36); less cash discount, 1/10, n/30; $127.81 [$165 − $36 = $129; freight charges totaled $10.00 ($129 − $10 = $119); $119.00 × .01 = $1.19; $129.00 − $1.19 = $127.81].

16 Bought merchandise for cash, Ck. No. 81, payable to James and Son, $200.

19 Received bill and issued Ck. No. 82 to Mullin Express for freight charges on merchandise purchased earlier from Adkins Manufacturing Company, $60.

23 Voided Ck. No. 83.

23 Issued Ck. No. 84 to Amco Fire Insurance Company for insurance premium for one year, $420.

25 Paid wages for two-week period, Ck. No. 85, $1,750 (previously recorded in the payroll entry).

27 Paid G. O. Fromer for merchandise he returned on a cash sale, Ck. No. 86, $51.

31 Issued Ck. No. 87 to Reilly and Peters in partial payment of invoice no. 982, net 30 days, $180.

Remember!

After posting to the accounts payable subsidiary ledger from the cash payments journal, record a check mark in the Post. Ref. column in the cash payments journal.

The transaction of August 19 (Mullin Express) increases the Freight In account because the transportation charges are for merchandise purchased.

CASH PAYMENTS JOURNAL   PAGE __26__

	DATE	CK. NO.	ACCOUNT DEBITED	POST. REF.	OTHER ACCOUNTS DEBIT	ACCOUNTS PAYABLE DEBIT	PURCHASES DISCOUNT CREDIT	CASH CREDIT	
1	20–								1
2	Aug.	8 76	Draper, Inc.	✓		4 5 0 00	8 40	4 4 1 60	2
3		10 77	Wages Payable	214	1 6 8 0 00			1 6 8 0 00	3
4		11 78	Adkins Manufacturing Company	✓		6 2 2 00	1 2 44	6 0 9 56	4
5		12 79	Supplies	115	7 0 00			7 0 00	5
6		15 80	Sullivan Products Company	✓		1 2 9 00	1 19	1 2 7 81	6
7		16 81	Purchases	551	2 0 0 00			2 0 0 00	7
8		19 82	Freight In	514	6 0 00			6 0 00	8
9		23 83	Void	—					9
10		23 84	Prepaid Insurance	114	4 2 0 00			4 2 0 00	10
11		25 85	Wages Payable	214	1 7 5 0 00			1 7 5 0 00	11
12		27 86	Sales Returns and Allowances	412	5 1 00			5 1 00	12
13		31 87	Reilly and Peters	✓		1 8 0 00		1 8 0 00	13
14		31			4 2 3 1 00	1 3 8 1 00	2 2 03	5 5 8 9 97	14
15					(X)	(2 2 1)	(5 1 3)	(1 1 1)	15
16									16

[handwritten annotations below table: "daily A/P-Daily daily monthly GL. monthly GL-monthly"]

FIGURE 5

Now let's record these transactions in the cash payments journal (Figure 5). Jackson Electric Supply's accountant then proves the equality of debits and credits:

Debit Totals		**Credit Totals**	
Other Accounts	$4,231.00	Cash	$5,589.97
Accounts Payable	1,381.00	Purchases Discount	22.03
	$5,612.00		$5,612.00

CHECK REGISTER

Objective 7

Journalize transactions in a check register.

Instead of using a cash payments journal as a book of original entry, you can use a check register. The **check register** is merely a large checkbook with perforations that make it easy to tear out the checks. The page opposite the checks has columns labeled for special accounts, such as Bank Credit (in place of Cash), Accounts Payable Debit, and so on. The checks are prenumbered, and each check issued is recorded on the columnar sheet. This is common practice for a small business in which the owner writes the checks personally. Transactions are posted directly from the check register.

Suppose Jackson Electric Supply had used a check register instead of the cash payments journal. Its August transactions would appear as they do in Figure 6.

CHECK REGISTER   PAGE _____

	DATE	CK. NO.	PAYEE	ACCOUNT DEBITED	POST. REF.	OTHER ACCOUNTS DEBIT	ACCOUNTS PAYABLE DEBIT	PURCHASES DISCOUNT CREDIT	CITY BANK CREDIT	
1	20—									1
2	Aug. 8	76	Draper, Inc.	Draper, Inc.	✓		4 5 0 00	8 40	4 4 1 60	2
3	10	77	Payroll	Wages Payable	214	1 6 8 0 00			1 6 8 0 00	3
4	11	78	Adkins	Adkins						4
5			Manufacturing Co.	Manufacturing	✓		6 2 2 00	1 2 44	6 0 9 56	5
6	12	79	Dillon Office							6
7			Supplies	Supplies	115	7 0 00			7 0 00	7
8	15	80	Sullivan	Sullivan						8
9			Products Co.	Products Co.	✓		1 2 9 00	1 19	1 2 7 81	9
10	16	81	James and Son	Purchases	511	2 0 0 00			2 0 0 00	10
11	19	82	Mullin Express	Freight In	514	6 0 00			6 0 00	11
12	23	83	Void	———————	—					12
13	23	84	Amco Fire	Prepaid						13
14			Insurance Co.	Insurance	114	4 2 0 00			4 2 0 00	14
15	25	85	Payroll	Wages Payable	214	1 7 5 0 00			1 7 5 0 00	15
16	27	86	G. O. Fromer	Sales Ret. and						16
17				Allowances	412	5 1 00			5 1 00	17
18	31	87	Reilly and Peters	Reilly and Peters	✓		1 8 0 00		1 8 0 00	18
19	31					4 2 3 1 00	1 3 8 1 00	2 2 03	5 5 8 9 97	19
20						(X)	(2 2 1)	(5 1 3)	(1 1 1)	20

FIGURE 6

Remember!

In the Post. Ref. column, a check mark indicates that the amount has been posted to the creditor's account in the accounts payable ledger; below the total of the Other Accounts Debit column, an (X) indicates that the total is not to be posted.

You can see that the difference between the cash payments journal and the check register is minor. The Bank Credit column substitutes for the Cash Credit column. The check register lists the payee of the check.

Two additional columns, Deposits and Bank Balance, can be added to give the current balance of the City Bank or Cash account. The posting process for each book of original entry is the same.

In a small business, the owner or manager usually signs all the checks. However, if the owner delegates the authority to sign checks to some other person, that person should *not* have access to the accounting records. Why? This helps prevent fraud, because a dishonest employee could conceal a cash disbursement in the accounting records. In other words, for a medium- to large-size business, a manager should keep a separate book, which in this case is the cash payments journal. One person writes the checks; another person records the checks in the cash payments journal; and a third person does the bank reconciliation. In this way, each person acts as a control on the others. There would have to be cooperation among the three people for embezzlement to take place. This precaution is consistent with a good system of internal control, because more than one person is involved in the process of recording cash payments. This system also provides protection against errors. One person can double-check the other person's work.

Comparison of Transactions for Two Companies' Purchases and Sales

Purchaser's Books— Able Company	Seller's Books— Baker Company
Bought merchandise from Baker Company, $500; terms 2/10, n/30.	Sold merchandise to Able Company, $500; terms 2/10, n/30.

Dr. Purchases, $500
  Cr. Accounts Payable, $500
	Dr. Accounts Receivable, $500
	  Cr. Sales, $500

Received credit memo from Baker Company for return of merchandise, $100.	Issued credit memo to Able Company for return of merchandise, $100.

Dr. Accounts Payable, $100
  Cr. Purchases Returns and
    Allowances, $100
	Dr. Sales Returns and Allowances, $100
	  Cr. Accounts Receivable, $100

Paid Baker Company within the discount period, $392 ($500 − $100 = $400; $400 × .02 = $8; $400 − $8 = $392).	Received cash from Able Company within the discount period, $392.

Dr. Accounts Payable, $400
  Cr. Cash, $392
  Cr. Purchases Discount, $8
	Dr. Cash, $392
	Dr. Sales Discount, $8
	  Cr. Accounts Receivable, $400

TRADE DISCOUNTS

Objective 8

Journalize transactions involving trade discounts.

Manufacturers and wholesalers of many lines of products publish annual catalogs listing their products at retail prices. These organizations offer their customers substantial reductions (often as much as 40 percent) from the list or catalog prices. The reductions from the list prices are called **trade discounts**. Trade discounts are not journalized. Remember, firms grant cash discounts for prompt payment of invoices. Trade discounts are *not related* to cash payments. Manufacturers and wholesalers use trade discounts to avoid the high cost of reprinting catalogs when selling prices change. To change prices, the manufacturer or wholesaler simply issues a sheet showing a new list of trade discounts to be applied to the catalog prices. Trade discounts can also be used to differentiate between classes of customers. For example, a manufacturer may use one schedule of trade discounts for wholesalers and another schedule for retailers.

Firms may quote trade discounts as a single percentage. *Example:* A distributor of furnaces grants a single discount of 40 percent off the listed catalog price of $8,000. In this case, the selling price is calculated as follows:

List or catalog price	$8,000
Less trade discount of 40% ($8,000 × .4)	3,200
Selling price	$4,800

Neither the seller nor the buyer records trade discounts in the accounts; they enter only the selling price. Using T accounts, the furnace distributor records the sale like this:

Accounts Receivable			Sales		
+	−			−	+
4,800					4,800

The buyer records the purchase as follows:

Purchases			Accounts Payable		
+	−			−	+
4,800					4,800

Firms may also quote trade discounts as a chain, or series, of percentages. For example, a distributor of automobile parts grants discounts of 30 percent, 10 percent, and 10 percent off the listed catalog price of $900. In this case, the selling price is calculated as follows:

List or catalog price	$900.00
Less first trade discount of 30% ($900 × .3)	270.00
Remainder after first discount	$630.00
Less second trade discount of 10% ($630 × .1)	63.00
Remainder after second discount	$567.00
Less third discount of 10% ($567 × .1)	56.70
Selling price	$510.30

Using T accounts, the automobile parts distributor records the sale as follows:

Accounts Receivable			Sales		
+	−			−	+
510.30					510.30

The buyer records the purchase as follows:

Purchases			Accounts Payable		
+	−			−	+
510.30					510.30

In the situation involving a chain of discounts, the additional discounts are granted for large-volume transactions, either in dollar amount or in size of shipment, such as carload lots.

Cash discounts could also apply in situations involving trade discounts. *Example:* Suppose that the credit terms of the preceding sale include a cash discount of 2/10, n/30, and that the buyer pays the invoice within ten days. The seller applies the cash discount to the selling price. The seller records the transaction as shown on the following page.

Cash		Sales Discount		Accounts Receivable	
+	–	+	–	+	–
500.09		10.21			510.30

The buyer records the transaction as follows:

Cash		Purchases Discount		Accounts Payable	
+	–	–	+	–	+
	500.09		10.21	510.30	

COMPARISON OF THE FIVE TYPES OF JOURNALS

We have now looked at four special journals and the general journal. It is very important for a business to select and use the journals that provide the most efficient accounting system possible. Figure 7 summarizes the applications of the journals we have discussed and correct procedures for using them.

FIGURE 7

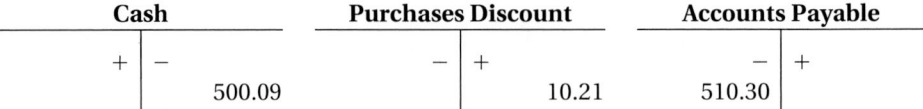

Types of Transactions

Sale of merchandise on account	Purchase of merchandise on account	Receipt of cash	Payment of cash	All other

Evidenced by Source Documents

Sales invoice	Purchase invoice	Credit card receipts Cash Checks	Check stub	Miscellaneous

Types of Journals

Sales journal	Purchases journal	Cash receipts journal	Cash payments journal	General journal

Posting to Ledger Accounts

Individual amounts posted daily to the accounts receivable ledger and the total posted monthly to the general ledger.	*Individual amounts posted daily to the accounts payable ledger and the totals of the special columns posted monthly to the general ledger.*	*Individual amounts in the Accounts Receivable Credit column posted daily to the accounts receivable ledger.* *Individual amounts in the Other Accounts columns posted daily to the general ledger.* *Totals of special columns posted monthly.*	*Individual amounts in the Accounts Payable Debit column posted daily to the accounts payable ledger.* *Individual amounts in the Other Accounts columns posted daily to the general ledger.* *Totals of special columns posted monthly.*	*Entries posted daily to the subsidiary ledgers and the general ledger.*

Recommended Order of Posting to the Subsidiary Ledgers and the General Ledger

To avoid errors and negative balances in accounts, post from the special journals in this order:

1. Sales journal
2. Purchases journal
3. Cash receipts journal
4. Cash payments journal

Posting of general journal entries depends on the dates of the specific transactions.

CHAPTER REVIEW

Review of Performance Objectives

1. Journalize transactions for a retail merchandising business in a cash receipts journal.

   A transaction for a retail merchandising business can be recorded on one line in a cash receipts journal. The cash receipts journal usually contains the following columns: Date, Account Credited, Post. Ref., Other Accounts Credit, Accounts Receivable Credit, Sales Credit, Sales Tax Payable Credit, Credit Card Expense Debit, and Cash Debit.

2. Post from a cash receipts journal to a general ledger and an accounts receivable ledger.

   The accountant posts daily from the Accounts Receivable Credit column to the individual charge customers' accounts in the accounts receivable ledger. After posting, the accountant puts a check mark (✓) in the Post. Ref. column. The accountant also posts the amounts in the Other Accounts Credit column daily and records the account numbers in the Post. Ref. column. The special columns are posted as totals at the end of the month. The accountant then writes the account numbers in parentheses under the totals. An (X) below the total of the Other Accounts Credit column shows that amounts are posted individually and the total is not posted.

3. Determine cash discounts according to credit terms, and record cash receipts from charge customers who are entitled to deduct the cash discount.

   The same cash discount is available to all the supplier's customers. The amount of the discount is determined by multiplying the invoice total (excluding freight charges and any returns and allowances) by the cash discount rate (usually 1 or 2 percent). The amount of the discount is recorded as a debit to Sales Discount.

4. Journalize transactions in a cash payments journal for a service enterprise.

   A cash payment by a service enterprise can be handled on one line in a cash payments journal. The cash payments journal usually contains the following columns: Date, Ck. No., Account Debited, Post. Ref., Other Accounts Debit, Accounts Payable Debit, and Cash Credit.

5. Post from a cash payments journal to a general ledger and an accounts payable ledger.

The accountant posts daily from the Accounts Payable Debit column to the individual suppliers' accounts in the accounts payable ledger. After posting, the accountant puts a check mark (✓) in the Post. Ref. column. The accountant also posts the amounts in the Other Accounts Debit column daily and records the account numbers in the Post. Ref. column. The special columns are posted as totals at the end of the month. The accountant then writes the account numbers in parentheses under the totals. An (X) below the total of the Other Accounts Debit column shows that amounts are posted individually and the total is not posted.

6. Journalize transactions involving cash discounts in a cash payments journal for a merchandising enterprise.

A cash payment by a merchandising enterprise that includes a purchase discount can be recorded on one line in a cash payments journal. The cash payments journal usually contains the following columns: Date, Ck. No., Account Debited, Post. Ref., Other Accounts Debit, Accounts Payable Debit, Purchases Discount Credit, and Cash Credit.

7. Journalize transactions in a check register.

Transactions can be recorded on one line in a check register. The check register is similar to the cash payments journal. However, the check register has an additional column entitled Payee, and instead of a Cash Credit column there is often a column with the name of the bank (City Bank Credit, for example).

8. Journalize transactions involving trade discounts.

In transactions involving trade discounts, the trade discounts are deducted from the list prices to arrive at the selling prices. Both sellers and buyers record the transactions at the selling prices.

Glossary

Bank charge card A bank credit card, like the credit cards used by millions of private citizens. The cardholder pays what she or he owes directly to the issuing bank. The business firm deposits the credit card receipts; the amount of the deposit equals the total of the receipts, less a discount deducted by the bank. (404)

Cash discount The amount a customer can deduct for paying a bill within a specified period of time; used to encourage prompt payment. Not all sellers offer cash discounts. (409)

Cash payments journal A special journal used to record all transactions involving cash payments or decreases. (412)

Cash receipts journal A special journal used to record all transactions involving cash receipts or increases. (404)

Check register A journal in which checks are listed as they are written. A check register replaces a cash payments journal. (418)

Credit period The time the seller allows the buyer before full payment on a charge sale has to be made. (409)

Notes Payable The account containing the balance of promissory notes. (407)

Promissory note A written promise to pay a specified amount at a specified time. (407)

Trade discount A substantial discount from the list or catalog prices of goods, granted by the seller; not recorded by the buyer or the seller. (420)

QUESTIONS, EXERCISES, AND PROBLEMS

Discussion Questions

1. What are the normal balances of (a) Purchases? (b) Sales Discount? (c) Purchases Returns and Allowances? (d) Sales? (e) Purchases Discount? (f) Sales Returns and Allowances?

2. What does an (X) below the total of a special journal's Other Accounts column signify?

3. Explain the following credit terms: (a) n/30; (b) 2/10, n/60; (c) 1/15, EOM, n/30.

4. In a cash receipts journal, both the Accounts Receivable Credit column and the Cash Debit column were mistakenly understated by $100. How will this error be discovered? *Bank Reconciliation*

5. If a cash payments journal is supposed to save writing, why are there so many entries in the Other Accounts Debit column?

6. Describe the posting procedure for a cash payments journal with an Other Accounts Debit column and several special columns, including an Accounts Payable Debit column.

7. An electronics business purchased speakers for resale. The total of the invoice is $3,600, and it is subject to trade discounts of 15 percent, 10 percent, and 5 percent. Compute the amount the dealer will pay for the speakers.

8. What is the difference between a cash discount and a trade discount?

Exercises

P.O. 1

Describe a recorded transaction involving sale of merchandise with sales tax, paid by credit card.

Exercise 12-1 Describe the transaction recorded.

Cash	Sales Tax Payable	Sales	Credit Card Expense
424.20	21.00	420.00	16.80

P.O. 1,3

Label column headings.

Exercise 12-2 Label the blanks in the column heads as either debit or credit.

CASH RECEIPTS JOURNAL   PAGE _____

DATE	ACCOUNT CREDITED	POST. REF.	OTHER ACCOUNTS *credit*	ACCOUNTS RECEIVABLE *credit*	SALES *credit*	SALES DISCOUNT *Debit*	CASH *Debit*

P.O. 6

Describe posted transactions.

Exercise 12-3 Describe the transactions recorded in the following T accounts.

	Cash		Accounts Payable			Purchases	
	(c) 1,479.80	(b)	170	(a) 1,680	(a)	1,680	
		(c)	1,510				

Purchases Returns and Allowances		Purchases Discount	
(b)	170	(c)	30.20

P.O. 6

Calculate amounts paid for merchandise purchases involving returns and cash discounts.

Exercise 12-4 For the following purchases of merchandise, determine the amount of cash to be paid:

Purchase	Invoice Date	Credit Terms	FOB	Amount of Purchase	Freight Charges	Total Invoice Amount	Returns and Allowances	Date Paid
a.	June 1	2/10, n/30	Destination	$460	—	$ 460	—	June 30
b.	June 12	1/10, n/30	Destination	700	—	700	$100	June 21
c.	June 14	2/10, n/30	Shipping point	860	$60	920	—	June 20
d.	June 21	n/30	Shipping point	930	70	1,000	130	July 12
e.	June 24	1/10, n/30	Shipping point	660	50	710	90	July 3

P.O. 1,6

Designate the appropriate journal.

Exercise 12-5 Indicate the journal in which each of the following transactions should be recorded. Assume a three-column purchases journal.

		Journal				
Transaction		S	P	CR	CP	J
a. Paid a creditor on account.					✓	
b. Bought merchandise on account.			✓			
c. Sold merchandise for cash.				✓		
d. Adjusted for insurance expired.						✓
e. Received payment on account from a charge customer.				✓		
f. Received a credit memo for merchandise returned.						✓
g. Bought equipment on credit.						✓
h. Sold merchandise on account.		✓				
i. Recorded a customer's NSF check.						✓
j. Invested personal noncash assets in the business.						✓
k. Withdrew cash for personal use.					✓	

P.O. 3

Journalize transactions involving sales and purchases of merchandise with returns and cash discounts.

Exercise 12-6 Journalize the following transactions in general journal form:

May 4 Sold merchandise on account to Secor, Inc.; 2/10, n/30; $690.
 10 Purchased merchandise on account from the Manly Company; 1/10, n/60; FOB shipping point; $940.
 11 Paid freight bill on merchandise purchased from the Manly Company, $37, to Golden Freight Lines.
 13 Received full payment from Secor, Inc.
 14 Received a credit memo from the Manly Company for defective merchandise returned, $104.
 19 Paid the Manly Company in full within the discount period.
 28 Bought merchandise on account from Beal Company, $910; 2/10, n/30; freight prepaid and added to the invoice, $37 (total, $947).

P.O. 3

Journalize transactions involving sale and purchase of merchandise, a return, and a cash discount.

Exercise 12-7 Journalize the following transactions in general journal form, first on the books of the seller (Rye Company) and then on the books of the buyer (Low Company).

Rye Company

a. Sold merchandise on account to Low Company; 2/10, n/30; $1,500.
b. Issued a credit memo to Low Company for damaged merchandise, $100.
c. Low Company paid the account in full within the discount period.

Low Company

a. Purchased merchandise on account from Rye Company; 2/10, n/30; $1,500.
b. Received a credit memo from Rye Company for damaged merchandise, $100.
c. Paid the Rye Company account in full within the discount period.

P.O. 8

Make correcting entries involving freight charges, returns, and trade discounts.

Exercise 12-8 Journalize general journal entries to correct the errors described below. Assume that the incorrect entries were posted in the same period in which the errors occurred.

a. A freight cost of $55 incurred on equipment purchased for use in the business was debited to Freight In.
b. The issuance of a credit memo to Sorino Company for $96 for merchandise returned was recorded as a debit to Purchases Returns and Allowances and a credit to Accounts Receivable, Sorino Company.
c. A cash purchase of $118 of store supplies for the business was recorded as office supplies.
d. A cash sale of $72 to M. A. Max was recorded as a sale on account.
e. A purchase of merchandise from Arms Company in the amount of $1,000 with a 30 percent trade discount was recorded as a debit to Purchases and a credit to Accounts Payable of $1,000 each.

CONSIDER AND COMMUNICATE

You are the manager of the Accounts Receivable Department for a merchandising business. Your billing clerk sent a bill for $2 to a customer who had charged $100 in goods with terms 2/10, n/30. The customer has called and indicated his displeasure; he can't understand an error like this, since he paid on time. Explain to your billing clerk why Accounts Receivable is credited for $100 and not $98. How was permission given to send less than the full amount?

CRITICAL THINKING ▪▪▪

You work for Dawson Plumbing Supply. You are responsible for training a new accounting clerk. He has the following questions for you to answer about this invoice:

Dawson Plumbing Supply			**No. 320**
1400 Jackson Avenue			
Chicago, Illinois 60612			

INVOICE

SOLD TO	C. P. Lind Company	DATE:	August 1, 20–
	5210 Gilman Avenue	ORDER NO.:	5384
	San Diego, CA 92102	SHIPPED BY:	Fast Freight
		TERMS:	2/10, n/30
		SALESPERSON:	H. M.

QUANTITY	DESCRIPTION	UNIT PRICE	TOTAL
6	Olin single-control tub shower faucet #44B652	51 50	309 00
6	Olin dual-control washerless lavatory faucet #59B641	22 20	133 20
12	Olin massage shower head, antique brass #37B411	11 56	138 72
	Subtotal		580 92
	Freight		63 80
	Total		644 72

1. Who is the buyer?
2. Who is paying the freight?
3. What is the customer's order number?
4. What percentage of the goods bought is the cost of the freight?
5. What are the credit terms and what do they mean?
6. How much will the buyer actually have to pay if it sends the money in ten days?
7. What is the dollar amount of the discount?
8. Who receives the discount?
9. What is the due date for payment to get the discount?
10. Why would a seller give a buyer a discount?

A MATTER OF ETHICS ▪▪▪

When the new accountant started work, the owner took him out to lunch each Friday to discuss problems, progress, and suggestions to improve the business. One Friday, the owner couldn't go to lunch with the accountant. The accountant took the money for his lunch from petty cash and charged it to the owner's drawing account. He reasoned that the owner always took him to lunch on Friday, and he didn't have money for lunch. This happened several Fridays during the year. Was this a fair assumption for the accountant to make? Was it ethical?

WEB WORK

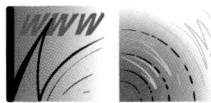

Using an Internet web browser, type the phrase for the home page of a company selling accounting software in the search box. Search for information about different brands of general ledger software. Compare the packages for features, modules, cost, the size of the company the software is designed to serve, the level of accounting knowledge needed by the user, and technical assistance. Discuss or write your findings in a memo to your supervisor.

PROBLEM SET A

For additional help, see the demonstration problem at the beginning of each chapter in your Working Papers.

P.O. 1,2

Problem 12-1A Freddy and Company, a retail carpet store, sells on the bases of (1) cash, (2) charge accounts, and (3) bank credit cards. The following transactions involved cash receipts for the firm during May of this year. The bank charges 4 percent on the total of the credit card sales plus sales tax. (For all sales involving credit cards, record credit card expense at the time of the sale.)

May 8 Total cash sales for the week, $1,380, plus $69 sales tax.

8 Total sales for the week paid for by bank credit cards, $1,600, plus $80 sales tax.

11 D. C. Colter, the owner, invested an additional $4,000.

11 Collected cash from N. D. Poyor, a charge customer, $82.50.

12 Sold store equipment at cost for cash, $270. D-cash misc Acct

15 Total cash sales for the week, $1,880, plus $94 sales tax.

15 Total sales for the week paid for by bank credit cards, $950, plus $47.50 sales tax.

19 Borrowed $2,500 from the bank, receiving the same in cash and giving the bank a promissory note.

21 Collected cash from R. Brace, a charge customer, $86.

22 Total cash sales for the week, $2,105, plus $105.25 sales tax.

22 Total sales for the week paid for by bank credit cards, $1,375, plus $68.75 sales tax.

24 Received cash as refund for the return of merchandise purchased, $152.60. misc acct

26 Collected cash from C. Fely, a charge customer, $158.

31 Total cash sales for the remainder of the month, $2,486, plus $124.30 sales tax.

31 Total sales for the remainder of the month paid for by bank credit cards, $1,050, plus $52.50 sales tax.

31 Collected cash from R. D. Thor, a charge customer, $157.60.

Instructions

1. Open the following accounts in the accounts receivable ledger and record the May 1 balances as given: R. Brace, $86; C. Fely, $188; S. R. Page, $114.72; N. D. Poyor, $82.50; R. D. Thor, $157.60; F. N. Wicks, $72.45. Place a check mark in the Post. Ref. column.
2. Record a balance of $701.27 in the Accounts Receivable controlling account as of May 1.
3. Journalize the transactions in the cash receipts journal beginning with page 62.
4. Post daily to the accounts receivable ledger.
5. Total and rule the cash receipts journal.
6. Prove the equality of debit and credit totals.
7. Post to the Accounts Receivable account in the general ledger.
8. Prepare a schedule of accounts receivable. Compare the total with the balance of the Accounts Receivable account.

P.O. 1,3

Problem 12-2A Pearson Company sells candy wholesale to vending machine operators. Terms of sales on account are 2/10, n/30, FOB shipping point. The following transactions involving cash receipts and sales of merchandise took place in May of this year:

May	1	Received $1,058.40 cash from L. Rich in payment of April 22 invoice of $1,080, less cash discount.
	4	Received $1,026 cash in payment of $950 note receivable and interest of $76.
	7	Received $882 cash from K. L. Shane in payment of April 29 invoice of $900, less cash discount.
	8	Sold merchandise on account to D. Pane, invoice no. 272, $572.
	16	Cash sales for first half of May, $4,741.
	17	Received cash from D. Pane in payment of invoice no. 272, less cash discount.
	20	Received $342 cash from L. N. Shay in payment of April 16 invoice, no discount.
	21	Sold merchandise on account to R. O. Wexel, invoice no. 285, $820.
	24	Received $371 cash refund for return of defective equipment that was originally bought for cash.
	27	Sold merchandise on account to R. Jones, invoice no. 292, $536.
	31	Cash sales for second half of May, $4,241.

Instructions

1. Journalize the transactions for May in the cash receipts journal and the sales journal.
2. Total and rule the journals.
3. Prove the equality of debit and credit totals.

P.O. 7

Problem 12-3A The Book Worm uses a check register to keep track of expenditures. The following transactions occurred during February of this year:

Feb.	3	Issued check no. 4312, $725.20, to Kent Company for the amount of its invoice no. 681 recorded previously for $740, less 2 percent cash discount.
	4	Paid freight bill to King Express Company, $58, for books purchased; issued check no. 4313.
	6	Paid rent for the month, $750; check no. 4314, to Mayer Company.

Feb. 11 Received and paid bill for advertising in the *Eastside News,* $155; check no. 4315.

11 Paid Conley Book Company $841.50, check no. 4316, for its invoice no. A331 recorded previously for $850 less 1 percent cash discount.

17 Paid wages recorded previously for first half of February, $550; check no. 4317.

21 R. D. Macky, the owner, withdrew $800 for personal use; check no. 4318.

26 Made payment on bank loan, $940; check no. 4319, consisting of $870 on the principal and $70 interest, Coast National Bank.

27 Paid Gary Publishing Company $1,200, check no. 4320, for its invoice no. 7768 recorded previously (no discount).

28 Voided check no. 4321.

28 Paid wages expense recorded previously for second half of February, $550; check no. 4322.

Check Figure

Total First Nat'l Bank Credit, $6,569.70

P.O. 1,2,3,5,6

Instructions

1. Journalize the transactions in the check register.
2. Total and rule the check register.
3. Prove the equality of the debit and credit totals.

Problem 12-4A The following transactions were completed by Hayden Auto Supply during January, which is the first month of this fiscal year. Terms of sale are 2/10, n/30.

Jan. 2 Paid rent for the month, $650; check no. 6981.

2 J. Helena, the owner, invested an additional $2,500 in the business.

4 Bought merchandise on account from Vicks and Company, $2,930; its invoice no. A691, dated January 2; terms 2/10, n/30.

4 Received check from Van Appliance for $1,176 in payment of $1,200 invoice less discount.

4 Sold merchandise on account to L. Parks, $950, invoice no. 6483.

6 Received check from Peters, Inc., for $735 in payment of $750 invoice less discount.

7 Issued check no. 6982, $686, to Franklin Company in payment of its invoice no. C1272 for $700 less discount.

7 Bought supplies on account from Dobson Office Supply, $108; its invoice no. 1906B; terms net 30 days.

7 Sold merchandise on account to Engle Company, $990, invoice no. 6484.

9 Issued credit memo no. 43 to L. Parks, $40, for merchandise returned.

11 Cash sales for January 1 to January 10, $4,943.

11 Paid Vicks and Company $2,871.40; check no. 6983, in payment of $2,930 invoice less discount.

14 Sold merchandise on account to Van Appliance, $2,140, invoice no. 6485.

18 Bought merchandise on account from Cross Products, $4,120; its invoice no. 7281D, dated January 16; FOB shipping point, freight prepaid and added to the invoice $150 (total invoice, $4,270); terms 2/10, n/60.

21 Issued check no. 6984, $370, to *The Shopper* for advertising not recorded previously (Miscellaneous Expense).

21 Cash sales for January 11 to January 20, $3,640.

Jan. 23 Received and paid invoice from Fast Freight; check no. 6985, $96, for freight charges on merchandise purchased on January 4.

23 Received credit memo no. 163, $315, from Cross Products for merchandise returned.

29 Sold merchandise on account to Byron Supply, $1,710, invoice no. 6486.

31 Cash sales, January 21 to January 31, $4,786.

31 Issued check no. 6986 for $56 payable to M. Dore for miscellaneous expenses.

31 Recorded payroll entry from the payroll register; total salaries, $6,200; employees' federal income tax withheld, $904; FICA tax withheld, $465.

31 Recorded the payroll taxes: FICA, $465; state unemployment tax, $334.80; federal unemployment tax, $49.60.

31 Issued check no. 6987, $4,831, for salaries for the month.

31 J. Helena, the owner, withdrew $900 for personal use, check no. 6988.

Check Figure

Trial balance totals, $63,328

Instructions

1. Journalize the transactions for January, using a sales journal, page 73; a purchases journal, page 56; a cash receipts journal, page 38; a cash payments journal, page 45; a general journal, page 100. The chart of accounts is as follows:

111 Cash	411 Sales
113 Accounts Receivable	412 Sales Returns and Allowances
114 Merchandise Inventory	413 Sales Discount
115 Supplies	
116 Prepaid Insurance	511 Purchases
121 Equipment	512 Purchases Returns and Allowances
	513 Purchases Discount
215 Salaries Payable	514 Freight In
216 Employees' Federal Income Tax Payable	
217 FICA Tax Payable	621 Salary Expense
218 State Unemployment Tax Payable	622 Payroll Tax Expense
	627 Rent Expense
219 Federal Unemployment Tax Payable	631 Miscellaneous Expense
221 Accounts Payable	

311 J. Helena, Capital
312 J. Helena, Drawing

2. Post daily all entries involving customer accounts to the accounts receivable ledger.

3. Post daily all entries involving creditor accounts to the accounts payable ledger.

4. Post daily those entries involving the Other Accounts columns and the general journal to the general ledger. Write the owner's name in the Capital and Drawing accounts.

5. Add the columns of the special journals, and prove the equality of debit and credit totals on scratch paper.

6. Post the appropriate totals of the special journals to the general ledger.
7. Prepare a trial balance.
8. Prepare a schedule of accounts receivable and a schedule of accounts payable. Do the totals equal the balances of the related controlling accounts?

Instructions for General Ledger Software

1. Journalize the transactions in the sales journal, purchases journal, cash receipts journal, cash payments journal, and general journal.
   a. For efficiency, analyze the transactions, indicate what journal each transaction goes into, and key the entries in five groups or batches, one for each journal.
   b. Because the program uses a single-column purchases journal, add the amount of the freight to the amount of purchases.
2. Print the journals.
3. Post the amounts from the sales, purchases, cash receipts, cash payments, and general journals.
4. Print a trial balance.
5. Print a schedule of accounts receivable and compare the total with the balance of the Accounts Receivable controlling account.
6. Print a schedule of accounts payable and compare the total with the balance of the Accounts Payable controlling account.

PROBLEM SET B

For additional help, see the demonstration problem at the beginning of each chapter in your Working Papers.

P.O. 1,2

Problem 12-1B Low-Cost Furniture, a home furnishings store, sells on the bases of (1) cash, (2) charge accounts, and (3) bank credit cards. The following transactions involve cash receipts for the firm for November of this year. The bank charges 4 percent of the total credit card sales plus tax. (For all sales involving credit cards, record credit card expense at the time of the sale.)

Nov.	7	Total cash sales for the week, $1,900, plus $95 sales tax.
	7	Total sales from bank credit cards for the week, $2,300, plus $115 sales tax.
	11	M. R. Vaa, the owner, invested an additional $4,500.
	12	Collected cash from T. R. Allard, a charge customer, $162.40.
	12	Sold office equipment for cash, $425.
	14	Total cash sales for the week, $2,734.60, plus $136.73 sales tax.
	14	Total sales from bank credit cards for the week, $1,980, plus $99 sales tax.
	18	Borrowed $5,000 from the bank, signing a promissory note.
	19	Collected cash from N. P. Troy, a charge customer, $192.40.
	21	Total cash sales for the week, $3,840, plus $192 sales tax.
	21	Total sales from bank credit cards for the week, $2,260, plus $113 sales tax.
	22	Low-Cost Furniture received cash as a refund for the return of merchandise it purchased, $271.

Nov. 24 Collected cash from C. E. Barry, a charge customer, $255.46.
30 Total cash sales for the remainder of the month, $4,531.50, plus $226.58 sales tax.
30 Total sales from bank credit cards for the remainder of the month, $397.10, plus $19.86 sales tax.
30 Collected cash from O. Harris, a charge customer, $182.17.

Check Figure

Total Sales Credit, $19,943.20

Instructions

1. Open the following accounts in the accounts receivable ledger and record the November 1 balances as given: T. R. Allard, $162.40; C. E. Barry, $255.46; L. R. Cao, $106.46; L. P. Drew, $179.52; O. Harris, $182,17; N. P. Troy, $192.40. Place a check mark in the Post. Ref. column.
2. Record a balance of $1,078.41 in the Accounts Receivable controlling account as of November 1.
3. Journalize the transactions in the cash receipts journal beginning with page 16.
4. Post daily to the accounts receivable ledger.
5. Total and rule the cash receipts journal.
6. Prove the equality of debit and credit totals.
7. Post to the Accounts Receivable account in the general ledger.
8. Prepare a schedule of accounts receivable. Compare the total with the balance of the Accounts Receivable account.

P.O. 1,3

Problem 12-2B The C. R. Mitchel Company sells candy wholesale, primarily to vending machine operators. Terms of sales on account are 2/10, n/30, FOB shipping point. The following transactions involving cash receipts and sales of merchandise took place in May of this year:

May 2 Received $823.20 cash from N. Rockney in payment of April 23 invoice of $840 less cash discount.
5 Received $594 cash in payment of $550 note receivable and interest of $44.
8 Sold merchandise on account to G. Sellers, invoice no. 862, $511.
9 Received $627.20 in cash from D. Marks in payment of April 30 invoice of $640, less cash discount.
15 Cash sales for first half of May, $3,857.
16 Received cash from G. Sellers in payment of invoice no. 862, less discount.
19 Received $353 in cash from R. O. Hays in payment of April 14 invoice, no discount.
22 Sold merchandise on account to N. T. Jakes, invoice no. 887, $684.
25 Received $218 cash refund for return of defective equipment bought in April for cash.
28 Sold merchandise on account to M. E. Mars, invoice no. 910, $818.
31 Cash sales for the second half of May, $3,449.

Check Figure

Total sales on account, $2,013

Instructions

1. Journalize the transactions for May in the cash receipts journal and the sales journal.
2. Total and rule the journals.
3. Prove the equality of debit and credit totals.

Problem 12-3B Newkirk Company uses a check register to keep track of expenditures. The following transactions occurred during February of this year:

Feb.
1   Issued check no. 4311 to Benson Company for its invoice no. 3113 recorded previously; $870 less cash discount of $17.40, $852.60.

2   Paid freight bill to The Express Company, $64, for merchandise purchased, issuing check no. 4312.

4   Paid rent for month of February, $550; check no. 4313 to Drexel Realty.

9   Received and paid bill for advertising in *Neighborhood News;* check no. 4314, $236.

10   Paid Delaney Company $1,202.85, check no. 4315, for its invoice no. D642 recorded previously in the amount of $1,215 less 1 percent cash discount.

15   Paid wages for first half of month, $1,562; check no. 4316 (payroll entry was previously recorded).

19   R. Newkirk, the owner, withdrew $700 for personal use; check no. 4317.

25   Made payment on bank loan, $648; check no. 4318, consisting of $600 on principal and $48 interest, Second National Bank.

27   Issued to Lacy Publishing Company check no. 4319, $528, for its invoice no. 6317 recorded previously (no discount).

28   Voided check no. 4320.

28   Paid wages recorded previously for second half of month; $1,562, check no. 4321.

Check Figure

Total First Nat'l Bank Credit, $7,905.45

Instructions

1. Journalize the transactions in the check register.
2. Total and rule the check register.
3. Prove the equality of the debit and credit totals.

Problem 12-4B The following transactions were completed by Top Restaurant Equipment during January, the first month of this fiscal year. Terms of sale are 2/10, n/30.

Jan.
2   Paid rent for the month, $675; check no. 6981.

2   E. Yu, the owner, invested an additional $2,500 in the business.

4   Bought merchandise on account from Vicks and Company, $2,430; its invoice no. A694, terms 2/10, n/30; dated January 2.

4   Received check from Van Appliance for $1,176 in payment of invoice for $1,200 less discount.

4   Sold merchandise on account to L. Parks, $860, invoice no. 6483.

6   Received check from Peters, Inc., for $735 in payment of $750 invoice less discount.

7   Issued check no. 6982, $686, to Franklin Company in payment of its invoice no. C127 for $700, less discount.

7   Bought supplies on account from Dobson Office Supply, $104.50, its invoice no. 1906B; terms net 30 days.

7   Sold merchandise on account to Engle Company, $910, invoice no. 6484.

9   Issued credit memo no. 43 to L. Parks, $45, for merchandise returned.

Jan. 11 Cash sales for January 1 to January 10, $4,120.18.

11 Paid Vicks and Company $2,381.40; check no. 6983, in payment of its $2,430 invoice, less discount.

14 Sold merchandise on account to Van Appliance, $1,830, invoice no. 6485.

18 Bought merchandise on account from Cross Products, $3,250; its invoice no. 7281, dated January 16; terms 2/10, n/60; FOB shipping point, freight prepaid and added to invoice, $110 (total invoice, $3,360).

21 Issued check no. 6984, $270, for advertising to Barclay Agency not recorded previously (Miscellaneous Expense).

21 Cash sales for January 11 through January 20, $3,911.

23 Received and paid invoice from Fast Freight; check no. 6985, $102, for freight charges on merchandise purchased January 4.

23 Received credit memo no. 163, $82, from Cross Products for merchandise returned.

29 Sold merchandise on account to Byron Supply, $1,720, invoice no. 6486.

31 Cash sales for January 21 through January 31, $4,104.

31 Issued check no. 6986, $55, to M. Dore for miscellaneous expenses not recorded previously.

31 Recorded payroll entry from the payroll register: total salaries, $6,050; employees' federal income tax withheld, $918; FICA tax withheld, $462.83.

31 Recorded the payroll taxes: FICA, $462.83; state unemployment tax, $326.70; federal unemployment tax, $48.40.

31 Issued check no. 6987, $4,669.17, for salaries for the month.

31 E. Yu, the owner, withdrew $800 for personal use, check no. 6988.

Check Figure

Trial balance totals, $60,701.04

Instructions

1. Journalize the transactions for January, using a sales journal, page 73; a purchases journal, page 74; a cash receipts journal, page 56; a cash payments journal, page 63; a general journal, page 119. The chart of accounts is as follows:

111 Cash	411 Sales
113 Accounts Receivable	412 Sales Returns and Allowances
114 Merchandise Inventory	413 Sales Discount
115 Supplies	
116 Prepaid Insurance	511 Purchases
121 Equipment	512 Purchases Returns and Allowances
	513 Purchases Discount
215 Salaries Payable	514 Freight In
216 Employees' Federal Income Tax Payable	
217 FICA Tax Payable	621 Salary Expense
218 State Unemployment Tax Payable	622 Payroll Tax Expense
219 Federal Unemployment Tax Payable	627 Rent Expense
221 Accounts Payable	631 Miscellaneous Expense
311 E. Yu, Capital	
312 E. Yu, Drawing	

2. Post daily all entries involving customer accounts to the accounts receivable ledger.
3. Post daily all entries involving creditor accounts to the accounts payable ledger.
4. Post daily those entries involving the Other Accounts columns and the general journal to the general ledger. Write the owner's name in the Capital and Drawing accounts.
5. Add the columns of the special journals, and prove the equality of debit and credit totals on scratch paper.
6. Post the appropriate totals of the special journals to the general ledger.
7. Prepare a trial balance.
8. Prepare a schedule of accounts receivable and a schedule of accounts payable. Do the totals equal the balances of the related controlling accounts?

Instructions for General Ledger Software

1. Journalize the transactions in the sales journal, purchases journal, cash receipts journal, cash payments journal, and general journal.
    a. For efficiency, analyze the transactions, indicate what journal each transaction goes into, and key the entries in five groups or batches, one for each journal.
    b. Because the program uses a single-column purchases journal, add the amount of the freight to the amount of purchases.
2. Print the journals.
3. Post the amounts from the sales, purchases, cash receipts, cash payments, and general journals.
4. Print a trial balance.
5. Print a schedule of accounts receivable and compare the total with the balance of the Accounts Receivable controlling account.
6. Print a schedule of accounts payable and compare the total with the balance of the Accounts Payable controlling account.

Continuous General Ledger Problem: Cash Receipts and Cash Payments Journals

During June and July, Like New added a sales journal and a purchases journal to the records to reduce writing and to save time. This month, August, Miracle has added a cash receipts journal (for all entries that increase cash) and a cash payments journal (for all entries that decrease cash). As the accountant for Like New, you are to journalize and post the following August transactions. All sales on account are 2/10, n/30.

Aug.

1   J. Miracle, the owner, invested a photocopy machine in the business, $350 (Office Equipment).

2   Paid the $1,140 interest (debit Interest Expense) and $261 on the principal of the mortgage (debit Mortgage Payable), $1,401, Ck. No. 1020.

3   Bought merchandise on account from Frame Co., Inv. no. 1054, $1,130; terms 2/10, n/30; dated August 3; freight prepaid and added to the invoice, $118 (total $1,248).

4   Received a check for $3,697.54 from Mike Wallen on account, $3,773 less 2% discount.

7   Received a check for $500 from Baker Inn on account, Sales Inv. 2011, no discount.

8   Issued a check for $1,605.50 to Au Furniture in payment of its invoice no. 494 for $1,605.50, Ck. No. 1021. Too late for discount.

9   Bought supplies on account from Office Ready, $43, invoice no. 416; terms net 30 days.

10   Sold merchandise on account to Baker Inn, Sales Inv. 2015, $1,788.

11   Cash sales for August 1 through August 10, $1,790.82 (Service Income) and $2,004.40 (Merchandise Income).

12   Paid Unique Furniture $1,325 in payment of its invoice no. 3455 for $1,325, Ck. No. 1022. Too late for the discount.

14   Bought merchandise on account from Au Furniture, Inv. no. 3474, $4,905; terms 2/10, n/30; dated August 14; freight prepaid and added to the invoice, $187 (total $5,092).

15   Sold merchandise on account to Mike Wallen, Sales Inv. 2016, $1,294.

16   Paid wages of part-time assistant for the first half of the month, $850, Ck. No. 1023.

18   Bought merchandise on account from Au Furniture, Inv. no. 502, $4,908; terms 2/10, n/30; dated July 23.

19   Issued a check for $876 for advertising to Castle Ads, Ck. No. 1024 (Advertising Expense).

19   Paid the utility bill, $125, Ck. No. 1025.

Note: The Continuous General Ledger Problem can be worked with Houghton Mifflin Windows General Ledger Package, Peachtree Release 5.01, QuickBooks 6.0, or other general ledger software packages.

Aug. 20 Cash sales for August 11 through August 20, $2,100 (Service Income) and $2,060 (Merchandise Income).

21 Received credit memo no. 24 for merchandise returned to Au Furniture, Inv. no. 502, $108.

24 Sold merchandise on account to Gail Murdock, Sales Inv. 2017, $1,916.

25 Received and paid invoice 2760 from WayFast Freight, Ck. No. 1026, $186, for freight purchased on August 18.

26 Issued Ck. No. 1027 to M. Pierce for $86 for flowers (Miscellaneous Expense).

27 J. Miracle, owner, withdrew $435 for personal use, Ck. No. 1028.

31 Cash sales for August 21 through August 31, $1,309 (Service Income) and $2,309 (Merchandise Income).

31 Paid wages of part-time assistant for the second half of the month, $850, Ck. No. 1029.

Instructions

1. Launch the general ledger software.
2. Open the likenew (July) file and rename it for August.
3. Add the following new accounts:

413 Sales Discount	625 Miscellaneous Expense
514 Freight In	613 Advertising Expense

4. Add the following vendor: Office Ready.
5. Journalize and post the transactions in either the general journal or one of the four special journals—Sales Journal, Purchases Journal, Cash Receipts Journal, or Cash Payments Journal.
6. Print a trial balance ($244,681.60).
7. Print a schedule of accounts receivable ($10,926.60). Compare the total with the Accounts Receivable account in the trial balance. They should be the same. If not, there is an error; reverse the process until you find the error.
8. Print a schedule of accounts payable ($14,131.94). Compare the total with the Accounts Payable account in the trial balance. They should be the same. If not, there is an error; reverse the process until you find the error.

Cumulative Self-Check: Chapters 10–12

PART I: COMPLETION

Complete each of the following statements by writing the appropriate word(s) in the spaces provided:

1. The normal balance of the Purchases Discount account is on the _____ side.

2. Entries in the Accounts Payable Debit column of a cash payments journal are posted daily to the _____.

3. The _____ is the amount a customer may deduct for paying a bill within a specified period of time.

4. The form sent to the supplier of merchandise is called a(n) _____.

5. The _____ account is used to record the buying of merchandise for resale only.

6. If the freight charges are FOB shipping point, the _____ pays the transportation charges.

7. Plans and procedures built into the accounting system to promote efficiency and prevent fraud and waste are called _____.

8. Increases in Sales Returns and Allowances are recorded on the _____ side.

9. The sales journal is used to record all _____.

10. The schedule of accounts receivable lists the balances of all the _____ customers' accounts at the end of the month.

PART II: MATCHING

For each numbered item, choose the appropriate journal, and write the identifying letter.

____ 1. Paid freight bill on merchandise purchased.

____ 2. Bought office equipment for our office on account.

____ 3. Received a credit memo for merchandise we returned.

____ 4. Journalized the adjustment for supplies used.

S   Sales journal
P   Purchases journal (3 columns)
CR   Cash receipts journal
CP   Cash payments journal
J   General journal

Note: Answers to Cumulative Self-Check begin on page A-1.

___ 5. Sold merchandise on account.

___ 6. Journalized the closing entries.

___ 7. Paid state sales tax to the state revenue department.

___ 8. Bought merchandise for resale on account.

___ 9. Sold merchandise for cash.

___ 10. Bought merchandise for resale for cash.

PART III: TRUE/FALSE

For each question circle T if it is True or circle F if it is False.

T   F   1. The Purchases Discount account is classified as a revenue account.

T   F   2. The normal balance of the Sales Discount account is on the debit side.

T   F   3. Check marks in the Post. Ref. column of the sales journal indicate that the amounts are not to be posted.

T   F   4. When you post directly from the purchases invoice, you eliminate the accounts payable ledger.

T   F   5. The purchases journal is used for the buying of merchandise for cash and on account.

13 Work Sheet and Adjusting Entries

WINDOWS ON **THE WORLD WIDE WEB**

How many videos do you watch in a year? Chances are you can find many of them at Blockbuster. Each store carries approximately 7,000 to 10,000 videos. And Blockbuster, Inc., is the only national video chain in the United States with more than 4,000 video stores. You can be sure to find your favorite drama, comedy, or action flick without traveling too far. Imagine taking inventory of all those videos. Would you use a periodic inventory system or a perpetual inventory system? How would you record supplies used, depreciation, and expired insurance for Blockbuster? What would you need to write on the work sheet? How would you make adjustments for unearned revenue? To find out fun stats about Blockbuster, visit **http://www.blockbuster.com/co/trivia.jhtml**.

Performance Objectives

After you have completed this chapter, you will be able to do the following:

1. Prepare an adjustment for merchandise inventory under the periodic inventory system.

2. Prepare an adjustment for unearned revenue.

3. Record the adjustment data in a work sheet (including merchandise inventory, unearned revenue, supplies used, expired insurance, depreciation, and accrued wages or salaries).

4. Complete the work sheet.

5. Journalize the adjusting entries for a merchandising business under the periodic inventory system.

6. Journalize the adjusting entry for merchandise inventory under the perpetual inventory system.

We have talked about the special journals and accounts kept by a merchandising business. Now we take another step toward completing the accounting cycle by presenting the related adjustments and the work sheet. Many of the adjustments made by a service business are also made by a merchandising firm. First, let's briefly review the adjusting entries described so far. To begin, look over the following accounts.

Supplies		Prepaid Insurance		Accumulated Depreciation		Wages Expense	
+	−	+	−	−	+	+	−
Bal. 600		Bal. 300			Bal. 1,000	Bal. 2,600	

Here are the data for the adjustments, along with the related adjusting entries:

Ending supplies inventory, $250. (Remember, subtract the amount left over to get the amount used: $600 − $250 = $350.)

Supplies				Supplies Expense		
	+	−			+	−
Bal.	600	Adj.	350	Adj.	350	
Bal.	250					

Insurance expired, $260. (The amount expired is the amount used.)

Prepaid Insurance				Insurance Expense		
	+	−			+	−
Bal.	300	Adj.	260	Adj.	260	
Bal.	40					

Additional depreciation, $280. (Add to both accounts.)

Depreciation Expense				Accumulated Depreciation		
	+	−		−	+	
Adj.	280				Bal.	1,000
					Adj.	280
					Bal.	1,280

Accrued wages (owed but not yet paid), $390. (Add to both accounts.)

Wages Expense				Wages Payable		
	+	−		−	+	
Bal.	2,600				Adj.	390
Adj.	390					
Bal.	2,990					

In this chapter, we introduce two more adjusting entries. One adjustment is for merchandise inventory, which is used exclusively for a merchandising business. Another adjustment is for unearned revenue, which could apply to either a merchandising or a service business. We also discuss how to handle the specialized accounts of a merchandising business in the work sheet. Finally, we briefly describe the perpetual inventory system and the accompanying adjustment.

ADJUSTMENT FOR MERCHANDISE INVENTORY USING THE PERIODIC INVENTORY SYSTEM

Objective 1

Prepare an adjustment for merchandise inventory under the periodic inventory system.

Under the **periodic inventory system,** we do not make an entry in the Merchandise Inventory account until an actual **physical inventory** or count of the stock of goods on hand has been taken. Instead, we record the purchase of merchandise as a debit to Purchases for the amount of the cost and the sale of the merchandise as a credit to Sales for the amount of the selling price. Finally, after a physical count of merchandise has been taken, one method of adjusting inventory is to make two adjusting entries to record the dollar amount of the inventory. The first adjusting entry is to remove the beginning inventory. The second entry is to enter the ending inventory.

Consider this example. A firm has a Merchandise Inventory balance of $37,000, which represents the cost of the inventory at the beginning of the fiscal period. At the end of the fiscal period, the firm takes an actual count of the stock on hand and determines the cost of the ending inventory to be $42,000. Naturally, in any business, goods are constantly being bought, sold, and replaced. The cost of the ending inventory is larger than the cost of the beginning inventory because the firm bought more than it sold. When we adjust the Merchandise Inventory account, we place the new figure of $42,000 in the account. This method can require two steps.

Step 1 Eliminate the amount of the beginning inventory from the Merchandise Inventory account by closing the account into Income Summary. This transfers the balance into Income Summary. (Remove the beginning inventory.)

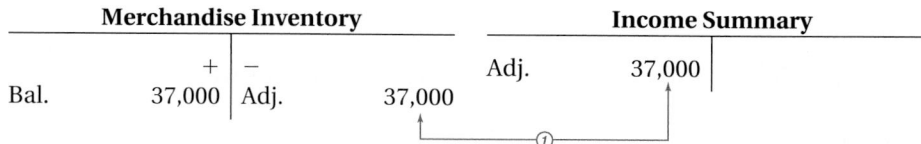

We handle this just as we handle the closing of any other account, by making the balance equal to zero. We treat the entry as a credit to Merchandise Inventory and then do the opposite to Income Summary, which means that we debit this account.

Step 2 Enter the ending Merchandise Inventory, because you must record on the books the cost of the asset remaining on hand. (Enter the ending inventory.)

Let's repeat the T accounts, showing step 1 and adding step 2.

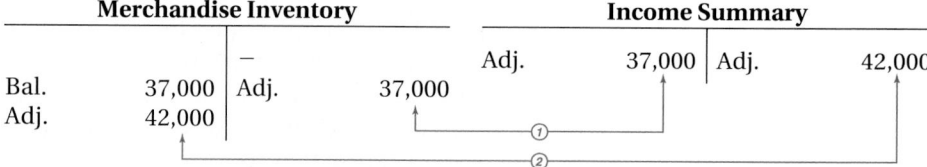

In step 2, we debit Merchandise Inventory (recording the asset on the plus side of the account) and do the opposite to Income Summary.

The reason for adjusting the Merchandise Inventory account in these two steps is that both the beginning and the ending amounts appear as distinct figures in the Income Statement columns of a work sheet, and these columns are used as the basis for preparing the income statement.

ADJUSTMENT FOR UNEARNED REVENUE

Objective 2

Prepare an adjustment for unearned revenue.

Now let's introduce another adjusting entry, **unearned revenue**, which is cash received in advance for goods or services to be delivered or performed later. This entry could pertain to a service business as well as to a merchandising business. Frequently, cash is received in advance for services to be performed in the future. For example, a professional sports team sells tickets in advance, a concert association sells season tickets in advance, a magazine publisher sells subscriptions in advance, and an insurance company receives premiums in advance. If the cash amounts received by each of these organi-

College students pay in advance to participate in a meal plan. Until all those meals are consumed, this money represents unearned revenue for the college or university dining hall services.

zations will be earned during the present fiscal period, the amounts should be credited to revenue accounts. On the other hand, if the amounts received will *not* be earned during the present fiscal period, the amounts should be credited to unearned revenue accounts. **An unearned revenue account is classified as a liability,** because an organization is liable for (owes) the amount received in advance until it is earned.

To illustrate, assume that on April 1, Bell Publishing Company receives $82,000 in cash for subscriptions covering two years and records them originally as debits to Cash and credits to Unearned Subscriptions. At the end of the year, Bell finds that $30,750 of the subscriptions have been earned. Accordingly, Bell's accountant makes an adjusting entry, debiting Unearned Subscriptions and crediting Subscriptions Income. In other words, the accountant takes the earned portion out of Unearned Subscriptions and adds it to Subscriptions Income. T accounts show the situation as follows:

Cash				Unearned Subscriptions		
	+	−		−	+	
April 1	82,000			Dec. 31 Adj. 30,750	April 1	82,000
				(9 months)	(24 months)	
					Bal.	51,250

Subscriptions Income	
−	+
	Dec. 31 Adj. 30,750
	(9 months)

FYI

The adjusting entries presented so far are end-of-the-fiscal-year adjustments. There may be other necessary changes or adjustments during the fiscal year.

Now, suppose that Jackson Electric Supply offers a course in wiring for homeowners and apartment managers. On October 1, Jackson Electric Supply receives $1,200 in fees for a four-month course. Because Jackson Electric Supply's present fiscal period ends on December 31, the four months' worth of fees received in advance will not all be earned during this fiscal period. Therefore, Jackson Electric Supply's accountant records the transaction as a debit to Cash of $1,200 and a credit to Unearned Course Fees of $1,200. Unearned Course Fees is a liability account because Jackson Electric Supply must complete the "how-to" course or refund a portion of the money it collected. **Any account beginning with the word *Unearned* is a liability.**

On December 31, because three months' worth of course fees have now been earned, Jackson Electric Supply's accountant makes an adjusting entry to transfer $900 (3/4 of $1,200) from Unearned Course Fees to Course Fees Income. Using T accounts, the situation looks like this:

Cash				Unearned Course Fees		
	+	−		−	+	
Oct. 1	1,200			Dec. 31 Adj. 900	Oct. 1	1,200
				(3 months)	(4 months)	
					Bal.	300

Course Fees Income	
−	+
	Dec. 31 Adj. 900
	(3 months)

Under the periodic inventory system, the Merchandise Inventory account is not adjusted until the goods on hand have actually been counted. This is called taking a physical inventory of the stock.

Before we demonstrate how to record adjustments, let's first look at the trial balance section of Jackson Electric Supply's work sheet (Figure 1).

FIGURE 1

Jackson Electric Supply
Work Sheet
For Year Ended December 31, 20—

	ACCOUNT NAME	TRIAL BALANCE DEBIT	TRIAL BALANCE CREDIT	ADJUSTMENTS DEBIT	ADJUSTMENTS CREDIT
1	Cash	21 1 5 4 00			
2	Notes Receivable	4 0 0 0 00			
3	Accounts Receivable	29 4 4 6 00			
4	Merchandise Inventory	77 0 0 0 00			
5	Supplies	1 4 4 0 00			
6	Prepaid Insurance	9 6 0 00			
7	Land	12 0 0 0 00			
8	Building	96 0 0 0 00			
9	Accumulated Depreciation, Building		32 0 0 0 00		
10	Equipment	33 6 0 0 00			
11	Accumulated Depreciation, Equipment		16 4 0 0 00		
12	Accounts Payable		36 4 0 0 00		
13	Notes Payable		3 0 0 0 00		
14	Unearned Course Fees		1 2 0 0 00		
15	Mortgage Payable		8 0 0 0 00		
16	N. C. Jackson, Capital		140 5 7 4 00		
17	N. C. Jackson, Drawing	48 9 0 0 00			
18	Sales		235 1 8 0 00		
19	Sales Returns and Allowances	8 4 0 00			
20	Sales Discount	1 8 8 0 00			
21	Interest Income		1 2 0 00		
22	Purchases	89 1 4 0 00			
23	Purchases Returns and Allowances		2 8 3 2 00		
24	Purchases Discount		1 2 4 8 00		
25	Freight In	2 4 6 0 00			
26	Wages Expense	55 8 0 0 00			
27	Taxes Expense	1 9 6 0 00			
28	Interest Expense	3 7 4 00			
29		476 9 5 4 00	476 9 5 4 00		

DATA FOR THE ADJUSTMENTS

Listing the adjustment data appears to be a relatively minor task. In a business situation, however, you must take actual physical counts of the inventories and match them with the recorded costs. You must check insurance policies to determine the amount of insurance that has expired. Finally, you must systematically write off, or depreciate, the cost of equipment and buildings.

For income tax and accounting purposes, land cannot be depreciated. Even if a building and lot were bought as one package for one price, the buyer must separate the cost of the building from the cost of the land. For real estate taxes, the county assessor appraises the building and the land separately. If there is no other qualified appraisal available, you can use the assessor's ratio or percentage as a basis for separating building cost and land cost.

Here are the adjustment data for Jackson Electric Supply recorded in T accounts.

a–b. Ending merchandise inventory, $64,900

Merchandise Inventory					Income Summary			
	+	–			**(a)** Adj.	77,000	**(b)** Adj.	64,900
Bal.	77,000	**(a)** Adj.	77,000					
(b) Adj.	64,900							
Bal.	64,900							

c. Course fees earned, $900

Unearned Course Fees					Course Fees Income		
	–	+			–	+	
(c) Adj.	900	Bal.	1,200			**(c)** Adj.	900
		Bal.	300				

d. Ending supplies inventory, $515

Supplies					Supplies Expense		
	+	–			+	–	
Bal.	1,440	**(d)** Adj.	925	**(d)** Adj.	925		
Bal.	515						

e. Insurance expired, $380

Prepaid Insurance					Insurance Expense		
	+	–			+	–	
Bal.	960	**(e)** Adj.	380	**(e)** Adj.	380		
Bal.	580						

In listing adjustment data, a business must check insurance policies to account for insurance that has expired as well as systematically write off, or depreciate, the cost of equipment.

f. Additional year's depreciation of building, $5,000

Accumulated Depreciation, Building				Depreciation Expense, Building		
−	+				+	−
	Bal.	32,000	**(f)**		5,000	
	(f)	5,000				
	Bal.	37,000				

g. Additional year's depreciation of equipment, $4,000

Accumulated Depreciation, Equipment				Depreciation Expense, Equipment		
−	+				+	−
	Bal.	16,400	**(g)** Adj.		4,000	
	(g) Adj.	4,000				
	Bal.	20,400				

h. Wages owed but not paid to employees at end of year, $1,220

Wages Payable				Wages Expense		
−	+				+	−
	(h)	1,220	Bal.		55,800	
			(h)		1,220	
			Bal.		57,020	

We now record these in the Adjustments columns of the work sheet, using the same letters to identify the adjustments (see Figure 2).

	ACCOUNT NAME	TRIAL BALANCE DEBIT	TRIAL BALANCE CREDIT	ADJUSTMENTS DEBIT	ADJUSTMENTS CREDIT
1	Cash	21 1 5 4 00			
2	Notes Receivable	4 0 0 0 00			
3	Accounts Receivable	29 4 4 6 00			
4	Merchandise Inventory	77 0 0 0 00		(b)64 9 0 0 00	(a)77 0 0 0 00
5	Supplies	1 4 4 0 00			(d) 9 2 5 00
6	Prepaid Insurance	9 6 0 00			(e) 3 8 0 00
7	Land	12 0 0 0 00			
8	Building	96 0 0 0 00			
9	Accumulated Depreciation, Building		32 0 0 0 00		(f) 5 0 0 0 00
10	Equipment	33 6 0 0 00			
11	Accumulated Depreciation, Equipment		16 4 0 0 00		(g) 4 0 0 0 00
12	Accounts Payable		36 4 0 0 00		
13	Notes Payable		3 0 0 0 00		
14	Unearned Course Fees		1 2 0 0 00	(c) 9 0 0 00	
15	Mortgage Payable		8 0 0 0 00		
16	N. C. Jackson, Capital		140 5 7 4 00		
17	N. C. Jackson, Drawing	48 9 0 0 00			
18	Sales		235 1 8 0 00		
19	Sales Returns and Allowances	8 4 0 00			
20	Sales Discount	1 8 8 0 00			
21	Interest Income		1 2 0 00		
22	Purchases	89 1 4 0 00			
23	Purchases Returns and Allowances		2 8 3 2 00		
24	Purchases Discount		1 2 4 8 00		
25	Freight In	2 4 6 0 00			
26	Wages Expense	55 8 0 0 00		(h) 1 2 2 0 00	
27	Taxes Expense	1 9 6 0 00			
28	Interest Expense	3 7 4 00			
29		476 9 5 4 00	476 9 5 4 00		
30	Income Summary			(a)77 0 0 0 00	(b)64 9 0 0 00
31	Course Fees Income				(c) 9 0 0 00
32	Supplies Expense			(d) 9 2 5 00	
33	Insurance Expense			(e) 3 8 0 00	
34	Depreciation Expense, Building			(f) 5 0 0 0 00	
35	Depreciation Expense, Equipment			(g) 4 0 0 0 00	
36	Wages Payable				(h) 1 2 2 0 00
37				154 3 2 5 00	154 3 2 5 00

FIGURE 2

COMPLETION OF THE WORK SHEET

Objective 4

Complete the work sheet.

When we introduced work sheets, we included the Adjusted Trial Balance columns as a means of verifying that the accounts were in balance after recording the adjusting entries. Now, to reduce the number of columns in the work sheet, we eliminate the Adjusted Trial Balance columns. The account balances after the adjusting entries are carried directly into the Income Statement and Balance Sheet columns. The completed work sheet looks like Figure 3 on pages 450–451.

Jackson Electric Supply
Work Sheet
For Year Ended December 31, 20—

	ACCOUNT NAME	TRIAL BALANCE	
		DEBIT	CREDIT
1	Cash	21 1 5 4 00	
2	Notes Receivable	4 0 0 0 00	
3	Accounts Receivable	29 4 4 6 00	
4	Merchandise Inventory	77 0 0 0 00	
5	Supplies	1 4 4 0 00	
6	Prepaid Insurance	9 6 0 00	
7	Land	12 0 0 0 00	
8	Building	96 0 0 0 00	
9	Accumulated Depreciation, Building		32 0 0 0 00
10	Equipment	33 6 0 0 00	
11	Accumulated Depreciation, Equipment		16 4 0 0 00
12	Accounts Payable		36 4 0 0 00
13	Notes Payable		3 0 0 0 00
14	Unearned Course Fees		1 2 0 0 00
15	Mortgage Payable		8 0 0 0 00
16	N. C. Jackson, Capital		140 5 7 4 00
17	N. C. Jackson, Drawing	48 9 0 0 00	
18	Sales		235 1 8 0 00
19	Sales Returns and Allowances	8 4 0 00	
20	Sales Discount	1 8 8 0 00	
21	Interest Income		1 2 0 00
22	Purchases	89 1 4 0 00	
23	Purchases Returns and Allowances		2 8 3 2 00
24	Purchases Discount		1 2 4 8 00
25	Freight In	2 4 6 0 00	
26	Wages Expense	55 8 0 0 00	
27	Taxes Expense	1 9 6 0 00	
28	Interest Expense	3 7 4 00	
29		476 9 5 4 00	476 9 5 4 00
30	Income Summary		
31	Course Fees Income		
32	Supplies Expense		
33	Insurance Expense		
34	Depreciation Expense, Building		
35	Depreciation Expense, Equipment		
36	Wages Payable		
37			
38	Net Income		
39			
40			
41			
42			

FIGURE 3

#	ADJUSTMENTS DEBIT	ADJUSTMENTS CREDIT	INCOME STATEMENT DEBIT	INCOME STATEMENT CREDIT	BALANCE SHEET DEBIT	BALANCE SHEET CREDIT
1					21 1 5 4 00	
2					4 0 0 0 00	
3					29 4 4 6 00	
4	(b) 64 9 0 0 00	(a) 77 0 0 0 00			64 9 0 0 00	
5		(d) 9 2 5 00			5 1 5 00	
6		(e) 3 8 0 00			5 8 0 00	
7					12 0 0 0 00	
8					96 0 0 0 00	
9		(f) 5 0 0 0 00				37 0 0 0 00
10					33 6 0 0 00	
11		(g) 4 0 0 0 00				20 4 0 0 00
12						36 4 0 0 00
13						3 0 0 0 00
14	(c) 9 0 0 00					3 0 0 00
15						8 0 0 0 00
16						140 5 7 4 00
17					48 9 0 0 00	
18			235 1 8 0 00			
19			8 4 0 00			
20			1 8 8 0 00			
21				1 2 0 00		
22			89 1 4 0 00			
23				2 8 3 2 00		
24				1 2 4 8 00		
25			2 4 6 0 00			
26	(h) 1 2 2 0 00		57 0 2 0 00			
27			1 9 6 0 00			
28			3 7 4 00			
29						
30	(a) 77 0 0 0 00	(b) 64 9 0 0 00	77 0 0 0 00	64 9 0 0 00		
31		(c) 9 0 0 00		9 0 0 00		
32	(d) 9 2 5 00		9 2 5 00			
33	(e) 3 8 0 00		3 8 0 00			
34	(f) 5 0 0 0 00		5 0 0 0 00			
35	(g) 4 0 0 0 00		4 0 0 0 00			
36		(h) 1 2 2 0 00				1 2 2 0 00
37	154 3 2 5 00	154 3 2 5 00	240 9 7 9 00	305 1 8 0 00	311 0 9 5 00	246 8 9 4 00
38			64 2 0 1 00			64 2 0 1 00
39			305 1 8 0 00	305 1 8 0 00	311 0 9 5 00	311 0 9 5 00
40						
41						
42						

Observe in particular the way we carry forward the figures for Merchandise Inventory and Income Summary. **Income Summary is the only account in which we don't combine the debit and credit figures. Instead, we carry them into the Income Statement columns in Figure 3 as two distinct figures.** As we said, the reason is that we need both figures to complete the income statement. The amount listed as Income Summary in the Income Statement Debit column is the beginning merchandise inventory. The amount listed as Income Summary in the Income Statement Credit column is the ending merchandise inventory.

When developing the work sheet, complete one stage at a time:

1. Record the trial balance, and make sure that the total of the Debit column equals the total of the Credit column.
2. Record the adjustments in the Adjustments columns, and make sure that the totals are equal.
3. Complete the Income Statement and Balance Sheet columns by recording the adjusted balance of each account. Here are the accounts and classifications pertaining to a merchandising business that appear in these columns:

INCOME STATEMENT		BALANCE SHEET	
DEBIT	CREDIT	DEBIT	CREDIT
Sales Returns and Allowances + Sales Discount + Purchases + Freight In + Expenses + Income Summary	Revenues (including Sales) + Purchases Returns and Allowances + Purchases Discount + Income Summary	Assets + Drawing	Accumulated Depreciation + Liabilities + Capital

Study the following example, noting especially the way we treat these special accounts for a merchandising business:

ACCOUNT NAME	INCOME STATEMENT		BALANCE SHEET	
	DEBIT	CREDIT	DEBIT	CREDIT
Merchandise Inventory			64 9 0 0 00	
Sales		235 1 8 0 00		
Sales Returns and Allowances	8 4 0 00			
Sales Discount	1 8 8 0 00			
Purchases	89 1 4 0 00			
Purchases Returns and Allowances		2 8 3 2 00		
Purchases Discount		1 2 4 8 00		
Freight In	2 4 6 0 00			
Income Summary	77 0 0 0 00	64 9 0 0 00		

ADJUSTING ENTRIES UNDER THE PERIODIC INVENTORY SYSTEM

Objective 5

Journalize the adjusting entries for a merchandising business under the periodic inventory system.

Figure 4 shows the way the adjusting entries look when they are taken from the Adjustments columns of the work sheet and recorded in the general journal.

FIGURE 4

	DATE		DESCRIPTION	POST. REF.	DEBIT	CREDIT	
1	20–		**Adjusting Entries**				1
2	Dec.	31	Income Summary		77 0 0 0 00		2
3			Merchandise Inventory			77 0 0 0 00	3
4							4
5		31	Merchandise Inventory		64 9 0 0 00		5
6			Income Summary			64 9 0 0 00	6
7							7
8		31	Unearned Course Fees		9 0 0 00		8
9			Course Fees Income			9 0 0 00	9
10							10
11		31	Supplies Expense		9 2 5 00		11
12			Supplies			9 2 5 00	12
13							13
14		31	Insurance Expense		3 8 0 00		14
15			Prepaid Insurance			3 8 0 00	15
16							16
17		31	Depreciation Expense, Building		5 0 0 0 00		17
18			Accumulated Depreciation,				18
19			Building			5 0 0 0 00	19
20							20
21		31	Depreciation Expense,				21
22			Equipment		4 0 0 0 00		22
23			Accumulated Depreciation,				23
24			Equipment			4 0 0 0 00	24
25							25
26		31	Wages Expense		1 2 2 0 00		26
27			Wages Payable			1 2 2 0 00	27
28							28

GENERAL JOURNAL PAGE 96

ADJUSTMENT FOR MERCHANDISE INVENTORY UNDER THE PERPETUAL INVENTORY SYSTEM

Objective 6

Journalize the adjusting entry for merchandise inventory under the perpetual inventory system.

Under the **perpetual inventory system**, a business continually maintains a record of each item in stock. **Under the perpetual inventory system, when merchandise is purchased, the Merchandise Inventory account (not the Purchases account) is debited for the cost of the merchandise and Accounts Payable or Cash is credited. When merchandise is sold, the Merchandise**

Inventory account is credited for the cost of the merchandise and the Cost of Goods Sold account is debited for the cost of the merchandise.

Many firms use electronic devices to keep track of stock items. For example, when a sale is made at a supermarket checkout counter, as the bar code on each item is scanned, the price and stock number are recorded. The cash register is connected to a computer that updates the inventory record and records the cost of the item. So the business perpetually (always) knows how much inventory it should have on hand.

However, to verify the inventory record, a physical count should be taken from time to time. The amount shown by the physical count may be less than the recorded amount as a result of errors, shrinkage, or shoplifting. If this is the case, an adjusting entry must be made to record the amount of the loss. This entry is a debit to the Cost of Goods Sold account (an expense account) and a credit to the Merchandise Inventory account.

Adjusting Entry Under the Perpetual Inventory System

Here is a comparison of entries in T-account form under both the periodic and the perpetual inventory systems. Assume a beginning inventory of $80,000.

1. Bought merchandise on account, $50,000.

Periodic Inventory				Perpetual Inventory		
Purchases		**Accounts Payable**		**Merchandise Inventory**		**Accounts Payable**
(1) 50,000		(1) 50,000	Bal. 80,000			(1) 50,000
			(1) 50,000			

2. Sold merchandise for $82,000 having a cost of $61,200.

Periodic Inventory				Perpetual Inventory		
Accounts Receivable		**Sales**		**Accounts Receivable**		**Sales**
(2) 82,000		(2) 82,000		(2) 82,000		(2) 82,000
				Cost of Goods Sold		**Merchandise Inventory**
				(2) 61,200	Bal. 80,000	(2) 61,200
					(1) 50,000	

■■■

Remember!

The ending inventory of one period becomes the beginning inventory of the next period.

3. Adjusting entry for ending inventory by physical count, $68,400. The recorded balance of the perpetual inventory is $68,800 ($80,000 + $50,000 − $61,200).

Periodic Inventory				Perpetual Inventory		
Income Summary		**Merchandise Inventory**		**Cost of Goods Sold**		**Merchandise Inventory**
(3a) Adj. 80,000	(3b) Adj. 68,400	Bal. 80,000	(3a) Adj. 80,000	(2) 61,200	Bal. 80,000	(2) 61,200
		(3b) Adj. 68,400		(3) Adj. 400	(1) 50,000	(3) Adj. 400

FIGURE 5

| | | | | GENERAL JOURNAL | | | PAGE | 96 | |

	DATE		DESCRIPTION	POST. REF.	DEBIT	CREDIT	
1	20–		**Adjusting Entries**				1
2	Dec.	31	**Cost of Goods Sold**		4 0 0 00		2
3			**Merchandise Inventory**			4 0 0 00	3
4			**or**				4
5		31	**Merchandise Inventory**		5 0 0 00		5
6			**Cost of Goods Sold**			5 0 0 00	6

FYI

This entry would have been previously listed in the Adjustments columns of the work sheet.

The difference of $400 ($68,800 − $68,400) is the adjustment amount under the perpetual inventory system (actual physical count versus the accounting records). The adjusting entry required to record the $400 loss is shown in Figure 5.

On the other hand, if the physical count of the stock of merchandise ($65,300) is more than the recorded amount ($64,800), the adjusting entry is to debit Merchandise Inventory and credit Cost of Goods Sold (account) for the difference ($65,300 − $64,800 = $500).

Additional adjusting entries would follow, such as those for supplies used, insurance expired, accrued wages, and other such expenses.

In the income statement, under the periodic inventory system, the Cost of Goods Sold account is listed under one line, rather than there being a Cost of Goods Sold section.

Here is a comparison of income statements under each of the two systems.

Periodic			**Perpetual**	
Sales		$82,000	Sales	$82,000
Cost of Goods Sold:			Cost of Goods Sold	61,600
Merchandise			Gross Profit	$20,400
Inventory				
(beginning)	$ 80,000			
Purchases (net)	50,000			
Goods Available				
for Sale	$130,000			
Less Merchandise				
Inventory (ending)	68,400			
Cost of Goods Sold		61,600		
Gross Profit		$20,400		

CHAPTER REVIEW

Review of Performance Objectives

1. Prepare an adjustment for merchandise inventory under the periodic inventory system.

   The adjustment for merchandise inventory under the periodic inventory system requires two adjusting entries. In the first adjusting entry (to remove the beginning inventory), debit Income Summary and credit Merchandise Inventory. In the second adjusting entry (to enter the ending inventory), debit Merchandise Inventory and credit Income Summary.

2. Prepare an adjustment for unearned revenue.

   For revenue received in advance, an adjustment is required to separate the portion that has been earned from the portion that is unearned. We assume that the amount of cash received in advance was originally recorded as unearned revenue, which is a liability. In the adjusting entry for the amount actually earned, debit the unearned revenue account (Unearned Course Fees) and credit the revenue account (Course Fees Income).

3. Record the adjustment data in a work sheet (including merchandise inventory, unearned revenue, supplies used, expired insurance, depreciation, and accrued wages or salaries).

   In the Adjustments columns of the work sheet, record the following adjusting entries:

   For merchandise inventory: first, debit Income Summary and credit Merchandise Inventory (to remove the beginning inventory); next, debit Merchandise Inventory and credit Income Summary (to enter the ending inventory).

   For unearned revenue: debit the unearned revenue account and credit the revenue account (to record revenue earned).

   For supplies used: debit Supplies Expense and credit Supplies.

   For expired insurance: debit Insurance Expense and credit Prepaid Insurance.

   For depreciation: debit Depreciation Expense and credit Accumulated Depreciation.

   For accrued salaries or wages: debit Salaries Expense or Wages Expense and credit Salaries Payable or Wages Payable.

4. Complete the work sheet.

   Carry the Income Summary account from the Adjustments columns into the Income Statement columns as two separate figures. For merchandise inventory, record the amount of the ending inventory in the Balance Sheet Debit column. For unearned revenue, record the unearned revenue account in the Balance Sheet Credit column and the revenue account in the Income Statement Credit column.

5. Journalize the adjusting entries for a merchandising business under the periodic inventory system.

   Take the adjusting entries recorded in the journal directly from the Adjustments columns of the work sheet.

6. Journalize the adjusting entry for merchandise inventory under the perpetual inventory system.

   Assuming that the amount of the physical count of the stock of merchandise is less than the recorded amount, the adjusting entry is a debit to Cost of Goods Sold (account) and a credit to Merchandise Inventory for the amount of the difference. On the other hand, if the physical count of the stock of merchandise is more than the recorded amount, the adjusting entry is to debit Merchandise Inventory and credit Cost of Goods Sold (accounts) for the amount of the difference.

Glossary

Periodic inventory system The system under which the buying of merchandise during the year is recorded as a debit to Purchases and a credit to Accounts Payable or Cash. At the end of the year, a physical count of the stock of goods is taken and adjusting entries are made to record the amount of the physical count. (443)

Perpetual inventory system The system under which the buying of merchandise during the year is recorded as a debit to Merchandise Inventory and a credit to Accounts Payable or Cash. When merchandise is sold, the cost of the merchandise is recorded as a debit to the Cost of Goods Sold account and a credit to Merchandise Inventory. At the end of the year, a physical count of the stock of goods is taken and an adjusting entry is made to record the difference between the amount of the count and the amount previously recorded. (453)

Physical inventory An actual count of the stock of goods on hand. (443)

Unearned revenue Revenue received in advance for goods or services to be delivered later; considered to be a liability until the revenue is earned. (444)

QUESTIONS, EXERCISES, AND PROBLEMS

Discussion Questions

1. What is a physical inventory? What does the word *periodic* mean in the term *periodic inventory?*
2. On the Income Summary line of a work sheet, $126,200 appears in the Income Statement Debit column, and $124,100 appears in the Income Statement Credit column. Which figure represents the beginning inventory?
3. Using the perpetual inventory system, what account is debited when a business buys more merchandise?
4. On a work sheet, where will the amount of the ending merchandise inventory be recorded?
5. What is meant by unearned revenue and why is it treated as a liability?
6. Why is it necessary to adjust the Merchandise Inventory account under a system of periodic inventories?
7. If a company begins the fiscal period with a $1,260 balance in Prepaid Insurance, would it be wrong to debit Insurance Expense for the next payment of an insurance premium?
8. When a college receives one semester's dormitory rent in advance, an entry is made debiting Cash and crediting Unearned Rent. At the end of the year, a large portion of the rent has been earned. What adjusting entry would you suggest?

Exercises

P.O. 1

Journalize adjustments for merchandise inventory.

Exercise 13-1 After adjusting entries are posted, the Merchandise Inventory account appears as on page 458. Journalize the complete entries that support these postings. The Income Summary account is numbered 313.

ACCOUNT **Merchandise Inventory**   ACCOUNT NO. **114**

	DATE		ITEM	POST. REF.	DEBIT	CREDIT	BALANCE DEBIT	BALANCE CREDIT	
1	2004								1
2	Dec.	31	Balance	✓			96 4 0 0 00		2
3	2005								3
4	Dec.	31	Adjusting	J112		96 4 0 0 00	——	——	4
5		31	Adjusting	J112	97 1 0 0 00		97 1 0 0 00		5
6									6
7									7
8									8

P.O. 2

Journalize the adjustment for unearned revenue.

Exercise 13-2 On October 31, the Igloos Hockey Club received $400,000 in cash in advance for season tickets for eight home games. The transaction was recorded as a debit to Cash and a credit to Unearned Admissions. By December 31, the end of the fiscal year, the team had played three home games and received an additional $50,000 cash admissions income at the gate.

a. Journalize the adjusting entry as of December 31.
b. List the title of the account and the related balance that will appear on the income statement.
c. List the title of the account and the related balance that will appear on the balance sheet.

P.O. 2

Determine the entries in an unearned revenue account.

Exercise 13-3 For the basketball federation's Unearned Season Tickets account, list the debits and credits for each amount posted to the account and briefly describe the transaction.

ACCOUNT **Unearned Season Tickets**   ACCOUNT NO. **214**

	DATE		ITEM	POST. REF.	DEBIT	CREDIT	BALANCE DEBIT	BALANCE CREDIT	
1	20–								1
2	Jan.	1	Balance	✓				10 2 0 0 00	2
3	Mar.	6		J71	10 2 0 0 00		——	——	3
4	Oct.	15		CR42		12 4 0 0 00		12 4 0 0 00	4
5	Nov.	1		CR43		22 1 0 0 00		34 5 0 0 00	5
6	Dec.	31	Adjusting	J99	22 5 0 0 00			12 0 0 0 00	6
7									7
8									8

P.O. 5

Determine entries in the Supplies account.

Exercise 13-4 For the Supplies ledger account on page 459, determine the debits and credits for each amount posted to the account and briefly describe each transaction. The entry of December 9 involved the return of defective goods. The purchases of December 17 involved the Beedle Company.

ACCOUNT **Supplies**   ACCOUNT NO. **115**

	DATE		ITEM	POST. REF.	DEBIT	CREDIT	BALANCE DEBIT	BALANCE CREDIT	
1	20–								1
2	Jan.	1	Balance	✓			4 2 0 00		2
3	Apr.	6		CP42	1 6 0 00		5 8 0 00		3
4	May	31		CP44	9 0 00		6 7 0 00		4
5	Nov.	21		CP53	2 2 5 00		8 9 5 00		5
6	Dec.	9		J77		4 2 00	8 5 3 00		6
7		17		J77	1 4 1 00		9 9 4 00		7
8		31	Adjusting	J78		2 2 0 00	7 7 4 00		8

P.O. 4

Place account balances in work sheet columns.

Exercise 13-5 Indicate the work sheet columns (Income Statement Debit, Income Statement Credit, Balance Sheet Debit, Balance Sheet Credit) in which the balances of the following accounts should appear:

a. F. Drexel, Drawing
b. Advertising Expense
c. Merchandise Inventory (ending)
d. Purchases Discount
e. Unearned Fees
f. Sales Returns and Allowances
g. Accumulated Depreciation, Building
h. Income Summary
i. Fees Income
j. Prepaid Rent

P.O. 2,3

Journalize adjustments for expired insurance, unearned revenue, and depreciation.

Exercise 13-6 Journalize the required adjusting entries for the year ended December 31 for Malloy Dance Studio. Begin on journal page 42.

a. On June 1 of this year, $600 was paid for a one-year insurance policy.
b. On October 1 of this year, $160 was paid for four months of advertising.
c. As of December 31, the balance of the Unearned Membership Fees account is $12,400. Of this amount, $8,200 has now been earned.
d. Equipment purchased on April 1 of this year for $3,400 is expected to have a useful life of five years and will have a trade-in value of $400. All the other equipment has been fully depreciated. The straight-line method is used.
e. As of December 31, two days' wages of $240 per day had accrued.

P.O. 2,3

Journalize adjusting entries.

Exercise 13-7 On December 31, the end of the year, the accountant for *Family Magazine* was called away suddenly because of an emergency. However, before leaving, the accountant jotted down a few notes pertaining to the adjustments. Record the necessary adjusting entries.

a. Subscriptions received in advance amounting to $136,400 were recorded as Unearned Subscriptions. At the end of the year, $90,200 has been earned.
b. Depreciation of equipment for the year is $18,600.
c. The amount of expired insurance for the year is $916.
d. The balance of Prepaid Rent is $2,800, representing four months' rent. Three months' rent has now expired.
e. Three days' salaries will be unpaid at the end of the year; total weekly (five days') salaries are $3,600.

P.O. 6
Journalize adjustment for merchandise inventory using the perpetual inventory system.

Exercise 13-8 On December 31, Benn Company took a physical count of its merchandise inventory. Benn Company operates under the perpetual inventory system. The physical count amounted to $178,400. The Merchandise Inventory account shows a balance of $180,200. Journalize the adjusting entry to Merchandise Inventory.

WHAT IF . . .

What would happen if a business spent the cash it had received in advance for services it promised to perform at a later date?

CRITICAL THINKING

On November 1, an exterior painting company received $3,420 for a paint job that will not be finished during this fiscal period. The bookkeeper inaccurately credited Painting Income instead of Unearned Painting Income. As of December 31, which is the end of the fiscal period, $1,200 worth of painting will have been completed. The bookkeeper intended to make the following adjustment at the end of the year:

Cash		Painting Income		Unearned Painting Income	
11/1 3,420		12/31 2,220	11/1 3,420		12/31 2,220

The owner wants to get a bank loan by December 1. The bank requires interim financial statements to be submitted as of December 1. How will the bookkeeper's entries affect the accuracy of the interim balance sheet and statements? What difference will the bookkeeper's methods make in the December 31 balance sheet and income statement?

A MATTER OF ETHICS

The owner of a bicycle shop allows his two sons to take bicycles home to try them out on different types of ground because he believes that they need to be familiar with the products they sell. Sometimes the bicycles are not returned to the store by the time the physical count of inventory takes place. Respond to this practice.

WEB WORK

Using an Internet web browser, type the phrase for the home page of a retail clothing company in the search box. How does it determine cost of goods sold? Discuss or write your findings in a memo to your instructor. Is cost of goods sold calculated or an amount in an account? Can you tell whether the company uses perpetual or periodic inventory?

PROBLEM SET A

For additional help, see the demonstration problem at the beginning of each chapter in your Working Papers.

P.O. 4

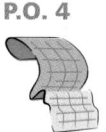

Problem 13-1A The trial balance of Tenson Company as of December 31, the end of its current fiscal year, is as follows:

Tenson Company
Work Sheet
For Year Ended December 31, 20—

	ACCOUNT NAME	TRIAL BALANCE	
		DEBIT	CREDIT
1	Cash	9 6 6 3 92	
2	Merchandise Inventory	63 4 2 2 84	
3	Store Supplies	1 5 4 1 12	
4	Prepaid Insurance	8 6 0 00	
5	Store Equipment	36 3 8 0 00	
6	Accumulated Depreciation, Store Equipment		24 2 2 0 00
7	Accounts Payable		14 4 7 8 80
8	Sales Tax Payable		3 4 3 36
9	G. O. Tenson, Capital		54 6 3 0 00
10	G. O. Tenson, Drawing	28 4 4 0 00	
11	Sales		178 0 3 6 74
12	Sales Returns and Allowances	1 3 4 3 04	
13	Purchases	76 4 6 8 46	
14	Purchases Returns and Allowances		1 7 7 8 94
15	Purchases Discount		1 5 9 7 90
16	Freight In	4 9 7 5 00	
17	Salary Expense	36 5 5 8 80	
18	Rent Expense	14 3 0 0 00	
19	Miscellaneous Expense	1 1 3 2 56	
20		275 0 8 5 74	275 0 8 5 74
21			

Here are the data for the adjustments.

a–b. Merchandise Inventory at December 31, $65,832.56.
c. Store supplies inventory, $486.40.
d. Insurance expired, $390.
e. Salaries accrued, $592.
f. Depreciation of store equipment, $2,880.

Check Figure

Net income, $44,128.72

Instructions

Complete the work sheet after entering the account names and balances into the work sheet.

Problem 13-2A The balances of the ledger accounts of Tallon Furniture as of December 31, the end of its fiscal year, are as follows:

Tallon Furniture
Work Sheet
For Year Ended December 31, 20—

	ACCOUNT NAME	TRIAL BALANCE DEBIT	TRIAL BALANCE CREDIT
1	Cash	11 692 00	
2	Accounts Receivable	42 862 00	
3	Merchandise Inventory	121 738 00	
4	Store Supplies	1 670 00	
5	Prepaid Insurance	1 528 00	
6	Store Equipment	37 024 00	
7	Accumulated Depreciation, Store Equipment		29 520 00
8	Office Equipment	9 536 00	
9	Accumulated Depreciation, Office Equipment		1 820 00
10	Accounts Payable		29 822 00
11	Unearned Rent		3 100 00
12	Notes Payable		5 000 00
13	P. Tallon, Capital		121 532 00
14	P. Tallon, Drawing	27 500 00	
15	Sales		650 500 00
16	Sales Returns and Allowances	9 648 00	
17	Purchases	518 474 00	
18	Purchases Returns and Allowances		13 340 00
19	Purchases Discount		7 734 00
20	Freight In	24 624 00	
21	Wages Expense	55 300 00	
22	Interest Expense	772 00	
23		862 368 00	862 368 00
24			

Data for the adjustments are as follows:

a–b. Merchandise Inventory at December 31, $102,676.
c. Store supplies inventory at December 31, $832.
d. Insurance expired during the year, $541.
e. Wages accrued at December 31, $1,256.
f. Depreciation of store equipment, $5,664.
g. Depreciation of office equipment, $1,532.
h. Rent earned, $2,200.

Check Figure

Net income, $36,063

Instructions

1. Complete the work sheet after entering the account names and balances into the work sheet.
2. Journalize the adjusting entries.

P.O. 4,5

Problem 13-3A The accounts in the ledger of Monty's Mountain Shop, with the balances as of December 31, the end of its fiscal year, are as follows:

Monty's Mountain Shop
Work Sheet
For Year Ended December 31, 20—

	ACCOUNT NAME	TRIAL BALANCE DEBIT	TRIAL BALANCE CREDIT
1	Cash	12 5 0 0 00	
2	Accounts Receivable	2 1 4 0 00	
3	Merchandise Inventory	120 5 0 0 00	
4	Store Supplies	1 5 2 0 00	
5	Prepaid Insurance	3 0 4 0 00	
6	Land	48 0 0 0 00	
7	Building	108 0 0 0 00	
8	Accumulated Depreciation, Building		16 6 0 0 00
9	Store Equipment	36 4 0 0 00	
10	Accumulated Depreciation, Store Equipment		11 6 0 0 00
11	Accounts Payable		14 6 5 0 00
12	Sales Tax Payable		4 1 9 2 00
13	Notes Payable		5 0 0 0 00
14	B. Monty, Capital		216 1 3 5 00
15	B. Monty, Drawing	44 2 0 0 00	
16	Sales		467 5 5 0 00
17	Sales Returns and Allowances	2 6 3 4 00	
18	Purchases	284 7 1 9 00	
19	Purchases Returns and Allowances		5 5 6 0 00
20	Purchases Discount		3 6 7 1 00
21	Freight In	7 8 6 8 00	
22	Salary Expense	58 6 7 3 00	
23	Advertising Expense	7 2 5 9 00	
24	Utilities Expense	5 8 9 5 00	
25	Miscellaneous Expense	8 4 0 00	
26	Interest Expense	7 7 0 00	
27		744 9 5 8 00	744 9 5 8 00

Data for the adjustments are as follows:

a–b. Merchandise Inventory at December 31, $104,682.
c. Store supplies inventory at December 31, $620.
d. Insurance expired during the year, $2,040.
e. Salaries accrued at December 31, $1,865.
f. Depreciation of building, $2,142.
g. Depreciation of store equipment, $2,731.

Check Figure

Net income, $82,627

Instructions

1. Complete the work sheet after entering the account names and balances into the work sheet.
2. Journalize the adjusting entries.

Instructions for General Ledger Software

1. Record the adjusting entries in the general journal.
2. Print the journal.
3. Post the general journal amounts to the general ledger.
4. Print a trial balance.
5. Print the income statement, statement of owner's equity, and balance sheet.

P.O. 4,5

Problem 13-4A A portion of the worksheet of Hurst Oxygen Company for the year ending December 31 is as follows:

	ACCOUNT NAME	INCOME STATEMENT		BALANCE SHEET		
		DEBIT	CREDIT	DEBIT	CREDIT	
1	Cash			9 3 4 0 00		1
2	Merchandise Inventory			76 9 4 0 00		2
3	Supplies			2 5 6 00		3
4	Prepaid Insurance			2 4 0 00		4
5	Store Equipment			39 2 8 0 00		5
6	Accumulated Depreciation, Store Equipment				26 2 2 0 00	6
7	Accounts Payable				14 6 0 0 00	7
8	P. R. Hurst, Capital				68 9 4 0 00	8
9	P. R. Hurst, Drawing			27 6 0 0 00		9
10	Sales		173 4 2 0 00			10
11	Sales Returns and Allowances	1 5 2 0 00				11
12	Purchases	82 3 1 2 00				12
13	Purchases Returns and Allowances		9 4 0 00			13
14	Purchases Discount		1 6 0 0 00			14
15	Freight In	1 9 4 8 00				15
16	Salary Expense	37 5 6 0 00				16
17	Rent Expense	14 8 0 0 00				17
18	Income Summary	65 6 8 0 00	76 9 4 0 00			18
19	Supplies Expense	9 4 4 00				19
20	Insurance Expense	7 6 0 00				20
21	Depreciation Expense, Store Equipment	4 0 4 0 00				21
22	Salaries Payable				5 6 0 00	22
23		209 5 6 4 00	252 9 0 0 00	153 6 5 6 00	110 3 2 0 00	23
24						24

Check Figure

Salaries accrued, $560

Instructions

1. Determine the entries that appeared in the Adjustments columns and present them in general journal form.
2. Determine the net income for the year.
3. What is the amount of the ending capital?

PROBLEM SET B

For additional help, see the demonstration problem at the beginning of each chapter in your Working Papers.

P.O. 4

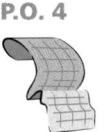

Problem 13-1B The trial balance of Halaka Company as of December 31, the end of its current fiscal year, is as follows:

Halaka Company
Work Sheet
For Year Ended December 31, 20—

	ACCOUNT NAME	TRIAL BALANCE DEBIT	TRIAL BALANCE CREDIT
1	Cash	9 0 3 6 54	
2	Merchandise Inventory	62 9 5 4 82	
3	Store Supplies	1 3 6 6 84	
4	Prepaid Insurance	1 1 2 0 00	
5	Store Equipment	37 2 4 0 00	
6	Accumulated Depreciation, Store Equipment		24 7 3 6 00
7	Accounts Payable		14 1 8 6 96
8	Sales Tax Payable		3 4 6 98
9	O. G. Halaka, Capital		54 7 5 9 00
10	O. G. Halaka, Drawing	28 9 0 0 00	
11	Sales		178 9 6 6 34
12	Sales Returns and Allowances	1 3 9 3 84	
13	Purchases	79 8 0 0 84	
14	Purchases Returns and Allowances		1 7 5 7 82
15	Purchases Discount		1 6 0 3 64
16	Freight In	2 7 3 7 00	
17	Salary Expense	36 4 6 8 86	
18	Rent Expense	14 3 0 0 00	
19	Miscellaneous Expense	1 0 3 8 00	
20		276 3 5 6 74	276 3 5 6 74

Here are the data for the adjustments:

a–b. Merchandise Inventory at December 31, $64,749.80.
c. Store supplies inventory, $504.32.
d. Insurance expired, $636.
e. Salaries accrued, $686.80.
f. Depreciation of store equipment, $3,810.

Check Figure

Net income, $42,388.92

Instructions

Complete the work sheet after entering the account names and balances into the work sheet.

P.O. 4,5

Problem 13-2B The balances of the ledger accounts of Balar Home Center as of June 30, the end of its fiscal year, are as follows:

Balar Home Center
Work Sheet
For Year Ended June 30, 20—

	ACCOUNT NAME	TRIAL BALANCE DEBIT	TRIAL BALANCE CREDIT
1	Cash	14 875 00	
2	Accounts Receivable	51 200 00	
3	Merchandise Inventory	72 800 00	
4	Supplies	1 570 00	
5	Prepaid Insurance	1 180 00	
6	Store Equipment	26 690 00	
7	Accumulated Depreciation, Store Equipment		16 300 00
8	Office Equipment	9 500 00	
9	Accumulated Depreciation, Office Equipment		4 715 00
10	Accounts Payable		29 922 00
11	Unearned Rent		3 100 00
12	Notes Payable		3 500 00
13	F. C. Balar, Capital		121 532 00
14	F. C. Balar, Drawing	25 800 00	
15	Sales		452 886 00
16	Sales Returns and Allowances	3 110 00	
17	Purchases	368 110 00	
18	Purchases Returns and Allowances		7 270 00
19	Purchases Discount		2 180 00
20	Freight In	13 590 00	
21	Salary Expense	52 250 00	
22	Interest Expense	730 00	
23		641 405 00	641 405 00

Here are the data for the adjustments:

a–b. Merchandise Inventory at June 30, $112,326.
c. Supplies inventory at June 30, $374.
d. Insurance expired during the year, $1,012.
e. Salaries accrued at June 30, $2,100.
f. Depreciation of store equipment, $3,645.
g. Depreciation of office equipment, $1,827.
h. Rent earned, $2,125.

Check Figure

Net income, $56,417

Instructions

1. Complete the work sheet after entering the account names and balances into the work sheet.
2. Journalize the adjusting entries.

P.O. 4,5

Problem 13-3B Here are the accounts in the ledger of Pollard's Jewel Box, with the balances as of December 31, the end of its fiscal year.

Pollard's Jewel Box
Work Sheet
For Year Ended December 31, 20—

	ACCOUNT NAME	TRIAL BALANCE DEBIT	TRIAL BALANCE CREDIT
1	Cash	11 3 8 0 00	
2	Accounts Receivable	1 4 5 4 00	
3	Merchandise Inventory	116 0 0 0 00	
4	Store Supplies	1 3 8 4 00	
5	Prepaid Insurance	2 1 8 6 00	
6	Land	16 0 0 0 00	
7	Building	77 0 0 0 00	
8	Accumulated Depreciation, Building		29 2 4 0 00
9	Store Equipment	77 5 9 0 00	
10	Accumulated Depreciation, Store Equipment		17 2 6 0 00
11	Accounts Payable		14 1 7 0 00
12	Sales Tax Payable		2 6 8 4 00
13	Notes Payable		5 0 0 0 00
14	L. Pollard, Capital		190 4 3 8 00
15	L. Pollard, Drawing	46 4 0 0 00	
16	Sales		379 3 5 4 00
17	Sales Returns and Allowances	3 7 8 8 00	
18	Purchases	250 8 6 8 00	
19	Purchases Returns and Allowances		3 1 6 1 00
20	Purchases Discount		4 5 1 0 00
21	Freight In	12 1 0 0 00	
22	Salary Expense	23 5 0 0 00	
23	Advertising Expense	2 0 2 6 00	
24	Utilities Expense	1 2 5 8 00	
25	Miscellaneous Expense	8 2 3 00	
26	Interest Expense	2 0 6 0 00	
27		645 8 1 7 00	645 8 1 7 00

Here are the data for the adjustments.

a–b. Merchandise Inventory at December 31, $115,327.
c. Store supplies inventory at December 31, $847.
d. Insurance expired during the year, $890.
e. Salaries accrued at December 31, $1,289.
f. Depreciation of building, $3,860.
g. Depreciation of store equipment, $4,182.

Check Figure

Net income, $79,171

Instructions

1. Complete the work sheet after entering the account names and balances into the work sheet.
2. Journalize the adjusting entries.

Instructions for General Ledger Software

1. Record the adjusting entries in the general journal.
2. Print the journal.
3. Post the general journal amounts to the general ledger.
4. Print a trial balance.
5. Print the income statement, statement of owner's equity, and balance sheet.

P.O. 4,5

Problem 13-4B A portion of the work sheet of Susan's Flowers for the year ending December 31 is as follows:

	ACCOUNT NAME	INCOME STATEMENT DEBIT	INCOME STATEMENT CREDIT	BALANCE SHEET DEBIT	BALANCE SHEET CREDIT	
1	Cash			7 7 3 6 00		1
2	Merchandise Inventory			74 2 9 8 00		2
3	Supplies			2 9 8 00		3
4	Prepaid Insurance			2 5 0 00		4
5	Store Equipment			37 9 6 0 00		5
6	Accumulated Depreciation, Store Equipment				29 4 4 0 00	6
7	Accounts Payable				13 7 6 0 00	7
8	S. R. Hale, Capital				75 1 4 2 00	8
9	S. R. Hale, Drawing			30 8 0 0 00		9
10	Sales		171 8 1 6 00			10
11	Sales Returns and Allowances	1 4 3 4 00				11
12	Purchases	85 9 3 4 00				12
13	Purchases Returns and Allowances		9 6 4 00			13
14	Purchases Discount		1 6 3 6 00			14
15	Freight In	2 6 5 8 00				15
16	Salary Expense	37 8 5 2 00				16
17	Rent Expense	14 4 0 0 00				17
18	Income Summary	68 2 2 8 00	74 2 9 8 00			18
19	Depreciation Expense, Store Equipment	4 3 6 0 00				19
20	Insurance Expense	5 5 2 00				20
21	Supplies Expense	8 8 4 00				21
22	Salaries Payable				5 8 8 00	22
23		216 3 0 2 00	248 7 1 4 00	151 3 4 2 00	118 9 3 0 00	23

Check Figure

Accrued salaries, $588

Instructions

1. Determine the entries that appeared in the Adjustments columns and present them in general journal form.
2. Determine the net income for the year.
3. What is the amount of the ending capital?

14 Financial Statements, Closing Entries, and Reversing Entries

Performance Objectives

After you have completed this chapter, you will be able to do the following:

1. Prepare a classified income statement for a merchandising firm.

2. Prepare a classified balance sheet for any type of business.

3. Compute working capital and current ratio.

4. Journalize the closing entries for a merchandising firm.

5. Determine which adjusting entries can be reversed, and journalize the reversing entries.

This chapter again demonstrates how to prepare financial statements directly from a work sheet. We also explain the functions of closing entries and reversing entries as means of completing the accounting cycle. Finally, we look at the financial statements in their entirety, and explain their various subdivisions.

FYI

Accountants sometimes number contra accounts as subaccounts. For example, Accumulated Depreciation, Building, is 122.1, Sales Returns and Allowances is 411.1, Sales Discount is 411.2, Purchases Returns and Allowances is 511.1, and so on.

First, here is the chart of accounts for Jackson Electric Supply.

Assets (100–199)

111 Cash
112 Notes Receivable
113 Accounts Receivable
114 Merchandise Inventory
115 Supplies
116 Prepaid Insurance
121 Land
122 Building
123 Accumulated Depreciation, Building
124 Equipment
125 Accumulated Depreciation, Equipment

Liabilities (200–299)

211 Wages Payable
213 Notes Payable
217 Unearned Course Fees
221 Accounts Payable
251 Mortgage Payable

Owner's Equity (300–399)

311 N. C. Jackson, Capital
312 N. C. Jackson, Drawing
313 Income Summary

Revenue (400–499)

411 Sales
412 Sales Returns and Allowances
413 Sales Discount
421 Course Fees Income
422 Interest Income

Cost of Goods Sold (500–599)

511 Purchases
512 Purchases Returns and Allowances
513 Purchases Discount
514 Freight In

Expenses (600–699)

621 Wages Expense
622 Depreciation Expense, Building
623 Supplies Expense
631 Depreciation Expense, Equipment
632 Taxes Expense
633 Insurance Expense
634 Interest Expense

THE INCOME STATEMENT

Objective 1

Prepare a classified income statement for a merchandising firm.

As you know, the work sheet is merely a tool used by accountants to prepare the financial statements. In Figure 1, we present the part of the work sheet for Jackson Electric Supply that includes the Income Statement columns. Of course, **each of the amounts that appear in the Income Statement columns of the work sheet will also be used in the income statement.** Notice that the amounts for the beginning and ending merchandise inventory appear separately on the Income Summary line. Figure 2 on page 472 shows the entire income statement. Pause for a while and look it over carefully; then we will break it down into its components.

The income statement follows a logical pattern that is much the same for any type of merchandising business. The ability to interpret the income statement and extract parts from it is very useful when gathering information for decisions. To realize the full value of an income statement, however, you need to know the basic format of an income statement. Let's look at the statement section by section.

Net Sales	$232,460
− Cost of Goods Sold	99,620
Gross Profit	$132,840
− Operating Expenses	69,285
Income from Operations	$ 63,555

Jackson Electric Supply
Work Sheet
For Year Ended December 31, 20—

	ACCOUNT NAME	TRIAL BALANCE DEBIT	TRIAL BALANCE CREDIT	ADJUSTMENTS DEBIT	ADJUSTMENTS CREDIT	INCOME STATEMENT DEBIT	INCOME STATEMENT CREDIT
1	Cash	21 1 5 4 00					
2	Notes Receivable	4 0 0 0 00					
3	Accounts Receivable	29 4 4 6 00					
4	Merchandise Inventory	77 0 0 0 00		(b) 64 9 0 0 00	(a) 77 0 0 0 00		
5	Supplies	1 4 4 0 00			(d) 9 2 5 00		
6	Prepaid Insurance	9 6 0 00			(e) 3 8 0 00		
7	Land	12 0 0 0 00					
8	Building	96 0 0 0 00					
9	Accumulated Depr.,						
10	Building		32 0 0 0 00		(f) 5 0 0 0 00		
11	Equipment	33 6 0 0 00					
12	Accumulated Depr.,						
13	Equipment		16 4 0 0 00		(g) 4 0 0 0 00		
14	Unearned Course Fees		1 2 0 0 00				
15	Accounts Payable		36 4 0 0 00				
16	Notes Payable		3 0 0 0 00				
17	Mortgage Payable		8 0 0 0 00	(c) 9 0 0 00			
18	N. C. Jackson, Capital		140 5 7 4 00				
19	N. C. Jackson, Drawing	48 9 0 0 00					
20	Sales		235 1 8 0 00				235 1 8 0 00
21	Sales Returns and						
22	Allowances	8 4 0 00				8 4 0 00	
23	Sales Discount	1 8 8 0 00				1 8 8 0 00	
24	Interest Income		1 2 0 00				1 2 0 00
25	Purchases	89 1 4 0 00				89 1 4 0 00	
26	Purchases Returns						
27	and Allowances		2 8 3 2 00				2 8 3 2 00
28	Purchases Discount		1 2 4 8 00				1 2 4 8 00
29	Freight In	2 4 6 0 00				2 4 6 0 00	
30	Wages Expense	55 8 0 0 00		(h) 1 2 2 0 00		57 0 2 0 00	
31	Taxes Expense	1 9 6 0 00				1 9 6 0 00	
32	Interest Expense	3 7 4 00				3 7 4 00	
33		476 9 5 4 00	476 9 5 4 00				
34	Income Summary			(a) 77 0 0 0 00	(b) 64 9 0 0 00	77 0 0 0 00	64 9 0 0 00
35	Course Fees Income				(c) 9 0 0 00		9 0 0 00
36	Supplies Expense			(d) 9 2 5 00		9 2 5 00	
37	Insurance Expense			(e) 3 8 0 00		3 8 0 00	
38	Depreciation Expense,						
39	Building			(f) 5 0 0 0 00		5 0 0 0 00	
40	Depreciation Expense,						
41	Equipment			(g) 4 0 0 0 00		4 0 0 0 00	
42	Wages Payable				(h) 1 2 2 0 00		
43				154 3 2 5 00	154 3 2 5 00	240 9 7 9 00	305 1 8 0 00
44	Net Income					64 2 0 1 00	
45						305 1 8 0 00	305 1 8 0 00
46							

FIGURE 1

To illustrate the concepts of **gross** and **net**, here is an example of a simple single-sale transaction.

Several years ago, Billie Reed bought an antique table at a second-hand store for $90. She decided to sell the table for $140. She advertised in the daily newspaper at a cost of $5. How much did she make as clear profit?

Sale of table	$140
Less cost of table	90
Gross Profit	$ 50
Less Advertising Expense	5
Net Income or Net Profit (gain on the sale)	$ 45

FIGURE 2

Jackson Electric Supply
Income Statement
For Year Ended December 31, 20—

Revenue from Sales:					
Sales			$ 235 1 8 0 00		
Less: Sales Returns and Allowances	$ 8 4 0 00				
Sales Discount	1 8 8 0 00	2 7 2 0 00			
Net Sales				$ 232 4 6 0 00	
Cost of Goods Sold:					
Merchandise Inventory, January 1, 20—			$ 77 0 0 0 00		
Purchases	$ 89 1 4 0 00				
Less: Purchases Returns and					
Allowances $2,832.00					
Purchases Discount 1,248.00	4 0 8 0 00				
Net Purchases	$ 85 0 6 0 00				
Add Freight In	2 4 6 0 00				
Delivered Cost of Purchases		87 5 2 0 00			
Goods Available for Sale		$ 164 5 2 0 00			
Less Merchandise Inventory, December 31, 20—		64 9 0 0 00			
Cost of Goods Sold				99 6 2 0 00	
Gross Profit				$ 132 8 4 0 00	
Operating Expenses:					
Wages Expense		$ 57 0 2 0 00			
Taxes Expense		1 9 6 0 00			
Supplies Expense		9 2 5 00			
Insurance Expense		3 8 0 00			
Depreciation Expense, Building		5 0 0 0 00			
Depreciation Expense, Equipment		4 0 0 0 00			
Total Operating Expenses				69 2 8 5 00	
Income from Operations				$ 63 5 5 5 00	
Other Income:					
Course Fees Income		$ 9 0 0 00			
Interest Income		1 2 0 00			
Total Other Income		$ 1 0 2 0 00			
Other Expenses:					
Interest Expense		3 7 4 00		6 4 6 00	
Net Income				$ 64 2 0 1 00	

Gross Profit is the profit on the sale of the table before any expenses have been deducted; in this case, it is $50. **Net Income**, or **Net Profit**, is the final or clear profit after all expenses have been deducted. In a single-sale situation such as this, we refer to the final outcome as the net profit. But for a business that has many sales and expenses, most accountants prefer the term *net income*. Regardless of which word you use, *net* refers to clear profit—after all expenses have been deducted.

Revenue from Sales

Now let's look at the Revenue from Sales section of the income statement for Jackson Electric Supply:

Revenue from Sales:								
Sales					$ 235 1 8 0 00			
Less: Sales Returns and Allowances	$	8 4 0 00						
Sales Discount	1 8 8 0 00			2 7 2 0 00				
Net Sales						$ 232 4 6 0 00		

When we introduced Sales Returns and Allowances and Sales Discount, we treated them as deductions from Sales. You can see that in the income statement, they are deducted from Sales to give us **Net Sales**. Note that we record these items in the same order in which they appear in the ledger.

Cost of Goods Sold

The section of the income statement that requires the greatest amount of concentration is the **Cost of Goods Sold** section, where the cost of the goods we sold is computed. Let's repeat it in its entirety:

Remember!
Returns and Allowances (Sales or Purchases) is listed on one line, and Discount (Sales or Purchases) is listed below.

Cost of Goods Sold:					
Merchandise Inventory, January 1, 20—			$ 77 0 0 0 00		
Purchases		$ 89 1 4 0 00			
Less: Purchases Returns and					
Allowances $2,832.00					
Purchases Discount 1,248.00		4 0 8 0 00			
Net Purchases		$ 85 0 6 0 00			
Add Freight In		2 4 6 0 00			
Delivered Cost of Purchases			87 5 2 0 00		
Goods Available for Sale			$ 164 5 2 0 00		
Less Merchandise Inventory, December 31, 20—			64 9 0 0 00		
Cost of Goods Sold				$ 99 6 2 0 00	

First, look closely at the Purchases section.

Purchases						$89	1	4	0	00					
Less: Purchases Returns															
and Allowances		$2,832.00													
Purchases Discount		1,248.00				4	0	8	0	00					
Net Purchases						$85	0	6	0	00					
Add Freight In						2	4	6	0	00					
Delivered Cost of Purchases											$87	5	2	0	00

Note the parallel to the Revenue from Sales section. To arrive at **Net Purchases**, we deduct the sum of Purchases Returns and Allowances and Purchases Discount from Purchases. To complete the Purchases section, we add Freight In to Net Purchases to get **Delivered Cost of Purchases**.

Now look at the full Cost of Goods Sold section. You might think of Cost of Goods Sold like this:

Amount we started with (beginning inventory)	$ 77,000
+ Net amount we purchased, including freight charges	87,520
Total amount that could have been sold (available)	$164,520
− Amount left over (ending inventory)	64,900
Cost of the goods that were actually sold	$ 99,620

Here's the Cost of Goods Sold expressed in proper wording.

Merchandise Inventory, January 1, 20—	$ 77,000
+ Delivered Cost of Purchases	87,520
Goods Available for Sale	$164,520
− Merchandise Inventory, December 31, 20—	64,900
Cost of Goods Sold	$ 99,620

The Cost of Goods Sold account begins with current inventory and adjusts for Purchases, Purchases Returns and Allowances, Discounts, and Freight In to arrive at a new inventory figure, from which the actual cost of goods sold can be determined.

Operating Expenses

Operating expenses, as the name implies, are the regular expenses of doing business. We list the accounts and their respective balances in the order in which they appear in the ledger.

Many firms use subclassifications of operating expenses, such as the following:

1. **Selling Expenses** Any expenses directly connected with the selling activity, such as

   - Sales Salaries Expense
   - Sales Commissions Expense
   - Advertising Expense
   - Store Supplies Expense
   - Delivery Expense
   - Depreciation Expense, Store Equipment

2. **General Expenses** Any expenses related to the office or administration, or any expense that cannot be directly connected with a selling activity:

   - Office Salaries Expense
   - Taxes Expense
   - Depreciation Expense, Office Equipment
   - Rent Expense
   - Insurance Expense
   - Office Supplies Expense

If the Cash Short and Over account has a debit balance (net shortage), the balance is added to and reported as Miscellaneous General Expense. Conversely, if the Cash Short and Over account has a credit balance (net overage), the balance is added to and reported as Miscellaneous Income, which is classified as Other Income.

Income from Operations

Now let's repeat the skeleton outline:

Net Sales
− Cost of Goods Sold
_____

Gross Profit
− Operating Expenses
_____

Income from Operations

If Operating Expenses are the regular, recurring expenses of doing business, then Income from Operations should be the regular or recurring income from normal business operations. When you compare the results of operations over a number of years, Income from Operations is the figure to use as a basis for comparison.

Other Income and Other Expenses

The Other Income classification, as the name implies, includes any revenue account other than Revenue from Sales. What we are trying to do is to isolate Sales at the top of the income statement as the major revenue account, so that the Gross Profit figure represents the profit made on the sale of merchandise *only*. Additional accounts that may appear under the heading of Other Income are Rent Income (the firm is subletting part of its premises),

Jackson Electric Supply
Work Sheet
For Year Ended December 31, 20—

	ACCOUNT NAME	TRIAL BALANCE DEBIT	TRIAL BALANCE CREDIT	ADJUSTMENTS DEBIT	ADJUSTMENTS CREDIT	BALANCE SHEET DEBIT	BALANCE SHEET CREDIT	
1	Cash	21 1 5 4 00				21 1 5 4 00		1
2	Notes Receivable	4 0 0 0 00				4 0 0 0 00		2
3	Accounts Receiv.	29 4 4 6 00				29 4 4 6 00		3
4	Merchandise Inven.	77 0 0 0 00		(b) 64 9 0 0 00	(a) 77 0 0 0 00	64 9 0 0 00		4
5	Supplies	1 4 4 0 00			(d) 9 2 5 00	5 1 5 00		5
6	Prepaid Insurance	9 6 0 00			(e) 3 8 0 00	5 8 0 00		6
7	Land	12 0 0 0 00				12 0 0 0 00		7
8	Building	96 0 0 0 00				96 0 0 0 00		8
9	Accum. Depr., Build.		32 0 0 0 00		(f) 5 0 0 0 00		37 0 0 0 00	9
10	Equipment	33 6 0 0 00				33 6 0 0 00		10
11	Accum. Depr., Equip.		16 4 0 0 00		(g) 4 0 0 0 00		20 4 0 0 00	11
12	Accounts Payable		36 4 0 0 00				36 4 0 0 00	12
13	Unearn. Course Fees		1 2 0 0 00	(c) 9 0 0 00			3 0 0 00	13
14	Notes Payable		3 0 0 0 00				3 0 0 0 00	14
15	Mortgage Payable		8 0 0 0 00				8 0 0 0 00	15
16	N. C. Jackson,							16
17	Capital		140 5 7 4 00				140 5 7 4 00	17
18	N. C. Jackson, Draw.	48 9 0 0 00				48 9 0 0 00		18
19	Sales		235 1 8 0 00					19
20	Sales Returns and							20
21	Allowances	8 4 0 00						21
22	Sales Discount	1 8 8 0 00						22
23	Interest Income		1 2 0 00					23
24	Purchases	89 1 4 0 00						24
25	Purchases Returns							25
26	and Allowances		2 8 3 2 00					26
27	Purchases Discount		1 2 4 8 00					27
28	Freight In	2 4 6 0 00						28
29	Wages Expense	55 8 0 0 00		(h) 1 2 2 0 00				29
30	Taxes Expense	1 9 6 0 00						30
31	Interest Expense	3 7 4 00						31
32		476 9 5 4 00	476 9 5 4 00					32
33	Income Summary			(a) 77 0 0 0 00	(b) 64 9 0 0 00			33
34	Course Fees Income				(c) 9 0 0 00			34
35	Supplies Expense			(d) 9 2 5 00				35
36	Insurance Expense			(e) 3 8 0 00				36
37	Depr. Expense,							37
38	Building			(f) 5 0 0 0 00				38
39	Depr. Expense,							39
40	Equipment			(g) 4 0 0 0 00				40
41	Wages Payable				(h) 1 2 2 0 00		1 2 2 0 00	41
42				154 3 2 5 00	154 3 2 5 00	311 0 9 5 00	246 8 9 4 00	42
43	Net Income						64 2 0 1 00	43
44						311 0 9 5 00	311 0 9 5 00	44
45								45

FIGURE 3

FIGURE 4

Jackson Electric Supply
Statement of Owner's Equity
For Year Ended December 31, 20—

N. C. Jackson, Capital, January 1, 20—								$	136	5	7	4	00
Additional Investment,													
August 26, 20—									4	0	0	0	00
Total Investment								$140	5	7	4	00
Net Income for the Year	$	64	2	0	1	00							
Less Withdrawals for the Year		48	9	0	0	00							
Increase in Capital													
N. C. Jackson, Capital,													
December 31, 20—								$	155	8	7	5	00

Remember!

The columns *do not* represent debit or credit columns. The columns are for making computations and listing totals.

Interest Income (the firm holds an interest-bearing note or contract), Gain on Disposal of Plant and Equipment (the firm makes a profit on the sale of plant and equipment), and Miscellaneous Income (the firm has an overage recorded in the Cash Short and Over account).

The classification Other Expenses records various nonoperating expenses, such as Interest Expense or Loss on Disposal of Plant and Equipment.

THE STATEMENT OF OWNER'S EQUITY AND THE BALANCE SHEET

Remember!

Net income appears on both the income statement and the statement of owner's equity.

Figure 3 is a partial work sheet for Jackson Electric Supply. Here again we find that **every figure in the Balance Sheet columns of the work sheet is used in either the statement of owner's equity or the balance sheet.**

Preparation of the financial statements follows the same order we presented before: first, the income statement; second, the statement of owner's equity; third, the balance sheet. The statement of owner's equity shows why the balance of the Capital account has changed from the beginning of the fiscal period to the end of it. In preparing the statement of owner's equity, always look into the ledger for the owner's Capital account to find any changes, such as additional investments, made during the year.

In Figure 4, observe that the balance of N. C. Jackson, Capital, listed on the work sheet is $140,574. Also note $4,000 in the completed statement of owner's equity, representing an additional investment. Therefore, the beginning balance of N. C. Jackson, Capital, was $136,574 ($140,574 − $4,000).

BALANCE SHEET CLASSIFICATIONS

Objective 2

Prepare a classified balance sheet for any type of business.

Balance sheet classifications are generally uniform for all types of business enterprises. You are strongly urged to take the time to learn the following definitions of the classifications and the order of accounts within them. As you read, refer to Figure 5 on the following page.

Jackson Electric Supply
Balance Sheet
December 31, 20—

Assets				
Current Assets:				
Cash			$ 21 1 5 4 00	
Notes Receivable			4 0 0 0 00	
Accounts Receivable			29 4 4 6 00	
Merchandise Inventory			64 9 0 0 00	
Supplies			5 1 5 00	
Prepaid Insurance			5 8 0 00	
Total Current Assets				$ 120 5 9 5 00
Plant and Equipment:				
Land			$ 12 0 0 0 00	
Building	$ 96 0 0 0 00			
Less Accumulated Depreciation	37 0 0 0 00		59 0 0 0 00	
Equipment	$ 33 6 0 0 00			
Less Accumulated Depreciation	20 4 0 0 00		13 2 0 0 00	
Total Plant and Equipment				84 2 0 0 00
Total Assets				$ 204 7 9 5 00
Liabilities				
Current Liabilities:				
Mortgage Payable (current portion)			$ 2 0 0 0 00	
Accounts Payable			36 4 0 0 00	
Notes Payable			3 0 0 0 00	
Wages Payable			1 2 2 0 00	
Unearned Course Fees			3 0 0 00	
Total Current Liabilities				$ 42 9 2 0 00
Long-Term Liabilities:				
Mortgage Payable				6 0 0 0 00
Total Liabilities				$ 48 9 2 0 00
Owner's Equity				
N. C. Jackson, Capital				155 8 7 5 00
Total Liabilities and Owner's Equity				$ 204 7 9 5 00

FIGURE 5

FYI

Some companies are so successful that they accumulate cash from earnings that is not needed to pay current obligations. Rather than leaving the cash in a bank account, companies may prefer to invest it in short-term government or corporate notes or bonds. These are called marketable securities. On the balance sheet, Marketable Securities is a separate account listed just below Cash.

Current Assets

Current Assets consist of cash and any other assets or resources that are expected to be realized in cash or to be sold or consumed during the normal operating cycle of the business (or one year, if the normal operating cycle is less than twelve months).

Accountants list current assets in the order of their convertibility into cash—in other words, their liquidity. (If you've got an asset such as a car or a stereo and you sell it quickly and turn it into cash, you are said to be turning it into a *liquid* state.) If the first four accounts shown under Current Assets in Figure 5 are present, they are always recorded in the same order: (1) Cash, (2) Notes Receivable, (3) Accounts Receivable, and (4) Merchandise Inventory.

The barn, the tractor, and the land this man is working are all classified as fixed assets in the Plant and Equipment account. Only the barn and tractor, however, are subject to depreciation.

Remember!

Since Accumulated Depreciation is a contra account, it is deducted from the appropriate asset.

Objective 3

Compute working capital and current ratio.

Notes Receivable (current) are short-term (one year or less) promissory notes (promise-to-pay notes) held by the firm. A note is generally received from a customer as a substitute for a charge account.

Supplies and Prepaid Insurance are considered prepaid items that will be used up or will expire within the following operating cycle or year. Generally, these prepaid items are not converted into cash and that's why they appear at the bottom of the Current Assets section. There is no particular reason to list Supplies before Prepaid Insurance. Prepaid Insurance could just as easily have preceded Supplies.

Plant and Equipment

Plant and Equipment are relatively long-lived assets that are held for use in the production or sale of other assets or services; some accountants refer to them as *fixed assets*. The three types of accounts that usually appear in this category are Land, Building, and Equipment (refer to Figure 5). Note that the Building and Equipment accounts are followed by their respective Accumulated Depreciation accounts. We list these assets in order of their length of life, with the longest-lived asset placed first.

Current Liabilities

Current liabilities are debts that will become due within the normal operating cycle of the business, usually within one year; they normally will be paid, when due, from current assets. List current liabilities in the order of their expected payment. Mortgage Payable is the payment one makes to reduce the principal of the mortgage in a given year. Accounts Payable are debts owed to creditors. Wages Payable and any other accrued liabilities, such as Commissions Payable and the current portion of unearned revenue accounts, usually fall at the bottom of the list of current liabilities.

Long-Term Liabilities

Long-term Liabilities are debts that are payable over a comparatively long period, usually longer than one year. Ordinarily, Mortgage Payable is the only account in this category for a sole-proprietorship (or one-owner) type of business. One single amount in a category can be placed in the column on the extreme right.

Working Capital and Current Ratio

Both the management and the short-term creditors of a firm are vitally interested in two questions:

1. Does the firm have a sufficient amount of capital to operate?
2. Does the firm have the ability to pay its debts?

Two measures used to answer these questions are a firm's working capital and its current ratio; the necessary data are taken from a classified balance sheet.

Working capital is determined by subtracting current liabilities from current assets; thus,

Working Capital = Current Assets − Current Liabilities

The normal operating cycle for most firms is less than one year. Because current assets equal cash—or items that can be converted into cash or used up within one year—and current liabilities equal the total amount that the company must pay out within one year, working capital is appropriately named. It is the amount of capital the company has available to use or to work with. The working capital for Jackson Electric Supply is as follows:

Working Capital = $120,595 − $42,920 = $77,675

The **current ratio** is useful in revealing a firm's ability to pay its bills. It is determined by dividing current assets by current liabilities:

$$\text{Current Ratio} = \frac{\text{Current Assets (amount coming in within one year)}}{\text{Current Liabilities (amount going out within one year)}}$$

The current ratio for Jackson Electric Supply is calculated like this:

$$\text{Current Ratio} = \frac{\$120{,}595}{\$\ 42{,}920} = 2.81 \qquad 42{,}920\overline{)\,120{,}595} = 2.8097$$

In the case of Jackson Electric Supply, $2.81 in current assets is available to pay every dollar currently due on December 31.

Chart of Accounts

When we introduced the chart of accounts and the account number arrangement, we said that the first digit represents the classification of an account. Since you are now acquainted with classified income statements and balance sheets, we can introduce the second digit. The second digit stands for the subclassification.

Assets	1--	Revenue	4--
Current Assets	11–	Revenue from Sales	41–
Plant and Equipment	12–	Other Income	42–
Liabilities	2--	Cost of Goods Sold	5--
Current Liabilities	21–	Purchases	51–
Long-Term Liabilities	22–	Expenses	6--
Owner's Equity	3--	Selling Expenses	61–
Capital	31–	General Expenses	62–
		Other Expenses	63–

The third digit indicates the placement of the account within the subclassification. For example, account number 411 represents Sales, which is the first account listed under Revenue. Account number 512 represents Purchases Returns and Allowances, which is the second account listed under Cost of Goods Sold. Account number 312 represents Drawing, which is the second account listed under Owner's Equity.

CLOSING ENTRIES

Now let's look at closing entries for a merchandising business. You follow the same four steps to close or zero out the revenue, expense, and Drawing accounts as for a service business.

	ACCOUNT NAME	TRIAL BALANCE DEBIT	TRIAL BALANCE CREDIT	INCOME STATEMENT DEBIT	INCOME STATEMENT CREDIT
1	Cash	21 1 5 4 00			
2	Notes Receivable	4 0 0 0 00			
3	Accounts Receivable	29 4 4 6 00			
4	Merchandise Inventory	77 0 0 0 00			
5	Supplies	1 4 4 0 00			
6	Prepaid Insurance	9 6 0 00			
7	Land	12 0 0 0 00			
8	Building	96 0 0 0 00			
9	Accumulated Depreciation, Building		32 0 0 0 00		
10	Equipment	33 6 0 0 00			
11	Accumulated Depreciation, Equipment		16 4 0 0 00		
12	Mortgage Payable		8 0 0 0 00		
13	Accounts Payable		36 4 0 0 00		
14	Notes Payable		3 0 0 0 00		
15	Unearned Course Fees		1 2 0 0 00		
16	N. C. Jackson, Capital		140 5 7 4 00		
17	N. C. Jackson, Drawing	48 9 0 0 00			
18	Sales		235 1 8 0 00		235 1 8 0 00
19	Sales Returns and Allowances	8 4 0 00		8 4 0 00	
20	Sales Discount	1 8 8 0 00		1 8 8 0 00	
21	Interest Income		1 2 0 00		1 2 0 00
22	Purchases	89 1 4 0 00		89 1 4 0 00	
23	Purchases Returns and Allowances		2 8 3 2 00		2 8 3 2 00
24	Purchases Discount		1 2 4 8 00		1 2 4 8 00
25	Freight In	2 4 6 0 00		2 4 6 0 00	
26	Wages Expense	55 8 0 0 00		57 0 2 0 00	
27	Taxes Expense	1 9 6 0 00		1 9 6 0 00	
28	Interest Expense	3 7 4 00		3 7 4 00	
29		476 9 5 4 00	476 9 5 4 00		
30	Income Summary			77 0 0 0 00	64 9 0 0 00
31	Course Fees Income				9 0 0 00
32	Supplies Expense			9 2 5 00	
33	Insurance Expense			3 8 0 00	
34	Depreciation Expense, Building			5 0 0 0 00	
35	Depreciation Expense, Equipment			4 0 0 0 00	
36	Wages Payable				
37				240 9 7 9 00	305 1 8 0 00
38	Net Income			64 2 0 1 00	
39				305 1 8 0 00	305 1 8 0 00
40					

FIGURE 6

Objective 4

Journalize the closing entries for a merchandising firm.

At the end of a fiscal period, you close the revenue and expense accounts so that you can start the next fiscal period with zero balances. You close the Drawing account because it, too, applies to one fiscal period. Recall that these accounts are called **temporary-equity accounts**, or *nominal accounts*.

Figure 6 shows the isolated Income Statement columns. After you have looked them over, let us look at the four steps of the closing procedure.

Four Steps in the Closing Procedure

These four steps should be followed when closing:

1. Close the revenue accounts and the other accounts that appear in the income statement and have credit balances (all temporary or nominal accounts with credit balances). **(Debit the figures that are credited in the Income Statement columns of the work sheet, except the figure on the Income Summary line.)** This entry is illustrated as follows:

GENERAL JOURNAL   PAGE __97__

	DATE		DESCRIPTION	POST. REF.	DEBIT	CREDIT	
1	20–		**Closing Entries**				1
2	Dec.	31	Sales		235 1 8 0 00		2
3			Interest Income		1 2 0 00		3
4			Purchases Returns and				4
5			Allowances		2 8 3 2 00		5
6			Purchases Discount		1 2 4 8 00		6
7			Course Fees Income		9 0 0 00		7
8			Income Summary			240 2 8 0 00	8

2. Close the expense accounts and the other accounts appearing in the income statement that have debit balances (all temporary or nominal accounts with debit balances). **(Credit the figures that are debited in the Income Statement columns of the work sheet, except the figure on the Income Summary line.)**

   Note that you close Purchases Discount and Purchases Returns and Allowances in step 1 along with the revenue accounts. Note also that in step 2 you close Sales Discount and Sales Returns and Allowances along with the expense accounts.

GENERAL JOURNAL   PAGE __97__

	DATE		DESCRIPTION	POST. REF.	DEBIT	CREDIT	
9	Dec.	31	Income Summary		163 9 7 9 00		9
10			Sales Returns and Allowances			8 4 0 00	10
11			Sales Discount			1 8 8 0 00	11
12			Purchases			89 1 4 0 00	12
13			Freight In			2 4 6 0 00	13
14			Wages Expense			57 0 2 0 00	14
15			Taxes Expense			1 9 6 0 00	15
16			Interest Expense			3 7 4 00	16
17			Supplies Expense			9 2 5 00	17
18			Insurance Expense			3 8 0 00	18
19			Depreciation Expense, Build.			5 0 0 0 00	19
20			Depreciation Expense, Equip.			4 0 0 0 00	20
21							21

3. Close the Income Summary account into N. C. Jackson, Capital. **(Debit Income Summary by the amount of the net income; credit it by the amount of a net loss.)**

		GENERAL JOURNAL				PAGE	97

	DATE		DESCRIPTION	POST. REF.	DEBIT	CREDIT	
22	Dec.	31	Income Summary		64 2 0 1 00		22
23			N. C. Jackson, Capital			64 2 0 1 00	23
24							24

Here is what the T accounts look like. Note that the Income Summary account already contains adjusting entries for merchandise inventory.

Like service businesses, merchandisers such as this CD store need to close entries to track net income.

Income Summary

Adjusting	77,000	Adjusting	64,900
(Beginning Merchandise		(Ending Merchandise	
Inventory)		Inventory)	
(Expenses and other debit		(Revenue and other credit	
balance accounts)	163,979	balance accounts)	240,280
(Net Income)	64,201		

N. C. Jackson, Capital

−	+	
	Balance	140,574
	(Net	
	Income)	64,201

4. Close the Drawing account into the Capital account.

		GENERAL JOURNAL				PAGE	97

	DATE		DESCRIPTION	POST. REF.	DEBIT	CREDIT	
25	Dec.	31	N. C. Jackson, Capital		48 9 0 0 00		25
26			N. C. Jackson, Drawing			48 9 0 0 00	26
27							27
28							28
29							29

Here is what the T accounts would look like:

N. C. Jackson, Drawing						N. C. Jackson, Capital		
	+	−				−	+	
Balance	48,900	Closing	48,900	(Drawing)	48,900	Balance	140,574	
						(Net Income)	64,201	

REVERSING ENTRIES

FYI

The use of reversing entries is optional.

Reversing entries are general journal entries that are the exact reverse of certain adjusting entries. A reversing entry enables the accountant to record routine transactions in the usual manner, *even though* an adjusting entry affecting one of the accounts involved in the transaction has intervened. We can understand this concept best by looking at an example.

Suppose there is an adjusting entry for accrued wages owed to employees at the end of the fiscal year. Assume that all the employees of a certain firm earn, altogether, $400 per day for a five-day week and that payday occurs every Friday throughout the year. When the employees get their checks at 5:00 P.M. on Friday, the checks include their wages for that day and for the preceding four days. And assume that, one year, the last day of the fiscal year happens to fall on Wednesday, December 31. A diagram of this situation would look like this:

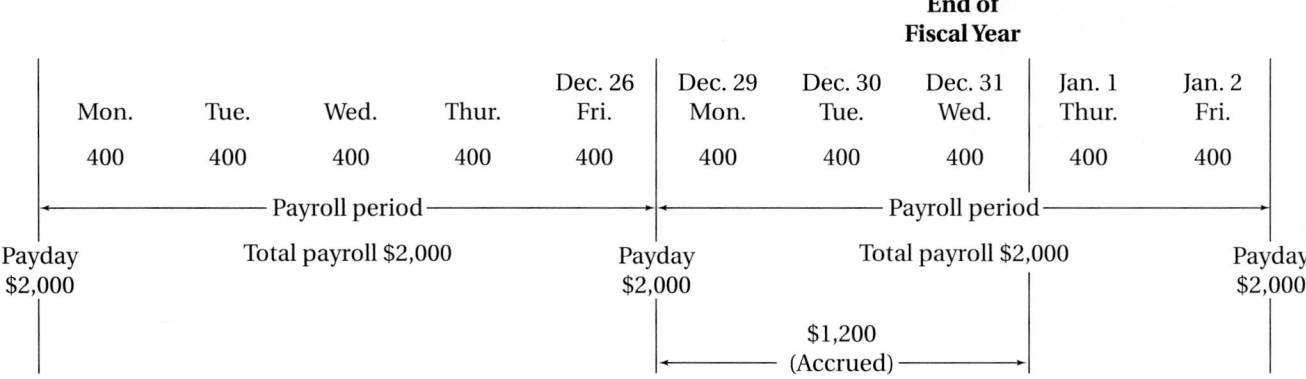

Each Friday during the year, the payroll has been debited to the Wages Expense account and credited to the Cash account. As a result, Wages Expense has a debit balance of $102,800. Here is the adjusting entry in T account form:

Wages Expense		
	+	−
Bal.	102,800	
Dec. 31 Adj.	1,200	

Wages Payable		
	−	+
		Dec. 31
		Adj. 1,200

Next, when all the expense accounts are closed, Wages Expense is closed by crediting it for $104,000. However, Wages Payable continues to have a credit balance of $1,200. The $2,000 payroll on January 2 must be split up by debiting Wages Payable $1,200, debiting Wages Expense $800, and crediting Cash $2,000.

The employee who records the payroll not only has to record this particular payroll differently from all other weekly payrolls for the year but also has to refer back to the adjusting entry to determine what portion of the $2,000 is debited to Wages Payable and what portion is debited to Wages Expense. In many companies, however, the employee who records the payroll does not have access to the adjusting entries.

There is a solution to this problem. The need to refer to the earlier entry and divide the debit total between the two accounts is eliminated *if a reversing entry is made on the first day of the following fiscal period.* You make an entry that is the exact reverse of the adjusting entry, as follows:

					GENERAL JOURNAL				PAGE	118	
	DATE		DESCRIPTION	POST. REF.		DEBIT			CREDIT		
27											27
28	20–		**Reversing Entries**								28
29	Jan.	1	**Wages Payable**			1 2 0 0 00					29
30			**Wages Expense**						1 2 0 0 00		30
31											31
32											32
33											33

Now let's bring the T accounts up to date.

Wages Expense

	+	−	
Balance	102,800	Dec. 31 Closing	104,000
Dec. 31 Adjust.	1,200		
		Jan. 1 Reversing	1,200

Wages Payable

	−	+	
Jan. 1 Reversing	1,200	Dec. 31 Adjust.	1,200

The reversing entry has the effect of transferring the $1,200 liability from Wages Payable to the credit side of Wages Expense. Wages Expense will temporarily have a credit balance until the next payroll is recorded in the routine manner. In our example, this occurs on January 2. See the T accounts on the following page.

Wages Expense

	+	−	
Balance	102,800	Dec. 31 Closing	104,000
Dec. 31 Adjust.	1,200		
Jan. 2	2,000	Jan. 1 Reversing	1,200

Wages Payable

	−	+	
Jan. 1 Reversing	1,200	Dec. 31 Adjust.	1,200

Cash

	+	−
Jan. 2		2,000

There is now a *net debit balance* of $800 in Wages Expense, which is the correct amount ($400 for January 1 and $400 for January 2). To see this, look at the following ledger accounts. December 26 was the last payday of one year, and January 2 is the first payday of the next year.

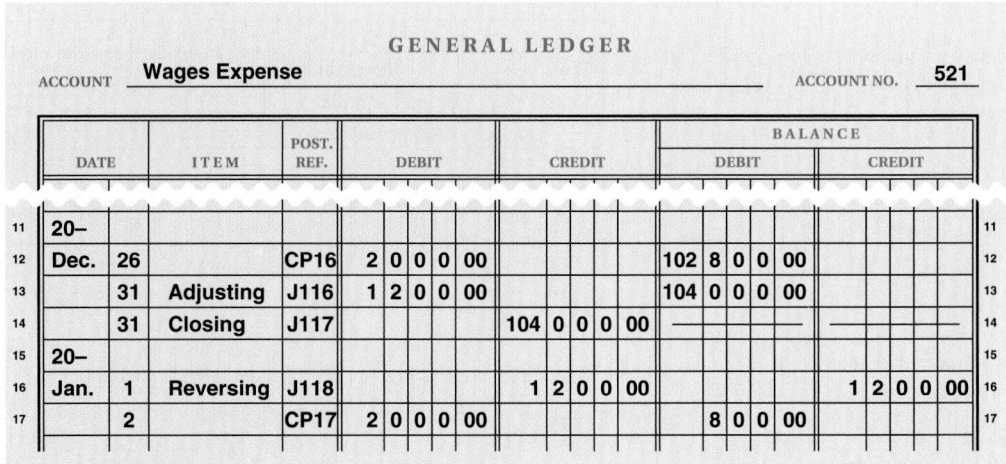

GENERAL LEDGER

ACCOUNT **Wages Expense**   ACCOUNT NO. **521**

	DATE		ITEM	POST. REF.	DEBIT	CREDIT	BALANCE DEBIT	BALANCE CREDIT	
11	20–								11
12	Dec.	26		CP16	2 0 0 0 00		102 8 0 0 00		12
13		31	Adjusting	J116	1 2 0 0 00		104 0 0 0 00		13
14		31	Closing	J117		104 0 0 0 00	—	—	14
15	20–								15
16	Jan.	1	Reversing	J118		1 2 0 0 00		1 2 0 0 00	16
17		2		CP17	2 0 0 0 00		8 0 0 00		17

ACCOUNT **Wages Payable**   ACCOUNT NO. **213**

	DATE		ITEM	POST. REF.	DEBIT	CREDIT	BALANCE DEBIT	BALANCE CREDIT	
1	20–								1
2	Dec.	31	Adjusting	J116		1 2 0 0 00		1 2 0 0 00	2
3									3
4	20–								4
5	Jan.	1	Reversing	J118	1 2 0 0 00		—	—	5

Objective 5

Determine which adjusting entries can be reversed, and journalize the reversing entries.

The reversing entry for accrued salaries or wages applies to service as well as merchandising companies. You can see that a reversing entry simply switches around an adjusting entry. The question is: Which adjusting entries should be reversed? Here are two handy rules for reversing. **If an adjusting entry is to be reversed, it must meet both of the following qualifications:**

1. **The adjusting entry increases an asset or liability account.**
2. **The asset or liability account did not have a previous balance.**

   With the exception of the first year of operations, Merchandise Inventory and contra accounts—such as Accumulated Depreciation—always have previous balances. Consequently, adjusting entries involving these accounts should never be reversed.

   Let's apply these rules to the adjusting entries for Jackson Electric Supply.

(Do not reverse; Merchandise Inventory is an asset, but it was decreased. Also, it has a previous balance.)

Merchandise Inventory				Income Summary			
	+	−					
Balance	77,000	Adjust.	77,000	Adjust.	77,000		

(Do not reverse; Merchandise Inventory is an asset, but it has a previous balance.)

Merchandise Inventory				Income Summary			
	+	−					
Balance	77,000	Adjust.	77,000	Adjust.	77,000	Adjust.	64,900
Adjust.	64,900						

(Do not reverse; Unearned Course Fees is a liability, but it was decreased. Also, it has a previous balance.)

Course Fees Income				Unearned Course Fees			
−		+		−		+	
		Adjust.	900	Adjust.	900	Balance	1,200

(Do not reverse; Supplies is an asset account, but it was decreased. Also, it has a previous balance.)

Supplies Expense				Supplies			
	+	−			+	−	
Adjust.	925			Balance	1,440	Adjust.	925

(Do not reverse; Prepaid Insurance is an asset account, but it was decreased. Also, it has a previous balance.)

Insurance Expense				Prepaid Insurance			
	+	−			+	−	
Adjust.	380			Balance	960	Adjust.	380

(Do not reverse; Accumulated Depreciation is a contra-asset, and it always has a previous balance after the first year.)

Depreciation Expense, Building				Accumulated Depreciation, Building			
	+	−		−		+	
Adjust.	5,000					Balance	32,000
						Adjust.	5,000

(Do not reverse; Accumulated Depreciation is a contra-asset, and it always has a previous balance after the first year.)

Depreciation Expense, Equipment				Accumulated Depreciation, Equipment			
	+	−		−		+	
Adjust.	4,000					Balance	16,400
						Adjust.	4,000

(Reverse; Wages Payable is a liability account. It was increased, and it had no previous balance.)

Wages Expense				Wages Payable			
	+	−		−		+	
Balance	45,800					Adjust.	1,220
Adjust.	1,220						

■ ■ ■

Remember!

Reversing entries are optional.

   Whenever we introduce additional adjusting entries, we will make it a point to state whether they can be reversed.

CHAPTER REVIEW

Review of Performance Objectives

1. Prepare a classified income statement for a merchandising firm.

   The outline of the income statement looks like this:

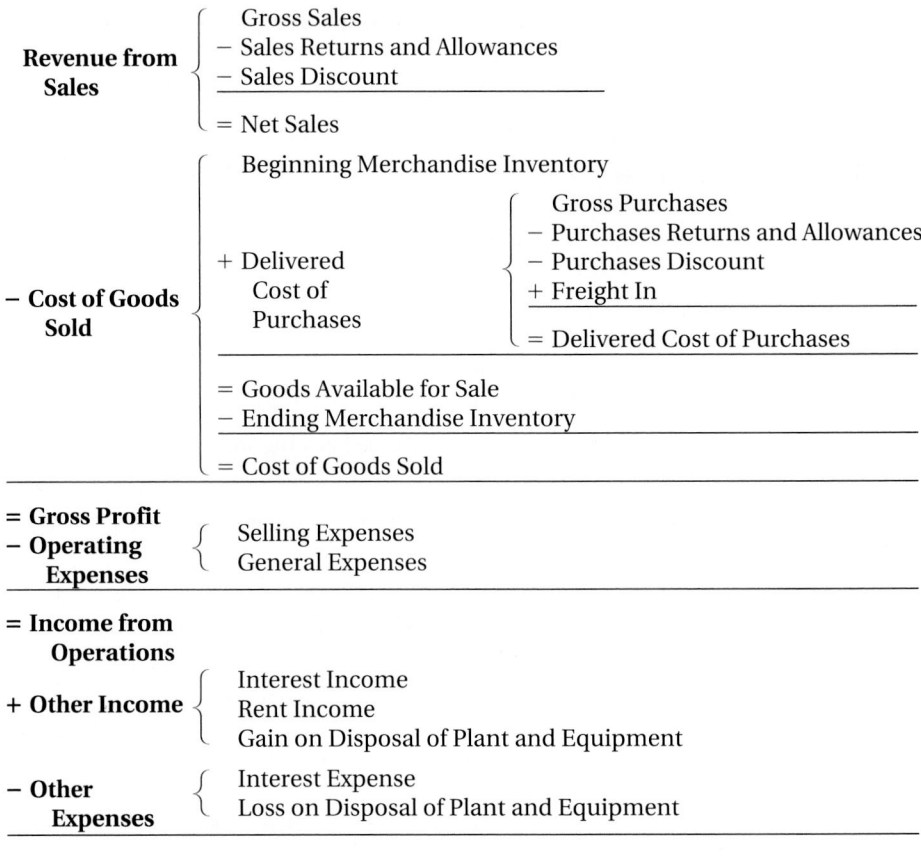

2. Prepare a classified balance sheet for any type of business.

   The outline of the balance sheet looks like this:

   Assets Current Assets (listed in the order of their convertibility into cash)

   1. Cash
   2. Notes Receivable
   3. Accounts Receivable
   4. Merchandise Inventory
   5. Prepaid items (Supplies; Prepaid Insurance)

   Plant and Equipment (listed in the order of their length of life; the asset with the longest life is placed first)

   1. Land
   2. Buildings
   3. Equipment

Liabilities Current Liabilities (listed in the order of their urgency of payment; the most pressing obligation is placed first)

1. Accounts Payable
2. Notes Payable
3. Accrued liabilities (Wages Payable; Commissions Payable)
4. Unearned Revenue
5. Mortgage Payable or Contracts Payable (current portion)

Long-Term Liabilities (Contracts Payable; Mortgage Payable)

Owner's Equity Capital balance at end of the fiscal year

3. Compute working capital and current ratio.

These two measures help analysts determine whether a firm has enough capital to operate and whether it can pay its debts.

Working capital = Current assets − Current liabilities

$$\text{Current ratio} = \frac{\text{Current assets}}{\text{Current liabilities}}$$

4. Journalize the closing entries for a merchandising firm.

There are four steps in making closing entries for a merchandising business:

Step 1. Close all revenue accounts, Purchases Returns and Allowances, and Purchases Discount into Income Summary (any accounts listed as credits in the work sheet Income Statement columns except Income Summary).

Step 2. Close all expense accounts, Sales Returns and Allowances, and Sales Discount into Income Summary (any accounts listed as debits in the work sheet Income Statement columns except Income Summary).

Step 3. Close Income Summary into Capital (transfer net income or net loss into the owner's Capital account). The Income Summary balance should now be zero.

Step 4. Close Drawing into Capital.

5. Determine which adjusting entries can be reversed, and journalize the reversing entries. The use of reversing entries is optional.

Reverse the adjusting entries that increase either asset or liability accounts and that do not have previous balances. A contra-account like Accumulated Depreciation should not be reversed. Reversing entries are dated as of the first day of the next fiscal period.

Glossary

Cost of Goods Sold A section of the income statement in which the amount of the cost of the goods we sold is calculated. Terms often used to describe the same thing are *cost of merchandise sold* and *cost of sales*.

Merchandise Inventory (beginning)
Plus Delivered Cost of Purchases
_____

Goods Available for Sale
Less Merchandise Inventory (ending)
_____

Cost of Goods Sold   (473)

Current Assets Cash and any other assets or resources that are expected to be realized in cash or to be sold or consumed during the normal operating cycle of the business (or one year, if the normal operating cycle is less than twelve months). (478)

Current liabilities Debts that will become due within the normal operating cycle of a business, usually within one year, and that are normally paid from current assets. (479)

Current ratio A firm's current assets divided by its current liabilities. Portrays a firm's short-term debt-paying ability. (480)

Delivered Cost of Purchases Net Purchases plus Freight In:

Net Purchases
Plus Freight In

Delivered Cost of Purchases (474)

General Expenses Expenses incurred in the administration of a business, including office expenses and any expenses that are not completely classified as Selling Expenses or Other Expenses. (475)

Gross Profit Net Sales minus Cost of Goods Sold, or profit before deducting expenses:

Net Sales
Less Cost of Goods Sold

Gross Profit (473)

Liquidity The ability of an asset to be quickly turned into cash, either by selling it or by putting it up as security for a loan. (478)

Long-term Liabilities Debts payable over a comparatively long period, usually more than one year. (479)

Net Income or **Net Profit** The final figure on an income statement after all expenses have been deducted from revenues. (473)

Net Purchases Purchases minus Purchases Returns and Allowances and minus Purchases Discount:

Purchases
Less Purchases Returns and Allowances
Less Purchases Discount

Net Purchases (474)

Net Sales Sales minus Sales Returns and Allowances and minus Sales Discount:

Sales
Less Sales Returns and Allowances
Less Sales Discount

Net Sales (473)

Notes Receivable (current) Written promises to pay the seller/lender the amount due in a period of less than one year. (479)

Plant and Equipment Long-lived assets that are held for use in the production or sale of other assets or services; also called *fixed assets*. (479)

Reversing entries The reverse of certain adjusting entries, recorded as of the first day of the following fiscal period. The use of reversing entries is optional. (484)

Selling Expenses Expenses directly connected with the selling activity, such as salaries of sales staff, advertising expenses, and delivery expenses. (475)

Temporary-equity accounts Accounts whose balances apply to one fiscal period only, such as revenues, expenses, and the Drawing account. Temporary-equity accounts are also called *nominal accounts*. (481)

Working capital A firm's current assets less its current liabilities. The amount of capital a firm has available to use or to work with during a normal operating cycle. (479)

QUESTIONS, EXERCISES, AND PROBLEMS

Discussion Questions

1. What is the difference between the cost of goods available for sale and the cost of goods sold?

2. What are the basic classifications found on an income statement for a merchandising business?

3. On an income statement, what is the difference between income from operations and net income? Which is more useful in comparing the results of operations over a number of years?

4. Explain the calculation of net sales and net purchases.

5. What is the order for listing accounts in the Current Assets section of the balance sheet?

6. On a balance sheet, what is the difference between Current Liabilities and Long-Term Liabilities? Give an example of an account in each classification.

7. In the closing procedure, what happens to (a) Purchases Discount, (b) Sales Returns and Allowances, (c) Freight In, (d) Gain on Disposal of Plant and Equipment?

8. What is the rule for recognizing whether or not an adjusting entry can be reversed?

P.O. 1

Provide missing amounts on an income statement.

Exercises

Exercise 14-1 Calculate the missing items in the following:

	Sales	Sales Returns and Allowances	Net Sales	Beginning Merchandise Inventory	Net Purchases	Goods Available for Sale	Ending Merchandise Inventory	Cost of Goods Sold	Gross Profit
a.	$249,000	$ 6,000	—	$148,000	$170,000	—	$136,000	$182,000	—
b.	304,000	—	$296,000	144,000	—	$404,000	196,000	208,000	—
c.	—	12,000	628,000	—	412,000	496,000	92,000	—	—

P.O. 1

Prepare Cost of Goods Sold section.

Exercise 14-2 Using the following information, prepare the Cost of Goods Sold section of an income statement.

Purchases Discount	$ 9,000
Merchandise Inventory, December 31	192,000
Purchases	480,000
Merchandise Inventory, January 1	188,000
Purchases Returns and Allowances	16,000
Freight In	27,000

P.O. 1

Classify income statement accounts.

Exercise 14-3 Identify each of the following items relating to sections of an income statement as Revenue from Sales (S), Cost of Goods Sold (CGS), Selling Expenses (SE), General Expenses (GE), Other Income (OI), or Other Expense (OE).

a. Advertising Expense
b. Rent Expense
c. Purchases Discount
d. Sales Returns and Allowances
e. Interest Income
f. Freight In
g. Depreciation Expense, Building
h. Interest Expense
i. Insurance Expense
j. Delivery Expense

P.O. 1

Prepare an income statement.

Exercise 14-4 The partial Income Statement columns of the June 30 (year-end) work sheet for Dahl Company are shown here. From the information given, prepare an income statement for the company. To save time and space, the expenses have been grouped together into two categories.

	ACCOUNT NAME	INCOME STATEMENT DEBIT	INCOME STATEMENT CREDIT
21	Income Summary	27 0 0 0 00	25 0 0 0 00
22	Sales		291 0 0 0 00
23	Sales Returns and Allowances	11 1 0 0 00	
24	Sales Discount	4 1 0 0 00	
25	Purchases	116 0 0 0 00	
26	Purchases Returns and Allowances		1 2 0 0 00
27	Purchases Discount		1 0 0 0 00
28	Freight In	7 5 0 0 00	
29	Selling Expenses	56 0 0 0 00	
30	General Expenses	49 0 0 0 00	
31		270 7 0 0 00	318 2 0 0 00
32	Net Income	47 5 0 0 00	
		318 2 0 0 00	318 2 0 0 00

P.O. 2

Classify balance sheet items.

Exercise 14-5 Identify each of the following items relating to sections of a balance sheet dated 2001 as Current Assets (CA), Plant and Equipment (PE), Current Liabilities (CL), Long-Term Liabilities (LTL), or Owner's Equity (OE).

a. Accounts Receivable
b. Building
c. Wages Payable
d. Prepaid Taxes
e. Mortgage Payable (current)
f. Supplies
g. Mortgage Payable (due May 31, 2008)
h. Unearned Fees
i. D. Deal, Capital
j. Notes Payable (due in 3 months)

P.O. 3

Determine working capital and current ratio.

Exercise 14-6 On December 31, 2001, the following selected accounts and amounts appeared in the balance sheet. Determine the amount of the working capital and the current ratio.

Building	$160,000
Prepaid Insurance	600
Merchandise Inventory	76,000
Store Equipment	14,000
Unearned Fees	700
Notes Payable (due within 12 months)	7,000
Accumulated Depreciation, Building	76,000
Accounts Payable	22,000
Land	40,000
Store Supplies	1,000
Cash	9,000
Accumulated Depreciation, Store Equipment	6,000
Notes Receivable (mature within 12 months)	4,000
Mortgage Payable (current portion)	4,400
Salaries Payable	2,000
C. Ray, Capital	101,500
Mortgage Payable (due June 30, 2010)	85,000

P.O. 4

Journalize closing entries.

Exercise 14-7 From the following T accounts, journalize the closing entries dated December 31:

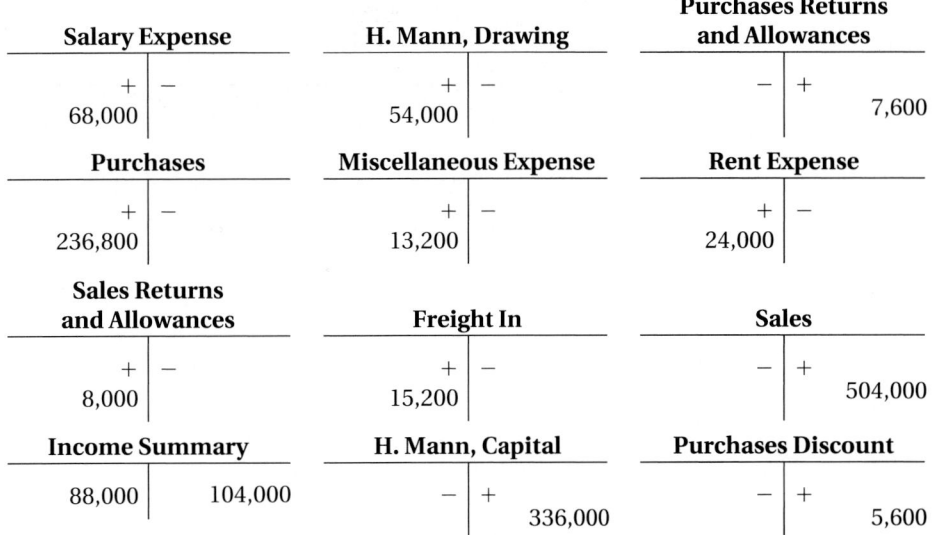

P.O. 4

From T accounts, prepare a statement of owner's equity.

Exercise 14-8 From the following information, journalize the last two closing entries, and present a statement of owner's equity for Rea Company:

T. H. Rea, Capital			Income Summary			
–	+		Dec. 31 Adj.	192,000	Dec. 31 Adj.	204,000
	Jan. 1 Balance	440,000	Dec. 31 Closing	410,000	Dec. 31 Closing	490,000
	Apr. 7	16,000				

T. H. Rea, Drawing		
	+	–
Mar. 1	42,000	
Dec. 9	37,000	

WHAT IF . . .

What if the freight charges on a new desk for the owner were journalized and posted to the Freight In account? Would this affect the Cost of Goods Sold section? If so, how?

CRITICAL THINKING

You are an owner/bookkeeper in a country whose economy has been nearly destroyed. Goods are scarce; in fact, you have no goods to sell at the start of each day. You go out early each morning to purchase goods and haul them back to sell. At the end of the day, you have sold everything. Prepare a Cost of Goods Sold section for a day when you purchased $400 in goods and assume you sold everything. What conclusion can you draw?

A MATTER OF ETHICS

Molly is an accountant. Sometimes printouts of financial statements have errors and are not usable. Molly doesn't like to waste anything. She even takes the unusable financial statements to her son's day care center to use as drawing paper. Explain why you think this is or is not unethical behavior.

WEB WORK

Using an Internet web browser, type the phrase for the home page of a retail organization or association in the search box. Find the balance sheet. Look for Current and Long-Term Assets and Liabilities on the balance sheet. Compute working capital. Compute the current ratio. Discuss your findings or write them in a memo to your instructor.

PROBLEM SET A

For additional help, see the demonstration problem at the beginning of each chapter in your Working Papers.

P.O. 1,4

Problem 14-1A A partial work sheet for Poe Music Store is presented here. The merchandise inventory at the beginning of the fiscal period was $49,584. F. L. Poe, the owner, withdrew $32,000 during the year.

Poe Music Store
Work Sheet
For Year Ended December 31, 20—

	ACCOUNT NAME	INCOME STATEMENT	
		DEBIT	CREDIT
21	Sales		326 5 9 2 80
22	Sales Returns and Allowances	5 2 2 9 20	
23	Sales Discount	1 9 0 8 00	
24	Interest Income		3 2 4 98
25	Purchases	195 1 9 1 00	
26	Purchases Returns and Allowances		1 6 5 6 00
27	Freight In	14 2 6 5 00	
28	Wages Expense	39 5 2 4 00	
29	Rent Expense	9 3 6 0 00	
30	Commissions Expense	9 4 4 0 00	
31	Interest Expense	6 5 6 32	
32	Income Summary	49 5 8 4 00	43 9 7 2 00
33	Supplies Expense	6 3 7 20	
34	Insurance Expense	9 3 6 00	
35	Depreciation Expense, Building	4 8 0 0 00	
36	Depreciation Expense, Equipment	3 3 4 0 00	
37		334 8 7 0 72	372 5 4 5 78
38	Net Income	37 6 7 5 06	
39		372 5 4 5 78	372 5 4 5 78
40			
41			
42			
43			
44			
45			
46			
47			
48			
49			

Check Figure

Cost of Goods Sold, $213,412

Instructions

1. Prepare an income statement.
2. Journalize the closing entries.

P.O. 2,3

Problem 14-2A Here is the partial work sheet for The Mountain Shop.

The Mountain Shop
Work Sheet
For Year Ended December 31, 20—

	ACCOUNT NAME	BALANCE SHEET DEBIT	BALANCE SHEET CREDIT	
1	Cash	9 7 2 3 00		1
2	Notes Receivable	3 6 0 0 00		2
3	Accounts Receivable	42 8 7 9 60		3
4	Merchandise Inventory	56 6 9 7 00		4
5	Supplies	4 7 4 00		5
6	Prepaid Taxes	6 1 3 50		6
7	Prepaid Insurance	6 3 0 00		7
8	Land	8 4 0 0 00		8
9	Building	63 0 0 0 00		9
10	Accumulated Depreciation, Building		21 6 0 0 00	10
11	Office Equipment	5 4 2 4 00		11
12	Accumulated Depreciation, Office Equipment		4 1 7 0 00	12
13	Store Equipment	6 5 7 0 00		13
14	Accumulated Depreciation, Store Equipment		4 9 9 5 00	14
15	Delivery Equipment	5 5 6 5 00		15
16	Accumulated Depreciation, Delivery Equipment		4 3 0 5 00	16
17	Mortgage Payable		55 7 1 3 00	17
18	Accounts Payable		29 5 9 1 70	18
19	Notes Payable		5 4 3 0 00	19
20	Mortgage Payable (current portion)		2 7 0 0 00	20
21	N. Olston, Capital		65 0 5 8 90	21
22	N. Olston, Drawing	25 1 9 4 00		22
23	Wages Payable		1 2 7 8 00	23
24		228 7 7 0 10	194 8 4 1 60	24
25	Net Income		33 9 2 8 50	25
26		228 7 7 0 10	228 7 7 0 10	26

Check Figure

Working capital, $75,617.40

Instructions

1. Prepare a statement of owner's equity (no additional investment).
2. Prepare a balance sheet.
3. Determine the amount of the working capital.
4. Determine the current ratio (carry to one decimal place).

P.O. 4,5

Problem 14-3A The following partial work sheet covers the affairs of Koto and Company for the year ending June 30:

Koto and Company
Work Sheet
For Year Ended June 30, 20—

	ACCOUNT NAME	INCOME STATEMENT DEBIT	INCOME STATEMENT CREDIT	BALANCE SHEET DEBIT	BALANCE SHEET CREDIT	
1	Cash			32 3 8 4 34		1
2	Accounts Receivable			104 6 3 4 54		2
3	Merchandise Inventory			119 4 5 6 00		3
4	Supplies			1 0 3 2 00		4
5	Prepaid Insurance			1 3 2 0 00		5
6	Delivery Equipment			12 9 2 0 00		6
7	Accumulated Depreciation, Delivery Equipment				6 4 8 0 00	7
8	Store Equipment			36 5 0 0 00		8
9	Accumulated Depreciation, Store Equipment				10 3 6 0 00	9
10	Accounts Payable				67 4 3 7 34	10
11	Salaries Payable				8 5 2 00	11
12	C. P. Koto, Capital				195 9 2 1 14	12
13	C. P. Koto, Drawing			37 4 4 0 00		13
14	Income Summary	115 2 2 6 00	119 4 5 6 00			14
15	Sales		536 3 5 2 40			15
16	Purchases	393 9 3 0 00				16
17	Purchases Returns and Allowances		7 8 2 8 00			17
18	Purchases Discount		5 7 4 6 00			18
19	Freight In	23 3 5 0 00				19
20	Salary Expense	51 4 0 0 00				20
21	Truck Expense	9 3 4 2 00				21
22	Supplies Expense	2 5 6 4 00				22
23	Insurance Expense	1 9 2 0 00				23
24	Depreciation Expense, Delivery Equipment	2 7 0 0 00				24
25	Depreciation Expense, Store Equipment	2 8 9 6 00				25
26	Miscellaneous Expense	1 4 1 8 00				26
27		604 7 4 6 00	669 3 8 2 40	345 6 8 6 88	281 0 5 0 48	27
28	Net Income	64 6 3 6 40			64 6 3 6 40	28
29		669 3 8 2 40	669 3 8 2 40	345 6 8 6 88	345 6 8 6 88	29

Check Figure

Reversing entry amount, $852

Instructions

1. Journalize the seven adjusting entries.
2. Journalize the closing entries.
3. Journalize the reversing entry.

P.O. 1,2,4,5

Problem 14-4A The following accounts appear in the ledger of The Short Company on January 31, the end of this fiscal year:

Cash	$ 5,400
Accounts Receivable	14,100
Merchandise Inventory	55,500
Store Supplies	690
Prepaid Insurance	1,080
Store Equipment	27,900
Accumulated Depreciation, Store Equipment	2,700
Accounts Payable	13,800
Wages Payable	—
M. R. Short, Capital	113,620
M. R. Short, Drawing	36,000
Income Summary	—
Sales	224,000
Sales Returns and Allowances	3,000
Purchases	170,000
Purchases Returns and Allowances	3,450
Purchases Discount	2,400
Freight In	7,000
Wages Expense	27,000
Advertising Expense	3,900
Depreciation Expense, Store Equipment	—
Store Supplies Expense	—
Rent Expense	8,400
Insurance Expense	—

The data needed for adjustments on January 31 are as follows:

a–b. Merchandise inventory, January 31, $53,400
c. Store supplies inventory, January 31, $390
d. Insurance expired for the year, $615
e. Depreciation for the year, $6,395
f. Accrued wages on January 31, $1,270

Check Figure

Net loss, $130

Instructions

1. Prepare a work sheet for the fiscal year ended January 31.
2. Prepare an income statement.
3. Prepare a statement of owner's equity. No additional investments were made.
4. Prepare a balance sheet.
5. Journalize the adjusting entries.
6. Journalize the closing entries.
7. Journalize the reversing entry.

Instructions for General Ledger Software

1. Record the adjusting entries in the general journal and print a copy of the entries.
2. Post the general journal amounts to the general ledger.
3. Print an adjusted trial balance and the general ledger after adjustments.
4. Print the income statement, statement of owner's equity, and balance sheet.

5. Record the closing entries in the general journal and print a copy of the entries.
6. Post the general journal amounts to the general ledger.
7. Print a post-closing trial balance.
8. Record the reversing entry in the general journal at the beginning of the next month.

PROBLEM SET B

For additional help, see the demonstration problem at the beginning of each chapter in your Working Papers.

P.O. 1,4

Problem 14-1B A partial work sheet for The Fall Shop is presented here. The merchandise inventory at the beginning of the year was $53,200. C. A. Fall, the owner, withdrew $26,500 during the year.

The Fall Shop
Work Sheet
For Year Ended December 31, 20—

	ACCOUNT NAME	INCOME STATEMENT DEBIT	INCOME STATEMENT CREDIT
21	Sales		328 0 0 0 00
22	Sales Returns and Allowances	4 4 8 0 00	
23	Sales Discount	3 7 0 7 32	
24	Interest Income		1 8 4 0 00
25	Purchases	199 4 9 0 00	
26	Purchases Returns and Allowances		2 9 8 0 00
27	Freight In	12 7 5 0 00	
28	Wages Expense	43 2 0 0 00	
29	Rent Expense	9 6 0 0 00	
30	Commissions Expense	10 3 2 0 00	
31	Interest Expense	9 6 4 22	
32	Income Summary	53 2 0 0 00	44 3 6 0 00
33	Supplies Expense	8 3 2 46	
34	Insurance Expense	1 0 4 0 00	
35	Depreciation Expense, Building	4 8 0 0 00	
36	Depreciation Expense, Equipment	3 6 0 0 00	
37		347 9 8 4 00	377 1 8 0 00
38	Net Income	29 1 9 6 00	
39		377 1 8 0 00	377 1 8 0 00

Check Figure

Cost of Goods Sold, $218,100

Instructions

1. Prepare an income statement.
2. Journalize the closing entries.

P.O. 2,3

Problem 14-2B Here is the partial work sheet for Haven Stereo.

Haven Stereo
Work Sheet
For Year Ended December 31, 20—

	ACCOUNT NAME	BALANCE SHEET DEBIT	BALANCE SHEET CREDIT	
1	Cash	12 9 1 5 00		1
2	Notes Receivable	6 3 0 0 00		2
3	Accounts Receivable	33 2 7 0 00		3
4	Merchandise Inventory	55 3 4 4 00		4
5	Supplies	4 2 0 00		5
6	Prepaid Taxes	6 3 0 00		6
7	Prepaid Insurance	5 4 0 00		7
8	Land	7 8 0 0 00		8
9	Building	60 0 0 0 00		9
10	Accumulated Depreciation, Building		18 9 0 0 00	10
11	Store Equipment	4 3 9 2 00		11
12	Accumulated Depreciation, Store Equipment		1 6 7 4 00	12
13	Testing Equipment	7 2 3 0 00		13
14	Accumulated Depreciation, Testing Equipment		5 4 2 4 00	14
15	Delivery Equipment	5 4 0 0 00		15
16	Accumulated Depreciation, Delivery Equipment		4 4 7 0 00	16
17	Mortgage Payable (current portion)		1 8 0 0 00	17
18	Accounts Payable		28 1 4 0 00	18
19	Notes Payable		4 2 1 5 00	19
20	Mortgage Payable		55 2 0 0 00	20
21	C. R. Gonza, Capital		67 3 1 4 00	21
22	C. R. Gonza, Drawing	22 4 4 0 00		22
23	Wages Payable		9 8 4 00	23
24		216 6 8 1 00	188 1 2 1 00	24
25	Net Income		28 5 6 0 00	25
26		216 6 8 1 00	216 6 8 1 00	26
27				27
28				28
29				29
30				30

Check Figure

Working capital, $74,280

Instructions

1. Prepare a statement of owner's equity (no additional investment).
2. Prepare a balance sheet.
3. Determine the amount of the working capital.
4. Determine the current ratio (carry to one decimal place).

P.O. 4,5

Problem 14-3B The following partial work sheet covers the affairs of Bessel and Company for the year ended June 30:

Bessel and Company
Work Sheet
For Year Ended June 30, 20—

	ACCOUNT NAME	INCOME STATEMENT DEBIT	INCOME STATEMENT CREDIT	BALANCE SHEET DEBIT	BALANCE SHEET CREDIT	
1	Cash			28 1 9 6 61		1
2	Accounts Receivable			92 0 0 6 00		2
3	Merchandise Inventory			112 4 0 0 00		3
4	Supplies			8 3 7 39		4
5	Prepaid Insurance			1 2 2 0 00		5
6	Delivery Equipment			12 4 0 0 00		6
7	Accumulated Depreciation, Delivery Equipment				5 8 0 0 00	7
8	Store Equipment			33 4 0 0 00		8
9	Accumulated Depreciation, Store Equipment				9 6 0 0 00	9
10	Accounts Payable				60 2 0 0 00	10
11	Salaries Payable				1 2 4 0 00	11
12	L. Bessel, Capital				167 8 2 0 00	12
13	L. Bessel, Drawing			28 0 0 0 00		13
14	Income Summary	109 2 0 0 00	112 4 0 0 00			14
15	Sales		520 0 0 0 00			15
16	Purchases	380 0 0 0 00				16
17	Purchases Returns and Allowances		7 6 0 0 00			17
18	Purchases Discount		4 8 0 0 00			18
19	Freight In	24 0 0 0 00				19
20	Salary Expense	48 0 0 0 00				20
21	Truck Expense	8 6 0 0 00				21
22	Supplies Expense	2 2 0 0 48				22
23	Insurance Expense	1 8 4 0 00				23
24	Depreciation Expense, Delivery Equipment	2 4 0 0 00				24
25	Depreciation Expense, Store Equipment	2 8 0 0 00				25
26	Miscellaneous Expense	1 9 5 9 52				26
27		581 0 0 0 00	644 8 0 0 00	308 4 6 0 00	244 6 6 0 00	27
28	Net Income	63 8 0 0 00			63 8 0 0 00	28
29		644 8 0 0 00	644 8 0 0 00	308 4 6 0 00	308 4 6 0 00	29
30						30
31						31
32						32

Check Figure

Reversing entry amount, $1,240

Instructions

1. Journalize the seven adjusting entries.
2. Journalize the closing entries.
3. Journalize the reversing entry.

P.O. 1,2,4,5

Problem 14-4B The following accounts appear in the ledger of Clos and Company as of June 30, the end of this fiscal year:

Cash	$ 4,349.76
Accounts Receivable	14,910.00
Merchandise Inventory	51,480.00
Store Supplies	735.52
Prepaid Insurance	975.00
Store Equipment	29,640.00
Accumulated Depreciation, Store Equipment	7,880.00
Accounts Payable	11,085.00
Wages Payable	—
D. E. Clos, Capital	102,195.00
D. E. Clos, Drawing	28,260.00
Income Summary	—
Sales	202,630.00
Sales Returns and Allowances	2,640.00
Purchases	137,050.00
Purchases Returns and Allowances	4,395.00
Purchases Discount	2,565.28
Freight In	9,260.00
Wages Expense	33,100.00
Advertising Expense	8,150.00
Depreciation Expense, Store Equipment	—
Store Supplies Expense	—
Rent Expense	10,200.00
Insurance Expense	—

The data needed for the adjustments on June 30 are as follows:

a–b. Merchandise inventory, June 30, $48,196
c. Store supplies inventory, June 30, $269.20
d. Insurance expired for the year, $640
e. Depreciation for the year, $6,290
f. Accrued wages on June 30, $472

Check Figure

Net loss, $1,962.04

Instructions

1. Prepare a work sheet for the fiscal year ended June 30.
2. Prepare an income statement.
3. Prepare a statement of owner's equity. No additional investments were made during the year.
4. Prepare a balance sheet.
5. Journalize the adjusting entries.
6. Journalize the closing entries.
7. Journalize the reversing entry.

Instructions for General Ledger Software

1. Record the adjusting entries in the general journal and print a copy of the entries.
2. Post the general journal amounts to the general ledger.
3. Print an adjusted trial balance and the general ledger after adjustments.

4. Print the income statement, statement of owner's equity, and balance sheet.
5. Record the closing entries in the general journal and print a copy of the entries.
6. Post the general journal amounts to the general ledger.
7. Print a post-closing trial balance.
8. Record the reversing entry in the general journal at the beginning of the next month.

Cumulative Self-Check: Chapters 13–14

PART I: COMPLETION

Complete each of the following statements by writing the appropriate word(s) in the spaces provided.

1. An actual count of a stock of goods is called a(n) _____.

2. Under the _____ system, entries to record the purchase of merchandise are recorded in the Merchandise Inventory account.

3. Unearned revenue is classified as a(n) _____.

4. Under the periodic inventory system, the first adjustment is to debit _____ for the amount of the beginning inventory.

5. Under the perpetual inventory system, after recording the sale of the goods, the accountant debits the _____ account and credits _____.

6. An increase in Rent Expense results in a(n) _____ to net income.

7. Gross Profit is calculated by subtracting _____ from Net Sales.

8. Current Assets minus Current Liabilities equals _____.

9. Gross Profit minus Total Operating Expenses equals _____.

10. Net Purchases plus _____ equals Delivered Cost of Purchases.

PART II: TRUE/FALSE

T   F   1. The second adjustment for Merchandise Inventory under the periodic inventory system is to debit Cost of Goods Sold and credit Merchandise Inventory.

T   F   2. Unearned Rental Income is classified as a revenue.

T   F   3. The perpetual inventory system requires that each sale of goods has two entries: one to reduce inventory and affix the cost of the goods sold and one to record the sale.

T   F   4. The periodic inventory system requires two adjusting entries: one to remove the old inventory amount and one to enter the latest inventory amount.

T   F   5. The adjustment to unearned revenue allows the correct amount of liability and revenue to be applied to each fiscal period involved.

T   F   6. Freight In is classified in the Operating Expenses section of an income statement.

T   F   7. Under the perpetual inventory system, the cost of goods sold is calculated by subtracting ending inventory from goods available for sale.

Note: Answers to Cumulative Self-Check begin on page A-1.

T   F   8. Reversing entries are optional, and only some adjusting entries are reversed.

T   F   9. Delivery Expense is added to net purchases to arrive at delivered cost of purchases.

T   F   10. Purchases Returns and Allowances increases Income from Operations.

PART III: APPLICATION

1. Alphonse Company uses the periodic inventory system. Employees have just taken a physical count of its inventory. This ending inventory has been valued at $136,000. The company's accounting records show the Merchandise Inventory account with a debit balance of $132,000. Journalize the entries on December 31 to adjust the records for this situation.

2. Regletto Company uses the perpetual inventory system. Employees have just taken a physical count of its inventory. This ending inventory has been valued at $146,000. The company's accounting records show the Merchandise Inventory account with a debit balance of $148,000. Journalize the entry on December 31 to adjust the records for this situation.

3. On December 1, Wesley Company collected $20,000 for a remodeling job that will be completed on March 31 of the following year. Wesley Company's fiscal period ends December 31. Make the entries to record the collection of the cash and the year-end adjustment to reflect the amount of revenue earned in December.

4. Yorkland Company has total assets of $250,000, of which non-current assets amount to $140,000. The company also has total liabilities of $130,000, of which $80,000 are long-term liabilities. Calculate (a) working capital and (b) current ratio.

Comprehensive Review Problem

You are to record transactions completed by Fine Fabrics during the month of February of this year. This company is located in Dallas. To gain practice in completing the steps in the accounting cycle, assume that the fiscal period consists of one month.

Assets

111 Cash
112 Petty Cash Fund
113 Accounts Receivable
114 Merchandise Inventory
117 Supplies
118 Prepaid Insurance
122 Equipment
123 Accumulated Depreciation, Equipment

Liabilities

221 Accounts Payable
226 Employees' Income Tax Payable
227 FICA Tax Payable
228 State Unemployment Tax Payable
229 Federal Unemployment Tax Payable
230 Salaries Payable

Owner's Equity

311 J. L. Fisher, Capital
312 J. L. Fisher, Drawing
399 Income Summary

Revenue

411 Sales
412 Sales Returns and Allowances

Cost of Goods Sold

511 Purchases
512 Purchases Returns and Allowances
513 Purchases Discount
514 Freight In

Operating Expenses

611 Salary Expense
612 Payroll Tax Expense
613 Rent Expense
614 Utilities Expense
616 Supplies Expense
617 Insurance Expense
618 Depreciation Expense, Equipment
619 Miscellaneous Expense

JOURNALS

Sales Journal, page 56
Purchases Journal, page 62
Cash Receipts Journal, page 69
Cash Payments Journal, page 75
General Journal, pages 89–92

ACCOUNTS RECEIVABLE

Hotel Bentnor
Jerome and Woods
Wilkes Decorators

ACCOUNTS PAYABLE

Byran, Inc.
Keller Textiles
Meldon Fabrics
Taylor Manufacturing Company

TRANSACTIONS

The following transactions were completed during February of this year.

Feb. 1 Reversed the adjusting entry for accrued salaries, $710.

1 Sold merchandise on account to Hotel Bentnor, $13,052.97, invoice no. 5221.

2 Issued Ck. No. 7216, $17,271.62, to Keller Textiles, in payment of its invoice no. D1739 for $17,624.10 less 2 percent discount.

5 Bought merchandise on account from Meldon Fabrics, $4,551.90; invoice no. RE275, dated February 2; terms 1/10, n/30; FOB Orlando; freight prepaid and added to the invoice, $147 (total, $4,698.90).

5 Received an electric bill and paid Regional Power, Ck. No. 7217, $121.

6 Received check from Jerome and Woods for $11,619.50 in payment of account.

7 Issued Ck. No. 7218, $9,519.84, to Meldon Fabrics, in payment of its invoice no. RE64 for $9,616 less 1 percent discount.

9 Cash sales for February 1 through February 9, $7,951.60.

12 **Recorded the payroll in the payroll register** for regular semi-monthly salaries for period ended February 12. Salaries: M. B. Corson, $2,730; K. L. Vickers, $2,240. Income tax withholdings are $382.20 for Corson and $313.60 for Vickers. Assume the following tax rates and taxable earnings limits (see payroll register for beginning cumulative earnings):

- Social Security taxable earnings, $68,400, with a rate of 6.2 percent.
- Medicare taxable earnings, all earnings, with a rate of 1.45 percent.

12 Recorded the payroll entry in the general journal, crediting Salaries Payable.

12 Issued Ck. No. 7219, $2,138.95, to M. B. Corson. Issued Ck. No. 7220, $1,755.04, to K. L. Vickers. Use two lines and debit Salaries Payable. (Verify these amounts.)

12 Recorded payroll taxes. Assume the following tax rates and taxable earnings:

- Federal unemployment taxable earnings, $7,000, with a rate of .8 percent.
- State unemployment taxable earnings, $7,000, with a rate of 5.4 percent. *Note:* Corson's taxable earnings for unemployment amount to $1,540 and Vickers's amount to $2,240.

12 Received a credit memo from Meldon Fabrics for defective merchandise, $542, credit memo no. 916.

Feb. 14 Issued Ck. No. 7221, $2,912.44, to State Bank for monthly deposit of January employees' federal income tax withheld, $1,391.60, and FICA taxes, $1,520.84.

14 Sold merchandise on account to Jerome and Woods, $15,692.50, invoice no. 5222.

14 Issued Ck. No. 7222, $4,116.80, to Meldon Fabrics in payment of its invoice no. RE275 less the credit memo for defective merchandise and less the discount ($40.10). *Note:* Debit Accounts Payable, $4,156.90, and credit Purchases Discount, $40.10. Verify these amounts: $4,698.90, less $147 freight, less $542 return, less 1 percent cash discount (cash discounts can't be taken on freight).

18 Bought merchandise on account from Byran, Inc., $20,488.20; invoice no. 164M, dated February 14; terms 2/10, n/30; FOB Miami; freight prepaid and added to the invoice, $1,152 (total, $21,640.20).

18 Cash sales for February 10 through February 18, $7,994.14.

19 Issued Ck. No. 7223 payable to Faster Printing for invoice forms, $327 (not previously recorded). (Debit Supplies.)

19 Received check from Wilkes Decorators for $4,920.14 in payment of account.

22 Issued Ck. No. 7224, $12,710, to Taylor Manufacturing Company, in payment of its invoice no. 9264D.

22 Sold merchandise on account to Wilkes Decorators, $16,721.42, invoice no. 5223.

24 Issued credit memo no. 214 to Wilkes Decorators, $156, for merchandise returned.

24 Bought merchandise on account from Keller Textiles, $16,448.01; invoice no. D1797, dated February 22; terms 2/10, n/30; FOB Memphis.

26 **Recorded the payroll in the payroll register** for regular semimonthly salaries for period ended February 26. Salaries: M. B. Corson, $2,730; K. L. Vickers, $2,240. Income tax withholdings are $382.20 for Corson and $313.60 for Vickers. *Note:* See the entry of February 12 for taxable earnings limits and tax rates. See payroll register for beginning cumulative earnings.

26 Recorded the payroll entry in the general journal, crediting Salaries Payable.

26 Issued Ck. No. 7225, $2,138.95, to M. B. Corson. Issued Ck. No. 7226, $1,755.04, to K. L. Vickers. Use two lines and debit Salaries Payable.

26 Ck. No. 7227 voided.

26 Recorded payroll taxes. *Note:* Vickers's taxable earnings for unemployment amount to $280.

27 Issued Ck. No. 7228, $994, to Greater Freight Line for transportation charge on merchandise purchased from Keller Textiles.

28 Issued Ck. No. 7229, $48.63, payable to Cash to reimburse the petty cash fund. Petty cash payments consist of Supplies, $27.16, and Miscellaneous Expense, $21.47.

28 Cash sales for February 19 through February 28, $7,685.20.

28 Issued Ck. No. 7230, $650, to Grandy Realty for monthly rent.

28 J. L. Fisher (owner) withdrew $3,000 for personal use, Ck. No. 7231.

INSTRUCTIONS

1. Journalize and post the transactions completed during February.

    a. Post the amounts in the Other Accounts columns of the special journals daily.
    b. Post the general journal daily.
    c. Post the totals of the special columns of the special journals at the end of the month.

2. Prepare a schedule of accounts receivable and a schedule of accounts payable.
3. Complete the work sheet for February.
   Data for the month-end adjustments are as follows:

    a–b. Merchandise inventory at February 28, $44,262
    c. Salaries accrued at February 28, $710
    d. Supplies inventory at February 28, $472
    e. Insurance expired during February, $40
    f. Depreciation of equipment during February, $105

4. Journalize and post the adjusting entries.
5. Prepare an income statement.
6. Prepare a statement of owner's equity. (No additional investment was made during the month.)
7. Prepare a balance sheet.
8. Journalize and post the closing entries.
9. Prepare a post-closing trial balance.

INSTRUCTIONS FOR GENERAL LEDGER SOFTWARE

1. Journalize and post the transactions completed during February.
2. Print the journals and the general ledger.
3. Print a trial balance.
4. Print a schedule of accounts receivable and a schedule of accounts payable.
5. Journalize and post the month-end adjustments:

    a–b. Merchandise inventory at February 28, $44,262
    c. Salaries accrued at February 28, $710
    d. Supplies inventory at February 28, $472
    e. Insurance expired during February, $40
    f. Depreciation of equipment during February, $105

6. Print the adjusting entries, an adjusted trial balance, and the general ledger after adjustments.
7. Print the income statement, the statement of owner's equity, and the balance sheet.
8. Journalize and post the closing entries.
9. Print the closing entries.
10. Print a post-closing trial balance.

Inventory Methods

Performance Objectives

After you have completed this appendix, you will be able to do the following:

1. Determine the amount of the ending merchandise inventory by the weighted-average-cost method.

2. Determine the amount of the ending merchandise inventory by the first-in, first-out method.

3. Determine the amount of the ending merchandise inventory by the last-in, first-out method.

To determine the dollar amount of the ending merchandise inventory, it is necessary to take a physical count of the various items in stock and match them up with their costs. In other words, the ending inventory consists of the number of units of each type of item on hand multiplied by the cost of each unit.

If each unit were purchased at exactly the same price, the job of determining the total cost of the inventory would be simple. For example, if there are 100 units of Product A on hand, and all 100 units were bought at $15, the total cost of the ending inventory is $1,500 (100 × $15). However, over a period of time, costs of individual purchases of units may differ. Changes in costs of individual units make the different methods of inventory valuation necessary.

We will use Casey Electronics, a distributor of compact disc (CD) players, to illustrate the three methods of inventory valuation. Casey's ending inventory consists of 182 Model M43 CD players acquired through various purchases, as follows:

Specific Purchase	Number of Units	Cost per Unit	Total Cost
Beginning inventory	34	$270	$ 9,180
First purchase	60	282	16,920
Second purchase	256	298	76,288
Third purchase	164	312	51,168
Total units available	514		$153,556

Of the 514 units available for sale, 182 units are still on hand and 332 have been sold (514 − 182).

Casey Electronics may choose any one of the three following methods of recording the total cost of the 182 units in the ending inventory of CD players.

WEIGHTED-AVERAGE-COST METHOD

Objective 1

Determine the amount of the ending merchandise inventory by the weighted-average-cost in Ending Inventory method.

$$\text{Average Cost per Unit} = \frac{\text{Total Cost}}{\text{Total Units Available}} = \frac{\$153,556}{514} = \$298.75 \text{ (rounded)}$$

Cost of 182 units = 298.75×182 units = \$54,373 (rounded)

Cost of 541 units sold = 298.75×332 units = 99.183 (rounded)

FIRST-IN, FIRST-OUT METHOD

Objective 2

Determine the amount of the ending merchandise inventory by the first-in, first-out method.

This method is based on the **assumption** that the first units of CD players purchased will be sold first. The costs of the units left will be those of the most recently purchased units. You may think of this as the way a grocery store sells milk. Because milk will sour, the oldest milk is moved to the front of the display shelf and is sold first. Consequently, the cartons of milk remaining on the shelf are the freshest milk.

Relating to our illustration of CD players,

Specific Purchase	Number of Units	Cost per Unit	Total Cost
Beginning inventory	34	$270	$ 9,180
First purchase	60	282	16,920
Second purchase	256	298	76,288
Third purchase	164	312	51,168
Total units available	514		$153,556

The cost of the 182 CD players on hand (most recently purchased) is as follows:

164 units (third purchase)	@ $312 each =	$51,168
18 units (second purchase)	@ $298 each =	5,364
182 units		$56,532

LAST-IN, FIRST-OUT METHOD

Objective 3

Determine the amount of the ending merchandise inventory by the last-in, first-out method.

This method is based on the **assumption** that the last units of CD players purchased will be sold first. The costs of the units left over will be those of the earliest purchased units. You may think of this as the way a coal yard sells coal. When the coal yard sells coal to its customers, it takes coal off the top of the pile. Consequently, the tons of coal in the ending inventory consist of those first few tons at the bottom of the pile.

Relating to our illustration of CD players shown above, the cost of the 182 CD players on hand (earliest purchased) is as follows:

34 units (beginning inventory) @ $270 each =	$ 9,180	
60 units (first purchase) @ $282 each =	16,920	
88 units (second purchase) @ $298 each =	26,224	
182 units	$52,324	

Comparison of Three Methods		
Method	Ending Inventory (182 units)	Cost of Goods Sold (Goods Available for Sale − Ending Inventory) (332 units = 514 − 182)
Weighted-average-cost	$54,373	$ 99,183 ($153,556 − $54,373)
First-in, first-out	56,532	97,024 ($153,556 − $56,532)
Last-in, first-out	52,324	101,232 ($153,556 − $52,324)

Assume that the CD players were sold for $380 each.

	Weighted-Average-Cost	First-in, First-out	Last-in, First-out
Sales (332 units × $380 each)	$126,160	$126,160	$126,160
Cost of Goods Sold	99,183	97,024	101,232
Gross Profit	$ 26,977	$ 29,136	$ 24,928

PROBLEMS

P.O. 1

Check Figure

Cost of ending inventory, $279.24

Problem C-1 Bermingham Nursery sells bark to its customers at retail. Bermingham buys bark from a plywood mill in bulk and transports the bark in its own trucks. Information relating to the beginning inventory and purchases of bark is as follows:

Beginning inventory	1,500 cubic yards @ $.20 per cubic yard
First purchase	2,100 cubic yards @ $.22 per cubic yard
Second purchase	1,400 cubic yards @ $.26 per cubic yard
Third purchase	1,000 cubic yards @ $.27 per cubic yard

Find the cost of 1,200 cubic yards in the ending inventory by the weighted-average-cost method. Carry average cost per cubic yard to four decimals.

P.O. 2

Check Figure

Cost of ending inventory, $322

Problem C-2 Using the information presented in Problem C-1, find the cost of the ending inventory by the first-in, first-out method.

P.O. 3

Check Figure

Cost of ending inventory, $240

Problem C-3 Using the information presented in Problem C-1, find the cost of the ending inventory by the last-in, first-out method.

D The Statement of Cash Flows

Performance Objectives

After you have completed this appendix, you will be able to do the following:

1. Classify cash flows as Operating Activities, Investing Activities, and Financing Activities.

2. Prepare a statement of cash flows.

The fourth major financial statement is the statement of cash flows. This statement explains in detail how the balance of Cash has changed between the beginning and the end of the fiscal period. Some accountants refer to the statement as the "where got, where gone" statement of cash.

SECTIONS OF THE STATEMENT OF CASH FLOWS

Objective 1

Classify cash flows as Operating Activities, Investing Activities, and Financing Activities.

The statement has three main sections: Operating Activities, Investing Activities, and Financing Activities. Cash flows are subdivided as cash inflows and cash outflows.

Operating Activities

This section covers cash received and used in carrying out the company's operations.

Cash Inflows
- Cash from selling of services or merchandise
- Miscellaneous income

Cash Outflows
- Payments for purchases of merchandise and supplies from suppliers
- Payments of salaries or wages
- Payments of rent, utilities, insurance
- Payment of interest to creditors

Investing Activities

This section covers cash used in or received from buying or selling of plant and equipment assets and all other noncurrent assets, such as long-term investments.

Cash Inflows
- Cash received from the sale of noncurrent assets

Cash Outflows
- Cash payments to buy noncurrent assets

Financing Activities

This section covers cash related to changes in the owner's equity accounts and long-term liabilities accounts.

Cash Inflows

- Investment of cash by the owner
- Borrowing from creditors

Cash Outflows

- Withdrawals of cash by the owner
- Repayment of loans to creditors

FINANCIAL STATEMENTS NEEDED FOR PREPARING THE STATEMENT OF CASH FLOWS

The financial statements required for preparing the statement of cash flows consist of the income statement and statement of owner's equity for the fiscal period, the balance sheet at the end of the fiscal period, and the balance sheet at the end of the previous fiscal period. Using the two balance sheets, we can prepare a comparative balance sheet for the two fiscal periods, showing the increases and decreases in the various accounts.

ILLUSTRATION OF THE STATEMENT OF CASH FLOWS

Objective 2

Prepare a statement of cash flows.

The financial statements for Morrow Company are shown here. To save space, we present the comparative balance sheet. Based on the comparative balance sheet, the first step is to record the increases and decreases in the accounts.

Morrow Company
Income Statement
For Year Ended December 31, 2001

Revenue from Sales:			
Net Sales	$ 647 0 0 0 00		
Less Cost of Goods Sold	500 0 0 0 00		
Gross Profit		$ 147 0 0 0 00	
Operating Expenses:			
Salary Expense	$ 70 0 0 0 00		
Rent Expense	10 0 0 0 00		
Depreciation Expense, Equipment	6 0 0 0 00		
Supplies Expense	1 0 0 0 00		
Total Operating Expenses		87 0 0 0 00	
Net Income		$ 60 0 0 0 00	

Morrow Company
Statement of Owner's Equity
For Year Ended December 31, 2001

B. Morrow, Capital, January 1, 2001		$ 120 0 0 0 00
Additional Investment, March 2, 2001		10 0 0 0 00
Total Investment		$ 130 0 0 0 00
Net Income for the Year	$60 0 0 0 00	
Less Withdrawals	50 0 0 0 00	
Increase in Capital		10 0 0 0 00
B. Morrow, Capital, Dec. 31, 2001		$ 140 0 0 0 00

Morrow Company
Comparative Balance Sheet
December 31, 2001, and December 31, 2000

	2001		2000		INCREASE OR DECREASE
Assets					
Cash		$ 12 0 0 0 00		$ 7 0 0 0 00	$ 5 0 0 0 00
Accounts Receivable		70 0 0 0 00		66 0 0 0 00	4 0 0 0 00
Merchandise Inventory		120 0 0 0 00		113 0 0 0 00	7 0 0 0 00
Supplies		3 0 0 0 00		4 0 0 0 00	(1 0 0 0 00)
Equipment	$72 0 0 0 00		$60 0 0 0 00		12 0 0 0 00
Less Accumulated Deprec.	(62 0 0 0 00)	10 0 0 0 00	(56 0 0 0 00)	4 0 0 0 00	(6 0 0 0 00)
Total Assets		$ 215 0 0 0 00		$ 194 0 0 0 00	$21 0 0 0 00
Liabilities					
Accounts Payable	$71 0 0 0 00		$69 0 0 0 00		$ 2 0 0 0 00
Salaries Payable	4 0 0 0 00		5 0 0 0 00		(1 0 0 0 00)
Total Liabilities		$ 75 0 0 0 00		$ 74 0 0 0 00	$ 1 0 0 0 00
Owner's Equity					
B. Morrow, Capital		140 0 0 0 00		120 0 0 0 00	20 0 0 0 00
Total Liabilities and					
Owner's Equity		$ 215 0 0 0 00		$ 194 0 0 0 00	$21 0 0 0 00

Note the $5,000 increase in Cash. First let's see how this increase comes about.

- Cash flows related to operating activities involve changes in current asset and current liability accounts.
- Cash flows related to investing activities involve changes in plant and equipment (long-term assets) accounts (with the exception of Accumulated Depreciation).
- Cash flows related to financing activities involve changes in owner's equity accounts and long-term liabilities accounts.

Now let's present the statement of cash flows.

Morrow Company
Statement of Cash Flows
For Year Ended December 31, 2001

Cash Flows from (Used by) Operating Activities																
Net Income	$	60	0	0	0	00										
Add (Deduct) Items to Convert Net Income from Accrual Basis to Cash Basis																
Depreciation Expense		6	0	0	0	00										
Increase in Accounts Receivable		(4	0	0	0	00)										
Increase in Merchandise Inventory		(7	0	0	0	00)										
Decrease in Supplies		1	0	0	0	00										
Increase in Accounts Payable		2	0	0	0	00										
Decrease in Salaries Payable		(1	0	0	0	00)										
Net Cash Flows from Operating Activities							$	57	0	0	0	00				
Cash Flows from (Used by) Investing Activities																
Purchase of Equipment	$	(12	0	0	0	00)										
Net Cash Flows Used by Investing Activities													(12	0	0	0	00)
Cash Flows from (Used by) Financing Activities																
Cash Investment by Owner	$	10	0	0	0	00										
Cash Withdrawals by Owner		(50	0	0	0	00)										
Net Cash Flows Used by Financing Activities													(40	0	0	0	00)
Net Increase (Decrease) in Cash							$	5	0	0	0	00				

EXPLANATION OF ITEMS IN THE STATEMENT OF CASH FLOWS

Cash Flows from Operating Activities

- Net income of $60,000, from the income statement, included such items as sale of services or merchandise, miscellaneous income, and payment of expenses such as salaries or wages, utilities, and interest.
- Depreciation of $6,000 was included as an expense on the income statement, but it did not result in the payment of cash to anyone. Since depreciation expense was deducted on the income statement, we now add $6,000 back in. Depreciation expense is always an addition under Cash Flows from Operating Activities.
- Accounts Receivable increased by $4,000. Of the amount shown as Sales on the income statement, $4,000 was in the form of additional charge account balances and therefore were not cash inflows. So we deduct $4,000 from Cash Flows from Operating Activities.
- Merchandise Inventory increased by $7,000. Because the inventory increased by $7,000 during the year (more merchandise was bought than was sold), we can assume that the change resulted in a $7,000 decrease in Cash Flows from Operating Activities.
- Decrease in Supplies of $1,000 means that the company used up supplies bought in a previous fiscal period and included the entire amount of supplies used as Supplies Expense on the income statement. In other words, the $1,000 of Supplies Expense shown on the income statement did not result in a payment of cash in the current period.
- Increase in Accounts Payable of $2,000 in this case means that $2,000 of the amount listed as Purchases on the income statement (not shown because

we included Purchases in Cost of Goods Sold) did not result in the payment of cash. So we add $2,000 to Cash Flows from Operating Activities.

- Decrease in Salaries Payable of $1,000 means that the amount listed as Salary Expense on the income statement is $1,000 less than the amount of cash spent by the company. So we deduct $1,000 from Cash Flows from Operating Activities.

Cash Flows from Investing Activities

Equipment increased by $12,000. We would have to look at the journal entry to determine how much cash was involved. In this case, we assume that the purchase of equipment resulted in a payment of $12,000 cash. So we deduct $12,000 from Cash Flows from Investing Activities.

Cash Flows from Financing Activities

- The owner's Capital account increased by $10,000 as a result of an additional investment. We would have to look at the journal entry to determine how much cash was involved. In this case, we assume that the investment was in the form of cash. So we add $10,000 to Cash Flows from Financing Activities.
- The owner's Drawing account increased by $50,000. We would have to look at the journal entries to determine how much cash was involved. In this case, we assume that the withdrawals were in the form of cash. So we deduct $50,000 from Cash Flows from Financing Activities.

Here are some handy guidelines for preparing a statement of cash flows.

Add to Net Income	
If Current Assets decrease	Why? If an account like Accounts Receivable decreases, this means that we received more cash than the amount listed as Net Sales.
If Current Liabilities increase	Why? If an account like Accounts Payable increases, this means that we bought more merchandise or supplies than we paid for in cash.
Deduct from Net Income	
If Current Assets increase	Why? If an account like Prepaid Insurance increases, this means that we paid more cash for insurance than the amount listed as Insurance Expense on the income statement.
If Current Liabilities decrease	Why? If an account like Notes Payable decreases, this means that we paid out cash to pay off the note.

PROBLEMS

P.O. 1,2

Problem D-1 Metter Company has the following financial statements for 2000 and 2001. Assume that the withdrawals were in the form of cash.

Check Figure

Net cash flows from operating
activities, $44,500

Instructions

Prepare a statement of cash flows for the year ended December 31, 2001.

Metter Company
Income Statement
For Year Ended December 31, 2001

Revenue:		
Income from Services		$ 134 000 00
Expenses:		
Wages Expense	$77 000 00	
Rent Expense	8 000 00	
Depreciation Expense, Equipment	5 000 00	
Supplies Expense	2 000 00	
Total Expenses		92 000 00
Net Income		$ 42 000 00

Metter Company
Statement of Owner's Equity
For Year Ended December 31, 2001

B. N. Metter, Capital, January 1, 2001		$94 000 00
Net Income for the Year	$42 000 00	
Less Withdrawals for the Year	40 000 00	
Increase in Capital		2 000 00
B. N. Metter, Capital, December 31, 2001		$96 000 00

Metter Company
Comparative Balance Sheet
December 31, 2001, and December 31, 2000

	2001		2000		INCREASE (DECREASE)
Assets					
Cash		$ 9 000 00		$ 6 500 00	$2 500 00
Supplies		5 000 00		2 500 00	2 500 00
Equipment	$100 000 00		$98 000 00		2 000 00
Less Accumulated Depreciation	(18 000 00)	82 000 00	(13 000 00)	85 000 00	(5 000 00)
Total Assets		$96 000 00		$94 000 00	$2 000 00
Owner's Equity					
B. N. Metter, Capital		$96 000 00		$94 000 00	$2 000 00
Total Liabilities and					
Owner's Equity		$96 000 00		$94 000 00	$2 000 00

P.O. 1,2

Problem D-2 The financial statements for Arms and Company are presented below. Assume that the additional investment and the withdrawals were both in the form of cash.

Check Figure

Net cash flows from operating activities, $77,000

Instructions

Prepare a statement of cash flows for the year ended December 31, 2001.

Arms and Company
Income Statement
For Year Ended December 31, 2001

Revenue:		
Income from Services		$ 270 0 0 0 00
Expenses:		
Wages Expense	$ 161 0 0 0 00	
Rent Expense	18 0 0 0 00	
Depreciation Expense, Equipment	12 0 0 0 00	
Supplies Expense	4 0 0 0 00	
Insurance Expense	1 0 0 0 00	
Total Expenses		196 0 0 0 00
Net Income		$ 74 0 0 0 00

Arms and Company
Statement of Owner's Equity
For Year Ended December 31, 2001

S. T. Arms, Capital, January 1, 2001		$ 150 0 0 0 00
Additional Investment		2 0 0 0 00
Total Investment		$ 152 0 0 0 00
Net Income for the Year	$74 0 0 0 00	
Less Withdrawals for the Year	70 0 0 0 00	
Increase in Capital		4 0 0 0 00
S. T. Arms, Capital, December 31, 2001		$ 156 0 0 0 00

Arms and Company
Comparative Balance Sheet
December 31, 2001 and December 31, 2000

	2001		2000		INCREASE (DECREASE)
Assets					
Cash		$ 11 8 0 0 00		$ 2 8 0 0 00	$ 9 0 0 0 00
Accounts Receivable		32 0 0 0 00		26 0 0 0 00	6 0 0 0 00
Supplies		10 0 0 0 00		9 4 0 0 00	6 0 0 00
Prepaid Insurance		3 2 0 0 00		6 0 0 00	2 6 0 0 00
Equipment	$145 4 0 0 00		$145 4 0 0 00		———
Less Accumulated Depreciation	(36 0 0 0 00)	109 4 0 0 00	(24 0 0 0 00)	121 4 0 0 00	(12 0 0 0 00)
Total Assets		$166 4 0 0 00		$160 2 0 0 00	$ 6 2 0 0 00
Liabilities					
Accounts Payable		$ 10 4 0 0 00		$ 10 2 0 0 00	$ 2 0 0 00
Owner's Equity					
S. T. Arms, Capital		156 0 0 0 00		150 0 0 0 00	6 0 0 0 00
Total Liabilities and					
Owner's Equity		$166 4 0 0 00		$160 2 0 0 00	$ 6 2 0 0 00

P.O. 1,2

Problem D-3 The financial statements for Torres Company are presented below. Assume that the withdrawals were in the form of cash.

Check Figure

Net cash flows used by financing activities, (70,000)

Instructions

Prepare a statement of cash flows for the year ended December 31, 2001.

Torres Company
Income Statement
For Year Ended December 31, 2001

Revenue from Sales:		
Net Sales	$ 942 0 0 0 00	
Less Cost of Goods Sold	753 6 0 0 00	
Gross Profit		$ 188 4 0 0 00
Operating Expenses:		
Salary Expense	$ 86 9 0 0 00	
Rent Expense	18 0 0 0 00	
Depreciation Expense, Equipment	10 0 0 0 00	
Supplies Expense	4 7 0 0 00	
Insurance Expense	2 8 0 0 00	
Total Operating Expenses		122 4 0 0 00
Net Income		$ 66 0 0 0 00

Torres Company
Statement of Owner's Equity
For Year Ended December 31, 2001

C. L. Torres, Capital, January 1, 2001		$ 196 0 0 0 00
Net Income for the Year	$ 66 0 0 0 00	
Less Withdrawals for the Year	70 0 0 0 00	
Decrease in Capital		4 0 0 0 00
C. L. Torres, Capital, December 31, 2001		$ 192 0 0 0 00

Torres Company
Comparative Balance Sheet
December 31, 2001 and December 31, 2000

	2001	2000	INCREASE (DECREASE)
Assets			
Cash	$ 9 4 0 0 00	$ 10 9 0 0 00	$ (1 5 0 0 00)
Accounts Receivable	56 0 0 0 00	48 6 0 0 00	7 4 0 0 00
Merchandise Inventory	104 6 0 0 00	104 4 0 0 00	2 0 0 00
Supplies	8 2 0 0 00	6 0 0 0 00	2 2 0 0 00
Prepaid Insurance	1 6 0 0 00	1 8 0 0 00	(2 0 0 00)
Equipment	$156 0 0 0 00	$156 0 0 0 00	—
Less Accumulated Depreciation	(76 4 0 0 00) 79 6 0 0 00	(66 4 0 0 00) 89 6 0 0 00	(10 0 0 0 00)
Total Assets	$259 4 0 0 00	$261 3 0 0 00	$ (1 9 0 0 00)
Liabilities			
Accounts Payable	$ 62 7 0 0 00	$ 60 4 0 0 00	$ 2 3 0 0 00
Salaries Payable	4 7 0 0 00	4 9 0 0 00	(2 0 0 00)
Total Liabilities	$ 67 4 0 0 00	$ 65 3 0 0 00	$ 2 1 0 0 00
Owner's Equity			
C. L. Torres, Capital	192 0 0 0 00	196 0 0 0 00	(4 0 0 0 00)
Total Liabilities and Owner's Equity	$259 4 0 0 00	$261 3 0 0 00	$ (1 9 0 0 00)

E Financial Statement Analysis

Performance Objectives

After you have completed this appendix, you will be able to do the following:

1. Determine gross profit percentage.

2. Determine merchandise inventory turnover.

3. Determine accounts receivable turnover.

4. Determine return on investment.

An important function of accounting is to provide tools for interpreting the financial statements or the results of operations. This appendix presents a number of percentages and ratios that are frequently used to analyze financial statements.

GROSS PROFIT PERCENTAGE

Objective 1

Determine gross profit percentage.

DeClerk Card Shop will serve as our example (see the comparative income statement on the next page).

For each year, net sales is the base (100 percent). All other items on the income statement can be expressed as a percentage of net sales for the particular year involved. For example, let's look at the following percentages:

$$\text{Gross Profit \% (2001)} = \frac{\text{Gross Profit for 2001}}{\text{Net Sales for 2001}} = \frac{\$150,000}{\$428,000} = .35 = 35\%$$

$$\text{Gross Profit \% (2000)} = \frac{\text{Gross Profit for 2000}}{\text{Net Sales for 2000}} = \frac{\$152,000}{\$400,000} = .38 = 38\%$$

$$\text{Sales Salary Expense \% (2001)} = \frac{\text{Sales Salary Expense for 2001}}{\text{Net Sales for 2001}}$$

$$= \frac{\$63,600}{\$428,000} = .1486 = 15\%$$

$$\text{Sales Salary Expense \% (2000)} = \frac{\text{Sales Salary Expense for 2000}}{\text{Net Sales for 2000}}$$

$$= \frac{\$58,000}{\$400,000} = .145 = 15\%$$

DeClerk Card Shop
Comparative Income Statement
For Years Ended January 31, 2001, and January 31, 2000

	2001 AMOUNT	2001 PERCENT	2000 AMOUNT	2000 PERCENT
Revenue from Sales:				
Sales	$ 453 6 0 0 00	106	$ 420 0 0 0 00	105
Less Sales Returns and Allowances	25 6 0 0 00	6	20 0 0 0 00	5
Net Sales	$ 428 0 0 0 00	100	$ 400 0 0 0 00	100
Cost of Goods Sold:				
Merchandise Inventory, February 1	$ 116 0 0 0 00	27	$ 64 0 0 0 00	16
Delivered Cost of Purchases	320 0 0 0 00	75	300 0 0 0 00	75
Goods Available for Sale	$ 436 0 0 0 00	102	$ 364 0 0 0 00	91
Less Merchandise Inventory, January 31	158 0 0 0 00	37	116 0 0 0 00	29
Cost of Goods Sold	$ 278 0 0 0 00	65	$ 248 0 0 0 00	62
Gross Profit	$ 150 0 0 0 00	35	$ 152 0 0 0 00	38
Operating Expenses:				
Sales Salary Expense	$ 63 6 0 0 00	15	$ 58 0 0 0 00	15
Rent Expense	24 0 0 0 00	6	24 0 0 0 00	6
Advertising Expense	21 4 0 0 00	5	16 0 0 0 00	4
Depreciation Expense, Equipment	20 0 0 0 00	5	18 0 0 0 00	4.5
Insurance Expense	2 0 0 0 00	—	2 0 0 0 00	.5
Store Supplies Expense	1 0 0 0 00	—	1 0 0 0 00	—
Miscellaneous Expense	1 0 0 0 00	—	1 0 0 0 00	—
Total Operating Expenses	$ 133 0 0 0 00	31	$ 120 0 0 0 00	30
Net Income	$ 17 0 0 0 00	4	$ 32 0 0 0 00	8

Here's how you might interpret a few of the percentages:

2001

- For every $100 in net sales, gross profit amounted to $35.
- For every $100 in net sales, sales salary expense amounted to $15.
- For every $100 in net sales, net income amounted to $4.

2000

- For every $100 in net sales, gross profit amounted to $38.
- For every $100 in net sales, sales salary expense amounted to $15.
- For every $100 in net sales, net income amounted to $8.

The gross profit percentage declined from 38% in 2000 to 35% in 2001 because the Cost of Goods Sold percentage increased from 62% in 2000 to 65% in 2001.

MERCHANDISE INVENTORY TURNOVER

Objective 2

Determine merchandise inventory turnover.

Merchandise inventory turnover is the number of times a firm's average inventory is sold during a given year.

$$\text{Merchandise Inventory Turnover} = \frac{\text{Cost of Goods Sold}}{\text{Average Merchandise Inventory}}$$

$$\text{Average Merchandise Inventory} = \frac{\text{Beginning Merchandise Inventory} + \text{Ending Merchandise Inventory}}{2}$$

	2001	2000
Beginning Merchandise Inventory (from the Cost of Goods Sold section of the income statement)	$116,000	$ 64,000
Ending Merchandise Inventory (from the Cost of Goods Sold section of the income statement or the balance sheet)	$158,000	$116,000

2001

$$\text{Average Merchandise Inventory} = \frac{\$116,000 + \$158,000}{2} = \frac{\$274,000}{2} = \underline{\$137,000}$$

$$\text{Merchandise Inventory Turnover} = \frac{\$278,000}{\$137,000} = \underline{2.03} \text{ times per year}$$

2000

$$\text{Average Merchandise Inventory} = \frac{\$64,000 + \$116,000}{2} = \frac{\$180,000}{2} = \underline{\$90,000}$$

$$\text{Merchandise Inventory Turnover} = \frac{\$248,000}{\$90,000} = \underline{2.76} \text{ times per year}$$

With each turnover of merchandise, the company makes a gross profit, so the higher the turnover, the better.

The inventory turnover deteriorated from 2.76 in 2000 to 2.03 in 2001 because the beginning inventory in 2000 of $64,000 nearly doubled to $116,000 at the end of 2000 and increased to $158,000 at the end of 2001. Over the same period net sales increased only 7% from $400,000 in 2000 to $428,000 in 2001.

ACCOUNTS RECEIVABLE TURNOVER

Objective 3

Determine accounts receivable turnover.

Accounts receivable turnover is the number of times charge accounts are turned over (paid off) during a given year. A turnover implies a sale on account followed by the cash collection of the amount owed to us.

$$\text{Accounts Receivable Turnover} = \frac{\text{Net Sales on Account}}{\text{Average Accounts Receivable}}$$

$$\text{Average Accounts Receivable} = \frac{\text{Beginning Accounts Receivable} + \text{Ending Accounts Receivable}}{2}$$

Going back to DeClerk Card Shop, let's assume the following information for 2001 and 2000.

	2001	2000
Net sales on account (from the sales journal)	$330,000	$302,000
Beginning accounts receivable (from Accounts Receivable account)	39,680	37,500
Ending accounts receivable (from Accounts Receivable account)	45,840	39,680

2001

$$\text{Average Accounts Receivable} = \frac{\$39,680 + \$45,840}{2} = \frac{\$85,520}{2} = \underline{\underline{\$42,760}}$$

$$\text{Accounts Receivable Turnover} = \frac{\$330,000}{\$42,760} = \underline{\underline{7.72}} \text{ times per year}$$

2000

$$\text{Average Accounts Receivable} = \frac{\$37,500 + \$39,680}{2} = \frac{\$77,180}{2} = \underline{\underline{\$38,590}}$$

$$\text{Accounts Receivable Turnover} = \frac{\$302,000}{\$38,590} = \underline{\underline{7.83}} \text{ times per year}$$

A lower turnover rate indicates that a firm is experiencing greater difficulty in collecting charge accounts. In addition, more investment capital is tied up in accounts receivable.

The receivable turnover deteriorated slightly from 7.83 to 7.72 in 2000, possibly because the seller granted easier credit terms or the buyers incurred cash flow problems because of a declining economy. From the end of 2000 to the end of 2001, the receivables balance increased 16% from $39,680 to $45,840. However, over the same period net sales increased only 7%. This provides further evidence of the company's deteriorating financial condition.

RETURN ON INVESTMENT (YIELD)

Objective 4

Determine return on investment.

Return on investment represents the earning power of the owner's investment in the business.

$$\text{Return on Investment} = \frac{\text{Net Income for the Year}}{\text{Average Capital}}$$

$$\text{Average Capital} = \frac{\text{Beginning Capital} + \text{Ending Capital}}{2}$$

Getting back to DeClerk Card Shop, let's assume the following information for 2001 and 2000:

	2001	2000
Beginning balance of owner's Capital account	$176,920	$181,440
Ending balance of owner's Capital account	184,780	176,920

2001

$$\text{Average Capital} = \frac{\$176,920 + \$184,780}{2} = \frac{\$361,700}{2} = \underline{\underline{\$180,850}}$$

$$\text{Return on Investment} = \frac{\$17,000}{\$180,850} = .094 = \underline{\underline{9.4\%}}$$

2000

$$\text{Average Capital} = \frac{\$181,440 + \$176,920}{2} = \frac{\$358,360}{2} = \underline{\underline{\$179,180}}$$

$$\text{Return on Investment} = \frac{\$32,000}{\$179,180} = .179 = \underline{\underline{17.9\%}}$$

As a result, we can state the following:

- In 2001, for an average investment of $100, the business earned $9.40.
- In 2000, for an average investment of $100, the business earned $17.90.

The return on investment deteriorated from 17.9% in 2000 to 9.4% in 2001 because net income declined 47% from $32,000 in 2000 to $17,000 in 2001.

PROBLEMS

P.O. 1

Problem E-1 Ross Company's abbreviated comparative income statement for years 2001 and 2000 is as follows:

Ross Company Comparative Income Statement For Years Ended December 31, 2001 and December 31, 2000		
	2001	2000
Net Sales	$ 487 2 0 0 00	$ 462 0 0 0 00
Cost of Goods Sold	287 4 0 0 00	277 2 0 0 00
Gross Profit	$ 199 8 0 0 00	$ 184 8 0 0 00
Total Operating Expenses	152 2 4 0 00	146 1 6 0 00
Net Income	$ 47 5 6 0 00	$ 38 6 4 0 00

Check Figure

Net income % (2000), 8.4%

Instructions

1. For the years 2001 and 2000, determine gross profit as a percentage of net sales.
2. For the years 2001 and 2000, determine net income as a percentage of net sales.

Problem E-2 Ross Company's merchandise inventory figures are:

	2001	**2000**
Beginning merchandise inventory (January 1)	$ 88,420	$106,110
Purchases	302,190	259,510
Ending merchandise inventory (December 31)	103,210	88,420

Check Figure

Cost of goods sold (2001),
$287,400

Instructions

Determine the merchandise inventory turnover for the years 2001 and 2000.

Problem E-3 A. L. Ross, Capital, account balances are as follows:

January 1, 2000	$375,670
January 1, 2001	$493,970
December 31, 2001	$526,820

Check Figure

Return on investment (2000),
8.9%

Instructions

Determine the return on investment for the years 2001 and 2000 if net income is $47,560 for 2001 and $38,640 for 2000.

15 Notes Payable

Performance Objectives

After you have completed this chapter, you will be able to do the following:

1. Define *promissory note.*

2. Calculate the interest on promissory notes.

3. Determine the due dates of promissory notes.

4. Make journal entries for (a) notes given to secure an extension of time on an open account; (b) payment of an interest-bearing note at maturity; (c) notes given in exchange for merchandise or other property purchased; (d) notes given to secure a cash loan, when the borrower receives the full face value of the note; (e) notes given to secure a cash loan, when the bank discounts the note; (f) payment of a non-interest-bearing note at maturity; and (g) renewal of a note at maturity.

5. Complete a notes payable register.

6. Make journal entries for (a) adjustment for accrued interest on notes payable, (b) adjustment for Discount on Notes Payable, and (c) conversion of Discount on Notes Payable to Interest Expense.

Credit plays an extremely important role in the operation of most business enterprises. Credit may be extended on a charge-account basis, with payment generally due in twenty-five to thirty days. This type of credit involves the Accounts Payable and Accounts Receivable accounts. Credit may also be granted by giving or receiving notes for specific transactions. This sort of credit involves the Notes Payable and Notes Receivable accounts. The notes, which represent formal instruments of credit, are known as *promissory notes*. They are customarily used as evidence of credit transactions for periods longer than thirty days. For example, promissory notes may be used in sales of equipment on the installment plan and for transactions involving large amounts of money.

Promissory notes are also used to grant extensions of credit beyond the original credit terms. For example, suppose that Eaton Company buys merchandise from Foster Company with terms of 2/10, n/30. Eaton Company finds that it can't pay its bill within the thirty-day period. To preserve its credit standing, Eaton Company offers a note. The advantages to Foster Company are as follows: (1) Foster now has specific evidence of the transaction, (2) the note may carry interest, and (3) Foster can borrow from the bank by pledging the note as security for a loan. Business concerns may also borrow from banks by issuing their own promissory notes.

Most companies become involved with notes at one time or another, either by issuing notes to creditors, by receiving notes from customers, or by issuing notes to banks in order to borrow money. Consequently, an accountant must be acquainted with the procedures for handling promissory notes.

PROMISSORY NOTES

Objective 1

Define *promissory note*.

A **promissory note**—usually referred to simply as a *note*—is a written promise to pay a certain sum at a fixed or determinable future time. Like a check, it must be payable to the order of a particular person or firm, known as the **payee**. It must also be signed by the person or firm making the promise, known as the **maker**. In Figure 1, Lund Manufacturing Company is the payee, and Jackson Electric Supply is the maker.

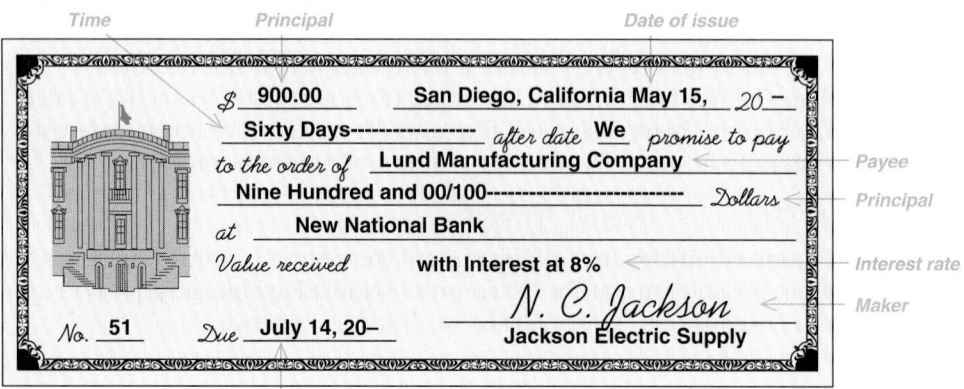

FIGURE 1

CALCULATING INTEREST

Objective 2

Calculate the interest on promissory notes.

Interest is a charge made for the use of money. To the maker of the note, interest is an expense. The amount of interest a maker pays is expressed as a certain percentage of the principal of the note for a period of one year (or less). The following formula is used to calculate interest:

Interest = **Principal** of note × **Rate** of interest × **Time** of note
(in dollars)   (in dollars)   (as a percentage   (expressed as a
                                of the principal)   year or fraction
                                                     of a year)

The **principal** is the face amount of the note. The *rate of interest* is a percentage of the principal, such as 10 percent or 11 percent. Since 1 percent equals $\frac{1}{100}$ or .01, then 10 percent equals $\frac{10}{100}$ or .10.

Time, or the length of life of the note, is expressed in days or months. It is the period between the note's date of issue (starting date) and its **maturity date** (the due date or interest payment date). It is stated in terms of a year or fraction of a year. Examples are

$$1 \text{ year} = 1 \qquad 6 \text{ months} = \frac{6}{12} \qquad 3 \text{ months} = \frac{3}{12}$$

$$90 \text{ days} = \frac{90}{360} \qquad 24 \text{ days} = \frac{24}{360}$$

The usual commercial practice is to use a 360-day year, making the denominator of the fraction 360. However, agencies of the federal government use the actual number of days in the year.

Example 1 $3,000, 8 percent, 1 year.

Interest = Principal × Rate × Time
Interest = $3,000 × .08 × 1 = $240

Example 2 $4,000, 9 percent, 3 months.

Interest = Principal × Rate × Time

$$\text{Interest} = \$4,000 \times .09 \times \frac{3}{12}$$

$$= \$4,000 \times .09 \times 3 \div 12 = \underline{\$90}$$

Example 3 $9,000, 7 percent, 60 days.

Interest = Principal × Rate × Time

$$\text{Interest} = \$9,000 \times .07 \times \frac{60}{360}$$

$$= \$9,000 \times .07 \times 60 \div 360 = \underline{\$105}$$

The liability incurred when borrowing money can be short-term or long-term in nature. Some debts last only a few days, whereas others last thirty years.

Remember!

A note is a formal written promise to pay an amount of money at a definite time, as opposed to the "open account" relationship in Accounts Receivable or Accounts Payable.

DETERMINING DUE DATES

Objective 3

Determine the due dates of promissory notes.

The period of time between a promissory note issue date and its maturity date is called the **duration** of the note. The duration of a note, as we have said, may be expressed in either days or months. If the time of the note is expressed in months, the maturity date is the corresponding day in the month after the specified number of months have elapsed. For example, a note dated March 15 with a time period of three months has a due date of June 15. In those cases in which there is no date in the month of maturity that corresponds to the issuance date, the due date becomes the last day of the month. For example, a three-month note dated March 31 would be due on June 30.

But suppose that the period of time a note has to run is expressed in days. When counting the number of days, begin with the day after the date the note was issued, since the note states "after date." The last day, however, is counted. Let's say that the due date of a promissory note is specified as 60 days after April 8. The due date is June 7.

April								May								June						
S	M	T	W	T	F	S		S	M	T	W	T	F	S		S	M	T	W	T	F	S
		1	2	3	4	5						1	2	3		1	2	3	4	5	6	7
6	7	8	9	10	11	12		4	5	6	7	8	9	10		8	9	10	11	12	13	14
13	14	15	16	17	18	19		11	12	13	14	15	16	17		15	16	17	18	19	20	21
20	21	22	23	24	25	26		18	19	20	21	22	23	24		22	23	24	25	26	27	28
27	28	29	30					25	26	27	28	29	30	31		29	30					

22 days
8th through the 30th
30 − 8 = 22 days left

+ 31 days

= 53 days have passed
60 − 53 = 7 days remaining after May 31
June 7 due date

The due date is determined by the following steps:

1. Determine the number of days remaining in the month of issue by subtracting the date of the note from the number of days in the month in which it is dated.
2. Add as many full months as possible without exceeding the number of days in the note, counting the full number of days in these months.
3. Determine the number of days remaining in the month in which the note matures by subtracting the total days counted so far from the number of days in the note, as shown here.

April (30 − 8)	= 22 days left in April
May	= 31 days
Total days so far	= 53 days
June (60 − 53)	= 7th day of June (due date)

Now, suppose you have a 120-day note dated May 20:

May (31 − 20)	= 11 days left in May
June	= 30 days
July	= 31 days
August	= 31 days
Total days so far	= 103 days
September (120 − 103)	= 17th day of September (due date)

TRANSACTIONS INVOLVING NOTES PAYABLE

The following types of transactions involve the issuance and payment of notes payable:

1. Note given to a supplier in return for an extension of time for payment of an open account (charge account)
2. Note given in exchange for merchandise or other property purchased
3. Note given as evidence of a loan
4. Note renewed at maturity

In our examples, we assume that all the notes are due within one year; thus they are classified on a balance sheet as Current Liabilities. However, if notes are not due within one year, that portion of the note that is due within one year is a Current Liability, and the remainder is classified as a Long-Term Liability. Interest Expense is classified on an income statement as Other Expense.

Note Given to Secure an Extension of Time on an Open Account

Objective 4a

Make journal entries for notes given to secure an extension of time on an open account.

Remember!

Accounts Payable is a controlling account. Notes Payable is not a controlling account like Accounts Payable and does not require the name of the maker following Notes Payable.

When a firm wishes to obtain an extension of time for the payment of an account, the firm may ask a supplier to accept a note for all or part of the amount due. For example, let's say that Jackson Electric Supply bought merchandise on account, $750, on April 15 from Nagle Company, with terms 2/10, n/30. Suppose that Jackson Electric prefers not to pay its open account with Nagle when it becomes due. Instead, Nagle agrees to accept a 60-day, 8 percent, $750 note from Jackson Electric Supply in settlement of the charge account.

Original Purchase In general journal form, the entry looks like this:

			GENERAL JOURNAL			PAGE 1	
	DATE		DESCRIPTION	POST. REF.	DEBIT	CREDIT	
1	20–						1
2	Apr.	15	Purchases		7 5 0 00		2
3			Accounts Payable, Nagle Co.			7 5 0 00	3
4			Terms 2/10, n/30.				4
5							5

Payment by Note On May 15, Jackson Electric Supply records the issuance of the note in its general journal.

	DATE		DESCRIPTION	POST. REF.	DEBIT	CREDIT	
1	20–						1
2	May	15	Accounts Payable, Nagle Co.		7 5 0 00		2
3			Notes Payable			7 5 0 00	3
4			Gave a 60-day, 8 percent				4
5			note in settlement of our				5
6			open account.				6
7							7

GENERAL JOURNAL   PAGE _____

By T accounts, the transactions look like this:

Purchases		
	+	−
Apr. 15	750	

Accounts Payable		
	−	+
May 15	750	Apr. 15 750

Notes Payable		
	−	+
		May 15 750

Observe that this entry cancels the Accounts Payable, Nagle Company account and substitutes Notes Payable. The note does not *pay* the debt; it merely changes the status of the liability from an account payable to a note payable. Nagle prefers the note to the open account because, in case of default and a subsequent lawsuit to collect, the possession of the note improves Nagle's legal position. The note is written evidence of the debt and the amount owed. In addition, Nagle will earn 8 percent interest on this note.

Payment of an Interest-bearing Note at Maturity

Objective 4b

Make journal entries for payment of an interest-bearing note at maturity.

When a note payable falls due, payment may be made directly to the holder, or it may be made to a bank with which the note was left for collection. The maker knows the identity of the original payee, of course, but he or she may not know who the holder of the note is at maturity. The payee may have transferred the note by endorsement to another party or may have left it with a bank for collection. When a note is left with a bank for collection, the bank usually mails the maker a notice of maturity specifying the terms, the due date of the note, and the maturity value (the principal of the note plus the interest). For example, Nagle Company turned the note over to its bank, the New National Bank, for collection. Accordingly, the bank sent Jackson Electric Supply a notice of maturity of the note.

A note may be given in exchange for merchandise or other property purchased, such as for an automobile to be used in the business. The portion of this woman's note that is payable this year is a current liability for her company. The balance is a long-term liability.

Jackson Electric Supply pays the note on July 14. In general journal form, the entry is as follows:

	DATE		DESCRIPTION	POST. REF.	DEBIT		CREDIT	
1	20–							1
2	July	14	Notes Payable		7 5 0 00			2
3			Interest Expense		1 0 00			3
4			Cash				7 6 0 00	4
5			Paid note to Nagle Co.					5
6								6

GENERAL JOURNAL   PAGE _____

Because Interest = Principal × Rate × Time, we perform this calculation:

$$Interest = \$750 \times .08 \times 60 \div 360 = \underline{\$10.00}$$

Cash				Notes Payable				Interest Expense		
	+	–			–	+			+	–
Bal.	10,000.00	July 14 760.00		July 14	750.00	May 15 750.00		July 14	10.00	

In practice, if special journals are used, transactions like this one are recorded directly in the cash payments journal rather than in the general journal. However, to simplify the discussion of the entries, all transactions are presented here in general journal form.

Objective 4c

Make journal entries for notes given in exchange for merchandise or other property purchased.

Note Given in Exchange for Assets Purchased

Occasionally, when the price of an item is high or the credit period is long, a buyer gives a note instead of buying the item on account. For example, Jackson Electric Supply issues a 90-day, 9 percent interest-bearing note for $4,500 to the Phelps Equipment Company in exchange for equipment purchased June 3 and records the transaction in the general journal as follows:

	DATE		DESCRIPTION	POST. REF.	DEBIT		CREDIT	
1	20–							1
2	June	3	Store Equipment		4 5 0 0 00			2
3			Notes Payable				4 5 0 0 00	3
4			Acquired shelves and					4
5			counters from Phelps					5
6			Equipment Co., 90 days,					6
7			9 percent.					7
8								8

By T accounts, the transaction looks like this:

Store Equipment		Notes Payable	
+	−	−	+
4,500			4,500

When Jackson Electric Supply pays the note at maturity, the entry in its books is the same as the entry it makes for the payment of any interest-bearing note. In general journal form, the entry is as follows:

	DATE		DESCRIPTION	POST. REF.	DEBIT	CREDIT	
1	20–						1
2	Sept.	1	Notes Payable		4 5 0 0 00		2
3			Interest Expense		1 0 1 25		3
4			Cash			4 6 0 1 25	4
5			Paid note to Phelps				5
6			Equipment Co.				6
7							7

Determining the Due Date

June (30 − 3)	= 27 days left in June	
July	= 31 days	
August	= 31 days	
Total days so far	= 89 days	
September (90 − 89)	= 1st day of September (due date)	

And because Interest = Principal × Rate × Time,

Interest = $4,500 × .09 × 90 ÷ 360 = $101.25

Note Given to Secure a Cash Loan

Businesses frequently need to stock up on merchandise in large amounts in order to meet seasonal demands. Sometimes their usual receipts from customers are not enough to cover the sudden volume of purchases. During such periods, firms customarily borrow money from banks, through the medium of short-term notes, to finance their operations.

Borrowing from a Bank When Borrower Receives Full Face Value of Note

In one type of bank loan, a business signs an interest-bearing note and receives the full face value of the note. The business (borrower) repays the principal plus interest. For example, on June 11, Jackson Electric Supply borrows $2,650 from Alpha National Bank for 120 days with interest of 7 percent payable at maturity. The entry to record the transaction is as follows:

	DATE		DESCRIPTION	POST. REF.	DEBIT					CREDIT				
1	20–														1
2	June	11	Cash		2	6	5	0	00						2
3			Notes Payable							2	6	5	0	00	3
4			Gave Alpha National Bank a												4
5			120-day, 7 percent note.												5
6															6

Note Paid to the Bank at Maturity

After Jackson Electric Supply has paid the note and interest, its accountant makes the following entry on the books:

	DATE		DESCRIPTION	POST. REF.	DEBIT					CREDIT				
1	20–														1
2	Oct.	9	Notes Payable		2	6	5	0	00						2
3			Interest Expense				6	1	83						3
4			Cash							2	7	1	1	83	4
5			Paid note to Alpha National												5
6			Bank.												6
7															7

Interest = Principal × Rate × Time

Interest = $2,650 × .07 × 120 ÷ 360 = $61.83

Borrowing from a Bank When Bank Discounts Note (Deducts Interest in Advance)

Banks assist businesses by providing loans to finance their operations. In exchange for a note payable, the bank makes the loan either with the interest payable at maturity or with the interest already deducted in advance.

In another type of bank loan, the bank deducts the interest in advance, which is called **discounting a note payable**. For example, on June 19, Jackson Electric Supply borrows $8,000 for 90 days from Northern National Bank, and the bank requires Jackson Electric Supply to sign a note. From the face value of the note, the bank deducts 8.5 percent interest for 90 days, so Jackson Electric Supply actually gets only $7,830. This interest deducted in advance by a bank is called the **discount**. The principal of the loan left after the discount has been subtracted is called the **proceeds**, which is the amount the borrower has available to use. Since all the interest is deducted at the time the loan is made, the note must state that only the face amount is to be paid at maturity. The calculation is as follows:

Interest = Principal × Rate × Time

Interest = $8,000 × .085 × 90 ÷ 360 = $170

The bank deducts the discount from the face amount of the note before making the money available to the borrower.

Principal	$8,000
− Discount	170
Proceeds	$7,830

Entry When Note Discounted at Bank Matures Before End of Fiscal Period

As long as a note begins and matures during the same fiscal period, the borrower may debit all the interest (or discount) to Interest Expense. The 90-day note that Jackson Electric Supply submits to the bank is dated June 19 and therefore matures September 17. Since Jackson Electric Supply's fiscal period is from January 1 to December 31, the company can include the entire amount of interest in Interest Expense. Accordingly, Jackson Electric Supply records the transaction as follows:

	DATE		DESCRIPTION	POST. REF.	DEBIT	CREDIT	
1	20–						1
2	June	19	Cash		7 8 3 0 00		2
3			Interest Expense		1 7 0 00		3
4			Notes Payable			8 0 0 0 00	4
5			Discounted our 90-day				5
6			non-interest-bearing note				6
7			at Northern National Bank,				7
8			discount rate 8.5 percent.				8
9							9

Note Paid to the Bank at Maturity

When the note becomes due, Jackson Electric Supply pays the bank only the *face value of the note* and records the transaction as follows:

	DATE		DESCRIPTION	POST. REF.	DEBIT	CREDIT	
1	20–						1
2	Sept.	17	Notes Payable		8 0 0 0 00		2
3			Cash			8 0 0 0 00	3
4			Paid Northern National Bank				4
5			on our note payable				5
6			discounted June 19.				6
7							7
8							8
9							9

Entry When Note Discounted at Bank Matures After End of Fiscal Period

Instead of the entire duration of the note (such as 90 or 60 days) being included in one 12-month fiscal period, assume that the duration extends into the next fiscal period. In this case, the journal entry must include a debit to Discount on Notes Payable instead of a debit to Interest Expense. In other words, Discount on Notes Payable is substituted for Interest Expense, using the same dollar amount.

Discount on Notes Payable is a contra-liability account; **it is a deduction from Notes Payable.** Recall that we defined the Accumulated Depreciation account as a contra-asset account—for example, a deduction from Equipment with the plus and minus signs reversed. Similarly, Discount on Notes Payable is a contra account—a deduction from Notes Payable with the plus and minus signs reversed. In T account form, these accounts look like this:

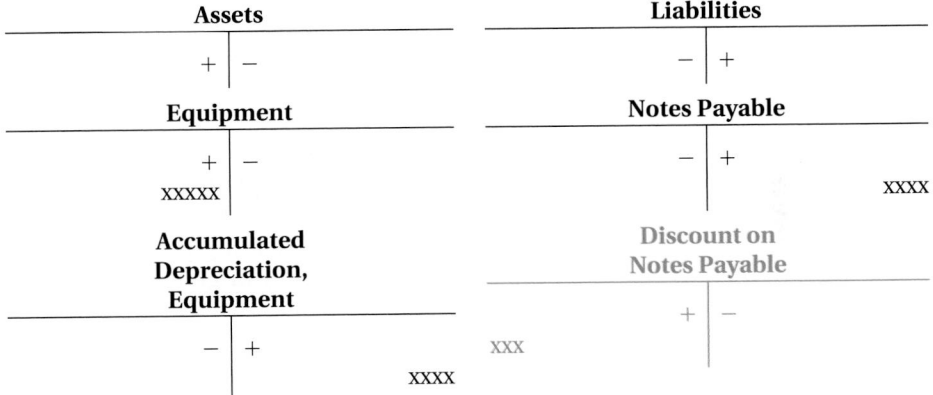

On a balance sheet, the contra account is deducted as follows:

Assets				
Plant and Equipment:				
Equipment	$xx x x x xx			
Less Accumulated Depreciation	x x x x xx	x x x x x xx		
Liabilities				
Current Liabilities:				
Notes Payable	$ x x x x xx			
Less Discount on Notes Payable	x x x x xx	$ x x x x xx		

At the end of the fiscal period, an adjusting entry must be made to record the accrued interest expense and the discount on notes payable for the time between the date the note is issued and the end of the fiscal period. The note is outstanding during the period. We will describe this type of adjusting entry as part of the section "End-of-Fiscal-Period Adjustments."

Let's say that on December 1, Jackson Electric Supply borrows $9,000 from Eastern State Bank for 120 days. The bank deducts 9 percent interest (in advance) for 120 days, $270, and gives Jackson Electric Supply $8,730.

Remember!

If a note payable discounted at a bank comes due *before* the end of the fiscal period, debit Interest Expense for the amount of the discount. If the note comes due *after* the end of the fiscal period, debit Discount on Notes Payable for the amount of the discount.

Remember!

In a discounted-note transaction, since all the interest is deducted at the time the loan is made, the note must state that only the face amount is to be paid at maturity.

Objective 4g

Make journal entries for renewal of a note at maturity.

Jackson Electric Supply's fiscal period is from January 1 through December 31, so the entry in the general journal is as follows:

	DATE		DESCRIPTION	POST. REF.	DEBIT	CREDIT	
1	20–						1
2	Dec.	1	Cash		8 7 3 0 00		2
3			Discount on Notes Payable		2 7 0 00		3
4			Notes Payable			9 0 0 0 00	4
5			Discounted our 120-day,				5
6			non-interest-bearing note at				6
7			Eastern State Bank;				7
8			discount rate 9 percent.				8
9							9

Renewal of Note at Maturity

A maker (or borrower) unable to pay a note in full at maturity may arrange to renew all or part of the note. At this time, he or she usually pays the interest on the old note. For example, assume that on June 27, Jackson Electric Supply issues a 45-day note to Bailey, Inc., for $9,800, with interest at 8 percent. The original entry in general journal form is as follows:

	DATE		DESCRIPTION	POST. REF.	DEBIT	CREDIT	
1	20–						1
2	June	27	Accounts Payable, Bailey, Inc.		9 8 0 0 00		2
3			Notes Payable			9 8 0 0 00	3
4			Issued a 45-day, 8 percent				4
5			note.				5
6							6

Renewal of Note with Payment of Interest

When a firm renews an interest-bearing note, while paying interest owed, the accountant first makes an entry for payment of the interest on the existing note up to the present date. This entry occurs on August 11, the maturity date of the note:

	DATE		DESCRIPTION	POST. REF.	DEBIT	CREDIT	
1	20–						1
2	Aug.	11	Interest Expense		9 8 00		2
3			Cash			9 8 00	3
4			Interest payment on note to				4
5			Bailey, Inc.				5
6							6

Interest = Principal × Rate × Time

Interest = \$9,800 × .08 × 45 ÷ 360 = \$98.00

The accountant then makes a separate entry for the issuance of the new note, to run for 30 days at 9 percent (the interest rate has been increased and the number of days decreased), as follows:

	DATE		DESCRIPTION	POST. REF.	DEBIT	CREDIT	
11	Aug.	11	Notes Payable		9 8 0 0 00		11
12			Notes Payable			9 8 0 0 00	12
13			Canceled note to Bailey, Inc.,				13
14			by issuing 30-day, 9 percent				14
15			note.				15

Renewal of Note with Payment of Interest and Part Payment of Principal

Remember!

For a renewal of a note payable, debit the old note to take it off the books, and credit the new note to put it on the books.

What if the maker decides to pay only *part* of a note at maturity? Let's assume that, instead of taking the course of action we have just described, Jackson Electric Supply pays \$1,600 on the principal of the note that is due (the old note), and also pays the entire interest on it. In other words, the maker pays the interest up to the present date for the old note, plus \$1,600 to reduce the principal from \$9,800 to \$8,200, and issues a *new* note for \$8,200.

	DATE		DESCRIPTION	POST. REF.	DEBIT	CREDIT	
11	Aug.	11	Notes Payable		1 6 0 0 00		11
12			Interest Expense		9 8 00		12
13			Cash			1 6 9 8 00	13
14			Interest payment on 45-day,				14
15			8 percent note to Bailey, Inc.,				15
16			and part payment on the				16
17			principal.				17
18							18
19		11	Notes Payable		8 2 0 0 00		19
20			Notes Payable			8 2 0 0 00	20
21			Canceled note to Bailey, Inc.,				21
22			by issuing 30-day, 9 percent				22
23			note.				23
24							24

Ordinarily, small businesses issue notes to relatively few creditors. These firms can record the details of the notes on stubs similar to check stubs, or they can just keep duplicate copies of the notes. However, if a firm issues many notes, it may be more convenient to keep a separate record listing the details of each note. This type of record is called a notes payable register.

In an abbreviated form, here's an illustration of a notes payable register for Jackson Electric Supply through August 11:

NOTES PAYABLE REGISTER

DATE		PAYEE	AMOUNT					TIME	RATE	INTEREST				DUE DATE	DATE PAID	REMARKS
20–																
May	15	Nagle Company		7	5	0	00	60 days	8%		1	0	00	7/14	7/14	Open account.
June	3	Phelps Equipment Co.	4	5	0	0	00	90 days	9%	1	0	1	25	9/1	9/1	Bought equipment.
	11	Alpha National Bank	2	6	5	0	00	120 days	7%		6	1	83	10/9	10/9	Loan, received full
																principal.
	19	Northern National	8	0	0	0	00	90 days	8.5%	1	7	0	00	9/17	9/17	Loan, discount
		Bank														$170.
	27	Bailey, Inc.		9	8	0	0	00	45 days	8%		9	8	00	8/11	Renewed	Open account.
Aug.	11	Bailey, Inc.		9	8	0	0	00	30 days	9%		7	3	50	9/10		Renewed June 27
																note.
		OR IF PARTIAL PAYMENT														
Aug.	11	Bailey, Inc.		8	2	0	0	00	30 days	9%		6	1	50	9/10		Renewed June 27
																note with part
																payment of $1,600.

More elaborate notes payable registers may include columns listing note numbers, addresses of payees, and similar information.

At the end of the fiscal period, the firm may prepare a schedule of notes payable by listing the unpaid notes that appear in the notes payable register. This schedule is similar to a schedule of accounts payable. The total of the schedule is compared with the balance of Notes Payable.

END-OF-FISCAL-PERIOD ADJUSTMENTS

When notes start in one fiscal period and mature in the next, adjusting entries must be made both for accrued interest and for discounts on notes payable. Otherwise, neither the expenses incurred by the business firm during a fiscal period nor its liabilities at the end of the fiscal period would be correctly stated.

Accrued Interest on Notes Payable

On all interest-bearing notes, interest expense *accrues*, or *accumulates*, daily. Consequently, if any notes payable are outstanding at the end of a fiscal period, the **accrued interest on notes payable** (that is, the interest due but not yet paid) should be calculated and recorded. For example, assume that a firm has two notes payable outstanding as of December 31, the end of the current fiscal period.

$3,000, 60 days, 8%, dated December 10
$7,200, 90 days, 7%, dated December 2

We can diagram the period of each note like this:

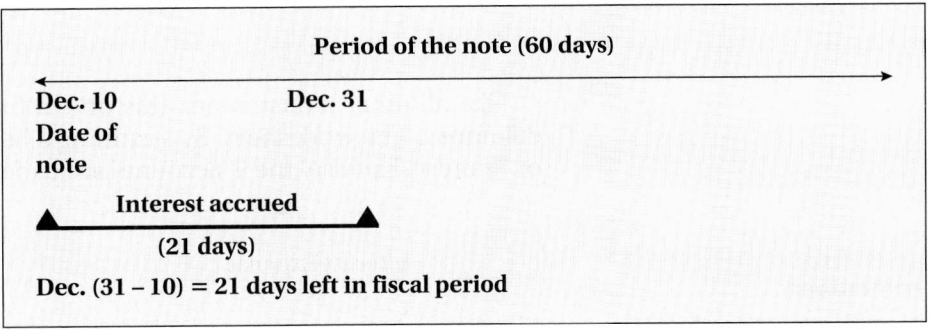

Interest = Principal × Rate × Time
Interest = $3,000 × .08 × 21 ÷ 360 = <u>$14.00</u>

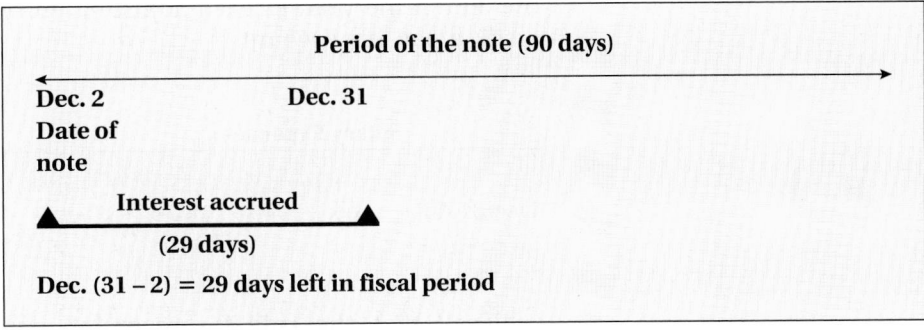

Interest = Principal × Rate × Time
Interest = $7,200 × .07 × 29 ÷ 360 = <u>$40.60</u>

Objective 6a

Make journal entries for adjustment for accrued interest on notes payable.

Obviously, both notes extend into the next fiscal period; if they didn't, there would be no need for an adjustment. When paying interest on notes—except for notes discounted at a bank—you usually pay the principal and interest together on the day the note matures, or becomes due. But since *these* notes have not matured, naturally the interest expense has been neither paid nor recorded. Therefore, the firm has to make an adjustment, because the accountant tries to portray the firm's expenses and liabilities for the current fiscal period as accurately as possible. In general journal form, the adjusting entry for the interest expense accrued on the two notes is as shown on the following page.

	DATE		DESCRIPTION	POST. REF.	DEBIT			CREDIT		
1	20–		**Adjusting Entry**							1
2	Dec.	31	Interest Expense		5	4	60			2
3			Interest Payable					5 4 60		3
4			($14.00 + $40.60)							4
5										5
6										6
7										7

Remember!

Calculations are included to show how the amounts were determined. They would not normally appear in journal entries.

Like all other adjustments, this one is first recorded in the Adjustments columns of the work sheet. By assuming a balance of $825 before adjustment of Interest Expense, the T accounts are as follows:

Remember!

Any account name ending in Payable is always a liability account.

Interest Expense			Interest Payable	
+	–		–	+
Dec. 31 Bal. 825.00				Dec. 31 Adj. 54.60
Dec. 31 Adj. 54.60				

This situation parallels the adjustment for accrued salaries, in which the objective is to record the additional amount of salaries incurred and owed at the end of the year. In each adjusting entry, debit an expense account and credit a payable account.

Salary Expense			Salaries Payable	
+	–		–	+
Dec. 31 Adj. xxx				Dec. 31 Adj. xxx

Remember!

Reversing entries are not required.

Recall that **the rule for reversing entries is: If an adjusting entry increases an asset or liability account that does not have a previous balance, then you may reverse the adjusting entry.** Entries involving contra accounts are never reversed.

Discount on Notes Payable

Remember!

Discount on Notes Payable is a contra-liability account and a deduction from Notes Payable.

When a note payable is discounted at a bank, the bank deducts the interest (based on the principal of the note) in advance. **If the note begins and ends during one fiscal period, the interest is recorded as Interest Expense, and no adjustment is needed. But if the note extends into the next fiscal period, the interest is recorded as Discount on Notes Payable.** An adjusting entry is needed to record the interest for the number of days the note was outstanding during the fiscal period.

Recall our original entry made on December 1, in which the firm discounted its note at the bank.

DATE		DESCRIPTION	POST. REF.	DEBIT	CREDIT	
20–						1
Dec.	1	Cash		8 7 3 0 00		2
		Discount on Notes Payable		2 7 0 00		3
		Notes Payable			9 0 0 0 00	4
		Discounted our 120-day,				5
		non-interest-bearing note at				6
		Eastern State Bank;				7
		discount rate 9 percent.				8
						9

Period of the note (120 days)

Dec. 1   Dec. 31

Dec. (31 – 1) = 30 days left in fiscal period

Interest = Principal $\times$ Rate $\times$ Time

Interest = $9,000 $\times$ .09 $\times$ 30 $\div$ 360 = $67.50

Objective 6b

Make journal entries for adjustment for Discount on Notes Payable.

Since there are 30 days between December 1 and December 31, Jackson Electric Supply's accountant has to make an adjusting entry to record the Interest Expense:

DATE		DESCRIPTION	POST. REF.	DEBIT	CREDIT	
20–		Adjusting Entry				1
Dec.	31	Interest Expense		6 7 50		2
		Discount on Notes Payable			6 7 50	3
						4

In T accounts, it looks this way:

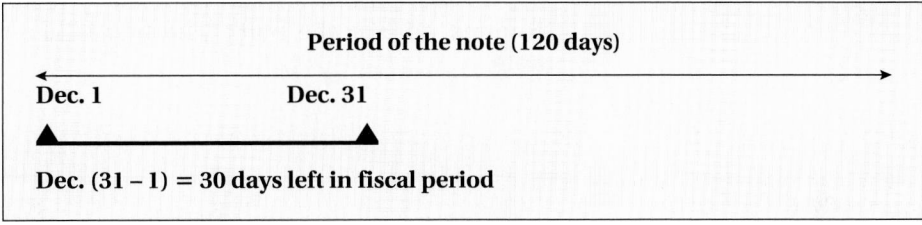

Interest Expense		Discount on Notes Payable	
+	–	+	–
Dec. 31 Adj. 67.50		Dec. 1 270.00	Dec. 31 Adj. 67.50

In addition to recording Interest Expense, the adjusting entry also reduces the balance of Discount on Notes Payable to its correct amount. This adjustment and the adjusting entry for accrued interest payable are shown on the partial worksheet in Figure 2 (page 546). At the end of the year, the Interest Expense account is closed along with all the other expense accounts.

FIGURE 2

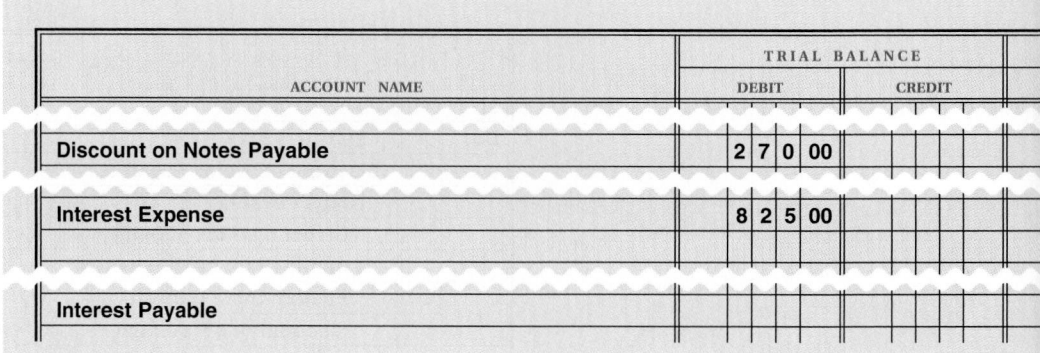

ACCOUNT NAME	TRIAL BALANCE	
	DEBIT	CREDIT
Discount on Notes Payable	2 7 0 00	
Interest Expense	8 2 5 00	
Interest Payable		

Two journal entries can be used to record the final payment of the discounted note to the bank. The first is like the payment of any discounted note.

	DATE		DESCRIPTION	POST. REF.	DEBIT	CREDIT	
1	20–						1
2	Mar.	31	Notes Payable		9 0 0 0 00		2
3			Cash			9 0 0 0 00	3
4			Paid the bank the 120-day,				4
5			non-interest-bearing note,				5
6			dated December 1 and				6
7			discounted at 9 percent.				7

◼◼◼

Objective 6c

Make journal entries for conversion of Discount on Notes Payable to Interest Expense.

The Discount on Notes Payable that was on the books has now become entirely an expense, and so it is converted into Interest Expense.

			DESCRIPTION		DEBIT	CREDIT	
9		31	Interest Expense		2 0 2 50		9
10			Discount on Notes Payable			2 0 2 50	10
11			To expense the discount for				11
12			the current year for the 120-				12
13			day note, dated December 1				13
14			and discounted at 9 percent.				14
15			($9,000 × .09 × 90/360)				15

In T accounts, the entries for the discounted note payable look like this:

Interest Expense				Discount on Notes Payable			
+		−			+	−	
Dec. 31 Adj.	67.50	Dec. 31 Clos.	67.50	Dec. 1	270	Dec. 31 Adj.	67.50
Mar. 31	202.50					Mar. 31	202.50

		ADJUSTMENTS		INCOME STATEMENT		BALANCE SHEET	
		DEBIT	CREDIT	DEBIT	CREDIT	DEBIT	CREDIT
	(b)		6 7 50			2 0 2 50	
(a)		5 4 60		8 9 1 70			
(b)		6 7 50					
	(a)		5 4 60				5 4 60

CHAPTER REVIEW

Review of Performance Objectives

1. Define *promissory note.*

   A promissory note is a written promise to pay a certain sum at a fixed or determinable future time.

2. Calculate the interest on promissory notes.

   The formula used to calculate interest is as follows:

   Interest = **Principal** of note × **Rate** of interest × **Duration** of note
   (in dollars)   (in dollars)   (as a percentage   (expressed as a year
                                        of the principal)   or fraction of a year)

3. Determine the due dates of promissory notes.

   Use the following steps to determine the due date:
   1. Determine the number of days remaining in the month of issue by subtracting the date of the note from the number of days in the month in which it is dated.
   2. Add as many full months as possible without exceeding the number of days in the note, counting the full number of days in these months.
   3. Determine the number of days remaining in the month in which the note matures by subtracting the total days counted so far from the number of days in the note.

4. Make journal entries for (a) notes given to secure an extension of time on an open account; (b) payment of an interest-bearing note at maturity; (c) notes given in exchange for merchandise or other property purchased; (d) notes given to secure a cash loan, when the borrower receives the full face value of the note; (e) notes given to secure a cash loan, when the bank discounts the note; (f) payment of a non-interest-bearing note at maturity; and (g) renewal of a note at maturity.

   (a) Notes given to secure an extension of time on an open account.

   May 15 Issued a 60-day, 8 percent note for $750, payable to Nagle Company, in place of the open-book account.

GENERAL JOURNAL   PAGE _____

	DATE		DESCRIPTION	POST. REF.	DEBIT	CREDIT	
1	20–						1
2	May	15	Accounts Payable, Nagle Co.		7 5 0 00		2
3			Notes Payable			7 5 0 00	3

(b) Payment of an interest-bearing note at maturity.

July 14 Paid at maturity the note given to Nagle Company.

CASH PAYMENTS JOURNAL   PAGE _____

	DATE	CK. NO.	ACCOUNT NAME	POST. REF.	OTHER ACCOUNTS DEBIT	ACCOUNTS PAYABLE DEBIT	PURCHASES DISCOUNT CREDIT	CASH CREDIT	
1	20–								1
2	July	14	Notes Payable		7 5 0 00				2
3			Interest Expense		1 0 00			7 6 0 00	3

(c) Notes given in exchange for merchandise or other property purchased.

June 3 Issued a 90-day, 9 percent note for $4,500, payable to the Phelps Equipment Company, for equipment.

GENERAL JOURNAL   PAGE _____

	DATE		DESCRIPTION	POST. REF.	DEBIT	CREDIT	
1	20–						1
2	June	3	Store Equipment		4 5 0 0 00		2
3			Notes Payable			4 5 0 0 00	3

(d) Notes given to secure a cash loan, when the borrower receives the full face value of the note.

June 11 Borrowed $2,650 from Alpha National Bank, giving in exchange a 120-day, 7 percent note (received full face amount).

CASH RECEIPTS JOURNAL   PAGE _____

	DATE	ACCOUNT NAME	POST. REF.	OTHER ACCOUNTS DEBIT	OTHER ACCOUNTS CREDIT	CASH DEBIT	
1	20–						1
2	June 11	Notes Payable			2 6 5 0 00	2 6 5 0 00	2
3							3

(e) Notes given to secure a cash loan, when the bank discounts the note.

June 19 Borrowed $8,000 from Northern National Bank for 90 days; discount rate is 8.5 percent; issued a note for $8,000.

CASH RECEIPTS JOURNAL   PAGE _____

	DATE	ACCOUNT NAME	POST. REF.	OTHER ACCOUNTS DEBIT	OTHER ACCOUNTS CREDIT	CASH DEBIT	
1	20–						1
2	June 19	Discount on Notes Payable		1 7 0 00			2
3		Notes Payable			8 0 0 0 00	7 8 3 0 00	3
4							4

(f) Payment of a non-interest-bearing note at maturity.

CASH PAYMENTS JOURNAL   PAGE _____

	DATE	CK. NO.	ACCOUNT NAME	POST. REF.	OTHER ACCOUNTS DEBIT	ACCOUNTS PAYABLE DEBIT	PURCHASES DISCOUNT CREDIT	CASH CREDIT	
1	20–								1
2	Sept. 17		Notes Payable		8 0 0 0 00			8 0 0 0 00	2
3									3

(g) Renewal of a note at maturity.

June 27 Cancelled a 45-day note payable to Bailey, Inc., for $9,800, with interest at 8 percent, by issuing a new note to run for 30 days at 9 percent.

GENERAL JOURNAL   PAGE _____

	DATE	DESCRIPTION	POST. REF.	DEBIT	CREDIT	
1	20–					1
2	June 27	Notes Payable		9 8 0 0 00		2
3		Notes Payable			9 8 0 0 00	3
4						4

5. Complete a notes payable register (see page 542).

For each note, list the date of the note, the payee, the amount, the time period, the interest rate, the amount of interest, the due date, the date paid, and relevant remarks.

6. Make journal entries for (a) adjustment for accrued interest on notes payable, (b) adjustment for Discount on Notes Payable, and (c) conversion of Discount on Notes Payable to Interest Expense.

   (a) Adjustment for accrued interest on notes payable (see page 544).

       When the time period of the note spans two fiscal periods, record interest expense incurred for the number of days the note is outstanding during the fiscal period.

   (b) Adjustment for Discount on Notes Payable (see page 546).

       If a discounted note extends into the next fiscal period, the Discount on Notes Payable is adjusted to reflect the portion of the discount that has become interest expense for the current fiscal period.

   (c) Conversion of Discount on Notes Payable to Interest Expense (see page 546).

       Upon payment of a discounted note spanning two fiscal periods, the remainder of the Discount on Notes Payable has become an expense and must be converted to Interest Expense.

Glossary

Accrued interest on notes payable The interest that is due (not yet paid) on notes payable that are outstanding at the end of the fiscal period. (543)

Contra-liability account A deduction from a liability, such as Discount on Notes Payable, which is a deduction from the balance of Notes Payable. (539)

Discount Interest deducted in advance by a bank that makes a loan. (537)

Discounting a note payable The procedure by which a bank deducts interest in advance when it loans money with a note. (537)

Duration The period of time a note is outstanding; the length of time in days from a note's issue date to its maturity date. (532)

Interest A charge made for the use of money. (531)

Maker An individual or firm that signs a promissory note. (530)

Maturity date The due date of a promissory note. (531)

Maturity value The principal of the note plus interest. (534)

Notes payable register An auxiliary record used for listing the details of notes issued. (542)

Notice of maturity A notice specifying the terms and due date of a promissory note that has been left with a bank for collection; mailed by the bank to the maker. (534)

Payee The party receiving payment, such as on a note receivable or an account receivable. (530)

Principal The face amount of a note. (531)

Proceeds The principal of a loan less the discount. (537)

Promissory note A written promise to pay a certain sum at a fixed or determinable future time. (530)

QUESTIONS, EXERCISES, AND PROBLEMS

Discussion Questions

1. Define *promissory note* and identify the two major parties involved.
2. How do you determine the maturity date of a note?
3. What is the basic formula for the calculation of interest on a note? Explain each element.
4. What is the difference between a regular note and a discounted note?
5. Explain the difference between the principal value of a note and the maturity value of a note.
6. Explain the difference in the entry for a note discounted at a bank in which the note matures before the end of the fiscal period and one in which the note matures after the end of the fiscal period. Is an adjusting entry required for each situation?
7. Explain the Discount on Notes Payable account. What is its classification?
8. Explain why it is necessary to make an adjusting entry for accrued interest on an interest-bearing note payable. Can the entry be reversed?

Exercises

P.O. 2,3

Determine interest amounts.

Exercise 15-1 Part A: Determine the interest on the following notes:

Principal	Interest Rate (percent)	Number of Days
1. $12,200	11	36 days
2. 1,200	10	45 days
3. 6,000	8	60 days
4. 9,600	10.5	90 days
5. 1,800	9	120 days

Determine maturity dates.

Part B: Determine the maturity dates on the following notes:

Date of Issue	Time Period
1. January 15	90 days
2. February 12	3 months
3. June 20	60 days
4. September 10	120 days
5. November 12	30 days

P.O. 2,3,4a,b

Determine interest and due date, and journalize entries to issue and pay the note.

Exercise 15-2 On April 3, B. M. Sibon gives a 60-day, 10 percent note, dated April 3, to Crosier Company, a creditor, in the amount of $6,430.

a. What is the due date of the note?
b. How much interest is to be paid on the note at maturity?

c. Write the entries in general journal form to record both issuance of the note by the maker and payment of the note at maturity as they would appear on Sibon's books.

P.O. 4e,f

Journalize issuance and payment of a discounted note.

Exercise 15-3 As a result of a loan from Plains State Bank, Akers Company signed a 120-day note, dated March 12, for $15,000 that the bank discounted at 8 percent. Write the entries for the maker in general journal form to record the following, assuming that the note is paid in the same fiscal period:

a. Issuance of the note on March 12.
b. Payment of the note at maturity.

P.O. 2,4d,e

Calculate interest and proceeds of a note.

Exercise 15-4 In arranging for a 90-day loan from a bank, Markey Company has the option of either (1) giving a $62,000, 10 percent interest-bearing note, dated November 3, that will be accepted at face value; or (2) giving a $62,000 note that will be discounted at 10 percent.

a. What is the amount of interest in each case?
b. What is the amount Markey Company actually receives in each case?

P.O. 2,3,5

Complete a notes payable register.

Exercise 15-5 Make entries in a notes payable register to document the following events. Show the computation of the interest and due dates.

Mar. 15 Gave a 30-day, 11 percent note, dated March 15, for $2,500, to Denley Company to apply on account.
Apr. 10 Borrowed $5,000 from Crew State Bank, giving a 90-day, 10.5 percent note, dated April 10 (received full face value).
  14 Paid Denley Company the amount owed on the note of March 15.
  20 Bought merchandise from Morris, Inc., with a $3,330, 45-day, 10 percent note, dated April 20.

P.O. 4b,c,g,6a

Journalize note renewal, partial payment, and adjusting entry.

Exercise 15-6 Gruner Supply Company completes the following transactions in November. Record them in general journal form.

a. Purchased merchandise for $18,300 on November 3, giving a 30-day, 8 percent note dated November 3 to Lester Company in exchange for the merchandise.
b. On December 3, Gruner is unable to pay the principal of the note due but pays the interest due.
c. On December 3, Gruner renews the $18,300 note for 60 days at 8.5 percent, dated December 3.
d. On December 31, Gruner makes the adjusting entry for accrued interest.

P.O. 4a,b,6a

Journalize note issuance, adjusting entry, reversing entry, and payment.

Exercise 15-7 On September 20, 2001, H. H. Hanson issued a 120-day, 10 percent note, dated September 20, to Swazey Construction, a creditor, for $9,600. Write the entries in general journal form to record the following transactions. Assume that closing entries were made at the appropriate time.

a. Issuance of the note on September 20.
b. Adjusting entry for accrued interest on December 31, the end of the fiscal year.
c. Reversing entry on January 1.
d. Payment of the note plus interest on January 18.

P.O. 4e,f,6b,c
Journalize note issuance, adjustment, payment, and conversion of Discount on Notes Payable to Interest Expense.

Exercise 15-8 On December 5, 2001, B. M. Moore borrowed $6,400 from Cosley State Bank for 45 days, with a discount rate of 9 percent. Accordingly, B. M. Moore signed a note for $6,400, dated December 5. The end of Moore's fiscal year is December 31. Write entries in general journal form to record the following transactions. Assume the closing entries were made at the appropriate time.

a. Issuance of the note on December 5.
b. Adjusting entry on December 31.
c. Payment of the note at maturity on January 19.
d. Conversion of the Discount on Notes Payable to Interest Expense for the current year.

CONSIDER AND COMMUNICATE ▪▪▪

Your friend needs to buy a $900 component to replace some essential sound equipment. He has neither that much cash nor credit available. He has heard of promissory notes and asks for your help. Explain the concept of a promissory note, what it will mean when your friend signs it, and why the total of the payments on the note at maturity will be greater than the original $900.

WHAT IF . . . ▪▪▪

The owner of a business told her accountant that she replaced an account payable with a 60-day, 8 percent note for $10,000. At the end of the 60 days, the owner told her accountant that she paid up the interest due and signed another 60-day, 8 percent note. Describe the entries that should be made by the accountant.

CRITICAL THINKING ▪▪▪

Your supervisor has asked you to audit some journal entries recorded by her client's bookkeeper. Review the following transactions. If there is an error, rejournalize the entry. If the bookkeeper's entry is correct, write OK next to the date on your paper. The fiscal period begins January 1 and ends on December 31.

Apr.	5	Borrowed $3,000 from Star Bank for 90 days, discount rate 9 percent. Signed a discounted note for $3,000 dated April 5.
June	30	Bought a new air conditioning system (Building), giving a 90-day, 9.5 percent note, dated June 30, to Weglin Company, $65,300.
July	4	Paid the $3,000 note to Star Bank dated April 5.
Sept.	28	Paid the entire interest due to Weglin Company as well as $30,000 toward the principal. Issued a new $35,300, 120-day, 9.5 percent note, dated September 28.
Nov.	20	Borrowed $4,000 from Larson Bank for 45 days, discount rate 9.5 percent. Signed a discounted note for $4,000 dated November 20.
Dec.	31	Journalized the adjusting entries for the outstanding notes owed to Weglin Company and Larson Bank.

GENERAL JOURNAL   PAGE _____

	DATE		DESCRIPTION	POST. REF.	DEBIT	CREDIT	
1	20–						1
2	Apr.	5	Cash		3 0 0 0 00		2
3			Interest Expense			6 7 50	3
4			Notes Payable			2 9 3 2 50	4
5							5
6	June	30	Building		65 3 0 0 00		6
7			Notes Payable			65 3 0 0 00	7
8							8
9	July	4	Notes Payable		3 0 0 0 00		9
10			Discount on Notes Payable		6 7 50		10
11			Cash			3 0 6 7 50	11
12							12
13	Sept.	28	Notes Payable		30 0 0 0 00		13
14			Cash			30 0 0 0 00	14
15							15
16		28	Notes Payable		35 3 0 0 00		16
17			Notes Payable			35 3 0 0 00	17
18							18
19	Nov.	20	Cash		3 9 5 2 50		19
20			Interest Expense		4 7 50		20
21			Notes Payable			4 0 0 0 00	21
22							22
23			Adjusting Entries				23
24	Dec.	31	Interest Expense		9 1 8 92		24
25			Interest Payable			9 1 8 92	25
26							26
27		31	Discount on Notes Payable		4 4 33		27
28			Interest Payable			4 4 33	28

WEB WORK

Using an Internet web browser, type *small business administration* in the search box and search for information about securing cash for small businesses by signing notes payable. Discuss your findings in a small group. Write a one-page summary of your findings.

PROBLEM SET A

For additional help, see the demonstration problem at the beginning of each chapter in your Working Papers.

P.O. 2,4a,b,d

Problem 15-1A The following were among the transactions of Tangas Appliances during the year, which uses a periodic inventory system:

Jan.   13   Bought merchandise on account from Huong Wholesalers, $4,540; terms 2/10, n/30.

Jan.	21	Paid Huong Wholesalers for the invoice of January 13.
Feb.	25	Bought merchandise on account from Marvin Company, $3,580; terms net 30 days.
Mar.	27	Gave a 60-day, 8 percent note for $3,580, dated March 27, to Marvin Company to apply on account.
May	26	Paid Marvin Company the amount owed on the note of March 27.
June	8	Borrowed $9,000 from Tower State Bank, giving a 90-day, 7.5 percent note, dated June 8, for that amount (received full face value).
Sept.	6	Paid Tower State Bank the amount due on the note of June 8.

Check Figure

May 26 Interest Expense, $47.73

P.O. 4a,b,c,e,g

Instructions

Record these transactions in a general journal (page 36).

Problem 15-2A The following were among the transactions of National Yarn Shop this year (January 1 through December 31), which uses a periodic inventory system:

Jan.	25	Bought merchandise on account from Geneva Mills, $2,950; terms net 30 days.
Feb.	24	Gave a 45-day, 10 percent note, dated February 24, for $2,950 to Geneva Mills to apply on account.
Apr.	10	Paid Geneva Mills the amount owed on the note of February 24.
May	4	Bought merchandise on account from Tildon Company, $8,300; terms net 30 days.
June	3	Gave a 30-day, 9.5 percent note, dated June 3, for $8,300 to Tildon Company to apply on account.
July	3	Paid Tildon Company the interest due on the note of June 3 and renewed the obligation by issuing a new 60-day, 9.5 percent note, dated July 3, for $8,300.
Sept.	1	Paid Tildon Company the amount owed on the note of July 3.
	25	Borrowed $11,500 from Valley Bank for 90 days; discount rate is 11 percent. Accordingly, signed a discounted note for $11,500, dated September 25. (Use Interest Expense because the note will mature in the present fiscal period.)
Dec.	24	Paid Valley Bank at maturity of loan.

Check Figure

April 10 Interest Expense, $36.88

Instructions

Record these transactions in a general journal (page 27).

Instructions for General Ledger Software

1. Journalize the entries in the general journal.
2. Print the journal entries.

P.O. 4a,b,c,e,g,5,6a

Problem 15-3A The following were among the transactions of Cliff Shop during this year. The firm, whose fiscal year ends on December 31, uses a periodic inventory system.

Jan.	12	Bought merchandise on account from Harkness Company, $3,895; terms net 30 days.
Feb.	11	Gave a 30-day, 10 percent note to Harkness Company, dated February 11, to apply on account, covering purchase of January 12, $3,895.

Mar. 13 Paid $1,895 as part payment on principal as well as the full interest on the note given to Harkness Company (Ck. No. 819). Issued new note for $2,000, 60 days, 10.5 percent, dated March 13.

May 10 Borrowed $10,100 from Washington Bank for 120 days; discount rate is 10.5 percent. Accordingly, signed a discounted note for $10,100, dated May 10.

12 Paid the amount owed on the note issued to Harkness Company dated March 13 (Ck. No. 911).

Sept. 7 Paid the amount owed on the note issued to Washington Bank, dated May 10 (Ck. No. 1051).

Nov. 20 Bought a laptop computer for $2,290 from Data Equipment. Issued a 90-day, 10 percent note, dated November 20.

Dec. 31 Recorded the adjusting entry for accrued interest on the note given to Data Equipment.

Jan. 1 Recorded the reversing entry. (Assume the closing entries were journalized and posted.)

Check Figure

Interest Expense, Adjusting entry, $26.08

Instructions

1. Record these transactions in one of the following journals: cash receipts journal (page 13), cash payments journal (page 18), and general journal (page 10).
2. Immediately after each journal entry, record each note in the notes payable register (page 5). Fill in the date paid after journalizing the entry to pay the note, or fill in "renewed" if not paid.

P.O. 4a,b,c,d,e,g,5,6a,b,c

Problem 15-4A The following were among the transactions of Kingley Company during the fiscal period ended December 31, which uses a periodic inventory system:

May 24 Gave a 60-day, 10 percent note for $60,300, dated May 24, to DeClerk Builders for additional office space.

June 20 Borrowed $14,200 from First Bank, signing a 3-month, 10 percent note for that amount, dated June 20 (received full face value).

July 15 Gave a note to Custom Carpentry for shelving units, $12,600 at 10 percent for 90 days, dated July 15. The invoice was not previously recorded.

23 Paid the amount due on the note given to DeClerk Builders.

Sept. 20 Paid interest on the note issued to First Bank; renewed the loan by issuing a new 60-day, 10.5 percent note, dated September 20.

Oct. 13 Paid the amount owed on the note given to Custom Carpentry.

27 Gave two notes to Chapman Company in settlement of its October 27 invoice for merchandise, as follows: $12,300 note for 30 days at 9.5 percent, dated October 27; $12,300 note for 60 days at 9.75 percent, dated October 27. The invoice was not previously recorded.

Nov. 19 Paid the note given to First Bank.

26 Paid the amount owed on the 30-day note given to Chapman Company.

Dec. 10 Issued a 60-day, 10 percent note, dated December 10, to McNeil Company in settlement of November 11 invoice for merchandise, $11,460. The invoice was previously recorded.

18 Borrowed $20,500 from Horner Bank for 60 days; discount rate is 10 percent; signed a discounted note for $20,500, dated December 18. (Debit Discount on Notes Payable, since note extends into next fiscal period.)

Dec. 26 Paid the amount owed on the 60-day note given to Chapman Company.

Instructions

1. Record these transactions in a general journal (page 26).
2. Immediately after each journal entry, record each note in the notes payable register (page 7). Fill in the date paid after journalizing the entry to pay the note, or fill in "renewed" if not paid.
3. On December 31, record the adjusting entries to adjust for accrued interest expense for the McNeil Company note and Discount on Notes Payable for the Horner Bank note.
4. On January 1, record the reversing entry. (Assume that closing entries have been made.)
5. On February 8, record the payment of the note to McNeil Company.
6. On February 16, record the payment of the note to Horner Bank.
7. On February 16, record the entry to expense the discount on the Horner Bank note.

PROBLEM SET B

For additional help, see the demonstration problem at the beginning of each chapter in your Working Papers.

P.O. 2,4a,b,d

Problem 15-1B The following were among the transactions of the Burdy Company, which uses a periodic inventory system:

Jan. 8 Bought merchandise on account from the Orvis Company, $4,250; terms 2/10, n/30.

18 Paid the Orvis Company for the invoice of January 8.

Feb. 12 Bought merchandise on account from Rolin Company, $3,800; terms net 30 days.

Mar. 14 Gave a 45-day, 10 percent note, dated March 14, for $3,800 to Rolin Company to apply on account.

Apr. 28 Paid Rolin Company the amount owed on the note of March 14.

May 24 Borrowed $10,800 from Kingston Bank, giving a 90-day, 9.5 percent note for that amount (received full face value), dated May 24.

Aug. 22 Paid Kingston Bank the amount due on the note of May 24.

Instructions

Record these transactions in the general journal (page 47).

P.O. 4a,b,e,g

Problem 15-2B The following were among the transactions of Jesolyn Company this year (January 1 through December 31), which uses a periodic inventory system:

Jan. 30 Bought merchandise on account from Rigdon Company, $2,860; terms net 30 days.

Mar. 1 Gave a 60-day, 9 percent note, dated March 1, for $2,860 to Rigdon Company to apply on account.

Apr. 30 Paid Rigdon Company the amount owed on the note of March 1.

May 5 Bought merchandise on account from Brent Company, $8,246; terms 2/10, n/30.

June	4	Gave a 45-day, 10 percent note, dated June 4, or $8,246 to Brent Company to apply on account.
July	19	Paid Brent Company the interest due on the note of June 4 and renewed the obligation by issuing a new 60-day, 10 percent note for $8,246 (2 entries).
Sept.	17	Paid Brent Company the amount owed on the note of July 19.
Oct.	15	Borrowed $15,300 from River Bank for 60 days; discount rate is 10 percent. Accordingly, signed a discounted note for $15,300, dated October 15.
Dec.	14	Paid River Bank at maturity of loan.

Check Figure

April 30 Interest Expense, $42.90

Instructions

Record these transactions in the general journal (page 36).

Instructions for General Ledger Software

1. Journalize the entries in the general journal.
2. Print the journal entries.

P.O. 3,4a,b,c,e,g,5,6a

Problem 15-3B The following were among the transactions of Kim's Crafts during this year. Kim's fiscal year ends on December 31 and the company uses a periodic inventory system.

Jan.	25	Bought merchandise on account from Ross Company, $3,980; terms 2/10, n/30.
Feb.	24	Gave a 30-day, 8 percent note to Ross Company, dated February 24, to apply on account, covering purchase of January 25, $3,980 (28 days in February).
Mar.	26	Paid $1,500 as part payment on principal as well as the full interest on the note given to Ross Company (Ck. No. 4120). Issued a new note for $2,480, 45 days, 8.5 percent, dated March 26 (2 entries).
May	10	Paid amount owed on the note dated March 26 (Ck. No. 4215).
June	20	Borrowed $6,960 from Old Bank for 90 days; discount rate is 9 percent. Accordingly, signed a discounted note for $6,960, dated June 20.
Sept.	18	Paid the amount owed on the note given to Old Bank, dated June 20 (Ck. No. 4310).
Oct.	28	Bought display racks for $1,980 from Cain's Fixtures. Issued a 90-day, 8 percent note, dated October 28.
Dec.	31	Recorded the adjusting entry for accrued interest on the note given to Cain's Fixtures.
Jan.	1	Recorded the reversing entry (assume closing entries were journalized and posted).

Check Figure

Adjusting Entry, Interest Expense, $28.16

Instructions

1. Record these transactions in one of the following journals: cash receipts journal (page 16), cash payments journal (page 21), and general journal (page 12).
2. Immediately following each journal entry, record each note in the notes payable register (page 5). Fill in the date paid after journalizing the entry to pay the note, or fill in "renewed" if not paid.

P.O. 4b,c,d,e,g,5,6a,b,c

Problem 15-4B The following were among the transactions of Grace Company during the year ended December 31, which uses a periodic inventory system:

June 10 Gave a 30-day, 9 percent note, dated June 10, to Baker, Inc., for $61,000, for an addition to the building.

15 Borrowed $26,100 from Mesa Bank, signing a 3-month, 8.5 percent note for that amount, dated June 15 (received full face value).

July 10 Paid the amount owed on the note given to Baker, Inc.

10 Gave a note to D. J., Inc., for the purchase of office equipment, $9,242, at 8.5 percent for 120 days, dated July 10. The invoice was not previously recorded.

Sept. 15 Paid interest on the note given to Mesa Bank; renewed loan by issuing note for 60 days at 8 percent, dated September 15.

Nov. 7 Paid the amount owed on the 120-day note given to D. J., Inc.

14 Gave two notes to NesCo in settlement of its November 14 invoice for merchandise, as follows: $11,200, 30 days, 8 percent, dated November 14; $11,200, 60 days, 8 percent, dated November 14. The invoice was not previously recorded.

14 Paid the note given to Mesa Bank.

Dec. 14 Paid the amount owed on the 30-day note given to NesCo.

17 Issued a 60-day, 8.5 percent note, dated December 17, payable to Hall Company, in settlement of November 17 bill for merchandise, $18,950. The invoice was previously recorded.

18 Borrowed $30,000 from Trent Bank for 30 days; discount rate is 8.5 percent; issued a discounted note, dated December 18, for $30,000 (debit Discount on Notes Payable since the note extends into the next fiscal period).

Check Figure

Adjusting Entry, Interest Payable, $179.62

Instructions

1. Record these transactions in a general journal (page 18).
2. Immediately following each journal entry, record each note in the notes payable register (page 7). Fill in the date paid after journalizing the entry to pay the note, or fill in "renewed" if not paid.
3. On December 31, record the adjusting entries to account for accrued interest expense for the NesCo and Hall notes, as well as the adjustment of Discount on Notes Payable on the Trent Bank note.
4. On January 1, record the reversing entry. (Assume closing entries have been made.)
5. On January 13, record the payment of the note to NesCo.
6. On January 17, record the payment of the note to Trent Bank.
7. On January 17, record the entry to expense the discount on the Trent note.
8. On February 15, record the payment of the note to Hall Company.

16 | Notes Receivable

THE WORLD WIDE WEB

What happens when a bagel company runs out of dough? When Bagel Brothers Bakery and Deli, Inc. failed to pay amounts it promised to Manhattan Bagel Company, Inc., as part of a previous agreement, Manhattan Bagel sued for, among other things, judgment on $6 million of promissory notes and guarantees. The $6 million would be a notes payable to Bagel Brothers, but a notes receivable to Manhattan Bagel. Normally, a notes receivable is considered an asset to the business. If the debt is not repaid, however, it becomes a bad debt. So, what happened between the two bagel bakers? How is Manhattan Bagel coping with this loss? For more info on the Manhattan Bagel Company's financials, check out **http://www.manhattanbagel.com/**.

Performance Objectives

After you have completed this chapter, you will be able to do the following:

1. Write the journal entries to record (a) receipt of a note from a charge customer; (b) receipt of payment of an interest-bearing note at maturity; (c) receipt of a note as a result of granting a personal loan; (d) receipt of a note in exchange for merchandise or other property; (e) renewal of a note at maturity and payment of interest; (f) renewal of a note with payment of interest and partial payment of principal; (g) a dishonored note receivable; (h) collection of a note receivable formerly dishonored; (i) discounting an interest-bearing note.

2. Complete a notes receivable register.

3. Write journal entries to record the adjustment for accrued interest on notes receivable.

FYI

Notes receivable may be written for short periods of time, even days or weeks. They can also be written for very long periods of time, as when a bank receives a 28-year mortgage note. The life of a note is whatever is agreed on by all parties.

FYI

Banks may grant loans for 100 percent of the face value of notes but a lesser percentage of the face value of open accounts.

Business firms receive promissory notes either regularly or occasionally for a variety of reasons. Sometimes a business firm accepts a promissory note from a customer at the time of sale. Companies frequently accept promissory notes from charge account customers who request an extension of time to settle past-due accounts. In effect, they substitute notes receivable for accounts receivable. The net result is that the charge customer gets an extension of time for the payment of a debt.

Obviously, getting a note receivable is not as good as having cash in hand. However, it offers several advantages to the company: (1) the note represents proof of the original transaction, (2) the note may bear interest, and (3) the note may be pledged as security for a loan from a bank. Banks, in fact, loan a higher proportion of the face value on notes (Notes Receivable) than on open accounts (Accounts Receivable).

Notes receivable also come into being when a company grants loans to employees or preferred customers or suppliers. In some industries, the credit period is often longer than thirty days; here, the transactions are frequently evidenced by notes rather than by open accounts. Examples are sales of farm machinery, construction equipment, and trucks.

Now let's see how to journalize transactions involving notes receivable. The accounts involved are Notes Receivable (classified as a current asset on the balance sheet in our examples, although it could be classified as a long-term asset if the repayment period is longer than a year) and Interest Income (classified as other income on the income statement).

Remember!

A note receivable on the books of the payee company is a note payable on the books of the company signing the note.

TRANSACTIONS FOR NOTES RECEIVABLE

First, let's say that all notes received are recorded in a single current asset account: Notes Receivable. Second, throughout this chapter, we are going to use Jackson Electric Supply to illustrate such transactions. All notes are payable at Alpha Bank.

Notes from Charge Customers to Extend Time on Their Accounts

Objective 1a

Write the journal entry to record receipt of a note from a charge customer.

On March 7, Jackson Electric Supply sold $960 worth of merchandise to Hazen and Son, with the customary terms of 2/10, n/30, and made the original entry in its sales journal. On April 6, Hazen and Son sent Jackson Electric Supply a note for $960, payable within 30 days, at 8 percent interest. The note, dated April 6, was in settlement of the transaction of March 7. Jackson Electric Supply recorded this new development in its general journal as follows:

Remember!

A note receivable and an account receivable differ in the strength of legal claim they represent and in the way interest is earned—a note is more formal.

Objective 1b

Write the journal entry to record receipt of payment of an interest-bearing note at maturity.

GENERAL JOURNAL   PAGE _____

	DATE		DESCRIPTION	POST. REF.	DEBIT	CREDIT	
1	20–						1
2	Apr.	6	Notes Receivable		9 6 0 00		2
3			Accounts Receivable, Hazen				3
4			and Son			9 6 0 00	4
5			Received a 30-day, 8 percent				5
6			note, dated April 6, in				6
7			settlement of open account.				7
8							8

T accounts for the transactions look like this:

Accounts Receivable		Sales		Notes Receivable	
+	–	–	+	+	–
Mar. 7	Apr. 6		Mar. 7	Apr. 6	
960.00	960.00		960.00	960.00	

Receipt of Payment of an Interest-Bearing Note at Maturity

On May 6, Hazen paid Jackson Electric Supply in full: principal plus interest. Jackson Electric Supply recorded the transaction in the general journal as follows:

	DATE		DESCRIPTION	POST. REF.	DEBIT	CREDIT	
1	20–						1
2	May	6	Cash		9 6 6 40		2
3			Notes Receivable			9 6 0 00	3
4			Interest Income			6 40	4
5			Received full payment of				5
6			Hazen and Son note.				6
7			($960 × .08 × 30/360)				7
8							8
9							9
10							10
11							11

Remember!

Calculations are included to show how the amounts were determined. They would not normally appear in journal entries.

Let's look at the T accounts for this entry:

Cash		
	+	−
May 6	966.40	

Notes Receivable			
	+	−	
Apr. 6	960.00	May 6	960.00

Interest Income	
−	+
	May 6 6.40

This transaction could be recorded directly in the cash receipts journal rather than in the general journal. But, for simplicity and clarity, we use the general journal format to illustrate entries throughout this chapter.

Businesses may accept a promissory note from a customer for several reasons. Customers may be making a large purchase or need an extension on a past-due account. A note receivable is a promise to pay the amount due, with interest, at a future date.

Notes Received as a Result of Granting Personal Loans

Objective 1c

Write the journal entry to record receipt of a note as a result of granting a personal loan.

Sometimes employees, preferred customers, or suppliers may want to borrow cash from the business. In this case, the business often accepts a note receivable. Let's say that Marian Kraft, an employee of Jackson Electric Supply, borrows $600 from her employer for 3 months at 6 percent. Her note is dated April 8. In general journal form, the entry is as follows:

	DATE		DESCRIPTION	POST. REF.	DEBIT	CREDIT	
1	20–						1
2	Apr.	8	Notes Receivable		6 0 0 00		2
3			Cash			6 0 0 00	3
4			Granted a loan to Marian				4
5			Kraft, 3 months, 6 percent,				5
6			dated April 8.				6
7							7

When the loan reaches maturity, Kraft pays the principal plus interest.

	DATE		DESCRIPTION	POST. REF.	DEBIT	CREDIT	
1	20–						1
2	July	8	Cash		6 0 9 00		2
3			Notes Receivable			6 0 0 00	3
4			Interest Income			9 00	4
5			Received full payment of				5
6			Marian Kraft's note, dated				6
7			April 8.				7
8			($600 × .06 × 3/12)				8
9							9
10							10

Note Received in Exchange for Merchandise or Other Property

Business firms that sell high-priced durable goods for which the credit period is longer than the normal thirty days may regularly accept notes from their customers.

Objective 1d

Write the journal entry to record receipt of a note in exchange for merchandise or other property.

On April 9, Jackson Electric Supply sold merchandise to C. L. Pihl and Company for $900. Pihl gave Jackson Electric Supply a promissory note, promising to pay the full amount within 60 days; the note specified 7 percent interest. When this type of transaction occurs occasionally, the transaction is recorded in the general journal as shown on the following page.

	DATE		DESCRIPTION	POST. REF.	DEBIT		CREDIT	
1	20–							1
2	Apr.	9	Notes Receivable		9 0 0 00			2
3			Sales				9 0 0 00	3
4			C. L. Pihl and Co.					4
5			60-day, 7 percent note, dated					5
6			April 9.					6
7								7
8								8

However, if this type of transaction were to occur frequently, Jackson Electric Supply would use a Notes Receivable Debit column in the sales journal to record such transactions.

Renewal of Note at Maturity and Payment of Interest

If the maker of a note is unable to pay the entire principal at maturity, he or she may be allowed to renew all or part of the note.

Suppose that C. L. Pihl and Company is not able to pay the note at maturity and offers to pay the interest on the current note and to issue a new note, for 30 days at 8 percent. Jackson Electric Supply makes the entries in the general journal as shown below. Note that two entries are required. One entry records the interest on the old note. The second entry cancels the old note and records the new note.

Objective 1e

Write the journal entries to record renewal of a note at maturity and payment of interest.

	DATE		DESCRIPTION	POST. REF.	DEBIT		CREDIT	
1	20–							1
2	June	8	Cash		1 0 50			2
3			Interest Income				1 0 50	3
4			Received payment of					4
5			interest on C. L. Pihl and Co.					5
6			note, dated April 9.					6
7			($900 × .07 × 60/360)					7
8								8
9		8	Notes Receivable		9 0 0 00			9
10			Notes Receivable				9 0 0 00	10
11			C. L. Pihl and Co.,					11
12			renewal of note, dated April					12
13			9; new note is dated June 8,					13
14			30 days, 8 percent.					14
15								15

Remember!

For a renewal of a note receivable, credit the old note to take it off the books, and debit the new note to put it on the books.

Actually, there is only one Notes Receivable ledger account. However, when a note is renewed, it is customary for the debtor or maker to pay the interest on the old note and then issue a new note.

Renewal of Note with Payment of Interest and Partial Payment of Principal

Objective 1f

Write the journal entries to record renewal of a note with payment of interest and partial payment of principal.

Sometimes the maker of a note cancels the original note by paying the interest plus part of the principal and issuing a new note. Suppose that, instead of paying the $900, 60-day, 7 percent note, Pihl gives Jackson Electric Supply $300 toward the principal and a new note for $600 in addition to the interest on the old note.

Jackson Electric Supply records the transactions in the general journal as follows:

	DATE		DESCRIPTION	POST. REF.	DEBIT	CREDIT	
1	20–						1
2	June	8	Cash		3 1 0 50		2
3			Notes Receivable			3 0 0 00	3
4			Interest Income			1 0 50	4
5			C. L. Pihl and Co.'s note,				5
6			dated April 9, partial				6
7			payment of the principal and				7
8			interest payment.				8
9							9
10		8	Notes Receivable		6 0 0 00		10
11			Notes Receivable			6 0 0 00	11
12			C. L. Pihl and Co.,				12
13			renewal of note dated April				13
14			9; the new note is dated				14
15			June 8, 30 days, 8 percent.				15
16							16

DISHONORED NOTES RECEIVABLE

Objective 1g

Write journal entries to record a dishonored note receivable.

When the maker of a note fails to pay the principal amount or to renew the note at maturity, the note is said to be a dishonored note receivable. The maker of the note is still obligated to pay the principal plus interest, and the creditor should take legal steps to collect the debt. However, the balance of the Notes Receivable account shows only the principal of notes that have not yet matured. A note that is past due, or dishonored, should be removed from the Notes Receivable account and added to the Accounts Receivable account; the amount listed should be the principal plus interest. In other words, once a note receivable comes due and is not collected, it's "dead." But the maker still owes us, so we put the amount owed (principal plus interest) back into Accounts Receivable.

For example, Jackson Electric Supply holds a 60-day, 7 percent note for $800, dated April 20, from Baker Company, which fails to pay by the due date. Thus the note is dishonored at maturity. Accordingly, Jackson Electric makes the following entry in its general journal to remove the dishonored note from the Notes Receivable account.

	DATE		DESCRIPTION	POST. REF.	DEBIT			CREDIT		
1	20–									1
2	June	19	Accounts Receivable, Baker Co.		8 0 9 33					2
3			Notes Receivable					8 0 0 00		3
4			Interest Income					9 33		4
5			Baker Co. dishonored its							5
6			60-day, 7 percent note for							6
7			$800, dated April 20.							7
8			($800 × .07 × 60/360)							8
9										9
10										10
11										11
12										12

Remember!

For a dishonored interest-bearing note receivable, interest income is recorded, and the note is removed from the Notes Receivable account.

Baker Company owes both the principal and the interest, and the account should reflect the full amount owed. Note particularly that Jackson Electric credits the Interest Income account, even though Baker did not pay the interest. This is consistent with the accrual basis of accounting: Revenue is recorded when it is *earned,* rather than when it is received. If Baker Company should ever ask Jackson Electric to act as a credit reference, or if Baker ever asks for credit in the future, subsidiary records will show all past dealings, including the dishonored note.

Collection of a Note Formerly Dishonored

Objective 1h

Write journal entries to record collection of a note receivable formerly dishonored.

Now suppose that 30 days after its note has been dishonored, Baker Company pays the balance of its account, plus an additional 30 days' interest at 7 percent on the amount owed. The entry in Jackson Electric Supply's general journal is as follows:

GENERAL JOURNAL   PAGE _____

	DATE		DESCRIPTION	POST. REF.	DEBIT			CREDIT		
1	20–									1
2	July	19	Cash		8 1 4 05					2
3			Accounts Receiv., Baker Co.					8 0 9 33		3
4			Interest Income					4 72		4
5			Baker Co. paid the							5
6			dishonored note, plus							6
7			interest for 30 days at							7
8			7 percent.							8
9			($809.33 × .07 × 30/360)							9
10										10
11										11

Jackson Electric Supply eventually receives its money, and it can now consider the matter closed.

DISCOUNTING NOTES RECEIVABLE

Objective 1i

Write the journal entry to record discounting an interest-bearing note receivable.

Instead of keeping notes receivable until they come due, a firm can raise cash by selling its notes receivable to a bank or finance company. This type of financing is called **discounting notes receivable** because the bank deducts the interest or discount from the maturity value of the note to determine the proceeds (that is, the amount of money received by the payee). The **maturity value** is the principal (face value) of the note plus interest from the date of the note until the due date.

In the process of discounting a note receivable, the payee endorses the note (as it would a check) and delivers it to the financial institution. The financial institution gives out cash now in exchange for the right to collect the principal and interest when the note comes due. The discount rate is the annual rate (percentage of maturity value) charged by the financial institution for buying the note. The financial institution generally discounts at a higher interest rate stated in the note because the financial institution assumes increased risk of the maker's possible default.

Sometimes notes receivable are discounted; that is, the lender sells the note to someone else to collect. The reason for doing this is the need for money before the borrower would pay his or her debt.

A Discounted Note: Example 1 Jackson Electric Supply granted an extension on an open account by accepting a 60-day, 8 percent note for $540, dated April 20, from Colmer Company. To raise cash to buy additional merchandise, Jackson Electric Supply sold the note to Alpha Bank on May 5. The bank charged a discount rate of 7 percent. A diagram of the situation looks like this:

Period of the note (60 days)		
Apr. 20 Date of note	**May 5** Date discounted	**Date of** **maturity**
Jackson Electric Supply holds note (15 days)	Bank holds note (discount period) (60 − 15 = 45 days)	

The **discount period** of the note consists of the interval between the date the note is given to the bank and the maturity date of the note. (In other words, the discount period is the time the note has left to run.)

Next we determine the value of the note at maturity and deduct the amount of the bank's discount from it, using the following formula.

Principal ($540)
+ Interest to maturity date (8%, 60 days)
_____

Value at maturity
− Discount (7%, 45 days)
_____

Proceeds

After we set up the problem, we can complete the calculation:

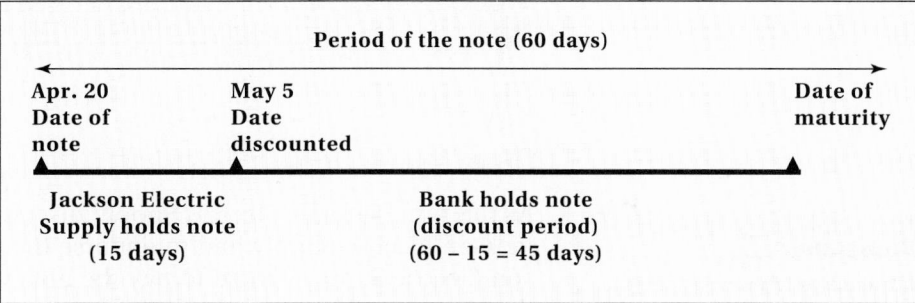

Principal	$540.00	Interest = Principal × Rate × Time
+ Interest (8%, 60 days)	7.20	Interest = $540 × .08 × $\frac{60}{360}$ = $7.20
Value at maturity	547.20	
− Discount (7%, 45 days)	4.79	Discount = $547.20 × .07 × $\frac{45}{360}$ = $4.79
Proceeds	$542.41	

Note that, in our calculations, we figure the discount on the value of the note at maturity ($547.20, 7 percent, 45 days). The proceeds are the amount that Jackson Electric Supply receives from the bank; this amount is therefore debited to Cash. *If the amount of the proceeds is greater than the amount of the principal, the difference represents Interest Income to Jackson Electric Supply. If the amount of the proceeds is less than the principal, the deficiency represents Interest Expense to Jackson Electric Supply.* Look at the entry in Jackson Electric Supply's general journal:

	DATE		DESCRIPTION	POST. REF.	DEBIT	CREDIT	
1	20–						1
2	May	5	Cash		5 4 2 41		2
3			Notes Receivable			5 4 0 00	3
4			Interest Income			2 41	4
5			Discounted at the bank				5
6			Colmer Company's note,				6
7			dated April 20. The bank				7
8			discount rate is 7 percent.				8
9							9
10							10
11							11
12							12
13							13

Contingent Liability

■■■
Remember!
If the maker dishonors the note, the endorser is liable to the bank to pay the note; thus, it is necessary to show such potential liability on the endorser's balance sheet.

At the time Jackson Electric Supply discounted Colmer's note at the bank, Jackson Electric Supply had to endorse the note. By this endorsement, Jackson Electric Supply agreed to pay the note when it became due if the maker did not pay it. Therefore the endorser has a **contingent liability** for payment of the note. A contingent liability is a liability that depends on certain conditions or events taking place. If the maker does not pay the note, the endorser is liable. In other words, the liability of the endorser is contingent on the possible dishonoring of the note by the maker. It follows that if the credit rating of the endorser of the note is good, a bank is usually willing to accept and discount a note. The endorser, by virtue of his or her endorsement or guarantee, agrees to pay the note at maturity *if* it is not paid by the maker. The fact that the note receivable is pledged as security, along with the amount of the contingent liability, should be shown as a footnote to the endorser's balance sheet.

Payment of a Discounted Note by the Maker

The bank collects the principal plus the interest on a discounted note directly from the maker. When the maker pays the bank, the endorser no longer has any contingent liability; the footnote to the endorser's balance sheet can be eliminated when the note is paid. A journal entry is not required.

A Discounted Note: Example 2 On April 25, Jackson Electric Supply received a 90-day, 6 percent, $1,800 note, dated April 24, from Files Service Company.

Remember!

The discount period is the time the note is held by the bank.

On May 4, Jackson Electric Supply discounted the note at Alpha Bank. The discount rate charged by the bank is 7 percent. In handling discounted notes receivable, you should follow a definite step-by-step procedure.

1. Diagram the situation.

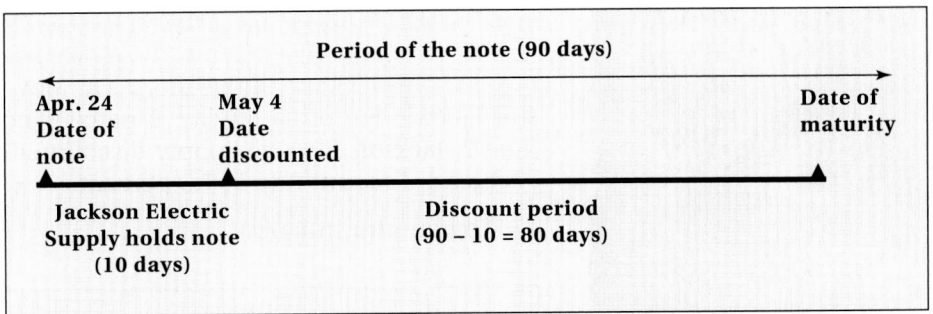

2. Determine the discount period.

April 30 − 24 = 6 days left in April
May = 4 days

Days held by = 10 days
endorser

Discount period (bank holds note),
(Total days − days held by endorser)
90 days − 10 days = 80 days

3. Record the formula.

Principal ($1,800)
+ Interest (6%, 90 days)

Value at maturity
− Discount (7%, 80 days)

Proceeds

4. Complete the formula.

Principal	$1,800.00	Interest = Principal × Rate × Time
+ Interest (6%, 90 days)	27.00	Interest = $1,800 × .06 × $\frac{90}{360}$ = $27.00
Value at maturity	$1,827.00	
− Discount (7%, 80 days)	28.42	Discount = $1,827.00 × .07 × $\frac{80}{360}$
Proceeds	$1,798.58	= $28.42

5. Make the entry, recognizing that the amount of the proceeds is a debit to Cash. If the amount of the proceeds is less than the principal, debit Interest Expense for the difference.

	DATE		DESCRIPTION	POST. REF.	DEBIT	CREDIT	
1	20–						1
2	May	4	Cash		1 7 9 8 58		2
3			Interest Expense		1 42		3
4			Notes Receivable			1 8 0 0 00	4
5			Discounted at the bank Files				5
6			Service Company's note,				6
7			dated April 24. The bank				7
8			discount rate is 7 percent.				8

Companies that specialize in seasonal merchandise such as skiing and other winter sports equipment may need to sign a promissory note for a certain period of time to increase their inventory prior to the time it will actually be sold.

A Discounted Note: Example 3 On May 10, Higgins Company gave Jackson Electric Supply a 60-day, 8 percent note for $2,640, dated May 9. On June 2, Jackson Electric Supply discounted the note at the bank. The bank charges a discount rate of 7.5 percent.

1. Diagram the situation.

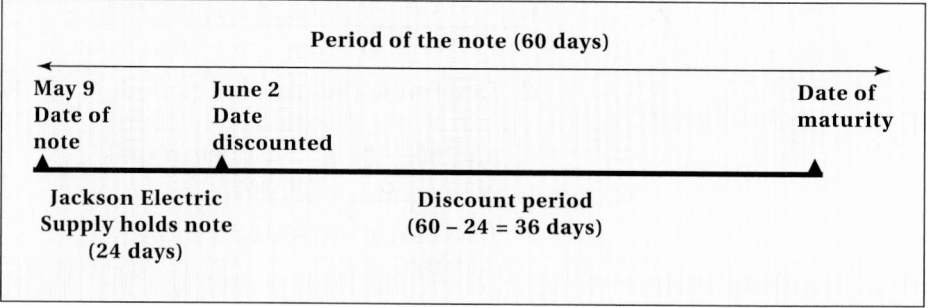

2. Determine the discount period.

May (31 − 9)	=	22 days left in May
June	=	2 days
Days held by endorser	=	24 days

Discount period (bank holds note),
(Total days − days held by endorser)
60 days − 24 days = 36 days

3. Record the formula.

Principal ($2,640)
+ Interest (8%, 60 days)

Value at maturity
− Discount (7½%, 36 days)

Proceeds

4. Complete the formula.

Principal	$2,640.00
+ Interest (8%, 60 days)	35.20
Value at maturity	$2,675.20
− Discount (7½%, 36 days)	20.06
Proceeds	$2,655.14

Interest = Principal × Rate × Time

Interest = $2,640 × .08 × $\dfrac{60}{360}$ = $35.20

Discount = $2,675.20 × .075 × $\dfrac{36}{360}$

= $20.06

5. Record the entry as shown. If the amount of the proceeds is greater than the principal, credit Interest Income for the difference.

	DATE		DESCRIPTION	POST. REF.	DEBIT	CREDIT	
1	20–						1
2	June	2	Cash		2 6 5 5 14		2
3			Notes Receivable			2 6 4 0 00	3
4			Interest Income			1 5 14	4
5			Discounted at bank the note				5
6			received from Higgins Co.				6
7			dated May 9; discount rate,				7
8			7.5 percent.				8
9							9

Notes Receivable Register

Companies that have a significant number of notes receivable may find it worthwhile to set up a separate list to keep track of them. This list is called a **notes receivable register** (see Figure 1). Information is taken from the face of each note. Columns are included to record the specifics of each note. At the end of the fiscal period, the accountant makes a schedule of notes receivable by listing the unpaid notes that appear in the notes receivable register. Also, the total of the schedule is compared with the balance of the Notes Receivable account. The two should match.

FIGURE 1

NOTES RECEIVABLE REGISTER

DATE		MAKER	WHERE PAYABLE	AMOUNT	TIME	RATE	INTEREST	DUE DATE	DISCOUNTED BANK	DATE	DATE PAID	REMARKS
20–												
Apr.	6	Hazen and Son	Alpha Bank	9 6 0 00	30 d	8%	6 40	5/6			5/6	Open account.
	8	Marian Kraft	Alpha Bank	6 0 0 00	3 m	6%	9 00	7/8			7/8	Employee loan.
	9	C. L. Pihl & Co.	Alpha Bank	9 0 0 00	60 d	7%	1 0 50	6/8			Ren.	Open account.
	20	Colmer Co.	Alpha Bank	5 4 0 00	60 d	8%	7 20	6/19	Alpha Bank	5/5	—	Discount. @ 7%, $542.41 proceeds.
	24	Files Service Co.	Alpha Bank	1 8 0 0 00	90 d	6%	2 7 00	7/23	Alpha Bank	5/4	—	Discount. @ 7%, $1,798.58 proc.
May	9	Higgins Co.	Alpha Bank	2 6 4 0 00	60 d	8%	3 5 20	7/8	Alpha Bank	6/2		Discount. @ 7.5%, $2,655.14 proc.
June	8	C. L. Pihl & Co.	Alpha Bank	9 0 0 00	30 d	8%	6 00	7/8				Renewed 4/9 note.
		Or if partial payment:										
June	8	C. L. Pihl & Co.	Alpha Bank	6 2 0 00	30 d	8%	4 00	7/8				Renewed 4/9 note with part. paymnt. of $300 plus interest.

END-OF-FISCAL-PERIOD ADJUSTMENTS: ACCRUED INTEREST ON NOTES RECEIVABLE

Accrued interest income on notes receivable is the interest that is due (not yet received) on notes receivable that are outstanding at the end of the fiscal period. Whenever a firm receives *or* issues an interest-bearing note, the interest accrues daily. As a result, any interest-bearing notes that overlap fiscal periods require adjusting entries in order for the financial statements to present a true picture of the firm's net income and financial condition.

For example, let's say that a firm has two notes receivable on December 31, the end of the fiscal period:

$6,000, 90 days, 8%, dated November 28
$5,200, 60 days, 7%, dated December 20

We can diagram the situation as follows:

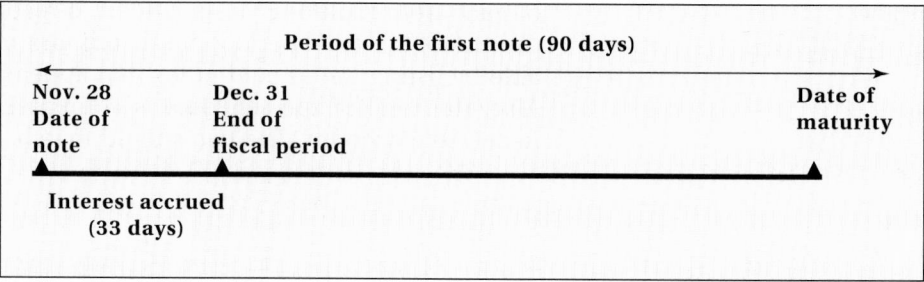

Nov. $(30 - 28) =$ 2 days left in November
Dec. $ = $ 31 days

Total 33 days left in the fiscal period

Interest $=$ Principal $\times$ Rate $\times$ Time

$$\text{Interest} = \$6{,}000 \times .08 \times \frac{33}{360} = \underline{\underline{\$44.00}}$$

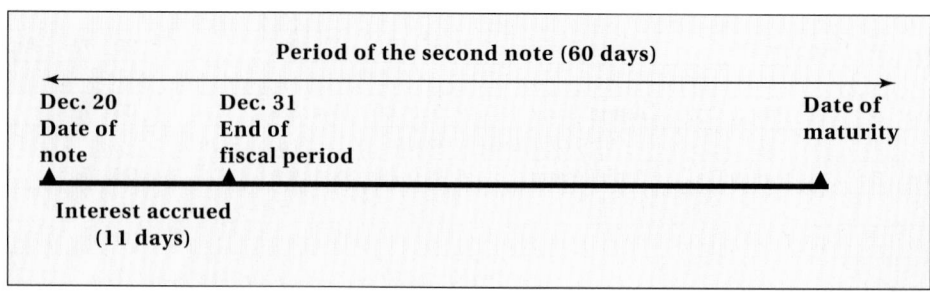

Dec. $(31 - 20) = 11$ days left in the fiscal period

Interest $=$ Principal $\times$ Rate $\times$ Time

$$\text{Interest} = \$5{,}200 \times .07 \times \frac{11}{360} = \underline{\underline{\$11.12}}$$

The maker doesn't ordinarily pay the interest until the note comes due. Since these notes have not matured, the interest income has been neither paid nor recorded ($44.00 + $11.12 = $55.12).

In the firm's general journal, the adjusting entry for the interest income accrued on the two notes looks like this:

	DATE		DESCRIPTION	POST. REF.	DEBIT	CREDIT	
1	20–		**Adjusting Entry**				1
2	Dec	31	Interest Receivable		5 5 12		2
3			Interest Income			5 5 12	3

GENERAL JOURNAL   PAGE _____

Like all other adjustments, this entry was first recorded in the Adjustments columns of the work sheet. Here is a T account picture of the situation, assuming a balance in Interest Income of $674.10 before adjustment:

Interest Receivable		Interest Income	
+	−	−	+
Dec. 31 Adj. 55.12			Dec. 31 Bal. 674.10
			Dec. 31 Adj. 55.12

The adjusting entry is this: debit Interest Receivable and credit Interest Income. On the work sheet shown in Figure 2, you can see the effect of this adjustment on the financial statements.

Remember that the interest accompanying notes receivable is Interest Income. On the balance sheet, Interest Receivable is classified as a current asset if it is to be received during the coming year.

The accountant may reverse this adjusting entry as of the first day of the next fiscal period because it increases a balance sheet account. When the note matures, the reversing entry makes it possible for the accountant to make the routine entry for the receipt of payment of an interest-bearing note: a debit to Cash, a credit to Notes Receivable, and a credit to Interest Income. This procedure is most convenient, especially when a significant number of notes is involved.

FIGURE 2

	TRIAL BALANCE		ADJUSTMENTS		INCOME STATEMENT		BALANCE SHEET
ACCOUNT NAME	DEBIT	CREDIT	DEBIT	CREDIT	DEBIT	CREDIT	DEBIT
Notes Receiv.	11 2 0 0 00						11 2 0 0 00
Int. Income		6 7 4 10		(a) 5 5 12		7 2 9 22	
Int. Receiv.			5 5 12				5 5 12

■
■■
■

CHAPTER REVIEW

Review of Performance Objectives

The performance objectives require you to write general journal entries, because those entries allow for the clearest analysis of the debits and credits in each transaction. We will repeat these entries, but to conserve space, we omit explanations. Ordinarily, any firm using a cash receipts and a cash payments journal would record any transactions involving cash in one of these journals.

FYI

Selected transactions are now repeated and shown in the appropriate journal.

1a. Write the journal entry to record receipt of a note from a charge customer.

April   6   Received a note for $960 from Hazen and Son, in settlement of the sale of March 7, 30 days, 8 percent.

GENERAL JOURNAL   PAGE _____

	DATE		DESCRIPTION	POST. REF.	DEBIT	CREDIT	
1	20–						1
2	Apr.	6	Notes Receivable		9 6 0 00		2
3			Accounts Receivable, Hazen				3
4			and Son			9 6 0 00	4

1b. Write the journal entry to record receipt of payment of an interest-bearing note at maturity.

May   6   Received payment at maturity of principal plus interest on Hazen and Son's note.

CASH RECEIPTS JOURNAL   PAGE _____

	DATE		ACCOUNT CREDITED	POST. REF.	OTHER ACCOUNTS CREDIT	ACCOUNTS RECEIVABLE CREDIT	SALES CREDIT	SALES DISCOUNT DEBIT	CASH DEBIT	
1	20–									1
2	May	6	Notes Receivable		9 6 0 00					2
3			Interest Income		6 40				9 6 6 40	3
4										4

1c. Write the journal entry to record receipt of a note as a result of granting a personal loan.

April   8   Granted a loan to Marian Kraft, an employee, for $600 for 3 months, 6 percent, dated April 8.

CASH PAYMENTS JOURNAL   PAGE _____

	DATE	CK. NO.	ACCOUNT NAME	POST. REF.	OTHER ACCOUNTS DEBIT	ACCOUNTS PAYABLE DEBIT	PURCHASES DISCOUNT CREDIT	CASH CREDIT	
1	20–								1
2	Apr. 8		Notes Receivable		6 0 0 00			6 0 0 00	2
3									3

1d. Write the journal entry to record receipt of a note in exchange for merchandise or other property.

April   9   Received a note for $900 from C. L. Pihl and Company for merchandise sold, 60 days, 7 percent, dated April 9.

GENERAL JOURNAL   PAGE _____

	DATE	DESCRIPTION	POST. REF.	DEBIT	CREDIT	
1	20–					1
2	Apr. 9	Notes Receivable		9 0 0 00		2
3		Sales			9 0 0 00	3

1e. Write the journal entries to record renewal of a note at maturity and payment of interest.

June   8   Received interest from C. L. Pihl and Company on its note of April 9.

CASH RECEIPTS JOURNAL   PAGE _____

	DATE	ACCOUNT CREDITED	POST. REF.	OTHER ACCOUNTS CREDIT	ACCOUNTS RECEIVABLE CREDIT	SALES CREDIT	SALES DISCOUNT DEBIT	CASH DEBIT	
1	20–								1
2	June 8	Interest Income		1 0 50				1 0 50	2

Then it was agreed to renew the note by issuing a new note, 30 days, 8 percent, dated June 8.

GENERAL JOURNAL   PAGE _____

	DATE	DESCRIPTION	POST. REF.	DEBIT	CREDIT	
1	20–					1
2	June 8	Notes Receivable		9 0 0 00		2
3		Notes Receivable			9 0 0 00	3
4						4

1f. Write the journal entries to record renewal of a note with payment of interest and partial payment of principal.

GENERAL JOURNAL PAGE _____

	DATE		DESCRIPTION	POST. REF.	DEBIT	CREDIT	
1	20–						1
2	June	8	Cash		3 1 0 50		2
3			Notes Receivable			3 0 0 00	3
4			Interest Income			1 0 50	4
5							5
6		8	Notes Receivable		6 0 0 00		6
7			Notes Receivable			6 0 0 00	7
8							8

CASH RECEIPTS JOURNAL PAGE _____

	DATE		ACCOUNT CREDITED	POST. REF.	OTHER ACCOUNTS CREDIT	ACCOUNTS RECEIVABLE CREDIT	SALES CREDIT	SALES DISCOUNT DEBIT	CASH DEBIT	
1	20–									1
2	June	8	Notes Receivable		3 0 0 00					2
3			Interest Income		1 0 50				3 1 0 50	3
4										4

1g. Write the journal entry to record a dishonored note receivable.

June 19 Baker Company dishonored its note of April 20 for $800 at 7 percent, for 60 days.

GENERAL JOURNAL PAGE _____

	DATE		DESCRIPTION	POST. REF.	DEBIT	CREDIT	
1	20–						1
2	June	19	Accounts Receivable, Baker Co.		8 0 9 33		2
3			Notes Receivable			8 0 0 00	3
4			Interest Income			9 33	4
5							5

1h. Write the journal entry to record collection of a note receivable formerly dishonored.

July 19 Baker Company paid its dishonored note, plus additional interest for 30 days at 7 percent.

CASH RECEIPTS JOURNAL   PAGE _____

	DATE		ACCOUNT CREDITED	POST. REF.	OTHER ACCOUNTS CREDIT	ACCOUNTS RECEIVABLE CREDIT	SALES CREDIT	SALES DISCOUNT DEBIT	CASH DEBIT	
1	20–									1
2	July	19	Baker Co.			8 0 9 33				2
3			Interest Income		4 72				8 1 4 05	3
4										4

1i. Write the journal entry to record discounting an interest-bearing note receivable.

> **May**   5   Discounted at Alpha Bank the note received from Colmer Company, dated April 20, $540; 8 percent, 60 days. The discount rate is 7 percent.

CASH RECEIPTS JOURNAL   PAGE _____

	DATE		ACCOUNT CREDITED	POST. REF.	OTHER ACCOUNTS CREDIT	ACCOUNTS RECEIVABLE CREDIT	SALES CREDIT	SALES DISCOUNT DEBIT	CASH DEBIT	
1	20–									1
2	May	5	Notes Receivable		5 4 0 00					2
3			Interest Income		2 41				5 4 2 41	3
4										4

2. Complete a notes receivable register.

   For each note, list the date, the maker, where the note is payable, the amount, the time period, the interest rate, the amount of interest, the due date, the date paid, and relevant remarks. See Figure 1 for a partial register.

3. Write journal entries to record the adjustment for accrued interest on notes receivable.

   Here is the adjusting entry for two notes: a $6,000, 90-day, 8 percent note dated November 28, and a $5,200, 60-day, 7 percent note dated December 20.

GENERAL JOURNAL   PAGE _____

	DATE		DESCRIPTION	POST. REF.	DEBIT	CREDIT	
1	20–		Adjusting Entry				1
2	Dec.	31	Interest Receivable		5 5 12		2
3			Interest Income			5 5 12	3
4							4
5							5

Glossary

Accrued interest income on notes receivable The interest that is due (not yet received) on notes receivable, which are outstanding at the end of the fiscal period. (572)

Contingent liability A liability that is dependent upon certain conditions or events taking place—for example, if a note receivable is discounted at a bank and then the maker does not pay. The payee or endorser of the dishonored note is then liable to pay the bank. (568)

Discounting notes receivable The process by which a firm may raise cash by selling a note receivable to a bank or finance company. The bank deducts the discount from the maturity value of the note to determine the proceeds (amount of money) that the firm receives. (567)

Discount period The time between the date a note receivable is discounted and the date it matures. (567)

Dishonored note receivable A note whose maker fails to pay the principal amount or to renew the note at maturity. (565)

Maturity value The principal (face value) of a note plus interest from the date of the note until the due date. (567)

Notes receivable register A supplementary record in which a firm lists details of notes received. (571)

QUESTIONS, EXERCISES, AND PROBLEMS

Discussion Questions

1. Explain what *contingent liability* means in relation to the endorser of a note.
2. From the point of view of a creditor, what are the advantages of having a note receivable over having an account receivable?
3. Describe the formula for calculating the proceeds of an interest-bearing note receivable discounted at a bank. Define the terms.
4. In discounting an interest-bearing note receivable, why is the discount figured on the maturity value of the note?
5. Explain how to record a discounted note receivable.
6. Explain why a business would sell its notes receivable to a bank or finance company.
7. What is the purpose of maintaining a notes receivable register?
8. When is it necessary to make an adjusting entry for accrued interest on an interest-bearing note receivable, and why? What is the adjusting entry? Can the adjusting entry be reversed?

Exercises

P.O. 1a,b

Calculate due date and interest, and journalize issuance and payment of note on the books of payee and maker.

Exercise 16-1 On March 9, the T. L. Reid Company received a 90-day, 8 percent note for $1,500, dated March 9, from D. Burris, a charge customer, to satisfy his open account receivable.

a. What is the due date of the note?
b. How much interest is due at maturity?

Given the preceding data, write entries in general journal form on the books of the T. L. Reid Company to record the following:

c. Receipt of the note from Burris in settlement of his account.
d. Receipt of the principal and interest at maturity.

Given the same data, write entries in general journal form on Burris's books to record the following:

e. Issuance of the note by Burris in settlement of his account.
f. Payment of the note at maturity.

P.O. 1b,c

Journalize entries to loan money with a note and collect the principal and interest.

Exercise 16-2 Prepare entries in general journal form to record the following:

May   5   Received a 2-month, 8 percent note from Pam Davis for a $250 personal loan.

July   5   Received the total amount due from Davis.

P.O. 1e,f

Renewal of note with payment of interest and full or partial payment of principal

Exercise 16-3 Prepare journal entries in general journal form to record the following:

June   4   Received payment from Barker Company of interest on a 30-day, 7 percent note for $9,000, dated May 5, and renewal of the note for 60 days at 7.5 percent.

July   8   Received payment of interest from Newkirk Company on a 60-day, 7.5 percent note for $7,000, dated May 9, and partial payment of $2,000 on the principal. Received an 8 percent, 30-day note for $5,000 dated July 8.

P.O. 1d,i

Discount a note at the bank.

Exercise 16-4 On May 8, the Baginski Company received a 90-day, 10 percent note for $7,500, dated May 8, for merchandise sold to the Burr Company. Baginski endorsed the note in favor of its bank on May 28. The bank discounted the note at 9 percent, paying the proceeds to Baginski. Determine the following facts:

a. Number of days the Baginski Company held the note
b. Number of days in the discount period
c. Face value
d. Maturity value
e. Discount
f. Proceeds
g. Interest income or expense recorded by the payee (the Baginski Company)

P.O. 1a,i

Journalize a sale on account, settlement of the account with a note, and discount of the note at the bank.

Exercise 16-5 Prepare entries in general journal form to record the following:

June   12   Sold merchandise on account to K. M. Free; terms 2/10, n/30; $1,640.

July   12   Received $380 in cash from K. M. Free and a 60-day, 10 percent note for $1,260, dated July 12.

Aug.   17   Discounted the note at the bank at 9 percent.

P.O. 1a,i

Describe transactions concerning sales on account and payments of those accounts.

Exercise 16-6 The T accounts below show a series of four transactions concerning a sale of merchandise on account and subsequent payment of the amount owed. Describe what happened in each transaction.

Cash			Accounts Receivable			Sales			Interest Income		
+	–		+	–		–	+		–	+	
(d) 1,090.02			(a) 1,200.00	(b) 120.00			(a) 1,200.00			(d) 10.02	
				(c) 1,080.00							

Sales Returns and Allowances			Notes Receivable		
+	–		+	–	
(b) 120.00			(c) 1,080.00	(d) 1,080.00	

P.O. 1g,h

Dishonored note and collection of dishonored note

Exercise 16-7 Prepare journal entries in general journal form to record the following:

Aug. 5   Wilcox Company failed to pay its 30-day, 7 percent note for $700, dated July 5. The note is thus dishonored at maturity.

Sept. 5   Wilcox Company pays the balance of its account, plus an additional 30 days' interest at 7 percent on the amount owed.

P.O. 1a,b,3

Journalize entries to receive a note, adjust for interest accrued, close, reverse, and record receipt of payment.

Exercise 16-8 Write entries in general journal form to record the following transactions for the Green Company, whose fiscal year ends on December 31:

Dec. 3   The Green Company received from BRB Enterprises an $8,000, 120-day, 10.5 percent note, dated December 3, as an extension of a charge account.

31   The adjusting entry for accrued interest.

31   The closing entry (for practice), assuming all other closing entries were made.

Jan. 1   The reversing entry.

Apr. 2   Receipt of the principal and interest at maturity.

CONSIDER AND COMMUNICATE

The term *discount* or *discounting* is used repeatedly in accounting. For example, it is common to see references to "a sales discount of 2 percent," "discounting our note at the bank," "discounting a customer's note at the bank," and "trade discount." Explain how discounting is similar in these cases and how these situations differ.

WHAT IF . . .

You loaned $15,000 to a close friend to buy an off-road vehicle. You planned to have him sign a note receivable, with the off-road vehicle becoming collateral or security for the note in case your friend failed to pay you. However, in the excitement and rush to get the vehicle, you forgot to have your friend sign the note, and you also forgot to make the arrangements for collateral. Nothing was signed prior to your giving your friend the cash. How should this transaction have been handled? What are the possible consequences of this transaction between you and your friend?

CRITICAL THINKING

A client would like you to explain some options he has regarding discounting of a 10 percent, 60-day, $2,100 note receivable. He wants to know what he will receive in proceeds and what will be his interest income (or expense) if he discounts the note (a) after 10 days with a discount rate of 10 percent, (b) after 50 days with a 10 percent discount rate, or (c) after 5 days with a discount rate of 12 percent. Please make the calculations for the client and explain the different outcomes to him.

WEB WORK

Using an Internet web browser, type *mortgage contract purchasing* in the search box and search for information about selling notes receivable. Discuss your findings in a small group. Write a one-page summary of your findings.

PROBLEM SET A

For additional help, see the demonstration problem at the beginning of each chapter in your Working Papers.

P.O. 1a,b,d

Problem 16-1A The Heeb Company carried out the following transactions this year:

Jan.	16	Sold merchandise on account to Ross Company; 2/10, n/30; $2,460.
	26	Received a check from Ross Company for the sale on January 16.
Feb.	23	Sold merchandise on account to Ryan Company; 2/10, n/30; $1,683.
Mar.	24	Received a 60-day, 9 percent note, dated this day, for $1,683 from Ryan Company for the amount owed on account.
May	23	Received a check from Ryan Company for the amount owed on the note of March 24.
June	8	Sold merchandise to Emily's Interiors for $4,327, receiving its 90-day, 10 percent note, dated June 8 (not previously recorded).
Sept.	6	Received payment from Emily's Interiors for the amount owed on its note of June 8.

Check Figure

Interest on Ryan Company note, $25.25

Instructions

Record these transactions in the general journal (page 23).

P.O. 1a,b,d,e,i,2

Problem 16-2A Hayashikawa, Inc. carried out the following transactions this year:

Jan.	11	Sold merchandise on account to Z. Frazier; 1/10, n/30; $3,424.
Feb.	10	Received a 30-day, 9 percent note, dated this day, for $3,424, from Z. Frazier on account. Assume 28 days in February.
Mar.	12	Z. Frazier paid the amount due on its note of February 10.
Apr.	28	Sold merchandise on account to Levin Gallery; 1/10, n/30; $3,900.

May   28   Received a 60-day, 10 percent note, dated this day, for $3,900 from Levin Gallery on account.

July   27   Levin Gallery paid the interest on its note of May 28 and renewed the obligation by issuing a new 60-day, 11 percent note for $3,900, dated July 27.

Sept. 25   Received check from Levin Gallery for the amount owed on its note of July 27.

Oct.   1   Sold merchandise to Newell, Inc., for $6,300, receiving a 30-day, 10 percent note, dated this day (not previously recorded).

      21   Discounted the note received from Newell, Inc., at Calkins Bank; discount rate, 9 percent.

Instructions

1. Record these transactions in the general journal (page 11).
2. Immediately after each journal entry, record each note receivable in the notes receivable register (page 7).

   a. All notes are payable at Calkins Bank.
   b. Fill in the date paid after journalizing the receipt of payment of the note, or fill in "renewed" or "discounted" when appropriate.

Check Figure

Interest Income on Frazier note, $25.68

P.O. 1a,b,d,f,i

Problem 16-3A Here are some selected transactions carried out by Atwater Nursery this year.

Jan.   6   Sold merchandise on account to Albin Gardens; 2/10, n/30; $4,850.

Feb.   5   Received a 30-day, 11 percent note from Albin Gardens for $4,850, dated February 5, to apply on account. Assume 28 days in February.

Mar.   7   Received $1,894.46 from Albin Gardens as payment on its note dated February 5: $1,850 as part payment on the principal, and $44.46 as interest on $4,850 for 30 days at 11 percent. Received a new 30-day, 10 percent note for $3,000, dated March 7.

Apr.   6   Received a check from Albin Gardens for the amount owed on its note dated March 7.

      13   Sold merchandise to K. T. Frank, receiving her 60-day, 10 percent note, dated April 13, in the amount of $2,100 (not previously recorded).

      21   Discounted the note received from K. T. Frank at Kundert Bank; discount rate, 10 percent.

May   23   Sold merchandise on account to Hogan Company; 2/10, n/30; $1,366.

June 22   Received a $1,366 note from Hogan Company for 90 days at 11 percent, dated June 22 for the amount owed on account.

Check Figure

Proceeds of the K. T. Frank note dated April 13, $2,104.16

Instructions

Record these transactions in one of the following journals: sales journal (page 37), cash receipts journal (page 32), or general journal (page 17).

Instructions for General Ledger Software

1. Journalize transactions in either the sales journal, the cash receipts journal, or the general journal.
2. Print the journal entries from each journal.

P.O. 1a,b,c,d,e,i,3

Problem 16-4A Epler's Printing Company completed the following transactions during the year ended December 31:

June	14	Received a 60-day, 9 percent note, dated June 14, for $1,840 from Wanaka Office Supply for the sale of services. (The sale was not previously recorded.)
	26	Received a 30-day, 10 percent note, dated June 26, for $3,452 from Dawson, Inc., a charge customer, for a sale recorded previously.
July	7	Received a 90-day, 10 percent note, dated July 7, for $4,980 from Colin Office Supply, a charge customer, for a sale recorded previously.
	26	Received a check from Dawson, Inc., in payment of principal and interest on its note.
Aug.	13	Received payment of interest from Wanaka Office Supply for its note of June 14 and also a new 30-day, 10 percent note, dated August 13, for $1,840.
	22	Received a 60-day, 9.5 percent note, dated August 22, for $2,600 from E. Morris and Company, a charge customer, for a sale recorded previously.
Sept.	12	Wanaka Office Supply paid its note dated August 13, principal plus interest.
	14	Discounted the note received from E. Morris and Company, dated August 22, at Harris Bank; discount rate, 10 percent.
Oct.	5	Received a check from Colin Office Supply in payment of principal and interest on its note.
Dec.	16	Received a 60-day, 10.5 percent note, dated December 16, for $5,820 from Largent and Ryan Company, a charge customer, for a sale recorded previously.
	18	Received a 45-day, 10 percent note for a personal loan, dated December 18, from B. Jorn, an employee, for $450.

Check Figure

Adjustment for interest
receivable, $27.09

Instructions

1. Record these transactions in the general journal (page 47).
2. Show the calculation of each due date.
3. Dec. 31 Record the adjusting entry to account for accrued interest receivable for the Largent and Ryan Company and B. Jorn notes, which are not due to be paid until the next fiscal period.
4. Jan. 1 Record the reversing entry. (Assume closing entries have been made.)
5. Feb. 1 Record the receipt of payment from Jorn on February 1 of the new fiscal period.

PROBLEM SET B

For additional help, see the demonstration problem at the beginning of each chapter in your Working Papers.

P.O. 1a,b,d

Problem 16-1B Following are selected transactions carried out by Bloomfield Company this year:

Jan.	12	Sold merchandise on account to J. Leeper; 2/10, n/30; $2,632.
	22	Received check from J. Leeper for the sale of January 12.

Feb. 17 Sold merchandise on account to L. Blessing; 2/10, n/30; $3,240.

Mar. 18 Received a 30-day, 9 percent note, dated this day, for $3,240 from L. Blessing, on account.

Apr. 17 Received check from L. Blessing for the amount owed on the note of March 18.

June 1 Sold merchandise to Maloney Company, $4,272, receiving a 90-day, 10 percent note, dated this day. (This sale was not previously recorded.)

Aug. 30 Received payment from Maloney Company for the amount owed on the note of June 1.

Check Figure

Interest on Blessing note, $24.30

Instructions

Record these transactions in the general journal (page 23).

P.O. 1a,b,d,e,i,2

Problem 16-2B Here are some of the transactions carried out by Alling Trading Company this year:

Jan. 6 Sold merchandise on account to Miller Imports: 2/10, n/30; $2,816.

Feb. 5 Received a 30-day, 9 percent note, dated this day, for $2,816 from Miller Imports on account. Assume 28 days in February.

Mar. 7 Miller Imports paid the amount due on its note of February 5.

Apr. 25 Sold merchandise on account to Klein's Gift Shop; 2/10, n/30; $3,152.

May 25 Received a 45-day, 11 percent note, dated May 25, for $3,152 from Klein's Gift Shop on account.

July 9 Klein's Gift Shop paid the interest on its note of May 25 and renewed the obligation by issuing a new 60-day, 12 percent note for $3,152, dated July 9.

Sept. 7 Received check from Klein's Gift Shop for the amount owed on its note of July 9.

14 Sold merchandise to Rikki Boe, Inc., $4,286, receiving its 30-day, 10 percent note. (The sale was not previously recorded.)

24 Discounted the note received from Rikki Boe, Inc., at Salem State Bank; discount rate, 9 percent.

Instructions

1. Record these transactions in the general journal (page 11).
2. Immediately after each journal entry, record each note receivable in the notes receivable register (page 7).

Check Figure

Interest Income on Miller Imports note, $21.12

a. All notes are payable at Salem State Bank.

b. Fill in the date paid after journalizing the receipt of payment of the note, or fill in "renewed" or "discounted" when appropriate.

P.O. 1a,b,d,f,i

Problem 16-3B Selected transactions of Lois's Center carried out this year are as follows:

Jan. 10 Sold merchandise on account to Osman Stores; 2/10, n/30; $5,230.

Feb. 9 Received a 30-day, 9 percent note from Osman Stores, $5,230, dated February 9, to apply on account. Assume 28 days in February.

Mar. 11 Received $2,269.23 from Osman Stores as part payment on its note dated February 9: $2,230 as part payment on the principal and $39.23 interest on $5,230 for 30 days at 9 percent. Received a new 30-day, 10 percent note, dated March 11, for $3,000.

Apr. 4 Sold merchandise to Fisher Sports, $2,790, receiving a 90-day, 9 percent note, dated April 4 (not previously recorded).

10 Received a check from Osman Stores for the amount owed on its note of March 11.

12 Discounted the note received from Fisher Sports at the Lundgren Bank; discount rate, 8 percent.

May 8 Sold merchandise on account to Laxtrom, Inc.; 2/10, n/30; $2,848.

June 7 Received a 45-day, 9 percent note for $2,848 from Laxtrom, Inc., dated June 7, to apply on account.

Check Figure

Proceeds of the Fisher Sports note dated April 4, $2,800.80

P.O. 1a,b,c,d,e,i,3

Instructions

Record these transactions in one of the following journals: sales journal (page 37), cash receipts journal (page 32), or general journal (page 17).

Instructions for General Ledger Software

1. Journalize transactions in either the sales journal, the cash receipts journal, or the general journal.
2. Print the journal entries from each journal.

Problem 16-4B Here are some selected transactions of Michael's Grocery Supply carried out during the year ended December 31:

June 9 Received a 60-day, 9 percent note, dated June 9, for $3,662 from Misty's Foods for merchandise. (The sale was not previously recorded.)

21 Received a 30-day, 10 percent note, dated June 21, for $2,838 from Lindsey Restaurants, a charge customer, for a sale recorded previously.

July 1 Received a 90-day, 10 percent note, dated July 1, for $1,980 from Armstrong, Inc., a charge customer, for a sale recorded previously.

21 Received a check from Lindsey Restaurants in payment of principal and interest on its note.

Aug. 8 Received payment of interest from Misty's Foods for its note of June 9 and signed a new 30-day, 9 percent note, for $3,662, dated August 8.

20 Received a 60-day, 9.5 percent note, dated August 20, from C. T. Tamparo, a charge customer, for $3,010, for a sale recorded previously.

Sept. 7 Misty's Foods paid its note, dated August 8, principal plus interest.

9 Discounted the note received from C. T. Tamparo, dated August 20, at the Hammond Bank; discount rate, 10 percent.

29 Received a check from Armstrong, Inc., in payment of principal and interest on its note.

Dec. 6 Received a 60-day, 9 percent note, dated December 6, from C. L. Chan, a charge customer, for $2,642, for a sale recorded previously.

8 Received a 30-day, 9.5 percent note, for a personal loan, dated December 8, from J. Brannon, an employee, for $380.

Check Figure

Adjustment for interest receivable, $18.82

Instructions

1. Record these transactions in the general journal (page 47).
2. Show the calculation of each due date.
3. Dec. 31 Record the adjusting entry to account for accrued interest receivable for the Chan and Brannon notes, which are not due to be paid until the next fiscal period.
4. Jan. 1 Record the reversing entry. (Assume closing entries have been made.)
5. Jan. 7 Record the receipt of payment on the Brannon note on January 7 of the new fiscal year.

Cumulative Self-Check: Chapters 15–16

PART I: NOTES PAYABLE

A. On September 20 of this year, A. Lake issued a 120-day, 9 percent note, dated September 20, to D. Cho, a creditor, for $12,000. Answer the following questions about the note:

1. What is the due date?
2. What is the face value?
3. How much is the total interest?
4. What is the maturity value?
5. What is the amount of the adjusting entry for interest expense on December 31?

B. On October 20 of this year, G. Fernandez borrowed $8,000 from the bank, signing a 90-day, discounted 8 percent note dated October 20. Answer the following questions about the note:

1. What is the due date?
2. What is the face value?
3. How much is the total interest?
4. On October 20, the entry to record the note includes a debit to Cash. Is the other debit to Interest Expense or to Discount on Notes Payable? How much is that debit?
5. What is the maturity value?
6. What is the amount of the adjusting entry on December 31?
7. What are the debit and the credit accounts in the December 31 adjusting entry?
8. On the date of payment of the note, besides debiting Notes Payable and crediting Cash for the face value of the note, what are the debit and credit accounts and amounts needed to report the entire amount of interest on the note?

PART II: NOTES RECEIVABLE

A. The Grandy Company received a $9,000, 60-day, 8.5 percent note, dated December 3 of this year, as an extension of a charge account for Fleshman Company. Determine the following:

1. The debit and credit accounts involved in recording the $9,000 note
2. The debit and credit accounts and amounts involved in the December 31 adjusting entry
3. The due date
4. The maturity value
5. The debit and credit accounts and amounts involved in the receipt of payment from the Fleshman Company, assuming a reversing entry was made on January 1

Note: Answers to the Cumulative Self-Check begin on page A-1.

B. On April 8 of this year, the Tauscher Company received a 90-day, 8 percent note for $6,500, dated April 8, for merchandise sold to the Walter Company. Tauscher endorsed the note in favor of its bank on April 28. The bank discounted the note at 8.5 percent, paying the proceeds to the Tauscher Company. Determine the following:

1. Number of days the Tauscher Company held the note
2. Number of days in the discount period
3. Face value
4. Maturity value
5. Discount
6. Proceeds
7. Will interest income or interest expense be recorded by the payee (the Tauscher Company)?
8. What is the amount of income or expense recorded by the payee (the Tauscher Company)?

17 Uncollectible Accounts

WINDOWS ON | THE WORLD WIDE WEB

If your company had uncollected accounts or bad debts, would you try to collect them before writing them off? If you did, you could use one of many collection services like Adams, Stevens & Bradley, Ltd., at **http:// www.baddebts.net/**, or Caine & Weiner, at **http://www.caine-weiner .com/collection.htm**. Debt collection is a thriving business, as you can see if you check out these web sites. But what if you still need to write off some customers' accounts and record the amount in a Bad Debt account? You would also write off these accounts receivable as uncollectible. Genzyme, maker of products such as cancer therapy, severe burn treatment, pharmaceuticals, and surgical items, recorded an allowance for doubtful accounts in past financials. For financial information about the human health-care products provider, go to **http://www.genzyme.com/company/**.

Performance Objectives

After you have completed this chapter, you will be able to do the following:

1. Make the adjusting entry to record estimated bad debt losses by using the allowance method of recording bad debts. (a) Determine the amount of the adjusting entry by aging Accounts Receivable. (b) Determine the amount of the adjusting entry by using a percentage of Accounts Receivable. (c) Calculate the amount of the adjusting entry by using a percentage of net sales or net credit sales.

2. Journalize the entries to write off accounts receivable as being uncollectible, using the allowance method of accounting for bad debt losses.

3. Journalize entries to reinstate accounts receivable previously written off, using the allowance method.

4. Journalize the entries to write off accounts receivable as being uncollectible, using the specific charge-off method.

5. Journalize entries to reinstate accounts receivable previously written off, using the specific charge-off method.

The use of credit for both buying and selling goods and services has become standard practice for businesses of all types and levels: retailers, wholesalers, and manufacturers. You have learned to record sales of goods on account as a debit to Accounts Receivable and a credit to Sales. You have also learned to record collections on account as a debit to Cash and a credit to Accounts Receivable.

Business firms selling goods or services on credit will find that not all the Accounts Receivable (charge accounts) are collected in full. As a result, the unpaid accounts must eventually be written off as uncollectible or as bad debts. In other words, a firm that grants credit will not collect from everyone, and therefore the firm needs to plan for these anticipated losses. In this chapter, we discuss ways to provide for losses as well as to write off customer accounts that are no longer collectible.

We examine two methods of accounting for uncollectible accounts: the *allowance method* and the *specific charge-off method*. The allowance method is consistent with the matching principle, in that it enables firms to match sales of one period with bad debt losses of the same period; and it is consistent with the accrual method of accounting required by generally accepted principles of accounting. The specific charge-off method traditionally has been used by small businesses. Now, in accordance with the Tax Reform Act of 1986, the specific charge-off method is the only method approved for federal income tax purposes. Many companies, especially larger firms, use the allowance method for their own accounting system for external reporting—that is, for their own financial statements. They use the specific charge-off method for federal income tax reporting. The adjustments required on their tax returns are not entered in the companies' books.

FYI

Write-off and *charge-off* mean the same thing.

THE CREDIT DEPARTMENT

The Credit Department has to keep a watchful eye on customers. It evaluates the debt-paying ability of prospective customers and determines the maximum amount of credit to extend to each customer. Retail stores selling to individuals rely on reports from local retail credit bureaus. When wholesalers and manufacturers grant credit to customers, they use reports from national credit-rating institutions, wholesale credit bureaus, and the financial statements of prospective customers. Firms that make many sales on credit find it worthwhile to subscribe to these credit bureaus or credit-rating agencies. These credit-reporting organizations maintain files of current financial information on charge customers, establish credit ratings for each charge customer, and conduct special investigations on request.

Incurring excessive credit losses is always unfavorable for a seller because any firm needs to be paid for its sales on account. Surprisingly, it may also be bad if a firm has no credit losses. Such a record may indicate that the firm is turning down applications for credit, even though most applicants would indeed pay their bills. If credit requirements are too rigid, the firm not only loses many immediate sales but may create considerable ill will. A sound credit policy should provide for a limited amount of credit losses. It is the responsibility of the Credit Department to keep these losses within acceptable limits.

Most companies, including major gas companies, lend money to customers by extending credit. This is a convenience to consumers, but some customers don't repay the debt. Businesses write off those accounts and record the amount in the Bad Debts Expense account.

MATCHING BAD DEBT LOSSES WITH SALES

Remember!

The matching principle attempts to match the amount of expenses incurred with the revenue earned for the same fiscal period.

A basic principle of the accrual basis of accounting is that revenue for a fiscal period be matched by the expenses incurred to earn that revenue. This **matching principle** is consistent with our earlier presentation of adjusting entries. For example, depreciation represents the allocation of cost of equipment to the particular periods or years benefited. In making the adjustment, we allocate this expense to that year. Thus, we debit Depreciation Expense, Equipment, and credit Accumulated Depreciation, Equipment. Similarly, when a firm sells merchandise on account to a customer who may eventually refuse to pay the bill for the merchandise, the firm has a bad debt loss potential. The firm must try to match the loss with the revenue earned for the year in which the sale is made.

At the time of making the sale, the company does not *know* that it has incurred a loss; it believes that the customer will pay the debt. If it did not, the company would not have extended credit to that customer in the first place. In other words, the firm making the credit sale has increased its revenue account, but it does not know at the time of the sale whether the money earned will be collected. As a matter of fact, the firm will not be certain of the loss until it has repeatedly failed in its attempts to collect the bill. The final recognition of the loss will probably occur many months after the sale. *In order to match the bad debt losses for the year with the sales for the same year, the firm must make an estimate of the losses as a means of providing for them in advance.* The allowance method of accounting for bad debt losses provides the means for matching bad debt losses with the applicable sales in the company's financial statements.

THE ALLOWANCE METHOD OF ACCOUNTING FOR BAD DEBTS

Most big firms use the **allowance method of accounting for bad debt losses** for financial reporting, which is consistent with the accrual method of accounting required by generally accepted accounting principles (GAAP). An adjusting entry is recorded first in the Adjustments columns of the work sheet—much like the adjustment for depreciation. In general journal and T account form, the adjusting entry for the estimated bad debt losses for Morgan Company is shown in the following examples.

	DATE		DESCRIPTION	POST. REF.	DEBIT	CREDIT	
1	20–		**Adjusting Entry**				1
2	Dec.	31	Bad Debts Expense		1 6 0 0 00		2
3			Allowance for Doubtful				3
4			Accounts			1 6 0 0 00	4

Bad Debts Expense			**Allowance for Doubtful Accounts**		
	+	−		−	+
Adj.	1,600			Bal.	2,200
				Adj.	1,600
					3,800

FIGURE 1

ACCOUNT NAME	TRIAL BALANCE	
	DEBIT	CREDIT
Accounts Receivable	60 0 0 0 00	
Allowance for Doubtful Accounts		2 2 0 0 00
Equipment	74 0 0 0 00	
Accumulated Depreciation, Equipment		22 0 0 0 00
Bad Debts Expense		
Depreciation Expense, Equipment		

■ ■ ■

Objective 1

Make the adjusting entry to record estimated bad debt losses by using the allowance method of recording bad debts.

The purpose of the adjusting entry is to increase Bad Debts Expense by the amount of the estimated loss and to produce a collectible figure for the book value of Accounts Receivable. **Allowance for Doubtful Accounts is classified as a deduction from Accounts Receivable. As such, it is a contra account, similar to Accumulated Depreciation.** Just as the book value of Equipment equals the cost of Equipment minus Accumulated Depreciation, Equipment, the **book value of Accounts Receivable** equals Accounts Receivable minus Allowance for Doubtful Accounts. Accountants also refer to the book value of Accounts Receivable as the **net expected realizable value of Accounts Receivable.**

Because a firm cannot know with certainty which accounts won't be fully collected, it's not possible to credit Accounts Receivable directly. However, on the basis of its experience, a firm is able to estimate what this year's bad debt losses will be. The firm bases its estimate on a year's sales, but it can't say with certainty *which* specific credit sales, by customer name, will not be paid.

Prior to the adjustments, the **Bad Debts Expense account has no previous balance, as the account is not used during the fiscal period.** The firm's accountant makes an adjusting entry to increase Bad Debts Expense and immediately closes the account along with all other expense accounts. Allowance for Doubtful Accounts, on the other hand, has a balance that is carried over from previous years and is not closed. Notice where these accounts appear in the partial work sheet shown in Figure 1.

Note that Accounts Receivable is recorded in the debit column, and Allowance for Doubtful Accounts is recorded in the credit column. The $1,600 adjustment is added to the previous credit balance of $2,200, resulting in $3,800 being recorded in the Balance Sheet Credit column. As you can see, Allowance for Doubtful Accounts is handled much like Accumulated Depreciation. Both are recorded as credits in the Adjustments and Balance Sheet columns of the work sheet; also, the adjustments are never reversed because both accounts have previous balances after the first year of operation.

■ ■ ■

Remember!

Allowance for Doubtful Accounts is a contra account. It is used to record an estimate of the accounts receivable that will not be collected in the future. Its signs are opposite to those of Accounts Receivable.

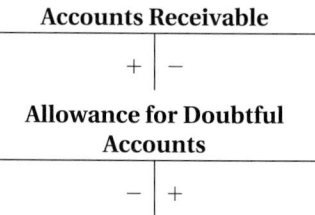

Bad Debts Expense and Allowance for Doubtful Accounts on Financial Statements

The Bad Debts Expense account appears on the income statement as an operating expense. Some firms subdivide operating expenses into selling expenses and general expenses, in which case they list Bad Debts Expense as a general expense. (*Reason:* The decision to grant credit is usually a function of the administrative rather than the sales staff.)

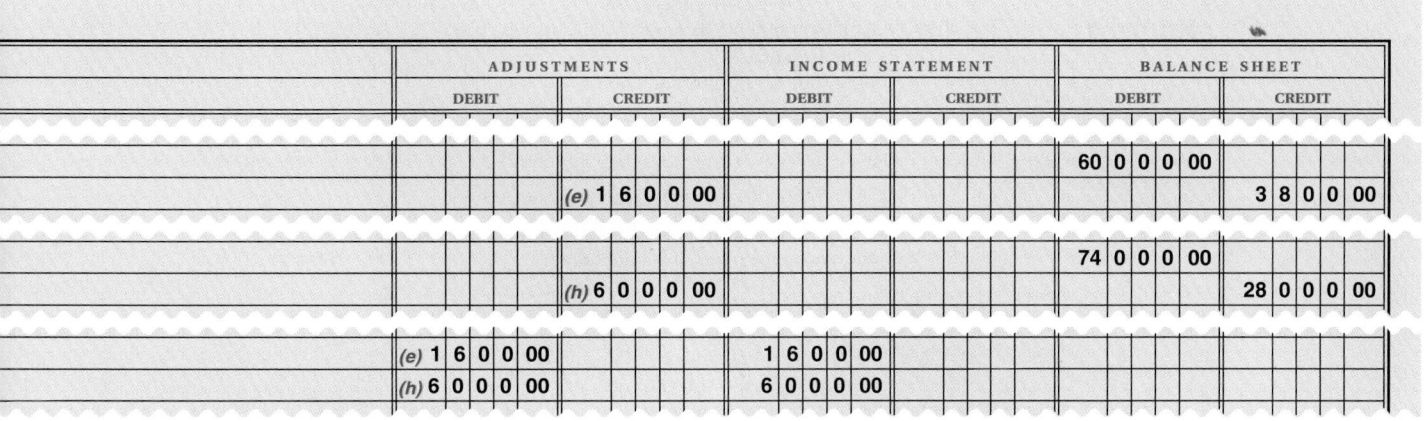

	ADJUSTMENTS		INCOME STATEMENT		BALANCE SHEET	
	DEBIT	CREDIT	DEBIT	CREDIT	DEBIT	CREDIT
		(e) 1 6 0 0 00			60 0 0 0 00	
						3 8 0 0 00
		(h) 6 0 0 0 00			74 0 0 0 00	
						28 0 0 0 00
	(e) 1 6 0 0 00		1 6 0 0 00			
	(h) 6 0 0 0 00		6 0 0 0 00			

Morgan Company
Balance Sheet
December 31, 20—

Assets				
Current Assets:				
Cash		$12 0 0 0 00		
Notes Receivable		8 0 0 0 00		
Accounts Receivable	$60 0 0 0 00			
Less Allowance for Doubtful Accounts	3 8 0 0 00	56 2 0 0 00		
Merchandise Inventory		96 0 0 0 00		
Supplies		4 0 0 00		
Total Current Assets			$172 6 0 0 00	
Plant and Equipment:				
Equipment	$74 0 0 0 00			
Less Accumulated Depreciation	28 0 0 0 00	$46 0 0 0 00		

FIGURE 2

Allowance for Doubtful Accounts is listed immediately below Accounts Receivable in the Current Assets section of the balance sheet, as shown in Figure 2.

The $56,200 ($60,000 − $3,800) represents the anticipated net realizable value of Accounts Receivable; this is also known as the *book value of Accounts Receivable*. The net realizable value is the amount of cash the seller eventually expects to collect from gross receivables. Allowance for Doubtful Accounts is classified as a *contra account*, because it is a deduction from an asset.

Estimating the Amount of Bad Debts Expense

Management—on the basis of its judgment and past experience—has to make a reasonable estimate of the amount of its uncollectible accounts. It stands to reason that any such estimate is modified by business trends. In a period of prosperity and high employment, you can usually expect fewer losses from uncollectible accounts than in a period of recession.

FIGURE 3

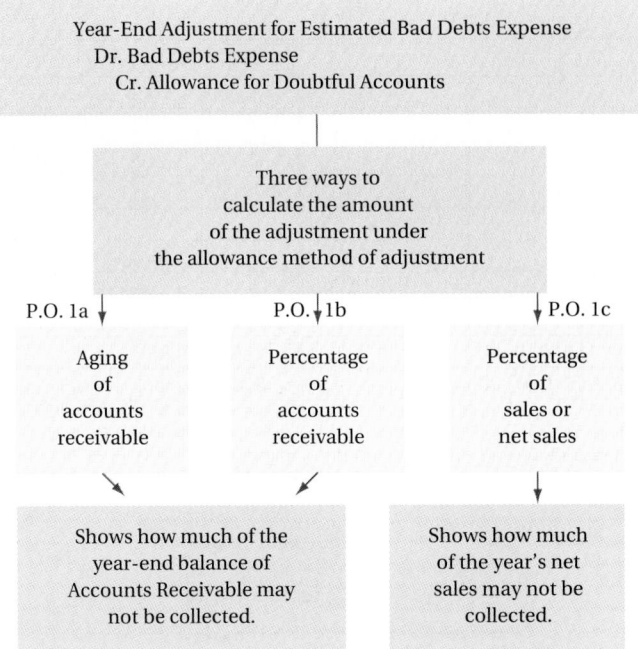

The next question is: "For the adjusting entry, how does management estimate the dollar amount of bad debts expense?" The estimate can be made in several ways; we present three methods here:

1. Aging Accounts Receivable
2. Using a percentage of Accounts Receivable
3. Using a percentage of Sales or net credit sales

Figure 3 illustrates the adjustment approaches to estimate the amount of bad debts expense.

Adjusting Entry Based on Aging Accounts Receivable

Objective 1a

Determine the amount of the adjusting entry by aging Accounts Receivable.

The most common technique for estimating the total uncollectible amount of Accounts Receivable is to **age** each charge customer's account by (1) determining the age, in number of days, of each account and (2) determining the number of days the account is past due. On a working paper, the accounts in a company's accounts receivable ledger are listed by name and amount. Columns are set up for various age groups. As an example, we use the accounts receivable of Rogers Company. Here is the partial aging schedule:

ANALYSIS OF ACCOUNTS RECEIVABLE BY AGE

CUSTOMER NAME	BALANCE	NOT YET DUE	DAYS PAST DUE					
			1–30	31–60	61–90	91–180	181–365	OVER 365
A. R. Adler	792.00	792.00						
B. N. Brandt	464.00				464.00			
C. L. Casey	136.90			136.90				
D. R. Dewey	914.00	914.00						
E. V. Eaton	593.10			593.10				
Total	94,000.00	78,200.00	8,030.00	3,280.00	1,975.00	1,260.00	834.00	421.00

Many companies offer credit opportunities to increase business, but they should screen their customers carefully. The longer an account is past due, the greater the possibility that it will be uncollectible.

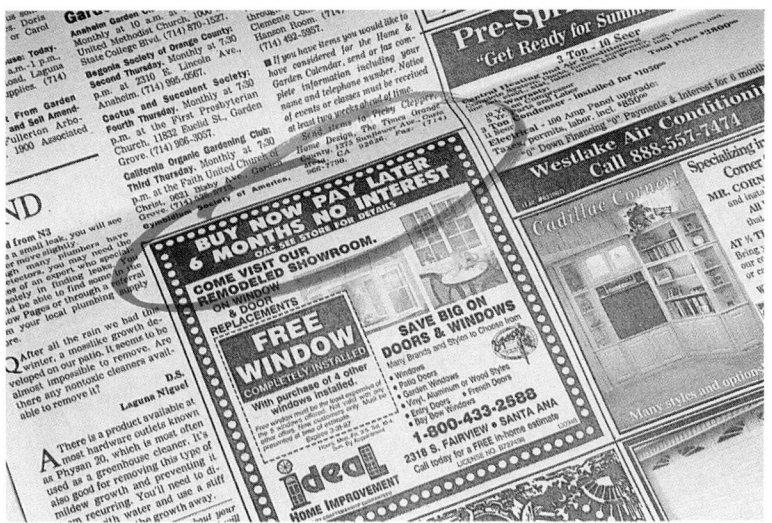

Remember!

The older the account, the greater the possibility that it is uncollectible.

Based on its past experience, a company can estimate that a given percentage of accounts in each age group will be uncollectible. Next, the accountant multiplies the total amount for each age group by the percentage for that group. This results in the amount estimated to be uncollectible for that group. Let's continue with the Accounts Receivable of Rogers Company.

Age of Accounts	Amount	Estimated Percentage Uncollectible	Allowance for Doubtful Accounts
Not yet due	$78,200	2	$78,200 × .02 = $1,564.00
1 to 30 days	8,030	4	8,030 × .04 = 321.20
31 to 60 days	3,280	10	3,280 × .10 = 328.00
61 to 90 days	1,975	20	1,975 × .20 = 395.00
91 to 180 days	1,260	30	1,260 × .30 = 378.00
181 to 365 days	834	50	834 × .50 = 417.00
Over 365 days	421	80	421 × .80 = 336.80
Total	$94,000		$3,740.00

FYI

The estimated percentage uncollectible can vary based on the economic health of an area and/or how strict a company is in granting credit.

In the ledger of Rogers Company, the new balance in Allowance for Doubtful Accounts should be $3,740 (the amount estimated by aging to be uncollectible). **The accountant now makes an adjusting entry large enough to make the balance of Allowance for Doubtful Accounts the same as the estimated uncollectible amount.** Rogers Company had a credit balance of $320 in Allowance for Doubtful Accounts. We now make an adjusting entry to bring the balance of the account up to $3,740. The amount of the adjusting entry is $3,420 ($3,740 − $320). This situation is illustrated by T accounts:

Bad Debts Expense			**Allowance for Doubtful Accounts**		
+	−		−	+	
Adj. 3,420				Bal.	320
				Adj.	3,420
					3,740

| ACCOUNT NAME | TRIAL BALANCE | |
	DEBIT	CREDIT
Accounts Receivable	94 0 0 0 00	
Allowance for Doubtful Accounts		3 2 0 00
Bad Debts Expense		

FIGURE 4

To sum up: The firm estimates that $3,740 of Accounts Receivable are uncollectible. *It now has to bring the balance of Allowance for Doubtful Accounts up to the desired figure of $3,740.* Allowance for Doubtful Accounts has a present credit balance of $320, so the firm adjusts for the difference, $3,420. After the accountant posts the adjusting entry, the footing of Allowance for Doubtful Accounts indicates the desired balance, as determined by the aging analysis. The adjusting data and their effect on the accounts are illustrated in Figure 4.

Bad Debts Expense ($3,420) appears on the income statement in the general expense portion of Operating Expenses. Like all expenses, it is closed into Income Summary at the end of the fiscal period. For emphasis, let's repeat the placement of the accounts in the balance sheet.

Rogers Company
Balance Sheet
December 31, 20x1

Assets			
Current Assets:			
Cash			$ 9 2 0 0 00
Notes Receivable			4 0 0 0 00
Accounts Receivable	$94 0 0 0 00		
Less Allowance for Doubtful Accounts	3 7 4 0 00		90 2 6 0 00

FYI

Aging of Accounts Receivable is easily accomplished by computer accounting programs.

Objective 1b

Determine the amount of the adjusting entry by using a percentage of Accounts Receivable.

Adjusting Entry Based on Estimating Bad Debts as a Percentage of Accounts Receivable

Some firms feel that the aging procedure is too time consuming; they prefer a quicker but less exact method for estimating the amount of uncollectible Accounts Receivable. These firms take an average of the actual bad debt losses of previous years as a percentage of Accounts Receivable. For example, the Romero Company calculated the following amount of the adjustment for uncollectible accounts:

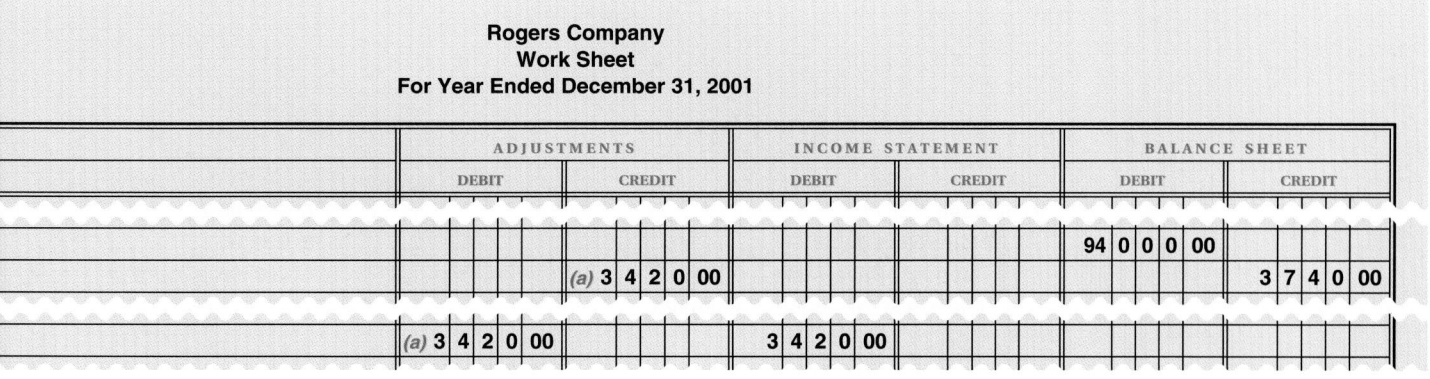

Rogers Company
Work Sheet
For Year Ended December 31, 2001

	ADJUSTMENTS		INCOME STATEMENT		BALANCE SHEET	
	DEBIT	CREDIT	DEBIT	CREDIT	DEBIT	CREDIT
					94 0 0 0 00	
		(a) 3 4 2 0 00				3 7 4 0 00
	(a) 3 4 2 0 00		3 4 2 0 00			

End of Year	Balance of Accounts Receivable	Total Actual Losses from Accounts Receivable (Accounts Receivable Written Off)
2001	$ 44,000	$1,540
2002	56,000	1,528
2003	48,000	1,372
	$148,000	$4,440

The firm's average loss over three consecutive years was 3 percent.

$$\frac{4{,}440}{148{,}000} = .03 = \underline{\underline{3\%}}$$

Assume that, at the end of 2004, the balance of Accounts Receivable is $59,200 and the credit balance of Allowance for Doubtful Accounts is $294. The amount of Accounts Receivable the company estimates to be uncollectible is $1,776 ($59,200 × .03 = $1,776). Since $1,776 is the desired figure, the amount of the adjustment is $1,482 ($1,776 − $294 = $1,482). As in the case of aging Accounts Receivable, when you figure the adjustment for bad debts as a percentage of Accounts Receivable, *you make an adjusting entry to bring the balance of Allowance for Doubtful Accounts up to the desired figure.* Notice how the adjusting entry looks in the following T accounts:

Remember!

No matter what method is used to determine the amount of the adjustment for bad debts, the resulting amount is an estimate only.

Bad Debts Expense			Allowance for Doubtful Accounts		
	+	−		−	+
Adj.	1,482			Bal.	294
				Adj.	1,482
					1,776

You would then record the adjustment in the work sheet as shown in Figure 5 on the following page.

ACCOUNT NAME	TRIAL BALANCE										
	DEBIT					CREDIT					
Cash	16	8	9	1	00						
Notes Receivable	1	6	0	0	00						
Accounts Receivable	59	2	0	0	00						
Allowance for Doubtful Accounts							2	9	4	00	
Bad Debts Expense											

FIGURE 5

Let's examine a portion of the balance sheet derived from the work sheet.

Romero Company
Balance Sheet
December 31, 2004

Assets											
Current Assets:											
Cash						$16	8	9	1	00	
Notes Receivable						1	6	0	0	00	
Accounts Receivable	$59	2	0	0	00						
Less Allowance for Doubtful Accounts	1	7	7	6	00	57	4	2	4	00	

In this statement, the book value of Accounts Receivable is shown as $57,424 ($59,200 − $1,776).

Adjusting Entry Based on Estimating Bad Debts as a Percentage of Net Sales or Net Credit Sales

Objective 1c

Calculate the amount of the adjusting entry by using a percentage of net sales or net credit sales.

Some businesses prefer a simplified method for determining the amount of the adjustment for Bad Debts Expense. They multiply the current year's sales by a set percentage rate and then record the adjusting entry for that amount.

Estimate Based on Net Sales For example, the actual losses from sales on account for the Loza Company have averaged approximately 1 percent of net sales (Sales less Sales Returns and Allowances and less Sales Discount). The firm makes virtually all sales on credit. Based on this information, the company computes the amount of the adjustment for bad debts expense as 1 percent of net sales.

The figure for net sales is shown in the partial income statement on page 599:

Romero Company
Work Sheet
For Year Ended December 31, 2004

| | ADJUSTMENTS | | INCOME STATEMENT | | BALANCE SHEET | |
	DEBIT	CREDIT	DEBIT	CREDIT	DEBIT	CREDIT
					16 8 9 1 00	
					1 6 0 0 00	
					59 2 0 0 00	
		(e) 1 4 8 2 00				1 7 7 6 00
	(e) 1 4 8 2 00		1 4 8 2 00			

Loza Company
Income Statement
For Year Ended June 30, 20—

Revenue from Sales:			
Sales		$711 0 0 0 00	
Less: Sales Returns and Allowances	$31 0 0 0 00		
Sales Discount	1 6 0 0 00	32 6 0 0 00	
Net Sales			$678 4 0 0 00

One percent of net sales is $6,784 ($678,400 × .01), **so the firm uses this amount directly for the adjusting entry, adding it to both accounts,** as shown in the T accounts below. In contrast to the previously illustrated aging and percentage of accounts receivable methods, the sales methods ignore any existing balance in the allowance account to calculate Bad Debt Expense.

Bad Debts Expense		Allowance for Doubtful Accounts	
+	−	−	+
Adj. 6,784			Bal. 196
			Adj. 6,784
			6,980

Figure 6 on the following pages shows how to record the adjustment in the work sheet. A portion of the balance sheet is as follows:

Remember!

Companies may change the percentage used for estimating bad debts based on changes in the economy.

Loza Company
Balance Sheet
June 30, 20—

Assets			
Current Assets:			
Accounts Receivable	$63 2 0 0 00		
Less Allowance for Doubtful Accounts	6 9 8 0 00	56 2 2 0 00	

FIGURE 6

ACCOUNT NAME	TRIAL BALANCE	
	DEBIT	CREDIT
Accounts Receivable	63 2 0 0 00	
Allowance for Doubtful Accounts		1 9 6 00
Sales		711 0 0 0 00
Sales Returns and Allowances	31 0 0 0 00	
Sales Discount	1 6 0 0 00	
Bad Debts Expense		

Estimate Based on Net Credit Sales Many companies that sell on both a cash and a credit basis compute the amount of their adjustment for bad debts on net credit sales only. As an example, we use the Rea Company. Charge sales, recorded in a sales journal, total $735,000. Sales Returns and Allowances and Sales Discounts relating to credit sales are $27,000 and $6,300, respectively. Rea Company records the adjustment for bad debts at ¾ percent of net credit sales. Look at the calculation and adjustment that follow:

Credit (charge) sales		$735,000
Less: Sales Returns and Allowances	$27,000	
Sales Discount	6,300	33,300
Net credit sales		$701,700

$701,700
× .0075

$5,262.75

By T accounts, the amount of the adjustment is added to both accounts as shown:

Bad Debts Expense		Allowance for Doubtful Accounts	
+	−	−	+
Adj. 5,262.75			Bal. 330.14
			Adj. 5,262.75
			5,592.89

Note that a firm using this simplified method multiplies net sales or net credit sales by the given percentage in order to determine the amount of the adjustment. **The present balance of Allowance for Doubtful Accounts is not involved in determining the amount of the adjustment.** If the given percentage does not adequately provide for the firm's losses (that is, if it yields either too little or too much), the firm merely changes the percentage.

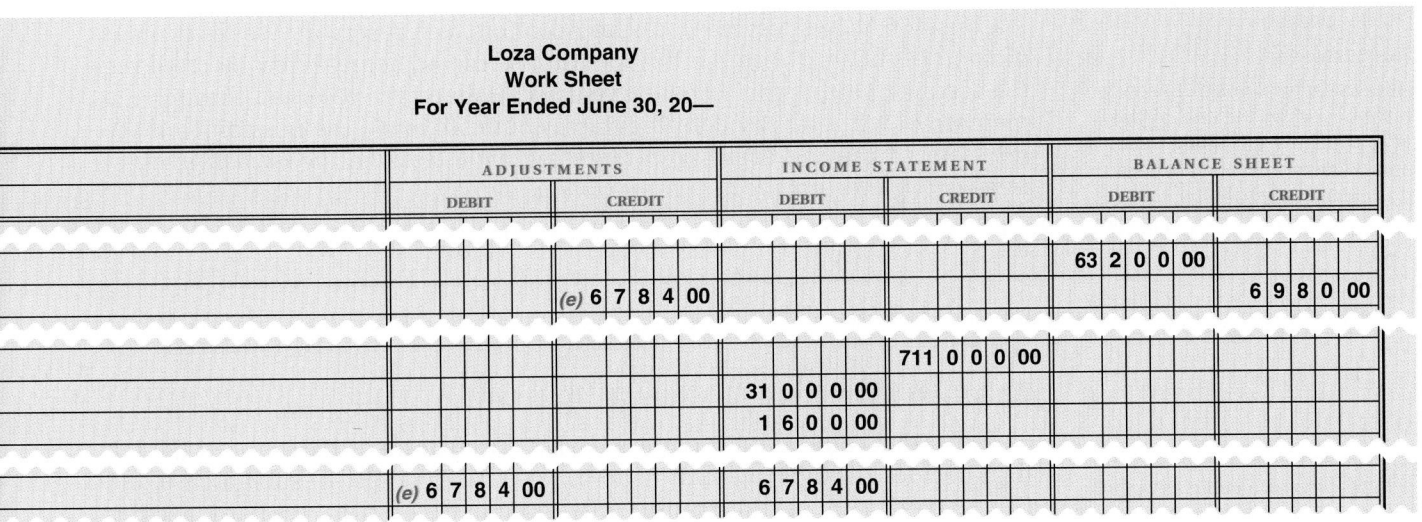

Loza Company
Work Sheet
For Year Ended June 30, 20—

	ADJUSTMENTS		INCOME STATEMENT		BALANCE SHEET	
	DEBIT	CREDIT	DEBIT	CREDIT	DEBIT	CREDIT
					63 2 0 0 00	
		(e) 6 7 8 4 00				6 9 8 0 00
				711 0 0 0 00		
			31 0 0 0 00			
			1 6 0 0 00			
	(e) 6 7 8 4 00		6 7 8 4 00			

CLOSING THE BAD DEBTS EXPENSE ACCOUNT

Up to now, we have seen that the firm's accountant first records the adjusting entry for bad debts in the appropriate columns of the work sheet. The T accounts for Rea Company are repeated here.

Bad Debts Expense			Allowance for Doubtful Accounts		
	+	**–**		**–**	**+**
Adj.	5,262.75				Bal. 330.14
					Adj. 5,262.75
					5,592.89

Next, the accountant closes Bad Debts Expense, along with all other expenses, into the Income Summary account. **The Bad Debts Expense account is not used during the year, so the only entries in it are the adjusting entry and the closing entry.** This represents the beginning and the end of Bad Debts Expense for the fiscal period. In other words, the only entry in Bad Debts Expense is the adjusting entry, and, as we said, this account is immediately closed out. After the adjusting entry and closing entry have been posted, the accounts look like this:

Bad Debts Expense				Allowance for Doubtful Accounts		
	+	**–**			**–**	**+**
Adj.	5,262.75	Clos.	5,262.75			Bal. 330.14
						Adj. 5,262.75
						5,592.89

Allowance for Doubtful Accounts

It is apparent that Allowance for Doubtful Accounts remains open. Rather than have the balance continually increase because of the successive adjustments on the credit side of the account, the accountant uses the debit side of the account to write off charge accounts that are considered uncollectible.

Remember!

Allowance for Doubtful Accounts increases when the end-of-the-year adjustment is made (credit) and decreases as write-offs occur during the year (debits).

Consider Allowance for Doubtful Accounts as a reservoir: We fill it up at the end of the year through the medium of the adjusting entry by crediting the account. During the following year, we drain off the reservoir through the medium of write-offs by debiting the account. To avoid the possibility of the reservoir's "running dry," *the accountant should make the adjusting entry large enough to provide for all possible write-offs.*

WRITING OFF ACCOUNTS AS UNCOLLECTIBLE

Objective 2

Journalize the entries to write off accounts receivable as being uncollectible, using the allowance method of accounting for bad debt losses.

Entry to Write Off a Charge Account in Full

Suppose that, after all attempts to collect a customer's debt have failed, a firm decides that the account is definitely uncollectible. In such a case, the firm should write off the amount due. Assume that Loza Company decides that the $271.40 account of a customer, C. N. Coe, is uncollectible. The accountant records the write-off by making the following entry:

GENERAL JOURNAL PAGE __116__

	DATE		DESCRIPTION	POST. REF.	DEBIT	CREDIT	
1	20–						1
2	July	1	Allowance for Doubtful Accounts		2 7 1 40		2
3			Accounts Receivable, C. N. Coe			2 7 1 40	3
4			Wrote off the account as				4
5			uncollectible.				5
6							6

By T accounts, the entry looks like this:

Accounts Receivable					**Allowance for Doubtful Accounts**			
	+	–				–	+	
Bal.	63,200.00	July 1	271.40	July 1	271.40	Bal.	6,980.00
Bal.	62,928.60			(Coe's write-off)				
						Bal.	6,708.60	

The accountant also posts the entry to the account of C. N. Coe in the accounts receivable subsidiary ledger.

NAME _____ C. N. Coe
ADDRESS _____ 217 Barclay Road
_____ Boston, MA 02101

DATE		ITEM	POST. REF.	DEBIT	CREDIT	BALANCE
20–						
May	1	Balance	✓			2 7 1 40
20–						
July	1	Written off	J116		2 7 1 40	—

Note that the entry just shown does not change the net realizable value or book value of Accounts Receivable.

Remember!

An entry to write off an account receivable does not change the book value of Accounts Receivable because Accounts Receivable and Allowance for Doubtful Accounts are reduced by the same amount.

Account Name	Balances Before Write-off	Balances After Write-off
Accounts Receivable	$63,200.00	$62,928.60
Less Allowance for Doubtful Accounts	6,980.00	6,708.60
Book value (net realizable value)	$56,220.00	$56,220.00

Also note that **the entry to write off an account does not involve an expense account.** The adjusting entry, which was made long before this time, provides for the expense. The estimated expense was recorded *during the year in which the sale was made,* even though this account is written off in a later year.

Compound Entry to Write Off a Number of Accounts as Uncollectible

Rather than writing off each uncollectible account separately during the year, a firm may write off a number of accounts at the end of the year by using a compound entry. For example, assume that on December 31, the Ortiz Company writes off the following accounts of charge customers as being uncollectible: C. D. Lem, $111.00; D. T. Rios, $94.00; O. C. Rose, $47.10; and M. A. See, $193.27. The accountant records the write-offs by making the following entry:

Remember!

With the allowance method, the Bad Debts Expense account is used only as part of the adjusting entry at the end of the fiscal period. Bad Debts Expense is not used during the period.

	DATE		DESCRIPTION	POST. REF.	DEBIT	CREDIT	
1	20–						1
2	Dec.	31	Allowance for Doubtful Accounts		4 4 5 37		2
3			Accounts Receivable, C. D. Lem			1 1 1 00	3
4			Accounts Receivable, D. T. Rios			9 4 00	4
5			Accounts Receivable, O. C. Rose			4 7 10	5
6			Accounts Receivable, M. A. See			1 9 3 27	6
7			Wrote off the accounts				7
8			as uncollectible.				8
9							9

Entry to Write Off a Charge Account Paid in Part

Sometimes a partial payment is involved in a write-off of an account. When this happens, it may be due to a bankruptcy settlement. The federal laws governing **bankruptcy** legally excuse a debtor from paying off certain obligations. For example, on April 21, the Loza Company received 10 cents on the dollar (10 percent) in settlement of a $442 account owed by its customer R. E. Linn, a bankrupt. In general journal form, the entry is as follows.

DATE		DESCRIPTION	POST. REF.	DEBIT	CREDIT	
1	20–					1
2	Apr.	21	Cash		4 4 20		2
3			Allowance for Doubtful Accounts		3 9 7 80		3
4			Accounts Receivable, R. E. Linn			4 4 2 00	4
5			Settlement in bankruptcy,				5
6			wrote off account balance				6
7			as uncollectible.				7
8							8

When a company does not have adequate cash to pay its bills, it may file for bankruptcy protection to reorganize or simply sell off its inventory and other assets and go out of business. If the company files for bankruptcy protection to reorganize, it may pay off only part of its debt to its creditors.

Write-offs Seldom Agree with Previous Estimates

The total amount of Accounts Receivable written off during a given year does not ordinarily agree with the estimate of uncollectible accounts previously debited to Bad Debts Expense and credited to Allowance for Doubtful Accounts. In the usual situation, the amounts written off as uncollectible turn out to be less than the estimated amount. At the end of a given year, there is normally a credit balance in Allowance for Doubtful Accounts. However, if the amounts written off are greater than the estimated amounts, Allowance for Doubtful Accounts temporarily has a debit balance. The debit balance is eliminated by the adjusting entry at the end of the year, which results in a credit to, or increase in, Allowance for Doubtful Accounts.

COLLECTION OF ACCOUNTS PREVIOUSLY WRITTEN OFF

Objective 3

Journalize entries to reinstate accounts receivable previously written off, using the allowance method.

Occasionally an account that was previously written off as uncollectible may later be recovered, either in part or in full. In such cases, the firm's accountant restores the account to the books, or reinstates it, by an entry that is the exact opposite of the write-off entry.

As an example, the Loza Company sells merchandise on account to P. E. Norris for $495 on May 5, 2000. Here is the entry in general journal form:

DATE		DESCRIPTION	POST. REF.	DEBIT	CREDIT	
1	2000						1
2	May	5	Accounts Receivable, P. E. Norris		4 9 5 00		2
3			Sales			4 9 5 00	3
4			Sold merchandise on account,				4
5			2/10, n/30.				5
6							6

The Loza Company makes many unsuccessful attempts to collect the Norris debt, and the **statute of limitations** finally expires. Since the statute of limitations is set at three years in many states, let's say that the Loza Company has not been able to collect any money at all from Norris during a three-year period and that Norris has remained within the jurisdiction of the court. This means that the debt is outlawed by the statute of limitations. In other words, the firm cannot use the courts to force the debtor to pay up. Accordingly, three years later, in 2003, the accountant for Loza Company writes off the account of P. E. Norris as uncollectible.

	DATE		DESCRIPTION	POST. REF.	DEBIT	CREDIT	
1	2003						1
2	June	10	Allowance for Doubtful Accounts		4 9 5 00		2
3			Accounts Receivable, P. E.				3
4			Norris			4 9 5 00	4
5			Wrote off the account as				5
6			uncollectible.				6

But on September 15, 2003, P. E. Norris suddenly pays her account in full! The entry to reinstate the account is the reverse of the entry used to write off the account.

	DATE		DESCRIPTION	POST. REF.	DEBIT	CREDIT	
1	2003						1
2	Sept.	15	Accounts Receivable, P. E. Norris		4 9 5 00		2
3			Allowance for Doubtful				3
4			Accounts			4 9 5 00	4
5			Reinstated the account.				5
6							6

The way is now clear to record the collection of the account.

	DATE		DESCRIPTION	POST. REF.	DEBIT	CREDIT	
1	2003						1
2	Sept.	15	Cash		4 9 5 00		2
3			Accounts Receivable, P. E.				3
4			Norris			4 9 5 00	4
5			Collection of account in full.				5
6							6

Now suppose that P. E. Norris had gone into bankruptcy and settled his account with the Loza Company by paying it 5 cents on the dollar. The Loza Company would realize that there was no hope of collecting any more, so the accountant would reinstate the account only for the amount collected, like this:

	DATE		DESCRIPTION	POST. REF.	DEBIT	CREDIT	
1	2003						1
2	Sept.	15	Accounts Receivable, P. E. Norris		2 4 75		2
3			Allowance for Doubtful				3
4			Accounts			2 4 75	4
5			Settlement in bankruptcy,				5
6			5 percent of $495 reinstated				6
7			the account to the extent of				7
8			the settlement.				8

The subsequent entry to record the cash payment would be as follows:

	DATE		DESCRIPTION	POST. REF.	DEBIT	CREDIT	
8	Sept.	15	Cash		2 4 75		8
9			Accounts Receivable, P. E.				9
10			Norris			2 4 75	10
11			Settlement in bankruptcy,				11
12			5 percent of $495.				12

SPECIFIC CHARGE-OFF OF BAD DEBTS

Objective 4

Journalize the entries to write off accounts receivable as being uncollectible, using the specific charge-off method.

The specific charge-off method of accounting for bad debt losses is a simpler system for writing off charge accounts determined to be uncollectible. No adjusting entry is made because there is no attempt to provide for bad debt losses in advance or to match revenue with related expenses. Instead, when a firm decides that a specific customer account is never going to be paid, the accountant makes an entry in the general journal debiting Bad Debts Expense and crediting Accounts Receivable. Thus Allowance for Doubtful Accounts does not exist in the firm's chart of accounts. Traditionally, this method has been used primarily by small companies and professional enterprises. As we stated previously, the specific charge-off method is required for federal income tax reporting, but is not allowed under GAAP.

For example, on April 16, 2000, the Roy Company sold merchandise on account to H. N. Morgan for $179.10, making the following entry in the general journal.

	DATE		DESCRIPTION	POST. REF.	DEBIT	CREDIT	
1	2000						1
2	Apr.	16	Accounts Receivable, H. N.				2
3			Morgan		1 7 9 10		3
4			Sales			1 7 9 10	4
5			Sale of merchandise on				5
6			account, n/30.				6

Morgan never paid his bill. Finally, three years later, on September 1, the account is written off as follows:

	DATE		DESCRIPTION	POST. REF.	DEBIT	CREDIT	
1	2003						1
2	Sept.	1	Bad Debts Expense		1 7 9 10		2
3			Accounts Receivable, H. N.				3
4			Morgan			1 7 9 10	4
5			To write off an uncollectible				5
6			account.				6

By T accounts, the entries look like this:

Accounts Receivable			Sales			Bad Debts Expense	
+	−		−	+		+	−
2000	2003		2000	2000		2003	
Apr. 16 179.10	Sept. 1 179.10		Dec. 31 Closed	Apr. 16 179.10		Sept. 1 179.10	

You can see that revenue does not match expenses for a particular year. The Roy Company counted the original sale of $179.10 in 2000, thereby overstating true revenue for that year. It counted Bad Debts Expense three years later, in 2003, thereby overstating expenses for that year. Note that the Roy Company did not use the account titled Allowance for Doubtful Accounts. In other words, if you wait until you consider an account to be a bad debt and then write it off, with no provision for realistically estimating the losses in advance, you are making unrealistic assumptions. On the balance sheet, Accounts Receivable is stated at the gross amount only; there is no book value or net realizable value. As a result, both asset and capital are overstated.

To reinstate an account previously written or charged off, let's say that on May 2, 2004, H. N. Morgan returns and pays his $179.10 bill. We show the entries in general journal form.

Objective 5

Journalize entries to reinstate accounts receivable previously written off, using the specific charge-off method.

GENERAL JOURNAL

	DATE		DESCRIPTION	POST. REF.	DEBIT	CREDIT	
1	2004						1
2	May	2	Accounts Receivable, H. N.				2
3			Morgan		1 7 9 10		3
4			Bad Debts Recovered			1 7 9 10	4
5			Reinstated the account.				5
6							6
7		2	Cash		1 7 9 10		7
8			Accounts Receivable, H. N.				8
9			Morgan			1 7 9 10	9
10			Collection of account in full.				10

With T accounts, the entries look like this:

Accounts Receivable		**Bad Debts Recovered**		**Cash**	
+	−	−	+		+ −
2004	2004		2004	2004	
May 2 179.10	May 2 179.10		May 2 179.10	May 2 179.10	

For a small company that uses the specific charge-off method alone, the account entitled Bad Debts Recovered is classified as a revenue account and would be listed in the Other Income section of an income statement. The Accounts Receivable account was placed back on the books, so that the firm would have a record of H. N. Morgan's account. Note that this method of accounting is not consistent with the accrual method. The following chart illustrates a comparison of journal entries involved in the allowance method and the specific charge-off method.

Comparison of Two Methods of Write-off, Reinstatement, and Collection		
	Allowance Method	**Specific Charge-off Method**
Original sale	Accounts Receivable, J. Smith Sales	Accounts Receivable, J. Smith Sales
Write-off	Allowance for Doubtful Accounts Accounts Receivable, J. Smith	Bad Debts Expense Accounts Receivable, J. Smith
Reinstatement	Accounts Receivable, J. Smith Allowance for Doubtful Accounts	Accounts Receivable, J. Smith Bad Debts Recovered (Other Income)
Collection	Cash Accounts Receivable, J. Smith	Cash Accounts Receivable, J. Smith

FEDERAL INCOME TAX REQUIREMENT

All firms except financial institutions are required to use the specific charge-off method for reporting on their federal income tax returns. A separate record should be maintained for reporting bad debt losses. For each account charged off, this record must contain the following:

1. A description of the debt, including the amount, and the date it became due
2. The name of the debtor
3. The efforts that have been made to collect the debt
4. Why it has been decided that the debt is worthless

CHAPTER REVIEW

Review of Performance Objectives

1. Make the adjusting entry to record estimated bad debt losses by using the allowance method of recording bad debts.

   The adjusting entry is a debit to Bad Debts Expense and a credit to Allowance for Doubtful Accounts.

   (a) **Determine the amount of the adjusting entry by aging Accounts Receivable.**
   Classify each charge customer's account according to the number of days past due (thirty days, sixty days, and so on).
      Multiply the total for each time period by a given percentage deemed to be uncollectible, and sum the totals.
      Assuming that the Allowance for Doubtful Accounts has a credit balance, subtract the amount of the credit balance from the amount estimated to be uncollectible to get the amount of the adjusting entry.

   (b) **Determine the amount of the adjusting entry by using a percentage of Accounts Receivable.**
   Multiply the balance of Accounts Receivable by the given percentage. Next, assuming that Allowance for Doubtful Accounts has a credit balance, subtract the amount of the credit balance from the percentage amount to get the amount of the adjusting entry.

   (c) **Calculate the amount of the adjusting entry by using a percentage of net sales or net credit sales.**
   Multiply the amount of net sales or net credit sales by the given percentage and make the adjusting entry for the amount determined.

2. Journalize the entries to write off accounts receivable as being uncollectible, using the allowance method of accounting for bad debt losses.

   Debit Allowance for Doubtful Accounts and credit Accounts Receivable.

3. Journalize entries to reinstate accounts receivable previously written off, using the allowance method.

   Debit Accounts Receivable and credit Allowance for Doubtful Accounts (the opposite of a write-off).

4. Journalize the entries to write off accounts receivable as being uncollectible, using the specific charge-off method.

   Debit Bad Debts Expense and credit Accounts Receivable.

5. Journalize entries to reinstate accounts receivable previously written off, using the specific charge-off method.

Debit Accounts Receivable and credit Bad Debts Recovered.

Glossary

Age (accounts receivable) To analyze the accounts receivable by classifying the outstanding balance of each charge customer's account according to the amount of time it has been outstanding. Multiply the total for each time period by a percentage deemed to be uncollectible and sum the totals to determine the balance of Allowance for Doubtful Accounts. (594)

Allowance method of accounting for bad debt losses A method that requires an adjusting entry to debit Bad Debts Expense and to credit Allowance for Doubtful Accounts to match losses from uncollectible accounts with sales of the same period. Write-offs of uncollectible accounts are debited to Allowance for Doubtful Accounts and credited to Accounts Receivable. (591)

Bankruptcy A condition governed by federal law in which a debtor is excused from certain obligations incurred. (603)

Book value of Accounts Receivable The balance of Accounts Receivable after deducting the balance of Allowance for Doubtful Accounts; also called the *net expected realizable value of Accounts Receivable*. The amount of cash expected to be collected eventually from gross receivables. (592)

Net expected realizable value of Accounts Receivable The balance of Accounts Receivable after deducting the balance of Allowance for Doubtful Accounts; also called the *book value of Accounts Receivable*. The amount of cash expected to be collected eventually from gross receivables. (592)

Specific charge-off method of accounting for bad debt losses A method of recognizing bad debts that requires no adjusting entry. The accountant debits Bad Debts Expense and credits Accounts Receivable. This method is required for federal income tax reporting but is not allowed under GAAP. (606)

Statute of limitations Laws that limit the period of time in which legal action may be taken; with regard to bad debts, laws limiting the period of time during which the courts may force a debtor to pay a debt, usually three years for charge accounts. (604)

QUESTIONS, EXERCISES, AND PROBLEMS

Discussion Questions

1. Explain what is meant by aging of Accounts Receivable.
2. How is the book value of Accounts Receivable calculated?
3. When an account is written off under the allowance method of accounting for bad debts, why doesn't the book value of Accounts Receivable decrease?
4. Explain the nature of Allowance for Doubtful Accounts, how it comes into existence, and what happens to it.
5. When the allowance method of accounting for bad debts is used to determine the amount of the adjusting entry, explain the difference between using a percentage of Accounts Receivable and a percentage of net sales.

6. Suppose that the estimate of bad debts is based on the aging method and that Allowance for Doubtful Accounts has a debit balance. Explain how this situation is handled.

7. Why is the allowance method of handling bad debts considered more effective than the specific charge-off method? Is the specific charge-off method ever acceptable?

8. Assume that a customer's account was previously written off as uncollectible and is paid at a later date. Under the allowance method, what journal entries are made on the seller's books? What entry is made on the buyer's books?

Exercises

P.O. 1a

Estimate uncollectible accounts based on aging and make the adjusting entry.

Exercise 17-1 The Nguyen Company uses the allowance method of estimating losses from bad debts. Management analyzed its accounts receivable balances on December 31 and determined the following aged balances.

Age of Accounts	Balance	Estimated Percentage Uncollectible	Allowance for Doubtful Accounts
Not yet due	$110,000	1	_____
30 to 60 days	18,000	2	_____
61 to 120 days	9,000	5	_____
121 to 365 days	1,200	30	_____
Over 365 days	4,200	60	_____
	$142,400		_____

Compute the estimate of the amount of uncollectible accounts. Write the adjusting entry for estimated credit losses on December 31. The credit balance of Allowance for Doubtful Accounts is $3,040.

P.O. 1b

Journalize the adjusting entry based on a percentage of Accounts Receivable.

Exercise 17-2 The Garber Company uses the allowance method of estimating losses from bad debts. Garber Company considers estimated losses to be 3 percent of Accounts Receivable. On December 31, the Accounts Receivable balance was $62,000, and Allowance for Doubtful Accounts had a credit balance of $320. Journalize the adjusting entry to record the estimated bad debt losses.

P.O. 1c

Journalize the adjusting entry based on a percentage of net sales.

Exercise 17-3 The Matlin Company uses the allowance method of estimating losses due to bad debts. On December 31, before any adjustments have been recorded, the ledger contains the following balances:

Sales	$180,000
Sales Returns and Allowances	27,000

The company estimates that bad debt losses will be ½ percent of net sales. Journalize the adjusting entry to record the estimated bad debt losses. The Allowance for Doubtful Accounts account has a credit balance of $320.

P.O. 1a,c

Journalize the adjusting entry based on (a) aging and (b) a percentage of net sales.

Exercise 17-4 The Greg Company uses the allowance method of handling losses due to bad debts. The Greg Company's Accounts Receivable account has a balance of $82,000. Net sales for the year total $104,000. Write the adjusting entry to record the estimated bad debt losses under each of the following conditions. Assume that Allowance for Doubtful Accounts has a credit balance of $650.

a. Aging of the charge accounts in the accounts receivable ledger indicates doubtful accounts of $1,570.
b. Bad debt losses are estimated at ¾ percent of net sales.

P.O. 2

Journalize the write-off of an account using the allowance method, compute net realizable value of Accounts Receivable, and prepare partial balance sheet.

Exercise 17-5 On June 1, Rich Supply's Accounts Receivable balance was $26,436. The balance of the contra account Allowance for Doubtful Accounts was $1,630. On June 20, the account balance of Mely Bakery of $480 was written off.

a. Journalize the write-off of the Mely account using the allowance method.
b. Using T accounts, determine what is now the net realizable value of Accounts Receivable. How would this be shown in the financial statements (the period ends December 31, 20—)?

P.O. 1c,2,3

Allowance method: write off, reinstate, and collect on an account; journalize adjusting entry based on percentage of net sales.

Exercise 17-6 McGregor Shop had the following selected transactions this year. Assuming that McGregor Shop uses the allowance method of accounting for bad debt losses, record the three transactions in general journal form. Allowance for Doubtful Accounts has a credit balance of $346.

a. Wrote off the account of D. Yarno as uncollectible, $280.
b. Reinstated the account of R. Nordal, which had been written off during the preceding year, $65; received $65 cash in full payment.
c. Estimated bad debt losses to be 1 percent of sales of $80,150.

P.O. 4,5

Specific charge-off method: write off, reinstate, and collect on an account.

Exercise 17-7 Using the same data as in Exercise 17-6, assume that McGregor Shop uses the specific charge-off method of accounting for bad debt losses. Record transactions *a* and *b* in general journal form.

P.O. 4,5

Journalize the write-off, the reinstatement, and the collection of an account using the specific charge-off method.

Exercise 17-8 With reference to Exercise 17-5:

a. Use the specific charge-off method of accounting for bad debt losses to write off the Mely account.
b. Reinstate the Mely account and collect the amount due.

CONSIDER AND COMMUNICATE

The owner of the business where you work is puzzled. He asks you how he can write off bad accounts. You know about the allowance method and the specific charge-off method.

Explain why the allowance method of accounting for bad debts is preferable to the specific charge-off method for financial reporting.

CRITICAL THINKING

Your supervisor has asked you to do some work for her on the Morton Company's accounts receivables.

Below is selected information from the Morton Company:

	12/31/00	12/31/01
Net Credit Sales	$250,000	$300,000
Accounts Receivable	48,000	65,000
Allowance for Doubtful Accounts (credit balance)	800	?

For each situation, your supervisor suggests you do the following:

1. Write the correct entry for Morton Company to record either estimated Bad Debts Expense or actual Bad Debts Expense, depending upon the method used to value Accounts Receivable.
2. Determine the amount of the Allowance for Doubtful Accounts account at the end of December 2001.
3. Tell the client whether the method is acceptable for financial statement preparation and/or for income tax preparation.

Situation A   The Morton Company ages Accounts Receivable to determine the amount of the adjustment for estimated Bad Debts Expense.

The following facts are available:

Age of Accounts	12/31/01 Balance	Estimated Percentage Uncollectible
Not yet due	$45,000	1
1 to 30 days	12,000	3
31 to 60 days	4,000	6
61 to 90 days	3,000	12
Over 90 days	1,000	30

Situation B   The Morton Company uses a percentage of Accounts Receivable to determine the amount of the adjustment for estimated Bad Debts Expense. The firm's average actual bad debt losses over the prior three consecutive years were 3 percent. The firm feels that this is a reasonable estimate of Bad Debts Expense.

Situation C   The Morton Company uses the percentage of net sales method to determine the amount of estimated Bad Debts Expense. The company determines that one-half of one percent (.005) of net credit sales will be uncollectible.

Situation D   The Morton Company uses the specific charge-off method to determine the amount of estimated Bad Debts Expense. The following Accounts Receivable are considered to be uncollectible: ABC Co., $750; Southern, Inc., $1,200.

A MATTER OF ETHICS

As the company bookkeeper reviewing delinquent accounts receivable, you find that a relative of yours has not paid his account amounting to $250. You know that he has been experiencing financial difficulties, and so you set his account aside and do not include it with the other past due accounts sent to a credit collection agency. Comment on this action.

WEB WORK

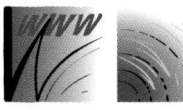

Using an Internet web browser, type *accounts receivable collections* in the search box and search for information about collecting on accounts receivable. Discuss your findings in a small group. Write a one-page summary of your findings.

PROBLEM SET A

For additional help, see the demonstration problem at the beginning of each chapter in your Working Papers.

P.O. 1,2

Problem 17-1A On December 31 of last year, the accountant for Bristol Co. prepared a balance sheet that included $197,900 in Accounts Receivable and $12,618 (credit) in Allowance for Doubtful Accounts. Selected transactions occurred during January of this year, as follows:

a. Sales of merchandise on account, $181,900.
b. Sales returns and allowances related to sales of merchandise on account, $4,922.
c. Cash payments by charge customers (no cash discounts), $168,461.24.
d. Account of Cooke Company written off as uncollectible, $1,217.27.
e. By the process of aging Accounts Receivable, on January 31 it was decided that Allowance for Doubtful Accounts should be adjusted to a balance of $20,011.14.
f. Closed Bad Debts Expense account.

Check Figure

Bad Debts Expense debit, $8,610.41

Instructions

1. Record the entries in general journal form, page 36. Record the letter in the Date column.
2. Record the balance in Allowance for Doubtful Accounts.
3. Post the appropriate entries to the accounts for Allowance for Doubtful Accounts and Bad Debts Expense.

Instructions for General Ledger Software

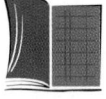

1. Account balances already appear in the general ledger.
2. Record the entries in the general journal. Record the letter in the Explanation.
3. Post the amounts in the general journal to the general ledger. Print the general ledger.

P.O. 1a

Problem 17-2A Malcolm Company uses the aging method of estimating bad debts as of December 31, the end of the fiscal year. Terms of sales are net 30 days. While preparing the aging schedule, the accountant became very ill and was unable to finish the job. The accountant's report, as he left it, appears below:

Customer Name	Balance	Not Yet Due	Days Past Due			
			1–30	31–60	61–90	More than 90
Balance Forward	$352,292	$192,800	$94,400	$37,452	$14,960	$12,680

The accountant still had to analyze the following accounts:

Account	Amount	Due Date
P. Noss	$3,480	January 12 (next year)
R. Novak	2,360	December 22
L. Pomeroy	7,820	November 2
C. Quinn	8,280	August 18
T. Renn	1,520	December 3
P. Roma	1,160	January 22 (next year)

From past experience, the company has found that the following percentages for estimated uncollectible accounts produce an adequate balance for Allowance for Doubtful Accounts:

Time Past Due	Estimated Percentage Uncollectible
Not yet due	2
1 to 30 days	4
31 to 60 days	20
61 to 90 days	30
Over 90 days	50

Prior to aging the accounts receivable, Allowance for Doubtful Accounts has a credit balance of $7,248.

Check Figure

Total of Allowance for Doubtful Accounts, $31,902.40

Instructions

1. Enter the Balance Forward balances and complete the aging schedule.
2. Complete the table for estimating an allowance for doubtful accounts.
3. Write the adjusting entry in general journal form.

P.O. 1c,2,3

Problem 17-3A On January 1 of this year, Ronald's Wholesale Meats had a credit balance of $4,234 in Allowance for Doubtful Accounts. During the year, the company completed the following selected transactions.

Feb. 8 Wrote off as uncollectible a $432 account of Seaforth Market, which had gone out of business, leaving no assets.

May 3 Wrote off the account of Marci's Catering as uncollectible, $250.80.

17 Collected 5 percent of the $1,444 owed by Lee Company, a bankrupt. Wrote off the remainder as worthless.

Aug. 2 Received $228.40 unexpectedly from Day Company, whose account had been written off two years earlier. Reinstated the account for $228.40 and recorded the collection.

Sept. 11 Received $162 from Marci's Catering as part payment of the account written off on May 3. She wrote a letter saying that she expects to pay the balance soon. Accordingly, reinstated the account for the amount of the original obligation, $250.80.

Dec. 30 Journalized a compound entry to write off the following accounts as uncollectible: C. D. Finch, $384.32; Southway Inn, $272.82; Hall's Drive-In, $566.30.

31 Recorded the adjusting entry for estimated bad debt losses at ½ percent of net sales of $584,260.

31 Closed the Bad Debts Expense account.

Check Figure

Balance of Allowance for Doubtful Accounts, $4,356.46

Instructions

1. Record the balance of Allowance for Doubtful Accounts in the ledger.
2. Record the entries in general journal form, page 73.
3. Post the entries to the ledger accounts for Allowance for Doubtful Accounts and Bad Debts Expense.

P.O. 1a,2,3

Problem 17-4A The following transactions were among those completed by Caldwell Wholesale Jewelers this year:

Feb. 15 Wrote off as uncollectible the account of Malin, Inc., $1,412.50. This company had gone out of business, leaving no assets.

Mar. 14 Reinstated the account of Golding, Inc., which had been written off in the preceding year; received $372.12 in full payment of account.

July 27 Received $214.26 unexpectedly from Craig and Son, whose account had been written off last year in the amount of $214.26. Reinstated the account and recorded the collection of $214.26.

Oct. 14 Reinstated the account of C. P. Stewart, which had been written off two years earlier, and received $614 in full payment.

Dec. 28 Journalized a compound entry to write off as uncollectible the following accounts: L. Browning, $315; C. Godfrey, $332.16; Engle and Burns, $716.42; Gable Jewelry, $2,739.60.

31 On the basis of an aged analysis of Accounts Receivable of $184,164.22, estimated that $5,514 will be uncollectible. Recorded the adjusting entry.

31 Recorded the entry to close the appropriate account to Income Summary.

Check Figure

Total Current Assets, $520,086.04

Instructions

1. Open the following accounts, recording the credit balances as of January 1 of this fiscal year:

114 Allowance for Doubtful Accounts $5,112.16
313 Income Summary   —
642 Bad Debts Expense   —

2. Record in general journal form, page 24, the transactions and the adjusting and closing entries described above. After each entry, post to the three selected ledger accounts.
3. Prepare the Current Assets section of the balance sheet. Other pertinent accounts are: Cash, $14,782.41; Notes Receivable, $2,720; Merchandise Inventory, $321,417; Supplies, $1,796.41; Prepaid Insurance, $720.

PROBLEM SET B

For additional help, see the demonstration problem at the beginning of each chapter in your Working Papers.

P.O. 1a,2

Problem 17-1B The balance sheet prepared by D. H. Allen Co. for December 31 of last year includes $206,400 in Accounts Receivable and $12,192 (credit) in Allowance for Doubtful Accounts. The following transactions occurred during January of this year:

a. Sales of merchandise on account, $193,400.
b. Sales returns and allowances related to sales of merchandise on account, $5,027.
c. Cash payments by charge customers (no cash discounts), $181,946.
d. Account of Sims and Towne written off as uncollectible, $1,216.
e. By the process of aging Accounts Receivable, on January 31 it was decided that Allowance for Doubtful Accounts should be adjusted to a balance of $19,412.
f. Closed Bad Debts Expense account.

Check Figure

Bad Debts Expense debit, $8,436

Instructions

1. Record the entries in general journal form, page 36. Record the letter in the Date column.
2. Record the balance in Allowance for Doubtful Accounts.
3. Post the appropriate entries to the accounts for Allowance for Doubtful Accounts and Bad Debts Expense.

Instructions for General Ledger Software

1. Account balances already appear in the general ledger.
2. Record the entries in the general journal. Record the letter in the Explanation.
3. Post the amounts in the general journal to the general ledger. Print the general ledger.

P.O. 1a

Problem 17-2B Johnson Company uses the aging method of estimating bad debts as of December 31, the end of the fiscal year. Terms of sales are net 30 days. While in the process of completing the aging schedule, the accountant became very ill and was unable to finish the job. The accountant's report, as far as she had done it, appears as follows:

Customer Name	Balance	Not Yet Due	Days Past Due			
			1–30	31–60	61–90	More than 90
Balance Forward	$389,900	$249,200	$76,280	$38,848	$15,032	$10,540

The accountant still had to analyze the following accounts:

Account	Amount	Due Date
B. Finch	$3,840	November 28
L. Flanagan	920	January 16 (next year)
C. Giller	6,480	November 6
L. Hernandez	9,420	January 27 (next year)
P. Lamb	3,700	September 20
C. Newman	1,160	October 16

From past experience, the company has found that the following percentages for estimated uncollectible accounts produce an adequate balance for Allowance for Doubtful Accounts:

Time Past Due	Estimated Percentage Uncollectible
Not yet due	2
1–30 days	4
31–60 days	20
61–90 days	30
Over 90 days	50

Prior to aging Accounts Receivable, Allowance for Doubtful Accounts has a credit balance of $4,346.

Check Figure

Total of Allowance for Doubtful Accounts, $30,053.20

P.O. 1c,2,3

Instructions

1. Enter the forward balances and complete the aging schedule.
2. Complete the table for estimating an allowance for doubtful accounts.
3. Record the adjusting entry in general journal form.

Problem 17-3B On January 1 of this year, Noss Company's Allowance for Doubtful Accounts account had a $1,926 credit balance. During the year Noss Company completed the following transactions:

Feb. 10 Wrote off the $654 account of Newton Company; the company had gone out of business, leaving no assets.

May 5 Wrote off the account of C. Tidwell as uncollectible, $348.32.

18 Received $182 unexpectedly from C. Weiss. The account had been written off two years earlier. Reinstated the account for $182 and recorded the collection of $182.

Aug. 3 Collected 10 percent of the $252 owed by C. C. Mack, a bankrupt. Wrote off the remainder as worthless.

Sept. 21 Received $180 from C. Tidwell as part payment of the account written off on May 5. He wrote a letter stating that he expects to pay the balance in the near future. Accordingly, reinstated the account for the amount of the original obligation, $348.32.

Dec. 29 Journalized a compound entry to write off the following accounts: N. C. Allen, $352.40; R. L. Barnes, $248.72; C. Ellis, $228.

Dec. 31 Recorded the adjusting entry for estimated bad debt losses at ½ percent of net sales of $303,426.

31 Closed the Bad Debts Expense account.

Instructions

1. Record the opening balance in the ledger account for Allowance for Doubtful Accounts.
2. Record the entries in general journal form, page 73.
3. Post the entries to the ledger accounts for Allowance for Doubtful Accounts and Bad Debts Expense.

P.O. 1a,2,3

Problem 17-4B The following are among the transactions completed by Wheeler Building Supplies this year:

Feb. 6 Wrote off the account of Malo, Inc., $1,211.17. The company went out of business, leaving no assets.

Mar. 12 Reinstated the account of L. Ward, which had been written off in the preceding year; received $217.16 in full payment.

Aug. 17 Received $144 unexpectedly from C. P. Beech. The account had been written off last year in the amount of $144. Reinstated the account and recorded the collection of $144.

Oct. 15 Reinstated the account of Dahl and Son, which had been written off two years earlier, and received $749.30 in full payment.

Dec. 29 Journalized a compound entry to write off the following accounts as uncollectible: D. C. Lang, $328; R. R. Mann, $752.28; N. Shearer, $1,274.41; D. Terry, $1,562.15.

31 On the basis of an aged analysis of Accounts Receivable, which amounted to $87,811.14, estimated that $4,991 will be uncollectible. Recorded the adjusting entry.

31 Recorded the entry to close the appropriate account to Income Summary.

Instructions

1. Open the following accounts, recording the credit balances as of January 1 of this fiscal year:

    114 Allowance for Doubtful Accounts $5,272.36
    313 Income Summary   —
    642 Bad Debts Expense   —

2. Journalize in general journal form, page 24, the transactions and the adjusting and closing entries described above. After each entry, post to the three selected ledger accounts.
3. Prepare the Current Assets section of the balance sheet. Other pertinent accounts are: Cash, $12,621.42; Merchandise Inventory, $144,567; Supplies, $1,940.50; Prepaid Insurance, $756.

18 Ending Merchandise Inventory

WINDOWS ON | **THE WORLD WIDE WEB**

How does "The Saving Place" record its cost of goods sold? Does Kmart Corporation use the LIFO or the FIFO method? What is Kmart's gross profit and net income for the past year? How would a change in ending merchandise inventory amount affect these gross profit and net income figures? How does Kmart know what is available in inventory and the cost of what has been sold? Does Kmart use the retail method or the gross-profit method of estimating the value of inventories? How does Kmart record property and equipment? In what portion of Kmart's annual report would you find answers to these questions? To look up Notes to Consolidated Financial Statements for the most recent Kmart Corporation annual report, go to **http://www.kmart.com/d_about/financials/index.htm** and look under the Annual Report's Table of Contents.

Performance Objectives

After you have completed this chapter, you will be able to do the following:

1. Determine the overstatement or understatement of cost of goods sold, gross profit, and net income resulting from a change in the ending merchandise inventory amount.

2. Determine unit cost, the value of the ending inventory, and the cost of goods sold by the following methods: (a) specific identification; (b) weighted-average-cost; (c) first-in, first-out; and (d) last-in, first-out.

3. Journalize transactions relating to perpetual inventories.

4. Complete a perpetual inventory record card.

One of the most important aspects of the operation of any merchandising business is the accounting for and valuation of the merchandise in stock. We define *merchandise inventory* as goods purchased by the company and held for resale to customers in the ordinary course of business. Merchandise Inventory and the related T accounts are as follows.

Assets	
+	−

Merchandise Inventory	
+	−
For Periodic Inventory record latest inventory in an adjusting entry at end of fiscal period.	For Periodic Inventory record beginning inventory in an adjusting entry at end of fiscal period.

Revenue	
−	+

Sales	
−	+
	Record the sale of merchandise at its selling price.

Expenses	
+	−

Purchases	
+	−
Record the purchase of merchandise at its cost.	

Sales Returns and Allowances	
+	−
Record the return of, or allowances on, merchandise previously sold at its selling price.	

Purchases Returns and Allowances	
−	+
	Record the return of, or allowances on, merchandise previously purchased at its cost.

Sales Discount	
+	−
Record cash discounts taken by customers.	

Purchases Discount	
−	+
	Record cash discounts taken on buying merchandise.

Freight In	
+	−
Record freight charges on incoming merchandise shipments at cost.	

Remember!

Contra accounts (like Sales Returns and Allowances or Purchases Discount) have signs opposite those of the accounts to which they are related.

Firms take a physical inventory at the end of their fiscal periods. At this time, the most up-to-date figure is included in the Adjustments columns of the work sheet. Remember, under the periodic inventory system, Merchandise Inventory requires two adjusting entries:

a. The first one closes off or "reverses out" the value of the beginning merchandise inventory.
b. The second adds in the value of the ending merchandise inventory.

Assume that a firm has a beginning merchandise inventory amounting to $177,000. The cost of the ending merchandise inventory is $195,000. The adjustment is described by T accounts as follows:

Merchandise Inventory			
	+	−	
Bal.	177,000	(a)	177,000
(b)	195,000		

Income Summary			
(a)	177,000	(b)	195,000

The same adjustment appears in the work sheet. In this example, the ending inventory figure of $195,000 is given. However, in a practical business situation, the cost of the ending inventory must be determined. Counting the goods on hand is a relatively easy although time-consuming procedure compared with the more difficult task of assigning a dollar amount to them in a time of changing prices. We talk mainly about the Merchandise Inventory account because of its relative importance. However, the same principle applies to other assets, such as supplies for a service business or raw materials for a manufacturer.

We examine the valuation of inventories in two ways: First, some merchandising firms take a physical inventory of merchandise on hand and then attach a value to it. This is known as a **periodic inventory system**, as shown in the example involving the two adjusting entries for Merchandise Inventory. Second, other merchandising firms keep continuous records of inventories by recording all transactions, so that at any given time they know what they should have on hand and the current cost of each item. This is known as a **perpetual inventory system**.

THE IMPORTANCE OF INVENTORY VALUATION

Objective 1

Determine the overstatement or understatement of cost of goods sold, gross profit, and net income resulting from a change in the ending merchandise inventory amount.

Merchandise Inventory is the only account that can appear on both major financial statements. On the balance sheet, it appears under Current Assets. On the income statement, it is listed under Cost of Goods Sold. Why is the valuation of merchandise inventory so important? In many firms, merchandise inventory is the asset with the largest dollar amount. Likewise, as a part of Cost of Goods Sold, it materially affects the net income because the cost of goods sold is the largest deduction from sales. As a result, inventory determination plays an important role in matching costs with revenue for a given period.

Differing costs of ending merchandise inventory have a dramatic effect on net income. We can see this in the partial income statements that follow (Figures 1 through 5).

Now assume that instead of the correct value for ending merchandise inventory of $185,000 (Figure 1), you in error set its value at $175,000, that

FIGURE 1

YEAR 1 — CORRECT ENDING INVENTORY STATED

Net Sales								$	505	0	0	0	00
Cost of Goods Sold:													
Merchandise Inventory (beginning)	$	177	0	0	0	00							
Purchases (net)		320	0	0	0	00							
Goods Available for Sale	$	497	0	0	0	00							
Less Merchandise Inventory (ending)		185	0	0	0	00							
Cost of Goods Sold									312	0	0	0	00
Gross Profit								$	193	0	0	0	00
Operating Expenses									127	0	0	0	00
Net Income								$	66	0	0	0	00

FIGURE 2

YEAR 1 — ENDING INVENTORY UNDERSTATED BY $10,000

Net Sales			$ 505 0 0 0 00
Cost of Goods Sold:			
Merchandise Inventory (beginning)	$ 177 0 0 0 00		
Purchases (net)	320 0 0 0 00		
Goods Available for Sale	$ 497 0 0 0 00		
Less Merchandise Inventory (ending)	175 0 0 0 00		
Cost of Goods Sold		322 0 0 0 00	
Gross Profit		$ 183 0 0 0 00	
Operating Expenses		127 0 0 0 00	
Net Income		$ 56 0 0 0 00	

∎∎∎

Remember!

The ending inventory of one year becomes the beginning inventory of the next year.

is, it was understated (too low by $10,000). The result would be a net income of only $56,000 (Figure 2). Of course, this would result in lower income taxes as well.

From Figures 1 and 2, you can see that if the ending merchandise inventory is understated (too low) by $10,000, the net income will be understated (too low) by $10,000 because the two are directly related to each other. Similarly, **if the ending merchandise inventory is overstated (too high), net income will be overstated (too high; Figure 3).**

From Figures 1 and 3 you can see that if the *ending* inventory is overstated (too high) by $10,000, net income is overstated (too high) by $10,000.

But there is something else you have to take into account. Because the *ending* inventory of one year becomes the beginning inventory of the following year, the net income of the following year is also affected, but in an opposite direction. Let's continue our examples into year 2. The understated $175,000 *ending* inventory of year 1 (Figure 2) becomes the *beginning* inventory of year 2 (Figure 4 on the following page). Similarly, if the *beginning* inventory (the *ending* inventory of the prior year) is understated by $10,000, the net income will be overstated because the two are inversely related to each other. Similarly, **if the beginning inventory is overstated, the net income will be understated.**

FIGURE 3

YEAR 1 — ENDING INVENTORY OVERSTATED BY $10,000

Net Sales			$ 505 0 0 0 00
Cost of Goods Sold:			
Merchandise Inventory (beginning)	$ 177 0 0 0 00		
Purchases (net)	320 0 0 0 00		
Goods Available for Sale	$ 497 0 0 0 00		
Less Merchandise Inventory (ending)	195 0 0 0 00		
Cost of Goods Sold		302 0 0 0 00	
Gross Profit		$ 203 0 0 0 00	
Operating Expenses		127 0 0 0 00	
Net Income		$ 76 0 0 0 00	

FIGURE 4

YEAR 2—UNDERSTATED ENDING INVENTORY ($175,000)
OF YEAR 1 BECOMES BEGINNING INVENTORY OF YEAR 2

Net Sales		$ 573 0 0 0 00
Cost of Goods Sold:		
Merchandise Inventory (beginning)	$ 175 0 0 0 00	
Purchases (net)	368 0 0 0 00	
Goods Available for Sale	$ 543 0 0 0 00	
Less Merchandise Inventory (ending)	200 0 0 0 00	
Cost of Goods Sold		343 0 0 0 00
Gross Profit		$ 230 0 0 0 00
Operating Expenses		125 0 0 0 00
Net Income		$ 105 0 0 0 00

FIGURE 5

YEAR 2—OVERSTATED ENDING INVENTORY ($195,000) OF
YEAR 1 BECOMES BEGINNING INVENTORY OF YEAR 2

Net Sales		$ 573 0 0 0 00
Cost of Goods Sold:		
Merchandise Inventory (beginning)	$ 195 0 0 0 00	
Purchases (net)	368 0 0 0 00	
Goods Available for Sale	$ 563 0 0 0 00	
Less Merchandise Inventory (ending)	200 0 0 0 00	
Cost of Goods Sold		363 0 0 0 00
Gross Profit		$ 210 0 0 0 00
Operating Expenses		125 0 0 0 00
Net Income		$ 85 0 0 0 00

Remember!

An error made in the ending inventory in one period will be carried to the next period in the beginning inventory. This is important because of the direct relationship between ending inventory and net income.

Now look at Figure 5 to see what happens when the overstated $195,000 ending inventory of year 1 becomes the beginning inventory of year 2.

If the *beginning* inventory is overstated by $10,000, the net income will be understated by $10,000, because the two are inversely related to each other. And similarly, **if the *beginning* inventory is overstated, the net income will be understated.**

In other words, over a two-year period, the total net income will be correct, because the overstatement of one year cancels out the understatement of the following year, and vice versa. At the end of a two-year period, the balance sheet is correct because *ending* inventory and *ending* capital are both correctly stated. We can summarize this in the following table:

Year	Ending Inventory of $195,000 ($10,000 overstatement)	Ending Inventory of $175,000 ($10,000 overstatement)
	Net Income	Net Income
1	$ 56,000	$ 76,000
2	105,000	85,000
Total	$161,000	$161,000

FYI

More and more companies stock fewer inventory items that in the past. Many companies use the just-in-time (JIT) method: Order the necessary inventory just in time to deliver it to the customer. This can save time and money.

If *ending* inventory is *overstated,* net income for the period will be *overstated.*

If *ending* inventory is *understated,* net income for the period will be *understated.*

If *beginning* inventory is *overstated,* net income for the period will be *understated.*

If *beginning* inventory is *understated,* net income for the period will be *overstated.*

THE NEED FOR AND THE TAKING OF INVENTORIES

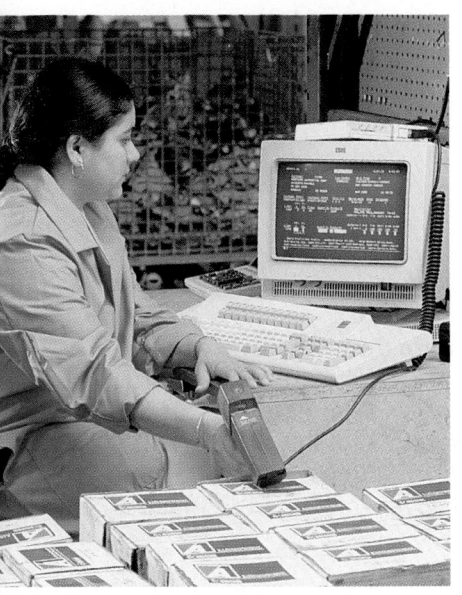

Inventory is taken both manually and by using electronic tools. A variety of scanning devices have made the job easier, faster, and more accurate.

Firms that want to satisfy their customers have to maintain large and varied inventories of goods. Efficient purchasing also requires that the company take advantage of quantity discounts and of special buys of seasonal or distressed merchandise.

Care should be taken to count all goods belonging to the firm. Sometimes the goods may not be physically present; this occurs while the goods are being transported. **From the seller's position, merchandise sold FOB destination should be included in the seller's inventory** because the seller is paying the freight charges. **From the buyer's position, merchandise purchased FOB shipping point should be included in the buyer's inventory** because the buyer is paying the freight charges. Title transfer or ownership of the goods depends on who has paid the freight.

Inventory Control

A small business such as a bicycle shop or an antique store may keep track of its inventories manually. However, to have up-to-date counts of inventory items on hand, most firms use computers. Software programs that record transactions and produce inventory reports are readily available. These reports include a description of each item in stock, the number of units on hand, the cost of each unit, and the number of units sold, as well as the number of units to be reordered. Also, management can use inventory reports to determine and analyze buying and selling trends.

METHODS OF ASSIGNING COSTS TO ENDING INVENTORY

Objective 2

Determine unit cost, the value of the ending inventory, and the cost of goods sold by the following methods:
(a) specific identification;
(b) weighted-average-cost;
(c) first-in, first-out; and
(d) last-in, first-out

After the items have been described and counted, the unit costs are inserted on the inventory sheet and the total costs are extended. How do you determine unit cost? You might think that this was rather elementary. Indeed, it would be *if* all the purchases of a given article had been made at the same price per unit. In that case, to determine the total unit cost, you would need only to look up one invoice, check the unit price, then multiply it by the number of items present. But nothing is ever that simple. A firm usually buys a number of batches of a given item during the year, and the unit costs can vary. A bottle of shampoo that cost $2.62 in January might cost $2.76 in October. Which unit cost should you assign to the goods on hand?

There are four main methods of assigning costs to goods in the ending inventory: (1) specific identification; (2) weighted-average-cost; (3) first-in, first-out; and (4) last-in, first-out.

Example of Inventory Evaluation Jackson Electric Supply keeps an inventory of safety switches (#810) purchased from Healy Company. This year, Jackson Electric Supply sold eighty of these switches and has twenty-six remaining in stock. The company started the year with twenty-two in stock and bought more as the year went on, as follows:

Jan. 1	Beginning inventory	22 units @ $57 each = $1,254
Mar. 16	Purchase	30 units @ 62 each = 1,860
July 29	Purchase	36 units @ 65 each = 2,340
Nov. 18	Purchase	18 units @ 68 each = 1,224
	Total available	106 units $6,678

Now let's compute the cost of goods sold (eighty switches) and the value of the ending inventory (twenty-six switches) using the four different methods.

Specific Identification Method

When a firm sells big-ticket items (cars, appliances, furniture, jewelry), the cost is low to keep track of the purchase price of each individual article and determine the exact cost of the goods sold. Such a firm uses the **specific identification method** of inventory control. Because the safety switches have imprinted manufacture date codes, Jackson Electric can identify each switch with a specific purchase invoice listing the unit cost. When Jackson Electric takes inventory at the end of the year, it finds that there are twenty-six safety switches left in stock; four of these were bought in March, ten were bought in July, and twelve were bought in November. Costs are assigned to the ending inventory as follows:

Mar. 16	Purchase	4 units @ $62 each = $ 248
July 29	Purchase	10 units @ 65 each = 650
Nov. 18	Purchase	12 units @ 68 each = 816
	Total	26 units $1,714

Jackson Electric Supply determines the cost of goods sold by subtracting the value of the ending inventory from the total available for sale:

Total safety switches available (106 units)	$6,678
Less ending inventory (26 units)	1,714
Cost of goods sold (80 units)	$4,964

Weighted-Average-Cost Method

An alternative to keeping track of the cost of each item purchased is to use the **weighted-average-cost method** to find the cost per unit of all like articles available for sale during the period. First, Jackson Electric finds the total cost of the switches it had on hand during the year by multiplying the number of units by their respective purchase costs.

Jan. 1	Beginning inventory	22 units @ $57 each = $1,254
Mar. 16	Purchase	30 units @ 62 each = 1,860
July 29	Purchase	36 units @ 65 each = 2,340
Nov. 18	Purchase	18 units @ 68 each = 1,224
	Total available	106 units $6,678

Accountants calculate the value of the ending inventory. These figures are needed not only to keep track of changing inventory but also to compute the cost of goods sold on the income statement.

Next Jackson Electric finds the average cost per switch.

Average Cost per Unit = Total Cost ÷ Total Units

Average Cost per Unit = $6,678 ÷ 106 units = $63 per unit

Value of Ending Inventory = Number of Units × Average Cost per Unit

Value of Ending Inventory = 26 × $63 = $1,638

According to this method, the beginning inventory is *weighted* (that is, multiplied by the number of units it comprises). Each purchase thereafter is weighted by the number of units involved in that purchase. In other words, the more you buy at a time, the more that purchase influences the average cost.

Total safety switches available (106 units)	$6,678
Less ending inventory (26 units)	1,638
Cost of goods sold (80 units)	$5,040

First-In, First-Out (FIFO) Method

Remember!

First-in, first-out refers to the assumed flow of costs. The ending inventory is assumed to consist of those items purchased most recently.

The **first-in, first-out (FIFO) method** is based on the flow-of-cost assumption that costs of merchandise sold should be charged against revenue in the order in which the costs were incurred. To determine the cost of goods sold, the accountant records the oldest (first) cost first, then the next-oldest cost, and so on. First-in, first-out is a logical way for a firm to rotate its stock of merchandise. Think of a grocery store selling milk. Because milk will sour, the oldest milk is moved up to the front of the shelf. As a result, the ending inventory consists of the freshest milk.

Again, let's return to Jackson Electric's safety switches. To repeat, 106 safety switches were available for sale during the year.

Jan. 1	Beginning inventory	22 units @ $57 each = $1,254
Mar. 16	Purchase	30 units @ 62 each = 1,860
July 29	Purchase	36 units @ 65 each = 2,340
Nov. 18	Purchase	18 units @ 68 each = 1,224
	Total available	106 units $6,678

Jackson Electric sold eighty units. The accountant calculates the total cost of the switches on a first-in, first-out (FIFO) basis, like the following.

Jan. 1	Beginning inventory	22 units @ $57 each = $1,254
Mar. 16	Purchase	30 units @ 62 each = 1,860
July 29	Purchase	28 units @ 65 each = 1,820
	Total	80 units $4,934

Jackson Electric has the twenty-six newest or most recently purchased units on hand in the ending inventory. The accountant records the ending inventory at the most recent costs, like this:

Nov. 18	Purchase	18 units @ $68 each = $1,224
July 29	Purchase	8 units @ 65 each = 520
	Total	26 units $1,744

The accountant now verifies the total cost of the eighty units sold:

Cost of Goods Sold = Total Available − Ending Inventory

$4,934   = $6,678   − $1,744

Last-In, First-Out (LIFO) Method

The **last-in, first-out (LIFO) method** is based on the flow-of-cost assumption that the most recently purchased articles are sold first and the articles remaining in the ending inventory are the oldest items. As an example, think of a coal yard selling coal. When the coal yard buys coal from its supplier, the new coal is added to the top of the pile. When the coal yard sells coal to its customer, coal is taken off the top of the pile. Consequently, the ending inventory consists of those first few tons at the bottom of the pile. And, unless the pile is exhausted, they will never be sold.

Meanwhile, back at Jackson Electric, the firm sold eighty units. The accountant calculates the cost of the switches on a last-in, first-out (LIFO) basis:

Nov. 18	Purchase	18 units @ $68 each = $1,224
July 29	Purchase	36 units @ 65 each = 2,340
Mar. 16	Purchase	26 units @ 62 each = 1,612
	Total	80 units $5,176

Jackson Electric has the twenty-six oldest units (or the units at the bottom of the pile) on hand in the ending inventory. The accountant records the ending inventory at the earliest costs, like this:

Jan. 1	Beginning inventory	22 units @ $57 each = $1,254
Mar. 16	Purchase	4 units @ 62 each = 248
	Total	26 units $1,502

The accountant now verifies the total cost of the eighty units sold:

Cost of Goods Sold = Total Available − Ending Inventory
$5,176   = $6,678   − $1,502

Comparison of Methods

Remember!

Goods do not always move as described in the FIFO, LIFO, and weighted-average-cost methods. The goods are assumed to move as described for the purpose of costing.

If prices don't change very much, all inventory methods give just about the same results. However, in a dynamic market where prices are constantly rising and falling, each method may yield different amounts. Here is a comparison of the results of the sale of the safety switches, using the four methods we described.

Method	Cost of Goods Sold (80 Units)	Ending Inventory (26 Units)
Specific identification	$4,964	$1,714
Weighted-average-cost	5,040	1,638
First-in, first-out	4,934	1,744
Last-in, first-out	5,176	1,502

Remember!

The method selected to cost inventory really has nothing to do with counting the inventory nor the actual flow of goods.

Assume that Jackson Electric sells the eighty safety switches for $90 apiece, for a total of $7,200. The four methods yield the following gross profits:

	Specific Identification	Weighted-Average-Cost	First-In, First-Out	Last-In, First-Out
Sales	$7,200	$7,200	$7,200	$7,200
Cost of goods sold	4,964	5,040	4,934	5,176
Gross profit	$2,236	$2,160	$2,266	$2,024

The effects of the methods are as follows:

1. Specific identification matches costs exactly with revenues.
2. Weighted-average cost is a compromise between LIFO and FIFO, both for the amount of the ending inventory and for the cost of goods sold.
3. FIFO provides the most realistic figure for ending merchandise inventory in the Current Assets section of the balance sheet. The ending inventory is valued at the most recent costs, referred to as replacement cost.
4. LIFO provides the most realistic figure for the Cost of Goods Sold section of the income statement, because the items that have been sold will have to be replaced at the most recent costs.

Tax Effect of LIFO

Remember!

The cost figure determined by the different methods may have nothing to do with the physical flow of goods.

In a period of rising prices, LIFO yields the lowest gross profit and hence the lowest income tax because the most recent (higher) costs are assigned to the cost of goods sold (expense). For the past forty years, prices in most industries have just kept going up, providing a built-in tax advantage for users of LIFO. In effect, a business using LIFO is postponing paying taxes. Since the money is not paid to the government, the business has the use of the money. Consequently, the money saved can be used to finance more inventory or to pay off interest-bearing debts. When prices fall, companies using LIFO are at a disadvantage from the standpoint of taxes.

Bear in mind that the cost figure determined by the different methods may have nothing to do with the physical flow of the goods. By physical flow, we mean the order in which specific items are taken out of inventory and sold.

The **consistency principle** is a fundamental principle of accounting. We have seen that a firm can increase or decrease its gross profit, and likewise its net income and income tax, by changing the flow-of-cost assumption from one method to another—from FIFO to LIFO, for example. Although a firm may change its method of assigning inventory costs, it may not change back and forth repeatedly. Consistency in the method of determining cost of goods sold and the related cost of the ending inventory is necessary to conform with generally accepted accounting principles. For one thing, the government has said that a firm cannot switch back and forth in order to evade some of its income tax. In addition, the firm must stick to a single method of reporting in financial statements to its owners and creditors. IRS approval is required before changing methods.

LOWER-OF-COST-OR-MARKET RULE

All the methods for determining the cost of ending inventory are based on cost per unit. In our examples, prices were generally rising. However, sometimes the replacement cost of items in stock is *less* than the original market cost. The word *market* refers to the current price charged in the market. It is the price at which, *at the time of taking the inventory,* the items could be bought through the usual channels and in the usual quantities. The current prices may be quoted in catalogs or reflect contract quotations.

The **lower-of-cost-or-market (LCM) rule** says that, under certain conditions, when the replacement or market cost is lower than the original cost, the inventory should be valued at the lower cost to comply with the accounting concept of conservatism. For example, the inventory of a store includes twenty leather vests originally purchased for $22 each (total, $440). At the time the inventory is being taken, the same type of leather vest may be purchased (replaced) for $18 each (total, $360). Under the lower-of-cost-or-market rule, the inventory is valued at $360. In this example, the original cost of $22 may have been determined by the specific identification method, the weighted-average-cost method, or the FIFO method. Under the tax law, the lower-of-cost-or-market rule may *not* be used when the original cost is determined by the LIFO method because this method already offers tax advantages.

PERPETUAL INVENTORIES

Objective 3

Journalize transactions relating to perpetual inventories.

Firms that sell a limited variety of products of relatively high value, such as equipment or appliance dealers, maintain records in real time of their inventories on hand. They *record additions to or deductions from their inventories directly in Merchandise Inventory accounts.* This is known as the perpetual inventory system because the firms perpetually (or continually) *know the amount* of goods on hand. With computers, many firms have adopted the perpetual inventory system. This system involves the following accounts:

Merchandise Inventory		Cost of Goods Sold		Sales	
+	−	+	−	−	+
Record the purchase of merchandise at cost.	Record the sale of merchandise at cost.	Record the sale of merchandise at cost.			Record the sale of merchandise at selling price.

FYI

Companies also have the option of eliminating the Purchases Discount account and making the credit to the Merchandise Inventory account.

The adjusting entries at the end of the year are the only entries firms using the periodic system make in Merchandise Inventory. But firms using the perpetual inventory system make entries directly in the Merchandise Inventory account throughout the year. The perpetual inventory system enables the firm to do away with the Purchases, Purchases Discount, and Purchases Returns and Allowances accounts.

To illustrate the perpetual inventory system, let's look at a series of entries in general journal form, with transactions recorded at the gross amount.

Feb. 14 Bought merchandise on account from Miller, Inc.; 2/10, n/30; $2,400.

Remember!

Under the perpetual inventory system, when goods are bought for resale, Merchandise Inventory is debited instead of Purchases. Similarly, when the goods are sold, Merchandise Inventory is credited for the amount of their cost.

	DATE		DESCRIPTION	POST. REF.	DEBIT	CREDIT	
1	20–						1
2	Feb.	14	Merchandise Inventory		2 4 0 0 00		2
3			Accounts Payable, Miller, Inc.			2 4 0 0 00	3
4			Terms 2/10, n/30.				4
5							5

Merchandise Inventory		Accounts Payable	
+	−	−	+
Feb. 14 2,400			Feb. 14 2,400

Feb. 24 Paid the invoice within the discount period.

	DATE		DESCRIPTION	POST. REF.	DEBIT	CREDIT	
1	20–						1
2	Feb.	24	Accounts Payable, Miller, Inc.		2 4 0 0 00		2
3			Cash			2 3 5 2 00	3
4			Merchandise Inventory			4 8 00	4
5			Paid invoice within discount				5
6			period.				6

Accounts Payable		Cash		Merchandise Inventory	
−	+	+	−	−	+
Feb. 24 2,400	Feb. 14 2,400		Feb. 24 2,352	Feb. 14 2,400	Feb. 24 48

Mar. 5 Sold the merchandise on account to S. P. Reems for $2,850. (The cost of the merchandise is $2,400. Two entries are required to record a sale under a perpetual inventory system.)

	DATE		DESCRIPTION	POST. REF.	DEBIT	CREDIT	
1	20–						1
2	Mar.	5	Accts. Receivable, S. P. Reems		2 8 5 0 00		2
3			Sales			2 8 5 0 00	3
4			Sold merchandise on acct.				4
5							5
6		5	Cost of Goods Sold		2 3 5 2 00		6
7			Merchandise Inventory			2 3 5 2 00	7
8			Relating to $2,850 sale to				8
9			S. P. Reems.				9

Accounts Receivable		Sales	
+	–	–	+
Mar. 5 2,850			Mar. 5 2,850

Cost of Goods Sold		Merchandise Inventory	
+	–	+	–
Mar. 5 2,352		Bal. 2,352	Mar. 5 2,352

For a firm using a perpetual inventory system, you can compare the Cost of Goods Sold account to an expense account: Both are increased by debits, and both are closed at the end of the year.

Apr. 2 S. P. Reems returned merchandise for credit having a sale price of $950 and a cost of $686.

Remember!

Under the perpetual inventory system, two entries are required for each sale—one for the sale and one for the cost.

	DATE		DESCRIPTION	POST. REF.	DEBIT	CREDIT	
1	20–						1
2	Apr.	2	Sales Returns and Allowances		9 5 0 00		2
3			Accts. Receivable, S. P. Reems			9 5 0 00	3
4			Issued credit memo for				4
5			the return of merchandise.				5
6							6
7		2	Merchandise Inventory		6 8 6 00		7
8			Cost of Goods Sold			6 8 6 00	8
9			Merchandise returned				9
10			by S. P. Reems.				10
11							11
12							12
13							13

Accounts Receivable				Sales Returns and Allowances		
+	−			+	−	
Bal. 2,850	Apr. 2	950	Apr. 2	950		

Cost of Goods Sold				Merchandise Inventory		
+	−			+	−	
Bal. 2,352	Apr. 2	686	Bal. 2,352		Mar. 5	2,352
			Apr. 2 686			

Firms may take physical inventories both during and at the end of the year to verify the book value of the perpetual inventory. If there is a difference between the book value and the physical count, an adjustment is made to the Merchandise Inventory account. In this adjustment, Cost of Goods Sold is used as the offsetting account. Suppose the book value figure for Merchandise Inventory is $52,756 and the physical count shows $51,980 of merchandise on hand. The ending inventory is short by $776 ($52,756 − $51,980). The adjusting entry looks like this:

	DATE	DESCRIPTION	POST. REF.	DEBIT	CREDIT	
1	20–	**Adjusting Entry**				1
2	June 30	**Cost of Goods Sold**		7 7 6 00		2
3		**Merchandise Inventory**			7 7 6 00	3
4						4

Using a scanner lets a store not only eliminate the tedious (and often error-ridden) process of entering code numbers, but also track inventory by maintaining a perpetual or up-to-the-moment count.

Here is a comparison of the periodic and perpetual inventory systems.

	Comparison: Periodic Versus Perpetual Inventory Systems	
Transaction	**Periodic Inventory System**	**Perpetual Inventory System**
Purchased merchandise from supplier on account, $2,000.	Purchases 2,000 　Accounts Payable 2,000	Merchandise Inventory 2,000 　Accounts Payable 2,000
Paid the invoice within the discount period	Accounts Payable, Miller, Inc. 2,400 　Cash 2,352 　Purchases Discount 48	Accounts Payable, Miller, Inc. 2,400 　Cash 2,352 　Merchandise inventory 48
Returned merchandise to supplier, $600.	Accounts Payable 600 　Purchases Returns 　and Allowances 600	Accounts Payable 600 　Merchandise Inventory 600
Sold merchandise to customer on account, $1,980, having a cost of $1,400.	Accounts Receivable 1,980 　Sales 1,980	Accounts Receivable 1,980 　Sales 1,980 Cost of Goods Sold 1,400 　Merchandise Inventory 1,400
Customer returned merchandise, $560, having a cost of $400.	Sales Returns and Allowances 560 　Accounts Receivable 560	Sales Returns and Allowances 560 　Accounts Receivable 560 Merchandise Inventory 400 　Cost of Goods Sold 400
Adjusting entries at end of fiscal period: Beginning merchandise inventory, $112,400. Ending merchandise inventory, $96,200. Book record of merchandise inventory (perpetual), $96,410.	Income Summary 112,400 　Merchandise 　Inventory 112,400 Merchandise Inventory 96,200 　Income Summary 96,200	Cost of Goods Sold 210 　Merchandise Inventory 210 　　Book inventory $96,410 　　Physical count 96,200 　Decrease in 　　Merchandise 　　Inventory $　210

Perpetual Inventory Record

Objective 4

Complete a perpetual inventory record card.

When a firm uses the perpetual inventory system, Merchandise Inventory is a controlling account. The firm maintains an individual record for each kind of product in the subsidiary ledger, recording the number of units received as "units received" and the number of units sold as "units sold." The firm records the remaining balance after each receipt or sale. Companies may keep perpetual inventories by any of the four methods. Assume that Jackson Electric Supply maintains a perpetual inventory on heaters on a LIFO basis, as shown in Figure 6.

The ending balance of twenty-six units amounts to $1,920 ($720 + $1,200). Eighteen heaters were sold at $120 each, for total sales of $2,160, and gross profit is $822.

INVENTORY RECORD CARD

ITEM Wall-mounted recessed heaters   LOCATION Warehouse, Heater Section

MAXIMUM 40   MINIMUM 8   METHOD LIFO

DATE	PURCHASED AT COST			SALES			COST OF GOODS SOLD			INVENTORY AT COST		
	UNITS	COST	TOTAL	UNITS	PRICE	TOTAL	UNITS	COST	TOTAL	UNITS	COST	TOTAL
1/2	Bal.									14	$72	$1,008
2/6				4	$120	$480	4	$72	$288	10	72	720
2/22	30	$75	$2,250							10	72	720
										30	75	2,250
3/14				6	120	720	6	75	450	10	72	720
										24	75	1,800
3/29				8	120	960	8	75	600	10	72	720
										16	75	1,200
Total	30	—	$2,250	18	—	$2,160	18	—	$1,338	—	—	

FIGURE 6

Sales (from sales journal)	$2,160
Less Cost of Goods Sold	1,338
Gross Profit	$ 822

FYI

Further discussion of moving averages is reserved for more advanced accounting texts.

The weighted-average-cost flow can be used with a perpetual inventory system. Rather than computing the average price for each inventory item at the end of a period, the firm calculates a new average each time a purchase is made. This average method is called a **moving average**. When goods are sold, their cost is determined by multiplying the number of units sold by the moving-average cost existing at that time.

Perpetual Inventory Records in Electronic Accounting Systems

Computers—which can retrieve an item of stored information in a fraction of a second—have enabled business firms to maintain perpetual inventories even when a wide variety of products and a large volume of transactions are involved. Think of the benefits a computer terminal would provide for a car parts store connected to its regional distribution center.

Each item of stock in the inventory is assigned a code number. Whenever the amount of an item changes, information concerning the change is fed into the computer by an on-line data entry terminal. The computer performs the arithmetic operations and determines the new balance in accordance with the inventory method in use: LIFO, FIFO, or moving-average. Thus the firm can determine the current status of any given item instantaneously. Whenever desired, the computer can list the balances of all the items in the inventory, in terms of both units and dollars.

As another illustration, in many department stores the cash registers (terminals) are linked directly to a computer center. When a sale is made, the salesperson punches in the item number, the quantity, and the price of the item. In other stores, clerks use a wand or gun to scan bar codes on individual tickets. And in supermarkets across the country, cashiers pass purchased items over scanners at the checkout register. With the information about the sale stored in the computer, management may obtain inventory quantities, costs, and total sales at any time as well as the program's prompting reordering of items that have reached a critical level.

Our discussion of perpetual inventories has been geared to merchandising firms. However, manufacturing concerns use perpetual inventories almost exclusively. A lumber mill, for example, uses the balances of daily inventories as a basis for deciding which sizes of lumber to cut: $2'' \times 4'' \times 8'$, $1'' \times 3'' \times 6'$, and so on.

CHAPTER REVIEW

Review of Performance Objectives

1. Determine the overstatement or understatement of cost of goods sold, gross profit, and net income resulting from a change in the ending merchandise inventory amount.

   The amounts of the beginning and ending merchandise inventories appear in the Cost of Goods Sold section of the income statement.

If the Ending Inventory Is	Net Income Will Be
Overstated	Overstated
Understated	Understated

If the Beginning Inventory Is	Net Income Will Be
Overstated	Understated
Understated	Overstated

2. Determine unit cost, the value of the ending inventory, and the cost of goods sold by the following methods: (a) specific identification; (b) weighted-average-cost; (c) first-in, first-out; and (d) last-in, first-out.

   (a) Specific identification: Used for high-value items when a firm can identify each item on hand with its respective price.
   (b) Weighted-average-cost: Number of Units of Each Purchase × Unit Price = Cost of Each Purchase. Cost of Beginning Inventory + Costs of All Purchases = Total Cost. Total Cost ÷ Total Units = Weighted-Average Cost per Unit.
   (c) First-in, first-out (FIFO): Costs are charged against revenue in the order in which they were incurred. This method produces the most realistic figure for the Current Assets section of the balance sheet.
   (d) Last-in, first-out (LIFO): Costs that are charged against revenue are the most recent costs. This method produces the most realistic figure for the Cost of Goods Sold section of the income statement.

In an era of rising prices, the LIFO method yields the lowest net income. Firms must be consistent in their use of inventory methods.

3. Journalize transactions relating to perpetual inventories.

Perpetual inventories are book records of what a firm has in stock. The Merchandise Inventory account is a controlling account. Merchandise Inventory is debited when goods are bought and credited when goods are sold. Cost of Goods Sold is an expense account.

4. Complete a perpetual inventory record card.

The perpetual inventory record card contains columns for the following information: date of purchase, number of units purchased, cost per unit purchased, total cost of purchase, number of units sold, selling price per unit of goods sold, total cost of units sold, cost per unit sold, total cost of goods sold, number of units in ending inventory, cost per unit of goods in ending inventory, and total cost of goods in ending inventory.

Glossary

Consistency principle An accounting principle that requires that a particular accounting procedure, once adopted, not be changed from one fiscal period to another. (630)

First-in, first-out (FIFO) method A procedure for assigning costs to merchandise sold based on the flow-of-cost assumption that units are sold in the order in which they were acquired. Unsold units on hand at date of inventory are assumed to be valued at the most recent costs. (627)

Last-in, first-out (LIFO) method A procedure for assigning costs to merchandise sold based on the flow-of-cost assumption that units sold are recorded at the costs of the most recently acquired units. Unsold units on hand at date of inventory are assumed to be valued at the earliest costs. (628)

Lower-of-cost-or-market (LCM) rule In cases where there is a difference between the original price and the market price of goods, using the lower price for determining the value of the ending inventory. The term *market price* means current replacement price. (630)

Moving average A modification of the weighted-average-cost method, used for computing the average cost of a perpetual inventory. The firm determines the moving-average unit price each time it buys more units. (635)

Periodic inventory system Determining the amount of goods on hand by periodically taking a physical count and then attaching a value to it. (622)

Perpetual inventory system A book record of the ending inventory showing the unit costs of the items received and the items sold. This gives the firm a running balance of the actual units on hand and the historical cost of each item. (622)

Specific identification method Counting the actual cost of each individual item in the ending inventory. (626)

Weighted-average-cost method A procedure for determining the cost of the ending inventory by multiplying the weighted-average cost per unit by the number of remaining units. (626)

QUESTIONS, EXERCISES, AND PROBLEMS

Discussion Questions

1. Explain the consistency principle. How can the consistency principle relate to inventory costing?
2. In periods of steadily rising prices, which inventory method (weighted-average-cost, FIFO, or LIFO) will give (a) the highest net income? (b) the lowest net income?
3. If the ending merchandise inventory of Year 1 is mistakenly understated by $4,000, what is the effect on the following:
   a. Year 1's net income?
   b. Year 1's balance sheet?
   c. Year 2's net income?
4. State an advantage and a disadvantage of LIFO.
5. What is meant by the specific identification method of pricing inventory? Give an example of a situation in which this method would be suitable.
6. Because of an error, goods costing $2,500 were omitted from the ending inventory. What effect does this omission have on the company's gross profit?
7. When a perpetual inventory system is in use, what are the necessary journal entries for buying merchandise on account and selling merchandise on account?
8. If the physical inventory count is less than the balance in the perpetual inventory record, what should be done?

Exercises

P.O. 1

Determine the effect of an error in ending inventory.

Exercise 18-1 An abbreviated income statement for Marged Company for this fiscal year is as follows:

Net Sales			$ 155 0 0 0 00
Cost of Goods Sold:			
Merchandise Inventory, January 1	$ 132 0 0 0 00		
Delivered Cost of Purchases	25 0 0 0 00		
Goods Available for Sale	$ 157 0 0 0 00		
Less Merchandise Inventory, Dec. 31	37 0 0 0 00		
Cost of Goods Sold		120 0 0 0 00	
Gross Profit		$ 35 0 0 0 00	
Expenses		18 0 0 0 00	
Net Income		$ 17 0 0 0 00	

An accountant discovers that the ending inventory is overstated by $5,800. What effect does this have on cost of goods sold, gross profit, and net income in this fiscal year?

P.O. 1

Correct errors on comparative income statements.

Exercise 18-2 Condensed income statements for Saunders Company for two years are presented here.

		2007		2006	
Net Sales			$91 0 0 0 00		$98 0 0 0 00
Cost of Goods Sold:					
Merchandise Inventory (beginning)	$13 0 0 0 00			$15 0 0 0 00	
Purchases (net)	47 0 0 0 00			49 0 0 0 00	
Goods Available for Sale	$60 0 0 0 00			$64 0 0 0 00	
Less Merchandise Inventory (ending)	14 0 0 0 00			13 0 0 0 00	
Cost of Goods Sold			46 0 0 0 00		51 0 0 0 00
Gross Profit			$45 0 0 0 00		$47 0 0 0 00
Operating Expenses			23 0 0 0 00		21 0 0 0 00
Net Income			$22 0 0 0 00		$26 0 0 0 00

After the end of 2007, it was discovered that an error had been made in 2006. Ending inventory in 2006 should have been $12,000 instead of $13,000. Determine the corrected net income for 2006 and 2007.

a. Did the error understate or overstate cost of goods sold for 2006?
b. Did the error understate or overstate net income for 2006?
c. What is the amount of total net income for the two-year period with the error ($13,000) and corrected ($12,000)?

P.O. 1

Calculate the value of ending inventory.

Exercise 18-3 The records of Belknap Company show the following data as of January 31, the end of the fiscal year. Determine the value of the ending merchandise inventory.

a. Cost of goods on hand, based on physical count, $204,330.
b. Cost of defective goods (to be thrown away) included in **a,** $328.
c. Cost of goods shipped out FOB destination on January 30, with an expected delivery date of approximately four days, $2,832; not included in **a.**
d. Goods purchased January 28, FOB shipping point, delivered to the transportation company on February 2, $1,120; not included in **a.**
e. Cost of goods sold to a customer on January 30, paid for in full and awaiting shipping instructions, $1,818; not included in **a.**

P.O. 2c,4

Calculate the cost of goods sold and the inventory value, using FIFO.

Exercise 18-4 Environco Systems keeps perpetual inventories on energy-efficient stoves, using the first-in, first-out method. Determine the cost of goods sold in each sale and the inventory balance after each sale for the following purchases and sales of energy-efficient stoves:

Jan.   1   Inventory of 35 units @ $430 each.
         25   Sold 16 units.
Mar.   4   Purchased 15 units @ $432 each.
          15   Sold 17 units.
June   5   Sold 10 units.
          22   Purchased 16 units @ $434 each.

P.O. 2b,c,d

Compute the value of ending inventory and cost of goods sold using three methods.

Exercise 18-5 Mclean's Mower Shop maintains an inventory of mower blades. Purchases of the blades during the year are as shown. (Round all computations to two decimal places.)

Jan.	1	Inventory of 25 units @ $250 each.
Mar.	8	Purchased 28 units @ $255 each.
May	15	Purchased 19 units @ $257 each.
	30	Purchased 12 units @ $258 each.

The ending inventory, by physical count, is 28 units. Determine the value of the ending inventory and the cost of goods sold by the following methods: weighted-average-cost; first-in, first-out; last-in, first-out.

P.O. 2b,c,d

Calculate the cost of ending inventory using three methods.

Exercise 18-6 Delannoy Office Supplies has a July beginning inventory of model 77 desk lamps consisting of 187 units at $87.50 each. Purchases and sales during July are as follows:

July	5	Sold 12 units.
	12	Purchased 8 units @ $88 each.
	14	Sold 15 units.
	25	Purchased 20 units @ $89 each.
	30	Sold 18 units.

Calculate the cost of the ending inventory under each of the following methods: weighted-average-cost; first-in, first-out; last-in, first-out. (Round all computations to two decimal places.)

P.O. 2

Calculate the gross profit using three methods.

Exercise 18-7 If the mower blades in Exercise 18-5 were sold during the year for $327 each, determine the gross profit using the weighted-average-cost; first-in, first-out; and last-in, first-out methods.

P.O. 3

Journalize adjusting entries under periodic and perpetual inventory methods.

Exercise 18-8 The Richter Company's fiscal year is from January 1 through December 31. The following figures are available:

Jan.	1	Inventory, $192,500 (by physical count).
Dec.	31	Inventory, $206,300 (by physical count).

a. Record the adjusting entries, assuming that the company uses the periodic inventory system.
b. Record the adjusting entry, assuming that the company uses the perpetual inventory system and that the book balance of the ending inventory is $206,820.

CONSIDER AND COMMUNICATE

A person you work for in the accounting department is confused about FIFO and LIFO as methods of charging costs of goods against revenue. Explain, for each method, which units are used to calculate the cost of the ending inventory and which financial statement is emphasized, and indicate which method results in a lower net income (assuming rising cost per unit).

CRITICAL THINKING

Your supervisor has asked you to evaluate the following situation and conditions:

Johnny's Music Store has taken inventory of the pianos, organs, and miscellaneous musical items that it sells retail. As the store's accountant, you gave your assistant instructions about taking the inventory and asked that unusual items be flagged for your review. Your assistant flagged the following items that need your review to determine if the item was correctly handled on the year-end inventory:

a. Last year's Model CX-2, Electronic Keyboard, is included in inventory at a cost of $468. (You happen to know that this outdated model can be purchased for $200, now that the new model is out.)

b. A purchase of 2 pianos at $750 each was sent by the supplier on 12/29, FOB destination. The shipment had not arrived and was not included in inventory.

c. A purchase of 2 organs at $950 each was sent by the supplier on 12/30, FOB shipping point. The shipment had not arrived and was not included in inventory.

d. You have received a credit memo for a defective amplifier, cost $237, from a supplier. The supplier issued the notice based on your promise to ship the defective unit back after the end of the year. The item is still in the warehouse, and the cost of $237 is included in the inventory.

e. A customer has paid $10,000 in full for a grand piano that cost $7,500. The customer requested that you deliver at the end of the first week of the new year. The value of the grand piano is included in the inventory, as no one remembered to put a "sold" tag on it.

f. For the holidays, the shop owner has taken home the newest model of the Electronic Keyboard. Retail value is $3,750; cost, $2,770. This item was not counted in inventory.

g. According to the company's layaway policy, a sale is not recorded until the merchandise is paid for in full, and then delivery is made. A customer has paid 25 percent of the $5,000 price of a spinet piano. The piano is set aside because the customer has put money down on it, and the $3,800 cost is not included in the inventory.

Instructions

1. What is the correct treatment for each item? Should you include it in inventory or exclude it? Why?

2. Was the item handled correctly by your assistant? If it was not correctly handled, what must be done to correct the inventory? Should you increase inventory (if so, by what amount) or decrease inventory (if so, by what amount)?

A MATTER OF ETHICS

A large computer retailer has taken year-end inventory and has valued 80 model XV computers at $800 each, or $64,000—the original cost of model XV. Current technologies have allowed the supplier to reduce the cost of model XV to $600, although the computer store has not purchased any model XVs at this price. Is the owner doing anything unethical by valuing the 80 model XVs at the original cost of $64,000?

WEB WORK

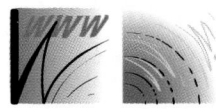

Using an Internet web browser, type *accounting for merchandise inventory* in the search box and search for information about merchandise inventory methods and procedures. Discuss your findings in a small group. Write a one-page summary of your findings.

PROBLEM SET A

For additional help, see the demonstration problem at the beginning of each chapter in your Working Papers.

P.O. 2b,c,d

Problem 18-1A Powell Chemical's inventory of NC221 on January 1 of one year was 7,000 gallons, costing $.52 per gallon. In addition to this beginning inventory, Powell Chemical made these purchases during the next six months:

Date	Quantity (Gallons)	Cost per Gallon	Total Cost
Jan. 1 Inventory	7,000	$.52	$3,640
26	10,000	.525	5,250
Feb. 4	12,000	.53	6,360
21	9,000	.53	4,770
Mar. 7	11,000	.535	5,885
24	8,000	.55	4,400
Apr. 19	9,000	.55	4,950
May 31	6,000	.55	3,300
June 15	4,000	.56	2,240

Powell Chemical's inventory on June 30 was 11,000 gallons. During this six-month period, the firm sold all its NC221 at $.69 per gallon. Assume that no liquid was lost through evaporation or leakage.

Check Figure

Ending inventory under FIFO, $6,090

Instructions

1. Find the cost of the ending inventory by the following methods:
   a. Weighted-average-cost (Round to two decimal places.)
   b. First-in, first-out
   c. Last-in, first-out

2. Determine the cost of goods sold according to the three methods of costing inventory.
3. Determine the amount of the gross profit according to the three methods of costing inventory.

P.O. 2b,c,d

Problem 18-2A Hoffman Stereo uses the periodic inventory system. Data for its inventories on January 1, the beginning of the fiscal year, purchases during the year, and the inventory count at December 31 are as follows.

	Model		
	JP314	CL247	9L21
Inventory, Jan. 1	6 @ $436	4 @ $692	17 @ $336
First purchase	9 @ 450	7 @ 722	21 @ 344
Second purchase	11 @ 460	8 @ 722	33 @ 344
Third purchase	8 @ 460	6 @ 736	14 @ 348
Fourth purchase	7 @ 466		
Inventory, Dec. 31	8	7	23

Instructions

1. Determine the cost of the inventory on December 31 by the weighted-average-cost method. (Round to two decimal places.)
2. Determine the cost of the inventory on December 31 by the first-in, first-out method.
3. Determine the cost of the inventory on December 31 by the last-in, first-out method.

P.O. 1,3

Problem 18-3A The McNeil Company carried out the following transactions during the year:

Jan.
  3 Bought merchandise on account from Sadler, Inc.; terms 2/10, n/30; FOB destination; $12,200.
  5 Received credit memo no. 1642 from Sadler, Inc., for the return of merchandise bought on January 3, $720.
  12 Issued check no. 2141, payable to Sadler, Inc., in payment of the invoice dated January 3.
  20 Sold merchandise on account to Schick and Son, $6,420; the cost of the merchandise was $5,292.
  30 Sold merchandise on account to O'Donnell and Company, $5,212; the cost of the merchandise was $3,744.

Dec.
  31 Made the following adjusting entries: The ending inventory determined by physical count is $225,814. The balance in the Inventory account under the perpetual inventory system is $225,975. The beginning inventory was $198,524. Accrued interest on notes payable is $79. Accrued interest on notes receivable is $112. Allowance for Doubtful Accounts is to be increased by $1,540.

Instructions

1. Assuming that McNeil Company uses the perpetual inventory system, record the transactions in general journal form, with purchases recorded at the gross amount.
2. Assuming that McNeil Company uses the periodic inventory system, record the transactions in general journal form, with purchases recorded at the gross amount.

Instructions for General Ledger Software

The Problem Menu lists two versions of this problem, one for each part.

1. Assuming that McNeil Company uses the perpetual inventory system, record the transactions in the general journal, with purchases recorded at the gross amount. Print the journal entries.
2. Assuming that McNeil Company uses the periodic inventory system, record the transactions in the general journal, with purchases recorded at the gross amount. Print the journal entries.

P.O. 4

Problem 18-4A The Brown Company's beginning inventory of C430 is 160 units at a cost of $88 each. Dates of purchases and sales for a three-month period are as follows.

	Purchases		Sales	
Date	Units	Cost per Unit	Units	Price per Unit
Jan. 16	220	$88.40		
18			70	$104.00
29			140	104.00
Feb. 2	180	92.00		
11			120	106.00
17	200	96.00		
27			170	112.00
Mar. 9			90	112.00
14	120	97.20		
22			75	112.00
29			70	112.80

Brown Company maintains a perpetual inventory record using the first-in, first-out method. Data for the month of January are recorded in the Working Papers.

Check Figure

Cost of goods sold, $66,888.00

Instructions

1. Record the data for purchases and sales of item C430 and for cost of goods sold in a perpetual inventory record using the first-in, first-out method for the months of February and March.
2. Determine the total cost of goods sold during the three-month period.
3. Determine the total sales for the three-month period.
4. Determine the gross profit from sales of item C430 for this period.

PROBLEM SET B

For additional help, see the demonstration problem at the beginning of each chapter in your Working Papers.

P.O. 2,b,c,d

Problem 18-1B Baisch and Company, on January 1 of one year, had an inventory of XN244 of 12,000 gallons, costing $.41 per gallon. In addition to this beginning inventory, purchases during the next six months were as follows.

Date	Quantity (Gallons)	Cost per Gallon	Total Cost
Jan. 1 Inventory	12,000	$.41	$4,920
14	9,000	.42	3,780
Feb. 21	8,000	.43	3,440
Mar. 7	6,000	.43½	2,610
Apr. 19	11,000	.43	4,730
May 5	8,000	.44	3,520
June 2	9,000	.45	4,050
29	7,000	.45	3,150

The inventory on June 30 was 16,000 gallons. During this six-month period, Baisch and Company sold XN244 for $.57 per gallon. Assume that no liquid was lost through evaporation or leakage.

Instructions

1. Find the cost of the ending inventory by the following methods:

   a. Weighted-average-cost (Round to two decimal places.)
   b. First-in, first-out
   c. Last-in, first-out

2. Determine the cost of goods sold according to the three methods of costing inventory.
3. Determine the amount of the gross profit according to the three methods of costing inventory.

P.O. 2b,c,d

Problem 18-2B Crown Jewelers uses the periodic inventory system. Data pertaining to the inventory on January 1, the beginning of the fiscal year, purchases during the year, and the inventory count on December 31 are as follows:

	Model		
	JP314	**CL247**	**9L21**
Inventory, Jan. 1	11 @ $432	3 @ $786	21 @ $318
First purchase	17 @ 444	7 @ 782	28 @ 322
Second purchase	22 @ 452	9 @ 788	30 @ 322
Third purchase	16 @ 452	6 @ 796	32 @ 330
Fourth purchase	12 @ 458		26 @ 332
Inventory, Dec. 31	15	7	31

Instructions

1. Determine the cost of the inventory on December 31 by the weighted-average-cost method. (Round to two decimal places.)
2. Determine the cost of the inventory on December 31 by the first-in, first-out method.
3. Determine the cost of the inventory on December 31 by the last-in, first-out method.

P.O. 1,3

Problem 18-3B The Golden Company made the following transactions during the year:

Jan.   2 Bought merchandise on account from Upton Products; terms 2/10, n/30; FOB destination; $7,640.

      4 Received credit memo no. 1421 from Upton Products for the return of merchandise bought on January 2, $426.

   11 Issued check no. 2912 to Upton Products, in payment of the invoice dated January 2.

   14 Sold merchandise on account to C. N. Lewis, $3,510; the cost of the merchandise was $2,492.

   30 Sold merchandise on account to S. T. Clark, $4,672; the cost of the merchandise was $3,317.

Dec. 31 Made adjusting entries: The ending merchandise inventory determined by physical count is $140,316. The beginning inventory was $137,294. The balance in the inventory account under the perpetual inventory system is $140,892. Accrued interest on notes payable is $221. Accrued interest on notes receivable is $118. Allowance for Doubtful Accounts is to be increased by $1,310.

Check Figure

First adjusting entry, periodic inventory system, $137,294

Instructions

1. Record the transactions in general journal form, assuming that Golden Company uses the perpetual inventory system and records purchases at the gross amount.
2. Record the transactions in general journal form, assuming that Golden Company uses the periodic inventory system and records purchases at the gross amount.

Instructions for General Ledger Software

The Problem Menu lists two versions of this problem, one for each part.

1. Assuming that Golden Company uses the perpetual inventory system, record the transactions in the general journal, with purchases recorded at the gross amount. Print the journal entries.
2. Assuming that Golden Company uses the periodic inventory system, record the transactions in the general journal, with purchases recorded at the gross amount. Print the journal entries.

P.O. 4

Problem 18-4B The Brady Company's beginning inventory of C215 is 160 units at a cost of $44 each. Dates of purchases and sales for a three-month period are shown here.

Date	Purchases			Sales	
	Units	**Cost per Unit**		**Units**	**Price per Unit**
Jan. 16	220	$44.20			
18				70	$52.00
29				140	52.00
Feb. 5	240	45.60			
14				130	53.00
22				190	53.00
26	220	46.20			
Mar. 4				70	54.00
11	150	48.00			
17				80	54.00
30				145	56.00

Brady Company maintains a perpetual inventory record using the first-in, first-out method. Data for the month of January are recorded in the Working Papers.

Check Figure

Cost of goods sold, $37,179

Instructions

1. Record the data for purchases and sales of item C215 and for cost of goods sold in a perpetual inventory record using the first-in, first-out method for the months of February and March.
2. Determine the total cost of goods sold during the three-month period.
3. Determine the total sales for the three-month period.
4. Determine the gross profit from sales of item C215 for the period.

Estimating the Value of Inventories

Performance Objectives

After you have completed this appendix, you will be able to do the following:

1. Estimate the value of inventory by the retail method.

2. Estimate the value of inventory by the gross-profit method.

To function efficiently, management must have interim income statements and balance sheets prepared monthly. Management needs a physical inventory at the end of the year, because inventory balance figures are an integral element of financial statements. However, because it is both time-consuming and expensive to take a physical inventory, management finds it more expedient to estimate the value of the ending inventory each month and to use these estimates on the monthly financial statements. Let's take a look at the two most frequently used methods of estimating the value of inventories: the retail method and the gross-profit method.

RETAIL METHOD OF ESTIMATING THE VALUE OF INVENTORIES

Objective 1

Estimate the value of inventory by the retail method.

This **retail method**, widely used by retail concerns, is based on both the cost and retail value of the goods. The retailer buys merchandise at cost, then adds the normal markup and prices the goods at the retail level. The **normal markup**—which is the normal amount, or percentage, that you add to the cost of an item to arrive at its selling price—covers operating expenses and profit. If a firm uses the retail method of estimating inventories, it must record the purchases-related accounts at both cost and retail values. The firm's accountant records retail values in supplementary records; he or she also records the physical inventory taken at the end of the previous year at both cost and retail values.

Example 1 Belver Company takes a physical inventory at the end of each year and estimates the value of the inventory at the end of each month for its monthly financial statements.

The accountant for Belver Company needs the following information to estimate the value of the ending merchandise inventory at cost:

• Cost value and retail value of merchandise on hand at the beginning of the month. (The inventory at the beginning of a given month is the same as the inventory at the end of the preceding month.)

	AT COST	AT RETAIL
Merchandise Inventory (beginning)	41 2 0 0 00	68 6 0 0 00

- Delivered cost of purchases during the month, both cost value and retail value. The retail figures include the cost plus the company's standard markup.

	AT COST			AT RETAIL	
Purchases			82 7 4 5 00			137 9 0 8 00
Less: Purchases Returns and Allowances	2 3 0 0 00			3 8 0 0 00	
Purchases Discount	1 9 0 0 00	4 2 0 0 00		3 2 0 0 00	7 0 0 0 00
Net Purchases		78 5 4 5 00			130 9 0 8 00
Add Freight In		4 3 5 5 00			7 2 5 9 00
Delivered Cost of Purchases		82 9 0 0 00			138 1 6 7 00

- Net sales for the month. All sales are recorded at retail price levels, as listed on sales slips and cash register tapes.

		AT RETAIL	
Sales			151 6 5 0 00
Less: Sales Returns and Allowances	7 0 0 0 00		
Sales Discount	2 6 5 0 00		9 6 5 0 00
Net Sales			142 0 0 0 00

The accountant can determine the cost value of the ending inventory by following these four steps:

1. Determine the dollar value of goods available for sale, at cost and at retail. The cost figures are the same as the Goods Available for Sale, which is part of the Cost of Goods Sold section of the income statement.

	At Cost	At Retail
Beginning inventory	$ 41,200	$ 68,600
Plus delivered cost of purchases	82,900	138,167
Goods available for sale	$124,100	$206,767

2. Find the ratio of the cost value of goods available for sale to the retail value of goods available for sale.

$$\frac{\text{Cost Value of Goods Available for Sale}}{\text{Retail Value of Goods Available for Sale}} = \frac{\$124,100}{\$206,767} = 60\%$$

3. Determine the retail value (selling price) of ending inventory.

Retail value of goods available	$206,767
Less net sales	142,000
Retail value of ending inventory	$ 64,767

Think of the retail value of the ending inventory this way: If the firm had $206,767 of goods available for sale, and $142,000 was actually sold, then the amount left over should be $64,767.

4. Convert the retail value of the ending inventory into the cost value of the ending inventory by using this formula and rounding to the nearest dollar:

$$\$64,767 \times 60\% = \$64,767 \times .6 = \underline{\underline{\$38,860}}$$

Therefore, on its income statement for the month, Belver Company records the value of the ending inventory as $38,860. If the retail value is $64,767 and 40 percent of this figure represents markup, the remaining 60 percent must be the cost.

Example 2 Corven Company has the following account balances, as shown by T accounts:

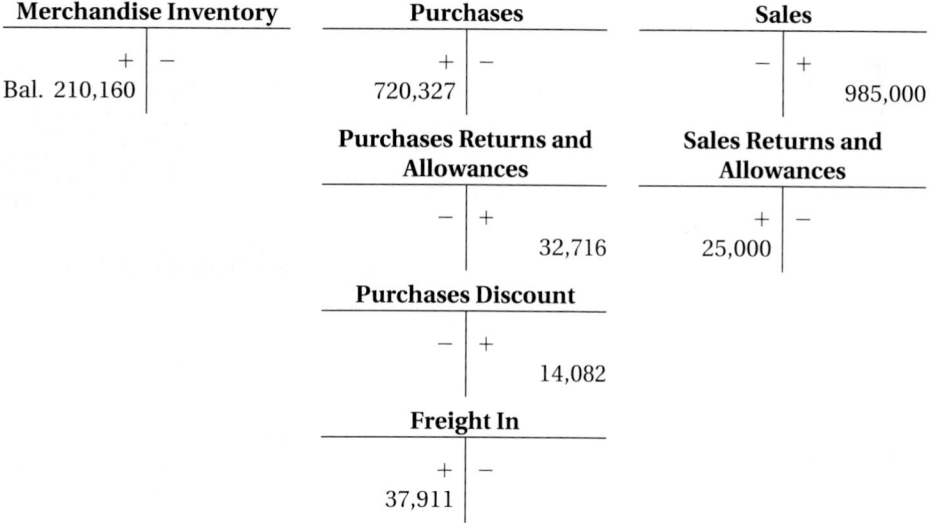

Merchandise Inventory			Purchases			Sales		
+	−		+	−		−	+	
Bal. 210,160			720,327				985,000	

Purchases Returns and Allowances		Sales Returns and Allowances	
−	+	+	−
	32,716	25,000	

Purchases Discount	
−	+
	14,082

Freight In	
+	−
37,911	

Retail value of beginning inventory is $296,000 (the accountant picks up this figure from a report dated the end of the preceding month).

$$\begin{aligned}
\text{Delivered Cost of Purchases} &= \text{Purchases} - \text{Purchases Returns and} \\
&\quad \text{Allowances} - \text{Purchases Discount} + \text{Freight In} \\
&= \$720,327 - \$32,716 - \$14,082 + \$37,911 \\
&= \underline{\underline{\$711,440}} \text{ Delivered Cost of Purchases}
\end{aligned}$$

Retail value of delivered cost of purchases is $1,001,708 (the normal markup is added to the cost figure).

$$\begin{aligned}
\text{Net Sales} &= \text{Sales} - \text{Sales Returns and Allowances} \\
&= \$985,000 - \$25,000 \\
&= \underline{\underline{\$960,000}}
\end{aligned}$$

Again, the information is obtained by following the four steps:

1. Determine the dollar value of goods available for sale, at cost and at retail.

	At Cost	At Retail
Beginning inventory	$210,160	$ 296,000
Plus delivered cost of purchases	711,440	1,001,708
Goods available for sale	$921,600	$1,297,708

2. Find the ratio of the cost value of goods available for sale to the retail value of goods available for sale.

$$\frac{\text{Cost Value of Goods Available for Sale}}{\text{Retail Value of Goods Available for Sale}} = \frac{\$921,600}{\$1,297,708} = 71\%$$

3. Find the retail value of ending inventory, as follows:

Retail value of goods available	$1,297,708
Less net sales	960,000
Retail value of ending inventory	$ 337,708

4. Convert retail value of ending inventory into cost value of ending inventory by using this formula:

$$\$337,708 \times 71\% = \$337,708 \times .71 = \underline{\$239,773}$$

These examples assume that the retailer maintains the normal markup. In other words, we are assuming that the composition or mix of the items in the ending inventory, in terms of the ratio of cost price to retail price, remains the same for the entire stock of goods available for sale.

Markups and Markdowns

In our examples, the retailers used normal markups, but some stores use additional markups and markdowns. Retailers impose additional markups on top of normal markups when the merchandise involved is in great demand. Because of the highly desirable nature of certain goods (such as up-to-the-minute fashion), a store may feel that it can get higher-than-normal prices for these goods. Conversely, a store uses markdowns to sell slow-moving merchandise during a clearance sale.

When a store using the retail inventory method imposes additional markups and markdowns, it must keep track of them, so that it can calculate the ratio of the cost value of merchandise available to the retail value of goods available. Look at the following example of how a store keeps track of markups and markdowns:

Step 1 Goods available for sale, at cost and at retail.

	At Cost	At Retail
Beginning inventory	$ 60,000	$ 90,000
Plus delivered cost of purchases	110,000	165,000
Plus additional markups		4,000
Goods available for sale	$170,000	$259,000

Step 2 Ratio of cost value of goods available for sale to retail value of goods available for sale is as follows:

$$\frac{\text{Cost Value of Goods Available for Sale}}{\text{Retail Value of Goods Available for Sale}} = \frac{\$170,000}{\$259,000} = 66\%$$

Step 3 Retail value of ending inventory.

Retail value of goods available for sale	$259,000
Less net sales	200,000
Less markdowns	3,000
Retail value of ending inventory	$ 56,000

Step 4 Convert retail value of ending inventory into cost value of ending inventory:

$$\$56,000 \times .66 = \$36,960$$

The accountant adds any additional markups in the retail column of his or her working paper because such markups result in an increase in the retail value of the goods available for sale. For example, let's say that the price of a popular item is $40, and a store seizes the opportunity and marks it up to $49; this is a $9 increase in the retail value of the goods available for sale. On the other hand, when a store marks down the price of an item, the accountant deducts the amount of the markdown from the retail value of the goods available for sale (step 3) to obtain the retail value of the merchandise inventory at the end of a given month. For example, say that the price tag of an item is $389, but nobody is buying, so the store marks it down to $359. This means that there has been a $30 decrease in the retail value of these goods available for sale.

END-OF-YEAR PROCEDURE

It is very important to take a physical inventory at the end of the year. Physical inventories may also be taken periodically during the year to spot-check the estimated inventories. Most retail stores record items in stock on the inventory sheets at retail prices (they take the total of all the price tags). It is then necessary to convert the total of the retail values into the total of the cost values, as in step 4. For example, suppose that the total retail value of the merchandise on all the inventory sheets is $96,000, and the ratio of cost value to retail value is

$$\frac{\text{Cost Value of Goods Available}}{\text{Retail Value of Goods Available}} = 70\%$$

The cost value of the goods is $96,000 × .7 = $67,200. The only difference between the steps taken to prepare the end-of-the-year statement and the steps taken to prepare the interim or monthly statements is that at the end of the year there is a physical count of the merchandise, and consequently you begin with step 4.

However, to find out the magnitude of shoplifting, or to verify the accuracy of the evaluation of the physical inventory, some firms go through the full procedure of estimating the value of the inventory at the end of the year. Then they take a physical count of the goods on hand and compare this value with the value of the estimated inventory.

GROSS-PROFIT METHOD OF ESTIMATING THE VALUE OF INVENTORIES

Objective 2

Estimate the value of inventory by the gross-profit method.

Sometimes a firm may find that the total of the retail prices of the beginning inventory and purchases is not readily available; in such cases, the firm naturally cannot use the retail method of estimating the value of the ending inventory. The **gross-profit method** is an alternative procedure that achieves the same objective. The key element in this method is that the percentage of gross profit earned in the prior year will remain the same for the present year.

The term *gross profit*, as used on income statements, represents net sales less cost of goods sold:

Net sales	$60,000
Less cost of goods sold	45,000
Gross profit	$15,000

You arrive at the figure for the percentage of gross profit by dividing the gross profit by the net sales:

$$\text{Percentage of Gross Profit} = \frac{\text{Gross Profit}}{\text{Net Sales}} = \frac{\$15,000}{\$60,000} = 25\%$$

A 25 percent gross-profit rate means that there is 25¢ of gross profit for every $1 of net sales. *Gross profit* is the profit earned on the sale of merchandise *before* other expenses are deducted. You can compute the gross-profit rate or percentage by using figures from a recent income statement, or you may compute the percentage of gross profit from income statements from past years, using averages of figures. The variation from year to year is usually relatively minor, unless marked changes in the firm's buying and selling policies have taken place.

You need the following information for the current year:

- Sales (balance of account to date)
- Sales Returns and Allowances (balance of account to date)
- Sales Discount (balance of account to date)
- Beginning Merchandise Inventory (ending inventory of the previous period)
- Purchases (balance of account to date)
- Purchases Returns and Allowances (balance of account to date)
- Purchases Discount (balance of account to date)
- Freight In (balance of account to date)

Example 1 On the night of April 29, the Chow Stop n' Shop was destroyed by fire. However, a heroic salesclerk ran into the building and rescued the company's books and records of transactions. For insurance purposes, the owner must estimate the value of the inventory by the gross-profit method. The owner knows that the average gross-profit percentage for the past five years is 32 percent. By journalizing and posting the transactions of the current month, the company's accounts can be brought up to date from these sources:

- Sales (from sales journal, cash receipts journal, and invoices for April 29)
- Sales Returns and Allowances (from cash receipts journal and general journal)
- Merchandise Inventory, December 31 (ending inventory of last fiscal period)
- Purchases (from purchases journal and invoices for April 29)
- Purchases Returns and Allowances (from general journal)
- Purchases Discount (from cash payments journal)
- Freight In (from purchases journal, cash payments journal, and invoices for April 29)

The owner of Chow Stop n' Shop arranges these figures in the customary income statement format, extending from Sales to Gross Profit (see Figure 1).

$$\text{Percentage of Gross Profit} = \frac{\text{Gross Profit}}{\text{Net Sales}} = \frac{\text{Gross Profit}}{\$200,000} = \underline{\underline{32\%}}$$

$$\text{Gross Profit} = .32 \times \$200,000 = \underline{\underline{\$64,000}}$$

Next fill in the Gross Profit blank in the income statement (see Figure 2 on page 654).

To find the value of the merchandise at the end (April 29), we work backward. The cost of goods sold is the difference between net sales and gross profit, or $136,000 ($200,000 − $64,000). The equation is as shown on the following page.

FIGURE 1

Chow Stop n' Shop
Partial Income Statement
For Period January 1 through April 29, 20—

Revenue from Sales:					
Sales				$217 0 0 0 00	
Less Sales Returns and Allowances				17 0 0 0 00	
Net Sales				$200 0 0 0 00	
Cost of Goods Sold:					
Merchandise Inventory, January 1, 20—			$ 72 0 0 0 00		
Purchases		$136 0 0 0 00			
Less: Purchases Returns and Allowances	$14 0 0 0 00				
Purchases Discount	2 4 0 0 00	16 4 0 0 00			
Net Purchases		$119 6 0 0 00			
Add Freight In		7 4 0 0 00			
Delivered Cost of Purchases			127 0 0 0 00		
Goods Available for Sale			$199 0 0 0 00		
Less Merchandise Inventory, April 29, 20—			⟨ ⟩		
Cost of Goods Sold				⟨ ⟩	
Gross Profit				$	

Chow Stop n' Shop
Partial Income Statement
For Period January 1 through April 29, 20—

Revenue from Sales:					
Sales					$217 0 0 0 00
Less Sales Returns and Allowances					17 0 0 0 00
Net Sales					$200 0 0 0 00
Cost of Goods Sold:					
Merchandise Inventory, January 1, 20—				$ 72 0 0 0 00	
Purchases		$136 0 0 0 00			
Less: Purchases Returns and Allowances	$14 0 0 0 00				
Purchases Discount	2 4 0 0 00	16 4 0 0 00			
Net Purchases		$119 6 0 0 00			
Add Freight In		7 4 0 0 00			
Delivered Cost of Purchases				127 0 0 0 00	
Goods Available for Sale				$199 0 0 0 00	
Less Merchandise Inventory, April 29, 20—					
Cost of Goods Sold					136 0 0 0 00
Gross Profit					$ 64 0 0 0 00

FIGURE 2

$$\text{Cost of Goods Sold} = \text{Net Sales} - \text{Gross Profit}$$
$$= \$200,000 - \$64,000$$
$$= \underline{\$136,000}$$

Now that we have filled in the figures for Gross Profit and Cost of Goods Sold, the partial income statement (from Goods Available for Sale through Gross Profit) looks like this:

Goods Available for Sale	$199,000.00
Less Merchandise Inventory, April 29, 20—	_____
Cost of Goods Sold	136,000.00
Gross Profit	$ 64,000.00

The value of the merchandise inventory on April 29 is the difference between the value of the goods available for sale and the cost of goods sold, or $63,000 ($199,000 − $136,000). The equation is as follows:

$$\text{Value of Ending Inventory} = \text{Value of Goods Available for Sale} - \text{Cost of Goods Sold}$$
$$= \$199,000 - \$136,000$$
$$= \$63,000$$

Goods Available for Sale	$199,000.00
Less Merchandise Inventory, April 29, 20—	63,000.00
Cost of Goods Sold	136,000.00
Gross Profit	$ 64,000.00

Haley Farm Supply
Partial Income Statement
For Period January 1 through May 31, 20—

Revenue from Sales:						
Sales					$314 7 1 9 00	
Less: Sales Returns and Allowances		$ 12 4 9 1 00				
Sales Discount		6 2 2 8 00		18 7 1 9 00		
Net Sales				$296 0 0 0 00		
Cost of Goods Sold:						
Merchandise Inventory, January 1, 20—		$ 83 1 1 8 00				
Purchases	$201 0 6 7 00					
Less: Purchases Returns and Allowances	$11 2 2 8 00					
Purchases Discount	3 7 1 5 00	14 9 4 3 00				
Net Purchases	$186 1 2 4 00					
Add Freight In	12 8 3 4 00					
Delivered Cost of Purchases		198 9 5 8 00				
Goods Available for Sale		$282 0 7 6 00				
Less Merchandise Inventory, May 31, 20—		86 7 1 6 00				
Cost of Goods Sold				195 3 6 0 00		
Gross Profit				$100 6 4 0 00		

FIGURE 3

The income statement is a very useful device in the box of tools that you have been accumulating. That is why we suggested earlier that you memorize the form to implant it firmly in your mind; then it will always be at your fingertips when you need it to do a specific job.

Example 2 Haley Farm Supply has an average gross-profit rate of 34 percent. Its account balances on May 31 of this year are shown by the following T accounts and by the partial income statement in Figure 3.

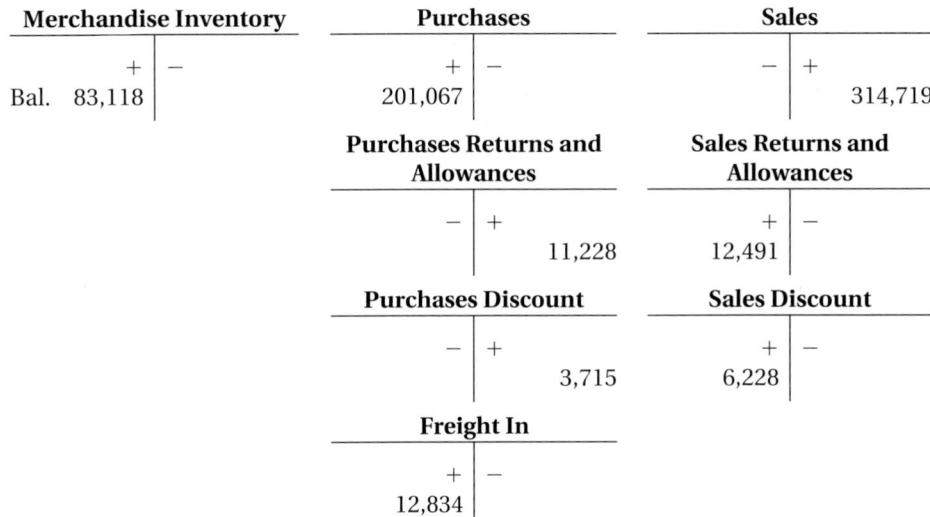

$$\text{Percentage of Gross Profit} = \frac{\text{Gross Profit}}{\text{Net Sales}} = \frac{\text{Gross Profit}}{\$296,000} = 34\%$$

$$\text{Gross Profit} = \text{Net Sales} \times .34 = \$296,000 \times .34 = \$100,640$$
$$\text{Cost of Goods Sold} = \text{Net Sales} - \text{Gross Profit}$$
$$= \$296,000 - \$100,640 = \$195,360$$

The cost of goods sold is equal to net sales minus gross profit, or $195,360 ($296,000 − $100,640). The ending merchandise inventory is the value of the goods available for sale minus the cost of goods sold, or $86,716 ($282,076 − $195,360).

$$\text{Ending Inventory} = \text{Goods Available for Sale} - \text{Cost of Goods Sold}$$
$$= \$282,076 - \$195,360 = \$86,716$$

Glossary

Gross-profit method An alternative procedure (vs. the retail method) to estimating the value of inventories. The key element in this method is that the percentage of gross profit earned in the prior year will remain the same for the present year. (652)

Normal markup The amount or percentage that is normally added to the cost of an item to arrive at its selling price. (647)

Retail method A widely used procedure for estimating the value of inventories. The key elements in this method are the cost of the goods and the retail value of the goods both being recorded. (647)

PROBLEMS

P.O. 1

Problem F-1 You are given the following information for Electric Toys at the end of its fiscal year, October 31:

	At Cost	At Retail
Sales		$264,789
Sales Returns and Allowances		10,659
Purchases	$152,806	254,600
Purchases Returns and Allowances	7,026	11,712
Merchandise Inventory (beginning)	59,172	98,640
Freight In	8,042	13,534

Check Figure

Amount of the loss, $1,225.80

Instructions

1. Determine the cost value of the ending merchandise inventory as of October 31, presenting details of your computations.
2. At the end of the year, Electric Toys takes a physical inventory at marked selling prices and finds that the retail stock totals $98,889. There is a possibility that the difference between the estimated ending inventory and the actual physical inventory is due to shoplifting. Convert the value of the physical inventory at retail into its value at cost, and determine the amount of the loss.

P.O. 2

Problem F-2 On May 10 of this year, a fire in the night destroyed the entire stock of merchandise of Kemp's Crafts. Most of the accounting records were destroyed also. However, from assorted statements and documents, the firm's accountant was able to piece together the balances of several accounts. Over the past three years, the percentage of gross profit averaged 40 percent.

Merchandise Inventory, January 1 (beginning of fiscal year)	$128,859
Account balances, as of May 10	
Purchases	163,970
Purchases Returns and Allowances	984
Freight In	7,906
Sales	219,540
Sales Returns and Allowances	660

Check Figure

Value of ending inventory, $168,423

Instructions

Determine the cost value of the ending merchandise inventory as of May 10, giving details of your computations.

P.O. 2

Problem F-3 On the morning of July 27, the owner of Sun Systems opened her store and discovered that a robbery had taken place over the weekend. A large part of the stock had been stolen. However, the following information for the period January 1 through July 27 was available. Each year during the past four years, the store had earned an average 34 percent gross profit on sales.

Merchandise Inventory, January 1 (beginning of fiscal year)	$190,389
Account balances, as of July 27	
Purchases	408,692
Purchases Returns and Allowances	10,986
Purchases Discount	8,244
Freight In	24,703
Sales	596,134
Sales Returns and Allowances	6,134

Check Figure

Value of ending inventory, $215,154

Instructions

1. Determine the cost value of the ending merchandise inventory as of July 27, giving details of your computations.
2. By physical count, the cost value of the remaining inventory on hand is $80,940. What is the amount of the loss to be claimed for insurance purposes?

19 Plant and Equipment

WINDOWS ON | **THE WORLD WIDE WEB**

What kind of plant and equipment costs did the Wright Brothers have to build their first airplane? Things have changed since then. Boeing, the largest aerospace company in the world, had net capital expenditures of $1,584 million at the end of the 1990s. How much is Boeing spending on plants and equipment to build its jets now? How are Boeing's commercial aircraft programs' costs of goods determined? What method does Boeing's accounting staff use to depreciate its plant and equipment? How does Boeing effectively amortize (or average) tooling and special equipment costs as well as unit production costs? For Boeing's financial information, check out **http://www.boeing.com/companyoffices/financial/**. Go to **http://www.boeing.com/companyoffices/financial/finreports/annual/98 annualreport/** to look at the annual report and see specific information on Boeing's depreciation methods.

Performance Objectives

After you have completed this chapter, you will be able to do the following:

1. Allocate costs to Land, Land Improvements, and Buildings accounts.

2. Calculate depreciation by the straight-line method, units-of-production method, double-declining-balance method, and sum-of-the-years'-digits method.

3. Differentiate among capital expenditures, revenue expenditures, and extraordinary-repairs expenditures.

4. Prepare journal entries for discarding of assets fully depreciated, discarding of assets not fully depreciated, sale of assets involving a loss, sale of assets involving a gain, exchange of assets involving a loss on the trade, and exchange of assets involving a gain on the trade.

5. Maintain a plant and equipment subsidiary ledger.

6. Calculate the allowable depreciation for federal income tax returns using the Modified Accelerated Cost Recovery System.

Assets in the Plant and Equipment category have a useful life longer than one year, and so they are often referred to as long-lived or fixed assets. Assets such as these are originally purchased for use in the business, unlike merchandise, which is bought for resale. Items most frequently classified as **plant and equipment** are equipment, furniture, machinery, tools, buildings, land improvements, and land.

INITIAL COSTS OF PLANT AND EQUIPMENT

The original cost of plant and equipment includes all normal expenditures necessary to acquire, install, and prepare the plant and equipment for its intended use. For example, the cost of a delivery van includes not only its invoice price (less any discount for paying cash) but also sales tax, freight charges, insurance costs while it is being transported, and costs of dealer preparation. If the buyer of the van pays these additional charges in cash, the accountant for the buyer debits Delivery Van and credits Cash. Suppose the firm buys a second-hand delivery van that needs repair before it can be used; the cost of the repairs are debited to the appropriate asset account, in this case Delivery Van.

Remember!

Normal costs of acquiring the asset, such as its transportation and installation, are debited to the asset account. Other expenditures, from abnormal causes, are debited to an expense account.

The accountant should debit only normal and necessary costs to the asset accounts; this rules out expenditures that result from carelessness, vandalism, and other abnormal causes. For example, suppose that an employee dented the van while parking it. The cost of the repair is not part of the cost of the van; that cost is debited to an expense account, such as Repair Expense. The cost is charged as an expense and not as an asset because the repair does not *add* to the usefulness of the asset—it simply restores its usefulness.

DIFFERENTIATING COSTS OF LAND, LAND IMPROVEMENTS, AND BUILDINGS

Objective 1

Allocate costs to Land, Land Improvements, and Buildings accounts.

A buyer usually buys a package including land, land improvements, and a building. In other words, the buyer pays one price for the package. So the question is: How should the price be allocated among the three elements?

When there is no qualified appraisal available, you accept the ratio established by the county or municipal tax assessor. For example, suppose that someone buys some real property, including land and a building, for $600,000. The assessor valued this property for tax purposes at $300,000: $60,000 for the land and $240,000 for the building. The percentage the assessor allocated to the land is $60,000/$300,000 = 20 percent. The percentage allocated to the building is $240,000/$300,000 = 80 percent. Therefore, the value that the buyer should allocate to the land is $600,000 × .2 = $120,000, and that to the building is $600,000 × .8 = $480,000. For bookkeeping purposes, you separate land improvements from buildings because of the different useful lives involved. There is no accounting recognition of depreciation of land because the useful life of land is infinite.

Land

Suppose that someone buys a piece of land—just land, no building. The cost of the land includes the amount paid for the land plus incidental charges connected with the purchase: real estate agents' commissions paid by the buyer, escrow and legal fees, delinquent taxes paid by the buyer, plus any costs of surveying, clearing, draining, or grading the land. In addition, the municipality or county—either at the time of purchase or later—may assess the buyer for such improvements as the installation of paved streets, curbs, sidewalks, and sewers. The buyer debits these items to the Land account, since the items are considered as permanent as the land. If a business entity buys land for a building site and the land happens to have old buildings standing on it, the firm debits the cost of the structures (as well as the costs of demolishing them) to the Land account.

Land Improvements

An accountant uses the asset account **Land Improvements** to record expenditures for improvements that have (1) a determinable or finite useful life or (2) are not directly associated with a building. Examples are driveways, parking lots, trees and shrubs, fences, and outdoor lighting systems.

Buildings

Remember!

If land and building are bought as a package, the assets on the land must be separated for accounting purposes.

The cost of a building includes not only labor and materials, but also architectural and engineering fees, insurance premiums during construction, interest on construction loans during the period of construction, and all other necessary and normal expenditures incurred to prepare the asset for its intended use.

THE NATURE AND RECORDING OF DEPRECIATION

Remember!

The purpose of depreciation is to spread the cost of plant and equipment over the years in which it is used to produce revenue—again, in keeping with the matching principle.

When accountants use the term *depreciation,* they mean loss in usefulness of long-lived assets (assets that will last longer than one year). Examples of long-lived assets are buildings, office furniture, store fixtures, machines, computers, trucks, and vehicles. Assets lose their usefulness for two reasons: (1) **physical depreciation**—simply wearing out or being used up, such as a vehicle's being beyond repair, and (2) **functional depreciation**—becoming obsolete or inadequate, such as a machine's being outdated because more efficient machines have been developed. Remember that depreciation represents a systematic procedure for spreading the cost of plant and equipment over the fiscal periods in which the company receives services from the assets.

An item of supplies is bought and used up in one fiscal period; its cost is charged to that fiscal period. In contrast, equipment is used over several fiscal periods. Thus, the cost of the equipment must be spread out over several periods, in accordance with the matching principle.

The firm records depreciation by debiting Depreciation Expense and crediting Accumulated Depreciation. It treats Accumulated Depreciation as a deduction from the related asset account. Accumulated Depreciation is thus a contra account. You can record depreciation as an adjusting entry at the end of each month or postpone recording it until the end of the fiscal year, except when there is a change in the assets, such as a sale or a trade-in. In that case, first record depreciation of the asset from the beginning of the fiscal year until the date of the change, and *then* make any other accounting entries to record the sale or trade-in.

Determining the Amount of Depreciation

To determine the depreciation of a long-lived asset, you must take into account three elements.

Machinery and equipment aren't the only assets that are depreciated. Professional sports teams and sponsors depreciate players as they age and become less useful to the organization.

1. The **depreciation base** is the full depreciation of an asset. Full depreciation is the total cost of an asset less its trade-in or salvage value.
2. The length of the useful life of the asset.
3. The method of depreciation chosen to allocate the depreciation base over the useful life of the asset.

Depreciation Base

When a business entity first puts an asset into service, it is hard to predict the amount of the trade-in or salvage (scrap) value, especially when such a trade-in will not take place for many years. Many firms make estimates based on their own experience or on data supplied by trade associations or government agencies. If the firm expects the salvage value to be insignificant in comparison with the cost of the asset, the accountant often assumes the salvage value to be zero.

Useful Life

The length of an asset's useful life is affected not only by the amount of physical wear and tear to which it is subjected, but also by technological change and innovation. For accounting purposes, the useful life of an asset is based on the expected use of the asset, in keeping with the company's replacement policy. An average car, for example, may have a useful life of five years. However, a car rental company may replace its cars every year in order to offer customers the latest models. A company operating a fleet of cars for its sales force may replace the cars every three years.

CALCULATING DEPRECIATION

Objective 2

Calculate depreciation by the straight-line method, units-of-production method, double-declining-balance method, and sum-of-the-years'-digits method.

The objective of recording depreciation is to systematically allocate the cost of a long-lived asset over the asset's useful life. However, a firm need not use the same method of depreciation for all its assets.

The four most common methods of computing depreciation are the (1) straight-line method, (2) units-of-production method, (3) double-declining-balance method, and (4) sum-of-the-years'-digits method. Methods 3 and 4 represent **accelerated depreciation**. In accelerated depreciation, depreciation is speeded up: Larger amounts of depreciation are taken during the early life of an asset, and smaller amounts are taken during the later years of an asset's life.

Remember!

Straight-line divides the depreciation into equal parts over the useful life of an asset, whereas some other methods (double-declining-balance and sum-of-the-years'-digits) are considered accelerated (they assign greater amounts of depreciation in the early years).

Straight-Line Method

A firm that uses the **straight-line method** to calculate depreciation charges an equal amount of depreciation for each year of service anticipated. The accountant computes the annual depreciation by dividing the depreciation base (cost minus trade-in value, if any) by the number of years of useful life predicted for the asset.

$$\text{Depreciation per Year} = \frac{\text{Cost} - \text{Trade-in Value}}{\text{Useful Life (in years)}}$$

The percentage rate of depreciation per year is determined by dividing the number of years of useful life into 1. For instance, take an asset with an estimated life of eight years:

$$\frac{1}{8 \text{ years}} = .125 \qquad .125 \times 100 = \underline{\underline{12.5\%}}$$

You always apply the depreciation rate against the depreciation base (cost less trade-in value).

Now let's look at two examples.

Example 1 A truck costs $30,000 and has a useful life of six years. The estimated trade-in value at the end of six years is $4,800.

$$\text{Depreciation per Year} = \frac{\$30,000 - \$4,800}{6} = \frac{\$25,200}{6} = \underline{\underline{\$4,200}}$$

$$\text{Depreciation Rate per Year} = \frac{1}{6 \text{ years}} = .1667 \qquad .1667 \times 100 = \underline{\underline{16.67\%}}$$

Example 2 A neon sign costs $3,200 and has a useful life of eight years. The estimated trade-in value at the end of eight years is zero.

$$\text{Depreciation per Year} = \frac{\$3,200 - 0}{8} = \frac{\$3,200}{8} = \underline{\underline{\$400}}$$

$$\text{Depreciation Rate per Year} = \frac{1}{8 \text{ years}} = .125 \qquad .125 \times 100 = \underline{\underline{12.5\%}}$$

A neon sign is a highly visible asset to a business. The useful life of a sign or another asset may be estimated using past experience and IRS guidelines. Useful life is the length of time the asset is appropriate for the business, not necessarily the actual life of the asset.

Units-of-Production Method

The **units-of-production method** allocates an asset's cost based on its usage or productivity within the period. You can obtain the depreciation charge per unit of production by dividing the depreciation base by the total estimated units of production.

$$\text{Depreciation per Unit of Production} = \frac{\text{Cost} - \text{Trade-in Value}}{\text{Estimated Units of Production}}$$

Example 1 A salesperson's car costs $19,000 and has a useful life of 60,000 miles. The estimated trade-in value at the end of 60,000 miles is $6,400. The car is driven 18,500 miles this year.

$$\text{Depreciation per Mile} = \frac{\$19,000 - \$6,400}{60,000 \text{ miles}} \quad \frac{\$12,600}{60,000 \text{ miles}}$$

$$= \underline{\$.21} \text{ per mile}$$

$$\text{Depreciation for 18,500 miles} = 18,500 \text{ miles} \times \$.21 \text{ per mile}$$

$$= \underline{\$3,885}$$

Remember!

Once you have computed the depreciation per unit (mile, hour, etc.), you must then multiply the unit amount by the number of units produced.

Example 2 A small bulldozer costs $82,000 and has a useful life of 4,000 hours. The estimated salvage value after 4,000 hours is $7,600. The firm uses the bulldozer for 380 hours this year.

$$\text{Depreciation per Hour} = \frac{\$82,000 - \$7,600}{4,000 \text{ hours}} = \frac{\$74,400}{4,000 \text{ hours}} = \underline{\$18.60} \text{ per hour}$$

$$\text{Depreciation for 380 hours} = 380 \text{ hours} \times \$18.60 \text{ per hour} = \underline{\$7,068}$$

Double-Declining-Balance Method

The **double-declining-balance method** is an accelerated method of depreciation allowing larger amounts of depreciation to be taken in the early years of an asset's life. Some accountants reason that the amount charged to depreciation should be higher during an asset's early years, when it is more productive and efficient, to offset the higher repair and maintenance expenses of the asset's later years. The total annual expense then tends to be equalized over the entire life of the asset.

For an asset that has a life of three years or more, this method allows a firm to calculate depreciation by *multiplying the book value (cost less accumulated depreciation) at the beginning of the year by* twice *the straight-line rate.*

Trade-in or salvage value is not counted in determining depreciation by the double-declining-balance method until the end of the depreciation schedule. As with other methods, an asset may not be depreciated below its salvage value.

To compute depreciation by the double-declining-balance method, follow these steps:

1. Calculate the straight-line depreciation rate.
2. Multiply the straight-line rate by 2.
3. Multiply the book value of the asset at the beginning of the year by double the straight-line rate.

During the first year, the book value of an asset is the same as its cost, because no depreciation has been taken. So for the first year only, multiply the cost by twice the straight-line rate.

FYI

Under the double-declining-balance method, book value never reaches zero. A company typically switches over to the straight-line method when the straight-line depreciation rate equals or exceeds the double-declining-balance rate.

Example 1 A firm's word processing equipment costs $40,000 and has a useful life of five years. The estimated trade-in value at the end of five years is zero.

1. Compute the straight-line depreciation rate:

$$\text{Straight-Line Depreciation Rate} = \frac{1}{5 \text{ years}} = .2 \quad .2 \times 100 = \underline{20\%}$$

2. Twice the straight-line rate $= .2 \times 2 = .4 \quad .4 \times 100 = \underline{40\%}.$
3. Depreciation per Year $=$ Book Value at Beginning of Year $\times$ .4.

Year	Beginning Book Value	Double-Declining-Balance Rate	Straight-Line Rate	Computation of Depreciation Expense	Ending Book Value
1	$40,000	.4	$\frac{1}{5} = .2$	$40,000 × .4 = $16,000	$40,000 − $16,000 = $24,000
2	24,000	.4	$\frac{1}{4} = .25$	24,000 × .4 = 9,600	24,000 − 9,600 = 14,400
3	14,400	.4	$\frac{1}{3} = .33$	14,400 × .4 = 5,760	14,400 − 5,760 = 8,640
4	8,640	.4	$\frac{1}{2} = .5$	8,640 × .5 = 4,320	8,640 − 4,320 = 4,320
5	4,320	.4	$\frac{1}{1} = 1$	4,320 × 1 = 4,320	4,320 − 4,320 = 0
Total				$40,000	

Computation of straight-line rate = 1 divided by the remaining number of years.

Notice that in the fourth year the straight-line depreciation rate is greater than the double-declining-balance rate. That is because a company typically switches over to the straight-line method when the straight-line depreciation rate equals or exceeds the double-declining-balance rate.

Example 2 A delivery van costs $24,000 and has a useful life of six years. The estimated trade-in value at the end of six years is $4,600.

1. Compute the straight-line depreciation rate:

$$\text{Straight-Line Depreciation Rate} = \frac{1}{6 \text{ years}} = .1667$$

$$.1667 \times 100 = 16.67\% = \frac{1}{6}$$

Since the decimal equivalent of $\frac{1}{6}$ has a remainder (.1667), it is more accurate to use the fraction.

2. Twice the straight-line rate = $\frac{1}{6} \times 2 = \frac{2}{6} = \frac{1}{3}$.

3. Depreciation per Year = Book Value at Beginning of Year × $\frac{1}{3}$.

FYI

The switch to straight-line is made whether or not a trade-in is expected on an asset.

Year	Beginning Book Value	Double-Declining-Balance Rate	Straight-Line Rate	Computation of Depreciation Expense	Ending Book Value
1	$24,000.00	$\frac{1}{3}$	$\frac{1}{6}$	$24,000.00 × $\frac{1}{3}$ = $ 8,000.00	$24,000.00 − $8,000.00 = $16,000.00
2	16,000.00	$\frac{1}{3}$	$\frac{1}{5}$	16,000.00 × $\frac{1}{3}$ = 5,333.33	16,000.00 − 5,333.33 = 10,666.67
3	10,666.67	$\frac{1}{3}$	$\frac{1}{4}$	10,666.67 × $\frac{1}{3}$ = 3,555.56	10,666.67 − 3,555.56 = 7,111.11
4	7,111.11	$\frac{1}{3}$	$\frac{1}{3}$	7,111.11 − 4,600.00 = 2,511.11 × $\frac{1}{3}$ = 837.04	7,111.11 − 837.04 = 6,274.07
5	6,274.07	$\frac{1}{3}$	$\frac{1}{2}$	6,274.07 − 4,600.00 = 1,674.07 × $\frac{1}{2}$ = 837.04	6,274.07 − 837.04 = 5,437.03
6	5,437.03	$\frac{1}{3}$	1	5,437.03 − 4,600.00 = 837.03 × 1 = 837.03	5,437.03 − 837.03 = 4,600.00
Total				$19,400.00	

Observe carefully that the trade-in or salvage value is not counted until the fourth year. When you use the double-declining-balance method and there is a trade-in value involved, the book value gradually declines until it reaches the amount of the trade-in value. *An asset must not be depreciated beyond its trade-in value.* For example, take the delivery van. During the fifth year, the normal depreciation would be one-third of the book value at the beginning of the year. Normally, depreciation for the year and the ending book value would be calculated:

Depreciation Expense $= \$6{,}274.07 \times \frac{1}{3} = \underline{\$2{,}091.36}$

Book Value at End of Year $= \$6{,}274.07 - \$2{,}091.36 = \underline{\underline{\$4{,}182.71}}$

Obviously, if you calculate depreciation in this manner, the book value of the van ($4,182.71) dips below the established trade-in value ($4,600). Notice in the chart that in this year, the straight-line rate exceeds the double-declining balance rate, so the former is used in this and the final year to bring the trade-in to the predetermined $4,600 amount.

Sum-of-the-Years'-Digits Method

The **sum-of-the-years'-digits method** is an accelerated method of depreciation and yields a large proportion of depreciation during the early years of an asset's life. It does this on a reducing-fraction basis. To compute depreciation by this method, follow these steps:

1. Determine the useful life in years. Then find the sum of the years' digits. For example, suppose the asset has an expected life of three years. Then add to find the sum of year 1, year 2, and year 3.

$$1 + 2 + 3 = 6$$

You can also determine the sum of the years by the following formula:

$$\frac{\text{Life}^2 + \text{Life}}{2}$$

For example, a life of three years would give

$$\frac{3^2 + 3}{2} = \frac{9 + 3}{2} = \frac{12}{2} = \underline{\underline{6}}$$

2. Record the years in reverse (or descending) order in the numerator (top) of the fraction and the sum of the years' digits in the denominator (bottom) of the fraction:

$$\frac{3}{6} + \frac{2}{6} + \frac{1}{6} = \frac{6}{6}$$

3. Multiply the decreasing fractions by the depreciation base (cost less trade-in value).

Example 1 A stamping machine costs $22,400 and has a useful life of five years. The estimated salvage value at the end of five years is $800. The depreciation base is $21,600 ($22,400 − $800).

Step 1*	Step 2	Step 3	
		Year	Depreciation Expense
1	$\frac{5}{15}$	1	$\frac{5}{15} \times \$21,600 = \$ 7,200$
2	$\frac{4}{15}$	2	$\frac{4}{15} \times 21,600 = 5,760$
3	$\frac{3}{15}$	3	$\frac{3}{15} \times 21,600 = 4,320$
4	$\frac{2}{15}$	4	$\frac{2}{15} \times 21,600 = 2,880$
5	$\frac{1}{15}$	5	$\frac{1}{15} \times 21,600 = 1,440$
15	$\frac{15}{15}$		$\$21,600$

*Step 1 can be calculated as follows: $\dfrac{5^2 + 5}{2} = \dfrac{25 + 5}{2} = \dfrac{30}{2} = 15.$

Example 2 A forklift costs $18,000 and has a useful life of six years. The estimated salvage value at the end of six years is $1,200.

Step 1*	Step 2	Step 3	
		Year	Depreciation Expense
1	$\frac{6}{21}$	1	$\frac{6}{21} \times \$16,800 = \$ 4,800$
2	$\frac{5}{21}$	2	$\frac{5}{21} \times 16,800 = 4,000$
3	$\frac{4}{21}$	3	$\frac{4}{21} \times 16,800 = 3,200$
4	$\frac{3}{21}$	4	$\frac{3}{21} \times 16,800 = 2,400$
5	$\frac{2}{21}$	5	$\frac{2}{21} \times 16,800 = 1,600$
6	$\frac{1}{21}$	6	$\frac{1}{21} \times 16,800 = 800$
21	$\frac{21}{21}$		$\$16,800$

*Step 1 can be calculated as follows: $\dfrac{6^2 + 6}{2} = \dfrac{36 + 6}{2} = \dfrac{42}{2} = 21.$

Accelerated depreciation may be used for certain types of assets, such as state-of-the-art computer systems, that become obsolete more quickly than other assets.

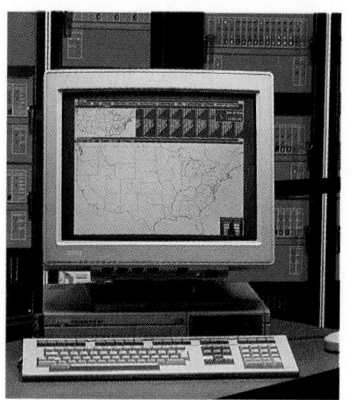

Comparison of Three Methods

You can see in the following charts that the double-declining-balance method and the sum-of-the-years'-digits method yield relatively large amounts of depreciation during the early years of use of an asset. For this reason they are examples of *accelerated depreciation*. In these charts, assume that a hoist costs $6,000 and has a useful life of four years. Estimated salvage value at the end of four years is $400.

Straight-Line Method			
Year	Depreciation Expense	Accumulated Depreciation	Book Value at End of Year
1	$\dfrac{\$6,000 - \$400}{4 \text{ years}} = \$1,400$	$\$1,400$	$\$6,000 - \$1,400 = \$4,600$
2	1,400	$\$1,400 + \$1,400 = \$2,800$	$6,000 - 2,800 = 3,200$
3	1,400	$2,800 + 1,400 = 4,200$	$6,000 - 4,200 = 1,800$
4	1,400	$4,200 + 1,400 = 5,600$	$6,000 - 5,600 = 400$
Total	$\$5,600$		

		Double-Declining-Balance Method (Based on Twice the Straight-Line Rate)*		
Year	Beginning Book Value	Depreciation Expense	Accumulated Depreciation	Book Value at End of Year
1	$6,000	$6,000 × .5 = $3,000	$3,000	$6,000 − $3,000 = $3,000
2	3,000	3,000 × .5 = 1,500	$3,000 + $1,500 = 4,500	6,000 − 4,500 = 1,500
3	1,500	1,500 × .5 = 750	4,500 + 750 = 5,250	6,000 − 5,250 = 750
4	750	$750 − $400 = 350	5,250 + 350 = 5,600	6,000 − 5,600 = 400
Total		$5,600		

$$*\frac{1}{4} \times 2 = \frac{2}{4} = .50.$$

	Sum-of-the-Year's-Digits Method*		
Year	Depreciation Expense	Accumulated Depreciation	Book Value at End of Year
1	$\frac{4}{10}$ × $5,600 = $2,240	$2,240	$6,000 − $2,240 = $3,760
2	$\frac{3}{10}$ × 5,600 = 1,680	$2,240 + $1,680 = 3,920	6,000 − 3,920 = 2,080
3	$\frac{2}{10}$ × 5,600 = 1,120	3,920 + 1,120 = 5,040	6,000 − 5,040 = 960
4	$\frac{1}{10}$ × 5,600 = 560	5,040 + 560 = 5,600	6,000 − 5,600 = 400
$\frac{10}{10}$	$\frac{10}{10}$ $5,600		

*The sum of the years' digits can be calculated as follows: $\frac{4^2 + 4}{2} = \frac{16 + 4}{2} = \frac{20}{2} = 10.$

A firm may calculate its regular depreciation by any of these methods: straight-line, double-declining-balance, units of production, or sum-of-the-years'-digits. For each separate asset, a company should use the same method of depreciation for each year, to follow the principle of consistency. Since depreciation is an expense, its amount will be subtracted from total revenue to arrive at net income. If the depreciation method is changed from year to year, it becomes impossible to compare the firm's performance from one year to the next.

DEPRECIATION FOR PERIODS OF LESS THAN A YEAR

Businesses do not buy nor sell or discard all their depreciable assets on the first and last days of their fiscal period. They buy and sell assets throughout the year. How, then, do they calculate depreciation? As you look at the examples in the following table, remember that when a business entity acquires a depreciable asset during the year, the accountant usually figures depreciation to the nearest whole month. If the firm held the asset for *less* than half a given month, the accountant doesn't count that month. But if the firm held it for half of a given month or more, the accountant counts it as a whole month. All of the examples in the table assume that the firm's fiscal year ends on December 31.

Date Acquired	Cost	Trade-in Value	Method	Useful Life	Depreciation for First Year
April 12	$9,000	$1,000	Straight-line	5 years	$\dfrac{\$9,000 - \$1,000}{5 \text{ years}} = \$1,600 \text{ per year}$ $\$1,600 \times \frac{9}{12} = \$1,200$ for 9 months
October 19	6,000	200	Double-declining-balance	8 years	$\$6,000 \times \frac{1}{4} = \$1,500$ for first year $\$1,500 \times \frac{2}{12} = \$250$ for 2 months
August 8	6,800	500	Sum-of-the-years'-digits	6 years	$\$6,300 \times \frac{6}{21} = \$1,800$ for first year $\$1,800 \times \frac{5}{12} = \$750$ for 5 months

Suppose a firm buys an asset on June 14. Depreciation is computed from June 1, counting the entire month. But if the firm buys that asset any time after June 15, no depreciation will be computed for the month of June. Software programs are readily available to calculate and keep track of depreciation by the various methods.

CAPITAL AND REVENUE EXPENDITURES

Objective 3

Differentiate among capital expenditures, revenue expenditures, and extraordinary-repairs expenditures.

The term *expenditure* refers to spending, either by paying cash now or by promising to pay in the future for services received or assets purchased. After paying the initial price for an asset, you often have to pay out more, either to maintain the asset's operating efficiency or to increase its capacity. So there are two classifications of expenditures: revenue and capital.

Capital expenditures include the initial costs debited to plant and equipment; they also include any costs of enlarging or increasing the capacity of assets. Capital expenditures benefit more than one accounting period. Examples are expenditures for buying a building, enlarging it, putting in air conditioning, and replacing a stairway with an elevator. All these expenditures result in debits to an asset account.

Revenue expenditures include the costs of maintaining the operation of an asset, such as the expense of making normal repairs. Examples are expenditures for painting, plumbing repairs, fuel, property taxes, and so on. These expenditures provide benefit only during the current accounting period and are recorded as debits to expense accounts.

EXTRAORDINARY-REPAIRS EXPENDITURES

Extraordinary-repairs expenditures refer to a major overhaul or reconditioning that either extends the useful life of an asset beyond its original estimated life or increases its estimated salvage value. An accountant usually records expenditures for extraordinary repairs as debits to Accumulated Depreciation and credits to Cash or Accounts Payable.

For example, on January 3, Year 1, a firm bought a used car for $12,000. The car's estimated useful life is four years and its trade-in value is $3,200;

straight-line annual depreciation expense is $2,200. On January 5, Year 4, the firm puts in a new engine and has other major repairs done, for which it spends $2,800 in cash. The entry in general journal form is as follows:

	DATE		DESCRIPTION	POST. REF.	DEBIT	CREDIT	
1	Year 4						1
2	Jan.	5	Accumulated Depreciation, Car		2 8 0 0 00		2
3			Cash			2 8 0 0 00	3
4			New engine installed in				4
5			company car.				5
6							6

This extraordinary repair extends the life of the car from the present one additional year to three additional years. Here are the balances, together with the $2,800 payment, as shown by T accounts:

Car	
+	−
Jan. 3, Year 1 12,000	

Accumulated Depreciation, Car		
−	+	
Jan. 5, Year 4 2,800	Dec. 31, Year 1	2,200
	Dec. 31, Year 2	2,200
	Dec. 31, Year 3	2,200

■ ■ ■
Remember!

When recording an extraordinary repair, debit Accumulated Depreciation. This maintains the original cost figure in the asset account, increases the book value, and yields a new depreciation base.

The car's book value before the extraordinary repair was $5,400 ($12,000 − $6,600). The accountant debits the Accumulated Depreciation account (rather than the asset account) to preserve the original cost figure in the asset account. Another reason is to partially offset the depreciation of previous years, since the estimated life is extended. In this example, the car cost $12,000, not $14,800. We can see this in the balance sheet as follows:

Plant and Equipment:			
Car	$12 0 0 0 00		
Less Accumulated Depreciation	3 8 0 0 00	$8 2 0 0 00	

When it comes to recording the remaining depreciation on this asset, the accountant now has a new cost base, which he or she uses to determine the new depreciation base. Assume that the trade-in value is still $3,200.

New book value ($12,000 − $3,800) $8,200
Less trade-in value   3,200

New depreciation base $5,000

5,000 ÷ 3 years = $1,666.67

The adjusting entry for depreciation of the car at the end of Year 4 is as shown on the following page.

Remember!

For an extraordinary-repair cost, debit Accumulated Depreciation instead of Repair Expense, and credit Cash or Accounts Payable.

	DATE		DESCRIPTION	POST. REF.	DEBIT	CREDIT	
1	Year 4		Adjusting Entry				1
2	Dec.	31	Depreciation Expense, Car		1 6 6 6 67		2
3			Accumulated Depreciation, Car			1 6 6 6 67	3
4							4

Assuming that no additional expenditures are made for extraordinary repairs, the adjusting entries for the remaining two years (Years 5 and 6) will be $1,666.67 for Year 5 and $1,666.66 for Year 6.

DISPOSITION OF PLANT AND EQUIPMENT

Objective 4

Prepare journal entries for discarding of assets fully depreciated, discarding of assets not fully depreciated, sale of assets involving a loss, sale of assets involving a gain, exchange of assets involving a loss on the trade, and exchange of assets involving a gain on the trade.

Sooner or later a business entity disposes of its long-lived assets by (1) discarding or retiring them, (2) selling them, or (3) trading them in for other assets. **If the assets are not fully depreciated, the accountant must first make an entry to bring the depreciation up to date.** Let's look at some examples. (Ordinarily entries involving Cash would be recorded in the cash journals; however, for simplification and clarity, we present all the following entries in general journal form.)

Discarding or Retiring Plant and Equipment

When long-lived assets are no longer useful to the business and have no market value, a firm discards them.

Discarding of Fully Depreciated Assets A display case that cost $1,920 and has been fully depreciated is given away as junk. The present status of the accounts is as follows:

Store Equipment		Accumulated Depreciation, Store Equipment	
+	−	−	+
Bal. 1,920			Bal. 1,920

The journal entry to record the disposal of the asset looks like this:

	DATE		DESCRIPTION	POST. REF.	DEBIT	CREDIT	
6	July	10	Accumulated Depreciation,				6
7			Store Equipment		1 9 2 0 00		7
8			Store Equipment			1 9 2 0 00	8
9			Discarded a fully depreciated				9
10			display case.				10
11							11

Although fully depreciated assets are retained on the books as long as they remain in use, the firm may not take any additional depreciation on them. Once an asset is fully depreciated, the asset's book value remains at its estimated salvage value unless an extraordinary repair is made or the company disposes of the asset.

Discarding an Asset Not Fully Depreciated A firm discards a time clock that cost $1,740. No salvage value is recognized. Accumulated Depreciation up to the end of the previous year is $1,370; depreciation for the current year is $190. The present balances of the accounts are as follows:

Office Equipment	Accumulated Depreciation, Office Equipment
+ | −	− | +
Bal. 1,740	Bal. 1,370

Record the entry to depreciate the asset up to date:

	DATE		DESCRIPTION	POST. REF.	DEBIT	CREDIT	
12	20–						12
13	Aug.	12	Depreciation Expense, Office				13
14			Equipment		1 9 0 00		14
15			Accumulated Depreciation,				15
16			Office Equipment			1 9 0 00	16
17			Depreciation on time clock				17
18			for the partial year.				18

The T accounts look like this:

Depreciation Expense, Office Equipment	Accumulated Depreciation, Office Equipment
+ | −	− | +
190	Bal. 1,370
	190
	1,560

Remember!

A gain occurs when the amount received for an asset is greater than the book value. A loss occurs when the amount received is less than the book value. To calculate the book value, the depreciation must be brought up to date before a sale, disposal, or trade-in.

The journal entry to record the disposal of the asset is as follows:

	DATE		DESCRIPTION	POST. REF.	DEBIT	CREDIT	
19		12	Accumulated Depreciation,				19
20			Office Equipment		1 5 6 0 00		20
21			Loss on Disposal of Plant and				21
22			Equipment		1 8 0 00		22
23			Office Equipment			1 7 4 0 00	23
24			Discarded a time clock.				24

The T accounts look like this:

Accumulated Depreciation, Office Equipment		Loss on Disposal of Plant and Equipment		Office Equipment	
−	+	+	−	+	−
1,560	Bal. 1,370	180		Bal. 1,740	1,740
	190				
	1,560				

Remember!

Gains or losses from disposal of assets go in either the Other Revenue or the Other Expenses section of the income statement.

The book value of the asset is $180 ($1,740 − $1,560). Because the firm realized nothing from the disposal of the asset, the loss is for the same amount as the book value.

Loss on Disposal of Plant and Equipment is an expense account that appears under Other Expenses on the income statement and is used when a firm sells or trades in an asset and receives an amount less than the book value of the asset.

Selling of Plant and Equipment

Remember!

Market value (the amount we could sell an asset for) often differs from book value (cost less accumulated depreciation).

Naturally, it is very hard to estimate the exact trade-in or salvage value of a long-lived asset. It is quite likely that when a firm sells or trades in such an asset, the amount realized will differ from the estimated amount.

Sale of an Asset at a Loss Suppose that a firm sells a used lathe for $220. This lathe originally cost $2,100; accumulated depreciation up to the end of the previous year (December 31) was $1,680. Yearly depreciation is $210. The lathe is sold on August 21.

The present balances of the accounts are as follows:

Factory Equipment		Accumulated Depreciation, Factory Equipment	
+	−	−	+
Bal. 2,100			Bal. 1,680

We record the depreciation of the asset to the present date:

Remember!

When disposing of plant and equipment that are not fully depreciated, an entry must first be made to bring the depreciation up to date. Then the entry to discard, sell, or trade the asset may be made.

	DATE		DESCRIPTION	POST. REF.	DEBIT	CREDIT	
1	20–						1
2	Aug.	21	Depreciation Expense, Factory				2
3			Equipment		1 4 0 00		3
4			Accumulated Depreciation,				4
5			Factory Equipment			1 4 0 00	5
6			Depreciation on lathe for				6
7			8 months, $140.				7
8			($210 × 8/12)				8

By T accounts, the situation looks like this:

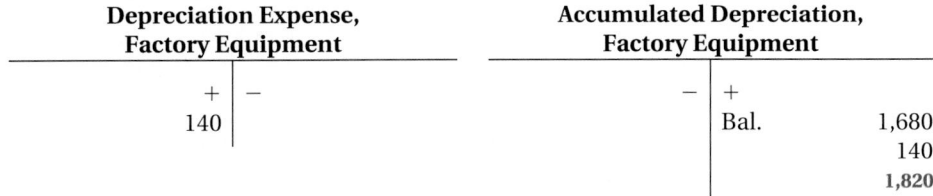

Depreciation Expense, Factory Equipment				Accumulated Depreciation, Factory Equipment		
+	–			–	+	
140					Bal.	1,680
						140
						1,820

The entry, in general journal form, to record the sale of the lathe is as follows:

	DATE	DESCRIPTION	POST. REF.	DEBIT	CREDIT	
9	21	Cash		2 2 0 00		9
10		Accumulated Depreciation,				10
11		Factory Equipment		1 8 2 0 00		11
12		Loss on Disposal of Plant and				12
13		Equipment		6 0 00		13
14		Factory Equipment			2 1 0 0 00	14
15		Sold a lathe for $220				15
16		having an orginal cost of				16
17		$2,100 and accumulated				17
18		depreciation of $1,820.				18
19						19

For purposes of illustration, let's record the above entry in the T accounts as follows:

Cash				Accumulated Depreciation, Factory Equipment		
+	–			–	+	
220				1,820	Bal.	1,680
						140
						1,820

Loss on Disposal of Plant and Equipment				Factory Equipment		
+	–			+	–	
60			Bal.	2,100		2,100

Note that the book value of the lathe is $280 ($2,100 − $1,820). When the firm sells it for $220, the loss is $60 because the amount received for the lathe is $60 less than its book value.

Sale of an Asset at a Gain Suppose that a firm sells an electronic analyzer for $620. The firm had originally paid $4,400; accumulated depreciation to the end of the previous year, December 31, was $3,960. Yearly depreciation is $360. The electronic analyzer is sold on October 18. The present balances of the accounts are as follows.

	Shop Equipment			Accumulated Depreciation, Shop Equipment	
	+	−		−	+
Bal.	4,400			Bal.	3,960

We record the depreciation of the asset to the present date:

	DATE		DESCRIPTION	POST. REF.	DEBIT	CREDIT	
1	20–						1
2	Oct.	18	Depreciation Expense, Shop				2
3			Equipment		3 0 0 00		3
4			Accumulated Depreciation,				4
5			Shop Equipment			3 0 0 00	5
6			Depreciation on electronic				6
7			analyzer for 10 months, $300.				7
8			($360 × 10/12)				8
9							9

Remember!

The calculations shown in the explanation are for illustration and would not normally appear in practice.

By T accounts, the situation looks like this:

	Depreciation Expense, Shop Equipment			Accumulated Depreciation, Shop Equipment	
	+	−		−	+
	300			Bal.	3,960
					300
					4,260

The general journal entry to record the sale of the electronic analyzer is as follows:

	DATE		DESCRIPTION	POST. REF.	DEBIT	CREDIT	
10		18	Cash		6 2 0 00		10
11			Accumulated Depreciation,				11
12			Shop Equipment		4 2 6 0 00		12
13			Shop Equipment			4 4 0 0 00	13
14			Gain on Disposal of Plant and				14
15			Equipment			4 8 0 00	15
16			Sold an electronic analyzer				16
17			for $620 having an orginal				17
18			cost of $4,400 and				18
19			accumulated depreciation of				19
20			$4,260.				20

The T accounts look like this:

Cash			Accumulated Depreciation, Shop Equipment		
+	−		−	+	
620			4,260	Bal.	3,960
					300
					4,260

Shop Equipment			Gain on Disposal of Plant and Equipment		
+	−		−	+	
Bal. 4,400	4,400				480

The revenue account **Gain on Disposal of Plant and Equipment** appears under Other Income in the income statement and is used when a firm sells or trades in an asset and receives an amount greater than the book value for that asset.

The book value of the electronic analyzer is $140 ($4,400 − $4,260). When the firm sells the electronic analyzer for $620, the firm's gain is $480 ($620 − $140). The amount received for the item is $480 more than its book value.

Exchange of Long-lived Assets for Other Similar Assets Without Recognition of Gain or Loss

Often a business trades in one asset for another, using the old item as part payment for the new one. The trade-in allowance may differ from the book value of the asset. If the trade-in allowance is greater than the book value, the firm has a gain; if the trade-in allowance is less than the book value, it has a loss. However, federal income tax laws state that when assets held for productive use are exchanged for similar assets, *no gain or loss is recognized.* In effect, the gain or loss is absorbed into the recorded cost of the new asset.

Exchange When Trade-in Value Is Less Than Book Value Suppose that a firm bought a delivery truck for $15,200. Four years later, the truck has accumulated depreciation of $13,100 (book value = $15,200 − $13,100 = $2,100). The firm buys a new truck, with a list price of $19,700, trading in the old one, for which the firm is allowed only $1,600, and paying the difference in cash. Assume that the depreciation for the year is already up to date. The present status of the accounts is as follows:

Delivery Equipment			Accumulated Depreciation, Delivery Equipment		
+	−		−	+	
Bal. 15,200				Bal.	13,100

When you use the income tax method of accounting, the loss is absorbed in the cost of the new equipment. (The recorded cost for the new asset is determined by adding the cash paid to the book value of the old asset [18,100 + 2,100 = 20,200].) In this case, the accountant added the loss of $500 ($2,100 book value − $1,600 trade-in value) to the price of the new equipment, as shown on the following page.

Cost of old equipment	$15,200
Less accumulated depreciation	13,100
Book value	$2,100
Less trade-in allowance	1,600
Loss	$ 500
Quoted price of new equipment	$19,700
Plus loss absorbed in recorded cost of new equipment	500
Recorded cost of new equipment	$20,200

The firm's accountant records the transaction by the following steps:

1. Credit Cash, $18,100 (quoted price of the new truck, $19,700, minus $1,600, which is the trade-in allowance on the old truck).
2. Close or clear the account of the old asset: credit Delivery Equipment, $15,200.
3. Close or clear the Accumulated Depreciation account of the old asset: debit Accumulated Depreciation, $13,100.
4. Calculate the loss and add it to the quoted price of the new equipment. Then debit the new asset for this amount.

The entry in general journal form (with the steps labeled) is as follows:

	DATE		DESCRIPTION	POST. REF.	DEBIT	CREDIT	
11	Nov.	(4)	Delivery Equipment		20 2 0 0 00		11
12		(3)	Accumulated Depreciation,				12
13			Delivery Equipment		13 1 0 0 00		13
14		(1)	Cash			18 1 0 0 00	14
15		(2)	Delivery Equipment			15 2 0 0 00	15
16			Bought a new delivery truck				16
17			having a list price of $19,700.				17
18			Received a trade-in				18
19			allowance of $1,600 on old				19
20			delivery truck, having an				20
21			original cost of $15,200 and				21
22			accumulated depreciation of				22
23			$13,100.				23

Remember!

For income tax purposes, gain or loss is not recognized when assets held for productive use are exchanged for similar assets—the gain or loss is absorbed into the recorded cost of the new asset.

You can also use this technique to verify the cost recorded for the new equipment. For income tax purposes, the firm cannot count the $500 loss at this time; however, the firm does have an additional $500 that it can take in depreciation in the future.

Exchange When Trade-in Value Is Greater Than Book Value A business bought a copier for $2,600. After some years, the business decides to trade it in on a new model. The old copier has accumulated depreciation of $2,480 *on the date of the trade-in,* leaving a book value of $120. The new copier has a list price of $3,410; however, the salesperson gives the firm a generous trade-in allowance of $310 on the old equipment, and the firm pays the difference in cash. The present status of the accounts is as follows:

Office Equipment		Accumulated Depreciation, Office Equipment	
+	−	−	+
Bal. 2,600			Bal. 2,480

The accountant records the cost of the new equipment at less than the list price, which indicates that a gain is involved. (The recorded cost for the new asset is determined by adding the cash paid to the book value of the old asset [3,100 + 120 = 3,220].) For income tax purposes, this gain has been absorbed in the price of the new equipment.

Cost of old equipment	$2,600
Less accumulated depreciation	2,480
Book value	$120
Trade-in allowance	$310
Less book value	120
Gain	$190
Quoted price of new equipment	$3,410
Less gain absorbed in recorded cost of new equipment	190
Recorded cost of new equipment	$3,220

The firm's accountant records the transaction by the following steps:

1. Credit Cash, $3,100 (quoted price of new copier, $3,410, minus the $310 trade-in allowance on the old model).
2. Close or clear the account of the old asset: credit Office Equipment, $2,600.
3. Close or clear the Accumulated Depreciation account of the old asset: debit Accumulated Depreciation, $2,480.
4. Calculate the gain and subtract it from the quoted price of the new equipment.

Here are the entries in general journal form with the steps labeled:

	DATE		DESCRIPTION	POST. REF.	DEBIT	CREDIT	
10	Nov.	(4)	Office Equipment		3 2 2 0 00		10
11		(3)	Accumulated Depreciation,				11
12			Office Equipment		2 4 8 0 00		12
13		(1)	Cash			3 1 0 0 00	13
14		(2)	Office Equipment			2 6 0 0 00	14
15			Bought a new copier having				15
16			a list price of $3,410.				16
17			Received a trade-in				17
18			allowance of $310 on old				18
19			copier, which had an original				19
20			cost of $2,600 and				20
21			accumulated depreciation of				21
22			$2,480.				22

For income tax purposes, the firm does not count the gain. However, the amount that the firm can take in depreciation in the future has been reduced by $190.

PLANT AND EQUIPMENT RECORDS

Objective 5

Maintain a plant and equipment subsidiary ledger.

Depreciation, which is regarded as an expense, vitally affects the net income of any business. Because net income is affected, the amount of income taxes owed is likewise affected, not only Depreciation Expense, but also Loss (or Gain) on Disposal affects net income. For income tax purposes, the business must be able to justify the amount of depreciation taken, as well as the gain or loss on disposal of assets.

We have discussed Plant and Equipment as a category on a classified balance sheet. Accountants use the term *plant* to include land, land improvements, and buildings.

Following is an illustration of the Plant and Equipment section of a balance sheet:

Plant and Equipment:			
Land		$ 6 0 0 0 00	
Land Improvements	$ 3 0 0 0 00		
Less Accumulated Depreciation	2 3 0 0 00	7 0 0 00	
Building	$40 0 0 0 00		
Less Accumulated Depreciation	28 0 0 0 00	12 0 0 0 00	
Office Equipment	$ 6 0 0 0 00		
Less Accumulated Depreciation	4 5 0 0 00	1 5 0 0 00	
Store Equipment	$18 0 0 0 00		
Less Accumulated Depreciation	14 0 0 0 00	4 0 0 0 00	
Delivery Equipment	$20 0 0 0 00		
Less Accumulated Depreciation	12 0 0 0 00	8 0 0 0 00	
Total Plant and Equipment			32 2 0 0 00

The Store Equipment account represents a functional group; it includes all types of equipment used in the operation of a store. Examples of store equipment are display cases, cash registers, counters, and storage shelves. Accountants maintain a separate depreciation record for each item in the plant and equipment ledger. The record may be in the form of a computer file or a card file. We will illustrate a card.

Store Equipment is a controlling account; the plant and equipment ledger is a subsidiary ledger. This relationship is like that of Accounts Receivable, which is a controlling account, and the accounts receivable ledger, which is a subsidiary ledger with an account for each individual charge customer. Figure 1 shows a record card in a firm's plant and equipment ledger. Posting to the subsidiary ledger will also be marked by a check mark in the journal's Post. Ref. column when the asset accounts and the related accumulated depreciation accounts are debited or credited.

PLANT AND EQUIPMENT RECORD

ITEM **Cash Register**　　　　　　　　　　　　　　　ACCOUNT NO. **128-1**

SERIAL NO. **ND37-4163**　　　　　　　　　　　　　MAKER **Security, Inc.**

FROM WHOM PURCHASED **Rogers Equipment Company**　　ESTIMATED

ESTIMATED LIFE **5**　　　　　　　　　　　　　　　SALVAGE VALUE **$300**

DEPRECIATION　　　　　DEPRECIATION　　　　　DEPRECIATION　　　　RATE OF

METHOD **Straight line**　PER YEAR **$900**　　PER MONTH **$75**　　DEPRECIATION **20%**

| DATE | EXPLANATION | ASSET | | | ACCUMULATED DEPRECIATION | | | BOOK VALUE |
		DEBIT	CREDIT	BALANCE	DEBIT	CREDIT	BALANCE	
7/3/Yr. 1		4,800		4,800				4,800
12/31/Yr. 1						450	450	4,350
12/31/Yr. 2						900	1,350	3,450
12/31/Yr. 3						900	2,250	2,550

FIGURE 1

Account 128 is the number of the general ledger account for Store Equipment. Account 128-1 is the first piece of equipment listed under Store Equipment in the plant and equipment ledger.

The plant and equipment record enables the accountant to calculate the total amount of the adjusting entry to be recorded on the company's work sheet. This total amount is found by adding the fiscal period's depreciation for each separate asset contained in the plant and equipment ledger. The amount of depreciation for each asset is determined by the schedule of depreciation for that asset. Also, plant and equipment records are valuable when a business has to submit insurance claims in the event of insured losses.

DEPRECIATION FOR FEDERAL INCOME TAX

Business firms are entitled to deduct depreciation on their income tax returns. However, the amount recorded on a company's income statement (involving the use of the straight-line, sum-of-the-years'-digits, units-of-production, or double-declining-balance method) may differ from the amount recorded on the company's income tax return.

For property acquired before 1981, companies could choose their own depreciation method for their income tax returns.

Accelerated Cost Recovery System

For property acquired between 1981 and 1986, companies used a set depreciation schedule called the Accelerated Cost Recovery System (ACRS) for their income tax returns. Under ACRS, assets were divided into classes according to length of life (three, five, ten, fifteen, or eighteen years). Percentages for annual depreciation of each class of assets were published in a series of tables developed by the federal government. Here are the tables for three types of assets:

	Classes of Assets (Property)		
Year	Three-Year Class	Five-Year Class	Ten-Year Class
1	25	15	8
2	38	23	14
3	37	21	12
4		21	10
5		21	10
6			10
7			9
8			9
9			9
10			9

The three-year class includes autos, light trucks, and some tools.
The five-year class includes equipment and machines.
The ten-year class includes pipelines and nuclear plants.
The fifteen- and eighteen-year classes are real estate.

Modified Accelerated Cost Recovery System

For property acquired after 1986, a revised schedule of depreciation called the **Modified Accelerated Cost Recovery System (MACRS)** was established. Under MACRS, assets are divided into eight classes. Here are the property classes as defined:

Property Class	Description
3-year property	Certain horses and tractor units for use over the road
5-year property	Autos, trucks, computers, typewriters, and copiers
7-year property	Office furniture and fixtures and any property that does not have a class life and that is not, by law, in any other class
10-year property	Vessels, barges, tugs, and similar water transportation equipment
15-year property	Wharves, roads, fences, and any municipal wastewater treatment plant
20-year property	Certain farm buildings and municipal sewers
27.5-year residential rental property	Rental houses and apartments
31.5-year real property	Office buildings and warehouses

Objective 6

Calculate the allowable depreciation for federal income tax returns using the Modified Accelerated Cost Recovery System.

Following are the approved schedules of percentage of cost allocated (written off or depreciated) each year for three-year, five-year, and seven-year property.

Year	Three-Year	Five-Year	Seven-Year
1	33.33	20.00	14.29
2	44.45	32.00	24.49
3	14.81	19.20	17.49
4	7.41	11.52	12.49
5		11.52	8.93
6	100.00	5.76	8.92
7			8.93
8		100.00	4.46
			100.00

FYI

Depreciation for five-year property is recorded over six fiscal years because under IRS guidelines, only a half-year's depreciation is taken during the first year.

To determine the depreciation for the year, multiply the cost of the asset by the percentage figure. For example, the first year's depreciation on a desk (classified as 7-year property) having a cost of $300 is $42.87 ($300 × .1429). Trade-in value is not counted.

CHAPTER REVIEW

Review of Performance Objectives

1. Allocate costs to Land, Land Improvements, and Buildings accounts.

   Land includes amounts paid for the land plus incidental charges connected with the purchase—for example, real estate agents' commissions, when the agent was retained by the buyer; legal fees; delinquent taxes paid by the buyer; surveying, clearing, and grading the land. *Land improvements* include costs of driveways, parking lots, trees and shrubs, and outdoor lighting systems. *Buildings* include amounts paid for labor and materials, architectural and engineering fees, premiums for insurance during construction, and interest on construction loans during the period of construction.

2. Calculate depreciation by the straight-line method, units-of-production method, double-declining-balance method, and sum-of-the-years'-digits method.

   The depreciation base is the cost of the asset less its trade-in or salvage value.

$$\text{Straight-Line Method} = \frac{\text{Cost} - \text{Trade-in Value}}{\text{Useful Life (in years)}}$$

$$\text{Units-of-Production Method} = \frac{\text{Cost} - \text{Trade-in Value}}{\text{Estimated Units of Production}} \times \text{Number of Units Produced}$$

$$\text{Double-Declining-Balance Method} = \text{Book Value at Beginning of Year} \times \text{Twice Straight-Line Rate}$$

$$\text{Sum-of-the-Years'-Digits Method} = \text{Reducing Fraction} \times (\text{Cost} - \text{Trade-in Value})$$

   Under the double-declining-balance method, book value never reaches zero. A company switches to the straight-line method when the double-declining-balance rate is equal to or exceeded by the straight-line rate. Also under the double-declining-balance method, the trade-in value is counted at the end of the schedule of depreciation. For the sum-of-the-years'-digits method, the numerator of the fraction is the years of the asset's life placed in reverse order. The denominator of the fraction is the sum of the years of the asset's life.

3. Differentiate among capital expenditures, revenue expenditures, and extraordinary-repairs expenditures.

   Capital expenditures include costs incurred to buy or increase the capacity of assets. Costs are debited to the asset accounts. *Revenue expenditures* include the costs of maintaining the operation of an asset, such as costs for fuel, painting, and normal repairs. Costs are debited to expense accounts. *Extraordinary-repairs expenditures* include the costs of prolonging the life of an asset or increasing its estimated salvage value, such as the cost of a new engine for a truck or a new roof for a building. Costs are debited to accumulated depreciation accounts.

4. Prepare journal entries for discarding of assets fully depreciated, discarding of assets not fully depreciated, sale of assets involving a loss, sale of assets involving a gain, exchange of assets involving a loss on the trade, and exchange of assets involving a gain on the trade.

   When a firm changes its Plant and Equipment accounts, as a result of selling, exchanging, or discarding its assets, the accountant must close or clear the asset accounts along with their respective Accumulated Depreciation accounts. When a firm discards, sells, or trades in an asset that has not yet been fully depreciated, the accountant must first depreciate the asset up to the present date. When the amount received for the old asset is less than the asset's book value, the accountant debits Loss on Disposal of Plant and Equipment. On the other hand, when a firm receives more for an asset than its book value, Gain on Disposal of Plant and Equipment is credited.

   When a firm trades in one asset for a similar asset, the entry must include the following four steps:

   a. Credit Cash or Accounts Payable for the difference between the quoted price of the new asset and the trade-in allowance.
   b. Credit the account of the old asset.
   c. Debit the Accumulated Depreciation account of the old asset.
   d. Debit the account of the new asset for the cash paid plus the book value of the old asset; or the recorded (adjusted) cost of the new equipment equals the price of the equipment plus the loss or minus the gain not recognized.

5. Maintain a plant and equipment subsidiary ledger.

   Plant and equipment records should consist of a controlling account and a subsidiary ledger. The subsidiary ledger should contain a card for each piece of equipment, listing the date acquired, cost, and depreciation taken to date. For income tax purposes, a subsidiary ledger is a must.

6. Calculate the allowable depreciation for federal income tax returns using the Modified Accelerated Cost Recovery System.

   First, determine the class of the property. Next, multiply the cost of the asset by the percentage listed in the schedule of depreciation for the Modified Accelerated Cost Recovery System.

Glossary

Accelerated depreciation Depreciation methods in which relatively larger amounts of depreciation are recorded during the early years of an asset's use and decreasing amounts in later years. (661)

Capital expenditures Costs incurred for the purchase of plant and equipment, as well as the cost of increasing the capacity or quality of assets; the firm receives services or benefits from this plant and equipment for more than one accounting period. (668)

Depreciation base Total cost of an asset less its trade-in or salvage value. (661)

Double-declining-balance method An accelerated method of depreciation; book value at the beginning of the year multiplied by twice the straight-line rate. (663)

Extraordinary-repairs expenditures Costs incurred for major overhauls or reconditioning of assets; repairs that either significantly prolong the life of the asset or increase its estimated salvage value. (668)

Gain on Disposal of Plant and Equipment The income account in which a gain is recorded when a firm sells or trades in an asset and receives an amount in excess of the book value for that asset; it appears under Other Income in the income statement. (675)

Land Improvements An asset account covering expenditures for improvements that are (1) not as permanent as the land or (2) not directly associated with a building. These include driveways, parking lots, trees and shrubs, fences, and outdoor lighting systems. (660)

Loss on Disposal of Plant and Equipment The account in which a loss is recorded when a firm sells or trades in an asset and receives an amount less than the book value for that asset; it appears under Other Expenses in the income statement. (672)

Modified Accelerated Cost Recovery System (MACRS) An accelerated method of depreciation that is used to determine allowable depreciation for federal income tax returns based on property acquired after 1986; assets are divided into eight classes. (680)

Revenue expenditures Costs incurred to maintain the operation of assets, such as normal repair expenses and fuel expenses. (668)

Straight-line method A method of depreciation that assigns equal amounts of depreciation to each year of the asset's depreciable life. (Cost minus trade-in value divided by useful life [in years].) (661)

Sum-of-the-years'-digits method An accelerated method of depreciation; a reducing fraction multiplied by cost minus trade-in value. (665)

Units-of-production method A method of depreciation that allocates an asset's costs based on its usage or productivity within the period. (Cost minus trade-in value divided by estimated units of production multiplied by the number of units produced.) (662)

QUESTIONS, EXERCISES, AND PROBLEMS

Discussion Questions

1. Define depreciation and list two ways in which assets lose their usefulness.

2. Explain how an asset's estimated trade-in or salvage value is treated in computing depreciation under the sum-of-the-years'-digits method, the double-declining-balance method, and the straight-line method.

3. What is meant by disposition of an asset? List the situations involving disposition of assets.

4. Explain the two entries usually involved in the disposition of an asset.

5. Give examples of possible expenditures that should be included in determining the total cost of an asset, such as a machine.

6. Distinguish between expenditures for ordinary repairs and expenditures for extraordinary repairs.

7. Explain how MACRS differs from other methods of depreciation.

8. Distinguish between capital expenditures and revenue expenditures. Give two examples of each type of expenditure for a truck.

Exercises

P.O. 1

Record amounts debited to Land.

Exercise 19-1 Kramer Manufacturing Company purchased land adjacent to its factory for the installation of a holding area for equipment. Expenditures by the company were as follows: purchase price, $132,000; paving, $4,200; title search and other fees, $650; grading, $3,900; demolition of a shack on the property, $3,800; lighting, $11,200; signs, $1,950; broker's fees, $9,240; landscaping, $8,000. Determine the amount that should be debited to the Land account.

P.O. 2,6

Determine depreciation using five methods.

Exercise 19-2 At the beginning of the fiscal year, Data Services bought a new computer for $16,000, with an estimated trade-in value of $2,500 and an estimated useful life of five years. Determine the amount of the depreciation for the first and second years by the following methods:

a. Straight-line
b. Double-declining-balance
c. Sum-of-the-years'-digits
d. Units-of-production Useful life is 10,400 hours. Year 1 use is 2,050 hours; Year 2 use, 1,800 hours. Compute depreciation per hour, then depreciation for Year 1 and Year 2.
e. MACRS (Assume the asset was purchased after 1986. Calculate the depreciation for income tax reporting.)

P.O. 3

Record an extraordinary-repair expenditure.

Exercise 19-3 Basehart Company just bought a piece of machinery for $8,000, with an estimated life of five years and an estimated trade-in value of $2,000; straight-line depreciation expense is $1,200. Record journal entries for the following transactions:

Jan. 12 Issued Ck. No. 5221 for $150 for inspection and lubrication of the equipment.
Oct. 15 Issued Ck. No. 5562 for $1,960 to replace the motor and rollers. Patterson Company estimates that this repair will extend the life of the machinery about two years.

P.O. 4

Record the disposal of a fully depreciated asset.

Exercise 19-4 On April 28, Muscle Mart discarded exercise equipment that cost $6,600. The Accumulated Depreciation account shows depreciation of $6,600 as of the previous December 31. Make the entry in general journal form to record the disposal of the asset.

P.O. 4

Record the update of depreciation and the discarding of office equipment at a loss.

Exercise 19-5 On July 25, Plouff Company discarded office equipment with no salvage value. The following details are taken from the subsidiary ledger: cost, $900; accumulated depreciation as of the previous December 31, $720; monthly depreciation, $15. Journalize entries to record the depreciation of the office equipment to date and to record the disposal of the office equipment.

P.O. 4

Record the update of depreciation and sale of an asset at a gain.

Exercise 19-6 On June 20, MB Communications sold editing equipment that cost $1,600 for $350. Accumulated depreciation up to the end of the previous year was $1,350. Monthly depreciation is $22.50. Make the necessary general journal entries.

P.O. 4

Record the update of depreciation and trade-in on a similar asset without recognizing a gain or loss.

Exercise 19-7 On September 20, Gilbert Florists traded in its old delivery van for a new one, which cost $16,000. Gilbert got a trade-in allowance of $3,000 on the old van and paid the difference in cash. The subsidiary account shows the following: cost (of old van), $12,000; accumulated depreciation as of last December 31, $9,600; monthly depreciation, $200. Without recognizing gain or loss, make entries in general journal form to record the depreciation of the old van to date and to record the trade-in and purchase of the new van.

P.O. 4

Record the update of depreciation and trade-in on a similar asset without recognizing a gain or loss.

Exercise 19-8 On June 25, Purkey Assemblers trades in a machine for a new one priced at $8,460, receiving a trade-in allowance of $1,500 on the old machine. Purkey makes a downpayment of $1,200 in cash and issues a 60-day, 9 percent note for the remainder. The subsidiary account shows the following: cost (of old machine), $6,000; accumulated depreciation as of last December 31, $4,800; monthly depreciation, $100. Without recognizing gain or loss, make entries in general journal form to record the depreciation of the old machine to date and to record the trade-in and purchase of the new machine.

CONSIDER AND COMMUNICATE

Jane Alex owns a small catering service. The company owns a delivery van as well as ovens and large cooking containers. She is confused about the different traditional depreciation methods she may use for financial reporting. Briefly explain to her the features and consequences of using each method.

WHAT IF . . .

Your employer, who is ordering equipment for a new office, has signed the purchase orders for new equipment without looking at them carefully. As you complete an invoice for items for the employee lunchroom, you are tempted to change the order from one microwave to two microwaves and quietly take the second one home to compensate yourself for all the hard work you have done on your own time to get the new office ready. You are a trusted employee; and you are sure that if your employer found out what you had done, there would be no real repercussions. What if you go ahead with this idea? How could it be discovered? Assume that you are the one who would accept shipment when the microwaves are delivered.

CRITICAL THINKING

Mike's Motorcycle Shop owns various depreciable assets, which were purchased beginning in 1996. The only record you can find on December 31, 2001 (prior to any depreciation adjustments for 2001) is the general ledger account for Equipment, which has a balance of $56,000, and the general ledger account for Accumulated Depreciation, Equipment, which has a balance of $30,179, plus the information listed below. You will need to prepare supporting schedules by asset classification and expense for each prior year before you can calculate the 2001 depreciation.

Depreciable Assets					
Asset	**Bought**	**Method**	**Life**	**Cost**	**Salvage Value**
Van #1	1/1/1996	DDB	5 yrs.	13,000	1,000
Office Desks	7/1/1996	SL	5 yrs.	2,500	500
Van #2	7/1/1998	DDB	5 yrs.	20,000	2,000
Display Ramps	7/1/2000	SYD	10 yrs.	5,500	—0—
Trailer	9/1/2000	DDB	5 yrs.	12,000	1,500
Computer	12/1/2000	SL	5 yrs.	3,000	—0—

Total Depreciation

1996	5,400
1997	3,520
1998	6,272
1999	7,923
2000	7,064

Instructions

1. Classify assets by type: Delivery Equipment, Showroom Equipment, or Office Equipment.
2. Recompute depreciation for 1996, 1997, 1998, 1999, and 2000. Round each year's depreciation expense to whole dollars.
3. Compute depreciation for 2001.

WEB WORK

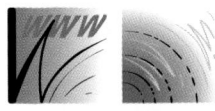

Using an Internet web browser, type *accounting for depreciation of plant and equipment* in the search box and search for information about depreciation methods and procedures. Discuss your findings in a small group. Write a one-page summary of your findings.

PROBLEM SET A

For additional help, see the demonstration problem at the beginning of each chapter in your Working Papers.

P.O. 2

Problem 19-1A At the beginning of a fiscal year, the Pretzel Company buys a truck for $18,000. The truck's estimated life is five years, and its estimated trade-in value is $3,000.

Check Figure

Double-declining-balance method, book value at end of year 5, $3,000

P.O. 2,3,4

Instructions

Using the following three methods, determine the annual depreciation for each of the estimated five years of life, the accumulated depreciation at the end of each year, and the book value of the truck at the end of each year.

a. Straight-line method
b. Double-declining-balance method
c. Sum-of-the-years'-digits method

Problem 19-2A During a three-year period, Braden Electric completed the following transactions related to its service truck:

Year 1

Jan.	4	Bought a used service truck for cash, $12,600.
Nov.	21	Paid garage for maintenance repairs to the truck, $146.
Dec.	31	Recorded the adjusting entry for depreciation for the fiscal year. The estimated life of the truck is four years, and it has an estimated trade-in value of $2,800. Braden uses the straight-line method of depreciation.
	31	Closed the expense accounts to the Income Summary account.

Year 2

Apr.	2	Paid garage for tune-up of truck, $76.
May	24	Paid $345 for tires for the truck.
Dec.	31	Recorded the adjusting entry for depreciation for the fiscal year.
	31	Closed the expense accounts to the Income Summary account.

Year 3

June	6	Paid garage for maintenance repairs to truck, $342.
	27	Traded in the used truck for a new truck that cost $21,600, receiving a trade-in allowance of $8,400 and paying the difference in cash. Made the entry to record the depreciation on the truck up to the present date. Made the entry to record the exchange, assuming gain or loss is not recognized.
Dec.	31	Recorded the adjusting entry for depreciation of the new truck for the fiscal year. The estimated life of the truck is six years, and it has an estimated trade-in value of $2,600. Braden Electric uses the straight-line method of depreciation.
	31	Closed the expense accounts to the Income Summary account.

Check Figure

Year 2 adjustment amount, $2,450

P.O. 2,3,4

Instructions

1. Record the transactions in general journal form, page 97.
2. After journalizing each entry, post to the following ledger accounts: Truck; Accumulated Depreciation, Truck; Truck Repair Expense; Depreciation Expense, Truck.

Problem 19-3A During a three-year period, Fowler Excavation completed the following transactions pertaining to its front-end loader:

Year 1

June	30	Bought a front-end loader, $42,640, paying $10,640 in cash and issuing a series of four notes for $8,000 each, to come due at six-month intervals. Payments are to include principal plus interest of 9 percent to maturity of each $8,000 note.

July 1 Paid transportation charges for the loader, $560.

Dec. 31 Paid the principal, $8,000, plus interest of $1,440 on $32,000 on the first note.

31 Made the adjusting entry to record depreciation for the fiscal year. The estimated life of the loader is four years; it has a salvage value of $4,000. Fowler's accountant uses the double-declining-balance method.

31 Closed the expense accounts to the Income Summary account.

Year 2

Mar. 14 Paid for normal mechanical repairs, $516.

June 30 Paid the principal, $8,000, plus interest of $1,080 on $24,000 on the second note.

Dec. 31 Paid the principal, $8,000, plus interest of $720 on $16,000 on the third note.

31 Recorded the adjusting entry for the fiscal year.

31 Closed the expense accounts to the Income Summary account.

Year 3

Apr. 21 Paid for normal mechanical repairs, $823.

June 30 Paid the principal, $8,000, plus interest of $360 on $8,000 on the fourth note.

Sept. 27 Fowler Excavation decided to get rid of its loader and use the services of an equipment rental firm in the future. Sold the loader for $8,400 cash. Made the entry to depreciate the loader to date ($6,075). Made the entry to account for the sale of the loader.

Dec. 31 Closed the expense accounts to the Income Summary account.

Check Figure

Year 3, Income Summary debit, $8,983

Instructions

1. Record the transactions in general journal form, page 192.
2. After making each journal entry, post to the following ledger accounts: Equipment; Accumulated Depreciation, Equipment; Depreciation Expense, Equipment; Equipment Maintenance Expense; Interest Expense; Loss on Disposal of Plant and Equipment.

P.O. 2,4,5

Problem 19-4A The general ledger of the Coski Personnel Service includes controlling accounts for Office Equipment and Accumulated Depreciation, Office Equipment. Coski's accountant also records the details of each item of office equipment in a subsidiary ledger. During a three-year period, the following transactions affecting office equipment took place:

Year 1

Jan. 5 Bought the following from Abingdon, Inc., for cash:
Filing cabinet, $240, account no. 123-1, expected life fifteen years, trade-in value zero.
Executive desk, $960, account no. 123-2, expected life twelve years, trade-in value zero.
Executive chair, $360, account no. 123-3, expected life twelve years, trade-in value zero.
(The above assets will be depreciated using the straight-line method.)

7 Paid Butler and Robbins $1,280 for a custom-made counter, account no. 123-4, expected life ten years, trade-in value zero; straight-line method.

Jan. 10 Bought for cash a laser printer, serial no. N-1522A, account no. 123-5, from Garland Office Supplies for $720, estimated life five years, estimated trade-in value $120; sum-of-the-years'-digits method.

Dec. 31 Made the adjusting entry to record depreciation of office equipment for the fiscal year (total depreciation, $454; verify this figure).

31 Closed the Depreciation Expense, Office Equipment account into the Income Summary account.

Year 2

June 29 Bought a carpet from Beel Floor Coverings on account, account no. 123-6, price $1,280, estimated life eight years, trade-in value zero; double-declining-balance method.

Dec. 31 Made the adjusting entry to record depreciation of office equipment for the fiscal year (depreciation for six months on the carpet; total depreciation, $574; verify this figure).

31 Closed the Depreciation Expense, Office Equipment account into the Income Summary account.

Year 3

June 30 Traded in the executive chair for a new one from Garcia and Wentz, account no. 123-7. The new chair cost $520, has an estimated life of eight years, and has a zero trade-in value, straight-line method. Coski Personnel Service received a trade-in allowance of $230 on the old chair and paid the balance in cash. Recorded the entry to depreciate the old chair to date. Made the entry to record the exchange of assets, without recognizing gain or loss.

Dec. 31 Made the adjusting entry to record depreciation of office equipment for the fiscal year (depreciation for six months on the chair; total depreciation, $659.94; verify this figure).

31 Closed the Depreciation Expense, Office Equipment account into the Income Summary account.

Check Figure

Year 3, Income Summary debit, $674.94

Instructions

1. Record the transactions in general journal form, page 136.
2. Each time Coski buys a new asset, open an account in the subsidiary ledger.
3. After each entry, post to the two controlling accounts and to the subsidiary ledger.
4. Make a list of the balances in the subsidiary ledger accounts at the end of year 3 and compare the totals with the balances of the two controlling accounts.

PROBLEM SET B

For additional help, see the demonstration problem at the beginning of each chapter in your Working Papers.

P.O. 2

Problem 19-1B The Hawkins Company, at the beginning of a fiscal year, buys a machine for $40,000. The machine has an estimated life of five years and an estimated trade-in value of $4,000.

Check Figure

Double-declining-balance method, book value at end of year 5, $4,000

Instructions

Using the following three methods, determine the annual depreciation of the machine for each of the expected five years of its life, the accumulated depreciation at the end of each year, and the book value of the machine at the end of each year.

a. Straight-line method
b. Double-declining-balance method
c. Sum-of-the-years'-digits method

P.O. 2,3,4

Problem 19-2B During a three-year period, Megan Motel completed the following transactions pertaining to its pickup truck:

Year 1

Jan.	11	Bought a used pickup truck for cash, $6,700.
Nov.	16	Paid garage for maintenance repairs to pickup truck, $138.
Dec.	31	Made the adjusting entry to record depreciation for the fiscal year, using the straight-line method of depreciation. The estimated life of the pickup truck is four years, and it has an estimated trade-in value of $1,200.
	31	Closed the expense accounts to the Income Summary account.

Year 2

Mar.	4	Paid garage for tune-up and minor repairs, $56.
May	27	Bought a tire, $69.
Dec.	31	Recorded the adjusting entry for depreciation.
	31	Closed the expense accounts to the Income Summary account.

Year 3

Feb.	13	Paid garage for maintenance repairs to pickup truck, $326.
June	22	Traded in the pickup truck for another pickup truck priced at $9,460, receiving a trade-in allowance of $1,040; paid the difference in cash. Recorded the entry to depreciate the old truck to date. Made the entry to record the exchange, assuming gain or loss is not recognized.
Dec.	31	Recorded adjusting entry for depreciation of the new pickup truck for the fiscal year, using the straight-line method of depreciation. The estimated life of the new truck is six years, and it has an estimated trade-in value of $1,500.
	31	Closed the expense accounts to the Income Summary account.

Check Figure

Year 2, adjustment amount, $1,375

Instructions

1. Record all these transactions in general journal form.
2. After journalizing each entry, post to the following ledger accounts: Truck; Accumulated Depreciation, Truck; Truck Repair Expense; Depreciation Expense, Truck.

P.O. 2,3,4

Problem 19-3B During a three-year period, the Bingham Construction Company completed the following transactions connected with its bulldozer:

Year 1

June	30	Bought a bulldozer, $120,400, paying $40,400 in cash, and issuing a series of four notes for $20,000 each, to come due at six-month intervals. Payments are to include principal plus 9 percent interest to maturity of each $20,000 note.

July	2	Paid transportation charges for the bulldozer, $3,600.
Dec.	31	Paid the principal, $20,000, plus interest of $3,600 on $80,000 on the first note.
	31	Made the adjusting entry to record depreciation on the bulldozer for the fiscal year, using the double-declining-balance method ($24,800; verify this figure). The estimated life of the bulldozer is five years, and it has an estimated salvage value of $11,600.
	31	Closed the expense accounts to the Income Summary account.

Year 2

Apr.	24	Paid for maintenance repairs to the bulldozer, $5,836.
June	30	Paid the principal, $20,000, plus interest of $2,700 on $60,000 on the second note.
Dec.	31	Paid the principal, $20,000, plus interest of $1,800 on $40,000 on the third note.
	31	Made the adjusting entry to record depreciation for the fiscal year.
	31	Closed the expense accounts to the Income Summary account.

Year 3

May	19	Paid for maintenance repairs to the bulldozer, $2,094.
June	30	Paid the principal, $20,000, plus interest of $900 on $20,000 on the fourth note.
Sept.	29	Bingham Construction decided to get rid of its bulldozer and use the services of an equipment rental firm in the future. Sold the bulldozer for $24,000, receiving cash. Made the entry to depreciate the bulldozer to date. Made the entry accounting for the sale of the machine.
Dec.	31	Closed the expense accounts to the Income Summary account.

Check Figure

Year 3, Income Summary debit, $41,214

P.O. 2,4,5

Instructions

1. Record the transactions in general journal form.
2. After making each journal entry, post to the following ledger accounts: Equipment; Accumulated Depreciation, Equipment; Depreciation Expense, Equipment; Equipment Maintenance Expense; Interest Expense; Loss on Disposal of Plant and Equipment.

Problem 19-4B The general ledger of the Laird Insurance Agency includes controlling accounts for Office Equipment and Accumulated Depreciation, Office Equipment. Laird's accountant also records the details of each item of office equipment in a subsidiary ledger. The following transactions affecting office equipment occurred during a three-year period:

Year 1

Jan.	4	Bought the following from Graham Office Supplies for cash: Executive desk, $810, account no. 123-1, estimated life ten years, trade-in value zero. Executive chair, $285, account no. 123-2, estimated life ten years, trade-in value zero. Filing cabinet, metal, $180, account no. 123-3, estimated life fifteen years, trade-in value zero. (The above assets will be depreciated using the straight-line method.)
	9	Paid Sears Cabinet Shop $1,080 for a custom-made counter, account no. 123-4, estimated life ten years, trade-in value zero; depreciation by straight-line method.

Jan. 12 Purchased for cash a laser printer from Regal Office Machines, $570, serial no. VPL2155, account no. 123-5, estimated life five years, estimated trade-in value, $75; depreciation by sum-of-the-years'-digits method.

Dec. 31 Made the adjusting entry to record depreciation of Office Equipment for the fiscal year (total depreciation, $394.50; verify this figure).

31 Closed the Depreciation Expense, Office Equipment account into the Income Summary account.

Year 2

June 27 Bought a rug from Franklin Furniture on account, $720, account no. 123-6, estimated life eight years, trade-in value zero; depreciation by double-declining-balance method.

Dec. 31 Recorded the adjusting entry for depreciation of office equipment for the fiscal year (depreciation for six months on the rug; total depreciation, $451.50; verify this figure).

31 Closed the Depreciation Expense, Office Equipment account into the Income Summary account.

Year 3

June 23 Traded in the executive desk for a new one, which cost $1,020, from Sellwood, Inc., account no. 123-7, receiving a trade-in allowance of $480 on the old desk and paying the balance in cash. Expected life of the new desk is eight years, with a zero trade-in value; depreciated using straight-line method. Made the entry to depreciate the old desk to date. Made the entry to record the exchange of assets, without recognizing gain or loss.

Dec. 31 Made the adjusting entry to record depreciation of office equipment for the fiscal year (depreciation for six months on the desk; total depreciation, $476.72; verify this figure).

31 Closed the Depreciation Expense, Office Equipment account into the Income Summary account.

Check Figure

Year 3, Income Summary debit, $517.22

Instructions

1. Record the transactions in general journal form.
2. With the purchase of each new asset, open an account in the subsidiary ledger.
3. After each entry, post to the two controlling accounts and to the subsidiary ledger.
4. Make a list of the balances in the subsidiary ledger accounts at the end of year 3 and compare the totals with the balances of the two controlling accounts.

Cumulative Self-Check: Chapters 17–19

PART I: TRUE/FALSE QUESTIONS

For each of the following statements, circle T if the statement is true and F if the statement is false.

T	F	1. The Allowance for Doubtful Accounts account is a current liability.
T	F	2. Under the allowance method of handling bad debt losses, accounts considered uncollectible are written off by debiting Allowance for Doubtful Accounts.
T	F	3. There is an adjusting entry required when the specific charge-off method is used to handle bad debt losses.
T	F	4. FIFO will result in the lowest net income during periods of rising prices.
T	F	5. An account called Cost of Goods Sold is included in the general ledger when the perpetual inventory system is used.
T	F	6. The income statement and the balance sheet both include the balance of the ending merchandise inventory for the same fiscal period.
T	F	7. When an extraordinary repair on an asset is made, the cost should be credited to the Accumulated Depreciation account.
T	F	8. When a business sells equipment for an amount greater than its book value, a loss is recorded.
T	F	9. Depreciation amounts are estimates of the loss of usefulness of an asset over a period of time.
T	F	10. The FIFO inventory valuation method assumes that the items on hand are the most recent ones purchased.

PART II: COMPLETION

Complete each of the following statements by writing the appropriate word(s) in the space provided.

1. The balance of Accounts Receivable after one has deducted the balance of Allowance for Doubtful Accounts is called the _____.

2. A method of accounting for bad debt losses that requires a debit to Bad Debts Expense and a credit to Accounts Receivable is called the _____ method.

3. A federal law excusing a debtor from certain obligations incurred is called _____.

4. A process of assigning costs to goods sold based on the flow-of-cost assumption that units sold are recorded at the costs of the most recently acquired goods is called _____.

Note: Answers to the Cumulative Self-Check problems begin on page A-1.

5. A method of inventory valuation requiring that the actual cost of each individual item in the ending inventory be used is called the _____ method.

6. The inventory system in which a running balance is kept of the inventory on hand and the current cost of each item is called the _____ system.

7. Expenditures for improvements that are not as permanent as the land or not directly associated with a building are debited to the _____ account.

8. The type of depreciation method that allows recording of larger amounts of depreciation in the early years of an asset's use is called a(n) _____ method.

9. The costs of normal day-to-day expenses associated with an asset are called _____.

10. The inventory system that requires a physical count and then attaches a value to that count is called the _____ inventory system.

PART III: MATCHING

For each numbered item, choose the matching term and write the identifying letter in the answer column.

_____ 1. The systematic expensing of the cost of equipment over its useful life.

_____ 2. Cost of major overhaul of an asset.

_____ 3. Cost less trade-in or salvage value.

_____ 4. Federal law excusing a debtor from certain obligations incurred.

_____ 5. Analysis of the composition of outstanding accounts receivable.

A. Perpetual system
B. Book value
C. Net realizable value
D. Periodic system
E. Depreciation
F. Aging
G. Capital expenditure
H. Revenue expenditure
I. Depreciation base
J. Specific identification
K. FIFO
L. LIFO
M. Weighted average
N. Bankruptcy
O. Extraordinary repair

_____ 6. Cost less accumulated depreciation.

_____ 7. Balance of Accounts Receivable minus Allowance for Doubtful Accounts.

_____ 8. Method of inventory valuation ideal for high-priced units.

_____ 9. Method of inventory valuation that yields the most realistic value of the asset.

_____ 10. Method of inventory valuation that yields lowest net income during a period of rising prices.

G The Voucher System of Accounting

Performance Objectives

After you have completed this appendix, you will be able to do the following:

1. Prepare vouchers.
2. Record vouchers in a voucher register.
3. Record payment of vouchers in a check register.
4. Record transactions involving canceling or altering an original voucher.

The voucher system is a means of achieving internal control and enabling the owner or manager to maintain contact with day-to-day transactions. This system promotes the delegation of duties and responsibilities.

OBJECTIVE OF THE VOUCHER SYSTEM

The objective of the voucher system is to control the incurrence of all liabilities and the payment of all expenditures—in other words, to control the purchase of (1) merchandise or materials, (2) other assets, and (3) services. The voucher system is suitable for companies of varying sizes that require a clear separation of duties. The voucher system has the following components: vouchers, voucher register, check register, unpaid voucher file, paid voucher file, and general journal.

VOUCHERS

The dictionary defines a voucher as a document that serves as proof of a transaction and, from a business point of view, also serves as a full description of the transaction. **When a business is using the voucher system, a voucher must be filled out for every invoice or bill received, whether it is to be paid immediately or in the future. The invoice or bill is usually stapled to the voucher.**

Characteristics of Vouchers

Just as the form of invoices varies from one company to another, so too the form of vouchers varies from one company to another. However, the following characteristics are usually present:

• Vouchers are numbered consecutively.
• The name and address of the payee or creditor appear on the voucher.

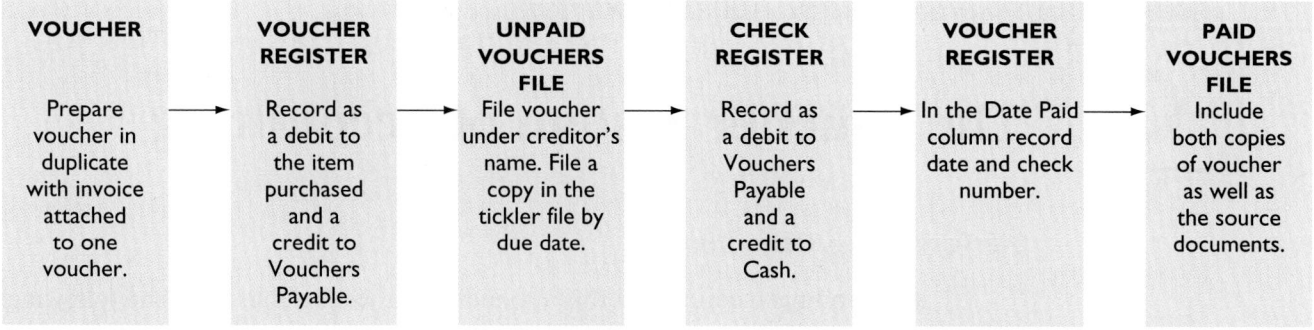

FIGURE 1

- The amount and credit terms of the invoice appear on the voucher.
- Vouchers state due dates so that firms can take advantage of possible cash discounts.
- For internal control, vouchers require signatures approving payment.
- Vouchers record payment: date paid and check number.

A completed voucher, with the invoice or bill stapled to it, describes an entire transaction as well as the procedure for processing the voucher. First, so that you can see the big picture, Figure 1 presents the steps involved in processing a voucher for a purchase of merchandise.

Preparation and Approval of Vouchers

Objective 1

Prepare vouchers.

To cite a familiar example, let's assume that Jackson Electric Supply has now achieved such a volume of business that it is using a voucher system. Let's also assume that Jackson has received from its supplier, Draper, Inc., the invoice shown here.

DRAPER, INC.
1614 Olivera Street
San Francisco, CA 94129

INVOICE

SOLD TO	Jackson Electric Supply	DATE:	October 1, 20—
	625 N.E. Manor Ave.	INVOICE NO.:	3394
	Portland, Oregon 97201	ORDER NO.:	9764
		SHIPPED BY:	Western Freight Line
		TERMS:	2/10, n/30

QUANTITY	DESCRIPTION	UNIT PRICE	TOTAL	
26	Butler Electronic Thermostats	26	70	694	20
	Freight			20	80
				715	00

Jackson Electric's accountant, using the invoice as the source of information, fills out the following voucher. The face of the voucher lists the details of the transaction.

JACKSON ELECTRIC SUPPLY   No. 118
625 N.E. Manor Avenue
Portland, Oregon 97201

VOUCHER

PAY TO: Draper, Inc.
1614 Olivera St.
San Francisco, CA 94129

DATE _____ 10/2/– _____

DATE OF INVOICE	TERMS	DESCRIPTION	AMOUNT	
10/1	2/10, n/30	Invoice No. 3394	694	20
		Less discount	13	88
		Subtotal	680	32
		Freight	20	80
		Net amount payable	701	12

APPROVAL	DATES	APPROVED BY
Extensions and footings verified	10/2	M. C. L.
Prices in agreement with purchase order	10/2	S. T.
Credit terms in agreement with purchase order	10/2	S. T.
Quantities in agreement with receiving report	10/2	J. D. S.
Approved for payment	10/7	R. L. R.

ACCOUNT DISTRIBUTION

VOUCHER NO.   118

ACCOUNT DEBITED	AMOUNT
Purchases	694.20
Freight In	20.80
Supplies	
Wages Expense	
Miscellaneous Expense	
Total Vouchers Payable Cr.	715.00

Due Date 10/8

Pay To   Draper, Inc.
1614 Olivera Street
San Francisco, CA 94129

SUMMARY OF CHARGES

Amount of invoice	$715.00
Less cash discount	13.88
Net amount	$701.12

RECORD OF PAYMENT

Paid by check no.	390
Date of check	10/8
Amount of check	701.12

ACCOUNT DISTRIBUTION by _____ R. R. H. _____

ENTERED IN VOUCHER REG. by _____ M. C. L. _____

The Account Distribution section is used to record the account titles and amounts to be debited, the total amount to be credited to Vouchers Payable, and the initials of the person authorized to determine the distribution.

THE VOUCHERS PAYABLE ACCOUNT

When you use a voucher system, you substitute the Vouchers Payable account for Accounts Payable. For example, when a firm buys merchandise on account, the accountant enters it as a debit to Purchases and a credit to Vouchers Payable. Similarly, when a firm buys store equipment on account, the accountant records it as a debit to Store Equipment and a credit to Vouchers Payable. Also, if a company incurs an expense on account, such as Advertising, the entry is a debit to Advertising Expense and a credit to Vouchers Payable.

	DATE	VOU. NO.	CREDITOR	PAYMENT DATE	CK. NO.	VOUCHERS PAYABLE CREDIT	PURCHASES DEBIT	
1	20–							
2	Oct. 1	117	Fast-Way Freight	10 1	383	7 3 00		
3	2	118	Draper, Inc.	10 8	390	7 1 5 00	6 9 4 20	
4	3	119	Donaldson and Farr	10 3	384	4 8 72		
5	5	120	Stable Ins. Co.	10 5	387	7 4 00		
6	9	121	Thomas and Son	10 18	404	3 2 8 00	3 0 6 00	
7	10	122	Payroll Bank Acc.	10 10	393	1 6 9 0 00		
8	12	123	Southland Journal			1 7 6 00		
9	12	124	Bradley Construction	10 12	395	1 1 6 00		
10	15	125	N. C. Jackson	10 15	399	5 0 0 00		
11	15	126	T. R. Wetzel	10 18	By note	4 2 1 00	4 2 1 00	
28	29	149	Adkins Mfg. Co.			7 1 4 00	7 1 4 00	
29	30	150	Safety Nat. Bank	10 30	412	1 5 0 7 50		
30								
31	31					10 7 2 0 70	4 3 6 2 92	
32						(2 1 2)	(5 1 1)	
33								
34								

Remember!

Since the check register replaces the cash payments journal and the voucher register replaces the purchases journal, the special-column totals from the voucher register must be posted before those from the check register.

	Debits
Purchases	$ 4,362.92
Freight In	212.30
Wages Payable	3,314.00
Supplies	121.79
Miscellaneous Expense	83.69
Other Accounts	2,626.00
	$10,720.70

When a check is issued in payment of a voucher, record the entry in the check register as a debit to Vouchers Payable and a credit to Cash. Again, we emphasize that *all* liabilities are recorded in the Vouchers Payable account.

THE VOUCHER REGISTER

Objective 2

Record vouchers in a voucher register.

The **voucher register** has the status of a journal; it is a book of original entry. All vouchers must be recorded in it, in numerical order. Think of it as a multicolumn purchases journal. The voucher register has only one credit column, Vouchers Payable Credit, but a number of debit columns. Headings for the debit columns are selected on the basis of their frequency of use. In addition to the special columns, the voucher register also has space for recording the voucher number, the name of the creditor, the date of payment, and the check number. The voucher register for Jackson Electric Supply is shown below.

VOUCHER REGISTER   PAGE __3__

FREIGHT-IN DEBIT	WAGES PAYABLE DEBIT	SUPPLIES DEBIT	MISCELLANEOUS EXPENSE DEBIT	OTHER ACCOUNTS DEBIT ACCOUNT	POST. REF.	AMOUNT	
							1
	73 00						2
	20 80						3
			48 72				4
				Prepaid Insurance	116	74 00	5
	22 00						6
		1690 00					7
				Advertising Expense	518	176 00	8
				Sales Returns and Allowances	412	116 00	9
				N. C. Jackson, Drawing	312	500 00	10
							11
							28
				Notes Payable	211	1500 00	29
				Interest Expense	534	7 50	30
212 30	3314 00	121 79	83 69			2626 00	31
(514)	(213)	(115)	(519)			(X)	32
							33
							34

Credit

Vouchers Payable $10,720.70

When you first record the voucher, leave the Payment Date and Ck. No. columns blank. After you have recorded the payment in the check register, go back to the voucher register and enter the date of payment and the number of the check.

Posting from the Voucher Register

Remember!

A voucher is prepared for every invoice or bill the company receives.

The entries in the Other Accounts columns are posted *daily* to the general ledger, just as the Other Accounts columns of the other special journals are posted daily. The (X) under the column total means "do not post." At the end of the month, total all the columns, and prove the equality of the debit and credit entries by comparing the combined total of the debit columns with the total of the Vouchers Payable Credit column.

THE CHECK REGISTER

Objective 3

Record payment of vouchers in a check register.

Any company or organization using a voucher system uses both the voucher register and the check register as books of original entry. Now let's look at the procedure for the check register. Since checks are issued only in payment of approved and recorded vouchers, the entry in the check register is always a debit to Vouchers Payable and a credit to Cash. A Vouchers Payable Debit column in the check register offsets the Vouchers Payable Credit column in the voucher register. Recall that after you record the entry in the check register, you enter the date and check number on the appropriate line in the voucher register and on the outside of the voucher in the Record of Payment section.

CHECK REGISTER PAGE 11

	DATE	CK. NO.	PAYEE	VOU. NO.	VOUCHERS PAYABLE DEBIT	PURCHASES DISCOUNT CREDIT	CASH CREDIT	
1	20–							1
2	Oct. 1	383	Fast-Way Freight	117	7 3 00		7 3 00	2
3	3	384	Donaldson and Farr	119	4 8 72		4 8 72	3
4	3	385	Spargo Products Company	114	2 0 6 00	2 06	2 0 3 94	4
5	4	386	Adkins Manufacturing Company	115	5 4 0 00	1 0 80	5 2 9 20	5
6	5	387	Stable Insurance Company	120	7 4 00		7 4 00	6
7	6	388	Void					7
8	6	389	Richter and Son	116	4 6 4 00	9 28	4 5 4 72	8
9	8	390	Draper, Inc.	118	7 1 5 00	1 3 88	7 0 1 12	9
24	30	412	Safety National Bank	150	1 5 0 7 50		1 5 0 7 50	24
25	31				6 5 2 5 98	1 7 5 42	6 3 5 0 56	25
26					(2 1 2)	(5 1 3)	(1 1 1)	26
27								27

Debits	Credits
$6,525.98	$ 175.42
	6,350.56
	$6,525.98

HANDLING OF UNPAID VOUCHERS

Firms usually prepare vouchers in duplicate. In the system used by Jackson Electric Supply, the invoice is attached to the original copy of the voucher. Then the voucher is circulated within the company for the necessary signatures. After a voucher is recorded in the voucher register, it is filed under the name of the creditor. (Other companies may prepare only one copy of the voucher and file it only under the date on which it is supposed to be paid.)

At Jackson Electric, the Unpaid Vouchers file contains all outstanding vouchers or credit memos. This file, organized by names of creditors, now acts as a subsidiary ledger. In fact, at Jackson Electric, this file substitutes for the accounts payable ledger.

The *second* copy of the voucher goes to the treasurer, who files it chronologically by due date. This tickler file (a file of unpaid vouchers filed by due date) helps the treasurer forecast the amount of cash that will be needed to pay outstanding bills and take advantage of cash discounts.

At the end of the month, the accountant lists all the vouchers payable, taking the information directly from the Unpaid Vouchers file.

Jackson Electric Supply
Schedule of Vouchers Payable
October 31, 20—

VOU. NO.	NAME OF CREDITOR	AMOUNT
123	Southland Journal	1 7 6 00
149	Adkins Manufacturing Company	7 1 4 00
	Total Vouchers Payable	$ 8 9 0 00

FILING PAID VOUCHERS

Now let's assume that the firm has paid its bill. The payment is recorded in the check register and in the Payment columns of the voucher register. Then the voucher is stapled to the copy in the tickler file, marked paid, and filed in numerical order in a Paid Vouchers file.

SITUATIONS REQUIRING SPECIAL TREATMENT

When a firm is using the voucher system, it inevitably runs into an occasional nonroutine transaction that does not fit into the fixed channels of the voucher system and therefore may require an entry in the general journal. You can consider such treatment as an adjustment to the voucher system.

Return of a Purchase Before Original Voucher Has Been Recorded

Normally, if a business with an efficient purchasing department is going to return any merchandise, it returns the merchandise before the vouchers are recorded in the voucher register. The accountant records the deduction right on the invoice and records the invoice in the voucher register for the net amount.

Return of a Purchase After Original Voucher Has Been Recorded

Assume that a business purchased merchandise for $566. The transaction was recorded in the voucher register as a debit to Purchases and a credit to Vouchers Payable. Later, the company returns $26 worth of defective merchandise. The return is recorded in the general journal as a debit to Vouchers Payable and a credit to Purchases Returns and Allowances. A notation "Return" is entered in the payment column of the voucher register.

Installment Payments Planned at Time of Original Purchase

In a voucher system, invoices not subject to cash discount are generally paid in full. Sometimes, however, management prefers to pay for an item in installments. When this happens, the company's accountant prepares a separate voucher for each installment and records each of these vouchers in the voucher register. Each voucher's due date corresponds to the date on which that installment is to be paid.

Installment Payments After Original Voucher Has Been Recorded

However, suppose that the buyer records the entire amount of the invoice on one voucher and *later* decides to pay the invoice in installments. The accountant must now cancel the original voucher by means of a general journal entry and issue a new voucher for each installment. A notation listing the new voucher numbers is made in the Payment column of the voucher register.

Correcting an Amount After Original Voucher Has Been Recorded

If an error in the purchase of merchandise is discovered after the voucher has been recorded in the voucher register, the original voucher must be canceled by means of a general journal entry debiting Vouchers Payable and crediting Purchases. Next, a new entry is made in the voucher register for the correct amount, debiting Purchases and crediting Vouchers Payable. A notation listing the new voucher number is made in the Payment column of the voucher register.

Issuing a Note Payable After Original Voucher Has Been Recorded

If a note is issued for the amount of an unpaid invoice after the voucher has been recorded, an entry must be made in the general journal to cancel the original voucher. The entry is a debit to Vouchers Payable and a credit to

Notes Payable. A notation, "by Note," is made in the Date Paid column of the voucher register. When the note is to be paid, a new voucher is issued for the amount of the principal and interest, debiting Notes Payable and Interest Expense and crediting Vouchers Payable.

PROBLEMS

P.O. 2,3

Problem G-1 The Crawford Company uses a voucher system in which it records invoices at the **gross amount.** The following vouchers were issued during February and were unpaid on March 1:

Voucher Number	Company	For	Date of Voucher	Amount
1729	Keaney Company	Merchandise, FOB destination	Feb. 26	$3,436
1732	F. N. Kell	Merchandise, FOB destination	Feb. 28	$4,710

The following transactions were completed during March:

Mar. 3 Issued voucher no. 1734 in favor of Leeds Company for March rent, $1,220.

3 Issued Ck. No. 1829 in payment of voucher no. 1734, $1,220.

5 Bought merchandise on account from Lipnik, Inc., $3,890; terms 2/10, n/30; FOB shipping point; freight prepaid and added to the invoice, $72 (total, $3,962). Issued voucher no. 1735.

5 Issued Ck. No. 1830 in payment of voucher no. 1729, $3,401.64 ($3,436 less 1 percent cash discount).

9 Issued voucher no. 1736 in favor of Manzer Electric Company for electric bill, $216.

9 Issued Ck. No. 1831 in payment of voucher no. 1736, $216.

9 Issued Ck. No. 1832 in payment of voucher no. 1732, $4,615.80 ($4,710 less 2 percent cash discount).

13 Issued Ck. No. 1833 in payment of voucher no. 1735, less the cash discount, $3,884.20. Recall that the freight portion is not eligible for discount.

16 Bought merchandise on account from Maple Manufacturing Company, $6,260; terms 2/10 EOM; FOB destination. Issued voucher no. 1737.

25 Issued voucher no. 1738 for note payable previously recorded in the general journal: principal, $4,000, plus $30 interest. The note is payable to the Southland State Bank.

25 Issued Ck. No. 1834 in payment of voucher no. 1737, $6,134.80 ($6,260 less 2 percent cash discount).

31 Issued voucher no. 1739 for wages payable, $4,985, in favor of the payroll bank account. (Assume that the payroll entry was previously recorded in the general journal.)

31 Paid voucher no. 1739 by issuing Ck. No. 1835, $4,985, to Payroll Bank Account.

Check Figure

Voucher Register, Vouchers
Payable Credit total, $20,673.00

Instructions

1. Using the voucher issue date, enter the unpaid invoices in the voucher register, beginning with voucher no. 1729. Then draw double lines across all columns to separate the vouchers of February from those of March.
2. Record the transactions for March in the voucher register (page 65). Also record the appropriate transactions in the check register (page 71).
3. Total and rule the voucher register and the check register.
4. Prove the equality of the debits and credits in the voucher register and the check register.

P.O. 2,3,4

Problem G-2 The Selig Company, which uses a voucher system, has the following unpaid vouchers on July 1. The firm follows the practice of recording vouchers at the **gross amount.**

Voucher Number	Company	For	Date of Voucher	Amount
4789	Doane and Son	Store equipment	June 15	$ 4,996
4795	Pauker and Company	Merchandise, FOB destination	June 28	$ 8,571
4797	K. P. Wigton Company	Merchandise, FOB destination	June 28	$10,710

The company made the following transactions during July:

July 1 Issued voucher no. 4800 in favor of Sound Insurance Company for a premium on a twelve-month fire insurance policy, $890.
  2 Paid voucher no. 4789 by issuing Ck. No. 8219, $4,996.
  2 Issued Ck. No. 8220 in payment of voucher no. 4800, $890.
  3 Issued voucher no. 4801 in favor of Quinn Quick Freight for transportation charges on merchandise purchases, $223.
  5 Paid voucher no. 4801 by issuing Ck. No. 8221, $223.
  7 Issued Ck. No. 8222 in payment of voucher no. 4795, $8,485.29 ($8,571 less 1 percent cash discount).
  8 Issued Ck. No. 8223 in payment of voucher no. 4797, $10,602.90 ($10,710 less 1 percent cash discount).
  11 Established a petty cash fund of $250. Issued voucher no. 4802.
  11 Paid voucher no. 4802 by issuing Ck. No. 8224, $250.
  13 Issued voucher no. 4803 in favor of G. L. Morsani Company for merchandise, $14,708; terms 2/10, n/30; FOB shipping point; freight prepaid and added to the invoice, $384 (total, $15,092).
  15 Received bill for advertising in the *Weekly Ad Pak.* Issued voucher no. 4804 in the amount of $410.
  17 Received a credit memo for $764 from G. L. Morsani Company for merchandise returned to them, credit memo no. 540 (pertaining to voucher no. 4803).
  20 Issued voucher no. 4805 in favor of Watcol County for six months' property tax (Prepaid Property Taxes), $2,272.
  20 Paid voucher no. 4805 by issuing Ck. No. 8225, $2,272.

July 21 Issued Ck. No. 8226 in payment of voucher no. 4803, $14,049.12 ($14,708 less $764 return, less cash discount, plus freight).

23 Bought merchandise on account from Lindros and Company, $6,039; terms 1/10, n/30; FOB destination. Issued voucher no. 4806.

27 Received a credit memo for $984 from Lindros and Company for damaged merchandise, credit memo no. 437 (pertaining to voucher no. 4806).

31 Issued voucher no. 4807 to reimburse petty cash fund. The charges were:

Supplies	$110.43
L. Selig, Drawing	75.00
Miscellaneous Expense	39.67

31 Issued Ck. No. 8227 in payment of voucher no. 4807, $225.10.

31 Issued voucher no. 4808 for Wages Payable, $8,448, in favor of the payroll bank account. (Assume that the payroll entry was recorded previously in the general journal.)

31 Paid voucher no. 4808 by issuing Ck. No. 8228, payable to Payroll Bank Account.

Check Figure

Check Register, Cash Credit total $50,441.41

Instructions

1. Using the voucher issue date, enter the unpaid invoices in the voucher register, beginning with voucher no. 4789. Then draw double lines across all columns to separate the vouchers of June from those of July.
2. Enter the transactions for July in the voucher register (page 75) at the **gross amount.** Also record the appropriate transactions in the check register (page 86) and the general journal (page 41).
3. Total and rule the voucher register and the check register for the transactions recorded during July.
4. Prove the equality of the debits and credits on the voucher register and the check register.

P.O. 2,3,4

Problem G-3 Beeler Systems uses a voucher system in which it records invoices at the **gross amount.** During October, it completed the following transactions:

Oct. 2 Prepared voucher no. 2632 in favor of Joiner and Browne for the purchase of merchandise with an invoice price of $5,831; terms 30 days; FOB shipping point; freight prepaid and added to the invoice, $192 (total, $6,023).

3 Prepared vouchers no. 2633 for $1,010, 2634 for $1,010, and 2635 for $1,010. The debt arose because Beeler Systems bought a personal computer, laser printer, and monitor from Interface, Inc. The terms are $1,010 cash on delivery, $1,010 in thirty days, and $1,010 in sixty days. (Use three lines.)

5 Issued Ck. No. 2725 in payment of voucher no. 2633, $1,010.

9 Issued voucher no. 2636 in favor of Wegner Company for the purchase of supplies, $360.50; terms 30 days.

12 Prepared voucher no. 2637 in favor of Gross Realty for rent for the month, $1,650.

12 Issued Ck. No. 2726 in payment of voucher no. 2637, $1,650.

16 Prepared voucher no. 2638 in favor of Brandon Cargo for freight charges on merchandise purchased, $104.

Oct. 16 Prepared voucher no. 2639 in favor of Grooms Company for the purchase of merchandise having a list price of $6,512 with a 25 percent trade discount (record voucher for $4,884); terms 2/10, n/30; FOB shipping point.

16 Issued Ck. No. 2727 in payment of voucher no. 2638, $104.00.

16 Canceled voucher no. 2632 because the invoice will be paid in two installments as follows: voucher no. 2640, payable November 1, $3,011.50; voucher no. 2641, payable November 15, $3,011.50. Prepared vouchers no. 2640 and 2641.

17 Received a credit memo from Grooms Company for merchandise returned, $352, credit memo no. 580, voucher no. 2639.

22 Prepared voucher no. 2642 in favor of Milton Telephone Company for telephone bill, $164.90.

22 Issued Ck. No. 2728 in payment of voucher no. 2642, $164.90.

23 Issued Ck. No. 2729 in payment of voucher no. 2639, $4,441.36. ($4,884 less $352 return, less cash discount.)

31 Prepared voucher no. 2643 for wages payable, $4,550, in favor of Payroll Bank Account. (Assume that the payroll entry was recorded previously in the general journal.)

31 Issued Ck. No. 2730 in payment of voucher no. 2643, $4,550.

31 Prepared voucher no. 2644 in favor of G. L. Beeler, the owner, for personal withdrawal, $1,400.

31 Issued Ck. No. 2731 for payment of voucher no. 2644.

Check Figure

Schedule of vouchers payable total, $8,403.50

Instructions

1. Record the transactions for October in the voucher register (page 32), the check register (page 34), and the general journal (page 18).
2. Total and rule the voucher register and the check register.
3. Prove the equality of the debits and credits on the voucher register and the check register.
4. Post the amounts from the registers and the general journal to the Vouchers Payable account.
5. Prepare a schedule of vouchers payable. Compare this total with the balance of the Vouchers Payable account.

20 Partnerships

WINDOWS ON | THE WORLD WIDE WEB

Who are Bobby's partners in the television law firm shown on *The Practice*? Who set the rules about the way the law firm started up, how it operates, and how the partnership may be dissolved? Unlike publicly held corporations, the financial statements of limited partnerships are not easily accessible. *The Practice* is fictional, but how would you obtain financial data on a partnership? Securities Pricing and Research, Inc. (SPAR), an organization that provides pricing and research on public-partnership trades and limited partnerships, may be able to help. For any partnership, keeping books involves journalizing initial investments and generating a statement of partners' equity. To reach SPARDATA.com, go to **http://www.spardata.com/spar.htm**. To find out who's who in Bobby's firm on *The Practice*, go to **http://abc.go.com/primetime/the_practice/prac_home.html**.

Performance Objectives

After you have completed this chapter, you will be able to do the following:

1. (a) Define *partnership* and list the main advantages and disadvantages of a partnership; (b) journalize initial investments.

2. Provide for the division of net income and loss on the basis of (a) fractional shares; (b) ratio of capital investments; and (c) salary and interest allowances.

3. Journalize the closing entries for a partnership.

4. Prepare a statement of partners' equity.

5. Journalize entries involving the sale of a partnership interest or withdrawal of a partner.

6. Journalize entries pertaining to the liquidation of a partnership involving the immediate sale of the assets for cash.

Up to now, we have been dealing entirely with sole proprietorships. We now turn our attention to partnerships. In the professions and in firms that stress personal service, partnerships are widely used. Each professional practitioner can maintain his or her own clientele, yet share with colleagues the expenses of operating an office or clinic. Partnerships are also popular in manufacturing and trade because they afford a means of combining the capital and abilities of two or more persons.

CHARACTERISTICS OF A PARTNERSHIP

Objective 1a

Define *partnership* and list the main advantages and disadvantages of a partnership.

A **partnership**, as defined by the Uniform Partnership Act, is an association of two or more persons to carry on, as co-owners, a business for profit. It is a voluntary association, entered into by the partners. Certain features of a partnership affect just the partners; other features affect both the partners and others who are not members of the partnership. Let's examine some of these features.

Co-ownership of Partnership Property

All partners are co-owners of the assets of the partnership. For example, Towne and Dillon formed a 50-50 partnership to run a fuel oil business. The partnership owns two tank trucks of equal value. According to the **co-ownership** concept, each partner owns half of each truck, as well as half of the other assets of the firm.

Limited Life

Remember!

Just because a partnership ends does not necessarily mean that the business ends. It can continue under a new partnership agreement.

A partnership may be ended by the death or withdrawal of any partner. Other factors that may bring about the end of a partnership include the bankruptcy or incapacity of a partner, the expiration of the period of time specified in the partnership agreement, or the completion of the project for which the partnership was formed.

Unlimited Liability

Each partner is personally liable to creditors for all the debts the partnership incurs during his or her membership in the firm. When a new partner joins an existing firm, he or she may or may not assume liability for debts incurred by the firm prior to admission. When a partner withdraws from a firm, he or she must give adequate public notice of withdrawal, or he or she may be held liable for debts the partnership incurs after his or her withdrawal.

Mutual Agency

Each partner can enter into binding contracts in the name of the firm for the purchase or sale of goods or services within the normal scope of the firm's business. If the partners agree among themselves to limit the right of any partner to enter into certain contracts in the name of the firm, this agreement is not binding on outsiders who are unaware of its existence.

Although accounting for partnerships is essentially the same as accounting for sole proprietorships, not all partnerships are small. All the major accounting firms, as well as many legal organizations, are partnerships.

ADVANTAGES OF A PARTNERSHIP

Here are four advantages of a partnership:

1. Partnerships offer the opportunity to pool the abilities and capital of two or more persons.
2. It is easy to form a partnership, the only requirement being an agreement or mutual understanding by the partners.
3. Legal restrictions are minimal. Although a partnership must have a legal purpose, there are no other limitations on types of business activities.
4. Federal income taxes are not levied against a partnership as an entity, although a partnership must file an information return (Form 1065) containing an income statement, balance sheet, and report of the distributive shares of income (the shares of the year's net income allocated to each partner). A partner has to file an individual income tax return and has to pay taxes on his or her share of the net income, whether or not this share is actually taken out of the business.

Remember!

Partnerships allow pooling of time, money, and talent. They can also have the same difficulties as any personal relationship. Therefore, a written agreement is extremely important.

DISADVANTAGES OF A PARTNERSHIP

Here are six disadvantages of a partnership:

1. **General partners** (those who actively and publicly participate in transactions of the firm) have unlimited liability.
2. A partnership has limited life.
3. The actions of one partner are binding on the other partners; this relationship is known as **mutual agency**. (This could also be an advantage.)
4. The raising of investment capital depends entirely on the partners themselves.
5. It is hard to transfer a partial or entire partnership interest to another person, as the transfer must be agreed to by all partners.
6. There may be some strain in personal relationships among partners as they carry out their daily responsibilities.

PARTNERSHIP AGREEMENTS

Although a partnership may be formed on the basis of an oral understanding, it is much better to have the partnership agreement based on a written contract. Although there is no standard form of partnership agreement, the following provisions are usually included:

• Effective date of the agreement
• Names and addresses of the partners
• Name, location, and nature of the business
• Duration of the agreement
• Investment of each partner
• Withdrawals to be allowed each partner
• Procedure for sharing profits and losses
• Provision for division of assets upon liquidation

FIGURE 1

Most law practices are partnerships. A partnership is like any other relationship between and among people—sometimes it works, and sometimes it doesn't. It requires the same care as other relationships, including attention to business detail. Prior to forming a partnership, an agreement that outlines the operations and liquidation plans is essential.

PARTNERSHIP AGREEMENT

J. C. Baron of San Diego, California, and D. S. Mallery of the same city and state agree as follows:

Recitals of Fact: The parties have this day formed a partnership for the purpose of engaging in and conducting a physical fitness business in the city of San Diego under the following stipulations, which are a part of this contract:

First: The partnership is to continue for a term of 20 years from January 1 of this year.

Second: The business is to be conducted under the firm name of Bayside Fitness, at 1424 West Sixth Street, San Diego, California.

Third: The investments are as follows: J. C. Baron, cash, $90,000; D. S. Mallery, cash, $90,000. These invested assets are partnership property in which the equity of each partner is the same.

Fourth: Each partner is to devote his or her entire time and attention to the business and to engage in no other business enterprise without the written consent of the other partner.

Fifth: During the operation of this partnership, neither partner is to become surety or bondsman for anyone without the written consent of the other partner.

Sixth: Each partner is to receive a salary of $39,000 a year, payable $1,625 in cash on the fifteenth and $1,625 on the last business day of each month. At the end of each annual fiscal period, the net income or the net loss shown by the income statement, after the salaries of the two partners have been allowed, is to be shared as follows: J. C. Baron, 50 percent; D. S. Mallery, 50 percent.

Seventh: Neither partner is to withdraw assets in excess of his or her salary, any part of the assets invested, or assets in anticipation of net income to be earned, without the written consent of the other partner.

Eighth: In the case of the death or the legal disability of either partner, the other partner is to continue the operations of the business until the close of the annual fiscal period on the following December 31. At that time the continuing partner is to be given an option to buy the interest of the deceased or incapacitated partner at the value of the deceased or incapacitated partner's proprietary interest as determined by the agreement of the continuing partner and the legal representative of the deceased or incapacitated partner. In the event they are unable to agree, then the determination of such value shall be submitted to arbitration in accordance with the rules of the American Arbitration Association. It is agreed that this purchase price is to be paid one half in cash and the balance in four equal installments payable quarterly.

Ninth: At the conclusion of this contract, unless it is mutually agreed to continue the operation of the business under a new contract, the assets of the partnership, after the liabilities are paid, are to be divided in proportion to the net credit of each partner's capital account on that date.

Dated _____ December 28, 20— _____   *J. C. Baron* (Seal)

D. S. Mallery (Seal)

A typical partnership agreement is shown in Figure 1.

ACCOUNTING ENTRIES FOR PARTNERSHIPS

The only difference between accounting for a sole proprietorship and accounting for a partnership is in the owners' equity accounts. The accountant uses the same types of asset, liability, revenue, and expense accounts that we discussed before. But, because there is more than one owner, each

Remember!

Accounting for a partnership is basically the same as accounting for other business entities. The major difference is that the partnership has a Capital and a Drawing account for each partner.

Objective 1b

Journalize initial investments.

partner has a Capital account and a Drawing account. As in sole proprietorships, the Capital accounts are involved only when there is a change in investments or when the Income Summary account and the Drawing accounts are closed.

Recording Investments

The accountant makes a separate entry for the investment of each partner. All assets contributed by a given partner are debited to the appropriate asset accounts. If the partnership assumes liabilities, the accountant credits the proper liability accounts. When the value of a partner's contributed assets exceeds the value of the partner's assumed liabilities, the partner's capital account is credited for the net amount.

Let's look at the recording of initial investments in a partnership: Ralph H. Coe and Rita L. Lopes decide to form a partnership on February 2 for the operation of a jewelry store. Coe presently owns and operates Coe Jewelers. He is contributing the assets and liabilities of his store to the new firm. Lopes's investment is $50,000 in cash; the entry on page 1 of the general journal to record this investment is as follows:

GENERAL JOURNAL   PAGE ___1___

	DATE		DESCRIPTION	POST. REF.	DEBIT	CREDIT	
1	20–						1
2	Feb.	2	Cash		50 0 0 0 00		2
3			Rita L. Lopes, Capital			50 0 0 0 00	3
4			To record the original				4
5			investment of Rita L. Lopes.				5
6							6

Both partners have to agree on the monetary amounts at which Coe's non-cash assets are to be recorded. Assume that Coe Jewelers has the following account balances:

Cash	$ 2,900
Accounts Receivable	18,000
Allowance for Doubtful Accounts	200
Merchandise Inventory	40,400
Equipment	16,000
Accumulated Depreciation, Equipment	4,500
Notes Payable	1,600
Accounts Payable	8,400

Furthermore, $400 of the Accounts Receivable have been determined to be uncollectible; the $400 should not be recorded on the books of the new partnership. Of the remaining $17,600 of Accounts Receivable, there is some doubt as to the collectibility of $500. Assume that these amounts have been determined by aging the accounts receivable. Since the values of the merchandise and equipment may be more or less than the amounts recorded on Coe's books, both parties agree to have an independent appraisal made. Assume that the present appraised value of Coe's merchandise is $41,000 and that of his equipment is $9,000. Therefore, the accountant records Coe's investment as follows:

DATE		DESCRIPTION	POST. REF.	DEBIT	CREDIT	
6						6
7	2	Cash		2 9 0 0 00		7
8		Accounts Receivable		17 6 0 0 00		8
9		Merchandise Inventory		41 0 0 0 00		9
10		Equipment		9 0 0 0 00		10
11		Allowance for Doubtful				11
12		Accounts			5 0 0 00	12
13		Notes Payable			1 6 0 0 00	13
14		Accounts Payable			8 4 0 0 00	14
15		Ralph H. Coe, Capital			60 0 0 0 00	15
16		To record the original				16
17		investment of Ralph H. Coe.				17
18						18

The accountant debits Accounts Receivable for the face amount of the accounts taken over by the new partnership and credits Allowance for Doubtful Accounts for the amount estimated to be uncollectible, which in this case is $500. Any definitely uncollectible customer accounts are excluded from those being taken over by the new business (in this case, $18,000 Accounts Receivable less $400 uncollectible).

The accountant debits the new firm's Merchandise Inventory and Equipment accounts for the amount of their present appraised values. The accumulated depreciation is not recorded because the appraised value represents the new book value for the partnership.

Remember!

An original investment by a partner may include liabilities as well as assets.

Additional Investments

Now let's say that eight months have gone by, and the new partnership needs more cash. On October 1, each partner invests an additional $7,000. The entry is as follows:

GENERAL JOURNAL   PAGE **28**

	DATE		DESCRIPTION	POST. REF.	DEBIT	CREDIT	
1	20–						1
2	Oct.	1	Cash		14 0 0 0 00		2
3			Ralph H. Coe, Capital			7 0 0 0 00	3
4			Rita L. Lopes, Capital			7 0 0 0 00	4
5			To record additional				5
6			investments.				6
7							7

FYI

Additional investments appear in the same place on the statement of partners' equity as on the statement of owner's equity.

At the end of the year, before the books are closed, the Capital accounts of the partners appear as shown here:

GENERAL LEDGER

ACCOUNT   Ralph H. Coe, Capital   ACCOUNT NO.   301

	DATE	ITEM	POST. REF.	DEBIT	CREDIT	BALANCE DEBIT	BALANCE CREDIT	
1	20–							1
2	Feb. 2		J1		60 0 0 0 00		60 0 0 0 00	2
3	Oct. 1		J28		7 0 0 0 00		67 0 0 0 00	3

ACCOUNT   Rita L. Lopes, Capital   ACCOUNT NO.   303

	DATE	ITEM	POST. REF.	DEBIT	CREDIT	BALANCE DEBIT	BALANCE CREDIT	
1	20–							1
2	Feb. 2		J1		50 0 0 0 00		50 0 0 0 00	2
3	Oct. 1		J28		7 0 0 0 00		57 0 0 0 00	3

Drawing Accounts

Drawing accounts of partners serve the same purpose as the Drawing account of the owner of a sole proprietorship. Debits to the Drawing accounts originate through transactions such as those listed here and illustrated in Figure 2.

- Withdrawal of cash by R. H. Coe, $620, March 17.
- Withdrawal of merchandise by R. L. Lopes, $742, May 4.

FIGURE 2

	DATE	DESCRIPTION	POST. REF.	DEBIT	CREDIT	
1	20–					1
2	Mar. 17	R. H. Coe, Drawing		6 2 0 00		2
3		Cash			6 2 0 00	3
4		To record a cash withdrawal.				4
5						5
6	May 4	R. L. Lopes, Drawing		7 4 2 00		6
7		Purchases			7 4 2 00	7
8		To record a merchandise				8
9		withdrawal at cost.				9
10						10

DIVISION OF NET INCOME OR NET LOSS

Objective 2

Provide for the division of net income and loss.

Recall that the closing entries for a sole proprietorship require the following steps:

1. Close the revenue accounts into the Income Summary account.
2. Close the expense accounts into the Income Summary account (the expense accounts do not include any payments to the owner).
3. Close the Income Summary account into the Capital account by the amount of the net income or loss.
4. Close the Drawing account into the Capital account.

The only differences between closing entries for a partnership and those for a sole proprietorship occur in steps 3 and 4. Instead of a single Capital account and a single Drawing account, in a partnership there are as many accounts of each type as there are partners. Income Summary is closed into the Capital accounts by the amount of the net income or loss, and the Drawing accounts are closed into the respective Capital accounts.

Let's look at step 3. The partnership agreement should specify the arrangement for the division of net income or net loss. However, if the partnership agreement fails to do this, from a legal standpoint, the partners should share any net income or loss equally. This is true regardless of differences in amounts invested, in special skills provided, or in time devoted to the business. The share of net income (or net loss) allocated to each partner is known as his or her **distributive share**.

Partners may use any one of a number of alternative methods of sharing partnership earnings, or they may use a combination of methods. The variety of methods reflects the different values of the services or investments contributed by individual partners. We discuss four methods for sharing earnings:

1. Division of income based on fractional shares
2. Division of income based on the ratio of capital investments
3. Division of income based on salary allowances
4. Division of income based on interest allowances

We look at two examples of each method.

In our first example, the partnership of Brock and Casey has a net *income* of $96,000. In the second, the partnership of Brock and Casey has a net *loss* of $4,000. We use the same balances in the Capital and Drawing accounts for each example and consider that each method used for dividing net income represents a separate partnership agreement.

The balances of the Capital accounts represent the partners' individual investments at the beginning of the year. The balances of the Drawing accounts represent the total personal withdrawals during the year. These are shown by T accounts as follows:

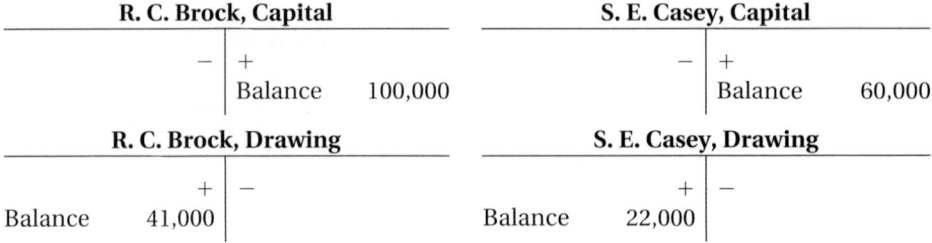

R. C. Brock, Capital		S. E. Casey, Capital	
−	+	−	+
	Balance 100,000		Balance 60,000

R. C. Brock, Drawing		S. E. Casey, Drawing	
+	−	+	−
Balance 41,000		Balance 22,000	

Closing entries for a partnership are similar to those of a sole proprietorship. The partnership agreement should detail the percentages of net income or net loss to attribute to each partner. In the case of Russ & Daughters, it would appear that there are at least three partners. They may divide the income based on fractional shares, the ratio of capital investments, salary allowances, or interest allowances.

Objective 2a

Provide for the division of net income and loss on the basis of fractional shares.

Division of Income Based on Fractional Shares

The simplest way to divide net income or loss is to allot each partner a stated fraction of the total. You can establish the size of the fraction by taking into consideration (1) the amount of each partner's investment and (2) the value of the services rendered by each partner. Assume that the partnership agreement stipulates that profits and losses are to be divided this way: three-fourths to Brock and one-fourth to Casey.

The accountant may present a report of the division of net income as a separate statement or record it on the income statement, immediately below Net Income.

Net Income of $96,000 If the accountant adopts the latter procedure, the division of net income appears as follows:

Brock and Casey
Partial Income Statement
For Year Ended December 31, 20—

	R. C. Brock	S. E. Casey	Total
Revenue from Sales:			
Net Income			$96 0 0 0 00
Division of Net Income	R. C. Brock	S. E. Casey	Total
Fractional Share	$72 0 0 0 00	$24 0 0 0 00	$96 0 0 0 00

Remember!

Financial statements for a partnership are basically the same as those of other business entities except for one main difference—the section showing the division of net income.

Objective 3

Journalize the closing entries for a partnership.

The division of net income is recorded as a closing entry in step 3 of the closing procedure, whether or not the partner has withdrawn his or her share. The entry is as follows:

	DATE		DESCRIPTION	POST. REF.	DEBIT	CREDIT	
1	20—		**Closing Entry**				1
2	Dec.	31	Income Summary		96 0 0 0 00		2
3			R. C. Brock, Capital			72 0 0 0 00	3
4			S. E. Casey, Capital			24 0 0 0 00	4
5							5
6							6

The entries for step 4, closing the Drawing accounts into the Capital accounts, are as follows:

	DATE	DESCRIPTION	POST. REF.	DEBIT	CREDIT	
6	Dec. 31	R. C. Brock, Capital		41 0 0 0 00		6
7		R. C. Brock, Drawing			41 0 0 0 00	7
8						8
9	31	S. E. Casey, Capital		22 0 0 0 00		9
10		S. E. Casey, Drawing			22 0 0 0 00	10
11						11
12						12

Now let's see what these entries look like in T accounts, with steps 3 and 4 labeled:

Income Summary

(3) Closing	96,000	Balance	96,000

R. C. Brock, Capital

	−	+	
(4)	41,000	Balance	100,000
		(3)	72,000

S. E. Casey, Capital

	−	+	
(4)	22,000	Balance	60,000
		(3)	24,000

R. C. Brock, Drawing

	+	−	
Balance	41,000	(4) Closing	41,000

S. E. Casey, Drawing

	+	−	
Balance	22,000	(4) Closing	22,000

Note that step 4 is the same for partnerships as for sole proprietorships.

Net Loss of $4,000 The lower portion of the income statement reflects the net loss. (The parentheses around the totals indicate that the figures are minus numbers.)

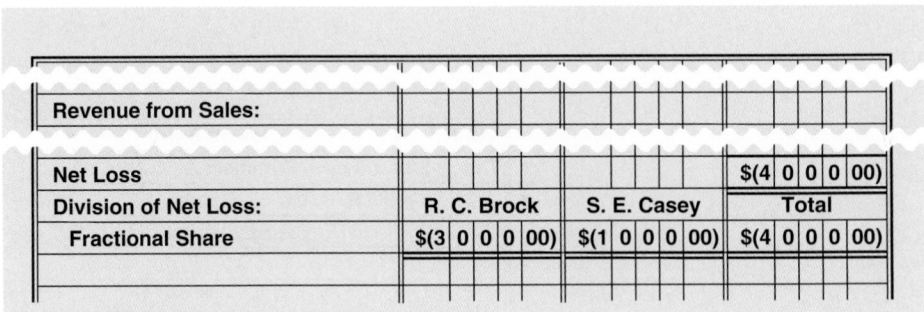

Revenue from Sales:				
Net Loss				$(4 0 0 0 00)
Division of Net Loss:	R. C. Brock	S. E. Casey	Total	
Fractional Share	$(3 0 0 0 00)	$(1 0 0 0 00)	$(4 0 0 0 00)	

Remember!

A net loss (like net income) is allocated according to the partnership agreement.

FIGURE 3

	DATE		DESCRIPTION	POST. REF.	DEBIT	CREDIT	
1	20–		**Closing Entries**				1
2	Dec.	31	R. C. Brock, Capital		3 0 0 0 00		2
3			S. E. Casey, Capital		1 0 0 0 00		3
4			Income Summary			4 0 0 0 00	4
5							5
6		31	R. C. Brock, Capital		41 0 0 0 00		6
7			R. C. Brock, Drawing			41 0 0 0 00	7
8							8
9		31	S. E. Casey, Capital		22 0 0 0 00		9
10			S. E. Casey, Drawing			22 0 0 0 00	10
11							11

The closing entries and posting to the ledger accounts are shown in Figure 3 and the T accounts that follow:

Income Summary

Balance	4,000	**(3)** Closing	4,000

R. C. Brock, Capital

	–	+	
(3)	3,000	Balance	100,000
(4)	41,000		

S. E. Casey, Capital

	–	+	
(3)	1,000	Balance	60,000
(4)	22,000		

R. C. Brock, Drawing

	+	–	
Balance	41,000	**(4)** Closing	41,000

S. E. Casey, Drawing

	+	–	
Balance	22,000	**(4)** Closing	22,000

When partners share net income on a fractional basis, this basis is often expressed as a ratio. We can express Brock's three-fourths and Casey's one-fourth as a 3:1 (3-to-1) ratio.

When you list the division of net income as a ratio and want to turn the ratio into a fraction, do it this way: First add the figures; then use the total as the denominator of the fraction.

3:1   (3 + 1 = 4)   ¾ and ¼

or (in the case of three partners):

5:3:1   (5 + 3 + 1 = 9)   5/9 and 3/9 and 1/9

or (in the case of four partners):

3:2:1:1   (3 + 2 + 1 + 1 = 7)   3/7 and 2/7 and 1/7 and 1/7

Division of Income Based on Ratio of Capital Investments

Allocating earnings to partners on the basis of the amounts of their investment often works well for enterprises whose earnings are closely related to the amount of money invested, such as real estate ventures, cattle feeding operations, and the like. Suppose that Brock and Casey have agreed to share earnings or losses according to the ratio of their investments at the beginning of the year. Let's say that Brock had $100,000 and Casey had $60,000 in their Capital accounts. You can calculate their respective shares as follows:

Brock	$100,000
Casey	60,000
Total	$160,000

Brock's share $= \dfrac{\$100,000}{\$160,000} = \dfrac{5}{8}$ or .625 (62.5%)

Casey's share $= \dfrac{\$60,000}{\$160,000} = \dfrac{3}{8}$ or .375 (37.5%)

Net Income of $96,000 When the partnership has a net income of $96,000, the accountant determines the distribution like this:

Brock's share of earnings $96,000 × ⅝ (or $96,000 × .625) = $60,000

Casey's share of earnings $96,000 × ⅜ (or $96,000 × .375) = $36,000

The section of the income statement showing the division of net income looks like this:

Revenue from Sales:			
Net Income			$96 0 0 0 00
Division of Net Income:	R. C. Brock	S. E. Casey	Total
Capital Investment Ratio	$60 0 0 0 00	$36 0 0 0 00	$96 0 0 0 00

The accompanying closing entries are as follows:

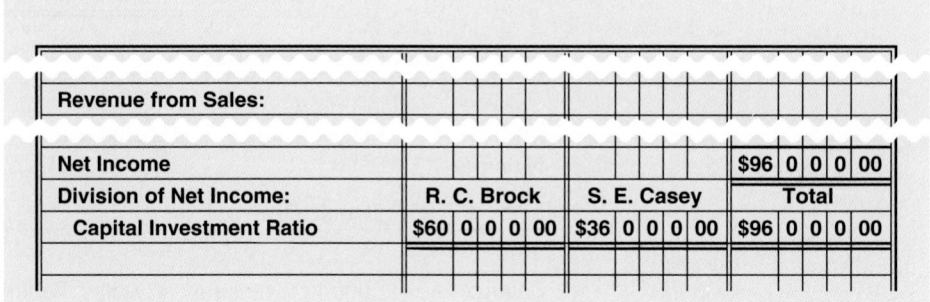

	DATE		DESCRIPTION	POST. REF.	DEBIT	CREDIT	
1	20–		**Closing Entries**				1
2	Dec.	31	Income Summary		96 0 0 0 00		2
3			R. C. Brock, Capital			60 0 0 0 00	3
4			S. E. Casey, Capital			36 0 0 0 00	4
5							5
6		31	R. C. Brock, Capital		41 0 0 0 00		6
7			R. C. Brock, Drawing			41 0 0 0 00	7
8							8
9		31	S. E. Casey, Capital		22 0 0 0 00		9
10			S. E. Casey, Drawing			22 0 0 0 00	10
11							11

Net Loss of $4,000 When the partnership has a net loss of $4,000, the accountant calculates the sharing of the loss as follows:

Brock's share of the loss $4,000 × ⅝ (or $4,000 × .625) = $2,500

Casey's share of the loss $4,000 × ⅜ (or $4,000 × .375) = $1,500

The section of the income statement showing the division of net loss and the accompanying closing entries looks like this:

■ ■ ■

Remember!

Closing the Drawing accounts into the Capital accounts is the same, regardless of whether a business produces a net income or a net loss.

	R. C. Brock	S. E. Casey	Total
Revenue from Sales:			
Net Loss			$(4 0 0 0 00)
Division of Net Loss:	R. C. Brock	S. E. Casey	Total
Capital Investment Ratio	$(2 5 0 0 00)	$(1 5 0 0 00)	$(4 0 0 0 00)

	DATE		DESCRIPTION	POST. REF.	DEBIT	CREDIT	
1	20–		Closing Entries				1
2	Dec.	31	R. C. Brock, Capital		2 5 0 0 00		2
3			S. E. Casey, Capital		1 5 0 0 00		3
4			Income Summary			4 0 0 0 00	4
5							5
6		31	R. C. Brock, Capital		41 0 0 0 00		6
7			R. C. Brock, Drawing			41 0 0 0 00	7
8							8
9		31	S. E. Casey, Capital		22 0 0 0 00		9
10			S. E. Casey, Drawing			22 0 0 0 00	10
11							11

Note that the entries for step 4—closing the Drawing accounts into the Capital accounts—are always the same, regardless of whether the firm finishes the year with a net income or a net loss.

Division of Income Based on Salary Allowances

■ ■ ■

Objective 2c

Provide for the division of net income and loss on the basis of salary and interest allowances.

Salary allowances are purely allocations of net income. They are used as a means of recognizing and rewarding differences in ability and in the amount of time devoted to the business. **Salary allowances are different from payments to the partners, which are recorded in the Drawing accounts.** They are also different from payments to employees, which are recorded as Salaries or Wages Expense. They may be thought of as guaranteed amounts determined without regard to the income of the partnership.

Suppose that Brock's and Casey's partnership agreement provides for yearly salaries of $24,000 and $16,000, respectively, with the remainder of the net income to be divided equally. (It would also be possible to divide the remainder on the basis of the ratio of investments or any other ratio agreed to by the partners.)

Net Income of $96,000 When there is a net income of $96,000, the Division of Net Income section of the income statement is as follows:

Revenue from Sales:			
Net Income			$96 0 0 0 00
Division of Net Income:	R. C. Brock	S. E. Casey	Total
Salary Allowances	$24 0 0 0 00	$16 0 0 0 00	$40 0 0 0 00
Remainder Allocated Equally	28 0 0 0 00	28 0 0 0 00	56 0 0 0 00
Net Income	$52 0 0 0 00	$44 0 0 0 00	$96 0 0 0 00

Remember!

If the partnership agreement does not stipulate the allocation of the net income or loss after allowances, it is assumed to be divided equally.

The accountant determines the allocation of the remainder as follows:

Net income	$96,000
Less amount allocated as salaries ($24,000 + $16,000)	40,000
Remainder	$56,000

$$\text{Remainder} \div 2 = \frac{\$56,000}{2} = \$28,000$$

Now look at the closing entries:

	DATE		DESCRIPTION	POST. REF.	DEBIT	CREDIT	
1	20–		**Closing Entries**				1
2	Dec.	31	Income Summary		96 0 0 0 00		2
3			R. C. Brock, Capital			52 0 0 0 00	3
4			S. E. Casey, Capital			44 0 0 0 00	4
5							5
6		31	R. C. Brock, Capital		41 0 0 0 00		6
7			R. C. Brock, Drawing			41 0 0 0 00	7
8							8
9		31	S. E. Casey, Capital		22 0 0 0 00		9
10			S. E. Casey, Drawing			22 0 0 0 00	10
11							11

Net Loss of $4,000 When salary allowances are stipulated in the partnership agreement, they must be allocated (not necessarily paid) regardless of whether there is enough net income to take care of them.

The accountant determines the remainder as follows:

Net loss	$(4,000)
Less amount allocated as salaries ($24,000 + $16,000)	40,000
Remainder	$(44,000)

$$\text{Remainder} \div 2 = \frac{\$(44,000)}{2} = \$(22,000)$$

The income statement and the closing entries appear as follows:

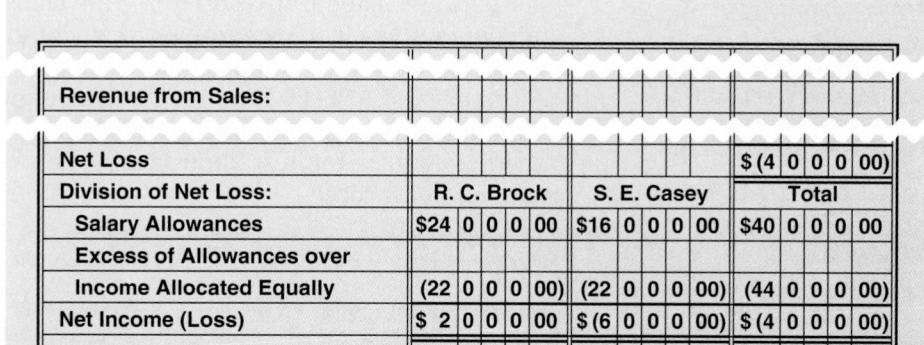

Revenue from Sales:				
Net Loss				$(40 0 0 00)
Division of Net Loss:		R. C. Brock	S. E. Casey	Total
Salary Allowances		$24 0 0 0 00	$16 0 0 0 00	$40 0 0 0 00
Excess of Allowances over				
Income Allocated Equally		(22 0 0 0 00)	(22 0 0 0 00)	(44 0 0 0 00)
Net Income (Loss)		$ 2 0 0 0 00	$(6 0 0 0 00)	$(4 0 0 0 00)

	DATE		DESCRIPTION	POST. REF.	DEBIT	CREDIT	
1	20–		**Closing Entries**				1
2	Dec.	31	S. E. Casey, Capital		6 0 0 0 00		2
3			Income Summary			4 0 0 0 00	3
4			R. C. Brock, Capital			2 0 0 0 00	4
5							5
6		31	R. C. Brock, Capital		41 0 0 0 00		6
7			R. C. Brock, Drawing			41 0 0 0 00	7
8							8
9		31	S. E. Casey, Capital		22 0 0 0 00		9
10			S. E. Casey, Drawing			22 0 0 0 00	10
11							11

After posting, the owners' equity accounts look like this:

Income Summary

Balance	4,000	(3) Closing	4,000

R. C. Brock, Capital

	–	+	
(4)	41,000	Balance	100,000
		(3)	2,000

S. E. Casey, Capital

	–	+	
(3)	6,000	Balance	60,000
(4)	22,000		

R. C. Brock, Drawing

	+	–	
Balance	41,000	(4) Closing	41,000

S. E. Casey, Drawing

	+	–	
Balance	22,000	(4) Closing	22,000

As a result of the $4,000 net loss for the year and the activity in the drawing accounts, Brock's Capital account decreased by $39,000 (credit $2,000 and debit $41,000), and Casey's Capital account decreased by $28,000 (debit $6,000 and debit $22,000).

Division of Income Based on Interest Allowances

Sometimes a partnership agreement stipulates an allowance for interest on the partners' capital investments. This clause acts as an incentive for partners not only to leave their investments in the business, but even to increase them. For example, suppose that Brock and Casey, in addition to their salary allowances of $24,000 and $16,000, are allowed 8 percent interest on their Capital balances at the beginning of the fiscal year; the remainder is to be divided equally. Interest allowances, like salary allowances, are just allocations of net income.

Interest allowance for Brock $100,000 \times .08 = \$8,000$

Interest allowance for Casey $60,000 \times .08 = \$4,800$

Net Income of $96,000 The section of the income statement relating to the division of a $96,000 net income appears as follows:

	R. C. Brock	S. E. Casey	Total
Revenue from Sales:			
Net Income			$96 0 0 0 00
Division of Net Income:	R. C. Brock	S. E. Casey	Total
Salary Allowances	$24 0 0 0 00	$16 0 0 0 00	$40 0 0 0 00
Interest Allowances	8 0 0 0 00	4 8 0 0 00	12 8 0 0 00
Remainder Allocated Equally	21 6 0 0 00	21 6 0 0 00	43 2 0 0 00
Net Income	$53 6 0 0 00	$42 4 0 0 00	$96 0 0 0 00

The accountant calculates the remainder in the following way:

Net income		$96,000
Less:		
Amount allocated as salaries ($24,000 + $16,000)	$40,000	
Amount allocated as interest ($8,000 + $4,800)	12,800	52,800
Remainder		$43,200

$$\text{Remainder} \div 2 = \frac{\$43,200}{2} = \$21,600$$

And the closing entries look like the following.

DATE		DESCRIPTION	POST. REF.	DEBIT	CREDIT	
20–		**Closing Entries**				1
Dec.	31	Income Summary		96 0 0 0 00		2
		R. C. Brock, Capital			53 6 0 0 00	3
		S. E. Casey, Capital			42 4 0 0 00	4
						5
	31	R. C. Brock, Capital		41 0 0 0 00		6
		R. C. Brock, Drawing			41 0 0 0 00	7
						8
	31	S. E. Casey, Capital		22 0 0 0 00		9
		S. E. Casey, Drawing			22 0 0 0 00	10
						11

Net Loss of $4,000 The accountant handles interest allowances the same way she or he handles salary allowances: Both must be allocated, whether or not there is enough net income to take care of them. The section of the income statement relating to the division of a $4,000 net loss appears as follows:

		R. C. Brock	S. E. Casey	Total
Revenue from Sales:				
Net Loss				$ (4 0 0 0 00)
Division of Net Loss:		R. C. Brock	S. E. Casey	Total
Salary Allowances		$24 0 0 0 00	$16 0 0 0 00	$40 0 0 0 00
Interest Allowances		8 0 0 0 00	4 8 0 0 00	12 8 0 0 00
Excess of Allowances over				
Income Allocated Equally		(28 4 0 0 00)	(28 4 0 0 00)	(56 8 0 0 00)
Net Income (Loss)		$ 3 6 0 0 00	$(7 6 0 0 00)	$ (4 0 0 0 00)

The accountant computes the remainder as follows:

Net loss		$(4,000)
Less:		
Amount allocated as salaries		
($24,000 + $16,000)	$40,000	
Amount allocated as interest		
($8,000 + $4,800)	12,800	52,800
Remainder		$(56,800)

$$\text{Remainder} \div 2 = \frac{\$(56,800)}{2} = \$(28,400)$$

And the closing entries look like those on the following page.

	DATE		DESCRIPTION	POST. REF.	DEBIT	CREDIT	
1	20–		**Closing Entries**				1
2	Dec.	31	S. E. Casey, Capital		7 6 0 0 00		2
3			Income Summary			4 0 0 0 00	3
4			R. C. Brock, Capital			3 6 0 0 00	4
5							5
6		31	R. C. Brock, Capital		41 0 0 0 00		6
7			R. C. Brock, Drawing			41 0 0 0 00	7
8							8
9		31	S. E. Casey, Capital		22 0 0 0 00		9
10			S. E. Casey, Drawing			22 0 0 0 00	10
11							11

Remember!

Income Summary is closed into the partners' Capital accounts by the amount of each partner's distributive share of net income or loss.

After posting, the owners' equity accounts look like this:

Income Summary

Balance	4,000	(3) Closing	4,000

R. C. Brock, Capital

	−	+	
(4)	41,000	Balance	100,000
		(3)	3,600

S. E. Casey, Capital

	−	+	
(3)	7,600	Balance	60,000
(4)	22,000		

R. C. Brock, Drawing

	+	−	
Balance	41,000	(4) Closing	41,000

S. E. Casey, Drawing

	+	−	
Balance	22,000	(4) Closing	22,000

FINANCIAL STATEMENTS FOR A PARTNERSHIP

Objective 4

Prepare a statement of partners' equity.

Changes in the balances of the partners' Capital accounts are recorded in the statement of partners' equity, which is just like a statement of owner's equity for a sole proprietorship, except that there is a separate column for each partner.

Brock and Casey
Statement of Partners' Equity
For Year Ended December 31, 20—

	R. C. Brock	S. E. Casey	Total
Capital, January 1, 20—	$100 0 0 0 00	$ 60 0 0 0 00	$160 0 0 0 00
Net Income for the Year	53 6 0 0 00	42 4 0 0 00	96 0 0 0 00
Total	$153 6 0 0 00	$102 4 0 0 00	$256 0 0 0 00
Less Withdrawals During the Year	41 0 0 0 00	22 0 0 0 00	63 0 0 0 00
Capital, December 31, 20—	$112 6 0 0 00	$ 80 4 0 0 00	$193 0 0 0 00

Remember!

A partner is taxed on the net income share, not on what the partner withdraws.

When a partner makes an additional permanent investment after the beginning of the fiscal period, the accountant records this amount right below the beginning balance of the Capital accounts.

Partners have to pay federal income taxes on the basis of each partner's distributive share (share of net income) in the business. For example, R. C. Brock's taxable income is $53,600, even though he withdrew only $41,000. He lists $53,600 on his personal income tax return. The Internal Revenue Code requires that details of the distributive share of each partner must be recorded on a U.S. Partnership Return of Income (Form 1065).

DISSOLUTION OF A PARTNERSHIP

One disadvantage of a partnership is its limited life. Any change in the personnel of the membership formally ends the partnership. When a partnership dissolves, the main visible result is a change in the names listed in the partnership agreement and a change in the division of net income; usually the routine transactions of the business continue. For example, suppose that a partnership originally consists of partners A, B, and C. Then C withdraws his or her investment from the firm, and a new partnership emerges: partners A and B. During the transition, business is continued. In other words, in a **dissolution**, the original partnership is dissolved by either the sale of one partner's interest in the firm to a new partner or the withdrawal of a partner. The firm continues to operate as before.

Sale of a Partnership Interest

Objective 5

Journalize entries involving the sale of a partnership interest or withdrawal of a partner.

When a partner retires, that partner may sell his or her interest to a person outside the firm who is acceptable to the remaining partners. Let's say that, at the end of a given year, S. E. Casey has a Capital balance of $63,520 and decides to sell his interest to D. N. Davis for $80,000. The accountant makes the following entry to account for the transfer of ownership:

	DATE		DESCRIPTION	POST. REF.	DEBIT	CREDIT	
1	20–						1
2	Dec.	31	S. E. Casey, Capital		63 5 2 0 00		2
3			D. N. Davis, Capital			63 5 2 0 00	3
4			To transfer Casey's equity				4
5			in the partnership to Davis.				5
6							6

The difference between $80,000 and $63,520 represents a personal profit to Casey, not to the firm. The new partner, buyer D. N. Davis, paid the $80,000 directly to the old partner, seller S. E. Casey, without affecting the partnership accounting records. *There has been no change in the partnership's assets or liabilities; consequently, there is no change in the total owners' equity.* However, if the firm is to continue, Brock (the other original partner) must be willing to accept Davis as a new partner.

Fern, Goll, and Horn
Balance Sheet
September 30, 20—

Assets																			
Current Assets																			
Cash								$28	0	0	0	00							
Accounts Receivable	$8	0	0	0	00													
Less Allowance for Doubtful Accounts		5	0	0	00		7	5	0	0	00							
Merchandise Inventory							47	5	0	0	00							
Total Current Assets												$83	0	0	0	00		
Plant and Equipment:																			
Equipment							$27	0	0	0	00							
Less Accumulated Depreciation							11	0	0	0	00		16	0	0	0	00
Total Assets												$99	0	0	0	00		
Liabilities																			
Accounts Payable												$ 7	0	0	0	00		
Partners' Equity																			
K. L. Fern, Capital							$46	0	0	0	00							
N. B. Goll, Capital							24	0	0	0	00							
J. C. Horn, Capital							22	0	0	0	00							
Total Partners' Equity												92	0	0	0	00		
Total Liabilities and Partners' Equity												$99	0	0	0	00		

FIGURE 4

Withdrawal of a Partner

The partnership agreement should outline a set procedure to follow if one of the partners withdraws. Such a procedure usually entails an audit of the books and a revaluation of the partnership's assets and liabilities to reflect current market values.

Partner Withdraws Book Value of His or Her Equity After Revaluation

> **Remember!**
>
> A loss or gain on revaluation is shared according to the ratio agreed upon in the partnership agreement.

Suppose that N. B. Goll is retiring from the partnership of Fern, Goll, and Horn. The partnership agreement stipulates that net income and net loss shall be shared on an equal basis; it also provides for an audit and revaluation of assets in the event that a partner retires. Figure 4 shows the firm's balance sheet immediately prior to the audit and revaluation.

At this point, an accountant (usually someone from an outside firm) audits the books and the firm's assets are appraised. This audit and appraisal indicate that Merchandise Inventory is undervalued by $9,800, that Allowances for Doubtful Accounts should be increased by $200, and that Equipment is overvalued by $2,400. The accountant allocates the net difference between debits and credits to the partners' Capital accounts, according to their basis for sharing profits and losses.

	DATE		DESCRIPTION	POST. REF.	DEBIT	CREDIT	
1	20–						1
2	Sept.	30	Merchandise Inventory		9 8 0 0 00		2
3			Allowance for Doubtful				3
4			Accounts			2 0 0 00	4
5			Equipment			2 4 0 0 00	5
6			K. L. Fern, Capital			2 4 0 0 00	6
7			N. B. Goll, Capital			2 4 0 0 00	7
8			J. C. Horn, Capital			2 4 0 0 00	8
9			To record the revaluation of				9
10			the assets; net increase in				10
11			owners' equity is $7,200.				11

After the entry has been posted, the partners' equity accounts look like this:

K. L. Fern, Capital			N. B. Goll, Capital			J. C. Horn, Capital	
–	+		–	+		–	+
	Balance	46,000		Balance	24,000		Balance	22,000
	Sept. 30	2,400		Sept. 30	2,400		Sept. 30	2,400

After the accountant has recorded the revaluation of the firm's assets, N. B. Goll withdraws cash from the partnership equal to her equity, which leads to the following entry:

Remember!

A partner has the right to leave a partnership. He or she may withdraw an amount equal to his or her equity or greater or less than the book value of his or her equity.

	DATE		DESCRIPTION	POST. REF.	DEBIT	CREDIT	
12	20–						12
13	Sept.	30	N. B. Goll, Capital		26 4 0 0 00		13
14			Cash			26 4 0 0 00	14
15			To record the withdrawal of				15
16			N. B. Goll.				16
17							17

Partner Withdraws More than Book Value of His or Her Equity

Sometimes a partner withdraws more cash than the amount of his or her Capital account. There are two possible reasons for this.

1. The business is prosperous and shows excellent potential for growth.
2. The remaining partners are so anxious for the partner to retire that they are willing to buy out the partner.

When Goll announced that she was going to retire, for example, Fern and Horn agreed to pay her $27,000 for her interest in the partnership. Because the balance of her Capital account after the revaluation is $26,400, the excess of $600 must be deducted from the Capital accounts of the remaining partners, in accordance with their basis for sharing profits and losses. The general journal entry appears as follows:

	DATE		DESCRIPTION	POST. REF.	DEBIT	CREDIT	
1	20–						1
2	Sept.	30	N. B. Goll, Capital		26 4 0 0 00		2
3			K. L. Fern, Capital		3 0 0 00		3
4			J. C. Horn, Capital		3 0 0 00		4
5			Cash			27 0 0 0 00	5
6			To record the withdrawal of				6
7			N. B. Goll.				7
8							8

Partner Withdraws Less than Book Value of His or Her Equity

Sometimes a partner may be so anxious to retire that he or she is willing to take less than the current value of his or her equity just to get out of the partnership or out of the business. In the firm of Fern, Goll, and Horn, let's say that Goll is willing to withdraw if she gets just $21,000 cash out of it. Because the balance of her Capital account after the revaluation is $26,400, the difference ($5,400) represents a bonus to the remaining partners. The entry to record this situation is as follows:

	DATE		DESCRIPTION	POST. REF.	DEBIT	CREDIT	
6	Sept.	30	N. B. Goll, Capital		26 4 0 0 00		6
7			K. L. Fern, Capital			2 7 0 0 00	7
8			J. C. Horn, Capital			2 7 0 0 00	8
9			Cash			21 0 0 0 00	9
10			To record the withdrawal of				10
11			N. B. Goll.				11
12							12

Death of a Partner

■ ■ ■

Remember!

The death of a partner automatically ends a partnership. The books must be closed to determine the net income or net loss.

The death of a partner automatically ends the partnership, and the partner's estate is entitled to receive the amount of his or her equity. The death of a partner makes it necessary to close the books immediately so that the accountant can determine the firm's net income for the current fiscal period. Partnership agreements usually provide for an audit and revaluation of the assets at this time. After the accountant has determined the current value of the deceased partner's Capital account, the remaining partners and the executor of the deceased partner's estate must agree on the method of payment. The journal entries are similar to those made for the withdrawal of a partner. To be certain that there is enough cash to meet such a demand, partners often carry life insurance policies.

Liquidation of a Partnership

Objective 6

Journalize entries pertaining to the liquidation of a partnership involving the immediate sale of the assets for cash.

A **liquidation** means an end, not only of the partnership, but of the business itself. This final winding-up process involves selling assets, paying off liabilities, and distributing the remaining cash to the partners. The closing entries are journalized and posted prior to the liquidation.

The accountant journalizes the entries for each step of the liquidation process as follows:

1. Sale of the assets, using the Loss or Gain from Realization account. The accountant debits this account for losses and credits it for gains. In this respect the account is comparable to the Cash Short and Over account. The word **realization** refers to the sale of the assets for cash.
2. Allocation of the loss or gain. The accountant closes the Loss or Gain from Realization account into the partners' Capital accounts according to the profit and loss ratio. It must be closed as a separate account because it came into being after the regular closing entries had been recorded.
3. Payment of the liabilities. The firm makes final settlement with all creditors.
4. Distribution of the remaining cash to the partners, in accordance with the balances of their Capital accounts.

Occasionally it takes a long time to convert merchandise inventory and other assets into cash; on the other hand, things can move quickly. It is impossible to predict how long liquidation operations may take. In the process, several things may happen. We will discuss only two possibilities here, although you can find more complex situations in more advanced books.

Remember!

On liquidation, creditors are first in line, before partners' interests.

Our first example concerns the partnership of Rice, Siba, and Tan. The partners share profits and losses as follows: Rice, one-half; Siba, one-fourth; Tan, one-fourth. Let's look at an abbreviated balance sheet for this firm (Figure 5).

FIGURE 5

Rice, Siba, and Tan
Balance Sheet
June 30, 20—

Assets			
Cash	$10 000 00		
Merchandise Inventory	80 000 00		
Other Assets	40 000 00		
Total Assets		$130 000 00	
Liabilities			
Accounts Payable		$ 7 000 00	
Partners' Equity			
G. P. Rice, Capital	$47 000 00		
C. L. Siba, Capital	44 000 00		
R. H. Tan, Capital	32 000 00	123 000 00	
Total Liabilities and Partners' Equity		$130 000 00	

Assets Are Sold at a Profit

Assume that the firm sells its merchandise inventory for $86,000 and the other assets for $48,000. Figure 6 shows the journal entries to cover this transaction. (Amounts in parentheses are purely explanatory.)

The T accounts for the Cash and Capital accounts look like this:

Cash					C. L. Siba, Capital			
	+	−				−	+	
Balance	10,000	(3)	7,000	(4)		47,500	Balance	44,000
(1)	134,000	(4)	137,000				(2)	3,500

G. P. Rice, Capital					R. H. Tan, Capital			
	−	+				−	+	
(4)	54,000	Balance	47,000	(4)		35,500	Balance	32,000
		(2)	7,000				(2)	3,500

FIGURE 6

	DATE		DESCRIPTION	POST. REF.	DEBIT	CREDIT	
1	20–						1
2	June	30	Cash ($86,000 + $48,000)		134 0 0 0 00		2
3			Merchandise Inventory			80 0 0 0 00	3
4	(1)		Other Assets			40 0 0 0 00	4
5			Loss or Gain from Realization			14 0 0 0 00	5
6			Sold the assets at a gain.				6
7							7
8		30	Loss or Gain from Realization		14 0 0 0 00		8
9			G. P. Rice, Capital (½)			7 0 0 0 00	9
10	(2)		C. L. Siba, Capital (¼)			3 5 0 0 00	10
11			R. H. Tan, Capital (¼)			3 5 0 0 00	11
12			To allocate the net gain to the				12
13			partners' Capital accounts				13
14			according to the profit and				14
15			loss ratio.				15
16							16
17		30	Accounts Payable		7 0 0 0 00		17
18			Cash			7 0 0 0 00	18
19	(3)		To pay the claims of creditors.				19
20							20
21		30	G. P. Rice, Capital		54 0 0 0 00		21
22			C. L. Siba, Capital		47 5 0 0 00		22
23	(4)		R. H. Tan, Capital		35 5 0 0 00		23
24			Cash			137 0 0 0 00	24
25			To distribute the remaining				25
26			cash to the partners				26
27			according to their account				27
28			balances.				28

Remember!

The balance of Cash before the final distribution to the partners should equal the total of the balances of their Capital accounts.

Assets Are Sold at a Loss: Partners' Capital Accounts Sufficient to Absorb Loss

Now suppose that the partnership of Rice, Siba, and Tan sells its merchandise inventory for only $76,000 and its other assets for $32,000. The journal entries would look like those in Figure 7.

The T accounts for the Cash and Capital accounts look like this:

Cash					C. L. Siba, Capital				
	+	–				–	+		
Balance	10,000	(3)	7,000		(2)	3,000	Balance	44,000	
(1)	108,000	(4)	111,000		(4)	41,000			

G. P. Rice, Capital					R. H. Tan, Capital				
	–	+				–	+		
(2)	6,000	Balance	47,000		(2)	3,000	Balance	32,000	
(4)	41,000				(4)	29,000			

FIGURE 7

	DATE		DESCRIPTION	POST. REF.	DEBIT	CREDIT	
1	20–						1
2	June	30	Cash ($76,000 + $32,000)		108 0 0 0 00		2
3			Loss or Gain from Realization		12 0 0 0 00		3
4	(1)		Merchandise Inventory			80 0 0 0 00	4
5			Other Assets			40 0 0 0 00	5
6			Sold the assets at a loss.				6
7							7
8		30	G. P. Rice, Capital (½)		6 0 0 0 00		8
9			C. L. Siba, Capital (¼)		3 0 0 0 00		9
10	(2)		R. H. Tan, Capital (¼)		3 0 0 0 00		10
11			Loss or Gain from Realization			12 0 0 0 00	11
12			To allocate the net loss to the				12
13			partners' Capital accounts				13
14			according to the profit and				14
15			loss ratio.				15
16							16
17		30	Accounts Payable		7 0 0 0 00		17
18			Cash			7 0 0 0 00	18
19	(3)		To pay the claims of creditors.				19
20							20
21		30	G. P. Rice, Capital		41 0 0 0 00		21
22			C. L. Siba, Capital		41 0 0 0 00		22
23	(4)		R. H. Tan, Capital		29 0 0 0 00		23
24			Cash			111 0 0 0 00	24
25			To distribute the remaining				25
26			cash to the partners				26
27			according to their account				27
28			balances.				28

Remember!

After liquidation, cash remaining is distributed to the partners according to their Capital account balances.

CHAPTER REVIEW

Review of Performance Objectives

1. (a) Define *partnership* and list the main advantages and disadvantages of a partnership; (b) journalize initial investments.

   A partnership is an association of two or more persons to carry on, as co-owners, a business for profit. The main advantages of a partnership are the combining of people's abilities and investments to carry on a business, and its ease of formation. The main disadvantages of a partnership are the unlimited liability of a general partner and mutual agency. The accountant makes a separate journal entry for the investment of each partner. The investments may include cash and other assets, along with any related liabilities.

2. Provide for the division of net income and loss on the basis of (a) fractional shares, (b) ratio of capital investments, and (c) salary and interest allowances.

   The division of net income or loss may be reported as a separate statement or shown at the bottom of the income statement below Net Income. For division by fractional shares, multiply net income or loss by each partner's fraction. For ratio of capital investments, multiply net income or loss by a fraction with the partner's beginning Capital balance in the numerator and the total of partners' Capital balances in the denominator. To calculate the division on the basis of salary and interest allowances, deduct the amounts of salary or interest allowances from the net income (or add them to the net loss) and divide the remainder by specified shares (usually equally).

3. Journalize the closing entries for a partnership.

   Close the revenue and expense accounts into Income Summary, then close Income Summary into the partners' Capital accounts. For a net income, debit Income Summary and credit each partner's Capital account. For a net loss, debit each partner's Capital account and credit Income Summary. Close the Drawing accounts by crediting each partner's Drawing account and debiting each partner's Capital account.

4. Prepare a statement of partners' equity.

   The format of a statement of partners' equity is the same as that for a statement of owner's equity. One column per partner is used to record each partner's beginning capital, additional investment, share of net income, withdrawals, and ending capital. A Total column is used to record the combined total for each line.

5. Journalize entries involving the sale of a partnership interest or withdrawal of a partner.

   Any change in the composition of partners results in a dissolution of the partnership. For the sale of a partnership interest, debit the Capital account of the old partner and credit the Capital account of the new partner. When a partner withdraws, there is a revaluation of the assets. Next, an entry is made debiting the partner's Capital account and crediting Cash.

6. Journalize entries pertaining to the liquidation of a partnership involving the immediate sale of the assets for cash.

   A liquidation requires four steps. First, for the sale of the assets, debit Cash, credit the assets, and debit or credit Loss or Gain from Realization. Next, close Loss or Gain from Realization into the partners' Capital accounts according to the partners' agreed-on profit and loss ratio. Next, pay off the liabilities. Last, distribute the remaining cash according to the partners' Capital account balances.

Glossary

Co-ownership A situation in which each party owns a fractional share of all the assets. (708)

Dissolution The ending of a partnership because of a change in the personnel of the membership and the forming of a new partnership. The transition results primarily in changes in the Capital accounts, with routine business being carried on as usual. (725)

Distributive share The share of the net income (or net loss) allocated to each partner. (714)

General partners Partners who actively and publicly participate in the transactions of the firm and have unlimited liability. (709)

Liquidation The ending of a partnership, involving the sale of the assets, payment of the liabilities, and distribution of the remaining cash to the partners. (729)

Mutual agency The ability of each partner to act as an agent of the firm, thereby committing the entire firm to a binding contract. (709)

Partnership An association of two or more persons to carry on, as co-owners, a business for profit. (708)

Realization Conversion into cash, as happens in the case of the sale of assets. (729)

QUESTIONS, EXERCISES, AND PROBLEMS

Discussion Questions

1. Is it possible for a partner to lose a greater amount than the amount of his or her investment in the partnership? Why?

2. What do accountants mean when they discuss the concept of co-ownership of partnership property?

3. To handle the provision for salary allowances used in allocating net income or loss, the accountant debited the Salary Expense account. Is the accountant correct? Why or why not?

4. Moore and Peel are considering forming a partnership. What do you consider the four most important factors to include in their partnership agreement?

5. When assets other than cash are invested in a partnership by one of the partners, at what value are these assets recorded on the books of the partnership?

6. What do you consider the greatest advantage and the greatest disadvantage of the partnership form of business organization?

7. Ash, Best, and Drake are partners. Drake dies, and her daughter claims the right to take her mother's place in the partnership. Explain why Drake's daughter either does or does not have the right to do this.

8. Describe how a dissolution of a partnership differs from a liquidation.

Exercises

P.O. 1b

Journalize the entry to record investment of a new partner.

Exercise 20-1 D. L. Holmes, as his original investment in the firm of Holmes and Little, contributes equipment originally recorded in his own business as costing $80,000, with accumulated depreciation of $52,000. The partners agree on a valuation of $38,000. They also agree to accept Holmes's Accounts Receivable of $40,000, collectible to the extent of 80 percent. Write the journal entry to record Holmes's investment in the partnership of Holmes and Little on June 15.

P.O. 2a,3

Calculate fractional shares and journalize closing entries for a partnership.

Exercise 20-2 Ardis and Rusk share profits and losses on a fractional-share basis, with three-fifths for Ardis and two-fifths for Rusk. This year the firm has a net income of $60,000. The beginning Capital balances for the year were $126,000 for Ardis and $84,000 for Rusk. The balances of the Drawing accounts are $32,000 for Ardis and $26,000 for Rusk. Journalize the entries to close Income Summary and the partners' Drawing accounts on December 31.

P.O. 2b

Calculate the division of net income or loss based on a ratio of capital investments.

Exercise 20-3 L. Embuscado, G. Renaldo, and C. Thomas agreed to share earnings or losses according to the ratio of their investments at the beginning of the year ($30,000, $25,000, and $45,000, respectively). Calculate the partners' shares under the following conditions:

a. $27,000 net income
b. $24,000 net loss

P.O. 2a,c

Calculate partners' shares with salary allowances and fractional shares of income.

Exercise 20-4 The partnership agreement of Beard and Froman provides for salary allowances of $28,000 per year for Beard and $24,000 per year for Froman. They share the remaining balance of net income on the basis of three-fifths for Beard and two-fifths for Froman. The net income amounts to $58,000; calculate the total share for each partner.

P.O. 5

Journalize entries to record a partner's retirement.

Exercise 20-5 Newman is retiring from the partnership of Korn, Morris, and Newman. The profit and loss ratio is 2:2:1, respectively. After the accountant has posted the revaluation and closing entries, the credit balances in the Capital accounts are: Korn, $54,000; Morris, $44,000; and Newman, $22,000. Journalize the entries to record the retirement of Newman under each of the following unrelated assumptions. Korn and Morris will split the difference evenly.

a. Newman retires, taking $22,000 of partnership cash for her equity.
b. Newman retires, taking $26,000 of partnership cash for her equity.

P.O. 5

Journalize the entry to record revaluation of assets upon the death of a partner.

Exercise 20-6 Bayer is the senior member of the partnership of Bayer, Caldwell, and Dillon. When Bayer dies, the firm's accountant revalues the assets. The following assets are to be increased in value by these amounts: Merchandise Inventory, $24,000; Building, $64,000. The value of the asset Equipment is to be decreased by $8,000. Assuming that the partnership profit and loss ratio is 2:2:1, respectively, write the journal entry to show the revaluation of the assets on May 6 prior to dissolution of the firm.

P.O. 6

Calculate gain or loss on realization and the cash distribution to partners.

Exercise 20-7 Rutledge and Williams are partners who share profits and losses equally. The credit balances of their Capital accounts before liquidation are $60,000 and $80,000, respectively. When they liquidate their partnership, they sell the noncash assets and pay all the partnership's liabilities, leaving a balance of $120,000 in cash. What is the amount of the gain or loss on realization? How much cash should be distributed to each partner?

P.O. 6

Journalize the entry to record the distribution of cash.

Exercise 20-8 The partners Markley, Piper, and Sawyer have a profit and loss ratio of 2:2:1, respectively. They decide to liquidate the firm and to sell off all its assets. After distribution of the firm's loss from realization, the credit balances of the Capital accounts are as follows: Markley, $84,000; Piper, $62,000; Sawyer, $74,000. The balance of Cash is $220,000. Write the entry the accountant would make on the books on April 3 to record the distribution of cash.

CONSIDER AND COMMUNICATE

A friend of yours is looking for a partner to begin a children's-wear boutique. She has fashion merchandising and sales education and experience, as well as cash and a good credit rating. She is enthusiastic and anxious to begin the new business. You have cash, a desire to own a business, and sales experience, and you feel you could get along well with this potential partner. Why would you hesitate? What should you discuss with your friend about partnerships?

CRITICAL THINKING

The following information concerns the partnership of Arken and Small.

The partnership agreement provides for salary allowances of $31,900 for Arken and $29,350 for Small. The agreement also stipulates interest of 10 percent on invested capital at the beginning of the year (Arken, $65,280, and Small, $53,040). There were no changes in the partners' Capital accounts during the year. The remainder of the net income is to be divided equally. Using this information, fill in the missing numbers in the partial income statement from net income through Division of Net Income for Arken and Small and in the statement of partners' equity.

Arken and Small
Partial Income Statement
For Year Ended December 31, 20—

	J. V. Arken	S. C. Small	Total
Net Income			$79 3 0 2 00
Division of Net Income:			
Salary Allowances	$	$	$
Interest Allowances			
Remaining Income			
Allocated Equally			6 2 2 0 00
Net Income	$41 5 3 8 00	$37 7 6 4 00	$79 3 0 2 00

Arken and Small
Statement of Partners' Equity
For Year Ended December 31, 20—

	J. V. Arken	S. C. Small	Total
Capital, January 1, 20—	$	$	$
Net Income for the Year			79 3 0 2 00
Total	$	$	$197 6 2 2 00
Less Withdrawals for the Year	30 1 9 2 00	29 3 7 6 00	
Capital, December 31, 20—	$	$	$

A MATTER OF ETHICS

Joe and Sam are partners. Joe wanted to purchase a newer model computer. Sam said it was too expensive and had capabilities that they did not need. While Sam was on vacation, Joe bought the computer anyway. He believed that if Sam saw how much quicker the newer computer would be, he would be convinced of its benefits. Did Joe act appropriately under the rules of a partnership? Is what Joe did ethical?

WEB WORK

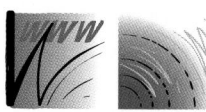

Using an Internet web browser, type different partnership conditions (formation, liquidation, dissolution, advantages, and disadvantages) in the search box and search for information about partnerships. Discuss your findings in a small group. Write a one-page summary of your findings.

PROBLEM SET A

For additional help, see the demonstration problem at the beginning of each chapter in your Working Papers.

P.O. 2c,3

Problem 20-1A The firm of B. N. Davis, F. M. Feldman, and G. W. Huber has a net income of $108,000 for this year. The balances in the Capital accounts of the partners at the beginning of the year were $42,000, $46,500, and $54,000, respectively. At the end of the year, the balances of the Drawing accounts are $21,000, $25,200, and $20,250, respectively. The partnership agreement stipulates salary allowances as follows: Davis, $21,000; Feldman, $25,500; Huber, $20,250. It also allows 10 percent interest on the balances of the partners' Capital accounts at the beginning of the year. The remainder of the net income, after salary and interest allowances, is divided equally.

Check Figure

For $108,000, Davis, Net Income, $34,200

Instructions

1. Prepare the section of the income statement on the division of net income for the current year.
2. Prepare entries to close the firm's Income Summary and Drawing accounts on December 31.
3. Assuming that the net income of the firm is $45,000, prepare the section of the income statement that deals with division of net income.

P.O. 2b,c

Problem 20-2A E. R. Halprin and H. O. Jayson, consulting engineers, are forming a partnership. Both plan to work in the firm on a full-time basis. Halprin's initial investment is $27,000; Jayson's investment is $45,000. They are considering the following plans for the division of net income:

a. Division in the same ratio as the balances of their Capital accounts.
b. Interest of 9 percent on the balances of their Capital accounts at the beginning of the year, and the remainder of the net income to be divided equally.

c. Salary allowances of $24,000 to Halprin and $20,000 to Jayson based on the value of their services, interest of 9 percent on the balances of their Capital accounts at the beginning of the year, and the remainder of the net income to be divided equally.

Check Figure

For $56,000, Plan (c), Jayson, Net Income, $26,810

Instructions

1. Record the distribution of net income for each of the plans, assuming (a) a net income of $56,000, and (b) a net income of $32,000.
2. Which plan is the fairest? Give reasons for your opinion.

P.O. 2c,4

Problem 20-3A The following are the adjusted account balances of Abel and Rist as of December 31, the end of this fiscal year.

M. B. Abel, Capital	$ 64,000
M. B. Abel, Drawing	29,600
Accounts Payable	69,416
Accounts Receivable	58,964
Accumulated Depreciation, Equipment	46,820
Allowance for Doubtful Accounts	2,148
Cash	3,742
Equipment	79,128
Freight In	26,834
General Expenses (control)	14,212
Interest Expense	2,942
Merchandise Inventory	126,236
Notes Payable	16,000
Prepaid Insurance	690
Purchases	509,846
Purchases Discount	4,428
Purchases Returns and Allowances	25,690
R. C. Rist, Capital	52,000
R. C. Rist, Drawing	28,800
Sales	684,836
Sales Returns and Allowances	35,872
Selling Expenses (control)	35,562

The merchandise inventory at the beginning of the year was $139,146, and there were no changes in the partners' Capital accounts during the year. The partnership agreement provides for salary allowances of $31,200 for Abel and $28,800 for Rist. The agreement also stipulates interest of 12 percent on invested capital at the beginning of the year. The remainder of the net income is to be divided equally.

Check Figure

Rist, Capital, $59,668

Instructions

1. Prepare an income statement for the year.
2. Prepare a statement of partners' equity for the year.
3. Prepare a classified balance sheet at the end of the year.

P.O. 6

Problem 20-4A The partnership of Hall, Lewis, and Madison is to be liquidated as of November 30 of this year. The partners share profits and losses in the ratio of 2:2:1, respectively. The firm's post-closing trial balance looks like the following.

Hall, Lewis, and Madison
Post-Closing Trial Balance
November 30, 20—

ACCOUNT NAME	DEBIT	CREDIT
Cash	37 4 0 0 00	
Merchandise Inventory	67 2 4 0 00	
Other Assets	48 1 6 0 00	
Accounts Payable		15 7 2 0 00
J. P. Hall, Capital		53 8 0 0 00
C. Y. Lewis, Capital		43 6 8 0 00
T. N. Madison, Capital		39 6 0 0 00
	152 8 0 0 00	152 8 0 0 00

The firm's realization and liquidation transactions are as follows:

Dec. 2 The merchandise inventory sold for $76,000; the other assets sold for $36,000.

2 The accountant allocated the loss or gain from realization to the partners' Capital accounts according to the profit and loss ratio.

2 The firm paid its creditors in full.

2 The firm distributed the remaining cash to the partners in accordance with the balances in their Capital accounts.

Check Figure

Madison, Capital, final entry, $38,920

Instructions

1. Record the balances in the selected ledger accounts.
2. Record the liquidating transactions in general journal form and post to the affected ledger accounts after each transaction.

PROBLEM SET B

For additional help, see the demonstration problem at the beginning of each chapter in your Working Papers.

P.O. 2c,3

Problem 20-1B The partnership of A. L. Banini, S. M. Canter, and R. D. Delaney has a net income of $92,850 for the current year. The balances in the Capital accounts of the partners at the beginning of the year were $34,500, $39,000, and $48,000, respectively. At the end of the year, the balances of the Drawing accounts are $16,500, $19,800, and $18,000, respectively. The partnership agreement stipulates salary allowances as follows: Banini, $16,500; Canter, $21,000; Delaney, $18,000. The partnership agreement also allows interest of 10 percent on the balances of the Capital accounts at the beginning of the year. The remainder (after salary and interest allowances) is divided equally among the three partners.

Check Figure

For $92,850, Banini, Net Income, $28,350

Instructions

1. Prepare the section of the income statement for the current year that deals with division of net income.

2. Prepare the entries to record the closing of the firm's Income Summary and Drawing accounts on December 31.
3. Assuming a net income of $40,650, prepare the section of the income statement that deals with division of net income.

P.O. 2b,c

Problem 20-2B W. A. Kim and M. C. Love are forming a partnership for a beauty salon and plan to work full time in the firm. Kim will make an initial investment of $30,000 and Love $45,000. They are considering the following plans for the division of net income:

a. Division in the same ratio as the balances of their Capital accounts.
b. Interest of 12 percent on the balances of their Capital accounts at the beginning of the year, and the remainder of the net income to be divided equally.
c. Salary allowances of $15,000 to Kim and $13,500 to Love based on the value of their services, interest of 9 percent on the balances of their Capital accounts at the beginning of the year, and the remainder of the net income to be divided equally.

Check Figure

For $45,000, Plan (c), Love, Net Income, $22,425

Instructions

1. Record the distributive shares of net income for each of the plans, assuming (a) a net income of $45,000, and (b) a net income of $26,000.
2. Which plan is the fairest? Give reasons for your opinion.

P.O. 2c,4

Problem 20-3B The following are the adjusted account balances of Allen and Wells as of December 31, the end of the current fiscal year:

Accounts Payable	$ 67,432
Accounts Receivable	53,438
Accumulated Depreciation, Equipment	45,380
R. M. Allen, Capital	60,000
R. M. Allen, Drawing	32,000
Allowance for Doubtful Accounts	1,842
Cash	3,658
Equipment	73,838
Freight In	22,047
General Expenses (control)	14,646
Interest Expense	3,432
Merchandise Inventory	129,452
Notes Payable	20,000
Prepaid Insurance	720
Purchases	529,133
Purchases Discount	4,220
Purchases Returns and Allowances	25,452
Sales	700,490
Sales Returns and Allowances	36,838
Selling Expenses (control)	37,832
C. C. Wells, Capital	48,000
C. C. Wells, Drawing	24,000

There were no changes in the partners' Capital accounts during the year. The merchandise inventory at the beginning of the year was $141,234. The partnership agreement provides for salary allowances of $32,000 for Allen and $28,000 for Wells. It also stipulates an interest allowance of 10 percent on invested capital at the beginning of the year, with the remainder of the net income to be divided equally.

Check Figure

Allen, Net Income, $39,826

Instructions

1. Prepare an income statement for the year.
2. Prepare a statement of partners' equity for the year.
3. Prepare a classified balance sheet for the partnership at the end of the year.

P.O. 6

Problem 20-4B The partnership of Hall, Lewis, and Madison is to be liquidated as of June 30 of this year. The partners share profits and losses in the ratio of 2:2:1, respectively. The firm's post-closing trial balance looks like this:

Hall, Lewis, and Madison
Post-Closing Trial Balance
June 30, 20—

ACCOUNT NAME	DEBIT	CREDIT
Cash	40 3 0 5 00	
Merchandise Inventory	58 8 7 5 00	
Other Assets	45 4 5 0 00	
Accounts Payable		12 6 3 0 00
J. P. Hall, Capital		54 0 0 0 00
C. Y. Lewis, Capital		42 0 0 0 00
T. N. Madison, Capital		36 0 0 0 00
	144 6 3 0 00	144 6 3 0 00

The firm's realization and liquidation transactions are as follows:

July 2   The merchandise inventory sold for $54,000; the other assets sold for $52,000.

     2   The accountant allocated the loss or gain from realization to the partners' capital accounts according to the profit and loss ratio.

     2   The firm paid its creditors in full.

     2   The firm distributed the remaining cash to the partners in accordance with the balances in their capital accounts.

Check Figure

Madison, Capital, 7/2 entry, $36,335

Instructions

1. Record the balances in the selected ledger accounts.
2. Record the liquidating transactions in general journal form and post to the affected ledger accounts after each transaction.

21 Corporate Organization and Capital Stock

Performance Objectives

After you have completed this chapter, you will be able to do the following:

1. Define *corporation.*

2. Name at least two advantages and two disadvantages of the corporate form.

3. Describe the formation of a corporation.

4. Journalize entries for the issuance of par-value stock.

5. Journalize entries for the issuance of no-par stock.

6. Journalize entries for the sale of stock on the subscription basis.

7. Prepare a classified balance sheet for a corporation, including Subscriptions Receivable, Organization Costs, Paid-in Capital, and Retained Earnings accounts.

Remember!

Sole proprietorships and partnerships are limited to the wealth of their few owners.

Business organizations are usually classified as sole proprietorships, partnerships, or corporations. Corporations are fewest in number, but they account for more business transactions than the other two types of organizations combined. Frequently a firm that begins as a sole proprietorship or a partnership needs more investment capital as it grows and prospers. To raise additional investment capital, the firm incorporates. Other businesses are organized as corporations from the outset. Because of the predominance of corporations, everyone entering the business world should be familiar with the corporate form of organization and its financial structure.

We consider corporations that issue stock and carry out business activities for the purpose of making profits and distributing the profits to their owners. Not-for-profit corporations generally do not issue stock or distribute profits, but carry out activities for charitable, educational, or other philanthropic purposes.

DEFINITION OF A CORPORATION

Objective 1
Define *corporation*.

In 1818, Chief Justice John Marshall defined a **corporation** as "an artificial being, invisible, intangible, and existing only in contemplation of the law." A corporation does indeed act as an artificial legal being, deriving its existence from its charter. In every respect it is a separate legal entity, having a continuous existence apart from that of its owners, the stockholders. As an entity, a corporation may own property, enter into contracts, sue in the courts, be sued, and so forth.

ADVANTAGES OF THE CORPORATE FORM

Objective 2
Name at least two advantages and two disadvantages of the corporate form.

Remember!
Compare the corporation with a partnership, in which the other partners have to give permission for changes in ownership in order for the business to continue.

Remember!
The owners of sole proprietorships and partnerships are personally liable for the entire debt of the business.

1. **Limited liability** As a separate legal entity, a corporation is responsible for its own debts. All that a stockholder can lose is the amount of his or her investment.

2. **Ease of raising capital** A corporation can accumulate more investment capital than a sole proprietorship or partnership because a corporation can sell stock. Some corporations have more than 1 million stockholders.

3. **Ease of transferring ownership rights** Ownership rights in a corporation are represented by shares of stock, which can readily be transferred from one person to another without the permission of other stockholders.

4. **Continuous existence** The length of life of a corporation is stipulated in its charter; when the charter expires, it may be renewed. The death, incapacity, or withdrawal of an owner does not affect the life of a corporation.

5. **No mutual agency** Stockholders who are not officers do not have the power to bind the corporation to contracts. Since owners need not participate in management, the corporation is free to employ the managerial talent it believes can best accomplish its objectives.

DISADVANTAGES OF THE CORPORATE FORM

The corporate form also has a number of disadvantages.

1. **Additional taxation** In addition to the usual property and payroll taxes, corporations must pay income taxes and charter fees. Since corporations are separate legal entities, they pay federal and state income taxes in their own names. Part of the corporation's net income goes to the stockholders

in the form of dividends; this money is personal income to the stockholders, and consequently the stockholders have to pay personal income taxes on it. This is known as **double taxation** to different entities (the corporation and the stockholders). It represents the corporate form's greatest disadvantage. Charter fees (fees paid for the corporation's right to exist) may be considered additional taxes because they are paid to a state in return for the issuance of a charter.

2. **Government regulation** Since states create corporations by granting charters, states can exercise closer control and supervision over corporations than over sole proprietorships and partnerships. States often regulate even the amount of net income that a corporation may retain, the extent to which it may buy back its own stock, and the amount of real estate it may own.

FORMATION OF A CORPORATION

Objective 3

Describe the formation of a corporation.

Remember!

One of the advantages of a corporation is ease of raising capital through the sale of stock.

Remember!

Corporations may be formed for small-, medium-, or large-sized businesses.

To organize a corporation, a person or persons must submit an application for a **charter**, which is a written permit for a corporation to exist. The charter is issued by the appropriate official (corporation commissioner or secretary of state) of the state in which the company is to be incorporated. The application is called the **articles of incorporation**. Application requirements vary depending on the state in which the company incorporates. They generally include at least the following points of information:

- Name and address of the corporation
- Nature of the business to be conducted
- Amount and description of the capital stock to be issued
- Name(s) of the promoter(s) or sole incorporator who will serve until the first meeting is held to elect a board of directors

The articles of incorporation must be accompanied by a charter fee, which is based on the dollar amount of maximum stock investment, or **authorized capital**.

When state officials approve the articles of incorporation, these articles become the charter or governing instrument of the corporation. Shortly after receiving the charter, the promoters or the sole promoter holds an initial meeting to elect an acting board of directors and formulate bylaws. The charter and the bylaws provide the basic rules for conducting the corporation's affairs. Next, the directors meet to appoint officers to serve as active managers of the business. Then the corporation issues **capital stock** to buyers of stock who have paid in full. The shares of stock are in the form of certificates. Since stockholders have come into existence at this point, they now elect a permanent board of directors.

The size of the corporation may vary in terms of number of stockholders and amount of investment. A corporation may be small, with only a few owners and a minimum investment of $1,000, or it may be a giant, with more than a million owners and an investment amounting to more than $1 billion. In a small corporation, the stockholders may also be the directors and officers. A corporation whose ownership is confined to a small group of stockholders is called a **closely held corporation**. A corporation whose ownership is widely distributed through a stock exchange or through over-the-counter markets to a large number of stockholders is called a **public corporation** or *open*.

Organization Costs

Let's suppose that a new corporation is being formed and the organizers call in an accountant to set up the books. The accountant debits the costs of organizing the corporation—such as fees paid to the state, attorneys' fees, promotional costs, travel outlays, costs of printing stock certificates—to an account titled **Organization Costs**. This account is classified as an **intangible asset**, an asset with no physical features. Intangible Assets appears as a separate section of the balance sheet, below Plant and Equipment. Organization Costs is like a prepaid expense account, such as Prepaid Insurance, in that it will be written off by means of adjusting entries over a minimum period of five years. Although organization costs are paid only once, they benefit the corporation throughout its entire life. Therefore, to expense organization costs entirely in the first year would violate the matching principle. Income tax laws allow a company to write off its organization costs over a period of five years or more. The adjusting entry is a debit to Organization Cost Expense or Miscellaneous General Expense and a credit to Organization Costs.

Stock Certificate Book

Remember!

Organization Costs is an asset account. As with Prepaid Insurance, the costs are eventually written off by means of adjusting entries.

One necessary element of organization costs is the printing of **stock certificates**. In a small corporation, the certificates often have stubs attached. The certificates and stubs are bound in a stock certificate book, rather like a checkbook. The corporation issues a stock certificate only when the stockholder has paid for the stock in full. On each blank certificate is written the name of the owner, the number of shares issued, and the date of issuance. The stub must show the name and address of the stockholder, the number of shares listed on the stock certificate, and the date of issuance. Both certificates and stubs are numbered consecutively. Figure 1 is an example of a stock certificate.

FIGURE 1

When a transfer of ownership takes place, the stockholder surrenders the stock certificate to the corporation; the corporation cancels it and also cancels the matching stub; and the corporation then issues one or more new certificates to the new owner(s) in place of these documents. This procedure enables the corporation to maintain an up-to-date record of the names of all the stockholders and the number of shares owned by each. A corporation needs this information when it pays out dividends and when it sends out notices of annual meetings or other information.

The law requires large corporations whose stocks are listed on major stock exchanges to have independent registrars and transfer agents maintain their records of stock ownership. Banks and trust companies perform this service.

STRUCTURE OF A CORPORATION

The stockholders own the corporation; they delegate authority to the board of directors, which manages the corporation's affairs. The board of directors, in turn, delegates authority to the officers, who do the actual work of running the business. The officers themselves may also be members of the board of directors. Figure 2 shows a typical organization chart for a corporation.

Dividends are the share of the corporation's earnings distributed to stockholders that can be paid in cash or with additional shares of stock. The sources of dividends are the current year's net income after income taxes and the retained earnings of prior years.

Suppose the corporation issues some new stock. Each original stockholder then may have the right to subscribe to additional shares in proportion to her or his present holding. This feature is known as the **preemptive right**. For example, assume that the corporation's new issue consists of 1,000

FIGURE 2

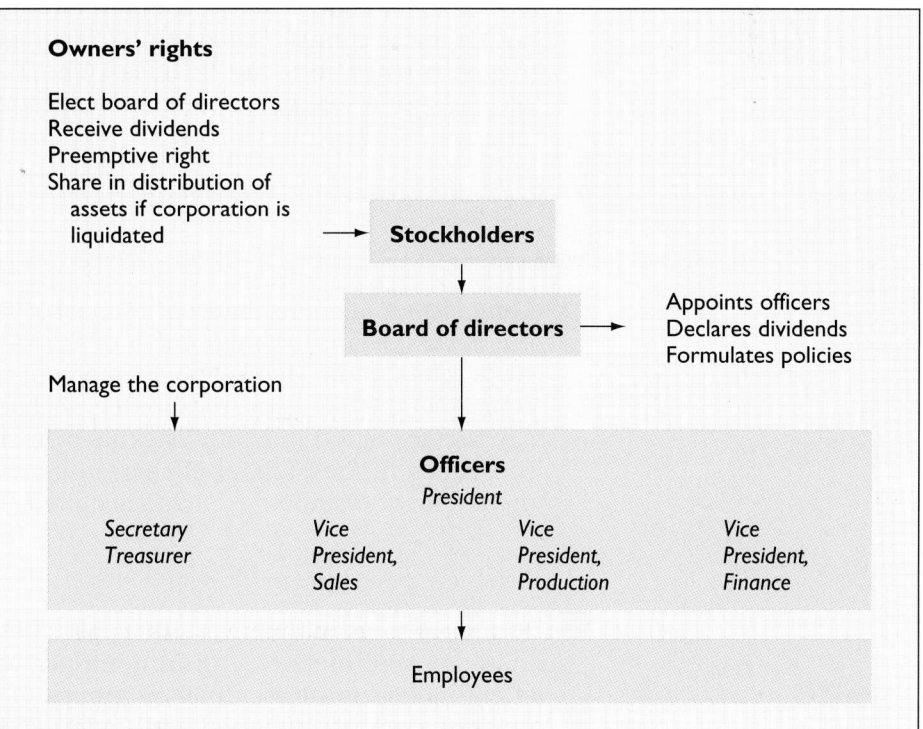

Owners' rights

Elect board of directors
Receive dividends
Preemptive right
Share in distribution of
  assets if corporation is
  liquidated → **Stockholders**

Board of directors → Appoints officers
Declares dividends
Formulates policies

Manage the corporation

Officers
President

*Secretary
Treasurer* *Vice
President,
Sales* *Vice
President,
Production* *Vice
President,
Finance*

Employees

FIGURE 3

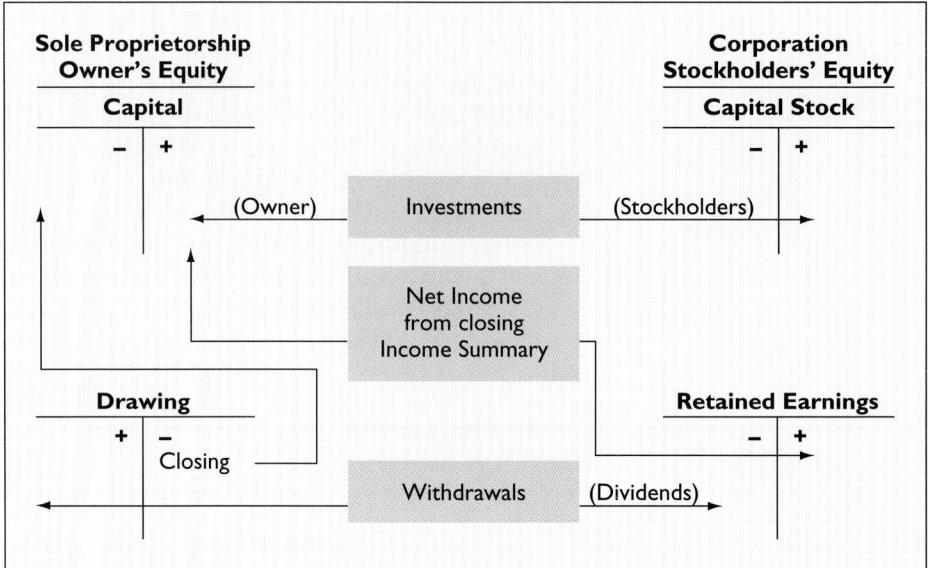

shares. The present amount of stock outstanding is 10,000 shares, of which Ruth Alber owns 2,000. Her proportion of stock held to stock outstanding is one-fifth (2,000/10,000). Therefore, she has the right to subscribe to 200 shares (one-fifth of 1,000 shares) of the new issue.

Stockholders' Equity

The owners' equity in a corporation is called **stockholders' equity**, or *capital.* Just as in sole proprietorships and partnerships, the equity of the owners represents the excess of assets over liabilities. Of the five major classifications of accounts, the main difference for a corporation occurs in the stockholders' equity classification, where capital stock accounts replace owners' Capital accounts. The **Retained Earnings** account is used to record earnings reinvested into the business. The T accounts in Figure 3 compare accounts for a sole proprietorship with those for a corporation.

CAPITAL STOCK

Capital stock refers to shares of ownership in a corporation. *Authorized capital stock* is the maximum number of shares designated in the charter. **Issued stock** refers to the shares apportioned out to the stockholders. Stock that is actually in the hands of stockholders is called **outstanding stock**. Occasionally, a corporation may buy back its own stock or receive it as a donation; consequently, the number of shares that have been issued may differ from the number outstanding. Such reacquired stock is known as **treasury stock**.

Classes of Capital Stock

To appeal to as many investors as possible, a corporation may issue more than one kind of stock, just as a refrigerator manufacturer, say, makes different models to please different groups of potential buyers. **The two main types of stock are *common* and *preferred.*** Each type may have a variety of characteristics. Some may be par-value stock (value printed on the stock certificate), and some may be no-par stock (no value printed on the stock certificate). We will refer to these types of stock frequently. Following is a brief comparison of par-value and no-par stock:

Par-value Stock	No-par Stock
• Has a par value (in dollars) printed on the face of the stock certificates.	• Has no dollar value printed on the face of the stock certificates.
• Has the par value listed in the corporation's charter.	• Has no dollar value per share of stock listed in the corporation's charter.
• The par value is used to record the shares of stock issued.	• The stated value is used to record the shares of stock issued.
• Par value can be changed only by amending the corporation's charter.	• Stated value is an arbitrary amount and can be changed during a meeting of the board of directors.
• Stock issued at an amount above par value is sold at a premium.	• Stock issued at an amount above stated value is sold **in excess of stated value.**
• Stock issued at an amount below par value is sold at a discount.	• Stock will not be issued at an amount below stated value, since the stated value can be changed readily.
• Total par value becomes the legal capital, which cannot be withdrawn by stockholders except in liquidation. (*Purpose:* to protect the corporation's assets for the creditors.)	• Total stated value becomes the legal capital, which cannot be withdrawn by stockholders except in liquidation.
• Contingent liability—in case of a liquidation, stockholders who bought stock below par value are liable for the corporation's debts to the extent of the discount.	• No contingent liability.

Some corporations are small privately held family businesses.

Common Stock

When a corporation issues only one type of stock, it is called common stock **and may be either par-value or no-par stock.** Common stocks are shares that may yield dividends, but only after owners of preferred stock have been paid. Holders of common stock have the rights listed in Figure 2, with voting privileges of one vote for each share of stock.

Preferred Stock

Preferred stock, **which is generally par-value stock,** has two preferences. (1) A preference as to dividends: corporations pay dividends on preferred stock (if dividends are declared at all) before they pay dividends on common stock. They pay dividends on preferred stock at a uniform rate—a disadvantage if a corporation is very successful because the preferred shareholder is limited to the stated rate of dividends. The dividend on preferred stock consists of a percentage of the par value of the stock. (2) If the corporation is liquidated, holders of preferred stock are paid off before holders of common stock. In most circumstances, however, holders of preferred stock do not have voting privileges. There are several specific types of preferred stock.

All corporations begin life by applying for a charter or permit. Whether the corporation is small, medium, or large, its articles of incorporation must include information about the nature of the business and a description of the capital stock structure. Many corporations start small and grow over time, which allows them to raise additional capital and grow even more.

Cumulative and Noncumulative Preferred Stock Suppose that a corporation has a bad year and finds that it is not able to pay the dividend on its preferred stock. In this case, the dividend is said to be *passed*. Dividends on **cumulative preferred stock** may accrue to stockholders. The corporation has to pay these dividends in full before it can pay any dividends to common stockholders. However, for stockholders who own **noncumulative preferred stock**, dividends do not accumulate. In other words, if the corporation passes dividends, they are gone forever. Since preferred stockholders naturally want a regular dividend, most preferred stock is cumulative.

Remember!

Since preferred stock can be cumulative or noncumulative, participating or nonparticipating, there are four possible combinations.

Participating and Nonparticipating Preferred Stock The dividend on preferred stock consists of an established percentage of the par value of that stock. Some preferred stock, however, provides for the possibility of dividends in excess of this established amount; this kind of preferred stock is called **participating preferred stock**. Holders of participating preferred stock first get the regular dividend that is due them. Then the corporation allocates a stipulated amount to holders of its common stock. And *then* the stockholders who own participating preferred stock are allowed to participate or share in the extra earnings if they are distributed as cash dividends. The dividends of **nonparticipating preferred stock**, on the other hand, are limited to the regular rate. Most preferred stock is nonparticipating.

ISSUING STOCK

Remember!

Authorized capital represents the maximum amount of stock that can be sold.

Objective 4

Journalize entries for the issuance of par-value stock.

Stock is issued when the buyer has paid for it in full or when the corporation has received noncash assets in exchange for its stock. A corporation may issue par-value stock at an amount equal to, above, or below its par value.

Issuing Stock at Par for Cash

There is a separate ledger account for each class of stock. The accountant records investments of cash as debits to Cash and credits to the Stock accounts for the total amount of the par value. Remember that par value is the face value printed on each stock certificate. This designation of par value is a convenient means of dividing the corporation's capital into units, with the ownership of each unit known.

For example, the Larson Corporation is organized on July 16 with authorized capital of 4,000 shares of $100-par preferred 8 percent stock and 20,000 shares of $50-par common stock. On August 1, Larson issues 2,000 shares of preferred 8 percent stock at par and 10,000 shares of common stock at par. In general journal form, the entry looks like this:

		GENERAL JOURNAL			PAGE 1	
	DATE	DESCRIPTION	POST. REF.	DEBIT	CREDIT	
1	20–					1
2	Aug. 1	Cash		700 0 0 0 00		2
3		Preferred 8 Percent Stock			200 0 0 0 00	3
4		Common Stock			500 0 0 0 00	4
5		Issued 2,000 shares of				5
6		preferred 8 percent stock at				6
7		par and 10,000 shares of				7
8		common stock at par.				8
9						9

In terms of T accounts, the situation looks like this:

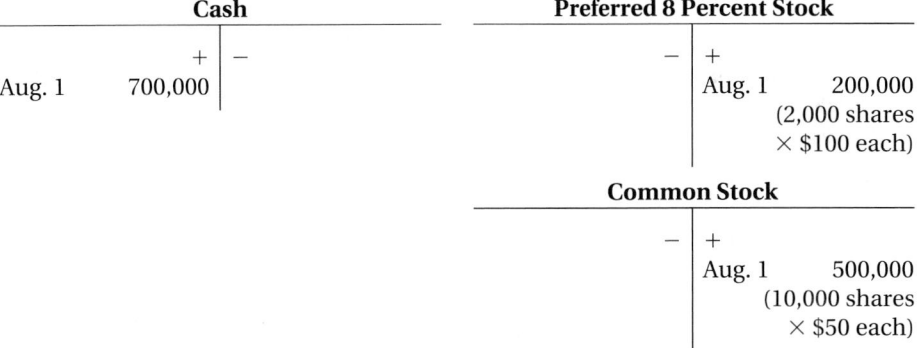

The capital stock accounts (Preferred 8 Percent Stock and Common Stock) are controlling accounts. The subsidiary ledger is known as the **stockholders' ledger**. The stockholders' ledger may consist of the stock certificate book or a supplementary record showing the name and address of each stockholder and the number of shares owned.

Remember!

Stock may be sold for cash or given in exchange for services or assets.

Issuing Stock at Par for Noncash Assets

Corporations often accept assets other than cash in exchange for their stock. The Larson Corporation received equipment, a building, and land in exchange for 1,720 shares of common stock, as in the following journal entry.

DATE		DESCRIPTION	POST. REF.	DEBIT	CREDIT	
20–						1
Aug.	1	Equipment		6 0 0 0 00		2
		Building		70 0 0 0 00		3
		Land		10 0 0 0 00		4
		Common Stock			86 0 0 0 00	5
		Exchanged 1,720 shares of				6
		common stock for equipment,				7
		building, and land.				8
						9

When a corporation accepts an asset other than cash, the accountant records the asset at its fair market value. The goal of the accountant is to have a realistic base on which to calculate future depreciation.

Now suppose that a corporation gives shares of its stock to its organizers in exchange for their services in organizing the corporation. In this instance, the corporation receives an intangible asset, Organization Costs. Suppose that the Larson Corporation issues 100 shares of common stock to its organizers. The accountant handles it this way:

DATE		DESCRIPTION	POST. REF.	DEBIT	CREDIT	
20–						1
Aug.	1	Organization Costs		5 0 0 0 00		2
		Common Stock			5 0 0 0 00	3
		Issued 100 shares to the				4
		promoters in exchange for				5
		their services in organizing				6
		the corporation.				7
						8

If the fair market value of the asset or service is not determinable, as in the case of organization costs, then the current market price of the stock on the date the asset or service is acquired is used.

Issuing Stock at a Premium or Discount

A newly organized corporation, such as the Larson Corporation, generally issues its stock at par. However, after the business has been operating for some time, the directors may realize that they need additional investment capital. Perhaps the business has been so successful that they want to expand it. Or perhaps they need to cover losses suffered during the early years of the business. So the directors decide to issue some new stock. The present market price of the original stock affects the price they can secure for the new shares. The market price of the stock of a corporation is usually influenced by the following factors.

The major stock exchanges for publicly held corporations are hubs of activity. Buyers are trying to buy low and sellers are trying to sell high.

■ ■ ■

Remember!

The recording of a premium or a discount may or may not reflect what is going on in the stock market, although the market may influence the price at which stock is issued.

1. The earnings record, financial condition, and dividend record of the corporation
2. The potential for growth in earnings of the corporation
3. The supply of and demand for money for investment purposes in the money market as a whole
4. General business conditions and prospects for the future

When a corporation issues stock at a price above par value, the stock is said to be issued at a **premium**; the premium is the amount by which the issuing price of the new stock exceeds the par value. The premium may exist because the corporation has performed successfully in the past and has good prospects for growth in earnings in the future. Conversely, when a corporation sells its stock at a price below par value, the stock is said to be issued at a **discount**; the discount is the amount by which the issuing price of the new stock falls below the par value. This discount may exist because the corporation incurred losses during its early period, or perhaps its prospects for the future are not too promising.

Premium on Stock

When a corporation issues stock at a price *above* its par value, the accountant debits Cash or other noncash assets for the amount received, credits the stock account for the par value, and credits a premium account for the difference between the amount received and the par value. Suppose Bannon Corporation issues 900 shares of $100-par cumulative preferred 9 percent stock at $103 on July 1. In general journal form, the entry looks like this:

	DATE		DESCRIPTION	POST. REF.	DEBIT	CREDIT	
1	20–						1
2	July	1	Cash		92 7 0 0 00		2
3			Preferred 9 Percent Stock			90 0 0 0 00	3
4			Premium on Preferred 9				4
5			Percent Stock			2 7 0 0 00	5
6			Issued 900 shares at $103				6
7			per share.				7
8							8

In terms of T accounts, the entry looks like this:

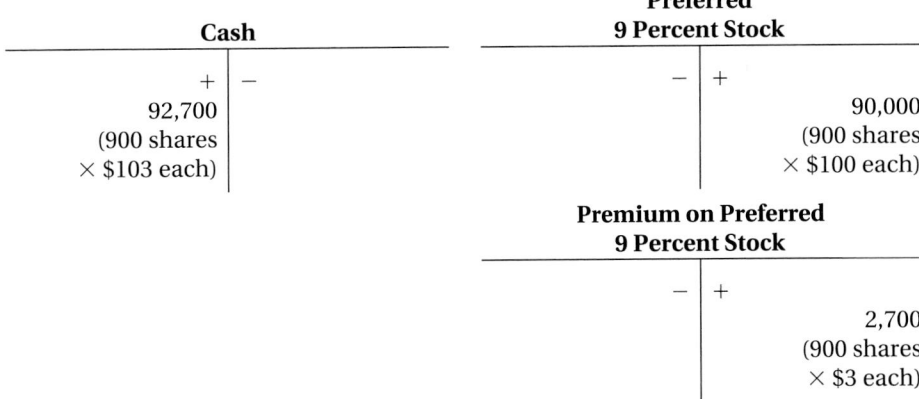

Cash		Preferred 9 Percent Stock	
+	–	–	+
92,700			90,000
(900 shares			(900 shares
× $103 each)			× $100 each)

	Premium on Preferred 9 Percent Stock	
	–	+
		2,700
		(900 shares
		× $3 each)

In the case of par-value stock, the stock account contains only the total par value of the stock. The Premium on Stock account is treated as an addition to stockholders' equity. Why would buyers be willing to pay a premium for Bannon's 9 percent preferred stock? The 9 percent rate may be higher than the current market rate for this type of stock. For example, other companies in comparable financial condition may be paying only 8 percent dividends on their stock.

Discount on Stock

When a corporation issues stock at a price *below* its par value, the accountant debits Cash or other assets for the amount received, credits the stock account for the par value, and debits a discount account for the difference between the amount received and the par value. Some states do not permit stock to be issued at a discount. In other states, it may be done only under certain conditions. However, since some states do indeed allow stock to be sold at a discount, we will proceed with an illustration.

Suppose that on July 1 Bannon Corporation issues 10,000 shares of $20-par common stock at $19. In general journal form, the entry is as follows:

	DATE		DESCRIPTION	POST. REF.	DEBIT	CREDIT	
1	20–						1
2	July	1	Cash		190 0 0 0 00		2
3			Discount on Common Stock		10 0 0 0 00		3
4			Common Stock			200 0 0 0 00	4
5			Issued 10,000 shares at $19				5
6			per share.				6
7							7

In T accounts, the entry looks like this:

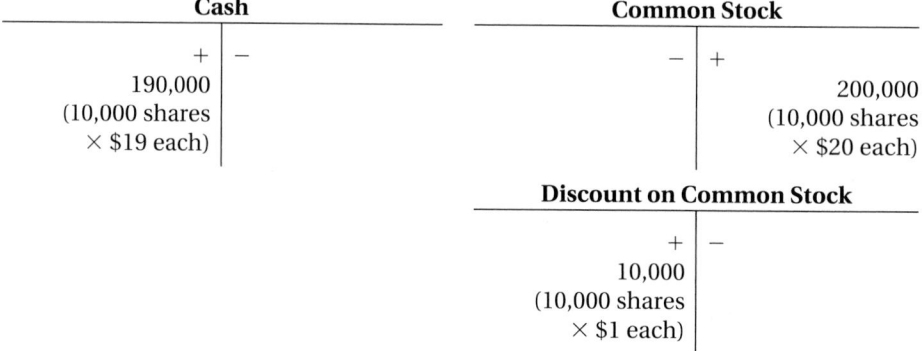

As in the case of par-value stock issued at a premium, the accountant records in the stock account the total *par* value of the stock issued. The

discount on the stock is treated as a deduction from stockholders' equity. It is a contra account. Note that whether the stock is issued at a premium or a discount, the amount recorded in the stock account is the total par value of the stock issued (10,000 shares × $20 per share).

Let's review the placement of the major accounts presented thus far in the fundamental accounting equation:

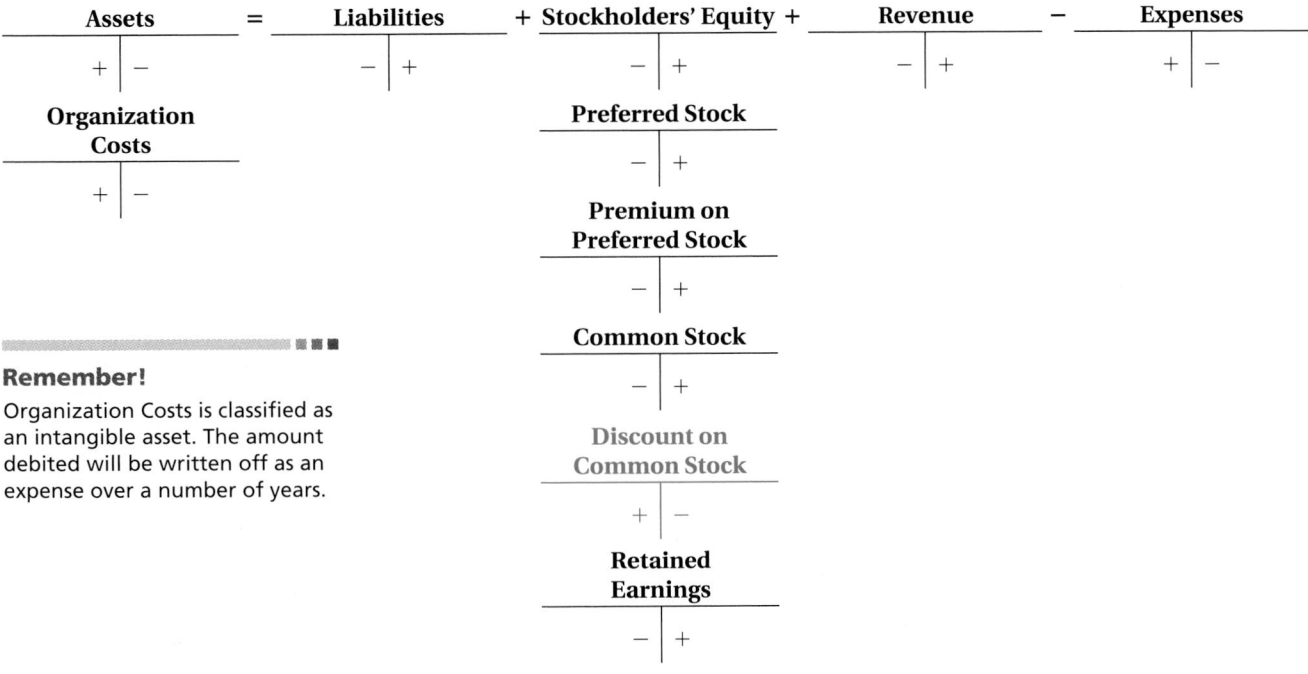

Assets	=	Liabilities	+	Stockholders' Equity	+	Revenue	−	Expenses
+ | −		− | +		− | +		− | +		+ | −

Organization Costs
+ \| −

Preferred Stock
− \| +

Premium on Preferred Stock
− \| +

Common Stock
− \| +

Discount on Common Stock
+ \| −

Retained Earnings
− \| +

Remember!
Organization Costs is classified as an intangible asset. The amount debited will be written off as an expense over a number of years.

Remember!
The Premium on Stock account is treated as an addition to stockholders' equity.

The Stockholders' Equity section of the balance sheet of the Bannon Corporation—showing the stock, premium, and discount accounts—looks like this:

Stockholders' Equity						
Paid-in Capital:						
Preferred 9 Percent Stock, cumulative, $100 par						
(2,000 shares authorized, 900 shares issued)	$ 90 0 0 0 00				
Premium on Preferred 9 Percent Stock	2 7 0 0 00	$ 92 7 0 0 00			
Common Stock, $20 par (20,000 shares authorized,						
10,000 shares issued)	$ 200 0 0 0 00				
Less Discount on Common Stock	10 0 0 0 00	190 0 0 0 00			
Total Paid-in Capital		$ 282 7 0 0 00			
Retained Earnings		45 0 0 0 00			
Total Stockholders' Equity			$ 327 7 0 0 00		

FYI

A corporation can also issue preferred stock at a discount or common stock at a premium.

Notice that the listing of the stock states the par value, the number of shares authorized, and the number of shares issued. The record also describes preferred stock as cumulative and participating. If the preferred stock is noncumulative or nonparticipating, the record does not mention it. Preferred stock is assumed to be noncumulative and nonparticipating unless otherwise stated.

Stockholders' Equity is divided into two major sections: **Paid-in Capital** and Retained Earnings. Paid-in or contributed capital includes the investments made by all the types of shareholders owning common and preferred stock in the corporation.

Concerning the Retained Earnings account, note that the amount is not necessarily in the form of cash. Retained earnings represents accumulated net income (not necessarily cash) kept in the company and not paid to stockholders in the form of dividends.

No-Par Stock

Preferred stock generally has a par value. However, common stock may or may not have a par value. If it does not have a par value, it is referred to as *no-par stock.* Corporations in all fifty states can issue no-par stock. The main advantages claimed for no-par stock are as follows:

1. Since it does not have a par value, no-par stock may be issued without a discount contingent liability.
2. No-par stock prevents any misconception on the part of naive stockholders as to the value of the stock. In the case of par stock, investors might believe that the stock is worth the amount printed on the face of the stock certificate. Actually, the market value of the stock may differ markedly from the par value, as a result of ups and downs in the corporation's past earnings and future prospects.

Stated Value and No-Par Stock

Remember!

Some states allow corporations to issue no-par, stated value stock. The stated value of the outstanding shares then becomes the legal capital of the corporation.

When all of a company's stock is of the par-value type, the par value of the shares represents the company's **legal capital**, which stockholders cannot withdraw. This law protects creditors. When various state legislatures passed laws permitting corporations to issue no-par stock, they tried to continue to protect creditors by stipulating that all or part of the amount the corporation receives for its no-par shares be exempt from withdrawal by stockholders. This amount is known as the stock's **stated value**. The minimum stated value per share of no-par stock varies from state to state. In some states the board of directors of the corporation, if it wishes, may choose a stated value for the company's no-par stock that is higher than the minimum required by the state law.

Established Amount of Stated Value

Objective 5

Journalize entries for the issuance of no-par stock.

Morris Optical is located in a state that allows the board of directors of a corporation to designate a stated value for its stock. Accordingly, the board of directors of Morris Optical chooses a stated value of $50 per share for its common stock. On June 20, Morris issues 1,000 shares at $56 per share, receiving cash. The accountant uses the account Paid-in Capital in Excess of Stated Value to record the amount received over and above the stated value.

The accountant's entry, in general journal form, is as follows:

	DATE		DESCRIPTION	POST. REF.	DEBIT	CREDIT	
1	20–						1
2	June	20	Cash		56 0 0 0 00		2
3			Common Stock			50 0 0 0 00	3
4			Paid-in Capital in Excess of				4
5			Stated Value			6 0 0 0 00	5
6			Issued 1,000 shares at $56				6
7			per share.				7

Next, on September 10, Morris Optical issues an additional 1,000 shares at $60 per share, receiving cash. The entry in general journal form is

	DATE		DESCRIPTION	POST. REF.	DEBIT	CREDIT	
1	20–						1
2	Sept.	10	Cash		60 0 0 0 00		2
3			Common Stock			50 0 0 0 00	3
4			Paid-in Capital in Excess of				4
5			Stated Value			10 0 0 0 00	5
6			Issued 1,000 shares at $60				6
7			per share.				7

In terms of T accounts, the entries look like this:

Cash			
	+	–	
June 20	56,000		
Sept. 10	60,000		

Common Stock			
	–	+	
		June 20	50,000 (stated value)
		Sept. 10	50,000 (stated value)

Paid-in Capital in Excess of Stated Value			
	–	+	
		June 20	6,000 (excess)
		Sept. 10	10,000 (excess)

Subscriptions and Stock Issuance

We have been talking about corporations that issue stock for which investors pay in full, either by giving cash or by giving noncash assets or organizational services. However, a corporation often sells its stock directly to investors on a subscription contract (installment) basis. This means that the investor enters into a contract with the corporation, promising to pay at a later date for a specified number of shares at an agreed-upon price. The corporation agrees to issue the shares when the investor has paid for them in full.

The accountant records the amount of the subscription, which is an asset, in the Subscriptions Receivable account and credits the par or stated value of the stock to Stock Subscribed, a stockholders' equity account. The accountant then records the difference between the subscription price and the par value under either Premium or Discount. In the case of no-par stock, the difference between the subscription price and the stated value is recorded under Paid-in Capital in Excess of Stated Value.

As the investor sends in payments, the accountant records them as debits to Cash and credits to Subscriptions Receivable. When the investor finishes paying for all the shares, the accountant records the issuance of the stock as a debit to Stock Subscribed and a credit to Common Stock or Preferred Stock. When investors want subscriptions to both common and preferred stock, the accountant uses separate accounts for each. We can best describe the procedure with some examples.

Subscription Transactions: No-Par Stock Delaney, Inc., a newly organized company, sets up its books with the following transactions involving its own stock:

May 1 Received subscriptions to 20,000 shares of common stock (stated value $10 per share) from various subscribers at $17 per share, with a downpayment of 50 percent of the subscription price (20,000 × $17 × .5 = $170,000).

June 1 Received an additional 30 percent of the subscription price from all subscribers (20,000 × $17 × .3 = $102,000).

July 1 Received an additional 20 percent of the subscription price from all subscribers; then issued the stock (20,000 × $17 × .2 = $68,000).

The general journal entries are shown in Figure 4 on the facing page. The items in parentheses are just explanations; they would not actually appear in the journal.

After the accountant has posted these transactions, the T accounts appear as follows:

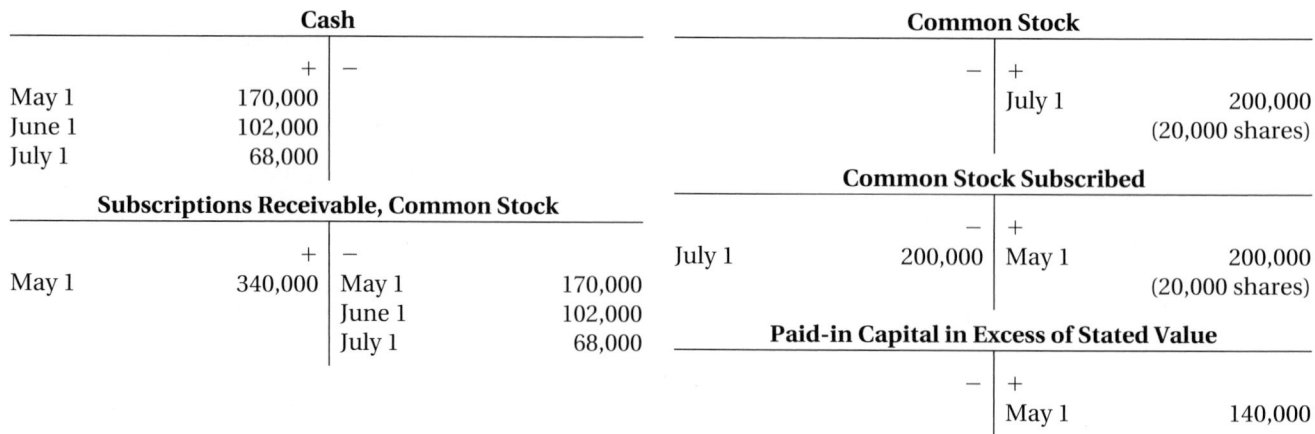

Common Stock Subscribed represents the total par value or stated value of the shares subscribed. It is a temporary account to handle subscribed shares that have not yet been paid for in full. When the investors finish

	DATE		DESCRIPTION	POST. REF.	DEBIT	CREDIT	
1	20–						1
2	May	1	Subscriptions Receivable,				2
3			Common Stock (20,000 shares				3
4			at $17 per share)		340 0 0 0 00		4
5			Common Stock Subscribed				5
6			(20,000 shares at $10 per				6
7			share)			200 0 0 0 00	7
8			Paid-in Capital in Excess of				8
9			Stated Value (20,000 shares				9
10			× $7)			140 0 0 0 00	10
11			Received subscriptions to				11
12			20,000 shares at $17 per				12
13			share.				13
14							14
15		1	Cash (20,000 shares × $17 per				15
16			share × .5)		170 0 0 0 00		16
17			Subscriptions Receivable,				17
18			Common Stock			170 0 0 0 00	18
19			Received 50 percent of the				19
20			subscription of May 1 on				20
21			20,000 shares.				21
22							22
23	June	1	Cash (20,000 shares × $17 per				23
24			share × .3)		102 0 0 0 00		24
25			Subscriptions Receivable,				25
26			Common Stock			102 0 0 0 00	26
27			Received 30 percent of the				27
28			subscription of May 1 on				28
29			20,000 shares.				29
30							30
31	July	1	Cash (20,000 shares × $17 per				31
32			share × .2)		68 0 0 0 00		32
33			Subscriptions Receivable,				33
34			Common Stock			68 0 0 0 00	34
35			Received 20 percent of the				35
36			subscription of May 1 on				36
37			20,000 shares.				37
38							38
39		1	Common Stock Subscribed		200 0 0 0 00		39
40			Common Stock (20,000 shares				40
41			× $10 per share)			200 0 0 0 00	41
42			Issued 20,000 shares.				42
43							43
44							44
45							45
46							46
47							47

GENERAL JOURNAL   PAGE 1

FIGURE 4

Remember!

For the sale of common stock on a subscription basis, use Common Stock Subscribed. Do not issue the stock until it is paid for in full.

Remember!

Stock may be paid for in installments, but is not issued until it is paid for in full. This requires two entries—one to record the final receipt of payment and one to issue the stock.

Remember

The "Item" column should be used to show the number of shares subscribed and shares issued.

paying for the shares, the accountant records the issuance of stock by debiting the Common Stock Subscribed account and crediting the Common Stock account.

In the ledger accounts for stock issued and subscribed, always list the number of shares in the Item column. Here is an example for Common Stock and Common Stock Subscribed:

ACCOUNT **Common Stock**   ACCOUNT NO. __314__

	DATE	ITEM	POST. REF.	DEBIT	CREDIT	BALANCE DEBIT	BALANCE CREDIT	
1	20–							1
2	July 1	20,000						2
3		shares	J1		200 0 0 0 00		200 0 0 0 00	3
4								4
5								5

ACCOUNT **Common Stock Subscribed**   ACCOUNT NO. __316__

	DATE	ITEM	POST. REF.	DEBIT	CREDIT	BALANCE DEBIT	BALANCE CREDIT	
1	20–							1
2	May 1	20,000						2
3		shares	J1		200 0 0 0 00		200 0 0 0 00	3
4	July 1		J1	200 0 0 0 00				4
5								5

FYI

Some states have authorized a hybrid organizational form that combines the tax benefits and organizational flexibility of a partnership with the liability-limiting characteristics of a corporation. It is called a limited liability partnership.

Subscription Transactions: Par-Value Stock Ortiz Insulation, Inc., a newly organized company, has the following transactions involving its own stock:

June 15 Received subscriptions to 4,000 shares of preferred 9 percent stock ($100 par value) from various subscribers at $104 per share, with a downpayment of 40 percent of the subscription price.

July 1 Received 30 percent of the subscription price from all subscribers (4,000 shares).

15 Received 30 percent of the subscription price from subscribers to 500 shares, and issued 500 shares.

The general journal is shown in Figure 5. The items in parentheses are explanations; they would not actually appear in the journal.

This illustrates that Preferred 9 Percent Stock Subscribed represents the total par value of the shares subscribed. **It also illustrates the fact that a firm does not issue stock until the investor has paid for it in full.** Since only 500 shares were paid for in full, the firm issued only 500 shares.

Controlling Accounts and Subsidiary Ledgers

Investors may finish paying for subscriptions at different times, and the firm issues stock when the individual subscriber has paid in full. Therefore, the firm's accountant has to maintain an account for each individual subscriber.

Remember!
Stock accounts are always credited at par value or stated value when stock is issued.

DATE		DESCRIPTION	POST. REF.	DEBIT	CREDIT	
20–						1
June	15	Subscriptions Receivable,				2
		Preferred 9 Percent Stock (4,000				3
		shares × $104 per share)		416 0 0 0 00		4
		Preferred 9 Percent Stock				5
		Subscribed (4,000 shares ×				6
		$100 per share)			400 0 0 0 00	7
		Premium on Preferred 9				8
		Percent Stock (4,000 shares				9
		× $4 per share)			16 0 0 0 00	10
		Received subscriptions to				11
		4,000 shares at $104 per				12
		share.				13
						14
	15	Cash (4,000 shares × $104 per				15
		share × .4)		166 4 0 0 00		16
		Subscriptions Receivable,				17
		Preferred 9 Percent Stock			166 4 0 0 00	18
		Received 40 percent of the				19
		subscription of June 15 on				20
		4,000 shares.				21
						22
July	1	Cash (4,000 shares × $104 per				23
		share × .3)		124 8 0 0 00		24
		Subscriptions Receivable,				25
		Preferred 9 Percent Stock			124 8 0 0 00	26
		Received 30 percent of the				27
		subscription of June 15 on				28
		4,000 shares.				29
						30
	15	Cash (500 shares × $104 per				31
		share × .3)		15 6 0 0 00		32
		Subscriptions Receivable,				33
		Preferred 9 Percent Stock			15 6 0 0 00	34
		Received 30 percent, the				35
		final installment of the				36
		subscription of June 15, on				37
		500 shares.				38
						39
	15	Preferred 9 Percent Stock				40
		Subscribed		50 0 0 0 00		41
		Preferred 9 Percent Stock (500				42
		shares × $100 per share)			50 0 0 0 00	43
		Issued 500 shares.				44
						45
						46
						47
						48

Remember!
Get the number of shares issued from the ledger account for the stock.

FIGURE 5

As a result, the books exhibit the following relationships between controlling accounts and subsidiary ledgers:

Controlling Account	Subsidiary Ledger
Subscriptions Receivable, Preferred 9 Percent Stock Subscriptions Receivable, Common Stock	Preferred 9 percent stock subscribers' ledger Common stock subscribers' ledger

These records are similar to the Accounts Receivable controlling account and the accounts receivable ledger.

The firm's accountant also has to keep an accurate record of the number of shares owned by each stockholder. Consequently, each stock account is a controlling account:

Controlling Account	Subsidiary Ledger
Preferred 9 Percent Stock	Preferred 9 percent stockholders' ledger
Common Stock	Common stockholders' ledger

As we have said, a small corporation may use its stock certificate book as a subsidiary ledger. Naturally, the accountant must see to it that the information is complete, so that the company can declare and pay dividends correctly. Cash dividends are paid on outstanding stock only.

ILLUSTRATION OF A CORPORATE BALANCE SHEET

Objective 7

Prepare a classified balance sheet for a corporation, including Subscriptions Receivable, Organization Costs, Paid-in Capital, and Retained Earnings accounts.

Remember!

The stockholders' equity items are each represented by a ledger account.

To reinforce your understanding of the accounts introduced in this chapter, examine the balance sheet shown in Figure 6 to see where each account is placed. Because this balance sheet covers so many of the concepts just discussed, you will probably want to refer back to it in the future. Notice that Retained Earnings is added separately to Total Paid-in Capital. In this case, the Retained Earnings account has a $170,000 credit balance. **This credit balance represents a surplus, and it is the normal balance. However, if a company had big losses, its Retained Earnings account could have a debit balance, which is called a deficit.** On a balance sheet, a Retained Earnings account with a debit balance is subtracted from Total Paid-in Capital.

NEW ACCOUNTS AND THE FUNDAMENTAL ACCOUNTING EQUATION

The placement and use of the accounts we have introduced in this chapter with respect to the fundamental accounting equation are shown in Figure 7 on page 762.

Landon, Inc.
Balance Sheet
June 30, 20—

Assets				
Current Assets:				
Cash			$ 27 0 0 0 00	
Notes Receivable			50 0 0 0 00	
Accounts Receivable	$ 419 0 0 0 00			
Less Allowance for Doubtful Accounts	12 0 0 0 00		407 0 0 0 00	
Subscriptions Receivable, Preferred 9 Percent Stock			14 0 0 0 00	
Subscriptions Receivable, Common Stock			30 0 0 0 00	
Merchandise Inventory			279 0 0 0 00	
Supplies			3 0 0 0 00	
Prepaid Insurance			5 0 0 00	
Total Current Assets				$ 810 5 0 0 00
Investments:				
Friedman Equipment Company 8 Percent Bonds				16 0 0 0 00
Plant and Equipment:				
Store Equipment	$ 82 0 0 0 00			
Less Accumulated Depreciation	19 0 0 0 00	$ 63 0 0 0 00		
Delivery Equipment	$ 60 0 0 0 00			
Less Accumulated Depreciation	40 0 0 0 00	20 0 0 0 00		
Total Plant and Equipment				83 0 0 0 00
Intangible Assets:				
Organization Costs				8 0 0 0 00
Total Assets				$ 917 5 0 0 00
Liabilities				
Current Liabilities:				
Accounts Payable			$ 281 5 0 0 00	
Notes Payable			20 0 0 0 00	
Salaries Payable			3 0 0 0 00	
Interest Payable			1 0 0 0 00	
Total Liabilities				$ 305 5 0 0 00
Stockholders' Equity				
Paid-in Capital:				
Preferred 7 Percent Stock, $50 par (2,000 shares authorized and issued)	$ 100 0 0 0 00			
Less Discount on Preferred 7 Percent Stock	1 0 0 0 00	$ 99 0 0 0 00		
Preferred 9 Percent Stock, $50 par (4,000 shares authorized, 1,500 shares issued)	$ 75 0 0 0 00			
Preferred 9 Percent Stock Subscribed (500 shares)	25 0 0 0 00			
Premium on Preferred 9 Percent Stock	3 0 0 0 00	103 0 0 0 00		
Common Stock, no-par, stated value $10 per share (20,000 shares authorized, 14,000 shares issued)	$ 140 0 0 0 00			
Common Stock Subscribed (2,000 shares)	20 0 0 0 00			
Paid-in Capital in Excess of Stated Value	80 0 0 0 00	240 0 0 0 00		
Total Paid-in Capital		$ 442 0 0 0 00		
Retained Earnings		170 0 0 0 00		
Total Stockholders' Equity				612 0 0 0 00
Total Liabilities and Stockholders' Equity				$ 917 5 0 0 00

FIGURE 6

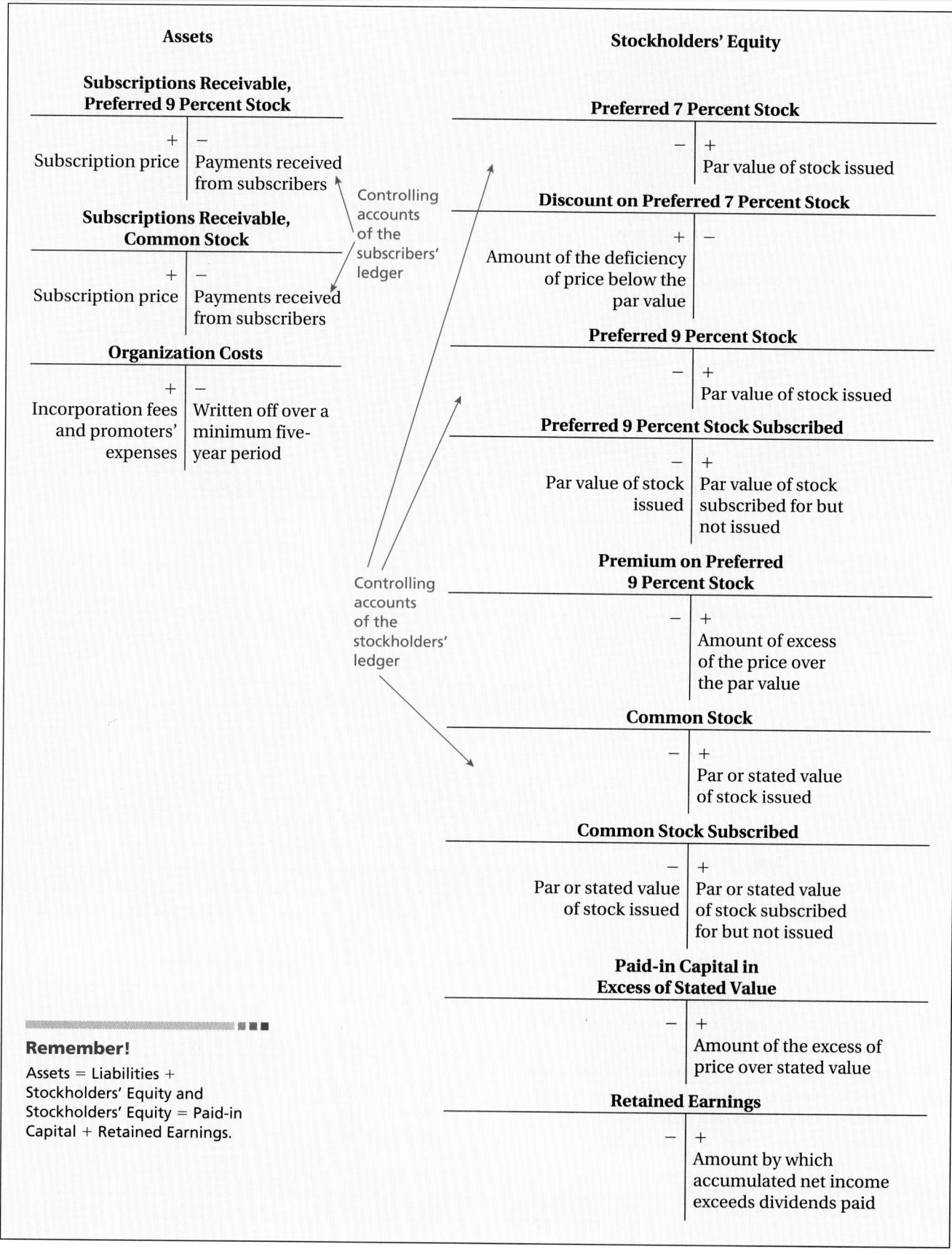

FIGURE 7

CHAPTER REVIEW

Review of Performance Objectives

1. Define *corporation.*

   A corporation is defined as "an artificial being, invisible, intangible, and existing only in contemplation of the law."

2. Name at least two advantages and two disadvantages of the corporate form.

   A corporation has the following advantages over a sole proprietorship or a partnership: limited liability, ease of raising capital, ease of transferring ownership rights, continuous existence, and no mutual agency. Two disadvantages of a corporation are additional taxation and increased government regulation.

3. Describe the formation of a corporation.

   To form a corporation, a person or persons must file articles of incorporation with the state. The corporation may be small (closely held) or large (public). Stock is sold to raise capital. Dividends (an amount per share owned) may be paid to stockholders. The capital stock accounts in a corporation replace owners' capital accounts in a sole proprietorship.

4. Journalize entries for the issuance of par-value stock.

   The entry for the issuance of par-value stock for cash is a debit to Cash and credits to the Stock accounts. When stock is exchanged for assets other than cash, those asset accounts are debited. When stock is issued for more than its par value, the accountant must credit a Premium account. For stock issued at a discount, a Discount account is debited.

5. Journalize entries for the issuance of no-par stock.

   When no-par stock with a stated value is issued, all the proceeds are credited to the Stock account. The entry credits a Paid-in Capital in Excess of Stated Value account for amounts higher than the stated value.

6. Journalize entries for the sale of stock on the subscription basis.

   The entry for the sale of stock on a subscription (installment) basis is a debit to a Subscriptions Receivable account (a current asset) and a credit to a Stock Subscribed account (a Paid-in Capital account). When the subscription is paid in full and the stock is issued, the entry is a debit to a Stock Subscribed account and a credit to a Stock account.

7. Prepare a classified balance sheet for a corporation, including Subscriptions Receivable, Organization Costs, Paid-in Capital, and Retained Earnings accounts.

   The accounts shown in Figure 7 are used to prepare a classified balance sheet. The classified balance sheet is presented in Figure 6.

Glossary

Articles of incorporation Application for a charter. (743)

Authorized capital The maximum number of shares that may be issued for each class of stock (common and preferred). (743)

Capital stock General term referring to shares of ownership in a corporation. (743)

Charter Written permit, issued by a state government, for a corporation to exist; state approved articles of incorporation. (743)

Closely held corporation A corporation having a relatively small group of owners. (743)

Common stock Stock whose owners are paid dividends only after owners of preferred stock have been paid (residual share); holders of common stock have voting privileges. (747)

Corporation "An artificial being, invisible, intangible, and existing only in contemplation of the law." As such, it is a separate legal entity. (742)

Cumulative preferred stock Preferred stock whose holders must be paid accumulated dividends or dividends in arrears (dividends that the firm has failed to pay in prior years) before any dividends can be paid to holders of common stock. (748)

Deficit A debit or negative balance in the Retained Earnings account. (760)

Discount The amount by which the issuing price of a stock falls below the par value. (751)

Dividends Distributions of earnings of a corporation, in the form of either cash or additional shares of stock. (745)

Double taxation Taxation of corporate income at two separate points. First, the net income of the corporation is taxed because the corporation is a separate entity. When the net income is distributed as dividends to stockholders, it becomes part of the personal income of the individual stockholder and is taxed a second time. (743)

Intangible asset An asset with no physical features; this classification includes such accounts as Organization Costs, Franchises, Patents, and Goodwill. (744)

Issued stock Stock issued by a corporation. (746)

Legal capital Minimum capital stock investment that a corporation must maintain; capital that is not subject to withdrawal by stockholders; usually equal to par or stated value. (747, 754)

Noncumulative preferred stock Preferred stock in which dividends in arrears do not accumulate; once they are passed, they are gone forever. (748)

Nonparticipating preferred stock Stock in which the dividends are limited to the regular rate. (748)

No-par stock Stock that has no value printed on the stock certificates. (747)

Organization Costs An intangible asset account used to record the cost of organizing a corporation, such as fees paid to the state, attorneys' fees, promotional costs, travel expenses, costs of printing stock certificates, and so on. (744)

Outstanding stock Stock actually in the possession of stockholders (issued stock less the number of shares reacquired by the company). (746)

Paid-in Capital A caption in the balance sheet listed immediately under Stockholders' Equity. The Paid-in Capital section includes the Stock accounts and their related Premium or Discount accounts. (754)

Participating preferred stock Preferred stock whose holders share in any extra dividends distributed by the corporation after the regular dividend has been paid to holders of preferred stock and a stipulated dividend has been paid to holders of common stock. (748)

Par-value stock Stock for which a uniform face value, indicating the amount per share to be entered in the Capital Stock account, is printed on the stock certificates. (747)

Preemptive right A stockholder's right to maintain the same proportionate ownership in a corporation in the future as she or he does originally, through the privilege of subscribing to a new issue of stock in the same proportion as her or his present ownership. (745)

Preferred stock Stock whose holders are paid dividends at a uniform rate before any dividends are paid to a holder of common stock. The holder of preferred stock also has preference in the distribution of assets in the event of a liquidation. (747)

Premium The amount by which the issuing price of a stock exceeds the par value. (751)

Public corporation A corporation having a large group of owners with shares traded on a stock exchange or in over-the-counter markets. Also called *open*. (743)

Retained Earnings A stockholders' equity account representing capital generated by the corporation's earnings that remain in the firm; the amount by which net income exceeds dividends paid over the life of the corporation. (746)

Stated value The amount per share of no-par stock that is recorded in the corporation's Stock accounts; an amount designated by law as not subject to withdrawal by stockholders. (754)

Stock certificates Documents giving evidence of ownership in shares of stock; issued only when the stockholder has paid for the shares in full. (744)

Stockholders' equity The owners' equity in a corporation. Also referred to as *capital*. (746)

Stockholders' ledger A record showing the name and address of each stockholder and the number of shares owned. (749)

Surplus A credit or positive balance in the Retained Earnings account. (760)

Treasury stock A corporation's own stock, which it has issued and which was at one time outstanding, that the firm reacquires. (746)

QUESTIONS, EXERCISES, AND PROBLEMS

Discussion Questions

1. Name the subsidiary ledgers for Common Stock and for Subscriptions Receivable, Common Stock.

2. In what respect is a corporation a separate legal entity?

3. Name three types of organization costs. How is the account Organization Costs classified on a balance sheet? What eventually happens to Organization Costs?

4. Identify four advantages and two disadvantages of the corporate form of business organization as compared to the sole proprietorship and partnership forms. In your opinion, which is the greatest advantage and which is the greatest disadvantage?

5. In regard to common stock, what is the difference between par value and stated value?

6. If a corporation sells its stock at a premium, does the amount of the premium represent revenue to the firm?

7. What is a stock subscription?

8. Classify each of the following accounts as asset, liability, stockholders' equity, revenue, or expense, and indicate the normal balance of each account:

a. Common Stock
b. Subscriptions Receivable, Common Stock
c. Common Stock Subscribed
d. Retained Earnings
e. Organization Costs
f. Discount on Preferred 8 Percent Stock
g. Preferred 8 Percent Stock
h. Premium on Common Stock

Exercises

P.O. 4

Describe stock transactions from T accounts.

Exercise 21-1 Describe the transactions recorded in the following accounts of the Gwynn Company:

Cash				Common Stock		
(1)	320,000	(2)	2,500		(1)	320,000
					(2)	1,500

Organization Costs	
(2)	4,000

P.O. 4

Journalize entries to sell common stock for cash and exchange it for other assets above par value.

Exercise 21-2 The Hecter Corporation is authorized to issue 40,000 shares of $85-par-value common stock. Record the following transactions in general journal form.

Feb. 10 Sold 7,000 shares of common stock at $86 per share; received cash.

27 Issued 2,150 shares of common stock in exchange for land with a fair market value of $90,000 and a building with a fair market value of $109,750.

Mar. 3 Sold 2,500 shares of common stock at $87 per share; received cash.

P.O. 4,5

Journalize entries to sell common and preferred stock for cash.

Exercise 21-3 On July 2, Fazio Corporation issued for cash 10,000 shares of no-par common stock (with a stated value of $13 per share) at $17. On July 17, it issued for cash 700 shares of $110-par preferred 10 percent stock at $112.

a. Write the entries for July 2 and July 17 in general journal form.
b. What is the total amount invested by all stockholders as of July 17?

P.O. 4

Journalize entries to sell common and preferred stock for cash and exchange it for services and assets.

Exercise 21-4 The Frame Corporation was organized on April 8 of this year. It was authorized to issue 900 shares of cumulative preferred 9 percent stock, $100 par value, and 9,000 shares of common stock, $30 par value. Record in general journal form the following transactions, completed during the firm's first year of operations:

Apr.	8	Sold 3,200 shares of common stock at par for cash.
	8	Issued 80 shares of common stock to an attorney in return for legal services pertaining to incorporation. The stock is selling at par.
May	7	Sold 500 shares of preferred stock at $107; received cash.
Aug.	12	Issued 2,800 shares of common stock in exchange for land with a fair market value of $84,000.

P.O. 5

Journalize entries to sell common stock above stated value for cash.

Exercise 21-5 Delicino, Inc., is authorized to issue 220,000 shares of no-par common stock, $12 stated value. Record the following transactions in general journal form.

May	23	Sold 4,000 shares of common stock at $15 per share for cash.
June	19	Sold 10,000 shares of common stock at $17 per share for cash.

P.O. 5

Journalize entries to receive subscriptions for stock, receiving periodic payments.

Exercise 21-6 Bob's Deli has authorized capital consisting of 25,000 shares of cumulative preferred 9 percent stock, $100 par value, and 25,000 shares of common stock, $30 par value. Record transactions a–c in general journal form:

a. Received subscriptions to 12,000 shares of preferred 9 percent stock at $102 per share, with a downpayment of 50 percent of the subscription price.
b. Received 30 percent of the subscription price from all subscribers.
c. Received 20 percent of the subscription price from all subscribers and issued the stock certificates.

P.O. 5,6

Describe stock transactions from T accounts.

Exercise 21-7 Describe the transactions recorded in the following ledger accounts of Metcalf Corporation:

	Cash				Common Stock	
(a)	25,000				(a)	22,000
(c)	34,500				(e)	45,000
(d)	25,500					

	Subscriptions Receivable, Common Stock				Common Stock Subscribed	
(b)	60,000	(c)	34,500	(e)	45,000	(b)	45,000
		(d)	25,500			

	Paid-in Capital in Excess of Stated Value	
	(a)	3,000
	(b)	15,000

P.O. 7

Prepare a Stockholders' Equity section of a balance sheet.

Exercise 21-8 Grace's Bakery, Inc., has a charter authorizing it to issue 3,000 shares of $40-par-value preferred 8 percent stock and 12,000 shares of no-par common stock (stated value $25). The following account balances are from the Balance Sheet columns of the work sheet:

Retained Earnings (debit balance)	$ 86,700
Common Stock Subscribed (2,500 shares)	62,500
Discount on Preferred 8 Percent Stock	2,400
Common Stock	150,000
Preferred 8 Percent Stock	60,000
Paid-in Capital in Excess of Stated Value	37,500

Prepare the Stockholders' Equity section of the balance sheet.

CONSIDER AND COMMUNICATE

Marvin is planning to open a fabric dyeing business. He plans to do large-scale dyeing of both fabric bolts and ready-to-wear garments. The source of business will be garment makers and cleaners. He has worked in this part of the fashion industry and knows how much capital he will need to buy the equipment required for this specialized activity.

He has some cash, and he is trying to decide whether to incorporate or to form a partnership. What would you say to him about the major advantages and disadvantages of chartering a corporation rather than forming a partnership?

WHAT IF . . .

After having been a partner in a personal services firm for five years, you decided to leave the partnership and form a corporation. After completing the necessary organization steps and forming a board of directors, you sold stock to raise the necessary capital. You have retained control of 51 percent of the stock. One day, one of your former partners (who owns 20 percent of the stock in your corporation) sends you a bill for $3,000 for a billboard campaign. He hired the public relations company to increase the visibility of the corporation in which he is a stockholder. Are you going to pay the $3,000 bill your former partner incurred?

CRITICAL THINKING

You asked your new assistant for the summer, a relative of your supervisor, to prepare the Stockholders' Equity section. A copy of the result is reproduced below. Check your assistant's work and comment on its accuracy and logic. Prepare a corrected stockholders' equity section.

Total Liabilities				$ 786 1 7 5 00
Stockholders' Equity				
Paid-in Capital:				
Preferred 9 Percent Stock, $100 par (3,500 shares authorized, 2,539 shares issued)	$ 603 9 0 0 00			
Preferred 9 Percent Stock Subscribed (520 shares)	52 0 0 0 00			
Premium on Preferred 9 Percent Stock	6 1 2 0 00	$ 662 0 2 0 00		
Common Stock, no-par, stated value $20 per share (35,000 shares authorized, 18,360 shares issued)	$1 067 2 0 0 00			
Common Stock Subscribed (4,590 shares)	91 8 0 0 00			
Paid-in Capital in Excess of Stated Value	114 7 5 0 00	1 273 7 5 0 00		
Total Paid-in Capital		$1 935 7 7 0 00		
Retained Earnings		284 5 8 0 00		
Total Stockholders' Equity			$1 651 1 9 0 00	
Total Liabilities and Stockholders' Equity			$2 437 3 6 5 00	

WEB WORK

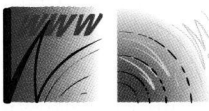

Using an Internet web browser, type a well-known company's name in the search box and search for information about common stock and preferred stock. Discuss your findings in a small group. Write a one-page summary of your findings.

PROBLEM SET A

For additional help, see the demonstration problem at the beginning of each chapter in your Working Papers.

P.O. 4

Problem 21-1A Bannister Pharmacy, organized on June 4 of this year, has a charter that stipulates the following authorized capital:

a. 6,000 shares of preferred 8 percent stock, $50 par value
b. 30,000 shares of common stock, $20 par value

During the first year of its operations, Bannister completed the following transactions:

June	14	Received subscriptions to 9,000 shares of common stock at $20 per share; collected 50 percent of the subscription price.
July	20	Sold 1,500 shares of preferred 8 percent stock for $48 per share, receiving cash.
Aug.	14	Subscribers to 9,000 shares of common stock paid an additional 30 percent of the subscription price.
Sept.	16	Subscribers to 9,000 shares of common stock paid an additional 20 percent of the subscription price. Bannister Pharmacy issued the 9,000 shares of stock.
Oct.	3	Sold 1,800 shares of preferred 8 percent stock for $47 per share, receiving cash.
Nov.	22	Received subscriptions to 1,600 shares of common stock at $22 per share; collected 25 percent of the subscription price.
Dec.	19	Received subscriptions to 1,200 shares of preferred 8 percent stock for $49 per share, collecting 10 percent of the subscription price.

Check Figure

Oct. 3 Discount, $5,400

Instructions

Record the above transactions in general journal form.

P.O. 4,7

Problem 21-2A Three people—Callas, Duncan, and Reeder—organized Freeze-it Cold Storage, Inc., with a charter providing for the following authorized capital:

a. 1,500 shares of preferred 9 percent stock, $50 par value
b. 15,000 shares of common stock, $10 par value

During its first year of operations, Freeze-it Cold Storage, Inc., completed the following transactions:

June	5	Issued 3,600 shares of common stock to Callas, at par, for cash.
	6	Paid an attorney $4,050 for performing services related to incorporation and for reimbursement of state fees.

June 6 Bought equipment from Reeder for $32,140. Reeder accepted 3,214 shares of common stock in exchange for the equipment.

6 Bought land and building from Duncan. It was determined that the fair market value of the land was $15,900 and of the building, $48,750. There is an outstanding mortgage on the property of $28,500 held by Trent Savings Bank. The corporation assumed responsibility for paying the mortgage. Duncan accepted common stock at par for his equity.

8 Issued 60 shares of common stock to Callas for organizational services. The stock is selling at par.

July 5 Issued 450 shares of preferred 9 percent stock at $53 per share to investors for cash.

31 Issued 300 shares of preferred 9 percent stock at $52 per share to investors for cash.

Check Figure

Total Stockholders' Equity, $187,480

Instructions

1. Record the above transactions in general journal form.
2. Post the entries to the following accounts: Preferred 9 Percent Stock, Premium on Preferred 9 Percent Stock, and Common Stock.
3. Prepare the Stockholders' Equity section of the balance sheet as of December 31, the end of the first year of operations. Net income after taxes for the year was $43,140, and no dividends were declared during the year. As a result, Retained Earnings has a credit balance of $43,140.

P.O. 7

Problem 21-3A Lang Freight-Forwarding Company, Inc., has an authorized capital of 3,000 shares of preferred 9 percent stock, $100 par value, and 30,000 shares of no-par common stock, stated value $20. The following account balances are from the Balance Sheet columns of the work sheet for the fiscal year ended December 31 of this year. The accounts are listed in alphabetical order.

Accounts Payable	$578,160
Accounts Receivable	704,340
Accumulated Depreciation, Building	80,700
Accumulated Depreciation, Equipment	131,190
Allowance for Doubtful Accounts	22,260
Building	396,000
Cash	89,880
Common Stock	360,000
Common Stock Subscribed	90,000
Equipment	289,350
Land	102,000
Merchandise Inventory	475,920
Mortgage Payable (long-term liability)	138,000
Notes Payable	54,600
Organization Costs	21,360
Paid-in Capital in Excess of Stated Value	112,500
Preferred 9 Percent Stock	249,000
Preferred 9 Percent Stock Subscribed	51,000
Premium on Preferred 9 Percent Stock	6,000
Retained Earnings (credit balance)	279,000
Subscriptions Receivable, Common Stock	48,600
Subscriptions Receivable, Preferred 9 Percent Stock	19,200
Supplies	5,760

Check Figure

Total Liabilities and Stockholders'
Equity, $1,918,260

Instructions

1. Determine the number of shares of preferred 9 percent stock issued and subscribed.
2. Determine the number of shares of common stock issued and subscribed.
3. Prepare a classified balance sheet.

P.O. 4,5,6

Problem 21-4A Stanski Corporation was organized on March 1 of this year, with a charter providing for the following authorized capital:

a. 3,000 shares of preferred 10 percent stock, $50 par value
b. 20,000 shares of no-par common stock, $25 stated value

During the first year of operations, Stanski Corporation completed the following transactions:

Mar. 2 Bought land from Stanski for $39,000. Stanski accepted 1,200 shares of common stock for the land (credit Paid-in Capital in Excess of Stated Value, $9,000).
     4 Received subscriptions to 4,500 shares of common stock at $26 per share, collecting 40 percent of the subscription price.
     6 Issued 100 shares of common stock to Stanski at $26 per share, in return for organizational services.
    10 Subscribers to 4,500 shares of common stock paid an additional 30 percent of the subscription price.
    13 Paid an attorney $3,940 for performing services needed for incorporating the firm and for reimbursement of state fees.
    14 Received subscriptions to 750 shares of preferred 10 percent stock at $52 per share, collecting 20 percent of the subscription price.
    21 Subscribers to 4,500 shares of common stock paid the remaining 30 percent of the subscription price; Stanski Corporation then issued the stock.

Apr. 9 Received subscriptions to 3,000 shares of common stock at $27 per share, collecting 50 percent of the subscription price.
    17 Subscribers to 750 shares of preferred 10 percent stock paid an additional 40 percent of the subscription price.
    23 Sold 300 shares of preferred 10 percent stock at $51 per share for cash.

Check Figure

Total paid-in capital, $293,900

Instructions

Record these transactions in general journal form. What is the total paid-in capital?

Instructions for General Ledger Software

1. Record the entries in the general journal.
2. Print the general journal. What is the total paid-in capital?

PROBLEM SET B

For additional help, see the demonstration problem at the beginning of each chapter in your Working Papers.

P.O. 4,6

Problem 21-1B The Grand-Way Food Service, Inc., was organized on April 4 of this year and has a charter that stipulates the following authorized capital:

a. 3,000 shares of preferred 7 percent stock, $100 par value
b. 40,000 shares of common stock, $25 par value

Grand-Way Food Service, Inc., completed the following transactions during its first year of operations:

Apr. 8 Received subscriptions to 12,000 shares of common stock at $25 per share; collected 60 percent of the subscription price.

14 Sold 1,000 shares of preferred 7 percent stock for $97 per share, receiving cash.

May 7 Subscribers to 12,000 shares of common stock paid an additional 20 percent of the subscription price.

June 6 Subscribers to 12,000 shares of common stock paid an additional 20 percent of the subscription price. Grand-Way Food Service, Inc., issued the 12,000 shares of stock.

July 5 Sold 600 shares of preferred 7 percent stock for $94 per share, receiving cash.

Aug. 14 Received subscriptions to 3,000 shares of common stock at $27 per share; collected 50 percent of the subscription price.

Sept. 21 Received subscriptions to 300 shares of preferred 7 percent stock for $97 per share; collected 20 percent of the subscription price.

Check Figure

July 5 Discount, $3,600

Instructions

Record the above transactions in general journal form.

P.O. 4,7

Problem 21-2B Three people—Kelly, Haglund, and Howard—organized Newburn Athletic Supply, Inc. The charter of this corporation authorizes capital consisting of the following:

a. 1,600 shares of preferred 9 percent stock, $50 par value
b. 20,000 shares of common stock, $10 par value

During its first year of operations, Newburn Athletic Supply, Inc., completed the following transactions:

May 1 Issued to Kelly 3,000 shares of common stock, at par, for cash.

2 Bought equipment from Haglund for $32,000. Haglund accepted 3,200 shares of common stock in exchange for the equipment.

2 Bought land and building from Howard. The fair market value of the land was $18,000 and of the building, $62,000. There is an outstanding mortgage on the property of $32,000, held by Regional Savings Bank. The corporation assumed responsibility for paying the mortgage. Howard accepted common stock at par for her equity.

5 Paid an attorney $4,200 for reimbursement of state fees and for performing services needed for incorporating the firm.

7 Issued 100 shares of common stock at par to Kelly for organizational services. The stock is selling at par.

June 7 Issued 600 shares of preferred 9 percent stock at $52 per share to investors for cash.

July 3 Issued 400 shares of preferred 9 percent stock at $51 per share to investors for cash.

Check Figure

Total Stockholders' Equity, $204,600

Instructions

1. Record the above transactions in general journal form.
2. Post the entries to the following accounts: Preferred 9 Percent Stock, Premium on Preferred 9 Percent Stock, and Common Stock.
3. Prepare the Stockholders' Equity section of the balance sheet as of December 31, the end of the first year of operations. Net income after taxes for the year was $42,000, and no dividends were declared during the year. As a result, Retained Earnings has a credit balance of $42,000.

P.O. 7

Problem 21-3B Delite Dairy, Inc., has an authorized capital of 3,000 shares of preferred 10 percent stock, $100 par value, and 25,000 shares of no-par common stock, stated value $20. The following account balances for the fiscal year ending June 30 of this year are taken from the Balance Sheet columns of the work sheet for the year. The accounts are listed in alphabetical order.

Accounts Payable	$375,280
Accounts Receivable	443,680
Accumulated Depreciation, Building	41,200
Accumulated Depreciation, Equipment	83,300
Allowance for Doubtful Accounts	13,840
Building	256,000
Cash	55,200
Common Stock	240,000
Common Stock Subscribed	40,000
Equipment	184,000
Land	60,000
Merchandise Inventory	289,000
Mortgage Payable (long-term liability)	84,000
Notes Payable	32,800
Organization Costs	12,840
Paid-in Capital in Excess of Stated Value	70,000
Preferred 10 Percent Stock	160,000
Preferred 10 Percent Stock Subscribed	20,000
Premium on Preferred 10 Percent Stock	3,600
Retained Earnings (credit balance)	168,000
Subscriptions Receivable, Common Stock	17,400
Subscriptions Receivable, Preferred 10 Percent Stock	10,200
Supplies	3,700

Check Figure

Total Liabilities and Stockholders' Equity, $1,193,680

Instructions

1. Determine the number of shares of preferred 10 percent stock issued and subscribed.
2. Determine the number of shares of common stock issued and subscribed.
3. Prepare a classified balance sheet.

P.O. 4,5,6

Problem 21-4B Gallatin Specialty Advertising was organized on September 1 of this year, with a charter providing for authorized capital as follows:

a. 2,000 shares of preferred 7 percent stock, $50 par value
b. 40,000 shares of no-par common stock, $10 stated value

During the first year of operations, Gallatin Specialty Advertising completed the following transactions:

Sept. 1 Received subscriptions to 8,000 shares of common stock at $12 per share, collecting 30 percent of the subscription price.

Sept. 3 Bought equipment from Gallatin, one of the promoters, for $32,000. Gallatin accepted 3,000 shares of common stock in return for the equipment. (Credit Paid-in Capital in Excess of Stated Value, $2,000.)

12 Subscribers to 8,000 shares of common stock paid an additional 30 percent of the subscription price.

14 Issued 100 shares of common stock to Gallatin at $12 per share in return for promotional services valued at $1,200.

18 Received subscriptions to 800 shares of preferred 7 percent stock at $47 per share, collecting 40 percent of the subscription price.

25 Paid an attorney $4,140 for paying state fees and for performing services needed for incorporating the firm.

29 Subscribers to 8,000 shares of common stock paid the remaining 40 percent of the subscription price, and Gallatin Specialty Advertising then issued the 8,000 shares.

Oct. 4 Received subscriptions to 3,000 shares of common stock at $14 per share, collecting 50 percent of the subscription price.

9 Subscribers to 800 shares of preferred 7 percent stock paid an additional 30 percent of the subscription price.

30 Subscribers to 3,000 shares of common stock paid the remaining 50 percent of the subscription price, and Gallatin Specialty Advertising issued the 3,000 shares.

Check Figure

Total paid-in capital, $208,800

Instructions

Record these transactions in general journal form. What is the total paid-in capital?

Instructions for General Ledger Software

1. Record the entries in the general journal.
2. Print the general journal. What is the total paid-in capital?

22 Corporate Work Sheets, Taxes, and Dividends

WINDOWS ON | *THE WORLD WIDE WEB*

Do you dream in Sony? By selling Sony Walkmans and digital camcorders, producing albums for Lauryn Hill and Mariah Carey, making films at Columbia Pictures, and producing game shows like *Jeopardy!* and soap operas like *Days of Our Lives*, Sony had net sales of more than $53 billion at the end of the 1990s. Sony Corporation has to pay corporate income taxes on those sales—as much as $1,594 million a year. How would you journalize entries for these taxes?

After paying taxes, Sony may declare and issue dividends to stockholders. Did Sony issue dividends last year? If so, were they cash dividends or stock dividends? What were Sony's retained earnings for the past year? How would you journalize entries for the appropriation of retained earnings? Read this chapter to learn how to journalize these entries. For current annual reports from Sony, go to **http://www.world.sony.com/IR/**, and then look up Annual Reports.

Performance Objectives

After you have completed this chapter, you will be able to do the following:

1. Journalize entries for corporate income taxes.

2. Journalize closing entries for a corporation.

3. Complete a work sheet for a corporation.

4. Journalize entries for the appropriation of Retained Earnings.

5. Journalize entries for the declaration and issuance of cash dividends.

6. Journalize entries for the declaration and issuance of stock dividends.

7. Complete a corporate statement of retained earnings and a balance sheet, including the following types of accounts: Appropriated Retained Earnings, Stock Dividends Distributable, Dividends Payable, and Income Tax Payable.

8. Describe guidelines for accounting reports.

L et's assume that the corporation is established. We now turn our attention to the year-to-year entries for taxes, dividends, and retained earnings.

PROCEDURE FOR RECORDING AND PAYING INCOME TAXES

Determining the net income of a corporation is simply a matter of

Revenue − Expenses = Net Income

You can compare most of the revenue and expense accounts of a corporation to those of sole proprietorships and partnerships. The net income of a sole proprietorship and the distributive shares of net income of a partnership are taxable as part of the owners' personal incomes. Since the corporation is a separate legal entity, however, it must pay income taxes in its own name. Corporations are subject to federal income taxes, and many states and cities also impose an income tax on them. We will talk about only the income tax levied by the federal government, but the same basic principles apply to state and city income taxes.

To place corporations on a pay-as-you-go basis, the law requires most of them to estimate in advance the amount of their federal income taxes for the forthcoming fiscal year. The corporation then pays the estimated amount in four quarterly installments during the year. The firm's accountant records each entry as a debit to Income Tax Expense and a credit to Cash. The Income Tax Expense account is handled like any other expense account, except that the accountant usually makes a separate entry closing Income Tax Expense into Income Summary.

At the end of the fiscal year, after the corporation determines the exact amount of its income, it calculates how much income tax it owes. If the amount of income tax the corporation has paid in advance exceeds its tax liability for the year, the accountant debits the amount of the overpayment to Prepaid Income Tax, a current asset account, and credits it to Income Tax Expense. Usually, however, the amount of income tax paid in advance is less than the amount of the tax liability. In this case, the accountant debits the amount of the underpayment to Income Tax Expense and credits it to Income Tax Payable, a current liability account. The corporation is required to make full payment of its final tax with its income tax return. The entry is a debit to Income Tax Payable and a credit to Cash.

FYI

The tax return is filed two and one-half months after the close of the fiscal year.

Corporate Income Tax Rates

Throughout this text, we assume that corporate income is subject to federal tax under a three-bracket, graduated-rate structure (the higher the income, the higher the tax rate), as follows:

Taxable Income	Tax Rate (%)
First $50,000	15
Next $25,000 ($50,001–$75,000)	25
Over $75,000	34

A 5 percent surtax (extra tax) is imposed on income between $100,000 and $335,000. In effect, the addition of the surtax causes corporations with taxable income above $335,000 to pay a flat 34 percent rate on all taxable income. Following are three examples.

Taxable Income of $77,000

Tax on the first $50,000 ($50,000 × .15)	$ 7,500
Tax on the next $25,000 ($25,000 × .25)	6,250
Tax on the next $2,000 ($2,000 × .34)	680
Total tax	$14,430

Remember!

Corporations are required to pay income taxes on the amount of their net income; sole proprietorships and partnerships are not taxed directly.

Taxable Income of $200,000

Tax on the first $50,000 ($50,000 × .15)	$ 7,500
Tax on the next $25,000 ($25,000 × .25)	6,250
Tax on the next $125,000 ($125,000 × .34)	42,500
Surtax on amount between $100,000 and $200,000 ($100,000 × .05)	5,000
Total tax	$61,250

Taxable Income of $460,000

Tax on the first $50,000 ($50,000 × .15)	$ 7,500
Tax on the next $25,000 ($25,000 × .25)	6,250
Tax on the next $385,000 ($385,000 × .34)	130,900
Surtax on amount between $100,000 and $335,000 ($235,000 × .05)	11,750
Total tax	$156,400

Or: Since the taxable income is above $335,000, use the flat tax rate of 34 percent: $460,000 × .34 = $156,400.

Income Tax Entries for a Corporation: First Year

Objective 1

Journalize entries for corporate income taxes.

Wahl, Inc., began operations on January 5. The corporation's fiscal year is from January 1 through December 31. Its authorized capital consists of 200,000 shares of $20-par-value common stock. For the fiscal year, the corporation estimates that its taxable income will be $116,000 and its income tax will be $28,490:

Tax on the first $50,000 ($50,000 × .15)	$ 7,500
Tax on the next $25,000 ($25,000 × .25)	6,250
Tax on the next $41,000 ($41,000 × .34)	13,940
Surtax on amount between $100,000 and $116,000 ($16,000 × .05)	800
Total tax	$28,490

Here is the way Wahl, Inc., records the payment of this tax:

	DATE		DESCRIPTION	POST. REF.	DEBIT	CREDIT	
1	Year 1						1
2	Apr.	15	Income Tax Expense		7 1 2 2 50		2
3			Cash			7 1 2 2 50	3
4			Paid first quarterly				4
5			installment of estimated				5
6			federal income tax for the				6
7			year (one-fourth of $28,490).				7
8							8

DATE		DESCRIPTION	POST. REF.	DEBIT	CREDIT	
1	Year 1					1
2	June	15	Income Tax Expense		7 1 2 2 50		2
3			Cash			7 1 2 2 50	3
4			Paid second quarterly				4
5			installment of estimated				5
6			federal income tax for the				6
7			year.				7

DATE		DESCRIPTION	POST. REF.	DEBIT	CREDIT	
1	Year 1					1
2	Sept.	15	Income Tax Expense		7 1 2 2 50		2
3			Cash			7 1 2 2 50	3
4			Paid third quarterly install-				4
5			ment of estimated federal				5
6			income tax for the year.				6
7							7

DATE		DESCRIPTION	POST. REF.	DEBIT	CREDIT	
1	Year 1					1
2	Dec.	15	Income Tax Expense		7 1 2 2 50		2
3			Cash			7 1 2 2 50	3
4			Paid fourth quarterly install-				4
5			ment of estimated federal				5
6			income tax for the year.				6
7							7

At the end of the year, the accountant prepares a work sheet and determines that the taxable income of the corporation for the year was $128,000 ($996,000 in revenues minus $868,000 in costs and expenses). Since the estimated taxable income was $116,000, the additional amount of taxable income is $12,000 ($128,000 − $116,000). The additional tax owed is $4,680, and this amount first appears as an adjusting entry on the work sheet.

Tax on the first $50,000 ($50,000 × .15)	$ 7,500
Tax on the next $25,000 ($25,000 × .25)	6,250
Tax on the next $53,000 ($53,000 × .34)	18,020
Surtax on amount between $100,000 and $128,000 ($28,000 × .05)	1,400
Total tax	$33,170
Less estimated tax paid previously	28,490
Additional tax owed	$ 4,680

The adjusting entry is as follows:

	DATE		DESCRIPTION	POST. REF.	DEBIT	CREDIT	
1	Year 1		**Adjusting Entry**				1
2	Dec.	31	Income Tax Expense		4 6 8 0 00		2
3			Income Tax Payable			4 6 8 0 00	3
4							4

Objective 2

Journalize closing entries for a corporation.

The accountant now records the closing entries. In this example, to save time, "Revenues" represents all temporary-equity accounts having a credit balance and "Expenses" represents all temporary-equity accounts having a debit balance.

	DATE		DESCRIPTION	POST. REF.	DEBIT	CREDIT	
1	Year 1		**Closing Entries**				1
2	Dec.	31	Revenues		996 0 0 0 00		2
3			Income Summary			996 0 0 0 00	3
4							4
5		31	Income Summary		868 0 0 0 00		5
6			Expenses			868 0 0 0 00	6
7							7
8		31	Income Summary		33 1 7 0 00		8
9			Income Tax Expense			33 1 7 0 00	9
10							10
11		31	Income Summary		94 8 3 0 00		11
12			Retained Earnings			94 8 3 0 00	12
13							13

Remember!

Examine these closing entries. There are no individual drawing accounts in a corporation. The new closing entry is to close Income Tax Expense. The Income Summary account is closed into Retained Earnings.

Let's summarize the steps for journalizing the closing entries of a corporation:

1. Close revenue accounts into Income Summary.
2. Close expense accounts into Income Summary.
3. Close Income Tax Expense into Income Summary by the amount of the actual income tax for the year.
4. Close Income Summary into Retained Earnings by the amount of the net income after income tax.

The Retained Earnings account is classified as a stockholders' equity account. It is a permanent or real account, as opposed to a temporary-equity or nominal account. After the accountant has finished posting to the Retained Earnings account, the account represents accumulated earnings if it has a credit balance. If the Retained Earnings account has a debit balance, it represents a deficit. In T account form, the entries for the year are as shown on the following page.

Cash

	+	−		
		Apr. 15		7,122.50
		June 15		7,122.50
		Sept. 15		7,122.50
		Dec. 15		7,122.50

Income Tax Expense

	+		−	
Apr. 15	7,122.50	Dec. 31 Clos.		33,170.00
June 15	7,122.50			
Sept. 15	7,122.50			
Dec. 15	7,122.50			
Dec. 31 Adj.	4,680.00			

Revenues

	−	+	
Dec. 31 Clos.	996,000	Balance	996,000

Expenses

	+	−	
Balance	868,000	Dec. 31 Clos.	868,000

Income Tax Payable

−	+	
	Dec. 31 Adj.	4,680

Income Summary

Dec. 31 (Exp.)	868,000	Dec. 31 (Rev.)		996,000
Dec. 31 (Inc. Tax)	33,170			
Dec. 31 Clos.	94,830			

Retained Earnings

−	+	
	Balance	
	Dec. 31	94,830

Income taxes are considered a necessary expense of conducting business, and the accountant handles the Income Tax Expense account much like any other expense account. However, it is common practice to make a separate entry closing Income Tax Expense into Income Summary rather than including the amount for income tax with the total amounts for all the other expenses. This procedure makes the amount of taxable income more evident from a quick analysis of Income Summary. Notice in the Income Summary T account that the balance of the account prior to transferring the Income Tax Expense balance is $128,000 ($996,000 − $868,000), the taxable income. If the amount of income tax were closed into Income Summary with all the other expenses, the amount of taxable income would not be as obvious.

Income Tax Entries for a Corporation: Second Year

The next year begins with a carryover of the income tax liability for the previous year. Wahl, Inc., estimates that its net income for this year will be $132,000 and that the related income tax will be $34,730. Here are the journal entries for Year 2:

	DATE		DESCRIPTION	POST. REF.	DEBIT	CREDIT	
1	Year 2						1
2	Mar.	15	Income Tax Payable		4 6 8 0 00		2
3			Cash			4 6 8 0 00	3
4			Paid tax liability for last				4
5			year, due two and one-half				5
6			months after the close of				6
7			the fiscal year.				7
8							8

One disadvantage of the corporate form is double taxation. Not only do the owners and employees pay income taxes based on their income, but the corporation itself, in this case Kinetic Concepts, has to pay taxes on its income as though it were a person. And like a person, the percentage of taxes is based on how much income it earns.

	DATE		DESCRIPTION	POST. REF.	DEBIT	CREDIT	
1	Year 2						1
2	Apr.	15	Income Tax Expense		8 6 8 2 50		2
3			Cash			8 6 8 2 50	3
4			Paid first quarterly install-				4
5			ment of estimated federal				5
6			income tax for the year				6
7			(one-fourth of $34,730).				7

	DATE		DESCRIPTION	POST. REF.	DEBIT	CREDIT	
1	Year 2						1
2	June	15	Income Tax Expense		8 6 8 2 50		2
3			Cash			8 6 8 2 50	3
4			Paid second quarterly				4
5			installment of estimated				5
6			federal income tax for the				6
7			year.				7

	DATE		DESCRIPTION	POST. REF.	DEBIT	CREDIT	
1	Year 2						1
2	Sept.	15	Income Tax Expense		8 6 8 2 50		2
3			Cash			8 6 8 2 50	3
4			Paid third quarterly install-				4
5			ment of estimated federal				5
6			income tax for the year.				6
7							7

	DATE		DESCRIPTION	POST. REF.	DEBIT	CREDIT	
1	Year 2						1
2	Dec.	15	Income Tax Expense		8 6 8 2 50		2
3			Cash			8 6 8 2 50	3
4			Paid fourth quarterly install-				4
5			ment of estimated federal				5
6			income tax for the year.				6
7							7

WORK SHEET FOR A CORPORATION

Objective 3

Complete a work sheet for a corporation.

FIGURE 1

The second-year work sheet for Wahl, Inc., is shown in Figure 1. When completing the work sheet, the accountant must give special treatment to the

Step 1: Record and total Trial Balance columns.

Step 2: Record all adjustments except income tax.

Step 3: Extend account balances into Income Statement columns.

Step 4: Determine taxable income and calculate tax.

Step 5: Record adjustment for income tax, and complete Adjustments columns totals.

Step 6: Record actual income tax in the Income Statement columns, and complete the section.

Step 7: Extend account balances into Balance Sheet columns, and total the columns.

	ACCOUNT NAME	TRIAL BALANCE DEBIT	TRIAL BALANCE CREDIT	
1	Cash	12 5 6 0 00		
2	Accounts Receivable	118 1 1 0 00		
3	Allowance for Doubtful Accounts		1 8 2 0 00	
4	Subscriptions Receivable, Common Stock	24 5 0 0 00		
5	Merchandise Inventory	180 5 0 0 00		
6	Prepaid Insurance	1 2 2 0 00		
7	Store Equipment	104 7 2 0 00		
8	Accumulated Depreciation, Store Equipment		27 2 5 0 00	
9	Office Equipment	28 9 2 0 00		
10	Accumulated Depreciation, Office Equipment		8 4 1 0 00	
11	Organization Costs	5 0 0 0 00		
12	Notes Payable		16 0 0 0 00	
13	Accounts Payable		62 7 5 0 00	
14	Common Stock		200 0 0 0 00	
15	Common Stock Subscribed		20 0 0 0 00	
16	Premium on Common Stock		2 4 0 0 00	
17	Retained Earnings		29 6 3 0 00	
18	Sales		1,062 0 0 0 00	
19	Purchases	729 2 3 4 00		
20	Purchases Discount		4 8 0 0 00	
21	Freight In	32 7 6 6 00		
22	Selling Expenses (control)	126 4 5 0 00		
23	General Expenses (control)	32 7 5 0 00		
24				
25				
26	Interest Expense	3 6 0 0 00		
27	Income Tax Expense	34 7 3 0 00		
28		1,435 0 6 0 00	1,435 0 6 0 00	
29	Income Summary			
30	Interest Payable		*Step 1*	
31	Income Tax Payable			
32	Organization Cost Expense			
33				
34	Net Income After Income Tax			
35				
36				
37				
38				
39				
40				

adjusting entry for the additional income tax. Before entering the adjustment for income tax, the accountant must do the following:

1. Enter and total the Trial Balance columns.
2. Enter all adjustments except the adjustment for income tax.

Wahl, Inc.
Work Sheet
For Year Ended December 31, Year 2

	ADJUSTMENTS		INCOME STATEMENT		BALANCE SHEET		
	DEBIT	CREDIT	DEBIT	CREDIT	DEBIT	CREDIT	
					12 5 6 0 00		1
					118 1 1 0 00		2
		(e) 1 6 8 0 00				3 5 0 0 00	3
					24 5 0 0 00		4
	(b) 189 8 8 0 00	(a) 180 5 0 0 00			189 8 8 0 00		5
		(f) 5 2 0 00			7 0 0 0 00		6
					104 7 2 0 00		7
		(c) 4 3 0 0 00				31 5 5 0 00	8
					28 9 2 0 00		9
		(d) 2 7 6 0 00				11 1 7 0 00	10
		(i) 1 0 0 0 00			4 0 0 0 00		11
						16 0 0 0 00	12
						62 7 5 0 00	13
						200 0 0 0 00	14
						20 0 0 0 00	15
						2 4 0 0 00	16
						29 6 3 0 00	17
				1,062 0 0 0 00			18
			729 2 3 4 00				19
				4 8 0 0 00			20
			32 7 6 6 00				21
	(c) 4 3 0 0 00		130 7 5 0 00				22
	(d) 2 7 6 0 00						23
	(e) 1 6 8 0 00						24
	(f) 5 2 0 00		37 7 1 0 00				25
	(g) 1 2 0 00		3 7 2 0 00				26
	(h) 3 5 1 0 00		38 2 4 0 00				27
							28
	(a) 180 5 0 0 00	(b) 189 8 8 0 00	180 5 0 0 00	189 8 8 0 00			29
		(g) 1 2 0 00				1 2 0 00	30
		(h) 3 5 1 0 00				3 5 1 0 00	31
	(i) 1 0 0 0 00		1 0 0 0 00				32
	384 2 7 0 00	384 2 7 0 00	1,153 9 2 0 00	1,256 6 8 0 00	483 3 9 0 00	380 6 3 0 00	33
			102 7 6 0 00			102 7 6 0 00	34
		Step 2	1,256 6 8 0 00	1,256 6 8 0 00	483 3 9 0 00	483 3 9 0 00	35
		Step 5					36
			Step 3		*Step 7*		37
			Step 4				38
			Step 6				39
							40

FYI

The accountant's objective is to determine the taxable income as a basis for calculating the actual amount of income tax owed. Thus, the trial balance amount for Income Tax Expense must not be extended at this time.

3. Extend account balances into the Income Statement columns and tentatively determine the net income before taxes, as shown below. Here are the Income Statement columns taken from the work sheet in Figure 1 on pages 782–783, showing revenue and expenses. From here we can determine the amount of the income before income tax, $141,000 ($1,256,680 − $1,115,680). Note that $1,153,920 (total of Income Statement Debit columns) less $38,240 (Income Tax Expense) gives $1,115,680. These totals do not include Income Tax Expense, whereas the totals in Figure 1 do.

	ACCOUNT NAME	INCOME STATEMENT	
		DEBIT	CREDIT
18	Sales		1,062 0 0 0 00
19	Purchases	729 2 3 4 00	
20	Purchases Discount		4 8 0 0 00
21	Freight In	32 7 6 6 00	
22	Selling Expenses (control)	130 7 5 0 00	
23	General Expenses (control)	37 7 1 0 00	
26	Interest Expense	3 7 2 0 00	
29	Income Summary	180 5 0 0 00	189 8 8 0 00
32	Organization Cost Expense	1 0 0 0 00	
33		1,115 6 8 0 00	1,256 6 8 0 00
34	Income Before Income Tax	141 0 0 0 00	
35		1,256 6 8 0 00	1,256 6 8 0 00
36			

Remember!

At the end of the fiscal period, the adjustment for additional income taxes owed is recorded on the work sheet as a debit to Income Tax Expense and as a credit to Income Tax Payable.

4. Calculate the amount of the income tax. The accountant figures the additional income tax this way. Since both estimated ($132,000) and actual ($141,000) taxable incomes fall in the bracket between $100,000 and $335,000, the 5 percent surtax is involved.

FYI

We present two methods here; take your pick.

Method 1 Compare the calculations for the taxes based on the estimated and actual taxable incomes.

Estimated Taxable Income $132,000

First $50,000 (15 percent)	$50,000 × .15 = $ 7,500
Next $25,000 (25 percent)	$25,000 × .25 = 6,250
Next $57,000 (34 percent)	$57,000 × .34 = 19,380
Surtax on amount over $100,000 (5 percent)	$32,000 × .05 = 1,600
Total estimated tax	$34,730

Actual Taxable Income $141,000

First $50,000 (15 percent)	$50,000 × .15 = $ 7,500
Next $25,000 (25 percent)	$25,000 × .25 = 6,250
Next $66,000 (34 percent)	$66,000 × .34 = 22,440
Surtax on amount over $100,000 (5 percent)	$41,000 × .05 = 2,050
Total actual tax	$38,240

The difference is $3,510 ($38,240 − $34,730).

Method 2 Calculate the additional income tax on the difference between estimated and actual taxable incomes ($10,000).

Regular rate, 34 percent of $9,000 = $9,000 × .34 = $3,060
Surtax rate, 5 percent of $9,000 = $9,000 × .05 = 450

Total additional income tax is $3,510

5. Enter the adjusting entry of $3,510 in the Adjustments columns of the work sheet, and add the column totals.
6. Enter the amount of the entire income tax in the Income Statement Debit column, and complete the Income Statement columns by determining the income after taxes: $102,760.
7. Extend all remaining figures, including Income Tax Payable and Net Income After Income Tax, into the Balance Sheet columns, and complete the Balance Sheet columns.

Financial Statements

Here is an abbreviated income statement for the second year:

Wahl, Inc.
Income Statement
For Year Ended December 31, Year 2

Revenue from Sales:																	
Sales										$1	062	0	0	0	00		
Income Before Income Tax											141	0	0	0	00		
Income Tax Expense											38	2	4	0	00		
Net Income After Income Tax									$		102	7	6	0	00		

The order of presentation of financial statements is similar to that for a sole proprietorship:

1. Income statement
2. Statement of retained earnings (counterpart in most respects to the statement of owner's equity)—showing the net income after income tax
3. Balance sheet—listing the ending balance of Retained Earnings

We look at a complete statement of retained earnings and balance sheet later in this chapter. The balance sheet includes Income Tax Payable as a current liability.

Adjusting and Closing Entries

Remember!
Income Tax Expense is closed separately into Income Summary.

The next step in the accounting cycle is to take the adjusting entries and closing entries directly from the Adjustments columns of the work sheet and record them in the general journal (Figure 2 on page 786).

Income Statement Net Income Versus Taxable Income

In our example, we assume that the accountant for Wahl, Inc., determined the income tax for the year by multiplying the corporation's income before taxes for the year (as shown on the income statement) by the tax rate. The accountant maintained that the corporation's income before taxes was its

	DATE		DESCRIPTION	POST. REF.	DEBIT		CREDIT		
1	Year 2		**Adjusting Entries**						1
2	Dec.	31	Income Summary		180 5 0 0 00				2
3			Merchandise Inventory				180 5 0 0 00		3
4									4
5		31	Merchandise Inventory		189 8 8 0 00				5
6			Income Summary				189 8 8 0 00		6
7									7
8		31	Selling Expenses (control)		4 3 0 0 00				8
9			Accumulated Depreciation, Store Equipment				4 3 0 0 00		9
10									10
11		31	General Expenses (control)		2 7 6 0 00				11
12			Accumulated Depreciation, Office Equipment				2 7 6 0 00		12
13									13
14		31	General Expenses (control)		1 6 8 0 00				14
15			Allowance for Doubtful Accounts				1 6 8 0 00		15
16									16
17		31	General Expenses (control)		5 2 0 00				17
18			Prepaid Insurance				5 2 0 00		18
19									19
20		31	Interest Expense		1 2 0 00				20
21			Interest Payable				1 2 0 00		21
22									22
23		31	Income Tax Expense		3 5 1 0 00				23
24			Income Tax Payable				3 5 1 0 00		24
25									25
26			**Closing Entries**						26
27		31	Sales		1,062 0 0 0 00				27
28			Purchases Discount		4 8 0 0 00				28
29			Income Summary				1,066 8 0 0 00		29
30									30
31		31	Income Summary		935 1 8 0 00				31
32			Purchases				729 2 3 4 00		32
33			Freight In				32 7 6 6 00		33
34			Selling Expenses (control)				130 7 5 0 00		34
35			General Expenses (control)				37 7 1 0 00		35
36			Interest Expense				3 7 2 0 00		36
37			Organization Cost Expense				1 0 0 0 00		37
38									38
39		31	Income Summary		38 2 4 0 00				39
40			Income Tax Expense				38 2 4 0 00		40
41									41
42		31	Income Summary		102 7 6 0 00				42
43			Retained Earnings				102 7 6 0 00		43

FIGURE 2

taxable income. In real life, things aren't quite that simple. The net income shown on the income statement may differ considerably from the income reported for tax purposes. Here are some of the reasons why:

1. The depreciation method used for income statement purposes may differ from the method used for tax purposes. For example, the firm might use

the straight-line method of depreciation for its income statement, but rates stipulated in the Tax Reform Act for tax purposes.

2. Some items listed in the income statement, such as interest on state and municipal bonds, are not taxable.

3. A corporation may list certain types of expenditures as assets and consequently not put them on the income statement. These same expenditures may be listed on the tax return as expenses. For example, a company might not include prepaid advertising on its income statement, whereas it would list it as an expense on its tax return.

FYI

Research and development and the treatment of bad debts are other examples.

REASONS FOR APPROPRIATING RETAINED EARNINGS

Objective 4

Journalize entries for the appropriation of Retained Earnings.

Since a corporation declares dividends out of its Retained Earnings, the *amount* of dividends is necessarily limited by the amount of Retained Earnings. However, rather than using the entire balance of Retained Earnings for cash or stock dividends, the board of directors may wish to earmark part of Retained Earnings for some specific purpose.

Such a restriction constitutes an **appropriation of Retained Earnings**. Let's say that the directors decide to provide for future expansion. The board passes a resolution, which is recorded in the minutes of a meeting, restricting or appropriating a certain amount of Retained Earnings for future expansion. The minutes of the meeting are the source document for the accounting entry. For example, Wahl, Inc., plans to erect its own building. To finance the project, it decides to restrict Retained Earnings for a total amount of $600,000 at the rate of $50,000 per year for twelve years. The accountant makes the entry to appropriate Retained Earnings at the end of each year, after the closing entries.

	DATE		DESCRIPTION	POST. REF.	DEBIT	CREDIT	
1	Year 2						1
2	Feb.	5	Retained Earnings		50 0 0 0 00		2
3			Retained Earnings				3
4			Appropriated for Building			50 0 0 0 00	4
5			To appropriate Retained				5
6			Earnings, as ordered by the				6
7			board of directors in meet-				7
8			ing of February 5, Year 2.				8
9							9

This appropriation of Retained Earnings does *not* represent a separate kitty or cash fund of $50,000. Look at cash dividends for a moment. If we consider the Retained Earnings account as a reservoir from which cash dividends are declared, then this reservoir has dried up by $50,000. **If the corporation does not declare and pay out these dividends, then the firm is preserving its net assets, particularly cash.** Of course, the $50,000 would not necessarily be in the form of cash. Perhaps the company can earn a higher return by putting the money into merchandise inventory or paying off its debts. By the term *net assets* we mean assets minus liabilities.

At the end of the twelve-year period, although the corporation does *not* have an actual $600,000 fund of cash, there is an additional $600,000 accumulated in net assets. The corporation can now formulate plans to convert the $600,000 increase in net assets into cash in order to put a downpayment on the building.

When the objective—buying or erecting the building—has been accomplished, the corporation no longer needs to restrict Retained Earnings. The accountant may then reverse the twelve previous entries as follows:

	DATE		DESCRIPTION	POST. REF.	DEBIT	CREDIT	
1	Year 14						1
2	Mar.	18	Retained Earnings				2
3			Appropriated for Building		600 0 0 0 00		3
4			Retained Earnings			600 0 0 0 00	4
5			To return to Retained				5
6			Earnings the balance in				6
7			the Retained Earnings				7
8			Appropriated for Building				8
9			account, as ordered by the				9
10			board of directors in the				10
11			meeting of March 18,				11
12			Year 14.				12
13							13

Other examples of appropriated Retained Earnings accounts include:

- Retained Earnings Appropriated for Plant Expansion (no specific objective stated)
- Retained Earnings Appropriated for Bonded Indebtedness (an obligation imposed by contract)
- Retained Earnings Appropriated for Self-Insurance (planning for possible casualty losses)
- Retained Earnings Appropriated for Inventory Losses (in the event of a price drop)
- Retained Earnings Appropriated for Contingencies (in the event of a "rainy day")

Each appropriated Retained Earnings is labeled "Retained Earnings Appropriated for _____." Therefore, the account Retained Earnings represents **unappropriated retained earnings**. These accounts appear in a statement of retained earnings (Figure 3 on page 794).

DECLARATION AND PAYMENT OF DIVIDENDS

A dividend is a distribution—of cash or other assets or shares of stock—that a corporation makes to its stockholders. Dividends are allocated to persons who own stock according to the number of shares they own and according to whether the stock is preferred or common. We discuss three types of dividends: cash dividends, stock dividends, and liquidating dividends. Cash dividends and stock dividends reduce Retained Earnings; liquidating dividends reduce Paid-in Capital.

Cash Dividends

A **cash dividend** is the most usual form of dividend. It ordinarily represents a share of the current earnings paid to stockholders as a reward for their investment. The board of directors declares dividends, generally paying up to a certain percentage of the firm's net income after income tax. The cash dividend is expressed as a specific amount per share—for example, $1.12 per share. A stockholder who owns 100 shares is thus entitled to $112.

Before a corporation can pay a cash dividend, three things are needed:

1. **Retained Earnings** The company must have a sufficient balance in the unappropriated Retained Earnings account.
2. **An adequate amount of cash** A corporation may have earned large profits, but not all profits are in cash. For example, the revenue may be in the form of charge accounts, such as Accounts Receivable. But this revenue becomes cash only when the company receives payments from charge customers.
3. **Formal declaration by the board of directors** The payment of dividends, although it may be a matter of policy, is not automatic. The board of directors must pass the declaration in the form of a motion and record it in the minute book—the source document for the accounting entry.

Dividend Dates

Three significant dates are involved in the declaration and payment of a dividend:

1. **Date of declaration** The date on which the board of directors votes to declare dividends. The entry recorded as of this date debits Retained Earnings and credits Dividends Payable.
2. **Date of record** The date as of which the ownership of shares is set. This date determines a person's eligibility for dividends and ordinarily is about three weeks after the date of declaration. No accounting entry is made; a memo entry is made in the minute book.
3. **Date of payment** The date on which payment is made; on this date, the accountant debits the amount to Dividends Payable and credits it to Cash.

For example, on January 20, the board of directors of Boyd Beauty Supply declares a quarterly cash dividend of $.76 per share (5,000 shares × $.76 = $3,800) to stockholders of record as of February 11, payable on February 20. (Dividends Payable is classified as a current liability.) The entries are as follows:

Stockholders sometimes receive dividend checks. The amount they receive depends on the number of shares owned at the time the dividend is declared. Some stockholders choose to reinvest the amount of the dividend and get more shares.

■ ■ ■
Remember!

The incentives for people to invest in corporation stock are the possibility of receiving cash dividends and/or the possibility of selling their stock at a gain.

■ ■ ■
Objective 5

Journalize entries for the declaration and issuance of cash dividends.

DATE		DESCRIPTION	POST. REF.	DEBIT	CREDIT	
1	**Year 2**					1
2	**Jan.**	**20**	Retained Earnings		3 8 0 0 00		2
3			Dividends Payable			3 8 0 0 00	3
4			To record declaration of				4
5			quarterly cash dividend on				5
6			common stock at the rate				6
7			of $.76 per share to				7
8			stockholders of record as				8
9			of February 11, payable				9
10			February 20, as ordered by				10
11			board of directors in				11
12			meeting of January 20.				12

	DATE		DESCRIPTION	POST. REF.	DEBIT	CREDIT	
1	Year 2						1
2	Feb.	20	Dividends Payable		3 8 0 0 00		2
3			Cash			3 8 0 0 00	3
4			Payment of quarterly				4
5			dividend declared on				5
6			January 20 to stockholders				6
7			of record as of February 11.				7
8							8

Remember!

Dividends Payable is a current liability (it must be paid in cash).

The Retained Earnings account before closing entries in Year 2 appears here. During the year, an appropriation was made for building, and regular cash dividends were declared and paid. To make the entries more understandable, we have included explanations in the Item column:

ACCOUNT **Retained Earnings**   ACCOUNT NO. **316**

	DATE		ITEM	POST. REF.	DEBIT	CREDIT	BALANCE DEBIT	BALANCE CREDIT	
1	Year 1								1
2	Dec.	31	Net income			94 8 3 0 00		94 8 3 0 00	2
3	Year 2								3
4	Jan.	20	Cash dividend		3 8 0 0 00			91 0 3 0 00	4
5	Feb.	5	Appropriation		50 0 0 0 00			41 0 3 0 00	5
6	Apr.	20	Cash dividend		3 8 0 0 00			37 2 3 0 00	6
7	July	20	Cash dividend		3 8 0 0 00			33 4 3 0 00	7
8	Oct.	20	Cash dividend		3 8 0 0 00			29 6 3 0 00	8
9									9

The balance of $29,630 would appear in the Trial Balance columns of the work sheet for the year ended December 31, Year 2.

Stock Dividends

Objective 6

Journalize entries for the declaration and issuance of stock dividends.

A **stock dividend** is a distribution, on a pro rata (proportional) basis, of additional shares of a company's stock to the stockholders. In other words, the dividend consists of shares of stock rather than cash. You could describe it as a dividend payable in stock. Generally, stock dividends consist of common stock distributed to holders of common stock. Stock dividends are usually issued by corporations that retain earnings in order to finance future expansion.

Suppose that the board of directors of Wahl, Inc., declared a 20 percent stock dividend on October 11 of Year 3 to stockholders of record as of November 1, payable on November 16. The ledger sheet for the Common Stock account on October 11 looks like this in T account form:

Common Stock

	Balance 200,000
	$40 per share
	(5,000 shares)

Number of shares in the stock dividend:

20 percent of 5,000 shares = <u>1,000</u> shares

The current market value of the shares is $47 per share (par value $40). The entries, in general journal form, are as follows:

	DATE		DESCRIPTION	POST. REF.	DEBIT	CREDIT	
1	Year 3						1
2	Oct.	11	Retained Earnings (1,000				2
3			shares × $47 each)		47 0 0 0 00		3
4			Stock Dividend Distributable				4
5			(1,000 shares × $40 each)			40 0 0 0 00	5
6			Premium on Common Stock			7 0 0 0 00	6
7			To record the declaration of				7
8			a 20 percent stock dividend				8
9			to stockholders of record				9
10			as of November 1; payable				10
11			November 16, as ordered				11
12			by board of directors in				12
13			meeting of October 11.				13

	DATE		DESCRIPTION	POST. REF.	DEBIT	CREDIT	
1	Year 3						1
2	Nov.	16	Stock Dividend Distributable		40 0 0 0 00		2
3			Common Stock			40 0 0 0 00	3
4			Issuance of a stock				4
5			dividend (1,000 shares)				5
6			declared on October 11 to				6
7			stockholders of record as				7
8			of November 1.				8

Some companies issue stock certificates indicating the number of shares bought and par or stated value. Selling shares of stock is one way a corporation raises capital.

Stock Dividend Distributable is a stockholders' equity account representing the total par value of the shares of stock to be issued. If the account is on the books at the time of the preparation of a balance sheet, the accountant lists it in the Paid-in Capital section, just below Common Stock.

A stock dividend—unlike a cash dividend—does *not* result in a reduction of assets. It transfers amounts among the stockholders' equity accounts. The stock dividend increases the Capital Stock accounts and decreases the Retained Earnings account without making any change in the total stockholders' equity.

The stock dividend has no effect on the proportionate share of ownership held by an individual stockholder. For example, Scott James owns 500 shares of the corporation's stock, which represents a one-tenth share in the corporation, since the total number of shares issued was 5,000. The corporation declares a 20 percent stock dividend. As his part of this dividend, James receives 100 shares (20 percent of 500 shares). His total stock now amounts to 600 shares; the corporation's total issued stock is now at 6,000 shares. Consequently, Scott James still has a one-tenth share in the ownership (600 shares ÷ 6,000 shares).

For accounting purposes, corporations make a distinction between a stock dividend of 25 percent or less (small) and a stock dividend of 26 percent or more (large). The preceding example represented a 20 percent stock dividend, in which the accountant debited Retained Earnings for the fair market value of the shares issued. If the stock dividend had been over 25 percent, the accountant would have debited Retained Earnings for the par or stated value of the shares to be issued instead of for the fair market value.

Reasons for Issuing Stock Dividends

Since a stockholder's proportionate share or equity in a company does not change when the company issues a stock dividend, why does a corporation bother with stock dividends? Here are a few reasons:

1. Stock dividends appease stockholders by giving them paper to hold onto. The corporation can conserve its cash and the stockholders feel partially rewarded. They didn't get cash, but at least they got something.
2. Stock dividends tend to reduce the market price of the stock. The supply of the stock increases, with no immediate offsetting change in the demand for it. Stock with a lower price per share is more easily sold to the public.
3. Stock dividends enable stockholders to postpone income tax liability until they sell the shares. Stock dividends are not considered to be income to the recipients. Therefore, the recipients do not have to pay any income tax on stock dividends.

Liquidating Dividends

A corporation pays a **liquidating dividend** when it is (1) going out of existence or (2) permanently reducing the size of its operations. It returns to the stockholders all or a part of their investment. For example, in the situation shown below, a corporation has returned all stockholders' investments:

	DATE		DESCRIPTION	POST. REF.	DEBIT	CREDIT	
1	20–						1
2	Mar.	10	Common Stock		240 0 0 0 00		2
3			Premium on Common Stock		10 0 0 0 00		3
4			Cash			250 0 0 0 00	4
5			To end the business affairs				5
6			of the corporation, the board				6
7			of directors during meeting				7
8			of August 12 authorized a				8
9			100 percent liquidation				9
10			dividend.				10

Remember!

The Stock Dividend Distributable account is used to record the par or stated value of a stock dividend that has been declared, but the stock has not yet been issued to stockholders.

Remember!

A stock dividend does not reduce total stockholders' equity; it is simply an exchange of Retained Earnings for stock.

STOCK SPLIT

When there is a stock split, a corporation splits or subdivides its stock, on the basis of its par or stated value, and issues a proportionate number of additional shares. For example, a corporation with 10,000 shares of $50-par-value stock outstanding may reduce the par value to $25 and increase the number of shares to 20,000 through a 2-for-1 stock split. If you own 200 shares before the split, you will own 400 shares after it. The company may call in all the old shares and issue certificates for new ones on a 2-for-1 basis, or it may issue an additional share for each old share. The accountant records a stock split by making the following entry.

	DATE		DESCRIPTION	POST. REF.	DEBIT	CREDIT	
1	20–						1
2	Oct.	15	Common Stock ($50 par value)		500 0 0 0 00		2
3			Common Stock ($25 par value)			500 0 0 0 00	3
4			The board of directors have				4
5			this day ordered a 2-for-1				5
6			stock split, increasing the				6
7			outstanding shares from				7
8			10,000 to 20,000, and				8
9			reducing the par value from				9
10			$50 to $25.				10
11							11
12							12
13							13

Remember!

A stock split does not change Retained Earnings because total paid-in capital remains the same after a split.

FYI

Par values are listed by way of explanation.

FYI

Some accountants record stock splits with a memorandum entry.

This 2-for-1 stock split reduces the market price per share by approximately half, thereby increasing the stock's salability. Since each share now costs less, more investors are able to afford the stock.

There is no change in Retained Earnings. The accountant changes the headings of the Capital Stock accounts in the ledger to show the new par or stated value per share and revises the stockholders' ledger to show the new distribution of shares.

Minute Book

The minute book is an important source document for any accounting entries involving the declaration of dividends and the appropriation of Retained Earnings. The minute book is just like the minute book of a club: It is a written narrative of all actions taken at official meetings of the board of directors. A corporation's minute book may also contain details relating to purchasing plant and equipment, obtaining bank loans, establishing officers' salaries, and so on.

STATEMENT OF RETAINED EARNINGS AND BALANCE SHEET FOR A CORPORATION

Objective 7

Complete a corporate statement of retained earnings and a balance sheet, including the following types of accounts: Appropriated Retained Earnings, Stock Dividend Distributable, Dividends Payable, and Income Tax Payable.

Remember!

The ending balances of unappropriated Retained Earnings and each appropriation account will appear in the Stockholders' Equity section of the corporation's balance sheet.

We have discussed a number of possible situations that would affect the status of retained earnings within a given period of time. These changes are reported on a separate financial statement called a *statement of retained earnings.* Generally, this statement lists only those items that represent significant changes. For example, the statement of retained earnings of Lester, Inc. (Figure 3), lists specific appropriations for plant expansion and possible price declines. The statement of retained earnings for a corporation may be compared, in some respects, to a statement of owner's equity for a sole proprietorship or partnership, with the ending balances appearing in the stockholders' or owner's equity section of a balance sheet.

To better visualize the relationship of the statement of retained earnings to the balance sheet, Figure 4 presents the balance sheet for Lester, Inc. The accountant may use the account Paid-in Capital from Donation to record a situation in which the corporation receives a material gift. For example, the city of Auburn gave Lester, Inc., an acre of land valued at $11,650 as an

Lester, Inc.
Statement of Retained Earnings
For Year Ended December 31, 20—

Unappropriated Retained Earnings:			
Unappropriated Retained Earnings, Jan. 1, 20—	$ 112 7 0 0 00		
Net Income for the Year	73 0 0 0 00	$ 185 7 0 0 00	
Less: Cash Dividends Declared	$ 20 0 0 0 00		
Stock Dividends Declared	39 5 0 0 00		
Transfer to Appropriation for Plant			
Expansion (see below)	4 0 0 0 00		
Transfer to Appropriation for			
Possible Price Declines (see below)	3 0 0 0 00	66 5 0 0 00	
Unappropriated Retained Earnings, Dec. 31, 20—			$ 119 2 0 0 00
Appropriated Retained Earnings:			
Appropriated for Plant Expansion, Jan. 1, 20—	$ 16 0 0 0 00		
Add Appropriation for the Year (see above)	4 0 0 0 00		
Appropriated for Plant Expansion, Dec. 31, 20—		$ 20 0 0 0 00	
Appropriated for Possible Price Declines,			
Jan. 1, 20—	$ 15 0 0 0 00		
Add Appropriation for the Year (see above)	3 0 0 0 00		
Appropriated for Possible Price Declines,			
Dec. 31, 20—		18 0 0 0 00	
Retained Earnings Appropriated, Dec. 31, 20—			38 0 0 0 00
Total Retained Earnings, Dec. 31, 20—			$ 157 2 0 0 00

FIGURE 3

Assets																
Current Assets:																
Cash							$	6	4	2	0	00				
Accounts Receivable	$	163	3	9	0	00										
Less Allowance for Doubtful Accounts		4	2	9	0	00		159	1	0	0	00				
Subscriptions Receivable, Common Stock								3	5	0	0	00				
Merchandise Inventory								320	2	2	0	00				
Supplies								1	2	5	0	00				
Total Current Assets													$	490	4	9	0	00
Plant and Equipment:																
Land							$	40	0	0	0	00				
Building	$	160	0	0	0	00										
Less Accumulated Depreciation		78	0	0	0	00		82	0	0	0	00				
Equipment	$	80	7	6	0	00										
Less Accumulated Depreciation		26	7	5	0	00		54	0	1	0	00				
Total Plant and Equipment													176	0	1	0	00
Intangible Assets:																
Organization Costs							$	7	2	0	0	00				
Patents								7	0	0	0	00				
Total Intangible Assets													14	2	0	0	00
Total Assets													$	680	7	0	0	00
Liabilities																
Current Liabilities:																
Accounts Payable	$	85	6	9	0	00										
Notes Payable		16	0	0	0	00										
Income Tax Payable		9	2	0	0	00										
Dividends Payable		4	0	0	0	00										
Interest Payable			9	6	0	00										
Total Current Liabilities							$	115	8	5	0	00				
Long-Term Liabilities:																
Mortgage Payable (due July 1, 20—)								54	0	0	0	00				
Total Liabilities													$	169	8	5	0	00
Stockholders' Equity																
Paid-in Capital:																
Preferred 7 Percent Stock, $25 par (5,000 shares authorized and issued)	$	125	0	0	0	00										
Less Discount on Preferred 7 Percent Stock		10	0	0	0	00	$	115	0	0	0	00				
Common Stock, no-par, stated value $10 per share (20,000 shares authorized, 16,000 shares issued)	$	160	0	0	0	00										
Stock Dividend Distributable (3,950 shares)		39	5	0	0	00										
Common Stock Subscribed (500 shares)		5	0	0	0	00										
Paid-in Capital in Excess of Stated Value		22	5	0	0	00		227	0	0	0	00				
Paid-in Capital from Donation								11	6	5	0	00				
Total Paid-in Capital							$	353	6	5	0	00				
Retained Earnings:																
Unappropriated Retained Earnings	$	119	2	0	0	00										
Appropriated:																
For Plant Expansion $20,000.00																
For Possible Price Declines 18,000.00		38	0	0	0	00										
Total Retained Earnings								157	2	0	0	00				
Total Stockholders' Equity														510	8	5	0	00
Total Liabilities and Stockholders' Equity													$	680	7	0	0	00

FIGURE 4

incentive to locate a manufacturing plant there. The accountant for Lester, Inc., debited Land and credited Paid-in Capital from Donation for $11,650 each at that time.

GUIDELINES FOR ACCOUNTING REPORTS

Objective 8

Describe guidelines for accounting reports.

We have called accounting the "language of business." This language is used in accounting reports or statements. Accountants want to make sure that their reports are clear and consistent. To make their reports consistent, accountants follow certain guidelines. Three of these fundamental guidelines are full disclosure, materiality, and conservatism.

Full Disclosure

To disclose means "to uncover or make known." The guideline of **full disclosure** requires that anyone preparing a financial statement include enough information so that the statement is complete. Leaving relevant information out of a report or including half-truths is not acceptable. Information included in the report must not lead the reader to wrong conclusions.

Example: At the end of its report, a business includes a footnote about a lawsuit in which it is involved. The report also states that the case has not been settled and that no financial claim has yet been made against the company. This note prepares the readers to expect a possible financial claim that the company may have to pay. The report would not meet the requirement of full disclosure if it failed to mention the lawsuit and the possible claim.

Materiality

If something is "material," it is important and carries weight. The guideline of **materiality** states that relatively important data are included in financial reports. Important data are material; unimportant data are immaterial. Accounting staffs deal with many different kinds of financial transactions involving small dollar amounts. These transactions may have very little effect on the results shown in financial statements and would not be likely to influence decisions made by users of the financial statements.

Example: In an annual report of a business reporting a profit of $14 million a year, the understatement of profit by $6,000 may be immaterial. The same understatement of profit for a business reporting profit of $22,000 would be material.

Conservatism

To be conservative means to take the safe route. When faced with a decision about which accounting procedures to apply, accountants generally follow the "safer" principle. According to the guideline of **conservatism**, they use the alternative that is the least likely to result in an overstatement of income or asset value.

Example: An accountant is estimating an amount of money to be received in the future. The accountant must choose between $12,000 and $14,000. Conservatism requires the accountant to choose the smaller amount.

CHAPTER REVIEW

Review of Performance Objectives

1. **Journalize entries for corporate income taxes.**

   A corporation has to estimate the federal income tax that it will have to pay for the forthcoming year. The amount of the estimate is to be paid in four quarterly installments. The entry when each installment is paid is a debit to Income Tax Expense and a credit to Cash. At the end of the year, when the exact amount of taxable income is known, an adjusting entry is made for the amount either underpaid or overpaid. If the tax is underpaid, the entry is a debit to Income Tax Expense and a credit to Income Tax Payable. The liability must be paid within two and one-half months. If the tax is overpaid, the entry is a debit to Prepaid Income Tax and a credit to Income Tax Expense.

2. **Journalize closing entries for a corporation.**

   The steps in the closing process for a corporation are as follows:
   (1) Close revenue accounts into Income Summary.
   (2) Close expense accounts into Income Summary.
   (3) Close Income Tax Expense into Income Summary.
   (4) Close Income Summary into Retained Earnings.

3. **Complete a work sheet for a corporation.**

   The Trial Balance and Adjustments columns are handled in the same manner as for all other businesses. After those columns are completed, the accountant first determines the amount of taxable income in the Income Statement columns. Next, the accountant backtracks to record the adjusting entry for income tax. Finally, the accountant extends all remaining current figures into the appropriate columns and completes the work sheet.

4. **Journalize entries for the appropriation of Retained Earnings.**

   An appropriation of Retained Earnings is a restriction of a portion of the Retained Earnings account, making the amount unavailable for dividends. The entry in each case is a debit to Retained Earnings and a credit to Retained Earnings Appropriated for _____ (some specific purpose). The Retained Earnings account by itself is unappropriated.

5. **Journalize entries for the declaration and issuance of cash dividends.**

   The entry for the declaration of a cash dividend is a debit to Retained Earnings and a credit to Dividends Payable. The entry for the payment of a cash dividend is a debit to Dividends Payable and a credit to Cash.

6. **Journalize entries for the declaration and issuance of stock dividends.**

   The entry for the declaration of a small stock dividend is a debit to Retained Earnings for the amount of the number of shares multiplied by the market value per share, a credit to Stock Dividend Distributable for the amount of the number of shares multiplied by the par or stated value per share, and a credit to Premium on Common Stock (or Paid-in Capital in Excess of Stated Value). The entry for the issuance of stock is a debit to Stock Dividend Distributable and a credit to Common Stock.

7. **Complete a corporate statement of retained earnings and a balance sheet, including the following types of accounts: Appropriated Retained Earnings, Stock Dividends Distributable, Dividends Payable, and Income Tax Payable.**

   A statement of retained earnings consists of two sections: Unappropriated Retained Earnings and Appropriated Retained Earnings. Unappropriated Retained

Earnings reflects the increases and decreases in the Retained Earnings account, consisting of net income, dividends, and transfers to Appropriated Retained Earnings accounts. The Appropriated Retained Earnings section consists of a listing of each Appropriated Retained Earnings account, including additions or deductions affecting each account.

On a corporate balance sheet, Stock Dividends Distributable is listed under Paid-in Capital. Dividends Payable and Income Tax Payable are listed under Current Liabilities.

8. Describe guidelines for accounting reports.

Three of the guidelines used to make accounting reports consistent are:

Full disclosure—to include enough information to make the statement complete, being sure not to leave out relevant information.

Materiality—to include important data or information.

Conservatism—to use accounting procedures that will result in a safer outcome by avoiding gross overstatements of revenues and assets or understatements of expenses and liabilities.

Glossary

Appropriation of Retained Earnings Designation of a portion of Retained Earnings for a specific purpose; the amount appropriated may not be used for cash or stock dividends. (787)

Cash dividend Distribution of a corporation's earnings to stockholders in the form of cash. (789)

Conservatism An accounting rule that means that, when accountants are faced with major uncertainties as to which alternative accounting procedure to apply, they should choose the procedure that is least likely to overstate a firm's revenues and assets or overstate its expenses and liabilities. (796)

Date of declaration The date on which the board of directors votes to declare dividends. (789)

Date of payment The date on which dividends are paid. (789)

Date of record The date as of which the ownership of shares is set determining a person's eligibility for dividends. (789)

Full disclosure An accounting rule requiring that financial statements and their accompanying footnotes contain all information that would influence a user's understanding of a firm's financial position. (796)

Liquidating dividend Distribution of assets to stockholders when a corporation is going out of existence or is permanently reducing the size of its operations. (792)

Materiality An accounting rule that refers to the inclusion in financial statements of important items that significantly affect a firm's financial position. (796)

Minute book A written narrative of all actions taken at official meetings of the board of directors; source document for dividend accounting entries. (793)

Stock dividend Distribution of a corporation's retained earnings to stockholders in the form of shares of the corporation's own stock. (790)

Stock split A deliberate reduction of the par value or stated value of a corporation's stock and the issuing of a proportionate number of additional shares. (793)

Unappropriated retained earnings The portion of Retained Earnings available for distribution as dividends to the stockholders. (788)

QUESTIONS, EXERCISES, AND PROBLEMS

Discussion Questions

1. What three things are needed before a corporation can pay a cash dividend?

2. What are the significant dates involved in the declaration and payment of a dividend?

3. Describe the difference between a stock dividend and a stock split.

4. What do the guidelines full disclosure, materiality, and conservatism have in common?

5. What are the journal entries that zero the following accounts: Income Tax Payable, Income Tax Expense?

6. Why aren't stock dividends considered taxable income for the receivers of the dividends at the time they are received?

7. List the possible titles of five accounts within the Paid-in Capital section of a balance sheet. Use 9 percent for preferred stocks.

8. Explain why an appropriation of retained earnings is not the same thing as setting aside cash. How does a corporation dispose of an appropriated retained earnings account, such as Retained Earnings Appropriated for Building?

Exercises

P.O. 1

Compute corporate income taxes.

Exercise 22-1 Assuming 15 percent tax on the first $50,000, 25 percent on the next $25,000 ($50,001–$75,000), 34 percent on the amount over $75,000, and a 5 percent surtax on amounts between $100,000 and $335,000, compute Ada Corporation's first-year total tax on a taxable income of $225,000.

P.O. 1,2

Describe entries from T accounts.

Exercise 22-2 Describe the entries recorded by letters in the T accounts.

Income Tax Expense		Cash		Revenues		Retained Earnings	
(a)	(e)	(a)			(c)		(f)
(b)							

Income Summary		Income Tax Payable		Expenses	
(d)	(c)		(b)	(d)	
(e)					
(f)					

P.O. 4

Journalize entries to appropriate retained earnings, purchase a warehouse, and release the appropriation.

Exercise 22-3 On January 3, the board of directors of Virgil Company, Inc., voted to appropriate $90,000 of the corporation's unappropriated retained earnings to Retained Earnings Appropriated for Plant Expansion. This is the fourth such appropriation; it gives a balance of $298,000 in Retained Earnings Appropriated for Plant Expansion. On September 1, the corporation bought a warehouse for $320,000 (building, $190,000; land, $130,000), paying $135,000 down and financing the remainder on a mortgage note. Write the entries to record the following.

a. The appropriation of retained earnings on January 3.
b. The purchase of the building and land on September 1.
c. The release of the $298,000 in Retained Earnings Appropriated for Plant Expansion on September 2.

P.O. 5

Journalize entries to declare and pay a cash dividend.

Exercise 22-4 The dates connected with a cash dividend of $115,000 on a corporation's common stock are April 12, April 29, and May 8. Present in general journal form the entries pertaining to the declaration and payment of the dividend.

P.O. 6

Journalize entries to record the declaration and issuance of a stock dividend.

Exercise 22-5 On December 31, the stockholders' equity of Marie's Auto Body Repair, Inc., is as follows:

Paid-in Capital:			
Common Stock, no-par, stated value $20 per share			
(30,000 shares authorized, 18,000 shares issued)	$ 360 0 0 0 00		
Paid-in Capital in Excess of Stated Value	54 0 0 0 00		
Total Paid-in Capital		$ 414 0 0 0 00	
Retained Earnings:			
Unappropriated	$ 205 0 2 0 00		
Appropriated for Contingencies	91 8 0 0 00		
Total Retained Earnings		296 8 2 0 00	
Total Stockholders' Equity			710 8 2 0 00

On March 6 of the following year, when the stock is selling at $38 per share, the board of directors votes a 20 percent stock dividend, distributable on May 28 to stockholders of record on March 22. Give the entries to record the declaration and distribution of the dividend.

P.O. 7

Calculate paid-in capital and total stockholders' equity.

Exercise 22-6 A corporation's balance sheet includes the following:

Preferred 9 Percent Stock	$137,700
Preferred 9 Percent Stock Subscribed	45,900
Subscriptions Receivable, Preferred 9 Percent Stock	22,700
Discount on Preferred 9 Percent Stock	1,900
Common Stock	229,500
Paid-in Capital in Excess of Stated Value	61,200
Retained Earnings (credit balance)	84,250

a. How much of the contributed capital is the result of the preferred 9 percent stock?
b. How much of the paid-in capital is the result of the common stock?
c. What is the total stockholders' equity?

P.O. 4,6,7

Indicate the effect of transactions on total Retained Earnings.

Exercise 22-7 Indicate the effect, if any, of each of the following transactions on total Retained Earnings of Thompson Company, Inc.:

a. Paid accounts payable.
b. Wrote off Accounts Receivable against Allowance for Doubtful Accounts.

c. Bought equipment on account, $58,000.

d. The board of directors declared a 20 percent stock dividend, to be issued thirty days from the present date.

e. The board of directors voted to appropriate $98,000 for future expansion.

f. Issued 2,500 shares of $25-par-value common stock, receiving $34 per share.

g. Issued the stock dividend declared in transaction **d.**

P.O. 7

Prepare the Stockholders' Equity section of a balance sheet.

Exercise 22-8 Prepare the Stockholders' Equity section of the balance sheet from the following account balances:

Retained Earnings	$143,000
Subscriptions Receivable, Preferred 10 Percent Stock	20,000
Common Stock, $40 par (30,000 shares authorized)	400,000
Preferred 10 Percent Stock, $50 par (2,000 shares authorized)	25,000
Premium on Common Stock	40,000
Preferred 10 Percent Stock Subscribed	20,000

WHAT IF . . .

Suppose that a stockholder who received notice of a 2-for-1 stock split told you that he had just doubled his money. Is the stockholder correct? If not, what has actually happened?

CRITICAL THINKING

You have just received the following note dated November 30 from one of your corporation's stockholders:

"Help! Please explain why I haven't received my dividend check. I own 100 shares that I bought at $30 and they are now selling for $35. I read in the annual report that the board of directors declared a 10 percent stock dividend, but I haven't received a dime yet. What is going on? Where is my dividend check? I was a stockholder of record on the declaration dates of the dividends." Assume that he was a stockholder of record for both dividends.

The following selected journal entries may help you answer.

GENERAL JOURNAL   PAGE __78__

	DATE	DESCRIPTION	POST. REF.	DEBIT	CREDIT	
1	20–					1
2	Sept. 15	Retained Earnings		98 0 0 0 00		2
3		Stock Dividend Distributable			65 0 0 0 00	3
4		Premium on Common Stock			33 0 0 0 00	4
5		To record the declaration of				5
6		a 10 percent stock dividend				6
7		to stockholders as of				7
8		September 30, payable				8
9		October 9.				9

(continued on page 802)

16	Oct.	9	Stock Dividend Distributable			65	0	0	0	00										16
17			Common Stock										65	0	0	0	00			17
18			Issuance of stock dividend																	18
19			declared on September 15 to																	19
20			stockholders as of																	20
21			September 30.																	21
22																				22
23	Nov.	17	Retained Earnings			74	8	0	0	00										23
24			Dividends Payable										74	8	0	0	00			24
25			Declared dividend of $6.80																	25
26			per share to stockholders of																	26
27			record on November 30,																	27
28			payable December 9.																	28
29																				29
30	Dec.	9	Dividends Payable			74	8	0	0	00										30
31			Cash										74	8	0	0	00			31
32			Paid cash dividend declared																	32
33			on November 17.																	33

A MATTER OF ETHICS

Your friend has been telling you that she knows someone in a publicly traded corporation who gives her information that lets her know when to buy and sell stock in that corporation. Consequently, your friend has made quite a bit of money. She has offered to share these inside tips with you for a small percentage of any gain you may make as a result. Her offer is very tempting to you. Are these friendly tips ethical?

WEB WORK

Using an Internet web browser, type *corporate taxes* or *corporate dividends* in the search box and search for information about taxes and dividends. Discuss your findings in a small group. Write a one-page summary of your findings.

PROBLEM SET A

For additional help, see the demonstration problem at the beginning of each chapter in your Working Papers.

P.O. 1,4,5,6

Problem 22-1A Some of the transactions of the Baldwin Video Corporation during this fiscal year are as follows:

Mar. 15 Paid balance due on the previous year's federal income tax, $44,940.

Apr. 15 Paid $62,100 for the first quarterly installment of estimated federal income tax for the current year.

June 15 Paid $62,100 for the second quarterly installment of estimated federal income tax for the current year.

Aug. 16 Declared a cash dividend of $68,400 ($6.84 per share on 10,000 shares, $75 par value) to stockholders of record as of August 31, payable September 10.

Sept. 10 Paid cash dividend.

15 Declared a 10 percent stock dividend on common stock outstanding to stockholders of record as of September 30, payable

on October 9. Current market value of stock: $108 per share (10,000 shares outstanding before stock dividend).

	15	Paid $62,100 for the third quarterly installment of estimated federal income tax for this year.
Oct.	9	Issued stock for stock dividend.
Nov.	17	Declared a cash dividend of $79,200 ($7.20 per share on 11,000 shares) to stockholders of record as of November 30, payable on December 9.
Dec.	9	Paid cash dividend.
	15	Paid $62,100 for the fourth quarterly installment of estimated federal income tax for this year.
	31	The board of directors authorized the appropriation of retained earnings for plant expansion, $29,400.
	31	Recorded $43,920 additional federal income tax allocable to taxable income for the year.

Check Figure

Adjusting entry, $43,920

Instructions

Record the above transactions in general journal form.

P.O. 3,7

Problem 22-2A The trial balance for Bell Luggage, Inc., dated May 31 of this year, is shown here.

Bell Luggage, Inc.
Trial Balance
May 31, 20—

ACCOUNT NAME	DEBIT	CREDIT
Cash	11 748 00	
Accounts Receivable	346 230 00	
Allowance for Doubtful Accounts		5 598 00
Subscriptions Receivable, Common Stock	78 000 00	
Merchandise Inventory	569 010 00	
Store Supplies	1 890 00	
Store Equipment	218 040 00	
Accumulated Depreciation, Store Equipment		34 860 00
Organization Costs	16 260 00	
Accounts Payable		153 120 00
Notes Payable		30 000 00
Preferred 8 Percent Stock ($100 par value)		120 000 00
Premium on Preferred 8 Percent Stock		6 000 00
Common Stock ($20 par value)		330 000 00
Common Stock Subscribed		90 000 00
Premium on Common Stock		42 000 00
Retained Earnings		154 800 00
Sales		3 048 900 00
Purchases	2 104 183 00	
Purchases Discount		15 960 00
Freight In	83 117 00	
Selling Expenses (control)	402 912 00	
General Expenses (control)	114 798 00	
Interest Expense	4 620 00	
Income Tax Expense	80 430 00	
	4 031 238 00	4 031 238 00

To reduce the number of accounts in the trial balance, Selling Expenses (control) is used in place of all selling expenses. Likewise, General Expenses (control) is used in place of all general expenses. The corporation's charter states that authorized preferred 8 percent stock amounts to 1,400 shares and authorized common stock amounts to 21,000 shares.

Data for the adjustments are as follows:

a.–b. Merchandise Inventory, May 31 (ending inventory), $582,660.
c. Additional depreciation of store equipment for the year amounts to $12,390; record depreciation expense under Selling Expenses (control).
d. Inventory of store supplies at May 31, $1,302. Use Selling Expenses (control).
e. Analysis of Accounts Receivable indicates that $10,470 is uncollectible; record estimated bad debt losses under General Expenses (control).
f. Accrued interest on Notes Payable, $420.
g. Additional income tax due for the current year, $28,260.
h. Amortization of Organization Costs, 5-year schedule at $3,252 per year.
i. No dividends were declared during the year.

Check Figure

Total Liabilities and Stockholders' Equity, $1,193,268

Instructions

1. Record the trial balance on the work sheet (leave two lines for Selling Expenses control) and complete the work sheet for the year.
2. Prepare an income statement.
3. Prepare a statement of retained earnings.
4. Prepare a classified balance sheet.

P.O. 2,4,5,6,7

Problem 22-3A The Stockholders' Equity section of the balance sheet of Peters Western Wear, Inc., as of January 1 is as follows:

Stockholders' Equity				
Paid-in Capital:				
Preferred 9 Percent Stock, $100 par (8,000 shares				
authorized, 6,750 shares issued)	$ 675 0 0 0 00			
Premium on Preferred 9 Percent Stock	27 0 0 0 00	$ 702 0 0 0 00		
Common Stock, no-par, stated value $20 per share				
(90,000 shares authorized, 54,000 shares issued)	$1 080 0 0 0 00			
Paid-in Capital in Excess of Stated Value	324 0 0 0 00	1 404 0 0 0 00		
Total Paid-in Capital		$2 106 0 0 0 00		
Retained Earnings:				
Unappropriated Retained Earnings	$ 630 0 0 0 00			
Appropriated for Expansion	126 0 0 0 00			
Total Retained Earnings		756 0 0 0 00		
Total Stockholders' Equity			2 862 0 0 0 00	

Some of the transactions that took place during the year are:

May   10   Declared the regular semiannual $4.50 per share dividend on the preferred stock and a $1.30 per share dividend on the common stock to stockholders of record as of June 1, payable on June 10.

June   2   Received subscriptions to 9,000 shares of common stock at $27 per share, collecting 70 percent of the subscription price.

10   Paid cash dividends declared on May 10.

26   Subscribers to 9,000 shares of common stock paid the remaining 30 percent of the subscription price; Peters Western Wear then issued the 9,000 shares.

Nov.   10   Declared the regular semiannual $4.50 per share dividend on the preferred stock and a $1.50 per share dividend on the common stock to stockholders of record as of December 1, payable on December 10.

Dec.   10   Paid cash dividends declared on November 10.

27   Declared a 5 percent stock dividend on common stock outstanding to stockholders of record as of January 14, payable on January 30. Current market value of the stock is $28 per share.

31   Increased the appropriation for expansion by $50,000.

31   After the accountant has closed all revenue, expense, and Income Tax Expense accounts, the Income Summary account has a credit balance of $333,000. Closed the Income Summary account.

Check Figure

Total Stockholders' Equity, $3,212,550

Instructions

1. Enter in the ledger accounts the balances appearing in the Stockholders' Equity section of the balance sheet as of January 1. In the Item column of the stock accounts, record the word *Balance* on the first line and the number of shares on the second line.
2. Journalize entries in general journal form to record the transactions that occurred during the year and post to the stockholders' equity accounts.
3. Prepare the Stockholders' Equity section of the balance sheet as of December 31.

P.O. 7

Problem 22-4A Here are the account balances taken from the general ledger and statement of retained earnings for Bristolware, Inc.:

a. Preferred 9 percent stock: 3,000 shares authorized, 2,280 shares issued
b. Common stock: 40,000 shares authorized, 36,000 shares issued

Accounts Payable	$ 338,280
Accounts Receivable	487,290
Accumulated Depreciation, Building	187,200
Accumulated Depreciation, Equipment	102,600
Allowance for Doubtful Accounts	16,920
Building	360,000
Cash	26,130
Common Stock, $15 stated value	540,000
Dividends Payable	24,600
Equipment	218,700
Income Tax Payable	61,800
Land	75,000
Merchandise Inventory	1,027,530
Mortgage Payable (due June 30, 2010)	145,800
Notes Receivable	37,800
Organization Costs	24,000
Paid-in Capital from Donation	21,600
Paid-in Capital in Excess of Stated Value	108,000
Preferred 9 Percent Stock, $100 par value	228,000
Preferred 9 Percent Stock Subscribed	72,000

Premium on Preferred 9 Percent Stock	6,000
Prepaid Insurance	2,880
Retained Earnings	320,100
Retained Earnings Appropriated for Inventory Losses	25,200
Retained Earnings Appropriated for Plant Expansion	48,000
Stock Dividend Distributable (3,330 shares)	49,950
Subscriptions Receivable, Preferred 9 Percent Stock	36,720

Check Figure

Total Assets, $1,989,330

Instructions

Prepare a classified balance sheet dated December 31.

PROBLEM SET B

For additional help, see the demonstration problem at the beginning of each chapter in your Working Papers.

P.O. 1,4,5,6

Problem 22-1B Some of the transactions of Alamo Air Service, Inc., during this year are as follows:

Mar.   15   Paid the balance due on the previous year's federal income tax, $22,500.

Apr.   15   Paid $38,520 for the first quarterly installment of estimated federal income tax for this year.

June   15   Paid $38,520 for the second quarterly installment of estimated federal income tax for this year.

Aug.   12   Declared a cash dividend of $50,400 ($5.04 per share on 10,000 shares, $60 par value) to stockholders of record as of August 22, payable on September 7.

Sept.   7   Paid the cash dividend.

15   Paid $38,520 for the third quarterly installment of estimated federal income tax for this year.

18   Declared 10 percent stock dividend on the common stock outstanding to stockholders of record as of September 28, payable on October 6. Current market value of stock: $74 per share.

Oct.   6   Issued stock for stock dividend.

Nov.   14   Declared a cash dividend of $55,440 ($5.04 per share on 11,000 shares) to stockholders of record as of November 30, payable on December 8.

Dec.   8   Paid the cash dividend.

15   Paid $38,520 for the fourth quarterly installment of estimated federal income tax for this year.

31   The board of directors authorized the appropriation of retained earnings for contingencies, $14,400.

31   Recorded $43,920 additional federal income tax allocable to taxable income for the year.

Check Figure

Adjusting entry, $43,920

Instructions

Record these transactions in general journal form.

P.O. 3,7

Problem 22-2B The trial balance of Brandon Beauty Supply, Inc., dated December 31 of this year, is shown here.

Brandon Beauty Supply, Inc.
Trial Balance
December 31, 20—

ACCOUNT NAME	DEBIT	CREDIT
Cash	14 0 4 0 00	
Notes Receivable	28 9 2 0 00	
Accounts Receivable	315 0 4 8 00	
Allowance for Doubtful Accounts		5 3 8 2 00
Subscriptions Receivable, Preferred 9 Percent Stock	25 8 0 0 00	
Merchandise Inventory	560 2 2 0 00	
Prepaid Insurance	2 5 9 2 00	
Equipment	170 2 2 0 00	
Accumulated Depreciation, Equipment		32 1 9 0 00
Organization Costs	19 2 0 0 00	
Accounts Payable		146 2 9 8 00
Preferred 9 Percent Stock ($100 par value)		150 0 0 0 00
Preferred 9 Percent Stock Subscribed		30 0 0 0 00
Premium on Preferred 9 Percent Stock		6 6 0 0 00
Common Stock ($20 stated value)		300 0 0 0 00
Paid-in Capital in Excess of Stated Value		36 0 0 0 00
Retained Earnings		156 0 0 0 00
Sales		3 535 2 0 0 00
Purchases	2 578 5 8 0 00	
Purchases Discount		15 6 0 0 00
Freight In	107 4 4 0 00	
Selling Expenses (control)	397 8 9 0 00	
General Expenses (control)	112 2 0 0 00	
Income Tax Expense	84 5 4 0 00	
Interest Income		3 4 2 0 00
	4 416 6 9 0 00	4 416 6 9 0 00

To reduce the number of accounts in the trial balance, Selling Expenses (control) is used in place of all selling expenses. Likewise, General Expenses (control) is used in place of all general expenses. The corporation's charter states that authorized preferred 9 percent stock amounts to 2,000 shares and authorized common stock amounts to 20,000 shares.

Data for the adjustments are as follows:

a.–b. Merchandise Inventory, December 31 (ending inventory), $576,570.

c. Additional depreciation of equipment for the year amounts to $12,870; record depreciation under Selling Expenses (control).

d. Insurance expired during the year, $1,542; record insurance expired under General Expenses (control).

e. Analysis of Accounts Receivable indicates that $10,560 is uncollectible; record estimated bad debt losses under General Expenses (control).

f. Accrued interest on Notes Receivable, $360.

g. Additional income tax due for this year, $25,680.

h. Amortization of Organizational Costs, 5-year schedule at $3,840 per year.

i. No dividends were declared during the year.

Check Figure

Total Liabilities and Stockholders' Equity, $1,091,748

Instructions

1. Record the trial balance on the work sheet (leave two lines for General Expenses control) and complete the work sheet for the year.
2. Prepare an income statement.
3. Prepare a statement of retained earnings.
4. Prepare a classified balance sheet.

P.O. 2,4,5,6,7

Problem 22-3B The Stockholders' Equity section of the balance sheet of Lido Auto Wholesale, Inc., as of January 1 is as follows:

Stockholders' Equity			
Paid-in Capital:			
Preferred 9 Percent Stock, $100 par (4,000 shares			
authorized, 2,250 shares issued)	$ 225 0 0 0 00		
Premium on Preferred 9 Percent Stock	9 0 0 0 00	$ 234 0 0 0 00	
Common Stock, no-par, stated value $20 per share			
(23,000 shares authorized, 18,000 shares issued)	$ 360 0 0 0 00		
Paid-in Capital in Excess of Stated Value	180 0 0 0 00	540 0 0 0 00	
Total Paid-in Capital		$ 774 0 0 0 00	
Retained Earnings:			
Unappropriated Retained Earnings	$ 191 2 5 0 00		
Appropriated for Expansion	40 5 0 0 00		
Total Retained Earnings		231 7 5 0 00	
Total Stockholders' Equity			1 005 7 5 0 00

Some of the transactions that took place during the year are:

Feb. 24 Declared the regular semiannual $4.50 per share dividend on the preferred stock and a $1.00 per share dividend on the common stock to stockholders of record as of March 15, payable on March 23.

Mar. 23 Paid cash dividends declared on February 24.

27 Received subscriptions to 1,000 shares of common stock at $31 per share, collecting 60 percent of the subscription price.

Apr. 19 Subscribers to 1,000 shares of common stock paid the remaining 40 percent of the subscription price; Lido Auto Wholesale, Inc., then issued the 1,000 shares.

Aug. 24 Declared the regular semiannual $4.50 per share dividend on the preferred stock and $1.20 per share dividend on the common stock to stockholders of record as of September 15, payable on September 23.

Sept. 23 Paid cash dividends declared on August 24.

Dec. 20 Declared a 10 percent stock dividend on common stock outstanding to stockholders of record as of January 15, payable on January 23. Fair market value of the stock is $33 per share.

Dec. 31 Increased the appropriation for expansion by $20,000.

31 After the accountant has closed all revenue, expense, and Income Tax Expense accounts, the Income Summary account has a credit balance of $162,000. Closed the Income Summary account.

Check Figure

Total Stockholders' Equity,
$1,137,700

Instructions

1. Enter in the ledger accounts the balances appearing in the Stockholders' Equity section of the balance sheet as of January 1. In the Item column of the stock accounts, record the word *Balance* on the first line and the number of shares on the second line.
2. Journalize entries in general journal form to record the transactions that occurred during the year and post to the stockholders' equity accounts.
3. Prepare the Stockholders' Equity section of the balance sheet as of December 31.

P.O. 7

Problem 22-4B The account balances taken from the general ledger and statement of retained earnings for Raymor Sales, Inc., are as follows:

a. Preferred 9 percent stock: 3,000 shares authorized, 2,400 shares issued
b. Common stock: 30,000 shares authorized, 20,400 shares issued

Accounts Payable	$294,780
Accounts Receivable	379,080
Accumulated Depreciation, Building	68,400
Accumulated Depreciation, Equipment	74,610
Allowance for Doubtful Accounts	13,860
Building	270,000
Cash	17,460
Common Stock, $15 stated value	306,000
Dividends Payable	14,400
Equipment	139,800
Income Tax Payable	43,800
Land	36,000
Merchandise Inventory	713,610
Mortgage Payable (due April 4, 2010)	126,000
Notes Receivable	36,000
Organization Costs	18,000
Paid-in Capital from Donation	36,000
Paid-in Capital in Excess of Stated Value	66,780
Preferred 9 Percent Stock, $100 par value	240,000
Preferred 9 Percent Stock Subscribed	60,000
Premium on Preferred 9 Percent Stock	3,000
Prepaid Insurance	2,580
Retained Earnings	230,700
Retained Earnings Appropriated for Inventory Losses	12,000
Retained Earnings Appropriated for Plant Expansion	24,600
Stock Dividend Distributable (1,860 shares)	27,900
Subscriptions Receivable, Preferred 9 Percent Stock	30,300

Check Figure

Total Assets, $1,485,960

Instructions

Prepare a classified balance sheet dated December 31.

23 Corporate Bonds

Performance Objectives

After you have completed this chapter, you will be able to do the following:

1. Journalize transactions involving the issuance of bonds at a premium or discount.

2. Journalize adjusting entries for amortization of bond premiums and discounts and accrued interest payable.

3. Journalize entries pertaining to the establishment of a bond sinking fund, the receipt of income from sinking fund investments, and the eventual payment of the principal of the bonds.

4. Journalize transactions involving the redemption of bonds.

In our discussions of corporations, we have assumed that the company got the money it needed for building and expansion by selling stock and retaining earnings. There is another possibility: A corporation can borrow money for a long period (five to forty years) by issuing bonds. A **bond** is a long-term obligation that provides capital. For all practical purposes, a bond is a long-term promissory note. A **bond issue** refers to the total number of bonds that a corporation issues at the same time. Bonds are issued in denominations of $1,000 or $5,000 each, with $1,000 being more common. You can get a better picture of bonds by comparing them with capital stock.

Bonds	Capital Stock
Bondholders are creditors; they receive interest and are eventually repaid the principal.	Stockholders are owners; they receive dividends.
Bonds Payable is classified as a long-term liability account.	Capital stock is subdivided into Common Stock and Preferred Stock accounts, which are stockholders' equity accounts.
Interest paid on bonds is an expense that must be paid year after year. Otherwise, bondholders may initiate bankruptcy proceedings against the debtor corporation.	Dividends are not expenses, they are distributions of net income.
Interest expense is deducted to arrive at net income.	Dividends are not deducted to arrive at net income. They are deducted from retained earnings.

CLASSIFICATION OF BONDS

Just as car manufacturers offer different models with various combinations of accessories, corporations have created a wide variety of bonds, each with a slightly different combination of characteristics, to appeal to different investors.

Bonds Classified as to Time of Payment

- **Term bonds** All term bonds of a particular issue have the same term, or time period to maturity. Thus, the entire issue of bonds comes due at the same time. For example, $1,000,000 worth of 10-year bonds issued January 1, 1997, all mature January 1, 2007.
- **Serial bonds** Serial bonds of a particular issue have a series of maturity dates. For example, $1,000,000 worth of bonds issued March 1, 1998, may mature as follows:

$100,000 on March 1, 2003	$100,000 on March 1, 2008
$100,000 on March 1, 2004	$100,000 on March 1, 2009
$100,000 on March 1, 2005	$100,000 on March 1, 2010
$100,000 on March 1, 2006	$100,000 on March 1, 2011
$100,000 on March 1, 2007	$100,000 on March 1, 2012

Bonds Classified as to Ownership

- **Registered bonds** When bonds are registered, the names of the owners are recorded with the issuing corporation. Title to such bonds is transferred when the bonds are sold, just as title to stock is transferred. The corporation pays interest by mailing checks to the registered owners.
- **Coupon bonds** These bonds derive their name from the interest coupons attached to each bond. The payee submits each coupon to a bank, and the interest is payable to the bearer of the coupon, usually every six months.

Today, corporations rarely issue coupon bonds because of Internal Revenue Service regulations. The IRS requires the corporation to submit a form listing each payee's name, address, tax identification number, and the amount of the interest paid. However, state and local governments do issue coupon bonds because the interest on their bonds is exempt from federal tax.

Bonds Classified as to Security

- **Secured bonds** When bonds are secured, they are covered or collateralized by mortgages on real estate or by titles to personal property. In case the corporation defaults in its payment of principal or interest, the bondholders, acting through a trustee, may take over the pledged assets.
- **Unsecured bonds** Unsecured bonds, also called *debenture bonds,* are backed only by the corporation's credit standing, or good name. Such bonds usually succeed only when issued by financially strong firms.

A bond can have characteristics of all three classifications. For example, if a corporation issues twenty-year mortgage bonds with coupons providing for the payment of interest, the bonds are term bonds, coupon bonds, and secured bonds.

WHY A CORPORATION ISSUES BONDS

A corporation that needs money on a long-term basis has the choice of raising the necessary funds by issuing (1) common stock, (2) preferred stock, or (3) bonds. Each choice has advantages and disadvantages. Since the holders of common stock control the corporation through their voting power, they choose the means of financing. Corporate boards of directors calculate the pros and cons of bonds as follows.

Advantages of Issuing Bonds

1. The bond-issuing corporation has the prospect of earning a greater return on the money it raises than it has to pay out in interest. This is known as **leverage**. For example, if a firm can borrow money at an interest rate of 8 percent and use this cash in the business to earn a net income of 15 percent after taxes, then the additional earnings of 7 percent (15 percent − 8 percent) are available to pay dividends to the holders of common stock. Thus, debt is used as a *lever* to raise the owners' rate of return.
2. Interest payments are tax-deductible expenses.
3. Bondholders cannot vote; therefore, the existing common stockholders retain control of the company's affairs.

Disadvantages of Issuing Bonds

1. Bondholders are creditors of the corporation, so interest payments must be made to bondholders each year. In contrast, a corporation pays dividends to stockholders only when it has enough money to do so and when the board of directors declares a dividend.
2. The corporation must eventually pay back the principal of the bonds it issues, but it does not have to repay the money it receives from issuing stock.

When a corporation is trying to decide whether to issue additional stock or to issue bonds, an important factor is estimated future earnings and the probable stability of these earnings. The advantages and disadvantages of issuing bonds become apparent in the following example.

Cook Development, which has 160,000 shares of $50-par-value common stock outstanding ($8,000,000), wishes to raise an additional $4,000,000 for expansion. Cook is considering three alternatives for raising the money:

- **Plan 1** Issue an additional $4,000,000 of common stock, thereby increasing the total stock outstanding from 160,000 to 240,000 shares.
- **Plan 2** Issue $4,000,000 of 8 percent cumulative preferred stock.
- **Plan 3** Issue $4,000,000 of 7 percent bonds.

Figure 1 shows how Cook Development comes out if it has a yearly income from operations of (1) $1,680,000 and (2) $300,000. (We assume that the combined federal and state income taxes amount to 40 percent.)

FIGURE 1

	Income from Operations $1,680,000			Income from Operations $300,000		
	Plan 1	**Plan 2**	**Plan 3**	**Plan 1**	**Plan 2**	**Plan 3**
Common stock now outstanding (160,000 shares)	$ 8,000,000	$ 8,000,000	$ 8,000,000	$ 8,000,000	$ 8,000,000	$ 8,000,000
Additional common stock, $50 par (80,000 shares)	4,000,000			4,000,000		
Preferred stock, 8% cumulative		4,000,000			4,000,000	
Bonds, 7%			4,000,000			4,000,000
Total capitalization	$12,000,000	$12,000,000	$12,000,000	$12,000,000	$12,000,000	$12,000,000
Income from operations (before income tax)	$ 1,680,000	$ 1,680,000	$ 1,680,000	$ 300,000	$ 300,000	$ 300,000
Deduct bond interest expense	0	0	280,000	0	0	280,000
Income (loss) before taxes	$ 1,680,000	$ 1,680,000	$ 1,400,000	$ 300,000	$ 300,000	$ 20,000
Deduct federal and state income taxes (40%)	672,000	672,000	560,000	120,000	120,000	8,000
Net income	$ 1,008,000	$ 1,008,000	$ 840,000	$ 180,000	$ 180,000	$ 12,000
Deduct preferred dividends		320,000			320,000	
Earnings available to common shareholders	$ 1,008,000	$ 688,000	$ 840,000	$ 180,000	$ (140,000)	$ 12,000
Earnings available to common shareholders	$ 1,008,000	$ 688,000	$ 840,000	$ 180,000	$ (140,000)	$ 12,000
Common stock shares outstanding	240,000	160,000	160,000	240,000	160,000	160,000
Earnings per share of common stock	$4.20	$4.30	$5.25	$.75	$(.875)	$.075

Money from the sale of bonds may finance a large project, like building construction.

You can see that plan 3 offers the greatest advantage to the original holders of common stock, provided that the company's earnings are large enough to pay the bondholders and still leave a sizable share for the holders of common stock. When the company has a *low* level of earnings, plan 1 is most advantageous to the holders of common stock because there are no prior claims of bondholders or preferred stockholders. The firm can use a combination of the three, but this entails larger financing costs.

ACCOUNTING FOR THE ISSUANCE OF BONDS

Objective 1

Journalize transactions involving the issuance of bonds at a premium or discount.

When a corporation issues bonds at face value, it records the transaction as a debit to Cash and a credit to Bonds Payable. Bonds Payable is a long-term liability account. If there is more than one bond issue, the company keeps a separate account for each issue. The listing in the balance sheet should identify the issue by stipulating its interest rate and due date.

Bonds Sold at a Premium

Remember!

Bonds Payable is a long-term liability. Its normal balance is a credit.

The corporation may receive a price for its bonds that is above or below their face value, depending on the rate of interest offered and the general credit standing of the company. If a corporation offers a rate of interest that is higher than the market rate for similar securities, investors may be willing to pay a **premium** for the bonds.

For example, on January 1, Roe Construction Corporation issues $500,000 of 9 percent, 10-year bonds at 103, with interest payable semiannually, on June 30 and December 31. The term "103" refers to the price of the bonds; it is a percentage of the face value of the bonds, with the percent symbol omitted. This is how the securities exchanges record bond prices. In this example, $500,000 of bonds at 103 means 103 percent of $500,000 ($500,000 × 1.03 = $515,000). Roe's entry to record the sale of the bonds, in general journal form, is shown at the top of the following page.

	DATE		DESCRIPTION	POST. REF.	DEBIT	CREDIT	
1	20—						1
2	Jan.	1	Cash		515 0 0 0 00		2
3			Bonds Payable			500 0 0 0 00	3
4			Premium on Bonds Payable			15 0 0 0 00	4
5			Sold 10-year, 9 percent				5
6			bonds, dated January 1, 20–,				6
7			at 103.				7
8							8

FYI

If $1,000,000 worth of bonds had been sold at 106, the amount received would have been $1,060,000 ($1,000,000 × 1.06 = $1,060,000).

Premium on Bonds Payable represents the amount received over and above the face value of the bonds. The accountant lists Premium on Bonds Payable right below the bond account in the Long-Term Liabilities section of the balance sheet. To illustrate the placement of Bonds Payable and Premium on Bonds Payable, a partial balance sheet on January 1 is shown here.

Roe Construction Corporation
Balance Sheet
January 1, 20—

Long-Term Liabilities:		
9 Percent Bonds Payable, due January 1, 20–	$500 0 0 0 00	
Add Premium on Bonds Payable	15 0 0 0 00	$515 0 0 0 00

Remember!

A premium exists because a bondholder paid more than the face value.

The corporation will write off or amortize Premium on Bonds Payable over the remaining life of the bond issue. The entries to pay the interest on the bonds, in general journal form, are

	DATE		DESCRIPTION	POST. REF.	DEBIT	CREDIT	
1	20—						1
2	June	30	Interest Expense		22 5 0 0 00		2
3			Cash			22 5 0 0 00	3
4			Semiannual interest				4
5			payment on bonds, face				5
6			value of $500,000, 9 percent.				6
7			($500,000 × .09 × $\frac{1}{2}$)				7
8							8
9							9
10							10

	DATE		DESCRIPTION	POST. REF.	DEBIT	CREDIT	
1	20–						1
2	Dec.	31	Interest Expense		22 5 0 0 00		2
3			Cash			22 5 0 0 00	3
4			Semiannual interest				4
5			payment on bonds, face				5
6			value of $500,000, 9 percent.				6
7							7

Adjusting Entry for Bonds Sold at a Premium

Objective 2

Journalize adjusting entries for amortization of bond premiums and discounts and accrued interest payable.

What is **amortization**? A company writes off, or *amortizes,* the Premium on Bonds Payable account over the remaining life of the bonds by debiting the account and using Interest Expense as the offsetting credit. The entry appears as an adjusting entry at the end of the fiscal period. It is first recorded in the Adjustments columns of the work sheet, like any other adjusting entry. Here is the entry to amortize or write off the $15,000 premium on the 10-year bonds issued by Roe Construction Corporation.

FYI

The calculation is recorded here purely as a demonstration.

	DATE		DESCRIPTION	POST. REF.	DEBIT	CREDIT	
1	20–		Adjusting Entry				1
2	Dec.	31	Premium on Bonds Payable		1 5 0 0 00		2
3			Interest Expense			1 5 0 0 00	3
4			($15,000 ÷ 10 years)				4
5							5

By T accounts, the entries for the year look like this:

Cash				Bonds Payable		
	+	−			−	+
Jan. 1	515,000	June 30	22,500			Jan. 1	500,000
		Dec. 31	22,500			

Interest Expense				Premium on Bonds Payable		
	+	−			−	+
June 30	22,500	Dec. 31 Adj.	1,500	Dec. 31 Adj.	1,500	Jan. 1	15,000
Dec. 31	22,500					

The adjusting entry reduces the balance of the Interest Expense account from $45,000 to $43,500. The accountant then closes Interest Expense into Income Summary in the amount of $43,500. The adjusting entry also has the effect of reducing the Premium on Bonds Payable account at the rate of $1,500 per year until it reaches zero, when the bonds come due.

In this illustration, we showed the amortization of the bond premium calculated by the straight-line method on an annual basis, which will also be used in the problems. This is like calculating depreciation by the straight-line method. (One can also record the amortization of the bond premium, just as one can record depreciation, on a monthly basis.) Many corporations, however, amortize premiums and discounts on bonds using the effective interest rate method, as required by the IRS.

Returning to our illustration, after the accountant records the adjusting entry, the balance of Interest Expense is $43,500. This amount represents the annual interest expense on the books. Here is another way of looking at it:

Cash to Be Paid

Face value of the bonds	$500,000	
Interest (20 payments of $22,500 each)	450,000	$950,000

Less Cash Received

Face value of the bonds	$500,000	
Premium on the bonds	15,000	515,000

Excess of Cash to Be Paid over Cash Received

(Interest expense for 10 years)	$435,000

$$\text{Interest Expense per Year} = \frac{\$435,000}{10 \text{ years}} = \$43,500$$

Example: Bonds Sold at a Premium, with Interest Payment Dates that Do Not Coincide with the End of the Fiscal Year On March 1, Gray Electronics issues $6,000,000 worth of 20-year, 9 percent bonds, at 104, dated March 1, with interest payable semiannually, on September 1 and March 1. The corporation's fiscal year ends on December 31. A diagram of the dates looks like this:

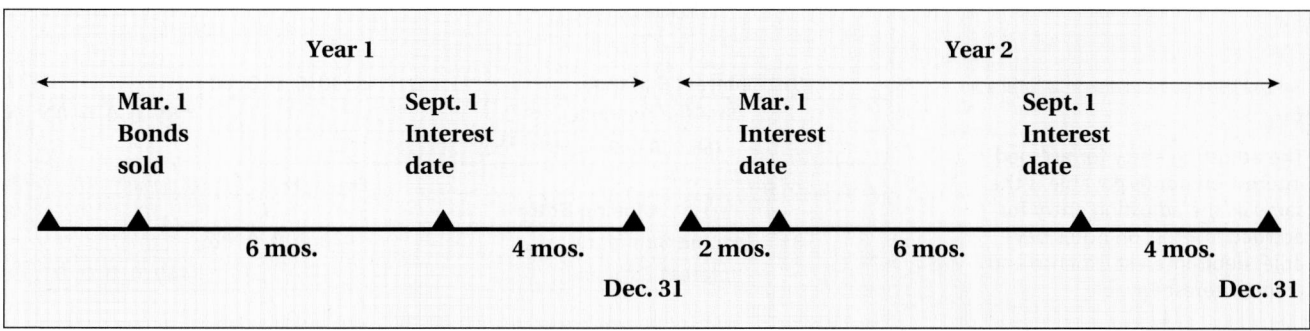

Since the date on which the interest has to be paid does not coincide with the end of the fiscal year, Gray Electronics has to make an adjusting entry for the accrued interest for the period from September 1 to December 31. The entries for the first year, in general journal form, are as follows.

	DATE		DESCRIPTION	POST. REF.	DEBIT	CREDIT	
1	Year 1						1
2	Mar.	1	Cash ($6,000,000 × 1.04)		6,240 0 0 0 00		2
3			Bonds Payable			6,000 0 0 0 00	3
4			Prem. on Bonds Payable			240 0 0 0 00	4
5			Sold 20-year bonds,				5
6			9 percent, dated March 1,				6
7			at 104.				7
8							8

	DATE		DESCRIPTION	POST. REF.	DEBIT	CREDIT	
1	Year 1						1
2	Sept.	1	Interest Expense		270 0 0 0 00		2
3			Cash			270 0 0 0 00	3
4			Semiannual interest on				4
5			bonds, face value of				5
6			$6,000,000, 9 percent.				6
7			($6,000,000 × .09 × $^{6}/_{12}$)				7
8							8

Remember!

Since Premium on Bonds Payable has a credit balance, we debit it to amortize it (write it off).

	DATE		DESCRIPTION	POST. REF.	DEBIT	CREDIT	
1	Year 1		Adjusting Entries				1
2	Dec.	31	Premium on Bonds Payable		10 0 0 0 00		2
3			Interest Expense			10 0 0 0 00	3
4			($240,000 ×				4
5			10 months/240 months)				5
6							6
7		31	Interest Expense		180 0 0 0 00		7
8			Interest Payable			180 0 0 0 00	8
9			($6,000,000 × .09 × $^{4}/_{12}$)				9
10							10
11			Closing Entry				11
12		31	Income Summary		440 0 0 0 00		12
13			Interest Expense			440 0 0 0 00	13
14							14

FYI

The adjusting entry for accrued interest on bonds payable is the same as the adjusting entry for accrued interest on notes payable: debit Interest Expense and credit Interest Payable.

Remember!

The premium or discount on a bond payable is spread over the life of the bond.

The amortization of the premium on December 31 is for only part of a year. The next year, amortization will be for a full year. The adjusting entry for accrued interest on a bond is like the one for accrued interest on an interest-bearing note payable. In T account form, the first-year entries look like the following:

Cash			
+		−	
Year 1		Year 1	
Mar. 1	6,240,000	Sept. 1	270,000

Interest Expense			
+		−	
Year 1		Year 1	
Sept. 1	270,000	Dec. 31 Adj.	10,000
Dec. 31 Adj.	180,000	Dec. 31 Clos.	440,000

Income Summary			
Year 1		Year 1	
(Int. Exp.)	440,000	Closed	xxxx

Bonds Payable			
−		+	
		Year 1	
		Mar. 1	6,000,000

Premium on Bonds Payable			
−		+	
Year 1		Year 1	
Dec. 31 Adj.	10,000	Mar. 1	240,000

Interest Payable			
−		+	
		Year 1	
		Dec. 31 Adj.	180,000

Because the adjusting entry for accrued interest opened a new balance sheet account, Interest Payable, Gray's accountant should make a reversing entry as of the first day of the next fiscal year. The reversing entry enables the accountant to follow the regular routine for the payment of six months' interest on March 1 without having to split up the interest for the period between September 1 of one year and March 1 of the following year.

DATE		DESCRIPTION	POST. REF.	DEBIT	CREDIT
Year 2		Reversing Entry			
Jan.	1	Interest Payable		180 000 00	
		Interest Expense			180 000 00

The entries for the rest of the second year are

DATE		DESCRIPTION	POST. REF.	DEBIT	CREDIT
Year 2					
Mar.	1	Interest Expense		270 000 00	
		Cash			270 000 00
		Semiannual interest on			
		bonds, face value of			
		$6,000,000, 9 percent.			
		($6,000,000 × .09 × $^{6}/_{12}$)			

	DATE		DESCRIPTION	POST. REF.	DEBIT	CREDIT	
1	Year 2						1
2	Sept.	1	Interest Expense		270 0 0 0 00		2
3			Cash			270 0 0 0 00	3
4			Semiannual interest on				4
5			bonds, face value of				5
6			$6,000,000, 9 percent.				6
7			($6,000,000 × .09 × $^6/_{12}$)				7
8							8

	DATE		DESCRIPTION	POST. REF.	DEBIT	CREDIT	
1	Year 2		Adjusting Entries				1
2	Dec.	31	Premium on Bonds Payable		12 0 0 0 00		2
3			Interest Expense			12 0 0 0 00	3
4			($240,000 ×				4
5			$^{12 months}/_{240 months}$)				5
6							6
7		31	Interest Expense		180 0 0 0 00		7
8			Interest Payable			180 0 0 0 00	8
9			($6,000,000 × .09 × $^4/_{12}$)				9
10							10
11			Closing Entry				11
12		31	Income Summary		528 0 0 0 00		12
13			Interest Expense			528 0 0 0 00	13
14							14

Remember!

If the interest payment date does not happen to be the same date as the end of a corporation's fiscal period, an adjusting entry must be made at the end of the fiscal period to record the accrued bond interest expense.

Here are the relevant T accounts from the previous year posted up to date:

Interest Expense

	+		–	
Year 1		Year 1		
Sept. 1	270,000	Dec. 31 Adj.		10,000
Dec. 31 Adj.	180,000	Dec. 31 Clos.		440,000
Year 2		Year 2		
Mar. 1	270,000	Jan. 1 Rev.		180,000
Sept. 1	270,000	Dec. 31 Adj.		12,000
Dec. 31 Adj.	180,000	Dec. 31 Clos.		528,000

Income Summary

Year 1		Year 1		
(Int. Exp.)	440,000	Closed		xxxx
Year 2		Year 2		
(Int. Exp.)	528,000	Closed		xxxx

Bonds Payable

	–		+	
		Year 1		
		Mar. 1		6,000,000

Premium on Bonds Payable

	–		+	
			Year 1	
Year 1		Year 1		
Dec. 31 Adj.	10,000	Mar. 1		240,000
Year 2				
Dec. 31 Adj.	12,000			

Interest Payable

	–		+	
		Year 1		
		Dec. 31 Adj.		180,000
Year 2		Year 2		
Jan. 1 Rev.	180,000	Dec. 31 Adj.		180,000

Bonds Sold at a Discount

When a corporation issues bonds that will pay a rate of interest that is less than the prevailing market rate of interest for comparable bonds, it sells its bonds at less than face value—or at a **discount**.

To demonstrate this, assume that on January 1, Connor, Inc., issues 6 percent, 20-year bonds with a face value of $700,000, at 96, with interest to be paid semiannually, on June 30 and December 31.

	DATE		DESCRIPTION	POST. REF.	DEBIT	CREDIT	
1	20–						1
2	Jan.	1	Cash ($700,000 × .96)		672 0 0 0 00		2
3			Discount on Bonds Payable		28 0 0 0 00		3
4			Bonds Payable			700 0 0 0 00	4
5			Sold 20-year bonds, 6 percent,				5
6			dated January 1, 20–, at 96.				6
7							7
8							8

Discount on Bonds Payable is a **contra-liability account**; it is listed on a classified balance sheet as a deduction from Bonds Payable. A partial balance sheet on January 1 is shown here.

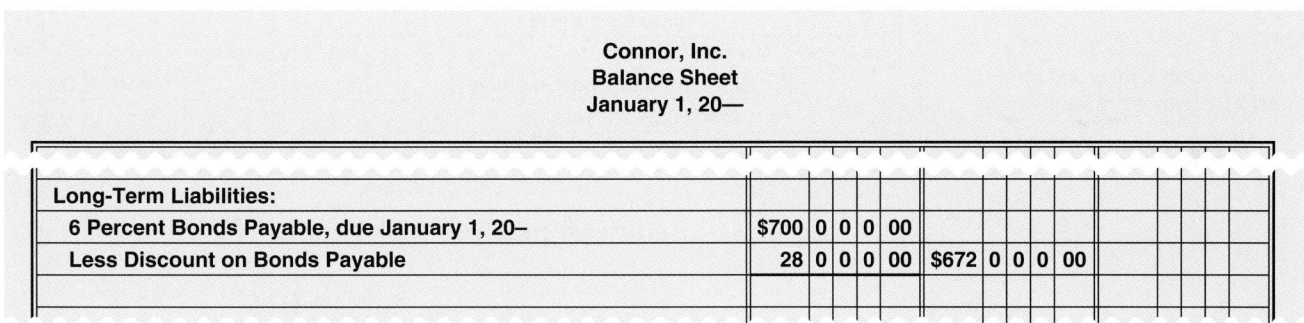

Connor, Inc.				
Balance Sheet				
January 1, 20—				
Long-Term Liabilities:				
6 Percent Bonds Payable, due January 1, 20–	$700 0 0 0 00			
Less Discount on Bonds Payable	28 0 0 0 00	$672 0 0 0 00		

The journal entries for the payment of interest are

	DATE		DESCRIPTION	POST. REF.	DEBIT	CREDIT	
1	20–						1
2	June	30	Interest Expense		21 0 0 0 00		2
3			Cash			21 0 0 0 00	3
4			Semiannual interest on				4
5			bonds, face value of				5
6			$700,000, 6 percent.				6
7			($700,000 × .06 × $^{6}/_{12}$)				7
8							8

	DATE		DESCRIPTION	POST. REF.	DEBIT	CREDIT	
1	20–						1
2	Dec.	31	Interest Expense		21 0 0 0 00		2
3			Cash			21 0 0 0 00	3
4			Semiannual interest on				4
5			bonds, face value of				5
6			$700,000, 6 percent.				6
7			($700,000 × .06 × $^{6}/_{12}$)				7
8							8

Adjusting Entry for Bonds Sold at a Discount

The corporation amortizes the Discount on Bonds Payable account, as it does the Premium on Bonds Payable account, over the remaining life of the bond issue. The write-off consists of an adjusting entry at the end of the fiscal period. Again, the accountant uses Interest Expense as the offsetting account in the adjusting entry. Here is the adjusting entry to amortize the $28,000 discount on the 20-year bonds issued by Connor, Inc.

	DATE		DESCRIPTION	POST. REF.	DEBIT	CREDIT	
1	20–		Adjusting Entry				1
2	Dec.	31	Interest Expense		1 4 0 0 00		2
3			Discount on Bonds Payable			1 4 0 0 00	3
4			($28,000 ÷ 20 years)				4

By T accounts, the entries for the year look like this:

Cash

	+	−	
Jan. 1	672,000	June 30	21,000
		Dec. 31	21,000

Interest Expense

	+	−
June 30	21,000	
Dec. 31	21,000	
Dec. 31 Adj.	1,400	

Bonds Payable

	−	+	
		Jan. 1	700,000

Discount on Bonds Payable

	+	−	
Jan. 1	28,000	Dec. 31 Adj.	1,400

The adjusting entry increases the balance of Interest Expense from $42,000 to $43,400. The accountant then closes Interest Expense into Income Summary in the amount of $43,400. The adjusting entry also has the effect of reducing the Discount on Bonds Payable account at the rate of $1,400 per year until it reaches zero, when the bonds come due.

Here is another way of looking at interest expense:

Cash to Be Paid

Face value of the bonds	$700,000	
Interest (40 payments of $21,000 each)	840,000	$1,540,000

Less Cash Received

Face value of the bonds	$700,000	
Less discount on the bonds	28,000	672,000

Excess of Cash to Be Paid over Cash Received

(Interest expense for 20 years)		$ 868,000

$$\text{Interest Expense per Year} = \frac{\$868,000}{20 \text{ years}} = \$43,400$$

BOND SINKING FUND

To provide greater security for bondholders, the bond agreement may specify that the issuing corporation make annual deposits of cash into a special fund—called a **sinking fund**—to be used to pay off the bond issue when it comes due. The company keeps the sinking fund separate from its other assets and puts the cash deposited in the sinking fund to work by investing it in income-producing securities. When the bonds mature, the total of the annual deposits plus the earnings on the investments should add up to approximately the face value of the bonds. The sinking fund may be controlled by either the corporation or a trustee—usually a bank.

Like a large corporation, the government may want to sell bonds to raise additional money for projects. The government may, at the same time, set up a bond sinking fund to provide reassurance to bondholders that the bonds will be paid when due. A sinking fund is similar to putting money aside for a specific future purchase.

When the corporation deposits cash in its sinking fund, it records the transaction as a debit to Sinking Fund Cash and a credit to Cash. When the corporation or the trustee invests the sinking fund cash, the transaction is recorded as a debit to Sinking Fund Investments and a credit to Sinking Fund Cash. **Both Sinking Fund Cash and Sinking Fund Investments are classified as investment accounts.** These accounts are classified as long-term assets because their use is restricted to paying off the bond issue—long-term liabilities. When the corporation receives interest or dividend income on the investments, it debits Sinking Fund Cash and credits Sinking Fund Income. Sinking Fund Income is classified as an Other Income account on the income statement.

For example, Lee Freight, Inc., issues $800,000 worth of 10-year bonds dated January 1, with the provision that at the end of each of the ten years, it will make an equal deposit into a sinking fund. Lee, which manages its own sinking fund, intends to invest this money in securities that will yield approximately 6 percent per year. Let's assume that, according to compound interest tables, an annual deposit of $60,693 will accumulate to approximately $800,000 in ten years, given the 6 percent annual interest rate.

The following are a few of the many routine transactions that affect the sinking fund during the ten-year period:

- **Annual deposits of cash in bond sinking fund**

DATE	DESCRIPTION	POST. REF.	DEBIT	CREDIT	
	Sinking Fund Cash		60 6 9 3 00		1
	Cash			60 6 9 3 00	2
	Annual deposit in bond				3
	sinking fund, according to				4
	bond agreement.				5
					6
					7

- **Purchase of investments** Time of purchase and amount invested may vary.

DATE	DESCRIPTION	POST. REF.	DEBIT	CREDIT	
	Sinking Fund Investments		59 7 3 0 00		1
	Sinking Fund Cash			59 7 3 0 00	2
	Bought $60,000 of Consoli-				3
	dated Steel 7 percent bonds				4
	at 99$^{1}/_{2}$, plus $30 brokerage				5
	commission.				6
	($60,000 × .995 = $59,700)				7
	($59,700 + $30 = $59,730)				8

- **Receipt of income from investments** Interest and dividends are received at different times during the year.

	DATE	DESCRIPTION	POST. REF.	DEBIT	CREDIT	
1		Sinking Fund Cash		6 5 7 0 00		1
2		Sinking Fund Income			6 5 7 0 00	2
3		Received interest and				3
4		dividends on sinking fund				4
5		investments.				5
6						6

- **Sale of investments** Investments may be sold and the proceeds reinvested.

	DATE	DESCRIPTION	POST. REF.	DEBIT	CREDIT	
1		Sinking Fund Cash		148 9 6 0 00		1
2		Sinking Fund Investments			147 2 0 0 00	2
3		Gain on Sale of Sinking Fund				3
4		Investments			1 7 6 0 00	4
5		Sold sinking fund investments,				5
6		yielding a profit of $1,760.				6
7						7
8						8
9						9
10						10
11						11

- **Payment of bonds** Cash available consists of the sinking fund after the sale of the investments plus the last annual deposit, which should bring the sinking fund up to approximately $800,000.

	DATE	DESCRIPTION	POST. REF.	DEBIT	CREDIT	
1		Bonds Payable		800 0 0 0 00		1
2		Sinking Fund Cash			800 0 0 0 00	2
3		Paid bond obligation with				3
4		sinking fund cash.				4
5						5
6						6

REDEMPTION OF BONDS

Objective 4

Journalize transactions involving the redemption of bonds.

To protect itself against a decline in market interest rates, a corporation may issue **callable bonds**. Callable bonds give the corporation the right—as stipulated in the bond **indenture**, or agreement—to **redeem** or buy back the bonds at a specified figure—the *call price*—that is ordinarily higher than the face value.

Costello, Inc., issues $2,000,000 worth of 10 percent, 20-year, callable bonds, with a call price of 104. Later, interest rates in general fall. Under the new market conditions, Costello could sell $2,000,000 worth of bonds at face value, with an interest rate of 7 percent. It would pay Costello, Inc., to buy back the bonds, even though it would have to pay $2,080,000 for them ($2,000,000 × 1.04), then turn around and issue new bonds at 7 percent. The annual savings in interest would amount to $60,000 (3 percent of $2,000,000). Even if a corporation's bonds are not callable, it may still buy its own bonds on the open market, if it can find any for sale.

When a corporation redeems its bonds at a price that is less than their book value, it realizes a gain. Conversely, if it redeems its bonds at a price that is more than their book value, it incurs a loss. The book value is the sum of the Bonds Payable account and the Premium on Bonds Payable account (or the Bonds Payable account less the Discount on Bonds Payable account).

For example, Sound, Inc., has $500,000 worth of callable bonds outstanding on December 31, with a call price of 105; there is an unamortized discount of $2,000. Sound pays the interest up to date on December 31 and exercises its option of calling in or redeeming the bonds on the same date, December 31. The entry is shown below in general journal form. The loss represents the difference between the book value and the price paid (also determined by the difference between debits and credits).

	DATE		DESCRIPTION	POST. REF.	DEBIT	CREDIT	
1	20–						1
2	Dec.	31	Bonds Payable		500 0 0 0 00		2
3			Loss on Redemption of Bonds		27 0 0 0 00		3
4			Cash			525 0 0 0 00	4
5			Discount on Bonds Payable			2 0 0 0 00	5
6			To record redemption of				6
7			bonds at 105.				7
8							8

Recall that, even if a corporation's bonds are not callable, the firm can buy back the bonds—all of them, or as many as it can find on the open market. For example, Erwin Fabrics has $1,000,000 worth of 7 percent bonds outstanding, on which there is an unamortized premium of $30,000. On July 15, Erwin buys $100,000 of bonds (one-tenth of the original issue) in the open market at 97, plus fifteen days' accrued interest. The entry, in general journal form, is as follows.

The phone company invests huge amounts of money in an effort to keep its cables well maintained and state-of-the-art. Such a company may issue bonds to produce the needed capital. To protect itself against market fluctuations, it may issue callable bonds, which allow the corporation to buy back the bonds at a certain price.

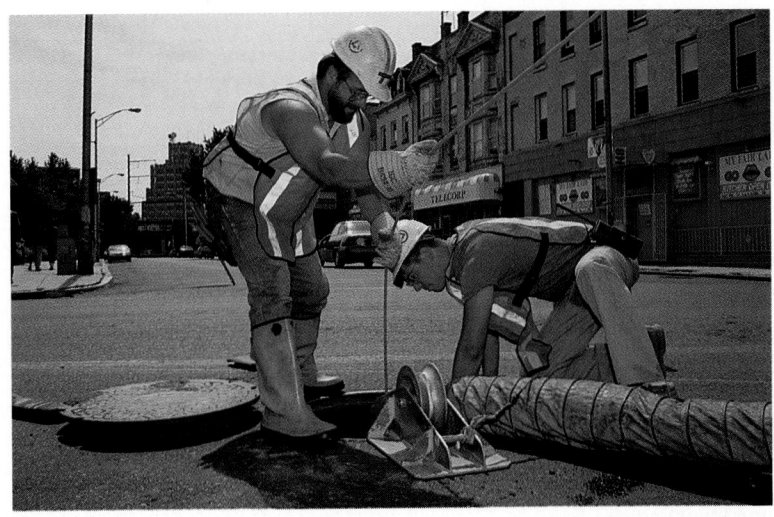

	DATE		DESCRIPTION	POST. REF.	DEBIT					CREDIT					
1	20–														1
2	July	15	Bonds Payable		100	0	0	0	00						2
3			Premium on Bonds Payable		3	0	0	0	00						3
4			Interest Expense ($100,000,												4
5			7 percent, 15 days)			2	9	1	67						5
6			Cash							97	2	9	1	67	6
7			Gain on Redemption of Bonds							6	0	0	0	00	7
8			To record redemption of bonds												8
9			at 97 plus accrued interest.												9
10			($100,000 × .07 × ^{15}/$_{360}$ =												10
11			$291.67)												11

Redemption in effect cancels all or a portion of the Bonds Payable account, as well as the accompanying premium or discount. **We list Gain (or Loss) on Redemption of Bonds in the income statement under the heading Other Income or Other Expense.** If the gains or losses are significant, they are listed (net of any related income tax effect) under the heading Extraordinary Items, a classification of accounts appearing at the bottom of an income statement. Extraordinary items are unusual in nature and do not occur with any regularity. They may include gains or losses on redemption of bonds, fire losses, expropriation of property by a foreign government, or a prohibition (a gain or loss resulting from the enactment of a new law).

BALANCE SHEET

The balance sheet of Mueller Company, Inc., shown in Figure 2 on the following page, shows how to place the accounts introduced in this chapter.

Mueller Company, Inc.
Balance Sheet
December 31, 20—

Assets					
Current Assets:					
Cash			$ 12 0 0 0 00		
Notes Receivable			30 0 0 0 00		
Accounts Receivable	$ 220 0 0 0 00				
Less Allowance for Doubtful Accounts	4 0 0 0 00		216 0 0 0 00		
Merchandise Inventory			647 0 0 0 00		
Supplies			2 0 0 0 00		
Total Current Assets				$ 907 0 0 0 00	
Investments:					
Sinking Fund Cash			$ 5 0 0 0 00		
Sinking Fund Investments			84 0 0 0 00		
Total Investments				89 0 0 0 00	
Plant and Equipment:					
Land			$ 70 0 0 0 00		
Building	$ 180 0 0 0 00				
Less Accumulated Depreciation	45 0 0 0 00		135 0 0 0 00		
Equipment	$ 222 0 0 0 00				
Less Accumulated Depreciation	32 0 0 0 00		190 0 0 0 00		
Total Plant and Equipment				395 0 0 0 00	
Intangible Assets:					
Goodwill			$ 20 0 0 0 00		
Organization Costs			8 0 0 0 00		
Total Intangible Assets				28 0 0 0 00	
Total Assets				$1 419 0 0 0 00	
Liabilities					
Current Liabilities:					
Accounts Payable			$ 70 0 0 0 00		
Income Tax Payable			8 0 0 0 00		
Dividends Payable			12 0 0 0 00		
Total Current Liabilities				$ 90 0 0 0 00	
Long-Term Liabilities:					
6 percent Bonds Payable, due December 31, 20–	$ 100 0 0 0 00				
Less Discount on Bonds Payable	3 0 0 0 00		$ 97 0 0 0 00		
8 percent Bonds Payable, due March 31, 20–	$ 200 0 0 0 00				
Add Premium on Bonds Payable	2 0 0 0 00		202 0 0 0 00		
Total Long-Term Liabilities				299 0 0 0 00	
Total Liabilities				$ 389 0 0 0 00	
Stockholders' Equity					
Paid-in Capital:					
Common Stock, $10 par (100,000 shares authorized,					
40,000 shares issued)	$ 400 0 0 0 00				
Premium on Common Stock	220 0 0 0 00				
Total Paid-in Capital			$ 620 0 0 0 00		
Retained Earnings:					
Unappropriated Retained Earnings	$ 310 0 0 0 00				
Appropriated For Plant Expansion	100 0 0 0 00				
Total Retained Earnings			410 0 0 0 00		
Total Stockholders' Equity				1 030 0 0 0 00	
Total Liabilities and Stockholders' Equity				$1 419 0 0 0 00	

FIGURE 2

CHAPTER REVIEW

Review of Performance Objectives

1. **Journalize transactions involving the issuance of bonds at a premium or discount.**

   A bond is sold at a premium when the stated rate of interest is higher than the market rate of interest. The entry for selling a bond at a premium is a debit to Cash, a credit to Bonds Payable, and a credit to Premium on Bonds Payable. A bond is sold at a discount when the stated rate of interest is less than the market rate of interest. The entry for selling a bond at a discount is a debit to Cash, a debit to Discount on Bonds Payable, and a credit to Bonds Payable.

2. **Journalize adjusting entries for amortization of bond premiums and discounts and accrued interest payable.**

   Premiums and discounts are written off, or amortized, over the remaining life of the bond from the time of the sale. The entry to write off a premium is a debit to Premium on Bonds Payable and a credit to Interest Expense. The entry to write off a discount is a debit to Interest Expense and a credit to Discount on Bonds Payable. Accrued interest represents the amount of interest incurred between the last interest-payment date and the end of the fiscal period. The entry to record accrued interest is a debit to Interest Expense and a credit to Interest Payable.

3. **Journalize entries pertaining to the establishment of a bond sinking fund, the receipt of income from sinking fund investments, and the eventual payment of the principal of the bonds.**

   The entry to establish a bond sinking fund is a debit to Sinking Fund Cash and a credit to Cash. The entry for the receipt of income from sinking fund investments is a debit to Sinking Fund Cash and a credit to Sinking Fund Income. The entry for the payment of the principal of the bonds is a debit to Bonds Payable and a credit to Sinking Fund Cash.

4. **Journalize transactions involving the redemption of bonds.**

   Assuming interest is paid up to date, the entry for the redemption of bonds is a debit to Bonds Payable, either a debit to Premium on Bonds Payable or a credit to Discount on Bonds Payable, either a debit to Loss on Redemption of Bonds or a credit to Gain on Redemption of Bonds, and a credit to Cash. If there is accrued interest on the bonds, the entry would also include a debit to Interest Expense.

Glossary

Amortization The systematic writing off of costs, discounts, or premiums over a period of years. (816)

Bond A long-term obligation that provides capital. (810)

Bond issue The total number of bonds that a corporation issues at one time, in denominations of $1,000 or $5,000 each. (810)

Callable bonds Bonds that give the corporation the right to redeem or buy back the bonds, prior to the date of maturity, at a specified figure, known as the *call price.* (826)

Contra-liability account A deduction from a liability, such as Discount on Bonds Payable, which is a deduction from the balance of Bonds Payable. (821)

Coupon bonds Bonds that have interest coupons attached to each bond. These coupons are payable to bearer and may be cashed on interest payment dates. (811)

Discount The amount by which the issue price is less than the face value of a bond. (821)

Extraordinary Items Significant transactions that appear at the bottom of an income statement (net of any related income tax effect) because they are unusual in nature and do not recur with any regularity. (827)

Indenture A bond agreement, or contract, between the corporation and its bondholders. (826)

Leverage The use of debt as a lever to raise the owners' rate of return by earning income on borrowed money at a higher rate than that paid to borrow the money (as, for example, borrowing money at 8 percent and using it to earn a 15 percent rate of return). (812)

Premium The excess of the price received over the face value of a bond. (814)

Redeem Buy back or repurchase bonds from bondholders. (826)

Registered bonds Bonds whose owners' names are registered with the corporation that issued the bonds. (811)

Secured bonds Bonds that are covered or backed by mortgages on real estate or by titles to personal property that may be claimed by the bondholders in the event that the issuing corporation defaults on its payment of principal or interest. (812)

Serial bonds Bonds of a particular issue that have a series of maturity dates. (811)

Sinking fund A special fund of cash accumulated over the life of a bond issue to enable the issuing corporation to pay off the bonds when they mature (come due). The fund is kept separate from other assets, and the cash is invested in income-producing securities. (823)

Term bonds Bonds of a particular issue that all have the same maturity date. (811)

Unsecured bonds Bonds backed only by the credit standing (good name) of the issuing corporation; also called *debenture bonds*. (812)

QUESTIONS, EXERCISES, AND PROBLEMS

Discussion Questions

1. How is a bond premium reported on the balance sheet?
2. What is the difference between term bonds and serial bonds?
3. What is the difference between a debenture and an indenture?
4. What do accountants mean by the redemption of callable bonds? What is involved in the journal entry?
5. What are two definite obligations a corporation incurs when it issues bonds?
6. What is a bond sinking fund, and what is its purpose?
7. If the market rate of interest is higher than the bond agreement's rate of interest, will the bonds be sold at a premium or a discount? Why?
8. How is a bond sinking fund classified on a balance sheet?

Exercises

Exercise 23-1 Journalize the following transactions for Fog Corporation:

July	10	Issued $800,000 of 8 percent, 20-year bonds at 102.
Oct.	5	Issued $600,000 of 9 percent, 10-year bonds at 103.

Exercise 23-2 Journalize the year-end adjusting entry to amortize the premium resulting from the issuance on January 5 of $200,000 of 10-year bonds at 104.

Exercise 23-3 Seng, Inc., issued $900,000 of 30-year, 9 percent bonds dated March 1. Interest is payable on March 1 and September 1. The fiscal year extends from January 1 through December 31. Journalize entries for the following:

Sept.	1	Payment of semiannual interest
Dec.	31	Adjustment for accrued interest expense

Exercise 23-4 On January 1, Moi, Inc., issued 7 percent, 20-year bonds with a face value of $800,000 at 96. Journalize:

a. The issuance of the bonds
b. The adjusting entry to amortize the discount

P.O. 1,2

Journalize bond issue, interest payment, and adjusting entries for discount and for accrued interest.

Exercise 23-5 On April 1, Borg Corporation issued $1,000,000 of 10-year, 9 percent bonds at 98, dated April 1, with interest payable semiannually on October 1 and April 1. The corporation's fiscal year ends on December 31. Journalize the issuance of the bonds, the payment of the semiannual interest on October 1, and the adjusting entries to amortize the Discount on Bonds Payable and record the accrued interest as of December 31.

Exercise 23-6 Describe the entries in the following T accounts:

Cash		
(1) 1,040,000	(2)	80,000

Premium on Bonds Payable		
(4) 2,000	(1)	40,000

Bonds Payable		
	(1)	1,000,000

Interest Payable		
(6) 20,000	(3)	20,000

Interest Expense			
(2)	80,000	(4)	2,000
(3)	20,000	(5)	98,000
(6)	20,000		

Income Summary	
(5) 98,000	

P.O. 3

Journalize sale of investments, sinking fund deposit, and payment of bonds.

Exercise 23-7 Link, Inc., has outstanding $650,000 of 10-year sinking fund bonds. At the end of the ninth year after it issued the bonds, the balance of Link's Sinking Fund Investments account is $598,600. List the entries to record the following:

a. The sale of the investments for $611,000
b. The final deposit in the sinking fund, bringing the balance of the account up to $650,000
c. The payment of the bonds

P.O. 4

Journalize bond redemption.

Exercise 23-8 The Mirez Corporation has the following account balances: Bonds Payable, $1,300,000, Premium on Bonds Payable, $40,000. As a step in redeeming the bond issue, Mirez buys $130,000 worth of its bonds on the open market at 97. Give the entry to record the redemption.

CONSIDER AND COMMUNICATE

A fellow student states that bond premium and bond discount are the same because (a) they are both reduced by amortization; (b) both occur because the cash received differs from the face value of the bond; and (c) both affect interest expense. Respond to the accuracy of this statement.

CRITICAL THINKING

Below is a partial Stockholders' Equity section of a corporate balance sheet. The preparer has carelessly left out several numbers. Please fill in the missing information.

Stockholders' Equity			
Paid-in Capital:			
1. Preferred 9 Percent Stock, $50 par (40,000 shares authorized, , shares issued)	$ 400,000		
2. Preferred 9 Percent Stock Subscribed (1,600 shares)	80,000	$,	
3. Common Stock, $ par (250,000 shares authorized, 58,000 shares issued)	$1,160,000		
4. Premium on Common Stock	40,000	, ,	
Paid-in Capital from Donation		16,000	
5. Total Paid-in Capital		$, ,	
Retained Earnings		189,000	
6. Total Stockholders' Equity			$, ,

A MATTER OF ETHICS

You walk into an unoccupied office to put something in the person's In Basket. As you do so, you cannot help noticing an open folder in which you see a list of names of people suggested for outplacement—a polite way of saying, "You are fired." You see that your name isn't on it and breathe a sigh of relief, but you also see the names of several people you know. What should you do?

WEB WORK

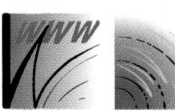

Using an Internet web browser, type *bonds* or *corporate bonds* in the search box and search for information about bonds as long-term liabilities. Discuss your findings in a small group. Write a one-page summary of your findings.

PROBLEM SET A

For additional help, see the demonstration problem at the beginning of each chapter in your Working Papers.

P.O. 1,2

Problem 23-1A During two consecutive years, Martino, Inc., completed the following transactions:

Year 1

Jan.	2	Issued $1,000,000 face value 20-year, 7 percent bonds, dated January 1 of this year, at 96. Interest is payable semiannually on June 30 and December 31.
June	30	Paid semiannual interest on bonds.
Dec.	31	Paid semiannual interest on bonds.
	31	Recorded adjusting entry for amortization of discount on bonds.
	31	Closed the Interest Expense account.

Year 2

June	30	Paid semiannual interest on bonds.
Dec.	31	Paid semiannual interest on bonds.
	31	Recorded adjusting entry for amortization of discount on bonds.
	31	Closed the Interest Expense account.

Check Figure

Year 2 adjustment debit, $2,000

Instructions

Record the transactions in general journal form.

P.O. 1,2

Problem 23-2A Price Hotel, Inc., completed the following selected transactions:

Year 1

Apr.	1	Issued $1,200,000 worth of 20-year, 10 percent bonds, dated April 1 of this year, at 105. Interest is payable semiannually on October 1 and April 1.
Oct.	1	Paid semiannual interest on bonds.
Dec.	31	Recorded adjusting entry for accrued interest payable.
	31	Recorded adjusting entry for amortization of premium on bonds.
	31	Closed the Interest Expense account.

Year 2

Jan.	1	Reversed adjusting entry for accrued interest payable.
Apr.	1	Paid semiannual interest on bonds.
Oct.	1	Paid semiannual interest on bonds.
Dec.	31	Made adjusting entry to record accrued interest payable.
	31	Made adjusting entry to record amortization of premium on bonds.
	31	Closed the Interest Expense account.

P.O. 1,2,3

Instructions

1. Record the transactions in general journal form.
2. Post the entries to the Interest Expense account. Label the adjusting, closing, and reversing entries.

Problem 23-3A During two consecutive years, the Weelen Freight Corporation completed the following transactions related to its $12,000,000 issue of 25-year, 8 percent bonds, dated May 1 of the first year. Interest is payable on May 1 and November 1. The corporation's fiscal year extends from January 1 through December 31.

Year 1

May	1	Sold bond issue at 98½.
Nov.	1	Paid semiannual interest on bonds.
Dec.	31	Deposited $173,250 in a bond sinking fund.
	31	Made adjusting entry to record accrued interest payable.
	31	Made adjusting entry to record amortization of bond discount.
	31	Closed the Interest Expense account.

Year 2

Jan.	1	Reversed adjusting entry for accrued interest payable.
	9	Bought various securities with sinking fund cash; cost, $168,600.
May	1	Paid semiannual interest on bonds.
Nov.	1	Paid semiannual interest on bonds.
Dec.	31	Recorded receipt of $12,994 of income derived from sinking fund investments, depositing cash in sinking fund.
	31	Deposited $258,000 in bond sinking fund.
	31	Made adjusting entry to record accrued interest payable.
	31	Made adjusting entry to record amortization of bond discount.
	31	Closed the Sinking Fund Income account.
	31	Closed the Interest Expense account.

Instructions

1. Record the transactions in general journal form.
2. Post the entries to the Interest Expense account and the Discount on Bonds Payable account. Label the adjusting, closing, and reversing entries.

P.O. 1,2,3

Problem 23-4A On May 1, the Mixler Corporation issued $9,000,000 worth of 25-year, 9 percent bonds, dated May 1, with interest payable May 1 and November 1. The corporation's fiscal year is the calendar year. The following transactions pertain to the bond issue for the first two years:

Year 1

May	1	Sold bond issue at 103.
Nov.	1	Paid semiannual interest on bonds.
Dec.	31	Deposited $160,500 in a bond sinking fund.
	31	Recorded adjusting entry for accrued interest payable.
	31	Recorded adjusting entry for amortization of bond premium.
	31	Closed the Interest Expense account.

Year 2

Jan.	1	Reversed adjusting entry for accrued interest payable.
	12	Bought various securities with sinking fund cash; cost, $157,400.

May	1	Paid semiannual interest on bonds.
July	1	Recorded receipt of $5,624 of income derived from sinking fund investments, depositing cash in sinking fund.
	2	Bought various securities with sinking fund cash, $7,290.
Nov.	1	Paid semiannual interest on bonds.
Dec.	31	Recorded receipt of $6,331 of income derived from sinking fund investments, depositing cash in sinking fund.
	31	Deposited $201,200 in bond sinking fund.
	31	Recorded adjusting entry for accrued interest payable.
	31	Recorded adjusting entry for amortization of bond premium.
	31	Closed the Sinking Fund Income account.
	31	Closed the Interest Expense account.

Check Figure

Year 2 adjustment, credit to Interest Payable, $135,000

Instructions

1. Record the transactions in general journal form.
2. Post entries to the Interest Expense account and the Premium on Bonds Payable account. Label the adjusting, closing, and reversing entries.

PROBLEM SET B

For additional help, see the demonstration problem at the beginning of each chapter in your Working Papers.

P.O. 1,2

Problem 23-1B During two consecutive years, Peters Corporation completed the following transactions:

Year 1

Jan.	2	Issued $2,000,000 face value 20-year, 9 percent bonds, dated January 1 of this year, at 102. Interest is payable semiannually on June 30 and December 31.
June	30	Paid semiannual interest on bonds.
Dec.	31	Paid semiannual interest on bonds.
	31	Recorded adjusting entry for amortization of premium on bonds.
	31	Closed the Interest Expense account.

Year 2

June	30	Paid semiannual interest on bonds.
Dec.	31	Paid semiannual interest on bonds.
	31	Recorded adjusting entry for amortization of premium on bonds.
	31	Closed the Interest Expense account.

Check Figure

Year 2 adjustment debit, $2,000

Instructions

Record the transactions in general journal form.

P.O. 1,2

Problem 23-2B Janco, Inc., completed the following selected transactions:

Year 1

Mar.	1	Issued $800,000 of 20-year, 9 percent bonds, dated March 1 of this year, at 104. Interest is payable semiannually on September 1 and March 1.

Sept.	1	Paid semiannual interest on bonds.
Dec.	31	Recorded adjusting entry for accrued interest payable.
	31	Recorded adjusting entry for amortization of premium on bonds.
	31	Closed the Interest Expense account.

Year 2

Jan.	1	Reversed adjusting entry for accrued interest payable.
Mar.	1	Paid semiannual interest on bonds.
Sept.	1	Paid semiannual interest on bonds.
Dec.	31	Made adjusting entry to record accrued interest payable.
	31	Made adjusting entry to record amortization of premium on bonds.
	31	Closed the Interest Expense account.

Check Figure

Year 2 adjustment, debit to Interest Expense, $24,000

Instructions

1. Record the transactions in general journal form.
2. Post entries to the Interest Expense account. Label the adjusting, closing, and reversing entries.

P.O. 1,2,3

Problem 23-3B During two consecutive years, the Eng Medical Clinic completed the following transactions relating to its $9,000,000 issue of 30-year, 8 percent bonds, dated April 1. Interest is payable on April 1 and October 1. The corporation's fiscal year extends from January 1 through December 31.

Year 1

Apr.	1	Sold the bond issue at 97.
Oct.	1	Paid semiannual interest on bonds.
Dec.	31	Deposited $79,500 in a bond sinking fund.
	31	Made adjusting entry to record accrued interest payable.
	31	Made adjusting entry to record amortization of bond discount.
	31	Closed the Interest Expense account.

Year 2

Jan.	1	Reversed adjusting entry for accrued interest payable.
	4	Bought various securities with sinking fund cash; cost, $73,940.
Apr.	1	Paid semiannual interest on bonds.
Oct.	1	Paid semiannual interest on bonds.
Dec.	31	Recorded receipt of $6,172 of income derived from sinking fund investments, depositing the cash in the sinking fund.
	31	Deposited $110,600 in bond sinking fund.
	31	Made adjusting entry to record accrued interest payable.
	31	Made adjusting entry to record amortization of bond discount.
	31	Closed the Sinking Fund Income account.
	31	Closed the Interest Expense account.

Check Figure

Year 2 adjustment, credit to Discount on Bonds Payable, $9,000

Instructions

1. Record the transactions in general journal form.
2. Post entries to the Interest Expense account and the Discount on Bonds Payable account. Label the adjusting, closing, and reversing entries.

P.O. 1,2,3

Problem 23-4B On June 1, Ryan, Inc., whose fiscal year is the calendar year, issued $12,000,000 of 20-year, 9 percent bonds, dated June 1, with interest payable on June 1 and December 1. The following transactions pertain to the bond issue for the first two years:

Year 1

June	1	Sold the bond issue at 101.
Dec.	1	Paid semiannual interest on bonds.
	31	Deposited $237,000 in a bond sinking fund.
	31	Recorded adjusting entry for accrued interest payable.
	31	Recorded adjusting entry for amortization of bond premium.
	31	Closed the Interest Expense account.

Year 2

Jan.	1	Reversed adjusting entry for accrued interest payable.
	9	Bought various securities with sinking fund cash; cost, $229,600.
June	1	Paid semiannual interest on bonds.
July	1	Recorded receipt of $8,114 of income derived from sinking fund investments, depositing the cash in the sinking fund.
	8	Bought various securities with sinking fund cash, $9,464.
Dec.	1	Paid semiannual interest on bonds.
	31	Recorded receipt of $15,992 of income derived from sinking fund investments, depositing the cash in the sinking fund.
	31	Deposited $335,000 in the bond sinking fund.
	31	Recorded adjusting entry for accrued interest payable.
	31	Recorded adjusting entry for amortization of bond premium.
	31	Closed the Sinking Fund Income account.
	31	Closed the Interest Expense account.

Check Figure

Year 2 adjustment, credit to Interest Payable, $90,000

Instructions

1. Record the transactions in general journal form.
2. Post entries to the Interest Expense account and the Premium on Bonds Payable account. Label the adjusting, closing, and reversing entries.

Cumulative Self-Check: Chapters 20–23

PART I: TRUE/FALSE QUESTIONS

T   F   1. A salary allowance represents a withdrawal by a partner for personal use when allocating partnership net income to partners.

T   F   2. Mutual agency means that each partner can enter into contracts in the name of the firm.

T   F   3. The primary difference between accounting for a sole proprietorship and accounting for a partnership is in the owners' equity accounts.

T   F   4. Stockholders' equity in a corporation can also be referred to as capital.

T   F   5. The Organization Costs account for a corporation is classified as an expense account.

T   F   6. Double taxation means that corporate net income is taxed first at the corporate level and then again as dividends to stockholders.

T   F   7. The issuance of a stock dividend results in a decrease in the assets of a corporation.

T   F   8. When retained earnings are appropriated for plant expansion, cash is set aside to pay for the expansion.

T   F   9. Dividends are declared only by a vote of the board of directors that is recorded in the minute book.

T   F   10. The limit of liability is the same for partners in a partnership as for stockholders in a corporation.

T   F   11. A premium on bonds payable is amortized over the period from the date of issue until the maturity date.

T   F   12. Discount on Bonds Payable is classified as a contra-liability account.

PART II: COMPLETION

1. _____ occurs when a partnership ends, the assets are sold, creditors are paid, and the remaining cash is distributed among the partners.

2. The ability of each partner to act as an agent of the firm, thereby committing the entire firm to a binding contract, is called _____.

3. A corporation's stock that is in the hands of its stockholders is called _____.

4. The owners of a corporation are referred to as _____.

5. A distribution of earnings of a corporation in the form of cash is called a(n) _____.

Note: Answers to the Cumulative Self-Check problems begin on page A-1.

6. A distribution of a corporation's retained earnings to stockholders in the form of shares of corporate stock is called a(n) _____.

7. A restriction of a portion of retained earnings designated for a specific purpose is called a(n) _____.

8. The systematic writing off of a bond premium or discount over the remaining life of the bond is called _____.

9. The _____ is the excess of the price received over the face value of a bond.

10. An account such as Discount on Bonds Payable, which represents a deduction from a liability, is called a(n) _____ account.

PART III: APPLICATION

A. Partnerships

Calculations Involving Division of Net Income

Lopez and Rell are partners in the Cruise Line Shop. Balances in the Capital accounts of Lopez and Rell at the beginning of the year are $90,000 and $70,000, respectively. The net income of the firm for the year is $80,000. Calculate each partner's share of net income under the specified conditions. The first answer is given as an example.

0. Equally.
1. Ratio of 3:1.
2. In the ratio of the balances of their Capital accounts at the beginning of the year.
3. Salary allowances of $30,000 to Lopez and $35,000 to Rell; the remainder divided equally.
4. Interest allowances of 9 percent on the balances of their Capital accounts at the beginning of the year; the remainder divided equally.
5. Salary allowances of $25,000 to Lopez and $30,000 to Rell and interest allowances of 10 percent on the balances of their Capital accounts at the beginning of the year; the remainder divided equally.

	Lopez's Share	Rell's Share
0.	$40,000	$40,000
1.		
2.		
3.		
4.		
5.		

B. Corporations

Stockholders' Equity

The charter of the Warder Corporation authorized the issuance of 20,000 shares of cumulative preferred 8 percent stock, $50 par, and 160,000 shares of common stock, $10 par. At the end of this year, the balances of the stockholders' equity accounts are as follows:

Common Stock	$750,000
Paid-in Capital from Donation	6,500
Preferred 8 Percent Stock	240,000
Preferred 8 Percent Stock Subscribed	30,000
Retained Earnings (credit balance)	240,000

Prepare the Stockholders' Equity section of the balance sheet, including descriptive details of stock accounts, for the end of this year.

Stockholders' Equity			
Paid-in Capital:			

24 The Statement of Cash Flows

Performance Objectives

After you have completed this chapter, you will be able to do the following:

1. Describe the statement of cash flows, and define *cash and cash equivalents*.

2. State the purpose of the statement of cash flows.

3. State the uses of the statement of cash flows by management, investors, and creditors.

4. Identify cash inflows and outflows as operating, investing, or financing activities.

5. Calculate amounts of cash inflows and outflows involving operating, investing, and financing activities.

6. Prepare a statement of cash flows using the direct method.

Certainly the financial statements presented in earlier chapters are important. Each statement serves a specific purpose. The income statement shows the results of operations. The statement of owner's or stockholders' equity shows additional investments by owners and payments to owners. The balance sheet portrays a company's financial condition. However, there are important questions that these statements do not answer. For example, what new assets did the firm invest in (buy) during the year? If liabilities increased during the year, where were the proceeds spent? Or, if liabilities decreased, how were they reduced? Did a corporation's operations for the year generate enough cash to pay dividends? If a corporation issued common stock during the year, where were the proceeds spent?

841

You may wonder why these questions can't be answered by the existing financial statements. The income statement is prepared on the accrual basis, and so it does not show the amounts of cash either generated or paid. The amounts of cash involved in changes in the balances of assets and liabilities during the year are not shown on the balance sheet. The statement of owner's or stockholders' equity shows only transactions that affect equity accounts. The statement of cash flows was developed to explain the reasons for the inflows and outflows of cash.

A BROAD LOOK AT THE STATEMENT OF CASH FLOWS

Definition

Objective 1

Describe the statement of cash flows, and define *cash and cash equivalents.*

The statement of cash flows is a financial statement that explains in detail how the balance of cash and cash equivalents has changed between the beginning and the end of a fiscal period. Some accountants refer to the statement of cash flows as the "where got, where gone" statement of cash. The Financial Accounting Standards Board, in its Statement of Financial Accounting Standards No. 95, requires a statement of cash flows as part of a full set of financial statements.

On the statement of cash flows, cash is defined to include both cash as you think of it and cash equivalents. Cash equivalents are short-term, highly liquid investments, including money market accounts, U.S. Treasury bills, and commercial paper, that mature within ninety days from the date acquired. When a company has more cash on hand than it needs immediately, it seems logical to put the excess cash to work earning interest. Money market accounts are interest-bearing accounts available at banks. U.S. Treasury bills may be considered short-term government bonds. Commercial paper is another corporation's short-term interest-bearing notes.

Cash, checking accounts, and CDs, as well as U.S. Treasury bills and commercial paper with a 90-day or less maturity, are all considered cash and cash equivalents.

Purpose

The main purpose of the statement of cash flows is to provide a summary of information concerning a company's cash receipts and payments during a fiscal period. A secondary purpose is to provide information about a firm's investing and financing activities during a fiscal period.

Uses of the Statement of Cash Flows

Management's Use of the Statement of Cash Flows Management uses the statement of cash flows to assess or determine the liquidity of the business, to determine dividend policy, and to evaluate possible investments and means of financing. Management asks the following questions:

Liquidity Is enough cash being generated to enable the company to pay its bills?
Dividend policy Is enough cash being generated to enable the corporation to establish a regular cash dividend policy?
Investment and financing If the firm borrows to buy an asset, is enough cash being generated to make the payments?

Investors' and Creditors' Use of the Statement of Cash Flows Investors (stockholders) are interested in a corporation's ability to pay dividends. Creditors are concerned with a company's ability to pay its liabilities. Both investors and creditors are interested in the firm's ability to generate future cash flows as well as its need for additional financing.

CLASSIFICATIONS OF CASH FLOWS

The statement of cash flows classifies cash receipts and payments into three categories: operating activities, investing activities, and financing activities.

Operating Activities

Operating activities is the first category on the statement of cash flows, and this category lists and classifies cash inflows and outflows from a variety of sources. *Cash inflows* include cash receipts from customers for the sale of merchandise and services and cash receipts in the form of interest and dividend income. Think of the items listed on an income statement; include the Revenue from Sales section, and then refer to the Other Income section to include interest income and dividend income.

Cash outflows include cash payments for merchandise purchases and operating expenses, such as Wages Expense and Rent Expense. Cash outflows for operating activities also include cash payments in the form of interest and taxes expense. Think of the items listed on an income statement; include merchandise purchases and the Operating Expenses (Selling and General) section, then refer to the Other Expenses section to include interest expense.

Incidentally, when you think about the income statement, you find the account Gain on Disposal of Plant and Equipment listed in the Other Income section and the account Loss on Disposal of Plant and Equipment listed in the Other Expenses section. These items generally arise because of investing activities; consequently, they are included with the sale or purchase of plant and equipment in the Investing Activities section.

Investing Activities

Investing activities include (1) buying and selling plant and equipment (long-term assets); (2) acquiring and selling investments other than cash equivalents; and (3) making and collecting loans. *Cash inflows* include the cash received from selling plant and equipment, from selling investments, and from collecting loans. *Cash outflows* include cash paid to purchase plant and equipment, cash invested in another corporation's stocks or bonds, and cash loaned to borrowers.

Financing activities include cash inflows from the sale of common or preferred stock or from the issuance of debt. Cash outflows from financing activities may be used to reacquire stock, to repay debt, or to pay dividends.

Financing Activities

Financing activities include cash transactions that involve borrowing from or repaying creditors, as well as additional cash investments from owners and transactions that reduce owners' investments. *Cash inflows* include proceeds received from short- or long-term borrowing (issuing notes or bonds) and those from issuing stock for cash. *Cash outflows* include repayments of loans (notes and bonds) and payments to owners, including personal withdrawals and cash dividends. Figure 1 illustrates the classification of cash inflows and outflows.

Classifying cash flows into three types of activities helps readers of financial statements interpret cash flow data. For example, in the following table, Companies A, B, and C are similar companies operating in the same industry. Each company has a positive cash flow.

	Company		
Positive Cash Flow	**A**	**B**	**C**
Net cash flows from operating activities: net sales, less cost of goods sold, less operating expenses (excluding depreciation), plus interest and dividend income, less interest expense and taxes	$180,000	0	0
Cash flows from investing activities: sale of equipment for cash	0	$210,000	0
Cash flows from financing activities: borrowing from a bank	0	0	$240,000
Net increase in cash	$180,000	$210,000	$240,000

If you were considering investing or loaning money, which company would you choose? If your decision were based only on these data, you would definitely select Company A. Company A's cash came from operating activities that can be expected to generate new cash during future years. Company B's cash came from the sale of equipment, which is a "one-shot deal." If the firm

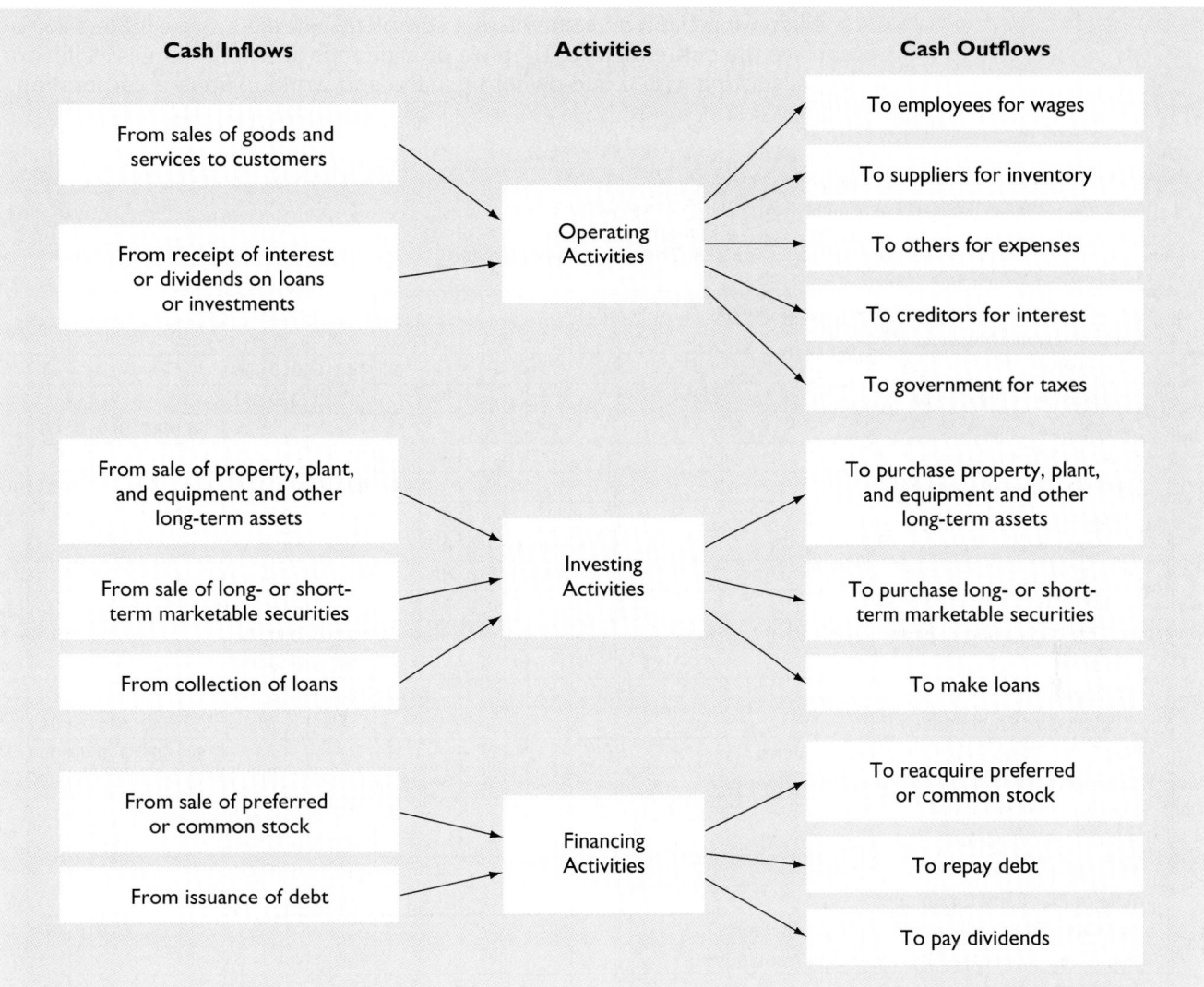

FIGURE 1

is planning to stay in business, it is not likely to generate cash regularly from this source in the future. Company C's cash came from borrowing, and the principal and interest will have to be paid in the future, resulting in a future drain on cash.

FORM OF THE STATEMENT OF CASH FLOWS

Objective 5

Calculate amounts of cash inflows and outflows involving operating, investing, and financing activities.

The statement of cash flows is divided into these three categories: operating activities, followed by investing activities, followed by financing activities. Within each activity, cash inflows and outflows are shown separately. For example, suppose that a company sells its used equipment for $5,000 in cash. Next, the company turns around and buys new equipment for $30,000, paying cash. Under investing activities, the sale of equipment, $5,000, is listed as an inflow of cash. The purchase of equipment, $30,000, is listed as an outflow of cash.

First, we present an example of a complete statement of cash flows so you can see the entire picture. Then we provide four other companies as illustrations, starting with a one-owner business and working up to a corporation.

Francis Corporation
Statement of Cash Flows
For Year Ended December 31, 2001

Cash Flows from (used by) Operating Activities:			
Cash Receipts from:			
Customers		$1 440 000 00	
Interest and Dividends		6 000 00	
Total Cash Receipts			$1 446 000 00
Cash Payments for:			
Merchandise Purchases		$ 520 000 00	
Operating Expenses:			
Employees	$ 190 000 00		
Supplies	14 000 00		
Insurance	3 000 00		
Total Operating Expenses		207 000 00	
Interest		20 000 00	
Income Tax		93 000 00	
Total Cash Payments			840 000 00
Net Cash Flows from Operating Activities			$ 606 000 00
Cash Flows from (used by) Investing Activities:			
Purchase of Investments		$ (10 000 00)	
Sale of Investments		20 000 00	
Purchase of Plant and Equipment		(30 000 00)	
Sale of Plant and Equipment		5 000 00	
Net Cash Flows used by Investing Activities			(15 000 00)
Cash Flows from (used by) Financing Activities:			
Issuance of Note		$ 10 000 00	
Issuance of Bonds		210 000 00	
Repayment of Bonds		(60 000 00)	
Issuance of Common Stock		140 000 00	
Payment of Dividends		(50 000 00)	
Net Cash Flows from Financing Activities			250 000 00
Net Increase (Decrease) in Cash			$ 841 000 00

■ ■ ■

FYI

The final pronouncement of SFAS No. 95 states that companies are encouraged to use the direct method, which is recognized as being more informative.

Actually, the statement of cash flows may be presented using either of two methods: the direct method and the indirect method. The FASB recommends the direct method, although the indirect method is also acceptable. **The direct method primarily involves converting each amount recorded on the income statement from the accrual basis to the cash basis.** The direct method shows the specific sources and uses of cash during a fiscal period.

The indirect method relies on a comparative balance sheet and uses the changes in the accounts to convert net income determined on the accrual basis to the cash basis. A comparative balance sheet presents totals for two years along with the amount of increase or decrease from the first to the second year.

DEVELOPING THE STATEMENT OF CASH FLOWS

Objective 6

Prepare a statement of cash flows using the direct method.

To describe the development of the statement of cash flows, we need the company's three basic financial statements for the present fiscal period, and its balance sheet at the end of the previous fiscal period (which is the same as the balance sheet at the beginning of the present fiscal period). From the balance sheets at the beginning and end of the fiscal period, we can compile a comparative balance sheet listing the increases and decreases in all accounts for each of our illustrations.

Illustration 1

Remember!

The three categories of cash flows relate to the three sections of the statement of cash flows: operating, investing, and financing activities.

Our first illustration shows conversions of Incomes from Services, Wages Expense, Supplies Expense, Insurance Expense, Depreciation Expense, and Drawing into cash flows. Nye Shoe Repair operates on a modified cash basis, in which revenue is counted only when it is received in cash and expenses are counted only when they are paid in cash. However, in keeping with Internal Revenue Service regulations, the firm makes adjusting entries for supplies used, insurance expired, and depreciation. The financial statements for Nye Shoe Repair are presented here.

Nye Shoe Repair
Income Statement
For Year Ended December 31, 2001

Revenue:		
Income from Services		$49 540 00
Expenses:		
Wages Expense	$12 000 00	
Supplies Expense	1 600 00	
Insurance Expense	240 00	
Depreciation Expense	13 200 00	
Total Expenses		27 040 00
Net Income		$22 500 00

Nye Shoe Repair
Statement of Owner's Equity
For Year Ended December 31, 2001

J. A. Nye, Capital, January 1, 2001		$41 200 00
Net Income	$22 500 00	
Less Withdrawals	20 000 00	
Increase in Capital		2 500 00
J. A. Nye, Capital, December 31, 2001		$43 700 00

Nye Shoe Repair
Comparative Balance Sheet
December 31, 2001 and December 31, 2000

	2001	2000	INCREASE OR (DECREASE)
Assets			
Cash	$16 4 5 0 00	$ 7 8 0 00	$15 6 7 0 00
Supplies	9 7 0 00	7 0 0 00	2 7 0 00
Prepaid Insurance	2 8 0 00	5 2 0 00	(2 4 0 00)
Equipment	50 0 0 0 00	50 0 0 0 00	0 00
Less Accumulated Depreciation	(24 0 0 0 00)	(10 8 0 0 00)	(13 2 0 0 00)
Total Assets	$43 7 0 0 00	$41 2 0 0 00	$ 2 5 0 0 00
Owner's Equity			
J. A. Nye, Capital	$43 7 0 0 00	$41 2 0 0 00	$ 2 5 0 0 00
Total Owner's Equity	$43 7 0 0 00	$41 2 0 0 00	$ 2 5 0 0 00

Remember!

Amounts in parentheses represent decreases.

Note the $15,670 increase in Cash in the comparative balance sheet ($16,450 − $780). The purpose of the statement of cash flows is to show how this increase in Cash came about ("where got, where gone"). In essence, the company's income statement must be converted from a modified cash basis to a pure cash basis.

Cash Flows from Operating Activities: Convert Revenue and Expenses to Cash Basis

1. **Convert Income from Services to Cash Receipts from Customers.** Since Nye Shoe Repair records revenue only when it is received in cash, the $49,540 listed as Income from Services on the income statement is the exact amount of cash received.

2. **Convert Wages Expense to Cash Payments to Employees.** Since Nye Shoe Repair records wages expense only when employees are paid, the $12,000 listed as Wages Expense on the income statement is the exact amount of cash paid.

3. **Convert Supplies Expense to Cash Payments for Supplies.** During 2001, Supplies increased from $700 to $970. Evidently, Nye Shoe Repair bought $270 more supplies than it used up during the year. So $270 more in cash was paid out than the $1,600 listed as Supplies Expense on the income statement. We calculate the cash payments like this:

Operating activities include cash inflows from selling goods and services to customers. This income has to be converted to a cash basis. Employee wages also have to be converted from Wages Expense to Cash Payments to Employees.

Supplies Expense	$1,600
+ Ending Supplies	970
= Total	$2,570
− Beginning Supplies	700
= Cash Payments for Supplies	$1,870

4. **Convert Insurance Expense to Cash Payments for Insurance.** During 2001, Prepaid Insurance decreased from $520 to $280. Evidently, Nye Shoe Repair did not buy any more insurance; instead, part of the prepaid insurance simply expired during the year. In other words, the company did not

pay any cash out for additional insurance. It simply used up what it had, so the $240 listed as Insurance Expense on the income statement did not cost the firm any cash. We calculate the cash payment like this:

Insurance Expense	$240
+ Ending Prepaid Insurance	280
= Total	$520
− Beginning Prepaid Insurance	520
= Cash Payments for Insurance	$ 0

5. **Convert Depreciation Expense to Cash Payments for Depreciation.** Because the $13,200 listed on the income statement as Depreciation Expense was not paid to anyone, it does not involve cash. Consequently, it is eliminated as an expense; depreciation is not recorded on a statement of cash flows.

Cash Flows from Investing Activities Investing activities are concerned with changes in plant and equipment. The balance of the Equipment account has not changed during the year. However, the balance of Accumulated Depreciation has gone from $10,800 to $24,000. This $13,200 change is accounted for by recording $13,200 as Depreciation Expense on the income statement. This amount is not paid to anyone. Since this is the only change we have, we can say that there have been no cash transactions involving investing activities.

Cash Flows from Financing Activities Financing activities include additions to or reductions in owner's equity. On the statement of owner's equity, we note a $20,000 withdrawal, which we assume is in the form of cash. The withdrawal results in a decrease in cash. We can easily check our assumption that the withdrawals involved cash by reviewing the transactions affecting the J. A. Nye, Drawing, account. Because there were no additional changes reported on the statement of owner's equity, we have gathered all the information we need to prepare our statement of cash flows for Nye Shoe Repair. Here it is:

Nye Shoe Repair
Statement of Cash Flows
For Year Ended December 31, 2001

Cash Flows from (used by) Operating Activities:			
Cash Receipts from Customers			$49 5 4 0 00
Cash Payments for Operating Expenses:			
Employees	$ 12 0 0 0 00		
Supplies	1 8 7 0 00		
Total Cash Payments		13 8 7 0 00	
Net Cash Flows from Operating Activities		$35 6 7 0 00	
Cash Flows from (used by) Financing Activities:			
Payment of Personal Withdrawals	$ (20 0 0 0 00)		
Net Cash Flows used by Financing Activities		(20 0 0 0 00)	
Net Increase (Decrease) in Cash		$15 6 7 0 00	

Summary of the Conversions in Illustration 1

- **For Prepaid Expenses** Prepaid expenses include items such as Supplies and Prepaid Insurance.

  Amount of the Expense Listed on the Income Statement + Ending Balance of the Prepaid Expense Account − Beginning Balance of the Prepaid Expense Account

- Each expense is listed individually in the operating expenses section under Cash Flows from (used by) Operating Activities.

- **For Depreciation** The amount of depreciation expense listed on the income statement is canceled out or eliminated.

- **For Personal Cash Withdrawals** The amount taken from the statement of owner's equity is listed as a negative amount (used by) under Cash Flows from (used by) Financing Activities.

Illustration 2

Remember!

The accrual basis means that revenue is recognized when it is earned, and expenses are recognized when they are incurred.

Our second illustration shows the conversion of Income from Services, Wages Expense, Supplies Expense, Depreciation Expense, purchase of equipment, and withdrawal. Mellon Company is a one-owner service business operating on the accrual basis. The financial statements for Mellon Company are presented here.

Mellon Company
Income Statement
For Year Ended December 31, 2001

Revenue:			
Income from Services			$70 0 0 0 00
Expenses:			
Wages Expense	$32 0 0 0 00		
Supplies Expense	4 0 0 0 00		
Depreciation Expense	5 0 0 0 00		
Total Expenses		41 0 0 0 00	
Net Income		$29 0 0 0 00	

Mellon Company
Statement of Owner's Equity
For Year Ended December 31, 2001

S. L. Mellon, Capital, January 1, 2001			$21 0 0 0 00
Net Income	$29 0 0 0 00		
Less Withdrawals	27 0 0 0 00		
Increase in Capital		2 0 0 0 00	
S. L. Mellon, Capital, December 31, 2001		$23 0 0 0 00	

Mellon Company
Comparative Balance Sheet
December 31, 2001 and December 31, 2000

	2001	2000	INCREASE OR (DECREASE)
Assets			
Cash	$ 7 3 7 0 00	$ 3 0 0 0 00	$4 3 7 0 00
Accounts Receivable	10 4 0 0 00	8 4 0 0 00	2 0 0 0 00
Supplies	9 3 0 00	1 0 0 0 00	(7 0 00)
Equipment	22 2 0 0 00	21 6 0 0 00	6 0 0 00
Less Accumulated Depreciation	(15 0 0 0 00)	(10 0 0 0 00)	(5 0 0 0 00)
Total Assets	$25 9 0 0 00	$24 0 0 0 00	$1 9 0 0 00
Liabilities			
Accounts Payable	$ 2 7 0 0 00	$ 2 7 0 0 00	$ 0 00
Wages Payable	2 0 0 00	3 0 0 00	(1 0 0 00)
Total Liabilities	$ 2 9 0 0 00	$ 3 0 0 0 00	$(1 0 0 00)
Owner's Equity			
S. L. Mellon, Capital	23 0 0 0 00	21 0 0 0 00	2 0 0 0 00
Total Liabilities and Owner's Equity	$25 9 0 0 00	$24 0 0 0 00	$1 9 0 0 00

Note the $4,370 increase in Cash shown in the comparative balance sheet ($7,370 − $3,000). To explain this increase, we must first convert the income statement of Mellon Company from the accrual basis to the cash basis. Then we look over the statement of owner's equity and the comparative balance sheet to note any possible cash received or paid out that has not shown up in the conversion of the income statement.

Cash Flows from Operating Activities

1. **Convert Income from Services to Cash Receipts from Customers.** Income from Services is in the form of cash and customer charge accounts. During 2001, Accounts Receivable increased from $8,400 to $10,400. Evidently, $2,000 more was recorded in the charge accounts than was collected in cash. Starting with the $70,000 listed as Income from Services on the income statement, we say that we collected the beginning balance of Accounts Receivable ($8,400) and did not collect the ending balance of Accounts Receivable ($10,400). The amount of cash received from customers is calculated as

Income from Services	$70,000
+ Beginning Accounts Receivable	8,400
= Total	$78,400
− Ending Accounts Receivable	10,400
= Cash Receipts from Customers	$68,000

Here's another way to picture the situation. Assume the company collects its beginning Accounts Receivable first. Next, of the $70,000 listed on the income statement as Income from Services, all but $10,400 (the ending balance of Accounts Receivable) was collected. The calculation looks like this:

		or		
Beginning Accounts Receivable	$ 8,400		Beginning Accounts Receivable	$ 8,400
+ Income from Services	70,000		+ Cash Income from Services ($70,000 − $10,400)	59,600
= Total	$78,400		= Cash Receipts from Customers	$68,000
− Ending Accounts Receivable	10,400			
= Cash Receipts from Customers	$68,000			

Remember!

You need the other three financial statements in order to prepare a statement of cash flows.

2. **Convert Wages Expense to Cash Payments to Employees.** Start with the amount shown on the income statement as Wages Expense, $32,000. During the first part of the year, Mellon Company also paid out to its employees the amount shown as the beginning balance of Wages Payable, $300. We add this amount to the $32,000. However, of the $32,000 listed as Wages Expense, $200 was not paid to the employees. The calculation for the amount paid in cash to employees looks like this:

Wages Expense	$32,000
+ Beginning Wages Payable	300
= Total	$32,300
− Ending Wages Payable	200
= Cash Payments to Employees	$32,100

Here's another way to picture the situation. Assume the company pays its beginning Wages Payable first. Next, of the $32,000 listed on the income statement as Wages Expense, all but $200 (the ending balance of Wages Payable) was paid. The calculation looks like this:

		or		
Beginning Wages Payable	$ 300		Beginning Wages Payable	$ 300
+ Wages Expense	32,000		+ Cash Wages Expense ($32,000 − $200)	31,800
= Total	$32,300		= Cash Payments to Employees	$32,100
− Ending Wages Payable	200			
= Cash Payments to Employees	$32,100			

3. **Convert Supplies Expense to Cash Payments for Supplies.** During 2001, Supplies decreased from $1,000 to $930. Evidently, Mellon Company bought fewer supplies than it used during the year. In other words, Mellon Company had to dip into its inventory of supplies to the extent of $70. So the $4,000 listed as Supplies Expense was $70 more than the amount of cash paid out. The calculation looks like this:

Supplies Expense	$4,000
+ Ending Supplies	930
= Total	$4,930
− Beginning Supplies	1,000
= Cash Payments for Supplies	$3,930

4. **Convert Depreciation Expense to Cash Payments for Depreciation.** Since no cash is involved in Depreciation Expense, it is eliminated.

Cash Flows from Investing Activities Look for clues to identify investment activities by examining changes in plant and equipment accounts. The comparative balance sheet shows that the balance of the Equipment account has increased from $21,600 to $22,200. When we review the Equipment ledger account, we see the posting reference for the one entry recorded this period. When we trace the entry to the journal page, we find a debit to Equipment for $600 and a credit to Cash for $600. Since this was a cash purchase, we list the purchase of equipment for $600 on the statement of cash flows as an outflow of cash.

Cash Flows from Financing Activities On the statement of owner's equity, we note a $27,000 personal withdrawal. After reviewing the journal entries affecting the S. L. Mellon, Drawing, account, we see that the $27,000 was paid in cash. On the statement of cash flows, $27,000 is listed as an outflow of cash. Here's the statement of cash flows for Mellon Company:

Mellon Company
Statement of Cash Flows
For Year Ended December 31, 2001

Cash Flows from (used by) Operating Activities:			
Cash Receipts from Customers			$68 000 00
Cash Payments for Operating Expenses:			
Employees	$ 32 100 00		
Supplies	3 930 00		
Total Cash Payments		36 030 00	
Net Cash Flows from Operating Activities		$31 970 00	
Cash Flows from (used by) Investing Activities:			
Purchase of Equipment	$ (600 00)		
Net Cash Flows used by Investing Activities		(600 00)	
Cash Flows from (used by) Financing Activities:			
Payment of Personal Withdrawals	$ (27 000 00)		
Net Cash Flows used by Financing Activities		(27 000 00)	
Net Increase (Decrease) in Cash		$ 4 370 00	

Summary of the Additional Conversions in Illustration 2

- **For Revenue Involving Accounts Receivable—like Income from Services**

  Amount of Revenue Listed on the Income Statement + Beginning Accounts Receivable − Ending Accounts Receivable.

- **For Accrued Expenses and Their Respective Liabilities—like Wages Expense and Wages Payable**

  Amount of Expense Listed on the Income Statement + Beginning Wages Payable − Ending Wages Payable.

- **For Purchases of Equipment for Cash** The amount credited to the Cash account in the journal entry for the transaction is listed as a negative amount (used by) under Cash Flows from (used by) Investing Activities.

Illustration 3

Our third example shows conversion of net sales, Income from Services, delivered cost of purchases, Salary Expense, Rent Expense, Depreciation Expense, Supplies Expense, Insurance Expense, and withdrawal. Ives Company is a one-owner merchandising business operating on the accrual basis. The financial statements for Ives Company are presented here.

Ives Company
Income Statement
For Year Ended December 31, 2000

Net Sales		$ 700 0 0 0 00
Cost of Goods Sold:		
Merchandise Inventory, January 1, 2000	$ 126 0 0 0 00	
Delivered Cost of Purchases	514 0 0 0 00	
Goods Available for Sale	$ 640 0 0 0 00	
Less Merchandise Inventory, December 31, 2000	130 0 0 0 00	
Cost of Goods Sold		510 0 0 0 00
Gross Profit		$ 190 0 0 0 00
Operating Expenses:		
Salary Expense	$ 100 0 0 0 00	
Rent Expense	20 0 0 0 00	
Depreciation Expense, Equipment	22 0 0 0 00	
Supplies Expense	1 6 0 0 00	
Insurance Expense	4 0 0 00	
Total Operating Expenses		144 0 0 0 00
Net Income		$ 46 0 0 0 00

Ives Company
Statement of Owner's Equity
For Year Ended December 31, 2000

R. A. Ives, Capital, January 1, 2000		$ 233 2 0 0 00
Net Income	$46 0 0 0 00	
Less Withdrawals	50 0 0 0 00	
Decrease in Capital		4 0 0 0 00
R. A. Ives, Capital, December 31, 2000		$ 229 2 0 0 00

Ives Company
Comparative Balance Sheet
December 31, 2000 and December 31, 1999

	2000	1999	INCREASE OR (DECREASE)
Assets			
Cash	$ 31 4 0 0 00	$ 35 0 0 0 00	$ (3 6 0 0 00)
Accounts Receivable	45 6 0 0 00	33 0 0 0 00	12 6 0 0 00
Merchandise Inventory	130 0 0 0 00	126 0 0 0 00	4 0 0 0 00
Supplies	6 0 0 00	9 0 0 00	(3 0 0 00)
Prepaid Insurance	1 7 0 0 00	5 0 0 00	1 2 0 0 00
Equipment	136 6 0 0 00	136 6 0 0 00	0 00
Less Accumulated Depreciation	(62 0 0 0 00)	(40 0 0 0 00)	(22 0 0 0 00)
Total Assets	$ 283 9 0 0 00	$ 292 0 0 0 00	$ (8 1 0 0 00)
Liabilities			
Accounts Payable	$ 51 5 0 0 00	$ 56 0 0 0 00	$ (4 5 0 0 00)
Salaries Payable	3 2 0 0 00	2 8 0 0 00	4 0 0 00
Total Liabilities	$ 54 7 0 0 00	$ 58 8 0 0 00	$ (4 1 0 0 00)
Owner's Equity			
R. A. Ives, Capital	229 2 0 0 00	233 2 0 0 00	(4 0 0 0 00)
Total Liabilities and Owner's Equity	$ 283 9 0 0 00	$ 292 0 0 0 00	$ (8 1 0 0 00)

Remember!

If Accounts Receivable has *increased* between the beginning and the end of the fiscal period, cash receipts from customers will be *less* than the revenue listed on the income statement. If Accounts Receivable has *decreased* between the beginning and the end of the fiscal period, cash receipts from customers will be *more* than the revenue listed on the income statement.

Remember!

If Accounts Payable has *increased* between the beginning and the end of the fiscal period, cash payments for merchandise purchases will be *less* than the delivered cost of purchases listed on the income statement. If Accounts Payable has *decreased* between the beginning and the end of the fiscal period, cash payments for merchandise purchases will be *more* than the delivered cost of purchases listed on the income statement.

Note the $3,600 decrease in cash. Let's start from the top.

Cash Flows from Operating Activities

1. **Convert Net Sales to Cash Receipts from Customers.** During 2000, Accounts Receivable increased from $33,000 to $45,600. Evidently, $12,600 more was recorded in the customer charge accounts than was collected in cash. The amount of cash received from customers is calculated like this:

Net Sales	$700,000
+ Beginning Accounts Receivable	33,000
= Total	$733,000
− Ending Accounts Receivable	45,600
= Cash Receipts from Customers	$687,400

2. **Convert Delivered Cost of Purchases to Cash Payments for Merchandise Purchases.** During 2000, Accounts Payable decreased from $56,000 to $51,500. Evidently, $4,500 more was paid in cash than was recorded as amounts owed to creditors. Starting with the $514,000 listed as Delivered Cost of Purchases on the income statement, we'll say that we paid the beginning Accounts Payable ($56,000) and did not pay the ending Accounts Payable ($51,500). The amount of cash paid to creditors is calculated in the following manner.

Delivered Cost of Purchases	$514,000
+ Beginning Accounts Payable	56,000
= Total	$570,000
− Ending Accounts Payable	51,500
= Cash Payments for Merchandise Purchases	$518,500

Here's another way to analyze the situation. Assume the company pays its beginning balance of Accounts Payable first. Next, of the $514,000 listed on the income statement as Delivered Cost of Purchases, all but $51,500 (the ending balance of Accounts Payable) was paid out. The calculation looks like this:

Beginning Accounts Payable	$ 56,000	or	Beginning Accounts Payable	$ 56,000
+ Delivered Cost of Purchases	514,000		+ Delivered Cost of Purchases Paid in Cash	
			($514,000 − $51,500)	462,500
= Total	$570,000		= Cash Payments for Merchandise Purchases	$518,500
− Ending Accounts Payable	51,500			
= Cash Payments for Merchandise Purchases	$518,500			

Operating Expenses In this section of the statement of cash flows, each expense is listed in the same order as it appears on the income statement.

1. **Convert Salary Expense to Cash Payments to Employees.** On the income statement, Salary Expense is $100,000. On the comparative balance sheet, Salaries Payable increased from $2,800 to $3,200. Evidently, $400 less than the $100,000 listed on the income statement was paid out in cash to employees. The calculation looks like this:

Salary Expense	$100,000
+ Beginning Salaries Payable	2,800
= Total	$102,800
− Ending Salaries Payable	3,200
= Cash Payments to Employees	$ 99,600

2. **Convert Rent Expense to Cash Payments for Rent.** Since there is no amount listed on the balance sheet as Prepaid Rent or Rent Payable, we can conclude that the $20,000 listed on the income statement was indeed paid in cash.

3. **Convert Depreciation Expense to Cash Payments for Depreciation.** Because the amount listed as Depreciation Expense is not paid to anyone, no cash is involved. Depreciation expense is a noncash expense—ignore it.

4. **Convert Supplies Expense to Cash Payments for Supplies.** During 2000, Supplies decreased from $900 to $600. Evidently, Ives Company used up $300 more in supplies than it bought during the year. The amount is listed as Supplies Expense on the income statement, $1,600, but $300 of that expense resulted from dipping into the company's stock of supplies. The calculation looks like this:

Supplies Expense	$1,600
+ Ending Supplies	600
= Total	$2,200
− Beginning Supplies	900
= Cash Payments for Supplies	$1,300

5. **Convert Insurance Expense to Cash Payments for Insurance.** During 2000, Prepaid Insurance increased from $500 to $1,700. Evidently, Ives Company bought more insurance than was used up (expired) during the year. So $1,200 more in cash than the $400 listed as Insurance Expense on the income statement was paid out. The calculation looks like this:

Insurance Expense	$ 400
+ Ending Prepaid Insurance	1,700
= Total	$2,100
− Beginning Prepaid Insurance	500
= Cash Payments for Insurance	$1,600

Cash Flows from Investing Activities There were no changes in the Equipment account balance between the beginning and end of the fiscal period. However, the Accumulated Depreciation account balance increased by the amount of the year's depreciation expense. No equipment was bought or sold, so no cash is involved.

Cash Flows from Financing Activities On the Statement of Owner's Equity, we note withdrawals of $50,000. We trace through the entries involving the Drawing account and note entries debiting R. A. Ives, Drawing, and crediting Cash for a total of $50,000 each. We record $50,000 as an outflow of cash. Putting these cash conversions all together, we have the statement of cash flows for Ives Company.

Ives Company
Statement of Cash Flows
For Year Ended December 31, 2000

Cash Flows from (used by) Operating Activities:			
Cash Receipts from Customers			$ 687 400 00
Cash Payments for:			
Merchandise Purchases		$ 518 500 00	
Operating Expenses:			
Employees	$99 600 00		
Rent	20 000 00		
Supplies	1 300 00		
Insurance	1 600 00		
Total Operating Expenses		122 500 00	
Total Cash Payments			641 000 00
Net Cash Flows from Operating Activities			$ 46 400 00
Cash Flows from (used by) Financing Activities:			
Payment of Personal Withdrawals		$ (50 000 00)	
Net Cash Flows used by Financing Activities			(50 000 00)
Net Increase (Decrease) in Cash			$ (3 600 00)

Summary of Additional Conversions in Illustration 3

- **Handling Delivered Cost of Purchases Involving Accounts Payable** This is figured as the amount of Delivered Cost of Purchases listed on the income statement + Beginning Accounts Payable − Ending Accounts Payable.

Illustration 4

Our final example shows the conversion of net sales, delivered cost of purchases, Wages Expense, Rent Expense, Depreciation Expense, Supplies Expense, Property Tax Expense, Insurance Expense, Interest Expense, sale of equipment, issuance of note payable (not a bank loan), issuance of stock, and payment of dividends into cash flows. Dean Corporation is a merchandising business operating on an accrual basis.

Dean Corporation
Income Statement
For Year Ended December 31, 2002

Revenue from Sales:			
Sales		$ 620 0 0 0 00	
Less Sales Returns and Allowances		6 0 0 0 00	
Net Sales			$ 614 0 0 0 00
Cost of Goods Sold:			
Merchandise Inventory, January 1, 2002		$ 224 0 0 0 00	
Purchases	$ 426 0 0 0 00		
Less Purchases Returns and Allowances	3 0 0 0 00		
Net Purchases	$ 423 0 0 0 00		
Add Freight In	47 0 0 0 00		
Delivered Cost of Purchases		470 0 0 0 00	
Goods Available for Sale		$ 694 0 0 0 00	
Less Merchandise Inventory, December 31, 2002		260 0 0 0 00	
Cost of Goods Sold			434 0 0 0 00
Gross Profit			$ 180 0 0 0 00
Operating Expenses:			
Wages Expense		$ 123 0 0 0 00	
Rent Expense		20 0 0 0 00	
Depreciation Expense, Equipment		24 0 0 0 00	
Supplies Expense		2 0 0 0 00	
Property Tax Expense		2 0 0 0 00	
Insurance Expense		1 0 0 0 00	
Total Operating Expenses			172 0 0 0 00
Income from Operations			$ 8 0 0 0 00
Other Income:			
Gain on Disposal of Plant and Equipment		$ 5 0 0 0 00	
Other Expenses:			
Interest Expense		26 0 0 0 00	(21 0 0 0 00)
Net Loss			$ (13 0 0 0 00)

Dean Corporation
Statement of Retained Earnings
For Year Ended December 31, 2002

Retained Earnings, January 1, 2002		$94 6 0 0 00
Less: Net Loss for the Year	$13 0 0 0 00	
Cash Dividends Declared	16 0 0 0 00	
Decrease in Retained Earnings		29 0 0 0 00
Retained Earnings, December 31, 2002		$65 6 0 0 00

Dean Corporation
Comparative Balance Sheet
December 31, 2002 and December 31, 2001

	2002	2001	INCREASE OR (DECREASE)
Assets			
Cash	$ 41 3 0 0 00	$ 33 4 0 0 00	$ 7 9 0 0 00
Accounts Receivable	58 4 0 0 00	69 0 0 0 00	(10 6 0 0 00)
Merchandise Inventory	260 0 0 0 00	224 0 0 0 00	36 0 0 0 00
Supplies	1 0 0 00	5 0 0 00	(4 0 0 00)
Prepaid Rent	3 0 0 0 00	3 0 0 0 00	0 00
Prepaid Insurance	9 0 0 00	4 0 0 00	5 0 0 00
Equipment	114 0 0 0 00	143 0 0 0 00	(29 0 0 0 00)
Less Accumulated Depreciation	(47 0 0 0 00)	(35 0 0 0 00)	(12 0 0 0 00)
Total Assets	$ 430 7 0 0 00	$ 438 3 0 0 00	$ (7 6 0 0 00)
Liabilities			
Accounts Payable	$ 31 6 0 0 00	$ 42 5 0 0 00	$ (10 9 0 0 00)
Notes Payable	24 0 0 0 00	0 00	24 0 0 0 00
Wages Payable	1 0 0 00	4 0 0 00	(3 0 0 00)
Dividends Payable	2 0 0 0 00	3 0 0 0 00	(1 0 0 0 00)
Property Tax Payable	3 0 0 00	1 0 0 00	2 0 0 00
Interest Payable	6 0 0 00	2 0 0 00	4 0 0 00
Total Liabilities	$ 58 6 0 0 00	$ 46 2 0 0 00	$ 12 4 0 0 00
Stockholders' Equity			
Common Stock	$ 306 5 0 0 00	$ 297 5 0 0 00	$ 9 0 0 0 00
Retained Earnings	65 6 0 0 00	94 6 0 0 00	(29 0 0 0 00)
Total Stockholders' Equity	$ 372 1 0 0 00	$ 392 1 0 0 00	$ (20 0 0 0 00)
Total Liabilities and Stockholders' Equity	$ 430 7 0 0 00	$ 438 3 0 0 00	$ (7 6 0 0 00)

Note the $7,900 increase in Cash. In spite of having a $13,000 net loss for the year, Dean Corporation winds up with a positive cash flow. Let's find out how this situation came about.

Cash Flows from Operating Activities

1. **Convert Net Sales to Cash Receipts from Customers.** During 2002, Accounts Receivable decreased from $69,000 to $58,400. Evidently, $10,600 more was collected in cash than was recorded as net sales. The calculation looks like this:

Net Sales	$614,000
+ Beginning Accounts Receivable	69,000
= Total	$683,000
− Ending Accounts Receivable	58,400
= Cash Receipts from Customers	$624,600

2. **Convert Delivered Cost of Purchases to Cash Payments for Merchandise Purchases.** During 2002, Accounts Payable decreased from $42,500 to

$31,600. Evidently, $10,900 more in cash was paid for merchandise purchases than the amount listed as delivered cost of purchases on the income statement. The amount of cash paid to creditors is calculated like this:

Delivered Cost of Purchases	$470,000
+ Beginning Accounts Payable	42,500
= Total	$512,500
− Ending Accounts Payable	31,600
= Cash Payments for Merchandise Purchases	$480,900

Operating and Other Expenses In preparing this section of the statement of cash flows, list each expense in its order shown on the income statement.

1. **Convert Wages Expense to Cash Payments to Employees.** During 2002, Wages Payable decreased from $400 to $100. Evidently, $300 more in cash was paid to employees than is recorded as Wages Expense. The calculation looks like this:

Wages Expense	$123,000
+ Beginning Wages Payable	400
= Total	$123,400
− Ending Wages Payable	100
= Cash Payments to Employees	$123,300

2. **Convert Rent Expense to Cash Payments for Rent.** Since the balance of the Prepaid Rent account has not changed during the year, the $20,000 recorded as Rent Expense on the income statement was paid to the landlord.
3. **Convert Depreciation Expense, Equipment, to Cash Payments for Depreciation.** Depreciation expense is a noncash expense, so it is eliminated.
4. **Convert Supplies Expense to Cash Payments for Supplies.** During 2002, Supplies decreased from $500 to $100. Evidently, Dean Corporation used up $400 more in supplies than it bought. The calculation looks like this:

Supplies Expense	$2,000
+ Ending Supplies	100
= Total	$2,100
− Beginning Supplies	500
= Cash Payments for Supplies	$1,600

5. **Convert Property Tax Expense to Cash Payments for Property Tax.** During 2002, Property Tax Payable increased from $100 to $300. Evidently, $200 less was paid out in cash than is recorded as Property Tax Expense. The calculation looks like this:

Property Tax Expense	$2,000
+ Beginning Property Tax Payable	100
= Total	$2,100
− Ending Property Tax Payable	300
= Cash Payments for Property Tax Expense	$1,800

6. **Convert Insurance Expense to Cash Payments for Insurance.** During 2002, Prepaid Insurance increased from $400 to $900. Evidently, $500

more was paid in cash than is recorded as Insurance Expense. The calculation looks like this:

Insurance Expense	$1,000
+ Ending Prepaid Insurance	900
= Total	$1,900
− Beginning Prepaid Insurance	400
= Cash Payments for Insurance	$1,500

7. **Convert Interest Expense to Cash Payments for Interest.** During 2002, Interest Payable increased from $200 to $600. Evidently, $400 less was paid in cash than is recorded as Interest Expense on the income statement. The calculation looks like this:

Interest Expense	$26,000
+ Beginning Interest Payable	200
= Total	$26,200
− Ending Interest Payable	600
= Cash Payments for Interest	$25,600

FYI

Note that this situation is similar to the relationship between Wages Expense and Wages Payable.

Before we continue, we should mention that if Dean Corporation had reported income tax expense on its income statement, we would need to convert that amount using the process we've just described. The cash payments for income would be listed below the cash payments for interest on the statement of cash flows.

Cash Flows from Investing Activities

1. **Record Cash Receipts from the Sale of Equipment.** During 2002, Equipment decreased from $143,000 to $114,000. On the income statement, a Gain on Disposal of Plant and Equipment of $5,000 is listed in the Other Income section. In addition, Depreciation Expense, Equipment, of $24,000 is listed in the income statement. Examine the general ledger accounts and journals to reconstruct the transactions. The following entry is found in the general journal:

DATE		DESCRIPTION	POST. REF.	DEBIT	CREDIT
2002					
Jan.	3	Cash		22 0 0 0 00	
		Accumulated Depreciation,			
		Equipment		12 0 0 0 00	
		Equipment			29 0 0 0 00
		Gain on Disposal of Plant and			
		Equipment			5 0 0 0 00
		To record the sale of			
		equipment.			

By reconstructing the entries, we spot the debit to Cash of $22,000. We list sale of equipment, $22,000, as a positive cash flow.

Cash Flows from Financing Activities

1. **Convert Notes Payable to Cash Receipts from the Issuance of a Note.** During 2002, Notes Payable increased from $0 to $24,000. We must examine the general ledger account and journals to reconstruct the transaction(s). The following entry is found in the general journal:

GENERAL JOURNAL   PAGE _____

	DATE		DESCRIPTION	POST. REF.	DEBIT	CREDIT	
1	2002						1
2	Oct.	2	Cash		24 0 0 0 00		2
3			Notes Payable			24 0 0 0 00	3
4			Borrowed from County Bank.				4
5			Issued 120-day, 10 percent				5
6			note dated October 2.				6

We list the issuance of the note for $24,000 as a positive cash flow under Financing Activities.

2. **Convert Common Stock to Cash Receipts from the Issuance of Common Stock.** During 2002, Common Stock increased from $297,500 to $306,500. Examine the general ledger account and journals to reconstruct the transaction(s). The following entry is found in the general journal:

GENERAL JOURNAL   PAGE _____

	DATE		DESCRIPTION	POST. REF.	DEBIT	CREDIT	
1	2002						1
2	June	16	Cash		9 0 0 0 00		2
3			Common Stock			9 0 0 0 00	3
4			To record the sale of 900				4
5			shares of $10 par value				5
6			common stock at par.				6

We list the sale of common stock as a positive cash flow under Financing Activities.

3. **Convert Dividends to Cash Payments of Dividends.** On the statement of retained earnings, we note $16,000 listed as cash dividends. During 2002, Dividends Payable decreased from $3,000 to $2,000. Evidently, $1,000 more was paid in cash than is recorded as cash dividends. The calculation looks like this:

Cash Dividends Declared	$16,000
+ Beginning Dividends Payable	3,000
= Total	$19,000
− Ending Dividends Payable	2,000
= Cash Payments of Dividends	$17,000

Let's put all these conversions together in the correct format to make up the statement of cash flows for Dean Corporation.

Dean Corporation
Statement of Cash Flows
For Year Ended December 31, 2002

Cash Flows from (used by) Operating Activities:				
Cash Receipts from Customers				$ 624 6 0 0 00
Cash Payments for:				
Merchandise Purchases		$ 480 9 0 0 00		
Operating Expenses:				
Employees	$ 123 3 0 0 00			
Rent	20 0 0 0 00			
Supplies	1 6 0 0 00			
Property Tax	1 8 0 0 00			
Insurance	1 5 0 0 00			
Total Operating Expenses		148 2 0 0 00		
Interest		25 6 0 0 00		
Total Cash Payments			654 7 0 0 00	
Net Cash Flows (used by) Operating Activities			$ (30 1 0 0 00)	
Cash Flows from (used by) Investing Activities:				
Sale of Equipment		$ 22 0 0 0 00		
Net Cash Flows from Investing Activities			22 0 0 0 00	
Cash Flows from (used by) Financing Activities:				
Issuance of Note		$ 24 0 0 0 00		
Issuance of Common Stock		9 0 0 0 00		
Payments of Dividends		(17 0 0 0 00)		
Net Cash Flows from Financing Activities			16 0 0 0 00	
Net Increase (Decrease) in Cash			$ 7 9 0 0 00	

Summary of Conversions in Illustration 4

- **For Sale of Equipment for Cash** The amount debited to the Cash account in the journal entry for the transaction is listed as a positive amount under Cash Flows from (used by) Investing Activities.
- **For Accrued Liabilities—like Interest Expense and Interest Payable** This is figured like accrued wages: Amount of Interest Expense Listed on the Income Statement + Beginning Balance of Interest Payable − Ending Balance of Interest Payable.
- **For Issuance of a Note** The amount debited to the Cash account in the journal entry for the transaction is listed as a positive amount under Cash Flows from (used by) Financing Activities.
- **For Issuance of Common Stock** The amount debited to the Cash account in the journal entry for the transaction is listed as a positive amount under Cash Flows from (used by) Financing Activities.
- **For Cash Dividend Payments** This is also similar to accrued wages: Amount taken from the statement of retained earnings listed as Cash Dividends Declared + Beginning Balance of Dividends Payable − Ending Balance of Dividends Payable.

INTERPRETING THE STATEMENT OF CASH FLOWS

Remember!

The statement of cash flows shows why cash changed, whereas a comparative balance sheet shows only by how much cash has changed.

Interpretation of the statement of cash flows begins with the net cash flows from operating activities. Is the net cash flow a positive amount, and how does it compare with net income on the income statement? It is useful to note the net cash flows from operating activities to see if the company is covering its cash outflows for dividends listed in the Financing Activities section. It is also useful to examine the Investing and Financing Activities sections to determine if the company is expanding and how the expansion is being financed. If the expansion is being financed primarily by long-term debt, we can be certain that, unless the expansion produces more cash revenue or a reduction in cash expenses, cash flows from operating activities will decline in the future as interest payments are made.

Anyone who uses financial statements can gather a great deal of information from the statement of cash flows. Let's take a closer look at Dean Corporation's statement of cash flows to see what we can find out.

Benefits to Users

Managers, investors, and creditors all use the statement of cash flows to judge how a company is doing. What kinds of conclusions could they draw about Dean Corporation from studying its financial statements?

Evidently, Dean Corporation is in a shaky financial position. The $7,900 increase in cash is not consistent with the $13,000 net loss. Users of the statement of cash flows are interested in the company's ability to generate enough cash to pay its bills and pay dividends.

Because of limited information, we will simply cite observations and pose questions. The negative $30,100 Net Cash Flows used by Operating Activities is bad news indeed. The $624,600 of cash receipts from customers is more than offset by the $654,700 of cash payments for operating activities. Evidently, a note payable with a principal of $24,000 was issued. However, the interest rates were quite high, resulting in an excessive amount of interest payments. Is the merchandise inventory salable? If so, can it be worked down to generate more cash? The $22,000 generated from the sale of equipment is a one-shot transaction. Will the equipment have to be replaced? If so, how will it be financed?

Remember!

Working Capital = Current Assets − Current Liabilities

Current Ratio = Current Assets ÷ Current Liabilities

Although the company had a comfortable beginning credit balance of $94,600 in Retained Earnings ($81,600 after closing the net loss into Retained Earnings), the declaration and payment of cash dividends were simply not feasible under the circumstances. Actually, Dean Corporation had to borrow funds to pay its dividends. Although dividends resulted in a cash outflow of $17,000, this is well below the $25,600 cash outflow for interest payments. Despite the fact that interest payments are tax-deductible, whereas dividends are not, will Dean Corporation be better off selling stock in the future to finance expansion?

Remember!

Quick Ratio = Quick Assets ÷ Current Liabilities (Quick assets = Cash + Accounts Receivable + Marketable Securities)

By using additional analytical tools, some interesting facts are discovered. Dean Corporation's working capital is $305,100 ($363,700 − $58,600); its current ratio is 6.21:1 ($363,700 ÷ $58,600); and its quick ratio is 1.70:1 ($99,700 ÷ $58,600). However, the firm is still not generating enough cash to pay its bills. Incidentally, the return on stockholders' equity is a dismal negative.

SCHEDULE OF NONCASH INVESTING AND FINANCING TRANSACTIONS

A company occasionally engages in significant transactions that do not affect cash directly. For example, a corporation may issue a long-term mortgage for the purchase of land and building. Or it may issue common stock for the land and building. These transactions represent important investing and financing activities, but they would not show up on a statement of cash flows because they do not involve either cash receipts or cash payments. However, since these transactions will affect future cash flows, the Financial Accounting Standards Board has determined that they should be presented in a separate schedule on the statement of cash flows. An example of such a schedule is shown here.

Schedule of Noncash Investing and Financing Transactions					
Issue of Mortgage Payable for Building	$	100	0	0	0	00

In this way, readers of the statement of cash flows will have a complete picture of a company's investing and financing activities.

CHAPTER REVIEW

Review of Performance Objectives

1. Describe the statement of cash flows, and define *cash and cash equivalents*.

   The statement of cash flows explains the changes in cash and cash equivalents between the beginning and the end of a fiscal period. Cash equivalents are short-term (mature ninety days or less from the date acquired) investments in money market accounts, U.S. Treasury bills, and commercial paper. Commercial paper consists of promissory notes issued by corporations.

2. State the purpose of the statement of cash flows.

   The statement of cash flows provides a summary of information concerning a company's cash receipts and payments during a fiscal period. A secondary purpose is to provide information about a firm's investing and financing activities during a fiscal period.

3. State the uses of the statement of cash flows by management, investors, and creditors.

   The statement of cash flows is useful to management, and also to investors and creditors, in assessing or evaluating the liquidity of a business, including the ability of the business to generate future cash flows and to pay its debts and dividends.

4. Identify cash inflows and outflows as operating, investing, or financing activities.

   Cash flows are classified as operating activities, investing activities, or financing activities. Operating activities include the cash effects of transactions that enter into the determination of net income after income tax. Investing activities include cash flows involving the making and collecting of loans, the buying and selling of investments, and the buying and selling of plant and equipment. Financing activities include cash flows involving the selling or retiring of bonds, the issuing or paying of notes, the issuing of stock, and payments of personal withdrawals or dividends.

5. Calculate amounts of cash inflows and outflows involving operating, investing, and financing activities.

   To calculate cash flows from operating activities:

   - Cash Receipts from Customers

     Net Sales + Beginning Accounts Receivable − Ending Accounts Receivable

   - Cash Payments for Merchandise Purchases

   Delivered Cost of Purchases + Beginning Accounts Payable − Ending Accounts Payable

   To determine cash payments for operating expenses:

   - Cash Payments to Employees

     Wages Expense + Beginning Wages Payable − Ending Wages Payable

   - Cash Payments for Prepaid Expenses (e.g., Supplies, Prepaid Insurance)

     Supplies Expense + Ending Supplies − Beginning Supplies

   - Cash Payments for Interest

     Interest Expense + Beginning Interest Payable − Ending Interest Payable

   - Cash Payments for Income Tax

   Income Tax Expense + Beginning Income Tax Payable − Ending Income Tax Payable

   - Depreciation

     Depreciation Expense does not cost cash—it is eliminated.

   To calculate cash flows from investing activities or financing activities:

   Changes in the balances of plant and equipment, investments, long-term liabilities, and owner's or stockholders' equity may indicate possible cash inflows or outflows. The amounts of cash involved are determined by exposing the related journal entries.

   - Cash Payments of Dividends

   Cash Dividends Declared + Beginning Dividends Payable − Ending Dividends Payable

6. Prepare a statement of cash flows using the direct method.

   Preparing the statement of cash flows involves converting a company's financial statements from an accrual to a cash basis. Starting with a company's balance sheet at the beginning and end of the accounting period, along with the income statement and statement of owner's equity for the period ended, we compile a comparative balance sheet listing the increases and decreases in all accounts. Then we convert changes in account balances to cash flows using the calculations presented in the chapter.

Glossary

Cash equivalents Items included in the broad definition of cash. Included are short-term, highly liquid investments, such as money market accounts, U.S. Treasury bills, and commercial paper, having maturities with a maximum of ninety days from the date acquired. (842)

Financing activities A category on the statement of cash flows (involving inflows and outflows) that includes borrowing money or repaying loans and additional cash investments or reductions of owners' investments through cash dividends or personal withdrawals. (844)

Investing activities A category on the statement of cash flows (involving inflows and outflows) that includes the buying and selling of plant and equipment, the acquiring and selling of investments other than cash equivalents, and the making and collecting of loans. (844)

Operating activities A category on the statement of cash flows (involving inflows and outflows) that includes cash receipts from customers for the sale of merchandise and services, cash receipts from interest and dividends, cash payments for merchandise purchases, cash payments for operating expenses, cash payments for interest, and cash payments for income taxes. (843)

Statement of cash flows A financial statement that explains in detail how the balance of cash and cash equivalents has changed between the beginning and the end of a fiscal period. A schedule on the statement presents important noncash investing and financing activities that occurred during the same period. (842)

QUESTIONS, EXERCISES, AND PROBLEMS

Discussion Questions

1. What are the three categories listed on the statement of cash flows? Give two examples of cash flows from each category.

2. What is included in *cash* as the term is used in a statement of cash flows?

3. What are the purposes of the statement of cash flows?

4. What are the effects of the following items on cash flows from operating activities?

   a. An increase in Accounts Receivable, $16,000
   b. An increase in Interest Payable, $500
   c. Depreciation Expense, $93,000

5. In which of the three categories listed on a statement of cash flows would each of the following appear? Also, state for each item whether it represents a cash inflow or outflow.

   a. Cash purchase of land
   b. Cash payment of wages
   c. Cash payment of dividends
   d. Cash sale of investments
   e. Cash proceeds from issuing stock
   f. Cash payment of interest

6. Kelley Company sold equipment at a gain of $1,000. The equipment cost $47,000 and had accumulated depreciation of $39,000. Describe how this event is handled in the statement of cash flows.

7. As a means of gaining a greater return on its cash balance, Hammond Company transferred $19,000 from its checking account to a money market account, purchased a $10,000 three-month U.S. Treasury bill, and bought $12,000 of another company's stock. How will each of these transactions affect the statement of cash flows?

8. Nevel, Inc., has a net loss of $111,000 for the fiscal year but a positive cash flow of $9,000. What are some conditions that might have caused this situation?

Exercises

P.O. 4

Classify operating, investing, and financing activities.

Exercise 24-1 Diravy, Inc., had the following transactions during the year. Classify each transaction as (O) an operating activity, (I) an investing activity, (F) a financing activity, or (X) a noncash transaction. Also classify each transaction as a plus (+) for inflow, a minus (−) for outflow, or zero (0) if neither inflow nor outflow.

1. Paid $10,000 for rent.
2. Purchased a bond for $5,000.
3. Paid $2,000 interest.
4. Sold equipment for $4,000.
5. Repaid the principal of a mortgage of $25,000.
6. Received cash from customers of $75,000.
7. Paid $3,000 of federal income tax.
8. Paid $7,500 for computer equipment.
9. Extended a customer's note of $1,400.

P.O. 5

Determine cash payments for insurance.

Exercise 24-2 The income statement of Vaa, Inc., for 2000 includes Insurance Expense of $11,480. The beginning balance of Prepaid Insurance amounted to $5,520, and the ending balance of Prepaid Insurance amounts to $6,380. Determine the cash payments for insurance by Vaa, Inc., for the year 2000.

P.O. 5

Determine cash receipts from customers.

Exercise 24-3 During 2000, Farley Company had net sales of $455,000. During the same year, the beginning balance of Accounts Receivable was $97,500, and the ending balance of Accounts Receivable was $93,750. Determine the amount of cash receipts from customers during the year 2000.

P.O. 5

Determine cash payments for merchandise purchases.

Exercise 24-4 During 2000, Top Optical had Delivered Cost of Purchases of $219,000. The beginning balance of Accounts Payable amounted to $63,000, and the ending balance of Accounts Payable amounted to $67,500. Determine the cash payments for merchandise purchases for the year 2000.

P.O. 5

Determine cash payments for income tax.

Exercise 24-5 Income Tax Expense for Marnely Corporation was $82,200 for the year 2000. Between the beginning and end of the year, Income Tax Payable increased by $6,000. Determine the amount of cash payments for income tax during 2000.

P.O. 5

Determine the cash payments for operating expenses.

Exercise 24-6 During 2000, Kozlo and Company had operating expenses of $197,400, including depreciation of $46,200. Also during 2000, the beginning balance of Supplies was $5,040, and the ending balance of Supplies was $5,880. The beginning balance of Wages Payable was $2,520, and the ending balance of Wages Payable was $2,100. Assume that operating expenses consisted only of Depreciation Expense, Supplies Expense, and Wages

Expense. Determine the total cash payments for operating expenses during the year 2000.

P.O. 4,5

Determine how transactions are to be recorded on the statement of cash flows.

Exercise 24-7 All transactions involving Notes Payable and Interest Payable for Rork Company during the year 2001 are presented in the general journal.

			GENERAL JOURNAL	PAGE ___			
	DATE		DESCRIPTION	POST. REF.	DEBIT	CREDIT	
1	2001		**Reversing Entry**				1
2	Jan.	1	Interest Payable		6 6 0 00		2
3			Interest Expense			6 6 0 00	3
4							4
5	Feb.	3	Notes Payable		28 0 5 0 00		5
6			Interest Expense		2 2 5 5 00		6
7			Cash			30 3 0 5 00	7
8			Repayment of note at				8
9			maturity.				9
10							10
11	Dec.	1	Cash		19 2 5 0 00		11
12			Notes Payable			19 2 5 0 00	12
13			Bank loan, receiving the full				13
14			principal.				14
15							15
16			**Adjusting Entry**				16
17		31	Interest Expense		4 1 2 50		17
18			Interest Payable			4 1 2 50	18

Determine the cash flow amounts (positive or negative) and describe how these transactions are to be recorded on the statement of cash flows (financing, operating, or investing activity).

P.O. 4,5

Compute amounts to be included in the statement of cash flows and determine where they should be shown.

Exercise 24-8 Following are the T accounts for Equipment and Accumulated Depreciation, Equipment for Rubens Company at the end of 2000:

Equipment				Accumulated Depreciation, Equipment			
Beg. Balance	75,600	Disposal	16,200	Disposal	8,100	Beg. Balance	55,800
Purchases	24,300					Adjusting	12,600
End. Balance	83,700					End. Balance	60,300

Loss on Disposal of Plant and Equipment

Disposal	5,400	

New equipment was bought for cash, and the used equipment was sold for cash. Compute the amounts to be included in the statement of cash flows, and indicate where these amounts should be shown.

CONSIDER AND COMMUNICATE

Your manager feels strongly that all he needs from the accountant are the income statement, statement of owner's equity, and balance sheet. He doesn't want to pay the additional fees charged for preparation of a statement of cash flows. Explain to your manager why this additional statement is important.

WHAT IF . . .

The new accountant can't understand why there is a need for a statement of cash flows. She says that a comparative balance sheet will show the change in the Cash account, and that that should be enough information. What is your response to this opinion?

CRITICAL THINKING

Following is a partially completed statement of cash flows for Cedrel Company. Selected line amounts have been left out because the accounting intern was not sure what to do. Fill in the missing amounts. The following information may be helpful:

Cash Receipts from Customers	
Net Sales	$656,780
Beginning Accounts Receivable	$ 45,820
Ending Accounts Receivable	$ 49,000

Insurance	
Beginning Prepaid Insurance	$ 400
Ending Prepaid Insurance	1,600
Insurance Expense	320

Supplies	
Beginning Supplies Inventory	$ 850
Ending Supplies Inventory	545
Supplies Expense	1,540

Employees	
Beginning Salaries Payable	$ 3,010
Ending Salaries Payable	2,890
Salary Expense	94,500

Cedrel Company
Statement of Cash Flows
For Year Ended December 31, 2000

Cash Flows from (used by) Operating Activities:						
Cash Receipts from Customers						
Cash Payments for:						
Merchandise Purchases			$ 492 5 7 5 00			
Operating Expenses:						
Employees						
Rent	19 0 0 0 00					
Supplies						
Insurance						
Total Operating Expenses						
Total Cash Payments					608 9 5 0 00	
Net Cash Flows from Operating Activities					$ 44 6 5 0 00	
Cash Flows from (used by) Financing Activities:						
Payment of Personal Withdrawals			$ (47 5 0 0 00)			
Net Cash Flows used by Financing Activities					(47 5 0 0 00)	
Net Increase (Decrease) in Cash					$ (2 8 5 0 00)	

WEB WORK

Using an Internet web browser, type *statement of cash flows* in the search box and search for information about sources and uses of cash. Discuss your findings in a small group. Write a one-page summary of your findings.

PROBLEM SET A

For additional help, see the demonstration problem at the beginning of each chapter in your Working Papers.

P.O. 5

Problem 24-1A The financial statements of Hoffman Realty are presented here.

Instructions

Prepare a statement of cash flows for 2001.

Check Figure

Net cash flows from operating activities, $36,670

Hoffman Realty
Income Statement
For Year Ended December 31, 2001

Revenue:											
Service Revenue							$71	1	9	0	00
Expenses:											
Commissions Expense	$20	6	4	0	00						
Advertising Expense	5	6	0	0	00						
Repairs Expense	1	2	5	0	00						
Rent Expense	3	6	0	0	00						
Telephone Expense		9	2	0	00						
Depreciation Expense, Automobile	2	2	8	0	00						
Depreciation Expense, Office Equip.	1	2	2	0	00						
Supplies Expense		4	1	0	00						
Utilities Expense	1	6	3	0	00						
Total Expenses							37	5	5	0	00
Net Income							$33	6	4	0	00

Hoffman Realty
Statement of Owner's Equity
For Year Ended December 31, 2001

L. A. Hoffman, Capital, January 1, 2001						$22	9	0	0	00
Net Income	$33	6	4	0	00					
Less Withdrawals	30	0	0	0	00					
Increase in Capital						3	6	4	0	00
L. A. Hoffman, Capital, December 31, 2001						$26	5	4	0	00

Hoffman Realty
Comparative Balance Sheet
December 31, 2001 and December 31, 2000

	2001					2000					INCREASE OR (DECREASE)				
Assets															
Cash	$16	9	6	0	00	$10	2	9	0	00	$6	6	7	0	00
Prepaid Rent		9	0	0	00		3	0	0	00		6	0	0	00
Supplies		6	2	0	00		7	5	0	00	(	1	3	0	00)
Automobile	11	4	0	0	00	11	4	0	0	00				0	00
Less Accumulated Depreciation	(4	5	6	0	00)	(2	2	8	0	00)	(2	2	8	0	00)
Office Equipment	6	1	0	0	00	6	1	0	0	00				0	00
Less Accumulated Depreciation	(4	8	8	0	00)	(3	6	6	0	00)	(1	2	2	0	00)
Total Assets	$26	5	4	0	00	$22	9	0	0	00	$3	6	4	0	00
Owner's Equity															
L. A. Hoffman, Capital	$26	5	4	0	00	$22	9	0	0	00	$3	6	4	0	00
Total Owner's Equity	$26	5	4	0	00	$22	9	0	0	00	$3	6	4	0	00

P.O. 5

Check Figure

Net cash flows from operating activities, $55,390

Problem 24-2A Benson Van and Storage's financial statements for the current year are presented here.

Instructions

Prepare a statement of cash flows for the year 2001.

Benson Van and Storage
Income Statement
For Year Ended December 31, 2001

Revenue:			
Income from Moving Services	$ 124 8 0 0 00		
Income from Storage Rentals	72 7 2 0 00		
Total Income		$ 197 5 2 0 00	
Expenses:			
Wages Expense	$ 117 1 0 0 00		
Truck Repair Expense	4 6 4 0 00		
Gas and Oil Expense	3 6 3 0 00		
Insurance Expense	2 8 5 0 00		
Supplies Expense	1 2 4 0 00		
Depreciation Expense, Building	9 6 2 0 00		
Depreciation Expense, Trucks	18 8 0 0 00		
Interest Expense	10 1 0 0 00		
Total Expenses		167 9 8 0 00	
Net Income		$ 29 5 4 0 00	

Benson Van and Storage
Statement of Owner's Equity
For Year Ended December 31, 2001

P. R. Benson, Capital, January 1, 2001		$ 228 0 4 0 00
Net Income	$29 5 4 0 00	
Less Withdrawals	27 0 0 0 00	
Increase in Capital		2 5 4 0 00
P. R. Benson, Capital, Dec. 31, 2001		$ 230 5 8 0 00

Benson Van and Storage
Comparative Balance Sheet
December 31, 2001 and December 31, 2000

	2001	2000	INCREASE OR (DECREASE)
Assets			
Cash	$ 36 800 00	$ 10 610 00	$ 26 190 00
Prepaid Insurance	2 660 00	920 00	1 740 00
Supplies	1 120 00	290 00	830 00
Land	32 200 00	32 200 00	0 00
Building	314 000 00	314 000 00	0 00
Less Accumulated Depreciation	(108 800 00)	(99 180 00)	(9 620 00)
Trucks	94 000 00	94 000 00	0 00
Less Accumulated Depreciation	(37 600 00)	(18 800 00)	(18 800 00)
Total Assets	$ 334 380 00	$ 334 040 00	$ 340 00
Liabilities			
Mortgage Payable	$ 103 800 00	$ 106 000 00	$ (2 200 00)
Owner's Equity			
P. R. Benson, Capital	230 580 00	228 040 00	2 540 00
Total Liabilities and Owner's Equity	$ 334 380 00	$ 334 040 00	$ 340 00

P.O. 5

Problem 24-3A Financial statements for The Style Touch are presented here.

Instructions

Prepare a statement of cash flows for the year 2001.

The Style Touch
Income Statement
For Year Ended December 31, 2001

Revenue from Sales:			
Net Sales		$ 742 6 0 0 00	
Cost of Goods Sold:			
Merchandise Inventory, Jan. 1, 2001	$ 133 6 7 0 00		
Net Purchases	545 2 8 0 00		
Goods Available for Sale	$ 678 9 5 0 00		
Less Merchandise Inventory,			
December 31, 2001	137 7 5 0 00		
Cost of Goods Sold		541 2 0 0 00	
Gross Profit		$ 201 4 0 0 00	
Operating Expenses:			
Salary Expense	$ 109 8 8 0 00		
Rent Expense	24 0 0 0 00		
Depreciation Expense, Equipment	29 6 0 0 00		
Supplies Expense	2 7 5 0 00		
Insurance Expense	1 2 0 0 00		
Total Operating Expenses		167 4 3 0 00	
Net Income		$ 33 9 7 0 00	

The Style Touch
Statement of Owner's Equity
For Year Ended December 31, 2001

C. D. Maki, Capital, January 1, 2001		$ 247 1 7 0 00
Net Income	$33 9 7 0 00	
Less Withdrawals	40 0 0 0 00	
Decrease in Capital		6 0 3 0 00
C. D. Maki, Capital, December 31, 2001		$ 241 1 4 0 00

The Style Touch
Comparative Balance Sheet
December 31, 2001 and December 31, 2000

	2001	2000	INCREASE OR (DECREASE)
Assets			
Cash	$ 37 6 4 0 00	$ 38 4 1 0 00	$ (7 7 0 00)
Accounts Receivable	51 1 3 0 00	42 1 6 0 00	8 9 7 0 00
Merchandise Inventory	137 7 5 0 00	133 6 7 0 00	4 0 8 0 00
Supplies	3 7 0 00	9 2 0 00	(5 5 0 00)
Prepaid Insurance	1 8 0 0 00	6 0 0 00	1 2 0 0 00
Equipment	154 9 0 0 00	154 9 0 0 00	0 00
Less Accumulated Depreciation	(118 4 0 0 00)	(88 8 0 0 00)	(29 6 0 0 00)
Total Assets	$ 265 1 9 0 00	$ 281 8 6 0 00	$ (16 6 7 0 00)
Liabilities			
Accounts Payable	$ 20 5 6 0 00	$ 31 9 5 0 00	$ (11 3 9 0 00)
Salaries Payable	3 4 9 0 00	2 7 4 0 00	7 5 0 00
Total Liabilities	$ 24 0 5 0 00	$ 34 6 9 0 00	$ (10 6 4 0 00)
Owner's Equity			
C. D. Maki, Capital	241 1 4 0 00	247 1 7 0 00	(6 0 3 0 00)
Total Liabilities and Owner's Equity	$ 265 1 9 0 00	$ 281 8 6 0 00	$ (16 6 7 0 00)

P.O. 5

Problem 24-4A Financial statements for Farley Corporation are presented here.

Additional information contained in the records revealed that equipment having a cost of $47,000 and accumulated depreciation of $35,600 was sold for $18,000 cash. Also, 4,700 shares of common stock having a par value of $10 per share were sold for $54,000 cash. The note receivable decrease was due to cash received, and the change in the note payable was due to principal that was paid.

Check Figure

Net cash flows from operating
activities, $3,310

Instructions

Prepare a statement of cash flows for the year 2001.

Farley Corporation
Income Statement
For Year Ended December 31, 2001

Revenue from Sales:			
Sales		$ 886 8 9 0 00	
Less Sales Returns and Allowances		10 7 8 0 00	
Net Sales			$ 876 1 1 0 00
Cost of Goods Sold:			
Merchandise Inventory, January 1, 2001		$ 352 6 2 0 00	
Net Purchases		625 7 6 0 00	
Goods Available for Sale		$ 978 3 8 0 00	
Less Merchandise Inventory, December 31, 2001		375 0 9 0 00	
Cost of Goods Sold			603 2 9 0 00
Gross Profit			$ 272 8 2 0 00
Operating Expenses:			
Salary Expense		$ 102 4 9 0 00	
Rent Expense		18 0 0 0 00	
Advertising Expense		6 4 0 0 00	
Depreciation Expense, Equipment		22 1 6 0 00	
Supplies Expense		2 7 1 0 00	
Miscellaneous Expense		9 2 0 00	
Total Operating Expenses			152 6 8 0 00
Income from Operations			$ 120 1 4 0 00
Other Income:			
Interest Income	$ 4 7 0 00		
Gain on Disposal of Plant and Equipment	6 6 0 0 00		
Total Other Income		$ 7 0 7 0 00	
Other Expenses:			
Interest Expense		3 2 0 00	6 7 5 0 00
Income Before Income Tax			$ 126 8 9 0 00
Income Tax Expense			38 6 7 0 00
Net Income			$ 88 2 2 0 00

Farley Corporation
Statement of Retained Earnings
For Year Ended December 31, 2001

Retained Earnings, January 1, 2001		$ 103 4 9 0 00
Net Income	$88 2 2 0 00	
Less Cash Dividends Declared	53 0 0 0 00	
Increase in Retained Earnings		35 2 2 0 00
Retained Earnings, December 31, 2001		$ 138 7 1 0 00

Farley Corporation
Comparative Balance Sheet
December 31, 2001 and December 31, 2000

	2001	2000	INCREASE OR (DECREASE)
Assets			
Cash	$ 24 8 0 0 00	$ 6 7 4 0 00	$ 18 0 6 0 00
Notes Receivable	0 00	2 8 7 0 00	(2 8 7 0 00)
Accounts Receivable	88 6 7 0 00	63 6 1 0 00	25 0 6 0 00
Merchandise Inventory	375 0 9 0 00	352 6 2 0 00	22 4 7 0 00
Prepaid Advertising	1 2 4 0 00	9 6 0 00	2 8 0 00
Supplies	4 3 0 00	2 1 0 00	2 2 0 00
Equipment	220 3 7 0 00	267 3 7 0 00	(47 0 0 0 00)
Less Accumulated Depreciation	(77 5 3 0 00)	(90 9 7 0 00)	13 4 4 0 00
Total Assets	$ 633 0 7 0 00	$ 603 4 1 0 00	$ 29 6 6 0 00
Liabilities			
Accounts Payable	$ 28 2 3 0 00	$ 79 3 2 0 00	$ (51 0 9 0 00)
Notes Payable	2 6 0 0 00	9 2 0 0 00	(6 6 0 0 00)
Salaries Payable	2 2 0 0 00	2 9 0 0 00	(7 0 0 00)
Income Tax Payable	4 8 3 0 00	5 2 6 0 00	(4 3 0 00)
Dividends Payable	3 9 5 0 00	4 4 7 0 00	(5 2 0 00)
Interest Payable	4 0 00	2 6 0 00	(2 2 0 00)
Total Liabilities	$ 41 8 5 0 00	$ 101 4 1 0 00	$ (59 5 6 0 00)
Stockholders' Equity			
Common Stock	$ 429 5 1 0 00	$ 382 5 1 0 00	$ 47 0 0 0 00
Premium on Common Stock	23 0 0 0 00	16 0 0 0 00	7 0 0 0 00
Retained Earnings	138 7 1 0 00	103 4 9 0 00	35 2 2 0 00
Total Stockholders' Equity	$ 591 2 2 0 00	$ 502 0 0 0 00	$ 89 2 2 0 00
Total Liabilities and Stockholders' Equity	$ 633 0 7 0 00	$ 603 4 1 0 00	$ 29 6 6 0 00

PROBLEM SET B

For additional help, see the demonstration problem at the beginning of each chapter in your Working Papers.

P.O. 5

Problem 24-1B The financial statements of Hern and Company are presented on the following page.

Instructions

Prepare a statement of cash flows for 2001.

Hern and Company
Income Statement
For Year Ended December 31, 2001

Revenue:				
Income from Services			$63 6 2 1 00	
Expenses:				
Wages Expense	$29 4 1 0 00			
Rent Expense	6 0 0 00			
Advertising Expense	4 2 0 00			
Utilities Expense	7 6 4 00			
Depreciation Expense, Equipment	8 2 1 0 00			
Supplies Expense	4 7 0 00			
Insurance Expense	2 4 0 00			
Miscellaneous Expense	3 2 2 00			
Total Expenses			40 4 3 6 00	
Net Income			$23 1 8 5 00	

Hern and Company
Statement of Owner's Equity
For Year Ended December 31, 2001

R. D. Hern, Capital, January 1, 2001			$65 0 1 8 00
Net Income	$23 1 8 5 00		
Less Withdrawals	36 0 0 0 00		
Decrease in Capital			12 8 1 5 00
R. D. Hern, Capital, December 31, 2001			$52 2 0 3 00

Hern and Company
Comparative Balance Sheet
December 31, 2001 and December 31, 2000

	2001	2000	INCREASE OR (DECREASE)
Assets			
Cash	$ 6 7 9 7 00	$ 11 5 1 7 00	$ (4 7 2 0 00)
Supplies	5 1 6 00	3 2 1 00	1 9 5 00
Prepaid Insurance	1 2 0 00	2 0 0 00	(8 0 00)
Equipment	69 4 0 0 00	69 4 0 0 00	0 00
Less Accumulated Depreciation	(24 6 3 0 00)	(16 4 2 0 00)	(8 2 1 0 00)
Total Assets	$ 52 2 0 3 00	$ 65 0 1 8 00	$ (12 8 1 5 00)
Owner's Equity			
R. D. Hern, Capital	$ 52 2 0 3 00	$ 65 0 1 8 00	$ (12 8 1 5 00)
Total Owner's Equity	$ 52 2 0 3 00	$ 65 0 1 8 00	$ (12 8 1 5 00)

P.O. 5

Problem 24-2B Marjean Hair Salon uses a modified cash basis. The financial statements for Marjean Hair Salon are presented below.

Instructions

Prepare a statement of cash flows for the year 2001.

Marjean Hair Salon
Income Statement
For Year Ended December 31, 2001

Revenue:				
Service Income			$ 117 1 3 0 00	
Expenses:				
Salary Expense	$65 4 2 0 00			
Rent Expense	12 0 0 0 00			
Supplies Expense	2 1 9 0 00			
Insurance Expense	4 6 0 00			
Utilities Expense	1 6 8 0 00			
Depreciation Expense, Equipment	1 9 2 0 00			
Depreciation Expense, Furniture	8 3 0 00			
Interest Expense	3 7 0 00			
Miscellaneous Expense	1 1 0 00			
Total Expenses			84 9 8 0 00	
Net Income			$ 32 1 5 0 00	

Marjean Hair Salon
Statement of Owner's Equity
For Year Ended December 31, 2001

M. C. Stein, Capital, January 1, 2001		$21 1 2 0 00
Net Income	$32 1 5 0 00	
Less Withdrawals	37 2 0 0 00	
Decrease in Capital		5 0 5 0 00
M. C. Stein, Capital, December 31, 2001		$16 0 7 0 00

Marjean Hair Salon
Comparative Balance Sheet
December 31, 2001 and December 31, 2000

	2001	2000	INCREASE OR (DECREASE)
Assets			
Cash	$ 9 6 8 0 00	$13 7 7 0 00	$(4 0 9 0 00)
Supplies	7 4 0 00	8 1 0 00	(7 0 00)
Prepaid Insurance	7 6 0 00	3 0 0 00	4 6 0 00
Equipment	9 6 0 0 00	9 6 0 0 00	0 00
Less Accumulated Depreciation	(5 7 6 0 00)	(3 8 4 0 00)	(1 9 2 0 00)
Furniture	5 8 4 0 00	5 8 4 0 00	0 00
Less Accumulated Depreciation	(2 4 9 0 00)	(1 6 6 0 00)	(8 3 0 00)
Total Assets	$18 3 7 0 00	$24 8 2 0 00	$(6 4 5 0 00)
Liabilities			
Notes Payable	$ 2 3 0 0 00	$ 3 7 0 0 00	$(1 4 0 0 00)
Owner's Equity			
M. C. Stein, Capital	16 0 7 0 00	21 1 2 0 00	(5 0 5 0 00)
Total Liabilities and Owner's Equity	$18 3 7 0 00	$24 8 2 0 00	$(6 4 5 0 00)

P.O. 5

Problem 24-3B Financial statements for Mangold Fine Clothes are presented below and on the following page.

Check Figure

Net cash flows from operating activities, $27,210

Instructions

Prepare a statement of cash flows for the year 2001.

Mangold Fine Clothes
Income Statement
For Year Ended December 31, 2001

Revenue from Sales:			
Net Sales			$ 854 6 0 0 00
Cost of Goods Sold:			
Merchandise Inventory, Jan. 1, 2001	$ 162 5 7 0 00		
Net Purchases	614 1 2 0 00		
Goods Available for Sale	$ 776 6 9 0 00		
Less Merchandise Inventory,			
December 31, 2001	122 6 5 0 00		
Cost of Goods Sold		654 0 4 0 00	
Gross Profit		$ 200 5 6 0 00	
Operating Expenses:			
Salary Expense	$ 137 9 5 0 00		
Rent Expense	27 0 0 0 00		
Depreciation Expense, Equipment	31 1 4 0 00		
Supplies Expense	3 2 1 0 00		
Insurance Expense	1 5 0 0 00		
Miscellaneous Expense	7 2 0 00		
Total Operating Expenses		201 5 2 0 00	
Net Loss		$ (9 6 0 00)	

Mangold Fine Clothes
Statement of Owner's Equity
For Year Ended December 31, 2001

F. R. Mangold, Capital, January 1, 2001			$ 292 1 4 0 00
Less: Net Loss	$ 9 6 0 00		
Withdrawals	15 0 0 0 00		
Decrease in Capital			15 9 6 0 00
F. R. Mangold, Capital, December 31,			
2001			$ 276 1 8 0 00

Mangold Fine Clothes
Comparative Balance Sheet
December 31, 2001 and December 31, 2000

	2001	2000	INCREASE OR (DECREASE)
Assets			
Cash	$ 43 7 7 0 00	$ 31 5 6 0 00	$ 12 2 1 0 00
Accounts Receivable	62 8 4 0 00	47 7 9 0 00	15 0 5 0 00
Merchandise Inventory	122 6 5 0 00	162 5 7 0 00	(39 9 2 0 00)
Supplies	7 1 0 00	6 9 0 00	2 0 00
Prepaid Insurance	2 4 0 0 00	8 0 0 00	1 6 0 0 00
Equipment	182 2 6 0 00	182 2 6 0 00	0 00
Less Accumulated Depreciation	(93 4 2 0 00)	(62 2 8 0 00)	(31 1 4 0 00)
Total Assets	$ 321 2 1 0 00	$ 363 3 9 0 00	$ (42 1 8 0 00)
Liabilities			
Accounts Payable	$ 42 0 8 0 00	$ 67 8 9 0 00	$ (25 8 1 0 00)
Salaries Payable	2 9 5 0 00	3 3 6 0 00	(4 1 0 00)
Total Liabilities	$ 45 0 3 0 00	$ 71 2 5 0 00	$ (26 2 2 0 00)
Owner's Equity			
F. R. Mangold, Capital	276 1 8 0 00	292 1 4 0 00	(15 9 6 0 00)
Total Liabilities and Owner's Equity	$ 321 2 1 0 00	$ 363 3 9 0 00	$ (42 1 8 0 00)

P.O. 5

Problem 24-4B Jordan Corporation's financial statements are presented on pages 883–884.

Additional information in the records revealed that equipment having a cost of $50,000 and accumulated depreciation of $44,000 was sold for $12,230 cash. Also, 5,000 shares of common stock having a par value of $10 per share were sold for $60,000 cash. The note receivable decrease was due to cash received, and the change in the note payable was due to the principal that was paid.

Check Figure

Net cash flows from operating activities, $27,540

Instructions

Prepare a statement of cash flows for the year 2001.

Jordan Corporation
Income Statement
For Year Ended December 31, 2001

Revenue from Sales:			
Sales	$ 994 2 6 0 00		
Less Sales Returns and Allowances	12 1 2 0 00		
Net Sales		$ 982 1 4 0 00	
Cost of Goods Sold:			
Merchandise Inventory, Jan. 1, 2001	$ 396 7 0 0 00		
Net Purchases	703 1 0 0 00		
Goods Available for Sale	$1 099 8 0 0 00		
Less Merchandise Inventory,			
December 31, 2001	421 4 5 0 00		
Cost of Goods Sold		678 3 5 0 00	
Gross Profit		$ 303 7 9 0 00	
Operating Expenses:			
Wages Expense	$ 126 4 0 0 00		
Rent Expense	20 0 0 0 00		
Depreciation Expense, Equipment	26 0 0 0 00		
Supplies Expense	2 9 5 0 00		
Insurance Expense	1 2 0 0 00		
Total Operating Expenses		176 5 5 0 00	
Income from Operations		$ 127 2 4 0 00	
Other Income:			
Gain on Disposal of Plant and			
Equipment	$ 6 2 3 0 00		
Other Expenses:			
Interest Expense	7 9 0 0 00	5 4 4 0 00	
Income Before Income Tax		$ 132 6 8 0 00	
Income Tax Expense		45 1 1 0 00	
Net Income		$ 87 5 7 0 00	

Jordan Corporation
Statement of Retained Earnings
For Year Ended December 31, 2001

Retained Earnings, January 1, 2001		$ 116 2 9 0 00	
Net Income	$87 5 7 0 00		
Less Cash Dividends Declared	60 0 0 0 00		
Increase in Retained Earnings		27 5 7 0 00	
Retained Earnings, December 31, 2001		$ 143 8 6 0 00	

Jordan Corporation
Comparative Balance Sheet
December 31, 2001 and December 31, 2000

	2001	2000	INCREASE OR (DECREASE)
Assets			
Cash	$ 36 920 00	$ 10 950 00	$ 25 970 00
Accounts Receivable	99 640 00	73 710 00	25 930 00
Merchandise Inventory	421 450 00	396 700 00	24 750 00
Supplies	5 20 00	7 90 00	(2 70 00)
Prepaid Rent	6 000 00	6 000 00	0 00
Prepaid Insurance	8 00 00	5 00 00	3 00 00
Equipment	250 980 00	300 980 00	(50 000 00)
Less Accumulated Depreciation	(88 700 00)	(106 700 00)	18 000 00
Total Assets	$ 727 610 00	$ 682 930 00	$ 44 680 00
Liabilities			
Accounts Payable	$ 31 720 00	$ 59 640 00	$ (27 920 00)
Notes Payable	10 400 00	24 200 00	(13 800 00)
Wages Payable	1 040 00	1 990 00	(950 00)
Income Tax Payable	11 280 00	10 460 00	8 20 00
Dividends Payable	12 000 00	12 000 00	0 00
Interest Payable	1 20 00	1 160 00	(1 040 00)
Total Liabilities	$ 66 560 00	$ 109 450 00	$ (42 890 00)
Stockholders' Equity			
Common Stock	$ 507 190 00	$ 457 190 00	$ 50 000 00
Premium on Common Stock	10 000 00	0 00	10 000 00
Retained Earnings	143 860 00	116 290 00	27 570 00
Total Stockholders' Equity	$ 661 050 00	$ 573 480 00	$ 87 570 00
Total Liabilities and Stockholders' Equity	$ 727 610 00	$ 682 930 00	$ 44 680 00

25 Comparative Financial Statements

WINDOWS ON | **THE WORLD WIDE WEB**

Having grown from a Finnish pulp mill in 1865 to a worldwide telecommunications company today, Nokia Corporation sells more than just wood pulp and cell phones. Headquartered in Finland, Nokia's annual report is available in three languages: English, Finnish, and Swedish. Until the late 1990s, the company's official accounting currency was the Finnish Markka. What is it now? Go to **www.nokia.com/investor/facts/index.html** to find out. How does Nokia present comparative financial statements? Which financial report will give you Nokia's earnings per share? What are the most recent earnings per share? Would this impress you if you were an investor in Nokia? Where would you look for total shareholders' equity and liabilities, and shareholder equity per share? Go to Nokia's annual report to find out at **http://www.nokia.com/investor/**.

Performance Objectives

After you have completed this chapter, you will be able to do the following:

1. Prepare a comparative income statement and balance sheet involving horizontal analysis.

2. Prepare a comparative income statement and balance sheet involving vertical analysis.

3. Express income statement data in trend percentages.

4. Compute (a) working capital, (b) current ratio, (c) quick ratio, (d) accounts receivable turnover, (e) merchandise inventory turnover, (f) ratio of stockholders' equity to liabilities, and (g) ratio of plant and equipment to long-term liabilities.

5. Calculate (a) equity per share, (b) rate of return on common stockholders' equity, (c) earnings per share of common stock, and (d) price-earnings ratio.

Accounting is the process of analyzing, classifying, recording, summarizing, and *interpreting* business transactions. We are now ready to interpret the information. How do you draw conclusions from financial data that have been summarized in financial statements?

The financial condition of a company and the results of operations of business enterprises are of interest not only to owners, employers, and managers, but also to creditors and to prospective owners and creditors. Everybody is interested in two aspects of an enterprise.

1. Its **solvency**, or its ability to pay its debts
2. Its **profitability**, or its ability to earn a reasonable profit on the owners' investment

This chapter explains the techniques used to determine solvency and profitability.

TYPES OF COMPARISON

To interpret a set of facts, you have to have similar data with which to compare it. In other words, a given set of facts by itself is not significant. If you are told that a certain corporation earned a net income of $56,000 during the past year, this figure by itself is not meaningful. Does this net income indicate a successful year or a poor year? Does it compare favorably or unfavorably with other years? Does it represent a reasonable return on sales and investment or not? How does it compare with the net income of other firms in the same industry?

A company's financial statements are meaningful only if you analyze them on a comparative basis. There are three useful bases for making such a comparison:

1. Statements of the same company for the current year and one or more prior years
2. Financial data for other companies in the same industry
3. Previously established financial standards or objectives

COMPARATIVE STATEMENTS

One technique for analyzing and interpreting financial data is the preparation of comparative statements. Two types of analysis—horizontal and vertical—are commonly used.

Horizontal Analysis

Objective 1

Prepare a comparative income statement and balance sheet involving horizontal analysis.

Income Statement Horizontal analysis is the comparison of the same item in a company's financial statements for two or more periods. Let's look at the comparative income statement (Figure 1) for Beacon Furniture, Inc., for 2001 and 2000.

Note that for each item in the income statement, the accountant expressed the difference—that is, the increase or decrease in 2001 over 2000—first in dollars and then in percentages. Look at the increase in Sales, on the second line, for example. Subtract Sales in 2000 from Sales in 2001.

$982,100	Sales for 2001
− 861,700	Sales for 2000
$120,400	Increase of 2001 over 2000

To calculate the *percentage* increase in Sales in 2001 over 2000, divide the dollar increase by the amount of Sales during the base year. Then round the answer to three decimal places and multiply by 100 to change the decimal to a percentage.

Beacon Furniture, Inc.
Comparative Income Statement
For Years Ended December 31, 2001 and December 31, 2000

	2001	2000	INCREASE OR (DECREASE) AMOUNT	PERCENT
Revenue from Sales:				
Sales	$ 982 1 0 0 00	$ 861 7 0 0 00	$ 120 4 0 0 00	14.0
Less Sales Returns and Allowances	15 2 0 0 00	13 1 0 0 00	2 1 0 0 00	16.0
Net Sales	$ 966 9 0 0 00	$ 848 6 0 0 00	$ 118 3 0 0 00	13.9
Cost of Goods Sold:				
Merchandise Inventory, January 1	$ 206 5 0 0 00	$ 138 7 0 0 00	$ 67 8 0 0 00	48.9
Delivered Cost of Purchases	804 8 0 0 00	636 6 0 0 00	168 2 0 0 00	26.4
Goods Available for Sale	$1 011 3 0 0 00	$ 775 3 0 0 00	$ 236 0 0 0 00	30.4
Less Merchandise Inventory, December 31	348 4 0 0 00	206 5 0 0 00	141 9 0 0 00	68.7
Cost of Goods Sold	$ 662 9 0 0 00	$ 568 8 0 0 00	$ 94 1 0 0 00	16.5
Gross Profit	$ 304 0 0 0 00	$ 279 8 0 0 00	$ 24 2 0 0 00	8.6
Operating Expenses:				
Selling Expenses:				
Sales Salary Expense	$ 114 6 5 0 00	$ 102 4 0 0 00	$ 12 2 5 0 00	12.0
Delivery Expense	14 7 0 0 00	13 7 0 0 00	1 0 0 0 00	7.3
Advertising Expense	7 9 0 0 00	6 9 0 0 00	1 0 0 0 00	14.5
Depreciation Expense, Equipment	6 8 0 0 00	6 6 0 0 00	2 0 0 00	3.0
Store Supplies Expense	7 5 0 00	6 0 0 00	1 5 0 00	25.0
Total Selling Expenses	$ 144 8 0 0 00	$ 130 2 0 0 00	$ 14 6 0 0 00	11.2
General Expenses:				
Office Salary Expense	$ 33 4 4 0 00	$ 27 6 8 0 00	$ 5 7 6 0 00	20.8
Depreciation Expense, Building	14 2 0 0 00	14 2 0 0 00	0 00	0
Bad Debts Expense	6 2 0 0 00	5 4 0 0 00	8 0 0 00	14.8
Taxes Expense	6 1 0 0 00	5 2 0 0 00	9 0 0 00	17.3
Insurance Expense	1 1 0 0 00	1 0 0 0 00	1 0 0 00	10.0
Miscellaneous General Expense	8 6 0 00	7 2 0 00	1 4 0 00	19.4
Total General Expenses	$ 61 9 0 0 00	$ 54 2 0 0 00	$ 7 7 0 0 00	14.2
Total Operating Expenses	$ 206 7 0 0 00	$ 184 4 0 0 00	$ 22 3 0 0 00	12.1
Income from Operations	$ 97 3 0 0 00	$ 95 4 0 0 00	$ 1 9 0 0 00	2.0
Other Expenses:				
Interest Expense	7 9 2 0 00	7 8 6 0 00	6 0 00	0.8
Income Before Income Tax	$ 89 3 8 0 00	$ 87 5 4 0 00	$ 1 8 4 0 00	2.1
Income Tax Expense	18 4 2 0 00	18 0 1 0 00	4 1 0 00	2.3
Net Income	$ 70 9 6 0 00	$ 69 5 3 0 00	$ 1 4 3 0 00	2.1

FIGURE 1

$$\frac{\$120,400}{\$861,700} = 861,700\overline{)120,400}^{.1397} = .140 \times 100 = \underline{\underline{14.0\%}}$$

Note: The expression **base year** means the year you are using as a basis for comparison, which is the earlier year.

Now look at the change in Sales Returns and Allowances:

$15,200   Sales Returns and Allowances for 2001
− 13,100   Sales Returns and Allowances for 2000
─────────
$ 2,100   Increase of 2001 over 2000

The percentage rate of increase is

$$\frac{\$2,100}{\$13,100} = 13,100\overline{)2,100}^{.1603} = .160 \times 100 = \underline{16.0\%}$$

■ ■ ■

Remember!

The percentage of increase is calculated by dividing the dollar amount of increase by the base year amount, rounding the answer to three decimal places, and multiplying by 100.

People appraising an income statement often use the percentage change in net sales as a basis for comparison. In other words, they compare all other percentage changes with the percentage change in net sales to determine reasonably whether the other percentage changes are out of line. If net sales increased 13.9 percent from 2000 to 2001, other percentage changes should also amount to approximately 13.9 percent. If they vary considerably from 13.9 percent, they may be out of line, and you should investigate to find the reasons for the difference. Let's look at the main items on the income statement.

Item	Percentage Change
Net Sales	13.9
Cost of Goods Sold	16.5
Gross Profit	8.6
Total Operating Expenses	12.1
Net Income	2.1

Horizontal analysis of an income statement lets management see the percentage of increase and decrease for each component of the income statement.

You can see that the percentage changes in Gross Profit and Net Income are considerably less than the percentage change in Net Sales. Since Gross Profit is determined by subtracting Cost of Goods Sold from Net Sales, you should investigate the entire Cost of Goods Sold section of the income statement. This is a starting point in accounting for the comparatively small percentage increase in Net Income. The percentage changes in items in the Cost of Goods Sold section are

Item	Percentage Change
Merchandise Inventory, January 1	48.9
Delivered Cost of Purchases	26.4
Merchandise Inventory, December 31	68.7

The merchandise inventory of January 1 was a carryover from the previous year, but why the large increase in Delivered Cost of Purchases? And look at the large increase in Merchandise Inventory at the end of the year. Buying all those goods required a large cash investment, which either increased debt and related interest expense or decreased investments and related interest income. In addition, carrying the larger inventory increased handling and storage expense plus the risk of an inventory loss write off due to obsolescence. Also, with such a large increase in Merchandise Inventory, we would expect a larger increase in sales. Is the increase in sales large enough?

Remember!

We are using the earlier year as the base year.

Incidentally, a percentage change can be calculated only when a positive amount is reported in the base year. For example, let's say a company had a net loss of $3,500 in Year 1 (base year) and a net income of $2,000 in Year 2. Because the $3,500 is not a positive amount, it is not possible to state the amount of the change as a percentage.

Balance Sheet Now look at the balance sheet in Figure 2 on page 890, which shows the comparison between 2001 and 2000. Again you see why changes are expressed in both dollars and percentages. Items showing either a large dollar change or a large percentage change really stand out. This time, some minus totals show up in the Amount of Increase or Decrease column.

The following items are based on data from the comparative balance sheet:

Item	Amount of Increase or Decrease	Percentage Increase or Decrease
Cash	$(16,900)	(43.7)
Merchandise Inventory	141,900	68.7
Accounts Payable	41,100	141.7

Recall that the comparative income statement already exposed the increase in the Merchandise Inventory account. You should also consider the effects of changes in the balances of other related accounts. The fact that Cash is down by 44 percent while Accounts Payable is up by 142 percent may indicate a pending financial crisis. To pay its bills, the firm may be forced to liquidate that large stock of goods by selling it at cost, or even less. The other current liabilities also show significant unfavorable increases. Note the 129 percent increase in Income Tax Payable, the 200 percent increase in Dividends Payable, and the 43 percent increase in Salaries Payable. One point in the company's favor, though, is the decrease in Accounts Receivable. The increase in Allowance for Doubtful Accounts, although relatively small in amount, could be considered unreasonable when expressed as a percentage (on the other hand, the increase may involve just one account).

Vertical Analysis

Objective 2

Prepare a comparative income statement and balance sheet involving vertical analysis.

Income Statement Another tool accountants can use to analyze financial statements is **vertical analysis**. Using this method, you can see in a single statement the relationship of each part to the whole. For an income statement, *the whole is net sales*. Although each percentage applies to a single item only, you can quickly see the relative importance of each item in the statement. Let's look first at the comparative income statement (Figure 3 on page 891) and then at the comparative balance sheet (Figure 4 on page 893) for Beacon Furniture, Inc.—this time, arranged for vertical analysis.

Beacon Furniture, Inc.
Comparative Balance Sheet
December 31, 2001 and December 31, 2000

	2001	2000	INCREASE OR (DECREASE) AMOUNT	PERCENT
Assets				
Current Assets:				
Cash	$ 21 800 00	$ 38 700 00	$ (16 900 00)	(43.7)
Accounts Receivable	79 700 00	81 400 00	(1 700 00)	(2.1)
Less Allowance for Doubtful Accounts	3 300 00	2 600 00	700 00	26.9
Merchandise Inventory	348 400 00	206 500 00	141 900 00	68.7
Prepaid Insurance	2 000 00	2 100 00	(1 00 00)	(4.8)
Total Current Assets	$ 448 600 00	$ 326 100 00	$ 122 500 00	37.6
Investments:				
Sinking Fund Cash	$ 4 100 00	$ 5 800 00	$ (1 700 00)	(29.3)
Sinking Fund Investments	61 700 00	59 400 00	2 300 00	3.9
Total Investments	$ 65 800 00	$ 65 200 00	$ 600 00	.9
Plant and Equipment:				
Land	$ 40 000 00	$ 40 000 00	$ 0 00	0
Building	160 000 00	160 000 00	0 00	0
Less Accumulated Depreciation	56 800 00	42 600 00	14 200 00	33.3
Equipment	88 600 00	86 000 00	2 600 00	3.0
Less Accumulated Depreciation	41 000 00	34 200 00	6 800 00	19.9
Total Plant and Equipment	$ 190 800 00	$ 209 200 00	$ (18 400 00)	(8.8)
Intangible Assets:				
Organization Costs	3 000 00	4 000 00	(1 000 00)	(25.0)
Total Assets	$ 708 200 00	$ 604 500 00	$ 103 700 00	17.2
Liabilities				
Current Liabilities:				
Accounts Payable	$ 70 100 00	$ 29 000 00	$ 41 100 00	141.7
Income Tax Payable	12 800 00	5 600 00	7 200 00	128.6
Dividends Payable	12 000 00	4 000 00	8 000 00	200.0
Salaries Payable	5 700 00	4 000 00	1 700 00	42.5
Total Current Liabilities	$ 100 600 00	$ 42 600 00	$ 58 000 00	136.2
Long-Term Liabilities:				
Bonds Payable, 6%, due Dec. 31, 2012	$ 100 000 00	$ 100 000 00	$ 0 00	0
Less Discount on Bonds Payable	2 200 00	2 400 00	200 00	(8.3)
Total Long-Term Liabilities	$ 97 800 00	$ 97 600 00	$ 200 00	.2
Total Liabilities	$ 198 400 00	$ 140 200 00	$ 58 200 00	41.5
Stockholders' Equity				
Paid-in Capital:				
Common Stock, $100 par (4,000 shares authorized, 3,000 shares issued)	$ 300 000 00	$ 300 000 00	$ 0 00	0
Premium on Common Stock	86 000 00	86 000 00	0 00	0
Total Paid-in Capital	$ 386 000 00	$ 386 000 00	$ 0 00	0
Retained Earnings:				
Unappropriated	$ 103 800 00	$ 66 300 00	$ 37 500 00	56.6
Appropriated for Plant Expansion	20 000 00	12 000 00	8 000 00	66.7
Total Retained Earnings	$ 123 800 00	$ 78 300 00	$ 45 500 00	58.1
Total Stockholders' Equity	$ 509 800 00	$ 464 300 00	$ 45 500 00	9.8
Total Liabilities and Stockholders' Equity	$ 708 200 00	$ 604 500 00	$ 103 700 00	17.2

FIGURE 2

Beacon Furniture, Inc.
Comparative Income Statement
For Years Ended December 31, 2001 and December 31, 2000

	2001 AMOUNT	2001 PERCENT*	2000 AMOUNT	2000 PERCENT*
Revenue from Sales:				
Sales	$982 1 0 0 00	101.6	$861 7 0 0 00	101.5
Less Sales Returns and Allowances	15 2 0 0 00	1.6	13 1 0 0 00	1.5
Net Sales	$966 9 0 0 00	100.0	$848 6 0 0 00	100.0
Cost of Goods Sold:				
Merchandise Inventory, January 1	$206 5 0 0 00	21.4	$138 7 0 0 00	16.3
Delivered Cost of Purchases	804 8 0 0 00	83.2	636 6 0 0 00	75.0
Goods Available for Sale	$1 011 3 0 0 00	104.6	$775 3 0 0 00	91.4
Less Merchandise Inventory, December 31	348 4 0 0 00	36.0	206 5 0 0 00	24.3
Cost of Goods Sold	$662 9 0 0 00	68.6	$568 8 0 0 00	67.0
Gross Profit	$304 0 0 0 00	31.4	$279 8 0 0 00	33.0
Operating Expenses:				
Selling Expenses:				
Sales Salary Expense	$114 6 5 0 00	11.9	$102 4 0 0 00	12.1
Delivery Expense	14 7 0 0 00	1.5	13 7 0 0 00	1.6
Advertising Expense	7 9 0 0 00	.8	6 9 0 0 00	.8
Depreciation Expense, Equipment	6 8 0 0 00	.7	6 6 0 0 00	.8
Store Supplies Expense	7 5 0 00	.1	6 0 0 00	.1
Total Selling Expenses	$144 8 0 0 00	15.0	$130 2 0 0 00	15.3
General Expenses:				
Office Salary Expense	$33 4 4 0 00	3.5	$27 6 8 0 00	3.3
Depreciation Expense, Building	14 2 0 0 00	1.5	14 2 0 0 00	1.7
Bad Debts Expense	6 2 0 0 00	.6	5 4 0 0 00	.6
Taxes Expense	6 1 0 0 00	.6	5 2 0 0 00	.6
Insurance Expense	1 1 0 0 00	.1	1 0 0 0 00	.1
Miscellaneous General Expense	8 6 0 00	.1	7 2 0 00	.1
Total General Expenses	$61 9 0 0 00	6.4	$54 2 0 0 00	6.4
Total Operating Expenses	$206 7 0 0 00	21.4	$184 4 0 0 00	21.7
Income from Operations	$97 3 0 0 00	10.1	$95 4 0 0 00	11.2
Other Expenses:				
Interest Expense	7 9 2 0 00	.8	7 8 6 0 00	.9
Income Before Income Tax	$89 3 8 0 00	9.2	$87 5 4 0 00	10.3
Income Tax Expense	18 4 2 0 00	1.9	18 0 1 0 00	2.1
Net Income	$70 9 6 0 00	7.3	$69 5 3 0 00	8.2

*There may be slight differences in the tenth's place due to the rounding methods of various calculators and computers. For the same reason, percentages may not add up exactly.

FIGURE 3

When you arrange an income statement for vertical analysis, you express each item as a *percentage of net sales.* In other words, you divide each item by net sales. Below is an illustration:

$$\text{Gross Profit \%} = \text{Gross Profit} \div \text{Net Sales}$$

$$\text{Gross Profit \% (2001)} = \frac{\$304,000}{\$966,900} = .3144 = \underline{\underline{31.4\%}}$$

$$\text{Gross Profit \% (2000)} = \frac{\$279,800}{\$848,600} = .3297 = \underline{\underline{33.0\%}}$$

$$\text{Income from Operations \%} = \text{Income from Operations} \div \text{Net Sales}$$

$$\text{Income from Operations \% (2001)} = \frac{\$97,300}{\$966,900} = .1006 = \underline{\underline{10.1\%}}$$

$$\text{Income from Operations \% (2000)} = \frac{\$95,400}{\$848,600} = .1124 = \underline{\underline{11.2\%}}$$

$$\text{Net Income After Income Tax \%} = \text{Net Income After Income Tax} \div \text{Net Sales}$$

$$\text{Net Income \% (2001)} = \frac{\$70,960}{\$966,900} = .0734 = \underline{\underline{7.3\%}}$$

$$\text{Net Income \% (2000)} = \frac{\$69,530}{\$848,600} = .0819 = \underline{\underline{8.2\%}}$$

You could also interpret the percentages as shown here:

2001

- For every $100 in net sales, gross profit was $31.40.
- For every $100 in net sales, income from operations was $10.10.
- For every $100 in net sales, net income was $7.30.

2000

- For every $100 in net sales, gross profit was $33.00.
- For every $100 in net sales, income from operations was $11.20.
- For every $100 in net sales, net income was $8.20.

Again we see the relative importance in 2001 of Delivered Cost of Purchases (83.2 percent of Net Sales) and ending Merchandise Inventory (36.0 percent of Net Sales). In the area of Selling Expenses, the percentage of Sales Salary Expense declined slightly from that of 2000. Advertising Expense as a percentage of Net Sales remained the same. (Is that necessarily a good sign?)

Balance Sheet When you perform a vertical analysis of a comparative balance sheet, you express the figure for each item as a *percentage of total assets,* or as a percentage of the total of liabilities and stockholders' equity, which is the same figure. (See Figure 4.) For example, suppose you want to find the percentage of total assets represented by Cash, Accounts Receivable, and Merchandise Inventory. (In referring to Accounts Receivable, we mean net Accounts Receivable [Accounts Receivable less Allowance for Doubtful Accounts].)

Major corporate advertisers reevaluate their advertising expense at least annually. By performing vertical analysis (and thus relating its advertising expense directly to net sales), a company is in a better position to assess the impact of one element upon another.

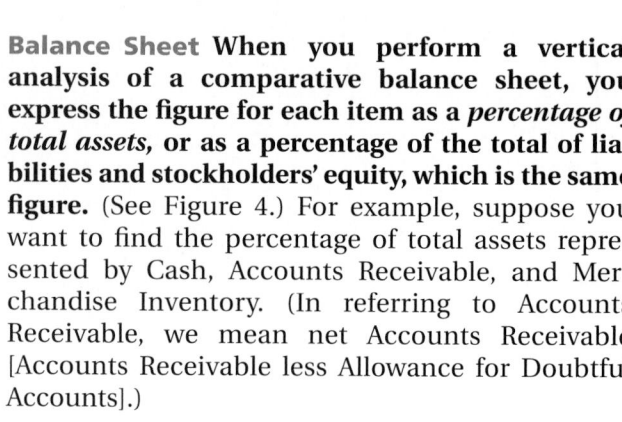

Beacon Furniture, Inc.
Comparative Balance Sheet
December 31, 2001 and December 31, 2000

	2001		2000	
	AMOUNT	PERCENT*	AMOUNT	PERCENT*
Assets				
Current Assets:				
Cash	$ 21 800 00	3.1	$ 38 700 00	6.4
Accounts Receivable	79 700 00	11.3	81 400 00	13.5
Less Allowance for Doubtful Accounts	3 300 00	.5	2 600 00	.4
Merchandise Inventory	348 400 00	49.2	206 500 00	34.2
Prepaid Insurance	2 000 00	.3	2 100 00	.3
Total Current Assets	$ 448 600 00	63.3	$ 326 100 00	53.9
Investments:				
Sinking Fund Cash	$ 4 100 00	.6	$ 5 800 00	1.0
Sinking Fund Investments	61 700 00	8.7	59 400 00	9.8
Total Investments	$ 65 800 00	9.3	$ 65 200 00	10.8
Plant and Equipment:				
Land	$ 40 000 00	5.6	$ 40 000 00	6.6
Building	160 000 00	22.6	160 000 00	26.5
Less Accumulated Depreciation	56 800 00	8.0	42 600 00	7.0
Equipment	88 600 00	12.5	86 000 00	14.2
Less Accumulated Depreciation	41 000 00	5.8	34 200 00	5.7
Total Plant and Equipment	$ 190 800 00	26.9	$ 209 200 00	34.6
Intangible Assets:				
Organization Costs	$ 3 000 00	.4	$ 4 000 00	.6
Total Assets	$ 708 200 00	100.0	$ 604 500 00	100.0
Liabilities				
Current Liabilities:				
Accounts Payable	$ 70 100 00	9.9	$ 29 000 00	4.8
Income Tax Payable	12 800 00	1.8	5 600 00	.9
Dividends Payable	12 000 00	1.7	4 000 00	.7
Salaries Payable	5 700 00	.8	4 000 00	.7
Total Current Liabilities	$ 100 600 00	14.2	$ 42 600 00	7.0
Long-Term Liabilities:				
Bonds Payable, 6%, due Dec. 31, 2012	$ 100 000 00	14.1	$ 100 000 00	16.5
Less Discount on Bonds Payable	2 200 00	.3	2 400 00	.4
Total Long-Term Liabilities	$ 97 800 00	13.8	$ 97 600 00	16.1
Total Liabilities	$ 198 400 00	28.0	$ 140 200 00	23.2
Stockholders' Equity				
Paid-in Capital:				
Common Stock, $100 par (4,000 shares authorized, 3,000 shares issued)	$ 300 000 00	42.4	$ 300 000 00	49.6
Premium on Common Stock	86 000 00	12.1	86 000 00	14.2
Total Paid-in Capital	$ 386 000 00	54.5	$ 386 000 00	63.9
Retained Earnings:				
Unappropriated	$ 103 800 00	14.7	$ 66 300 00	11.0
Appropriated for Plant Expansion	20 000 00	2.8	12 000 00	2.0
Total Retained Earnings	$ 123 800 00	17.5	$ 78 300 00	13.0
Total Stockholders' Equity	$ 509 800 00	72.0	$ 464 300 00	76.8
Total Liabilities and Stockholders' Equity	$ 708 200 00	100.0	$ 604 500 00	100.0

*Percentages may not add up exactly due to rounding.

FIGURE 4

$$\text{Cash \%} = \text{Cash} \div \text{Total Assets}$$

$$\text{Cash \% (2001)} = \frac{\$21,800}{\$708,200} = .0308 = \underline{3.1\%}$$

$$\text{Cash \% (2000)} = \frac{\$38,700}{\$604,500} = .0640 = \underline{6.4\%}$$

$$\text{Accounts Receivable \%} = \text{Net Accounts Receivable} \div \text{Total Assets}$$

$$\text{Accounts Receivable \% (2001)} = \frac{\$76,400}{\$708,200} = .1079 = \underline{10.8\%}$$

$$\text{Accounts Receivable \% (2000)} = \frac{\$78,800}{\$604,500} = .1304 = \underline{13.0\%}$$

$$\text{Merchandise Inventory \%} = \text{Merchandise Inventory} \div \text{Total Assets}$$

$$\text{Merchandise Inventory \% (2001)} = \frac{\$348,400}{\$708,200} = .4920 = \underline{49.2\%}$$

$$\text{Merchandise Inventory \% (2000)} = \frac{\$206,500}{\$604,500} = .3416 = \underline{34.2\%}$$

One could also interpret the above percentages as follows:

2001

- Of every $100 in total assets, $3.10 was in cash.
- Of every $100 in total assets, $10.80 was net accounts receivable.
- Of every $100 in total assets, $49.20 was merchandise inventory.

2000

- Of every $100 in total assets, $6.40 was in cash.
- Of every $100 in total assets, $13.00 was net accounts receivable.
- Of every $100 in total assets, $34.20 was merchandise inventory.

FYI

On an income statement arranged for vertical analysis, each dollar amount is expressed as a percentage of net sales. On a balance sheet arranged for vertical analysis, each dollar amount is expressed as a percentage of total assets or total liabilities and stockholders' equity.

These percentages accentuate Beacon Furniture's poor status with respect to Cash and Merchandise Inventory, as well as its favorable status with respect to Accounts Receivable. Also striking a warning note are that

- Percentage of plant and equipment declined during 2001.
- Percentage of Accounts Payable more than doubled during 2001.

Our illustrations show full income statements and balance sheets. But sometimes accountants prepare financial statements in condensed form and put the details in supporting schedules. In this case, the figures are taken from the supporting schedules, and the percentages are worked out in the same way. Since the percentages are rounded, the Percent column may not always add to exactly 100 in vertical analysis. (The Percent column is never added in horizontal analysis because it does not involve a common base.)

TREND PERCENTAGES

Objective 3

Express income statement data in trend percentages.

You may also use percentages to determine trends, or general directions that become evident only when you make a comparison covering a period of years. Trend percentages are calculated by dividing a specific item in an income statement by the corresponding item in the base year income statement. Here is the way to calculate the percentages:

1. Select a representative year as the base year.
2. Label the base year 100 percent.
3. Express all other years as percentages of the base year.

Let's say that you have been able to pull the following figures from the income statements for Beacon Furniture, Inc., for 1997 through 2001.

Item	Year				
	1997	**1998**	**1999**	**2000**	**2001**
Net Sales	$714,200	$782,380	$806,400	$848,600	$966,900
Cost of Goods Sold	466,150	519,180	540,300	568,800	662,900
Gross Profit	248,050	263,200	266,100	279,800	304,000

Trend percentages, a form of horizontal analysis, use a particular year as a base from which to compare previous or subsequent years. Rising college tuition and fees are easier to compare using this method.

You establish 1997 as the base year and calculate the trend percentages for Net Sales by dividing the Net Sales for each year by the Net Sales for 1997.

For 1998: $\dfrac{\$782,380}{\$714,200} = 714,200\overline{)782,380}^{\,1.095} = 1.095 \times 100 = \underline{\underline{109.5\%}}$

For 1999: $\dfrac{\$806,400}{\$714,200} = 714,200\overline{)806,400}^{\,1.129} = 1.129 \times 100 = \underline{\underline{112.9\%}}$

For 2000: $\dfrac{\$848,600}{\$714,200} = 714,200\overline{)848,600}^{\,1.188} = 1.188 \times 100 = \underline{\underline{118.8\%}}$

For 2001: $\dfrac{\$966,900}{\$714,200} = 714,200\overline{)966,900}^{\,1.354} = 1.354 \times 100 = \underline{\underline{135.4\%}}$

You determine trend percentages for Cost of Goods Sold and Gross Profit the same way. Here are the results, with the percentages rounded off as before.

Item	Year				
	1997	**1998**	**1999**	**2000**	**2001**
Net Sales	100.0%	109.5%	112.9%	118.8%	135.4%
Cost of Goods Sold	100.0%	111.4%	115.9%	122.0%	142.2%
Gross Profit	100.0%	106.1%	107.3%	112.8%	122.6%

Observe that, over the five-year period, the trend of Net Sales is upward. However, Cost of Goods Sold is going up at a more rapid rate. In other words, over the five years, Cost of Goods Sold increased faster than Net Sales, resulting in smaller increases in Gross Profit. This is fine if the company's plan is to achieve a greater volume of sales accompanied by more moderate profits. But if this shrinking Gross Profit is *not* consistent with company policy, then it may be a sign that the company is not passing along its increased costs to its customers.

INDUSTRY COMPARISONS

Vertical analysis, using percentage figures, is very useful when you wish to compare the figures for one company with the average figures for the given industry. The format of the financial statement defines it as a **common-size statement**. You express all items as percentages of a common base. Common-size statements can be used to compare one company with another as well as with industry averages. For the income statement, the common base is again net sales. Net sales is set at 100 percent, and all other items are expressed as a percentage of net sales. Trade and marketing associations often gather information and publish common-size statements.

ANALYSIS BY CREDITORS AND MANAGEMENT

Because management is vitally interested in increasing the company's solvency and profitability, managers are concerned with all types of analytical tools and techniques. Because creditors want assurance of being repaid, they are concerned first with the company's solvency and second with its profitability.

How Do Short-Term Creditors and Management Analyze an Enterprise?

FYI

Current means within one year or the operating cycle, whichever is longer.

Bankers and other short-term creditors are primarily interested in the *current* position of a given firm: Does the firm have enough money coming in to meet its current operating needs and to pay its current debts promptly? Let's use as an example some calculations derived from the comparative financial statements of Beacon Furniture, Inc., for 2001 and 2000.

Objective 4a

Compute working capital.

Working Capital **Working capital** is the excess of current assets over current liabilities. One determines the working capital for Beacon Furniture, Inc., as shown in the following equations:

Remember!

Working capital equals current assets minus current liabilities.

$$\text{Working Capital} = \text{Current Assets} - \text{Current Liabilities}$$

Working Capital (2001) = \$448,600 − \$100,600 = $\underline{\$348,000}$

Working Capital (2000) = \$326,100 − \$42,600 = $\underline{\$283,500}$

Beacon Furniture has \$348,000 of capital available to work with during 2001, compared with \$283,500 of capital available to work with during 2000.

Objective 4b

Compute current ratio.

Current Ratio The relationship of a company's current assets to its current liabilities is its **current ratio**. You arrive at this figure by dividing current assets by current liabilities.

$$\text{Current Ratio} = \frac{\text{Current Assets}}{\text{Current Liabilities}}$$

$$\textbf{Current Ratio (2001)} = \frac{\$448,600}{\$100,600} = \underline{\underline{4.46:1}}$$

$$\textbf{Current Ratio (2000)} = \frac{\$326,100}{\$42,600} = \underline{\underline{7.65:1}}$$

Remember!

To compute the current ratio, divide current assets by current liabilities.

A firm's current ratio reveals its current debt-paying ability. Beacon Furniture's current ratio of 4.46:1 in 2001 indicates that there is $4.46 of cash coming in within a year from now for every dollar Beacon has to pay out within a year. But the firm was better off in 2000, because in that year, it had $7.65 coming in within the year for every dollar to be paid out within the year.

From the point of view of bankers and other creditors, the adequacy of a company's current ratio depends on what type of business the firm is in. A favorable ratio for a merchandising business is generally 2:1—higher if the type of merchandise the firm sells is subject to abrupt changes in design or technology that create higher risk. But a public utility, which has no inventories other than supplies, is considered solvent even if its current ratio is less than 1:1. But notice that a current ratio of 4.46:1 for Beacon Furniture only indicates that current assets (not cash inflows) at one point in time (year-end date, for example) exceed current liabilities (not cash outflows). (*Note:* If the company has changed inventory valuation methods from one year to another—for example, if it has switched from FIFO to LIFO—a restatement should be made in the costs of merchandise inventories; otherwise, there is no common base for making a comparison.)

Objective 4c

Compute quick ratio.

Quick Ratio The relationship of a company's current assets that can be quickly converted into cash to its current liabilities is known as its **quick ratio** or *acid-test ratio*. **Quick assets** are Cash, current Notes Receivable, net Accounts Receivable (that is, Accounts Receivable less Allowance for Doubtful Accounts), Interest Receivable, and Marketable Securities. They do not include inventories and prepaid expenses because these are less easily converted into cash than are other current assets. Determine the quick ratio by dividing quick assets by current liabilities.

$$\text{Quick Ratio} = \frac{\text{Quick Assets}}{\text{Current Liabilities}}$$

$$\textbf{Quick Ratio (2001)} = \frac{\$21,800 + (\$79,700 - \$3,300)}{\$100,600} = \frac{\$98,200}{\$100,600} = \underline{\underline{.98:1}}$$

$$\textbf{Quick Ratio (2000)} = \frac{\$38,700 + (\$81,400 - \$2,600)}{\$42,600} = \frac{\$117,500}{\$42,600} = \underline{\underline{2.76:1}}$$

Remember!

Quick assets do not include inventories or prepaid expenses—only assets quickly convertible to cash.

Beacon Furniture's quick ratio of .98:1 in 2001 indicates that there are 98 cents in cash coming in quickly—without involving the liquidation of inventory—for every dollar it has to pay out on that date. For 2000, there was $2.76 that the firm could realize quickly for every dollar it had to pay out on a given date.

A quick ratio of 1:1 is normally considered satisfactory. However, the quick ratio for Beacon Furniture exposes a precarious short-term financial position. Consider this quick ratio in conjunction with the company's working capital and its current ratio. Although working capital and current ratio are two indicators of a firm's ability to meet its current obligations, they don't reveal the *composition of its current assets*—a very important factor.

Relationship of Each Current Asset to Total Current Assets Suppose that you are asked to find out the proportionate position of each item in the list of current assets of Beacon Furniture. Your first step is to compile a schedule of each current asset as it relates to total current assets, as shown in the following illustration:

	DECEMBER 31, 2001		DECEMBER 31, 2000	
	AMOUNT	PERCENT	AMOUNT	PERCENT
Current Assets:				
Cash	$ 21 800 00	4.9	$ 38 700 00	11.9
Accounts Receivable (net)	76 400 00	17.0	78 800 00	24.2
Merchandise Inventory	348 400 00	77.7	206 500 00	63.3
Prepaid Insurance	2 000 00	.4	2 100 00	.6
Total Current Assets	$ 448 600 00	100.0	$ 326 100 00	100.0

As an example, cash as a percentage of total current assets is calculated like this:

$$\frac{\$21,800}{\$448,600} = .0486 = \underline{\underline{4.9\%}}$$

We have already commented on the large increase in the proportion of merchandise inventory (it was 63 percent of current assets in 2000 but amounts to 78 percent of current assets in 2001). This change, coupled with the decline in the cash position (12 percent of current assets for 2000; only 5 percent of current assets for 2001), reinforces the message we got from the decline in the quick ratio: The firm may have a hard time paying its current debts.

Objective 4d

Compute accounts receivable turnover.

Accounts Receivable Turnover Since money tied up in accounts receivable does not yield any revenue, any firm tries to collect accounts receivable promptly and to keep them at a minimum. It can use the cash it gets from collection of accounts receivable to reduce bank loans or to take advantage of cash discounts. This action reduces the amount of interest it has to pay and the cost of the merchandise it buys. It also reduces the risk of loss from bad debts.

Accounts receivable turnover is the number of times charge accounts are turned over (or paid off) per year. A turnover implies a sale on account followed by payment of the debt in cash. Compute this by *dividing net sales on account by average net accounts receivable*. If possible, use the average of the monthly balances of Accounts Receivable because this allows for seasonal fluctuations. If you don't have figures for monthly balances, use the average of the balances at the beginning and the end of the year. Here is how accounts receivable turnover looks for Beacon Furniture. (You have to take the beginning balance of net Accounts Receivable for 2000, which was $61,460, from the 1999 balance sheet. Net sales on account, taken from the sales journal, were $773,020 for 2001 and $678,880 for 2000.)

$$\text{Accounts Receivable Turnover} = \frac{\text{Net Sales on Account}}{\text{Average Accounts Receivable (Net)}}$$

$$\text{Average Accounts Receivable} = \frac{\text{Beginning Accounts Receivable} + \text{Ending Accounts Receivable}}{2}$$

$$\text{Accounts Receivable Turnover (2001)} = \frac{\$773,020}{\dfrac{\$78,800 + \$76,400}{2}} = \frac{\$773,020}{\$77,600} = 9.96 \text{ times/per year}$$

$$\text{Accounts Receivable Turnover (2000)} = \frac{\$678,880}{\dfrac{\$61,460 + \$78,800}{2}} = \frac{\$678,880}{\$70,130} = 9.68 \text{ times/per year}$$

You can use the accounts receivable turnover to determine the number of days that the receivables were on the books. Calculate this by dividing 365 days by the turnover figure:

$$\text{Year (2001)} = \frac{365 \text{ days}}{9.96 \text{ times per year}} = 36.65 \text{ or } 37 \text{ days}$$

$$\text{Year (2000)} = \frac{365 \text{ days}}{9.68 \text{ times per year}} = 37.71 \text{ or } 38 \text{ days}$$

It took an average of one day less to collect accounts receivable in 2001 than it did in 2000. This reduction represents a slight improvement in collections for Beacon Furniture. Since the company's credit terms are net 30 days, 37 or 38 days is reasonable.

Objective 4e

Compute merchandise inventory turnover.

Merchandise Inventory Turnover **Merchandise inventory turnover** is the number of times a company's average inventory is sold during a given year. Calculate this by *dividing Cost of Goods Sold by average Merchandise Inventory*. Here is the calculation for Beacon Furniture (beginning Merchandise Inventory for 2000, taken from the 1999 balance sheet, was $138,700):

$$\text{Merchandise Inventory Turnover} = \frac{\text{Cost of Goods Sold}}{\text{Average Merchandise Inventory}}$$

$$\text{Average Merchandise Inventory} = \frac{\text{Beginning Merchandise Inventory} + \text{Ending Merchandise Inventory}}{2}$$

$$\text{Merchandise Inventory Turnover (2001)} = \frac{\$662,900}{\dfrac{\$206,500 + \$348,400}{2}} = \frac{\$662,900}{\$277,450} = 2.39 \text{ times/per year}$$

$$\text{Merchandise Inventory Turnover (2000)} = \frac{\$568,800}{\dfrac{\$138,700 + \$206,500}{2}} = \frac{\$568,800}{\$172,600} = 3.30 \text{ times/per year}$$

If possible, you should use the average of the monthly balances of Merchandise Inventory (add them and divide by 12). The figure for merchandise inventory turnover varies depending on the type of product involved. You can compare the figure for merchandise inventory turnover for one company with figures for the rest of the industry as a test of merchandising efficiency. Each turnover yields a gross profit or markup to the company. Note that there has been a serious decline in the rate of merchandise inventory turnover for Beacon Furniture. This is something to investigate further with management and monitor for future corrective action.

You may also use the figure for merchandise inventory turnover to determine the number of days that the merchandise was kept in stock. Calculate this the same way you calculate the number of days that the receivables were collectible: dividing 365 days by the turnover figure.

$$\text{Year (2001)} = \frac{365 \text{ days}}{2.39 \text{ times per year}} = 152.72 = \underline{\underline{153}} \text{ days}$$

$$\text{Year (2000)} = \frac{365 \text{ days}}{3.30 \text{ times per year}} = 110.61 = \underline{\underline{111}} \text{ days}$$

Note that Beacon Furniture's merchandise remained in stock 42 days longer in 2001 than it did in 2000. This fact surely calls for an investigation of the company's sales and purchasing practices.

In addition to yielding a higher gross profit, rapid merchandise inventory turnover has other advantages. The money invested in the inventory is tied up for a shorter period of time; storage costs are lower; there is less risk of spoilage (if the merchandise is perishable); there is less risk of change in demand (if the merchandise is affected by changes in style or in business conditions).

How Do Long-Term Creditors and Management Analyze an Enterprise?

Remember!

A corporation's bonds are classified as long-term liabilities.

Long-term creditors include mortgage holders and bondholders. Whenever specific property has been pledged or mortgaged, long-term creditors have first claim on the property in the event that the company cannot keep up its payments. Even in the case of debentures (unsecured bonds), the bondholders have a prior claim to the general assets of the company, a claim that takes precedence over that of the stockholders. Management is concerned with taking care of the company's present obligations, as well as preserving its credit standing, and hence its ability to borrow in the future.

Two ratios are particularly useful from the standpoint of long-term creditors:

Objective 4f

Compute ratio of stockholders' equity to liabilities.

Ratio of stockholders' equity to liabilities The ratio of stockholders' equity to liabilities is the ratio of the stockholders' investment to the creditors' claims.

In calculating any ratio, we mean the ratio *of* one thing *to* something else. When we write the ratio as a fraction, we put the *of* part in the numerator and the *to* part in the denominator. Look at this calculation for Beacon Furniture.

$$\text{Ratio of Stockholders' Equity to Liabilities} = \frac{\text{Stockholders' Equity}}{\text{Liabilities}}$$

$$\text{Ratio of Stockholders' Equity to Liabilities (2001)} = \frac{\$509,800}{\$198,400} = \underline{\underline{2.57{:}1}}$$

$$\text{Ratio of Stockholders' Equity to Liabilities (2000)} = \frac{\$464,300}{\$140,200} = \underline{\underline{3.31{:}1}}$$

In 2001, for every $2.57 of stockholders' investment, the creditors have loaned $1. Beacon Furniture's ratio of stockholders' equity to liabilities shows a decline since 2000, from 3.31:1 to 2.57:1. Creditors like to see a high proportion of stockholders' equity because stockholders' equity, or owners' equity, acts as a buffer in case the company has to absorb losses. Also, owners often prefer a high proportion of equity to liabilities.

Objective 4g

Compute ratio of plant and equipment to long-term liabilities.

Ratio of plant and equipment to long-term liabilities There is another factor that provides a margin of safety to mortgage holders and bondholders—the ratio of the value of a firm's total plant and equipment to its long-term liabilities. This ratio also indicates the potential ability of the enterprise to borrow more money on a long-term basis. Let's look at the calculation for Beacon Furniture.

$$\text{Ratio of Plant and Equipment to Long-Term Liabilities} = \frac{\text{Plant and Equipment}}{\text{Long-Term Liabilities}}$$

$$\text{Ratio of Plant and Equipment to Long-Term Liabilities (2001)} = \frac{\$190,800}{\$97,800} = \underline{\underline{1.95:1}}$$

$$\text{Ratio of Plant and Equipment to Long-Term Liabilities (2000)} = \frac{\$209,200}{\$97,600} = \underline{\underline{2.14:1}}$$

But in 2000, there was $2.14 book value of plant and equipment for every dollar of long-term liabilities. In 2001, there is $1.95 book value of plant and equipment for every dollar of long-term liabilities. This ratio, too, has deteriorated.

As we have seen, a firm's creditors and managers may use any of eight devices to determine the financial position of a firm:

Remember!

To find the ratio of . . . to . . . , divide the "of . . ." amount by the "to . . ." amount. Put a colon and the number 1 to the right of the answer.

- Working capital
- Current ratio
- Quick ratio
- Relationship of each current asset to total current assets
- Accounts receivable turnover
- Merchandise inventory turnover
- Ratio of stockholders' equity to liabilities
- Ratio of plant and equipment to long-term liabilities

ANALYSIS BY OWNERS AND MANAGEMENT

In addition to being concerned about the solvency and profitability of a company, owners and managers are vitally interested in the value of and return on investment in the company. In many cases, the owners are the managers. In other situations, managers are employed by the owners. What diagnostic tools do owners and managers use to determine the financial health of their company?

Equity per Share

Objective 5a

Calculate equity per share.

When you examine the annual report of a corporation, you encounter the term *equity per share,* also referred to as *book value per share.* If a corporation has only one class of common stock outstanding, equity per share is determined by dividing the total stockholders' equity by the number of shares of stock issued. Here are the calculations for Beacon Furniture:

$$\text{Equity per Share} = \frac{\text{Total Stockholders' Equity Available to a Class of Stock}}{\text{Number of Shares Issued and Outstanding}}$$

$$\text{Equity per Share (2001)} = \frac{\$509,800}{3,000 \text{ shares}} = \underline{\underline{\$169.93}} \text{ per share}$$

$$\text{Equity per Share (2000)} = \frac{\$464,300}{3,000 \text{ shares}} = \underline{\underline{\$154.77}} \text{ per share}$$

When there are shares of preferred stock outstanding, you must deduct the liquidation value of the preferred stockholder's equity, including any dividends in arrears on cumulative preferred stock, to arrive at the stockholders' equity available to holders of common stock.

The term *equity per share* does *not* mean the cash value or market value of a share; it means the amount that would be distributed per share of stock *if* the corporation were to **liquidate** (wind up its affairs by paying off its creditors and selling its assets for cash) without incurring any expenses, gains, or losses in selling its assets and paying its liabilities. The equity per share increases as a firm retains net income. This concept of equity per share is important in contracts involving the sale of stock. For example, a large stockholder might obtain an option to buy the shares of small stockholders at the value of the equity per share as of a certain future date.

Rate of Return on Common Stockholders' Equity

A corporation exists first and foremost to earn a net income for its stockholders. Therefore, the rate of return on the common stockholders' equity is important as a means of measuring how good or bad the investment is. This rate is calculated by dividing the net income available to holders of common stock by the *average value* of their equity. Here's the calculation for Beacon Furniture (beginning common stock equity for 2000 was $422,100):

Rate of Return on Common Stockholders' Equity

$$= \frac{\text{Net Income Available to Common Stock}}{\dfrac{\text{Beginning Common Stock Equity} + \text{Ending Common Stock Equity}}{2}}$$

Rate of Return on Common Stockholders' Equity (2001)

$$= \frac{\$70,960}{\dfrac{\$464,300 + \$509,800}{2}} = \frac{\$70,960}{\$487,050} = .1457 = \underline{\underline{14.6\%}}$$

Rate of Return on Common Stockholders' Equity (2000)

$$= \frac{\$69,530}{\dfrac{\$422,100 + \$464,300}{2}} = \frac{\$69,530}{\$443,200} = .1569 = \underline{\underline{15.7\%}}$$

The rate of return on common stockholders' equity declined 1.1 percent. Management should look into the matter to uncover the possible causes. Again, begin by investigating the large increase in merchandise inventory because it represents 49.2 percent of total assets in 2001.

Earnings per Share of Common Stock

Objective 5c

Calculate earnings per share of common stock.

Remember!

Dividends on preferred stock are paid before those on common.

You often see earnings per share of stock listed in the financial columns of newspapers. If a corporation has no preferred stock outstanding, compute the earnings per share of common stock by dividing net income by the average number of common stock shares outstanding during the year. When there is preferred stock, you must first deduct any dividends on preferred stock to arrive at the amount available to common stock. Here is the calculation of earnings per share of common stock for Beacon Furniture:

$$\text{Earnings per Share of Common Stock} = \frac{\text{Net Income Available to Common Stock}}{\text{Average Number of Shares of Common Stock Outstanding}}$$

$$\text{Earnings per Share of Common Stock (2001)} = \frac{\$70,960}{3,000 \text{ shares}} = \underline{\$23.65} \text{ per share}$$

$$\text{Earnings per Share of Common Stock (2000)} = \frac{\$69,530}{3,000 \text{ shares}} = \underline{\$23.18} \text{ per share}$$

Any big change during the year in the *number* of shares outstanding naturally has a significant impact on the amount of earnings per share. That's why a company must disclose (or show) the average number of shares outstanding and disclose any information relating to stock dividends and stock splits.

Price-Earnings Ratio

Objective 5d

Calculate price-earnings ratio.

The **price-earnings ratio** is a measure commonly used to determine whether the market price of a corporation's stock is reasonable. You calculate the price-earnings ratio of a company's stock by dividing the market price per share by the annual earnings per share. Suppose that the market price of a share of common stock of Beacon Furniture at the end of 2001 is $141, and that at the end of 2000, it was $137. Here is how you figure out the price-earnings ratio:

$$\text{Price-Earnings Ratio} = \frac{\text{Market Price per Share}}{\text{Earnings per Share}}$$

$$\text{Price-Earnings Ratio (2001)} = \frac{\$141}{\$23.65} = 5.962 = \underline{5.96{:}1}$$

$$\text{Price-Earnings Ratio (2000)} = \frac{\$137}{\$23.18} = 5.910 = \underline{5.91{:}1}$$

What constitutes a reasonable price-earnings ratio varies from one industry to another and with the state of the economy. Stocks quoted in the Dow Jones Average usually have about a 25:1 to 30:1 price-earnings ratio. Corporations that have shown a large continued growth in earnings over a period of years may have a ratio of more than 30:1.

You may also use the price-earnings ratio in this manner: If the acceptable price-earnings ratio for a given stock is 15:1 and the earnings per share equal $2.50, it follows that the maximum reasonable price you ought to pay for the stock is $37.50 (that is, $2.50 × 15). But what if the stock is selling for only $20? You may well consider it to be undervalued.

CHAPTER REVIEW

Review of Performance Objectives

1. Prepare a comparative income statement and balance sheet involving horizontal analysis.

   Horizontal analysis involves the comparison of the same item in an income statement or balance sheet for two or more periods. First, determine the difference between the two periods. Next, express the difference as a percentage of the base period (usually the earliest period).

2. Prepare a comparative income statement and balance sheet involving vertical analysis.

   In vertical analysis, each item in a financial statement is expressed as a percentage of a base amount. For an income statement, the base amount is net sales. For a balance sheet, the base amount is total assets or total liabilities and stockholders' equity.

3. Express income statement data in trend percentages.

   Income statement data shown in trend percentages involve a comparison of the same item over a number of periods. One period or year (usually the earliest) is designated as the base period and the amount for this period is set at 100 percent. Each amount in later years is expressed as a percentage of the amount for the base period.

4. Compute (a) working capital, (b) current ratio, (c) quick ratio, (d) accounts receivable turnover, (e) merchandise inventory turnover, (f) ratio of stockholders' equity to liabilities, and (g) ratio of plant and equipment to long-term liabilities.

   Short-term creditors and management use the following techniques:

   $$\text{Working Capital} = \text{Current Assets} - \text{Current Liabilities}$$

   $$\text{Current Ratio} = \frac{\text{Current Assets}}{\text{Current Liabilities}}$$

   $$\text{Quick Ratio} = \frac{\text{Quick Assets}}{\text{Current Liabilities}}$$

   $$\text{Accounts Receivable Turnover} = \frac{\text{Net Sales on Account}}{\text{Average Accounts Receivable (Net)}}$$

   $$\text{Merchandise Inventory Turnover} = \frac{\text{Cost of Goods Sold}}{\text{Average Merchandise Inventory}}$$

   Long-term creditors and management use the following ratios:

   $$\text{Ratio of Stockholders' Equity to Liabilities} = \frac{\text{Stockholders' Equity}}{\text{Liabilities}}$$

   $$\text{Ratio of Plant and Equipment to Long-Term Liabilities} = \frac{\text{Plant and Equipment}}{\text{Long-Term Liabilities}}$$

5. Calculate (a) equity per share, (b) rate of return on common stockholders' equity, (c) earnings per share of common stock, and (d) price-earnings ratio.

Owners and managers use the following measures:

$$\text{Equity per Share} = \frac{\text{Total Stockholders' Equity Available to a Class of Stock}}{\text{Number of Shares Issued and Outstanding}}$$

$$\text{Rate of Return on Common Stockholders' Equity} = \frac{\text{Net Income Available to Common Stock}}{\text{Average Common Stock Equity}}$$

$$\text{Earnings per Share of Common Stock} = \frac{\text{Net Income Available to Common Stock}}{\text{Average Number of Shares of Common Stock Outstanding}}$$

$$\text{Price-Earnings Ratio} = \frac{\text{Market Price per Share}}{\text{Earnings per Share}}$$

Glossary

Accounts receivable turnover The number of times charge accounts are paid off per year; a turnover is a sale on account and subsequent repayment. (898)

Base year The year used as a basis for comparison. (887)

Common-size statement A financial statement using vertical analysis with all items expressed as percentages; allows comparison of one company with another as well as with industry averages. (896)

Current ratio Current assets divided by current liabilities. (896)

Horizontal analysis Comparing the same item in the financial statements of an enterprise for two or more periods. (886)

Liquidate To wind up the affairs of a business by paying off the creditors and selling the assets for cash. (902)

Merchandise inventory turnover The number of times a company's average inventory is sold during a given year. (899)

Price-earnings ratio A common measure for deciding whether a stock's market price is reasonable; calculated by dividing the market price per share by the annual earnings per share. (903)

Profitability An enterprise's ability to earn a reasonable profit on the owners' investment. (886)

Quick assets Cash, current Notes Receivable, net Accounts Receivable, Interest Receivable, and Marketable Securities. (897)

Quick ratio Quick assets divided by current liabilities. Also called *acid-test ratio.* (897)

Solvency An enterprise's ability to pay its debts. (886)

Trend percentages Percentages calculated by dividing a specific item in an income statement by the corresponding item in the base year income statement. (894)

Vertical analysis Portraying items in financial statements as percentages (or proportional parts) of a given item on the same financial statement. (889)

Working capital The excess of current assets over current liabilities. (896)

■ QUESTIONS, EXERCISES, AND PROBLEMS

Discussion Questions

1. A company has a net income percentage of 10 percent. What does this mean?
2. What does an increase in the accounts receivable turnover indicate as far as a company is concerned?
3. What is the difference between a firm's solvency and its profitability?
4. How does a company's current ratio differ from its quick ratio?
5. Why is a high merchandise inventory turnover more desirable than a low turnover?
6. Describe the difference between horizontal analysis and vertical analysis with regard to comparative balance sheets.
7. For each of the following types of business, would you expect a high or a low merchandise inventory turnover?
   a. Furniture store
   b. Women's clothing boutique
   c. Jeweler
   d. Gift shop
   e. Grocery
   f. Florist
8. Why are creditors interested in the ratio of stockholders' equity to liabilities? Is it more desirable to have a high ratio or a low ratio?

Exercises

P.O. 1

Calculate the percentage of increase and decrease—horizontal analysis.

Exercise 25-1 Calculate the percentages of increase and decrease for the following items (horizontal analysis). Round off to one decimal place.

	2001	2000
Cash	$ 72,500	$ 80,000
Notes Receivable	51,000	40,000
Equipment (net)	179,600	182,500
Retained Earnings	117,200	115,000

P.O. 2

Prepare a comparative income statement—vertical analysis.

Exercise 25-2 Using the following revenue and expense data, prepare a comparative income statement, expressing each item for both 2001 and 2000 as a percentage of net sales (vertical analysis). Round off to one decimal place. Comment on the results.

	2001	2000
Sales (net)	$702,000	$645,000
Cost of Goods Sold	502,000	452,145
Selling Expenses	40,100	39,000
General Expenses	21,540	20,500
Income Tax Expense	47,125	45,340

P.O. 3

Calculate trend percentages and comment on the trends.

Exercise 25-3 Calculate trend percentages for the following items, and comment on the trends. Use 1999 as the base year. Round off to one decimal place. Comment on the results.

	1999	2000	2001	2002
Net Sales	$687,000	$663,000	$630,000	$600,000
Cost of Goods Sold	369,000	363,000	391,000	360,000
Merchandise Inventory	76,000	70,000	66,000	63,000

P.O. 4a,b,c

Compute working capital, current ratio, and quick ratio.

Exercise 25-4 The following items are from the balance sheets of Blessing Company as of December 31, 2000 and 1999.

	2000	1999
Current Assets:		
Cash	$ 98 0 0 0 00	$ 89 0 0 0 00
Notes Receivable	15 0 0 0 00	13 0 0 0 00
Accounts Receivable (net)	67 0 0 0 00	58 0 0 0 00
Merchandise Inventory	272 0 0 0 00	235 0 0 0 00
Supplies	1 0 0 0 00	1 0 0 0 00
Total Current Assets	$ 453 0 0 0 00	$ 396 0 0 0 00
Current Liabilities	$ 228 0 0 0 00	$ 182 0 0 0 00

Calculate the following items for each year. Round off to one decimal place.

a. Working capital
b. Current ratio
c. Quick ratio

P.O. 4a,b,c

Compute working capital, current ratio, and quick ratio.

Exercise 25-5 The following items are taken from the balance sheet of the Masty Company:

Cash	$125,000
Accounts Receivable (net)	376,000
Merchandise Inventory	122,000
Prepaid Expenses	3,750
Accounts Payable	176,000
Notes Payable (current)	17,200
Salaries Payable	2,700

Compute the following items. Round off to one decimal place.

a. Working capital
b. Current ratio
c. Quick ratio

P.O. 2,4d,e

Calculate gross profit percentage, accounts receivable turnover, and merchandise inventory turnover.

Exercise 25-6 The following data on page 908 are taken from the financial statements of the Mory Company. For 2000, calculate the gross profit percentage, the accounts receivable turnover, and the merchandise inventory turnover. Round off to one decimal place.

	2000	1999
Sales (net on account)	$820,000	$700,000
Cost of Goods Sold	617,000	520,000
Merchandise Inventory (at end of year)	139,400	130,000
Accounts Receivable (at end of year)	99,600	102,500

P.O. 4d,e,g,5b

Compute turnovers, ratio, and rate of return.

Exercise 25-7 The following items are taken from the financial statements of the Berg Company. All sales are made on account. Common stock is the only stock issued by Berg.

	2001	2000
Accounts Receivable	$ 420,000	$ 390,000
Merchandise Inventory	310,000	287,000
Plant and Equipment	2,500,000	2,200,000
Long-Term Liabilities	1,010,000	1,000,000
Stockholders' Equity	3,970,000	3,640,000
Sales (net) on account or credit	1,850,000	1,670,000
Gross Profit	560,000	517,000
Net Income	199,000	187,000

Compute the following for 2001. Round off to one decimal place.

a. Accounts receivable turnover
b. Merchandise inventory turnover
c. Ratio of plant and equipment to long-term liabilities
d. Rate of return on common stockholders' equity

P.O. 5a,b,c,d

Calculate equity of common stock per share, earnings per share, price-earnings ratio, and rate of return on common stockholders' equity.

Exercise 25-8 The Stockholders' Equity section of the balance sheet of the Pavel Corporation is as follows:

Stockholders' Equity		
Paid-in Capital:		
Common Stock, $5 par (100,000 shares authorized, 80,000 shares issued and outstanding)	$ 400 0 0 0 00	
Premium on Common Stock	140 0 0 0 00	
Total Paid-in Capital	$ 540 0 0 0 00	
Retained Earnings	290 0 0 0 00	
Total Stockholders' Equity		$ 830 0 0 0 00

Net income for the year is $125,000. Stockholders' equity was $880,000 at the beginning of the year. The present market price of the stock is $44 per share.

The number of outstanding shares did not change during the year. Determine the following items, rounding to one decimal place:

a. Equity per share
b. Earnings per share of common stock
c. Price-earnings ratio
d. Rate of return on common stockholders' equity

WHAT IF . . .

What if you see that purchases discounts for this year are 5 percent lower than for last year? Who would you talk to about it? What is happening? How has it affected your "bottom line"?

CRITICAL THINKING

The following data were analyzed by the new accounting assistant:

Gross sales	$102,000	Cost of goods sold	$54,540
Sales returns and allowances	$4,804	Operating expenses	$36,890
Sales discounts	$1,040		

The accounting assistant concluded the following:

The gross profit percentage for the year is 40.8 percent.
The income from operations percentage for the year is 4.63 percent.

You are suspicious of the percentages reported. Check the numbers. If there are errors, do you have any suggestions for the next step?

A MATTER OF ETHICS

A manager of a company is evaluated on the gross profit percentage of his department. To boost sales, in spite of potential higher uncollectible accounts expense, he unduly extends more credit. Comment on this tactic as well as the board of directors' buying back significant blocks of stock at the end of the year so that stock is not outstanding when earnings per share is calculated.

WEB WORK

Using an Internet web browser, type *comparative financial statements* in the search box and search for information about the uses of comparative financial statement analysis. Discuss your findings in a small group. Write a one-page summary of your findings.

PROBLEM SET A

For additional help, see the demonstration problem at the beginning of each chapter in your Working Papers.

P.O. 1

Problem 25-1A During 2000, Martin's Floor Coverings put on a sales promotion campaign that cost $17,090 more than Martin's usually spent on advertising. A condensed comparative income statement for the fiscal years ended December 31, 2000, and December 31, 1999, is shown here.

Martin's Floor Coverings
Comparative Income Statement
For Years Ended December 31, 2000 and December 31, 1999

	2000	1999
Revenue from Sales:		
Sales	$ 470 5 6 0 00	$ 346 0 0 0 00
Less Sales Returns and Allowances	36 4 0 0 00	26 0 0 0 00
Net Sales	$ 434 1 6 0 00	$ 320 0 0 0 00
Cost of Goods Sold	278 1 6 0 00	195 2 0 0 00
Gross Profit	$ 156 0 0 0 00	$ 124 8 0 0 00
Operating Expenses:		
Selling Expenses	$ 89 9 6 0 00	$ 69 2 0 0 00
General Expenses	22 4 4 0 00	20 4 0 0 00
Total Operating Expenses	$ 112 4 0 0 00	$ 89 6 0 0 00
Income from Operations	$ 43 6 0 0 00	$ 35 2 0 0 00
Other Expenses	5 6 0 00	4 0 0 00
Net Income	$ 43 0 4 0 00	$ 34 8 0 0 00

Check Figure

Amount of increase in Net Income, $8,240

Instructions

1. Using horizontal analysis, prepare a comparative income statement for the two-year period. Round off to one decimal place.
2. Comment on the percentages of increase or decrease.

P.O. 2

Problem 25-2A Use the comparative income statement for Martin's Floor Coverings presented in Problem 25-1A.

Check Figure

Net Income percentage for 2000, 9.9%

Instructions

1. Using vertical analysis, prepare a comparative income statement for the two-year period. Round off to one decimal place.
2. Comment on the percentage figures.

P.O. 3

Problem 25-3A On the next page is the condensed comparative income statement of the Seahorn Manufacturing Corporation.

Seahorn Manufacturing Corporation
Comparative Income Statement
For Years Ended December 31, 1999, 2000, 2001 (thousands of dollars)

	1999	2000	2001
Sales (net)	$ 16 0 0 0 00	$ 17 6 0 0 00	$ 20 0 0 0 00
Cost of Goods Sold	11 4 0 0 00	12 8 0 0 00	15 0 0 0 00
Gross Profit	$ 4 6 0 0 00	$ 4 8 0 0 00	$ 5 0 0 0 00
Operating Expenses:			
Selling Expenses	$ 2 3 6 8 00	$ 2 5 5 4 00	$ 2 6 8 8 00
General Expenses	1 5 6 0 00	1 5 6 0 00	1 5 7 2 00
Total Operating Expenses	$ 3 9 2 8 00	$ 4 1 1 4 00	$ 4 2 6 0 00
Income Before Income Tax	$ 6 7 2 00	$ 6 8 6 00	$ 7 4 0 00
Income Tax Expense	2 2 8 00	2 3 8 00	2 5 3 00
Net Income	$ 4 4 4 00	$ 4 4 8 00	$ 4 8 7 00

Check Figure

Net Income After Income Tax,
2000, 100.9%

P.O. 4a,b,c,e;5b,c,d

Instructions

1. Express the income statement data in trend percentages. Round off to the nearest tenth of a percent (one decimal place).
2. Comment on any significant relationships revealed by the percentages.

Problem 25-4A Below and on the following page are the year-end financial statements of Henkel Music Store:

Henkel Music Store
Income Statement
For Year Ended December 31, 2000

Revenue from Sales:		
Sales		$ 810 0 0 0 00
Cost of Goods Sold:		
Merchandise Inventory, Jan. 1, 2000	$ 120 0 0 0 00	
Delivered Cost of Purchases	504 6 0 0 00	
Goods Available for Sale	$ 624 6 0 0 00	
Less Merchandise Inventory,		
Dec. 31, 2000	132 9 0 0 00	
Cost of Goods Sold		491 7 0 0 00
Gross Profit		$ 318 3 0 0 00
Operating Expenses:		
Selling Expenses (control)	$ 168 7 5 0 00	
General Expenses (control)	82 9 5 0 00	
Total Operating Expenses		251 7 0 0 00
Income from Operations		$ 66 6 0 0 00
Other Expenses:		
Interest Expense		11 4 0 0 00
Income Before Income Tax		$ 55 2 0 0 00
Income Tax Expense		9 5 0 0 00
Net Income		$ 45 7 0 0 00

Henkel Music Store
Balance Sheet
December 31, 2000

Assets										
Current Assets:										
Cash					$	21 3 0 0 00				
Notes Receivable						6 0 0 0 00				
Accounts Receivable (net)						77 7 0 0 00				
Merchandise Inventory						132 9 0 0 00				
Prepaid Expenses						1 8 0 0 00				
Total Current Assets								$ 239 7 0 0 00		
Plant and Equipment:										
Store Equipment (net)					$	46 3 5 0 00				
Office Equipment (net)						14 1 0 0 00				
Delivery Equipment (net)						74 5 5 0 00				
Total Plant and Equipment								135 0 0 0 00		
Total Assets								$ 374 7 0 0 00		
Liabilities										
Current Liabilities:										
Accounts Payable	$	50 7 0 0 00								
Notes Payable		3 6 0 0 00								
Total Current Liabilities					$	54 3 0 0 00				
Long-Term Liabilities:										
Mortgage Payable (due June 30, 2013)						115 2 0 0 00				
Total Liabilities								$ 169 5 0 0 00		
Stockholders' Equity										
Common Stock, $15 par (10,000 shares authorized and issued)					$	150 0 0 0 00				
Retained Earnings						55 2 0 0 00				
Total Stockholders' Equity								205 2 0 0 00		
Total Liabilities and Stockholders' Equity								$ 374 7 0 0 00		

The market price of the stock on December 31, 2000, is $50 per share. At the beginning of the year, stockholders' equity was $175,000. The number of shares did not change during the year.

Check Figure

Price-earnings ratio, 10.94:1

Instructions

Determine the following items, showing the figures you used in your calculations (round off to two decimal places):

1. Working capital
2. Current ratio
3. Quick ratio
4. Merchandise inventory turnover
5. Number of days merchandise inventory is kept in stock
6. Rate of return on common stockholders' equity
7. Earnings per share of common stock
8. Price-earnings ratio

PROBLEM SET B

For additional help, see the demonstration problem at the beginning of each chapter in your Working Papers.

P.O. 1

Problem 25-1B During 2000, Whaley's Fashion Shoppe put on a big sales promotion campaign that cost $13,200 more than Whaley's usually spent for advertising. The condensed comparative income statement for the fiscal years ended December 31, 2000, and December 31, 1999, is shown here.

Whaley's Fashion Shoppe
Comparative Income Statement
For Years Ended December 31, 2000 and December 31, 1999

	2000	1999
Revenue from Sales:		
Sales	$ 427 6 8 0 00	$ 324 0 0 0 00
Less Sales Returns and Allowances	35 0 4 0 00	24 0 0 0 00
Net Sales	$ 392 6 4 0 00	$ 300 0 0 0 00
Cost of Goods Sold	223 0 2 0 00	177 0 0 0 00
Gross Profit	$ 169 6 2 0 00	$ 123 0 0 0 00
Operating Expenses:		
Selling Expenses	$ 74 8 9 6 00	$ 60 4 0 0 00
General Expenses	22 0 8 0 00	19 2 0 0 00
Total Operating Expenses	$ 96 9 7 6 00	$ 79 6 0 0 00
Income from Operations	$ 72 6 4 4 00	$ 43 4 0 0 00
Other Expenses	7 5 0 00	6 0 0 00
Net Income	$ 71 8 9 4 00	$ 42 8 0 0 00

Check Figure

Amount of increase in Net Income, $29,094

Instructions

1. Using horizontal analysis, prepare a comparative income statement for the two-year period. Round off percentages to one decimal place.
2. Comment on the percentages of increase or decrease.

P.O. 2

Problem 25-2B Use the comparative income statement for Whaley's Fashion Shoppe presented in Problem 25-1B.

Check Figure

Net Income percentage for 2000, 18.3%

Instructions

1. Using vertical analysis, prepare a comparative income statement for the two-year period. Round off percentages to one decimal place.
2. Comment on the percentage figures.

P.O. 3

Problem 25-3B On the next page is the condensed comparative income statement of the Central Electric Corporation:

Central Electric Corporation
Comparative Income Statement
For Years Ended December 31, 1999, 2000, 2001 (thousands of dollars)

	1999	2000	2001
Sales (net)	$9 3 0 0 00	$10 2 0 0 00	$11 4 0 0 00
Cost of Goods Sold	6 6 0 0 00	7 4 4 0 00	8 4 4 5 00
Gross Profit	$2 7 0 0 00	$ 2 7 6 0 00	$ 2 9 5 5 00
Operating Expenses:			
Selling Expenses	$1 3 9 5 00	$ 1 4 1 3 00	$ 1 5 8 1 00
General Expenses	9 1 5 00	9 3 0 00	9 3 0 00
Total Operating Expenses	$2 3 1 0 00	$ 2 3 4 3 00	$ 2 5 1 1 00
Income Before Income Tax	$ 3 9 0 00	$ 4 1 7 00	$ 4 4 4 00
Income Tax Expense	1 4 0 00	1 4 3 00	1 5 6 00
Net Income	$ 2 5 0 00	$ 2 7 4 00	$ 2 8 8 00

Check Figure

Net Income After Income Tax, 2000, 109.6%

P.O. 4a,b,c,e;5b,c,d

Instructions

1. Express the income statement data in trend percentages. Round off to the nearest tenth of a percent (one decimal place).
2. Comment on any significant relationships revealed by the percentages.

Problem 25-4B Below and on the following page are the income statement and balance sheet of Hudson Corporation.

Hudson Corporation
Income Statement
For Year Ended December 31, 2000

Revenue from Sales:			
Sales			$ 705 0 0 0 00
Cost of Goods Sold:			
Merchandise Inventory, Jan. 1, 2000	$ 114 0 0 0 00		
Delivered Cost of Purchases	460 2 0 0 00		
Goods Available for Sale	$ 574 2 0 0 00		
Less Merchandise Inventory,			
Dec. 31, 2000	121 8 0 0 00		
Cost of Goods Sold			452 4 0 0 00
Gross Profit			$ 252 6 0 0 00
Operating Expenses:			
Selling Expenses (control)	$ 139 0 5 0 00		
General Expenses (control)	69 3 0 0 00		
Total Operating Expenses			208 3 5 0 00
Income from Operations			$ 44 2 5 0 00
Other Expenses:			
Interest Expense			7 8 0 0 00
Income Before Income Tax			$ 36 4 5 0 00
Income Tax Expense			8 2 5 0 00
Net Income After Income Tax			$ 28 2 0 0 00

Hudson Corporation
Balance Sheet
December 31, 2000

Assets			
Current Assets:			
Cash		$ 17 250 00	
Notes Receivable		6 000 00	
Accounts Receivable (net)		80 550 00	
Merchandise Inventory		121 800 00	
Prepaid Expenses		2 100 00	
Total Current Assets			$ 227 700 00
Plant and Equipment:			
Store Equipment (net)		$ 46 800 00	
Office Equipment (net)		13 650 00	
Delivery Equipment (net)		77 100 00	
Total Plant and Equipment			137 550 00
Total Assets			$ 365 250 00
Liabilities			
Current Liabilities:			
Accounts Payable	$ 32 250 00		
Notes Payable	3 000 00		
Total Current Liabilities		$ 35 250 00	
Long-Term Liabilities:			
Mortgage Payable (due June 30, 2013)		120 000 00	
Total Liabilities			$ 155 250 00
Stockholders' Equity			
Common Stock, $15 par (10,000 shares authorized and issued)		$ 150 000 00	
Retained Earnings		60 000 00	
Total Stockholders' Equity			210 000 00
Total Liabilities and Stockholders' Equity			$ 365 250 00

The market price of the stock on December 31, 2000, is $46 per share. At the beginning of the year, stockholders' equity was $193,800. The number of shares issued did not change during the year.

Check Figure

Price-earnings ratio, 16.31:1

Instructions

Determine the following items, showing the figures you used in your calculations (round off to two decimal places):

1. Working capital
2. Current ratio
3. Quick ratio
4. Merchandise inventory turnover
5. Number of days merchandise inventory is kept in stock
6. Rate of return on common stockholders' equity
7. Earnings per share of common stock
8. Price-earnings ratio

Departmental Accounting

Performance Objectives

After you have completed this chapter, you will be able to do the following:

1. Compile a departmental income statement extended through Gross Profit.

2. Compile a departmental work sheet.

3. Compile a departmental income statement extended through Income from Operations.

4. Apportion operating expenses among various operating departments.

5. Compile a departmental income statement extended through departmental margin.

A company that carries on a number of different business activities should be divided into a number of subdivisions or departments. This enables the company's management to delegate authority to departmental managers, who are held responsible for their respective departments, and to measure the profitability of each department. It is the element of profitability that we discuss in this chapter.

Large companies have greater opportunities to use departmental accounting than small ones. However, even a small business—if it carries on more than one type of business activity—may benefit from departmental accounting. For example, Ross and Robins operate a real estate and insurance firm and account separately for real estate and insurance commissions. At the end of the fiscal year, Ross and Robins can compare the profitability of each activity with the amount of time and attention they had to devote to that activity.

With these comparisons, they may decide to spend more time on one activity and less on the other.

For large business firms—those that engage in service, merchandising, or manufacturing—departmental accounting is a must. The accounting reports consist of several levels of income statements recorded on a departmental basis and extended from sales through gross profit or income from operations or departmental margin.

GROSS PROFIT BY DEPARTMENTS

A department's gross profit depends on its sales volume and its markup on the goods sold:

Net Sales − Cost of Goods Sold = Gross Profit

Gross profit, in the same context, consists of the items listed in the income statement shown in Figure 1. To determine the gross profit of a given department, you need a separate set of figures for the department for each element entering into the gross profit. There are two ways to obtain these figures:

1. Keep separate general ledger accounts for each item affecting gross profit, such as a Sales account for each department, a Sales Returns and Allowances account for each department, and so on. Then record the balances of these accounts on the income statement, OR
2. Keep only one general ledger account for each item affecting gross profit, and apportion the balance to the various departments. For example, maintain one Sales account and one Sales Returns and Allowances account for the company, and in addition keep a breakdown of sales and sales returns for each department. Then record the figures for each department on the income statement.

FIGURE 1

INCOME STATEMENT

Revenue from Sales:				
Sales				$120 0 0 0 00
Less: Sales Returns and Allowances		$ 6 0 0 0 00		
Sales Discounts		3 0 0 0 00		9 0 0 0 00
Net Sales				$111 0 0 0 00
Cost of Goods Sold:				
Merchandise Inventory (beginning)		$ 48 0 0 0 00		
Purchases	$76 4 0 0 00			
Less: Purchases Returns				
and Allowances	$4 0 0 0 00			
Purchases Discount	2 0 0 0 00	6 0 0 0 00		
Net Purchases	$70 4 0 0 00			
Add Freight In	4 6 0 0 00			
Delivered Cost of Purchases		75 0 0 0 00		
Goods Available for Sale		$123 0 0 0 00		
Less Merchandise Inventory (ending)		52 0 0 0 00		
Cost of Goods Sold				71 0 0 0 00
Gross Profit				$ 40 0 0 0 00

							SALES CREDIT				
DATE	INV. NO.	CUSTOMER'S NAME	POST. REF.	ACCOUNTS RECEIVABLE DEBIT	DEPT. A	DEPT. B	DEPT. C	DEPT. D	DEPT. E		
20–											1
Sept. 1	1698	Cora Bule	✓	1 6 5 00	1 6 5 00						2
3	1702	Rob Carler	✓	3 7 6 00			3 7 6 00				3
3	1704	Steve Krane	✓	7 1 6 00		7 1 6 00					4
30				14 9 3 3 00	2 6 8 1 00	8 6 4 00	4 7 9 4 00	3 7 1 6 00	2 8 7 8 00		16
				(1 1 4)	(4 1 1)	(4 1 2)	(4 1 3)	(4 1 4)	(4 1 5)		17

SALES JOURNAL   PAGE **12**

FIGURE 2

Keeping Separate Accounts by Department

Keeping separate accounts by department yields the most accurate accounting data. You need separate accounts for each department for Sales, Sales Returns and Allowances, Sales Discounts, Purchases, Purchases Returns and Allowances, Purchases Discount, Freight In, and Merchandise Inventory. For example, Riggs Hardware has five departments and uses five Sales accounts, five Sales Returns and Allowances accounts, five Sales Discount accounts, five Merchandise Inventory accounts, and so forth. The special journals contain columns for each departmental account, as in the sales journal in Figure 2.

The accountant posts each total to a separate account, as indicated by the ledger account numbers. A company that has many departments and keeps a separate journal column for each may find that the journal becomes quite cumbersome. In a situation like this, it is better to post from the sales invoices directly to the departmental sales accounts. Another alternative is to establish a controlling account in the general ledger and to record each department in a subsidiary ledger.

Maintaining One General Ledger Account

When a company keeps only one general ledger account for each item involved in gross profit, the accountant has to distribute the total amount among the various departments at the end of the accounting period. To do so, the accountant has to accumulate departmental information on supplementary records. Winn's Pharmacy, for example, has pharmacy, cosmetics, gifts, and cards departments. Winn's uses a counter scanner that reads bar codes on products to record sales by department electronically. Products without bar codes may be entered by key pad. At the end of each day, the sales are recorded in a journal, with the totals taken from the cash register tapes. Sales are also recorded on a departmental analysis sheet.

Businesses use separate analysis sheets for sales returns, purchases, purchases returns and allowances, purchases discounts, and so forth. At the end of the accounting period, these analysis sheets give departmental breakdowns for each item.

Gross Profit by Departments

Objective 1

Compile a departmental income statement extended through Gross Profit.

Corson Company, Inc., has two departments, A and B, and keeps separate accounts for each. The income statement for the fiscal year ending December 31, showing departmental reporting only through Gross Profit, appears in Figure 3 on pages 920–921. An outline of this process is as follows:

From Sales Through Gross Profit

Revenue from Sales
Less Cost of Goods Sold

> Based on separate departmental accounts or supplementary analysis sheets

Gross Profit
Less Operating Expenses

Income from Operations
Add Other Income
Less Other Expenses

Income Before Income Tax
Less Income Tax Expense

Net Income

INCOME FROM OPERATIONS BY DEPARTMENTS

A company may extend departmental reporting of income through Income from Operations. Corson Company, Inc., keeps separate accounts for each item that enters into gross profit and apportions the operating expenses between Gross Profit and Income from Operations to Department A or Department B on a logical basis. Let's look at the outline of the income statement:

From Sales Through Income from Operations

Departmentalized

Revenue from Sales
Less Cost of Goods Sold

> Separate departmental accounts or supplementary analysis sheets

Gross Profit
Less Selling Expenses
Less General Expenses

> Account balances are apportioned

Income from Operations

Nondepartmentalized

Add Other Income
Less Other Expenses

Income Before Income Tax
Less Income Tax Expense

Net Income

Corson Company, Inc.
Income Statement
For Year Ended December 31, 20—

		DEPARTMENT A	
1	Revenue from Sales:		
2	Sales	$ 560 0 0 0 00	
3	Less Sales Returns and Allowances	14 2 0 0 00	
4	Net Sales		$ 545 8 0 0 00
5	Cost of Goods Sold:		
6	Merchandise Inventory, Jan. 1, 20—	$ 96 4 0 0 00	
7	Purchases	$ 312 1 1 5 00	
8	Less: Purchases Returns and Allowances $9,580.00		
9	Purchases Discount 5,740.00	15 3 2 0 00	
10	Net Purchases	$ 296 7 9 5 00	
11	Add Freight In	13 0 0 5 00	
12	Delivered Cost of Purchases	309 8 0 0 00	
13	Goods Available for Sale	$ 406 2 0 0 00	
14	Less Merchandise Inventory, Dec. 31, 20—	110 0 0 0 00	
15	Cost of Goods Sold		296 2 0 0 00
16	Gross Profit		$ 249 6 0 0 00
17			
18	Operating Expenses:		
19	Selling Expenses:		
20	Sales Salary Expense		
21	Advertising Expense		
22	Depreciation Expense, Store Equipment		
23	Miscellaneous Selling Expense		
24	Total Selling Expenses		
25	General Expenses:		
26	Office Salary Expense		
27	Rent Expense		
28	Utilities Expense		
29	Insurance Expense		
30	Bad Debts Expense		
31	Miscellaneous General Expense		
32	Total General Expenses		
33	Total Operating Expenses		
34	Income from Operations		
35			
36	Other Income:		
37	Interest Income		
38	Other Expenses:		
39	Interest Expense		
40	Income Before Income Tax		
41	Income Tax Expense		
42	Net Income		
43			

FIGURE 3

Row	DEPARTMENT B			TOTAL		
1						
2		$ 240 0 0 0 00			$ 800 0 0 0 00	
3		5 8 0 0 00			20 0 0 0 00	
4			$ 234 2 0 0 00			$ 780 0 0 0 00
5						
6		$ 82 7 4 0 00			$ 179 1 4 0 00	
7	$ 161 1 7 5 00			$ 473 2 9 0 00		
8	4 7 5 6 00			14 3 3 6 00		
9	3 2 7 4 00			9 0 1 4 00		
10	$ 153 1 4 5 00			$ 449 9 4 0 00		
11	6 7 1 5 00			19 7 2 0 00		
12		159 8 6 0 00			469 6 6 0 00	
13		$ 242 6 0 0 00			$ 648 8 0 0 00	
14		90 0 0 0 00			200 0 0 0 00	
15			152 6 0 0 00			448 8 0 0 00
16		$ 81 6 0 0 00				$ 331 2 0 0 00
17						
18						
19						
20				$ 140 8 2 5 00		
21				17 6 0 0 00		
22				3 3 0 0 00		
23				4 2 7 0 00		
24					$ 165 9 9 5 00	
25						
26				$ 32 1 0 0 00		
27				16 4 0 0 00		
28				4 8 4 0 00		
29				4 4 0 0 00		
30				2 5 7 0 00		
31				9 2 0 00		
32					61 2 3 0 00	
33						227 2 2 5 00
34						$ 103 9 7 5 00
35						
36						
37					$ 3 6 2 4 00	
38						
39					2 4 0 0 00	1 2 2 4 00
40						$ 105 1 9 9 00
41						24 2 7 8 00
42						$ 80 9 2 1 00
43						

Work Sheet for Departmental Accounting

Objective 2

Compile a departmental work sheet.

Each department assumes its share of overhead expenses. Recall once again the sequential steps of the accounting cycle: Record the trial balance in the first columns of the work sheet, formulate and record the adjustments, complete the work sheet, and then use the work sheet to prepare the income statement. The Income Statement columns of the work sheet for a company that keeps track of income by departments contain debit and credit columns for each department, as well as debit and credit columns titled Nondepartmental. These last two columns include Other Income and Other Expenses accounts that are not directly assigned to a department. By the time the accountant gets to the income statement, she or he has already performed the calculations apportioning the expenses, which are accordingly subdivided on the work sheet. A sample portion of the work sheet for the Corson Company is shown in Figure 4 on pages 924–927. Various asset, liability, and owners' equity accounts are not shown, but they are included in the totals.

Income Statement for Departmental Accounting

Objective 3

Compile a departmental income statement extended through Income from Operations.

The income statement contains a set of columns for each department, as well as a set of columns for the combined total of all departments. The income statement in Figure 5 on pages 928–929, which is extended through Income from Operations, is a more representative example than the one in Figure 3. A discussion of the apportionment of operating expenses between the two departments follows.

Apportionment of Operating Expenses

Objective 4

Apportion operating expenses among various operating departments.

Apportionment of expenses is a crucial element of departmental accounting. It consists of allocating operating expenses among operating departments. You can readily identify some operating expenses as belonging to a given department. For example, if a salesperson makes sales in one department only, the accountant assigns that salesperson's salary or commission directly to that department. However, other operating expenses, such as Miscellaneous Selling Expense or Utilities Expense, cannot be restricted to one department and must be divided on some equitable basis. Let's look at the operating expenses of the Corson Company and see how they are apportioned.

Sales Salary Expense Corson allocates the salespersons' salaries to Department A or Department B according to the payroll register, which lists each employee by department. Department A's share is $88,625; Department B's is $52,200.

Advertising Expense Corson advertises in three media: billboards, newspapers, and radio. The cost breakdown is as follows:

Billboard advertising	$ 1,600
Newspaper advertising	9,600
Radio advertising	6,400
Total	$17,600

The billboard advertising displays the name of the company and tells where it is, but it doesn't advertise the products of Department A or Depart-

Although Volkswagen markets several products, this billboard is solely advertising its new Beetle. The expense for this advertising piece may be billed to that department alone. If it had shown more than one model, the expense would have been allocated to more than one department, either equally or based on gross sales. Compare this to newspaper advertising, which is generally billed to each department based on column inches, or to radio, which is based on air time.

ment B. Since no specific department is featured, Corson's accountant apportions the cost of these billboard ads according to gross sales, as follows:

Sales for Department A	$560,000
Sales for Department B	240,000
Total Sales	$800,000

Dept. A's sales as percentage of total: $\dfrac{\$560,000}{\$800,000} = \underline{\underline{70\%}}$

Dept. B's sales as percentage of total: $\dfrac{\$240,000}{\$800,000} = \underline{\underline{30\%}}$

Dept. A's share of cost of billboard advertising: 70% of $1,600 = $1,600 × .7 = $\underline{\underline{\$1,120}}$

Dept. B's share of cost of billboard advertising: 30% of $1,600 = $1,600 × .3 = $\underline{\underline{\$480}}$

Corson allocates the cost of its newspaper advertising according to the number of column inches each department uses. In a year, Corson buys 3,200 inches of newspaper advertising, divided according to departments as follows:

Advertising for Dept. A: 1,920 column inches or $\dfrac{1,920}{3,200} = \underline{\underline{60\%}}$

Advertising for Dept. B: 1,280 column inches or $\dfrac{1,280}{3,200} = \underline{\underline{40\%}}$

Dept. A's share of cost of newspaper advertising: 60% of $9,600 = $9,600 × .6 = $\underline{\underline{\$5,760}}$

Dept. B's share of cost of newspaper advertising: 40% of $9,600 = $9,600 × .4 = $\underline{\underline{\$3,840}}$

Corson Company, Inc.
Work Sheet
For Year Ended December 31, 20—

	ACCOUNT NAME	TRIAL BALANCE DEBIT	TRIAL BALANCE CREDIT	ADJUSTMENTS DEBIT	ADJUSTMENTS CREDIT	DEPARTMENT A INCOME STATEMENT DEBIT	DEPARTMENT A INCOME STATEMENT CREDIT
3	Accounts Receivable	82 0 4 0 00					
4	Allowance for						
5	Doubtful Accounts		8 6 2 00		(f) 2 5 7 0 00		
6	Merchandise						
7	Inventory						
8	Department A	96 4 0 0 00		(b)110 0 0 0 00	(a) 96 4 0 0 00		
9	Department B	82 7 4 0 00		(d) 90 0 0 0 00	(c) 82 7 4 0 00		
10	Prepaid Insurance	5 5 4 0 00			(e) 4 4 0 0 00		
11	Store Equipment	32 4 0 0 00					
12	Accumulated Depre-						
13	ciation, Store						
14	Equipment		21 6 0 0 00		(g) 3 3 0 0 00		
27	Sales						
28	Department A		560 0 0 0 00				560 0 0 0 00
29	Department B		240 0 0 0 00				
30	Sales Returns and						
31	Allowances						
32	Department A	14 2 0 0 00				14 2 0 0 00	
33	Department B	5 8 0 0 00					
34	Purchases						
35	Department A	312 1 1 5 00				312 1 1 5 00	
36	Department B	161 1 7 5 00					
37	Purchases Returns						
38	and Allowances						
39	Department A		9 5 8 0 00				9 5 8 0 00
40	Department B		4 7 5 6 00				
41	Purchases Discount						
42	Department A		5 7 4 0 00				5 7 4 0 00
43	Department B		3 2 7 4 00				
44	Freight In						
45	Department A	13 0 0 5 00				13 0 0 5 00	
46	Department B	6 7 1 5 00					
47	Sales Salary						
48	Expense	140 8 2 5 00				88 6 2 5 00	
49	Advertising Expense	17 6 0 0 00				10 3 3 6 00	
50	Misc. Selling						
51	Expense	4 2 7 0 00				2 9 8 9 00	
52	Office Salary						
53	Expense	32 1 0 0 00				22 4 7 0 00	
54	Rent Expense	16 4 0 0 00				10 2 5 0 00	
55	Utilities Expense	4 8 4 0 00				3 0 2 5 00	
56	Totals carried forward	1,468 5 4 4 00	1,490 4 9 0 00	200 0 0 0 00	189 4 1 0 00	477 0 1 5 00	575 3 2 0 00

FIGURE 4

	DEPARTMENT B INCOME STATEMENT		NONDEPARTMENTAL INCOME STATEMENT		BALANCE SHEET		
	DEBIT	CREDIT	DEBIT	CREDIT	DEBIT	CREDIT	
					82 0 4 0 00		3
							4
						3 4 3 2 00	5
							6
							7
					110 0 0 0 00		8
					90 0 0 0 00		9
					1 1 4 0 00		10
					32 4 0 0 00		11
							12
							13
						24 9 0 0 00	14
							27
							28
		240 0 0 0 00					29
							30
							31
							32
	5 8 0 0 00						33
							34
							35
	161 1 7 5 00						36
							37
							38
							39
		4 7 5 6 00					40
							41
							42
		3 2 7 4 00					43
							44
							45
	6 7 1 5 00						46
							47
	52 2 0 0 00						48
	7 2 6 4 00						49
							50
	1 2 8 1 00						51
							52
	9 6 3 0 00						53
	6 1 5 0 00						54
	1 8 1 5 00						55
	252 0 3 0 00	248 0 3 0 00	0	0	1,118 7 6 1 00	1,035 8 1 2 00	56

(continued)

ACCOUNT NAME	TRIAL BALANCE DEBIT	TRIAL BALANCE CREDIT	ADJUSTMENTS DEBIT	ADJUSTMENTS CREDIT	DEPARTMENT A INCOME STATEMENT DEBIT	DEPARTMENT A INCOME STATEMENT CREDIT	
1 Totals brought forward	1,468 5 4 4 00	1,490 4 9 0 00	200 0 0 0 00	189 4 1 0 00	477 0 1 5 00	575 3 2 0 00	
2 Misc. General							
3 Expense	9 2 0 00				6 4 4 00		
4 Income Tax Expense	22 2 5 0 00		(h) 2 0 2 8 00				
5 Interest Income		3 6 2 4 00					
6 Interest Expense	2 4 0 0 00						
7	1,494 1 1 4 00	1,494 1 1 4 00					
8 Inc. Summary, A			(a) 96 4 0 0 00	(b) 110 0 0 0 00	96 4 0 0 00	110 0 0 0 00	
9 Inc. Summary, B			(c) 82 7 4 0 00	(d) 90 0 0 0 00			
10 Insurance Expense			(e) 4 4 0 0 00		2 5 4 0 00		
11 Bad Debts Expense			(f) 2 5 7 0 00		1 7 9 9 00		
12 Depreciation							
13 Expense, Store							
14 Equipment			(g) 3 3 0 0 00		1 8 4 0 00		
15 Income Tax Payable				(h) 2 0 2 8 00			
16			391 4 3 8 00	391 4 3 8 00	580 2 3 8 00	685 3 2 0 00	
17 Net Income (Loss)							
18 by Department					105 0 8 2 00		
19					685 3 2 0 00	685 3 2 0 00	
20 Net Income							
21							
22							
23							
24							

FIGURE 4 (continued)

Corson allocates cost of radio advertising to the two departments according to the amount of air time each department uses. In a year, Corson buys
1,250 minutes of radio time, divided according to departments as shown here:

Advertising for Dept. A: 675 minutes or $\frac{675}{1,250} = \underline{\underline{54\%}}$

Advertising for Dept. B: 575 minutes or $\frac{575}{1,250} = \underline{\underline{46\%}}$

Dept. A's share of cost of radio advertising: 54% of $6,400 = $6,400 \times .54 = \underline{\underline{\$3,456}}$

Dept. B's share of cost of radio advertising: 46% of $6,400 = $6,400 \times .46 = \underline{\underline{\$2,944}}$

Here is a summary of the Corson Company's allocation of advertising
expense:

Expense	Department A	Department B	Total
Billboard advertising	$ 1,120	$ 480	$ 1,600
Newspaper advertising	5,760	3,840	9,600
Radio advertising	3,456	2,944	6,400
	$10,336	$7,264	$17,600

	DEPARTMENT B INCOME STATEMENT		NONDEPARTMENTAL INCOME STATEMENT		BALANCE SHEET		
	DEBIT	CREDIT	DEBIT	CREDIT	DEBIT	CREDIT	
	252 0 3 0 00	248 0 3 0 00	0	0	1,118 7 6 1 00	1,035 8 1 2 00	1
							2
	2 7 6 00						3
			24 2 7 8 00				4
				3 6 2 4 00			5
			2 4 0 0 00				6
							7
							8
	82 7 4 0 00	90 0 0 0 00					9
	1 8 6 0 00						10
	7 7 1 00						11
							12
							13
	1 4 6 0 00						14
						2 0 2 8 00	15
	339 1 3 7 00	338 0 3 0 00					16
							17
		1 1 0 7 00		103 9 7 5 00			18
	339 1 3 7 00	339 1 3 7 00	26 6 7 8 00	107 5 9 9 00	1,118 7 6 1 00	1,037 8 4 0 00	19
							20
			80 9 2 1 00			80 9 2 1 00	21
			107 5 9 9 00	107 5 9 9 00	1,118 7 6 1 00	1,118 7 6 1 00	22
							23
							24

Depreciation Expense, Store Equipment Corson keeps a plant and equipment ledger that notes the department in which each piece of equipment is located. The total year's depreciation of the equipment used in Department A is $1,840; the total year's depreciation of the equipment used in Department B is $1,460.

Office Salary Expense People who work in the office of the company get paid a total of $32,100 per year. Corson apportions the amount of money that is paid in salaries to office workers on the basis of the amount of time the office personnel have to spend on each department. Management estimates that 70 percent of the office force's time is devoted to Department A and 30 percent to Department B:

Dept. A's share: 70% of $32,100 = $32,100 × .7 = $22,470

Dept. B's share: 30% of $32,100 = $32,100 × .3 = $9,630

Remember!

To apportion or to allocate means to divide up.

Rent Expense and Utilities Expense The Corson Company rents 40,000 square feet of floor space and allocates the expenses of rent and utilities on the basis of floor space occupied by each department, as follows. (Yearly expense for rent is $16,400; yearly expense for utilities is $4,840.)

Corson Company, Inc.
Income Statement
For Year Ended December 31, 20—

#			DEPARTMENT A		
1	Revenue from Sales:				
2	Sales		$ 560 0 0 0 00		
3	Less Sales Returns and Allowances		14 2 0 0 00		
4	Net Sales			$ 545 8 0 0 00	
5	Cost of Goods Sold:				
6	Merchandise Inventory, Jan. 1, 20–		$ 96 4 0 0 00		
7	Purchases	$ 312 1 1 5 00			
8	Less: Purchases Returns and Allowances $9,580.00				
9	Purchases Discount 5,740.00	15 3 2 0 00			
10	Net Purchases	$ 296 7 9 5 00			
11	Add Freight In	13 0 0 5 00			
12	Delivered Cost of Purchases		309 8 0 0 00		
13	Goods Available for Sale		$ 406 2 0 0 00		
14	Less Merchandise Inventory, Dec. 31, 20–		110 0 0 0 00		
15	Cost of Goods Sold			296 2 0 0 00	
16	Gross Profit			$ 249 6 0 0 00	
17					
18	Operating Expenses:				
19	Selling Expenses:				
20	Sales Salary Expense	$ 88 6 2 5 00			
21	Advertising Expense	10 3 3 6 00			
22	Depreciation Expense, Store Equipment	1 8 4 0 00			
23	Miscellaneous Selling Expense	2 9 8 9 00			
24	Total Selling Expenses		$ 103 7 9 0 00		
25	General Expenses:				
26	Office Salary Expense	$ 22 4 7 0 00			
27	Rent Expense	10 2 5 0 00			
28	Utilities Expense	3 0 2 5 00			
29	Insurance Expense	2 5 4 0 00			
30	Bad Debts Expense	1 7 9 9 00			
31	Miscellaneous General Expense	6 4 4 00			
32	Total General Expenses		40 7 2 8 00		
33	Total Operating Expenses			144 5 1 8 00	
34	Income (Loss) from Operations			$ 105 0 8 2 00	
35					
36	Other Income:				
37	Interest Income				
38	Other Expenses:				
39	Interest Expense				
40	Income Before Income Tax				
41	Income Tax Expense				
42	Net Income				
43					

FIGURE 5

	DEPARTMENT B			TOTAL			
1							
2		$ 240 000 00			$ 800 000 00		
3		5 800 00			20 000 00		
4			$ 234 200 00			$ 780 000 00	
5							
6		$ 82 740 00			$ 179 140 00		
7	$ 161 175 00			$ 473 290 00			
8	4 756 00			14 336 00			
9	3 274 00			9 014 00			
10	$ 153 145 00			$ 449 940 00			
11	6 715 00			19 720 00			
12		159 860 00			469 660 00		
13		$ 242 600 00			$ 648 800 00		
14		90 000 00			200 000 00		
15			152 600 00			448 800 00	
16			$ 81 600 00			$ 331 200 00	
17							
18							
19							
20	$ 52 200 00			$ 140 825 00			
21	7 264 00			17 600 00			
22	1 460 00			3 300 00			
23	1 281 00			4 270 00			
24		$ 62 205 00			$ 165 995 00		
25							
26	$ 9 630 00			$ 32 100 00			
27	6 150 00			16 400 00			
28	1 815 00			4 840 00			
29	1 860 00			4 400 00			
30	771 00			2 570 00			
31	2 76 00			9 20 00			
32		20 502 00			61 230 00		
33			82 707 00			227 225 00	
34			$ (1 107 00)			$ 103 975 00	
35							
36							
37					$ 3 624 00		
38							
39					2 400 00	1 224 00	
40						$ 105 199 00	
41						24 278 00	
42						$ 80 921 00	
43							

Rent and utilities expenses are often allocated on the basis of square feet of floor space occupied by a department or production area.

Dept. A occupies 25,000 square feet or $\dfrac{25,000}{40,000} = 62.5\%$

Dept. B occupies 15,000 square feet or $\dfrac{15,000}{40,000} = 37.5\%$

Dept. A's share of rent: 62.5% of $16,400 = $10,250

Dept. B's share of rent: 37.5% of $16,400 = $6,150

Dept. A's share of utilities: 62.5% of $4,840 = $3,025

Dept. B's share of utilities: 37.5% of $4,840 = $1,815

In this case, for simplicity, we assume that all floor space is of equal value. However, when apportioning the rent expense in a multistory building, you have to take into account differences in the value of the various floors and locations.

Insurance Expense The Corson Company carries insurance policies to cover losses that might result from (1) damage to merchandise or equipment (annual cost $3,600) and (2) injury incurred by customers while on the premises (annual cost, $800). The allocation of the cost of the insurance on merchandise and equipment is based on the average cost of the assets held by each department. The average is equal to the cost of assets on hand at the beginning of the year plus the cost of assets on hand at the end of the year, divided by 2. Following are the computations presented in tabular form:

Computations for Insurance Expense				
Item	**Department A**		**Department B**	**Total**
Merchandise Inventory				
Balance, Jan. 1	$ 96,400		$ 82,740	
Balance, Dec. 31	110,000		90,000	
Total	2)$206,400		2)$172,740	
Average (Total ÷ 2)	$103,200	$103,200	$ 86,370	$86,370	
Store Equipment				
Balance, Jan. 1	$ 19,440		$ 12,960	
Balance, Dec. 31	19,440		12,960	
Total	2)$ 38,880		2)$ 25,920	
Average (Total ÷ 2)	$ 19,440	19,440	$ 12,960	12,960	
Total		$122,640		$99,330	$221,970

Remember!

The allocation of insurance for damage to merchandise or inventory is based on the average cost of assets held by a department. But the allocation of liability insurance due to injury to customers is again based on gross sales.

The balances for the Store Equipment in the two departments are contained in the plant and equipment ledger.

Dept. A's percentage: $\dfrac{\$122,640}{\$221,970} = 55\%$

Dept. B's percentage: $\dfrac{\$99,330}{\$221,970} = 45\%$

Dept. A's share of property insurance: 55% of $3,600 = $1,980

Dept. B's share of property insurance: 45% of $3,600 = $1,620

The allocation of the cost of liability insurance (in case of personal injury to customers) is based on sales. Using the same percentages as for billboard advertising, Corson apportions the cost of liability insurance as follows:

Dept. A's share of liability insurance: 70% of $800 = $560

Dept. B's share of liability insurance: 30% of $800 = $240

A summary of the way Corson allocates its insurance expense is shown here.

Type of Insurance	Department A	Department B	Total
Property Insurance	$1,980	$1,620	$3,600
Liability Insurance	560	240	800
	$2,540	$1,860	$4,400

Bad Debts Expense, Miscellaneous Selling Expense, and Miscellaneous General Expense Bad Debts Expense and the miscellaneous expense accounts vary according to the volume of sales. Accordingly, Corson apportions them on this basis, 70% for Department A and 30% for Department B. Division of these expense accounts by department is as follows:

Dept. A's share of Bad Debts Expense: 70% of $2,570 = $1,799

Dept. B's share of Bad Debts Expense: 30% of $2,570 = $771

Dept. A's share of Miscellaneous Selling Expense: 70% of $4,270 = $2,989

Dept. B's share of Miscellaneous Selling Expense: 30% of $4,270 = $1,281

Dept. A's share of Miscellaneous General Expense: 70% of $920 = $644

Dept. B's share of Miscellaneous General Expense: 30% of $920 = $276

Item	Department A	Department B	Total
Bad Debts Expense	$1,799	$ 771	$2,570
Miscellaneous Selling Expense	2,989	1,281	4,270
Miscellaneous General Expense	644	276	920
	$5,432	$2,328	$7,760

DEPARTMENTAL MARGIN

Objective 5

Compile a departmental income statement extended through departmental margin.

Departmental margin is a measurement of the contribution that a given department makes to the income of the firm—gross profit of a department minus the department's direct expenses. When a company breaks down its expense figures on a departmental-margin basis, its income statement indicates the contribution each department makes toward the overhead expenses incurred on behalf of the business as a whole. You can divide operating expenses into two classes: (1) direct expenses, which are incurred for the sole benefit of a given department and are under the control of the department head but not necessarily under the department being considered; and (2) indirect expenses, which are incurred as overhead expenses of the entire business and thus are not under the control of one department head. For example, Sales Salary Expense is a direct expense because it is incurred purely for the benefit of one department. Property tax on real estate, on the other hand, is an overhead expense incurred for the business as a whole; it is not directly chargeable to one department.

Some operating expenses may be partially direct and partially indirect. For example, Corson Company's Advertising Expense consisted partially of billboard advertising, which stresses the name and location of the company, and partially of newspaper and radio advertising, which directly benefits separate departments of the company. So the part of the advertising budget that went to billboard advertising is an indirect expense, and the part that went to newspaper and radio advertising is a direct expense. Costs of insurance on merchandise inventories and store equipment are a direct expense; costs of liability insurance are an indirect or overhead expense. When you classify an expense as direct or indirect, use this rule of thumb to identify direct expenses: **If the department were not in existence, then the expense would not be in existence.** The expense must be directly related to the department.

Here is an outline of an income statement that emphasizes departmental margin:

Remember!

In any departmental accounting system, it is necessary to keep separate accounts or supplementary records by department for each account involved in determining gross profit on sales.

From Sales Through Departmental Margin

Revenue from Sales
Less Cost of Goods Sold
⎰ Based on separate departmental accounts
⎱ or supplementary analysis sheets

Gross Profit
Less Direct Departmental Expenses
⎰ Expenses that are directly related to the
⎱ department

Departmental Margin
Less Indirect Expenses

Income from Operations
Add Other Income
Less Other Expenses

Income Before Income Tax
Less Income Tax Expense

Net Income

The income statement shown in Figure 6 on pages 934–935 presents the same figures that we saw in Figure 5 for the Corson Company. This time, however, they are in the departmental-margin format. It is interesting to compare the two.

The Meaning of Departmental Margin

Departmental margin is the most realistic portrayal of the profitability of a department. **If the company closes the department, the company's income before taxes will decrease or increase by the amount of the departmental margin.** For example, in the case of the Corson Company, Department B had a positive departmental margin of $18,765; if Corson eliminated the department, its income before taxes would be reduced by $18,765 (assuming that Corson didn't create a new department to take the place of Department B or expand Department A to occupy the void).

In the company's work sheet (Figure 4), in which operating expenses were apportioned to departments, Department B showed a net loss from operations of $1,107. Department B sustained this loss because it was assigned a number of indirect expenses. If Corson eliminates Department B, these indirect expenses, or overhead, will still exist and will therefore be assigned entirely to Department A, thereby accounting in part for the reduction in income before taxes of $18,765 for the company as a whole (the amount of the departmental margin). Therefore, Department B should continue to operate because it has a positive departmental (or contribution) margin whereby incremental Department B sales exceed incremental (direct) Department B expenses by $18,765.

The Usefulness of Departmental Margin

Income statements that show departmental margin are extremely useful when it comes to controlling a company's direct expenses, because the company can hold the head of a given department accountable for expenses directly chargeable to that department. If a department head reduces direct expenses, this action will have a favorable effect on the departmental margin.

A company that manufactures a number of different products can also use the concept of departmental margin to determine the profitability of a particular product. This is clearly one of the most important uses of departmental margin.

Management can use an income statement showing departmental margin as a tool for making future plans and analyzing future operations. Sometimes such an income statement may even lead to the elimination of a department. For example, the Rivera Company, Inc., has five departments. Its income from operations for last year was $120,000, which is about the same as it has been for the past four years. Rivera's partial income statement, in which all operating expenses are apportioned to the various departments, shows that Department E has a Loss from Operations of $9,000. In an abbreviated departmental-margin format, the results of the fiscal year are shown in the following table.

Item	Department E (only)	Departments A to D (only)	Total, Departments A to E	Total, Departments A to D (with E eliminated)
Sales	$120,000	$1,480,000	$1,600,000	$1,480,000
Cost of Goods Sold	72,000	880,000	952,000	880,000
Gross Profit	$ 48,000	$ 600,000	$ 648,000	$ 600,000
Direct Departmental Expense	32,000	336,000	368,000	336,000
Departmental Margin	$ 16,000	$ 264,000	$ 280,000	$ 264,000
Indirect Expenses	25,000	135,000	160,000	160,000
Income (Loss) from Operations	$ (9,000)	$ 129,000	$ 120,000	$ 104,000

Corson Company, Inc.
Income Statement
For Year Ended December 31, 20—

			DEPARTMENT A		
1	Revenue from Sales:				
2	Sales		$ 560 0 0 0 00		
3	Less Sales Returns and Allowances		14 2 0 0 00		
4	Net Sales			$ 545 8 0 0 00	
5	Cost of Goods Sold:				
6	Merchandise Inventory, Jan. 1, 20—		$ 96 4 0 0 00		
7	Purchases	$ 312 1 1 5 00			
8	Less: Purchases Returns and Allowances	$9,580.00			
9	Purchases Discount	5,740.00	15 3 2 0 00		
10	Net Purchases	$ 296 7 9 5 00			
11	Add Freight In	13 0 0 5 00			
12	Delivered Cost of Purchases		309 8 0 0 00		
13	Goods Available for Sale		$ 406 2 0 0 00		
14	Less Merchandise Inventory, Dec. 31, 20—		110 0 0 0 00		
15	Cost of Goods Sold			296 2 0 0 00	
16	Gross Profit			$ 249 6 0 0 00	
17					
18	Direct Departmental Expenses:				
19	Sales Salary Expense		$ 88 6 2 5 00		
20	Advertising Expense		9 2 1 6 00		
21	Insurance Expense		1 9 8 0 00		
22	Depreciation Expense, Store Equipment		1 8 4 0 00		
23	Bad Debts Expense		1 7 9 9 00		
24	Total Direct Departmental Expenses			103 4 6 0 00	
25	Departmental Margin			$ 146 1 4 0 00	
26					
27	Indirect Expenses:				
28	Office Salary Expense				
29	Rent Expense				
30	Utilities Expense				
31	Advertising Expense (billboard)				
32	Insurance Expense (liability)				
33	Miscellaneous Selling Expense				
34	Miscellaneous General Expense				
35	Total Indirect Expenses				
36	Income from Operations				
37					
38	Other Income:				
39	Interest Income				
40	Other Expenses:				
41	Interest Expense				
42	Income Before Income Tax				
43	Income Tax Expense				
44	Net Income				
45					

FIGURE 6

	DEPARTMENT B			TOTAL			
		$ 240 0 0 0 00			$ 800 0 0 0 00		2
		5 8 0 0 00			20 0 0 0 00		3
			$ 234 2 0 0 00			$ 780 0 0 0 00	4
							5
		$ 82 7 4 0 00			$ 179 1 4 0 00		6
$ 161 1 7 5 00				$ 473 2 9 0 00			7
4 7 5 6 00				14 3 3 6 00			8
3 2 7 4 00				9 0 1 4 00			9
$ 153 1 4 5 00				$ 449 9 4 0 00			10
6 7 1 5 00				19 7 2 0 00			11
		159 8 6 0 00			469 6 6 0 00		12
		$ 242 6 0 0 00			$ 648 8 0 0 00		13
		90 0 0 0 00			200 0 0 0 00		14
			152 6 0 0 00			448 8 0 0 00	15
			$ 81 6 0 0 00			$ 331 2 0 0 00	16
							17
							18
		$ 52 2 0 0 00			$ 140 8 2 5 00		19
		6 7 8 4 00			16 0 0 0 00		20
		1 6 2 0 00			3 6 0 0 00		21
		1 4 6 0 00			3 3 0 0 00		22
		7 7 1 00			2 5 7 0 00		23
			62 8 3 5 00			166 2 9 5 00	24
			$ 18 7 6 5 00			$ 164 9 0 5 00	25
							26
							27
					$ 32 1 0 0 00		28
					16 4 0 0 00		29
					4 8 4 0 00		30
					1 6 0 0 00		31
					8 0 0 00		32
					4 2 7 0 00		33
					9 2 0 00		34
						60 9 3 0 00	35
						$ 103 9 7 5 00	36
							37
							38
					$ 3 6 2 4 00		39
							40
					2 4 0 0 00	1 2 2 4 00	41
						$ 105 1 9 9 00	42
						24 2 7 8 00	43
						$ 80 9 2 1 00	44
							45

Now suppose that Rivera eliminates Department E. Because Department E's departmental margin amounts to $16,000, the Income from Operations of the entire firm will decrease by $16,000 ($120,000 − $104,000 = $16,000). Another factor Rivera has to consider is possible "spillover sales" of Department E; that is, customers of Department E may buy things in other departments. Also, any change in income will cause a change in the amount of income tax paid by Rivera. However, to simplify our analysis, we have omitted income tax from our discussion.

CHAPTER REVIEW

Review of Performance Objectives

1. Compile a departmental income statement extended through Gross Profit.

From Sales Through Gross Profit

Based on separate departmental accounts or supplementary analysis sheets
{
  Revenue from Sales
  − Cost of Goods Sold

  = Gross Profit
  − Operating Expenses
}

= Income from Operations
+ Other Income
− Other Expenses

= Income Before Income Tax
− Income Tax Expense

= Net Income

2. Compile a departmental work sheet.

Accountants use work sheets with separate Income Statement columns for each department to facilitate the correct apportionment of revenues and expenses.

3. Compile a departmental income statement extended through Income from Operations.

From Sales Through Income from Operations

Based on separate departmental accounts or supplementary analysis sheets
{
  Revenue from Sales
  − Cost of Goods Sold

  = Gross Profit
  − Operating Expenses
}
One ledger account for each expense apportioned to various departments

= Income from Operations
+ Other Income
− Other Expenses

= Income Before Income Tax
− Income Tax Expense

= Net Income

4. Apportion operating expenses among various operating departments.

Operating expenses may be apportioned or subdivided on a variety of bases, such as gross sales, advertising space, floor space, amounts in the payroll register, amounts in the equipment ledger, and so on.

5. Compile a departmental income statement extended through departmental margin.

From Sales Through Departmental Margin

Based on separate departmental accounts or supplementary analysis sheets

Revenue from Sales
− Cost of Goods Sold

= Gross Profit
− Direct Departmental Expenses

= Departmental Margin
− Indirect Expenses

= Income from Operations
+ Other Income
− Other Expenses

= Income Before Income Tax
− Income Tax Expense

= Net Income

Expenses that are directly related to the department

Glossary

Apportionment of expenses Allocating operating expenses among operating departments. (922)

Departmental margin The contribution that a given department makes to the income of the firm—gross profit of a department minus the department's direct expenses. (931)

Direct expenses Expenses that benefit only one department and are controlled by the head of the department. (932)

Indirect expenses Overhead expenses that benefit several departments or the business as a whole and are not under the control of any one department head. (932)

QUESTIONS, EXERCISES, AND PROBLEMS

Discussion Questions

1. Explain two ways in which Purchases Returns and Allowances may be recorded in a departmentalized company.
2. Explain the three types of departmentalized income statements illustrated in the chapter.
3. Describe the difference between direct and indirect operating expenses.
4. For a retail store, what is the logical basis for allocating advertising expense?

5. In what ways may departmental accounting information be useful?

6. What is departmental margin, and why is a positive departmental margin important?

7. How does a departmentalized income statement differ from one that is not departmentalized?

8. You have been hired as the new manager of an athletic supply store. Previously, the income statement listed total revenue and operating expenses only. The company can be divided into two departments: clothing and shoes. You need to know the gross profit for each department. Describe the changes in the accounting system that will be required.

Exercises

P.O. 1

Determine amount of gross profit.

Exercise 26-1 The ski department of Down Sports buys all its products FOB destination and has the following account balances:

Merchandise Inventory (beginning)	$ 69,600
Merchandise Inventory (ending)	62,400
Purchases	220,800
Purchases Discount	4,800
Purchases Returns and Allowances	7,200
Sales	412,800
Sales Returns and Allowances	9,600

Determine the amount of the gross profit.

P.O. 4

Allocate office salaries expense to three operating departments.

Exercise 26-2 Rascin Electronics has annual expenses for salaries of office staff of $34,560 that it allocates to the various departments on the basis of gross sales for each department. Sales by department are as follows:

Department	Gross Sales
Cellular phones	$488,000
CD players	424,000
VCRs	48,000
Total	$960,000

Determine what share of the office salaries expense each of the three operating departments should bear. (On a calculator, select the floating decimal setting or the maximum number of decimal places.)

P.O. 4

Apportion rent expense to five departments.

Exercise 26-3 Bailey Sports occupies an area of 22,500 square feet. The departments and the floor space each department occupies are as follows:

Department	Floor Space
Basketball	900 square feet
Skiing	15,075 square feet
Skating	2,700 square feet
Baseball	1,800 square feet
Receiving and Storage	2,025 square feet
Total	22,500 square feet

Bailey Sports leases the building for $40,000 per year. Apportion the rent expense to the five departments.

P.O. 4

Allocate insurance costs to three operating departments.

Exercise 26-4 The premium for public liability insurance for the electronics company in Exercise 26-2 is $1,710, and the premium for fire and theft insurance on the inventory is $2,160. The average balances of the inventories for the period are as follows:

Department	Average Inventory
Cellular phones	$160,000
CD players	120,000
VCRs	40,000
Total	$320,000

How much of the insurance costs should be allocated to each department, given that public liability insurance is apportioned on the basis of gross sales and that property insurance is allocated on the basis of the values of the average inventories?

P.O. 4

Determine the apportionment of depreciation expense and insurance expense to three operating departments.

Exercise 26-5 Tesson Company apportions depreciation on equipment on the basis of the average cost of the equipment. Insurance expense is apportioned on the basis of average cost of the merchandise inventory. Depreciation expense on equipment was $27,000. Insurance expense was $10,800. Determine the apportionment of the depreciation expense and the insurance expense based on the following information. Round to the nearest dollar amount.

Department	Average Cost Equipment	Inventory
A	$135,000	$ 450,000
B	270,000	540,000
C	135,000	270,000
Total	$540,000	$1,260,000

P.O. 5

Determine the amount of the departmental margin.

Exercise 26-6 The following figures apply to McCabe's hardware department:

Direct Departmental Expenses	$148,200
Freight In	31,293
Indirect Expenses	88,350
Interest Expense	5,700
Merchandise Inventory (beginning)	188,100
Merchandise Inventory (ending)	216,600
Purchases	490,257
Purchases Returns and Allowances	8,550
Sales	701,100
Sales Returns and Allowances	11,400

Determine the amount of the departmental margin.

P.O. 5

Determine the departmental margin on a department considered for closing.

Exercise 26-7 Morrow, Inc., is considering eliminating its Drapery Department. Management does not believe that the indirect expenses and the level of operations in the other departments will be affected if the Drapery Department closes. Information from Morrow's income statement for the fiscal year ended December 31, which is considered a typical year, is shown here.

	Drapery Department	All Other Departments	Total of All Departments (including Drapery)
Sales	$74,000	$562,000	$636,000
Cost of Goods Sold	48,000	396,000	444,000
Gross Profit	$26,000	$166,000	$192,000
Operating Expenses	30,000	111,000	141,000
Income (Loss) from Operations	$(4,000)	$ 55,000	$ 51,000

Morrow considers that $18,000 of the operating expenses of the Drapery Department are direct expenses. What is the departmental margin of the Drapery Department?

P.O. 3

Prepare an income statement assuming the department in Exercise 26-7 is closed.

Exercise 26-8 For Morrow, Inc., in Exercise 26-7, prepare an income statement for the forthcoming year, assuming that Morrow discontinues the Drapery Department.

CONSIDER AND COMMUNICATE

You work for a sports equipment company that has three departments: the Swim Shop, the Climbing Corner, and the Pedal Room. This company is continuing to grow, but it has not set up departmentalized accounting procedures. The owner is not sure that the benefits of departmentalized information will outweigh the additional paperwork and potential employee retraining. Briefly describe the benefits of changing to departmentalized accounting and producing departmentalized income statements through departmental margin.

WHAT IF . . .

As a result of company-wide remodeling, several hundred square feet that had been a part of Department A became a part of Department B. This detail, however, escaped the new accountant, who allocated the rent expense (based on the floor space) the same way it had been allocated in the prior year. Comment on this situation.

CRITICAL THINKING

The following is a table that your company is using to analyze the possibility of eliminating Department A. Because of a defective printer, some of the numbers are missing. Complete the table and give an analysis of the impact of eliminating Department A.

Item	Department A (only)	Departments B to D (only)	Total, Departments A to D	Total, Departments B to D (A gone)
Sales	$121,800	$	$1,624,000	$
Cost of Goods Sold		875,500	958,300	
Gross Profit	39,000	626,700		
Direct Departmental Expenses		302,000	327,200	
Departmental Margin	13,800		338,500	
Indirect Expenses	18,750	101,250		
Income (Loss) from Operations	$	$223,450	$	$204,700

WEB WORK

Using an Internet web browser, type *departmental accounting* in the search box and search for information about departmental accounting and apportionment of expenses. Discuss your findings in a small group. Write a one-page summary of your findings.

PROBLEM SET A

For additional help, see the demonstration problem at the beginning of each chapter in your Working Papers.

P.O. 1

Problem 26-1A Hendricks Lumber, a sole proprietorship, has two sales departments: lumber and hardware. Hendricks's accountant prepared the adjusted trial balance shown at the end of the fiscal year, after all adjustments, including adjustments for merchandise inventory, had been recorded and posted.

Check Figure

Net Income, $180,906

Instructions

Prepare an income statement showing gross profit for each department and income from operations and net income for the business. Beginning merchandise inventory balances are: lumber, $235,848; hardware, $217,446.

Hendricks Lumber
Adjusted Trial Balance
December 31, 20—

ACCOUNT NAME	DEBIT	CREDIT
Cash	9 6 2 4 00	
Accounts Receivable	135 5 6 7 00	
Allowance for Doubtful Accounts		4 8 6 0 00
Merchandise Inventory, Lumber Dept.	258 3 5 7 00	
Merchandise Inventory, Hardware Dept.	204 5 8 5 00	
Store Supplies	1 5 4 2 00	
Store Equipment	59 0 1 0 00	
Accumulated Depreciation, Store Equipment		38 3 0 4 00
Accounts Payable		143 9 5 5 00
L. T. Hendricks, Capital		361 8 6 0 00
L. T. Hendricks, Drawing	61 2 0 0 00	
Income Summary	235 8 4 8 00	258 3 5 7 00
	217 4 4 6 00	204 5 8 5 00
Sales, Lumber Department		1,120 6 7 7 00
Sales, Hardware Department		945 7 2 0 00
Sales Returns and Allowances, Lumber Department	21 4 2 3 00	
Sales Returns and Allowances, Hardware Department	19 4 2 8 00	
Purchases, Lumber Department	1,011 7 6 0 00	
Purchases, Hardware Department	697 4 0 4 00	
Purchases Returns and Allowances, Lumber Department		15 8 5 2 00
Purchases Returns and Allowances, Hardware Department		13 1 5 2 00
Purchases Discount, Lumber Department		20 5 2 3 00
Purchases Discount, Hardware Department		14 8 8 0 00
Freight In, Lumber Department	31 2 9 2 00	
Freight In, Hardware Department	33 6 2 7 00	
Sales Salary Expense	86 3 7 0 00	
Depreciation Expense, Store Equipment	13 1 4 6 00	
Miscellaneous Selling Expense	5 2 8 00	
Office Salary Expense	17 6 4 0 00	
Rent Expense	14 4 0 0 00	
Utilities Expense	8 6 5 8 00	
Bad Debts Expense	7 2 6 00	
Miscellaneous General Expense	3 6 0 00	
Interest Expense	2 7 8 4 00	
	3,142 7 2 5 00	3,142 7 2 5 00

P.O. 3

Problem 26-2A Bryan Book and Software has two sales departments: book and software. After recording and posting all adjustments, including the adjustments for merchandise inventory, the accountant prepared the following adjusted trial balance at the end of the fiscal year:

Bryan Book and Software
Adjusted Trial Balance
December 31, 20—

ACCOUNT NAME	DEBIT	CREDIT
Cash	11 2 8 0 00	
Accounts Receivable	104 6 4 0 00	
Allowance for Doubtful Accounts		5 6 8 0 00
Merchandise Inventory, Book Department	160 6 7 2 00	
Merchandise Inventory, Software Department	74 9 6 2 00	
Prepaid Insurance	1 9 6 8 00	
Store Supplies	1 5 9 6 00	
Store Equipment	128 4 4 0 00	
Accumulated Depreciation, Store Equipment		97 8 5 6 00
Accounts Payable		96 8 4 0 00
Sales Tax Payable		2 6 8 4 00
Income Tax Payable		3 4 9 7 00
Common Stock		223 8 9 0 00
Retained Earnings	27 4 5 0 00	
Income Summary	157 8 5 6 00	160 6 7 2 00
	72 4 4 8 00	74 9 6 2 00
Sales, Book Department		952 0 0 0 00
Sales, Software Department		408 0 0 0 00
Sales Returns and Allowances, Book Dept.	24 4 8 2 00	
Sales Returns and Allowances, Software Department	1 6 5 2 00	
Purchases, Book Department	599 6 8 6 00	
Purchases, Software Department	288 8 1 8 00	
Purchases Returns and Allowances, Book Department		8 4 5 2 00
Purchases Returns and Allowances, Software Department		2 5 9 2 00
Purchases Discount, Book Department		11 7 6 8 00
Purchases Discount, Software Department		8 5 6 0 00
Freight In, Book Department	21 7 5 0 00	
Freight In, Software Department	8 6 2 6 00	
Sales Salary Expense	243 5 6 4 00	
Advertising Expense	32 0 0 0 00	
Depreciation Expense, Store Equipment	31 6 0 0 00	
Store Supplies Expense	1 2 1 2 00	
Miscellaneous Selling Expense	1 0 4 0 00	
Rent Expense	19 2 0 0 00	
Utilities Expense	7 2 0 0 00	
Insurance Expense	1 6 8 0 00	
Bad Debts Expense	4 4 0 0 00	
Miscellaneous General Expense	1 5 6 0 00	
Interest Expense	3 6 2 4 00	
Income Tax Expense	24 0 4 7 00	
	2,057 4 5 3 00	2,057 4 5 3 00

Merchandise inventories at the beginning of the year were as follows: book department, $157,856; software department, $72,448. The bases (and sources of figures) for apportioning expenses to the two departments are as follows:

- Sales Salary Expense (payroll register): book department, $136,676; software department, $106,888
- Advertising Expense (newspaper column inches): book department, 1,200 inches; software department, 800 inches
- Depreciation Expense, Store Equipment (plant and equipment ledger): book department, $23,284; software department, $8,316
- Store Supplies Expense (requisitions): book department, $640; software department, $572
- Miscellaneous Selling Expense (volume of gross sales): book department, $728; software department, $312 (verify these figures)
- Rent Expense and Utilities Expense (floor space): book department, 5,000 square feet; software department, 3,000 square feet
- Insurance Expense (average cost of merchandise inventory, rounded): book department, $1,148; software department, $532 (verify these figures)
- Bad Debts Expense (volume of gross sales): book department, $3,080; software department, $1,320 (verify these figures)
- Miscellaneous General Expense (volume of gross sales): book department, $1,092; software department, $468 (verify these figures)

Check Figure

Net Income, $80,561

Instructions

Prepare an income statement to show income from operations by department and a nondepartmentalized income statement (using the Total columns) to show net income for the entire company.

P.O. 2

Problem 26-3A Capra's Cycle, a sole proprietorship, has two departments, bicycle and clothing. The trial balance as of October 31, the end of the fiscal year, is shown on the opposite page.

The data for the adjustments are as follows:

a.–d. Merchandise inventories, October 31, the end of the fiscal period: bicycle department, $60,000; clothing department, $36,000
e. Depreciation of store equipment for the year, $7,230
f. Estimated uncollectible customer charge accounts (based on a percentage of charge sales), $2,190
g. Insurance expired, $585
h. Accrued wages and commissions, $555
i. Accrued interest payable, $216

The bases for apportioning expenses to the two departments are as follows:

- Wages and Commissions Expense (time sheets): bicycle department, $45,540; clothing department, $19,515
- Advertising Expense (space): bicycle department, $7,680; clothing department, $1,920
- Depreciation Expense (equipment ledger): bicycle department, $5,061; clothing department, $2,169
- Rent Expense, Utilities Expense, Miscellaneous Expense, Bad Debts Expense, Insurance Expense (sales): bicycle department, 60 percent; clothing department, 40 percent

Capra's Cycle
Trial Balance
October 31, 20—

ACCOUNT NAME	DEBIT	CREDIT
Cash	9 3 0 0 00	
Accounts Receivable	59 4 0 0 00	
Allowance for Doubtful Accounts		1 5 6 0 00
Merchandise Inventory, Bicycle Department	63 0 0 0 00	
Merchandise Inventory, Clothing Department	42 0 0 0 00	
Prepaid Insurance	9 0 0 00	
Store Equipment	27 3 0 0 00	
Accumulated Depreciation, Store Equipment		12 2 1 0 00
Accounts Payable		58 0 8 0 00
C. D. Capra, Capital		99 4 2 0 00
C. D Capra, Drawing	21 0 0 0 00	
Sales, Bicycle Department		180 0 0 0 00
Sales, Clothing Department		120 0 0 0 00
Purchases, Bicycle Department	86 4 0 0 00	
Purchases, Clothing Department	66 2 4 0 00	
Freight In, Bicycle Department	3 6 0 0 00	
Freight In, Clothing Department	2 7 6 0 00	
Wages and Commissions Expense	64 5 0 0 00	
Advertising Expense	9 6 0 0 00	
Rent Expense	10 8 0 0 00	
Utilities Expense	2 1 7 5 00	
Miscellaneous Expense	1 6 3 5 00	
Interest Expense	6 6 0 00	
	471 2 7 0 00	471 2 7 0 00

Check Figure

Net Income, $31,854

P.O. 5

Instructions

Complete the work sheet.

Problem 26-4A Modern Decorators is a sole proprietorship. After the firm has recorded adjustments, it has the balances shown in the work sheet for revenue and expense accounts and merchandise inventories for its two departments on December 31, the end of the fiscal year (see page 946). The values of merchandise inventory on January 1 (beginning) are: carpets, $146,130; draperies, $72,420. Essential data for direct expenses (and sources of figures) are as follows:

a. Sales Salary Expense (sales personnel work in one department only) is allocated as follows: carpets, $97,140; draperies, $41,640.
b. Advertising: newspaper advertising is allocated as follows: carpets, $10,080; draperies, $2,520.
c. Depreciation: Depreciation of store equipment is apportioned on the basis of the average cost of equipment in each department. The average cost of store equipment is $15,000 for carpets and $5,000 for draperies.
d. Bad Debts Expense: Department managers are responsible for granting credit on net sales made by their respective departments. Bad Debts Expense is allocated as follows: carpets, $4,104; draperies, $1,596.

Modern Decorators
Work Sheet
For Year Ended December 31, 20—

ACCOUNT NAME	ADJUSTED TRIAL BALANCE	
	DEBIT	CREDIT
Merchandise Inventory, Carpets	157 9 8 0 00	
Merchandise Inventory, Draperies	68 9 4 0 00	
Sales, Carpets		569 5 6 8 00
Sales, Draperies		222 4 3 2 00
Sales Returns and Allowances, Carpets	14 4 4 8 00	
Sales Returns and Allowances, Draperies	6 5 5 2 00	
Purchases, Carpets	316 2 3 5 00	
Purchases, Draperies	124 9 3 5 00	
Purchases Returns and Allowances, Carpets		4 9 4 4 00
Purchases Returns and Allowances, Draperies		2 0 1 0 00
Purchases Discount, Carpets		3 5 4 6 00
Purchases Discount, Draperies		2 2 2 0 00
Freight In, Carpets	20 1 8 5 00	
Freight In, Draperies	4 9 3 5 00	
Sales Salary Expense	138 7 8 0 00	
Advertising Expense	12 6 0 0 00	
Depreciation Expense, Store Equipment	9 6 0 0 00	
Miscellaneous Selling Expense	1 1 7 0 00	
Bad Debts Expense	5 7 0 0 00	
Office Salary Expense	25 5 6 0 00	
Rent Expense	25 2 0 0 00	
Utilities Expense	3 7 8 0 00	
Insurance Expense	1 2 6 0 00	
Miscellaneous General Expense	1 0 2 0 00	
Interest Expense	1 8 6 2 00	

Check Figure

Net Income, $99,268

Instructions

Prepare an income statement to show each department's departmental margin.

PROBLEM SET B

For additional help, see the demonstration problem at the beginning of each chapter in your Working Papers.

P.O. 1

Problem 26-1B Bella's Garden Shop, a sole proprietorship, has two sales departments: plants and tools. After recording and posting all adjustments, including the adjustments for merchandise inventory, the accountant presented the adjusted trial balance shown at the end of the fiscal year.

Bella's Garden Shop
Adjusted Trial Balance
September 30, 20—

ACCOUNT NAME	DEBIT	CREDIT
Cash	4 6 5 6 00	
Accounts Receivable	46 8 4 4 00	
Allowance for Doubtful Accounts		2 2 8 2 00
Merchandise Inventory, Plants	50 3 0 2 00	
Merchandise Inventory, Tools	35 5 3 9 00	
Store Supplies	9 6 2 00	
Store Equipment	23 1 0 2 00	
Accumulated Depreciation, Store Equipment		15 0 8 2 00
Accounts Payable		30 9 5 9 00
B. R. Ogdahl, Capital		85 5 4 2 00
B. R. Ogdahl, Drawing	22 9 2 2 00	
Income Summary	57 0 4 0 00	50 3 0 2 00
	32 1 0 6 00	35 5 3 9 00
Sales, Plants		370 1 3 6 00
Sales, Tools		257 4 6 2 00
Sales Returns and Allowances, Plants	7 1 4 2 00	
Sales Returns and Allowances, Tools	6 1 1 8 00	
Purchases, Plants	302 6 8 5 00	
Purchases, Tools	208 6 6 3 00	
Purchases Returns and Allowances, Plants		7 0 4 2 00
Purchases Returns and Allowances, Tools		5 1 3 6 00
Purchases Discount, Plants		5 1 5 0 00
Purchases Discount, Tools		4 3 1 0 00
Freight In, Plants	9 3 6 1 00	
Freight In, Tools	6 4 5 6 00	
Sales Salary Expense	27 1 6 2 00	
Depreciation Expense, Store Equipment	4 3 0 6 00	
Miscellaneous Selling Expense	5 4 8 00	
Office Salary Expense	12 3 2 2 00	
Rent Expense	5 9 2 2 00	
Utilities Expense	2 4 1 4 00	
Bad Debts Expense	6 3 8 00	
Miscellaneous General Expense	5 0 6 00	
Interest Expense	1 2 2 6 00	
	868 9 4 2 00	868 9 4 2 00

Check Figure

Net Income, $50,462

P.O. 3

Instructions

Prepare an income statement showing gross profit for each department and income from operations and net income for the entire business. Beginning balances of merchandise inventory are as follows: plants, $57,040; tools, $32,106.

Problem 26-2B Hiram Foster, Inc., has two departments: luggage and accessories. Foster's accountant prepared the adjusted trial balance shown at the end of the fiscal year, after all adjustments, including the adjustments for merchandise inventory, have been recorded and posted.

Hiram Foster, Inc.
Adjusted Trial Balance
January 31, 20—

ACCOUNT NAME	DEBIT	CREDIT
Cash	9 6 5 2 00	
Accounts Receivable	137 7 8 0 00	
Allowance for Doubtful Accounts		5 2 4 0 00
Merchandise Inventory, Luggage Department	168 2 8 4 00	
Merchandise Inventory, Accessory Department	82 2 7 6 00	
Prepaid Insurance	1 6 8 0 00	
Store Supplies	1 5 2 4 00	
Store Equipment	107 3 6 4 00	
Accumulated Depreciation, Store Equipment		83 6 2 0 00
Accounts Payable		77 3 6 0 00
Sales Tax Payable		2 5 6 8 00
Income Tax Payable		3 4 6 5 00
Common Stock		138 8 8 8 00
Retained Earnings		83 7 5 0 00
Income Summary	165 5 2 0 00	168 2 8 4 00
	81 4 4 0 00	82 2 7 6 00
Sales, Luggage Department		819 6 0 0 00
Sales, Accessory Department		546 4 0 0 00
Sales Returns and Allowances, Luggage Department	23 3 7 0 00	
Sales Returns and Allowances, Accessory Department	3 4 3 2 00	
Purchases, Luggage Department	503 6 9 4 00	
Purchases, Accessory Department	330 4 8 4 00	
Purchases Returns and Allowances, Luggage Department		9 2 3 6 00
Purchases Returns and Allowances, Accessory Department		3 5 8 4 00
Purchases Discount, Luggage Department		10 9 9 2 00
Purchases Discount, Accessory Department		5 9 2 8 00
Freight In, Luggage Department	26 5 1 0 00	
Freight In, Accessory Department	13 7 7 0 00	
Sales Salary Expense	246 4 4 0 00	
Advertising Expense	28 0 0 0 00	
Depreciation Expense, Store Equipment	26 8 7 2 00	
Store Supplies Expense	1 4 8 4 00	
Miscellaneous Selling Expense	1 3 6 0 00	
Rent Expense	16 0 0 0 00	
Utilities Expense	6 4 0 0 00	
Insurance Expense	1 8 0 0 00	
Bad Debts Expense	3 6 0 0 00	
Miscellaneous General Expense	1 6 4 0 00	
Interest Expense	5 6 0 0 00	
Income Tax Expense	45 2 1 5 00	
	2,041 1 9 1 00	2,041 1 9 1 00

Merchandise inventories at the beginning of the year were as follows: luggage department, $165,520; accessory department, $81,440. The bases for apportioning expenses and the sources of the figures are as follows:

- Sales Salary Expense (payroll register): luggage department, $149,600; accessory department, $96,840
- Advertising Expense (newspaper column inches): luggage department, 1,200 inches; accessory department, 800 inches
- Depreciation Expense, Store Equipment (plant and equipment ledger): luggage department, $19,232; accessory department, $7,640
- Store Supplies Expense (requisitions): luggage department, $836; accessory department, $648
- Miscellaneous Selling Expense (volume of gross sales): luggage department, $816; accessory department, $544 (verify these figures)
- Rent Expense and Utilities Expense (floor space): luggage department, 5,000 square feet; accessory department, 3,000 square feet
- Insurance Expense (average cost of merchandise inventory, rounded): luggage department, $1,208; accessory department, $592 (verify these figures)
- Bad Debts Expense (volume of gross sales): luggage department, $2,160; accessory department, $1,440 (verify these figures)
- Miscellaneous General Expense (volume of gross sales): luggage department, $984; accessory department, $656 (verify these figures)

Check Figure

Net Income, $113,669

Instructions

Prepare an income statement to show income from operations by department and a nondepartmentalized income statement (using the Total columns) to show net income for the entire company.

P.O. 2

Problem 26-3B The Athletic Station, a sole proprietorship, has two departments: bicycle and clothing. The trial balance, as of April 30, the end of the fiscal year, is as shown on the following page.

The data for the adjustments are as follows:

a.–d. Merchandise inventories, April 30, the end of the fiscal period: bicycle department, $61,420; clothing department, $43,226
e. Insurance expired, $615
f. Estimated uncollectible customer charge accounts (based on an analysis of accounts), $3,662
g. Depreciation of store equipment for the year, $7,290
h. Accrued wages and commissions, $512
i. Accrued interest payable, $206

The bases for apportioning expenses to the two departments are as follows:

- Advertising Expense (column inches of space): bicycle department, $7,920; clothing department, $1,980
- Depreciation Expense (equipment ledger): bicycle department, $5,024; clothing department, $2,266
- Wages and Commissions Expense (time sheets): bicycle department, $47,681; clothing department, $25,981
- Rent Expense, Utilities Expense, Miscellaneous Expense, Bad Debts Expense, Insurance Expense (sales): bicycle department, 60 percent; clothing department, 40 percent

The Athletic Station
Trial Balance
April 30, 20—

ACCOUNT NAME	DEBIT	CREDIT
Cash	10 2 1 0 00	
Accounts Receivable	60 1 8 0 00	
Allowance for Doubtful Accounts		1 5 6 4 00
Merchandise Inventory, Bicycle Department	66 1 0 0 0 00	
Merchandise Inventory, Clothing Department	47 3 0 0 0 00	
Prepaid Insurance	8 7 0 00	
Store Equipment	26 9 4 0 00	
Accumulated Depreciation, Store Equipment		12 1 6 5 00
Accounts Payable		58 1 1 0 00
S. E. Olson, Capital		99 1 2 0 00
S. E. Olson, Drawing	23 2 5 0 00	
Sales, Bicycle Department		192 0 0 0 00
Sales, Clothing Department		128 0 0 0 00
Purchases, Bicycle Department	85 8 2 4 00	
Purchases, Clothing Department	65 9 5 2 00	
Freight In, Bicycle Department	3 5 7 6 00	
Freight In, Clothing Department	2 7 4 8 00	
Wages and Commissions Expense	73 1 5 0 00	
Advertising Expense	9 9 0 0 00	
Rent Expense	10 8 0 0 00	
Utilities Expense	2 1 3 0 00	
Miscellaneous Expense	1 3 3 5 00	
Interest Expense	6 9 4 00	
	490 9 5 9 00	490 9 5 9 00

Check Figure

Net Income, $44,416

P.O. 5

Instructions

Complete the work sheet.

Problem 26-4B Ingalls Interiors is a sole proprietorship. After the firm has recorded adjustments, it has the balances shown in the work sheet for revenue and expense accounts and merchandise inventories for its two departments on December 31, the end of the fiscal year.

The values of merchandise inventory on January 1 (beginning) are: carpets, $143,460; and draperies, $71,838. Essential data for direct expenses (and sources of figures) are as follows:

a. Sales Salary Expense (sales personnel work in one department only) is allocated as follows: carpets, $95,580; draperies, $40,920.
b. Advertising Expense: Newspaper advertising is allocated as follows: carpets, $9,840; draperies, $2,490.
c. Depreciation: Depreciation of store equipment is apportioned on the basis of the average cost of equipment in each department. The average cost of store equipment is as follows: carpets, $22,500; draperies, $7,500.
d. Bad Debts Expense: Department managers are responsible for granting credit on sales made by their respective departments. Bad Debts Expense is allocated as follows: carpets, $3,888; draperies, $1,572.

Ingalls Interiors
Work Sheet
For Year Ended December 31, 20—

ACCOUNT NAME	ADJUSTED TRIAL BALANCE	
	DEBIT	CREDIT
Merchandise Inventory, Carpets	153 0 9 0 00	
Merchandise Inventory, Draperies	65 3 4 6 00	
Sales, Carpets		562 2 4 8 00
Sales, Draperies		221 7 8 4 00
Sales Returns and Allowances, Carpets	14 3 4 6 00	
Sales Returns and Allowances, Draperies	6 0 1 8 00	
Purchases, Carpets	315 7 6 7 00	
Purchases, Draperies	125 0 3 3 00	
Purchases Returns and Allowances, Carpets		7 9 2 0 00
Purchases Returns and Allowances, Draperies		2 0 5 2 00
Purchases Discount, Carpets		5 9 4 0 00
Purchases Discount, Draperies		2 1 6 0 00
Freight In, Carpets	20 1 5 5 00	
Freight In, Draperies	4 9 3 9 00	
Sales Salary Expense	136 5 0 0 00	
Advertising Expense	12 3 3 0 00	
Depreciation Expense, Store Equipment	9 6 0 0 00	
Miscellaneous Selling Expense	1 1 2 2 00	
Bad Debts Expense	5 4 6 0 00	
Office Salary Expense	25 8 0 0 00	
Rent Expense	25 2 0 0 00	
Utilities Expense	3 7 2 0 00	
Insurance Expense	1 1 7 0 00	
Miscellaneous General Expense	1 0 6 8 00	
Interest Expense	2 2 4 4 00	

Check Figure

Net Income, $94,770

Instructions

Prepare an income statement to show each department's departmental margin.

27 Manufacturing Accounting

Performance Objectives

After you have completed this chapter, you will be able to do the following:

1. Prepare a statement of cost of goods manufactured.

2. Complete a work sheet for a manufacturing enterprise and journalize closing entries.

3. Define *job-order cost accounting system* and make related entries.

4. Define *process cost accounting system* and make related entries.

Now let's turn to another type of business operation: manufacturing. The accounting principles we have already discussed pertain to manufacturing concerns, but manufacturers also have special procedures to account for manufacturing costs. In this chapter, we describe how manufacturers determine the total cost of goods manufactured during each accounting period. To acquaint you with the end results, early in the chapter we present a statement of cost of goods manufactured. This statement will enable you to understand the function of the work sheet and its relationship to the financial statements. This chapter is only an introduction to accounting for manufacturing operations. As you continue your accounting education, you will have the opportunity to deal with more advanced systems and procedures.

COMPARISON OF INCOME STATEMENTS FOR MERCHANDISING AND MANUFACTURING ENTERPRISES

FYI

The main difference between accounting for a merchandising business and for a manufacturing business is in determining the cost of goods sold.

Manufacturing and merchandising companies have the same type of revenue accounts. However, a merchant buys goods in a finished condition and later sells them at a higher price in the same condition. A manufacturer, on the other hand, buys raw materials, transforms them into finished goods, and later sells the finished goods.

To compare the two types of companies, study the portions of income statements for a merchandising firm and for a manufacturing firm shown in Figure 1.

FIGURE 1

A Merchandising Company
Income Statement
For Year Ended December 31, 20—

Sales (net)			$2 000 000 00
Cost of Goods Sold:			
Merchandise Inventory, Jan. 1, 20—	$ 390 000 00		
Delivered Cost of Purchases	1 200 000 00		
Goods Available for Sale	$1 590 000 00		
Less Merchandise Inventory,			
December 31, 20—	250 000 00		
Cost of Goods Sold		1 340 000 00	
Gross Profit		$ 660 000 00	

A Manufacturing Company, Inc.
Income Statement
For Year Ended December 31, 20—

Sales (net)			$2 000 000 00
Cost of Goods Sold:			
Finished Goods Inv., Jan. 1, 20—	$ 390 000 00		
Cost of Goods Manufactured	1 200 000 00		
Goods Available for Sale	$1 590 000 00		
Less Finished Goods Inventory,			
December 31, 20—	250 000 00		
Cost of Goods Sold		1 340 000 00	
Gross Profit		$ 660 000 00	

Merchandising Firm	**Manufacturing Firm**
Beginning Merchandise Inventory Plus Delivered Cost of Purchases	Beginning Finished Goods Inventory Plus Cost of Goods Manufactured
Goods Available for Sale Less Ending Merchandise Inventory	Goods Available for Sale Less Ending Finished Goods Inventory
Cost of Goods Sold	Cost of Goods Sold

Wendt Manufacturing Company, Inc.
Statement of Cost of Goods Manufactured
For Year Ended December 31, 20—

Work-in-Process Inventory, January 1, 20—			$ 140 0 0 0 00
Raw Materials:			
Raw Materials Inventory, January 1, 20—	$ 90 0 0 0 00		
Raw Materials Purchases (net)	230 0 0 0 00		
Cost of Raw Materials Available for Use	$ 320 0 0 0 00		
Less Raw Materials Inventory, December 31, 20—	100 0 0 0 00		
Cost of Raw Materials Used		$ 220 0 0 0 00	
Direct Labor		565 0 0 0 00	
Factory Overhead:			
Indirect Labor	$ 120 0 0 0 00		
Supervisory Salaries	110 0 0 0 00		
Heat, Light, and Power	42 0 0 0 00		
Depreciation Expense, Factory Equipment	32 0 0 0 00		
Depreciation Expense, Factory Building	25 0 0 0 00		
Repairs and Maintenance	24 0 0 0 00		
Factory Insurance Expired	22 0 0 0 00		
Factory Supplies Used	14 0 0 0 00		
Miscellaneous Factory Costs	16 0 0 0 00		
Total Factory Overhead		405 0 0 0 00	
Total Manufacturing Costs			1 190 0 0 0 00
Total Cost of Work-in-Process During Period			$1 330 0 0 0 00
Less Work-in-Process Inventory, December 31, 20—			130 0 0 0 00
Cost of Goods Manufactured			$1 200 0 0 0 00

FIGURE 2

Cost of Goods Manufactured for a manufacturer is the equivalent of Delivered Cost of Purchases for a merchandiser.

STATEMENT OF COST OF GOODS MANUFACTURED

Objective 1

Prepare a statement of cost of goods manufactured.

As an illustration, we'll use the statement of cost of goods manufactured for Wendt Manufacturing Company, Inc., shown in Figure 2 above. **Because Cost of Goods Manufactured is included in the income statement, the accountant naturally prepares the statement of cost of goods manufactured first.**

ELEMENTS OF MANUFACTURING COSTS

No matter what type of product a manufacturer produces, the three elements that make up the cost of the goods manufactured are *raw materials used, direct labor,* and *factory overhead.*

Manufacturing plants maintain more than one inventory—they have raw materials, work-in-process, and finished goods inventories. Raw materials are also called direct materials because they directly become a part of the finished product.

Remember!

The cost of manufacturing any product consists of direct (raw) materials, direct labor, and factory overhead.

Raw Materials Used

Raw materials are the materials that enter directly into—and become a part of—the finished product. The delivered cost of these materials is Cost of Raw Materials Used. For example, if you are manufacturing tables, you need wood, glue, hardware, finishing materials, etc. Raw materials are also called *direct materials.*

Direct Labor

Direct labor consists of the wages paid to factory employees who work—with machines or hand tools—directly on the materials to convert them into finished products. The manufacturer debits the Direct Labor account for the gross wages of those who work directly on the raw materials. The cost of direct labor varies directly with the level of production.

Factory Overhead

Factory overhead consists of manufacturing costs (other than raw materials used and direct labor) that cannot be traced directly to products being manufactured. A manufacturer uses Factory Overhead as a control account. The specific titles of accounts in the factory overhead subsidiary ledger vary from company to company. In Figure 2, the accounts in the factory overhead ledger are Indirect Labor; Supervisory Salaries; Heat, Light, and Power; Depreciation Expense, Factory Equipment; Depreciation Expense, Factory Building; Repairs and Maintenance; Factory Insurance Expired; Factory Supplies Used; and Miscellaneous Factory Costs.

Indirect labor is the wages paid to those people who keep the plant in operation, rather than directly working on production. Examples are operations personnel, maintenance workers, and timekeepers.

The balance of *Factory Supplies Used* reveals the cost of materials used to keep the plant in operation (oil, grease, and so on). These items are also called **indirect materials**.

Other items that may be included in Factory Overhead are workers' compensation insurance, payroll taxes on wages of factory employees, pension contributions for factory employees, taxes on factory building and equipment, taxes on raw materials and work-in-process inventories, patents written off, and small tools written off.

WORK SHEET FOR A MANUFACTURING FIRM

Objective 2

Complete a work sheet for a manufacturing enterprise and journalize closing entries.

A manufacturer's work sheet must include two extra columns headed Statement of Cost of Goods Manufactured.

Let's examine the work sheet for Wendt Manufacturing Company, Inc., shown in Figure 3 (pages 956–959). First, notice that all accounts in the Trial Balance columns representing manufacturing costs have debit balances, just as expense accounts have debit balances. Next, look at the adjusting entries for inventories. (We are assuming that Wendt uses a periodic inventory system.) A manufacturer, like a merchandiser, takes two steps to adjust inventory: The accountant (1) takes off (or closes off) the beginning inventory and (2) adds on the ending inventory. However, in manufacturing accounting, three inventories are involved: Raw Materials, Work-in-Process, and Finished Goods.

	ACCOUNT NAME	TRIAL BALANCE DEBIT	TRIAL BALANCE CREDIT	ADJUSTMENTS DEBIT	ADJUSTMENTS CREDIT
1	Cash	24 000 00			
2	Notes Receivable	50 000 00			
3	Accounts Receivable	180 000 00			
4	Allowance for Doubtful Accounts		2 500 00		(l) 3 500 00
5	Raw Materials Inventory	90 000 00		(b) 100 000 00	(a) 90 000 00
6	Work-in-Process Inventory	140 000 00		(d) 130 000 00	(c) 140 000 00
7	Finished Goods Inventory	390 000 00		(f) 250 000 00	(e) 390 000 00
8	Prepaid Insurance	25 000 00			(i) 22 000 00
9	Factory Supplies	16 000 00			(j) 14 000 00
10	Land	100 000 00			
11	Factory Building	500 000 00			
12	Accumulated Deprec., Factory Building		250 000 00		(h) 25 000 00
13	Factory Equipment	360 000 00			
14	Accumulated Deprec., Factory Equipment		218 000 00		(g) 32 000 00
15	Office Equipment	62 000 00			
16	Accumulated Deprec., Office Equipment		40 000 00		(k) 5 000 00
17	Notes Payable		40 000 00		
18	Accounts Payable		55 550 00		
19	Dividends Payable		12 000 00		
20	Bonds Payable		280 000 00		
21	Common Stock		310 000 00		
22	Premium on Common Stock		100 000 00		
23	Retained Earnings		214 900 00		
24	Sales (net)		2,000 000 00		
25	Raw Materials Purchases	230 000 00			
26	Direct Labor	565 000 00			
27	Indirect Labor	120 000 00			
28	Supervisory Salaries	110 000 00			
29	Heat, Light, and Power	42 000 00			
30	Repairs and Maintenance	24 000 00			
31	Miscellaneous Factory Costs	16 000 00			
32	Selling Expenses (control)	300 000 00			
33	General Expenses (control)	123 500 00		(k) 5 000 00	
34				(l) 3 500 00	
35	Interest Expense	18 000 00			
36	Income Tax Expense	37 450 00		(m) 16 000 00	
37		3,522 950 00	3,522 950 00		
38	Totals carried forward			504 500 00	721 500 00
39					
40					
41					

FIGURE 3

Wendt Manufacturing Company, Inc.
Work Sheet
For Year Ended December 31, 20—

	STATEMENT OF COST OF GOODS MANUFACTURED		INCOME STATEMENT		BALANCE SHEET		
	DEBIT	CREDIT	DEBIT	CREDIT	DEBIT	CREDIT	
					24 0 0 0 00		1
					50 0 0 0 00		2
					180 0 0 0 00		3
						6 0 0 0 00	4
					100 0 0 0 00		5
					130 0 0 0 00		6
					250 0 0 0 00		7
					3 0 0 0 00		8
					2 0 0 0 00		9
					100 0 0 0 00		10
					500 0 0 0 00		11
						275 0 0 0 00	12
					360 0 0 0 00		13
						250 0 0 0 00	14
					62 0 0 0 00		15
						45 0 0 0 00	16
						40 0 0 0 00	17
						55 5 5 0 00	18
						12 0 0 0 00	19
						280 0 0 0 00	20
						310 0 0 0 00	21
						100 0 0 0 00	22
						214 9 0 0 00	23
				2,000 0 0 0 00			24
	230 0 0 0 00						25
	565 0 0 0 00						26
	120 0 0 0 00						27
	110 0 0 0 00						28
	42 0 0 0 00						29
	24 0 0 0 00						30
	16 0 0 0 00						31
			300 0 0 0 00				32
							33
			132 0 0 0 00				34
			18 0 0 0 00				35
			53 4 5 0 00				36
							37
	1,107 0 0 0 00	0 00	503 4 5 0 00	2,000 0 0 0 00	1,761 0 0 0 00	1,588 4 5 0 00	38
							39
							40
							41

(continued)

	ACCOUNT NAME	TRIAL BALANCE		ADJUSTMENTS		
		DEBIT	CREDIT	DEBIT	CREDIT	
1	Totals brought forward			504 5 0 0 00	721 5 0 0 00	
2	Manufacturing Summary			(a) 90 0 0 0 00	(b) 100 0 0 0 00	
3				(c) 140 0 0 0 00	(d) 130 0 0 0 00	
4	Income Summary			(e) 390 0 0 0 00	(f) 250 0 0 0 00	
5	Depreciation Expense, Factory Equipment			(g) 32 0 0 0 00		
6	Depreciation Expense, Factory Building			(h) 25 0 0 0 00		
7	Factory Insurance Expired			(i) 22 0 0 0 00		
8	Factory Supplies Used			(j) 14 0 0 0 00		
9	Income Tax Payable				(m) 16 0 0 0 00	
10				1,217 5 0 0 00	1,217 5 0 0 00	
11	Cost of Goods Manufactured					
12						
13	Net Income After Income Tax					
14						
15						

FIGURE 3 (continued)

Since Raw Materials Inventory and Work-in-Process Inventory appear in the statement of cost of goods manufactured, the accountant adjusts them using the **Manufacturing Summary** account, an account similar to Income Summary used to make adjustments to Raw Materials and Work-in-Process Inventory accounts. Since Finished Goods Inventory appears in the income statement, the accountant adjusts it using the Income Summary account. Finished Goods Inventory for a manufacturing firm is equivalent to Merchandise Inventory for a merchandising firm.

Data for the adjustments are as follows:

a.–b. Raw materials inventory at December 31, $100,000
c.–d. Work-in-process inventory at December 31, $130,000
 e.–f. Finished goods inventory at December 31, $250,000

In T account form, the adjusting entries for the inventory accounts are:

Remember!

The raw materials inventory and the work-in-process inventory are adjusted using the Manufacturing Summary account.

Raw Materials Inventory

+	–
Bal. 90,000	(a) 90,000
(b) 100,000	

Work-in-Process Inventory

+	–
Bal. 140,000	(c) 140,000
(d) 130,000	

Manufacturing Summary

(a) 90,000	(b) 100,000
(c) 140,000	(d) 130,000

Finished Goods Inventory

+	–
Bal. 390,000	(e) 390,000
(f) 250,000	

Income Summary

(e) 390,000	(f) 250,000

g. Depreciation of factory equipment, $32,000
h. Depreciation of factory building, $25,000
 i. Expired factory insurance, $22,000 (assuming the unexpired portion had already been calculated)

	STATEMENT OF COST OF GOODS MANUFACTURED		INCOME STATEMENT		BALANCE SHEET		
	DEBIT	CREDIT	DEBIT	CREDIT	DEBIT	CREDIT	
	1,107 0 0 0 00	0 00	503 4 5 0 00	2,000 0 0 0 00	1,761 0 0 0 00	1,588 4 5 0 00	1
	90 0 0 0 00	100 0 0 0 00					2
	140 0 0 0 00	130 0 0 0 00					3
			390 0 0 0 00	250 0 0 0 00			4
	32 0 0 0 00						5
	25 0 0 0 00						6
	22 0 0 0 00						7
	14 0 0 0 00						8
						16 0 0 0 00	9
	1,430 0 0 0 00	230 0 0 0 00					10
		1,200 0 0 0 00	1,200 0 0 0 00				11
	1,430 0 0 0 00	1,430 0 0 0 00	2,093 4 5 0 00	2,250 0 0 0 00	1,761 0 0 0 00	1,604 4 5 0 00	12
			156 5 5 0 00			156 5 5 0 00	13
			2,250 0 0 0 00	2,250 0 0 0 00	1,761 0 0 0 00	1,761 0 0 0 00	14
							15

FYI

The adjustments other than those for the inventory accounts are like the ones we have already seen.

Remember!

Cost of Goods Manufactured is the equivalent of Delivered Cost of Purchases for a merchandising firm.

j. Cost of the remaining factory supplies inventory, $2,000
k. Depreciation of office equipment, $5,000
l. Estimated uncollectible accounts, $6,000 (determined by an aging analysis)
m. Income tax, $53,450 (based on a taxable income before income tax of $180,000; the accountant determined this by completing the Income Statement columns of the work sheet without including income tax).

Notice how the figures in the Adjustments columns are transferred to the remaining columns of the work sheet. Just as the accountant transfers the figures on the Income Summary line into the Income Statement columns as separate figures, he or she also transfers the four figures on the Manufacturing Summary lines into the Statement of Cost of Goods Manufactured columns as separate figures, like this:

	ACCOUNT NAME	ADJUSTMENTS		STATEMENT OF COST OF GOODS MANUFACTURED		INCOME STATEMENT	
		DEBIT	CREDIT	DEBIT	CREDIT	DEBIT	CREDIT
22	Manufacturing						
23	Summary	(a) 90 0 0 0 00	(b) 100 0 0 0 00	90 0 0 0 00	100 0 0 0 00		
24		(c) 140 0 0 0 00	(d) 130 0 0 0 00	140 0 0 0 00	130 0 0 0 00		
25	Income						
26	Summary	(e) 390 0 0 0 00	(f) 250 0 0 0 00			390 0 0 0 00	250 0 0 0 00
27							

On the work sheet, the accountant transfers the cost of goods manufactured ($1,200,000, the difference between the debit and credit totals in the Statement of Cost of Goods Manufactured columns) to the Income Statement Debit column as shown in the following section of Wendt Manufacturing's work sheet.

| ACCOUNT NAME | STATEMENT OF COST OF GOODS MANUFACTURED | | INCOME STATEMENT | |
	DEBIT	CREDIT	DEBIT	CREDIT
28	1,430 0 0 0 00	230 0 0 0 00		
29 Cost of Goods Manufactured		1,200 0 0 0 00	1,200 0 0 0 00	
30	1,430 0 0 0 00	1,430 0 0 0 00	2,093 4 5 0 00	2,250 0 0 0 00
31			156 5 5 0 00	
32			2,250 0 0 0 00	2,250 0 0 0 00

Closing Entries

Here are the steps to take in making the closing entries for a manufacturer:

■■■

Remember!

Manufacturing Summary is closed into Income Summary by the amount of the Cost of Goods Manufactured.

1. Close the costs that appear in the statement of cost of goods manufactured into the Manufacturing Summary account.
2. Close the Manufacturing Summary account into the Income Summary account (by the amount of the cost of goods manufactured).
3. Close the revenue accounts into the Income Summary account.
4. Close the expense accounts into the Income Summary account.
5. Close the Income Tax Expense account into the Income Summary account.
6. Close the Income Summary account into the Retained Earnings account (by the amount of the net income after income tax).

Following are T accounts for Manufacturing Summary and Income Summary, labeled so that you can readily identify the manufacturing accounts recorded. The end-of-month entries are shown in Figure 4 (pages 961–962).

Manufacturing Summary

Raw Materials Inventory, Jan. 1	90,000	Raw Materials Inventory, Dec. 31	100,000
Work-in-Process Inventory, Jan. 1	140,000	Work-in-Process Inventory, Dec. 31	130,000
Raw Materials Purchases	230,000	Closing	1,200,000
Direct Labor	565,000	(To Income Summary)	
Indirect Labor	120,000		
Supervisory Salaries	110,000		
Heat, Light, and Power	42,000		
Repairs and Maintenance	24,000		
Miscellaneous Factory Costs	16,000		
Deprec. Expense, Factory Equipment	32,000		
Deprec. Expense, Factory Building	25,000		
Factory Insurance Expired	22,000		
Factory Supplies Used	14,000		
	1,430,000		1,430,000

Income Summary

Finished Goods Inventory, Jan. 1	390,000	Finished Goods Inventory, Dec. 31	250,000
(From Manufacturing Summary)	1,200,000		

FIGURE 4

GENERAL JOURNAL   PAGE _____

	DATE		DESCRIPTION	POST. REF.	DEBIT	CREDIT	
1	20–		**Adjusting Entries**				1
2	Dec.	31	Manufacturing Summary		90 0 0 0 00		2
3			Raw Materials Inventory			90 0 0 0 00	3
4							4
5		31	Raw Materials Inventory		100 0 0 0 00		5
6			Manufacturing Summary			100 0 0 0 00	6
7							7
8		31	Manufacturing Summary		140 0 0 0 00		8
9			Work-in-Process Inventory			140 0 0 0 00	9
10							10
11		31	Work-in-Process Inventory		130 0 0 0 00		11
12			Manufacturing Summary			130 0 0 0 00	12
13							13
14		31	Income Summary		390 0 0 0 00		14
15			Finished Goods Inventory			390 0 0 0 00	15
16							16
17		31	Finished Goods Inventory		250 0 0 0 00		17
18			Income Summary			250 0 0 0 00	18
19							19
20		31	Depreciation Expense, Factory				20
21			Equipment		32 0 0 0 00		21
22			Accumulated Depreciation,				22
23			Factory Equipment			32 0 0 0 00	23
24							24
25		31	Depreciation Expense, Factory				25
26			Building		25 0 0 0 00		26
27			Accumulated Depreciation,				27
28			Factory Building			25 0 0 0 00	28
29							29
30		31	Factory Insurance Expired		22 0 0 0 00		30
31			Prepaid Insurance			22 0 0 0 00	31
32							32
33		31	Factory Supplies Used		14 0 0 0 00		33
34			Factory Supplies			14 0 0 0 00	34
35							35
36		31	General Expenses (control)		5 0 0 0 00		36
37			Accumulated Depreciation,				37
38			Office Equipment			5 0 0 0 00	38
39							39
40		31	General Expenses (control)		3 5 0 0 00		40
41			Allowance for Doubtful Accts.			3 5 0 0 00	41
42							42
43		31	Income Tax Expense		16 0 0 0 00		43
44			Income Tax Payable			16 0 0 0 00	44
45							45
46							46

(continued)

**FIGURE 4
(continued)**

		GENERAL JOURNAL			PAGE _____	
	DATE	DESCRIPTION	POST. REF.	DEBIT	CREDIT	
1	20–	**Closing Entries**				1
2	Dec. 31	Manufacturing Summary		1,200 0 0 0 00		2
3		Raw Materials Purchases			230 0 0 0 00	3
4		Direct Labor			565 0 0 0 00	4
5		Indirect Labor			120 0 0 0 00	5
6		Supervisory Salaries			110 0 0 0 00	6
7		Heat, Light, and Power			42 0 0 0 00	7
8		Repairs and Maintenance			24 0 0 0 00	8
9		Misc. Factory Costs			16 0 0 0 00	9
10		Depreciation Expense,				10
11		Factory Equipment			32 0 0 0 00	11
12		Depreciation Expense,				12
13		Factory Building			25 0 0 0 00	13
14		Factory Insurance Expired			22 0 0 0 00	14
15		Factory Supplies Used			14 0 0 0 00	15
16						16
17	31	Income Summary		1,200 0 0 0 00		17
18		Manufacturing Summary			1,200 0 0 0 00	18
19						19
20	31	Sales (net)		2,000 0 0 0 00		20
21		Income Summary			2,000 0 0 0 00	21
22						22
23	31	Income Summary		450 0 0 0 00		23
24		Selling Expenses (control)			300 0 0 0 00	24
25		General Expenses (control)			132 0 0 0 00	25
26		Interest Expense			18 0 0 0 00	26
27						27
28	31	Income Summary		53 4 5 0 00		28
29		Income Tax Expense			53 4 5 0 00	29
30						30
31	31	Income Summary		156 5 5 0 00		31
32		Retained Earnings			156 5 5 0 00	32
33						33
34						34
35						35

DETERMINING THE VALUE OF ENDING INVENTORIES

A manufacturer has to record the costs of the ending inventories for (1) raw materials, (2) work-in-process, and (3) finished goods. The manufacturer first lists these costs in the Adjustments columns of the work sheet and then carries the figures forward into the financial statement columns. Now let's consider raw materials inventory and work-in-process inventory separately, because each poses a slightly different set of problems.

Computers have become essential in compiling the data needed to compute the cost of goods manufactured.

Raw Materials Inventory

The items that make up the raw materials inventory are in the same form they were in when the manufacturer bought them; nothing has been done to them yet. So the accountant first determines the quantities on hand and the unit costs and then figures the value of the inventory. The value of the ending inventory may be calculated by either FIFO, LIFO, or weighted-average method. You may also use the lower-of-cost-or-market rule. These alternatives involve periodic and perpetual inventory systems.

A manufacturer may choose to use a *perpetual inventory system,* which provides a continuous or running balance of the firm's inventory. When a firm that uses a perpetual inventory system buys raw materials, it immediately debits Raw Materials Inventory for the cost of these materials. When the materials are put into production, the manufacturer credits Raw Materials Inventory for the cost of the materials used and debits Work-in-Process Inventory. The same debiting and crediting process goes on in the Work-in-Process Inventory and the Finished Goods Inventory accounts as the materials go through the manufacturing process. If a company keeps a perpetual inventory, it verifies the balance of the account periodically by physically counting the goods on hand. Any discrepancy that exists can be handled by an adjusting entry either debiting or crediting the Inventory account and either debiting or crediting the Cost of Goods Sold account.

Work-in-Process Inventory

How do you calculate the cost of the work-in-process inventory? We have seen that the cost of manufacturing any product consists of (1) *raw materials used,* (2) *direct labor expended,* and (3) *factory overhead.* Therefore the manufacturer keeps a record of the amount and cost of raw materials placed in production. The manufacturer also records the cost of direct labor expended on the ending work-in-process inventory.

The third item, factory overhead, consists of a group of accounts such as Heat, Light, and Power; Repairs and Maintenance; and Miscellaneous Factory Costs; to name a few. The manufacturer cannot calculate the *exact* cost of factory overhead included in the ending work-in-process inventory and must therefore estimate this cost. The firm does this by using a percentage of the direct labor cost involved in the ending inventory. The reasoning here is that since factory overhead is closely related to the level of production, and since the level of production varies directly with the amount of direct labor, the cost of factory overhead should be regarded as a percentage of direct labor. For example, Heat, Light, and Power is part of factory overhead and varies directly with the level of production.

You may determine the percentage for factory overhead from the most recent statement of cost of goods manufactured. The factory overhead rate for the Wendt Manufacturing Company, Inc., is as follows:

$$\text{Factory Overhead Rate} = \frac{\text{Factory Overhead}}{\text{Direct Labor}} = \frac{\$405,000}{\$565,000} = .72 = \underline{\underline{72\%}}$$

COST ACCOUNTING SYSTEMS FOR MANUFACTURING OPERATIONS

There are two principal cost accounting systems: (1) the job-order cost accounting system and (2) the process cost accounting system.

Job-Order Cost Accounting System

Objective 3

Define *job-order cost accounting system* and make related entries.

In a **job-order cost accounting system**, costs, materials, labor, and overhead costs are accumulated *by the job* or batch on a job order cost sheet as the batch is transferred through the various production departments. The job order may originate from a customer's request or be initiated by the company itself to increase its inventory of finished products. After the job is completed and included in the finished goods inventory, the cost per unit can be calculated by dividing the total costs of materials, labor, and overhead accumulated from each department by the total units completed in the job or batch. For each job order, there is a definite beginning and, when the objective has been achieved, a definite ending.

For example, one of the products made by Ace Manufacturing Company is bicycle pumps. The company has an order for 5,000 pumps. Ace sets up a subsidiary Work-in-Process Inventory account in the work-in-process subsidiary ledger and titles it Work in Process—Job Order 72. Work-in-Process Inventory is a control account, and the subsidiary ledger contains an account for each job order number. Below are typical entries pertaining to Job Order 72. These entries relate to a perpetual inventory system.

a. Purchased raw materials, $100,000, paying cash. (For simplicity, assume that all payments are made in cash.)

GENERAL JOURNAL   PAGE _____

	DATE	DESCRIPTION	POST. REF.	DEBIT	CREDIT	
1		Raw Materials Inventory		100 0 0 0 00		1
2		Cash			100 0 0 0 00	2

b. Placed $80,000 of raw materials into production.

DATE	DESCRIPTION	POST. REF.	DEBIT	CREDIT	
	Work-in-Process Inventory		80 0 0 0 00		1
	Raw Materials Inventory			80 0 0 0 00	2

c. Issued checks for direct labor, $40,000.

DATE	DESCRIPTION	POST. REF.	DEBIT	CREDIT	
	Work-in-Process Inventory		40 0 0 0 00		1
	Cash			40 0 0 0 00	2

■ ■ ■

Remember!

We pay for factory overhead (debit Factory Overhead and credit Cash), and then we distribute (apply) the factory overhead.

d. Applied factory overhead at the rate of 70 percent of direct labor.

DATE	DESCRIPTION	POST. REF.	DEBIT	CREDIT	
	Work-in-Process Inventory		28 0 0 0 00		1
	Factory Overhead			28 0 0 0 00	2

e. Transferred completed production to Finished Goods Inventory.

DATE	DESCRIPTION	POST. REF.	DEBIT	CREDIT	
	Finished Goods Inventory		148 0 0 0 00		1
	Work-in-Process Inventory			148 0 0 0 00	2

To carry on its production, Ace Manufacturing must keep a variety of raw materials. Consequently, Raw Materials Inventory (sometimes called Materials) is a control account, and the materials ledger contains a separate account for each type of material. As mentioned before, since Ace Manufacturing may be working on a number of job orders at the same time, Work-in-Process Inventory is also a control account. Finally, Finished Goods Inventory is a control account, and the finished goods ledger contains a separate account for bicycle pumps as well as a separate account for each other product manufactured.

The following page shows the entries involving the inventories in T account form.

General Ledger

Raw Materials Inventory		Work-in-Process Inventory		Finished Goods Inventory		Factory Overhead		Cash	
Bal. xxx	**(b)** 80,000	Bal. xxx	**(e)**	Bal. xxx		Bal. xxx	**(d)** 28,000	Bal. xxx	**(a)**
(a)		**(b)** 80,000	148,000	**(e)**					100,000
100,000		**(c)** 40,000		148,000					**(c)** 40,000
		(d) 28,000							

Materials Ledger			Work-in-Process Ledger			Finished Goods Ledger	

Material A

Bal.	xx	**(b)**	60,000
(a)	100,000		

Material B

Bal.	xx	**(b)**	10,000

Material C

Bal.	xx	**(b)**	10,000

Job Order 72

Bal.	xx	**(e)**	148,000
(b)	80,000		
(c)	40,000		
(d)	28,000		

Job Order 73

Bal.	xx

Job Order 74

Bal.	xx

Product No. 1

Bal.	xx
(e)	148,000

Product No. 2

Bal.	xx

Product No. 3

Bal.	xx

Since the Factory Overhead account is a control account, it will be debited when actual expenses are paid. Note that a variety of materials are used for Job Order 72. Note the output of Job Order 72 is Product No. 1.

Process Cost Accounting System

■ ■ ■

Objective 4

Define *process cost accounting system* and make related entries.

Companies whose product is homogeneous, such as this wheat processing plant, use a process cost accounting system. In this plant, one bag of wheat is indistinguishable from the next.

A **process cost accounting system** is used by manufacturers of homogeneous units (items that are exactly the same and are not distinguishable from one another) in a continuous production process. For example, the production of cement or flour is the result of a continuous process. Also, in the case of cement, one 90-pound bag of cement is the same as another 90-pound bag.

Production of such goods is continuous and is completed in stages, with one department completing one stage and another department completing the next stage. Each department accumulates the costs of materials, labor, and overhead. As a result, in a process cost accounting system, costs are accumulated by department, in contrast to the job-order cost system, where costs are accumulated by the job or batch. The cost per unit of output in a process cost system is calculated by dividing each department's costs of materials, labor, and overhead by the equivalent units of output processed in each department. The calculations of equivalent units and equivalent unit costs are complex calculations covered in a more advanced managerial or cost accounting text.

There is a Work-in-Process Inventory account for each department that is debited for the costs of materials, labor, and overhead used by that department. In the continuous process, the production of the first department is passed on to the second department. The first department's total cost is debited to the second department's Work-in-Process

Inventory account. For example, assume that the production of rolled roofing takes place in two departments. The flow of production from Department 1 to Department 2 and ending up in Finished Goods Inventory is illustrated in T accounts using symbolic amounts. Note that additional raw materials have been added in Department 2.

Work-in-Process Inventory—Department 1			
Raw Materials	100	To Department 2	200
Direct Labor	50		
Factory Overhead	50		

Work-in-Process Inventory—Department 2			
From Department 1	200	To Finished Goods	270
Raw Materials	10		
Direct Labor	20		
Factory Overhead	40		

Finished Goods Inventory		
From Department 2	270	

CHAPTER REVIEW

Review of Performance Objectives

1. Prepare a statement of cost of goods manufactured.

   The statement of cost of goods manufactured includes the beginning work-in-process inventory, plus the cost of raw materials used, plus direct labor, plus factory overhead, less the ending work-in-process inventory.

2. Complete a work sheet for a manufacturing enterprise and journalize closing entries.

   A work sheet for a manufacturing company contains an extra pair of columns entitled "Statement of Cost of Goods Manufactured." Manufacturing costs—Raw Materials Purchases, Direct Labor, and Factory Overhead account balances—are recorded in the Debit column. Debit amounts recorded in the Manufacturing Summary account (representing the beginning balances of Raw Materials Inventory and Work-in-Process Inventory) are listed in the Statement of Cost of Goods Manufactured Debit column. Credit amounts recorded in the Manufacturing Summary account (representing the ending balances of Raw Materials Inventory and Work-in-Process Inventory) are listed in the Statement of Cost of Goods Manufactured Credit column. The difference between the Statement of Cost of Goods Manufactured Debit and Credit columns is the amount of the cost of goods manufactured, and this amount is recorded as a credit to balance off the columns. The amount of the cost of goods manufactured is also recorded in the Income Statement Debit column.

3. Define *job-order cost accounting system* and make related entries.

   A job-order cost accounting system is used by manufacturers producing distinctive products in batches of a specified number of units. Each batch of units is given a job-order number. The costs of production (raw materials, direct labor, and factory overhead) are debited to the account for that job-order number in the work-in-process subsidiary ledger. When the job is completed, the Finished Goods Inventory account is debited and the Work-in-Process Inventory account is credited.

4. Define *process cost accounting system* and make related entries.

   A process cost accounting system is used by manufacturers whose production involves a continuous process. The output consists of homogeneous units. The production flows from one department to another department. A Work-in-Process

Inventory account is set up for each department to record the costs of production. The entry to record the passing on of production from one department to another is a debit to the second department's Work-in-Process Inventory account and a credit to the first department's Work-in-Process Inventory account. Upon completion of the last stage of production, the entry is a debit to Finished Goods Inventory and a credit to the last department's Work-in-Process Inventory account.

Glossary

Direct labor Wages paid to factory employees who work—with machines or hand tools—directly on raw materials to convert them into finished products. (955)

Factory overhead All manufacturing costs that cannot be traced directly to products being manufactured. Examples: heat, light, and power; repairs and maintenance; indirect labor; indirect materials. (955)

Indirect labor The cost of work performed by workers who keep the plant in operation—such as operations personnel, factory maintenance workers, and timekeepers—rather than by workers who are directly occupied with production; considered part of factory overhead. (955)

Indirect materials Factory supplies, such as oil, grease, and cleaning fluids, used to keep the plant in operation; considered part of factory overhead. (955)

Job-order cost accounting system A product costing system used by companies making products in batches. Raw materials, direct labor, and factory overhead costs are assigned to specific job orders. (964)

Manufacturing Summary An account used to make adjustments to Raw Materials Inventory and Work-in-Process Inventory accounts. (958)

Process cost accounting system A product costing system used by companies that maintain a continuous production flow. Manufacturing costs are assigned to departments that complete successive stages of production. (966)

Raw materials The materials (also called *direct materials*) that enter directly into and become a part of the finished product. (955)

QUESTIONS, EXERCISES, AND PROBLEMS

Discussion Questions

1. In manufacturing operations, how do raw materials differ from indirect materials?
2. How do job-order and process cost accounting systems differ?
3. Compare the Manufacturing Summary account with the Income Summary account.
4. Why is cost of goods manufactured entered in the Statement of Cost of Goods Manufactured Credit and the Income Statement Debit columns on a work sheet?
5. Compare cost of goods manufactured for a manufacturing business with cost of goods sold for a merchandising business.
6. List six examples of factory overhead accounts.
7. Is it possible for paint to be considered an indirect material for one company and a direct material for another company?

8. Does the Manufacturing Summary account have a balance during the fiscal period? Explain your answer.

Exercises

P.O. 1

Determine cost of goods manufactured.

Exercise 27-1 From the following balances, determine the cost of goods manufactured:

Costs of Goods Sold	$3,825,000
Finished Goods Inventory, March 1	900,000
Finished Goods Inventory, March 31	675,000

P.O. 1

Prepare a statement of cost of goods manufactured.

Exercise 27-2 Prepare a statement of cost of goods manufactured, using any of the following balances that you need:

Raw Materials Purchases	$630,000
Raw Materials Inventory, June 30	75,000
Raw Materials Inventory, June 1	45,000
Work-in-Process Inventory, June 1	225,000
Work-in-Process Inventory, June 30	300,000
Finished Goods Inventory, June 30	120,000
Direct Labor	900,000
Factory Overhead	675,000
Finished Goods Inventory, June 1	135,000

P.O. 1

Prepare a statement of cost of goods manufactured.

Exercise 27-3 The Statement of Cost of Goods Manufactured columns and the Income Statement columns of the work sheet for the R. W. Manufacturing Company for the year ended December 31 are as shown. R. W.'s beginning inventory of raw materials is $8,000; its beginning inventory of work-in-process is $38,400. Prepare a statement of cost of goods manufactured.

	STATEMENT OF COST OF GOODS MANUFACTURED		INCOME STATEMENT	
ACCOUNT NAME	DEBIT	CREDIT	DEBIT	CREDIT
Sales				360 0 0 0 00
Raw Materials Purchases	64 0 0 0 00			
Direct Labor	160 0 0 0 00			
Indirect Labor	3 2 0 0 00			
Heat, Light, and Power	1 6 0 0 00			
Miscellaneous Factory Costs	8 0 0 00			
Selling Expenses (control)			34 0 0 0 00	
General Expenses (control)			14 0 0 0 00	
Income Tax Expense			22 4 8 0 00	
Manufacturing Summary	8 0 0 0 00	12 0 0 0 00		
	38 4 0 0 00	40 0 0 0 00		
Income Summary			32 0 0 0 00	36 0 0 0 00
	276 0 0 0 00	52 0 0 0 00		
Cost of Goods Manufactured		224 0 0 0 00	224 0 0 0 00	
	276 0 0 0 00	276 0 0 0 00	326 4 8 0 00	396 0 0 0 00
Net Income			69 5 2 0 00	
			396 0 0 0 00	396 0 0 0 00

P.O. 1

Determine cost of raw materials used.

Exercise 27-4 From the following balances, determine the cost of the raw materials used:

Raw Materials Purchases	$1,800,000
Raw Materials Inventory, August 31	480,000
Raw Materials Inventory, August 1	360,000

P.O. 2

Journalize the closing entries.

Exercise 27-5 From the information in Exercise 27-3, journalize the closing entries for the R. W. Manufacturing Company.

P.O. 2

Calculate total manufacturing costs.

Exercise 27-6 From the following balances, calculate the total manufacturing costs, which contain the following three elements:

Raw materials used	$240,000
Direct labor	275,000
Factory overhead (60% of direct labor cost)	

P.O. 3

Prepare journal entries.

Exercise 27-7 Everett Printers received an order to print 10,000 brochures for Channing Cruise Line. Record the following transactions in general journal form for Job Order 716.

a. Purchased paper stock on account, $4,000, from Delta Pulp and Paper.
b. Placed all the paper into production.
c. Issued a check payable to the payroll bank account for direct labor, $1,000.
d. Applied factory overhead at 200 percent of direct labor.

P.O. 4

Prepare journal entries.

Exercise 27-8 Bingham Company manufactures a special soap. The processing takes place in two departments, Department 1 and Department 2. Record the following transactions in general journal form.

a. Raw materials costing $400,000 are transferred from inventory to Department 1 to be placed in production.
b. Direct labor costs amounting to $100,000 are recorded and charged to Department 1 (Wages Payable).
c. Factory overhead is allocated to Department 1 at the rate of 20 percent of direct labor.
d. Production is completed in Department 1 and transferred to Department 2.
e. Direct labor costs amounting to $40,000 are recorded and charged to Department 2 (Wages Payable).
f. Factory overhead is allocated to Department 2 at the rate of 20 percent of direct labor.
g. Production is completed in Department 2 and the products are transferred to Finished Goods Inventory.

WHAT IF . . .

The Tender Loving Toy Company manufactures plush animals that move and talk. The accountant is trying to set up the accounting records. These animals need to be kept dust-free until they are sold so that they will look crisp and clean. To accomplish this, the animals are put into boxes with cellophane windows. They are boxed by hand because they need to be attached to the inside of the boxes. The accountant is not certain whether this boxing work is direct labor or indirect labor because the animals are completely finished before they are boxed. How would you classify it?

CRITICAL THINKING

Following is a statement of cost of goods manufactured for Pabrucy Manufacturing, Inc. Since the records that support this statement were destroyed by water damage caused by a collapsed roof, fill in the missing amounts.

Pabrucy Manufacturing, Inc.
Statement of Cost of Goods Manufactured
For Year Ended December 31, 20—

	Col 1	Col 2	Col 3
Work-in-Process Inventory, January 1, 20—			$
Raw Materials:			
Raw Materials Inventory, January 1, 20—	$ 135 000 00		
Raw Materials Purchases (net)			
Cost of Raw Materials Available for Use	$ 399 500 00		
Less Raw Materials Inventory, December 31, 20—			
Cost of Raw Materials Used		$ 253 000 00	
Direct Labor		553 700 00	
Factory Overhead:			
Indirect Labor	$		
Supervisory Salaries	112 000 00		
Heat, Light, and Power	45 300 00		
Depreciation Expense, Factory Building	27 400 00		
Depreciation Expense, Factory Equipment	30 700 00		
Repairs and Maintenance	18 430 00		
Factory Supplies Used	11 200 00		
Factory Insurance Expired	24 800 00		
Miscellaneous Factory Costs	12 520 00		
Total Factory Overhead		414 350 00	
Total Manufacturing Costs			
Total Cost of Work-in-Process During Period			$1 364 050 00
Less Work-in-Process Inventory, December 31, 20—			
Cost of Goods Manufactured			$1 239 050 00

A MATTER OF ETHICS

The accountant at Orin Manufacturing is afraid that he will be fired if he is not able to show management what they want to see—higher profits. Part of the raw materials inventory is stored off the property, and he is considering inflating its value. If he does so, the cost of goods manufactured will be lower and the gross profit higher. Comment on this practice.

WEB WORK

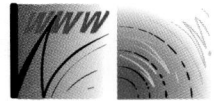

Using an Internet web browser, type *manufacturing accounting, job-order cost accounting,* or *process cost accounting* in the search box and search for information on manufacturing accounting. Discuss your findings in a small group. Write a one-page summary of your findings.

PROBLEM SET A

For additional help, see the demonstration problem at the beginning of each chapter in your Working Papers.

P.O. 2,3

Problem 27-1A Here is the statement of cost of goods manufactured for the Epler Manufacturing Company:

Epler Manufacturing Company
Statement of Cost of Goods Manufactured
For Year Ended June 30, 20—

Work-in-Process Inventory, July 1, 20—			$ 80 0 0 0 00
Raw Materials:			
Raw Materials Inventory, July 1, 20—	$ 136 0 0 0 00		
Raw Materials Purchases (net)	197 5 0 0 00		
Cost of Raw Materials Available for Use	$ 333 5 0 0 00		
Less Raw Materials Inventory, June 30, 20—	130 0 0 0 00		
Cost of Raw Materials Used		$ 203 5 0 0 00	
Direct Labor		291 0 0 0 00	
Factory Overhead:			
Indirect Labor	$ 54 2 0 0 00		
Supervisory Salaries	38 0 5 0 00		
Depreciation Expense, Factory Equipment	36 0 0 0 00		
Depreciation Expense, Factory Building	10 9 0 0 00		
Heat, Light, and Power	9 3 0 0 00		
Repairs and Maintenance	7 2 0 0 00		
Factory Supplies Used	6 9 5 0 00		
Factory Insurance Expired	3 8 0 0 00		
Property Tax on Factory Building	3 7 5 0 00		
Miscellaneous Factory Costs	3 5 5 0 00		
Total Factory Overhead		173 7 0 0 00	
Total Manufacturing Costs			668 2 0 0 00
Total Cost of Work-in-Process During Period			$ 748 2 0 0 00
Less Work-in-Process Inventory, June 30, 20—			87 5 0 0 00
Cost of Goods Manufactured			$ 660 7 0 0 00

Check Figure

Amount needed to close Manufacturing Summary into Income Summary, $660,700

Instructions

1. Journalize the adjusting entries for the Raw Materials Inventory and the Work-in-Process Inventory.
2. Journalize the closing entries for manufacturing costs.
3. Post the entries to the Manufacturing Summary account.

4. Journalize and post the entry to close the Manufacturing Summary account.

Problem 27-2A The trial balance of the Bonnard Manufacturing Corporation as of December 31 of this year is shown here.

Bonnard Manufacturing Corporation
Trial Balance
December 31, 20—

ACCOUNT NAME	DEBIT	CREDIT
Cash	4 3 5 0 00	
Accounts Receivable	34 7 0 0 00	
Allowance for Doubtful Accounts		1 3 5 0 00
Raw Materials Inventory	45 8 0 0 00	
Work-in-Process Inventory	71 0 5 0 00	
Finished Goods Inventory	69 2 0 0 00	
Prepaid Factory Insurance	2 1 0 0 00	
Factory Supplies	3 0 0 0 00	
Machinery	85 5 0 0 00	
Accumulated Depreciation, Machinery		43 2 0 0 00
Accounts Payable		27 4 5 0 00
Common Stock		100 0 0 0 00
Paid-in Capital in Excess of Stated Value		25 0 0 0 00
Retained Earnings		65 4 0 5 00
Sales		645 7 0 0 00
Raw Materials Purchases	69 9 5 0 00	
Direct Labor	210 6 4 0 00	
Indirect Labor	80 7 3 0 00	
Heat, Light, and Power	16 2 0 0 00	
Machinery Repairs	9 8 0 0 00	
Selling Expenses (control)	141 7 1 0 00	
General Expenses (control)	59 3 7 5 00	
Income Tax Expense	4 0 0 0 00	
	908 1 0 5 00	908 1 0 5 00

You are given the following information for the adjustments:

a.–f. Year-end inventories: raw materials, $42,700; work-in-process, $64,200; finished goods, $70,350.

g. Estimated depreciation of factory machinery, $9,250.

h. A study of the company's insurance policies shows that $1,550 of factory insurance expired during the year.

i. Allowance for Doubtful Accounts is to be increased by $775 (debit General Expenses [control]).

j. Accrued direct labor, $360; accrued indirect labor, $120; accrued sales commissions, $140 (credit Wages and Commissions Payable).

k. Ending factory supplies inventory, $1,100.

l. Additional income tax, $1,160.

Check Figure

Cost of goods manufactured, $410,450

P.O. 1,2

Instructions

1. Prepare a work sheet.
2. Prepare a statement of cost of goods manufactured.
3. Prepare an income statement.

Problem 27-3A Here are the columns reflecting the statement of cost of goods manufactured and the income statement in the work sheet of the Sero Pump Corporation as of December 31, the end of the fiscal year. Beginning inventory of raw materials is $142,920; beginning inventory of work-in-process is $253,400.

	ACCOUNT NAME	STATEMENT OF COST OF GOODS MANUFACTURED DEBIT	STATEMENT OF COST OF GOODS MANUFACTURED CREDIT	INCOME STATEMENT DEBIT	INCOME STATEMENT CREDIT	
1	Sales				3,016 4 8 0 00	1
2	Sales Returns and Allowances			25 2 0 0 00		2
3	Sales Discount			24 0 0 0 00		3
4	Selling Expenses (control)			373 9 0 0 00		4
5	General Expenses (control)			147 2 2 0 00		5
6	Raw Materials Purchases	764 0 0 0 00				6
7	Direct Labor	973 8 0 0 00				7
8	Indirect Labor	221 6 8 0 00				8
9	Heat, Light, and Power	55 2 4 0 00				9
10	Factory Supervision	53 8 6 0 00				10
11	Rent, Factory	36 0 0 0 00				11
12	Machinery Repairs	35 8 4 0 00				12
13	Depreciation Expense, Machinery	34 7 6 0 00				13
14	Factory Supplies Used	9 8 0 0 00				14
15	Factory Insurance Expired	7 2 0 0 00				15
16	Small Tools Expense	2 4 8 0 00				16
17	Miscellaneous Factory Costs	1 3 0 0 00				17
18	Loss on Disposal of Equipment			16 0 0 0 00		18
19	Interest Expense			15 2 0 0 00		19
20	Income Tax Expense			83 0 0 0 00		20
21	Manufacturing Summary	142 9 2 0 00	147 6 4 0 00			21
22		253 4 0 0 00	265 6 8 0 00			22
23	Income Summary			369 2 0 0 00	385 6 0 0 00	23
24		2,592 2 8 0 00	413 3 2 0 00			24
25	Cost of Goods Manufactured		2,178 9 6 0 00	2,178 9 6 0 00		25
26		2,592 2 8 0 00	2,592 2 8 0 00	3,232 6 8 0 00	3,402 0 8 0 00	26
27	Net Income			169 4 0 0 00		27
28				3,402 0 8 0 00	3,402 0 8 0 00	28

Check Figure

Gross profit, $804,720

Instructions

1. Prepare a statement of cost of goods manufactured.
2. Prepare an income statement.
3. Journalize the adjusting entries for the inventories.
4. Journalize the closing entries.

P.O. 1

Problem 27-4A Here are adjusting and closing entries that appear on the books of the Bailor Cedar Shingle Company at the end of the fiscal year, December 31.

	DATE		DESCRIPTION	POST. REF.	DEBIT	CREDIT	
1	20–		**Adjusting Entries**				1
2	Dec.	31	Manufacturing Summary		88 7 7 0 00		2
3			Raw Materials Inventory			88 7 7 0 00	3
4							4
5		31	Raw Materials Inventory		90 6 1 8 00		5
6			Manufacturing Summary			90 6 1 8 00	6
7							7
8		31	Manufacturing Summary		112 8 2 0 00		8
9			Work-in-Process Inventory			112 8 2 0 00	9
10							10
11		31	Work-in-Process Inventory		116 8 4 0 00		11
12			Manufacturing Summary			116 8 4 0 00	12
13							13
14			**Closing Entries**				14
15		31	Purchases Discount		4 2 1 0 00		15
16			Manufacturing Summary			4 2 1 0 00	16
17							17
18		31	Manufacturing Summary		794 8 7 0 00		18
19			Raw Materials Purchases			254 9 6 0 00	19
20			Direct Labor			339 4 6 0 00	20
21			Indirect Labor			38 4 8 0 00	21
22			Supervision			58 6 4 0 00	22
23			Depreciation of Machinery			42 0 0 0 00	23
24			Depreciation of Factory Bldg.			24 0 0 0 00	24
25			Heat, Light, and Power			12 8 2 0 00	25
26			Repairs and Maintenance			9 6 8 0 00	26
27			Property Tax, Machinery			1 2 7 0 00	27
28			Property Tax, Factory Bldg.			1 8 4 0 00	28
29			Factory Supplies Used			9 4 7 0 00	29
30			Factory Insurance Expired			1 2 0 0 00	30
31			Miscellaneous Factory Costs			1 0 5 0 00	31
32							32
33		31	Income Summary		784 7 9 2 00		33
34			Manufacturing Summary			784 7 9 2 00	34
35							35
36							36
37							37
38							38
39							39

Check Figure

Cost of goods manufactured, $784,792

Instructions

Prepare a statement of cost of goods manufactured for the year.

PROBLEM SET B

For additional help, see the demonstration problem at the beginning of each chapter in your Working Papers.

P.O. 2,3

Problem 27-1B Here is the statement of cost of goods manufactured for the Sarbo Manufacturing Company:

Sarbo Manufacturing Company
Statement of Cost of Goods Manufactured
For Year Ended December 31, 20—

Work-in-Process Inventory, January 1			$ 240 0 0 0 00
Raw Materials:			
Raw Materials Inventory, January 1	$ 500 0 0 0 00		
Raw Materials Purchases (net)	780 0 0 0 00		
Cost of Raw Materials Available for Use	$1 280 0 0 0 00		
Less Raw Materials Inventory, December 31	530 0 0 0 00		
Cost of Raw Materials Used		$ 750 0 0 0 00	
Direct Labor		1 200 0 0 0 00	
Factory Overhead:			
Indirect Labor	$ 220 0 0 0 00		
Supervisory Salaries	190 0 0 0 00		
Depreciation Expense, Factory Equipment	130 0 0 0 00		
Depreciation Expense, Factory Building	37 6 0 0 00		
Heat, Light, and Power	38 0 0 0 00		
Repairs and Maintenance	28 4 0 0 00		
Factory Supplies Used	24 0 0 0 00		
Factory Insurance Expired	17 6 0 0 00		
Property Tax on Factory Building	14 4 0 0 00		
Miscellaneous Factory Costs	12 8 0 0 00		
Total Factory Overhead		712 8 0 0 00	
Total Manufacturing Costs			2 662 8 0 0 00
Total Cost of Work-in-Process During Period			$2 902 8 0 0 00
Less Work-in-Process Inventory, December 31			520 0 0 0 00
Cost of Goods Manufactured			$2 382 8 0 0 00

Check Figure

Amount needed to close Manufacturing Summary into Income Summary, $2,382,800

Instructions

1. Journalize the adjusting entries for the Raw Materials Inventory and the Work-in-Process Inventory.
2. Journalize the closing entries for manufacturing costs.
3. Post the entries to the Manufacturing Summary account.
4. Journalize and post the entry to close the Manufacturing Summary account.

P.O. 1,2

Problem 27-2B The trial balance of the McBain Products Company, Inc., as of December 31 of this year, is shown on the facing page.

McBain Products Company, Inc.
Trial Balance
December 31, 20—

ACCOUNT NAME	DEBIT	CREDIT
Cash	4 2 0 0 00	
Accounts Receivable	35 8 0 0 00	
Allowance for Doubtful Accounts		1 4 5 0 00
Raw Materials Inventory	45 0 0 0 00	
Work-in-Process Inventory	71 3 0 0 00	
Finished Goods Inventory	68 2 0 0 00	
Prepaid Factory Insurance	1 8 0 0 00	
Factory Supplies	3 0 0 0 00	
Machinery	84 0 0 0 00	
Accumulated Depreciation, Machinery		42 0 0 0 00
Accounts Payable		29 3 0 0 00
Common Stock		100 0 0 0 00
Paid-in Capital in Excess of Stated Value		20 0 0 0 00
Retained Earnings		70 0 0 0 00
Sales		638 7 5 0 00
Raw Materials Purchases	70 0 0 0 00	
Direct Labor	209 7 0 0 00	
Indirect Labor	79 9 0 0 00	
Heat, Light, and Power	16 0 0 0 00	
Machinery Repairs	9 0 0 0 00	
Selling Expenses (control)	139 9 5 0 00	
General Expenses (control)	60 0 5 0 00	
Income Tax Expense	3 6 0 0 00	
	901 5 0 0 00	901 5 0 0 00

You are given the following information for the adjustments:

a.–f. Year-end inventories: raw materials, $43,000; work-in-process, $63,400; finished goods, $69,250.

g. Allowance for Doubtful Accounts to be increased by $800 (debit General Expenses [control]).

h. Cost of the factory supplies inventory, $1,000.

i. Estimated depreciation of factory machinery, $8,750.

j. A study of the company's insurance policies shows that $1,200 of factory insurance expired during the year.

k. Accrued direct labor, $300; accrued indirect labor, $100; accrued sales commissions, $100 (credit Wages and Commissions Payable).

l. Additional income tax, $1,208.

Check Figure

Cost of goods manufactured, $406,850

Instructions

1. Prepare a work sheet.
2. Prepare a statement of cost of goods manufactured.
3. Prepare an income statement.

P.O. 1,2

Problem 27-3B The columns reflecting the statement of cost of goods manufactured and the income statement from the work sheet of Nesta Sporting Goods Company, Inc., as of December 31, the end of the fiscal year, are shown here. Beginning inventory of raw materials is $138,240; beginning inventory of work in process is $248,800.

	ACCOUNT NAME	STATEMENT OF COST OF GOODS MANUFACTURED DEBIT	STATEMENT OF COST OF GOODS MANUFACTURED CREDIT	INCOME STATEMENT DEBIT	INCOME STATEMENT CREDIT	
1	Sales				2,999 9 2 0 00	1
2	Sales Returns and Allowances			24 8 0 0 00		2
3	Sales Discount			23 6 0 0 00		3
4	Selling Expenses (control)			358 9 8 0 00		4
5	General Expenses (control)			145 7 2 0 00		5
6	Raw Materials Purchases	769 0 0 0 00				6
7	Direct Labor	965 8 0 0 00				7
8	Indirect Labor	221 2 4 0 00				8
9	Heat, Light, and Power	53 9 6 0 00				9
10	Factory Supervision	53 9 0 0 00				10
11	Rent, Factory	32 0 0 0 00				11
12	Machinery Repairs	31 8 0 0 00				12
13	Depreciation Expense, Machinery	31 6 8 0 00				13
14	Factory Supplies Used	12 4 0 0 00				14
15	Factory Insurance Expired	7 6 0 0 00				15
16	Small Tools Expense	2 5 2 0 00				16
17	Miscellaneous Factory Costs	1 3 6 0 00				17
18	Loss on Disposal of Equipment			17 2 0 0 00		18
19	Interest Expense			13 6 0 0 00		19
20	Income Tax Expense			86 0 0 0 00		20
21	Manufacturing Summary	138 2 4 0 00	143 2 0 0 00			21
22		248 8 0 0 00	252 9 8 0 00			22
23	Income Summary			362 8 0 0 00	373 4 4 0 00	23
24		2,570 3 0 0 00	396 1 8 0 00			24
25	Cost of Goods Manufactured		2,174 1 2 0 00	2,174 1 2 0 00		25
26		2,570 3 0 0 00	2,570 3 0 0 00	3,206 8 2 0 00	3,373 3 6 0 00	26
27	Net Income			166 5 4 0 00		27
28				3,373 3 6 0 00	3,373 3 6 0 00	28
29						29

Check Figure

Gross profit, $788,040

Instructions

1. Prepare a statement of cost of goods manufactured.
2. Prepare an income statement.
3. Journalize the adjusting entries for the inventories.
4. Journalize the closing entries.

P.O. 1

Problem 27-4B The following page shows the adjusting and closing entries on the books of Maynard Paint Company at the end of the fiscal year, May 31.

	DATE		DESCRIPTION	POST. REF.	DEBIT					CREDIT					
1	20–		**Adjusting Entries**												1
2	May	31	**Manufacturing Summary**		86	7	0	0	00						2
3			Raw Materials Inventory							86	7	0	0	00	3
4															4
5		31	Raw Materials Inventory		78	4	9	0	00						5
6			Manufacturing Summary							78	4	9	0	00	6
7															7
8		31	Manufacturing Summary		110	7	4	0	00						8
9			Work-in-Process Inventory							110	7	4	0	00	9
10															10
11		31	Work-in-Process Inventory		106	4	2	0	00						11
12			Manufacturing Summary							106	4	2	0	00	12
13															13
14			**Closing Entries**												14
15		31	Purchases Discount		3	8	4	0	00						15
16			Manufacturing Summary							3	8	4	0	00	16
17															17
18		31	Manufacturing Summary		954	5	3	0	00						18
19			Raw Materials Purchases							236	7	0	0	00	19
20			Direct Labor							488	9	4	0	00	20
21			Indirect Labor							48	7	4	0	00	21
22			Supervision							69	4	8	0	00	22
23			Depreciation of Machinery							50	0	0	0	00	23
24			Depreciation of Factory Bldg.							20	0	0	0	00	24
25			Heat, Light, and Power							14	2	0	0	00	25
26			Repairs and Maintenance							12	7	9	0	00	26
27			Property Tax, Machinery							1	8	5	0	00	27
28			Property Tax, Factory Bldg.							2	2	0	0	00	28
29			Factory Supplies Used							6	8	7	0	00	29
30			Factory Insurance Expired							1	8	0	0	00	30
31			Miscellaneous Factory Costs								9	6	0	00	31
32															32
33		31	Income Summary		963	2	2	0	00						33
34			Manufacturing Summary							963	2	2	0	00	34
35															35
36															36
37															37
38															38
39															39
40															40

Check Figure

Cost of goods manufactured, $963,220

Instructions

Prepare a statement of cost of goods manufactured for the year.

Cumulative Self-Check: Chapters 24–27

PART I: TRUE/FALSE

T   F   1. A company acquired a long-lived asset by issuing $480,000 par-value common stock. This event is listed under Financing Activities in a statement of cash flows.

T   F   2. It is possible for a business to have a net loss and still have a positive cash flow.

T   F   3. Money market accounts are listed as a part of cash on a statement of cash flows.

T   F   4. Generally, the lower the current ratio, the lower the risk to creditors.

T   F   5. Presenting each asset as a percentage of total assets is an example of horizontal analysis.

T   F   6. When percentage analysis is applied to the income statement, net sales is used as the base.

T   F   7. The only accounts that companies must keep departmentalized to compute gross profit by department are Sales and Purchases.

T   F   8. If a department covers its direct expenses, but not all its indirect expenses, the business can increase its income before taxes if it discontinues the department.

T   F   9. Departmental margin equals gross profit minus direct expenses.

T   F   10. The statement of costs of goods manufactured supports the income statement by providing the figure for cost of goods sold.

T   F   11. The Manufacturing Summary account is closed by an entry debiting the Income Summary account and crediting the Manufacturing Summary account.

T   F   12. Supervisory salaries are part of factory overhead.

PART II: COMPLETION

1. If a company's income statement lists Delivered Cost of Purchases as $440,000, beginning Accounts Payable (trade) as $54,000, and ending Accounts Payable (trade) as $51,500, the amount of cash paid for merchandise purchased is ——————.

Note: Answers to the Cumulative Self-Check problems begin on page A-1.

2. If a company's income statement lists Income from Services as $85,300, beginning Accounts Receivable as $8,400, and ending Accounts Receivable as $9,700, the amount of cash received from customers is _____.

3. If income tax is listed on a corporation's income statement as $36,800 and the balance of Income Tax Payable increased by $2,800 between the beginning and the end of the year, the amount of cash paid for income tax is _____.

4. Merchandise Inventory Turnover $= \dfrac{(\text{_____})}{\text{Average Merchandise Inventory}}$.

5. Quick Ratio $= \dfrac{(\text{_____})}{\text{Current Liabilities}}$.

6. Accounts Receivable Turnover $= \dfrac{(\text{_____})}{\text{Average Accounts Receivable}}$.

7. Those expenses that benefit only one department and are controlled by the head of that department are called _____ expenses.

8. The gross profit of a department minus the department's direct expenses is known as _____.

9. The _____ consists of all manufacturing costs that cannot be traced directly to products being manufactured.

10. Raw materials and work-in-process inventories are adjusted using the _____ account.

PART III: APPLICATION

A. Statement of cash flows

1. Compute the amount of cash paid for insurance if a company's income statement lists Insurance Expense as $640, and its balance sheet lists beginning Prepaid Insurance as $820 and ending Prepaid Insurance as $920.

2. Compute the amount of cash paid for Rent Expense if a company's income statement lists Rent Expense as $24,000 and the balance of Prepaid Rent decreased by $1,800 between the beginning and the end of the year.

B. Financial statement analysis

1. Compute the current ratio if current assets are $210,000 and current liabilities are $202,000.

2. Compute working capital if total liabilities equal $400,000, long-term liabilities are $200,000, and current assets are $500,000.

C. Departmental accounting

If a company's property taxes of $4,000 are apportioned on the basis of floor space, and Department X has 4,000 square feet, Department Y has 5,000 square feet, and Department Z has 6,000 square feet, what would be the amount of tax per department?

Cumulative Self-Check Solutions

CHAPTERS 1–3

Part I: 1. d; 2. e; 3. d; 4. b; 5. e; 6. a

Part II: 1.

			GENERAL JOURNAL		PAGE	31	

	DATE		DESCRIPTION	POST. REF.	DEBIT	CREDIT	
1	20–						1
2	Dec.	1	Cash	111	10 0 0 0 00		2
3			D. Stanfill, Capital	311		10 0 0 0 00	3
4			Invested an additional				4
5			amount, Deposit Slip No.				5
6			41372.				6
7							7
8		4	Rent Expense	513	9 0 0 00		8
9			Cash	111		9 0 0 00	9
10			Ck. No. 2331.				10
11							11
12		11	Cash	111	1 8 6 0 00		12
13			Accounts Receivable	112		1 8 6 0 00	13
14			Cash on account from				14
15			customers, Cash Receipt				15
16			Nos. 1430-1438.				16
17							17
18		19	Accounts Receivable	112	2 1 5 0 00		18
19			Service Income	411		2 1 5 0 00	19
20			M. Linares, Sales Inv. No.				20
21			2591.				21
22							22
23		22	Utilities Expense	512	1 9 7 00		23
24			Cash	111		1 9 7 00	24
25			Ck. No. 2332.				25
26							26
27		23	Supplies	113	2 4 8 00		27
28			Accounts Payable	221		2 4 8 00	28
29			Staple Works, Inv. No. 2606.				29
30							30
31		31	Wages Expense	511	1 6 6 5 00		31
32			Cash	111		1 6 6 5 00	32
33			Paid month's wages, Ck. No.				33
34			2333.				34
35							35
36		31	D. Stanfill, Drawing	312	1 8 0 0 00		36
37			Cash	111		1 8 0 0 00	37
38			Ck. No. 2334.				38

2, 3, 4.

Assets	=	Liabilities	+	Owner's Equity	+	Revenue	−	Expenses

+	−
Debit	Credit

Cash   111

+	−
Debit	Credit
Bal. 18,900	12/4 900
12/1 10,000	12/22 197
12/11 1,860	12/31 1,665
30,760	12/31 1,800
26,198	4,562

Accounts Receivable   112

+	−
Debit	Credit
Bal. 6,300	12/11 1,860
12/19 2,150	
8,450	
Bal. 6,590	

Supplies   113

+	−
Debit	Credit
Bal. 870	
12/23 248	
Bal. 1,118	

Prepaid Insurance   114

+	−
Debit	Credit
Bal. 1,230	

Equipment   124

+	−
Debit	Credit
Bal. 31,200	

Accounts Payable   221

−	+
Debit	Credit
	Bal. 6,340
	12/23 248
	Bal. 6,588

D. Stanfill, Capital   311

−	+
Debit	Credit
	Bal. 49,590
	12/1 10,000
	Bal. 59,590

D. Stanfill, Drawing   312

+	−
Debit	Credit
Bal. 11,200	
12/31 1,800	
Bal. 13,000	

Service Income   411

−	+
Debit	Credit
	Bal. 39,600
	12/19 2,150
	Bal. 41,750

Wages Expense   511

+	−
Debit	Credit
Bal. 10,450	
12/31 1,665	
Bal. 12,115	

Utilities Expense   512

+	−
Debit	Credit
Bal. 2,760	
12/22 197	
Bal. 2,957	

Rent Expense   513

+	−
Debit	Credit
Bal. 12,620	
12/4 900	
Bal. 13,520	

5.

Stanfill Services
Trial Balance
December 31, 20—

ACCOUNT NAME	DEBIT	CREDIT
Cash	26 1 9 8 00	
Accounts Receivable	6 5 9 0 00	
Supplies	1 1 1 8 00	
Prepaid Insurance	1 2 3 0 00	
Equipment	31 2 0 0 00	
Accounts Payable		6 5 8 8 00
D. Stanfill, Capital		59 5 9 0 00
D. Stanfill, Drawing	13 0 0 0 00	
Service Income		41 7 5 0 00
Wages Expense	12 1 1 5 00	
Utilities Expense	2 9 5 7 00	
Rent Expense	13 5 2 0 00	
	107 9 2 8 00	107 9 2 8 00

6.

Stanfill Services
Income Statement
For Year Ended December 31, 20—

Revenue:		
Service Income		$41 7 5 0 00
Expenses:		
Wages Expense	$12 1 1 5 00	
Utilities Expense	2 9 5 7 00	
Rent Expense	13 5 2 0 00	
Total Expenses		28 5 9 2 00
Net Income		$13 1 5 8 00

7.

Stanfill Services
Statement of Owner's Equity
For Year Ended December 31, 20—

D. Stanfill, Capital, December 1, 20—	$49 5 9 0 00		
Additional Investment	10 0 0 0 00		
Total Investment		$59 5 9 0 00	
Net Income	$13 1 5 8 00		
Less Withdrawals	13 0 0 0 00		
Increase in Capital			1 5 8 00
D. Stanfill, Capital, December 31, 20—		$59 7 4 8 00	

8.

Stanfill Services
Balance Sheet
December 31, 20—

Assets			
Cash	$26 1 9 8 00		
Accounts Receivable	6 5 9 0 00		
Supplies	1 1 1 8 00		
Prepaid Insurance	1 2 3 0 00		
Equipment	31 2 0 0 00		
Total Assets		$66 3 3 6 00	
Liabilities			
Accounts Payable		$6 5 8 8 00	
Owner's Equity			
D. Stanfill, Capital		59 7 4 8 00	
Total Liabilities and Owner's Equity		$66 3 3 6 00	

CHAPTERS 4–5

Part I

1. b;   2. d;   3. d;   4. a;   5. a;   6. b;   7. c;   8. c

Part II

	DATE		DESCRIPTION	POST. REF.	DEBIT	CREDIT	
1	20–		**Closing Entries**				1
2							2
3	Dec.	31	Income from Services		25 9 0 0 00		3
4			Income Summary			25 9 0 0 00	4
5							5
6		31	Income Summary		8 5 0 0 00		6
7			Wages Expense			1 5 0 0 00	7
8			Rent Expense			2 4 0 0 00	8
9			Utilities Expense			1 0 0 0 00	9
10			Depreciation Expense,				10
11			Equipment			5 0 0 00	11
12			Supplies Expense			2 2 0 0 00	12
13			Miscellaneous Expense			9 0 0 00	13
14							14
15		31	Income Summary		17 4 0 0 00		15
16			T. L. Hanley, Capital			17 4 0 0 00	16
17							17
18		31	T. L. Hanley, Capital		16 4 0 0 00		18
19			T. L. Hanley, Drawing			16 4 0 0 00	19

GENERAL JOURNAL   PAGE ___1___

Part III

1. b;   2. h;   3. m;   4. q;   5. d;   6. k;   7. u;   8. w;   9. o;   10. s;   11. e;
12. f;   13. i;   14. n;   15. a;   16. t;   17. x;   18. p;   19. y;   20. v;   21. j;   22. c;
23. r;   24. l;   25. g

CHAPTERS 7–9

Part I

1. canceled; 2. deposit in transit or late deposit; 3. endorsement; 4. payee; 5. petty cash fund.

Part II

1. $1,775 per month × 12 months = $21,300 per year
   $21,300 per year ÷ 52 weeks = $409.62 per week
   $409.62 per week ÷ 40 hours = $10.24 per regular hour
   $10.24 per regular hour × 1.5 = $15.36 per overtime hour

   Earnings for 45 hours:

   Forty hours at straight time = 40 × $10.24 = $409.60
   Five hours overtime = 5 × $15.36 =   76.80

   Total gross pay $486.40

2.

GENERAL JOURNAL   PAGE _____

	DATE		DESCRIPTION	POST. REF.	DEBIT	CREDIT	
1	20–						1
2	June	30	Cleaning Salaries Expense		9 0 0 0 00		2
3			Office Salaries Expense		3 0 0 0 00		3
4			Employees' Federal Income Tax Payable			1 5 0 0 00	4
5			FICA Tax Payable ($12,000 × .062) + ($12,000 × .0145)			9 1 8 00	5
6			Savings Bonds Payable			5 0 0 00	6
7			Medical Insurance Payable			9 6 2 00	7
8			Salaries Payable			8 1 2 0 00	8

3.

GENERAL JOURNAL   PAGE _____

	DATE		DESCRIPTION	POST. REF.	DEBIT	CREDIT	
1	20–						1
2	Dec.	31	Payroll Tax Expense		12 4 7 7 50		2
3			FICA Tax Payable ($143,000 × .062) + ($155,000 × .0145)			11 1 1 3 50	3
4			State Unemployment Tax Payable ($22,000 × .054)			1 1 8 8 00	4
5			Federal Unemployment Tax Payable ($22,000 × .008)			1 7 6 00	5

Part III

1. T;   2. F;   3. F;   4. T;   5. F

CHAPTERS 10–12

Part I

1. credit; 2. accounts payable ledger; 3. cash discount; 4. purchase order; 5. Purchases; 6. buyer; 7. internal controls; 8. debit; 9. sales of merchandise on account; 10. charge customers.

Part II

1. CP; 2. J; 3. J; 4. J; 5. S; 6. J; 7. CP; 8. P; 9. CR; 10. CP

Part III

1. F; 2. T; 3. F; 4. F; 5. F

CHAPTERS 13–14

Part I

1. physical inventory; 2. perpetual inventory; 3. current liability; 4. Income Summary; 5. Cost of Goods Sold, Merchandise Inventory; 6. decrease; 7. Cost of Goods Sold; 8. working capital; 9. Income from Operations; 10. Freight In.

Part II

1. F; 2. F; 3. T; 4. T; 5. T; 6. F; 7. F; 8. T; 9. F; 10. T

Part III

1.

GENERAL JOURNAL   PAGE _____

	DATE		DESCRIPTION	POST. REF.	DEBIT	CREDIT	
1	20–		**Adjusting Entries**				1
2	Dec.	31	Income Summary		132 0 0 0 00		2
3			Merchandise Inventory			132 0 0 0 00	3
4							4
5		31	Merchandise Inventory		136 0 0 0 00		5
6			Income Summary			136 0 0 0 00	6

2.

GENERAL JOURNAL   PAGE _____

	DATE		DESCRIPTION	POST. REF.	DEBIT	CREDIT	
1	20–		**Adjusting Entries**				1
2	Dec.	31	Cost of Goods Sold		2 0 0 0 00		2
3			Merchandise Inventory			2 0 0 0 00	3

3.

	DATE		DESCRIPTION	POST. REF.	DEBIT	CREDIT	
1	20–						1
2	Dec.	1	Cash		20 0 0 0 00		2
3			Unearned Revenue			20 0 0 0 00	3
4			To record collection of cash				4
5			for a four-month job.				5
6							6
7			Adjusting Entry				7
8		31	Unearned Revenue		5 0 0 0 00		8
9			Remodeling Revenue			5 0 0 0 00	9
10			To record one month's				10
11			revenue earned.				11

GENERAL JOURNAL   PAGE ———

4. a. $250,000 total assets − $140,000 plant and equipment = $110,000 current assets
$130,000 total liabilities − $80,000 long-term liabilities = $50,000 current liabilities
$110,000 current assets − $50,000 current liabilities = $60,000 working capital

b. $\dfrac{\$110,000 \text{ current assets}}{\$50,000 \text{ current liabilities}} = 2.2{:}1$ current ratio

CHAPTERS 15–16

Part I

A. 1. January 18 of the next year; 2. $12,000; 3. $360; 4. $12,360; 5. $306
B. 1. January 18 of the next year; 2. $8,000; 3. $160; 4. Discount on Notes Payable, $160; 5. $8,000; 6. $128; 7. Debit Interest Expense, credit Discount on Notes Payable; 8. Debit Interest Expense, $32.00; credit Discount on Notes Payable, $32.00

Part II

A. 1. Debit Notes Receivable, $9,000; credit Accounts Receivable, Fleshman Company, $9,000; 2. Debit Interest Receivable, $59.50; credit Interest Income, $59.50; 3. February 1 of the next year; 4. $9,127.50; 5. Debit Cash, $9,127.50; credit Notes Receivable, $9,000; credit Interest Income, $127.50
B. 1. 20 days; 2. 70 days; 3. $6,500; 4. $6,630; 5. $109.58; 6. $6,520.42; 7. Interest Income; 8. $20.42

CHAPTERS 17–19

Part I

1. F; 2. T; 3. F; 4. F; 5. T; 6. T; 7. F; 8. F; 9. T; 10. T

Part II

1. book value or net realizable value; 2. specific charge-off; 3. bankruptcy; 4. LIFO; 5. specific identification; 6. perpetual inventory; 7. Land Improvements; 8. accelerated; 9. revenue expenditures; 10. periodic

Part III

1. E; 2. O; 3. I; 4. N; 5. F; 6. B; 7. C; 8. J; 9. K; 10. L

CHAPTERS 20–23

Part I

1. F; 2. T; 3. T; 4. T; 5. F; 6. T; 7. F; 8. F; 9. T; 10. F; 11. T; 12. T

Part II

1. Liquidation; 2. mutual agency; 3. outstanding stock; 4. stockholders; 5. cash dividend; 6. stock dividend; 7. appropriation of retained earnings; 8. amortization; 9. premium; 10. contra-liability

Part III

A. Partnerships

	Lopez's Share	Rell's Share
0.	$40,000	$40,000
1.	60,000	20,000
2.	45,000	35,000
3.	37,500	42,500
4.	40,900	39,100
5.	38,500	41,500

B. Corporations

Stockholders' Equity			
Paid-in Capital:			
1. Preferred 8 Percent Stock, $50 par (20,000 shares authorized, 4,800 shares issued)	$240,000		
2. Preferred 8 Percent Stock Subscribed (600 shares)	30,000	$ 270,000	
3. Common Stock, $10 par (160,000 shares authorized, 75,000 shares issued)		750,000	
4. Paid-in Capital from Donation		6,500	
5. Total Paid-in Capital		$1,026,500	
6. Retained Earnings		240,000	
7. Total Stockholders' Equity			$1,266,500

CHAPTERS 24–27

Part I

1. F; 2. T; 3. T; 4. F; 5. F; 6. T; 7. F; 8. F; 9. T; 10. F; 11. T; 12. T

Part II

1. $442,500; 2. $84,000; 3. $34,000; 4. Cost of Goods Sold; 5. Quick Assets; 6. Net Sales on Account; 7. direct; 8. departmental margin; 9. factory overhead; 10. Manufacturing Summary

Part III

A. 1. $740; 2. $22,200

B. 1. 1.04:1; 2. $300,000

C. Department X = $1,066.67, Y = $1,333.33, Z = $1,600

Credits

(credits continued from p. iv)

Chapter 18

p. 625, Steve Wenrebe/Stock Boston; p. 627, Richard Pasley/Stock Boston; p. 633, Jeff Greenberg/Photo Edit.

Chapter 19

p. 661, Rudi Van Briel/Photo Edit; p. 662, Stuart Cohen/The Image Works; p. 666, Matthew Borkoski/Stock Boston.

Chapter 20

p. 708, Bill Aaron/Photo Edit; p. 710, Michael Newman/Photo Edit; p. 715, Mark Antman/The Image Works.

Chapter 21

p. 747, Gale Zucker/Stock Boston; p. 748, Steve Rubin/The Image Works; p. 751, C. Savino/The Image Works.

Chapter 22

p. 781, Bob Daemmrich/The Image Works; p. 789, Ziggy Kaluzny/Tony Stone Images; p. 791, B. D. Lanphere/Stock Boston.

Chapter 23

p. 814, Joe Sohm/The Image Works; p. 823, Sandra Daves/The Image Works; p. 827, James Nubile/The Image Works.

Chapter 24

p. 842, Robert Brenner/Photo Edit; p. 844, Rhoda Sidney/Photo Edit; p. 848, Michael Newman/Photo Edit.

Chapter 25

p. 888, Bob Daemmrich/Stock Boston; p. 892, J. Griffin/The Image Works; p. 895, Lee Snider/The Image Works.

Chapter 26

p. 918, Billy Barnes/Photo Edit; p. 923, David Young Wolff/Photo Edit; p. 930, Jon Feingersh/Stock Boston.

Chapter 27

p. 955, M. Douglas/Stock Boston; p. 963, C. Crandall/The Image Works; p. 966, Cary Wolinsky/Stock Boston.

Index

Note: *Boldface* indicates a key term and the page where it is defined.

The Accounting Cycle

During the accounting period

At the end of the accounting period

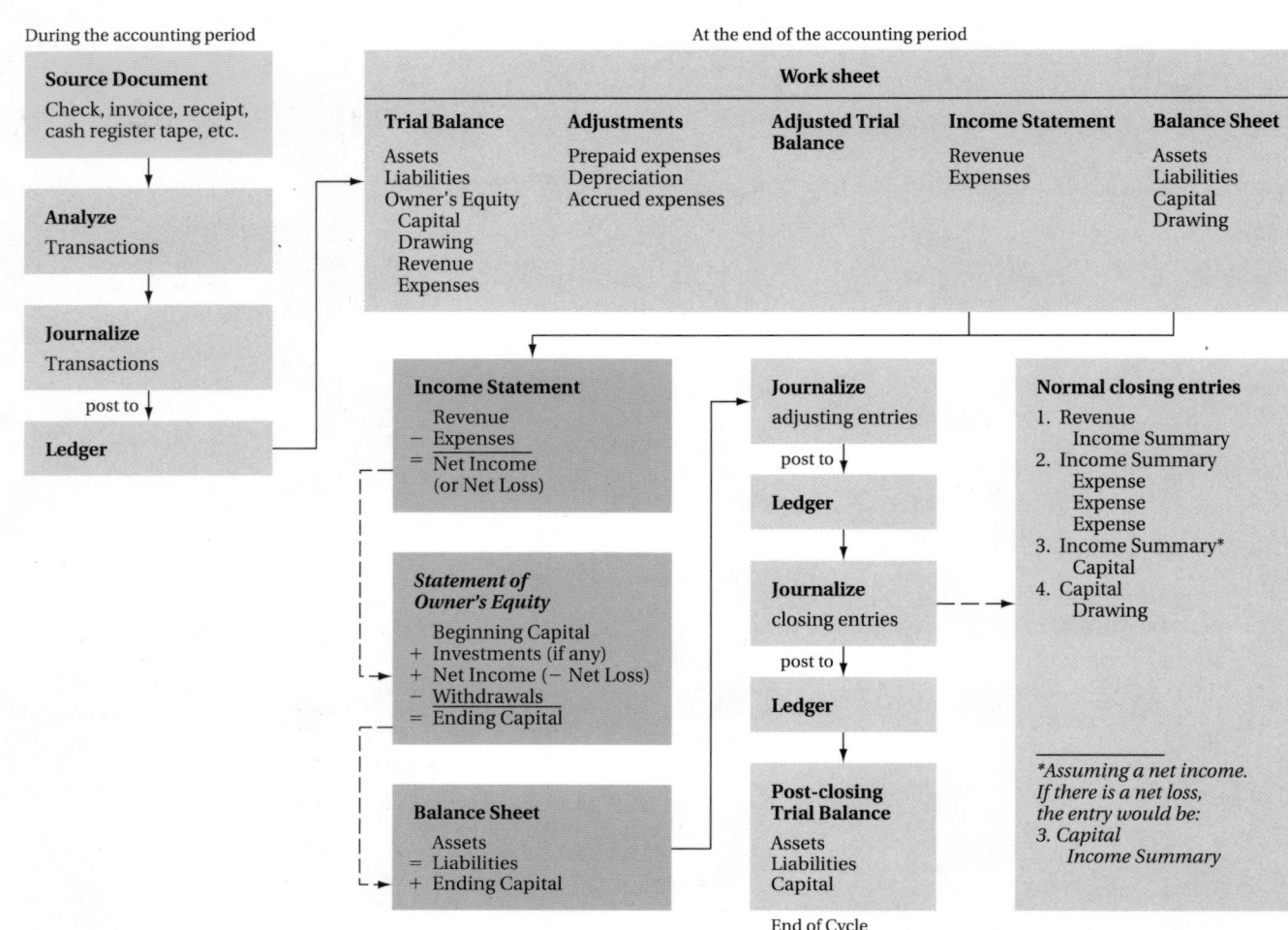

Source Document

Check, invoice, receipt, cash register tape, etc.

Analyze

Transactions

Journalize

Transactions

post to

Ledger

Work sheet

Trial Balance	**Adjustments**	**Adjusted Trial Balance**	**Income Statement**	**Balance Sheet**
Assets	Prepaid expenses		Revenue	Assets
Liabilities	Depreciation		Expenses	Liabilities
Owner's Equity	Accrued expenses			Capital
Capital				Drawing
Drawing				
Revenue				
Expenses				

Income Statement

   Revenue
− Expenses
= Net Income
   (or Net Loss)

Statement of Owner's Equity

   Beginning Capital
+ Investments (if any)
+ Net Income (− Net Loss)
− Withdrawals
= Ending Capital

Balance Sheet

   Assets
= Liabilities
+ Ending Capital

Journalize

adjusting entries

post to

Ledger

Journalize

closing entries

post to

Ledger

Post-closing Trial Balance

Assets
Liabilities
Capital

End of Cycle

Normal closing entries

1. Revenue
    Income Summary
2. Income Summary
    Expense
    Expense
    Expense
3. Income Summary*
    Capital
4. Capital
    Drawing

_____

*Assuming a net income. If there is a net loss, the entry would be:
3. Capital
    Income Summary